CONTEMPORARY LINGUISTICS

AN INTRODUCTION

CONTEMPORARY LINGUISTICS

AN INTRODUCTION

Fourth Edition

Edited by

William O'Grady
University of Hawaii at Manoa

and

John Archibald
University of Calgary

U.S. edition prepared by

Mark Aronoff
State University of New York at Stony Brook

and

Janie Rees-Miller
Marietta College

Bedford/St. Martin's
Boston ♦ New York

For Bedford/St. Martin's

Senior Editor: Talvi Laev
Production Editor: Harold Chester
Senior Production Supervisor: Cheryl Mamaril
Marketing Manager: Richard Cadman
Art Direction and Cover Design: Lucy Krikorian
Text Design: Kyle Gell
Graphics: Allan Moon, Valentino Sanna
Cover Art: The Stock Illustration Source, Inc., Joel Nakamura
Composition: the dotted i
Printing and Binding: RR Donnelley & Sons Company

President: Charles H. Christensen
Editorial Director: Joan E. Feinberg
Editor in Chief: Nancy Perry
Director of Marketing: Karen R. Melton
Director of Editing, Design, and Production: Marcia Cohen
Managing Editor: Erica T. Appel

Library of Congress Control Number: 00-104679

Manufactured in the United States of America.

6 5 4 3 2 1
f e d c b a

For information, write: Bedford/St. Martin's, 75 Arlington Street, Boston, MA 02116 (617-399-4000)

ISBN: 0-312-24738-9

Acknowledgments

Acknowledgments and copyrights appear at the back of the book on page 734, which constitutes an extension of the copyright page.

Convinced at once that, in order to break loose from the beaten paths of opinions and systems, it was necessary to proceed in my study of man and society by scientific methods, and in a rigorous manner, I devoted one year to philology and grammar; linguistics, or the natural history of speech, being, of all the sciences, that which best suited the researches which I was about to commence.

–PIERRE-JOSEPH PROUDHON, *What Is Property?* (1840)

PREFACE

It has been our goal since *Contemporary Linguistics* was first published in 1989 to provide a comprehensive, engaging, and readable introductory linguistics text that will convey to students the fascinating aspects of language study. By including up-to-date coverage of all the important areas of linguistics—from phonology, morphology, syntax, and semantics to cross-curricular topics such as sociolinguistics and psycholinguistics—we aim to prepare students for further work in the subject. At the same time, we strive for a clear, direct presentation of the material so that students at differing levels, and with differing goals for taking the course, can come to understand and appreciate how language works. To our gratification, feedback from users of previous editions indicates that *Contemporary Linguistics* has succeeded at both tasks.

In addition to the text's comprehensiveness and accessibility, other features of *Contemporary Linguistics* that have proven popular with instructors include the following:

A flexible organization to match instructors' teaching needs. While the subject of linguistics is treated as a cohesive whole, the text's flexible organization and self-contained chapters enable instructors to teach the topics in the order they prefer.

The knowledge of working experts in the field. Each chapter is written by an expert or team of experts on a particular topic, providing the most current and in-depth information available.

Extensive support for students. To help students master concepts, each chapter concludes with a summary, a list of key terms and ideas, additional source information, recommended readings, and questions that test and reinforce the material presented in the chapter.

"For the Student Linguist" boxes. Written by a student, these thought-provoking boxes take an inquisitive, sometimes playful, look at language and help other students gain a richer perspective on the subject.

New to This Edition

As with the previous three editions, this fourth U.S. edition of *Contemporary Linguistics* follows closely on the heels of the corresponding edition of its Canadian counterpart and contains the improvements included in that edition, as well as changes designed specifically to meet the needs of readers in the United States.

A unique new chapter on Native American languages. *Contemporary Linguistics* is the first and only introductory linguistics text to give serious attention to the early languages of North America, with a full new chapter (Chapter 9, "Indigenous Languages of North America") written by Victor Golla, a leading scholar in the field.

A completely revised sociolinguistics chapter. Chapter 14, "Language in Social Contexts," now includes an extensive treatment of discourse, conversation, and text analysis. The discussion integrates issues of solidarity and power, introduces methods of studying sociolinguistic variation, and incorporates material on code-switching. It also includes an expanded treatment of American regional dialects and African American Vernacular English.

An updated chapter on computational linguistics. In Chapter 17, "Computational Linguistics," coverage of underlying technologies has been updated, and the discussion of applications of computational linguistics has been expanded to include smart search engines and automatic summarizers.

Extensive revisions to the core chapters. All of the chapters on core issues (Chapters 1–6)—particularly Chapter 5, "Syntax: The Analysis of Sentence Structure"—have been thoroughly revised to reflect recent developments in the field.

More extensive pedagogical aids. We have responded to requests from instructors by placing at the start of each chapter a list of ***Objectives*** to guide students as they work through the chapter. Furthermore, the ***Key Terms*** following each chapter are organized for more effective review, with related terms now grouped together.

An expanded ancillary package. For instructors, we now offer an expanded ***Instructor's Resource Manual,*** which includes teaching advice and answers to the exercises in each chapter, and **103 transparency masters,** featuring key charts and other teaching aids from the main text. A **companion Web site** at <www.bedfordstmartins.com/literature/linguistics> offers links to useful materials.

As in previous editions, some of the specifically Canadian references and factual material have been deleted or replaced (though not where a Canadian example serves its pedagogical purpose as well as another might), and some specifically American material has been added, especially in the chapter on language in social contexts, where American dialects and social phenomena have replaced discussion of the national languages of Canada.

The greatest changes for both the fourth Canadian and U.S. editions concern the editors. On the Canadian side, Michael Dobrovolsky, coeditor for the first three editions, has taken up other pursuits, and John Archibald, professor of linguistics at the University of Calgary, has joined the team as new coeditor. Stateside, Janie Rees-Miller, chair of modern languages at Marietta College in Ohio, who served as chief editorial assistant for both the second and third U.S. editions, has moved to the editorial front lines. We extend our thanks to Michael Dobrovolsky for his many contributions to the first three editions of the book, and we welcome our new colleagues aboard.

Acknowledgments

Since its inception, *Contemporary Linguistics* has benefited from the generous comments and advice of numerous colleagues. In addition to the many individuals whose assistance is acknowledged in the first three editions and whose names are listed below, the editors would particularly like to acknowledge the help we received in preparing this edition of our book.

A special debt of gratitude is owed to Keira Ballentyne, who carefully read through drafts of several chapters, noting many problems and inconsistencies. The editors are also grateful to Denise Devenuto, Alice Harris, Kevin Gregg, Terry Pratt, and Byron Bender for valuable comments and suggestions.

The assistance of the many individuals who contributed comments and advice on the first three editions continues to manifest itself in our fourth edition. Heartfelt thanks are owed to: Howard Aronson, Peter Avery, Derek Bickerton, Robert Blust, Patrick Bruke, Vit Bubenik, Gary Byma, Steven Carey, Andrew Carnie, Jack Chambers, Shuji Chiba, Vanna Condax, Eung-Do Cook, Lynda Costello, John Davison, John DeFrancis, Nicole Domingue, Elan Dresher, Matthew Dryer, Sheila Embleton, Robert

Fisher, Michael Forman, Donald Frantz, Donna Gerdts, John Haiman, John Hewson, Joyce Hildebrand, Robert Hsu, David Ingram, Ricky Jacobs, Kazue Kanno, Brian King, Margaret Larock, Gary Libben, Anatole Lyovin, Barry Meislin, Yves-Charles Morin, Woody Mott, Robert Murray, Michael O'Grady, George Patterson, Mary Pepper, Marilyn Phillips, R. Radhakrishnan, Laurence Reid, Keren Rice, Lorna Rowsell, Yataka Sato, Coral Sayce, Albert Schütz, Peter Seyffert, Patricia Shaw, Stanley Starosta, the students in Terry Pratt's linguistics course at the University of Prince Edward Island, Ronald Southerland, Allison Teasdale, Charles Ulrich, Tim Vance, Theo Venneman, Douglas Walker, Lydia White, Norio Yamada, and Nava Zaig.

For this fourth U.S. edition, we are indebted to the following reviewers, whose comments and suggestions were especially helpful to us: Sharon Hargus (University of Washington), Uptal Lahiri (University of California–Irvine), Joyce McDonough (University of Rochester), Thomas Purnell (University of Wisconsin–Madison), Lori Repetti (SUNY–Stony Brook), Lynn Santelmann (Portland State University), and Mehmet Yavas (Florida International University).

We would like to thank Lyle Campbell (University of Canterbury, New Zealand), Marianne Mithun (University of California–Santa Barbara), and Douglas R. Parks (Indiana University) for contributing thoughtful, detailed comments on a draft of the new Chapter 9, "Indigenous Languages of North America," on very short notice.

Bedford/St. Martin's has been the publisher of the U.S. edition since its inception. We are happy that Nancy Perry, who was so instrumental in getting the project off the ground many years ago, has now returned as editor in chief. We are grateful to publishers Chuck Christensen and Joan Feinberg for their support of this edition. We thank project editors Kathy Moreau and Harold Chester and senior production supervisor Cheryl Mamaril for their assistance with the later stages of the book's production. We are especially grateful to Harold, who did a meticulous job of checking data and shepherding the page proofs through to publication. Last but not least, we acknowledge the contribution of Talvi Laev, senior development editor, who has been our mainstay through the last two editions. She is the sort of editor one reads about in books about the good old days of publishing—a true lover of learning, and, most of all, a real friend.

Mark Aronoff
Janie Rees-Miller

PREFACE TO THE FIRST EDITION

Thanks to the application of rigorous analysis to familiar subject matter, linguistics provides students with an ideal introduction to the kind of thinking we call "scientific." Such thinking proceeds from an appreciation of problems arising from bodies of data, to hypotheses that attempt to account for those problems, to the careful testing and extension of the hypotheses. But science is more than a formal activity. One of the great pleasures offered introductory students of linguistics is the discovery of the impressive body of subconscious knowledge that underlies language use. This book attempts to emphasize the extent of this knowledge as well as to introduce the scientific methodology used in linguistic analysis.

Although this is the first linguistics textbook designed primarily for a Canadian readership, we have tried to do much more than simply provide coverage of linguistic phenomena peculiar to Canada. As the title suggests, we have attempted an introduction to linguistic analysis as it is practiced at this stage in the development of our discipline. While we do not ignore or reject other fruitful approaches to linguistics, we have taken the generative paradigm as basic for two reasons. First, generative linguistics provides a relatively coherent and integrated approach to basic linguistic phenomena. Phonetics, phonology, morphology, syntax, and semantics are viewed within this framework as perhaps in no other as fully integrated and interrelated. Secondly, the generative approach has been widely influential in its application to a broad range of other linguistic phenomena over the past twenty years.

The extent of our "contemporariness" has been limited by the inevitable compromise between the need to present basic concepts and the demands of sophisticated and competing recent approaches. In many cases, early versions of our chapters were judged "too contemporary" by instructors who were not specialists in the subfields in question. This led to substantial revisions and a somewhat more traditional approach to certain issues than was originally intended. Where possible, however, later sections of the chapters are used to present more contemporary material. In this way, we have attempted to provide what is promised by the title—an introductory text that provides a solid grounding in basic linguistic concepts, but one that also prepares the student to go on to current work in the discipline. For this reason, the student is introduced to multilevelled phonology (in preparation for further tiered analysis), allophonic/morphophonemic distinctions (in preparation for lexical phonology), interaction among components of the grammar (in preparation for a more extended modular approach), word-formation rules in morphology, and examples of parametric variation in syntax.

To the extent possible, we have attempted to integrate the basic mechanisms outlined in the first five chapters of the book into our discussion of phenomena in later chapters. Thus, our discussion of semantics, historical linguistics, first and second language acquisition, and neurolinguistics draws to some degree on the notions presented in our introduction to generative grammar.

No textbook can be all things to all users. We hope that this book will provide students not only with a springboard to the realm of scientific linguistic analysis, but with a greater appreciation for the wonder of human language, the variety and complexity of its structure, and the subtlety of its use.

We gratefully acknowledge the assistance of Jack Chambers and Sheila Embleton, both of whom read the manuscript in its entirety and provided invaluable comments. Thanks are also due to those who have read and commented upon individual chapters and sections, including Steven Carey, Matthew Dryer, David Ingram, Gary Byma, Gary Libben, Robert Murray, R. Radhakrishnan, Ronald Southerland, Mary Pepper, Derek Bickerton, Robert Blust, Ricky Jacobs, Don Frantz, John Haiman, John Hewson, Nicole Domingue, Lydia White, George Patterson, Donna Gerdts, Elan Dresher, Keren Rice, Robert Fisher, Marilyn Philips, Lorna Rowsell, and Joyce Hildebrand. For assistance in the planning, editing, and production of the manuscript, we are grateful to Coral Sayce, Lynda Costello, Joyce Hildebrand, Brian Henderson, Patrick Burke, Les Petriw, and our project editor at Copp Clark, Margaret Larock.

CONTENTS

Preface vii
Preface to the First Edition xi
List of Technical Abbreviations xxv

one

LANGUAGE: A PREVIEW **1**

1 Specialization for Language 1
2 A Creative System 2
3 Grammar and Linguistic Competence 5
3.1 Generality: All Languages Have a Grammar 6
3.2 Parity: All Grammars Are Equal 7
3.3 Universality: Grammars Are Alike in Basic Ways 8
3.4 Mutability: Grammars Change over Time 9
3.5 Inaccessibility: Grammatical Knowledge Is Subconscious 10
Summing Up 11
Key Terms 11
Sources 11
Recommended Reading 12
Questions 12

two

PHONETICS: THE SOUNDS OF LANGUAGE **15**

1 Phonetic Transcription 16
1.1 Units of Representation 17
1.2 Segments 17
2 The Sound-Producing System 18
2.1 The Lungs 18
2.2 The Larynx 19
2.3 Glottal States 19
3 Sound Classes 21
3.1 Vowels, Consonants, and Glides (Syllabic and Nonsyllabic Elements) 21
4 Consonant Articulation 22
4.1 The Tongue 22
4.2 Places of Articulation 23
5 Manners of Articulation 25
5.1 Oral versus Nasal Phones 25
5.2 Stops 25

5.3 Fricatives 26
5.4 Affricates 27
5.5 Voice Lag and Aspiration 28
5.6 Liquids 30
5.7 Syllabic Liquids and Nasals 31
5.8 Glides 31
6 Vowels 32
6.1 Simple Vowels and Diphthongs 33
6.2 Basic Parameters for Describing Vowels 33
6.3 Tense and Lax Vowels 35
7 Phonetic Transcription of American English Consonants and Vowels 36
8 Suprasegmentals 38
8.1 Pitch: Tone and Intonation 38
8.2 Length 42
8.3 Stress 42
9 Processes 43
9.1 Coarticulation 44
9.2 Processes and Efficiency 45
9.3 Processes and Clarity 46
9.4 Articulatory Processes 46
10 Other Vowels and Consonants *(Advanced)* 50
10.1 Vowels 50
10.2 Consonants 51
Summing Up 54
Key Terms 54
Sources 56
Recommended Reading 57
Appendix: The International Phonetic Alphabet (condensed) 57
Questions 58
For the Student Linguist: "Don't Worry about Spelling" 61

three

PHONOLOGY: THE FUNCTION AND PATTERNING OF SOUNDS **63**
1 Segments in Contrast 65
1.1 Minimal Pairs 65
1.2 Language-Specific Contrasts 67
2 Phonetically Conditioned Variation: Phonemes and Allophones 68
2.1 Complementary Distribution 68
2.2 Phonemes and Allophones 69
2.3 Classes and Generalization in Phonology 71
2.4 Canadian Raising 72
2.5 English Mid Vowels and Glides 74
2.6 Language-Specific Patterns 75
3 Phonetic and Phonemic Transcription 76

3.1 Phonetic and Phonemic Inventories 78
4 Above the Segment: Syllables 79
4.1 Defining the Syllable 79
4.2 Onset Constraints and Phonotactics 80
4.3 Accidental and Systematic Gaps 82
4.4 Setting Up Syllables 83
4.5 Syllabic Phonology 87
5 Features 91
5.1 Why We Use Features 91
5.2 Feature Representations 95
5.3 The Feature Hierarchy *(Advanced)* 103
6 Derivations and Rules 106
6.1 Derivations 107
6.2 Rule Application 108
6.3 The Form and Notation of Rules 109
7 Representations *(Advanced)* 112
7.1 Assimilation and the Feature Hierarchy 113
7.2 Autosegmental Principles 113
7.3 Tonal Assimilation as a Representation 115
7.4 Processes, Rules, and Representations: A Last Word 116
Summing Up 116
Key Terms 117
Sources 118
Recommended Reading 118
Appendix: Hints for Solving Phonology Problems 119
Questions 121
For the Student Linguist: "The Feature Presentation" 128

four

MORPHOLOGY: THE ANALYSIS OF WORD STRUCTURE **131**
1 Words and Word Structure 132
1.1 Morphemes 133
1.2 Analyzing Word Structure 135
1.3 Some Common Morphological Phenomena 137
2 Derivation 142
2.1 English Derivational Affixes 143
2.2 Two Classes of Derivational Affixes *(Advanced)* 146
3 Compounding 147
3.1 Properties of Compounds 148
3.2 Endocentric and Exocentric Compounds 149
3.3 Compounds in Other Languages 150
4 Other Types of Word Formation 151
4.1 Conversion 151
4.2 Clipping 152

4.3 Blends 152
4.4 Backformation 153
4.5 Acronyms 154
4.6 Onomatopoeia 154
4.7 Other Sources 154
5 Inflection 155
5.1 Inflection in English 155
5.2 Inflection versus Derivation 156
6 Further Examples of Inflection *(Advanced)* 158
6.1 Number 158
6.2 Noun Class 159
6.3 Case 160
6.4 Person and Number Agreement 162
6.5 Tense 163
7 Morphophonemics 164
7.1 Deriving Allomorphs 165
7.2 Conditioning by Morphological Class 167
Summing Up 169
Key Terms 169
Sources 170
Recommended Reading 171
Appendix: How to Identify Morphemes in Unfamiliar Languages 172
Questions 173
For the Student Linguist: "Bambification" 179

five

SYNTAX: THE ANALYSIS OF SENTENCE STRUCTURE **183**
1 Categories and Structure 184
1.1 Categories of Words 185
1.2 Phrase Structure 187
1.3 Sentences 192
1.4 Tests for Phrase Structure 193
1.5 X' Categories *(Advanced)* 194
2 Complement Options 196
2.1 Complement Options for Verbs 197
2.2 Complement Options for Other Categories 198
2.3 Complement Clauses 200
3 Transformations 202
3.1 *Yes-No* Questions 203
3.2 *Wh* Movement 207
3.3 Deep Structure and Surface Structure 211
3.4 Constraints on Transformations *(Advanced)* 213
4 Universal Grammar and Parametric Variation 214
4.1 Variation in Phrase Structure 214

4.2 Variation in the Use of Transformations 216
5 Some Extensions *(Advanced)* 221
5.1 Modifiers 221
5.2 Case: The Interaction between Syntax and Morphology 223
6 Other Types of Syntactic Analysis 226
6.1 The Transformational Analysis 227
6.2 The Relational Analysis 228
6.3 The Functional Analysis 230
Summing Up 231
Key Terms 231
Sources 232
Recommended Reading 233
Appendix: How to Build Tree Structures 233
Questions 236
For the Student Linguist: "Backwards" 242

six

SEMANTICS: THE ANALYSIS OF MEANING **245**
1 The Nature of Meaning 246
1.1 Semantic Relations among Words 246
1.2 Semantic Relations Involving Sentences 248
1.3 What Is Meaning? 250
2 The Conceptual System 253
2.1 Fuzzy Concepts 253
2.2 Metaphor 255
2.3 The Lexicalization of Concepts 256
2.4 Grammaticization 260
3 Syntax and Sentence Interpretation 261
3.1 Constructional Meaning 261
3.2 Structural Ambiguity 263
3.3 Thematic Roles 264
3.4 The Interpretation of Pronouns *(Advanced)* 268
4 Other Factors in Sentence Interpretation 271
4.1 The Role of Beliefs and Attitudes 271
4.2 Setting 272
4.3 Discourse 273
4.4 Conversational Maxims 275
Summing Up 277
Key Terms 278
Sources 279
Recommended Reading 280
Questions 280
For the Student Linguist: "Elvis's Biggest Fan Cleans Out Bank—Accomplice Launders the Dough" 285

seven

Historical linguistics: the study of language change 289

1 The Nature of Language Change 290
1.1 Systematicity of Language Change 291
1.2 Causes of Language Change 291
2 Sound Change 293
2.1 Sequential Change 294
2.2 Segmental Change 301
2.3 Auditorily Based Change 301
2.4 Phonetic versus Phonological Change 302
2.5 Explaining Phonological Shift 304
2.6 Sound Change and Rule Ordering 306
3 Morphological Change 306
3.1 Addition of Affixes 306
3.2 Loss of Affixes 307
3.3 From Synthetic to Analytic to Synthetic 309
3.4 Analogy 309
3.5 Reanalysis 310
4 Syntactic Change 311
4.1 Word Order 311
4.2 Inversion in the History of English 314
5 Lexical and Semantic Change 314
5.1 Addition of Lexical Items 315
5.2 Loss of Lexical Items 318
5.3 Semantic Change 319
6 The Spread of Change 320
6.1 Diffusion through the Language 321
6.2 Spread through the Population 322
7 Language Reconstruction 323
7.1 Comparative Reconstruction 324
7.2 Techniques of Reconstruction 325
7.3 Internal Reconstruction 330
7.4 The Discovery of Indo-European 331
7.5 Reconstruction and Typology 334
8 Language Change and Naturalness 336
Summing Up 337
Key Terms 337
Notes 339
Sources 339
Recommended Reading 340
Questions 341

eight

The classification of languages 347

1 Some Preliminaries 347

1.1 Dialect and Language 348
1.2 Types of Classification 348
2 Typological Classification 349
2.1 Phonology 350
2.2 Morphology 355
2.3 Syntax 358
2.4 Explaining Universals 362
3 Genetic Classification 365
3.1 The Indo-European Family 366
3.2 Some Other Families 371
3.3 North, Central, and South America 379
3.4 Language Phyla 381
Summing Up 383
Key Terms 384
Sources 384
Recommended Reading 386
Questions 386

nine

INDIGENOUS LANGUAGES OF NORTH AMERICA **391**
1 Origin and Classification 392
1.1 Ultimate Origins 392
1.2 Historical Relationships in North America 393
2 Phonetics and Phonology 395
2.1 Velar, Uvular, and Pharyngeal Articulations 395
2.2 Lateral Fricatives 395
2.3 Glottalized Stops and Affricates (Ejectives) 396
2.4 Vowels and Suprasegmental Features 396
2.5 Sounds Not Frequently Found 397
3 Morphology and Syntax 397
3.1 The Structure of Words 397
3.2 Grammatical Categories 400
3.3 Noun Classification 403
4 The Future of Indigenous North American Languages 405
Summing Up 406
Key Terms 406
Sources 407
Recommended Reading 407

ten

FIRST LANGUAGE ACQUISITION **409**
1 The Study of Language Acquisition 410
1.1 Methods 410
2 Phonological Development 412

2.1 Babbling 413
2.2 The Developmental Order 413
2.3 Early Phonetic Processes 414
3 Vocabulary Development 417
3.1 Strategies for Acquiring Word Meaning 418
3.2 Meaning Errors 419
4 Morphological Development 423
4.1 Overgeneralization 423
4.2 A Developmental Sequence 424
4.3 Word-Formation Processes 426
5 Syntactic Development 427
5.1 The One-Word Stage 427
5.2 The Two-Word Stage 427
5.3 The Telegraphic Stage 429
5.4 Later Development 430
5.5 The Interpretation of Sentence Structure *(Advanced)* 432
6 What Makes Language Acquisition Possible? 434
6.1 The Role of Adult Speech 434
6.2 The Role of Feedback 436
6.3 The Role of Cognitive Development 437
6.4 The Role of Inborn Knowledge 439
6.5 Is There a Critical Period? 441
Summing Up 442
Key Terms 442
Sources 442
Recommended Reading 445
Questions 445

eleven

SECOND LANGUAGE ACQUISITION **449**

1 The Study of Second Language Acquisition 450
1.1 The Role of the First Language 450
1.2 The Role of the L2 451
1.3 The Nature of an Interlanguage 452
1.4 The Final State 453
1.5 Variation in Performance 455
2 Interlanguage Grammars 457
2.1 L2 Phonology 457
2.2 L2 Syntax 463
2.3 L2 Morphology 467
3 Factors Affecting SLA 469
3.1 Age 469
3.2 Individual Differences 471
3.3 The Good Language Learner 473
4 The L2 Classroom 474

4.1 Modified Input 474
4.2 Modified Interaction 475
4.3 Focus on Form 475
4.4 Bilingual Education 477
Summing Up 479
Key Terms 480
Appendix: L2 Pedagogy 480
Sources 481
Recommended Reading 482
Questions 482

twelve

PSYCHOLINGUISTICS: THE STUDY OF LANGUAGE PROCESSING **485**

1 Methods of Psycholinguistic Research 486
1.1 Slips of the Tongue 486
1.2 Experimental Methods: Words in the Mind 488
1.3 Experimental Methods: Sentence Processing 491
1.4 Brain Activity: Event-Related Potentials 493
2 Language Processing and Linguistics 494
2.1 Phonetics and Phonology 495
2.2 Morphological Processing 498
2.3 Syntax 500
3 Putting It All Together: Psycholinguistic Modeling 503
3.1 The Use of Metaphors in Psycholinguistic Modeling 504
3.2 Which Model Is Right? 507
Summing Up 508
Key Terms 509
Sources 509
Recommended Reading 510
Questions 511

thirteen

BRAIN AND LANGUAGE **513**

1 The Human Brain 514
1.1 The Cerebral Cortex 514
1.2 The Cerebral Hemispheres 514
1.3 The Lobes of the Cortex 517
2 Investigating the Brain 518
2.1 Autopsy Studies 518
2.2 Images of the Living Brain 519
2.3 Learning from Hemispheric Connections and Disconnections 521
3 Aphasia 522

3.1 Nonfluent Aphasia 523
3.2 Fluent Aphasia 525
4 Acquired Dyslexia and Dysgraphia 527
4.1 Reading and Writing Disturbances in Aphasia 527
4.2 Acquired Dyslexia as the Dominant Language Deficit 527
5 Linguistic Theory and Aphasia 528
5.1 Features, Rules, and Underlying Forms 529
5.2 Agrammatism 529
5.3 Function Words 530
5.4 The Loss of Syntactic Competence 530
5.5 Agrammatism in Other Languages 531
6 Where Is Language? 531
Summing Up 532
Key Terms 532
Sources 533
Recommended Reading 534
Questions 534

fourteen

Language in social contexts **537**

1 The Sociolinguistics of Language 538
1.1 Discourse Analysis 538
1.2 Solidarity and Power 547
2 The Sociolinguistics of Society 553
2.1 Sociolinguistic Norms 553
2.2 Methods of Studying Variation 559
2.3 Social Influence on Variation 563
2.4 Variable Use of Varieties 578
Summing Up 582
Key Terms 583
Sources 584
Recommended Reading 587
Questions 587
For the Student Linguist: "When Language Goes Bad" 588

fifteen

Writing and language **591**

1 Types of Writing 592
1.1 Logographic Writing 592
1.2 Phonographic Writing 592
2 The Early History of Writing 593
2.1 Prewriting 593
2.2 Pictograms 594

3 The Evolution of Writing 595
3.1 Rebuses and the Emergence of Writing 596
3.2 Toward Syllabic Writing 597
3.3 Another Middle Eastern Writing System: Hieroglyphics 598
3.4 The Emergence of Alphabets 599
3.5 Other Developments, East and West 602
4 Some Non-European Writing Systems 605
4.1 Chinese Writing 605
4.2 Japanese Writing 607
4.3 Korean Writing 609
4.4 American Scripts 610
4.5 Some African Scripts 612
4.6 Some Indian Scripts 613
5 English Orthography 614
5.1 Irregularities 614
5.2 Obstacles to Reform 616
6 Writing and Reading 619
Summing Up 620
Key Terms 620
Sources 621
Recommended Reading 622
Questions 623

sixteen

ANIMAL COMMUNICATION **625**
1 Nonvocal Communication 626
2 Communication Structure: The Study of Signs 627
2.1 Signs 628
2.2 Types of Signs 629
2.3 Sign Structure 632
2.4 A View of Animal Communication 633
3 The Bees 635
3.1 The System 635
3.2 Bees and Humans 637
4 The Birds 638
4.1 Bird Vocalization 638
4.2 Birds and Humans 641
5 Nonhuman Primates 641
5.1 Some Functions of Nonhuman Primate Communication 643
5.2 Prosimian Communication 643
5.3 Monkeys 644
5.4 Gibbons, Orangutans, and Chimpanzees 646
6 Testing Nonhuman Primates for Linguistic Ability 647
6.1 Some Experiments 648
6.2 Nonsigning Experiments 649

6.3 The Clever Hans Controversy 650
6.4 The Great Ape Debate 651
6.5 Implications 654
7 Comparing Communication Systems: Design Features 655
Summing Up 658
Key Terms 659
Picture Credits 660
Sources 660
Recommended Reading 661
Questions 661

seventeen

COMPUTATIONAL LINGUISTICS **663**
1 Computational Phonetics and Phonology 665
1.1 The Talking Machine: Speech Synthesis 665
1.2 Speech Recognition or Speech Analysis 669
2 Computational Morphology 670
2.1 Morphological Processes 671
2.2 Some Problems in Computational Morphology 674
3 Computational Syntax 675
3.1 Natural Language Analysis 675
3.2 Natural Language Generation 681
4 Computational Lexicology 682
5 Computational Semantics 687
5.1 Pragmatics 689
6 Practical Applications of Computational Linguistics 690
6.1 Indexing and Concordances 691
6.2 Information Accessing and Retrieval 692
6.3 Machine Translation 693
6.4 Automatic Summarization 696
6.5 Speech Recognition 696
6.6 Speech Synthesis 697
Summing Up 698
Key Terms 698
Recommended Reading 699
Questions 699
For the Student Linguist: "One Second" 701

Glossary 705
Language Index 735
Index 739

LIST OF TECHNICAL ABBREVIATIONS

*	(in historical linguistics) proto-form
*	(in syntactic rules) one or more
*	(in front of words or sentences) unacceptable
#	word boundary
1	first person
1	primary stress
2	second person
2	secondary stress
3	third person
A	adjective
AAVE	African American Vernacular English
Abl	ablative case
Abs	absolutive case
Acc	accusative case
Adv	adverb
AdvP	adverb phrase
Af	affix
ag	agent
AP	adjective phrase
Aux	auxiliary verb
C	complementizer
C	consonant
caus	cause
CG	constricted glottis
cmpl	completed action
C_o	any number of consonants
Co	coda
CP	complementizer phrase
CT	computerized axial tomography
DA	derivational affix
Dat	dative case
Deg	degree word
DR	delayed release
Erg	ergative case
ERP	event-related potential
ESL	English as a second language
fMRI	functional magnetic resonance imaging
Fut	future tense
Gen	genitive case
go	goal
H	high tone
IA	inflectional affix
IL	interlanguage
indic	indicative
IP	inflectional phrase (= S)
IPA	International Phonetic Alphabet
L	low tone
L1	first language
L2	second language
LN	last name
Loc	location
Loc	locative case
M	man
M	mid tone
N	(first) name
N	noun
N	nucleus
Nom	nominative case
NP	noun phrase
O	(direct) object
O	onset
Obl	oblique
OE	Old English
P	preposition, postposition
Pass	passive
PC	Principal Component
PCA	Principal Components Analysis
PET	positron emission tomography
PIE	Proto-Indo-European
PL	plural
PP	prepositional phrase
PR	phonetic representation
Prs	present tense
Pst	past tense
R	rhyme
R	rounded
REA	right ear advantage
recip	recipient
S	sentence
S	subject
σ	syllable
SES	socioeconomic status
SG	spread glottis
SG	singular
SLA	second language acquisition
T	title alone
th	theme
TLN	title + last name
Top	topic
UG	Universal Grammar
UR	underlying representation
UR	unrounded
V	verb
V	vowel
VP	verb phrase
W	woman
Wd	word

CONTEMPORARY LINGUISTICS

AN INTRODUCTION

one

LANGUAGE: A PREVIEW

William O'Grady

The gift of language is the single human trait that marks us all genetically, setting us apart from the rest of life.

– LEWIS THOMAS, *The Lives of a Cell*

OBJECTIVES

In this chapter, you will learn:

- that human beings are specialized for language
- that all human languages are creative, have a grammar, and change over time
- that grammatical knowledge is subconscious in all native speakers of a language

Language is many things—a system of communication, a tool for thought, a medium for self-expression, a social institution, a source of ethnic pride and political controversy. All normal human beings have at least one language, and it is difficult to imagine much significant social, intellectual, or artistic activity taking place in the absence of language.

The centrality of language to virtually every aspect of human life gives each of us a reason to want to understand more about its nature and use. This book takes a first step in that direction by providing a basic introduction to **linguistics**—the discipline that studies language.

1 SPECIALIZATION FOR LANGUAGE

Modern *Homo sapiens* (our species) made their appearance 200,000 years ago, by many estimates. Our ancestors were anatomically just like us—they had large brains and vocal tracts capable of producing speech. Archaeological evidence (such as tools, carvings, and cave paintings) suggest that they also had the type of intellect that could support language.

Hundreds of thousands of years of evolution created a special capacity for language in humans not found in any other species. The evidence is literally inside us. For example, our speech organs (the lungs, larynx, tongue, teeth, lips, soft palate, and nasal passages) were—and still are—directly concerned with breathing and eating. However, they have also all become highly specialized for use in language. Their structure and shape are unique to our species, as is the highly developed network of neural pathways that exercises control over them during speech production.

Table 1.1 Dual functions of the speech organs

Organ	*Survival function*	*Speech function*
Lungs	to exchange CO_2 and oxygen	to supply air for speech
Vocal cords	to create seal over passage to lungs	to produce vibrations for speech sounds
Tongue	to move food to teeth and back into throat	to articulate vowels and consonants
Teeth	to break up food	to provide place of articulation for consonants
Lips	to seal oral cavity	to articulate vowels and consonants
Nose	to assist in breathing	to provide nasal resonance during speech

Breathing during speech is associated with higher lung pressure and a longer exhalation time than ordinary respiration. Abdominal muscles that are not normally employed for respiration are brought into play in order to regulate the air pressure needed for speech.

Human beings are also specially equipped for the perception of speech. Newborns respond differently to human voices than to other types of sounds, and six-month-old infants are able to perceive subtle differences among sounds in languages that they have never heard before (this is discussed in more detail in Chapter 10).

Even the ability to deal with nonvocal, cognitive aspects of language—such as word formation, sentence building, and the interpretation of meaning—seems to be the product of neurological specialization. Particular parts of the brain tend to be associated with specific types of linguistic phenomena (see Chapter 13 for discussion), and species with different types of brains appear to be unable to acquire or use human language (see Chapter 16).

2 A CREATIVE SYSTEM

Knowing that human beings are especially suited for language only increases the mystery that surrounds this phenomenon. What, precisely, is language? What does it mean to know a language? To answer these questions, it is first necessary to understand the resources that a language makes available to its **native speakers**, those who have acquired it as children in a natural setting (say, a home rather than a classroom).

The breadth and diversity of human thought and experience place great demands on language. Because communication is not restricted to a fixed set of topics, language must do something more than provide a package of ready-made messages; it must enable us to produce and understand new words and sentences as the need arises. In short, human language must be creative—allowing novelty and innovation in response to new thoughts, experiences, and situations.

The **creativity** of language goes hand in hand with a second defining characteristic—the presence of systematic constraints that establish the boundaries within which innovation can occur. As a preliminary illustration of this, let us consider the process that creates verbs from nouns in English. (For now, you can think of verbs as words that name actions and nouns as words that name things.)

Table 1.2 Nouns used as verbs

Noun use	*Verb use*
pull the boat onto the *beach*	*beach* the boat
keep the airplane on the *ground*	*ground* the airplane
tie a *knot* in the string	*knot* the string
put the wine in *bottles*	*bottle* the wine
catch the fish with a *spear*	*spear* the fish
clean the floor with a *mop*	*mop* the floor

As the following sentences show, there is a great deal of freedom to innovate in the formation of such verbs.

1)

a. I *wristed* the ball over the net.
b. He would try to *stiff-upper-lip* it through.
c. She *Houdini'd* her way out of the locked closet.

However, there are also limits on this freedom. For instance, a new verb is rarely coined if a word with the intended meaning already exists. Although we say *jail the robber* to mean 'put the robber in jail', we do not say *prison the robber* to mean 'put the robber in prison'. This is because the well-established verb *imprison* already has the meaning that the new form would have.

There are also special constraints on the meaning and use of particular subclasses of these verbs. One such constraint involves verbs that are created from time expressions such as *summer*, *vacation,* and so on.

2)

a. Julia *summered* in Paris.
b. Harry *wintered* in Mexico.
c. Bob *vacationed* in France.
d. Harry and Julia *honeymooned* in Hawaii.

Although the sentences in *2* are all natural-sounding, not all time expressions can be used in this way. (Throughout this book, an asterisk is used to indicate that an utterance is unacceptable.)

3)

a. *Jerome *midnighted* in the streets.
b. *Andrea *nooned* at the restaurant.
c. *Philip *one o'clocked* at the airport.

These examples show that when a verb is created from a time expression, it must be given a very specific interpretation—roughly paraphrasable as 'to be somewhere for the period of time X'. Thus, *to summer in Paris* is 'to be in Paris for the summer', *to vacation in France* is 'to be in France for a vacation', and so on. Since *noon* and *midnight* express *points* in time rather than extended *periods* of time, they cannot be used to create new verbs of this type.

Systematic constraints are essential to the viability of the creative process. If well-established words were constantly being replaced by new creations, a language's vocabulary would be so unstable that communication could be jeopardized. A similar danger would arise if there were no constraints on the meaning of words newly derived from other words. If *They winter in Hawaii* could mean 'They make it snow in Hawaii' or 'They wish it were winter in Hawaii' or any other arbitrary thing, the production and interpretation of new forms would be chaotic and unsystematic, undermining the usefulness of language for communication.

Some other examples

Systematic creativity is the hallmark of all aspects of language. For instance, consider the way in which sounds are combined to form words. Certain patterns of sounds, like the novel forms in *4,* have the "look" of English words—we recognize that they could become part of the language and be used as names for new products or processes, for example.

4)

a. prasp
b. flib
c. traf

In contrast, the forms in *5* contain combinations of sounds that English just does not permit. As a result, they simply do not have the shape of English words.

5)

a. *psapr
b. *bfli
c. *ftra

Still other constraints determine how new words can be created from already existing forms with the help of special endings. Imagine, for example, that the word *soleme* entered the English language (used perhaps for a newly discovered atomic particle). As a speaker of English, you would then automatically know that something with the properties of a soleme could be called *solemic.* You would also know that to make something solemic is to *solemicize* it, and you would call this process *solemicization*. Further, you would know that the *c* is pronounced as *s* in *solemicize* but as *k* in *solemic*. Without hesitation, you would also recognize that *solemicize* is pronounced with the stress on the second syllable (you would say *soLEmicize,* not *SOlemicize* or *solemiCIZE*).

Nowhere is the ability to deal with novel utterances more obvious than in the production and comprehension of sentences. Apart from a few fixed expressions and greetings, much of what you say, hear, and read in the course of a day consists of sentences that are new to you. In conversations, lectures, newscasts, and textbooks, you are regularly exposed to novel combinations of words, unfamiliar ideas, and new information. Consider, for instance, the paragraph that you are currently reading. While each sentence is no doubt perfectly comprehensible to you, it is extremely unlikely that you have ever seen any of them before.

Not all new sentences are acceptable, however. For example, the words in *6* are all familiar, but they are simply not arranged in the right way to make a sentence of English.

6)

*Frightened dog this the cat that chased mouse a.
(cf. This dog frightened the cat that chased a mouse.)

As with other aspects of language, the ability to form and interpret sentences is subject to systematic limitations. One of the principal goals of contemporary linguistic analysis is to identify and understand these limitations.

3 GRAMMAR AND LINGUISTIC COMPETENCE

As we have just seen, speakers of a language are able to produce and understand an unlimited number of utterances, including many that are novel and unfamiliar. At the same time, they are able to recognize that certain utterances are not acceptable and simply do not belong in their language. This ability, which is often called **linguistic competence**, constitutes the central subject matter of linguistics and of this book.

In investigating linguistic competence, linguists focus on the mental system that allows human beings to form and interpret the sounds, words, and sentences of their language. Linguists call this system a **grammar** and often break it down into the following components.

Table 1.3 The components of a grammar

Component	*Domain*
Phonetics	the articulation and perception of speech sounds
Phonology	the patterning of speech sounds
Morphology	word formation
Syntax	sentence formation
Semantics	the interpretation of words and sentences

As you can see, the term *grammar* is used in a special way within linguistics. A linguist's grammar is not a book and it is not concerned with just the form of words and sentences. Rather, it is an intricate system of knowledge that encompasses sound and meaning as well as form and structure.

The study of grammar lies at the core of our attempts to understand what language is and what it means to know a language. Five simple points should help clarify why the investigation of grammatical systems is so important to contemporary linguistic analysis.

3.1 Generality: All languages have a grammar

One of the most fundamental claims of modern linguistic analysis is that all languages have a grammar. It could not be any other way. If a language is spoken, it must have a phonetic and a phonological system; since it has words and sentences, it must also have a morphology and a syntax; and since these words and sentences have systematic meanings, there must obviously be semantic principles as well. Of course, these are the very things that make up a grammar.

It is not unusual to hear it remarked that a particular language—say, Puerto Rican Spanish, Navajo, or Swahili—"has no grammar." (This is especially common in the case of languages that are not written or are not taught in schools and universities.) To an untrained observer, unfamiliar languages sometimes appear to have no grammar simply because their grammatical systems are different from those of better-known languages. In Walbiri (an indigenous language of Australia), for example, the relative ordering of words is so free that the English sentence *The two dogs now see several kangaroos* could be translated by the equivalent of any of the following sentences.

7)

a. Dogs two now see kangaroos several.
b. See now dogs two kangaroos several.
c. See now kangaroos several dogs two.
d. Kangaroos several now dogs two see.
e. Kangaroos several now see dogs two.

Although Walbiri may not restrict the order of words in the way English does, its grammar imposes other types of requirements. For example, in the sentence types we are considering, Walbiri speakers must place the ending *lu* on the word for 'dogs' to indicate that it names the animals that do the seeing rather than the animals that are seen. In English, by contrast, this information is conveyed by placing *two dogs* in front of the verb and *several kangaroos* after it.

Rather than showing that Walbiri has no grammar, such differences simply demonstrate that it has a grammar that is unlike the grammar of English in certain respects. This point holds across the board: although no two languages have exactly the same grammar, there are no languages without a grammar.

A similar point can be made about different varieties of the same language. To some extent, for instance, each of the many varieties of English spoken in today's world (Appalachian English, Jamaican English, Boston English) has its own characteristic pronunciation, vocabulary, and sentence patterns. Crucially, though, these differences exist not because the various varieties of English have no grammar but rather because they have grammars that differ from each other in particular ways.

3.2 Parity: all grammars are equal

Contrary to popular belief, there is no such thing as a "primitive" language, even in places untouched by modern science and technology. Indeed, some of the most complex linguistic phenomena we know about are found in societies that have neither writing nor electricity.

Moreover, there is no such thing as a "good grammar" or a "bad grammar." In fact, all grammars do essentially the same thing: they tell speakers how to form and interpret the words and sentences of their language. The form and meaning of those words and sentences vary from language to language and even from community to community, but there is no such thing as a language that doesn't work for its speakers.

Linguists sometimes clash over this point with people who are upset about the use of "nonstandard" varieties of English that permit sentences such as *I seen that, They was there, He didn't do nothing, He ain't here,* and so forth. Depending on where you live and who you talk to, speaking in this way can have negative consequences: it may be harder to win a scholarship, to get a job, to be accepted in certain social circles, and so forth. This is an undeniable fact about the social side of language and we'll return to it in Chapter 14. From a purely linguistic point of view, however, there is absolutely nothing wrong with grammars that permit such structures. They work for their speakers, and they deserve to be studied in the same objective fashion as the varieties of English spoken by the rich and educated.

The bottom line for linguistics is that the analysis of language must reflect the way it is actually used, not someone's idealized vision of how it should be used. The linguist Steven Pinker offers the following illustration to make the same point.

> Imagine that you are watching a nature documentary. The video shows the usual gorgeous footage of animals in their natural habitats. But the voiceover reports some troubling facts. Dolphins do not execute their swimming strokes properly. White-crowned sparrows carelessly debase their calls. Chickadees' nests are incorrectly constructed, pandas hold bamboo in the wrong paw, the song of the humpback whale contains several well-known errors, and the monkey's cries have been in a state of chaos and degeneration for hundreds of years. Your reaction would probably be, What on earth could it mean for the song of the humpback whale to contain an "error"? Isn't the song of the humpback whale whatever the humpback whale decides to sing? . . .

As Pinker goes on to observe, language is like the song of the humpback whale. The way to determine whether a particular sentence is permissible is to find people who speak the language and observe how they use it.

In sum, linguists don't even think of trying to rate languages as good or bad, simple or complex. Rather, they investigate language in much the same way that other scientists study snails or stars—with a view to simply figuring out how it works. This same point is sometimes made by noting that linguistics is **descriptive**, not **prescriptive**. Its goal is to describe and explain the facts of language, not to change them by prescribing one way of speaking as "correct."

3.3 Universality: grammars are alike in basic ways

In considering how grammars can differ from each other, it is easy to lose sight of something even more intriguing and important—the existence of principles and properties shared by all human languages.

For example, all spoken languages use a small set of contrastive sounds that help distinguish words from each other (like the *t* and *d* sounds that allow us to recognize *to* and *do* as different words). Not all languages use the same sounds, but there are real constraints on which ones they can and cannot use. For instance, all languages have more consonant sounds (*p*, *t*, *d*, etc.) than vowel sounds (*a*, *e*, *i*); any language that has an *f* sound also has an *s* sound; and all languages have a vowel that sounds like the 'ah' in *father.* (For more on this, see Chapter 8.)

There are also universal constraints on how words can be put together to form sentences. For example, no language can use the second of the sentences in *8* for a situation in which *he* refers to *Ned.*

8)

a. Ned lost his wallet.
b. He lost Ned's wallet.

Moreover, even when languages do differ from each other, there are often constraints on how much variation is possible. For example, some languages (like English) place question words at the beginning of a sentence.

9)

Mary sees a book. *What* do you see?

Other languages, like Mandarin, make no such changes.

10)

Mali kanjian shu. Ni kanjian *sheme*?
Mary sees book you see what
'Mary sees a book. What do you see?'

No language, however, uniformly places question words at the end of a sentence.

In other cases, variation is constrained by strong tendencies rather than absolute prohibitions. Take a three-word sentence such as *Canadians like hockey*, for instance. There are only six possible orders for such a sentence.

11)

a. Canadians like hockey.
b. Canadians hockey like.
c. Like Canadians hockey.

d. Like hockey Canadians.
e. Hockey like Canadians.
f. Hockey Canadians like.

All other things being equal, we would expect to find each order employed in about one-sixth of the world's languages. In fact, though, more than 95 percent of the world's languages adopt one of the first three orders for basic statements (and the vast majority of those use one or the other of the first two orders). Only a handful of languages use any of the last three orders as basic.

These are not isolated examples. As later chapters will show, languages—like the people who use them—are fundamentally alike in important ways.

3.4 Mutability: grammars change over time

The features of language that are not universal and fixed are subject to change over time. Indeed, within these limits, the grammars of all languages are constantly changing. Some of these changes are relatively minor and occur very quickly (for example, the addition of new words such as *morphing, Internet, email,* and *cyberspace* to the vocabulary of English). Other changes have a more dramatic effect on the overall form of the language and typically take place over a long period of time. One such change involves the manner in which we negate sentences in English. Prior to 1200, English formed negative constructions by placing *ne* before the verb and a variant of *not* after it.

12)

a. I *ne* seye *not.* ('I don't say.')
b. He *ne* speketh *nawt.* ('He does not speak.')

By 1400 or thereabouts, *ne* was used infrequently and *not* (or *nawt*) typically occurred by itself after the verb.

13)

a. I seye *not* the wordes.
b. He saw *nawt* the knyghtes.

It was not until several centuries later that English adopted its current practice of allowing *not* to occur after only certain types of verbs (such as *do, have, will,* and so on).

14)

a. I will *not* say the words. (versus *I will say not the words.)
b. He did *not* see the knights. (versus *He saw not the knights.)

These changes illustrate the extent to which grammars can be modified over time. The structures exemplified in *13* are archaic by today's standards and those in *12* sound completely foreign to most speakers of modern English.

Through the centuries, those who believed that certain varieties of language were better than others frequently expressed concern over what they perceived to be the deterioration of English. In 1710, for example, the writer Jonathan Swift (author of *Gulliver's Travels*) lamented "the continual Corruption of our English Tongue."

Among the corruptions to which he objected were contractions such as *he's* for *he is*, although he had no objection to *'Tis* for *It is*.

In the nineteenth century, Edward S. Gould, a columnist for the New York *Evening Post*, published a book entitled *Good English; or, Popular Errors in Language*, in which he accused newspaper writers and authors of "sensation novels" of ruining the language by introducing "spurious words" like *jeopardize, leniency*, and *underhanded*. The tradition of prescriptive concern about the use of certain words continues to this day in the work of such popular writers as Edwin Newman and John Simon, who form a kind of self-appointed language police.

Linguists reject the view that languages attain a state of perfection at some point in their history and that subsequent changes lead to deterioration and corruption. As noted above, there are simply no grounds for claiming that one language or variety of language is somehow superior to another.

3.5 Inaccessibility: Grammatical Knowledge Is Subconscious

Knowledge of a grammar differs in important ways from knowledge of arithmetic, traffic rules, and other subjects that are taught explicitly at home or in school: it is largely subconscious and not accessible to introspection (that is, you can't figure out how it works just by thinking about it). As an example of this, consider your pronunciation of the past tense ending written as *ed* in the following words.

15)

a. hunted
b. slipped
c. buzzed

You probably didn't notice it before, but the *ed* ending has a different pronunciation in each of these words. Whereas you say *id* in *hunted*, you say *t* in *slipped* and *d* in *buzzed*. Moreover, if you heard the new verb *flib*, you would form the past tense as *flibbed* and pronounce the ending as *d*. If you are a native speaker of English, you acquired the grammatical subsystem regulating this aspect of speech when you were a child and it now exists subconsciously in your mind, allowing you to make the relevant contrasts automatically.

The same is true for virtually everything else about language. Once we go beyond the most obvious things (like whether words like *the* and *a* come before or after a noun), there is not much that the average person can say about how language works. For example, try explaining to someone who is not a native speaker of English why we can say *I went to school* but not **I went to movie*. Or try to figure out for yourself how the word *too* works. Notice that it sounds perfectly natural in sentences like the following.

16)

a. Mary ate a cookie, and then Johnnie ate a cookie too.
b. Mary ate a cookie, and then she ate some cake too.

For some reason, though, it doesn't sound so natural in the following sentence.

17)

*Mary ate a cookie, and then Johnnie ate some cake too.

You may be thinking that that is because Mary and Johnnie didn't eat the same thing. But if that's so, then why does *too* sound natural in the next sentence, even though Johnnie didn't have a cookie for his snack?

18)

Mary ate a cookie, and then Johnnie had a snack too.

Speakers of a language know what sounds right and what doesn't sound right, but they are not sure how they know.

Because most of what we know about our language is subconscious, the analysis of human linguistic systems requires considerable effort and ingenuity. As is the case in all science, information about facts that can be observed (the pronunciation of words, the interpretation of sentences, and so on) must be used to draw inferences about the sometimes invisible mechanisms (atoms, cells, or grammars, as the case may be) that are ultimately responsible for these phenomena. A good deal of this book is concerned with the findings of this research and with what they tell us about the nature and use of human language and how it is represented in the mind.

Summing up

Human language is characterized by **creativity**. Speakers of a language have access to a **grammar**—a mental system that allows them to form and interpret both familiar and novel utterances. The grammar governs the articulation, perception, and patterning of speech sounds; the formation of words and sentences; and the interpretation of utterances. All languages have grammars that are equal in their expressive capacity, and all speakers of a language have (subconscious) knowledge of its grammar. The existence of such linguistic systems in humans is the product of unique anatomical and cognitive specialization not found in other species.

Key terms

creativity
descriptive (grammar)
grammar
linguistic competence
linguistics
native speakers
prescriptive (grammar)

Sources

The discussion of word creation is based on an article by Eve Clark and Herb Clark, "When Nouns Surface as Verbs," *Language* 55 (1979): 767–811. The Walbiri data are based on K. Hale's article "Person Marking in Walbiri," in *A Festschrift for Morris Halle*, edited by S. Anderson and P. Kiparsky (New York: Holt, Rinehart and Winston, 1973). The quote at the end of Section 3.2 is from the book by Steven Pinker (p. 370) cited below. The Gould book is cited in Dennis Baron's *Grammar and Good Taste* (New Haven: Yale University Press, 1982). The data on the word order preferences are from *Typology and Universals* by William Croft (New York: Cambridge University Press, 1990), p. 46. The books by Bickerton and Pinker, cited below, provide different views of the emergence of language in the human species.

The exercises for this chapter were prepared by Joyce Hildebrand.

Recommended reading

Bickerton, Derek. 1990. *Language and Species*. Chicago: University of Chicago Press.

Crystal, David. 1997. *Cambridge Encyclopedia of the English Language*. New York: Cambridge University Press.

Pinker, Steven. 1994. *The Language Instinct: How the Human Mind Creates Language*. New York: Morrow.

Questions

1. The following sentences contain verbs created from nouns in accordance with the process described in Section 1 of the chapter. Describe the meaning of each of these new verbs.
   a) We punk-rocked the night away.
   b) She dog-teamed her way across the Arctic.
   c) We MG'd to Oregon.
   d) They Concorded to London.
   e) He Gretzky'd his way to the net.
   f) We Greyhounded to Toronto.
   g) We'll have to Ajax the sink.
   h) He Windexed the windows.
   i) You should Clairol your hair.
   j) Let's carton the eggs.

2. Using the examples in the preceding exercise as a model, create five new verbs from nouns. Build a sentence around each of these new verbs to show its meaning.

3. Which of the following forms are possible words of English? Solicit the help of an acquaintance and see if you agree on your judgments.

a) mbood	e) sproke
b) frall	f) flube
c) coofp	g) wordm
d) ktleem	h) bsarn

4. Imagine that you are an advertising executive and that your job involves inventing new names for products. Create four new forms that are possible words of English and four that are not.

5. Part of linguistic competence involves the ability to recognize whether novel utterances are acceptable. Consider the following sentences and determine which are possible sentences in English. For each unacceptable sentence, change the sentence to make it acceptable, and compare the two.
   a) Jason's mother left himself with nothing to eat.
   b) Miriam is eager to talk to.
   c) This is the man who I took a picture of.
   d) Colin made Jane a sandwich.
   e) Is the dog sleeping the bone again?
   f) Wayne prepared Zena a cake.
   g) Max cleaned the garden up.
   h) Max cleaned up the garden.
   i) Max cleaned up it.
   j) I desire you to leave.
   k) That you likes liver surprises me.

6. Consider the following sentences, each of which is acceptable to some speakers of English. Try to identify the prescriptive rules that are violated in each case.
   a) He don't know about the race.
   b) You was out when I called.
   c) There's twenty horses registered in the show.
   d) That window's broke, so be careful.
   e) Jim and me are gonna go campin' this weekend.
   f) Who did you come with?
   g) I seen the parade last week.
   h) He been lost in the woods for ten days.
   i) My car needs cleaned 'cause of all the rain.
   j) Julie ain't got none.
   k) Somebody left their book on the train.
   l) Murray hurt hisself in the game.

   What is the reaction of linguists to the claim that sentences of this sort are "wrong"?

two

PHONETICS: THE SOUNDS OF LANGUAGE

Michael Dobrovolsky

Heavenly labials in a world of gutturals

– WALLACE STEVENS

OBJECTIVES

In this chapter, you will learn:

- how we use special symbols to represent all the different sounds in human languages, beginning with English
- how to write down your own speech using these symbols
- how we use articulators in the vocal tract to produce specific sounds
- how we can group language sounds into classes
- how human languages use tone, intonation, and sound length to create meaning
- how language sounds in context can be modified by neighboring sounds
- what vowel and consonant sounds exist in other languages

We do not need to speak in order to use language. Language can be written, broadcast from tapes and CDs, and even produced by computers in limited ways. Nevertheless, speech remains the primary way humans encode and broadcast language. Our species spoke long before we began to write, and as we saw in the first chapter of this book, this long history of spoken language is reflected in our anatomical specialization for it. Humans also appear to have specialized neural mechanisms for the perception of speech sounds. Because language and speech are so closely linked, we begin our study of language by examining the inventory and structure of the sounds of speech. This branch of linguistics is called **phonetics**.

Human languages display a wide variety of sounds, called **phones** (from Greek *phōnē* 'sound, voice') or **speech sounds**. There are a great many speech sounds, but not an infinite number of them—the class of possible speech sounds is finite, and a portion of the total set will be found in the inventory of any human language. Certain sounds that humans are capable of producing with the vocal tract do not occur in speech, such as the sound made by inhaling through one corner of the mouth, or the "raspberry" produced by sticking out the tongue and blowing hard across it. Nonetheless, a very wide range of sounds is found in human language, including such sounds as the click made by drawing the tongue hard away from the upper molars on one side of the mouth, or the sound made by constricting the upper part of the throat as we breathe out. The class of possible speech sounds is universal and can be learned by any human—child or adult.

There are two ways of approaching phonetics. One approach studies the physiological mechanisms of speech production. This is known as **articulatory phonetics**. The other, known as **acoustic phonetics**, is concerned with measuring and analyzing the physical properties of the sound waves we produce when we speak. Both approaches are indispensable to an understanding of phonetics. This chapter focuses on articulatory phonetics, but also makes reference to the acoustic properties of sounds and to acoustic analysis.

1 PHONETIC TRANSCRIPTION

Since the sixteenth century, efforts have been made to devise a universal system for transcribing the sounds of speech. The best-known system, the **International Phonetic Alphabet (IPA)**, has been developing since 1888. This system of transcription attempts to represent each sound of human speech with a single symbol. These symbols are enclosed in brackets [ ] to indicate that the transcription is phonetic and does not represent the spelling system of a particular language. For example, the sound spelled *th* in English *this* is transcribed as [ð] (pronounced *eth*, as in *weather*). The IPA uses this symbol to represent the sound in whichever language it is heard, whether it is English, Spanish, Turkmen (a Turkic language spoken in Central Asia and generally written with the Cyrillic alphabet), or any other (see Table 2.1).

Table 2.1 Use of [ð] in the International Phonetic Alphabet

Language	*Spelling*	*IPA*	*Meaning*
English	this	[ðɪs]	'this'
Spanish	boda	[bɔða]	'wedding'
Turkmen	aдak	[aðak]	'foot'

The use of a standardized phonetic alphabet enables linguists to transcribe languages consistently and accurately. In North American (NA) usage, though, some phonetic symbols differ from those employed by IPA transcription. For example, the sound heard at the beginning of the English word *shark* is transcribed as [ʃ] in IPA, but usually as [š] in North America. This book employs IPA transcription but notes common North American symbols where relevant.

If you wish to start practicing the phonetic transcription of English, turn to Tables 2.16 and 2.17, pages 36–38, for examples.

1.1 Units of representation

Anyone who hears a language spoken for the first time finds it hard to break up the flow of speech into individual units. Even when hearing our own language spoken, we do not focus attention on individual sounds as much as we do on the meanings of words, phrases, and sentences. Many alphabets, including the IPA, represent speech in the form of **segments**—individual phones like [p], [s], or [m]. Using segments, however, is only one way to represent speech. The **syllable**, presented in Chapter 3, is also represented in some writing systems (see Chapter 15, Sections 1.2, 3.2, and 4.2). In one form of Japanese writing, for example, signs such as か [ka], と [ko], and み [mo] represent syllables without recourse to segmental transcription.

Segments are produced by coordinating a number of individual articulatory gestures including jaw movement, lip shape, and tongue placement. Many of these individual activities are represented as smaller subunits called **features**, which segments are assumed to be made up of. Even though features are almost never represented in writing systems, they are important elements of linguistic representation. Features reflect individual aspects of articulatory control or acoustic effects produced by articulation. This chapter presents segmental transcription, since it is the most widely used way of representing speech. Features and syllables are introduced in the following chapter.

1.2 Segments

We have defined the segment as an individual speech sound (phone). There are several kinds of evidence that suggest that speakers have the linguistic knowledge that makes it possible to break down a stream of speech into sound segments.

Errors in speech production provide one kind of evidence for the existence of segments. Slips of the tongue such as *Kolacodor* for *Kodacolor* and *melcome wat* for *welcome mat* show segments shifting and reversing position within and across words. This suggests that segments are individual units of linguistic structure and can be represented individually in a system of transcription.

The relative invariance of speech sounds in human language also suggests that segmental phonetic transcription is a well-motivated way of transcribing speech. It is impossible to represent all variants of human speech sounds, since no one says the same sound in exactly the same way twice. Nonetheless, the sounds of speech remain invariant enough from language to language for us to transcribe them consistently. A *p* sound is much the same in English, Russian, or Uzbek. The fact that when producing a *p* sound, English speakers press their lips together but Russian speakers draw theirs slightly inward does not make the sounds different enough to warrant separate symbols. But the sounds *p* and *t* are distinct enough from each other in languages the world over to be consistently transcribed with separate symbols.

2 THE SOUND-PRODUCING SYSTEM

Sound is produced when air is set in motion. Think of the speech production mechanism as consisting of an air supply, a sound source that sets the air in motion in ways specifically relevant to speech production, and a set of filters that modifies the sound in various ways. The air supply is provided by the lungs. The sound source is in the **larynx**, where a set of muscles called the **vocal folds** (or **vocal cords**) are located. The filters are the organs above the larynx: the tube of the throat between the larynx and the oral cavity, which is called the **pharynx**; the oral cavity; and the nasal cavity. These passages are collectively known as the **vocal tract**.

2.1 THE LUNGS

In order to produce the majority of sounds in the world's languages, we take air into the lungs and then expel it during speech. (A small number of phones are made with air as it flows into the vocal tract.) A certain level of air pressure is needed to keep the speech mechanism functioning steadily. The pressure is maintained by the

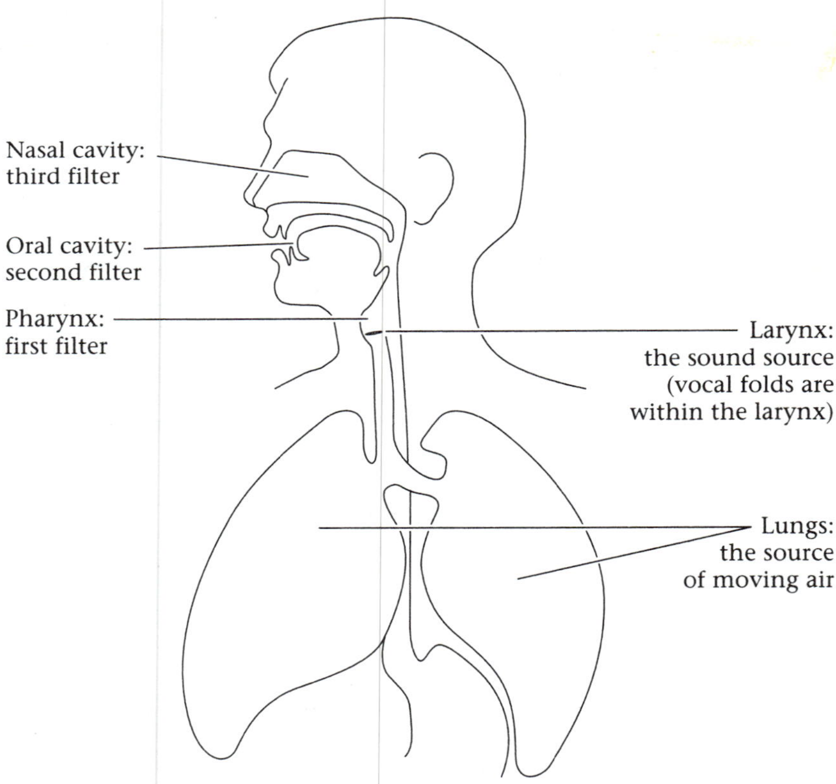

Figure 2.1 The sound-producing system

action of various sets of muscles coming into play during the course of an utterance. The muscles are primarily the **intercostals** (the muscles between the ribs) and the **diaphragm** (the large sheet of muscle separating the chest cavity from the abdomen).

2.2 The larynx

As air flows out of the lungs up the **trachea** (windpipe), it passes through a box-like structure made of cartilages and muscle; this is the larynx (commonly known as the voice box or Adam's apple). The main portion of the larynx is formed by the **thyroid cartilage**, which spreads outward like the head of a plow. The thyroid cartilage rests on the ring-shaped **cricoid cartilage**. Fine sheets of muscle flare from the inner sides of the thyroid cartilage, forming the paired vocal folds (vocal cords). The inner edges of the vocal folds are attached to the vocal ligaments. The vocal folds can be pulled apart or drawn closer together, especially at their back or posterior ends, where each is attached to one of two small cartilages—the **arytenoids**. The arytenoids are opened, closed, and rotated by several pairs of small muscles (not shown in Figure 2.2). As air passes through the space between the vocal folds, which is called the **glottis**, different glottal states are produced, depending on the positioning of the vocal folds.

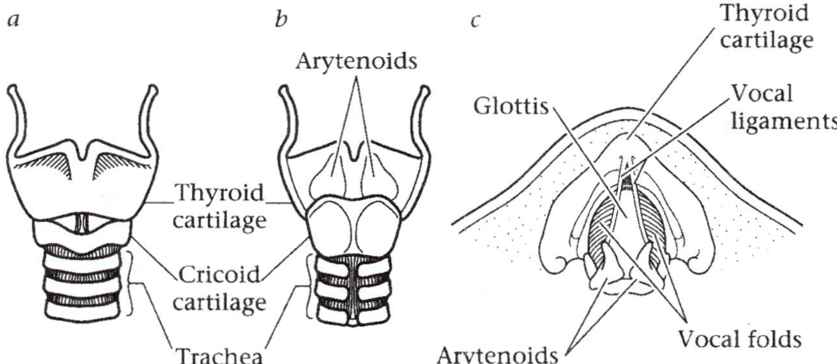

Figure 2.2 The larynx: *a* from the front; *b* from the back; *c* from above, with the vocal folds in open position. The striated lines indicate muscles, a number of which have been eliminated from the drawings in order to show the cartilages more clearly.

2.3 Glottal states

The vocal folds may be positioned in a number of ways to produce different glottal states. The first two glottal states presented in Figure 2.3 are commonly encountered in most of the world's languages. The third diagram depicts the glottal state that underlies a common speech phenomenon, and the fourth illustrates one of a number of glottal states not encountered in English.

Voicelessness

When the vocal folds are pulled apart as illustrated in Figure 2.2, air passes directly through the glottis. Any sound made with the vocal folds in this position is said to be **voiceless**. You can confirm a sound's voicelessness by touching your fingers to the larynx as you produce it. You will not feel any vibration from the vocal folds being transmitted to your fingertips. The initial sounds of *fish*, *sing*, and *house* are all voiceless. Voicelessness is a true speech state; the vocal folds are not as far apart as they are in silent breathing.

Voicing

When the vocal folds are brought close together but not tightly closed, air passing between them causes them to vibrate, producing sounds that are said to be **voiced**. (See Figure 2.3, where the movement of the vocal folds during voicing is indicated by the wavy lines.) You can determine whether a sound is voiced in the same way you determined voicelessness. By lightly touching the fingers to the larynx as you produce an extended version of the initial sounds of the words *zip* or *vow*, or any vowel, you can sense the vibration of the vocal folds within the larynx.

Whisper

Another glottal state produces a **whisper**. Whispering is voiceless, but as shown in Figure 2.3, the vocal folds are adjusted so that the anterior (front) portions are pulled close together, while the posterior (back) portions are apart.

Murmur

Yet another glottal state produces a **murmur**, also known as **whispery voice**. Sounds produced with this glottal configuration are voiced, but the vocal folds are relaxed to allow enough air to escape to produce a simultaneous whispery effect.

These four glottal states represent only some of the possibilities of sound production at the glottis. Combined with various articulations made above the larynx, they produce a wide range of phones. The total number of glottal states is still undecided, but it is over a dozen. Recent research suggests that there is a special glottal state—

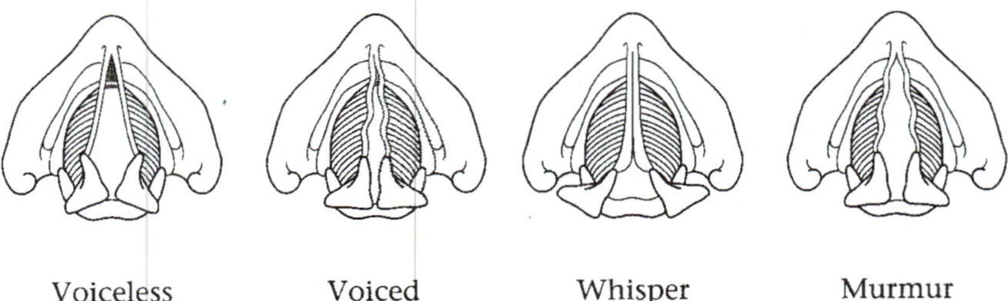

Figure 2.3 Four glottal states: the stylized drawing represents the vocal folds and glottis from above; the anterior portion at the larynx is toward the top. The small triangles represent the arytenoid cartilages, which help spread or close the vocal folds.

prephonation—preceding a voiceless unaspirated stop. Before examining phones in more detail, we will first consider the three major classes of speech sound.

3 SOUND CLASSES

The sounds of language can be grouped into **sound classes** based on the phonetic properties that they share. You have already seen what some of these properties can be. All **voiced sounds**, for example, form a class, as do all **voiceless sounds**. The most basic division among sounds is into two major classes—**vowels** and **consonants**. Another class of sounds, the **glides**, shares properties of both vowels and consonants. Each of these classes of sounds has a number of distinguishing features.

3.1 VOWELS, CONSONANTS, AND GLIDES (SYLLABIC AND NONSYLLABIC ELEMENTS)

Vowels, consonants, and glides can be distinguished on the basis of differences in articulation, or by their acoustic properties. We can also distinguish among these elements with respect to whether they function as **syllabic** or **nonsyllabic** elements.

The articulatory difference

Consonantal sounds, which may be voiced or voiceless, are made with either a complete closure or narrowing of the vocal tract. The airflow is either blocked momentarily or restricted so much that noise is produced as air flows past the constriction. Vowels are produced with little obstruction in the vocal tract and are usually voiced.

The acoustic difference

As a result of the difference in articulation, consonants and vowels differ in the way they sound. Vowels are more **sonorous** (acoustically powerful) than consonants, and so we perceive them as louder and longer lasting.

Syllabic and nonsyllabic sounds

The greater sonority of vowels allows them to form the basis of syllables. A syllable can be defined as a peak of sonority surrounded by less sonorous segments. For example, the words *a* and *go* each contain one syllable, the word *laughing* two syllables, and the word *telephone* three syllables. In counting the syllables in these words, we are in effect counting the vowels. A vowel is thus said to form the **nucleus** of a syllable. In Section 5.7, it will be shown that certain types of consonants can form syllabic nuclei as well. It is a good idea, therefore, to think of vowels and consonants not simply as types of articulations but as elements that may or may not be syllabic. In *1*, the initial sounds of the words in the left column are all consonants; those on the right are all vowels.

1)

take	above
cart	at
feel	eel
jump	it
think	ugly
bell	open

Table 2.2 sums up the differences between consonants and vowels.

Table 2.2 Major differences between syllabic and nonsyllabic elements

Vowels (and other syllabic elements)	Consonants (nonsyllabic elements)
• are produced with relatively little obstruction in the vocal tract	• are produced with a complete closure or narrowing of the vocal tract
• are more sonorous	• are less sonorous

Glides

A type of sound that shows properties of both consonants and vowels is called a glide. Glides may be thought of as rapidly articulated vowels—this is the auditory impression they produce. While glides are produced with an articulation like that of a vowel, they move quickly to another articulation, as do the initial glides in *yet* or *wet*, or quickly terminate, as do the word-final glides in *boy* and *now*.

Even though they are vowel-like in articulation, glides pattern as consonants. For example, glides can never form the nucleus of a syllable. Since glides show properties of both consonants and vowels, the terms *semivowel* and *semiconsonant* may be used interchangeably with the term *glide*.

4 CONSONANT ARTICULATION

Airflow is modified in the vocal tract by the placement of the tongue and the positioning of the lips. These modifications occur at specific **places** or **points of articulation**. The major places of articulation used in speech production are outlined in this section. Figure 2.4 provides a midsagittal section, or cutaway view, of the vocal tract on which each place of articulation has been indicated.

4.1 The tongue

The primary articulating organ is the tongue. It can be raised, lowered, thrust forward or drawn back, and even rolled back. The sides of the tongue can also be raised or lowered.

Phonetic description refers to five areas of the tongue. The **tip** is the narrow area at the front. Just behind the tip lies the **blade**. The main mass of the tongue is called

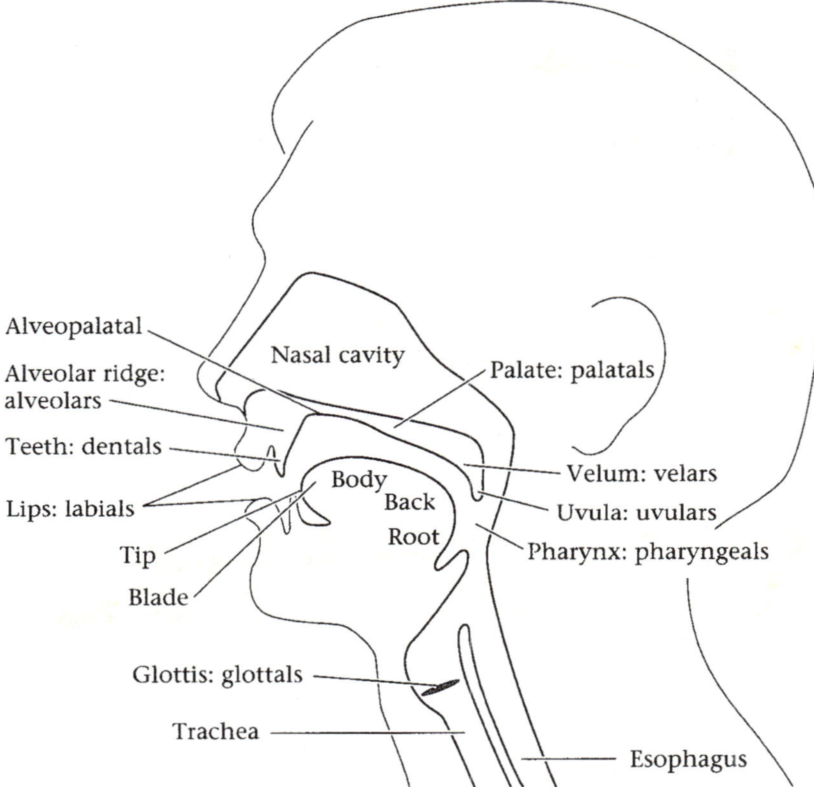

Figure 2.4 The vocal tract

the **body**, and the hindmost part of the tongue that lies in the mouth is called the **back**. The body and back of the tongue can also be referred to jointly as the **dorsum**. The **root** of the tongue is contained in the upper part of the throat (pharynx).

4.2 Places of articulation

Each point at which the airstream can be modified to produce a different sound is called a place of articulation. Places of articulation are found at the lips, within the oral cavity, in the pharynx, and at the glottis.

Labial

Any sound made with closure or near-closure of the lips is said to be **labial**. Sounds involving both lips are termed **bilabial**; sounds involving the lower lip and upper teeth are called **labiodentals**. English includes the bilabials heard word-initially in *peer*, *bin*, and *month*, and the labiodentals heard initially in *fire* and *vow*.

Dental and interdental

Some phones are produced with the tongue placed against or near the teeth. Sounds made in this way are called **dentals**. European French has dental sounds at the beginning of the words *temps*, *dire*, *sept*, and *zizi*.

If the tongue is placed between the teeth, the sound is said to be **interdental**. Interdentals in English include the initial consonants of the words *this* and *thing*. (Some English speakers produce *s* and *z* as dentals; see Section 5.3 for more details.)

Alveolar

Within the oral cavity, a small ridge protrudes from just behind the upper front teeth. This is called the **alveolar ridge**. The tongue may touch or be brought near this ridge. Alveolar sounds are heard at the beginning of the following English words: *top, deer, soap, zip, lip,* and *neck*. Some languages, such as Spanish, have an *r* that is made by touching the tongue to the alveolar ridge.

Alveopalatal and palatal

Just behind the alveolar ridge, the roof of the mouth rises sharply. This area is known as the **alveopalatal** area (palatoalveolar in some books).

The highest part of the roof of the mouth is called the **palate**, and sounds produced with the tongue on or near this area are called **palatals**. The word-initial phone in *yes* is a palatal glide. Alveopalatal consonants are heard in the following English words: *show, measure, chip,* and *judge*.

Velar

The soft area toward the rear of the roof of the mouth is called the **velum**. Sounds made with the tongue touching or near this position are called **velars**. Velars are heard in English at the beginning of the words *call* and *guy*, and at the end of the word *hang*. The glide heard word-initially in *wet* is called a **labiovelar**, since the tongue is raised near the velum and the lips are rounded at the same time.

Uvular

The small fleshy flap of tissue known as the **uvula** hangs down from the velum. Sounds made with the tongue near or touching this area are called **uvulars**. English has no uvulars, but the *r* sound of standard European French is uvular.

Pharyngeal

The area of the throat between the uvula and the larynx is known as the pharynx. Sounds made through the modification of airflow in this region by retracting the tongue or constricting the pharynx are called **pharyngeals**. Pharyngeals can be found in many dialects of Arabic but not in English.

Glottal

Sounds produced using the vocal folds as primary articulators are called **glottals**. The sound at the beginning of the English words *heave* and *hog* is made at the glottis.

5 MANNERS OF ARTICULATION

The lips, tongue, velum, and glottis can be positioned in different ways to produce different sound types. These various configurations are called the **manners of articulation**.

5.1 Oral versus nasal phones

A basic distinction in manner of articulation is between **oral** and **nasal phones**. When the velum is raised, cutting off the airflow through the nasal passages, oral sounds are produced. The velum, however, can be lowered to allow air to pass through the nasal passages, producing a sound that is nasal. Both consonants and vowels can be nasal, in which case they are generally voiced. (Unless otherwise noted, all nasals represented in this chapter are voiced.) The consonants at the end of the English words *sun, sum,* and *sung* are nasal. For many speakers of English, the vowels of words such as *bank* and *wink* are also nasal.

5.2 Stops

Stops are made with a complete and momentary closure of airflow through the vocal tract. In the world's languages, stops are found at bilabial, dental, alveolar, palatal, velar, uvular, and glottal points of articulation.

In English, bilabial, alveolar, and velar oral and nasal stops occur in the words shown in Table 2.3. Note that [ŋ] does not occur word-initially in English.

Table 2.3 English stops and their transcription

Bilabial		*Transcription*
Voiceless	span	[p]
Voiced	ban	[b]
Nasal	man	[m]
Alveolar		
Voiceless	stun	[t]
Voiced	dot	[d]
Nasal	not	[n]
Velar		
Voiceless	scar	[k]
Voiced	gap	[g]
Nasal	wing	[ŋ]
Glottal		
Voiceless	(see p. 26)	[ʔ]

The glottal stop is commonly heard in English in the expression *uh-uh* [ʔʌ̃ʔʌ̃], meaning 'no'. The two vowels in this utterance are each preceded by a momentary closing of the airstream at the glottis. In some British and American dialects, the glottal stop is commonly heard in place of the [t] in a word like *bottle*. This glottal stop is often spelled with an apostrophe *(bo'l)*.

A grid for stops

Table 2.4 presents a grid on which the stop consonants of English are arranged horizontally according to point of articulation. As you can see, each stop, with one exception, has voiced and voiceless counterparts. The glottal stop is always voiceless. It is produced with the vocal folds drawn firmly together and the arytenoids drawn forward, and since no air can pass through the glottis, the vocal folds cannot be set in motion.

Table 2.4 English stop consonants

	Bilabial	*Alveolar*	*Velar*	*Glottal*
Voiceless	[p]	[t]	[k]	[ʔ]
Voiced	[b]	[d]	[g]	
Nasal	[m]	[n]	[ŋ]	

5.3 Fricatives

Fricatives are consonants produced with a continuous airflow through the mouth. They belong to a large class of sounds called **continuants** (a class that also includes vowels and glides), all of which share this property. The fricatives form a special class of continuants; during their production, they are accompanied by a continuous audible noise, due to air passing through a very narrow opening either at the glottis or in the vocal tract.

English fricatives

English has voiceless and voiced labiodental fricatives at the beginnings of the words *fat* and *vat*, voiceless and voiced interdental fricatives heard word-initially in the words *thin* and *those*, alveolar fricatives heard word-initially in *sing* and *zip*, and a voiceless alveopalatal fricative heard word-initially in *ship*. The voiced alveopalatal fricative is rare in English. It is the first consonant in the word *azure*, and is also heard in the words *pleasure* and *rouge*. The voiceless glottal fricative of English is heard in *hotel* and *hat*.

Special note must be taken of the alveolar fricatives [s] and [z]. There are two ways that English speakers commonly produce these sounds. Some speakers raise the tongue tip to the alveolar ridge (or to just behind the upper front teeth) and allow the air to pass through a grooved channel in the tongue. Other speakers form this same channel using the blade of the tongue; the tip is placed behind the lower front teeth.

Table 2.5 The transcription of English fricatives

Glottal state	*Point of articulation*	*Transcription*
	Labiodental	
Voiceless	fan	[f]
Voiced	van	[v]
	Interdental	
Voiceless	thin	[θ]
Voiced	then	[ð]
	Alveolar	
Voiceless	sun	[s]
Voiced	zip	[z]
	Alveopalatal	
Voiceless	ship	[ʃ]
Voiced	azure	[ʒ]
	Glottal	
Voiceless	hat	[h]

A grid for fricatives

Table 2.6 presents a grid on which the fricative consonants of English are ranged according to point of articulation. As in Table 2.5, dentals are not distinguished from alveolars, since most languages have sounds with either one or the other point of articulation, not both. Note that IPA [ʃ] and [ʒ] correspond respectively to North American [š] and [ž].

Table 2.6 English fricatives

	Labiodental	*Interdental*	*Alveolar*	*Alveopalatal*	*Glottal*
Voiceless	[f]	[θ]	[s]	[ʃ]	[h]
Voiced	[v]	[ð]	[z]	[ʒ]	

5.4 Affricates

When a stop articulation is released, the tongue moves rapidly away from the point of articulation. Some noncontinuant consonants show a slow release of the closure; these sounds are called **affricates**. English has only two affricates, both of which are alveopalatal. They are heard word-initially in *church* and *jump*, and are transcribed as [tʃ] and [dʒ], respectively.

A grid for affricates

Table 2.7 presents a grid showing the two English affricates. Note that IPA [tʃ] and [dʒ] correspond to North American [č] and [ǰ], respectively.

Table 2.7 English affricates

	Alveopalatal
Voiceless	[tʃ]
Voiced	[dʒ]

Stridents and sibilants

At the beginning of this chapter, it was noted that acoustic as well as articulatory criteria are sometimes used in describing speech sounds. An acoustic criterion comes into play to describe fricatives and affricates. These sounds are subdivided into two types, some of which are distinctly louder than others. The noisier fricatives and affricates are called **stridents** (see Table 2.8). Their quieter counterparts, such as [θ] or [ð], which have the same or nearly the same place of articulation, are called **non-stridents**. Stridents are also known as **sibilants**.

Table 2.8 Strident fricatives and affricates in English

Place of articulation	*Strident*	
	Voiceless	*Voiced*
Alveolar	[s]	[z]
Alveopalatal	[ʃ]	[ʒ]
	[tʃ]	[dʒ]

5.5 Voice lag and aspiration

After the release of certain voiceless stops in English, you can sometimes hear a lag or brief delay before the voicing of a following vowel. Since the lag in the onset of vocalic voicing is accompanied by the release of air, the traditional term for this phenomenon is **aspiration**. It is transcribed with a small raised [ʰ] after the aspirated consonant. Table 2.9 provides some examples of aspirated and unaspirated consonants in English (some vowel symbols are introduced here as well). Notice that the sounds that have both aspirated and unaspirated varieties are all voiceless stops. In other languages, voiceless fricatives and affricates may also be aspirated or unaspirated.

Table 2.9 Aspirated and unaspirated consonants in English

Aspirated		*Unaspirated*	
[pʰæt]	pat	[spæt]	spat
[tʰʌb]	tub	[stʌb]	stub
[kʰowp]	cope	[skowp]	scope

Figure 2.5 shows how aspiration of a voiceless consonant takes place, using the aspirated consonant [pʰ] as an example. Though the sequence of articulations takes place continuously, the figure illustrates only certain moments.

a) As articulation of the voiceless consonant is begun, the glottis is open.

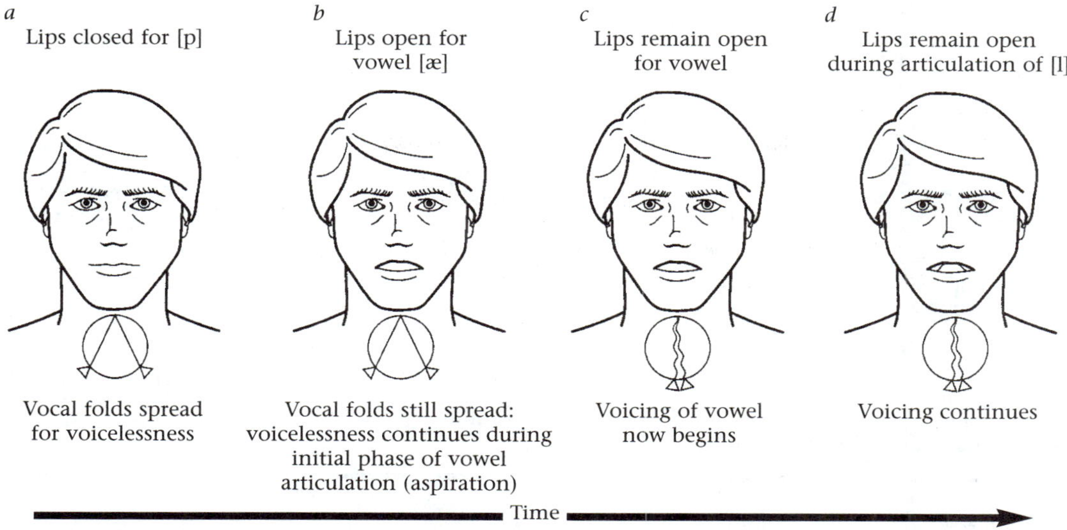

Figure 2.5 Aspirated consonant production (English *pal*)

b) The closure for the consonant is released and the vowel articulation begins; however, the glottis is not yet closed enough to permit voicing to begin. Because of this, the vowel is briefly voiceless, giving the impression of an extra release of air that we call aspiration.
c) After a short delay, measurable in milliseconds, voicing of the vowel begins.
d) The lips remain open and voicing continues during the articulation of the final consonant of the word.

Figures 2.6 and 2.7 show the relation between articulation and voicing for unaspirated and voiced consonants. The unaspirated consonant, such as the [p] of English

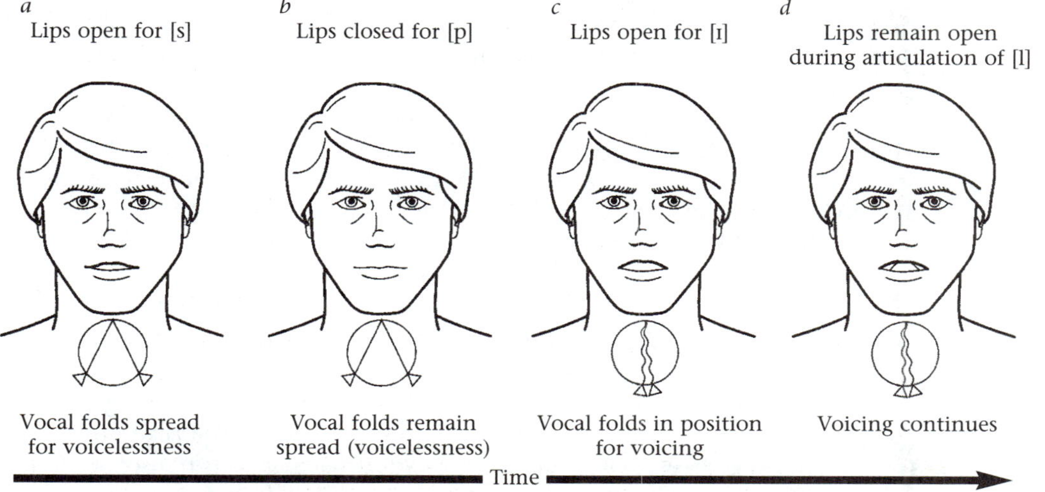

Figure 2.6 Unaspirated consonant production (English *spill*)

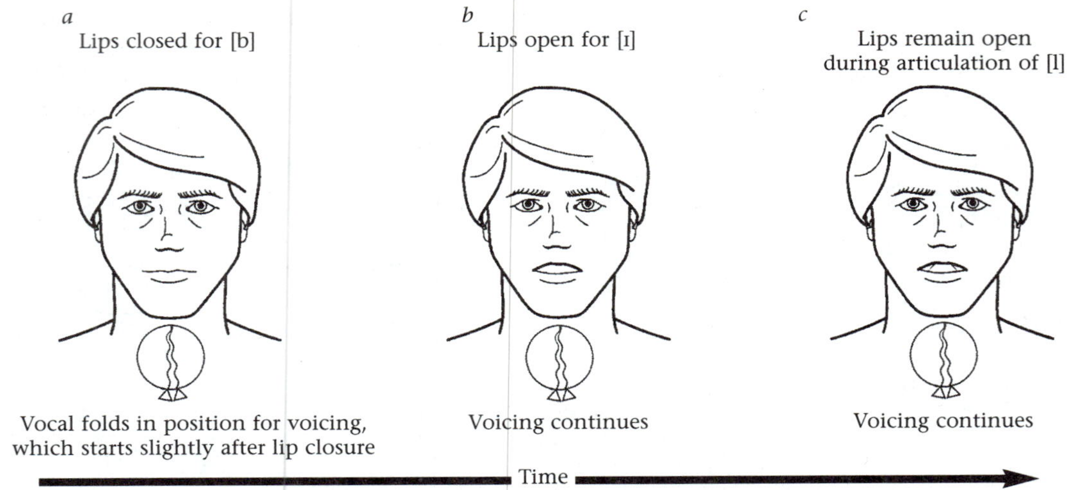

Figure 2.7 Voiced consonant release (English *bill*)

spill, shows voicing of the vowel starting very soon after release of the consonant articulation. The voiced initial [b] of English *bill* shows voicing starting just before the release of the bilabial articulation. In Figure 2.7, note how voicing precedes the release of the labial articulators.

5.6 Liquids

Among the sounds commonly found in the world's languages are *l* and *r* and their numerous variants. They form a special class of consonants known as **liquids**.

Laterals

Varieties of *l* are called **laterals**. As laterals are articulated, air escapes through the mouth along the lowered sides of the tongue. When the tongue tip is raised to the dental or alveolar position, the dental or alveolar laterals are produced. Both may be transcribed as [l].

Because laterals are generally voiced, the term *lateral* used alone usually means 'voiced lateral'. Still, there are instances of voiceless laterals in speech. The voiceless dental or alveolar lateral is written with an additional phonetic symbol, called a **diacritic**. In this case, the diacritic is a circle beneath the symbol: [l̥]. Voiceless laterals can be heard in the pronunciation of the English words *please* and *clear*.

English *r*'s

Numerous varieties of *r* are also heard in the world's languages. This section describes the types found in English.

The *r* of English as it is spoken in North America is made either by curling the tongue tip back into the mouth or by bunching the tongue upward and back in the mouth. This *r* is known as a **retroflex** *r* and is heard in *ride* and *car*. It is transcribed as [r] in this book. IPA transcription favors [ɹ] for this sound, though it also offers the symbol [r].

Another sound commonly identified with *r* is the **flap**. The flap is produced when the tongue tip strikes the alveolar ridge as it passes across it. It is heard in the North American English pronunciation of *bitter* and *butter*, and in some British pronunciations of *very*. It is commonly transcribed as [ɾ] and is generally voiced. Table 2.10 presents the laterals, *r*, and the flap of American English.

Table 2.10 English liquids

		Alveolar	
Laterals		voiced	[l]
		voiceless	[l̥]
r's	retroflex	voiced	[r]
		voiceless	[r̥]
	flap		[ɾ]

5.7 Syllabic liquids and nasals

Liquids and nasals are more sonorous than other consonants and in this respect are more like vowels than are the other consonants. In fact, they are so sonorous that they may function as syllabic nuclei. When they do so, they are called **syllabic liquids** and **syllabic nasals** (see Table 2.11). Syllabic liquids and nasals are found in many of the world's languages, including English. In transcription, they are usually marked with a short diacritic line underneath. Unfortunately for beginning linguistics students, North American transcription is not always consistent here. The syllabic *r* sound heard in words like *bird* and *her* is often transcribed in North America as a vowel-*r* sequence: [ər]. (The vowel symbol is presented in Section 6.2 of this chapter.) The IPA symbol for this sound is [ɚ].

Table 2.11 Syllabic liquids and nasals in English

	Syllabic		*Nonsyllabic*
bottle	[bɑɾl̩]	lift	[lɪft]
funnel	[fʌnl̩]	pill	[pʰɪl]
bird	[bərd], [bɚd], or [br̩d]	rat	[ræt]
her	[hər], [hɚ], or [hr̩]	car	[kʰɑr]
button	[bʌtn̩]	now	[naw]
'm-m'	[ʔm̩ʔm̩] (meaning 'no')	mat	[mæt]

5.8 Glides

Recall that a glide is a very rapidly articulated nonsyllabic segment. The two glides of North American English are the jod [jɑd] (North American 'y-glide') [j] of *yes* and *boy*, and the w-glide [w] of *wet* and *now*. The [j] in IPA transcription corresponds to the [y] of North American transcription.

The [j] is a palatal glide (often cited as alveopalatal as well) whose articulation is virtually identical to that of the vowel [i] of *see*. You can verify this by pronouncing a [j] in an extended manner; it will sound very close to an [i].

The glide [w] is made with the tongue raised and pulled back near the velum and with the lips protruding, or rounded. For this reason, it is sometimes called a labiovelar. The [w] corresponds closely in articulation to the vowel [u] of *who*. This can be verified by extending the pronunciation of a [w]. We will consider [w] a rounded velar glide for purposes of description. Some speakers of English also have a voiceless (labio)velar glide, transcribed [ʍ], in the words *when*, *where*, and *which* (but not in *witch*).

Given that nonsyllabic [j] corresponds closely in articulation to syllabic [i], and nonsyllabic [w] corresponds closely in articulation to syllabic [u], we could argue that nonsyllabic [r] is the glide counterpart of syllabic [r̩] in English. (No such claim has been made for [l]/[l̩]). However, since most linguistics books clearly place [r] among the liquids and not the glides, we will continue to do so here.

English consonants

Table 2.12 provides a summary of the places and manners of articulation of English consonants.

Table 2.12 English consonants: places and manners of articulation

		Place of articulation						
Manner of articulation		*Labial*	*Labiodental*	*Interdental*	*Alveolar*	*Alveopalatal*	*Velar*	*Glottal*
Stop	voiceless	p			t		k	ʔ
	voiced	b			d		g	
Fricative	voiceless		f	θ	s	ʃ		h
	voiced		v	ð	z	ʒ		
Affricate	voiceless					tʃ		
	voiced					dʒ		
Nasal	voiced	m			n		ŋ	
Liquid	voiced lateral				l			
	voiced retroflex				r			
Glide	voiced	w				j	w	
	(voiceless)	(ʍ)					(ʍ)	

6 VOWELS

Vowels are sonorous, syllabic sounds made with the vocal tract more open than it is for consonant and glide articulations. Different vowel sounds (also called **vowel qualities**) are produced by varying the placement of the body of the tongue and shaping the lips. The shape of the vocal tract can be further altered by protruding the lips to produce rounded vowels, or by lowering the velum to produce nasal vowels. Finally, vowels may be tense or lax, depending on the degree of vocal tract constriction during their articulation.

The following section on vowels provides an introduction to most of the basic vowels of English. Additional phonetic detail will be introduced in the following chapter.

6.1 SIMPLE VOWELS AND DIPHTHONGS

English vowels are divided into two major types—**simple vowels** and **diphthongs**. Simple vowels do not show a noticeable change in quality during their articulation. The vowels of *pit, set, cat, dog, but, put,* and the first vowel of *suppose* are all simple vowels.

Diphthongs are vowels that exhibit a change in quality within a single syllable. English diphthongs show changes in quality that are due to tongue movement away from the initial vowel articulation toward a glide position. This change in vowel quality is clearly perceptible in words such as *say, buy, cow, ice, lout, go,* and *boy*. The change is less easy to hear, and in fact is not made by all English speakers, in the vowels of words like *heed* and *lose*. Because the glides on these vowels—if present—are so weak as to be virtually inaudible, we do not show the vowels in *heed* and *lose* as diphthongs in this book. Table 2.13 presents the simple vowels and diphthongs of English. The diphthongs are transcribed as vowel-glide sequences.

Table 2.13 Some simple vowels and diphthongs of American English

Simple vowel		*Diphthong*		*Simple vowel*		*Diphthong*	
pit	[ɪ]	heat	[i] or [ij]	cut	[ʌ]	lose	[u] or [uw]
set	[ɛ]	say	[ej]	bought	[ɔ]	grow	[ow]
mat	[æ]	my	[aj]	put	[ʊ]	boy	[ɔj]
pot	[ɑ]	now	[aw]	suppose	[ə]		

In all cases, the diphthongs are somewhat longer than the simple vowels. Notice that the diphthongs [aj] and [aw] are transcribed with a low back unrounded vowel symbol that is different from the one used to transcribe the vowel of, say, *hot*: [ɑ]. This symbol represents a vowel that is both lax and less back than [ɑ]. Try to pronounce the vowel [ɑ] in place of the [a] in these diphthongs; you will hear why a different vowel symbol is needed.

6.2 BASIC PARAMETERS FOR DESCRIBING VOWELS

Vowel articulations are not as easy to feel at first as consonant articulations, since the vocal tract is not narrowed as much. To become acquainted with vowel articulation, alternately pronounce the vowels of *he* and *ah*. You will feel the tongue move from a **high** front to a **low** back position. Once you feel this tongue movement, alternate between the vowels of *ah* and *at*. You will feel the tongue moving from the low **back** to low **front** position. Finally, alternate between the vowels of *he* and *who*. You will notice that in addition to moving your tongue from the high front to the high back position, you are also **rounding** your lips for the [u]. Figure 2.8 shows

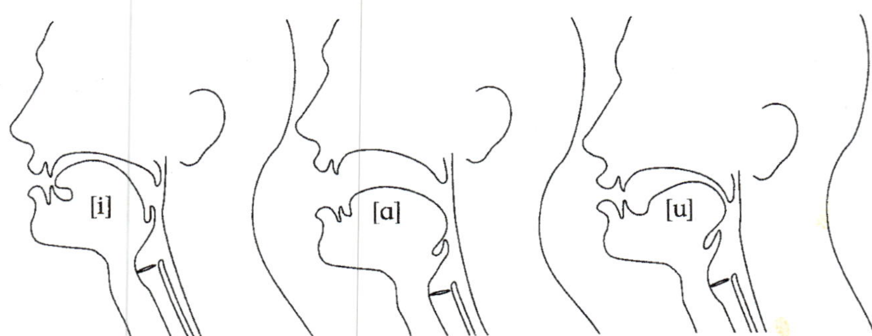

Figure 2.8 Tongue position and transcription for three English vowels

a midsagittal view of the tongue position for the vowels [i], [ɑ], and [u] based on X-ray studies of speech.

Vowels for which the tongue is neither raised nor lowered are called **mid vowels**. The front vowel of English *made* or *fame* is mid, front, and unrounded. The vowel of *code* and *soak* is mid, back, and rounded. In the case of diphthongs, the articulatory descriptions refer to the tongue position of the vowel nucleus. The vowels presented so far in this section are summed up in Table 2.14. Note that in describing the vowels, the articulatory parameters are presented in the order *height, backness, rounding*.

Table 2.14 Basic phonetic parameters for describing American English vowels

heat	[i]	high front unrounded
fate	[ej]	mid front unrounded
mad	[æ]	low front unrounded
Sue	[u]	high back rounded
boat	[ow]	mid back rounded
caught	[ɔ]	mid back rounded
sun	[ʌ]	mid back unrounded
cot	[ɑ]	low back unrounded

In some dialects of North American English, there is no difference between the vowels of a pair of words like *cot* [ɑ] and *caught*, whose vowel is also [ɑ]. In other dialects of North American English, as well as in many other dialects of English worldwide, the vowel of *caught* (and certain other words such as *law*) is the mid back rounded lax vowel [ɔ].

Tongue positions for these vowels are illustrated in Figure 2.9. The trapezoid corresponds roughly to the space within which the tongue moves, which is wider at the top of the oral cavity and more restricted at the bottom. Nonfront vowels are traditionally divided into central and back vowels (see Figures 2.9 and 2.10); often the term back alone is used for all nonfront vowels.

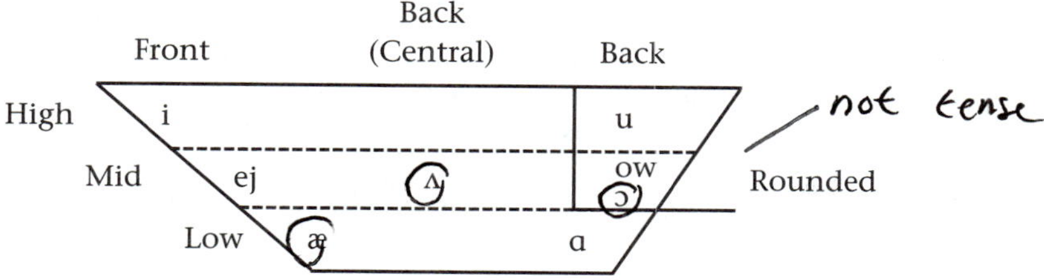

Figure 2.9 Basic tongue positions for English vowels

6.3 Tense and lax vowels

All of the vowels illustrated in Figure 2.9 except [æ], [ʌ], and [ɔ] are **tense vowels**; they are produced with a placement of the tongue that results in greater vocal tract constriction than that of nontense vowels; as well, tense vowels are longer than nontense vowels. Some vowels of English are made with roughly the same tongue position as the tense vowels, but with a less constricted articulation; they are called **lax vowels**.

Table 2.15 Tense and lax vowels in American English

	Tense		*Lax*
heat	[i]	hit	[ɪ]
mate	[ej]	met	[ɛ]
—	—	mat	[æ]
shoot	[u]	should	[ʊ]
coat	[ow]	ought	[ɔ] (in some dialects)
—	—	cut	[ʌ]
—	—	Canada	[ə]
lock	[ɑ]	—	—
lies	[aj]		
loud	[aw]		

Table 2.15 provides examples from English comparing tense and lax vowels. Note that not all the vowels come in tense/lax pairs.

The difference in two vowels illustrated in Table 2.15 is often not easy to hear at first. Both the vowel [ʌ] in *cut, dud, pluck,* and *Hun,* and the vowel [ə] of *Canada, about, tomahawk,* and *sofa* are mid, back, unrounded, and lax. The vowel of the second set of examples, called **schwa**, is referred to as a **reduced vowel**. In addition to being lax, it is characterized by very brief duration (briefer than that of any of the other vowels).

There is a simple test that helps determine whether vowels are tense or lax. In English, monosyllabic words spoken in isolation do not end in lax vowels (except for [ɔ]). We find *see* [si], *say* [sej], *Sue* [su], *so* [sow], and *spa* [spɑ] in English, but not *s[ɪ], *s[ɛ], *s[æ], *s[ʊ], or *s[ʌ]. Schwa, however, frequently appears in unstressed positions in polysyllabic words like *sofa* [ə] and *Canada* [ə]. It should be pointed out—especially for those who think their ears are deceiving them—that many speakers produce the final vowel in the last two examples not as [ə] but as [ʌ].

The representation of vowels and their articulatory positions (Figure 2.9) is expanded in Figure 2.10 to include both tense and lax vowels.

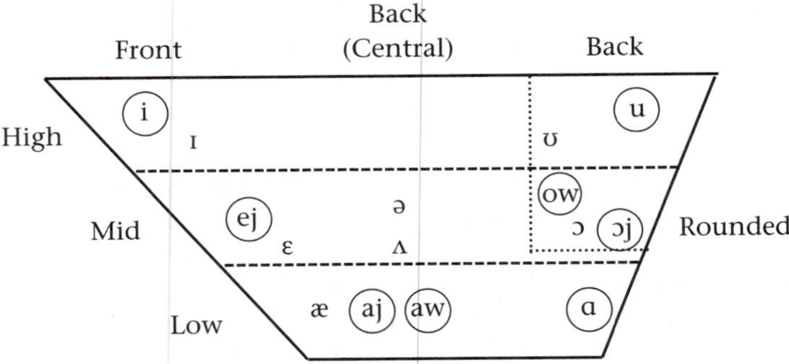

Figure 2.10 American English vowels (tense vowels are circled)

This rather formidable crowd of vowels should not intimidate you. If you are a native speaker of English, you have been using these vowels (and others, some of which you will be introduced to in the next chapter) most of your life. Learning to hear them consciously and transcribe them is not a difficult task. The next section provides more examples of the transcription of English consonants and vowels.

7 PHONETIC TRANSCRIPTION OF AMERICAN ENGLISH CONSONANTS AND VOWELS

Tables 2.16 and 2.17 show the phonetic symbols for consonants and vowels commonly used to transcribe American English. To show how each symbol is used, one word is transcribed completely, and then some other words in which the same sound is found are given. You will notice that in the example words, the spelling of the sound may vary. Be careful of this when you transcribe words phonetically—the sound of a word, not its spelling, is what is transcribed!

Table 2.16 Transcribing English consonants

Symbol	*Word*	*Transcription*	*More examples*
[pʰ]	pit	[pʰɪt]	pain, upon, apart
[p]	spit	[spɪt]	spar, crispy, upper, Yuppie, culprit, bumper
[tʰ]	tick	[tʰɪk]	tell, attire, terror, Tutu
[t]	stuck	[stʌk]	stem, hunter, nasty, mostly

Table 2.16 (continued) Transcribing English consonants

Symbol	Word	Transcription	More examples
[kʰ]	keep	[kʰip]	cow, kernel, recur
[k]	skip	[skɪp]	scatter, uncle, blacklist, likely
[tʃ]	chip	[tʃɪp]	lunch, lecher, ditch, belch
[dʒ]	judge	[dʒʌdʒ]	germ, journal, budge, wedge
[b]	bib	[bɪb]	boat, liberate, rob, blast
[d]	dip	[dɪp]	dust, sled, draft
[ɾ]	butter	[bʌɾər]	madder, matter, hitting, writer, rider
[g]	get	[gɛt]	gape, mugger, twig, gleam
[f]	fit	[fɪt]	flash, coughing, proof, phlegmatic, gopher
[v]	vat	[væt]	vote, oven, prove
[θ]	thick	[θɪk]	thought, ether, teeth, three, bathroom
[ð]	though	[ðow]	then, bother, teethe, bathe
[s]	sip	[sɪp]	psychology, fasten, lunacy, bass, curse, science
[z]	zap	[zæp]	Xerox, scissors, desire, zipper, fuzzy
[ʃ]	ship	[ʃɪp]	shock, nation, mission, glacier, wish
[ʒ]	azure	[æʒər]	measure, rouge, visual, garage (for some speakers), Taj Mahal
[h]	hat	[hæt]	who, ahoy, forehead, behind
[j]	yet	[jɛt]	use, few, yes
[w]	witch	[wɪtʃ]	wait, weird, queen, now
[ʍ]	which	[ʍɪtʃ]	what, where, when (only for some speakers)
[l]	leaf	[lif]	loose, lock, alive, hail
[l̩]	huddle	[hʌdl̩]	bottle, needle (for many speakers)
[r]	reef	[rif]	prod, arrive, tear
[r̩]	bird	[br̩d] [bɚd], [bərd]	early, hurt, stir, purr, doctor
[m]	moat	[mowt]	mind, humor, shimmer, sum, thumb
[m̩]	'm-m'	[ʔm̩ʔm̩]	bottom, random
[n]	note	[nowt]	now, winner, angel, sign, wind
[n̩]	button	[bʌtn̩]	Jordan, batten
[ŋ]	sing	[sɪŋ]	singer, longer, bank, twinkle

Table 2.17 Transcribing English vowels

Symbol	Word	Transcription	More examples
[i]	fee	[fi]	she, cream, believe, receive, serene, amoeba, highly
[ɪ]	fit	[fɪt]	hit, income, definition, been (for some speakers)
[ej]	fate	[fejt]	they, clay, grain, gauge, engage, great, sleigh
[ɛ]	let	[lɛt]	led, head, says, said, sever, guest
[æ]	bat	[bæt]	panic, racket, laugh, Nantucket
[u]	boot	[but]	to, two, loose, brew, Louise, Lucy, through

Table 2.17 (continued) Transcribing English vowels

Symbol	*Word*	*Transcription*	*More examples*
[ʊ]	book	[bʊk]	should, put, hood
[ow]	note	[nowt]	no, throat, though, slow, toe, oaf, O'Conner
[ɔj]	boy	[bɔj]	voice, boil, toy
[ɔ]	fought	[fɔt]	caught, normal, all
[ɑ]	rot	[rɑt]	cot, father, rob
[ʌ]	shut	[ʃʌt]	other, udder, tough, lucky, was, flood
[ə]	roses	[rowzəz]	collide, hinted, telegraph, (to) suspect
[aw]	crowd	[krawd]	(to) house, plow, bough
[aj]	lies	[lajz]	my, tide, thigh, buy

8 SUPRASEGMENTALS

All phones have certain inherent **suprasegmental** or **prosodic properties** that form part of their makeup no matter what their place or manner of articulation. These properties are **pitch**, **loudness**, and **length**.

All sounds give us a subjective impression of being relatively higher or lower in pitch. Pitch is the auditory property of a sound that enables us to place it on a scale that ranges from low to high. Pitch is especially noticeable in sonorous sounds like vowels, glides, liquids, and nasals. Even stop and fricative consonants convey different pitches. This is particularly noticeable among the fricatives, as you can hear by extending the pronunciation of [s] and then of [ʃ]; the [s] is clearly higher pitched. All sounds have some degree of intrinsic loudness as well or they could not be heard. Moreover, all sounds occupy a certain stretch of time—they give the subjective impression of length.

8.1 PITCH: TONE AND INTONATION

Speakers of any language have the ability to control the level of pitch they speak on. This is accomplished by controlling the tension of the vocal folds and the amount of air that passes through the glottis. The combination of tensed vocal folds and greater air pressure results in higher voice pitch on vowels and sonorant consonants, while less tense vocal folds and lower air pressure result in lower voice pitch. Two kinds of controlled pitch movement found in human language are called **tone** and **intonation**.

Tone

A language is said to have tone or be a **tone language** when differences in word meaning are signaled by differences in pitch. Pitch on forms in tone languages functions very differently from the movement of pitch in a non-tone language. When a speaker of English says *a car?* with a rising pitch, the word *car* does not mean anything different from the same form pronounced on a different pitch level or with a different pitch contour. In contrast, when a speaker of a tone language such as Mandarin pronounces the form *ma* with a falling pitch [mà], it means 'scold', but when the same form is pronounced with a rising pitch [má], the meaning is 'hemp' (see Figure 2.13). There is no parallel to anything like this in nontone languages such as English and French.

Some tone languages show tones at only certain pitch levels. Sarcee, an Athapaskan language spoken in Canada, has tones heard at high, mid, and low pitch levels. In Figure 2.11, the uppercase letters H, M, and L stand for high, mid, and low tones, respectively. An **association line**, drawn from the letters to the vowel, links the segments with their respective tones. This type of notation is known as **autosegmental notation** (see Chapter 3, Section 7.2).

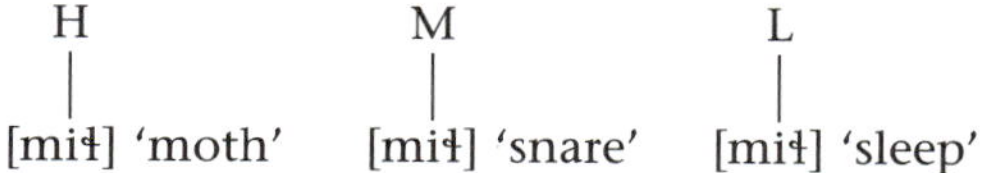

Figure 2.11 Sarcee level tones ([ɬ] is a voiceless lateral fricative)

Level tones that signal meaning differences are called **register tones**: two or three register tones are the norm in most of the world's register-tone languages, though four have been reported for Mazatec, a language spoken in Mexico.

A single tone may be associated with more than one syllabic element. In Mende, a language spoken in West Africa, there are certain polysyllabic forms that show the same tone on each syllable (here, the diacritic [´] indicates a high tone and the diacritic [`] indicates a low tone).

Table 2.18 High-tone and low-tone words in Mende

pɛ́lɛ́	'banana'
háwámá	'waistline'
kpàkàlì	'tripod chair'

Autosegmental notation and association lines allow us to represent the tone as characteristic of an entire form. The single underlying tone unit is associated with all vowels.

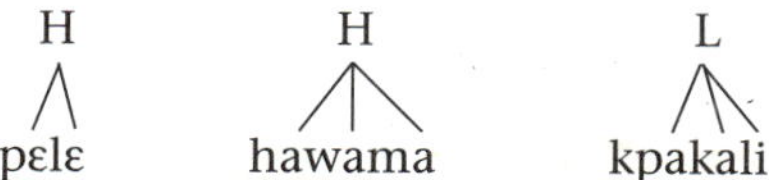

Figure 2.12 Tone as a word feature

In some languages, tones change pitch on single syllabic elements. Moving pitches that signal meaning differences are called **contour tones**. In Mandarin, both register and contour tones are heard. Contour tones are shown by pitch level notation lines that converge above the vowel, as shown in Figure 2.13. In Figure 2.13, there is one (high) register tone. The other tones are all contour tones.

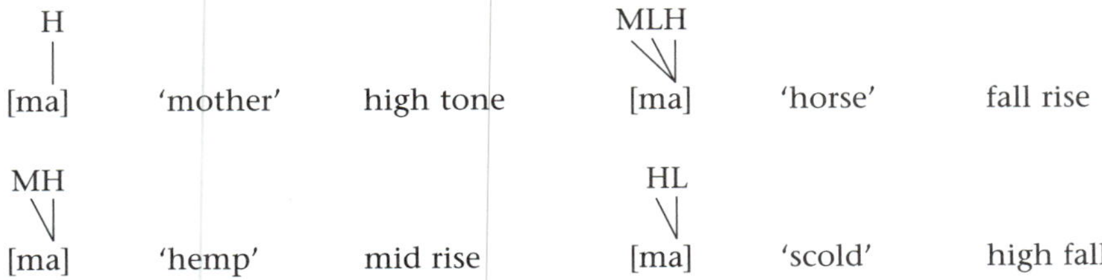

Figure 2.13 Register and contour tones in Mandarin

In other languages, tone can have a grammatical function. In Bini, a language spoken in Nigeria, tone can signal differences in the tense of a verb (such as past versus present), as Figure 2.14 shows.

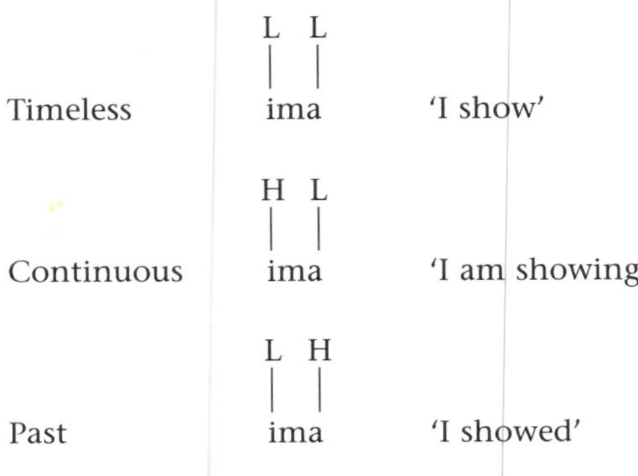

Figure 2.14 Tense and tone in Bini

Although tones may seem exotic to native speakers of Western European languages, they are very widespread. Tone languages are found throughout North and South America, sub-Saharan Africa, and the Far East.

Intonation

Pitch movement in spoken utterances that is not related to differences in word meaning is called intonation. It makes no difference to the meaning of the word *seven*, for example, whether it is pronounced with a rising pitch or a falling pitch.

Intonation often does serve to convey information of a broadly meaningful nature, however. For example, the falling pitch we hear at the end of a statement in English such as *Fred parked the car* signals that the utterance is complete. For this reason, falling intonation at the end of an utterance is called a **terminal (intonation) contour**. Conversely, a rising or level intonation, called a **nonterminal (intonation) contour**, often signals incompleteness. Nonterminal contours are often heard in the nonfinal forms found in lists and telephone numbers.

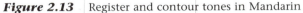

Sally Fred Helen and Joe

two eight four two five one three

Figure 2.15 Rising nonterminal intonations in a list and a telephone number

In questions, final rising intonations also signal a kind of incompleteness in that they indicate that a conversational exchange is not finished.

Did you have a nice time

Figure 2.16 Nonterminal intonation in a question

However, English sentences that contain question words like *who, what, when,* and *how* (for example, *What did you buy?*) do not ordinarily have rising intonation. It is as if the question word itself is enough to indicate that an answer is expected.

Intonation can be represented graphically as in Figures 2.15 and 2.16. A more formal way of representing intonation is shown in Figure 2.17. Here, as in tonal representation, L and H are relative terms for differences in pitch. The letters HL are placed above the syllabic elements on which the pitch change occurs. The dotted lines indicate that the lowering pitch spreads across the remaining pitch-bearing elements.

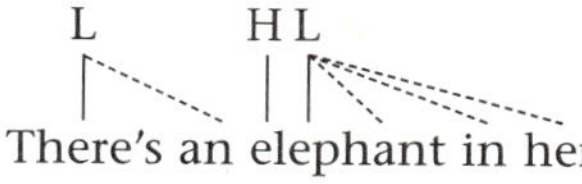

L HL

There's an elephant in here.

Figure 2.17 A terminal contour

Rising intonation on names or requests is common when people are being addressed. Its use indicates that the speaker is opening a conversation or that some further action is expected from the addressee.

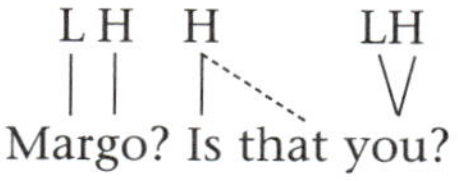

LH H LH

Margo? Is that you?

Figure 2.18 Two nonterminal contours

The complex uses of intonation have just been touched on here. Consider, for example, that rising intonation is often used to express politeness, as in *Please sit down.* Some linguists think that this use is an extension of the "open-ended mode" of intonation, and that since a rising intonation indicates that further response is expected (but not demanded) of the addressee, a sentence uttered with a rising intonation sounds less like an order and therefore is more polite.

Intonation and tone

Tone and intonation are not mutually exclusive. Tone languages show intonation of all types. This is possible since the tones are not absolute but relative pitches. A tone is perceived as high if it is high relative to the pitches around it. As long as this relative difference is maintained, the pitch distinctions will also be maintained. Figure 2.19 shows this graphically. It represents the overall pitch of a declarative sentence in Igbo, a West African language with register tones. Note how an Igbo speaker clearly maintains the distinction among the pitch registers even as the overall pitch of the utterance falls. Each high tone is always lower than the preceding high tone, but higher than the low tone that immediately precedes it. This phenomenon is known as **downdrift**.

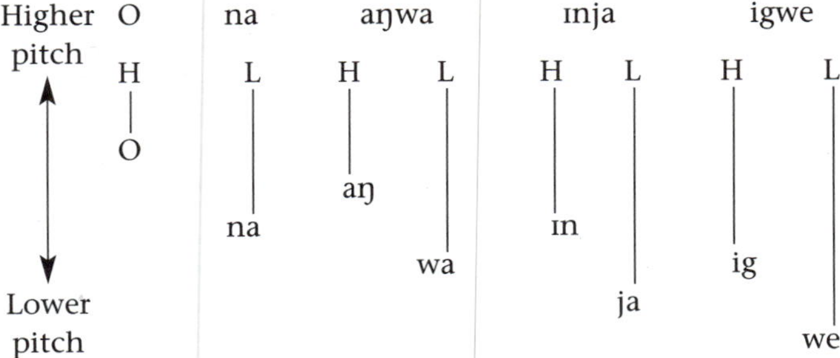

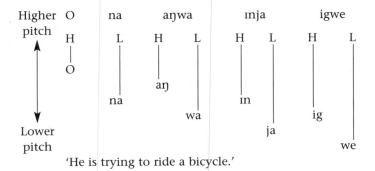

'He is trying to ride a bicycle.'

Figure 2.19 Tone and intonation: downdrift in Igbo

8.2 Length

In many languages there are both vowels and consonants whose articulation takes longer relative to that of other vowels and consonants. This phenomenon, known as length, is widespread in the world's languages. Length is indicated in phonetic transcription by the use of an IPA style colon [ː] (or simply a colon in North American transcription [:]) placed after the segment in question.

Italian, Hungarian, German, Cree, and Finnish are a few of the many languages that have short and long vowels. Table 2.19 shows short and long vowels in pairs of words in Yap, a language spoken on the island of Yap in the Western Pacific.

Table 2.19 Short and long vowels in Yap

[θis]	'to topple'	[θiːs]	'(a) post'
[pul]	'to gather'	[puːl]	'moon'
[ʔer]	'near you'	[ʔeːr]	'part of a lagoon'

Table 2.20 shows short and long consonants in pairs of words in Italian. Long and short consonants are also found in many other languages, including Finnish, Turkish, and Hungarian.

Table 2.20 Short and long consonants in Italian

fato	[fato]	'fate'	fatto	[fatːo]	'fact'
fano	[fano]	'grove'	fanno	[fanːo]	'they do'
casa	[kasa]	'house'	cassa	[kasːa]	'box'

8.3 Stress

In any utterance, some vowels are perceived as more prominent than others. In a word such as *telegraphic* [tʰɛ̀ləgrǽfɪk], the two vowel nuclei that are more prominent than the others are [ɛ] and [æ]. Syllabic segments perceived as relatively more prominent are stressed. **Stress** is a cover term for the combined effects of pitch, loudness, and length—the result of which is perceived prominence. In each language, the effect of these prosodic features varies. In general, English stressed vowels are higher in pitch, longer, and louder than unstressed ones. But this is not always the case. The example word *telegraphic* could just as well be pronounced with the stressed syllables lower than the unstressed ones. The important thing is that they be prominent with respect to the syllables around them, and this is usually accomplished by a relatively large shift in one, two, or all three of the parameters of pitch, loudness, and length.

In some languages, the impression of vowel prominence results from an interaction of the prosodic parameters that is different from that found in English. In Modern Greek, for example, syllables tend to be of equal length. Stress, therefore, is manifested by a change only in pitch and loudness and not in syllable length. Tone languages do not change the pitch level or contour of tones to mark stress. In many of these languages, relative prominence is marked by exaggerating the vowel length or pitch contour.

There are various ways to mark stress in phonetic transcription. North American transcription commonly uses an acute accent [´] placed over the vowel nucleus in question to mark the most prominent or **primary stress**, and a grave accent [`] to mark the second most prominent or **secondary stress** or stresses. (This should not be confused with the use of the same diacritics to mark tone in tone languages.) Stress can also be marked by placing numbers above the stressed vowels, usually 1 for a primary stress and 2 for a secondary stress. The word *telegraphic* is transcribed as either of the following:

2)

[tʰɛ̀ləgrǽfɪk] or [tʰɛ²ləgræ¹fɪk]

The examples in Table 2.21 show some differences in English stress placement.

Table 2.21 Differing stress placement in English

(an) éxport	[ɛ́kspɔrt]	(to) expórt	[ɛkspɔ́rt]
(a) présent	[prɛ́zənt]	(to) presént	[prəzɛ́nt]
télegràph	[tʰɛ́ləgræ̀f]		
telégraphy	[tʰəlɛ́grəfì]		
tèlegráphic	[tʰɛ̀ləgrǽfɪk]		

In these examples, you can also see that the quality of certain vowels varies depending on whether they are stressed or unstressed. This phenomenon is common in English, Russian, Palauan, and many other languages but is not universal.

9 PROCESSES

Speech production is not a series of isolated events. The process of articulation is a complex one. The articulatory organs are operating independently of each other, and many fine adjustments are carried out very rapidly as we speak. As a consequence, speech production often results in the articulation of one sound affecting that of another sound.

9.1 Coarticulation

Figures 2.5 to 2.7 showed how aspiration results from **coarticulation**. Figure 2.20 shows more complex aspects of coarticulation. Here, some of the articulatory organs involved in the production of the word *pan* are represented. Reading from top to bottom, the actions of the lips, tongue, velum, and glottis are shown. The bold black line in each box represents the state of articulation listed to the right of the box.

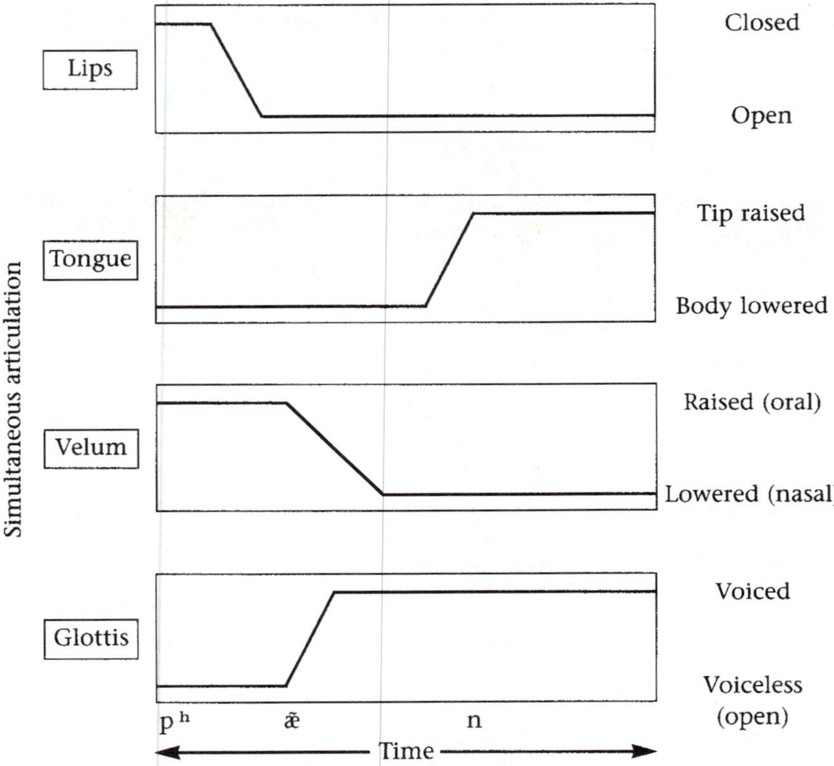

Figure 2.20 Coarticulation among several articulatory parameters of the word *pan*

Lips

The raised line in the upper box indicates that the lips are closed for the articulation of the initial [p] of *pan*. In order to articulate the vowel, the lips are opened—represented by the change in the position of the line—and they stay open during the articulation of the [n].

Tongue

The tongue body is lowered in anticipation of the low front vowel [æ] during articulation of the word-initial consonant. As the vowel articulation ends, the tongue tip is raised to articulate the final [n] of the word.

Velum

You have seen how nasal consonants are produced with the velum lowered to allow air to pass through the nasal cavities. The raising and lowering of the velum is not always precisely coordinated with other speech production activity. Speakers often anticipate lowering the velum for nasal consonants and, consequently, produce a nasal vowel before a nasal consonant. Many English speakers do this consistently in fluent speech when they pronounce words like *pan* [pʰæ̃n] or *bank* [bæ̃ŋk] (the tilde [˜] over the vowel indicates nasality). This is reflected in Figure 2.20. The line representing the velum closure changes to the open (lowered) position during the articulation of the vowel, before the tongue tip raises to articulate the word-final [n].

Glottis

You have already seen in Section 5.5 how aspiration results from a delay in voicing after the release of a voiceless stop. Aspiration is shown in Figure 2.20 by the black line remaining in the voiceless position even after the lips have opened and the vowel articulation is in place.

Consonant coarticulation with vowels

All speech is characterized by the kind of complex coarticulation among the articulatory organs illustrated in Figure 2.20. Another typical coarticulation phenomenon occurs when we pronounce the sound [k] before the vowel [i] in English in words such as *keys* and *keel*. The [k] we articulate before [i] is pronounced with the back of the tongue so far forward it nearly touches the palate (and is transcribed as [k̑]). It is scarcely a velar articulation at all for many speakers. The [k] we pronounce before the vowels [ɑ] and [ow] in words such as *cot* and *cold* is articulated further back and is a true velar. These adjustments are made in anticipation of the tongue position that will be needed for the vowel in question: front for the [i] and back for the [ɑ] and [ow]. The [k] pronounced before the vowel [u] in a word such as *cool* also shows lip rounding in anticipation of the following (back) rounded vowel and is transcribed as [kʷ].

9.2 PROCESSES AND EFFICIENCY

Articulatory adjustments that occur during the production of connected speech are called **processes**. Their cumulative effect often results in making words easier to articulate, and in this sense they are said to make speech more efficient. For example, when speakers of English nasalize the vowel of *bank*, they do not delay lowering the velum until the exact moment the nasal consonant articulation is reached. Most English speakers begin lowering the velum for a nasal consonant almost as soon as they articulate the vowel that precedes it.

In a parallel manner, when speakers pronounce [k̑] as more palatal in a word such as *key*, they are speaking more efficiently from the point of view of articulation since they are making a less drastic adjustment in moving from the articulation of a more palatal [k̑] to that of a high front vowel than they would make in moving from a velar [k] to a high front vowel. Even more drastically, a speaker of English who says [pr̥ejd] for *parade* is making a major adjustment that results in a more efficient articulation: the two syllables of a careful pronunciation of *parade* are reduced to one by dropping the unstressed vowel of the first syllable; the tongue position for [r] can be anticipated during pronunciation of the [p]; finally, the voicelessness of the initial stop is carried on through the [r̥].

9.3 Processes and clarity

Some processes appear to make articulation less rather than more efficient. For example, English speakers often lengthen consonants and vowels when they are asked to repeat a word that someone has not heard clearly. The following kind of exchange is typical.

3)

"It's Fred."
"Did you say, 'It's red'?"
"No, I said, 'Fffreeed!'"

Lengthening segments results in a greater articulatory effort, but the process results in a form being more distinct and therefore easier to perceive.

Another process that results in more easily perceivable speech adds a segment under certain conditions. When speaking slowly and carefully in a noisy environment, for example, English speakers often insert a vowel inside a group of consonants. This breaks up the sequence of consonants into separate syllables. Judging from the use people often make of this process when they wish to be clearly understood, it may well make words easier to perceive.

4)

"Stop screaming!"
"What?"
"I said, 'Stop sc[ə]reaming.'"

These examples show that there are two basic reasons for the existence of articulatory processes. Some processes result in a more efficient articulation of a series of sounds in that the precise timing and coordination of speech is relaxed to various degrees. Other processes result in a more distinct output, which is easier to perceive than fluent or rapid everyday speech. Although these two types of processes might at first appear to be contradictory, each serves a particular end in speech production.

9.4 Articulatory processes

Only a finite number of processes operate in language, though the end result is a great deal of linguistic variability. In this section, we survey some of the most common of these processes.

Assimilation

A number of different processes, collectively known as **assimilation**, result from the influence of one segment on another. Assimilation always results from a sound becoming more like another nearby sound in terms of one or more of its phonetic characteristics.

Nasalization of a vowel before a nasal consonant is caused by speakers anticipating the lowering of the velum in advance of a nasal segment. The result is that the preceding segment takes on the nasality of the following consonant as in [k^{h}æ̃nt] *can't*. This type of assimilation is known as **regressive assimilation**, since the nasalization is, in effect, moving *backward* to a preceding segment.

The nasalization of vowels following nasal consonants in Scots Gaelic (see Table 2.22) is an example of **progressive assimilation**, since the nasality moves *forward* from the nasal consonant onto the vowel. This results from not immediately raising the velum after the production of a nasal stop.

Table 2.22 Progressive nasalization of vowels in Scots Gaelic

[mõːr]	'big'
[nĩ]	'cattle'
[mũ]	'about'
[nẽːl]	'cloud'

Voicing assimilation is also widespread. For many speakers of English, voiceless liquids and glides occur after voiceless stops in words such as *please* [pl̥iz], *proud* [pr̥awd], and *pure* [pj̊uwr]. These sounds are said to be devoiced in this environment. **Devoicing** is a kind of assimilation. Here, the vocal folds are not set in motion immediately after the release of the voiceless consonant closure. The opposite of devoicing is voicing. In Dutch, voiceless fricatives assimilate to the voicing of the stops that follow them, in anticipation of the voiced consonant. For example, the word *af* [ɑf] 'off, over' is pronounced with a [v] in the words *afbelen* 'to ring off' and *afdeken* 'to cover over'.

Assimilation for place of articulation is also widespread in the world's languages. Nasal consonants are very likely to undergo this type of assimilation, as shown in Table 2.23.

Table 2.23 Assimilation for place of articulation in English

possible	impossible
potent	impotent
tolerable	intolerable
tangible	intangible

The negative form of each of these words is made with either *im* or *in*. In both cases, the form shows a nasal consonant that has the same place of articulation as the stop consonant that follows it: labial in the case of *possible* and *potent*, and alveolar in the case of *tolerable* and *tangible*. In informal speech, many English speakers pronounce words like *inconsequential* and *inconsiderate* with an [ŋ] where the spelling shows *n*. Assimilation can also be heard in pronunciations such as *Va*[ŋ]*couver* and *Ba*[ɱ]*ff* (the symbol [ɱ] represents a labiodental nasal). Assimilation may even cross the boundaries between words. In rapid speech, it is not uncommon to hear people pronounce phrases such as *in code* as [ɪŋk^{h}owd].

The preceding English example shows regressive assimilation to place of articulation. The following example, taken from German, shows progressive assimilation that again affects nasal consonants. In careful speech, certain German verb forms are pronounced with a final [ən], as in *laden* 'to invite', *loben* 'to praise', and *backen* 'to bake'. In informal speech, the final [ən] is reduced to a syllabic nasal, which takes on the point of articulation of the preceding consonant. (Recall that the diacritic line under the phonetically transcribed nasals indicates that they are syllabic.)

Table 2.24 Progressive assimilation in German

Careful speech		*Informal speech*	
laden	[laːdən]	[laːdn̩]	'to invite'
loben	[loːbən]	[loːbm̩]	'to praise'
backen	[bakən]	[bakŋ̍]	'to bake'

Flapping is a process in which a dental or alveolar stop articulation changes to a flap [ɾ] articulation. In American English, this process applies to both [t] and [d] and occurs between vowels, the first of which is generally stressed. Flaps are heard in the casual speech pronunciation of words such as *butter, writer, fatter, wader,* and *waiter*, and even in phrases such as *I bought it* [ajbɔ́ɾɪt]. The alveolar flap is always voiced. Flapping is considered a type of assimilation since it changes a noncontinuant segment (a stop) to a continuant segment in the environment of other continuants (vowels). In addition, we may note that voicing assimilation also occurs in the change of the voiceless [t] to the voiced [ɾ].

Dissimilation

Dissimilation, the opposite of assimilation, results in two sounds becoming less alike in articulatory or acoustic terms. The resulting sequence of sounds is easier to articulate and distinguish. It is a much rarer process than assimilation. One commonly heard example of dissimilation in English occurs in words ending with three consecutive fricatives, such as *fifths*. Many speakers dissimilate the final [fθs] sequence to [fts], apparently to break up the sequence of three fricatives with a stop.

Deletion

Deletion is a process that removes a segment from certain phonetic contexts. Deletion occurs in everyday rapid speech in many languages. In English, a schwa [ə] is often deleted when the next vowel in the word is stressed.

Table 2.25 Deletion of [ə] in English

Slow speech	*Rapid speech*	
[pʰəréjd]	[pr̥éjd]	parade
[kʰərówd]	[kr̥ówd]	corrode
[səpʰówz]	[spówz]	suppose

Deletion also occurs as an alternative to dissimilation in words such as *fifths*. Many speakers delete the [θ] of the final consonant cluster and say [fɪfs]. In very rapid speech, both the second [f] and [θ] are sometimes deleted, resulting in [fɪs].

Epenthesis

Epenthesis is a process that inserts a syllabic or a nonsyllabic segment within an existing string of segments. For example, in careful speech, the words *warmth* and *something* are pronounced [wɔrmθ] and [sʌ̃mθĩŋ] (see Table 2.26). It is common in casual speech for speakers to insert a [p] between the *m* and the *th* and pronounce the words [wɔrmpθ] and [sʌ̃mpθĩŋ]. Consonant epenthesis of this type is another example of a coarticulation phenomenon. In English, the articulatory transition from a sonorant consonant to a nonsonorant consonant appears to be eased by the insertion of a consonant that shares properties of both segments. Notice that the epenthesized consonants are all nonsonorant, have the same place of articulation as the sonorant consonant before them, and have the same voicing as the nonsonorant consonant after them.

Table 2.26 Some examples of English consonant epenthesis

Word	*Nonepenthesized pronunciation*	*Epenthesized pronunciation*
something	[sʌ̃mθĩŋ]	[sʌ̃mpθĩŋ]
warmth	[wɔrmθ]	[wɔrmpθ]
length	[lɛ̃ŋθ]	[lɛ̃ŋkθ]
prince	[prĩns]	[prĩnts]
tenth	[tɛ̃nθ]	[tɛ̃ntθ]

Vowels may also be epenthesized. In Turkish, a word may not begin with two consonants. When words are borrowed into Turkish, an epenthetic vowel is inserted between certain sequences of two initial consonants, creating a new and permissible sequence (see Table 2.27). (The reason for the differences among the vowels need not concern us here; note, though, that the vowel is always high; see Section 10.1 for further presentation of these and other unfamiliar symbols.)

Table 2.27 Vowel epenthesis in Turkish

Source word	*Turkish form*
train	[tiren]
club	[kylʏp]
sport	[sɯpor]

Metathesis

Metathesis is a process that reorders a sequence of segments. Metathesis often results in a sequence of phones that is easier to articulate. It is common to hear metathesis in the speech of children, who often cannot pronounce all the consonant sequences that adults can. For example, some English-speaking children pronounce *spaghetti* as *pesghetti* [pəskɛɾi]. In this form, the initial sequence [spə], which is often difficult for children to pronounce, is metathesized to [pəs].

The pronunciations of *prescribe* and *prescription* as *perscribe* and *perscription* are often-cited examples of metathesis in adult speech. In these cases, metathesis appears to facilitate the pronunciation of two successive consonant-*r* sequences in each word.

Vowel reduction

In many languages, the articulation of vowels may move to a more central position when the vowels are unstressed. This process is known as **(vowel) reduction**. Typically, the outcome of vowel reduction is a schwa [ə]; this can be observed in pairs of related words that show different stress placement, such as *Canada* [kʰǽnədə] versus *Canadian* [kʰənéjdijən]. Note that the first vowel of the words *Canada/Canadian* is [æ] when stressed but a schwa when unstressed, while the second vowel is [ej] when stressed but a schwa when unstressed. Since we cannot predict what vowel a schwa may "turn into" when it is stressed, we assume that [æ] and [ej] are basic to the words in question and are reduced in unstressed positions.

10 OTHER VOWELS AND CONSONANTS *(ADVANCED)*

This chapter has considered only the vowels and consonants of English, many of which are found in other languages. There are also many speech sounds found in the world's languages that are not heard in English. Since phonetic descriptions are universally valid, once the basic articulatory parameters have been mastered it is not too difficult to describe and even to pronounce less familiar sounds. This section presents a number of speech sounds found in other languages.

10.1 VOWELS

Front vowels, which in English are always unrounded, can also be rounded. A high front tense rounded vowel is heard in French *pur* 'pure', German *Bücher* 'books', and Turkish *düğme* 'button'. It is transcribed as [y] in IPA transcription but as [ü] in North America—a difference that sometimes leads to confusion. A rounded high front lax vowel, transcribed as [ʏ], is heard in Canadian French *lune* 'moon' and *duc* 'duke'. A rounded mid front tense vowel, transcribed as [ø] (NA [ö]), is found in French *peu* 'few' and German *schön* 'beautiful'. A rounded mid front lax vowel, transcribed as [œ], is heard in French *œuf* 'egg' and *peur* 'fear', German *örtlich* 'local', and Turkish *göl* 'lake'. Back vowels may be unrounded; a high back unrounded vowel, transcribed as [ɯ], is heard in Russian words like *byl* 'was', and Rumanian *mînă* 'hand'. These vowels, as well as other "exotic" ones, are found in many other languages as well. Table 2.28 illustrates the vowels presented in this chapter (UR = unrounded; R =

rounded). Note carefully that the tense vowels are presented without glides. This is intentional; whereas certain English tense vowels are followed by glides, the tense vowels of the languages cited here (and many others) are not.

Table 2.28 Articulatory grid of vowels presented in this chapter

	Front		*Back (Central)*		*Back*	
	UR	*R*	*UR*	*R*	*UR*	*R*
High	i	y			ɯ	u tense
	ɪ	ʏ				ʊ lax
Mid	e	ø	ə (reduced)			o tense
	ɛ	œ	ʌ			ɔ lax
Low	æ (lax)		a (lax)		ɑ (tense)	

Nasal vowels

Nasal vowels, like nasal consonants, are produced with a lowered velum. Air passes simultaneously through the oral and nasal cavities. Nasal vowels can be heard in English, French, Portuguese, Polish, Hindi, and a wide variety of other languages (see Table 2.29). They are often transcribed with a tilde [˜] over the vowel symbol.

Table 2.29 Some nasal vowels

English	win	[wĩn]	'win'
French	pain	[pɛ̃]	'bread'
Portuguese	cento	[sẽntu]	'one hundred'
Polish	ząb	[zɔ̃p]	'tooth'

10.2 Consonants

The same consonants found in English are widespread in other languages. A few additional consonants are introduced in this section.

Stops

In many European languages, we find not the alveolar stops [t], [d], and [n], but the dental stops [t̪], [d̪], and [n̪]. Although this seems like a very slight difference in articulation, it can be readily observed in the speech of French, Spanish, or Italian speakers.

Other stop positions are common in the world's languages. Serbo-Croatian has both a voiceless and a voiced palatal stop in words like *ćaśa* 'dish' and *đak* 'pupil'. These are transcribed as [c] and [ɟ], respectively. Inuktitut dialects show a voiceless and voiced uvular stop pair in words like *imaq* 'sea' and *ugsik* 'cow'. These are transcribed as [q] and [ɢ], respectively. A nasal stop is also made at the palatal point of articulation, as in Spanish *año* 'year' (transcribed as [ɲ] in IPA and as [ñ] in North America), and at the uvula as well, where it is transcribed as [ɴ].

We now return to the glottal state known as whispery voice or murmur that was introduced in Section 2.3. In Hindi there is a series of stops sometimes incorrectly referred to as "voiced aspirated stops" that make use of whispery voice (murmur). These stops are traditionally represented with a following *h* (e.g., *bh, dh, sh*); the double underdots of IPA standard are used here.

In Table 2.30, examples of non-English stop articulations and glottal states are laid out. The distinction between dentals and alveolars is not indicated in the transcription, since most of the world's languages have either dental or alveolar stop articulations, but not both. Sounds found in English are set off in boxes.

Table 2.30 Stops

	Bilabial	*Dental/ alveolar*	*Palatal*	*Velar*	*Uvular*	*Glottal*
Voiceless	[p]	[t]	[c]	[k]	[q]	[ʔ]
Voiced	[b]	[d]	[ɟ]	[g]	[ɢ]	
Murmured	[b̤]	[d̤]	[ɟ̤]	[g̤]		
Nasal	[m]	[n]	[ɲ]	[ŋ]	[ɴ]	

Fricatives

Fricatives other than those of English are found in the world's languages. A bilabial fricative, produced by drawing the lips almost together and forcing the airstream through the narrow opening, is found in many languages. The voiceless bilabial fricative [ɸ] is heard word-initially in the Japanese word *Fuji* (the mountain). The voiced bilabial fricative [β] is found in Spanish words like *deber* 'to owe'. A voiceless palatal fricative [ç] is found in Standard German as in the word *ich* 'I'. Velar fricatives are not found in English but are widespread in the world's languages. The voiceless velar fricative [x] is common in German and Russian. (The composer Bach's name, pronounced in German, has this sound.) A voiced velar fricative [ɣ] is commonly heard in Spanish words like *agua* 'water'.

Table 2.31 presents a grid on which some common fricative consonants are ranged according to point and manner of articulation. As in Table 2.30, dentals are not distinguished from alveolars, as most languages have sounds with either one or the other point of articulation, but not both. Sounds found in English are set off in boxes.

Table 2.31 Fricatives

	Bilabial	*Labio-dental*	*Inter-dental*	*Alveolar*	*Alveo-palatal*	*Palatal*	*Velar*	*Glottal*
Voiceless	[ɸ]	[f]	[θ]	[s]	[ʃ]	[ç]	[x]	[h]
Voiced	[β]	[v]	[ð]	[z]	[ʒ]	[ʝ]	[ɣ]	

Affricates

Affricates are found at most points of articulation. In German, a voiceless labiodental affricate transcribed as [p^f] is heard at the beginning of the word *Pferd* 'horse.' Some New York speakers produce voiceless and voiced dental (or alveolar) affricates [t^s] and [d^z] in words like *time* and *dime*.

Table 2.32 presents a grid including the two English affricates and some others commonly found in other languages. The English sounds are again set off in a box.

Table 2.32 Affricates

	Labiodental	*Alveolar*	*Alveopalatal*	*Velar*
Voiceless	[p^f]	[t^s]	[tʃ]	[kx]
Voiced	[b^v]	[d^z]	[dʒ]	[gɣ]

Liquids

As with the stops, laterals may be dental as well as alveolar. Laterals can also be made with the tongue body raised to the palate. Such a sound is called a palatal lateral, and is transcribed with the symbol [ʎ]. It is heard in some pronunciations of the Spanish words *caballo* 'horse' and *calle* 'street', and in the Serbo-Croatian words *dalje* 'farther' and *ljudi* 'people'. The palatal lateral may also be voiceless, in which case it is transcribed as [ʎ̥].

Lateral fricatives are produced when a lateral is made with a narrow enough closure to be classified as a fricative. This sound is transcribed as [lʒ] when voiced and [ɬ] when voiceless. Lateral fricatives can be heard in many American Indian languages, in Welsh, and in the languages spoken in the Caucasus. Table 2.33 shows some examples of voiceless alveolar lateral fricatives in Welsh.

Table 2.33 Voiceless lateral fricatives in Welsh

llan	[ɬan]	'clan'
ambell	[ambɛɬ]	'some'

Other *r*-like sounds are widely heard in the world's languages. A common one is the **trill**, which is made by passing air over the raised tongue tip and allowing it to vibrate. Trills are commonly transcribed as [r] (IPA), but as [r̃] in North American. They can be heard in the Spanish words *perro* 'dog' and *río* 'river', and the Italian words *carro* 'wagon' and *birra* 'beer'. A similar trilling effect can be made with the uvula and is called a uvular trill. Its IPA symbol is [ʀ].

A uvular *r* made without trilling is more commonly heard, however. This is the voiced *r* of Standard European French, and is also widespread in German. IPA transcription classifies this sound along with the fricatives. It is transcribed as [χ] when voiceless and as [ʁ] when voiced.

Table 2.34 presents the liquids. As before, sounds found in English are set off in boxes. Flaps and trills can be voiceless as well. Voicelessness for these sounds is usually indicated by a small open circle beneath the symbol, as in [r̥̃] or [ʀ̥].

Table 2.34 Liquids

		Dental/alveolar	Palatal	Uvular
Laterals				
	Voiced	[l]	[ʎ]	
	Voiceless	[l̥]	[ʎ̥]	
Lateral fricatives				
	Voiced	[ɮ]		
	Voiceless	[ɬ]		
r's				
	Retroflex	[r]		
	Flap	[ɾ]		
	Trill	[r̃]		[ʀ]

Glides

Other glides are found in the world's languages. A commonly heard one is made with the tongue position of [j] but with the lips rounded. It is transcribed as [ɥ] and can be heard in French words such as [ɥit] *huit* 'eight', [ɥil] *huile* 'oil', and [ɥitχ] *huître* 'oyster'.

Summing up

The study of the sounds of human language is called **phonetics**. These sounds are widely transcribed by means of the **International Phonetic Alphabet**.

The sounds of language are commonly described in **articulatory** and **acoustic** terms, and fall into two major types: syllabic sounds (**vowels**, **syllabic liquids**, and **syllabic nasals**) and nonsyllabic sounds (**consonants** and **glides**). Sounds may be **voiced** or **voiceless**, and **oral** or **nasal**. Consonants are produced at various **places of articulation**: labial, dental, alveolar, alveopalatal, palatal, velar, uvular, glottal, and pharyngeal. At the places of articulation, the airstream is modified by different **manners of articulation** and the resulting sounds are **stops**, **fricatives**, or **affricates**. Vowels are produced with less drastic closure and are described with reference to tongue position (**high**, **low**, **back**, and **front**), tension (**tense** or **lax**), and lip rounding (**rounded** or **unrounded**). Language also exhibits **suprasegmental** phenomena such as **tone**, **intonation**, and **stress**.

Key terms

General terms

acoustic phonetics
articulatory phonetics
diacritic
features
International Phonetic Alphabet (IPA)
phones

phonetics
segments
speech sounds
syllable

Parts of the vocal tract below the mouth

arytenoids
cricoid cartilage
diaphragm
glottis
intercostals
larynx
pharynx
thyroid cartilage
trachea
vocal folds (vocal cords)
vocal tract

Terms concerning glottal states

murmur
voiced (sounds)
voiceless (sounds)
whisper
whispery voice

Terms concerning sound classes

consonants
glides
nonsyllabic
sonorous (sounds)
sound classes
syllabic
vowels

Terms concerning the mouth

alveolar ridge
dorsum
palate
tongue back
tongue blade
tongue body
tongue root
tongue tip
uvula
velum

Types of sounds based on places (points) of articulation

alveopalatal
bilabial (sounds)
dentals
glottals
interdental (sounds)
labial (sounds)
labiodentals
labiovelar (sounds)
palatals
pharyngeals
uvulars
velars

General terms concerning manners of articulation

manners of articulation
nasal phones
oral phones

Terms for consonant sounds based on manner of articulation

affricates
aspiration
continuants
flap
fricatives
laterals
liquids
nonstridents
retroflex
sibilants
stops
stridents
syllabic liquids
syllabic nasals

Terms used for vowel sounds

back
diphthongs
front
high
lax vowels
low
mid vowels
reduced vowel
rounding
schwa
simple vowels
tense vowels
vowel qualities

Terms concerning suprasegmental properties

association line
autosegmental notation
contour tones
downdrift
intonation
length
loudness
nonterminal (intonation) contour
nucleus
pitch
primary stress
prosodic properties
register tones
secondary stress
stress
suprasegmental
syllable
terminal (intonation) contour
tone
tone language

Terms concerning sounds in context

assimilation
coarticulation
deletion
devoicing
dissimilation
epenthesis
flapping
metathesis
nasalization
processes
progressive assimilation
regressive assimilation
voicing assimilation
(vowel) reduction

Sounds in world languages

lateral fricatives
nasal vowels
trill

Sources

Information on the International Phonetic Alphabet can be obtained from the International Phonetic Association, University College, Gower Street, London, WC1E 6BT, England (Web site: http://www.arts.gla.ac.uk/IPA/ipa.html). Sarcee data are taken from E.-D. Cook, "Vowels and Tones in Sarcee," *Language* 47:164–79; Gaelic data are courtesy of James Galbraith. Bini data are adapted from Ladefoged (cited below). For a discussion of glottal states, see Jimmy G. Harris, "The State of the Glottis for Voiceless Plosives," *Proceedings of the 14th International Congress of Phonetic Sciences* 3:2041–2044. More detailed reading on the phonetics of English and other languages is reported below.

Recommended reading

Catford, J. C. 1977. *Fundamental Problems in Phonetics*. Bloomington, IN: Indiana University Press.

Cruttenden, Alan. 1986. *Intonation*. Cambridge, UK: Cambridge University Press.

Fromkin, V. A., ed. 1978. *Tone: A Linguistic Survey*. New York: Academic Press.

Ladefoged, P. 1982. *A Course in Phonetics*. 2nd ed. Toronto: Harcourt Brace Jovanovich.

Ladefoged, P., and I. Maddieson. 1995. *The Sounds of the World's Languages*. Cambridge, MA: Blackwell.

Pullum, G. K., and W. A. Ladusaw. 1986. *Phonetic Symbol Guide*. Chicago: University of Chicago Press.

Rogers, H. 1991. *Theoretical and Practical Phonetics*. Toronto: Copp Clark Pitman.

Shearer, William M. 1968. *Illustrated Speech Anatomy*. Springfield, IL: Charles C. Thomas.

Walker, Douglas C. 1984. *The Pronunciation of Canadian French*. Ottawa: University of Ottawa Press.

Appendix: The International Phonetic Alphabet (condensed)

CONSONANTS

	Bilabial	Labiodental	Dental	Alveolar	Postalveolar	Retroflex	Palatal	Velar	Uvular	Pharyngeal	Glottal
Plosive	p b			t d		ʈ ɖ	c ɟ	k g	q ɢ		ʔ
Nasal	m	ɱ		n		ɳ	ɲ	ŋ	ɴ		
Trill	ʙ			r					ʀ		
Tap or Flap				ɾ		ɽ					
Fricative	ɸ β	f v	θ ð	s z	ʃ ʒ	ʂ ʐ	ç ʝ	x ɣ	χ ʁ	ħ ʕ	h ɦ
Lateral fricative				ɬ ɮ							
Approximant		ʋ		ɹ		ɻ	j	ɰ			
Lateral approximant				l		ɭ	ʎ	ʟ			
Ejective stop	p'			t'		ʈ'	c'	k'	q'		

Where symbols appear in pairs, the one to the right represents a voiced consonant. Shaded areas denote articulations judged impossible.

VOWELS

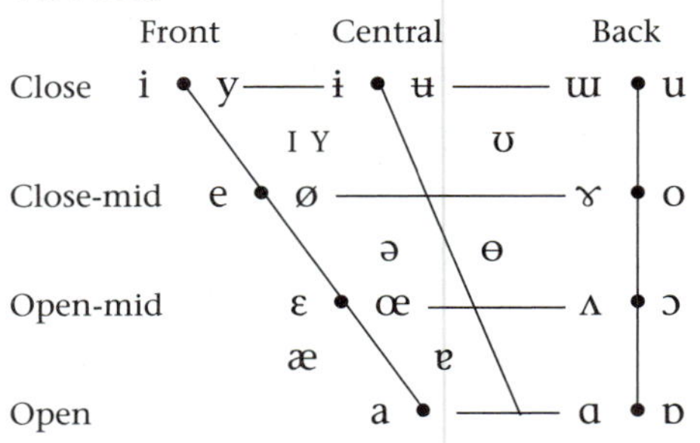

Where symbols appear in pairs, the one to the right represents a rounded vowel. The symbols for vowels used in this book sometimes differ from IPA usage.

QUESTIONS

1. In order to become more aware of the differences between spelling and pronunciation, answer the following questions about English spelling.
   a) Find four words that show four alternative spellings of the sound [f].
   b) Find six words that have the letter <a> pronounced differently.
   c) Find four words in which different groups of letters represent only one sound.
   d) Find two words in which two different sounds are pronounced but not spelled out.

2. How many segments are there in the following words?

a) at	e) psychology
b) math	f) knowledge
c) cure	g) mailbox
d) hopping	h) awesome

3. Is the first sound in each of the following words voiced or voiceless?

a) though	e) zoom	i) huge	m) when (*may vary*)
b) thought	f) silk	j) choose	n) ghetto
c) form	g) pan	k) judge	o) pneumatic
d) view	h) boat	l) buns	p) winced

4. Using the words presented in question 3, state whether the last sound of each word is voiced or voiceless.

5. For each of the following pairs of sounds, state whether they have the same or a different place of articulation. Then identify the place of articulation for each sound.

a) [s] : [l]	e) [m] : [n]	i) [b] : [f]
b) [k] : [ŋ]	f) [dʒ] : [ʃ]	j) [tʃ] : [dʒ]
c) [p] : [g]	g) [f] : [h]	k) [s] : [v]
d) [l] : [r]	h) [w] : [j]	l) [θ] : [t]

6. For each of the following pairs of sounds, state whether they have the same or a different manner of articulation. Then identify the manner of articulation for each sound.

a) [s] : [θ]	e) [l] : [t]	i) [r] : [w]
b) [k] : [g]	f) [ð] : [v]	j) [tʃ] : [dʒ]
c) [w] : [j]	g) [tʃ] : [s]	k) [h] : [ʔ]
d) [f] : [ʃ]	h) [m] : [ŋ]	l) [z] : [dʒ]

7. After each of the following articulatory descriptions, write the sound described in phonetic brackets.

a) voiceless velar stop	e) voiced velar nasal
b) voiced labiodental fricative	f) voiceless interdental fricative
c) voiced alveopalatal affricate	g) high back rounded lax vowel
d) voiced palatal glide	h) low front unrounded vowel

8. Which of the following pairs of words show the same vowel sound? Mark each pair "same" or "different." Then transcribe the vowels of each word.

a) back	sat	h) hide	height
b) cot	caught	i) least	heed
c) bid	key	j) drug	cook
d) luck	flick	k) sink	fit
e) ooze	deuce	l) oak	own
f) cot	court	m) pour	port
g) fell	fail	n) mouse	cow

9. Using descriptive terms like sibilant, fricative, and so on, provide a single phonetic characteristic that all the segments in each group share. Try to avoid over-obvious answers such as "consonant" or "vowel."
Example: [b d g œ m j] are all voiced.

a) [p t k g ʔ]	e) [ʌ ə ʊ a]	i) [l r m n ŋ j w]
b) [i e ɛ æ]	f) [h ʔ]	j) [t d l r n s z]
c) [tʃ ʒ ʃ dʒ]	g) [u o]	
d) [p b m f v]	h) [s z tʃ dʒ ʃ ʒ]	

10. Transcribe the following sets of words. You may use these words to practice transcribing aspiration.

a) tog	i) peel	q) spell
b) kid	j) stun	r) cord
c) attain	k) Oscar	s) accord
d) despise	l) cooler	t) astound
e) elbow	m) sigh	u) pure
f) haul	n) hulk	v) wheeze
g) juice	o) explode	w) remove
h) thimble	p) tube	x) clinical

11. Using H, L, and association lines, transcribe the intonation of the following English phrases. Compare your results with the transcriptions of several class-

mates. Are they the same? If they aren't, discuss what aspects of intonation (such as emotion or speech context) might account for the differences in transcription.

a) "Hi, Alice."
b) "Three people got off the bus at the last stop."
c) "My uncle likes to mountain climb."

12. Mark primary and secondary (where present) stresses on the following words. It is not necessary to transcribe them.

a) sunny	f) arrive	k) secret
b) banana	g) defy	l) exceed
c) blackboard	h) summary	m) summery
d) Canada	i) Canadian	n) Canadianize
e) (to) reject	j) (a) reject	o) difficult

13. Find a fluent speaker of a language other than English and transcribe phonetically ten words of that language. If you encounter any sounds for which symbols are not found in this chapter, attempt to describe them in phonetic terms and then invent diacritics to help you transcribe them.

14. Using Figure 2.20 as your model, provide coarticulation diagrams for the following words. Be sure that your diagrams capture the movement of the lips, tongue, velum, and glottis as in the model.

a) had	c) please
b) snap	d) dome

15. Compare the careful speech and rapid speech pronunciations of the following English words and phrases. Then, name the process or processes that make the rapid speech pronunciation different from the careful speech. (Stress is omitted here.)

	Careful speech	*Rapid speech*
a) in my room	[ɪn maj rum]	[ɪm maj rum]
b) I see them	[aj si ðɛm]	[aj siəm]
c) I see him	[aj si hɪm]	[aj siəm]
d) within	[wɪθɪn]	[wɪðɪn]
e) balloons	[bəlunz]	[blunz]
f) popsicle	[p^{h}ɑpsɪkəl]	[p^{h}ɑpskl̩]
g) sit down	[sɪt dawn]	[sɪɾawn]
h) my advice	[maj ədvajs]	[maj əvajs]
i) Scotch tape	[skɑtʃ t^{h}ejp]	[k^{h}ɑtʃstejp]
j) protection	[pr̥owt^{h}ɛkʃən]	[pərt^{h}ɛkʃən]
k) hand me that	[hænd mi ðæt]	[hæ̃miðæt]
l) Pam will miss you	[pæm wɪl mɪs juw]	[pæml̩mɪʃjə]

For the Student Linguist

DON'T WORRY ABOUT SPELLING

What if you had to choose: either nobody would read and write ever again, or nobody would speak or hear language? This is a total nonchoice for me—I'd pitch out liner notes and lyric sheets in a second, but would be really upset about losing all my Ella Fitzgerald CDs. Not that it would be easy to function without reading and writing. Road signs, for example, are pretty important, and even linguistics textbooks have their uses. But the point is, I think spoken language is more fundamental than reading or writing. Let's assume it is, but let's also assume that writing is pretty important to modern society. The question, then, is how closely writing should resemble speaking.

Current spelling is much closer to the way English *used* to be spoken than the way it's spoken today, and for years various folks have been proposing spelling reforms. Would learning to read be easier if you didn't have to deal with spelling nightmares like *night, though, tough, cough, two, due, who, threw, shoe, through,* or *answer?* Some of these words are already being changed informally in advertising, pop music, and casual writing. For example, when my best friend sends me letters, she always writes *nite, tho, tuff, cough, 2, due, who, threw, shoe, thru,* and *anser.* Are these spellings any better? For someone who's learning to read English, it could be hard to figure out that *tho* and *who* aren't supposed to rhyme but *2, due, who, threw, shoe,* and *thru* are supposed to rhyme, although there's now a difference in spelling for the nonrhyming *tho* and *tuff.*

Phonetic transcription—using the IPA—is unambiguous about what rhymes with what. For every sound there's exactly one symbol (except for a couple of substitutions for different keyboards), and for every symbol there's exactly one sound. Thus the word list becomes: najt, ðow, tʰʌf, kʰɔf, tʰuw, duw, huw, θruw, ʃuw, θruw, and ænsər. Making the changeover from standard spelling to IPA would be a nightmare, though. We'd have to reconfigure our keyboards, for starters. Instead of five vowel symbols (and many combinations of them) and twenty-one consonants, we'd have about eighteen vowels and twenty-five consonants.

Imagine all the changeover details could be taken care of (including instantly teaching everyone the IPA). Think about how much richer writing could be if it included all the information you get from hearing someone speak. You'd have information about the writer's regional background and class, plus information about the level of formality of the piece you were reading. Depending on how detailed the writing system was, you would be able to read all sorts of nuances of stress and intonation.

I've transcribed the same piece of dialogue in several different systems below. The first system is probably the hardest to read, and the following systems get progressively easier. Try to figure out the dialogue from the first system, checking the later ones for clarification if you get stuck. Also try to figure out the stylistic differences among the different versions of the dialogue.

1. *ʃijləˀejtʰejlardʒpʰʌmpkʰɪnpʰaj ˀəwɛrðæt ˀælənwəzwɑtʃɪŋ o̥:w̥ ˀæ̥l̥ə̥n̥ ʃijsɛdbrɛθɪlij pʰæ̥sm̥i̥j̥ ð̥i̥j̥ w̥ɪ̥ptʰ kʰr̥i̥j̥m̥ ʃijlə hijwajnd ˀajmtʃrajiŋ tʰuwfɪnɪʃgrajndɪŋðijkɔfij*
2. ʃijləˀejɾəla:dʒpʰʌmpkʰɪnpʰaj ˀəwɛrðæˀæln̩wəzwɑtʃn̩ o:w ˀælən̩ ʃijsɛˀbrɛθlij pʰæsmijðəwɪpkʰrijm ʃijlə hijwajnd ˀajmtʃrajn̩tʰəfɪnɪʃgrajndn̩ðəkɔfij
3. ʃíjləˀejɾəla:dʒpʰʌmpkʰɪnpʰáj ˀəwɛrðæˀǽln̩wəzwɑ́tʃn̩ o:w ˀǽln̩ ʃijsɛˀbrɛ́θlij pʰæsmijðəwɪpkʰríjm ʃíjlə hijwájnd ˀajmtʃrájn̩tʰəfɪnɪʃgrájndn̩ðəkɔ́fij
4. ʃijlə ejt ej lardʒpʰʌmpkʰɪn pʰaj ˀəwɛr ðæt ˀælən wəz wɑtʃɪŋ o:w ˀælən ʃij sɛd brɛθɪlij pʰæs mij ðij wɪptʰ kʰrijm ʃijlə hij wajnd ˀajm tʃrajiŋ tʰuw fɪnɪʃ grajndɪŋ ðij kɔfij
5. ʃijlə ejt ej lardʒ pʰʌmpkʰɪn pʰaj, ˀəwɛr ðæt ˀælən wəz wɑtʃɪŋ. "o:w ˀælən," ʃij sɛd brɛθɪlij, "pʰæs mij ðij wɪptʰ kʰrijm." "ʃijlə," hij wajnd, "ˀajm tʃrajiŋ tʰuw fɪnɪʃ grajndɪŋ ðij kɔfij."

The downside of this type of writing is that there'd be so much variability. For instance, you might care about the accent or tone of a character in a novel, but do you really need to know where the journalist who wrote this morning's article on the economy was raised? And what if his or her editor were from someplace else? Whose accent would get printed? Not to mention the difficulties of something like a GRE exam or SAT test written in someone else's dialect.

Of course, the degree of variability depends on how extreme the system is. There's a wide gap between standard spelling and the fairly narrow (detailed) transcription system used in examples *1* through *3*. Writing could be more phonetic than it is now, but we don't have to force people to include every minor variation in pronunciation. We could forget about stress marks and anything to show intonation—except for a few simple things like question marks and exclamation points. We could also leave off fairly predictable things like aspiration (you'll discover how predictable aspiration is in the next chapter). Examples *4* and *5* are probably a lot easier to understand than *1* through *3,* since *4* and *5* are not as detailed (broad transcription) and, most importantly, because they have spaces between the words. Putting in spaces makes the writing less like the actual pronunciation, but it also takes away the ambiguity of figuring out whether something like [ʃijla] is supposed to be *she lo . . .* (as in *she locked the door . . .*) or *Sheila.*

In fact, the new writing system could keep punctuation, keep word spaces, and have nothing but the bare minimum to distinguish the way one word sounds from the way other words sound. The trick, then, is to figure out what the bare minimum is. It's a pretty difficult question, and before you can answer it, you'll need to read about phonology and morphology. You'll also need to figure out what exactly a word *is,* anyway. So, read the next two chapters and then come back to this section and read it again. Then devise the perfect writing system, use it for your senior thesis, patent it, market it, make a fortune off of it, and retire to a lovely little tropical island (with good food) where they don't speak English.

three

PHONOLOGY: THE FUNCTION AND PATTERNING OF SOUNDS

Michael Dobrovolsky
Ewa Czaykowska-Higgins

A person's tongue is a twisty thing, there are plenty of words there of every kind, and the range of words is wide, and their variation.
– HOMER, *The Iliad,* 20

OBJECTIVES

In this chaper, you will learn:

- how we know which language sounds are distinctive in a particular language
- how distinctive sounds in a particular language can vary systematically according to the context in which they occur
- how we use transcription to represent distinctive sounds and systematic variations of these sounds
- how syllables are constructed and the influence of language-specific syllable structure
- how individual sounds can be broken down further, according to specific features
- how we can construct rules to explain systematic variations in the production of sounds
- how we can group, organize, and illustrate features of sounds

We saw in Chapter 2 that human beings can produce and perceive a large number of speech sounds. No human language exploits all of these phonetic possibilities. Instead, every language makes its own particular selection from the range of all possible speech sounds and organizes them into a more or less regular system. The component of grammar that determines the selection of speech sounds and governs both the sound patterns and the systematic phonetic variation found in language is known as **phonology**.

Speakers have (at least) some subconscious knowledge of the phonetic patterns that make up phonological systems. For example, as we saw in Chapter 1, speakers of English recognize without being taught that certain combinations of consonants are acceptable in English, even if those combinations occur in forms that are not real words, while other combinations are not acceptable; thus, *slish* and *screnk* are acceptable to English speakers, while *srish* and *screpk* are not. In fact, speakers can do more than recognize that certain forms are unnatural in their system; they can even correct unnatural forms to make them conform to the patterns that are acceptable in their own language. Without knowing exactly why, most English speakers would pronounce a form like *srish* as [səɹɪʃ]—breaking up the unacceptable consonant combination with a vowel, rather than, say, deleting one of the consonants to form [sɪʃ] or [ɹɪʃ]. The task of phonologists, then, is (1) to discover and describe the systematic phonetic patterns found in individual languages and (2) to discover the general principles that underlie the patterning of sounds across all human languages. In doing this, phonologists hope to uncover the largely subconscious knowledge that speakers have of sound patterns.

The existence of phonological patterns in language is a result of the organization of certain basic elements or units that combine to make up these patterns. In our discussion of phonology we will examine three of the major phonological units: the **feature**, the **segment**, and the **syllable**.

We are already acquainted with the idea that the flow of speech can be divided into segments and that segments are characterized by specific phonetic properties. In this chapter, we will investigate the types of patterned phonetic variation that segments exhibit in individual languages and cross-linguistically. We will also learn that segments are composed of features. Features correspond to articulatory or acoustic categories such as [voice] or [strident]. They are the smallest building blocks of phonological structure, and as we will see, the types of phonological patterns found in language are directly related to the properties of the features that make up segments. Finally, we will learn about the ways in which segments combine to form syllables. Syllables consist of a syllabic element—usually a vowel—and any preceding or following segments that are associated with it. As the representation of the word *segment* in Figure 3.1 illustrates, features, segments, and syllables are organized into hierarchical levels, each of which is composed of units from the level beneath it. In Figure 3.1, *segment* is a word-level unit represented by the abbreviation *Wd*. This word in turn consists of two syllables, each of which is represented by the Greek

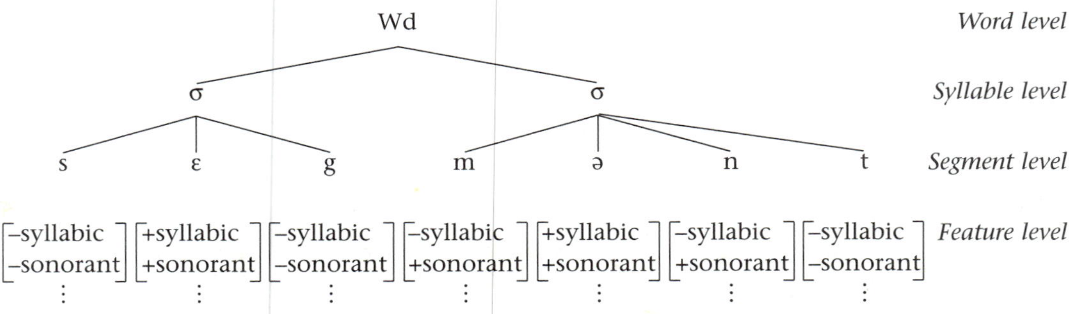

Figure 3.1 Partial phonological representation of *segment*

letter σ (sigma). Each syllable itself consists of several segments. Finally, each segment is composed of features. (For purposes of illustration, only a few features are provided for each segment and the internal hierarchical structure of syllables and segments is not represented; these are treated later, in Sections 4, 5.2, and 5.3, respectively.)

As units of phonological structure, syllables, segments, and features play major roles in the processes we investigated in the previous chapter and, in combination with certain general principles of phonology, produce the sound patterns of language. In the next sections we examine these sound patterns and the phonological knowledge that enables speakers to distinguish among forms and to deal with the systematic phonetic variation found in the pronunciation of speech sounds.

1 SEGMENTS IN CONTRAST

All speakers know which segments of their language **contrast** and which do not. Segments are said to contrast (or to be *distinctive* or be in *opposition*) in a particular language when their presence alone may distinguish forms with different meanings from each other. Thus, for instance, in the English words *sip* and *zip*, the phonetically distinct segments [s] and [z] are in contrast; similarly, in *hit*, *hate*, and *hot*, the vowels are in contrast.

In this section we will consider how to determine which segments contrast in a language. In Section 2 we will consider the systematic patterns associated with phonetically similar segments when they do not contrast.

1.1 Minimal pairs

Since knowledge of segmental contrasts is fundamental to knowing any language, the first step in an analysis of the phonology of a language is to establish which sounds in that language are in contrast with each other. In order to establish contrasts, it is necessary to examine the distribution of sounds in words and to compare word meanings. The most straightforward way to accomplish this examination is by way of the **minimal pair** test.

A minimal pair consists of two forms with distinct meanings that differ by only one segment found in the same position in each form. The examples [sɪp] *sip* and [zɪp] *zip* given previously form a minimal pair and show that the sounds [s] and [z] contrast in English.

A number of minimal pairs that demonstrate consonant contrasts for English are given in Table 3.1; it is important to remember that it is on the basis of *sound* and not spelling that minimal pairs are established. In displaying contrasts, contrasting words are often placed along the horizontal axis with respect to their place of articulation, reading from left to right (labial, alveolar, and so on), and vertically with respect to their manner of articulation, in order to show which places and manners of articulation are exploited by the language in question.

Table 3.1 Contrasts among consonants in English

Labial		*Interdental*		*Alveolar*		*Alveopalatal*		*Velar*		*Glottal*	
Stops and affricates (noncontinuants)											
tap	[p]			pat	[t]	match	[tʃ]	pick	[k]		
tab	[b]			pad	[d]	Madge	[dʒ]	pig	[g]		
Continuants											
leaf	[f]	thigh	[θ]	sip	[s]	mesher	[ʃ]			hip	[h]
leave	[v]	thy	[ð]	zip	[z]	measure	[ʒ]				
Nasals											
sum	[m]			sun	[n]			sung	[ŋ]		
Liquids and glides											
wet	[w]					yet	[j]		[w]		
				leer	[l]						
				rear	[r]						

The phonetic context in which a sound occurs is called its **environment**. Pairs that have segments in nearly identical environments—such as *assure* [əʃʊ́r]/*azure* [ǽʒər], which contrast [ʃ] and [ʒ], or *author* [ɔ́θər]/*either* [íðər], which contrast [θ] and [ð]—are called **near-minimal pairs**. They can be used to establish contrasts if no minimal pairs for a particular set of segments can be found.

Once you have established the existence of a minimal or near-minimal pair for a set of two segments, you may assume that those two segments contrast or are distinctive. Segments that contrast with each other in a particular language are said to belong to separate **phonemes** (contrastive phonological units) of that language. Thus, all the consonants in Table 3.1 belong to separate phonemes in English, since all of them are contrastive in the language.

When looking for the contrastive sounds of a language, it is in fact rare to find minimal pairs for all such sounds, since the historical evolution of every language has led to some sounds being used more frequently than others or being eliminated from some environments. For example, you will find no minimal pairs involving [h] and [ŋ] in word-initial or word-final position in English because there are no words that begin with [ŋ] or end in [h]. It is also difficult to find minimal pairs in English that have the phone [ʒ], which occurs for the most part in words borrowed from French, such as *azure* and *mirage*.

Vowel contrasts in English

Vowel contrasts in English can be established with a few sets of examples. We assume in Table 3.2 that English vowel-glide sequences like [ej] and [ow] are single vowels. From this perspective, we can say that the vowels [ej] and [ɛ] and [aw] and [aj], and so on, contrast.

Table 3.2 Vowel contrasts in American English

beet	[bit]	[i]
bit	[bɪt]	[ɪ]
bait	[bejt]	[ej]
bet	[bɛt]	[ɛ]
bat	[bæt]	[æ]
cooed	[kʰud]	[u]
could	[kʰʊd]	[ʊ]
code	[kʰowd]	[ow]
caught	[kʰɔt]	[ɔ]
cod	[kʰɑd]	[ɑ]
cud	[kʰʌd]	[ʌ]
lewd	[lud]	[u]
loud	[lawd]	[aw]
lied	[lajd]	[aj]
Lloyd	[lɔjd]	[ɔj]

1.2 Language-specific contrasts

Whether or not segments contrast with each other is determined on a language-particular basis. In other words, just because two sounds are phonetically distinct, it does not mean that they necessarily behave as phonologically distinct or contrastive. Therefore, sounds that are contrastive in one language will not necessarily be contrastive in another. For example, the difference between the two vowels [ɛ] and [æ] is crucial to English, as we can see from minimal pairs like *Ben* [bɛn] and *ban* [bæn] (see Table 3.3). But in Turkish, this difference in pronunciation is not distinctive. A Turkish speaker may pronounce the word for 'I' as [bɛn] or [bæn], and it will make no difference to the meaning.

Table 3.3 Language-specific vowel contrasts: English versus Turkish

English		*Turkish*	
[bɛn]	Ben	[bɛn]	'I'
[bæn]	ban	[bæn]	'I'

Conversely, sounds that do not contrast in English, such as long and short vowels, may be distinctive in another language. There are no minimal pairs of the type [hæt]:[hæ:t] or [lus]:[lu:s] in English. But in Japanese and Finnish, short and long vowels contrast, as the examples in Table 3.4 show.

Establishing the contrasting segments in a language is a first step in phonological analysis. However, in every language there are many sounds that never contrast. The following section deals with this aspect of phonology.

Table 3.4 Short/long vowel contrasts in Japanese and Finnish

Japanese			
[tori]	'bird'	[tori:]	'shrine gate'
[kibo]	'scale'	[kibo:]	'hope'
Finnish			
[tuli]	'fire'	[tu:li]	'wind'
[hætæ]	'distress'	[hæ:tæ:]	'to evict'

2 PHONETICALLY CONDITIONED VARIATION: PHONEMES AND ALLOPHONES

Everyday speech contains a great deal of phonetic variation that speakers pay little or no attention to. Some of this variation arises from nonlinguistic factors such as fatigue, excitement, orthodontic work, gum chewing, and the like. This kind of variation is not part of the domain of phonology. But much phonetic variation is systematic. It occurs most often among phonetically similar segments and is conditioned by the phonetic context or environment in which the segments are found. This variation occurs because segments are affected and altered by the phonetic characteristics of neighboring elements or by the larger phonological context in which they occur. We rarely notice this kind of variation unless we are trained to do so, because every speaker has the ability to factor it out in order to focus attention on only those contrasts of the language that affect meaning. In this section we will consider the patterns of variation exhibited by noncontrastive sounds, how to analyze these patterns, and the conclusions that can be drawn from them.

2.1 Complementary distribution

When first learning phonetic transcription, English speakers are often surprised that all the *l*s they pronounce are not identical. In Table 3.5, the *l*s in column A are voiced, while those in column B are voiceless (indicated here by a subscript ̥). Many speakers of English are unaware that they routinely produce this difference in articulation, which can be heard clearly when the words in column B are pronounced slowly.

Table 3.5 Voiced and voiceless *l* in English

A		*B*	
blue	[blu]	plow	[pl̥aw]
gleam	[glim]	clap	[kl̥æp]
slip	[slɪp]	clear	[kl̥ir]
flog	[flɑg]	play	[pl̥ej]
leaf	[lif]		

In fact, as it turns out, the two *l*s never contrast in English: there are no minimal pairs like [plej] and [pl̥ej] in which the phonetic difference between [l] and [l̥] functions to signal a difference in meaning.

Moreover, when one examines the distribution of the two *l*s, it becomes apparent that voiced and voiceless *l*s vary systematically: all of the voiceless [l̥]s occur after the class of voiceless stops in English, while the voiced [l]s never occur after voiceless stops. The voicelessness of the *l*s in column B is thus a consequence of their phonetic environment; it is also a predictable property of the phonology of English in the sense that in English, only voiceless [l̥]s occur after voiceless stops.

Since no voiced [l] ever occurs in the same phonetic environment as a voiceless one (and vice versa), we say that the two variants of *l* are in **complementary distribution**.

In the data in Table 3.5, voiced [l] occurs in a greater number of different phonetic environments (after voiced stops, after voiceless fricatives, and in word-initial position) than does voiceless [l̥], and in addition those different environments for voiced [l] cannot be easily described as they do not naturally fall together as a class. Therefore, when two (or more) segments are in complementary distribution, the term *elsewhere* is used, as in Table 3.6, to indicate the kind of wider distribution exhibited by [l] in Table 3.5. Specifically, we find [l̥] after voiceless stops, and [l] elsewhere.

Table 3.6 Complementary distribution of [l] and [l̥] in English

	[l]	[l̥]
After voiceless stops	no	yes
Elsewhere	yes	no

In spite of these differences in their phonetic environments, native speakers of English consider the two *l*s to be instances of the same segment, since they are not contrastive but are nevertheless similar phonetically (they are both types of *l*s) and since the differences between them are systematic and predictable. We can sum up the relationship that the two *l*s bear to each other by stating that, for speakers of English, although the two *l*s are *phonetically* distinct, they are *phonologically* the same because of the sound system of English, given their phonetic similarity, predictable distribution, and noncontrastiveness.

2.2 Phonemes and Allophones

When two (or more) segments are phonetically distinct but phonologically the same, they are referred to as **allophones** (predictable variants) of one **phoneme** (contrastive phonological unit). The ability to group phonetically distinct sounds into the phonological units known as phonemes is shared by all speakers of all languages. Phonologists represent this phonological knowledge formally by distinguishing two levels of representation: the **phonetic representation** that consists of predictable variants or allophones, and the **phonemic** (or phonological) **representation** that consists of the phonemes to which the allophones belong. A representation of the relationship between phonemes and their allophones is given in Figure 3.2.

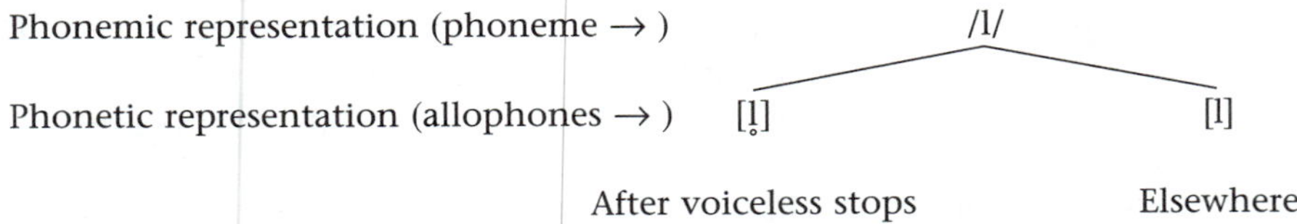

Figure 3.2 The phoneme /l/ and its allophones [l̥] and [l] in English

In Figure 3.2 the symbols for allophones are enclosed in square brackets, while the symbol for the phoneme is placed between slashes. This is standard notation in phonology. Notice that the phoneme /l/ in Figure 3.2 is the same as its voiced allophone [l]. In most cases the elsewhere variant or allophone of a phoneme can be chosen to represent the phoneme itself.

As we have seen, segments that can be considered to be allophones of one phoneme are phonetically similar and occur in phonetically predictable environments. In fact, it is frequently the case that allophones of one phoneme are in complementary distribution with each other. Consequently, we can use the fact that allophones occur in complementary distribution as a way of testing whether or not two (or more) segments should be considered to be allophones of one phoneme.

Allophonic variation is found throughout language. In fact, every speech sound we utter is an allophone of some phoneme and can be grouped together with other phonetically similar sounds into a class that is represented by a phoneme on a phonological level of representation. An important part of phonological analysis thus deals with discovering inventories of the phonemes of languages and accounting for allophonic variation.

Some problematic distributions

At this point, some other considerations in determining phonemes and allophones must be taken into account. So far, we have seen that a minimal pair test is a quick and direct way of establishing that two sounds belong to separate phonemes in a language. If the sounds contrast, they are members of different phonemes. We have also seen that if certain sounds are noncontrastive and in complementary distribution, they may be considered allophones of one phoneme. In some cases, however, we must go beyond these procedures to discover the phonemic inventory of a language.

As noted in Section 1.1, certain patterns of distribution prevent some sounds in a language from ever contrasting with each other. In cases like these, we can establish the phonemic status of a sound by default. If the sound cannot be grouped together with any other phonetically similar sounds as an allophone of a phoneme, we may assume that it has phonemic status. The following data from English help to illustrate this point.

1)

*[ŋowp]	(does not exist)	[howp]	*hope*
*[ŋejt]	(does not exist)	[hejt]	*hate*

We can see here that [h] and [ŋ] do not contrast in initial position in English. The following examples show that they do not contrast in final position either.

2)

[lɔŋ]	*long*	*[lɔh]	(does not exist)
[sɪŋ]	*sing*	*[sɪh]	(does not exist)
[kl̥æŋ]	*clang*	*[kl̥æh]	(does not exist)

These lists could be extended for pages, but a minimal pair involving [h] and [ŋ] could never be found in English. Additionally, as *1* and *2* have shown, [h] and [ŋ] are in complementary distribution. Do these facts taken together not lead us to conclude that [h] and [ŋ] are allophones of one phoneme? No. Since [h] and [ŋ] are so distinct phonetically, we assume that each one is a member of a separate phoneme and that the pattern of distribution is of secondary importance in this instance.

Minimal pairs or near-minimal pairs help us establish which sounds contrast in a language; phonetic similarity and complementary distribution help us decide which sounds are allophones of a particular phoneme. But not all examples of variation among sounds can be dealt with through these approaches.

In some cases, phonetically similar sounds are neither in complementary distribution nor are they found to contrast. It is still possible, nevertheless, to determine which phonemes these sounds belong to. A case in point is the variation in English voiceless stops when they are found in word-final position, as in the word *stop.* Sometimes an English speaker releases the articulation of these sounds rather forcefully. Let us represent this with a diacritic sign [!]. At other times, the same speaker may keep the articulators closed for a moment after the articulation; the diacritic [˺] can represent this. Some speakers may even coarticulate a glottal closure (represented here with the raised symbol for a glottal stop following the consonant in question) and produce the word as [stɑp^{ʔ}]. Thus we can find at least three pronunciations of *stop:* [stɑp!], [stɑp˺], and [stɑp^{ʔ}]. Since there is no difference in the meaning of these forms and since the final consonants are phonetically similar, we say that these sounds are in **free variation**, and that they are all allophones of the phoneme /p/. The same pattern holds for the other voiceless stops of English.

2.3 CLASSES AND GENERALIZATION IN PHONOLOGY

Phonological analysis permits us to account for the great amount of phonetic variation in everyday speech. This variation, which is usually systematic, is found throughout language. Evidence of its systematic nature comes from the fact that allophones in languages do not pattern piecemeal but rather according to their membership in phonetic classes. This point can be illustrated by comparing the patterns of distribution of *r*s and glides in English to the patterning of *l*s that was illustrated earlier in Table 3.5.

The data in Table 3.7 show that in English, voiceless [r̥] occurs after voiceless stops, while voiced [r] occurs elsewhere. Based on this information we can conclude that there is an /r/ phoneme in English with (at least) two allophones—one voiced, the other voiceless, and that the allophones of English /r/ thus pattern like those of /l/. But if we were to stop there, we would overlook an important point. The

Table 3.7 Voiced and voiceless allophones of English /r/

A		*B*	
brew	[bru]	prow	[pr̥aw]
green	[grin]	trip	[tr̥ɪp]
drip	[drɪp]	creep	[kr̥ip]
frog	[frɑg]	pray	[pr̥ej]
shrimp	[ʃrɪmp]		

phonemes /r/ and /l/ belong to the same class of sounds: both are *liquids*. By taking this information into account, we can state a general fact about English.

3)

In English, liquids have voiceless allophones after voiceless stops, and voiced allophones elsewhere.

Now examine the data in Table 3.8.

Table 3.8 Voiced and voiceless allophones of English glides

A		*B*	
beauty	[bjuɾi]	putrid	[pj̥utr̥ɪd]
Duane	[dwejn]	twin	[tw̥ɪn]
Gwen	[gwɛn]	quick	[kw̥ɪk]
view	[vju]	cute	[kj̥ut]
swim	[swɪm]		
thwack	[θwæk]		

These forms demonstrate that the contrasting glides /j/ and /w/ pattern like the liquids. We can now extend our general statement even further.

4)

In English, liquids and glides have voiceless allophones after voiceless stops, and voiced allophones elsewhere.

When we consider the fact that liquids and glides all belong to the same phonetic class, namely the class of non-nasal sonorant consonants, we can understand why the allophones of liquids and glides pattern similarly. One of the major goals of phonological description is the discovery of such broad patterns of variation, and the formulation of the most general statements possible to capture these broad patterns.

2.4 Canadian Raising

Another example of allophonic variation is taken from English. In most Canadian and some American dialects, pronunciations like those illustrated in Table 3.9 are common.

Table 3.9 Low and central vowel allophones in raising dialects

[ajz]	eyes	[ʌjs]	ice
[lajz]	lies	[lʌjs]	lice
[tr̥ajd]	tried	[tr̥ʌjt]	trite
[tr̥ajb]	tribe	[tr̥ʌjp]	tripe
[hawz]	(to) house (verb)	[hʌws]	house (noun)
[lawd]	loud	[lʌwt]	lout
[kaw]	cow	[skʌwt]	scout
[flaj]	fly	[flʌjt]	flight

In Table 3.9, the vowels [aj] and [ʌj] are in complementary distribution. The [aj] occurs before the class of voiced consonants or in word-final position, and the [ʌj] occurs before the class of voiceless consonants. The two are allophones of the single phoneme /aj/. The same relationship holds between the vowels [aw] and [ʌw], which are allophones of /aw/.

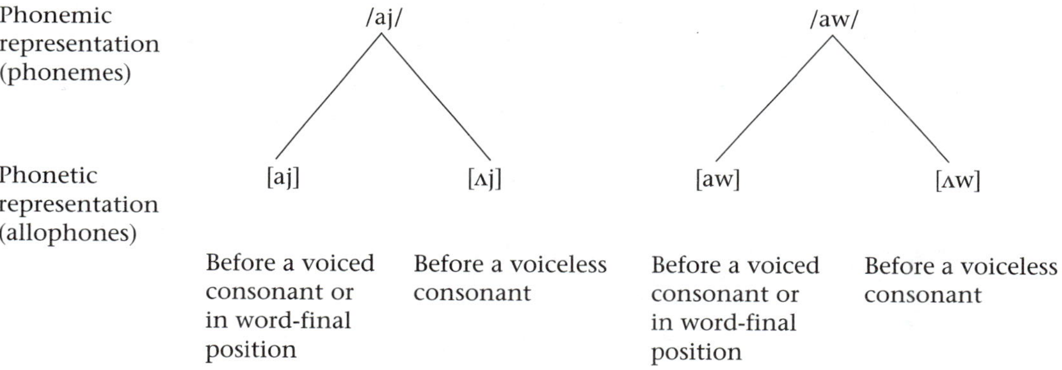

Figure 3.3 Allophones of /aj/ and /aw/ in raising dialects

Again, we see this phonological fact reflected in everyday language use. Most speakers of these dialects find it difficult to distinguish between these allophones, even when the difference is pointed out to them. This is because the difference is not contrastive. On the other hand, many people who speak varieties of English that do not have the [ʌj] or [ʌw] allophones are very much aware of their presence in Canadian English. To them, a Canadian speaker sounds markedly different, even though they may be confused about the nature of the difference.

> *I don't agree he was an American. . . . Where all other English-speaking people pronounce OU as a diphthong, the Canadian . . . makes a separate sound for each letter. The word* about, *for instance, he pronounces as* ab-oh-oot.
>
> Philip MacDonald, *The List of Adrian Messenger*

This phenomenon is sometimes referred to as Canadian Raising, since the allophones [ʌj] and [ʌw] have higher vowel components than the elsewhere variants [aj] and [aw].

2.5 English mid vowels and glides

The vowels that exhibit the Canadian Raising alternation are all and only the central (unreduced) vowels of raising dialects; the two mid allophones [ʌj] and [ʌw] both occur before voiceless consonants, while the two low allophones [aj] and [aw] both occur elsewhere. Just as in the case of the liquid and glide patterns seen in Section 2.3, the allophones that participate in the Canadian Raising pattern are distributed according to their membership in phonetic classes. A final example of predictable variation that refers to classes of segments but that differs crucially from examples seen so far is again taken from English.

Table 3.2 showed contrasts among English vowels. In most dialects of English, the mid tense vowels [ej] and [ow] are always diphthongized and thus end in the glide [j] or [w]. Significantly, the nonback (i.e., front) vowel [e] is always followed by the palatal glide [j], which is a nonback unrounded segment, while the back rounded vowel [o] is always followed by the labiovelar glide [w], which is a back rounded segment. These facts are summed up in Table 3.10.

Table 3.10 Tense vowel-glide combinations in English

Vowel	*Glide*			*Vowel*	*Glide*		
(both non-back and unrounded)				*(both back and rounded)*			
e	j	[fejt]	fate	o	w	[bowt]	boat
		[kejn]	cane			[kown]	cone

In other words, the occurrence of the glides following the mid tense vowels is predictable. The following generalization states the distribution of the two glides.

5)

The mid tense vowels of English are predictably followed by a glide that has the same backness and roundness as the vowel.

The data in Table 3.10 show parallels with the **allophonic distribution** we have considered so far in the sense that certain elements in it are predictable under certain systematically statable phonetic conditions. However, there is a difference between allophonic distribution and the kind of distribution exhibited by the glides. Specifically, in Table 3.10, instead of a number of variants of one phoneme, we have two segments, [ej] and [ow], whose pronunciation is always the same: the mid tense vowels of English are always followed by glides of the same backness and roundness. When certain sounds are found predictably in a given environment, they are not included in phonemic representations. Thus, although the phonetic representations of English mid vowels include the glides, the corresponding phonemic representations do not.

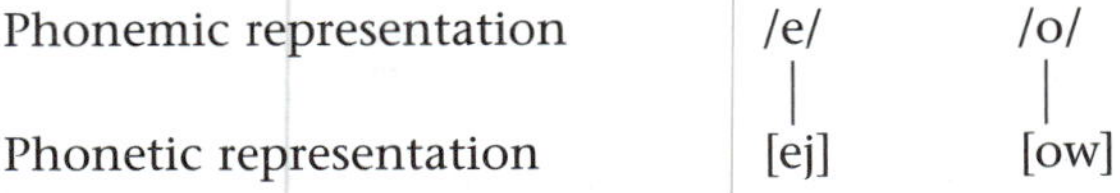

Figure 3.4 Two representations of mid vowels in English

2.6 LANGUAGE-SPECIFIC PATTERNS

The phenomenon of allophonic variation is universal. However, just as the phonemic contrasts found in each language are specific to that language, the actual patterning of phonemes and allophones is also language-specific. Thus, whatever distribution we discover for one language may not hold true for another.

Language-specific variation in allophonic nasalization

Some languages have nasal as well as oral vowels and glides. It is usual in such languages for nasal vowel (and nasal glide) allophones to occur near nasal consonants, but as Tables 3.11 and 3.12 illustrate, the details of the patterning may vary from language to language.

In Scots Gaelic, for instance, whenever a nasal consonant occurs in a word, the vowel adjacent to it appears as nasalized. Glides do not get nasalized.

Table 3.11 Nasal and oral vowels in Scots Gaelic

[mõːr]	'big'
[nĩ]	'cattle'
[nẽːl]	'cloud'
[mũ]	'about'
[rũːn]	'secret'
[ʃalak]	'hunting'

The generalization governing the distribution of nasal vowels in Scots Gaelic is stated as follows.

6)

Vowels are nasal in Scots Gaelic when preceded or followed by a nasal consonant.

Malay, a language spoken in Malaysia and Singapore, has both nasalized vowels and glides. In Malay, all vowels and glides following a nasal are predictably nasalized until an obstruent (stop or fricative), liquid, or glottal ([h], [ʔ]) is reached.

Table 3.12 Nasalization in Malay

[mẽw̃ãh]	'luxurious'
[mãj̃ãn]	'stalk'
[mãrah]	'scold'
[nãẽʔ]	'ascend'
[mə̃laran]	'forbid'
[mãkan]	'eat'
[rumãh]	'house'
[kəreta]	'car'

For Malay, then, the generalization governing nasalization is different from the Scots Gaelic case both in the direction and the targets of nasalization.

7)

In Malay, all vowels and glides following a nasal consonant and not separated from it by a nonnasal consonant are nasalized.

Language-specific variation in allophonic distribution

In Section 1.2 we saw that a phonemic contrast in one language may not prove to be a phonemic contrast in another. This means that the relationship of phonemes to allophones may vary. A comparison of the contrasts among stops in English and Khmer (Cambodian) in Table 3.13 illustrates this point. In both languages, aspirated and unaspirated phones can be heard.

Table 3.13 Stop phones in English and Khmer

English		*Khmer*	
[p]	[pʰ]	[p]	[pʰ]
[t]	[tʰ]	[t]	[tʰ]
[k]	[kʰ]	[k]	[kʰ]

In English, aspirated and unaspirated stops are allophones of their respective phonemes (the distribution is explained in Section 4.5 of this chapter); there are no contrasting forms like [pɪk] and [pʰɪk]. In Khmer, though, unaspirated and aspirated voiceless stops contrast (see Table 3.14).

Table 3.14 Khmer contrastive voiceless stops

[pɔːŋ]	'to wish'	[pʰɔːŋ]	'also'
[tɔp]	'to support'	[tʰɔp]	'be suffocated'
[kat]	'to cut'	[kʰat]	'to polish'

The phonological contrasts of the two languages are different, even though the phones are not (see Figure 3.5). These distributions are the same for the other voiceless stops in both languages.

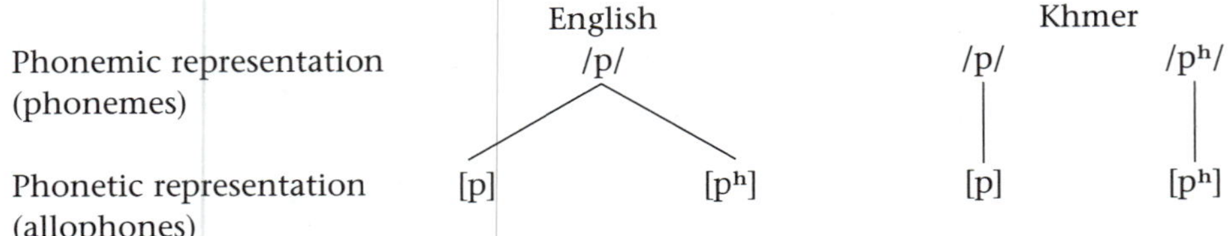

Figure 3.5 English and Khmer voiceless bilabial stop phonemes and allophones

3 PHONETIC AND PHONEMIC TRANSCRIPTION

We have seen so far that each language has a set of contrastive phonemes (which can be established largely by means of the minimal pair test) and that phonemes themselves can have predictable variants or allophones (which are usually in complementary distribution with each other). We have also suggested that there are two distinct levels of representation: the phonemic (or phonological) and the phonetic. We can now illustrate more clearly the types of transcription used at each level of representation.

The phonetic level of representation includes both predictable and unpredictable phonetic information. In contrast, the phonemic level includes all and only those aspects of a representation that are unpredictable; all predictable information is excluded. The examples in Table 3.15 show this difference for the classes of sounds in English that we have examined so far.

Table 3.15 Phonetic and phonemic transcription of English

Phonetic transcription	*Phonemic transcription*	*Word*	*Predictable property(s) not represented in phonemic transcription*
[pl̥aw]	/plaw/	plow	voicelessness of liquid
[kr̥ip]	/krip/	creep	voicelessness of liquid
[kw̥ɪk]	/kwɪk/	quick	voicelessness of liquid
[lejt]	/let/	late	glide after mid tense vowel
[lɛt]	/lɛt/	let	—
[tʰajd]	/tajd/	tied	aspiration
[tʰʌjt]	/tajt/	tight	aspiration; Canadian Raising

In the phonemic transcriptions in Table 3.15, the words are transcribed using only phonemes; in the phonetic transcriptions, however, the allophones of each phoneme are transcribed (in the environments in which they predictably occur). There is thus more phonetic information in the phonetic transcriptions than in the phonemic ones. If one compares the two transcriptions of *tight*, for instance, one sees that the phonetic transcription indicates the aspiration of the initial *t*, and the raised pronunciation of the vowel. In the corresponding phonemic transcription, the aspiration is left out because its occurrence is predictable, and the [ʌj] allophone of /aj/ is replaced by its phoneme.

The contrast between phonetic and phonemic representation is even more striking for the Malay forms given earlier, as shown in Table 3.16.

Table 3.16 Phonetic and phonemic transcription of Malay nasal vowels

Phonetic transcription	*Phonemic transcription*	*Word*	*Predictable property(s) not represented in phonemic transcription*
[mẽw̃ãh]	/mewah/	'luxurious'	nasalization
[mãj̃ãn]	/majan/	'stalk'	nasalization
[nãɛ̃ʔ]	/naɛʔ/	'ascend'	nasalization

Here, nasalization on all vowel and glide segments is predictable and is therefore omitted from the phonemic representation.

3.1 Phonetic and phonemic inventories

All languages have both a phonetic level of representation and a phonemic one. The phonetic level represents the allophones of a language. The phonemic level represents the language's phonemes. What this means is that each language has two inventories of sounds: one, used for phonetic transcription, is the inventory of the allophones of the language; the other, used for phonemic transcription, is the inventory of the phonemes of the language. Since every language has more allophones of phonemes than it has phonemes, phonetic inventories of sounds are always larger than phonemic ones. Table 3.17 illustrates a partial phonetic inventory and the phonemic inventory for the vowels of English. Only those allophones that we have discussed so far in this chapter are listed (the phonetic inventory is thus obviously incomplete).

Table 3.17 Phonetic and phonemic inventories of the vowels of English

Phonetic inventory				*Phonemic inventory*		
i			u	i		u
ɪ			ʊ	ɪ		ʊ
ej			ow	e		o
ɛ	ʌ	ʌj	ɔj	ɛ	ʌ	ɔj
		ʌw	ɔ			ɔ
	ə				ə	
æ		aj	ɑ	æ	aj	ɑ
		aw			aw	

Table 3.18 illustrates a partial phonetic inventory (again based on allophones discussed so far) and the phonemic inventory of English consonants.

Since there are two levels of representation—the phonetic and the phonemic—one obvious question to ask is how they are related to each other. In Sections 6 and 7 we consider in detail the nature of the relationship between phonetic and phonemic levels and inventories and show how to formalize this relationship.

Table 3.18 Phonetic and phonemic inventories of the consonants of English

Phonetic inventory						*Phonemic inventory*					
p		t		k		p		t		k	
p^h		t^h		k^h							
b		d		g		b		d		g	
			tʃ						tʃ		
			dʒ						dʒ		
	f	s	ʃ		h		f	s	ʃ		h
	v	z	ʒ				v	z	ʒ		
m		n		ŋ		m		n		ŋ	
w		l	j			w		l	j		
w̥		l̥	j̊								
		r						r			
		r̥									

4 ABOVE THE SEGMENT: SYLLABLES

So far we have been discussing the distributional properties of segments, and have established the existence of the segmental units of phonological analysis known as phonemes and their allophones. We have also seen that allophonic variation may be conditioned by neighboring segments. We turn now to a different unit of phonological representation, namely the **syllable**. We will see that syllables are composed of segments, and thus impose an organization on segments; in this sense syllables are **suprasegmental** (above the segment) units. We will also see that the shapes of syllables are governed by universal and language-specific constraints. Finally, we will examine examples of allophonic variation that is conditioned by syllable structure rather than by neighboring segments.

4.1 Defining the syllable

As we saw in Chapter 2, vowels, glides, liquids, and nasals are **sonorants** (singable sounds); **obstruents**, in contrast, are not sonorant. Of the sonorant sounds, vowels are most sonorous, and glides, liquids, and nasals are correspondingly less sonorous. A syllable consists of a sonorous element and its associated nonsyllabic (less sonorous) segments. Since vowels are the most sonorous sounds, syllables usually have a vowel nucleus at their core; less sonorous sounds may appear on either side of a nucleus. Thus the word *telegraph* has three syllables because it has three vowels that serve as syllable nuclei.

Native speakers of a language demonstrate their awareness of the sonority values of segments and of the syllable as a unit of phonological structure whenever they count syllables in a word. No English speaker would hesitate to say that the words *telegraph* and *accident* have three syllables, and most speakers would feel confident that the words could be broken up into the syllables /tɛ.lɛ.græf/ and /æk.sə.dənt/ (the "." marks syllable divisions informally).

Speakers also know that syllables have internal subsyllabic structure as well. This internal organization of the syllable unit is shown in Figure 3.6 with the monosyllabic English word *sprint*. As you can see, a syllable (σ) consists of an **onset** and a **rhyme**; the rhyme, in turn, consists of the **nucleus** or syllable core, and a **coda**. The onset (O) is made up of those elements that precede the rhyme (R) in the same syllable. The nucleus (N) is the syllable's only obligatory member. The coda (Co) consists of those elements that follow the nucleus in the same syllable.

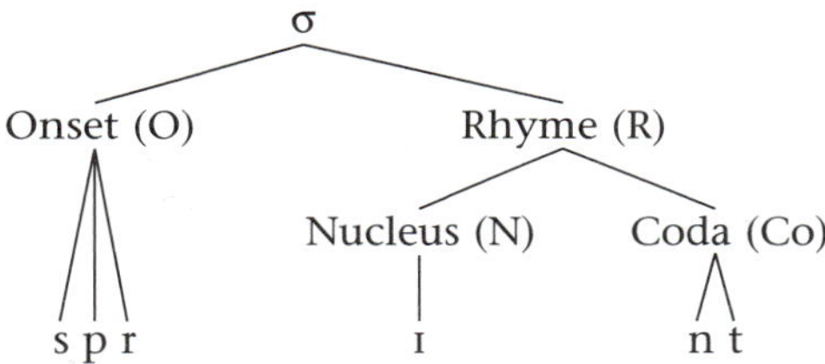

Figure 3.6 Internal structure of a syllable

We will see later on in this chapter that some allophonic variation makes reference to internal subsyllabic structure such as the coda.

There are other kinds of evidence that subsyllabic structure is part of speakers' knowledge. In English rhyming verses, for instance, it is always the rhymes of syllables that match each other (in other words, that rhyme), while onsets may vary: thus *sprite* and *fright* rhyme by virtue of having identical rhyme (nucleus and coda) constituents, but the onsets of each are different. In addition, one version of the English language game known as Pig Latin is played by displacing the onset of the first syllable of a word to the end of the word and then tacking on the rhyme *ay* [ej]: thus *strong* becomes *ong-str-ay,* and *swivel* become *ivel-sw-ay.*

Furthermore, when speakers are asked to syllabify words, they are able to do so in ways that are neither random nor variable. The word *extreme* /ɛkstrim/ would never be syllabified as /ɛ.kstrim/ in English, for example. Instead, syllables comply with certain constraints that prohibit them from beginning with a sequence like *kstr* and thus result in the actual syllabification /ɛk.strim/. The examples here are all from English, but similar kinds of evidence for the existence of subsyllabic constituents can be found in many other languages as well.

Table 3.19 Some examples of English syllables

/ə.plɔd/	applaud
/di.klajn/	decline
/ɛk.splen/	explain
/ɪm.prə.vajz/	improvise

All languages have syllables. The shapes of these syllables are governed by various kinds of constraints, but certain universal tendencies are observable: (1) syllable nuclei usually consist of one vowel (V); (2) syllables usually begin with onsets; (3) syllables may end with codas; (4) onsets and codas usually consist of one consonant (C). Putting these tendencies together, we find that the most common types of syllables found in languages throughout the world take the shapes CV and CVC. These are general tendencies, not absolute laws, and languages may, and often do, violate them. But even when a language violates the universal tendencies, the types of syllables that do occur are governed by other constraints on the shapes of the subsyllabic units O, N, and Co. To illustrate this, we turn to the constraints that govern the phonological shape of consonant sequences in onsets in English.

4.2 Onset constraints and phonotactics

Native speakers of any language intuitively know that certain words that come from other languages sound unusual and they often adjust the segment sequences of these words to conform with the pronunciation requirements of their own language. These intuitions are based on a tacit knowledge of the permissible syllable structures of the speaker's own language. For example, English-speaking students learning Russian have difficulty pronouncing a word like *vprog* /fprɔk/ 'value, good', since the sequence /fpr/ is never found in English onsets. Since speakers typically adjust an impermissible sequence by altering it to a permissible one, many English speakers would pronounce the Russian word [fprɔk] as [fəprɔk], or even delete the initial /f/ and say [prɔk] in order to adjust the impermissible sequence /fpr/ to a permissible English onset. **Phonotactics**, the set of constraints on how sequences of segments pattern, forms part of a speaker's knowledge of the phonology of his or her language.

Some English onsets

English is a language that allows onsets to contain more than one consonant; in this sense, English permits syllables that are more complex than those found in many languages. Nevertheless, there are very strict phonotactic constraints on the shapes of English onsets. Table 3.20 contains examples of the possible syllable-initial consonant sequences of English that contain a voiceless stop consonant. These sequences are all illustrated in word-initial position to make them easier to pick out. (Stress marking and phonetic details such as liquid-glide devoicing that are not relevant to the present discussion are omitted here.)

Table 3.20 Initial consonant clusters in English containing a voiceless stop

Labial + sonorant		*Alveolar + sonorant*		*Velar + sonorant*	
[pl]	please	[tl]	—	[kl]	clean
[pr]	proud	[tr]	trade	[kr]	cream
[pw]	—	[tw]	twin	[kw]	queen
[pj]	pure	[tj]	tune (British; Southern)	[kj]	cute
[spl]	splat	[stl]	—	[skl]	sclerosis
[spr]	spring	[str]	strip	[skr]	scrap
[spw]	—	[stw]	—	[skw]	squeak
[spj]	spew	[stj]	stew (British; Southern)	[skj]	skewer

The examples in Table 3.20 show that the first segment of a word-initial three-consonant cluster in English is always *s*; the second consonant in the series is always a voiceless stop, and the third is either a liquid or a glide. These sound patterns can be formally represented as follows:

$$\sigma\ [\text{s}\quad \begin{Bmatrix}\text{p}\\ \text{t}\\ \text{k}\end{Bmatrix} \quad \begin{Bmatrix}\text{(l)}\\ \text{r}\\ \text{(w)}\\ \text{j}\end{Bmatrix}$$

In this formalization, σ indicates the boundary of a syllable and the curly braces designate 'either/or'. The sounds in parentheses are not found in all combinations. An important observation about the types of onsets that are allowed in English is that the consonant combinations are not random; in fact: (1) the consonant combinations are dependent primarily on the manners of articulation of the consonants and (2) sonorant consonants (here liquids and glides) are closer to the nucleus than are stops and fricatives. Both these phonotactic constraints reflect universal restrictions on consonant combinations and are found in other languages that allow complex onsets.

4.3 Accidental and systematic gaps

Although there are twenty-four possible two- and three-consonant syllable-initial sequences in English containing a voiceless stop, not all of these combinations are exploited in the vocabulary of the language.

Some gaps in the inventory of possible English words include *snool, splick, sklop, flis, trok,* and *krif,* although none of these forms violates any constraints on onset combinations found in English. Gaps in a language's vocabulary that correspond to nonoccurring but possible forms are called **accidental gaps**. Occasionally, an accidental gap will be filled by the invention of a new word. The word *Kodak* is one such invented word; its shape conforms to the phonotactic constraints of English, but it only became part of English vocabulary in this century. Borrowed words such as *perestroika* (from Russian), *taco* (from Spanish), and *Zen* (from Japanese) are readily accepted by English speakers when, as is the case in these three examples, their syllable structures conform to the phonotactic patterns of the language.

Table 3.20 has shown which syllable-initial consonant clusters involving voiceless stops are permissible in English. Gaps in the occurring syllable structures of a language that result not by accident but from the exclusion of certain sequences are called **systematic gaps**. Certain onset sequences like /bz/, /pt/, and /fp/ are systematic gaps in the pattern of English. They are unacceptable to English speakers and never occur in spoken English. Instead, such sequences will be adjusted phonologically when they are pronounced in spontaneous speech. This can be seen in the case of borrowings from other languages into English. Many Greek words beginning with *ps-* and *pt-* have been absorbed into English, as the spellings of *psychology, psoriasis,* and *pterodactyl* attest. In all of them the impermissible syllable-initial clusters **ps-* and **pt-* have been reduced to *s-* or *t-* in onsets of spoken English. However, when these same forms occur word-internally, where their syllabification is different, the "lost" segments may resurface. For example, the *pter* of *pterodactyl* means 'wing'; both consonants are heard in the word *helicopter,* where English syllabification has resulted in a structure *he.li.cop.ter* in which the members of the cluster *pt* belong to different syllables.

There are other words that violate phonotactic constraints but that nonetheless do commonly appear in spoken English, such as *pueblo* [pwɛblow] and *Tlingit* [tl̥ɪŋɪt]. The fact that such words and pronunciations do occur in spoken English even though they violate phonotactic constraints is due to the fact that some phonotactic constraints are stronger than others and thus less likely to be violated. Thus, the sequences **ps-, *pt-,* and **bz-* are excluded from the initial position of English syllables because English has a very strong and thus absolute constraint against allowing stop-stop or stop-fricative clusters in onsets. In contrast, the restriction against sequences like **pw-* and **tl-* in English onsets is due to a weaker and thus violable constraint on stop-sonorant onset sequences with the same place of articulation: for example, a labiovelar glide is not usually permitted to occur after a labial consonant, and an alveolar stop such as /t/ is not usually permitted to precede an alveolar /l/ in English words.

Language-specific phonotactics

It is important to emphasize again that certain aspects of the particular constraints discussed in the previous section are universal and thus form part of human linguistic knowledge, whereas others are language-specific. An onset like *pl* is found in many languages besides English (for example, in Russian, Thai, and French), while an onset sequence like *lp* is never found. We may therefore say that no restrictions against an onset like *pl* appear to exist as part of human universal linguistic knowledge, while the nonexistence of onsets like **lp* suggests that something in their phonetic makeup disqualifies them from occurring in language. Language-specific constraints, on the other hand, hold true for individual languages such as English, and they may or may not be found in other languages. Each language has its own set of restrictions on the phonological shapes of its syllable constituents. Speakers of Russian, for example, are quite accustomed to pronouncing onset sequences such as *ps-*, *fsl-*, and *mgl-*, which are not found in English (see Table 3.21).

Table 3.21 Some onset sequences in Russian

[psa]	'dog's'
[fslux]	'aloud'
[mgla]	'fog'

Phonotactic constraints of the kind that we have seen for English represent one kind of phonological knowledge. You might, however, wonder what prevents English words like *extreme, applaud, decline, explain,* and *improvise* from being syllabified as the incorrect */ɛks.trim/, */ʌp.lɔd/, */dik.lajn/, */ɛks.plen/, and */ɪmp.rəv.ajz/, instead of the correct /ɛk.strim/, /ʌ.plɔd/, /di.klajn/, /ɛk.splen/, and /ɪm.prə.vajz/. In the incorrect syllabifications, the syllable divisions do not violate any phonotactic constraints, so the question to consider is why the syllabifications are nevertheless incorrect. The answer to this question is that such syllabifications are prevented by a universal constraint on general syllable shapes, rather than by a phonotactic constraint on segment sequences. As mentioned in Section 4.1, there is a universal syllable-shape constraint that encourages languages to make syllables with onsets; as a result, onsets in languages tend to be as large as possible. The next section illustrates the way this universal constraint works by providing a procedure for establishing the association of consonants and vowels within syllables.

4.4 Setting up syllables

Each language defines its own syllable structure through the interaction of universal and language-specific constraints. The process for setting up syllables in a given language involves three steps: (a) nucleus formation, (b) onset formation, and (c) coda formation; a fourth step, word level construction, ensures that syllables are incorporated into word-level units. The first step reflects the universal tendency for syllables to have a sonorant core; the second step reflects the tendency for syllables to have onsets, and the third step reflects the tendency for syllables to have codas. Ordering onset formation before coda formation reflects the cross-linguistic tendency of *Onsets before codas* (in a sequence of VCV, the consonant C will always be syllabified as an onset rather than a coda) and ensures that onsets gather up as many consonants as possible before any codas are formed.

- **Step a** *Nucleus formation:* Since the syllable nucleus is the only obligatory constituent of a syllable, it is constructed first. Each vowel segment in a word makes up a syllabic nucleus. To represent this, link a vowel to an N above it by drawing an **association line**. Above each nucleus symbol, place an R (for rhyme—in Section 4.1 we saw that the rhyme consists of the nucleus plus the coda), which is filled out in step c below. Above each R, place the symbol σ; link all with association lines.

Figure 3.7

- **Step b** *Onset formation:* The longest sequence of consonants to the left of each nucleus that does not violate the phonotactic constraints of the language in question is the onset of the syllable. Link these consonants to an O and join it to the same syllable as the vowel to the right. Note that there is no onset in the first syllable of *extreme*.

Figure 3.8

- **Step c** *Coda formation:* Any remaining unassociated consonants to the right of each nucleus form the coda, and are linked to a Co above them. This Co is associated with the syllable nucleus to its left in the rhyme. A syllable with a coda is called a **closed syllable** (a syllable without a coda is an **open syllable**).

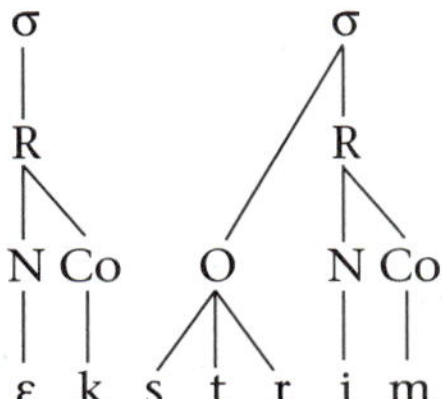

Figure 3.9

- **Step d** *Word-level construction:* Syllables that make up a single form (usually a word) branch out from the representation *Wd* (this step is frequently omitted from phonological representations to save space; the complete representation is understood even when *Wd* is not written out).

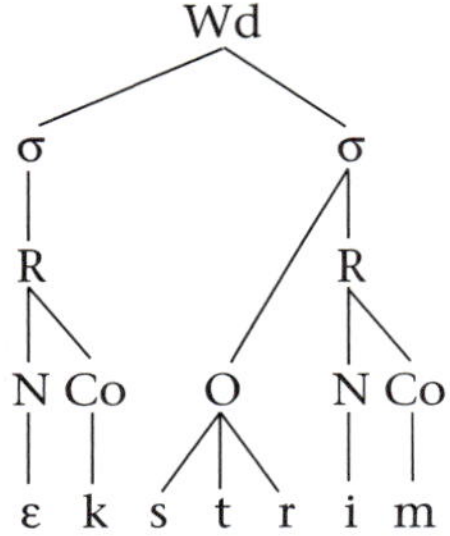

Figure 3.10

The steps in the procedure just outlined reflect universal constraints on syllable shapes. These interact with universal and language-specific phonotactic constraints. Given the procedure and the phonotactic constraints, we can now explain why words such as *applaud* and *explain* are syllabified as /ʌ.plɔd/ and /ɛk.splen/. In accordance with step b, onset formation, all the consonants in the clusters between the two vowel nuclei in each word (*pl* and *kspl,* respectively) could be syllabified as onsets of the second syllable. Thus *pl* is a possible candidate for an onset. According to the phonotactic constraints that are active in English, it is also a permissible onset, so both consonants are syllabified as part of the second syllable onset. In contrast, *kspl* is not a permissible onset in English because of the strong constraint against stop-fricative clusters in onsets; *spl* is a permissible onset, however, so the last three consonants of *kspl* are syllabified as part of the second syllable onset, and the first consonant *k* is left to be syllabified as a coda to the preceding syllable.

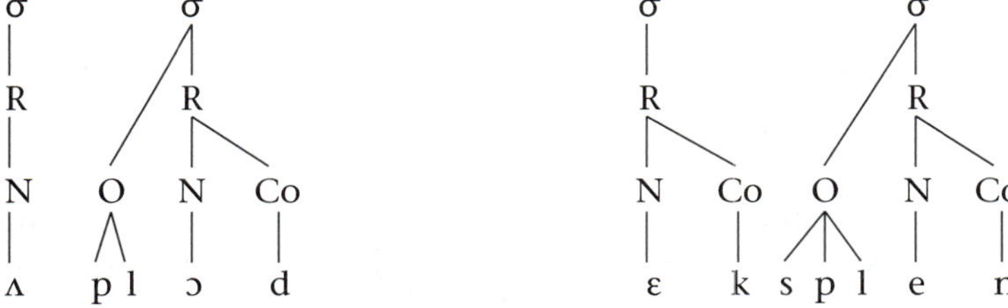

Figure 3.11 Syllabification: onsets before codas and phonotactic constraints

Some further syllabification

This procedure is used to syllabify forms in any language. An example from Turkish demonstrates in more detail how this universal syllabification procedure works. Turkish has different syllable structure constraints than English. As in English, onsets are optional in Turkish, but when present, they may consist of no more than one segment—clearly not a constraint found in English. A nucleus may consist of a long vowel (which is equivalent to two short vowels in length) or a short vowel. Codas can be no more than two segments long, and are largely limited to the following combinations: fricative-stop (for example, $-ft_\sigma$) or sonorant-obstruent (for example, $-rp_\sigma$).

The following words can be syllabified in the steps given above (steps c and d have been collapsed here). Note how the procedure leads to different syllabifications of the word *alt* 'bottom' in steps b and c of the examples.

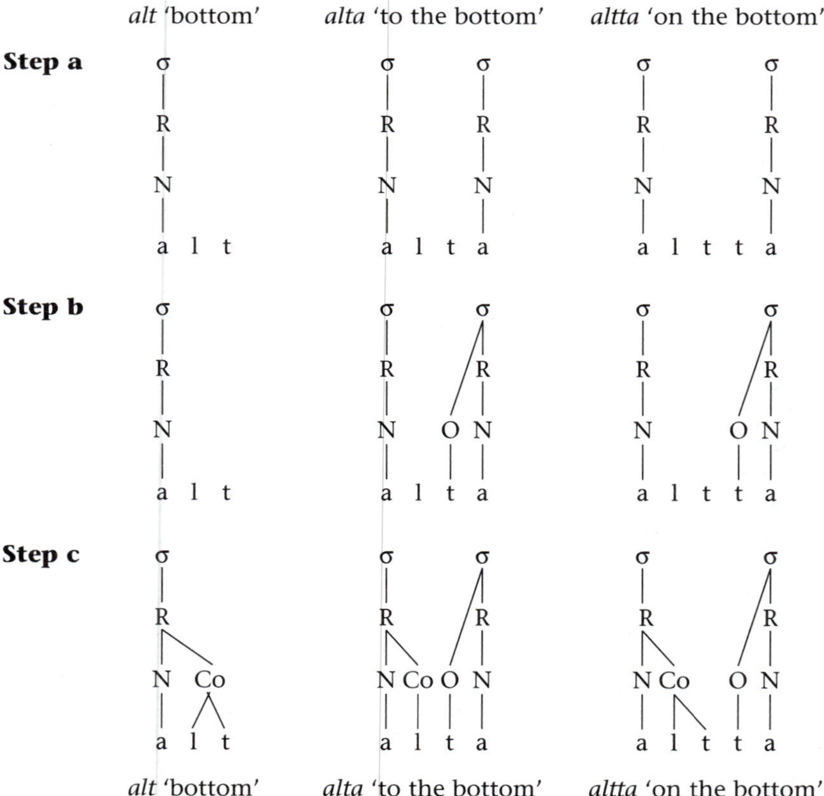

Figure 3.12 Examples of syllabification in Turkish

In these examples, the *t* of *alt* 'bottom' is assigned to the coda of the first syllable, since there is no syllable with an available onset position following it. However, the same phoneme *t* in *alta* 'to the bottom' is assigned to the onset of the second syllable, since onsets are filled first and *t* is available to fill the position. In *altta* 'on the bottom', the two *t*s fill the available coda and onset positions of their respective syllables.

As a final example of the procedure, the following figure demonstrates the syllabification of the English words *slim*, *decline*, and *scrimp*.

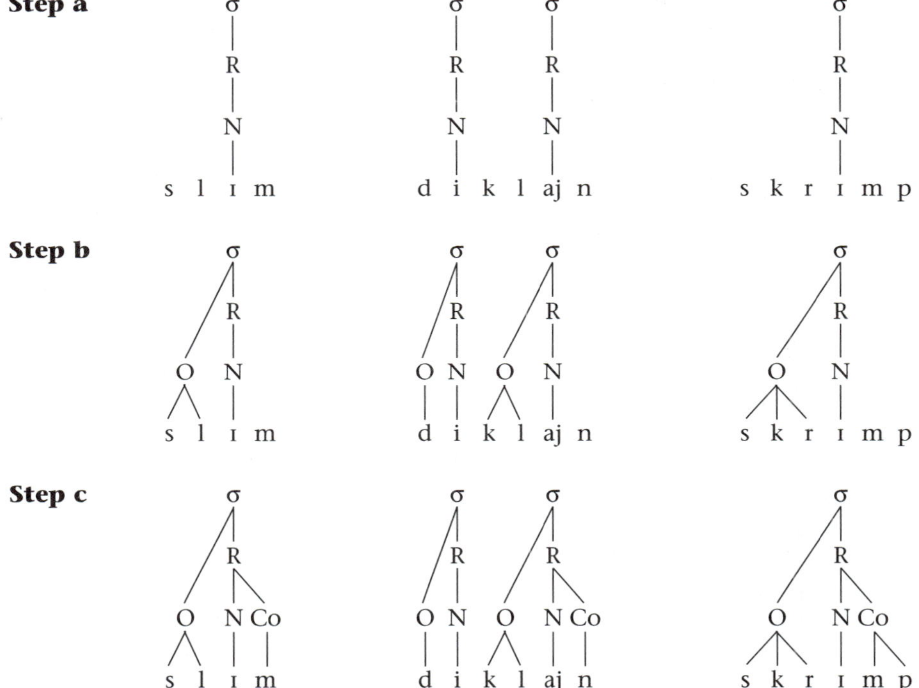

Figure 3.13 Examples of syllabification in English

With this method in mind, we can now consider the relevance of syllables to phonological description.

4.5 Syllabic phonology

One reason that syllables are treated as units of phonological structure is that they are relevant to stating generalizations about the distribution of allophonic features. The next sections provide examples of the role of syllables and subsyllabic constituents in phonological patterns. The fact that syllables and their internal constituents have such a role is thus evidence that they are part of the knowledge that speakers have of the phonology of their language.

Aspiration in English

As Table 3.22 shows, the voiceless stops of English each have an aspirated and an unaspirated allophone.

Table 3.22 English aspiration

A		B		C	
[pʰǽn]	pan	[spǽn]	span	[slǽp]	slap
[pʰéjn]	pain	[spéjn]	Spain	[slɑ́t]	slot
[pʰówk]	poke	[spówk]	spoke	[blɑ́k]	block
[tʰówn]	tone	[stówn]	stone		
[kʰín]	kin	[skín]	skin		
[pʰərspájr]	perspire	[splǽt]	splat		
[tʰəméjɾow]	tomato	[ʌpsɛ́t]	upset		
[kʰənúw]	canoe				
[əpʰɔ́n]	upon				
[ətʰǽk]	attack				
[tʰəkʰílə]	tequila				

The distribution of aspiration can be stated generally by referring to syllable structure and, in the case of the distribution of unaspirated stops, by referring to the subsyllabic units onset and coda.

Table 3.23 Distribution of aspirated stops in English

Aspirated stops	*Unaspirated stops*
• syllable-initially	Elsewhere, i.e.: • in a syllable onset preceded by *s* (whether another C follows or not) • in a coda

The phonemic representations of the three English stops are unaspirated, since aspiration is predictable. The environments where aspiration occurs can be stated very generally by referring to syllable structure.

8)

English voiceless stops are aspirated syllable-initially.

This statement accounts for all the data in column A of Table 3.22, where voiceless stops appear syllable-initially. No aspiration is found in the forms in columns B and C, since the voiceless stops appear either as the second member of the syllable onset (in *span, Spain, spoke, stone,* and *skin*) or in a coda, as in *upset.*

Phonetic length in English vowels

English offers a second example of the phonological relevance of syllables. Phonetic length is predictable in English vowels, as the next examples show. English vowels are shorter before voiceless consonants, before sonorant consonants, and in word-final position; they are longer before voiced nonsonorant consonants as long as these nonsonorant consonants are in coda-position in the same syllable. As the next

Table 3.24 Phonetic length in English: long vowels before voiced coda consonants

A		*B*	
bad	[bæːd]	bat	[bæt]
Abe	[eːjb]	ape	[ejp]
phase	[feːjz]	face	[fejs]
leave	[liːv]	leaf	[lif]
tag	[tʰæːg]	tack	[tʰæk]
brogue	[broːwg]	broke	[browk]
		tame	[tʰẽjm]
		meal	[mil]
		soar	[sɔr]
		show	[ʃow]

examples show, if vowels are followed by nonsonorant consonants that are onsets of the following syllable, the vowels are short. Thus, in Table 3.25, the first-syllable vowels all precede voiced, nonsonorant consonants, but they are short since the voiced consonant is in the following syllable.

Table 3.25 Phonetic length in English: Short vowels before voiced onset consonants in English

obey	[ow.bej]	/obe/
redo	[ri.du]	/ridu/
regard	[ri.gɑrd]	/rigɑrd/
ogre	[ow.gər]	/ogər/

In order for an English vowel to be long, it must be followed by a voiced obstruent in the same syllable. The following generalization can now be made.

9)

English vowels are long when followed by a voiced obstruent in the coda position of the same syllable.

As the analyses of the distribution of aspiration and vowel length in English have shown, the use of syllabic representations in phonology permits us to make more general statements about certain allophonic patterns in language than if we used only statements that do not make reference to syllable structure.

Syllables and stress in English

English provides a final example of the relevance of syllabic units to phonological analysis. Recall (from Chapter 2, Section 8.3) that stress is defined as the perceived prominence of one or more syllabic elements over others in a word. In some languages—English among them—the structure of individual syllables plays a role in determining which vowel is stressed. Consider the data in Table 3.26.

Table 3.26 English noun stress

A	B	C
agénda	aróma	cínema
consénsus	Manitóba	cábinet
appéndix	horízon	vénison
synópsis	aréna	América
veránda	Minnesóta	jávelin

The words in columns A and B are all stressed on the next-to-last (penultimate) syllable, while the words in column C are all stressed on the third syllable from the end of the word (the antepenultimate syllable), as the form *America* makes clear. Although the stressing of the words at first may seem arbitrary, reference to syllable structure makes clear that there is some system underlying the assignment of stress here.

Syllabifying the words in each column reveals what stress assignment is based on. Figure 3.14 provides the syllabification of one word from each column. Words are provided in phonetic transcription.

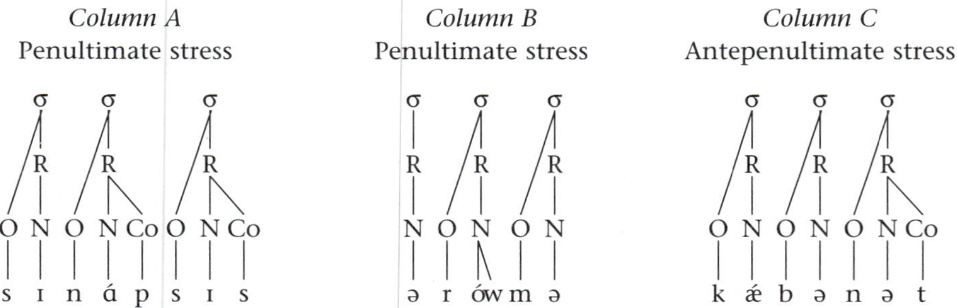

Figure 3.14 Syllable-based stress in English

All the words in column A share a correlation between their syllabification and their stress: the stressed penultimate syllable has a coda (recall that a syllable with a coda is said to be closed). All the words in column B also share a syllabic characteristic: their nucleus contains a tense vowel. Although the syllable is not closed, the nucleus vowel with two elements in it (the vowel-glide sequence) is now represented as branching. Tense vowels, in other words, have the same effect on stress assignment in English as closed syllables. Both closed syllables and syllables with two elements in the nucleus are referred to as **heavy syllables**. Compare these words with the representative item from column C. We see that the penultimate syllable is not heavy: it is neither closed nor does it contain a branching nucleus. With these facts before us, we can state our generalization. We will be careful to limit it to English *nouns*—that is, words that label or describe some thing or state (see Chapter 5, Section 1).

10)

English nouns are stressed on the penultimate syllable when it is heavy; otherwise, they are stressed on the antepenultimate syllable.

We have limited our generalization to English nouns because the full stress pattern of English is rather elaborate. Nevertheless, there is no doubt that syllabification plays a central role in determining stress placement in English.

5 FEATURES

In the previous section, we saw the role that syllable structure plays in verse, language games, and especially in allophonic variation. We also saw that universal and language-specific constraints govern the ways in which segment units combine to form the suprasegmental units of structure known as syllables. In this section we will discover that segments themselves are composed of even smaller, subsegmental, phonological units known as **features**. In fact, features are like atoms: they are the smallest units of phonology and as such are the basic building blocks of human speech sounds.

5.1 WHY WE USE FEATURES

There are a number of reasons why linguists consider features to be the most basic units of phonology.

Features as independent and coordinated phonetic elements

We have already seen in Chapter 2 that speech is produced by a number of independent but coordinated articulatory activities such as voicing, tongue position, and lip rounding. For example, when we produce the voiceless labial stop [p], the vocal cords in the larynx are open and not vibrating (hence the sound is voiceless), and the lips are actively pressed together to form a complete constriction (hence the sound is a labial stop). Each sound is thus the result of the coordinated articulatory activity of the larynx, and the various articulators—such as the tongue body, the tongue blade, the lips, and the velum—found in the oral and nasal cavities of the vocal tract. We assume that segments are themselves composed of smaller units known as features as a way of modeling this phonetic reality.

Features reflect the articulatory basis of speech in the sense that each feature encodes one of the independently controllable aspects of speech production. For example, in the case of [p], the feature [–voice] reflects laryngeal activity; the feature [LABIAL] reflects the activity of the lips; and the feature [–continuant] reflects the stop manner of articulation (note that features are written in square brackets; the use of '+' and '–' signs and capital versus lowercase letters is explained below); an 'o' before a feature indicates place of articulation.

As a further example, consider the sound [ɑ]. This sound is produced with a low, back, and tense tongue body (dorsal) position, with no rounding of the lips (therefore no labial activity) and little constriction. It is a vowel, and therefore is voiced and sonorant as well. All these phonetic properties are represented in terms of separate features in the feature representation in Figure 3.15. In this representation, the features of the segment are listed in an array called a **matrix**. This is a common way of presenting sets of features.

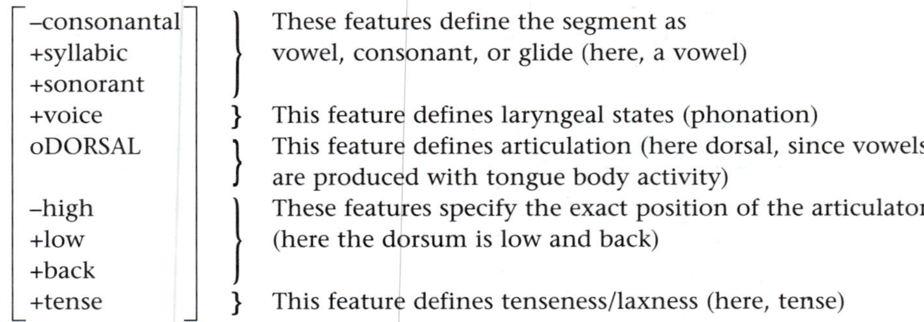

[ɑ]
–consonantal
+syllabic
+sonorant
These features define the segment as vowel, consonant, or glide (here, a vowel)
+voice
This feature defines laryngeal states (phonation)
oDORSAL
This feature defines articulation (here dorsal, since vowels are produced with tongue body activity)
–high
+low
+back
These features specify the exact position of the articulator (here the dorsum is low and back)
+tense
This feature defines tenseness/laxness (here, tense)

Figure 3.15 Feature representation for the English vowel /ɑ/

Features and natural classes

A second reason for viewing segments as composed of features is that doing so gives us an economical way of characterizing segments as members of natural classes. **Natural classes** are classes of sounds that share a feature or features and that pattern together in sound systems.

To see what is meant by this, consider the set of English sounds /p/, /t/, /k/, /f/, /s/, /ʃ/, and the set /b/, /d/, /g/, /v/, /z/, /ʒ/ given in Figure 3.16. All these sounds belong to the class of obstruents (/tʃ/, /dʒ/, /θ/, and /ð/ are also obstruents, but we will ignore them for now). In order to capture this fact, we can say that they are all [–sonorant] (the '–' means 'not' in this context; definitions of the features are given in Section 5.2). In addition, a subset of the members of this [–sonorant] class, namely /p/, /t/, /k/, /f/, /s/, and /ʃ/, all of which differ in place and (in part) in manner of articulation, can be readily distinguished from the subset /b/, /d/, /g/, /v/, /z/, and /ʒ/ by the single feature [voice] alone. Finally the feature [continuant] (which refers to whether or not a sound is produced with continuous, free airflow) can distinguish all the (noncontinuous) stops in the obstruent class, /p/, /t/, /k/, /b/, /d/, and /g/, from all the (continuous) fricatives, /f/, /s/, /ʃ/, /v/, /z/, and /ʒ/.

[–sonorant]

[–voice]	[+voice]	
p t k	b d g	[–continuant]
f s ʃ	v z ʒ	[+continuant]

Figure 3.16 Natural classes: obstruents in English

Using these three features, we are able to capture nine different natural classes of sounds; these are given in Table 3.27.

Table 3.27 Nine natural classes: obstruents in English

[–sonorant]	[–sonorant –continuant]	[–sonorant +continuant]	[–sonorant –voice]	[–sonorant +voice]	[–sonorant –continuant –voice]	[–sonorant –continuant +voice]	[–sonorant +continuant –voice]	[–sonorant +continuant +voice]
p t k	p t k	f s ʃ	p t k	b d g	p t k	b d g	f s ʃ	v z ʒ
b d g	b d g	v z ʒ	f s ʃ	v z ʒ				
f s ʃ								
v z ʒ								

Any natural class requires fewer features to define it than to define any one of its members. Thus in Table 3.27, the largest class, that of the obstruents, is defined by only one feature, while the four classes containing three segments each are defined by three features each.

Every set of sounds that is characterized by one or more features and that therefore constitutes a natural class has the potential to pattern together in some way in the phonology of a language. For instance, we saw above that aspiration in English affects /p/, /t/, and /k/, the [–sonorant, –continuant, –voice] sounds of the language. All and only these sounds are affected by the aspiration process. An interesting point about features is that their use allows us to exclude sounds from (as well as to include them in) natural classes. Thus, because /b/ is [+voice], it does not belong to the class of [–voice] stops in English, which includes /p/, /t/, and /k/. As a result /b/ is not affected by aspiration.

Table 3.28 provides an additional illustration of the use of features to distinguish natural classes—in this case, the class of front and back vowels in English. Again we see that fewer features are needed to define the larger class of English front vowels than to capture the vowel /æ/ alone.

Table 3.28 Two natural classes: front and back vowels in English

[–consonantal +syllabic +sonorant oDORSAL –back]	[–consonantal +syllabic +sonorant oDORSAL +back]	[–consonantal +syllabic +sonorant oDORSAL –back –high +low –tense –reduced]
i	u	æ
ɪ	ʊ	
e	o	
ɛ	ʌ	
	ɔ	
æ	ɑ	

In preceding sections, we listed those segments of English that contrast and that therefore are the phonemes of English. Because features define natural classes, it is not just individual phonemes such as /p/, /b/, /k/, and /g/ that contrast in English; in fact, the entire class of voiced stops contrasts with the class of voiceless stops. All the contrasts found in the English sound system (and in the sound system of any language) can be defined in terms of the features that make up those phonemes. Thus, the distinctions between /p/ and /b/, /t/ and /d/, and /k/ and /g/ all reside in the feature [voice]. In addition, words like *pit* and *bit*, which constitute a minimal pair, contrast in the segments /p/ and /b/, and /p/ and /b/ themselves contrast in the feature [voice]. What these examples show us, then, is that features as well as segments can be contrastive. When a feature is the source of phonemic contrasts in a language, we say that it is a **distinctive feature** in the language. Thus, [voice] is a distinctive feature in English.

Other features provide for other contrasts. For example, we can capture the contrast between /t/ and /s/ in English with the feature [continuant]. Both /t/ and /s/ are voiceless and have an alveolar point of articulation. By viewing the relevant distinctive feature as [continuant], we can use the same feature to distinguish between /p/ and /f/, /b/ and /v/, and /d/ and /z/.

Table 3.29 Stop-fricative contrasts as a feature

[–continuant]	[+continuant]
p	f
b	v
t	s
d	z

By systematically examining the phonemic contrasts of a language, we can extract the distinctive features and use these irreducible linguistic elements to describe the phonemic inventory.

Features, processes, and allophonic variation

A third reason for using features is that reference to features enables us to understand the nature of allophonic variation more exactly. Viewed from the perspective of features, allophonic variation is seen to be not simply the substitution of one allophone for another, but rather the environmentally conditioned change or specification of a feature or features. The liquid-glide devoicing that occurs in English words like *tree* and *twinkle*, for example, is a change in the value of the feature [voice] from [+voice] to [–voice] after voiceless (i.e., [–voice]) stop consonants. Similarly, the vowel and glide nasalization that occurs in Malay forms like /mewah/ [mẽw̃ãh] 'luxurious' is a change in the value of the feature [nasal] from [–nasal] to [+nasal] following a nasal (i.e., [+nasal]) consonant (see *7*).

We saw above that features reflect the fact that speech is produced by a number of independent but coordinated articulatory activities. Certain features, however, reflect classes of sounds that are not always reflected in the traditional descriptive terminology of phonetics that was introduced in Chapter 2, but that are nevertheless relevant to phonological patterning. For example, the feature [CORONAL] (the use of capitals as opposed to lowercase letters here reflects a difference in feature type that will be clarified below) refers to the class of sounds made with the tongue tip or blade raised; this class includes sounds made with interdental, alveolar, and alveopalatal places of articulation. It turns out that just this feature is required to state a constraint on the selection of consonant sequences in coda position in English: according to this constraint, when a vowel is tense and followed by two consonants (*pint*), or when a vowel is lax and followed by three consonants (*next* [nɛkst]), the final consonant in the coda must always be [CORONAL] (t, d, s, z, θ, ð, ʃ, ʒ, tʃ, or dʒ). Although the feature [CORONAL] does not reflect a traditional phonetic term, it plays a very important role in the phonologies of many languages. This fact shows us that features reflect articulatory reality in a way that is more than just a different guise for traditional phonetic descriptions.

5.2 Feature representations

We have seen that segments are composed of subsegmental units or features and that features reflect phonetic reality. Since features are considered to be the basic building blocks of speech sounds, and thus of phonology, linguists have attempted to state all possible phonological facts about language with the fewest number of features possible. Only a limited number of features—currently around twenty-four—have been proposed. Features thus constitute an important part of a theory of what is possible (and what is not possible) in the phonological behavior of human beings. In this section we present and define all the features that are needed to characterize the sounds of English, as well as of many other languages.

Defining the features of English

Most features have labels that reflect traditional articulatory terms, such as [voice], [consonantal], and [nasal]. These features require little further description. A few features have less familiar labels, such as [CORONAL] and [anterior]. From this point on, features will be used to describe classes of sounds. At the same time, we will continue throughout the book to use terms such as *consonant, glide,* and *obstruent* (a fricative, an affricate, or a nonnasal stop) in phonetic description. The traditional terminology will be maintained because it is still widely used in phonetic description.

Features are organized into groups that reflect natural classes. The following headings indicate what these classes are and how the features represent them. Most of the features given below are written in lowercase and can have one of two values, + or –, each of which defines a particular class of sounds. For example, [+voice] sounds involve vibration or voicing in the larynx, while [–voice] sounds involve an open glottis and therefore no vibration or voicing. Three of the features ([LABIAL], [CORONAL], and [DORSAL]), are written in uppercase and do not have + and – values. Why this is so will be made clear below.

- **Major class features** *features that represent the classes consonant, obstruent, and sonorant (nasal, liquid, glide, vowel)*

[±consonantal] Sounds that are [+consonantal] are produced with a major obstruction in the vocal tract. All nonsonorant consonants as well as liquids and nasals are [+consonantal]. Glides and vowels are [–consonantal].

[±syllabic] Sounds that can act as syllable peaks are [+syllabic]; this includes vowels, and syllabic liquids or syllabic nasals. All other sounds are [–syllabic].

[±sonorant] All and only those sounds that are "singable" are [+sonorant]; this includes vowels, glides, liquids, and nasals (even if the [+sonorant] sounds are voiceless). All nonsingable sounds (obstruents) are [–sonorant].

Table 3.30 illustrates how the major class features are used to divide sounds into classes. Note that nasals and liquids have the same values for the three major class features; to distinguish these two classes from each other, additional (manner) features are needed.

Table 3.30 Use of major class features

	Obstruents	*Nasals*	*Liquids*	*Glides*	*Vowels*
[±consonantal]	+	+	+	–	–
[±syllabic]	–	–	–	–	+
[±sonorant]	–	+	+	+	+
Examples:	p d v tʃ	m n	l r	j w	i a

The features given next represent manners of articulation. Their use is particularly important in distinguishing the following classes: stops/affricates from fricatives ([±continuant]); affricates from stops ([±delayed release]); nasals from nonnasals ([±nasal]); and laterals from nonlaterals ([±lateral]).

- **Manner features** *features that represent manner of articulation*

  [±continuant] Sounds produced with free or nearly free airflow through the center of the oral cavity are [+continuant]; these include vowels, glides, the nonlateral liquid *r*, and fricatives. All other sounds are [–continuant]; these include nasal and oral stops, and the lateral liquid *l*.

  [±delayed release] ([±DR]) In the stop portion [t] of an affricate sound such as [tʃ], the tongue is slower in leaving the roof of the mouth than when a stop like [t] is produced on its own. Hence affricates are said to be produced with "delayed release." All affricates, such as [tʃ] and [dʒ], are [+delayed release]; all other sounds are [–delayed release].

  [±nasal] Sounds produced with a lowered velum are [+nasal]; this includes nasal stops and all nasalized sounds. Sounds that are oral, and thus produced with a raised velum, are [–nasal].

  [±lateral] All and only varieties of *l* are [+lateral]. All other sounds are [–lateral].

Voicing, aspiration, and glottal constriction are all the result of laryngeal activity. To represent different laryngeal states, we use the features [±voice], [±spread glottis], and [±constricted glottis].

- **Laryngeal features** *features that represent laryngeal activity*

  [±voice] All voiced sounds are [+voice]; all voiceless sounds are [–voice].

  [±spread glottis] ([±SG]) All aspirated consonants are [+SG]; all others are [–SG].

  [±constricted glottis] ([±CG]) All sounds made with a closed glottis are [+CG]; all others are [–CG]. In English, only the glottal stop [ʔ] is [+CG].

The last set of features is used to represent the supralaryngeal (above the larynx) articulatory activity, which determines place of articulation. There are two types of articulatory features. The first type includes the features [LABIAL], [CORONAL], and [DORSAL], which are used specifically to represent and to distinguish the articulators that are active at particular places of articulation. For instance, the sound [k] is produced when the dorsum or body of the tongue touches the velum (soft palate) to form a constriction. [k] thus has a velar place of articulation; this place of articulation is activated by moving the dorsal (tongue body) articulator. The second type of articulatory feature includes all the other place of articulation features (e.g., [high], [back]) listed below. These features are used to distinguish different settings for each of the active articulators and are in this sense specific to individual articulators. For instance, when [k] is pronounced, the tongue body is always positioned high and back in the oral cavity, and therefore the [k] is [+high] and [+back] as well as being [DORSAL].

- **Place of articulation features** *features that represent supralaryngeal activity*

  [LABIAL] This feature represents the labial articulator; any sound that is produced with involvement of one or both of the lips is [LABIAL].

    [±round] A sound produced with the labial articulator may be produced by protruding the lips; such sounds are [+round]; labial sounds made with no lip protrusion are [–round]. Rounded vowels and the rounded labiovelar glide [w] are [+round] labial sounds. Sounds like [p, b, f, v] are [–round] labial sounds.

  [CORONAL] This feature represents the coronal articulator; any sound that is produced with involvement of the tongue tip or blade raised is [CORONAL].

    [±anterior] All coronal sounds articulated in front of the alveopalatal region (interdentals and alveolars) are [+anterior]; coronal sounds articulated at or behind the alveopalatal region (alveopalatals) are [–anterior].

    [±strident] All "noisy" coronal fricatives and affricates ([s, z, ʃ, ʒ, tʃ, dʒ]) are [+strident]; all other coronal fricatives and affricates ([θ, ð]) are [–strident].

  [DORSAL] This feature represents the dorsal articulator; any sound that is produced with involvement of the body of the tongue is [DORSAL].

    [±high] Dorsal consonants (velars or palatals) or vowels produced with the tongue body raised from a central position in the oral cavity are [+high]. Sounds produced with a neutral or lowered tongue body are [–high].

    [±low] Vowels produced with the tongue body lowered from a central position in the oral cavity are [+low]. All other vowels are [–low].

[±back] Dorsal consonants or vowels produced with the tongue body behind the palatal region (hard palate) in the oral cavity are [+back]. Sounds produced with the tongue body at or in front of the palatal region are [–back].

[±tense] Vowels that are tense are [+tense]; vowels that are lax are [–tense].

[±reduced] The vowel schwa ([ə]) is a lax and exceptionally brief vowel and is therefore [+reduced]; all other vowels are [–reduced].

To set the articulator features apart from other features, they are written with capitals. They do not have + and – values associated with them because if they are not being used to execute an articulation, they are simply inactive and are therefore absent from a representation. In other words, if a sound is a velar [k], it is produced with the tongue body, not with the lips or the tongue blade or tip. Consequently, the lips and the tongue blade or tip are not actively involved in the production of the sound and therefore the feature specification for [k] does not include the articulator features [LABIAL] and [CORONAL].

Features like [±round], [±anterior], or [±high], which are executed by particular articulators, are used only to distinguish sounds produced by those articulators. Thus, for instance, only sounds like [k] that are produced with the tongue body and that are thus [DORSAL] may be [±high], [±low], or [±back]. No sounds made with other articulators are represented with values for these features.

To see exactly how the articulation features are used to represent the various places of articulation of the consonants found in English, let us look at Table 3.31. In the feature representations, o indicates that the relevant articulator is active in the production of a sound. Where no o is present, it means that the articulator is inactive.

Table 3.31 Use of place of articulation features in representing some English consonants

	Labials		*Dentals*	*Alveolars*	*Alveopalatals*	*Palatals*	*Velars*
	p	w	θ	s	ʃ	j	k
LABIAL	o	o					
[±round]	–	+					
CORONAL			o	o	o		
[±anterior]			+	+	–		
[±strident]			–	+	+		
DORSAL		o				o	o
[±high]		+				+	+
[±back]		+				–	+
[±low]		–				–	–

The feature representations in Table 3.31 can be understood as follows:

- [p] is produced with the lips in an unrounded state. It is therefore a [LABIAL], [–round] sound. The tongue blade and the tongue body are not used in the production of [p] and therefore it has no feature specifications for the coronal and dorsal articulators nor for [CORONAL] or [DORSAL] features.

- [θ, s, ʃ] are all [CORONAL] sounds because they are produced with the tongue blade. [θ, s] are produced with the tongue blade before or at the alveolar ridge and are therefore [+anterior], while [ʃ] is produced with the tongue blade behind the alveolar ridge and is therefore [–anterior]. [θ] is produced with a quiet airflow and so is [–strident], while [s, ʃ] are produced with noisy airflow and so are [+strident]. Since neither the lips nor the tongue body are used to produce these sounds, they have no specifications for the labial and dorsal articulators nor for [LABIAL] or [DORSAL] features.
- [j, k] are both produced with the tongue body and are therefore [DORSAL] sounds. Both have a raised tongue body and so are [+high], but [j] is pronounced with the tongue body at the hard palate and so is [–back], while [k] is pronounced with the tongue body behind the hard palate and so is [+back]. Since sounds cannot have both a raised and a lowered tongue body simultaneously, and since [j] and [k] are both [+high], they are also both [–low]. Finally, since neither the lips nor the tongue blade are used to produce these sounds, they have no specifications for the labial and coronal articulators nor for [LABIAL] or [CORONAL] features.
- [w] is a labiovelar sound and is thus coarticulated: it is produced with both a tongue body that is raised and behind the hard palate, *and* with lip rounding. This means that both the dorsum and the lips are used to produce [w], so it is executed with two articulators acting simultaneously. It is therefore both [LABIAL] and [DORSAL]; as a [LABIAL] sound it is [+round], and as a [DORSAL] sound it is [+high, +back, –low]. Since the tongue blade is not used to produce this sound, it has no specifications for the [CORONAL] articulator or for coronal features.

Table 3.32 exemplifies how the place of articulation features are used to represent vowels in English. All the vowels in the table are produced with an active tongue body and therefore are [DORSAL]; this is true of all vowels—in English and in all

Table 3.32 Use of place of articulation features in representing some English vowels

	ɛ	ə	u	ɑ
LABIAL			o	
[±round]			+	
DORSAL	o	o	o	o
[±high]	–	–	+	–
[±low]	–	–	–	+
[±back]	–	+	+	+
[±tense]	–	–	+	+
[±reduced]	–	+	–	–

other languages. Vowels that involve lip rounding are also produced with the [LABIAL] articulator. [CORONAL] is never used in the feature representations of vowels. All vowels except schwa are unreduced and therefore specified as [–reduced].

- [ɛ] is a mid, front (nonback), unrounded, lax vowel. Since it is unrounded, it does not use the labial articulator. As a mid vowel, it has neither a raised nor a lowered tongue body, so it is [DORSAL] and specified as both [–high] and [–low]. As a front vowel, it is [–back] and as a lax vowel, it is [–tense].

- [ə] is a mid, central, unrounded, lax, and reduced vowel. As a mid vowel, it is [DORSAL, –high] and [–low]. As a central and therefore nonfront vowel, it is [+back]. (All central vowels are always [+back] in feature representations.) Being unrounded, it does not involve the labial articulator. Because it is a lax, reduced vowel, it is [–tense] and [+reduced].

- [u] is a high, back, tense vowel, and is therefore specified as [+high], [+back], and [+tense]. Since it is rounded, it is [LABIAL, +round] in addition to being [DORSAL]. Since it is [+high], it is also [–low]. (As in the case of consonants, the tongue body cannot be both raised and lowered at the same time, so all [+high] vowels are also [–low].)

- [ɑ] is a low, back, unrounded, tense vowel. Since it is produced with a lowered tongue body, it is [DORSAL, +low]; because a lowered tongue body cannot be simultaneously raised, it is also [–high]. Since it is back, it is [+back]. Being tense, it is [+tense], and being unrounded, it has no labial specifications.

Feature notation does not provide a convenient way to distinguish diphthongs such as [aj], [aw], and [ɔj] from the other vowels. These diphthongs may be treated as vowel-glide sequences when using features.

Determining feature representations

We have now defined the phonological features used to represent sounds, and have illustrated the feature specifications of some of the consonants and vowels of English. Unlike in the case of constructing syllables, there is no straightforward algorithm for setting up feature representations. It is possible, however, to simplify the task of determining feature representations for individual sounds by going through the process in a step-wise fashion, asking certain key questions in a particular order.

I. What is the manner of articulation of the sound?
To determine the answer to this question, use the *major class features* and the *manner features*.
1. Start by asking yourself if the sound is [+sonorant] or [–sonorant].
2. Is it [–consonantal] or [+consonantal]?
3. Is it [+continuant] or [–continuant]?
4. Is it [+syllabic] or [–syllabic]?
5. Is it [–nasal] or [+nasal]?

6. If [+sonorant, +consonantal, –nasal], is it [–lateral] or [+lateral]?
7. If [–sonorant, +consonantal, –continuant], is it [+DR] or [–DR]?

Once the major class divisions have been determined, the next step is to go on to the laryngeal features.

II. What is the laryngeal setting of the sound?
To determine the answer to this question, use the *laryngeal features*.
1. Is it [+voice] or [–voice]?
2. Is it [+CG] or [–CG]? This question is only relevant to [ʔ].
3. Is it [+SG] or [–SG]? This question is only relevant to [h] and aspirated sounds.

Finally, place of articulation must be determined.

III. What is the place of articulation of the sound?
To determine the answer to this question, use the *place of articulation features*.
1. Which articulator is active in producing the sound?
2. If [LABIAL], is the sound [+round] or [–round]?
3. If [CORONAL], is the sound [+anterior] or [–anterior]
[+strident] or [–strident]?
4. If [DORSAL], is the sound [+high] or [–high]
[+low] or [–low]
[+back] or [–back]
[+tense] or [–tense]
[+reduced] or [–reduced]? } These questions are only for vowels.

To illustrate how these questions lead one to the right feature representations, consider the sounds [t], [m], and [i].

- [t] is an oral stop (obstruent), is voiceless, and has an alveolar place of articulation.

Manner of articulation: As an obstruent, it is [–sonorant], and since all [–sonorant] sounds are also always consonants, it is [+consonantal, –syllabic]. As an oral stop, it is [–nasal], [–continuant], and [–DR].
Laryngeal setting: As a voiceless sound, it is [–voice], and since it is not a glottal stop or [h], it is [–CG, –SG].
Place of articulation: As an alveolar, it is produced with the tongue blade at the alveolar ridge with no obvious noise, so it is [CORONAL, +anterior, –strident].

- [m] is a nasal stop, is voiced, and has a labial place of articulation.

Manner of articulation: As a nasal, it is a sonorant consonant, and therefore, it is [+sonorant] and [+consonantal], and [–syllabic] (unless it is a syllabic nasal). Nasals are always stops; therefore it is [–continuant]. It is also crucially [+nasal].
Laryngeal setting: Like all sonorant sounds, in the normal case it is [+voice] and [–CG, –SG].
Place of articulation: As a labial, it is produced with the lips but with no lip rounding and is therefore [LABIAL, –round].

- [i] is an oral vowel, which is high, front, unrounded, and tense.

  Manner of articulation: It is nonconsonantal, sonorant, syllabic, and a continuous sound, and therefore is [+sonorant, –consonantal, +syllabic, +continuant]. It is also [–nasal].

  Laryngeal setting: Like all sonorant sounds, in the normal case it is [+voice] and [–CG, –SG].

  Place of articulation: As an unrounded vowel, it is produced only with the tongue body and is therefore [DORSAL, +high, –low, –back, +tense, –reduced].

To illustrate what complete feature representations look like, Figure 3.17 gives feature matrices for [t, m, i]. In the matrices, features are listed following the same basic order as the one we have just followed to arrive at the feature representations: the major class features are followed by the manner features; the manner features are followed by laryngeal features; and, finally, laryngeal features are followed by place of articulation features with the articulator feature given first.

t	m	i	
+consonantal	+consonantal	–consonantal	Major class features
–syllabic	–syllabic	+syllabic	
–sonorant	+sonorant	+sonorant	
–continuant	–continuant	+continuant	Manner features
–DR	–DR	–DR	
–nasal	+nasal	–nasal	
–lateral	–lateral	–lateral	
–voice	+voice	+voice	Laryngeal features
–CG	–CG	–CG	
–SG	–SG	–SG	
oCORONAL	oLABIAL	oDORSAL	Place of articulation features
+anterior	–round	+high	
–strident		–low	
		–back	
		+tense	
		–reduced	

Figure 3.17 Feature matrices for three English sounds

In the feature matrices in Figure 3.17, a complete set of features is given for every phoneme. However, it is not always necessary to give a complete set of features for a sound, and so in some cases in this chapter we leave predictable features out. The reason for this is that in some situations certain features are inherently predictable and so can be left out of feature representations. For example, as we saw above, segments that are [+high] are always [–low] because the two tongue positions represented by these features are mutually exclusive. Conversely, segments that are [+low] are always [–high]. When giving feature representations for [+high] segments, therefore, it is not absolutely necessary to include the feature [–low], since this feature is predictable; similarly, for [+low] segments it is not necessary to include the feature [–high] in the representation, since [–high] is predictable. The phoneme /l/ is another example: this segment is the only [+lateral] sound in the language; therefore it is sufficient to represent it simply as [+lateral]. All its other features are predictable. Other examples of features that are predictable include [+voice] on sonorant consonants and vowels and [–nasal] on vowels. Since sonorant consonant and vowel phonemes are always [+voice] (unless they become devoiced by a phonological process such as liquid-glide devoicing), [+voice] can be left out of the feature representations for these phonemes. Similarly, since vowel phonemes in English are never contrastively nasal, they are always [–nasal]; therefore, [–nasal] does not have to be part of the representation of vowel phonemes.

Tables 3.33 and 3.34 provide the feature representations for all the vowels and consonants of English. Go through them, keeping in mind the basic questions that need to be answered when determining the feature representation of any sound.

Table 3.33 Feature matrix for English vowels

		i	ɪ	e	ɛ	æ	ʌ	ə	u	ʊ	o	ɔ	ɑ
Major class features	[consonantal]	–	–	–	–	–	–	–	–	–	–	–	–
	[sonorant]	+	+	+	+	+	+	+	+	+	+	+	+
	[syllabic]	+	+	+	+	+	+	+	+	+	+	+	+
Manner feature	[continuant]	+	+	+	+	+	+	+	+	+	+	+	+
Laryngeal features	[voice]	+	+	+	+	+	+	+	+	+	+	+	+
Place of articulation features	LABIAL								o	o	o	o	
	[round]								+	+	+	+	
	DORSAL	o	o	o	o	o	o	o	o	o	o	o	o
	[high]	+	+	–	–	–	–	–	+	+	–	–	–
	[low]	–	–	–	–	+	–	–	–	–	–	–	+
	[back]	–	–	–	–	–	+	+	+	+	+	+	+
	[tense]	+	–	+	–	–	–	–	+	–	+	–	+
	[reduced]	–	–	–	–	–	–	+	–	–	–	–	–

5.3 The feature hierarchy *(Advanced)*

In the preceding subsection the features of any one segment are listed in a matrix, which has no internal structure of any kind. Listing features in a matrix has long been the most common way to represent the featural composition of segments. It is also possible, however, to group features together into a **feature hierarchy**. Hierarchical feature representations are useful for several reasons: first, they are an even better mirror of vocal tract activity than feature matrices are; and, second, they represent more directly than matrices do how features are related to one other.

Table 3.34 Feature matrix for English consonants

		Stops									*Fricatives*								*Affricates*		*Nasals*			*Liquids*		*Glides*			*Laryngeals*	
		p	pʰ	b	t	tʰ	d	k	kʰ	g	f	v	θ	ð	s	z	ʃ	ʒ	tʃ	dʒ	m	n	ŋ	l	r	j	w	ʍ	h	ʔ
Major class features	[consonantal]	+	+	+	+	+	+	+	+	+	+	+	+	+	+	+	+	+	+	+	+	+	+	+	+	−	−	−	−	−
	[sonorant]	−	−	−	−	−	−	−	−	−	−	−	−	−	−	−	−	−	−	−	+	+	+	+	+	+	+	+	−	−
	[syllabic]	−	−	−	−	−	−	−	−	−	−	−	−	−	−	−	−	−	−	−	−	−	−	−	−	−	−	−	−	−
Manner features	[nasal]	−	−	−	−	−	−	−	−	−	−	−	−	−	−	−	−	−	−	−	+	+	+	−	−	−	−	−	−	−
	[continuant]	−	−	−	−	−	−	−	−	−	+	+	+	+	+	+	+	+	−	−	−	−	−	−	+	+	+	+	+	−
	[lateral]	−	−	−	−	−	−	−	−	−	−	−	−	−	−	−	−	−	−	−	−	−	−	+	−	−	−	−	−	−
	[delayed release]	−	−	−	−	−	−	−	−	−	−	−	−	−	−	−	−	−	+	+	−	−	−	−	−	−	−	−	−	−
Laryngeal features	[voice]	−	−	+	−	−	+	−	−	+	−	+	−	+	−	+	−	+	−	+	+	+	+	+	+	+	+	−	−	−
	[CG]	−	−	−	−	−	−	−	−	−	−	−	−	−	−	−	−	−	−	−	−	−	−	−	−	−	−	−	−	+
	[SG]	−	+	−	−	+	−	−	+	−	−	−	−	−	−	−	−	−	−	−	−	−	−	−	−	−	−	−	+	−
Place of articulation features	LABIAL	o	o	o							o	o									o						o	o		
	[round]	−	−	−							−	−									−						+	+		
	CORONAL				o	o	o						o	o	o	o	o	o	o	o		o		o	o					
	[anterior]				+	+	+						+	+	+	+	−	−	−	−		+		+	+					
	[strident]				−	−	−						−	−	+	+	+	+	+	+		−		−	−					
	DORSAL							o	o	o													o			o	o	o		
	[high]							+	+	+													+			+	+	+		
	[back]							+	+	+													+				+	+		

Note: [low], [tense], and [reduced] are not used for English consonants.

Figure 3.18 illustrates the kind of hierarchical representation that features can be grouped into:

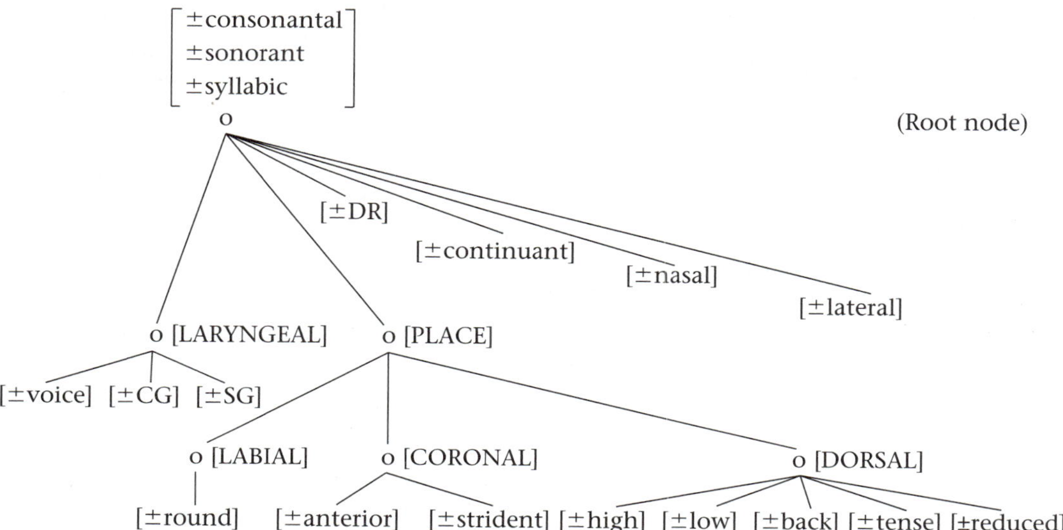

Figure 3.18 The feature hierarchy

In addition to the features themselves (for definitions, see Section 5.2), three **class nodes** are included in the feature tree: these are the **root node**, the **laryngeal node**, and the **place node**. Each feature grouping in the hierarchy is represented by one of these nodes (the node symbol is a small circle: o). Beneath each node are found the feature or features that make up that grouping. For instance, grouped beneath each of the articulators [LABIAL], [CORONAL], and [DORSAL] are all those features that further specify the positioning of the articulators ([±round] for [LABIAL]; [±anterior] and [±strident] for [CORONAL]; etc.). Thus, the nodes and features are ranked on levels, or **tiers,** that reflect their relation to each other.

Nodes serve three functions in the hierarchy. First, they represent the articulatory organization of the feature hierarchy: the laryngeal node represents laryngeal activity; the place node represents supralaryngeal articulations; the root node groups the major class features together, thus defining whether a segment is a vowel, consonant, or glide; and each articulator node groups together all those features that the articulator is able to produce. Second, the nodes function to group together and label natural classes of features. And third, nodes, like features themselves, may be referred to directly when attempting to describe sound patterns and processes. This property of the hierarchy is illustrated in some detail in Section 7.

The manner features are not grouped together under one node, but instead are all linked individually to the root node; this is because segments of each type of place of articulation ([LABIAL], [CORONAL], and [DORSAL]) can have different values for any one of the manner features individually. For instance, a [CORONAL, +anterior] segment can be [±continuant], [±nasal], or [±lateral]. Thus, manner features always seem to pattern individually rather than as a group.

Figure 3.19 illustrates how the feature hierarchy is used to represent the feature specifications of individual segments. No representation of an actual segment makes use of all the features in the hierarchy simultaneously.

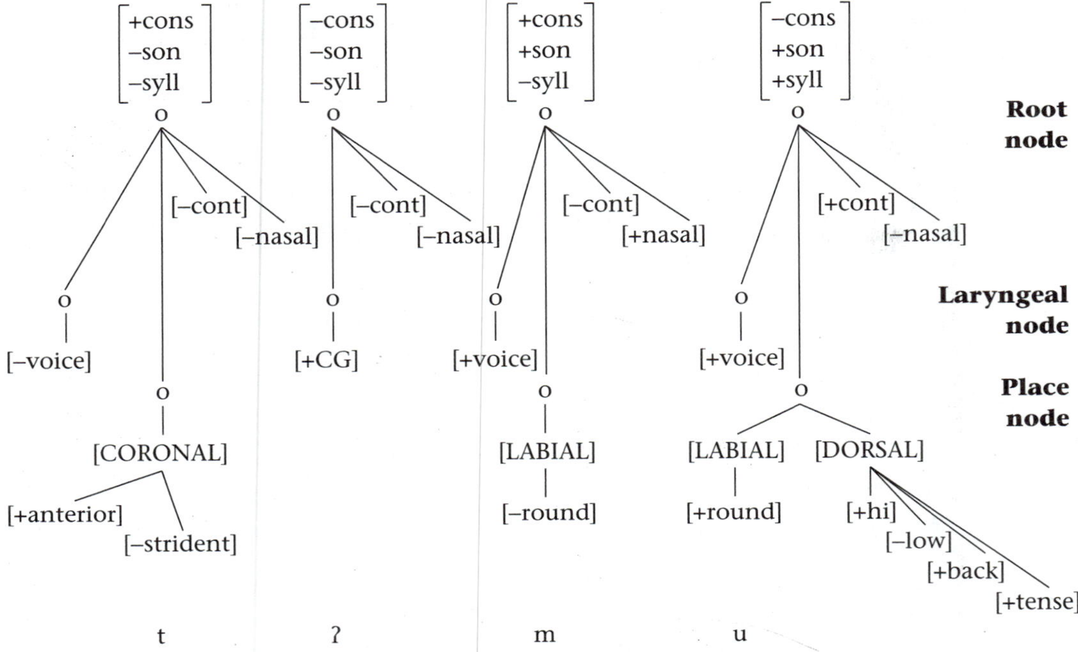

Figure 3.19 The feature hierarchical representations of some English sounds

Notice that in the representation for /ʔ/ there is no place node. Only glottal sounds, which are produced with no supralaryngeal articulation, are represented without this feature. Features like [±lateral], [±DR], and [±reduced] have been left out of the structures to simplify them somewhat.

While this kind of feature representation may at first look more complex and clumsy than a strictly segmental representation, it is in fact very useful. It allows us to capture contrasts at the level of the feature, instead of listing individual sets of contrastive phonemes. Much allophonic variation can be represented as the addition, loss, or change of a few features. The influence of the conditioning environment is also made more obvious with this type of representation, as shown in Section 7 of this chapter.

6 DERIVATIONS AND RULES

To this point we have established the existence of related levels of phonological structure. In this model, phonological units from a lower level of structure are organized and grouped into higher-level structural units. Thus, features are grouped into segments, which in turn are organized into syllables. We have established that segments can be contrastive and hence function as separate phonemes, or noncontrastive and hence function as predictable allophonic variants of phonemes. We have also seen that general statements referring to natural classes and to syllable structure can account for the patterning of noncontrastive elements. Finally, we have seen that there are two levels of representation associated with the difference between contrastive and noncontrastive segments: the phonemic level represents unpredictable, phonemic properties and units of a language, while the phonetic level represents predictable, allophonic properties and units. In this section and in Section 7, we will explore the relationship between the phonemic and phonetic levels of representation and illustrate how this relationship is formalized.

Phonologists assume that phonemic representations are equivalent to the mental representations that speakers have of the words in their language, while phonetic representations are equivalent to the actual phonetic outputs that are produced in the course of speech. In this sense, phonemic representations are understood to be the basic representations of units such as the word. The unpredictable phonological information represented in a phonemic representation thus underlies all actual phonetic forms; for this reason, phonemic representations are also called **underlying representations** (or forms), and **phonetic representations** are also called **surface representations** (or forms).

Phonemic representations become phonetic representations as a result of being acted upon by **phonological processes** such as the devoicing of liquids and glides following voiceless stops in English, the aspiration of voiceless stops at the beginnings of syllables in English, and the lengthening of English vowels preceding voiced coda obstruents. Thus we say that phonetic or surface forms are derived from phonemic or underlying forms by means of the action of phonological processes. These phonological processes are formalized in two ways: as **phonological rules** (formalized statements of phonological processes) or as **phonological representations** (graphic presentations of phonological processes). In this section, we focus on understanding how rules act in derivations and how they should be formalized. Section 7 focuses on phonological representations.

6.1 Derivations

Underlying representations are composed of phonemes (it is important to keep in mind that all phonemes are themselves composed of distinctive features). Phonetic forms are derived by allowing phonological processes—formalized as rules—to operate on underlying representations in those contexts where the processes are relevant.

The **derivation** of three phonetic representations (PRs) from underlying representations (URs) is presented in Figure 3.20. Here, the underlying representation is on the top line (the crosshatch # symbolizes a word boundary); reading downward, each rule applies in sequence, and the underlying representation is adjusted as required. Where a rule fails to apply, the form remains unchanged; this information is conveyed by dashes. The resulting output then serves as the input to the following rule. Finally, when all rules relevant to the derivation in question have applied, a phonetic representation is provided. The two rules presented in the following example are aspiration and vowel lengthening (see Section 4.5).

UR	#slæp# slap	#tæp# tap	#pæd# pad
Aspiration	—	#tʰæp#	#pʰæd#
V-length	—	—	#pʰæːd#
PR	[slæp]	[tʰæp]	[pʰæːd]

Figure 3.20 The phonological derivation of three English words

In this example, two rules have applied (since the words being derived are all monosyllabic, the syllable boundaries are equivalent to word boundaries and so are not indicated here). The first accounts for aspiration. Since the initial consonant of the URs #tæp# and #pæd# are voiceless stops found in onset position, they fulfill the conditions under which English stops become aspirated. We therefore indicate that aspiration occurs by providing an intermediate form on a new line.

We have also seen that in English, vowels are predictably long when they occur before a voiced stop in the same syllable. In Figure 3.20, the /æ/s of *slap* and *tap* occur before voiceless stops and so are not lengthened. The vowel of *pad*, however, occurs in just the environment associated with long vowels and so is predictably lengthened.

The use of such derivations underscores the fact that allophonic variation is the result of processes that apply in the course of language use. Underlying representations capture the knowledge that speakers have about the nature of their phonological system, rules reflect the application of allophonic processes, and the phonetic representation reflects the speech output. The relationship between phonemic or underlying representations and phonetic or surface representations is the result of the action of phonological processes.

6.2 Rule application

We have seen that more than one rule may be employed in a derivation. Consequently, we must now ask how several rules are applied to a given underlying form when these rules interact.

Unordered rule application and feeding

In Figure 3.20 we saw the application of the rules of English aspiration and vowel lengthening, which apply to voiceless stops and vowels, respectively. Note that the environments in which each of these rules applies (onset and pre-coda position, respectively) are entirely different. Therefore, these rules do not interact or affect each other in any way; the order in which they are applied makes no difference to the outcome of the derivation. Figure 3.21 shows the same rules applied in reverse order; there is no difference in the outcome.

We therefore say that the rules of aspiration and vowel lengthening are **unordered** with respect to each other.

UR	#slæp#	slap	#tæp#	tap	#pæd#	pad
V-length	—		—		#pæːd#	
Aspiration	—		#tʰæp#		#pʰæːd#	
PR	[slæp]		[tʰæp]		[pʰæːd]	

Figure 3.21 Unordered rule application

A second type of rule ordering is called **feeding**. Rules are said to be in a feeding order when the application of one rule creates an environment that makes possible the application of another rule that could otherwise not apply. The rules of English schwa deletion and liquid-glide devoicing (given in example *4*) are in a feeding relationship in the casual speech pronunciation of a word like *parade*. In this word, the schwa between *p* and *r* gets deleted because it is unstressed. After the schwa has been lost, through schwa deletion, a liquid or glide that follows the schwa in the underlying representations gets positioned directly after a voiceless stop and, therefore, becomes subject to liquid-glide devoicing. This is shown in Figure 3.22. The arrows, which are normally not written in derivations, indicate feeding relationships. Notice that before schwa deletion, a rule has to apply to assign stress to the final vowel.

UR	#pəred#	parade
Stress	#pəréd#	
→ Schwa deletion	#préd#	
→ Liquid-glide devoicing	#pr̥éd#	
Diphthongization	#pr̥éjd#	
Vowel lengthening	#pr̥éːjd#	
PR	[pr̥éːjd]	

Figure 3.22 Feeding order in a derivation

Notice now that no incorrect forms would result if, say, the schwa-deletion rule attempted to apply before the stress rule. Because its environment is not present, the schwa-deletion rule would simply fail to apply. However, once the stress rule was applied, the schwa-deletion rule could then follow in its turn, ultimately leading to a correct phonetic representation. What these facts suggest is that rules in a feeding relationship may apply in free order, each attempting to apply wherever the required conditions are met. The result will be the desired phonetic output.

6.3 The form and notation of rules

General statements about allophonic distribution are formalized as rules. These rules are written so as to reflect the dynamic nature of processes (Chapter 2, Section 9.4).

Rules

Rules take the following form.

11)

$A \rightarrow B \,/\, X \,\_\_\_\, Y$

In this notation, *A* stands for an element in the underlying representation, *B* for the change it undergoes, and *X* and *Y* for the conditioning environment. Either *X* or *Y* may be absent (null) if the conditioning environment is found only on one side of the allophone. The __ (focus bar) indicates the position of the segment undergoing the rule. The slash separates the statement of the change from the statement of the conditioning environment. This rule is read as *A becomes B between X and Y*.

As an example of rule writing, we return to the distribution of liquid-glide devoicing in English (Section 2.4): in English, liquids and glides have voiceless allophones after syllable-initial voiceless stops, and voiced allophones elsewhere. The rule statement operates on the voiced allophones of liquids and glides as basic (underlying) and changes the feature [+voice] to [–voice] in the appropriate environment. This rule is read as follows:

12)

Liquids and glides become voiceless after syllable-initial voiceless stops.

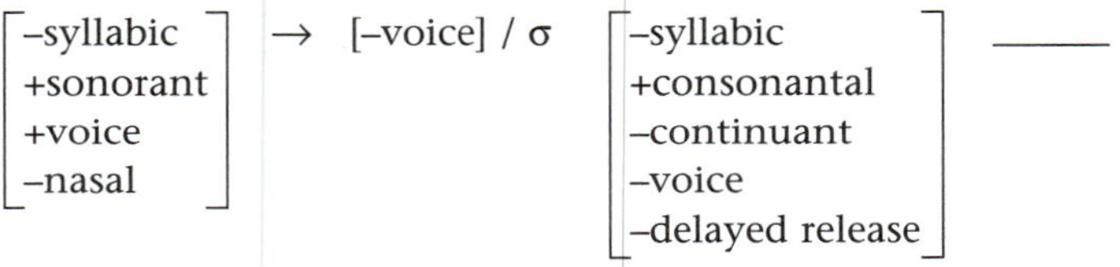

Figure 3.23 Liquid-glide devoicing in English expressed as a rule

Rule and feature notation formally represents the origin of allophones in phonetic processes that arise in the course of speech. For example, the devoicing of liquids and glides in English is a typical process of assimilation. The rule notation in Figure 3.23 shows explicitly how this change of [+voice] to [–voice] occurs in a specific class of sounds following the class of sounds that is [–voice]. Features in Figure 3.23 and others below are listed in matrices (between square brackets) rather than trees, to simplify the forms of the rules.

Deletion as a rule

We have already seen that English speakers (optionally) drop a schwa [ə] in an open syllable when it is followed by a stressed syllable, as in *police* [pl̥is] and *parade* [pr̥ejd]. The rule can be formalized as in Figure 3.24. Here, $C_ø$ is an abbreviation for any number of successive consonants from zero on up and the σ represents a syllable boundary.

$$[\text{ə}] \rightarrow ø \,/\, C_ø \,\_\_\_\, \sigma\, C_ø \underset{[+\text{stress}]}{V}$$

Figure 3.24 Schwa deletion in English

The English schwa-deletion rule interacts with the constraint on possible consonant sequences. It automatically fails to apply when an impermissible sequence would result. Since $_\sigma$[pt^h and $_\sigma$[dl are impermissible onsets in English, there are no forms like *[pt^héjɾow] *potato* or *[dlít] *delete* (except in extremely fast speech).

Epenthesis and alpha rules

Recall that epenthesis involves the insertion of a segment (Chapter 2, Section 9.4) into a sequence of other segments. In Section 2.5 we saw that the glides following English tense nonlow vowels are predictable by a general rule: the tense mid [–back] vowel /e/ is followed by the [–back] glide /j/; the tense mid [+back] vowel /o/ is followed by the [+back] glide /w/.

In order to represent this epenthesis, we can make use of a type of notation called **alpha notation**. Here, the Greek letter α is a variable (like *x* in algebra) that can stand for either feature value. For example, a feature statement like [α round] can be read as either [+round] or [–round], but the alpha variable or variables used in a rule must match. Whenever the alpha is used in a rule, it must have the same value wherever it occurs. Since alpha notation is used to capture two rules, alphas are read twice, once as '+' and once as '–'. When the first alpha is read as '+', all other alphas in the same rule must be read as '+'; when it is read as '–', all other alphas in the same rule must be read as '–'.

With alpha notation, we can capture the variability of the glide insertion in English as follows.

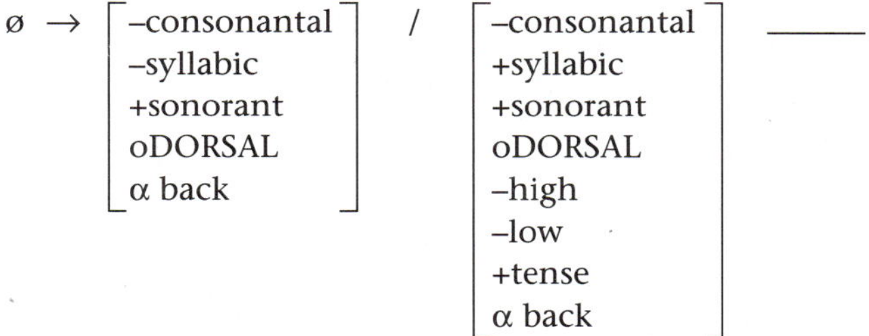

Figure 3.25 Alpha notation in English glide epenthesis

Remember: in reading an alpha, you are reading a rule twice—once with the plus value for the alpha feature and once with the minus value. The rule in Figure 3.25 states that a [+back] glide is inserted after a [+back] mid tense vowel and that a [–back] glide is inserted after a [–back] mid tense vowel. Since there are only two glides in the phonological inventory of English, [+back] /w/ and [–back] /j/, the correct glide will be inserted by the rule.

Rules that refer to syllable structure

The rule of vowel lengthening in English makes reference to syllable structure. The boundary of the syllable may be represented by a syllable marker σ. Recall the rule of vowel lengthening in English.

13)

English vowels are long when followed by a voiced obstruent consonant in the same syllable.

The corresponding rule (in Figure 3.26) states that an underlying short vowel is lengthened in the appropriate context.

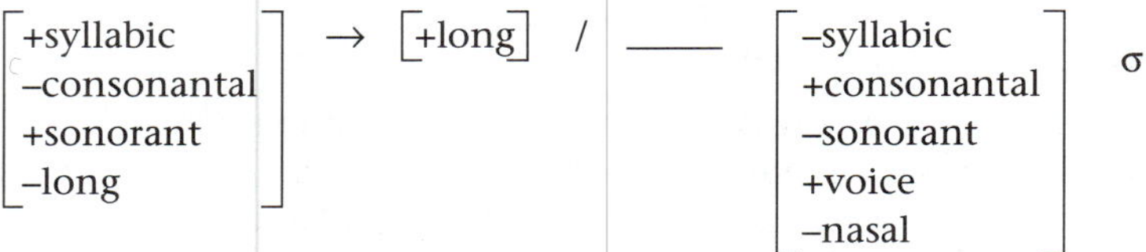

Figure 3.26 Vowel lengthening in English

Notice here that the onset of the syllable is irrelevant to the statement of the rule and so is not included in the formalization.

Vowel epenthesis

Vowel epenthesis is frequently triggered when an impermissible phonotactic structure is encountered in a borrowed word, as in the English pronunciation of the name *Dmitri*. It is also the case that in some dialects of English, a coda consisting of *l* and another consonant is not permitted. In these dialects, *milk* is pronounced [mɪlək] and *film* [fɪləm]. This change can be represented in rule format, as in Figure 3.27.

$$\emptyset \rightarrow [\text{ə}] \; / \; [\text{+lateral}] \; \_\_\_ \begin{bmatrix} \text{–syllabic} \\ \text{+consonantal} \end{bmatrix} \sigma$$

Figure 3.27 Schwa epenthesis in English as a rule

A more complete representation of this process requires showing the change of syllable structure, as in Figure 3.28.

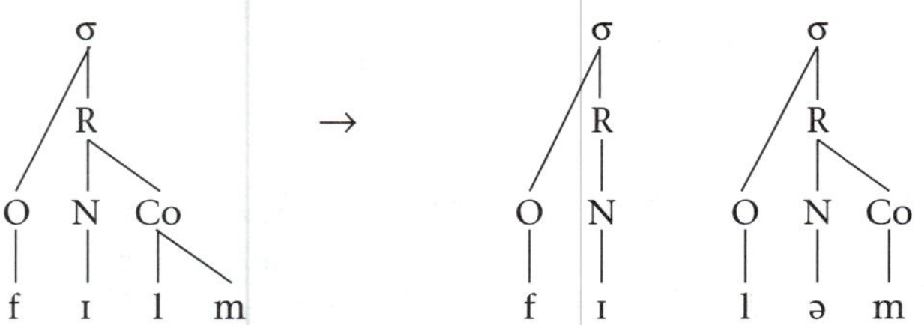

Figure 3.28 Syllabic representation of schwa epenthesis in English

7 REPRESENTATIONS *(ADVANCED)*

In recent years, the formalization of rules has become more graphic. This change has taken place because certain types of processes, especially processes of assimilation (where one segment becomes similar in one or more features to a neighboring segment), have been viewed as the **spreading** of features from one segment (represented as a feature hierarchy) to another. It has also been claimed that a simple set of principles governs the way in which features spread.

These graphic presentations of feature changes are referred to as **representations**. The features themselves are referred to as **autosegments**—the label suggesting that each feature has a certain autonomy in its operation.

7.1 Assimilation and the feature hierarchy

Assimilation processes are particularly amenable to **autosegmental representation** using the feature hierarchy. This is the case because the overlapping production typical of coarticulation (see Chapter 2, Section 9.1) is neatly represented by the spread of individual features from one segment to another.

Assimilation of [+nasal]

In English, a vowel nasalizes when it is immediately followed by a nasal consonant in the same syllable. One or more consonants may follow the nasal consonant. (For some speakers, the vowels must also be stressed.) The words *banks*, *shunted*, and *nimble*, for example, are pronounced [bæ̃ŋks], [ʃʌ̃ntəd], and [nĩmbəl]. This regressive nasalization in English can be represented as in Figure 3.29 (the symbol σ following the feature matrices indicates the boundary of the syllable—that is, that the nasal consonant is in the coda; the change undergone by the word *bank* is provided below the representation).

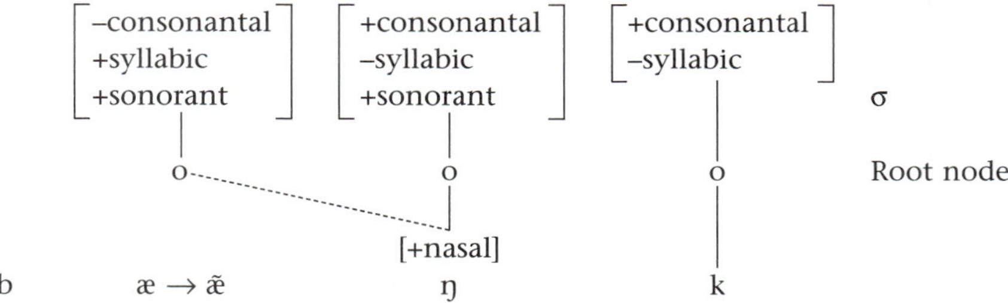

Figure 3.29 Vowel nasalization in English (regressive assimilation)

Note that the English nonnasal vowel is represented as having no feature [nasal]. This fact will be very important in our discussion of representations below. With autosegmental representations, there is no need to list individual segments or even to write a rule. The next section outlines the principles that govern the spreading of features.

7.2 Autosegmental principles

It is claimed that only three principles account for the many processes that can be represented with **autosegmental notation**.

- **Association: feature-to-segment** Each autosegment (feature) is associated with at least one segment by an association line.

- **Association: segment-to-feature** Each segment is associated with at least one autosegment (feature) by an association line.
- **Crossing** Association lines do not cross.

Feature spreading

We are now in a position to understand how English nasalization can be viewed as a form of feature spreading. Since English vowels never contrast for the feature [nasal], they can be unspecified for nasality (in other words, the feature [+nasal] can be left out of their representations). Our principles note that each feature must be associated with at least one segment, and vice versa. But nasality is not part of the specification of English vowels. A language-specific rule of English allows leftward spreading. The feature [nasal] on /n/ will therefore "automatically" spread leftward whenever it finds a vowel that is not specified for nasality. This spreading is not accomplished by a rule, but by a general principle.

Compare nasal spreading in English with nasal spreading in Scots Gaelic (see Figure 3.30). Remember that nasal assimilation in Scots Gaelic can occur progressively (see Section 2.6). To capture this fact autosegmentally, we do not have to write a new rule; we merely state that spreading in Scots Gaelic can operate rightward. The general principles take care of the rest.

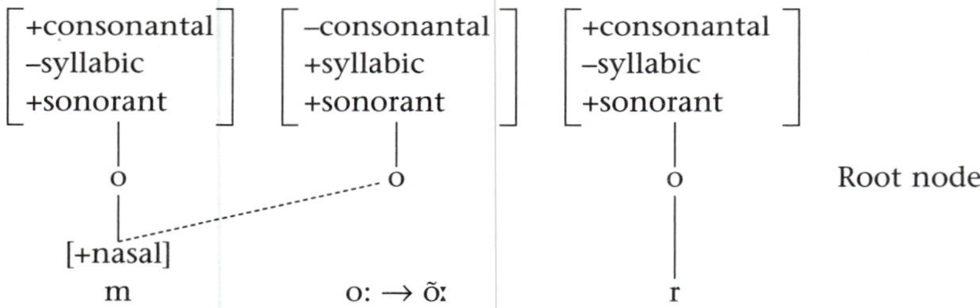

Figure 3.30 Nasal spreading in Scots Gaelic

The spreading of autosegments need not apply only to the feature [nasal]. In theory, just about any feature should follow the same principles. The next section shows how spreading can apply to voicing features.

Laryngeal assimilation: English liquid-glide devoicing revisited

We have already seen (Figure 3.23) how English liquid-glide devoicing is stated in rule format. This particular variation is in fact assimilatory, in the sense that the liquids and glides take on the voiceless quality of a preceding voiceless stop. For this reason, devoicing lends itself well to statement as a representation (see Figure 3.31).

The root node and manner features represent the leftmost class as stops and the class to its right as liquids or glides. The place node is not represented since the place of articulation of both the stops and the liquids and glides is irrelevant to the process in question here as it is not affected by the rule. The dotted line represents the spreading of the laryngeal node feature [–voice] from the voiceless stop to the liquid or glide.

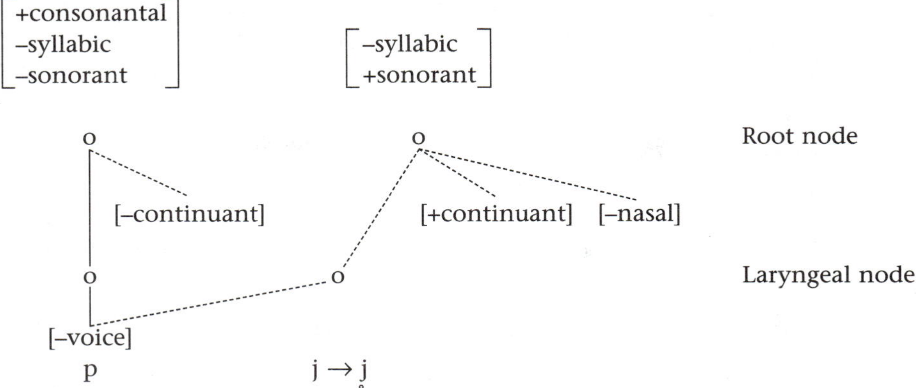

Figure 3.31 Liquid-glide devoicing in English as a representation

7.3 Tonal assimilation as a representation

In Chapter 2, we saw how tone is represented on separate levels or tiers of phonological description. Association lines link the tone to the appropriate vowel. A representation of the word *tunko* 'sheep' from Duwai, a language spoken in West Africa, is shown in Figure 3.32, where L indicates low tone, and H high tone.

```
L   H
|   |
t u n k o
```

Figure 3.32 Representing tone

This type of representation has the advantage of being able to show explicitly certain facts about tone languages. Tones, like other phonological phenomena, are subject to contextually conditioned variation. A good example of this comes from Duwai (see Figure 3.33). In Duwai, many words show the tonal pattern LH (low-high).

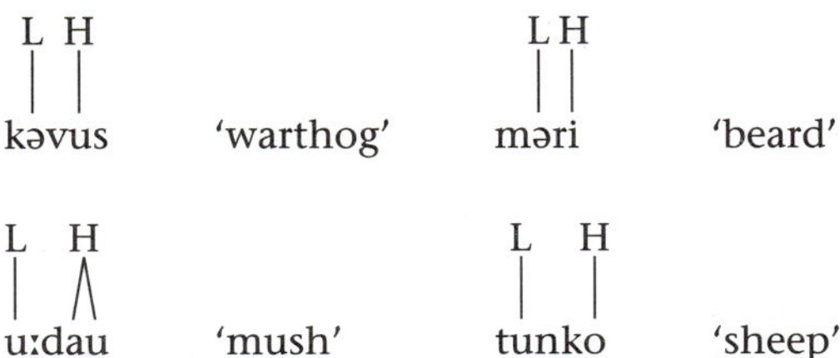

Figure 3.33 Low-high tonal patterns in Duwai

When a word with an LH tonal pattern is followed by a word with an L tone, such as the form *bàì* '(is) not', the H tone of the first word becomes L: *kə̀vús* 'warthog' becomes *kə̀vùs bàì* 'it's not a warthog'; *mə̀rí* 'beard' becomes *mə̀rì bàì* 'it's not a beard', and so on.

This tonal change is a kind of assimilation, and parallels common processes of assimilation of segmental features. This assimilation is viewed as a spreading of the L tone backwards from the word *bài* to the final vowel of the preceding word, and is represented by drawing a dotted association line, as in Figure 3.34 (which represents the change in tone), and breaking the original association line from the vowel to the former tone value (the short double lines indicate the loss of association).

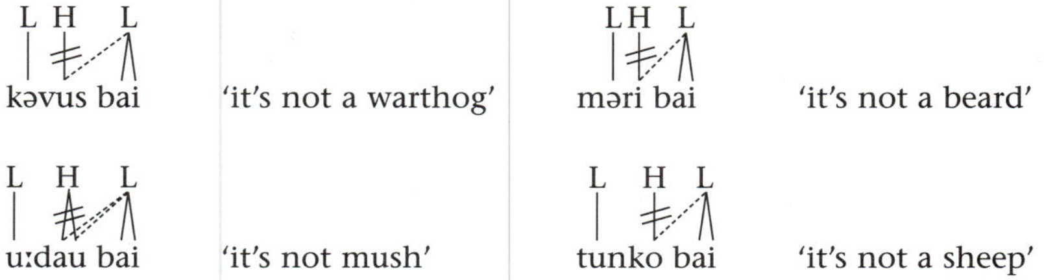

L H L kəvus bai	'it's not a warthog'	L H L məri bai	'it's not a beard'
L H L u:dau bai	'it's not mush'	L H L tunko bai	'it's not a sheep'

Figure 3.34 Tone assimilation in Duwai

Thus, both features and tonal material are handled by the same type of representation and the same principles.

7.4 Processes, rules, and representations: a last word

The combined use of features and processes in phonological description reflects the dynamic nature of linguistic behavior. First, the use of features reflects a basic level of phonological activity—contrasts take place on the feature level, not on the level where segments are represented. Secondly, the use of process notation and formalization with rules and representations reflects the realities of linguistic production, in which sounds are affected by the context in which they are pronounced as we speak.

Overall, the patterning of phonological units is seen to be based on the interaction of a universal set of features, universal and language-specific phonotactic constraints and syllabification procedures, and the use of rules and representations. This current theory of phonology is based on principles that are applicable to the study of any human language.

Summing up

Phonology deals with the sequential and phonetically conditioned patterning of sounds in language. To account for this patterning, three units of phonological representation have been established: the **feature**, the **phoneme**, and the **syllable**. Phonemes are contrastive segmental units composed of distinctive features. Phonetically conditioned variants of phonemes are called **allophones**.

Phonology makes use of **underlying forms**, **derivations**, **phonological rules**, and **representations** in its formal notation. Some rules apply in **free** order. **Autosegments**—features that are autonomous to varying degrees—spread or delete on the basis of a limited number of principles.

Key terms

General terms

accidental gaps
environment
feature
phonology
segment
syllable
systematic gaps

Distinctive sounds and their variations

allophones
allophonic distribution
complementary distribution
contrast
free variation
minimal pair
near-minimal pairs
phonemes
phonemic representation
phonetic representation

Terms concerning syllable structure

association line
closed syllable
coda
heavy syllable
nucleus
onset
open syllable
phonotactics
rhyme
suprasegmental
syllable

General terms concerning classes of sounds and features

class nodes
consonantal
distinctive feature
feature hierarchy
features
laryngeal node
matrix
natural classes
obstruents
place node
root node
sonorants
syllabic
tiers

Manner features

continuant
delayed release (DR)
lateral
nasal

Laryngeal features

constricted glottis (CG)
spread glottis (SG)
voice

Place features

anterior
back
CORONAL
DORSAL
high
LABIAL
low
reduced
round
strident
tense

Terms concerning rules, representations, and processes

alpha notation
assimilation
autosegmental notation
autosegmental representation
autosegments
derivation
epenthesis
feeding
phonetic representations
phonological processes
phonological representations
phonological rules
representations
spreading
surface representations
underlying representations
unordered (rule application)

Sources

A classic and still valuable presentation of phonemic analysis is found in H. A. Gleason, Jr.'s *An Introduction to Descriptive Linguistics* (Toronto: Holt, Rinehart and Winston, 1961). Tone data on Mende are from W. R. Leben's "The Representation of Tone" and on Duwai from R. G. Schuh's "Tone Rules," both in *Tone: A Linguistic Survey*, edited by V. A. Fromkin (New York: Academic Press, 1978). Syllabification, tone, and autosegmental analysis are drawn from numerous sources, all summarized recently in Goldsmith (cited below). The Malay data are adapted from M. Kenstowicz and C. Kisseberth, *Generative Phonology* (New York: Academic Press, 1979), with additional examples provided by S. L. Lee (personal communication).

Data sources for problems are as follows: for Inuktitut, B. Harnum (personal communication); for Mokilese, S. Harrison's *Mokilese Reference Grammar* (Honolulu: University of Hawaii Press, 1976); for Tamil, R. Radhakrishnan (personal communication); for Gascon, R. C. Kelly's *A Descriptive Analysis of Gascon* (Amsterdam: Mouton, 1978); for Plains Cree, Y. Carifelle and M. Pepper (personal communication); for Canadian French, D. C. Walker's *The Pronunciation of Canadian French* (Ottawa: University of Ottawa Press, 1984) and A. Teasdale (personal communication); for English fast speech, G. Zhang, *Phonological Representation and Analyses of Fast Speech Phenomena in English*, M.A. thesis, Memorial University of Newfoundland, 1994; for Moru, A. N. Tucker, *The Eastern Sudanic Languages* (London: Dawsons, 1976/1940), pp. 112, 271.

Recommended reading

Anderson, Stephen R. 1985. *Phonology in the Twentieth Century.* Chicago: University of Chicago Press.

Carr, Philip. 1993. *Phonology.* London: Macmillan.

Clements, George N., and Samuel Jay Keyser. 1983. *CV Phonology*. Cambridge, MA: MIT Press.

Goldsmith, John. 1990. *Autosegmental and Metrical Phonology.* Cambridge, MA: Blackwell.

Goldsmith, John, ed. 1995. *The Handbook of Phonological Theory.* Cambridge, MA: Blackwell.

Hayes, Bruce. 1995. *Metrical Stress Theory: Principles and Case Studies.* Chicago: University of Chicago Press.

Hyman, Larry M. 1975. *Phonology: Theory and Analysis.* New York: Holt, Rinehart and Winston.

Keating, Patricia. 1988. "The Phonology-Phonetics Interface." In *Linguistics: The Cambridge Survey.* Ed. F. Newmeyer. Vol. 1. London: Cambridge University Press, 1988. 218–302.

Kenstowicz, Michael. 1994. *Phonology in Generative Grammar.* Cambridge, MA: Blackwell.

Stampe, David. 1980. *A Dissertation on Natural Phonology.* New York: Garland.

APPENDIX: HINTS FOR SOLVING PHONOLOGY PROBLEMS

The task of solving a phonology problem is made easier if certain facts presented in this chapter and summarized here are kept in mind. The data that we consider below are taken from Tagalog, a language spoken in the Philippines.

1. In the following data, consider the phones [h] and [ʔ] and determine whether they contrast or whether they are allophones of one phoneme.

a)	kahon	'box'	d)	ʔari	'property'
b)	hariʔ	'king'	e)	kaʔon	'to fetch'
c)	ʔumagos	'to flow'	f)	humagos	'to paint'

   In order to determine whether the phones contrast, we begin by looking for minimal pairs. These establish which segments are contrastive. For example, in the data in a through f, minimal pairs occur in items a/e and c/f; the pair b/d is a near-minimal pair. The existence of minimal and near-minimal pairs of words indicates here that [h] and [ʔ] contrast. Therefore we can conclude that /h/ and /ʔ/ are separate phonemes.

2. Now consider the following data, and determine whether the two sounds [d] and [r] contrast or whether they are allophones of one phoneme.

a)	datiŋ	'to arrive'	f)	daraʔiŋ	'will complain'
b)	dami	'amount'	g)	marumi	'dirty'
c)	dumi	'dirt'	h)	marami	'many'
d)	daratiŋ	'will arrive'	i)	daʔiŋ	'to complain'
e)	mandurukot	'pickpocket'	j)	mandukot	'to go pickpocketing'

   Since there are no minimal pairs in the data that contrast [d] and [r], we proceed to check whether the two sounds are in complementary distribution. Normally, when two sounds are in complementary distribution and therefore allophones of one phoneme, they must be phonetically similar. In Tagalog, [d] and [r] are both voiced alveolar segments; thus they are sufficiently similar phonetically to be viewed as potential allophones of one phoneme.

To check whether two (or more) sounds are in complementary distribution, the best thing to do is to list the environments in which the sounds occur:

[d] occurs:	[r] occurs:
–word-initially (e.g., *dami*)	–between two vowels (e.g., *marami*)
–following a nasal (e.g., *mandukot*)	

[d] never occurs between two vowels, and [r] never occurs word-initially or following a nasal. The two sounds never occur in identical environments; therefore, they are in complementary distribution and their distributions are predictable.

3. If two potential allophones of one phoneme are in complementary distribution, we can be reasonably sure that they are allophones of one phoneme. We can therefore make a general statement about their distribution, in terms of some natural phonological class. For example:

   Tagalog [d] and [r] are in complementary distribution and are allophones of one phoneme. The allophone [r] occurs between vowels; [d] occurs elsewhere—in 2 above, word-initially, as in items a, b, c, f, and so on, and after nasal consonants, as in items e and j.

4. Once we have determined that two sounds are allophones of one phoneme, we need to determine the phoneme that they are both derived from. Usually this can be done by selecting one of the allophones as basic. In most cases, the allophone chosen as the phoneme is the one with the widest distribution (the elsewhere variant). In the Tagalog case, the elsewhere variant is [d], so we posit the phoneme /d/, which has two allophones, [d] and [r]. It may be helpful to set up a traditional phoneme-allophone diagram to illustrate this (see Figure 3.2).

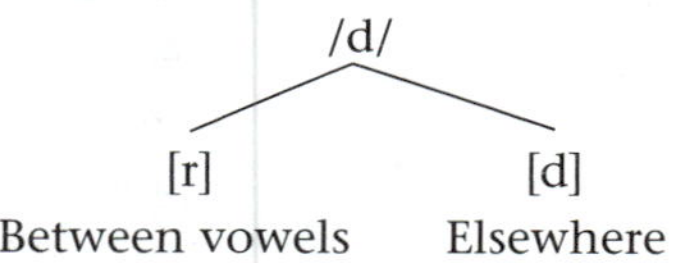

5. Now that we know that [d] and [r] are allophones of the phoneme /d/, we need to determine the phonological rule or the representation that accounts for the predictable features of the other allophones. Our rule or representation is probably correct if it describes a common linguistic process (such as assimilation) in terms of natural classes of sounds interacting with neighboring segments and/or syllable structure.

   For example, for the above: d → r / V___V

   Here the process that leads to the allophony is a form of assimilation, in that an underlying voiced stop consonant becomes a continuant when found between two continuants (vowels).

6. We can assume that segments are phonemic if there are no minimal pairs for them but they cannot be shown to be allophones of one phoneme. In such a case, we can conclude that the data simply did not provide minimal pairs.

QUESTIONS

Assume phonetic transcription of the data in all exercises.

1. *Inuktitut* (Eastern) (Native Canadian)

a)	iglumut	'to a house'	h)	pinna	'that one up there'
b)	ukiaq	'late fall'	i)	ani	'female's brother'
c)	aiviq	'walrus'	j)	iglu	'(snow)house'
d)	aniguvit	'if you leave'	k)	panna	'that place up there'
e)	aglu	'seal's breathing hole'	l)	aivuq	'she goes home'
f)	iglumit	'from a house'	m)	ini	'place, spot'
g)	anigavit	'because you leave'	n)	ukiuq	'winter'

i) List all the minimal pairs in this data. Based on the minimal pairs you have found, list all the contrastive pairs of vowels.

ii) Using the vowel charts in Figures 2.9 and 2.10 as your models, make a chart of Inuktitut vowel phonemes.

iii) Now consider the data again; here it is transcribed in more phonetic detail. In it, there are phonetically similar segments that are in complementary distribution. Look for them and then answer the question that follows the data.

aa)	iglumut	'to a house'	hh)	pinna	'that one up there'
bb)	ukiaq	'late fall'	ii)	anɪ	'female's brother'
cc)	aivɪq	'walrus'	jj)	iglʊ	'(snow)house'
dd)	aniguvit	'if you leave'	kk)	panna	'that place up there'
ee)	aglʊ	'seal's breathing hole'	ll)	aivʊq	'she goes home'
ff)	iglumit	'from a house'	mm)	inɪ	'place, spot'
gg)	anigavit	'because you leave'	nn)	ukiʊq	'winter'

iv) List the phonetically similar segments that are in complementary distribution. State their distribution in words.

2. *Hindi* (Hindi is a language of the Indo-European family spoken in India)
Consider the segments [b] and [b̤] in the data below and answer the questions that follow. The segment transcribed [b̤] is a murmured voiced stop; it was presented in Chapter 2, Section 10.2.

a)	[bara]	'large'	f)	[b̤ɛd]	'disagreement'
b)	[b̤ari]	'heavy'	g)	[bais]	'twenty-two'
c)	[bina]	'without'	h)	[b̤əs]	'buffalo'
d)	[b̤ir]	'crowd'	i)	[bap]	'father'
e)	[bori]	'sackcloth'	j)	[b̤ag]	'part'

i) Are the segments [b] and [b̤] allophones of the same phoneme or do they belong to separate phonemes? If you believe they belong to separate phonemes, give evidence from the data to support your analysis. If you believe they are allophones of the same phoneme, list the conditioning environments.

3. *Mokilese* (Mokilese is an Austronesian language of the South Pacific)
Examine the following data from Mokilese carefully, taking note of where voiceless vowels occur.

a) pi̥san 'full of leaves'
b) tu̥pu̥kta 'bought'
c) pu̥ko 'basket'
d) ki̥sa 'we two'
e) su̥pwo 'firewood'
f) kamwɔki̥ti 'to move'
g) uduk 'flesh'
h) kaskas 'to throw'
i) poki 'to strike something'
j) pil 'water'
k) apid 'outrigger support'
l) ludʒuk 'to tackle'

i) The vowel phonemes of Mokilese are /i e ɛ u o ɔ a/. In Mokilese, [i̥] is an allophone of /i/, and [u̥] is an allophone of /u/. No other vowels have voiceless allophones. State in words the conditioning factors that account for this. Be as general as possible in referring to classes of sounds.

ii) If you have completed the section on rule formalization, write a rule (using features) that accounts for the derived allophones.

4. *Gascon* (Gascon is spoken in southwest France)
The phones [b], [β], [d], [ð], [g], and [ɣ] are all found in Gascon, as the following examples show. The phone [β] is a voiced bilabial fricative; [ɣ] is a voiced velar fricative (see Chapter 2, Section 10.2).

a) brẽn 'endanger'
b) bako 'cow'
c) ũmbro 'shadow'
d) krãmbo 'room'
e) dilys 'Monday'
f) dũŋko 'until'
g) duso 'sweet'
h) taldepãn 'leftover bread'
i) pũnde 'to lay eggs'
j) dudze 'twelve'
k) guteʒa 'flow'
l) ẽŋgwãn 'this year'
m) puðe 'to be able'
n) gat 'cat'
o) lũŋg 'long'
p) saliβo 'saliva'
q) noβi 'husband'
r) aβe 'to have'
s) ʃiβaw 'horse'
t) byðɛt 'gut'
u) eʃaðo 'hoe'
v) biɣar 'mosquito'
w) riɣut 'he laughed'
x) agro 'sour'
y) ʒuɣɛt 'he played'

i) Which pairs among the phones [b], [β], [d], [ð], [g], and [ɣ] are the most phonetically similar? Support your claim with phonetic descriptions of the similar pairs.

ii) List the environments in which the phones [b], [β], [d], [ð], [g], and [ɣ] are found. You may ignore word-final position in your consideration.

iii) Is there any evidence for grouping these pairs of sounds into phonemes? State the evidence for each pair.

iv) Make a general statement about the patterning of the phonemes you have established.

v) Following your analysis, write the following forms in phonemic transcription.

a) [puɣo] b) [deðat] c) [ʃiβaw] d) [krãmbo]

5. *Plains Cree* (Plains Cree is a Native Canadian language of the Algonquian family)
The following data from Plains Cree show a number of different voiced and voiceless consonantal segments.

a)	niska	'goose'	l)	nisto	'three'
b)	kodak	'another'	m)	tʃi:gahigan	'axe'
c)	asaba:p	'thread'	n)	a:dim	'dog'
d)	wasko:w	'cloud'	o)	mi:bit	'tooth'
e)	paskwa:w	'prairie'	p)	pime:	'lard'
f)	ni:gi	'my house'	q)	mide	'heart'
g)	ko:gos	'pig'	r)	o:gik	'these'
h)	tahki	'often'	s)	tʃihtʃij	'finger'
i)	namwa:tʃ	'not at all'	t)	wa:bos	'rabbit'
j)	ospwa:gan	'pipe'	u)	na:be:w	'man'
k)	midʒihtʃij	'hand'	v)	mi:dʒiwin	'food'

i) Do [p] and [b] belong to separate phonemes or are they allophones of one phoneme? If you think they belong to separate phonemes, list data to support your case. If you think they are allophones, first state the conditioning factors in words, and then, using features, write a rule that accounts for their distribution.

ii) Do the same for [t] and [d], [k] and [g], and [tʃ] and [dʒ].

iii) Can you make a general statement about the relationship among all the consonantal pairs whose distribution you have examined?

iv) Using Figure 3.17 as your model, provide complete derivations of the forms for (k) *hand*, (m) *axe*, and (o) *tooth*.

6. There are a number of natural classes in the vowel and consonant data below. Circle three natural classes in each set of data. Indicate which feature or features define the class, as in the example.

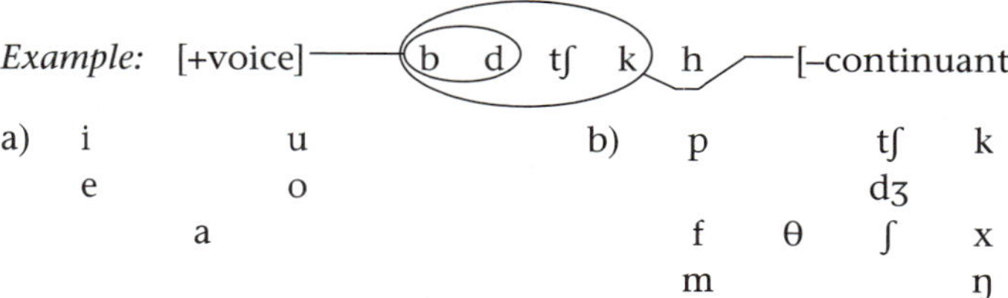

7. Name the single feature that distinguishes the following pairs of sounds.

a) [θ] : [ð]	e) [b] : [m]	i) [ʌ] : [ə]
b) [p] : [f]	f) [s] : [ʃ]	j) [s] : [θ]
c) [u] : [ʊ]	g) [ɪ] : [i]	k) [e] : [ɛ]
d) [i] : [e]	h) [k] : [x]	l) [u] : [o]

8. Complete the feature matrix for each of the sounds indicated. The V abbreviates the features [+syllabic, –consonantal], and the C abbreviates the features [–syllabic, +consonantal].

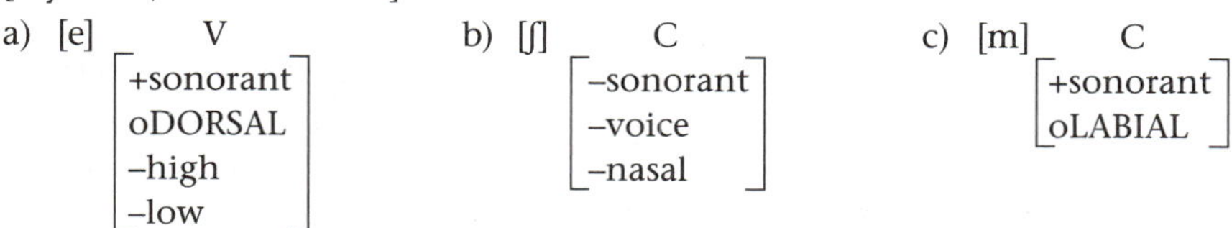

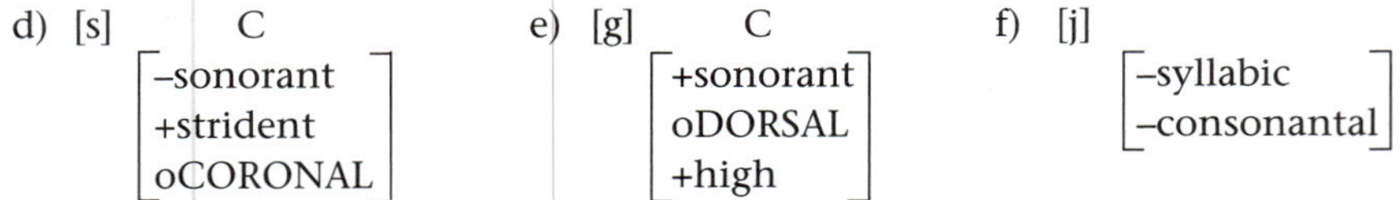

Using the appropriate features, represent each segment on a feature hierarchy tree.

9. *English/Korean*

As we have seen, phonological adaptation of loanwords may reflect facts about syllable structure. Recently, the Korean automobile name *Hyundai* has been adapted into English in various ways, one of which follows. Given the Korean form and the English adaptation provided, state two reasons based on syllable structure conditions that explain why the English form is pronounced the way it is.

Korean form		*English form*	
/hjʌndæ/	→	/hʌnde/	[hʌndej]

10. *English*

Many speakers of English have two variants of [l]. One, called *clear l*, is transcribed as [l] in the following data. The other, called *dark l*, is transcribed as [ɫ]. Examine the data, and answer the questions that follow.

a)	[lajf]	'life'	g)	[pʰɪɫ]	'pill'
b)	[lip]	'leap'	h)	[fiɫ]	'feel'
c)	[lu:z]	'lose'	i)	[hɛɫp]	'help'
d)	[ilowp]	'elope'	j)	[bʌɫk]	'bulk'
e)	[dəlajt]	'delight'	k)	[sowɫd]	'sold'
f)	[slip]	'sleep'	l)	[fʊɫ]	'full'

Do [l] and [ɫ] belong to separate phonemes or are they allophones of the same phoneme? If you think they belong to separate phonemes, answer question *i*. If you think they are allophones of the same phoneme, answer questions *ii–iv*.

i) List the evidence that makes your case for considering [l] and [ɫ] as separate phonemes.
ii) State the distribution of [l] and [ɫ] in words.
iii) Which variant makes the best underlying form? Why?
iv) Can you make reference to syllable structure in your distribution statement? If you can, do so in rule form.

11. *Canadian French*

For the purposes of this problem, you may assume that syllables in Canadian French have the following structure:

- Maximum number of consonants in an onset: 2. Where there are two onset consonants, the first must be an obstruent, the second a sonorant or a fricative.
- Each vowel forms a syllable nucleus.
- Maximum number of consonants in a coda: 2.

i) With these stipulations in mind, syllabify the following forms:

a)	bukan	'smoke'	c)	pudrœri	'snowstorm'
b)	erite	'to inherit'	d)	liɔ̃	'lion'

In the following data from Canadian French, each pair of phones is in complementary distribution.

[i] and [ɪ] are allophones of one phoneme
[y] and [ʏ] are allophones of a second phoneme
[o] and [ɔ] are allophones of a third phoneme
[u] and [ʊ] are allophones of a fourth phoneme

It is possible to make a general statement about the distribution of the vowel allophones that accounts for all four phonemes.

Examine the data and answer the questions that follow.

a) pilʏl 'pill'
b) griʃe 'to crunch'
c) grɪʃ 'it crunches'
d) pətsi 'little (masc.)'
e) pətsɪt 'little (fem.)'
f) vitamɪn 'vitamin'
g) saly 'hi'
h) ʒʏp 'skirt'
i) fyme 'smoke'
j) lynɛt 'glasses'
k) frole 'to skim'
l) pɔrt 'door'
m) bote 'beauty'
n) bɔt 'boot'
o) fo 'false'
p) tɔrdzy 'twisted'
q) zero 'zero'
r) pɔm 'apple'
s) lʏn 'moon'
t) pɪp 'pipe'
u) grimas 'grimace'
v) fini 'finished'
w) fɪj 'girl'
x) dzʏr 'hard'
y) tryke 'to fake'
z) fʊl '(a) crowd'
aa) plʏs 'more'
bb) fɔl 'crazy (fem.)'
cc) ru 'wheel'
dd) rʊt 'road'
ee) suvã 'often'
ff) trupo 'herd'
gg) sʊp 'flexible'
hh) tʊʃ 'touch'
ii) fu 'crazy (masc.)'
jj) trʏk '(a) trick'

ii) Provide a statement of the distribution of [i] and [ɪ], [y] and [ʏ], [o] and [ɔ], [u] and [ʊ] in words. Make your statement as general as possible, but be precise.

iii) If you have completed the section on rule formalization, write a single rule that derives the allophones of each phoneme from the underlying form. Use features. Be sure to give your rule a mnemonic name; use this name in the answer to question *iv*.

iv) Provide derivations for the following underlying forms.

UR	# # 'vitamin'	# # 'glasses'
PR	[vitamɪn]	[lynɛt]

12. *English*

The following data contain both careful speech and fast speech forms. Note the differences and answer the questions that follow. Some phonetic detail irrelevant to the question has been omitted from the transcription. Remember that an asterisk before a form indicates that it is not acceptable to (most) native speakers.

Careful speech	*Fast speech*	*Spelled form*
a) [ǽspərən]	k) [ǽsprən]	aspirin
b) [pɔ́rsələn]	l) [pɔ́rslən]	porcelain
c) [nǽʃənəlàjz]	m) [nǽʃnəlàjz]	nationalize
d) [rízənəbl̩]	n) [ríznəbl̩]	reasonable
e) [ɪmǽdʒənətɪv]	o) [ɪmǽdʒnətɪv]	imaginative
f) [sɛ̀pərəbílɪɾi]	p) [sɛ̀prəbílɪɾi]	separability
g) [mɛ́θəd]	q) [mɛ́θəd] *[mɛ́θd]	method
h) [féjməs]	r) [féjməs] *[féjms]	famous
i) [mɛ́məràjz]	s) [mɛ́məràjz] *[mɛ́mràjz]	memorize
j) [kʰənsìdəréjʃən]	t) [kʰənsìdəréjʃən] *[kʰənsìdréjʃən]	consideration

i) The schwa deletion between the careful speech forms and the rapid speech forms in items a–f is systematic. State in words the phonetic conditions that account for the deletion.

ii) The same pattern that occurs between the careful speech forms and the rapid speech forms in items a–f does not occur in items g–j. State in words the phonetic difference between these sets of forms that accounts for the lack of schwa deletion.

iii) Now that you have taken items g–j into account, will you have to change your original statement about the phonetic conditions governing schwa deletion in the fast speech form? If so, do this in words.

iv) If you have completed the section on rule formalization, convert your statement in *iii* into formal notation.

13. The English data below provide examples of stress placement on certain verbs.

A	*B*	*C*
appéar	adápt	astónish
collíde	collápse	consíder
eráse	eléct	imágine
caróuse	obsérve	detérmine
corróde	tormént	prómise

i) Describe in words the stress placement on these verbs. Be sure to make reference to syllable structure in your statement.

ii) Provide syllabified representations of the words *collide, elect,* and *consider* in order to illustrate your conclusions about stress placement on these forms.

14. State each of the following rules in English, making reference to natural classes and common linguistic processes.

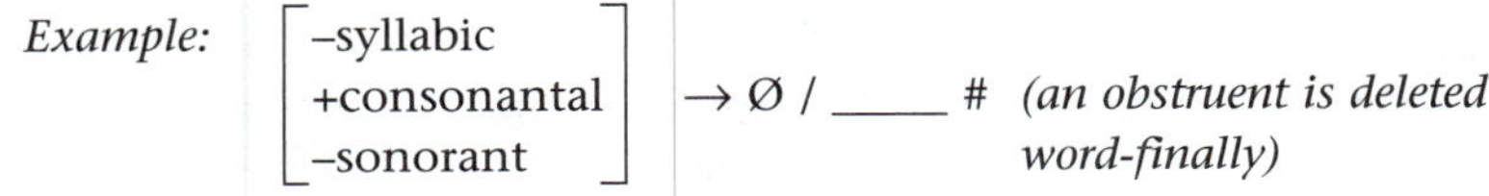

Example: $\begin{bmatrix} -\text{syllabic} \\ +\text{consonantal} \\ -\text{sonorant} \end{bmatrix} \rightarrow \varnothing \ / \ \_\_\_\_ \ \#$ *(an obstruent is deleted word-finally)*

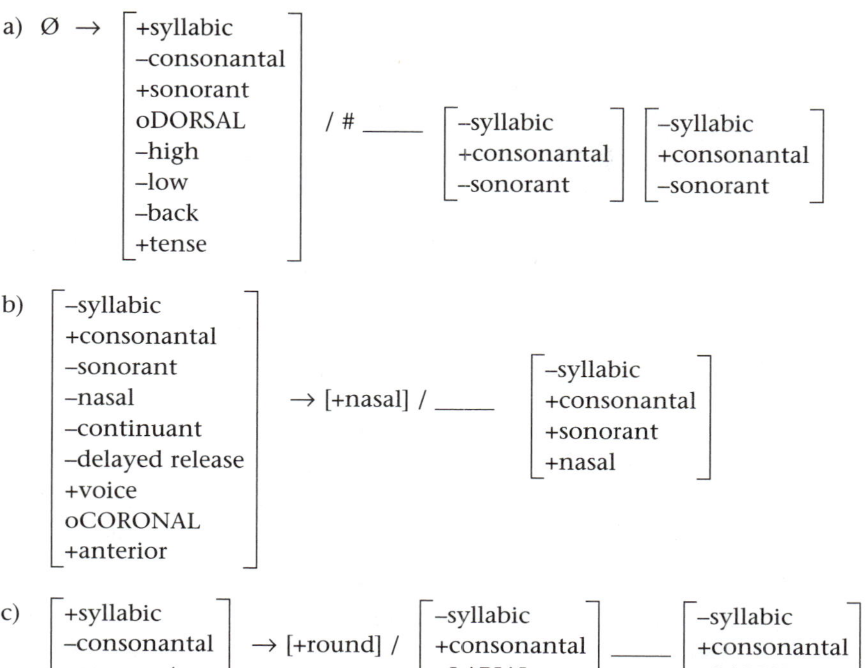

15. Change the following statements into rule notation. Be sure to name the process in question for each case.
    a) Voiceless stops become corresponding fricatives between vowels.
    b) A schwa is inserted between a voiced stop and a word-final voiced fricative.
    c) Low unrounded vowels become rounded before *m*.

16. *Tamil* (Tamil is a Dravidian language spoken in South India and Sri Lanka)
    In the following Tamil data, some words begin with glides and others do not. The symbol [ɖ] represents a voiced retroflex stop, and the diacritic [̪] indicates dentals.

Initial j-glide			*Initial w-glide*			*No initial glide*		
a)	jeli	'rat'	f)	woɖi	'break'	k)	arivu	'knowledge'
b)	jiː	'fly'	g)	woːlaj	'palm leaf'	l)	ain̪t̪u	'five'
c)	jilaj	'leaf'	h)	wuːsi	'needle'	m)	aːsaj	'desire'
d)	jeŋgeː	'where'	i)	wujir	'life'	n)	aːru	'river'
e)	jiɖuppu	'waist'	j)	woːram	'edge'	o)	aːdi	'origin'

i) The occurrence of these glides is predictable. Using your knowledge of natural classes, make a general statement about the distribution of the glides.

ii) Assuming the glides are not present in the underlying representations, name the process that accounts for their presence in the phonetic forms.

iii) Using features, write a rule using alpha notation that formalizes this process. Show the derivation of the forms for *fly* and *break*.

17. *Mende* (Mende is spoken in Liberia and Sierra Leone)
    In Mende, the forms that mean 'on' (*ma*) and 'in' (*hu*) are suffixes (they are attached to a preceding word; see Chapter 4, Section 1.3). Notice in the data below that suffixes all bear tone, but that the tone varies on different words. In the examples, ˊ indicates a high tone, ˋ a low tone, and ˆ a falling (high-to-low) tone.

a)	kɔ́	'war'	kɔ́má	'on war'	kɔ́hú	'in war'
b)	pɛ́lɛ́	'house'	pɛ́lɛ́má	'on (the) house'	pɛ́lɛ́hú	'in (the) house'
c)	bɛ̀lɛ̀	'trousers'	bɛ̀lɛ̀mà	'on trousers'	bɛ̀lɛ̀hù	'in trousers'
d)	ngílà	'dog'	ngílàmà	'on (the) dog'	ngílàhù	'in (the) dog'

i) Can you account for the differences in tone on the suffixes for 'on' and 'in' in Mende? Provide a solution using autosegmental notation. (*Hint:* Assume that the suffixes have no tone to begin with but that the words to which they are attached do have tone.)

ii) Assuming that you have answered question *i* successfully, account for the tones of the suffixes meaning 'on' and 'in' in the remaining examples.

e)	mbû	'owl'	mbúmà	'on (the) owl'	mbúhù	'in (the) owl'
f)	njàhâ	'woman'	njàhámà	'on (the) woman'	njàháhù	'in (the) woman'

18. *Moru* (Miza dialect; Moru is a Sudanic language)
    In Moru, contour tones are not found on short vowels in underlying representations. However, phonetic forms of combined lexical items do show contour tones. Can you represent this using autosegmental notation? (*Hint:* A segmental process is involved as well as a typical suprasegmental process, and the two processes must be ordered.) In the data provided, ˊ indicates a high tone, ˋ a low tone, ˆ a falling (high-to-low) tone, and ˇ a rising (low-to-high) tone. Vowels with no tone mark need not be considered.

a)	màá we	→	[mǎ]	'we'
b)	ká ùmu he runs	→	[kûmu]	'he runs'
c)	ká ɔ̀ŋga he jumps	→	[kɔ̂ŋga]	'he jumps'
d)	njá àdì ùzi ja you call who?	→	[njâdùzi ja]	'who are you calling?'

For the Student Linguist

THE FEATURE PRESENTATION

You've already read that features are the fundamental building blocks of phonemes. By writing rules with features, you can describe simply a change that happens to an entire class of sounds. You also make a stronger statement when you use features in a rule. For example, rule *1* says something about all the stops in a language, but rule *2* only says something about a list of sounds.

1. [–continuant] → [–voice] / ___ #
(stops become voiceless at the end of a word)
2. {p,t,k,b,d,g} → {p,t,k,p,t,k} / ___ #
(p "becomes" p at the end of a word;
b becomes p at the end of a word; etc.)

If you're just listing sounds, nothing requires them to have anything in common with each other. The sounds in the list could be a totally random selection of sounds turning into another totally random selection of sounds, as in rule *3*, and you'd have no way of predicting that *3* should be less common than *2*.

3. {e,t,w,b,n,h} → {ʃ,p,tʃ,g,a,m} / ___ #
(e becomes ʃ at the end of a word; etc.)

If you use features, you can predict that the set of changes described by rule *2* should be common (because once the rule is translated to features, it's merely rule *1*, a delightfully simple rule), but the set of changes described by rule *3* should be weird and unlikely. To describe rule *3* with features, you'd have to write six different rules, and each rule would be ugly and complicated. (I'm assuming that the more features you have to include in a rule, the more complicated it is.) For example, the first rule, changing [e] to [ʃ], would be:

4.
$$\begin{bmatrix} \text{–consonantal} \\ \text{+voice} \\ \text{–high} \\ \text{–low} \\ \text{–back} \\ \text{+tense} \end{bmatrix} \rightarrow \begin{bmatrix} \text{+consonantal} \\ \text{–voice} \\ \text{oCORONAL} \\ \text{+continuant} \\ \text{+strident} \\ \text{–anterior} \\ \text{–delayed release} \end{bmatrix} \; / \; \_\_\_ \; \#$$

However, you can accept the brilliance of features without buying the idea of using a matrix of binary features (like you've done so far) or a hierarchy of binary features. Features could have only one value (these are called "monovalent" or "privative" features). So instead of, say, [–nasal] and [+nasal], there'd only be [nasal]. Sounds that had [nasal] in the matrix/representation would be nasal; everything else would be oral. How is that any different from using a binary feature? The difference is that with a binary feature, you can write rules about things that are [–nasal]. You could write a rule like this:

5.
$$\begin{bmatrix} \text{–continuant} \\ \text{–nasal} \end{bmatrix} \rightarrow [\text{–voice}] \; / \; \_\_\_ \; \#$$
(oral stops become voiceless at the end of a word)

But if [–nasal] didn't exist, the only rule you could write would be:

6. [–continuant] → [–voice] / ___ #
(all stops, including nasal stops, become voiceless at the end of a word)

If [–nasal] did exist, you could write rule *5 or* rule *6*. Monovalent features, then, give you fewer possible rules. That's great if you can still write all the rules you need for every language, but awful if you can't write every rule you need.

Having fewer possible rules isn't important just because it would make this unit of linguistics easier. It's also important because, theoretically, if there are fewer possible rules in a language, it's easier for a child trying to learn the language to figure out how the sound system in that language works. He or she has fewer options to consider.

What if features could have three values? Or four? Or an infinite number of values? For example, there could be four features for the different laryngeal states: [A laryngeal], for glottal stops; [B laryngeal], for voiced sounds; [C laryngeal], for voiceless unaspirated sounds; and [D laryngeal], for voiceless aspirated sounds. Just like nothing can be both [+voice] and [–voice] at the same time, nothing could be [A laryngeal] and [B laryngeal] at the same time (or [A laryngeal] and [C laryngeal], etc.). Place of articulation could be handled the same way: [A place] for labials, [B place] for dentals, [C place] for alveolars, etc.

With this type of multivalued system, none of the subgroups (like dentals and alveolars) could be lumped together in a rule. Thus, for the place system I described, you couldn't talk about all of the coronals at once—you could only talk about the dentals or the alveolars or the alveopalatals and so forth. Once again, whether this is good or bad depends on how well it describes actual languages. (You might want to try out a multivalued feature system for place on some of the phonology problems you've already solved for homework or in class discussions, and see if they're harder or easier to do this way than with a binary feature system.)

These are just a couple of the possible variations on feature systems. I haven't even begun to question the merit of these *features*—that is, do we *really* need [voice]? Or [strident]? Or [delayed release]? Think about this as you work on a few phonology problems, and see if you can come up with a better feature system. There's a lot of room for change here.

four

MORPHOLOGY: THE ANALYSIS OF WORD STRUCTURE

William O'Grady
Videa de Guzman

Carve every word before you let it fall.
– OLIVER WENDELL HOLMES SR.

OBJECTIVES

In this chapter, you will learn:

- how we analyze the structure of words
- how we form words by adding prefixes, suffixes, and infixes
- how we form words by putting two or more existing words together
- how we form words by less common means
- how we mark words to show grammatical concepts such as number, case, agreement, and tense
- how the processes of word formation interact with phonology

Nothing is more important to language than words. Unlike phonemes and syllables, which are simply elements of sound, words carry meaning in addition to their phonological form. And unlike sentences, which are made up as needed and then discarded, words are permanently stored in a speaker's mental dictionary or **lexicon**. They are arguably the fundamental building blocks of language.

The average high school student knows about 60,000 basic words—items such as *read, language, on, cold,* and *if,* whose form and meaning cannot be predicted from anything else. Countless other words can be constructed and comprehended by the application of general rules to these and other elements. For example, any speaker of English who knows the verb *fax* recognizes *faxed* as its past tense form, and can construct and interpret words such as *faxable* (for things that can be faxed) and *fax machine* (for the device that sends and receives faxes). Linguists use the term **morphology** to refer to the part of the grammar that is concerned with word formation and word structure.

1 WORDS AND WORD STRUCTURE

As literate speakers of English, we rarely have difficulty segmenting a stream of speech sounds into words or deciding where to leave spaces when writing a sentence. What, though, is a word?

Linguists define the **word** as the smallest **free form** found in language. A free form is simply an element that does not have to occur in a fixed position with respect to neighboring elements; in many cases, it can even appear in isolation. Consider the words making up the following sentence.

1)

The birds left.

The plural marker *-s* is not a free form (and therefore not a word) since it never occurs in isolation and cannot be separated from the noun to which it belongs. (Elements that must be attached to another category are written here with a hyphen.)

2)

*The bird left -s.

In contrast, *birds* is a word since it can occur in isolation, as in the following example.

3)

Speaker A: What are those things in the tree?
Speaker B: Birds.

Moreover, even when *birds* occurs as part of a larger sentence, it is not attached to anything else. This is why it can appear in different positions within a sentence, as illustrated in *4*.

4)

a. *birds* occurring in front of a verb:
   Birds avoid cats.
b. *birds* occurring after a verb:
   Cats chase birds.

Some words—like *the* in sentence *1*—normally do not occur in isolation. However, they are still free forms since their positioning with respect to neighboring words is not entirely fixed. As shown by the following example, *the* can be separated from an accompanying noun by an intervening word.

5)

the birds
the young birds
the very young birds

1.1 Morphemes

Like syllables and sentences, words have an internal structure consisting of smaller units organized with respect to each other in a particular way. The most important component of word structure is the **morpheme**—the smallest unit of language that carries information about meaning or function. The word *builder*, for example, consists of two morphemes: *build* (with the meaning of 'construct') and *-er* (which indicates that the entire word functions as a noun with the meaning 'one who builds'). Similarly, the word *houses* is made up of the morphemes *house* (with the meaning of 'dwelling') and *-s* (with the meaning 'more than one').

Some words consist of a single morpheme. For example, the word *train* cannot be divided into smaller parts (say, *tr* and *ain* or *t* and *rain*) that carry information about its meaning or function. Such words are said to be **simple words** and are distinguished from **complex words**, which contain two or more morphemes (see Table 4.1). It is important to keep in mind that a morpheme is neither a meaning nor a stretch of sound, but a meaning and a stretch of sound joined together. For example, there are at least two morphemes spelled *top* and pronounced /tɑp/ in English, one with the approximate meaning of 'upper part or surface' and the other meaning 'a toy designed to be spun.' In each case, the morpheme is not the meaning or the sound, but the two together. Morphemes are usually arbitrary—there is no natural connection between their sound and their meaning. So, there is nothing about the sound /kæt/ and the meaning 'domesticated feline' that makes the two go together naturally. We could just as easily call a cat /billi/ as in Hindi, or /neko/ as in Japanese. When we want to distinguish the sound of a morpheme from the entire morpheme, we may use the term **morph**. The English plural and possessive morphemes, for example, may be said to share a single morph, the suffix /-s/.

Table 4.1 Words consisting of one or more morphemes

One	*Two*	*Three*	*More than three*
and			
boy	boy-s		
hunt	hunt-er	hunt-er-s	
act	act-ive	act-iv-ate	re-act-iv-ate

Free and bound morphemes

A morpheme that can be a word by itself is called a **free morpheme** whereas a morpheme that must be attached to another element is said to be a **bound morpheme**. The morpheme *boy*, for example, is free, since it can be used as a word on its own; plural *-s*, on the other hand, is bound.

Concepts that are expressed by free morphemes in English do not necessarily have the same status in other languages. For example, in Hare (an Athapaskan language spoken in Canada's Northwest Territories), morphemes that indicate body parts must always be attached to a morpheme designating a possessor (see Table 4.2). (The diacritic ´ marks a high tone.)

Table 4.2 Some body part names in Hare

Without a possessor		*With a possessor*	
*fí	'head'	sefí	'my head'
*bé	'belly'	nebé	'your belly'
*dzé	'heart'	ʔedzé	'someone's heart/a heart'

In English, of course, these body part names are free morphemes and do not have to be attached to another element.

Conversely, there are also some bound forms in English whose counterparts in other languages are free. For example, the notion 'past' or 'completed' is expressed by the bound morpheme *-ed* in English, but by the free morpheme *lɛɛw* in Thai. As the following sentence shows, this morpheme can even be separated from the verb by an intervening word. (Tone is not marked here.)

6)

Boon thaan khaaw lɛɛw.
Boon eat rice past
'Boon ate rice.'

Allomorphs

Morphemes do not always have an invariant form. The morpheme used to express indefiniteness in English, for instance, has two forms—*a* before a word that begins with a consonant and *an* before a word that begins with a vowel.

7)

an orange	a building
an accent	a car
an eel	a girl

The variant forms of a morpheme are called its **allomorphs**.

Another example of allomorphic variation is found in the pronunciation of the plural morpheme *-s* in the following words.

8)

cats
dogs
judges

Whereas the plural is /s/ in the first case, it is /z/ in the second, and /əz/ in the third. Here again, selection of the proper allomorph is dependent on phonological facts. We will examine this phenomenon in more detail later in this chapter.

Other examples of patterns in which a morpheme's form changes when it combines with another element are easy to find in English. The final segment in *assert*, for instance, is /t/ when this morpheme stands alone as a separate word but /ʃ/ when it combines with the morpheme *-ion* in the word *assertion*. Similar alternations are found in words such as *permit/permiss-ive, include/inclus-ive, electric/electric-ity, impress/impress-ion*, and so on.

It is important not to confuse spelling changes with allomorphic variation. For example, the final *e* in the spelling of *create* and *ride* is dropped in *creat-ive* and *rid-ing*. However, since there is no change in pronunciation, this is not allomorphic variation.

1.2 Analyzing word structure

In order to represent the internal structure of words, it is necessary not only to identify each of the component morphemes but also to classify them in terms of their contribution to the meaning and function of the larger word.

Roots and affixes

Complex words typically consist of a **root** morpheme and one or more **affixes**. The root constitutes the core of the word and carries the major component of its meaning. Roots typically belong to a **lexical category**, such as noun (N), verb (V), adjective (A), or preposition (P). These categories will be discussed in more detail in Chapter 5, Section 1.1. For now it suffices to note that nouns typically refer to concrete and abstract "things" (*tree, intelligence*); verbs tend to denote actions (*treat, teach*); adjectives usually name properties (*kind, red*); and prepositions encode spatial relations (*in, near*).

Unlike roots, affixes do not belong to a lexical category and are always bound morphemes. For example, the affix *-er* is a bound morpheme that combines with a verb such as *teach*, giving a noun with the meaning 'one who teaches'. The internal structure of this word can be represented in diagram form as in Figure 4.1. (The symbol *Af* stands for affix.)

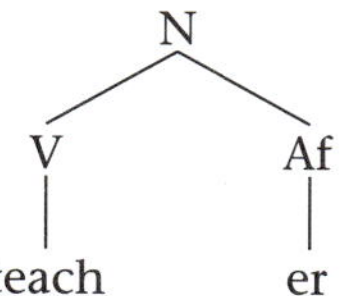

Figure 4.1 The internal structure of the word *teacher*

Figure 4.2 on page 136 provides some additional examples of word structure.

The structural diagrams in Figures 4.1 and 4.2 are often called **tree structures**. The information they depict can also be represented by using labeled bracketing—$[_A [_{Af}$ un$] [_A$ kind$]]$ for *unkind* and $[_N [_N$ book$] [_{Af}$ s$]]$ for *books*. (This is somewhat harder to read, though, and we will generally use tree structures in this chapter.) Where the details of a word's structure are irrelevant to the point being considered, it is traditional to use a much simpler system of representation that indicates only the location of the morpheme boundaries: *un-kind, book-s*, and so on.

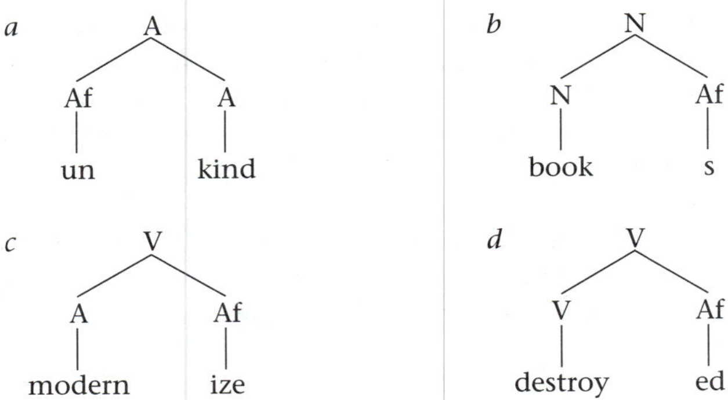

Figure 4.2 Some other words with an internal structure consisting of a root and an affix

Bases

A **base** is the form to which an affix is added. In many cases, the base is also the root. In *books,* for example, the element to which the affix *-s* is added corresponds to the word's root. In other cases, however, the base can be larger than a root. This happens in words such as *blackened,* in which the past tense affix *-ed* is added to the verbal base *blacken*—a unit consisting of the root morpheme *black* and the suffix *-en* (see Figure 4.3).

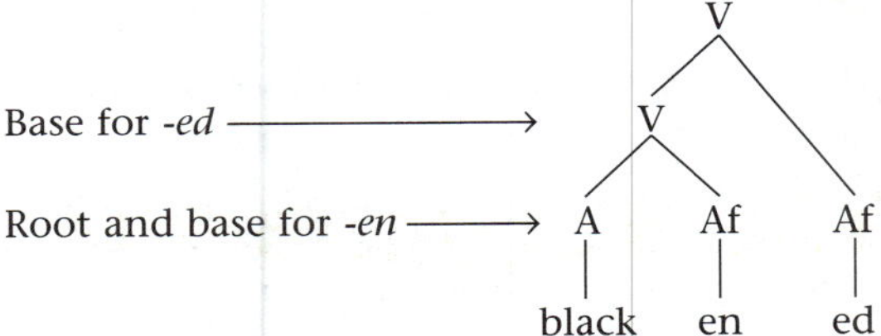

Figure 4.3 A word illustrating the difference between a root and a base

In this case, *black* is not only the root for the entire word but also the base for *-en.* The unit *blacken,* on the other hand, is simply the base for *-ed.*

Problematic cases *(Advanced)*

The majority of complex words in English are built from roots that are free morphemes. In the words *re-do* and *treat-ment*, for example, the root (*do* and *treat*, respectively) is a V that can appear elsewhere in the language without an affix. Because most complex words are formed from a root that can itself be a word, English morphology is said to be **word-based**.

Not all languages work this way, however. In Japanese and Spanish, for instance, verbal roots must always appear with an affix; they never stand alone as separate words.

English too has some bound roots. For example, the word *unkempt* seems to consist of the prefix *un-* (with the meaning 'not') and the root *kempt* (meaning 'groomed'), even though *kempt* cannot be used by itself. Other common words of this type include *in-ept, venge-ance*, and *salv-ation*, to name but a few.

There is a good historical explanation for why English has words of this type. For example, there was once a word *kempt* in English (with the meaning 'combed'), and it was to this base that the affix *un-* was originally attached. However, *kempt* later disappeared from the language, leaving behind the word *unkempt* in which an affix appears with a bound root.

Still other words with bound roots were borrowed into English as whole words. *Inept*, for instance, comes from Latin *ineptus* 'unsuited'. Its relationship to the word *apt* may have been evident at one time, but it now seems to consist of a prefix and a bound root.

Another class of words that are notoriously problematic for morphological analysis includes items such as *receive, deceive, conceive,* and *perceive* or *permit, submit,* and *commit.* These items were borrowed into English from Latin (usually via French) as whole words and their component syllables have no identifiable meaning of their own. (The *re* of *receive*, for instance, does not have the sense of 'again' that it does in *redo.*) For this reason, we will assume that words of this type consist of a single morpheme.

An interesting fact about these forms is that although *ceive* and *mit* have no identifiable meaning, they undergo certain alternations that suggest that they have a special status in the language. For instance, the *ceive* in words like *receive* and *deceive* becomes *cept* in *receptive* and *deceptive*, and the *mit* in words like *submit* and *permit* becomes *miss* in *submissive* and *permissive*. (For further discussion of this point, see *Word Formation in Generative Grammar* by Mark Aronoff [Cambridge, MA: MIT Press, 1976].)

1.3 Some common morphological phenomena

Words can be extended and modified in a variety of ways—sometimes by adding an additional morpheme and sometimes by making an internal change. As the next step in our survey of word structure, we will examine some of the more common of these morphological processes.

Compounding

One of the most common and important word-building processes in language involves **compounding**, the combination of two or more existing words to create a new word. The effects of compounding can be seen in countless English words, including the examples in Table 4.3.

Table 4.3 Some examples of English compounds

Noun + noun	*Adjective + noun*	*Verb + noun*	*Preposition + noun*
street light	bluebird	swear word	overlord
campsite	happy hour	washcloth	outhouse
bookcase	high chair	scrub board	in-group

Compounding plays a central role in word formation in many languages, as we will see in more detail in Section 3.

Affixation

Another extremely common morphological process in language is **affixation**, the addition of an affix. Normally, linguists distinguish among three types of affixes. An affix that is attached to the front of its base is called a **prefix**, whereas an affix that is attached to the end of its base is termed a **suffix**. Both types of affix occur in English, as Table 4.4 shows.

Table 4.4 Some English prefixes and suffixes

Prefixes	*Suffixes*
de-activate	vivid-*ly*
re-play	govern-*ment*
il-legal	hunt-*er*
in-accurate	kind-*ness*

We will consider the nature and properties of English affixes in more detail in Sections 2.1 and 5.

Far less common than prefixes and suffixes are **infixes**—a type of affix that occurs within a base. The data in Table 4.5 from the Philippine language Tagalog contains examples of the infix -*in*-, which is inserted after the first consonant of the base to mark a completed event.

Table 4.5 Some Tagalog infixes

Base		*Infixed form*	
bili	'buy'	b-*in*-ili	'bought'
basa	'read'	b-*in*-asa	'read' (past)
sulat	'write'	s-*in*-ulat	'wrote'

Beginning students sometimes think that a morpheme such as -*ish* in *boy-ish-ness* is an infix since it occurs between two other morphemes (*boy* and -*ness*), but this is not so. To be an infix, an affix must occur inside its base (as when -*in*- in Tagalog occurs inside *sulat* 'write'). Nothing of this sort happens in the case of -*ish*, since its base is *boy*—not the impossible **boyness*.

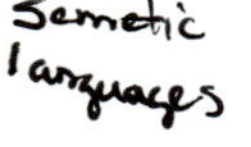

A very special type of infixing system is found in Arabic, in which a typical root consists simply of three consonants. Affixes consisting of two vowels are then inserted into this root in a manner that intersperses the vowels among the consonants. (In the examples that follow, the segments of the root are written in boldface.)

9)

ka**t**a**b**	**k**u**t**i**b**	a**kt**u**b**	u**kt**a**b**
'write'	'have been written'	'be writing'	'being written'

One way to represent the structure of such words is shown in Figure 4.4, with the root and affix assigned to different **tiers**, or levels of structure, that are intercalated in the actual pronunciation of the word.

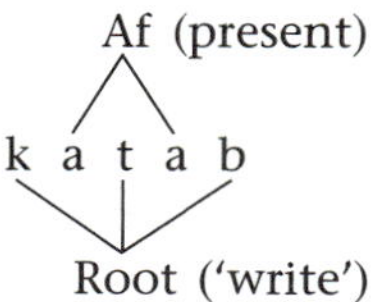

Figure 4.4 Two tiers are used to represent the structure of infixed words in Arabic.

Cliticization

Some morphemes behave like words in terms of their meaning and function, but are unable to stand alone as independent forms for phonological reasons. Called **clitics**, these elements must be attached to another word (known as a **host**). A good example of this can be found in English, where certain verb forms have reduced variants (*'m* for *am*, *'s* for *is*, and *'re* for *are*) that cannot stand alone since they no longer constitute a syllable. Cliticization occurs, attaching these elements to the preceding word.

10)

a. I*'m* leaving now.
b. Mary*'s* going to succeed.
c. They*'re* here now.

Cliticization is also common in French, which has a set of unstressed clitic pronouns that must be attached to the verb. (Although not evident in the written language, the clitic and the verb are pronounced as if they formed a single word.)

11)

Suzanne *les* voit.
Suzanne them-sees
'Suzanne sees them.'

Clitics that attach to the end of their host (as in the English examples) are called **enclitics**; those that attach to the beginning of their host (as in the French example) are known as **proclitics**.

The effects of cliticization can bear a superficial resemblance to affixation since in both cases an element that cannot stand alone is attached to a base. The key difference is that—unlike affixes—clitics are members of a lexical category such as verb, noun (or pronoun), or preposition.

Internal change

Internal change is a process that substitutes one nonmorphemic segment for another to mark a grammatical contrast, as illustrated in the pairs of words in Table 4.6.

Table 4.6 Internal change in English

sing (present)	sang (past)
sink (present)	sank (past)
drive (present)	drove (past)
foot (singular)	feet (plural)
goose (singular)	geese (plural)

Verbs such as *sing, sink*, and *drive* form their past tense by changing the vowel (e.g., from *i* to *a* in the first two examples). The term **ablaut** is often used for vowel alternations that mark grammatical contrasts in this way.

Some internal changes reflect phonologically conditioned alternations from an earlier stage in the language's history. The irregular plurals *geese* and *feet* came about in this way: the original vowel in the words *goose* and *foot* was fronted under the influence of the front vowel in the old plural suffix /i/, which was subsequently dropped. This type of change in English and other Germanic languages is known as **umlaut**.

12)

Old singular form of *goose*:	/gos/
Old plural form:	/gos-i/
Umlaut:	/gœs-i/
Loss of the plural suffix:	/gœs/
Other changes (see Ch. 7)	/ges/ and then /gis/ 'geese'

Internal change differs from infixing in important ways. As shown by the Tagalog examples in Table 4.5, the base into which a real infix is inserted typically exists as a separate form elsewhere in the language (compare *sulat* 'write' with *s-in-ulat* 'wrote'). Matters are quite different in the case of alternations such as *foot/feet* or *sing/sang* in English, since we have no form *ft* meaning 'lower extremity of the leg' or *sng* meaning 'produce words in a musical tone'. Moreover, in contrast to the situation in either Tagalog or Arabic, the segments affected by internal change are not themselves morphemes: the *a* of *ran* and the *o* of *drove* do not in general carry the meaning 'past' in English any more than the *ee* of *geese* normally carries the meaning 'plural'.

The existence of internal change and of infixing illustrates an important point about word structure: morphology is not always **concatenative**. That is, not all word structure is built by assembling morphemes in an additive, linear fashion. The morphological processes considered in the remainder of this section provide additional illustrations of this point.

Suppletion

Suppletion is a morphological process that replaces a morpheme with an entirely different morpheme in order to indicate a grammatical contrast (see Table 4.7). Examples of this phenomenon in English include the use of *went* as the past tense form of the verb *go* and *was* and *were* as the past tense forms of *be.*

Table 4.7 Suppletion in some European languages

Language	*Basic form*		*Suppletive form*	
French	avoir	'to have'	eu	'had'
Spanish	ir	'to go'	fue	'(s/he) went'
German	ist	'is'	sind	'are'
Russian	/xoroʃo/	'good'	/lutʃʃe/	'better' ('more good')

In some cases, it is hard to distinguish between suppletion and internal change. For example, is the past tense of *think (thought)* and *seek (sought)* an instance of suppletion or internal change? Because the initial phoneme of these verbs remains unchanged and because the phenomenon shows up in several words (see also *catch/caught* and *wreak/wrought*), this type of alternation is often treated as an extreme form of internal change. (However, the term **partial suppletion** is used by some linguists for these cases.)

Reduplication

A common morphological process in some languages involves **reduplication**, which marks a grammatical or semantic contrast by repeating all or part of the base to which it applies. Repetition of the entire base yields **full reduplication**, as in the data in Table 4.8 from Turkish and Indonesian.

Table 4.8 Some examples of full reduplication

Base		*Reduplicated form*	
Turkish			
tʃabuk	'quickly'	tʃabuk tʃabuk	'very quickly'
javaʃ	'slowly'	javaʃ javaʃ	'very slowly'
iji	'well'	iji iji	'very well'
gyzel	'beautifully'	gyzel gyzel	'very beautifully'
Indonesian			
oraŋ	'man'	oraŋ oraŋ	'all sorts of men'
anak	'child'	anak anak	'all sorts of children'
maŋga	'mango'	maŋga maŋga	'all sorts of mangoes'

In contrast, **partial reduplication** copies only part of the base. In the data from Tagalog in Table 4.9, for instance, reduplication affects only the first consonant-vowel sequence.

Table 4.9 Reduplication in Tagalog

Base		*Reduplicated form*	
takbuh	'run'	tatakbuh	'will run'
lakad	'walk'	lalakad	'will walk'
piliʔ	'choose'	pipiliʔ	'will choose'

English makes limited use of reduplication—for example, in diminutive expressions such as *teeny-weeny* and *itsy-bitsy*.

Stress and tone placement

Sometimes a base can undergo a change in the placement of stress or tone to reflect a change in its category. In English, for example, there are pairs of words—such as those in Table 4.10 on page 142—in which the verb has stress on the final syllable while the corresponding noun is stressed on the first syllable. (Stress is represented here by ´.)

In the language Mono-Bili (spoken in the Congo in Africa; see Table 4.11), tone is used to make the distinction between past and future tense. (A high tone is marked by ´ and a low tone by `.)

Table 4.10 Stress placement in English

Verb	*Noun*
implánt	ímplant
impórt	ímport
presént	présent
subjéct	súbject
contést	cóntest

Table 4.11 Past versus future in Mono-Bili

Past		*Future*	
dá	'spanked'	dà	'will spank'
zɨ́	'ate'	zɨ̀	'will eat'
wó	'killed'	wò	'will kill'

As you can see, high tone is associated with the past tense and low tone with the future.

Of the morphological operations we have been considering, two deserve special attention because of the crucial role they play in the formation of new words in English and many other languages—derivation (a special type of affixation) and compounding. The next sections of this chapter focus on these processes.

2 DERIVATION

Derivation is an affixational process that forms a word with a meaning and/or category distinct from that of its base. Table 4.12 contains words formed by adding the suffix *-er* to a verb to form a noun with the meaning 'one who does X'. (Do not confuse this suffix with the *-er* that applies to a noun in cases such as *New Yorker* and *islander* or the *-er* that combines with an adjective in cases such as *taller* and *smarter*.)

Table 4.12 The *-er* affix

Verb base	*Resulting noun*
sell	sell-er
write	writ-er
teach	teach-er
sing	sing-er
discover	discover-er

Once formed, derived words become independent lexical items that receive their own entry in a speaker's mental dictionary. As time goes by, they often take on special senses that are not predictable from the component morphemes. The word *writer*, for example, is often used not just for someone who can write but rather for someone who writes for a living (e.g., *He's a writer*); *comparable* (with stress on the first syllable) means 'similar' rather than 'able to be compared'; *profession* usually denotes a career rather than the act of professing; and so on.

2.1 English derivational affixes

Table 4.13 lists some English derivational affixes, along with information about the category of their usual base (ignoring bound roots) and of the resulting new word. The first entry states that the affix *-able* applies to a verb base and converts it into an

Table 4.13 Some English derivational affixes

Affix	*Change*	*Examples*
Suffixes:		
-able	V → A	fix-able, do-able, understand-able
-al	V → N	refus-al, dispos-al, recit-al
-ant	V → N	claim-ant, defend-ant
-(at)ion	V → N	realiz-ation, assert-ion, protect-ion
-er	V → N	teach-er, work-er
-ing$_1$	V → N	the shoot-ing, the danc-ing
-ing$_2$	V → A	the sleep-ing giant, a blaz-ing fire
-ive	V → A	assert-ive, impress-ive, restrict-ive
-ment	V → N	adjourn-ment, treat-ment, amaze-ment
-ful	N → A	faith-ful, hope-ful, dread-ful
-(i)al	N → A	president-ial, nation-al
-(i)an	N → A	Arab-ian, Einstein-ian, Minnesot-an
-ic	N → A	cub-ic, optimist-ic, moron-ic
-ize$_1$	N → V	hospital-ize, crystal-ize
-less	N → A	penni-less, brain-less
-ous	N → A	poison-ous, lecher-ous
-ate	A → V	activ-ate, captiv-ate
-en	A → V	dead-en, black-en, hard-en
-ity	A → N	stupid-ity, prior-ity
-ize$_2$	A → V	modern-ize, national-ize
-ly	A → Adv	quiet-ly, slow-ly, careful-ly
-ness	A → N	happi-ness, sad-ness
Prefixes:		
de-	V → V	de-activate, de-mystify
dis-	V → V	dis-continue, dis-obey
mis-	V → V	mis-identify, mis-place
re-	V → V	re-think, re-do, re-state
un$_1$-	V → V	un-tie, un-lock, un-do
anti-	N → N	anti-abortion, anti-pollution
ex-	N → N	ex-president, ex-wife, ex-friend
in-	A → A	in-competent, in-complete
un$_2$-	A → A	un-happy, un-fair, un-intelligent

adjective. Thus, if we add the affix *-able* to the verb *fix*, we get an adjective (with the meaning 'able to be fixed').

It is sometimes difficult to determine the category of the base to which an affix is added. In the case of *worker*, for instance, the base (*work*) is sometimes used as a verb (as in *they work hard*) and sometimes as a noun (as in *the work is time consuming*). How can we know which of these forms serves as the base for *-er*? The key is to find words such as *teacher* and *writer*, in which the category of the base can be unequivocally determined. Because *teach* and *write* can only be verbs, we can infer that the base with which *-er* combines in the word *worker* is also a verb.

Words formed by derivation exhibit the type of internal structure illustrated in Figure 4.5.

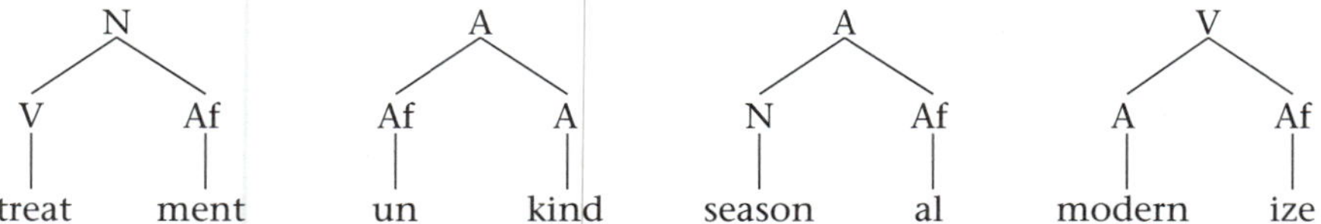

Figure 4.5 Some words formed by derivation

In each of these structures, an affix combines with a base of a particular type to give a new word, in accordance with the properties listed in Table 4.13. In the case of *treatment,* for instance, the affix *-ment* combines with the verb *treat* to give the noun *treatment.*

Complex derivations

Since derivation can apply more than once, it is possible to create multiple levels of word structure, as in Figure 4.6.

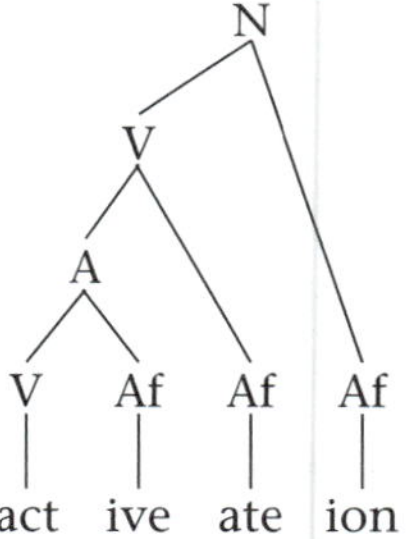

Figure 4.6 A word with a multilayered internal structure

The word *activation* contains several layers of structure, each of which reflects the attachment of an affix to a base of the appropriate type. In the first layer, the affix *-ive* combines with the verbal base *act* to give an adjective. (As noted in Table 4.13, *-ive* is the type of affix that converts a verb into an adjective.) In the next layer, the affix *-ate* combines with this adjective and converts it into a verb (*activate*). At this point, the affix *-ion* is added, converting the verb into a noun and producing the word *activation.*

In some cases, the internal structure of a complex word is not so obvious. The word *unhappiness*, for instance, could apparently be analyzed in either of the ways indicated in Figure 4.7.

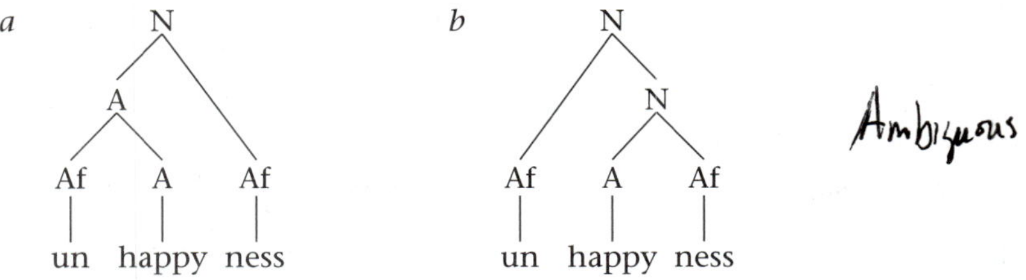

Figure 4.7 Two possible structures for the word *unhappiness*

However, by considering the properties of the affixes *un-* and *-ness*, it is possible to find an argument that favors Figure 4.7a over 4.7b. The key observation is that the prefix *un-* combines quite freely with adjectives, but not with nouns.

Table 4.14 The prefix *un-*

un + A	*un + N*
unable	*unknowledge
unkind	*unhealth
unhurt	*uninjury

This suggests that *un-* must combine with the adjective *happy* before it is converted into a noun by the suffix *-ness*, exactly as depicted in Figure 4.7a.

By contrast, in a word such as *unhealthy*, the prefix *un-* can be attached only AFTER the suffix *-y* has been added to the root. That is because *-y* turns nouns into adjectives, creating the type of category with which *un-* can combine.

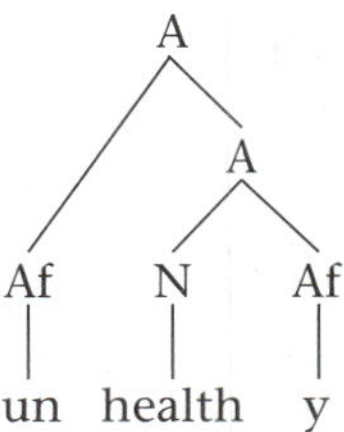

Figure 4.8 The internal structure of the word *unhealthy*

Constraints on derivation

Derivation is often subject to special constraints and restrictions. For instance, the suffix *-ant* (see Table 4.13) can combine with bases of Latin origin such as *assist* and *combat*, but not those of native English origin such as *help* and *fight*. Thus, we find words such as *assistant* and *combatant*, but not **helpant* and **fightant*.

Sometimes, a derivational affix is able to attach only to bases with particular phonological properties. A good example of this involves the suffix *-en*, which can combine with some adjectives to create verbs with a causative meaning (*whiten* means roughly 'cause to become white').

Table 4.15 Restrictions on the use of *-en*

Acceptable	*Unacceptable*
whiten	*abstracten
soften	*bluen
madden	*angryen
quicken	*slowen
liven	*greenen

The contrasts illustrated in Table 4.15 reflect the fact that *-en* can only combine with a monosyllabic base that ends in an obstruent. Thus, it can be added to *white*, which is both monosyllabic and ends in an obstruent. But it cannot be added to *abstract*, which has two syllables, or to *blue*, which does not end in an obstruent.

2.2 Two classes of derivational affixes *(Advanced)*

It is common to distinguish between two types of derivational affixes in English. **Class 1 affixes** often trigger changes in the consonant or vowel segments of the base and may affect stress placement. In addition, they often combine with bound roots, as in the last of the following examples (see Table 4.16).

Table 4.16 Typical effects of Class 1 affixes

Affix	*Sample word*	*Change triggered by affix*
-ity	san-ity	vowel in the base changes from /e/ to /æ/ (cf. *sane*)
	public-ity	final consonant of the base changes from /k/ to /s/; stress shifts to second syllable (cf. *públic* vs. *publícity*)
-y	democrac-y	final consonant of the base changes from /t/ to /s/; stress shifts to second syllable (cf. *démocrat* vs. *demócracy*)
-ive	product-ive	stress shifts to second syllable (cf. *próduct* vs. *prodúctive*)
-(i)al	part-ial	final consonant of the base changes from /t/ to /ʃ/ (cf. *part*)
-ize	public-ize	final consonant of the base changes from /k/ to /s/ (cf. *public*)
-ion	nat-ion	final consonant of the base changes from /t/ to /ʃ/ (cf. *native*)

In contrast, **Class 2 affixes** tend to be phonologically neutral, having no effect on the segmental makeup of the base or on stress placement (see Table 4.17).

Table 4.17 Some typical Class 2 affixes

Affix	*Sample word*	*Change triggered by affix*
-ness	prompt-ness	None
-less	hair-less	None
-ful	hope-ful	None
-ly	quiet-ly	None
-er	defend-er	None
-ish	self-ish	None

When both types of affix appear in the same word, the Class 1 affix must normally occur closer to the root than does the Class 2 affix. As the following examples help illustrate, forms in which a Class 2 affix appears closer to the root are typically not possible words.

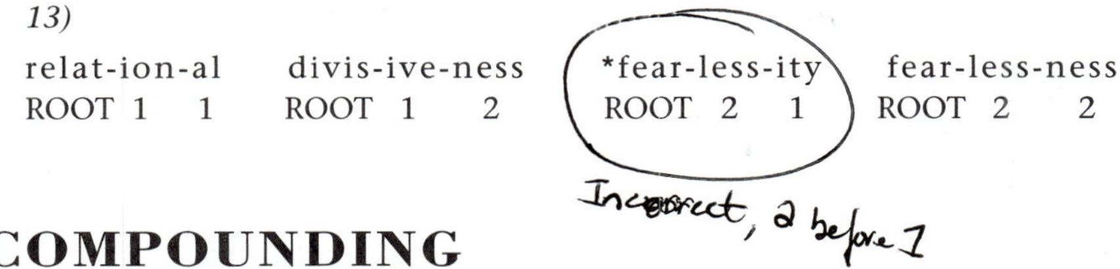

13)

relat-ion-al	divis-ive-ness	*fear-less-ity	fear-less-ness
ROOT 1 1	ROOT 1 2	ROOT 2 1	ROOT 2 2

3 COMPOUNDING

Another common technique for word building in English involves compounding—the combination of two already existent words. With very few exceptions, the resulting **compound word** is a noun, a verb, or an adjective (see Figure 4.9). (Possible examples of compound prepositions include the words *into* and *onto*.)

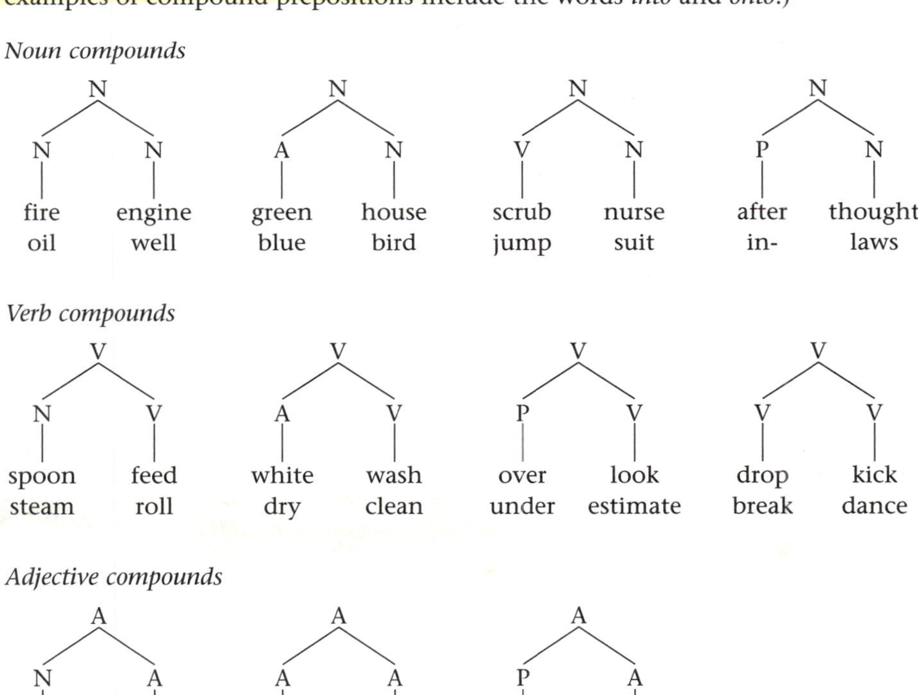

Figure 4.9 Some English compounds

In these and most other compounds of this type, the rightmost morpheme determines the category of the entire word. Thus, *greenhouse* is a noun because its rightmost component is a noun, *spoonfeed* is a verb because *feed* also belongs to this category, and *nationwide* is an adjective just as *wide* is. The morpheme that determines the category of the entire word is called the **head**.

Once formed, compounds can be combined with other words to create still larger compounds, as the examples in Figure 4.10 help show.

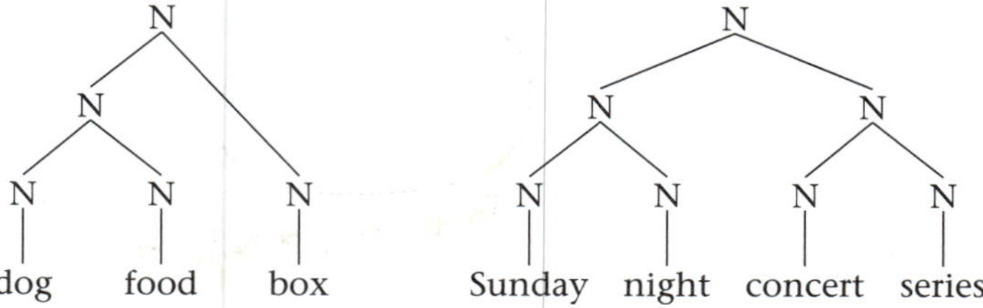

Figure 4.10 Compounds formed from smaller compounds

In addition, compounding can interact with derivation, yielding forms such as *abortion debate*, in which the first word in the compound is the result of derivation (see Figure 4.11).

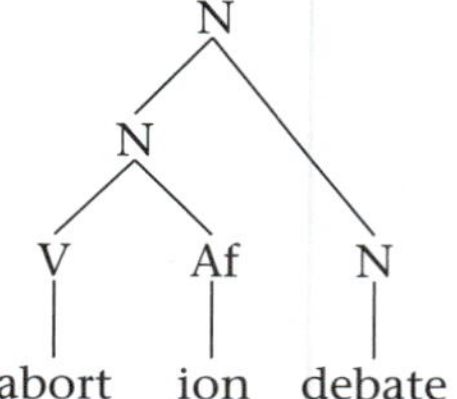

Figure 4.11 The interaction of derivation with compounding

3.1 Properties of compounds

English orthography is not consistent in representing compounds, which are sometimes written as single words, sometimes with an intervening hyphen, and sometimes as separate words. In terms of pronunciation, however, there is an important generalization to be made (see Table 4.18). In particular, adjective-noun compounds are characterized by a more prominent stress on their first component. In noncompounds consisting of an adjective and a noun, in contrast, the second element is generally stressed.

Table 4.18 Compounds versus noncompounds

Compound word		*Noncompound expressions*	
greénhouse	'a glass-enclosed garden'	green hoúse	'a house painted green'
bláckboard	'a chalkboard'	black boárd	'a board that is black'
wét suit	'a diver's costume'	wet suít	'a suit that is wet'

A second distinguishing feature of compounds in English is that tense and plural markers cannot typically be attached to the first element, although they can be added to the compound as a whole. (There are some exceptions, however, such as *passers-by* and *parks supervisor.*)

14)

*The player [dropped kick] the ball through the goal posts.
The player [drop kick]ed the ball through the goal posts.

15)

*The [foxes hunter] didn't have a license.
The [fox hunter]s didn't have a license.

Compounds whose first element is an adjective (*greenhouse, wet suit*) can be identified with the help of a different test. As illustrated in the following example, the adjectival component of a compound cannot be preceded by a word such as *very*.

16)

Compound with *very*:
*We live next to a very [greenhouse].

In contrast, an adjective that is not part of a compound can typically be accompanied by this type of word.

17)

very with an adjective that is not part of a compound:
We live next to a very green house.

3.2 Endocentric and exocentric compounds

Compounds are used to express a wide range of meaning relationships in English. Table 4.19 contains examples of some of the semantic patterns found in noun–noun compounds.

In most cases, a compound denotes a subtype of the concept denoted by its head (the rightmost component). Thus *dog food* is a type of food, a *cave man* is a type of man, *sky blue* is a type of blue, and so on. Such compounds, including all the examples in Table 4.19, are called **endocentric compounds**. In a smaller number of cases, however, the meaning of the compound does not follow from the meanings of its parts in this way. Thus, a *redhead* is not a type of head; rather, it is a person with red hair. Similarly, a *redneck* is a person and not a type of neck. Such compounds are said to be **exocentric compounds**.

Table 4.19 Some noun–noun compounds

Example	*Meaning*
steamboat	'a boat powered by steam'
airplane	'a conveyance that travels through the air'
air hose	'a hose that carries air'
air field	'a field where airplanes land'
fire truck	'a vehicle used to put out fires'
fire drill	'a practice in the event of a fire'
bath tub	'a place in which to bathe'
bath towel	'a towel used after bathing'

A very striking difference between English endocentric and exocentric compounds sometimes shows up in cases where the head is a word like *tooth* or *foot*, which has an irregular plural form. Consider this in the following examples.

Table 4.20 Pluralization in English compounds

In endocentric compounds	*In exocentric compounds*
wisdom teeth	saber tooths (extinct species of carnivore)
club feet	bigfoots (mythical creatures; 'Sasquatch')
policemen	Walkmans (a type of portable radio)
oak leaves	Maple Leafs (Toronto's NHL hockey team)

Notice that whereas the endocentric compounds employ the usual irregular plural (*teeth, feet,* etc.), the exocentric compounds permit the plural suffix *-s* for words such as *tooth, foot,* and *man.*

3.3 Compounds in other languages

Although the rules for forming compounds differ from language to language, the practice of combining lexical categories to build a word is very widespread. As the examples in Table 4.21 help illustrate, compound nouns are especially common. With the exception of Tagalog, in which compounds are left-headed, the languages exemplified in Table 4.21 all have compounds in which the rightmost element is the head.

A special type of compounding process involves **incorporation**, the combination of a word (usually a noun) with a verb to form a compound verb. Although incorporation is not a productive word formation process in English, it is common in other languages. The following examples are from Chukchee, spoken in northeastern Siberia, and the Micronesian language Ponapean. (As these examples help illustrate, incorporation often involves phonological adjustments to the noun and/or the verb.)

Table 4.21 Noun compounds in various languages

Korean		
kot elum straight ice 'icicle'	isul pi dew rain 'drizzle'	nwun mwul eye water 'tears'
Tagalog		
tubig ulan water rain 'rainwater'	tanod bayan guard town 'policeman'	anak araw child sun 'albino'

Table 4.21 (continued) Noun compounds in various languages

German		
Gast-hof guest inn 'hotel'	Wort-bedeutungs-lehre word meaning theory 'semantics'	Fern-seher far seer 'television'
Finnish		
lammas-nahka-turkki sheep skin coat 'sheepskin coat'	elin-keino-tulo-vero-laki life's means income tax law 'income tax law'	
Tzotzil		
piʃ-xól wrap-head 'hat'	méʔ-k'ínobal mother-mist 'rainbow'	ʔóra-tʃón rightaway-snake 'deadly viper'

18)

a. Chukchee

Without incorporation	*With incorporation*
tə-pelarkən qoraŋə.	tə-qora-pelarkən
I leave reindeer	I-reindeer-leave
'I'm leaving the reindeer.'	'I'm in the process of reindeer-leaving.'

b. Ponapean

Without incorporation	*With incorporation*
I pahn pereki lohs	I pahn perek-los
I will unroll mats	I will unroll-mats
'I will unroll the mats.'	'I will engage in mat unrolling.'

4 OTHER TYPES OF WORD FORMATION

Derivation and compounding are the two most common types of word formation in English, but they are not the only ones. As the examples presented in this section will show, there are various other ways to create new words.

4.1 CONVERSION

Conversion is a process that assigns an already existing word to a new syntactic category. Even though it does not add an affix, conversion is often considered to be a type of derivation because of the change in category and meaning that it brings about. For this reason, it is sometimes called **zero derivation**.

Table 4.22 contains examples of the three most common types of conversion in English. (As noted in Section 1.3 above, nouns derived from verbs sometimes undergo stress shift, which moves the stress to the initial syllable. The effects of this phenomenon can be seen in the first three examples in the middle column of Table 4.22.)

Table 4.22 Some examples of conversion

V derived from N	*N derived from V*	*V derived from A*
ink (a contract)	(a building) pérmit	dirty (a shirt)
butter (the bread)	(an exciting) cóntest	empty (the box)
ship (the package)	(a new) súrvey	better (the old score)
nail (the door shut)	(a brief) report	right (a wrong)
button (the shirt)	(an important) call	total (a car)

Less common types of conversion can yield a noun from an adjective (*the poor, gays*) and even a verb from a preposition (*down a beer, up the price*).

Conversion is usually restricted to words containing a single morpheme, although there are a few exceptions such as *propos-ition* (noun and verb), *refer-ee* (noun and verb), and *dirt-y* (adjective and verb). In some cases, conversion can even apply to a compound, as when the noun *grandstand* is used as a verb in the sense of 'show off' (*he likes to grandstand*).

4.2 Clipping

Clipping is a process that shortens a polysyllabic word by deleting one or more syllables. Some of the most common products of clipping are names—*Liz, Ron, Rob, Sue,* and so on. Clipping is especially popular in the speech of students, where it has yielded forms like *prof* for *professor, phys-ed* for *physical education, poli-sci* for *political science*, and *burger* for *hamburger.* However, many clipped forms have also been accepted in general usage: *doc, ad, auto, lab, sub, deli, porn, demo,* and *condo.*

In some cases, speakers may not even realize that a particular word is the product of clipping: the word *zoo*, for instance, was formed in this manner from *zoological garden.* A more recent example of this sort that has become part of general English vocabulary is *fax*, from *facsimile* (meaning 'exact copy or reproduction').

4.3 Blends

Blends are words that are created from non-morphemic parts of two already existing items, usually the first part of one and the final part of the other. Familiar examples include *brunch* from *breakfast* and *lunch, smog* from *smoke* and *fog, spam* from *spiced* and *ham, telethon* from *telephone* and *marathon, aerobicise* from *aerobics* and *exercise, chunnel* (for the underwater link between Britain and the continent) from *channel* and *tunnel,* and *infomercial* from *information* and *commercial.*

In some languages, blending can bring together parts of three words. The following examples are from Malay.

19)

pembangunan lima tahun > pelita 'five-year plan'
development five year

universeti utara malaysia > unitama 'University of North Malaysia'
university north Malaysia

Some blends have become so integrated into the standard vocabulary of English that speakers are unaware of their status. For example, relatively few people know that blending has produced *chortle* (coined by author Lewis Carroll) from *chuckle* and *snort*, *motel* from *motor* and *hotel*, *bit* (in computer jargon) from *binary* and *digit*, and *modem* from *modulator* and *demodulator*.

Sometimes a word is formed by a process that is on the borderline between compounding and blending in that it combines all of one word with part of another. Examples of this in English include *perma-press* (for *permanent-press*), *workaholic*, *medicare*, *guesstimate*, and *threepeat* (used by sports fans to refer to the winning of a championship in three successive years).

4.4 Backformation

Backformation is a process that creates a new word by removing a real or supposed affix from another word in the language. *Resurrect* was originally formed in this way from *resurrection*. Other backformations in English include *enthuse* from *enthusiasm*, *donate* from *donation*, *orient* or *orientate* from *orientation*, and *self-destruct* from *self-destruction*. Sometimes backformation involves an incorrect assumption about a word's form: for example, the word *pea* was derived from the singular noun *pease*, whose final /z/ was incorrectly interpreted as the plural suffix.

Words that end in *-or* or *-er* have proven very susceptible to backformation in English. Because hundreds of such words are the result of affixation (*runner, walker, singer*, etc.), any word with this shape is likely to be perceived as a verb + *er* combination. The words *editor, peddler*, and *swindler* were (mis)analyzed in just this way, resulting in the creation of the verbs *edit, peddle*, and *swindle* (see Table 4.23). A more recent backformation of this type is the verb *lase*, produced by backformation from *laser*, which itself had an unusual origin (see Section 4.5).

Backformation continues to produce new words in modern English. For instance, the form *attrit*, from *attrition*, was used by military officials during the 1991 Gulf War (as in *The enemy is 50 percent attritted*). Among the backformations noticed by the authors of this chapter are *liposuct* (from *liposuction*, seen in a magazine article), *orate* (from *oration*, used in a newspaper editorial), and *tuit* (from *intuition*, heard on the radio).

Table 4.23 Some examples of backformation

Original word	*Misanalysis*	*Verb formed by backformation*
editor	edit + or	edit
peddler	peddle + er	peddle
swindler	swindle + er	swindle

4.5 Acronyms

Acronyms are formed by taking the initial letters of (some or all) the words in a phrase or title and pronouncing them as a word. This type of word formation is especially common in names of organizations and in military and scientific terminology. Common examples include UNICEF for United Nations International Children's Emergency Fund, NASA for National Aeronautics and Space Administration, NATO for North Atlantic Treaty Organization, and AIDS for acquired immune deficiency syndrome.

In some cases, speakers may not know that a word in their vocabulary originated as an acronym. Three commonly used words of this type are *radar* (from radio detecting and ranging), *scuba* (self-contained underwater breathing apparatus), and *laser* (light amplification by stimulated emission of radiation).

4.6 Onomatopoeia

All languages have some words that have been created to sound like the thing that they name. Examples of such **onomatopoeic words** in English include *buzz, hiss, sizzle,* and *cuckoo.* Since onomatopoeic words are not exact phonetic copies of noises, their form can differ from language to language (see Table 4.24).

Table 4.24 Onomatopoeia across languages

English	*Japanese*	*Tagalog*
cock-a-doodle-doo	kokekokko	kuk-kukaok
meow	nyaa	ngiyaw
chirp	pii-pii	tiririt
bow-wow	wan-wan	aw-aw

English does not always have an equivalent for the onomatopoeic words found in other languages. The Athapaskan language Slavey, for instance, has the onomatopoeic word *sah sah sah* for 'the sound of a bear walking unseen not far from camp', *ðik* for 'the sound of a knife hitting a tree', and *tɬóòtʃ* for 'the sound of an egg splattering'.

4.7 Other sources

Sometimes a word may be created from scratch. Called **word manufacture** or **coinage**, this phenomenon is especially common in the case of product names, including *Kodak, Dacron, Orlon,* and *Teflon.* (Notice how the *-on* of the final three words makes them more scientific-sounding, perhaps because an affix of this form occurs in words of Greek origin such as *phenomenon* and *automaton.*)

New words can also be created from names. Familiar words of this type include *watt, curie, fahrenheit,* and *boycott,* all of which originated from the names of the inventors or discoverers of the things to which they refer. In still other cases, brand names can become so widely known that they are accepted as generic terms for the product with which they are associated. The words *kleenex* for 'facial tissue' and *xerox* for 'photocopy' are two obvious examples of this.

5 INFLECTION

Virtually all languages have contrasts such as **singular** versus **plural** and past versus nonpast. Such contrasts are often marked with the help of **inflection**—the modification of a word's form (through affixation, internal change, reduplication, or suppletion) to indicate the grammatical subclass to which it belongs. (The base to which an inflectional affix is added is sometimes called a **stem**.) Affixation is the dominant inflectional process in language, and many languages (e.g., Japanese, Swahili, Inuktitut, and Finnish) have dozens of inflectional affixes.

5.1 Inflection in English

With only eight inflectional affixes (all suffixes), English is not a highly inflected language. Table 4.25 gives a complete list of English inflectional affixes.

Table 4.25 English inflectional affixes

Nouns	
Plural *-s*	the books
Possessive *-'s*	John's book
Verbs	
3rd person SG nonpast *-s*	He reads well.
Progressive *-ing*	He is working.
Past tense *-ed*	He worked.
Past participle *-en/-ed*	He has eaten/studied.
Adjectives	
Comparative *-er*	the smaller one
Superlative *-est*	the smallest one

Although most inflection in English involves regular affixation, some words mark inflectional contrasts in less regular ways. This is most obvious in the case of verbs, a number of which indicate past tense by internal changes of various sorts and even by suppletion: *come-came, see-saw, fall-fell, eat-ate, drink-drank, lose-lost, think-thought, is-was, go-went,* and so on.

Regular and irregular inflection appear to operate in fundamentally different ways: whereas regular inflected forms are constructed as needed in accordance with a general morphological rule (such as "Add *-ed* to mark the past tense"), irregular forms must be stored permanently in the language user's memory. Evidence for this difference comes from studies of how long it takes speakers to utter the past tense form of a verb when presented with the base. For irregular forms, there is a correlation between response time and frequency of the verb: thus it takes less time to recall the past form of frequent verbs such as *see* and *find* than it does for infrequent verbs such as *stride* and *bid*—presumably because it takes longer to locate infrequently used forms in one's memory. For regular verbs, in contrast, response time is independent of frequency: because the past tense is formed by a regular rule, there is no need to "look up" the word in the mental dictionary and all verbs—frequent ones like *walk* and infrequent ones like *discern*—can be handled with equal speed.

5.2 Inflection versus Derivation

Because inflection and derivation are both marked by affixation, the distinction between the two can be a subtle one and it is sometimes unclear which function a particular affix has. Three criteria are commonly used to help distinguish between inflectional and derivational affixes.

Category change

First, inflection does not change either the grammatical category or the type of meaning found in the word to which it applies (see Figure 4.12).

Figure 4.12 The output of inflection: there is no change in either the category of the base or the type of meaning it denotes.

The form produced by adding the plural suffix *-s* in Figure 4.12a is still a noun and has the same type of meaning as the base. Even though *books* differs from *book* in referring to several things rather than just one, the type of thing(s) to which it refers remains the same. Similarly, a past tense suffix such as the one in Figure 4.12b indicates that the action took place in the past, but the word remains a verb and it continues to denote the same action.

In contrast, derivational suffixes characteristically change the category and/or the type of meaning of the form to which they apply and are therefore said to create a new word. Consider the examples of derivation in Figure 4.13.

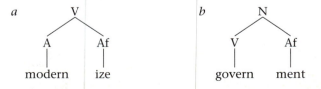

Figure 4.13 The output of derivation: there is a change in the category of the base and/or the type of meaning it denotes.

Figure 4.13 Continued

As Figure 4.13a shows, *-ize* makes a verb out of an adjective, changing the type of meaning it expresses from a property (*modern*) to an action (*modernize*). Parallel changes in category and type of meaning are brought about by *-ment* (V to N) and *-al* (N to A). Matters are a little different in the case of *-dom*, which does not bring about a **category change** in the word *kingdom* (since both the base and the resulting word are nouns). However, *-dom* does modify the type of meaning from 'person' (for *king*) to 'place' (for *kingdom*).

Order

A second property of inflectional affixes has to do with the order in which they are combined with a base relative to derivational affixes. As Figure 4.14 illustrates, a derivational affix must combine with the base before an inflectional affix does (IA = inflectional affix; DA = derivational affix).

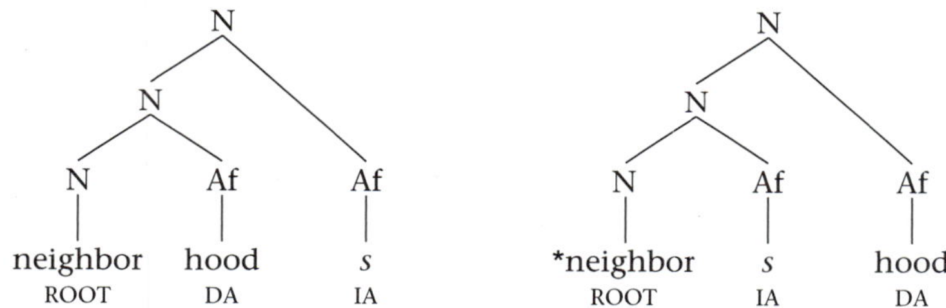

Figure 4.14 The relative positioning of derivational and inflectional affixes: the derivational affix must be closer to the root.

The positioning of inflectional affixes outside derivational affixes in these examples reflects the fact that inflection takes place after derivation.

Productivity

A third criterion for distinguishing between inflectional and derivational affixes has to do with **productivity**—the relative freedom with which they can combine with bases of the appropriate category. Inflectional affixes typically have relatively few exceptions. The suffix *-s*, for example, can combine with virtually any noun that allows a plural form (aside from a few exceptions such as *oxen* and *feet*). In contrast, derivational affixes characteristically apply to restricted classes of bases. Thus, *-ize* can combine with only certain adjectives to form a verb.

20)

modern-ize	*new-ize
legal-ize	*lawful-ize
final-ize	*permanent-ize

In the case of verbs, matters are somewhat more complicated, since many English verbs have irregular past tense forms (*saw, left, went*, and so on). Nonetheless, the distribution of the inflectional affix *-ed* is still considerably freer than that of a derivational affix such as *-ment*. In Table 4.26, for example, all the verbs can take the regular past tense ending, but only those in the first three rows are able to take the *-ment* suffix.

Table 4.26 Compatibility of verb bases with inflectional *-ed* and derivational *-ment*

Verb	*With* -ed	*With* -ment
confine	confined	confinement
align	aligned	alignment
treat	treated	treatment
arrest	arrested	*arrestment
straighten	straightened	*straightenment
cure	cured	*curement

6 FURTHER EXAMPLES OF INFLECTION (*ADVANCED*)

As we have already seen, language uses inflection to mark grammatical information of various sorts. Some of this information, such as the contrast between past and nonpast or singular and plural, is familiar to English speakers. However, as we will see in this section, inflection can also be used to mark less familiar sorts of contrasts.

6.1 Number

Number is the morphological category that expresses contrasts involving countable quantities. The simplest number contrast consists of a two-way distinction between singular (one) and plural (more than one). This is the contrast found in English, where a noun usually takes the suffix *-s* if it refers to two or more entities.

Although most languages express number, not all do. In Nancowry (spoken in India's Nicobar Islands), for example, number is not marked on nouns at all. A sentence such as that in *21* is therefore ambiguous since *nɔ́t* 'pig' can refer to one or more pigs.

21)

sák nɔ́t ʔin tsiʔə́j.
spear pig the we
'We speared the pig(s).'

In Inuktitut (spoken in northern Canada), on the other hand, there is a three-way number contrast involving singular, dual (two and only two), and plural (more than two).

22)

iglu	'a house'
iglu-k	'two houses'
iglu-t	'three or more houses'

6.2 Noun class

Some languages divide nouns into classes based on shared phonological and/or semantic properties. For example, the so-called gender system of French divides nouns into two classes—masculine and feminine. (Despite the noun class names, the gender system of French is not based on a male–female contrast, since it applies even to nouns with inanimate referents: *monde* 'world' and *livre* 'book' are masculine while *chaise* 'chair' and *lune* 'moon' are feminine.) Other languages have far more elaborate noun classes—Latin recognized six classes, for instance, and the Bantu language SiSwati distinguishes among more than a dozen.

Noun class can be marked in a variety of ways. In some languages, the determiner (the equivalent of words such as *the* and *a*) is inflected to indicate the class of the noun. For example, singular nouns in French take the definite determiner *le* if masculine but *la* if feminine. In other languages, inflectional affixes are used to indicate the gender class of the noun. For instance, Russian employs one set of suffixes for nouns in the feminine, animate class and another set for nouns in the masculine, animate class. The examples in Table 4.27 show the gender inflection for nouns that function as the subject of a sentence.

Table 4.27 Gender distinctions in Russian

Class	*Suffix*	*Example*	
Masculine	-Ø	dom	'house'
Feminine	-a	ulic-a	'street'
Neuter	-o	tʃuvstv-o	'sensation'

SiSwati makes use of prefixes to distinguish among its noun classes. (Tone is not represented in the examples in Table 4.28.)

Table 4.28 Some noun classes in SiSwati

Prefix	*Description of class*	*Example*	
um(u)-	persons	um-fana	'boy'
li-	body parts, fruit	li-dvolo	'knee'
s(i)-	instruments	si-tja	'plate'
in-	animals	in-ja	'dog'
bu-	abstract properties	bu-bi	'evil'
pha-	locations	pha-ndle	'outside'

6.3 CASE

Still another type of inflectional contrast associated with nouns in many languages involves **case**—a category that encodes information about an element's grammatical role (subject, direct object, and so on). As an illustration of this, consider the set of related nominal forms (called a **nominal paradigm** or **declension**) for the Turkish word *ev* 'house' in Table 4.29. The contrasts represented in the Turkish case system are intermediate in complexity compared to Finnish, which has fifteen distinct case categories, and to Rumanian, which has only two.

Table 4.29 Turkish case

Case	*Form*	*Type of element that it marks*
Nominative	ev-Ø	the subject
Accusative	ev-i	the direct object
Dative	ev-e	the recipient
Genitive	ev-in	the possessor
Locative	ev-de	a place or location
Ablative	ev-den	direction away from somewhere

The following sentences illustrate the use of these case suffixes.

23)

a. Adam-Ø ev-i Ahmed-e gœster-di.
man-Nom house-Acc Ahmed-Dat show-past.
'The man showed the house to Ahmed.'

b. Ev-in rengi-Ø maːvidir.
house-Gen color-Nom blue
'The house's color is blue.'

c. Adam-Ø ev-de kaldɨ.
man-Nom house-Loc stayed
'The man stayed in the house.'

d. Adam-Ø ev-den tʃiktɨ.
man-Nom house-Abl went
'The man went from the house.'

In the final sentence, for example, *adam* 'man' bears the zero ending of the nominative to indicate that it is the subject of the sentence, while *ev* 'house' bears the ablative suffix indicating the place from which the man went.

Case is most often manifested as affixation on nouns and pronouns, as in Turkish. In some languages, though, it is expressed through changes in the form of the determiner.

24)

German
Der Mann sieht *den* Hund.
The (Nom) man sees the (Acc) dog
'The man sees the dog.'

Because case provides a reliable way to distinguish between subjects and direct objects, there is no need to rely on word order for this purpose. For this reason, languages with case often have relatively free word order. (In the following example, Nom = nominative case, Acc = accusative case, Pst = past.)

25)

Japanese

a. subject-direct object-verb order:
Yumiko-ga sono kodomo-o sikat-ta.
Yumiko-Nom that child-Acc scold-Pst
'Yumiko scolded the child.'

b. direct object-subject-verb order:
Sono kodomo-o Yumiko-ga sikat-ta.
that child-Acc Yumiko-Nom scold-Pst
'Yumiko scolded the child.'

Ergative case marking

Some languages use case marking to encode grammatical contrasts quite unlike those found in familiar European languages. In the Australian language Yidin^y, for instance, the case system groups together the subject of an **intransitive verb** and the direct object of a **transitive verb** (both of which receive a zero ending) while using a special marker (*-ngu*) for the subject of a transitive verb. (A verb is transitive if it takes a direct object; otherwise, it is intransitive. We will talk more about this in Chapter 5.)

26)

a. Yidin^y sentence with a transitive verb:
Wagudya-ngu dyugi-Ø gundal.
man-Erg tree-Abs is cutting.
'The man is cutting the tree.'

b. Yidin^y sentence with an intransitive verb:
Wagudya-Ø gundal.
man-Abs is cutting
'The man is cutting.'

In this type of system, the case associated with the subject of the transitive verb, *wagudya* 'man' in *26a*, is called the **ergative** (abbreviated as Erg in *26*). The case associated with the direct object (*dyugi* 'tree' in the first sentence) and with the subject of an intransitive verb (*wagudya* in the second sentence) is called the **absolutive** (abbreviated as Abs).

Ergative case marking is found in a varied set of languages, including Basque (in Spain), Tagalog (in the Philippines), Tabassaran (in the Caucasus), Inuktitut (in northern Canada and Greenland), and Halkomelem (on the west coast of Canada). Ergative case marking is far less common than the nominative-accusative pattern, which groups together the subjects of transitive and intransitive verbs, distinguishing them from direct objects. Nominative-accusative case marking is found in Turkish, German, Russian, Japanese, Korean, and many other languages.

English nouns and pronouns

At one time, English nouns and determiners (words such as *the*) were inflected for case (see discussion in Chapter 7). In modern English, however, the only remnant of this case system is the genitive suffix *-'s*, used to mark possessors (*the man's book*). Neither nouns nor determiners are inflected to mark grammatical relations such as subject and direct object.

27)

a. *the man* in subject position:
The man left. The man read the book.

b. *the man* in direct object position:
A noise frightened the man.

However, English pronouns do exhibit case contrasts, distinguishing a nominative (*I, they, he*), an accusative (*me, them, him*), and a genitive (*my, their, his*).

28)

Nominative: *He* left. *He* read the book.
Accusative: A noise frightened *him.*
Genitive: Sam took *his* car.

These contrasts follow the nominative-accusative pattern: the same form of the pronoun is used for the subject of an intransitive verb (*leave*) and the subject of a transitive verb (*read*) and this form differs from the one used for direct objects.

We will have more to say about case in Section 5.2 of Chapter 5.

6.4 Person and number agreement

A widely attested type of verbal inflection in human language involves **person**—a category that typically distinguishes among the first person (the speaker), the second person (the addressee), and the third person (anyone else). In many languages, the verb is marked for both the person and number (singular or plural) of the subject. When one category is inflected for properties (such as person and number) of another, the first category is said to agree with the second.

A quite rich system of **agreement** is found in Italian, which exhibits the following contrasts in the present tense (see Table 4.30). (The set of inflected forms associated with a verb is called a **verbal paradigm** or a **conjugation**.)

Table 4.30 The Italian present tense paradigm

	Singular		*Plural*	
1st person	parl-o	'I speak'	parl-iamo	'we speak'
2nd person	parl-i	'you speak'	parl-ate	'you speak'
3rd person	parl-a	'she, he speaks'	parl-ano	'they speak'

Because inflectional affixes in languages like Italian provide so much information about the person and number of the subject phrase, this element need not be overtly present. Thus, *parla italiano* 'speaks Italian' can make up a complete sentence with the meaning 'He/she speaks Italian'.

Modern English has a much more impoverished system of person and number agreement in the verb, and an inflectional affix is used only for the third person singular in the nonpast tense (see Table 4.31).

Table 4.31 The English verbal paradigm (nonpast forms)

	Singular	*Plural*
1st person	I speak	we speak
2nd person	you speak	you speak
3rd person	she, he, or it speaks	they speak

Except for commands, formal English differs from Italian and many other languages with rich verbal inflection in requiring an overtly expressed subject in a complete sentence.

29)

*Speaks English.

6.5 TENSE

Tense is the category that encodes the time of an event with reference to the moment of speaking. There are many different types of tense systems in the languages of the world. For example, English makes a two-way contrast between past (before the moment of speaking) and nonpast, which can be used for both present and future events (see Figure 4.15).

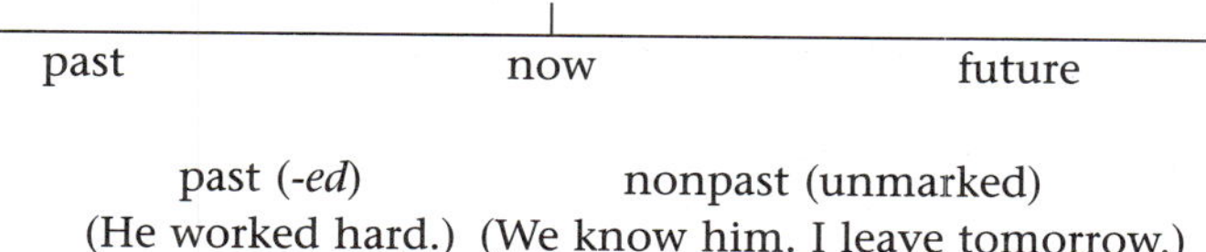

Figure 4.15 Tense in English

In the Australian language Dyirbal, in contrast, there is a two-way distinction between future and nonfuture. As the following examples show, the nonfuture form can be used for both present and past events.

30)

a. Future:	*b.* Nonfuture:
bani-ɲ	bani-ɲu
'will come'	'came, is coming'

In Spanish and Lithuanian, on the other hand, inflectional endings are used to express a three-way contrast involving past, present, and future.

31)

	Spanish	*Lithuanian*
a.	Juan habl-ó bien. 'John spoke well.'	Dirb-au. 'I worked.'
b.	Juan habl-a bien. 'John speaks well.'	Dirb-u. 'I work.'
c.	Juan habl-ar-á bien. 'John will speak well.'	Dirb-siu. 'I will work.'

A still richer system of contrasts is found in the Bantu language ChiBemba, which uses its inflectional system to distinguish degrees of pastness and futurity. (In Table 4.32, the diacritics mark tone; affixes expressing tense contrasts are underlined.)

Table 4.32 Tense in ChiBemba

Past	*Future*
Remote past (before yesterday) ba-àlí-bomb-ele 'They worked.'	Remote future (after tomorrow) ba-ká-bomba 'They'll work.'
Removed past (yesterday) ba-àlíí-bomba 'They worked.'	Removed future (tomorrow) ba-kà-bomba 'They'll work.'
Near past (earlier today) ba-àcí-bomba 'They worked.'	Near future (later today) ba-léé-bomba 'They'll work.'
Immediate past (just happened) ba-á-bomba 'They worked.'	Immediate future (very soon) ba-áláá-bomba 'They'll work.'

7 MORPHOPHONEMICS

As we saw in Chapter 3, a word's pronunciation is often sensitive to the particular phonetic context in which phonemes occur. For instance, an /æ/ that occurs before a nasal consonant will be nasalized (e.g., [kæ̃nt] *can't* vs. [kæt] *cat*), an /æ/ that occurs before a voiced consonant will be longer than one that occurs before a voiceless consonant (e.g., [hæːd] *had* vs. [hæt] *hat*), and so on. Pronunciation can also be sensitive to morphological factors, including a word's internal structure. The study of this phenomenon is known as **morphophonemics** (or **morphophonology**).

Morphophonemic phenomena are extremely common in language. A quite straightforward example from English involves the way that we pronounce the plural suffix *-s*. As first noted in Chapter 1, the morpheme can be pronounced as [s], [z], or [əz].

32)

lip[s]
pill[z]
judg[əz]

We know that this is a morphophonemic alternation because it occurs only in certain morphologically defined contexts. It is perfectly possible to pronounce an [s] sound after an [l] in English—as in a word like *else*, for instance—but for some reason the plural *-s* has to be pronounced as [z] when it occurs after an [l], as in *pill*-[z]. The fact that this phenomenon is found only in particular morphological contexts underlines its morphophonemic character.

7.1 DERIVING ALLOMORPHS

When linguists find that the same morpheme has more than one form (or allomorph), they often seek to set up a single underlying representation for the morpheme and to formulate rules that will derive the appropriate pronunciation for any particular context. To see how this works, let us consider in more detail the precise environments in which the different allomorphs of the English plural morpheme occur (see Table 4.33).

Table 4.33 English plural allomorphs

[-s]		Environment
tops	[tɑps]	• base ends in a voiceless consonant that is not strident
mitts	[mɪts]	
backs	[bæks]	
puffs	[pʌfs]	
baths	[bæθs]	
[-z]		Environment
cobs	[kɑbz]	• base ends in a vowel or a voiced consonant that is not strident
lids	[lɪdz]	
lads	[lædz]	
doves	[dʌvz]	
lathes	[lejðz]	
pins	[pɪnz]	
bums	[bʌmz]	
wings	[wɪŋz]	
teas	[tiz]	
days	[dejz]	
[-əz]		Environment
hisses	[hɪsəz]	• base ends in a consonant that is strident (s, z, ʃ, ʒ, tʃ, dʒ)
buzzes	[bʌzəz]	
crutches	[krʌtʃəz]	
judges	[dʒʌdʒəz]	
wishes	[wɪʃəz]	

As you can see, the choice of plural allomorph is determined by the final segment of the base. Bases that end in a nonstrident voiceless consonant take the [-s] allomorph. Bases that end in a vowel or a nonstrident voiced consonant take the [-z] allomorph. And bases that end in a strident (sibilant) consonant occur with the [-əz] allomorph.

In selecting the underlying representation of a morpheme, it is common to choose the allomorph with the widest distribution. This happens to be [-z] in the case of the English plural morpheme, since it occurs after most voiced consonants and after all vowels (which are also voiced). This is no accident, of course, since [-z] too is voiced.

The words *lips, pills,* and *glasses* therefore have the underlying representations depicted in *33*.

33)

lɪp-z 'lips'   pɪl-z 'pills'   glæs-z 'glasses'

Two rules are now required to derive the correct final form of these words. The first rule, which we will call Coda Epenthesis, inserts a schwa whenever the [-z] appears after a base that ends in a strident consonant.

34)

$$\varnothing \rightarrow \begin{bmatrix}\text{+syllabic}\\ \text{+reduced}\end{bmatrix} \;/\; [\text{+strident}]\;\_\_\_\_\;\text{-z}$$

This rule has a solid perceptual and articulatory motivation since it helps ensure that the resulting word will obey the general phonotactic constraint prohibiting a sequence of strident consonants in the same coda in English. Notice that English permits double strident sequences across word boundaries (as in *crash site* [kræʃ sajt] and *buzz saw* [bʌz sɔ] and across syllable boundaries (as in *posture* [pɑstʃər]), but never within a coda. Our rule of Coda Epenthesis helps rule out illegal codas by applying whenever the plural morpheme [-z], a type of strident, is attached to a base that ends in a strident consonant.

The second rule needed to ensure that the plural morpheme has the right form devoices [-z] when it occurs after a voiceless consonant in the same coda.

35)

Devoicing

$$\text{-z} \rightarrow [\text{-voice}] \;/\; [\text{-voice}]\;\_\_\_\_\;]_{\sigma}$$

Like Coda Epenthesis, Devoicing helps ensure that English plurals comply with the usual phonotactic constraints of the language: no English words contain a coda in which a voiceless consonant is followed by a voiced one.

Figure 4.16 illustrates the derivations of all three plural allomorphs.

	lips	*pills*	*glasses*
Underlying representation:	lɪp-z	pɪl-z	glæs-z
Coda Epenthesis:	lɪp-z	pɪl-z	glæs-əz
Devoicing:	lɪp-s	pɪl-z	glæs-əz

Figure 4.16 Underlying representations and derivations for the three plural allomorphs in English

Notice that the ordering of the rules is crucial here. If Devoicing applied first, the plural ending of forms such as *glasses* would incorrectly end up as */glæs-s/, since Coda Epenthesis would not apply (see Figure 4.17).

Underlying representation:	glæs-z
Devoicing:	glæs-s
Coda Epenthesis:	does not apply

Figure 4.17 Derivation for *glasses* in which Devoicing incorrectly applies before Coda Epenthesis

7.2 Conditioning by morphological class

A second type of morphophonemic phenomenon is manifested in just a subclass of morphemes rather than in the entire class. This too can be illustrated with the help of English plurals.

As the examples in Table 4.34 show, English includes a limited class of words in which an /f/ in the base alternates with /v/ in the plural.

Table 4.34 Alternating base-final /f/ and /v/ in English

The f-v *alternation (irregular forms)*		*No alternation (regular forms)*	
wife	wives	whiff	whiffs
thief	thieves	chief	chiefs
leaf	leaves	fife	fifes
knife	knives	laugh	laughs

The alternating class is unproductive, and new words with final [f] entering English do not exhibit the *f-v* alternation. That is why a hypothetical new word such as *nif* would have [nɪfs] rather than *[nɪvz] as its plural form.

We can formulate the process that is responsible for the *f-v* alternation as follows:

36)

f → v / ___]-plural

Notice that this rule is morphophonemic in two ways. First, it applies only when the plural morpheme is present: there is no *f-v* alternation with the possessive morpheme *-'s*, which is why we say *my wife-'[s] car*, not **my wive-'[z] car*. Second, only certain root morphemes (e.g., *thief*, but not *chief*) can undergo the rule.

This second characteristic illustrates a frequent feature of morphophonemic rules: they often have exceptions. In this, they contrast with allophonic rules, which apply very generally. Thus, all vowels occurring before a nasal in the same syllable are nasalized; all vowels occurring before a voiced consonant in the same syllable are lengthened; and so on. But only some base-final /f/s are converted to /v/ in the plural.

Figure 4.18 illustrates how the plural forms of *thief* and *chief* are derived from the appropriate underlying representations.

	thieves	*chiefs*
Underlying representation:	θif-z	tʃif-z
The */f/-to-/v/* rule:	θiv-z	tʃif-z
Devoicing:	θiv-z	tʃif-s
Other rules:	θi:v-z	tʃif-s

Figure 4.18 Underlying representations and derivations for *thieves* and *chiefs* (The */f/-to-/v/* rule applies only to *thieves*.)

Once again, rule ordering is important here. Unless the */f/-to-/v/* rule applies before Devoicing, the final form of *thieves* will be *[θi:v-s], with the [-s] allomorph of the plural (see Figure 4.19).

Underlying representation:	θif-z
Devoicing:	θif-s
The */f/-to-/v/* rule:	*θiv-s
Other rules:	*θi:v-s

Figure 4.19 Derivation for *thieves* in which Devoicing incorrectly applies before the */f/-to-/v/* rule

Abstract underlying representations

As the preceding examples help show, the underlying representations needed to account for morphophonemic phenomena may be quite unlike a word's phonetic form. For example, the word *thieves* is pronounced [θi:vz], but its underlying representation is /θif-z/. Representations that differ from phonetic forms in this way are said to be **abstract**.

In some cases, a morpheme's underlying representation can be very abstract indeed. For example, in order to account for the alternation in the pronunciation of the morpheme *electric* in words like *electrical* and *electricity*, linguists often posit the underlying representations given in *37*.

37)

ilɛktrɪk-əl ilɛktrɪk-ɪti

A morphophonemic rule then converts the /k/ of the base to [s] in front of the affix *-ity*. This rule is clearly morphophonemic in character since it applies only before the [ɪ] of *-ity* rather than before any [ɪ]. (Notice that we don't pronounce *kill* as *sill*.)

The variant of the base that ends in *k* is chosen as underlying for two reasons. First, the base *electri*[k] has a wider distribution than the allomorph *electri*[s], since it occurs in words such as *electrical* as well as in the unsuffixed form. Second, a rule that fronts a /k/ to [s] before the high front vowel of the suffix is phonetically more natural than a rule that changes an /s/ to [k] in final position or before the suffix *-al*.

A more complicated example involves the three-way alternation involving *permit, permissive,* and *permission* (see Figure 4.20). The underlying representation for the root morpheme is /pərmɪt/, with a *t-to-s* rule accounting for the [s] in the second form and a *t-to-ʃ* rule giving the [ʃ] in the third word.

	permit	*permissive*	*permission*
UR	pərmɪt	pərmɪt - ɪv	pərmɪt - ən
t-to-s		pərmɪsɪv	
t-to-ʃ			pərmɪʃən

Figure 4.20 Derivations for *permit, permissive,* and *permission*

Although very abstract, this sort of analysis has proven to be very popular over the years, primarily because it allows us to posit a single underlying representation for each morpheme and to find general rules that predict its actual pronunciation in particular contexts.

Summing up

This chapter has focused on the structure and formation of **words** in human language. Many words consist of smaller formative elements, called **morphemes**. These elements can be classified in a variety of ways (**free** versus **bound**, **root** versus **affix**, **prefix** versus **suffix**) and can be combined and modified under various conditions to build words. Operations that can combine and modify morphemes include **compounding**, **affixation**, **cliticization**, **internal change**, **suppletion**, and **reduplication**.

The two basic types of word formation in English are **derivation** and **compounding**. Less common types of word formation include **conversion**, **blending**, **clipping**, and **backformation**. Once formed, words may be **inflected** to mark grammatical contrasts in **number**, **gender**, **case**, **person**, and **tense**.

Key terms

General terms

allomorphs
bound morpheme
complex words
free form
free morpheme
lexicon
morph
morpheme
morphology
simple words
word

General terms concerning morphological analysis

affixes
base
infixes
lexical category
prefix
root
suffix
tiers
tree structures
word-based (morphology)

Terms concerning inflection and derivation

ablaut
affixation
category change
Class 1 affixes
Class 2 affixes
clitics
concatenative (morphology)
derivation
enclitics
full reduplication
host
inflection
internal change
partial reduplication
partial suppletion
proclitics
productivity
reduplication
stem
suppletion
umlaut

Terms concerning compounding

compound word
compounding
endocentric compounds
exocentric compounds
head
incorporation

Other kinds of word formation

acronyms
backformation
blends
clipping
coinage
conversion
onomatopoeic words
word manufacture
zero derivation

Terms for morphological analysis of world languages

absolutive
agreement
case
conjugation
declension
ergative
intransitive verb
nominal paradigm
noun class
number
person
plural
singular
tense
transitive verb
verbal paradigm

Terms concerning the interaction of morphology and phonology

abstract (representation)
morphophonemics
morphophonology

Sources

The estimate that the average high school student knows 60,000 "basic" words comes from *The Language Instinct* by S. Pinker (New York: Morrow & Co.), p. 150. The introduction to words and morphemes draws on the classic treatments found in L. Bloomfield's *Language* (New York: Holt, Rinehart and Winston, 1933), Gleason's *An Introduction to Descriptive Linguistics* (cited on the next page), and C. F. Hockett's

A Course in Modern Linguistics (New York: Macmillan, 1958). The discussion of word formation seeks to portray those aspects of recent and current work that represent widely accepted views and are appropriate for presentation in an introductory textbook. Much of this work is summarized in the books by Jensen, Katamba, and Spencer (cited below) and the many references cited therein. For a detailed discussion on nonconcatenative morphology, see *A-Morphous Morphology* by S. Anderson (New York: Cambridge University Press, 1992).

The Arabic examples in Section 1.3 are from p. 17 of the book by Spencer cited below. The tier-based analysis of Arabic word structure is based on work by John McCarthy, including his article "A Prosodic Theory of Nonconcatenative Morphology," *Linguistic Inquiry* 12 (1981): 373–418. The facts concerning the requirement that *-ant* combine with a base of Latin origin (Section 2.2) are noted on p. 71 of the book by Katamba cited below.

The example of the Chukchee compound in Section 3.3 is from p. 15 of the book by Spencer cited below. The Ponapean example is from p. 212 of *A Ponapean Reference Grammar* by Kenneth Rehg (Honolulu: University of Hawaii Press, 1981).

The examples of conversion given in Section 4.1 come largely from the discussion in the books by Jensen (pp. 92–93) and Bauer (pp. 229–31) cited below. The examples of Malay blends come from "Malay Blends—CV or Syllable Templates" by M. Dobrovolsky, unpublished ms., University of Calgary. The data on Slavey onomatopoeia is from "Slavey Expressive Terms" by M. Pepper, *Kansas Working Papers in Linguistics* 10 (1985): 85–100.

The definition of *stem* introduced in Section 5 is from the article by S. Anderson cited below (p. 163). The discussion of the difference between regular and irregular inflection draws on information from "Rules of Language" by S. Pinker (*Science* 253 [August 1991]: 530–35). The Nancowry example in the section on number was provided by R. Radhakrishnan. The data in the section on tense come principally from "Tense, Aspect and Mood" by S. Chung and A. Timberlake, in *Language Typology and Syntactic Description*, vol. 3, edited by T. Shopen (London: Cambridge University Press, 1985), pp. 202–58.

The examples used in the section on morphophonemics were taken from the discussion of this subject written by Michael Dobrovolsky for the third edition of this book. Exercises 1 to 19 were prepared by Joyce Hildebrand and exercise 20 by Michael Dobrovolsky. The data in problem 7 is from *Writing Transformational Grammars* by A. Koutsoudas (New York: McGraw-Hill, 1966).

Recommended reading

Anderson, Stephen. 1988. "Morphological Theory." In *Linguistics: The Cambridge Survey*. Vol. 1. Edited by F. Newmeyer, 146–91. New York: Cambridge University Press.

Bauer, L. 1983. *English Word-Formation*. New York: Cambridge University Press.

Gleason, H. 1955/1961. *An Introduction to Descriptive Linguistics*. New York: Holt, Rinehart and Winston.

Jensen, John. 1990. *Morphology: Word Structure in Generative Grammar*. Amsterdam: John Benjamins.

Katamba, Francis. 1993. *Morphology*. London: Macmillan.
Spencer, Andrew. 1991. *Morphological Theory*. Cambridge, MA: Blackwell.

Appendix: How to identify morphemes in unfamiliar languages

An important part of morphological analysis involves identifying morphemes in unfamiliar languages and determining the nature of the information that they carry. (A number of the problems in the set of exercises that follow this chapter will give you an opportunity to practice this type of analysis.) The key procedure to follow in working on this sort of problem can be stated simply as follows:

- Identify recurring strings of sounds and match them with recurring meanings.

Consider in this regard the small sample of data in Table 4.35 from Turkish, consisting of four words along with their English translations. (A more realistic data sample would not only be much larger but would also include sentences in which it might well be unclear where the word boundaries should be placed.)

Table 4.35 Some Turkish words

/mumlar/	'candles'
/toplar/	'guns'
/adamlar/	'men'
/kitaplar/	'books'

As you can probably see, the syllable /lar/ occurs in all four items in our sample. From the translations of these items, you can see that a particular feature of meaning—namely, plurality—is present in all four cases as well. Using the procedure just stated, we therefore hypothesize that /lar/ is the morpheme marking plurality in Turkish. Once this has been determined, we can then infer that /mum/ in /mumlar/ is also a morpheme (with the meaning 'candle'), that /top/ in /toplar/ is a morpheme (with the meaning 'gun'), and so on. A larger sampling of Turkish data would confirm the correctness of these inferences.

In doing morphological analysis in unfamiliar languages, there are a number of pitfalls to avoid. For the type of data normally investigated at the introductory level, the following guidelines are especially important.

- Do not assume that the morpheme order in the language you are analyzing is the same as in English. In Korean, for example, morphemes indicating location (the rough equivalent of 'at', 'in', and so forth) follow rather than precede the noun (*hakkyo-eyse* 'at school' is literally 'school at').

- Do not assume that every semantic contrast expressed in English will also be manifested in the language you are analyzing. In Turkish, for instance, there is no equivalent for English *the* and *a*. In Mandarin Chinese, the same pronoun form can be used to refer to a male or a female (there is no *he-she* distinction).

- Do not assume that every contrast expressed in the language you are analyzing is manifested in English. For example, some languages distinguish more than two number categories (Inuktitut distinguishes singular, dual, and plural; see Section 6.1) and some languages make multiple tense contrasts (ChiBemba, discussed in Section 6.5, has an eight-way distinction).
- Remember that a morpheme can have more than one form (allomorph). For example, further study of Turkish would reveal that the plural suffix in this language can also be realized as /ler/, depending on the vowel in the base to which the suffix is attached.

Questions

1. Consider the following words and answer the questions below.

a) fly	f) reuse	k) spiteful	p) preplan
b) desks	g) triumphed	l) suite	q) optionality
c) untie	h) delight	m) fastest	r) prettier
d) tree	i) justly	n) deform	s) mistreat
e) dislike	j) payment	o) disobey	t) premature

   i) For each word, determine whether it is simple or complex.
   ii) Circle all of the bound morphemes. Underline all of the roots.

2. All of the following Persian words consist of two or more morphemes. (*Note*: *xar* means 'buy' and *-id* designates the past tense.)

a) xaridam	'I bought'
b) xaridi	'you (sg) bought'
c) xarid	'(he) bought'
d) naxaridam	'I did not buy'
e) namixaridand	'they were not buying'
f) naxaridim	'we did not buy'
g) mixarid	'(he) was buying'
h) mixaridid	'you (pl) were buying'

   i) Try to match each of the following notions with a morpheme in the Persian data.

a) I	e) they
b) you (sg)	f) not
c) we	g) was/were + -ing (continuous)
d) you (pl)	

   ii) How would you say the following in Persian?
   a) They were buying.
   b) You (sg) did not buy.
   c) You (sg) were buying.

3. Consider the following data from Turkish.

a) lokanta	'a restaurant'	lokantada	'in/at a restaurant'
b) kapɨ	'a door'	kapɨda	'in/at a door'
c) randevu	'an appointment'	randevuda	'in/at an appointment'
d) baʃ	'a head'	baʃta	'in/at a head'
e) kitap	'a book'	kitapta	'in/at a book'
f) koltuk	'an armchair'	koltukta	'in/at an armchair'
g) taraf	'a side'	tarafta	'in/at a side'

i) Does the Turkish morpheme meaning 'in/at' have more than one allomorph?
ii) If so, what are the allomorphs? Describe their distribution as generally as possible.

4. Consider the following words.

a) desks	e) triumphed	i) preplan (V)	m) optionality
b) untie	f) ageless	j) fastest	n) prettier
c) invalid (A)	g) justice	k) reuse	o) mistreat
d) dislike (V)	h) payment	l) disobey	p) preview (V)

i) Draw a tree structure for each word.
ii) For the word *optionality*, what is the base for the affix *-ion*? What is the base for the suffix *-ity*? Are either of these bases also the root for the entire word? If so, which one?

5. Each of the following columns illustrates a different morphological process.

Column 1	*Column 2*	*Column 3*
a) mouse/mice	f) go/went	k) récord/recórd
b) dive/dove	g) is/was	l) ímport/impórt
c) take/took	h) good/better	m) cónvict/convíct
d) man/men	i) she/her	n) ímprint/imprínt
e) eat/ate	j) am/are	o) óutrage/outráge

i) What morphological process is at work in column 1? column 2? column 3?
ii) Describe in your own words the difference between the process exemplified in column 1 versus that in column 2.
iii) Think of at least one more English example to add to each column.

6. The following words can be either nouns or verbs.

a) record	f) outline	k) report
b) journey	g) convict	l) assault
c) exchange	h) imprint	m) answer
d) remark	i) reply	n) import
e) surprise	j) retreat	o) cripple

i) For each word, determine whether stress placement can be used to make the distinction between noun and verb.
ii) Think of two more English examples illustrating the process of stress shift to mark a category distinction.

7. The following Samoan data illustrate one of the morphological processes discussed in this chapter.

a)	mate	'he dies'	mamate	'they die'
b)	nofo	'he stays'	nonofo	'they stay'
c)	galue	'he works'	galulue	'they work'
d)	tanu	'he buries'	tatanu	'they bury'
e)	alofa	'he loves'	alolofa	'they love'
f)	taoto	'he lies'	taooto	'they lie'
g)	atamaʔi	'he is intelligent'	atamamaʔi	'they are intelligent'

i) What morphological process is illustrated by these data?
ii) Describe the process in your own words.
iii) If 'he is strong' in Samoan is *malosi*, how would you say 'they are strong' in Samoan?

8. The following data from Agta (spoken in the Philippines) illustrate a specific type of affix.

a)	dakal	'big'	dumakal	'grow big, grow up'
b)	darag	'red'	dumarag	'redden'
c)	furaw	'white'	fumuraw	'become white'

i) What is the affix in Agta meaning 'become X'?
ii) What type of affix is it?
iii) Describe its placement.

9. The following words from Chamorro, spoken in Guam and the Mariana Islands, illustrate some of the morphological processes described in this chapter. (Data are presented in the orthography of Chamorro, not in phonetic transcription.)

I.	*Root*		*Derived word*	
a)	adda	'mimic'	aadda	'mimicker'
b)	kanno	'eat'	kakanno	'eater'
c)	tuge	'write'	tutuge	'writer'
II.	*Root*		*Derived word*	
d)	atan	'look at'	atanon	'nice to look at'
e)	sangan	'tell'	sanganon	'tellable'
f)	guaiya	'love'	guaiyayon	'lovable'
g)	tulaika	'exchange'	tulaikayon	'exchangeable'
h)	chalek	'laugh'	chalekon	'laughable'
i)	ngangas	'chew'	ngangason	'chewable'
III.	*Root*		*Derived word*	
j)	nalang	'hungry'	nalalang	'very hungry'
k)	dankolo	'big'	dankololo	'very big'
l)	metgot	'strong'	metgogot	'very strong'
m)	bunita	'pretty'	bunitata	'very pretty'

i) What morphological process is involved in I? in II? in III?
ii) What changes in lexical category take place in I? in II? in III?
iii) Formulate a general statement as to how the derived words in I are formed. Do for the same for III.

iv) Does the affix in II have more than one allomorph? If so, what are the allomorphs? What is their distribution?

10. In this chapter, an argument was presented in favor of the following structure for the word *unhappiness*.

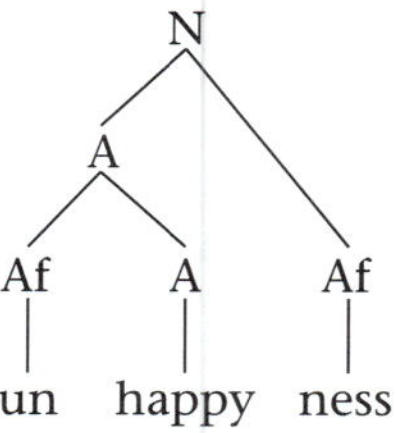

Using the same type of argument, justify tree structures for the words *inexpensive, redisposal*, and *disinvestment*. (*Hint:* This will involve determining the type of syntactic category with which the affixes in these words can combine; see Table 4.13.)

11. In English, the suffix *-er* can be added to a place name. Examine the words in the two columns below.

Column 1	*Column 2*
Long Islander	*Denverer
Vermonter	*Philadelphiaer
New Yorker	*San Franciscoer
Newfoundlander	*Torontoer
Londoner	*Miamier

i) In general terms, what does the suffix *-er* mean in these words?
ii) How is this *-er* different in meaning from the *-er* found in the words *skater* and *walker*?
iii) As is shown in column 2, the distribution of *-er* in the above data is restricted in some way. State the constraint in your own words.
iv) Does this constraint also apply to the type of *-er* used in the word *skater*? (*Hint*: What would you call 'one who discovers' or 'one who rows'?)

12. The following words have all been formed by compounding. Draw a tree structure for each word. If you are in doubt as to the lexical category of the compound, remember that the category of the head determines the category of the word.

a) football	i) tree trunk	q) hockey match
b) billboard	j) lead free	r) coffee table
c) sunspot	k) shortstop	s) flower girl
d) in-crowd	l) girlfriend	t) blueprint
e) fast food	m) city center	u) Greenpeace
f) software	n) fail-safe	v) spaceship
g) freeze-dry	o) potato peel	w) brain dead
h) overbook	p) bittersweet	x) kill-joy

13. In this chapter, several ways of identifying compounds were discussed. Using the tests given in the left-hand column, verify the compound status of the forms in the right-hand column.

Test	*Compound*
past tense	blow-dry
compatibility with *very*	loudmouth
plural	headlight
stress	poorhouse

14. Examine the following compounds and answer the questions below.

Column 1	*Column 2*
a) loudmouth	h) cutthroat
b) skinhead	i) pickpocket
c) kill-joy	j) spoilsport
d) bath towel	k) crybaby
e) death blow	l) brain dead
f) birdbrain	m) blow-dry
g) Walkman	n) armchair

i) For each of the compounds in column 1, determine whether it is endocentric or exocentric.

ii) How do you form the plural of *Walkman* and *loudmouth*? (*Hint:* see Table 4.20. Also, pay special attention to the pronunciation of *mouth*. Is it any different here than when it is an independent word?)

15. The words in column 2 have been created from the corresponding words in column 1. Indicate the word formation process responsible for the creation of each item in column 2.

	Column 1		*Column 2*
a)	automation	→	automate
b)	humid	→	humidifier
c)	information, entertainment	→	infotainment
d)	love, seat	→	loveseat
e)	prógress	→	progréss
f)	typographical error	→	typo
g)	aerobics, marathon	→	aerobathon
h)	act	→	deactivate
i)	curve, ball	→	curve ball
j)	methamphetamine	→	meth
k)	(a) comb	→	comb (your hair)
l)	beef, buffalo	→	beefalo
m)	random access memory	→	RAM
n)	megabyte	→	meg
o)	Federal Express	→	FedEx
p)	influenza	→	flu
q)	They have finished	→	They've finished

16. Here are five instances where a new word is needed. Create a word for each of these definitions using the word formation process suggested. Fill in the blanks with your new words.
    a) Use an acronym . . . for your uncle's second oldest brother.
       "We visited my ____________ at Christmas."
    b) Use onomatopoeia . . . for the sound of a dishwasher in operation.
       "I can't concentrate because my dishwasher is ___________ing."
    c) Use conversion . . . for wrapping something breakable in bubble wrap.
       "You'd better ___________ that ornament or else it might break."
    d) Use a compound . . . for the annoying string of cheese stretching from a slice of hot pizza to one's mouth.
       "As the ______________ hung precariously from my lips, our eyes met!"
    e) Use backformation . . . for the action of backformation.
       "We had to _________________ words in Linguistics today."

17. Create new words for each of the following situations.
    a) Use a product name . . . for the act of scrubbing with Ajax.
       "I _________ed the tub after giving Fido a bath."
    b) Use a proper name . . . for the act of breaking dishes, which Jonathan does regularly.
       "He's going to ____________ all of my best dishes."
    c) Use clipping . . . for a course in ovinology (the study of sheep).
       "Have you done your ____________ assignment yet?"
    d) Use derivation . . . for being able to be contacted.
       "The counselor is not very ______________."
    e) Use a blend . . . for a hot drink made with chocolate and ginseng.
       "I'll have a ___________ and two peanut butter cookies, please."

18. Determine whether the words in each of the following groups are related to one another by processes of inflection or derivation.
    a) go, goes, going, gone
    b) discover, discovery, discoverer, discoverable, discoverability
    c) lovely, lovelier, loveliest
    d) inventor, inventor's, inventors, inventors'
    e) democracy, democrat, democratic, democratize

19. The following sentences contain both derivational and inflectional affixes. Underline all of the derivational affixes and circle the inflectional affixes.
    a) The farmer's cows escaped.
    b) It was raining.
    c) Those socks are inexpensive.
    d) Jim needs the newer copy.
    e) The strongest rower continued.
    f) The pitbull has bitten the cyclist.
    g) She quickly closed the book.
    h) The alphabetization went well.

20. The following data provide the possible forms of the regular past tense morpheme of English.
    a) walked /wɔkt/
    b) cracked /krækt/
    c) flipped /flɪpt/
    d) hissed /hɪst/
    e) huffed /hʌft/
    f) hushed /hʌʃt/

g) munched	/mʌntʃt/	o) flitted	/flɪtəd/
h) drubbed	/drʌbd/	p) butted	/bʌtəd/
i) dragged	/drægd/	q) padded	/pædəd/
j) jogged	/dʒɑgd/	r) loaded	/lodəd/
k) fudged	/fʌdʒd/	s) collided	/kəlajdəd/
l) heaved	/hivd/	t) allowed	/ʌlawd/
m) wheezed	/wizd/	u) sowed	/sod/
n) fined	/fajnd/		

i) List the alternate forms of the past tense morpheme.

ii) Which alternate makes the best underlying form? Why?

iii) State in words the conditioning factors that account for the presence of the alternate forms of the past tense morpheme.

For the Student Linguist

BAMBIFICATION

Well, of course, language is productive. You can't possibly read this chapter without being completely convinced of how very easy it is to make up new words. Morphological productivity is mildly interesting when you're creating transparent new words, such as when you have a verb like *fax* and create a new verb like *refax* (fax again) or *speed-fax* (fax fast) or an adjective like *faxable* (can be faxed), but it's not exactly earth-shattering.

What amazes me, though, is running across a new word, knowing it's a perfectly good word in English, knowing exactly how to pronounce it, and not having a clue about what it means. I'm not talking about knowing *frete* could be a word because it doesn't break any phonological rules of English. I'm talking about a word whose meaning remains mysterious even though that word can be broken down into recognizable, meaningful parts. Take the word *Brazilification,* which appears in Douglas Coupland's novel *Generation X. Brazilification* might appear in a sentence like "The recent Brazilification seen in the United States will have a large impact on tax reform plans." *Brazilification* could mean 'the replacement of forests with cattle ranches' or 'the improved quality of coffee' or many other things; it actually means 'the widening gulf between the rich and the poor and the accompanying disappearance of the middle classes' (p. 11). From this, the meaning of *Brazilify* is transparent: make the gulf between the rich and the poor wider, thereby causing the disappearance of the middle classes.

Now consider *Bambification,* another morphologically complex word from Coupland's book. It means 'make like X', where X is a variable that can be replaced by *Brazil,* or *Bambi,* or some other noun. *Bambification* doesn't mean 'make like Bambi's economic system', although theoretically it could. It means 'the mental conversion of flesh and blood living creatures into cartoon characters possessing bourgeois Judeo-Christian attitudes and morals' (p. 48).

Morphology is even more interesting when you look at compounds. The four words below, also gleaned from *Generation X,* could each be interpreted in a few ways. For each word, I've given the real definition and my own, made-up definition (Coupland's are made-up too, but his were first, so I count them as the real definitions). I've also given the morphological structure that matches one of the definitions. Your task is to figure out if and how the structure would be different for the other definition.

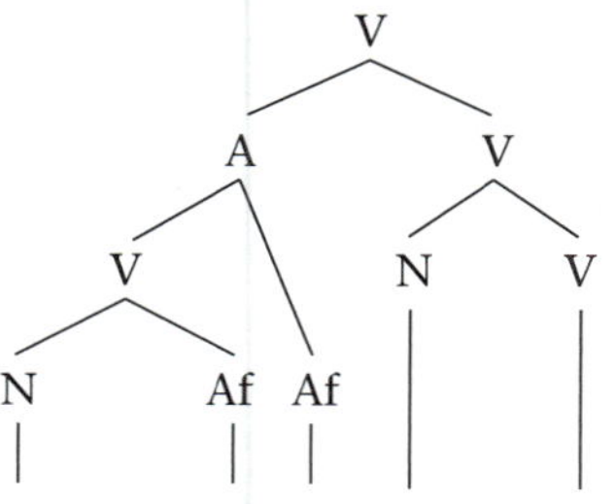

VACCIN ATE D TIME TRAVEL
To fantasize about traveling backward in time, but only with the proper vaccinations. (p. 11)

VACCINATED TIME TRAVEL
To travel freely in time, but only to times and places worth going to.

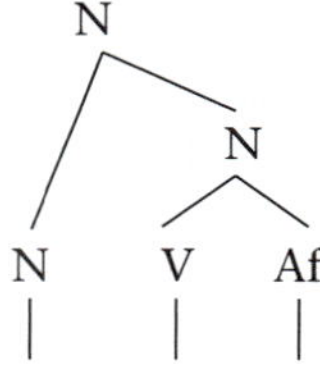

GREEN DIVISION
Sorting waste into chic recycling bins, showing how environmentally aware you are to all your friends.

GREEN DIVIS ION
Knowing the difference between envy and jealousy. (p. 150)

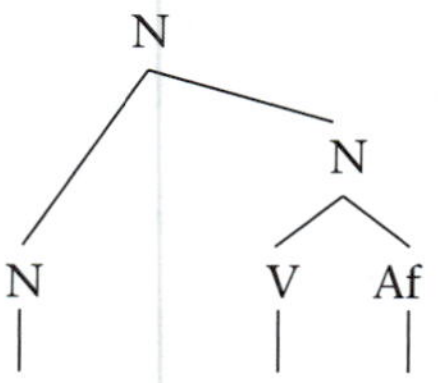

DUMPSTER CLOCK ING
The tendency when looking at objects to guesstimate the amount of time they will take to eventually decompose: *"Ski boots are the worst. Solid plastic. They'll be around till the sun goes supernova."* (p. 162)

DUMPSTER CLOCKING
Reckoning time by the amount and nature of the contents of the dumpster. *"An old couch, three textbooks, and twenty pounds of notebooks beneath a case of empties. Must be late May."*

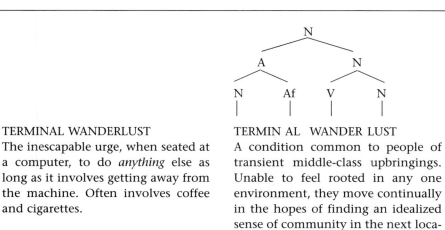

TERMINAL WANDERLUST
The inescapable urge, when seated at a computer, to do *anything* else as long as it involves getting away from the machine. Often involves coffee and cigarettes.

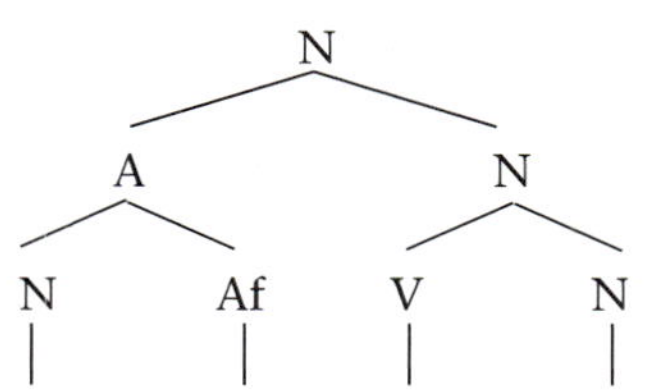

TERMIN AL WANDER LUST
A condition common to people of transient middle-class upbringings. Unable to feel rooted in any one environment, they move continually in the hopes of finding an idealized sense of community in the next location. (p. 171)

five

SYNTAX: THE ANALYSIS OF SENTENCE STRUCTURE

William O'Grady

. . . the game is to say something new with old words
– RALPH WALDO EMERSON, *Journals* (1849)

OBJECTIVES

In this chapter, you will learn:

- how we categorize words
- how words can be combined into phrases and sentences according to a systematic schema
- that words "choose" what they can combine with in the same phrase
- how questions are derived from statements
- how all languages are alike in the way sentences are constructed
- how languages can differ systematically in the way sentences are constructed
- how different theories account for human ability to construct and understand sentences

Not much can be said with a single word. If language is to express complex thoughts and ideas, there has to be a way to combine words to form sentences. In this chapter, we will consider how this is done by focusing on the component of the grammar that linguists call **syntax**.

As we noted in Chapter 1, speakers of a language are able to combine words in novel ways, forming sentences that they have neither heard nor seen before. However, not just any combination of words will result in a well-formed sentence. English speakers recognize that the pattern in *1* is not permissible even though the same words can be combined in a different way to form the acceptable sentence in *2*.

1)

*House painted student a the.

2)

A student painted the house.

We say that an utterance is **grammatical** if native speakers judge it to be a possible sentence of their language.

The study of syntax lies very close to the heart of contemporary linguistic analysis, and work in this area is notorious both for its diversity and for its complexity. New ideas are constantly being put forward and there is considerable controversy over how the properties of sentence structure should be described and explained.

This chapter will introduce a simple version of **transformational** (or **generative**) **grammar**. Although many linguists disagree with various features of this approach, it is very widely used in linguistics and other disciplines concerned with language (especially cognitive science). For this reason, it is the usual point of departure for introductions to the study of sentence structure. Section 6 provides a brief discussion of some alternatives to transformational analysis.

An intriguing aspect of work within transformational syntax is the emphasis on **Universal Grammar (UG)**, the system of categories, operations, and principles that are shared by all languages. The key idea is that despite the many superficial differences among languages, there are certain commonalities with respect to the manner in which sentences are formed. As things now stand, it is widely believed that the syntactic component of any grammar must include at least two subcomponents. The first of these is a **lexicon**, or mental dictionary, that provides a list of the language's words along with information about each word's pronunciation, form, and meaning.

The second subcomponent consists of what can be called a **computational system**—by which we simply mean a system that can carry out operations on words to combine them and arrange them in particular ways. As we will see a little later in this chapter, the two key structure-building operations made available by Universal Grammar are **Merge** (which combines elements to create phrases and sentences) and **Move** (which transports an element to a new position within a particular sentence).

We will begin our discussion of these matters in Section 1 by introducing some of the most common categories of words found in language and by investigating how they can be combined into larger structural units. Subsequent sections describe other aspects of sentence structure, using examples and phenomena drawn from English and other languages.

1 CATEGORIES AND STRUCTURE

A fundamental fact about words in all human languages is that they can be grouped together into a relatively small number of classes, called **syntactic categories**. This classification reflects a variety of factors, including the type of meaning that words express, the type of affixes that they take, and the type of structures in which they can occur.

1.1 Categories of words

Table 5.1 provides examples of the word-level categories that are most central to the study of syntax.

Table 5.1 Syntactic categories

Lexical categories	*Examples*
Noun (N)	Harry, boy, wheat, policy, moisture, bravery
Verb (V)	arrive, discuss, melt, hear, remain, dislike
Adjective (A)	good, tall, old, intelligent, beautiful, fond
Preposition (P)	to, in, on, near, at, by
Adverb (Adv)	silently, slowly, quietly, quickly, now
Nonlexical categories	*Examples*
Determiner (Det)	the, a, this, these
Degree word (Deg)	too, so, very, more, quite
Qualifier (Qual)	always, perhaps, often, never, almost
Auxiliary (Aux)	will, can, may, must, should, could
Conjunction (Con)	and, or, but

The four most studied syntactic categories are **noun (N)**, **verb (V)**, **adjective (A)**, and **preposition (P)**. These elements, which are often called **lexical categories**, play a very important role in sentence formation, as we will soon see. A fifth and less studied lexical category consists of **adverbs (Adv)**, most of which are derived from adjectives.

Languages may also contain **nonlexical** or **functional categories**, including **determiners (Det)**, **auxiliary verbs (Aux)**, **conjunctions (Con)**, and **degree words (Deg)**. Such elements generally have meanings that are harder to define and paraphrase than those of lexical categories. For example, the meaning of a determiner such as *the* or an auxiliary such as *would* is more difficult to describe than the meaning of a noun such as *hill* or *vehicle*.

A potential source of confusion in the area of word classification stems from the fact that some items can belong to more than one category.

3)

comb used as a noun:
The woman found a comb.

comb used as a verb:
The boy should comb his hair.

4)

near used as a preposition:
The child stood near the fence.

near used as a verb:
The runners neared the finish line.

near used as an adjective:
The end is nearer than you might think.

How then can we determine a word's category?

Meaning

One criterion involves meaning. For instance, nouns typically name entities, including individuals (*Harry, Sue*) and objects (*book, desk*). Verbs, on the other hand, characteristically designate actions (*run, jump*), sensations (*feel, hurt*), and states (*be, remain*). Consistent with these tendencies, *comb* in *3* refers to an object when used as a noun but to an action when used as a verb.

The meanings associated with nouns and verbs can be elaborated in various ways. The typical function of an adjective, for instance, is to designate a property or attribute of the entities denoted by nouns. Thus, when we say *that tall building,* we are attributing the property 'tall' to the building designated by the noun.

In a parallel way, adverbs typically denote properties and attributes of the actions, sensations, and states designated by verbs. In the following sentences, for example, the adverb *quickly* indicates the manner of Janet's leaving and the adverb *early* specifies its time.

5)

Janet left quickly.
Janet left early.

A word's category membership does not always bear such a straightforward relationship to its meaning, however. For example, there are nouns such as *difficulty, truth,* and *likelihood,* which do not name entities in the strict sense. Moreover, even though words that name actions tend to be verbs, nouns may also denote actions (*push* is a noun in *give someone a push*). Matters are further complicated by the fact that in some cases, words with very similar meanings belong to different categories. For instance, the words *like* and *fond* are very similar in meaning (as in *Mice like/are fond of cheese*), yet *like* is a verb and *fond* an adjective.

Inflection

Most linguists believe that meaning is only one of several criteria that enter into determining a word's category. As Table 5.2 shows, inflection can also be very useful

Table 5.2 Lexical categories and their inflectional affixes

Category	*Inflectional affix*	*Examples*
Noun	plural *-s* possessive *-'s*	books, chairs, doctors John's, (the) man's
Verb	past tense *-ed* progressive *-ing*	hunted, watched, judged hunting, watching, judging
Adjective	comparative *-er* superlative *-est*	taller, faster, smarter tallest, fastest, smartest

for distinguishing among different categories of words. (For a discussion of inflection, see Chapter 4, Section 5.) However, even inflection does not always provide the information needed to determine a word's category. In English, for example, not all adjectives can take the comparative and superlative affixes (**intelligenter, *beautifulest*) and some nouns cannot be pluralized (**moistures, *braveries, *knowledges*).

Distribution

A third and often more reliable criterion for determining a word's category involves the type of elements (especially functional categories) with which it can co-occur (its **distribution**). For example, nouns can typically appear with a determiner, verbs with an auxiliary, and adjectives with a degree word, in the sort of patterns illustrated in Table 5.3.

Table 5.3 Distributional properties of Nouns, Verbs, and Adjectives

Category	*Distributional property*	*Examples*
N	occurrence with a determiner	a car, the wheat
V	occurrence with an auxiliary	has gone, will stay
A	occurrence with a degree word	very rich, too big

Of course, a verb cannot occur with a determiner or degree word in these sorts of patterns and a noun cannot occur with an auxiliary.

6)

a verb with a determiner:
*the destroy

a verb with a degree word:
*very arrive

a noun with an auxiliary:
*will destruction

Distributional tests for category membership are simple and highly reliable. They can be used with confidence when it is necessary to categorize unfamiliar words.

1.2 Phrase structure

Sentences are not formed by simply stringing words together like beads on a necklace. Rather, they have a hierarchical design in which words are grouped together into successively larger structural units. For this reason, the structure of a sentence is often visualized as an "inverted tree," whose branches reflect the sentence's internal architecture (see Figure 5.1).

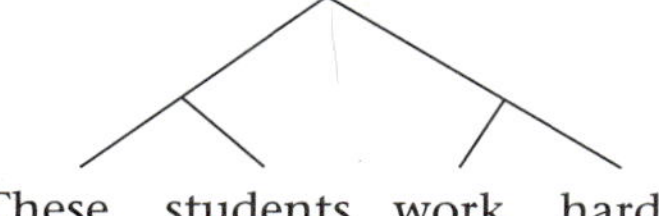
These students work hard

Figure 5.1 A tree structure illustrating the design of the sentence *These students work hard*

This section will focus on the structure of **phrases**, which are the units that stand between words and sentences in syntactic structure.

Heads

Phrases are built around a nucleus called the **head**—a noun in the case of noun phrases (NPs), a verb in the case of verb phrases (VPs), and so on (see Figure 5.2). (Qual stands for **qualifier**, a type of adverb.)

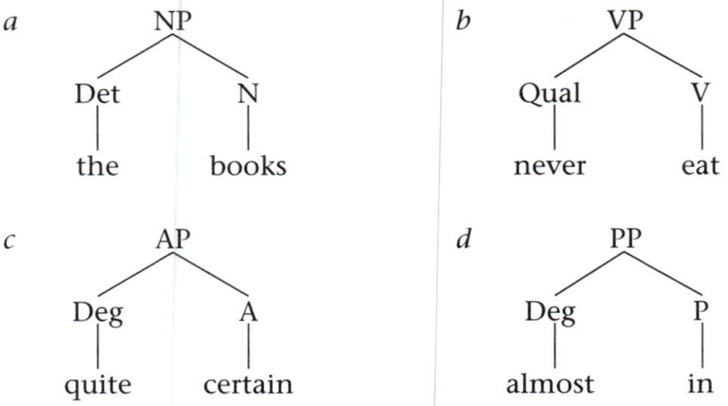

Figure 5.2 Some simple phrases

Although phrases usually consist of two or more words, a head may form a phrase all by itself.

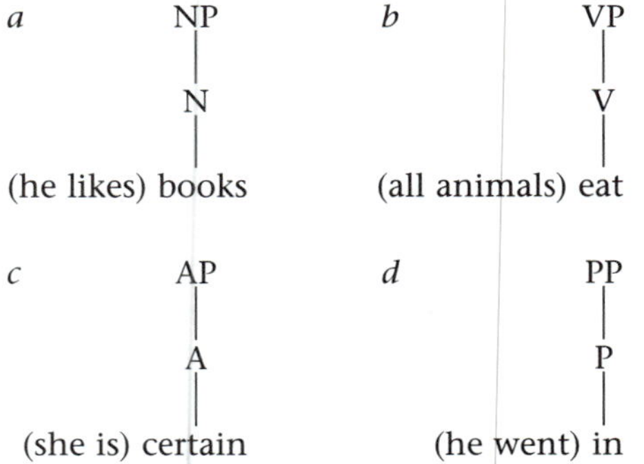

Figure 5.3 Phrases consisting of just a head

Specifiers

Let's go back now to the two-word phrases in Figure 5.2. We have already identified the head in these phrases, but we have said nothing about the status of the other word. Determiners (*the* and *a*), qualifiers (*never* and *often*), and degree words (*quite* or *almost*) function as **specifiers**. Semantically, specifiers help to make the meaning of the head more precise. Hence, the determiner (Det) *the* in *a* indicates that the speaker has in mind specific books, the qualifier (Qual) *never* in *b* indicates a non-occurring event, and the degree words (Deg) *quite* and *almost* in *c* and *d* indicate the extent to which a particular property or relation is manifested.

Syntactically, specifiers typically mark a phrase boundary. In English, specifiers occur at the left boundary (the beginning) of their respective phrases, as illustrated in Figure 5.3. However, as we will see in Section 4, some languages (Thai, for example) place specifiers in other positions.

The syntactic category of the specifier differs depending on the category of the head. As the examples in Figure 5.2 and Table 5.4 help show, determiners serve as the specifiers of Ns while qualifiers typically function as the specifiers of Vs and degree words as the specifiers of As and (some) Ps.

Table 5.4 Some specifiers

Category	*Typical function*	*Examples*
Determiner (Det)	specifier of N	the, a, this, those, no
Qualifier (Qual)	specifier of V	never, perhaps, often, always
Degree word (Deg)	specifier of A or P	very, quite, more, almost

Question 3 at the end of the chapter provides practice in identifying specifiers and heads.

Complements

Consider now some examples of slightly more complex phrases.

7)

a. [$_{NP}$ the books about the war]
b. [$_{VP}$ never eat a hamburger]
c. [$_{AP}$ quite certain about Mary]
d. [$_{PP}$ almost in the house]

In addition to a specifier and the underlined head, the phrases in *7* also contain a **complement**. These elements, which are themselves phrases, provide information about entities and locations whose existence is implied by the meaning of the head. For example, the meaning of *eat* implies an object that is eaten, the meaning of *in* implies a location, and so on.

8)

A vegetarian would never eat [a hamburger].
↑ ↑
head *complement naming the thing eaten*

9)

in [the house]
↑ ↑
head *complement naming a location*

Complements are attached to the right of the head in English (but to the left in many other languages—see Section 4). Figure 5.4 illustrates the structure of a phrase consisting of a specifier, a head, and a complement. (The NP serving as complement of a V is often called a **direct object**; a verb taking a direct object is referred to as **transitive**.)

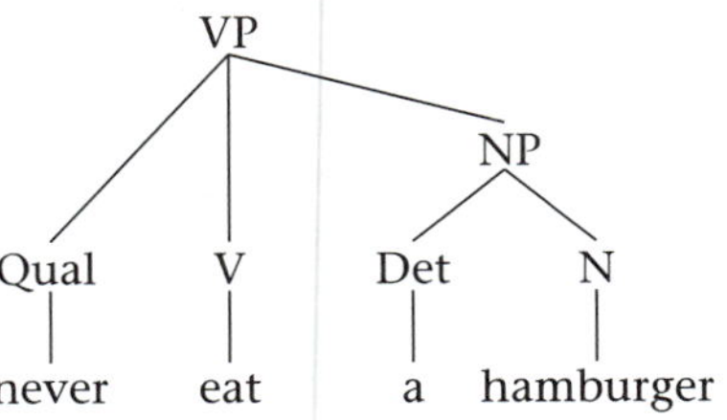

Figure 5.4 A VP consisting of a specifier, a head, and a complement

As we noted above, complements are themselves phrases. Thus, the complement of the V *eat* is an NP that itself consists of a determiner (*a*) and a head (*hamburger*). This phrase then combines with the verb and its specifier to form a still larger structural unit.

NPs, APs, and PPs have a parallel internal structure, as the examples in Figure 5.5 illustrate. (In order to save space, we do not depict the internal structure of the complement phrases in these examples.) Question 4 at the end of the chapter provides practice in identifying complements.

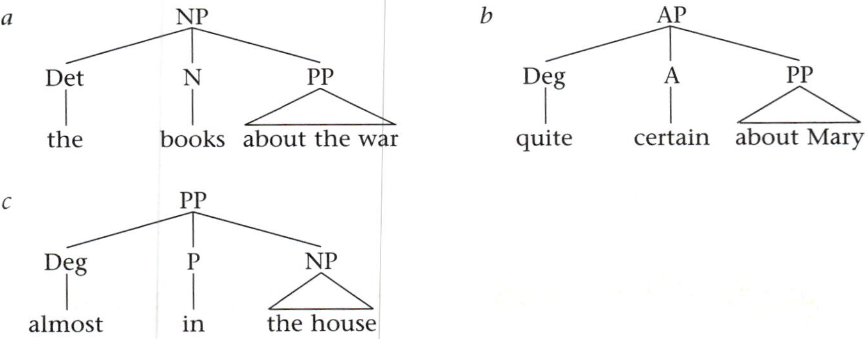

Figure 5.5 Other phrases consisting of a specifier, a head, and a complement

The blueprint

How does the grammar ensure that specifiers, heads, and complements occupy the appropriate positions in a language's sentences? In early work in transformational syntax, a special mechanism known as a **phrase structure rule** was used to describe the composition of phrases. (The arrow in the following sample rules can be read as 'consists of' or 'branches into'. Parentheses are used to indicate that a particular element is optional.)

10)

NP → (Det) N (PP)
VP → (Qual) V (NP)
AP → (Deg) A (PP)
PP → (Deg) P (NP)

The first of these rules states that an NP can consist of a determiner, an N head, and a PP complement (as in Figure 5.5a); the second rule captures the fact that a VP can be composed of an optional qualifier, a V, and an NP complement (as in Figure 5.4); and so on.

There are very obvious structural similarities among the phrase types referred to by these rules. As you can see by reconsidering the trees in Figures 5.4 and 5.5, the specifier is attached to the left of the head while the complement is attached to the right in all four cases. In more recent work, these similarities have been summarized with the help of the following general rule, in which X stands for N, V, A, or P.

11)

The XP Rule

XP → (Specifier) X (Complement)

Put even more explicitly, we can say that the internal structure or "architecture" of a phrase must comply with the following blueprint, or **phrase structure schema** (see Figure 5.6).

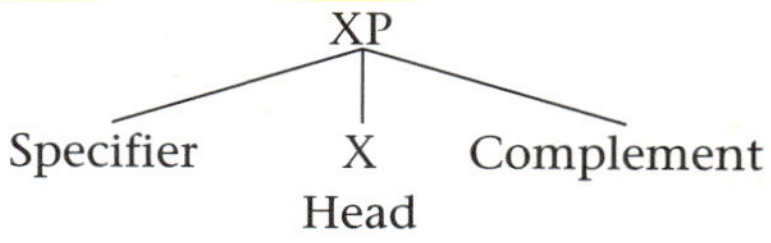

Figure 5.6 The phrase structure schema

We can now formulate the following operation for sentence building.

12)

Merge

Combine words in a manner compatible with the phrase structure schema.

The Merge operation is able to take a determiner such as *the* and combine it with a noun such as *house* to form the NP *the house*. It is then able to take a head such as the preposition *in* and combine it with the NP *the house* to form the PP *in the house* (see Figure 5.7).

Step 1: Merge applies to the determiner and the noun.

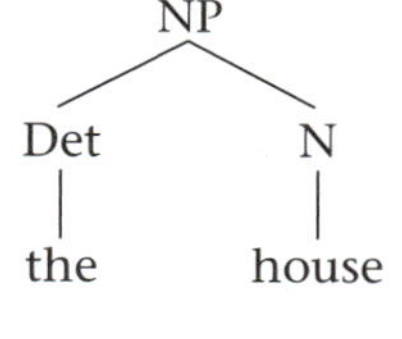

Step 2: Merge applies to the preposition and the NP formed in Step 1.

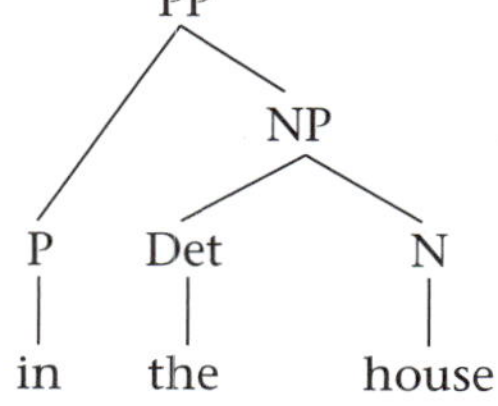

Figure 5.7 The Merge operation in action

Continued application of the Merge operation to additional words can lead to the formation of phrases and sentences of unlimited complexity.

1.3 Sentences

The largest unit of syntactic analysis is the sentence (S). Traditionally, sentences are taken to consist of an NP (often called the **subject**) and a VP (sometimes called the **predicate**) to yield structures such as the one in Figure 5.8.

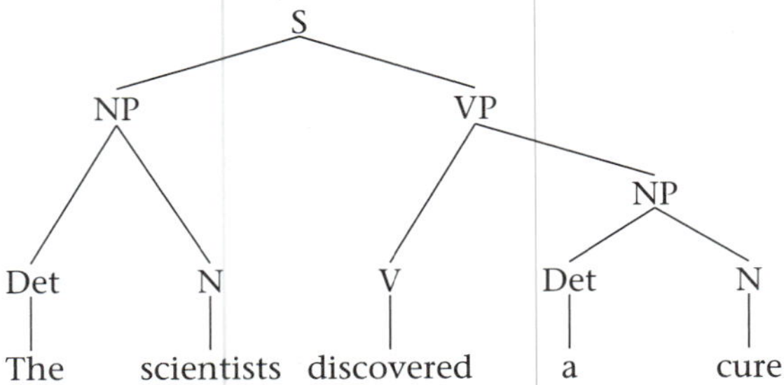

Figure 5.8 The structure of S (traditional view)

This traditional analysis assumes that S is special in not having an internal structure like other phrases (with a head, a complement, and a specifier). However, many linguists now believe that S has the structure depicted in Figure 5.9 (Pst = past).

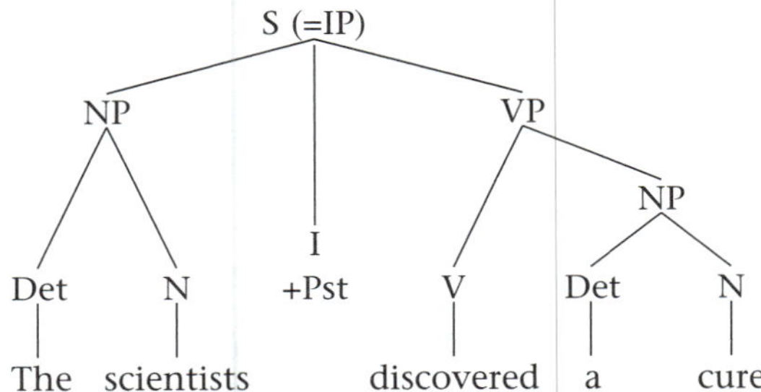

Figure 5.9 The structure of S (popular contemporary view)

The key idea is that sentences have as their head an abstract category dubbed "I" or "Infl" (for "inflection"), which indicates the sentence's tense. It is commonly assumed that the I node also contains information about subject-verb agreement, which—like tense—is often realized as verbal inflection (see Chapter 4, Section 6.4). Because I, like all heads, is obligatory, this automatically accounts for the fact that all sentences of English have tense (e.g., they are either past or nonpast). Other important aspects of sentence structure follow from the fact that the I category takes a VP as its complement and an NP (the subject) as its specifier.

Although somewhat abstract, this analysis has the advantage of giving sentences the same internal structure as other phrases, making them consistent with the phrase structure schema. It also provides us with a natural place in syntactic structure for words such as *can, may,* and *will*, which are inherently associated with a particular tense. (These particular elements are invariably nonpast, as shown by the unacceptability of patterns such as **He can/may/will work yesterday.*) Although traditionally analyzed as "auxiliary verbs," these words are commonly treated as instances of the I category in contemporary linguistic analysis and are placed in the I position, as depicted in Figure 5.10.

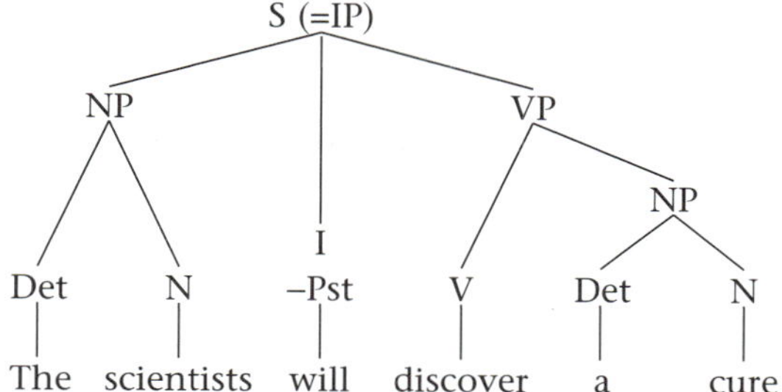

Figure 5.10 An S with an auxiliary in the I position

This neatly accounts not only for the fact that these elements have an inherent tense, but also for their occurrence between the subject (the specifier) and the VP (the complement)—the position reserved for the head of the sentence. (It must be admitted, however, that the use of the term *inflection* by syntacticians to include free morphemes is unfortunate.)

For the reasons just outlined, we will adopt the view that sentences have I as their head and that this element may be realized as either a tense label (past or nonpast) or an auxiliary. Nonetheless, for the sake of exposition, we will also follow the common practice of using the label S rather than IP to designate sentences.

The appendix at the end of the chapter outlines a procedure that should help you assign sentences an appropriate structure. Question 5 provides an opportunity to practice this procedure.

1.4 TESTS FOR PHRASE STRUCTURE

The words that make up a sentence form intermediate structural units called phrases. How can linguists be sure that they have grouped words together into phrases in the right way? The existence of the syntactic units, or **constituents**, found in tree structures can be independently verified with the help of special tests. We will briefly consider three such tests here. Not every test will work for every constituent.

The substitution test

Evidence that phrases are syntactic units comes from the fact that they can often be replaced by an element such as *they, it*, or *do so*. This is illustrated in *13*, where *they* replaces the NP *the children* and *do so* replaces the VP *stop at the corner*. (This is called a **substitution test**.)

13)

[$_{NP}$The children] will [$_{VP}$ stop at the corner] if *they* see us *do so*.
(*they* = the children; *do so* = stop at the corner)

The substitution test also confirms that a PP such as *at the corner* is a unit since it can be replaced by a single word in a sentence such as *14*.

14)

The children stopped [$_{PP}$ at the corner] and we stopped *there* too.
(*there* = at the corner)

Elements that do not form a constituent cannot be replaced in this way. Thus, there is no word in English that we can use to replace *children stopped,* for example, or *at the*.

The movement test

A second indication that *at the corner* forms a constituent is that it can be moved as a single unit to a different position within the sentence. (This is called a **movement test**.) In *15*, for instance, *at the corner* can be moved from a position after the verb to the beginning of the sentence.

15)

They stopped [$_{PP}$ at the corner] → [$_{PP}$ At the corner], they stopped.

Of course, *at the*, which is not a syntactic unit, cannot be fronted in this manner (**At the, they stopped corner*).

The coordination test

Finally, we can conclude that a group of words forms a constituent if it can be joined to another group of words by a conjunction such as *and*, *or*, or *but*. (This is known as the **coordination test**, since patterns built around a conjunction are called **coordinate structures**.) The sentence in *16* illustrates how coordination can be used to help establish that *stopped at the corner* is a constituent.

16)

The children [$_{VP}$ stopped at the corner] and [$_{VP}$ looked both ways].

1.5 X' CATEGORIES *(ADVANCED)*

Up until now, we have been assuming that the architecture of phrase structure complies with the blueprint in Figure 5.11 (identical to Figure 5.6).

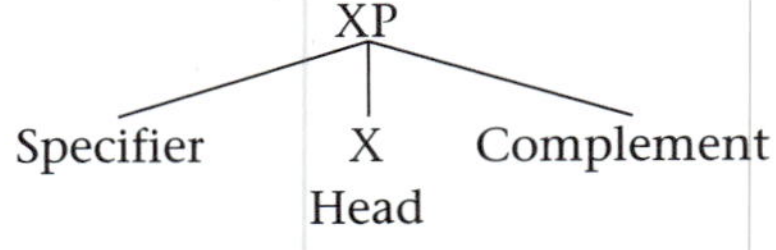

Figure 5.11 The phrase structure schema

In fact, however, this may be a simplification since many syntacticians believe that there is an intermediate level of structure within phrases, as depicted in Figure 5.12.

The intermediate level of structure is represented by the symbol X' (pronounced *X-bar*).

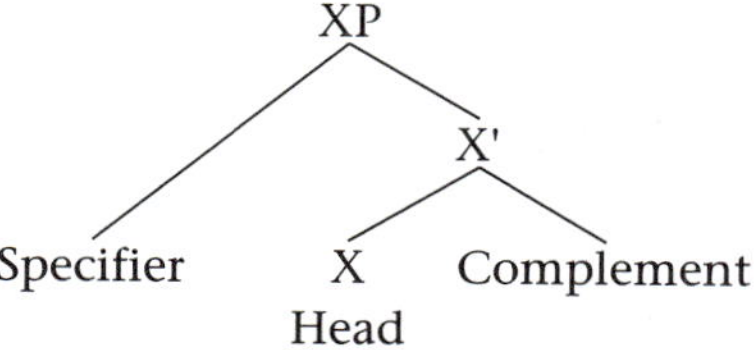

Figure 5.12 The phrase structure template (revised)

According to this viewpoint, the Merge operation combines the head and its complement to form an X'-level constituent, which can then be combined with a specifier to create an XP. Figure 5.13 provides an example of an entire sentence analyzed in this way.

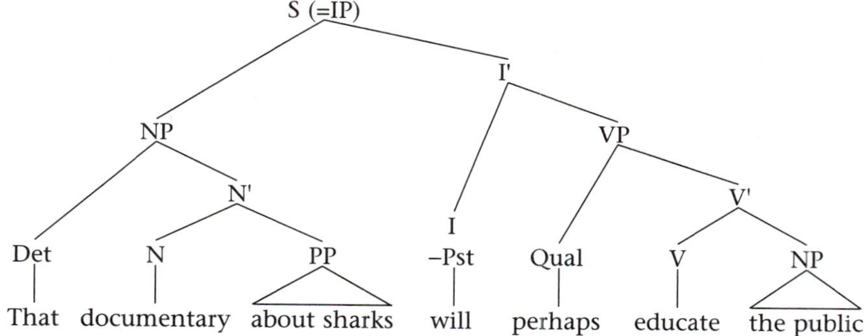

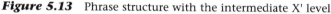

Figure 5.13 Phrase structure with the intermediate X' level

The existence of X' categories can be verified with the help of the same sort of constituency tests discussed in Section 1.4. Consider, for example, the V' *educate the public* in Figure 5.13. As the following sentence shows, this constituent can be replaced by *do so*, in accordance with the substitution test.

17)

That documentary about sharks will perhaps [$_{V'}$ educate the public], but media reports never *do so*. (*do so* = educate the public)

Now consider the N' *documentary about sharks* in Figure 5.13. As the next sentence shows, this unit can be replaced by the element *one* (the substitution test again).

18)

That [$_{N'}$ documentary about sharks] is more informative than the previous *one*. (*one* = documentary about sharks)

The fact that *one* can replace *documentary about sharks* in this manner confirms that it is a syntactic unit, consistent with the structure in Figure 5.13.

Finally, the coordination test can be used to provide evidence for the existence of the I' constituent in Figure 5.13.

19)

That documentary about sharks [$_{I'}$ will perhaps educate the public] and [$_{I'}$ may even save the species from extinction].

In order to accommodate these new three-level structures, it is necessary to replace our original XP rule by the pair of rules in *20*. As before, X can stand for any one of a number of categories, including N, V, A, P, or I.

20)

a. XP → (Specifier) X'
b. X' → X (Complement)

The first of these rules stipulates that XP categories of any type consist of an optional specifier and an X'. The second rule then states that an X' consists of a head, X, and its complements (if any). Taken together, these two rules form the three-level structures illustrated in Figure 5.13, as desired.

Because three-level structures take up a considerable amount of space and can be tedious to draw, we will not make further use of them here. In order to do more advanced syntactic analysis, though, you need to be familiar with the X' level.

2 COMPLEMENT OPTIONS

How can we be sure that individual words will occur with a complement of the right type in the syntactic structures that we have been building? Information about the complements permitted by a particular head is included in its entry in a speaker's lexicon. For instance, the lexicon for English includes an entry for *devour* that indicates its syntactic category (V), its phonological representation, its meaning, and the fact that it takes an NP complement.

21)

devour: category: V
phonological representation: /dəvawər/
meaning: EAT HUNGRILY, . . .
complement: NP

The term **subcategorization** is used to refer to information about a word's complement options.

Subcategorization information helps ensure that lexical items appear in the appropriate types of tree structures. For example, because *devour* belongs to the subcategory of verbs that require an NP complement, it is permitted in the tree structure depicted in Figure 5.14a (where there is an NP complement) but not in the tree structure in Figure 5.14b.

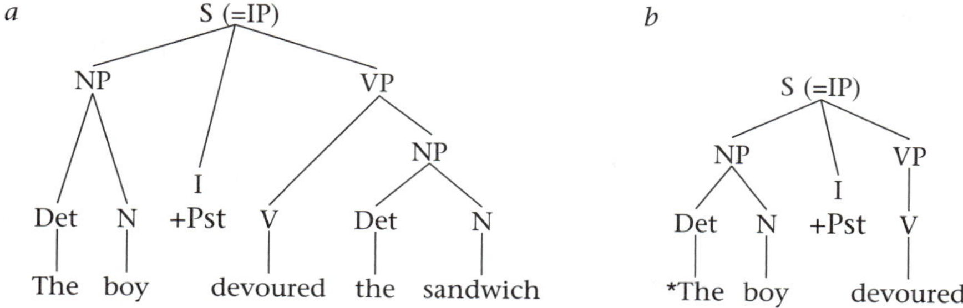

Figure 5.14 Subcategorization determines the type of syntactic structure in which *devour* can occur.

Thanks to subcategorization information, heads occur only in tree structures where they have compatible complement phrases.

2.1 Complement options for verbs

Table 5.5 illustrates some of the more common complement options for verbs in English. The subscripted prepositions indicate subtypes of PP complements where relevant. *Loc* stands for any preposition expressing a location (such as *near, on, under*).

Table 5.5 Some examples of verb complements

Complement option	*Sample heads*	*Example*
Ø	vanish, arrive, die	The rabbit vanished __.
NP	devour, cut, prove	The professor proved [$_{NP}$ *the theorem*].
AP	be, become	The man became [$_{AP}$ *very angry*].
PP_{to}	dash, talk, refer	The dog dashed [$_{PP}$ *to the door*].
NP NP	spare, hand, give	We handed [$_{NP}$ *the woman*] [$_{NP}$ *a map*].
NP PP_{to}	hand, give, send	She gave [$_{NP}$ *a diploma*] [$_{PP}$ *to the student*].
NP PP_{for}	buy, cook, reserve	We bought [$_{NP}$ *a hat*] [$_{PP}$ *for Andy*].
NP PP_{loc}	put, place, stand	She put [$_{NP}$ *the muffler*] [$_{PP}$ *on the car*].
PP_{to} PP_{about}	talk, speak	I talked [$_{PP}$ *to a doctor*] [$_{PP}$ *about Sue*].
NP PP_{for} PP_{with}	open, fix	We opened [$_{NP}$ *the door*] [$_{PP}$ *for John*] [$_{PP}$ *with a crowbar*].

The verbs in the first line of Table 5.5 (*vanish, arrive*, and *die*) can occur without any complement, those in the second line occur with an NP complement, and so on.

A word can belong to more than one subcategory. The verb *eat*, for example, can occur either with or without an NP complement and therefore belongs to both of the first two subcategories in our table.

22)

After getting home, they ate (the sandwiches).

However, not all verbs exhibit this flexibility. Although *devour* is similar in meaning to *eat*, it requires an explicitly stated complement NP and therefore belongs only to the second subcategory in our table.

23)

devour with a complement:
After getting home, they devoured the sandwiches.

devour without a complement:
*After getting home, they devoured.

As the examples in Table 5.5 also show, some heads can take more than one complement. The verb *put* is a case in point, since it requires both an NP complement and a PP complement.

24)

put with an NP complement and a PP complement:
The librarian put [$_{NP}$ the book] [$_{PP}$ on the shelf].

25)

put without an NP complement:
*The librarian put [$_{PP}$ on the shelf].

26)

put without a PP complement:
*The librarian put [$_{NP}$ the book].

The VP *put the book on the shelf* has the structure in Figure 5.15, in which the VP consists of the head *put* and its two complements—the NP *the book* and the PP *on the shelf*.

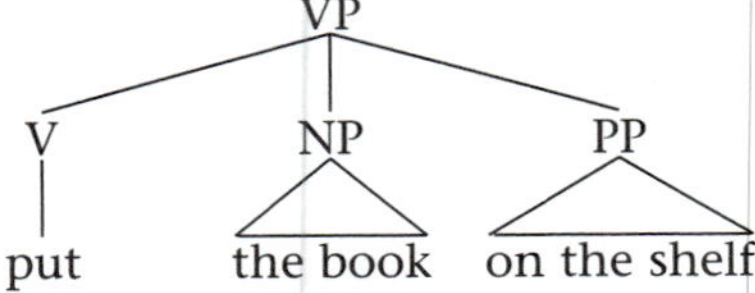

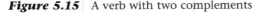

Figure 5.15 A verb with two complements

We can therefore revise our XP rule as follows, using an asterisk after the complement to indicate that one or more of these elements is permitted.

27)

The XP Rule (revised)
XP → (Specifier) X (Complement*)

2.2 Complement options for other categories

Various complement options are also available for Ns, As, and Ps. Tables 5.6, 5.7, and 5.8 provide examples of just some of the possibilities.

Table 5.6 Some examples of noun complements

Complement option	*Sample heads*	*Example*
Ø	car, boy, electricity	the car __
PP_{of}	memory, failure, death	the memory [$_{PP}$ *of a friend*]
PP_{of} PP_{to}	presentation, description, donation	the presentation [$_{PP}$ *of a medal*] [$_{PP}$ *to the winner*]
PP_{with} PP_{about}	argument, discussion, conversation	an argument [$_{PP}$ *with Stella*] [$_{PP}$ *about politics*]

Table 5.7 Some examples of adjective complements

Complement option	*Sample heads*	*Example*
Ø	tall, green, smart	very tall __
PP_{about}	curious, glad, angry	curious [$_{PP}$ *about China*]
PP_{to}	apparent, obvious	obvious [$_{PP}$ *to the student*]
PP_{of}	fond, full, tired	fond [$_{PP}$ *of chocolate*]

Table 5.8 Some examples of preposition complements

Complement option	*Sample heads*	*Example*
Ø	near, away, down	(she got) down __
NP	in, on, by, near	in [$_{NP}$ *the house*]
PP	down, up, out	down [$_{PP}$ *into the cellar*]

Here again subcategorization ensures that particular heads can appear in tree structures only if there is an appropriate type of complement. Thus, the adjective *curious* (Table 5.7) can occur with an *about*-PP, but the adjective *fond* cannot.

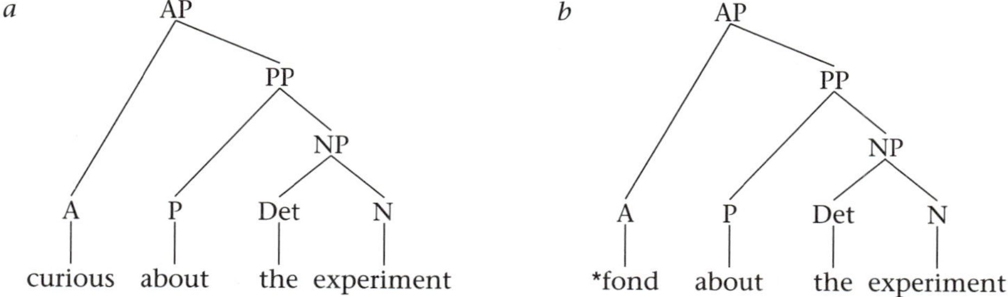

Figure 5.16 Subcategorization permits *curious*, but not *fond*, to take an *about*-PP as complement

As you can see, a good deal of what we know about our language consists of information about words and the type of complement with which they can appear. Much of this information must be learned, memorized, and stored in the lexicon since it cannot be predicted from a word's meaning. For example, there seems to be nothing about the meaning of *devour* to predict why it—but not *eat*—must occur with an NP complement. And there is apparently nothing about the meaning of *tired* and *bored* that predicts that the first one takes an *of*-PP (*tired of cafeteria food*) as its complement whereas the second one takes a *with*-PP (*bored with cafeteria food*).

2.3 Complement clauses

In addition to the complement options considered to this point, all human languages allow sentence-like constructions to function as complements. A simple example of this from English is given in *28*.

28)

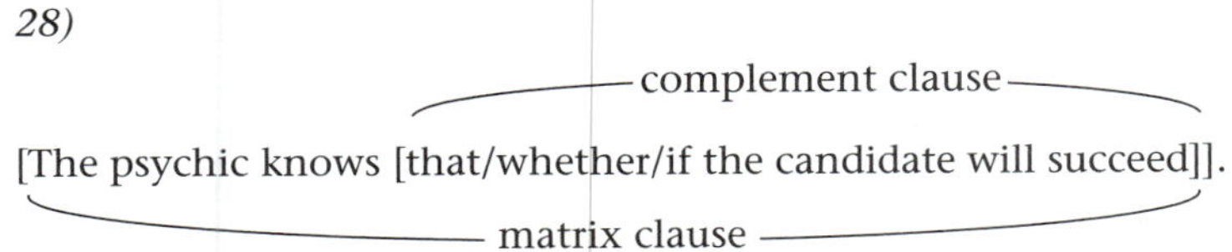

The smaller bracketed phrase in *28* is called a **complement clause**; the larger phrase in which it occurs is called the **matrix clause**.

Words such as *that*, *whether*, and *if* are known as **complementizers** (Cs). They take an S (IP) complement, forming the CP (complementizer phrase) structure depicted in Figure 5.17.

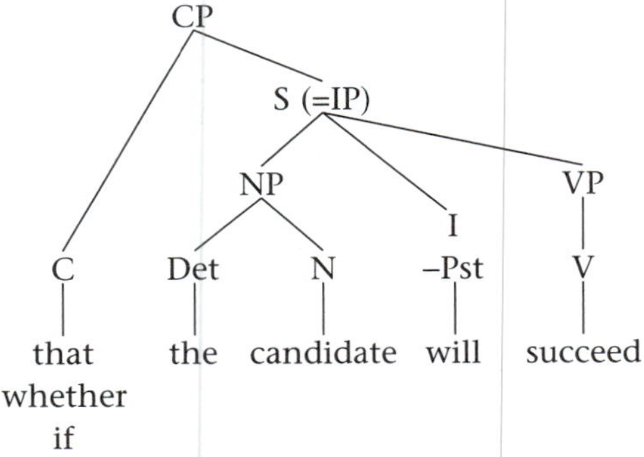

Figure 5.17 The structure of a CP

As we will see in Section 3.2, there is even a type of element that can occur in the specifier position under CP.

When a CP occurs in a sentence such as *28*, in which it serves as complement of the verb *know*, the entire sentence has the structure shown in Figure 5.18. Table 5.9 provides examples of some of the verbs that are commonly found with this type of complement.

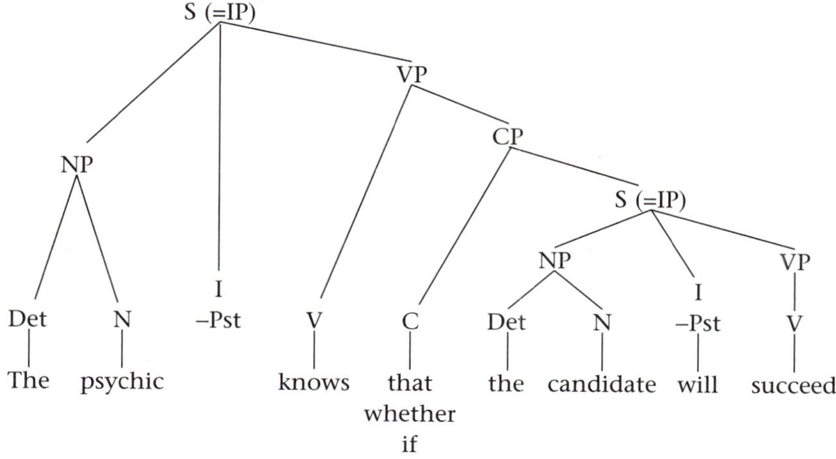

Figure 5.18 The structure of a sentence with an embedded CP

Table 5.9 Some verbs permitting CP complements

Complement(s)	*Sample heads*	*Example*
CP	believe, know, think, remember	They believe [$_{CP}$ *that Mary left*].
NP CP	persuade, tell, convince, promise	They told [$_{NP}$ *Eric*] [$_{CP}$ *that Mary had left*].
PP_{to} CP	concede, admit	They admitted [$_{PP}$ *to Eric*] [$_{CP}$ *that Mary had left*].

There is no limit on the number of embedded clauses that can occur in a sentence, as Figure 5.19 helps show.

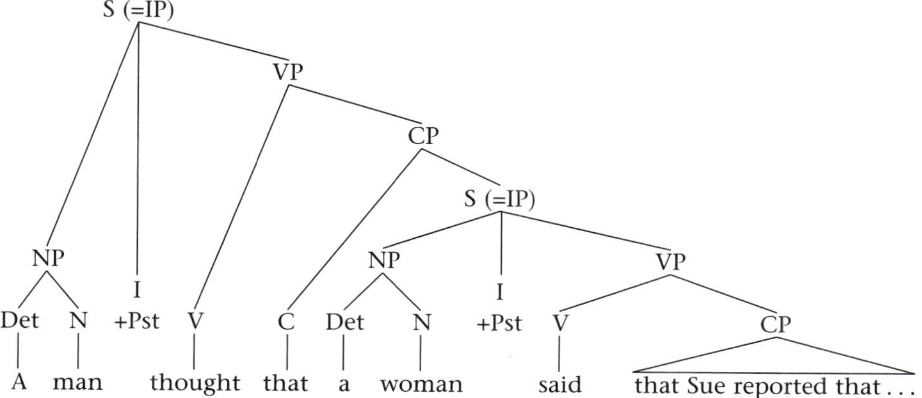

Figure 5.19 The structure of a sentence with more than one embedded CP

This structure is made possible by the fact that any CP can contain a verb that itself takes a complement CP. The topmost clause in our example contains the verb *think*, whose complement clause contains the verb *say*, whose complement clause contains *report*, and so on.

Other categories with CP complements

So far, the embedded CPs in our examples have all occurred as complements of a verb. However, as the examples in Figure 5.20 show, a CP may also serve as a complement to an N, an A, or a P.

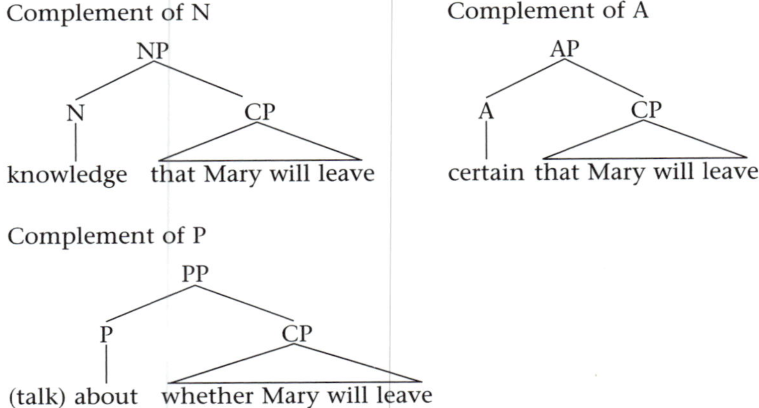

Figure 5.20 An N, an A, and a P with a CP complement

Table 5.10 gives examples of some other adjectives, nouns, and prepositions that can take CP complements.

Table 5.10 Some As, Ns, and Ps permitting CP complements

Items	*Example with CP complement*
Adjectives	
afraid, certain, aware, confident	They are afraid [$_{CP}$ *that Mary left*].
Nouns	
claim, belief, fact, knowledge, proof	They lack proof [$_{CP}$ *that Mary left*].
Prepositions	
over, about	They argued over [$_{CP}$ *whether Mary had left*].

3 TRANSFORMATIONS

As we have seen, it is possible to build a very large number of different sentences by allowing the Merge operation to combine words and phrases in accordance with the phrase structure schema and the subcategorization properties of individual words. Nonetheless, there are still a number of sentence types that we cannot build. This section considers two such patterns and discusses the sentence-building operation needed to accommodate them.

3.1 *Yes-no* questions

To begin, let us consider the question sentences exemplified in *29*. (Such structures are called ***yes-no* questions** because the expected response is usually "yes" or "no.")

29)

a. *Will* the girl leave?
b. *Can* the cat climb this tree?

A curious feature of these sentences is that the auxiliary verb occurs before the subject rather than in its more usual position after the subject, as illustrated in *30*.

30)

a. The boy *will* leave.
b. The cat *can* climb this tree.

Given that auxiliary verbs such as *will* and *can* are instances of the I category, the phrase structure schema dictates that they should occur in the position depicted in Figure 5.21.

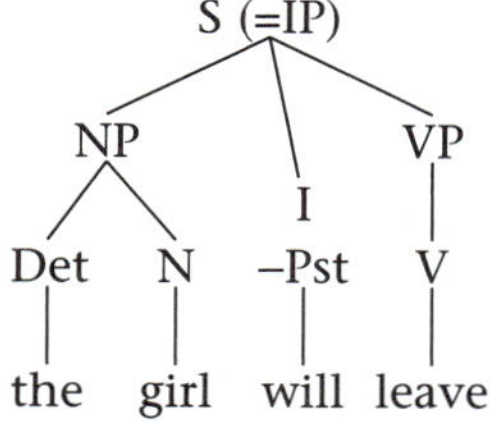

Figure 5.21 *Will* occurring in the head position between the subject (its specifier) and the VP (its complement)

How, then, does the word order found in *29* come about?

The formation of question structures requires the use of a structure-building operation that we can call **Move**. Traditionally known as a **transformation** because it transforms an existing structure, Move applies to structures such as the one in Figure 5.21 and moves the auxiliary verb in the I position to a new position in front of the subject.

31)

Will the girl __ leave?
↑__________|

The transformational analysis has at least two advantages. First, it allows us to avoid the conclusion that there are two types of auxiliary verbs in English: one that occurs in the usual I position between the subject and the VP and one that occurs in front of the subject. Under the transformational analysis, all auxiliaries occur in the I position, consistent with the analysis proposed in Section 1.2. Sentences that have an auxiliary verb in front of the subject simply undergo an "extra" process—the Move operation that transports the I category in front of the subject in order to signal a question.

Second, the transformational analysis automatically captures the fact—known to all speakers of English—that the sentence *Will the girl leave?* is the question structure corresponding to *The girl will leave*. According to the analysis presented here, both sentences initially have the same basic structure. They differ only in that the Move operation has applied to the I category in the question structure.

A landing site for I

In what position does the auxiliary verb "land" when it is moved in front of the subject? If we assume that sentences such as *31* are simple Ss (IPs), no position is available in front of the subject. However, the problem can be solved if we assume that all Ss (IPs) occur within larger CPs, as depicted in Figure 5.22.

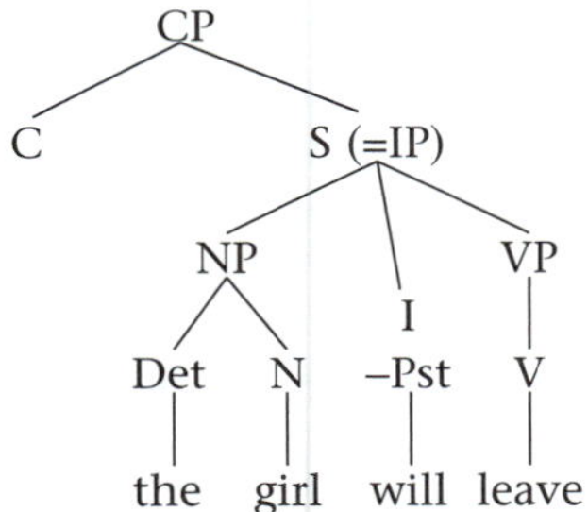

Figure 5.22 An S inside a CP "shell"

By adopting this structure, we take the position that *all* Ss (IPs) occur within a CP, whether they are embedded or not. It may help to think of the CP category as a "shell" that forms an outer layer of structure around an S (=IP). When embedded within a larger sentence, the CP can contain an overt complementizer such as *that* or *whether*. Elsewhere, the C position simply contains information about whether the sentence is a statement or a question. For the sake of illustration, let us use the symbol '+Q' to indicate a question; sentences with no such symbol in their C position will be interpreted as statements.

In some languages, the **Q feature** is "spelled out" as a separate morpheme (see Section 4.2 following). In languages like English, where there is no such morpheme, the feature must attract another element to its position. The auxiliary verb in the I position is that element. This is illustrated in Figure 5.23, where the Q feature in the C position attracts the auxiliary verb in the I position, causing it to move to the beginning of the sentence.

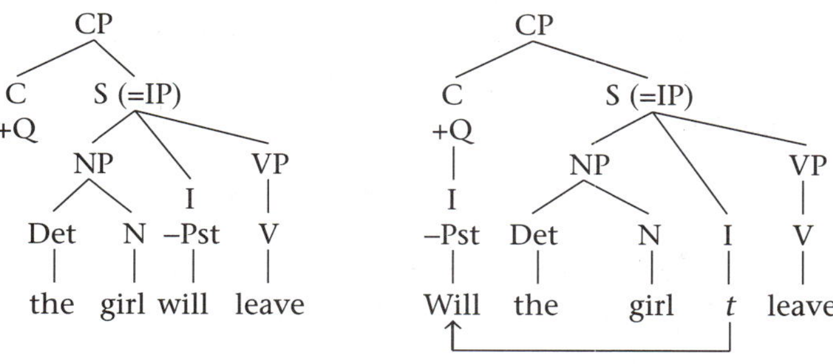

Figure 5.23 Movement of an auxiliary from the I position to C

A transformation (i.e., a Move operation) can do no more than change an element's position. It does not change the categories of any words and it cannot eliminate any part of the structure created by the Merge operation. Thus, *will* retains its I label even though it is moved into the C position, and the position that it formerly occupied remains in the tree structure. Called a **trace** and marked by the symbol *t*, it records the fact that the moved element comes from the head position within S (IP).

The Move operation used for *yes-no* questions is often informally called **Inversion** and formulated as follows.

32)

Inversion:
Move I to C.

Is there any way to be sure that this idea is on the right track and that the auxiliary verb in the I position really does move to the C position? Some interesting evidence comes from the analysis of the embedded CPs in sentences such as the following.

33)

a. The coach wonders [$_{CP}$ if the girl should stay].
b. A fan asked [$_{CP}$ whether the team will win].

The underlined elements in these CPs are complementizers and therefore occur in the C position. Assuming that there can be no more than one element in each position in a tree structure, there should be no room for the moved auxiliary under the C label in the embedded CPs in *33*. We therefore predict that Inversion should not be able to apply in these cases. The ungrammaticality of the sentences in *34* shows that this is correct.

34)

Inversion in embedded CPs that include complementizers:
a. *The coach wonders [$_{CP}$ if-should the girl *t* stay].
b. *A fan asked [$_{CP}$ whether-will the team *t* win].

Interestingly, the acceptability of Inversion in embedded CPs improves quite dramatically when there is no complementizer and the C position is therefore open to receive the moved auxiliary. (These sentences sound most natural when the embedded clause is interpreted as a sort of quotation.)

35)

Inversion in embedded CPs that do not have complementizers:

a. The coach wonders [$_{CP}$ should the girl *t* stay].

b. A fan asked [$_{CP}$ will the team *t* win].

Although some speakers prefer not to apply Inversion in embedded clauses at all (especially in formal speech), most speakers of English find the sentences in *35* to be much more natural than those in *34*. This is just what we would expect if Inversion moves the auxiliary to an empty C position, as required by our analysis.

To summarize before continuing, we have introduced two changes into the system of syntactic analysis used until now. First, we assume that all Ss (IPs) occur inside CPs. Second, we assume that the Inversion transformation moves the auxiliary from the I position within S (IP) to an empty C position in front of the subject NP. This not only gives the correct word order for question structures but helps explain why the inversion pattern sounds so unnatural when the C position is already filled by another element, as in *34*.

Do Insertion

As we have just seen, formation of *yes-no* questions in English involves moving the I category, and the auxiliary verb that it contains, to the C position. How, then, do we form the questions corresponding to sentences such as those in *36*, which contain no auxiliary?

36)

a. The students liked the movie.
b. Those birds sing.

Since the I category in these sentences contains only an abstract tense marker (see Figure 5.24a), applying the Inversion transformation would have no visible effect and there would be no indication that the sentence was being used as a question. English circumvents this problem by adding the special auxiliary verb *do*.

37)

a. *Did* the students like the movie?
b. *Do* those birds sing?

As these examples show, *do* is inserted into sentences that do not already have an auxiliary verb, thereby making Inversion possible. We can capture this fact by formulating an **insertion rule**—an operation that adds an element to a tree structure.

38)

Do Insertion
Insert interrogative *do* into an empty I position.

The sentence in *37b* can now be analyzed in the manner shown in Figure 5.24.

a Structure formed by Merge

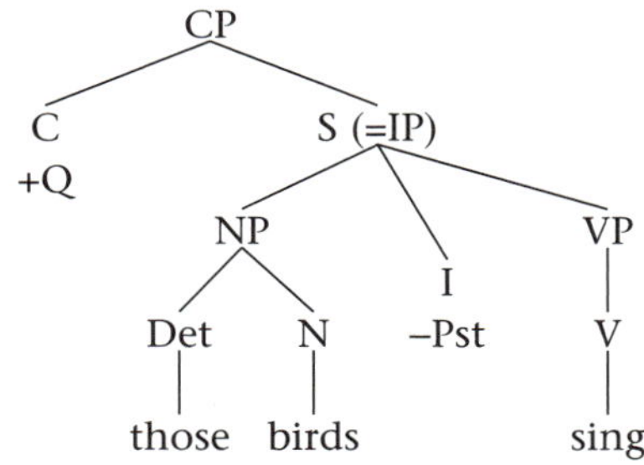

b After Do *Insertion*

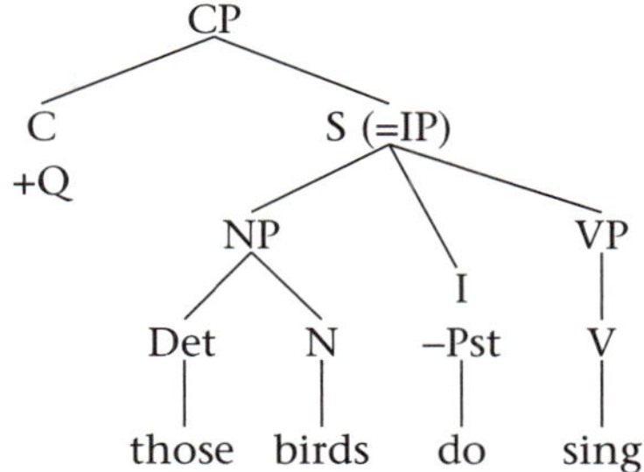

c After Inversion

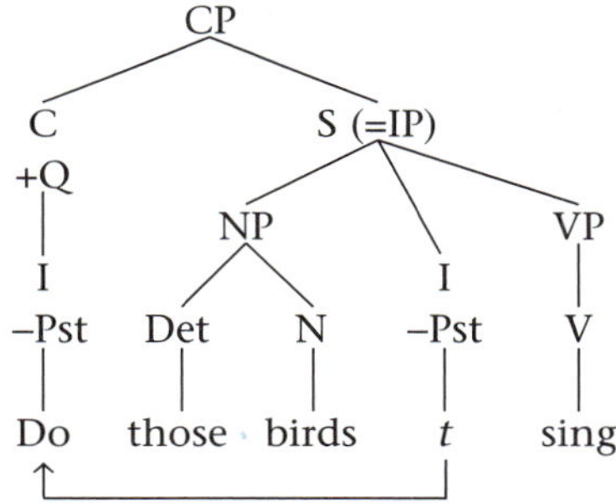

Figure 5.24 A sentence formed with the help of *Do* Insertion

As these tree structures show, the sentence *Do those birds sing*? is built in three steps. In the initial step, the Merge operation interacts with the phrase structure schema to give the structure in Figure 5.24a, which contains no auxiliary verb in the I position. The ***Do* Insertion rule** then adds the special interrogative auxiliary *do*, at which point it can be moved to the C position.

3.2 *Wh* Movement

Consider now the set of question constructions exemplified in *39*. These sentences are called ***wh* questions** because of the presence of a question word beginning with *wh*.

39)

a. Which car should the man fix?
b. What can the child sit on?

There is reason to believe that the *wh* elements at the beginning of these sentences have been moved there from the positions indicated in Figure 5.25. (Notice that we take *which* to be a determiner and *what* to be a noun in these sentences.)

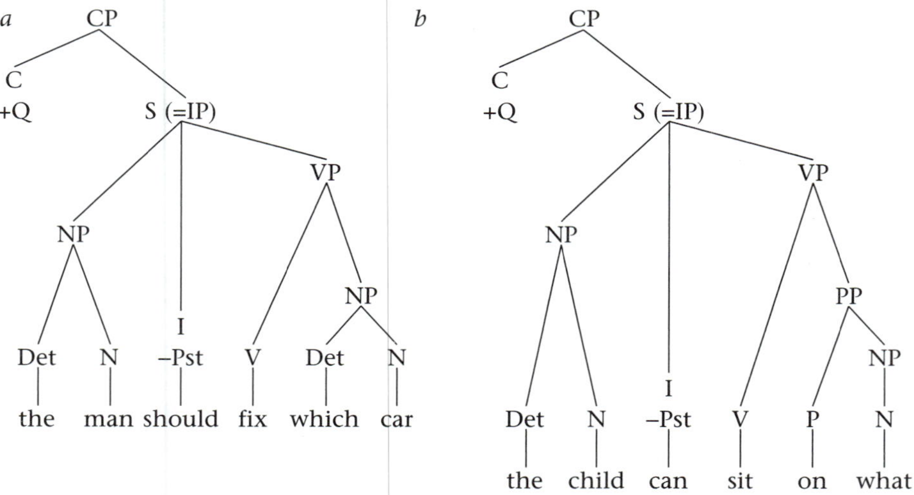

Figure 5.25 Structures depicting the original positions of the *wh* expressions in *39*

Notice that *which car* occurs as complement of the verb *fix* while *what* appears as complement of the preposition *on*. This captures an important fact about the meanings of these sentences, since *which car* asks about the thing that was fixed in the first case while *what* asks about the location where the child can sit in the second case. We will return to this point in Section 3.3 of Chapter 6.

A second argument in favor of this analysis involves subcategorization. Consider the sentences in *40*, which are incomplete without an NP after *fix* and *on*.

40)

a. *The man should fix.
b. *The child can sit on.

Crucially, however, there is no such problem with the *wh* questions in *39*, which suggests that the *wh* phrases must be fulfilling the complement function in these sentences. The structures in Figure 5.25 capture this fact by treating the *wh* phrase as complement of the verb in the first pattern and complement of the preposition in the second.

How then do the *wh* phrases end up at the beginning of the sentence? The answer is that they are attracted there by the Q feature, which results in the application of a second Move operation. (Recall that we have already posited one Move operation, which we have been calling Inversion.)

41)

Which car should the man *t* fix *t*?

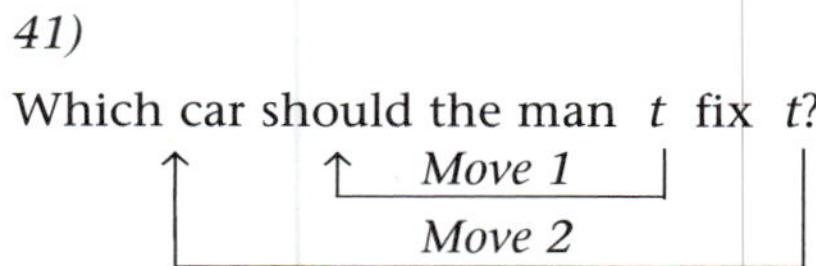

Application of the same two transformations to the structure in Figure 5.25b yields the *wh* question in *42*.

42)

What can the child *t* sit on *t*?

Move 1

Move 2

A landing site for *wh* words

As the examples in *41* and *42* help illustrate, the Move operation carries the *wh* phrase to the beginning of the sentence, to the left even of the fronted auxiliary. But where precisely does the *wh* phrase land?

Given that the moved auxiliary is located in the C position (see Figure 5.23 or 5.24, for example), it seems reasonable to conclude that the fronted *wh* phrase ends up in the specifier position of CP. Not only is this the only position in syntactic structure to the left of the C, but it is available to receive the moved *wh* phrase—because there is no class of words that serves as specifier of C, this position is empty prior to the application of the Move operation.

We can make this idea precise by formulating the Move operation that applies to *wh* phrases (***Wh* Movement**) as follows.

43)

Wh Movement:
Move a *wh* phrase to the specifier position under CP.

The sentence *Which car should the man fix?* can now be analyzed in steps, the first of which involves formation of the structure in Figure 5.26 by the Merge operation. Consistent with our earlier assumption, the S (IP) here occurs within a CP shell.

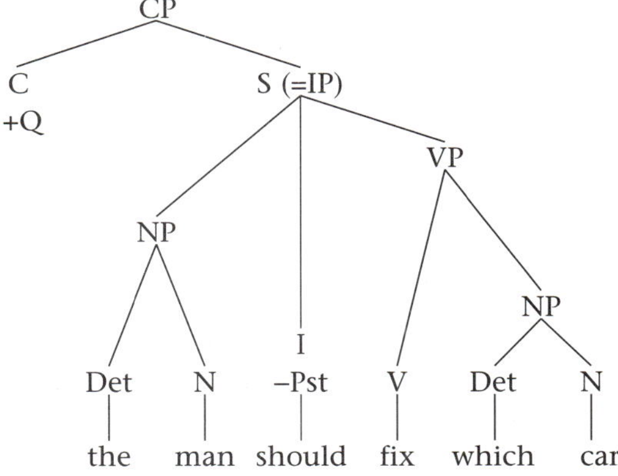

Figure 5.26 Deep structure for *Which car should the man fix?*

Wh Movement and Inversion then apply to this structure, yielding the structure in Figure 5.27.

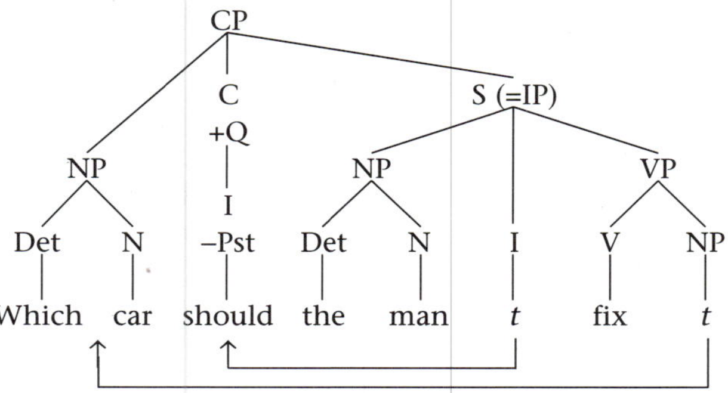

Figure 5.27 Structure for *Which car should the man fix?* The I category moves to the C position and the *wh* phrase moves to the specifier position under CP.

Like other transformations, *Wh* Movement cannot eliminate any part of the previously formed structure. The position initially occupied by the *wh* phrase is therefore not lost. Rather, it remains as a trace (an empty category), indicating that the moved element corresponds to the complement of the verb *fix*.

In the examples considered so far, the *wh* word originates as complement of a verb or preposition. In sentences such as the following, however, the *wh* word asks about the subject (the person who does the criticizing).

44)

Who criticized Maxwell?

In such patterns, the *wh* word originates in the subject position and subsequently moves to the specifier position within CP even though the actual order of the words in the sentence does not change as a result of this movement. (For reasons that are not fully understood, there is no *Do* Insertion or Inversion in this type of question structure, except for purposes of emphasis, as in *Who DID criticize Maxwell?*)

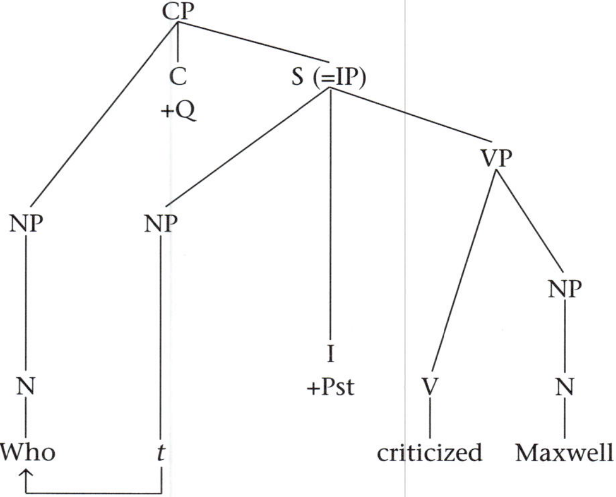

Figure 5.28 Movement of a subject *wh* word. Since there is nothing for the *wh* word to move over in such cases, there is no visible change in word order.

3.3 Deep structure and surface structure

The preceding examples show that at least some sentences must be analyzed with the help of two distinct types of mechanisms. The first of these is the Merge operation, which creates tree structures by combining categories in a manner consistent with their subcategorization properties and the phrase structure schema. The second is the Move operation, which can modify these tree structures by moving an element from one position to another. The process whereby a syntactic structure is formed by these operations is called a **derivation**.

In traditional work in transformational syntax, all instances of the Merge operation take place before any instances of the Move operation. As a result, the derivation for a sentence typically yields two distinct levels of syntactic structure. The first, called **deep structure** (or **D-structure**), is formed by the Merge in accordance with the head's subcategorization properties and the phrase structure schema. As we shall see in the chapter on semantics, deep structure plays a special role in the interpretation of sentences.

The second level of syntactic structure corresponds to the final syntactic form of the sentence. Called **surface structure** (or **S-structure**), it results from applying whatever transformations are appropriate for the sentence in question.

The deep structure for the question *Which apple will the boy pick?* is given in Figure 5.29.

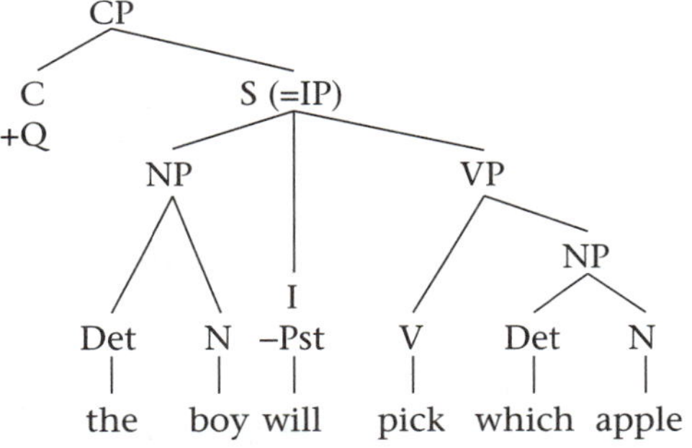

Figure 5.29 Deep structure for the question *Which apple will the boy pick?*

The surface structure for the question pattern is then formed by applying Inversion and *Wh* Movement, yielding Figure 5.30.

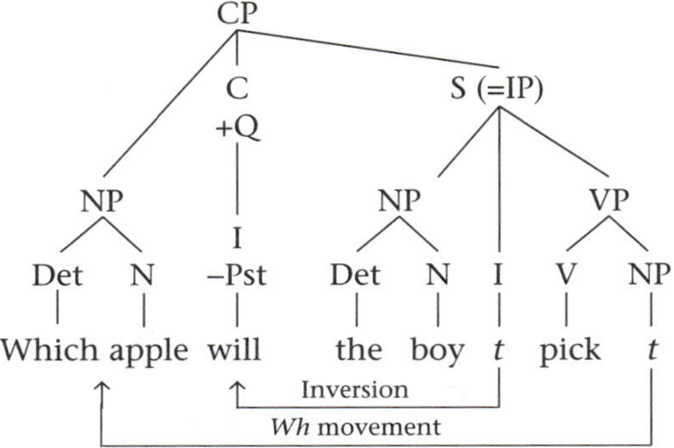

Figure 5.30 Surface structure for *Which apple will the boy pick?*

The organization of the syntactic component of the grammar according to the view put forward in traditional work on transformational syntax can be depicted as follows.

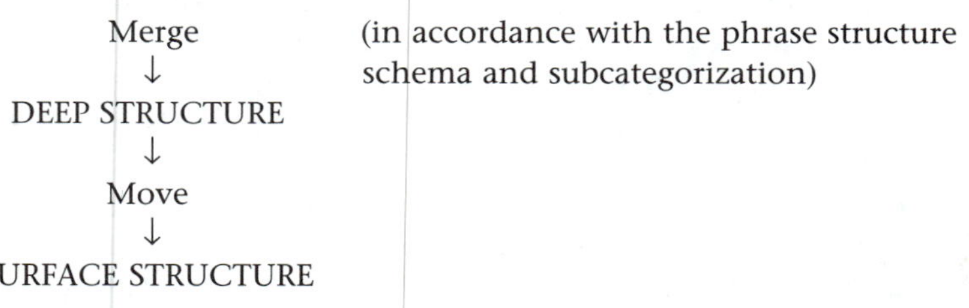

Figure 5.31 The path followed by a derivation

A recent development (*Advanced*)

Within the last few years, matters have changed considerably and it is now believed that the Merge and Move operations interact with each other freely. One consequence of this simpler picture is that derivations no longer include a level of deep structure per se. This is easiest to see if we consider the formation of a two-clause sentence such as the following.

45)

$[_{CP}$ The country wonders $[_{CP}$ what the president will decide]].

In traditional work, this sentence had the following derivation.

46)

The result of all applications of the Merge operation (deep structure):
$[_{CP}$ The country wonders $[_{CP}$ the president will decide what]].

47)

The result of applying the Move operation (surface structure):
$[_{CP}$ The country wonders $[_{CP}$ what the president will decide *t*]].

However, according to the more recent conception, Merge operations first build just the lower clause. The Move operation then moves the *wh* word to the specifier of CP position in that clause and the Merge operations resume, building the rest of the sentence.

48)

A first series of applications of the Merge operation builds the embedded clause:
$[_{CP}$ the president will decide what].

The Move operation applies:
$[_{CP}$ what the president will decide *t*].

A second series of applications of the Merge operation builds the rest of the sentence:
$[_{CP}$ The country wonders $[_{CP}$ what the president will decide *t*]].

Although the newer derivation produces no deep structure per se for the entire sentence, it does not constitute a complete break with the past either. There are still operations (Merge) that build structure in accordance with the phrase structure schema and other operations (Move) that can change it in the course of the derivation.

3.4 Constraints on transformations *(Advanced)*

A good deal of research in the field of syntax in recent years has been devoted to determining constraints on the Move operation. One such constraint has been dubbed **Shortest Move**.

49)

Shortest Move
Moves should be as short as possible.

The effects of Shortest Move can be seen by considering the following structure, which contains two *wh* words.

50)

$[_{CP}$ $[_{IP}$ Marvin should give *what* to *whom*]]

There is only room for one *wh* word in the specifier position under CP, but which one is attracted to that position? As the contrast between the following two sentences shows, it is the nearer *wh* word that moves.

51)

a. The nearer *wh* word moves to the specifier of CP position:
$[_{CP}$ What should $[_{IP}$ Marvin *t* give *t* to who(m)]]
(Inversion: should ← *t*; *Wh* Movement: What ← *t*)

b. The more distant *wh* word moves to the specifier of CP position:
*$[_{CP}$ Who should $[_{IP}$ Marvin *t* give what to *t*]]
(Inversion: should ← *t*; *Wh* Movement: Who ← *t*)

For most speakers of English, *51a* is more acceptable than *51b*. This is the result that we would expect, given Shortest Move.

The effects of Shortest Move can also be seen by considering the application of Inversion to a structure such as the following.

52)

$[_{CP}$ $[_{IP}$ The visitors should have stayed longer]]

This structure contains two auxiliary verbs—*should* and *have*. Crucially, it is the nearer one that is attracted to the C position, as the contrast between the following two sentences shows.

53)

a. The nearer auxiliary verb moves to the C position:
$[_{CP}$ Should $[_{IP}$ the visitors *t* have stayed longer]]
(Should ← *t*)

b. The more distant auxiliary moves to the C position:
*[$_{CP}$ Have [$_{IP}$ the visitors should *t* stayed longer]]

As *53* shows, moving the closer auxiliary produces a grammatical sentence, whereas moving the further auxiliary yields an ungrammatical sentence.

Shortest Move is sometimes referred to as an **economy constraint**, since it has the effect of making moves as short as possible, which in turn reduces the "computational cost" of the derivation. A good deal of current research focuses on the notion of derivational economy and its role in explaining syntactic phenomena.

4 UNIVERSAL GRAMMAR AND PARAMETRIC VARIATION

Thus far, our discussion has focused on English. Before looking at any further phenomena in this language, it is important to extend the scope of our analysis to other languages.

As noted at the beginning of this chapter, recent work on Universal Grammar suggests that all languages are fundamentally alike with respect to the basics of syntax. For instance, all languages use the Merge operation to combine words on the basis of their syntactic category and subcategorization properties, creating phrases that comply with the phrase structure schema. Moreover, Move operations are available in all languages and appear to be universally subject to economy constraints such as Shortest Move.

The fact that certain syntactic properties are universal does not mean that languages must be alike in all respects. Universal Grammar leaves room for variation, allowing individual languages to differ with respect to certain **parameters**. (You can think of a parameter as the set of options that UG permits for a particular phenomenon.) We will consider a few examples of this now, beginning with variation in phrase structure. Some additional instances of cross-linguistic differences in syntax are considered in Section 2.3 of Chapter 8.

4.1 Variation in phrase structure

Even where languages have the same categories, there can be variation in terms of how they are assembled. Part of this variation can be traced to a head position parameter that offers three options—head-initial, head-medial, and head-final. In Japanese, for example, heads consistently occur in the final position within their phrase. Thus, the noun comes at the end of the NP, the verb at the end of the VP, and so on (see Figure 5.32). Because Ps occur at the end of the PP, they are called **postpositions** rather than prepositions. (Nom = nominative, the subject marker; we ignore CP here to save space.)

These word-order differences reflect the positioning of heads with respect to the other elements in their phrases, not the presence of an entirely new type of syntac-

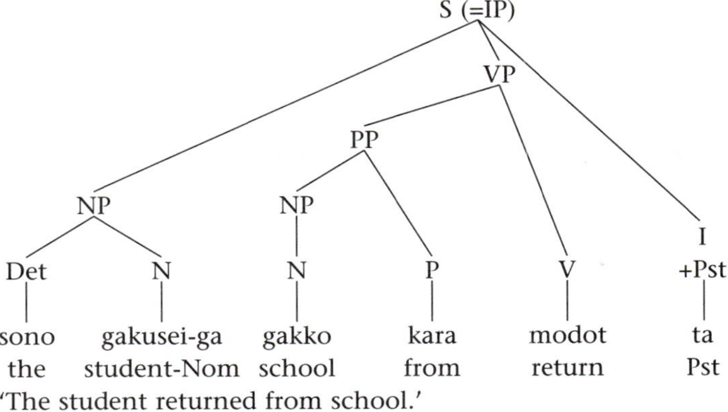

Figure 5.32 Japanese phrase structure: the head is always final.

tic system. We can account for these facts by formulating the following phrase structure rule for Japanese.

54)

XP → (Specifier) (Complement) X

As this rule indicates, the head uniformly follows its specifier and complement(s) in Japanese. In English, on the other hand, the head follows its specifier but precedes any complements.

55)

XP → (Specifier) X (Complement*)

Matters are not always so simple, however. In Thai, for instance, heads precede both complements and specifiers (the head-initial option) within phrases other than S (IP) (see Figure 5.33). Thus, Ns appear at the beginning of NPs, Ps at the beginning of PPs, Vs at the beginning of VPs, and so on. (Tones have been omitted here.)

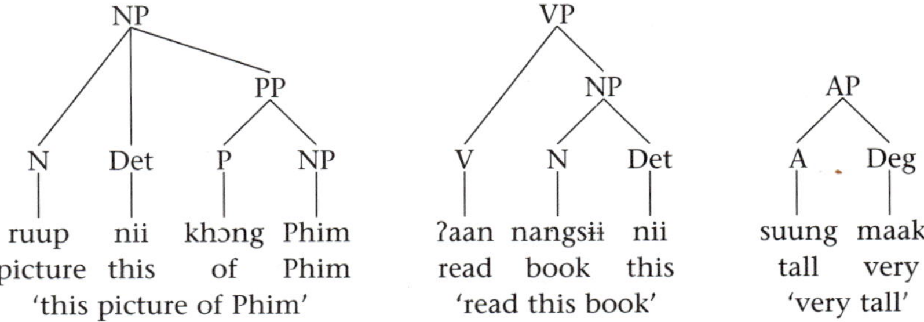

Figure 5.33 Thai phrase structure: the head is initial in phrases other than S.

Within S (IP), however, the specifier (the subject NP) comes first, just as it does in English (see Figure 5.34).

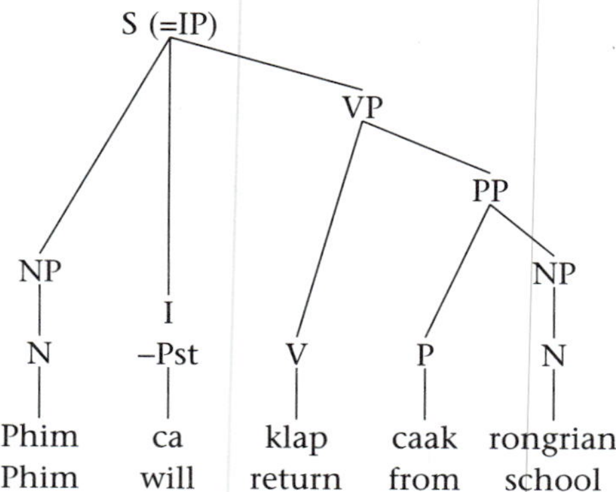

Figure 5.34 Thai sentence structure: the specifier (subject) precedes the head.

4.2 Variation in the use of transformations

Languages often differ from each other in the kinds of rules they use to form a particular sentence type. To illustrate this point we will consider four phenomena involving the Move operation.

Yes-no questions

In Tamil (a language of India), *yes-no* questions are signaled by the presence of the morpheme *-ā* at the end of the sentence, rather than by an Inversion transformation. (The diacritic ̪ indicates a dental point of articulation; the diacritic ¯ marks a long vowel; ɭ is a retroflex liquid.)

56)

a. Mut̪t̪u paɭam parit̪t̪ān.
Muttu fruit picked
'Muttu picked the fruit.'

b. Mut̪t̪u paɭam parit̪t̪ān-ā.
Muttu fruit picked -Ques
'Did Muttu pick the fruit?'

The morpheme *-ā* "spells out" the Q feature in the complementizer position, which occurs at the end of the sentence since Tamil is a head-final language. As depicted in Figure 5.35, corresponding to sentence *56b*, the V comes at the end of the VP, I at the end of S (IP), and C (containing the question morpheme) at the end of CP.

Wh questions

Just as some languages form *yes-no* questions without the help of the Inversion transformation, so do some languages form *wh* questions without using *Wh* Movement. Languages of this type include Japanese, Korean, Tamil, Chinese, and Thai. Example *57* is from Thai.

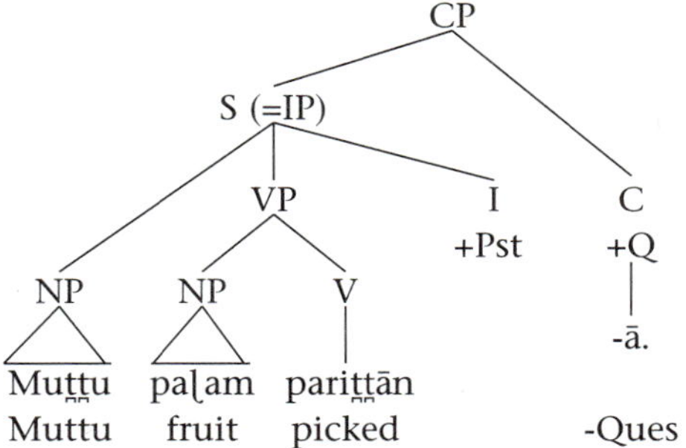

Figure 5.35 A question structure in Tamil

57)

Khun ʔaan ʔaray?
you read what
'What did you read?'

It seems that the Q feature in languages such as Thai is not "strong" enough to attract *wh* words, with the result that *wh* questions are formed without the help of a Move operation.

Verb Raising

Consider now the contrast between the following two English sentences.

58)

a. Paul always works.
b. *Paul works always.

This ungrammaticality of the second sentence is expected since the preverbal qualifier *always* functions as specifier of the verb and therefore should occur to its left, as in *58a*. Surprisingly, however, qualifiers must follow the verb in French.

59)

a. *Paul toujours travaille. (= English *58a*)
Paul always works

b. Paul travaille toujours. (= English *58b*)
Paul works always

Why should this be? One possibility is that the tense feature in the I category somehow attracts the verb to that position in French, just as the Q feature can attract verbs to the C position in some languages. As a result, French has the **Verb Raising transformation** outlined in *60*.

60)

Verb Raising
Move V to I.

This Move operation brings about the change depicted in Figure 5.36.

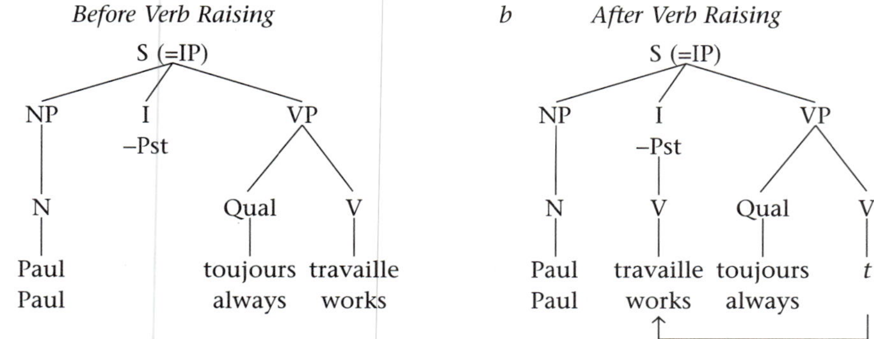

Figure 5.36 Verb Raising in French: the verb moves from within the VP to the I position.

A fascinating piece of independent evidence for the existence of Verb Raising in French comes from the operation of the Inversion transformation in that language. As we have already seen (Section 3.1), this transformation moves the I category to the C position. Now, in English only auxiliary verbs occur in the I position, which explains why only they can undergo Inversion.

61)

a. Inversion of an auxiliary verb in English:
Will you *t* stay for supper?
↑____|

b. Inversion of a nonauxiliary verb in English:
*Stay you *t* for supper?
↑____|

In French, however, regular verbs can also occur in the I position, thanks to the Verb Raising transformation. This predicts that Inversion should be able to apply to these Vs in French as well as to auxiliaries. This is correct. Like English, French can form a question by moving an auxiliary leftward, as *62* illustrates.

62)

Inversion of an auxiliary:
As-tu *t* essayé?
↑___|
Have you tried?

However, unlike English, French also allows inversion of nonauxiliary Vs.

63)
Inversion of a nonauxiliary verb:
Vois-tu *t* le livre?
↑___|
see you the book
'Do you see the book?'

Figure 5.37 depicts the interaction between Verb Raising and Inversion needed to form this sentence. (We treat the pronoun *tu* 'you' as a type of NP.)

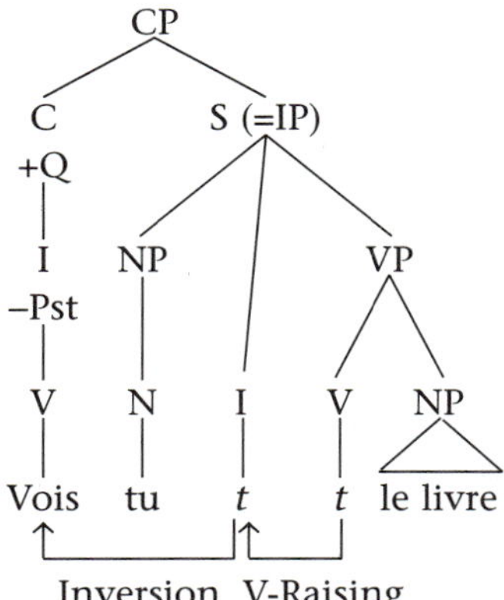

Figure 5.37 The interaction of Verb Raising and Inversion in French

Although Verb Raising is generally not found in English, there is reason to believe that it applies to the "copula" verb *be* as a special case. As shown in the following example, *be* sounds more natural when it occurs in front of a qualifier such as *always*.

64)

a. *be* in front of the specifier:
Jane *is* always on time.

b. *be* after the specifier:
?*Jane always *is* on time.

This suggests that *be* can be moved leftward to the I position by the Verb Raising transformation.

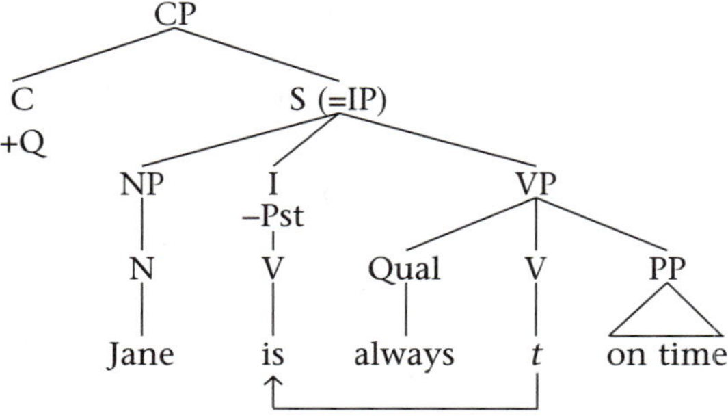

Figure 5.38 Raising of copula *be* in English

As expected, *be* is also able to undergo subsequent movement to the C position (Inversion) in *yes-no* questions, yielding sentences such as *65*.

65)

Is Jane *t* always *t* on time?

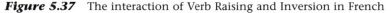

Verb-initial languages

Languages in which the verb is the first element in the sentence provide a special challenge for syntactic analysis. The following example is from Welsh.

66)

Lladdodd y ddraig y dyn
killed the dragon the man
'The dragon killed the man.'

At first glance, it seems impossible to build a legal structure for these sentences, since the subject occurs in the middle of the sentence rather than on the left or right margin.

In order to get around this problem, it has been necessary to consider a radical idea—namely, that the subject originates in the specifier position of VP in all languages. (If this is right, qualifiers have to be reanalyzed as something else—perhaps modifiers; see Section 5.1.) This idea is usually implemented in conjunction with the more detailed version of the phrase structure schema discussed in Section 1.5, and we will follow this practice here (see Figure 5.39). To save space, we ignore the internal structure of NPs.

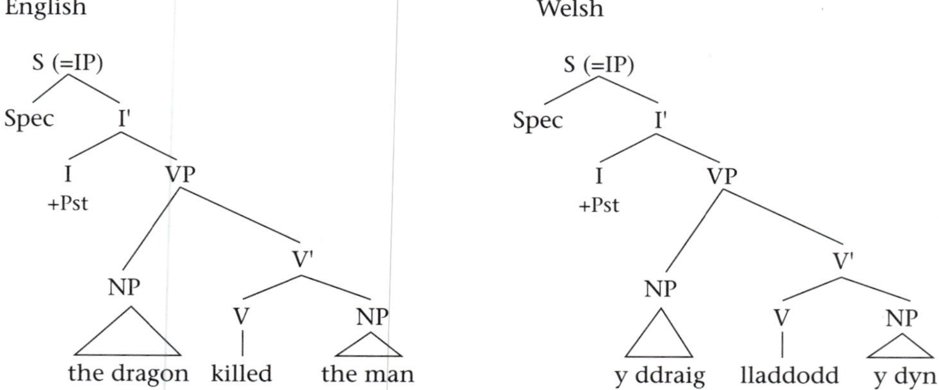

Figure 5.39 The deep structure of a typical transitive sentence in English and Welsh. In both languages, the subject occurs as specifier of VP.

In a verb-medial language such as English, the subject raises from the specifier position within VP to the specifier position of S (IP) in surface structure. In a verb-initial language such as Welsh, by contrast, the subject remains in the specifier position within VP, but the verb raises to the I position (just as it does in French). As illustrated in Figure 5.40, this gives the correct final order for both types of language. This analysis has two immediate advantages. First, it allows us to extend the X' template to verb-initial languages, which is clearly desirable since this template is supposed to be part of Universal Grammar. Second, it allows us to account for the differences between verb-medial and verb-initial languages in terms of the application of Move operations that are independently attested in human language. We have already seen that the verb-raising operation is needed to account for word

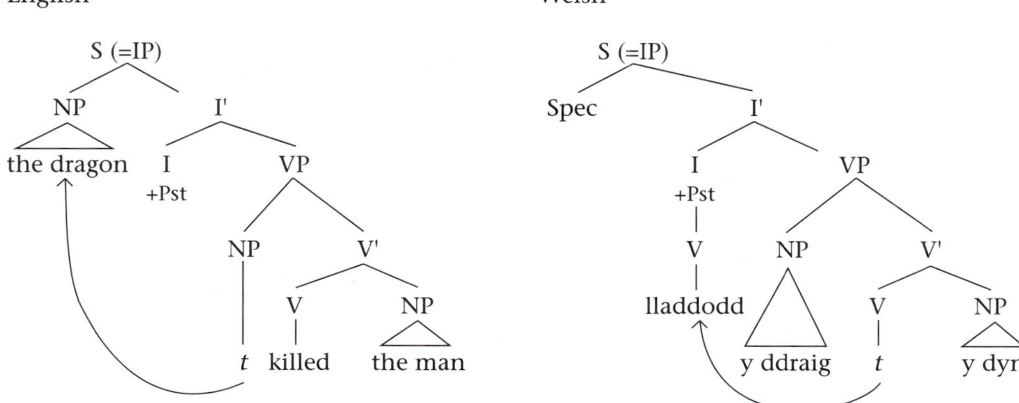

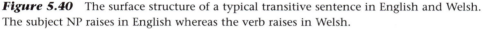

Figure 5.40 The surface structure of a typical transitive sentence in English and Welsh. The subject NP raises in English whereas the verb raises in Welsh.

order in French, and we will see in Section 6 that evidence for an NP-raising operation can be found in English and many other languages.

5 SOME EXTENSIONS *(ADVANCED)*

Now that we have considered some of the basic mechanisms of sentence formation found in human language, it is possible to broaden our treatment of English syntax by briefly examining additional phenomena. We focus in this section on two such phenomena—modifier constructions and case.

5.1 Modifiers

Thus far, our treatment of phrase structure has ignored **modifiers**—a class of elements that encode optionally expressible properties of heads. Although all lexical categories can have modifiers, we will focus here on the types of categories that can modify Ns and Vs.

Adjective phrases (APs) make up the single most commonly used class of modifiers in English. As the following examples show, the principal function of APs is to serve as modifiers of Ns.

67)

APs serving as modifiers of N:
A *very tall* man walked into the room.
She made *exceptional* progress.

The most common modifiers of Vs are adverb phrases (AdvPs) and PPs that describe manner or time.

68)

AdvPs serving as modifiers of V:

describing manner:	Ellen left *quickly.*
	Ellen *quickly* left.
describing time:	We arrived *very early.*

PPs serving as modifiers of V:

describing manner:	Ellen proceeded *with care.*
describing time:	He stayed *for three days.*

As the examples in Table 5.11 show, English modifiers vary in terms of their position with respect to the head. APs precede the N while PPs follow the verb, and many AdvPs can occur either before or after the verb that they modify.

Table 5.11 Some modifiers in English

Modifier	*Position*	*Examples*
AP	precedes the head	[very tall] buildings
PP	follows the head	work [with care]
AdvP	precedes or follows the head	walk [carefully] or [carefully] walk

A rule for modifiers

How do modifiers fit into phrase structure? For the purposes of this introduction to syntax, we will attach modifiers at the XP level of phrase structure, in accordance with the following expanded XP rule.

69)

The Expanded XP Rule
XP → (Spec) (Mod) X (Complement) (Mod)

This rule allows a modifier to occur either before the head (as in Figure 5.41a) or after it (as in Figure 5.41b).

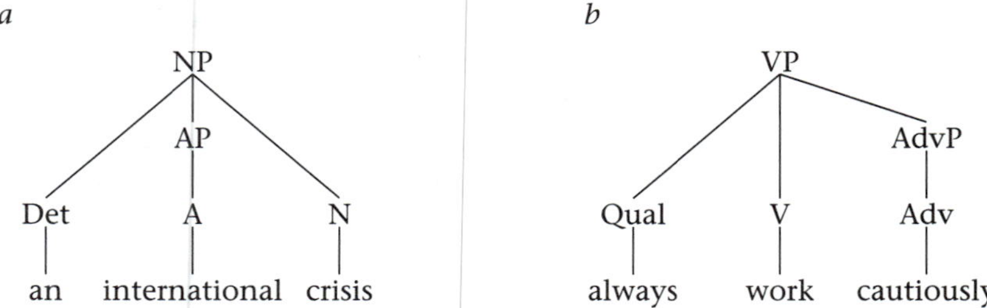

Figure 5.41 Phrases containing modifiers

Where there is a complement, a modifier that occurs after the head will normally occur to the right of the complement as well. This is illustrated in Figure 5.42.

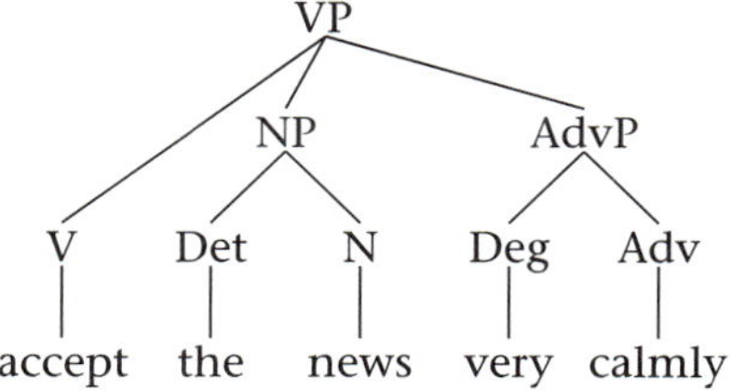

Figure 5.42 A phrase in which both the complement and the modifier occur after the head. In such cases, the modifier occurs after the complement.

5.2 Case: the interaction between syntax and morphology

Many linguistic phenomena reflect the interaction of the morphological and syntactic components of the grammar. An important example of this interaction involves **case**, which indicates an NP's grammatical role in the sentence (see Chapter 4, Section 6.3).

The sole case marker used with nouns in Modern English is *-'s*, which marks an NP that occupies the specifier position within a larger NP, as depicted in Figure 5.43. (We extend our system of phrase structure by allowing an NP to serve as specifier of an N.)

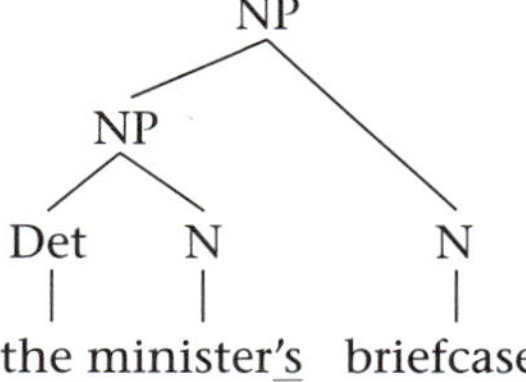

Figure 5.43 The genitive case marks an NP that functions as specifier of an N.

However, a richer system of contrasts is found in English pronouns, whose forms reflect a three-way case distinction (see Table 5.12).

Table 5.12 Case contrasts for the third person singular masculine pronoun in English

Case	*Form*	*Function*	*Example*
Nominative	he	subject	*He* left.
Genitive	his	specifier of N	*his* book
Accusative	him	complement of V or P	Mary saw *him*. Mary sat near *him*.

Contemporary transformational syntax accounts for these contrasts by treating the various cases as features that are associated with particular syntactic positions. We capture this idea by having heads of particular types assign case features to NPs in their specifier or complement positions.

70)

The Case Rules for English NPs
a. I assigns a nominative case feature to the subject NP.
b. V and P assign an accusative case feature to their complement NP.
c. N assigns a genitive case feature to an NP in its specifier position.

To see how this works, consider the sentence *She saw him*, with the structure depicted in Figure 5.44. (Case features are written as subscripts.)

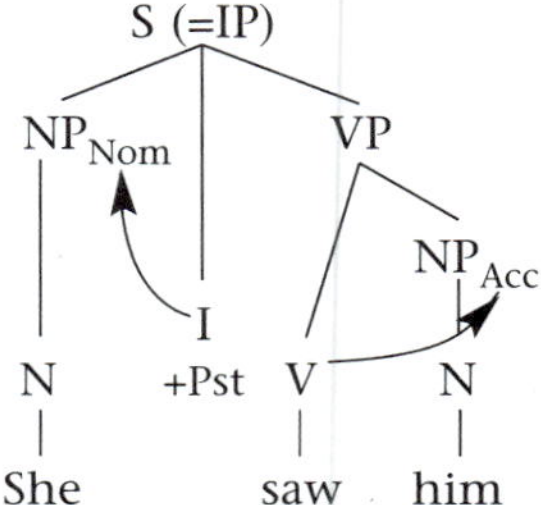

Figure 5.44 An example of case assignment in English

This sentence is well formed, since the pronoun in the subject position has the nominative form required by *70a* and the pronoun in the complement position has the accusative form required by *70b*. Had we used the accusative form in the subject position and the nominative in the direct object position (**Her saw he*), the sentence would have been ungrammatical because of the mismatch between the pronoun's form and the case feature that is assigned to the position it occupies.

The Case Filter

You may have noticed that the case rules are formulated in such a way that any NP occurring in the right position—not just a pronoun—will receive case. This means that in a sentence such as *Roberta saw Jean*, *Roberta* will be assigned nominative case and *Jean* will receive accusative case, even though there is no inflection to show this. Case that need not have visible effects is known as **abstract case**.

Contemporary versions of transformational syntax require all NPs to have a case feature, even if it is not expressed inflectionally. This requirement is known as the **Case Filter.**

71)

The Case Filter
Every NP in a grammatical sentence must be assigned a case feature.

A major advantage of the Case Filter is that it helps explain why NPs can occur in some positions but not in others. As you may have already noticed, the case rules do not assign a case feature to every imaginable position in syntactic structure. For instance, while V and P assign accusative case to their complements (rule *70b*), A and N do not assign case to their complements. Since each NP requires a case feature, this helps explain why NPs can occur as complements of V and P, but not of A or N.

72)

V with NP complement: criticize $[_{NP}$ the girl]	P with NP complement: near $[_{NP}$ the girl]
N with NP complement: *criticism $[_{NP}$ the girl]	A with NP complement: *critical $[_{NP}$ the girl]

Phrases such as *criticize the girl* and *near the girl*, shown in Figure 5.45, satisfy the Case Filter since the NP *the girl* can receive an accusative case feature in that position, in accordance with *70b*.

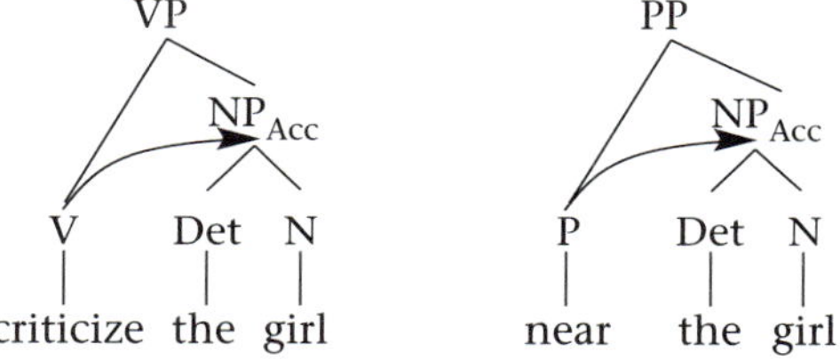

Figure 5.45 Case assignment to the complement of V and P

In contrast, the ill-formed phrases **criticism the girl* and **critical the girl* in *72* violate the Case Filter, since the NP *the girl* is not in a position to which a case feature is assigned.

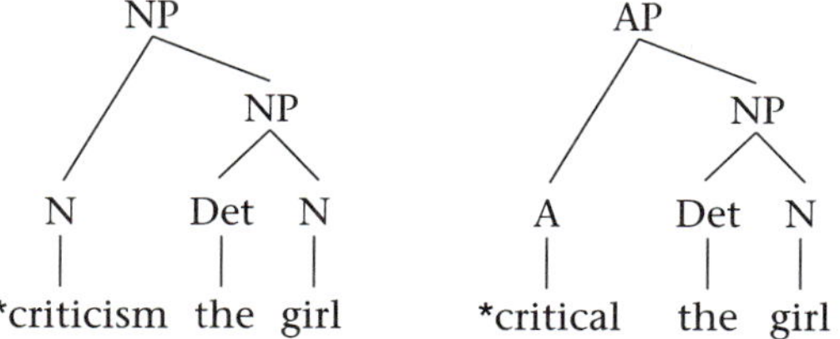

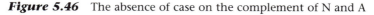

Figure 5.46 The absence of case on the complement of N and A

In order for these phrases to be grammatical, the complement must be realized as a PP (see Figure 5.47).

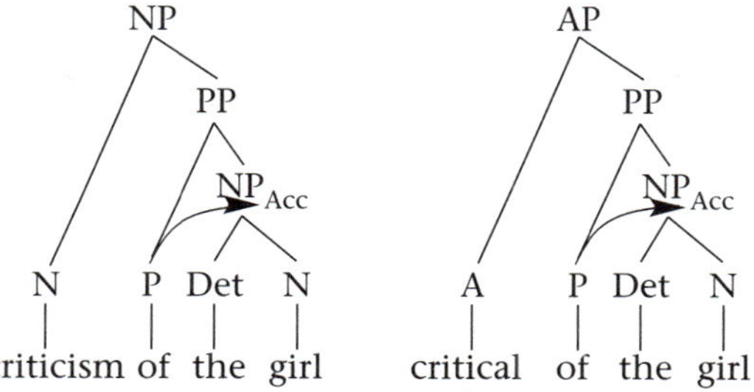

Figure 5.47 Case assignment when the complement of N and A is realized as a PP

As you can see, this structural pattern avoids the problem found in Figure 5.46, since the complement of P can have accusative case checked in that position, according to the rules in *70*.

Sometimes an NP's case is determined by its position prior to movement. A good example of this involves *wh* questions, in which the *wh* word appears in a position (the specifier of CP) to which no case feature is assigned. Under such circumstances, the NP must receive its case feature in the position that it occupies prior to *Wh* Movement. Direct evidence for this comes from conservative varieties of English, in which *who* is associated with the subject position and the special accusative form *whom* with the direct object position.

73)

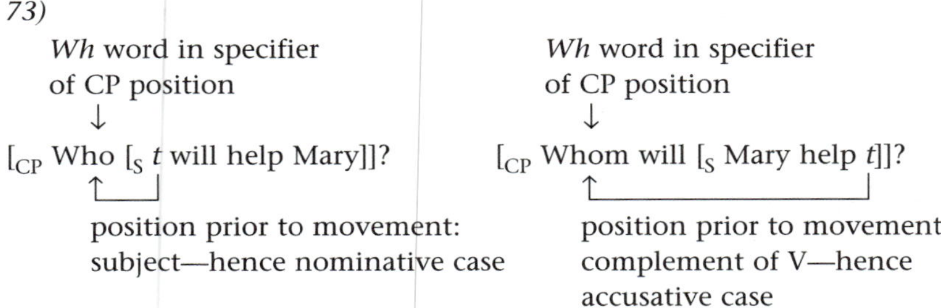

In summary, then, although case is a morphological category, it encodes syntactic information. This is captured by means of the rules outlined in *70*, which associate each of the various case forms of English with a different position in syntactic structure (subject, specifier of N, complement of V, and so on). Taking this idea and extending it one step further, the Case Filter then ensures that NP must occupy a position to which a case feature is assigned at some point in the derivation. This explains why an NP may serve as complement of a V or P (Figure 5.45), but not of an N or A (Figure 5.46).

6 OTHER TYPES OF SYNTACTIC ANALYSIS

Thus far in this chapter, we have focused our attention on the theory of sentence formation known as transformational syntax. As mentioned at the outset, however, this is not the only type of syntactic analysis used in contemporary linguistics. In this section, we will briefly consider two other approaches to syntax—one focusing on grammatical relations such as subject and direct object, and the other focusing on the way in which syntactic structure is used to communicate information.

In order to illustrate how these approaches work, it is helpful to consider how they—and transformational syntax—deal with the contrast between the two types of sentences illustrated in *74* and *75*.

74)

a. The thief took the painting.
b. The painting was taken by the thief.

75)

a. The dog chased the truck.
b. The truck was chased by the dog.

In order to describe the differences and similarities between these two sentences, it is necessary to distinguish between the **agent** (the doer of the action designated by the verb) and the **theme** (the entity directly affected by that action). (These notions are discussed in more detail in Chapter 6.)

76)

a. active sentence:
The thief took the painting.
agent *theme*

b. passive sentence:
The painting was taken (by the thief).
theme *agent*

The *a* sentence is called **active** because the agent is the subject of the sentence while the *b* sentence is called **passive** in recognition of the fact that the theme is the subject.

The analysis of the relationship between active and passive sentences is an important part of all syntactic theories and therefore provides an ideal "testing ground" for comparing competing approaches to syntax.

6.1 The transformational analysis

The key generalizations that the transformational analysis of passive sentences tries to capture are as follows:

77)

a. The agent, which functions as subject in active sentences, is "downgraded" to a less prominent position in passive sentences.

b. The vacancy in the subject position is filled in passive sentences by the theme NP, which normally functions as direct object in active sentences.

In a transformational analysis, the first of these generalizations is captured with the help of the deep structure illustrated in Figure 5.48. Note that auxiliary *be* can be treated as a V that takes a VP complement.

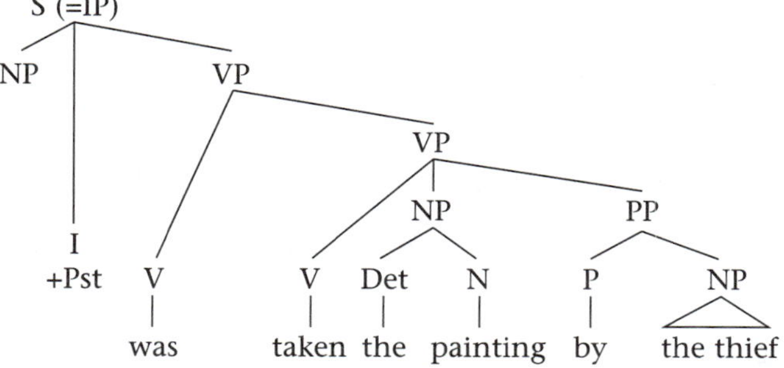

Figure 5.48 Deep structure for *The painting was taken by the thief*

The second generalization is captured by moving the theme NP from the direct object position to the subject position in surface structure. The Move operation needed to bring about this result can be stated as follows.

78)

NP Movement
Move NP into the subject position.

This transformation applies to the deep structure in Figure 5.48 to give the surface structure depicted in Figure 5.49.

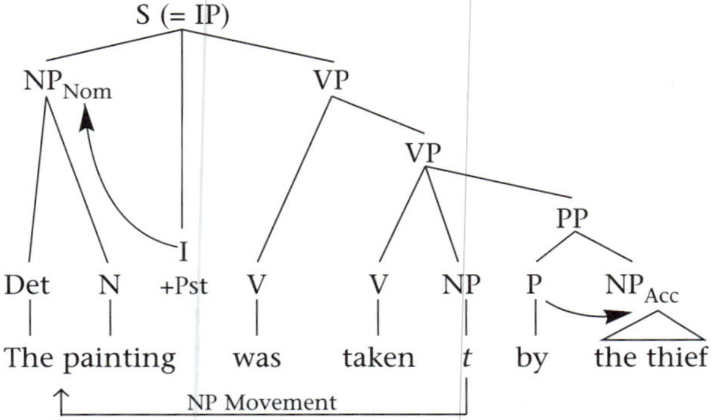

Figure 5.49 Surface structure resulting from NP Movement

What ensures that **NP Movement** takes place and that the subject position is not simply left empty in the surface structure of a passive sentence? The answer may well lie in the Case Filter discussed in Section 5.2.

The key idea is simply that a passive verb is unable to assign a case feature to its complement. Since only transitive verbs are able to assign case, this is just another way of saying that passive verbs are **intransitive**. In fact, it is often suggested that the *-en* or *-ed* suffix found on the passive forms of the verb has a detransitivizing function.

Given that a passive verb cannot assign a case feature to its complement, the direct object must find its case elsewhere if it is to satisfy the Case Filter. As illustrated in Figure 5.49, it is "attracted" to the empty subject position due to the availability of nominative case there and is transported to that position by the NP Movement operation.

6.2 The relational analysis

The transformational analysis works well for English and for other languages in which passivization is marked by a combination of verbal affixation (indicating a loss of the ability to assign case) and a change in the position of the theme (indicating movement). However, not all languages have passives of this type. In Tzotzil (a Mayan language of Mexico), for instance, the relative order of the agent and the theme is the same in active and passive constructions.

79)

a. active sentence:
Lá snákan ti vĩnike ti xpétule.
theme *agent*
seated the man the Peter
'Peter seated the man.'

b. passive sentence:
Inákanat ti vĩnike yuʔun ti xpétule.
theme *agent*
was seated the man by the Peter
'The man was seated by Peter.'

Here the passive is signaled by a change in the form of the verb and the appearance of the preposition *yuʔun* 'by' before the agent, but there is no change in the relative order of the agent and theme.

Mandarin Chinese employs yet another option.

80)

a. active sentence:
Zhū lǎoshī pīyuè le wǒde kǎoshì.
agent *theme*
Zhu professor mark PAST my test
'Professor Zhu marked my test.'

b. passive sentence:
Wǒde kǎoshì bèi Zhū lǎoshī pīyuè le.
theme *agent*
my test by Zhu professor mark PAST
'My test was marked by Professor Zhu.'

Here, the passive is marked by a change in word order and by the appearance of the preposition *bèi* 'by' before the agent, but the verb has exactly the same form in both patterns.

This has led some linguists to believe syntactic phenomena are best described in terms of grammatical relations such as subject and direct object rather than case or movement. According to proponents of **relational analysis**, the key facts about the contrast between active and passive sentences should be stated as follows in Table 5.13. (An NP that occurs with a preposition is said to be **oblique**.)

Table 5.13 Properties of passive structures

Active pattern		*Passive pattern*
subject	→	oblique
direct object	→	subject

This works straightforwardly for English, as the following example helps illustrate.

81)

a. active sentence: The thief took the painting.
subject *direct object*

subject *oblique*
b. passive sentence: The painting was taken (by the thief).

Notice that the direct object in the active *81a* (*the painting*) is the subject in the passive *81b,* while the subject in *81a* (*the thief*) occurs as part of a PP in *81b*—just as the relational generalization say they should.

Since the criteria used to identify subjects and direct objects differ from language to language, relational changes can be associated with a variety of structural effects. In English, where the direct object appears after the verb and the subject before it, a change in an NP's grammatical relation will also involve a change in its linear position. In other languages, word order may not be so important and the relational changes may be indicated in other ways—by verbal affixation, by case, or by the use of a preposition (as in Tzotzil). By analyzing passivization in terms of processes that affect subjects and direct objects, it is possible to go beyond these differences and to capture the universal properties of this important phenomenon.

Notions like subject and direct object have an important role to play in syntactic analysis, and they are often used to describe phenomena in a way that can be understood by linguists of all theoretical orientations. We will see additional examples of this in Chapter 8.

6.3 The functional analysis

Some syntactic analysis focuses on the relationship between a sentence's form and the way in which it is used to communicate information. This type of analysis is often called **functional**, since it seeks to understand syntactic phenomena in terms of their communicative function. The contrast between active and passive sentences is especially instructive in this regard. Although both sentence types have the same basic meaning, they differ from each other in terms of how they present the situation that they describe. Put another way, they differ from each other in how they package the information to be communicated. Two differences can be noted here.

First, passive sentences tend to de-emphasize the role of the agent in the situation being described. In fact, the vast majority of passive sentences do not mention the agent at all. In English, for instance, we can say simply *The painting was taken* or *The dishes were broken*, without attributing responsibility for these events to any particular person.

Second, passive sentences foreground the theme by making it the subject of the sentence. As a result, the situation is presented from the perspective of that person or thing. (As we will see in Chapter 6, the subject usually introduces the entity that the rest of the sentence is about.) Consider in this regard the following passage.

82)

Gretzky raced down the ice, stole the puck, and passed it out in front of the net. An instant later, *he was hit by the defenseman.* (Compare: An instant later, *the defenseman hit him.*)

The italicized passive sentence sounds more natural than the corresponding active sentence, since it brings to the foreground the pronoun *he*, which refers to the person (Gretzky) from whose perspective the entire series of events is being described.

In contrast, the passive is not nearly so natural in the following context.

83)

Gretzky raced down the ice, circled the net, and stopped. *The puck was then stolen by Gretzky* from the defenseman. (Compare: *He then stole the puck* from the defenseman.)

Here the passive sentence seems somewhat less natural, since it suddenly foregrounds the puck even though the rest of the passage is about Gretzky. This abrupt shift in the flow of information could be avoided by using the active sentence, with a pronoun referring to Gretzky in the subject position.

As this example illustrates, the functional analysis of the passive pattern focuses on the way in which it packages information compared to active sentences, placing the emphasis on how it is used rather than just on its structure. The key claim is that the function of the passive construction is to de-emphasize the agent (often deleting it entirely) and to draw attention to the theme NP. By analyzing syntactic structures functionally, it is often possible to gain insights into why human language has the particular syntactic patterns that it does, and how these patterns contribute to the larger task of communication.

Summing up

Universal Grammar provides all languages with the same general type of syntactic mechanisms. As we have seen, this includes a **Merge** operation that combines words in accordance with their **syntactic category** and their **subcategorization** properties, creating a representation called **deep structure**. Deep structure must comply with the **phrase structure schema**, which stipulates the place of **heads**, **specifiers, complements**, and **modifiers** in phrase structure.

Move operations (**transformations**) can modify deep structure by moving words and phrases in ways to produce a **surface structure**. But not just any movement is permitted, since transformations are constrained by economy principles such as **Shortest Move**.

Although the form of sentences can vary considerably from language to language, such differences can for the most part be attributed to a small set of **parameters**, each of which makes available a variety of alternatives from which individual languages may choose.

Key terms

General terms

computational system
grammatical
lexicon
syntax
transformational (generative) grammar
Universal Grammar (UG)

Terms concerning syntactic categories

adjective (A)
adverbs (Adv)
auxiliary verbs (Aux)
conjunctions (Con)
degree words (Deg)
determiners (Det)
distribution
lexical categories
nonlexical (functional) categories
noun (N)
preposition (P)
qualifier (Qual)
syntactic categories
verb (V)

Terms concerning combining words into phrases

complement
complement clause
complementizers
direct object
head
matrix clause
Merge
phrases
phrase structure rule
phrase structure schema
predicate
specifiers
subcategorization
subject
transitive

Terms concerning constituency tests

constituents
coordinate structures
coordination test
movement test
substitution test

Terms concerning mechanisms of sentence formation in world languages

deep structure (D-structure)
derivation
Do Insertion rule
economy constraint
insertion rule
Inversion
Move
parameters
postpositions
Q feature
Shortest Move
surface structure (S-structure)
trace
transformation
Verb Raising transformation
Wh Movement
wh questions
yes-no questions

Terms concerning modifiers and case

abstract case
active
agent
case
Case Filter
intransitive
modifiers
NP Movement
oblique
passive
theme

Other types of syntactic analysis

functional analysis
relational analysis

Sources

Transformational syntax is the most popular of the half-dozen major contemporary syntactic theories. Traditionally, it is the theory taught in introductory linguistics courses, both because it is so widely used and because many of the other approaches that exist today have developed in response to it. The particular system outlined here involves a variety of simplifications to make it appropriate for presentation in an introductory course.

The system of subcategorization employed here is loosely based on the one outlined in *Generalized Phrase Structure Grammar* by G. Gazdar, E. Klein, G. Pullum, and I. Sag (Cambridge, MA: Harvard University Press, 1979), which describes a non-transformational approach to syntax.

The discussion of the relational analysis of passive sentences is intended to be neutral between Lexical Functional Grammar, as outlined in *The Mental Representation of Grammatical Relations*, edited by Joan Bresnan (Cambridge, MA: MIT Press, 1978), and Relational Grammar, as described in "Toward a Universal Characterization of Passivization" by D. Perlmutter and P. Postal, in *Studies in Relational Grammar I*, edited by D. Perlmutter (Chicago: University of Chicago Press, 1983); the Chinese and Tzotzil examples cited in Section 6.2 were taken from this paper. The functional analysis of passives draws on the discussion in *Functional Syntax* by Susumu Kuno (Chicago: University of Chicago Press, 1981) and *Functional Syntax and Universal Grammar* by W. Foley and R. Van Valin (New York: Cambridge University Press, 1980).

The exercises for this chapter were prepared by Joyce Hildebrand.

Recommended reading

Haegeman, Liliane. 1994. *Introduction to Government and Binding Theory*. 2nd ed. Cambridge, MA: Blackwell.

Palmer, F. R. 1994. *Grammatical Roles and Relations*. New York: Cambridge University Press.

Payne, Thomas. 1997. *Describing Morphosyntax: A Guide for Field Linguists*. New York: Cambridge University Press.

Radford, Andrew. 1997. *Syntax: A Minimalist Introduction*. New York: Cambridge University Press.

Shopen, Timothy, ed. 1985. *Language Typology and Syntactic Description*. Vols. 1–3. New York: Cambridge University Press.

Appendix: How to build tree structures

Although it is relatively easy to check a tree structure to see if it complies with the phrase structure schema, it is somewhat harder to build a tree structure from scratch when trying to analyze a new phrase or sentence. In such cases, you will probably find it easiest to proceed in steps, working from the bottom up and from right to left. As an illustration, let us first consider the phrase *near the door.*

The first step involves assigning each word to the appropriate category, as depicted in Figure 5.50.

Figure 5.50 The first step: determining the word-level categories

Then, working from right to left, the appropriate XPs are built above each head (see Figure 5.51). Thus, we first build an NP above the N *door*. There is clearly no complement here, but there is a specifier (the determiner *the*), which combines with the N in accordance with the phrase structure schema.

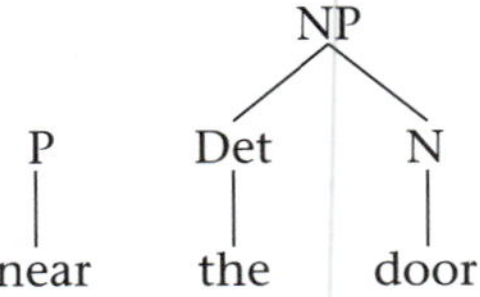

Figure 5.51 Building the NP

Next, we carry out the same procedure for the P *near*. The NP to the right of the P clearly functions as its complement, since it names the location entailed by the meaning of *near*. We therefore combine the P and the NP, forming the structure depicted in Figure 5.52.

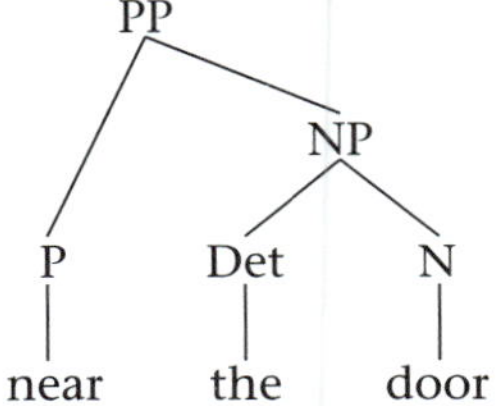

Figure 5.52 The complete PP

A sentential example

Consider now how we proceed in the case of a complete sentence such as *The dog might bite that man*. Assignment of each word to the appropriate category gives the structure depicted in Figure 5.53.

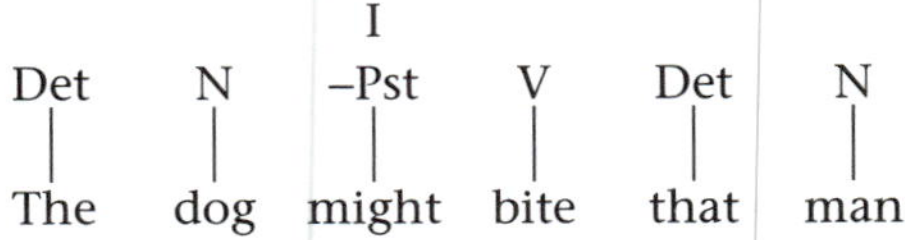

Figure 5.53 The categories for each word in the sentence

Working from right to left, it is easy to see that the noun *man* heads an NP that contains a specifier but no complement (see Figure 5.54).

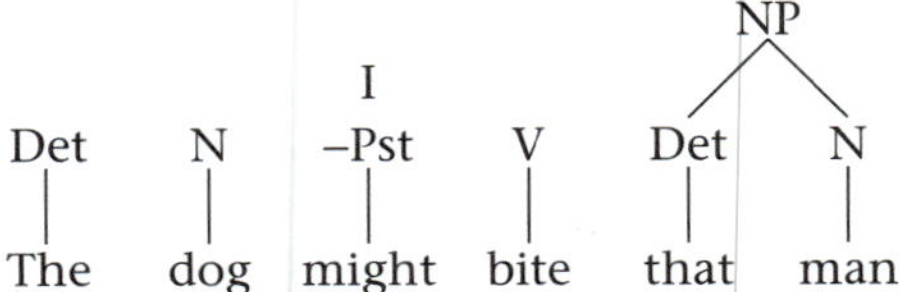

Figure 5.54 The structure of the rightmost NP

Next, we focus on the V *bite*, building the required VP and attaching the complement NP *that man* (see Figure 5.55).

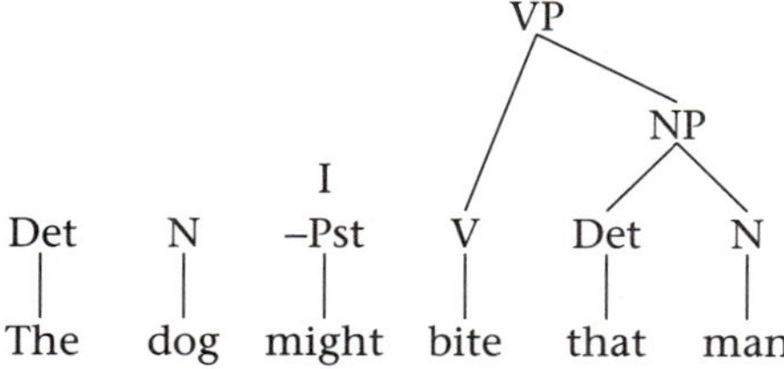

Figure 5.55 Adding the VP level above the V head

As an instance of the I category, the auxiliary *might* is the head of S (IP), with the VP to the right serving as its complement and the NP to the left functioning as its specifier. This yields the complete sentence illustrated in Figure 5.56.

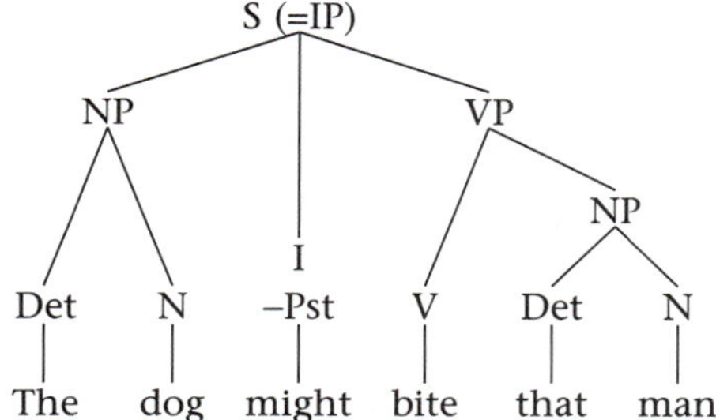

Figure 5.56 The complete sentence

The entire sentence is then embedded in a CP "shell," giving the tree in Figure 5.57.

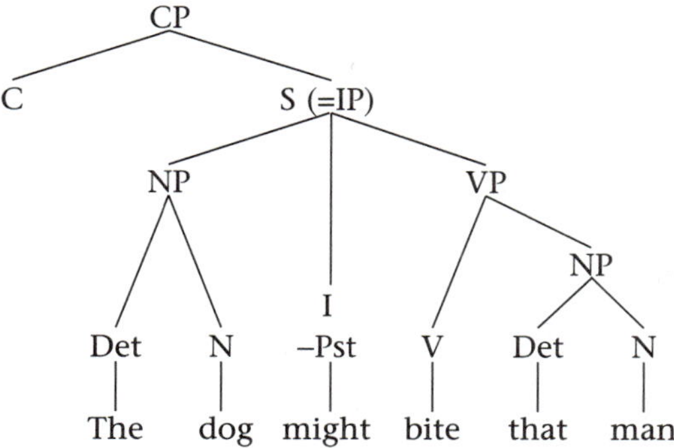

Figure 5.57 The sentence embedded in a CP shell

Transformations

As explained in Section 3, the syntactic analysis of some sentences involves the Move operation in addition to Merge. Recognizing that one of the transformations used in this chapter has applied is relatively simple: if a sentence contains an auxiliary verb to the left of the subject, then Inversion has applied; if it begins with a *wh* word, then *Wh* Movement has applied. Consequently, in the sentence *What should the farmers plant?* both of these transformations have applied.

In order to determine the deep structure, we must "return" the auxiliary verb to its position under I and must determine the position from which the *wh* word has been moved. Since the *wh* word in the sentence *What should the farmers plant?* asks about the complement of the verb (the thing that is planted), we place *what* in the complement position within VP in deep structure. This gives the deep structure depicted in Figure 5.58.

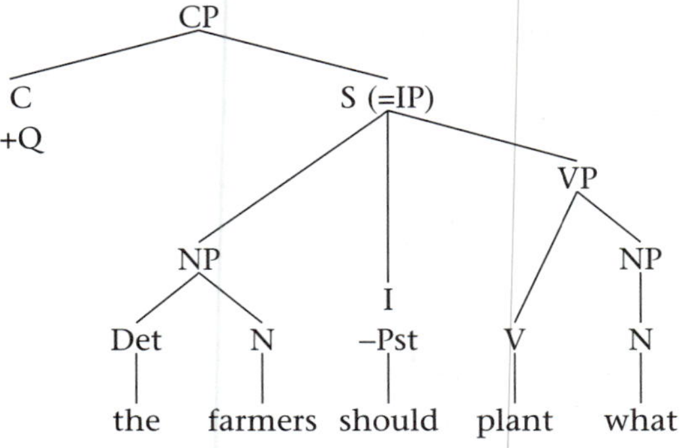

Figure 5.58 The deep structure for the sentence *What should the farmers plant?*

Attracted by the +Q feature, the auxiliary *should* then moves to the C position (Inversion) and *what* to the specifier position under CP (*Wh* Movement), yielding the complete surface structure depicted in Figure 5.59.

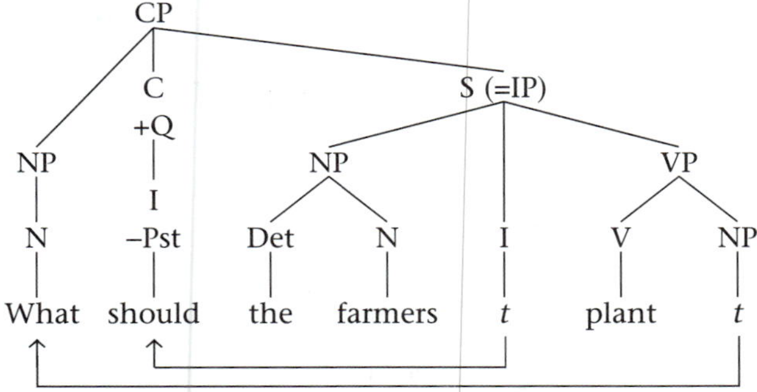

Figure 5.59 The surface structure for *What should the farmers plant?*

Questions

1. Place an asterisk next to any of the sentences that are ungrammatical for you. Can you figure out what makes these sentences ungrammatical?
   a) The instructor told the students to study.
   b) The instructor suggested the students to study.
   c) The customer asked for a cold beer.

d) The customer requested for a cold beer.
e) He gave the Red Cross some money.
f) He donated the Red Cross some money.
g) The pilot landed the jet.
h) The jet landed.
i) A journalist wrote the article.
j) The article wrote.
k) Jen is bored of her job.
l) Jen is tired of her job.

2. Indicate the category of each word in the following sentences. (It may help to refer back to Section 1.1.)
   a) That glass suddenly broke.
   b) A jogger ran toward the end of the lane.
   c) These dead trees are blocking the road.
   d) The detective hurriedly looked through the records.
   e) The peaches never appear quite ripe.
   f) Jeremy will play the trumpet and the drums in the orchestra.

3. Each of the following phrases consists of a specifier and a head. Use the Merge operation to create the appropriate tree structure for each example.
   a) the zoo
   b) always try
   c) so witty
   d) perhaps pass
   e) less bleak
   f) this house
   g) very competent
   h) quite cheap
   i) never surrender
   j) those books

4. The following phrases include a head, a complement, and (in some cases) a specifier. Use the Merge operation to create the appropriate tree structure for each example. For now, there is no need to depict the internal structure of complements. (See the tree diagrams in Figures 5.4 and 5.5 in the chapter.)
   a) into the house
   b) fixed the telephone
   c) full of mistakes
   d) more toward the window
   e) a film about pollution
   f) always study this material
   g) perhaps earn the money
   h) that argument with Owen
   i) the success of the program

5. After carefully reading the first two sections of the appendix, use the Merge operation to create phrase structure trees for each of the following sentences.
   a) Those guests should leave.
   b) Maria never ate a brownie.
   c) That shelf will fall.
   d) The glass broke.
   e) The student lost the debate.
   f) The manager may offer a raise.
   g) The judge often jails shoplifters.
   h) The teacher often organized a discussion.
   i) A psychic will speak to this group.
   j) Marianne could become quite fond of Larry.

6. Apply the substitution test to determine which of the bracketed sequences in the following sentences form constituents. Rewrite each sentence with the substitution. Is the sequence a constituent?
   a) [The tragedy] upset the entire family.
   b) They hid [in the cave].
   c) The [computer was very] expensive.
   d) [The town square and the civic building] will be rebuilt.
   e) Jane has [left town].

7. Apply the movement test to determine which of the bracketed sequences in the following sentences form constituents. Rewrite each sentence so that the bracketed sequence has been moved. Is the sequence a constituent?
   a) We ate our lunch [near the river bank].
   b) Steve looked [up the number] in the book.
   c) The [island has been] flooded.
   d) I love [peanut butter and bacon sandwiches].
   e) The environmental [movement is gaining momentum].
   f) The goslings [swam across] the lake.

8. Lexical categories are divided into subcategories on the basis of their complements. For each of the following words, two potential complement options are given. For each of the words:
   i) Determine which one of the two options better matches the subcategorization requirements of the verb, noun, or adjective.
   ii) Justify your choice by creating a sentence using that complement option.

	Verb	*Options*		*Verb*	*Options*
a)	expire	Ø *or* NP NP	e)	clean	NP PP_{for} *or* NP NP
b)	destroy	NP *or* Ø	f)	mumble	NP *or* NP NP
c)	observe	NP *or* PP_{to} PP_{about}	g)	throw	Ø *or* NP PP_{loc}
d)	discuss	NP *or* Ø	h)	paint	NP PP_{to} *or* NP PP_{for}

	Noun	*Options*
a)	debate	PP_{of} PP_{to} *or* PP_{with} PP_{about}
b)	hammer	Ø *or* PP_{with} PP_{about}
c)	success	PP_{of} PP_{to} *or* PP_{of}
d)	transfer	PP_{with} PP_{about} *or* PP_{of} PP_{to}
e)	sickness	Ø *or* PP_{with} PP_{about}

	Adjective	*Options*
a)	strong	Ø *or* PP_{about}
b)	sick	NP *or* PP_{of}
c)	bored	PP_{with} *or* PP_{on}
d)	knowledgeable	PP_{to} *or* PP_{about}
e)	small	PP_{of} *or* Ø

9. *i)* The following sentences all contain embedded clauses that function as complements of a verb. Draw a tree structure for each sentence.
   a) The reporter said that an accident injured a woman.

b) The fishermen think that the company polluted the bay.
c) Bill reported that a student asked whether the eclipse would occur.

ii) The following sentences all contain embedded clauses that function as complements of an adjective, a preposition, or a noun. Draw a tree structure for each sentence.
d) The police appeared happy that the criminal would surrender.
e) That officer was sure that Gerry often speeds down the highway.
f) Ray wondered about whether the exam would cover that section.
g) Scientists will never accept the claim that the earth is flat.

10. The derivations of the following sentences involve the Inversion transformation. Draw tree diagrams to show the deep structure and the surface structure for each sentence (*Hint:* see the appendix).
   a) Will the boss hire Hilary?
   b) Can the dog fetch the Frisbee?
   c) Should the student report the incident?
   d) Must the musician play that music?
   e) Might that player leave the team?

11. The following sentences involve the rules of *Wh* Movement and Inversion. Draw tree diagrams to show the deep structure and the surface structure for each sentence.
   a) Who should the director call?
   b) Who should call the director?
   c) What can Joanne eat?
   d) Who will the visitors stay with?
   e) What might Terry bake for the party?
   f) What could Anne bring to the gathering?

12. The following data is from Igbo, a tone language spoken in Nigeria.

a) Nwáànyĭ̀áhŭ̀	b) ŭ́lŭ́ à
woman that	house this
'that woman'	'this house'

   i) Draw tree diagrams to show the phrase structure for each of the Igbo phrases.

13. The following data is from Malagasy, spoken on the island of Madagascar.

a) Entin' kafe izy	b) Mankany amin' ny restauranta izy.
brings coffee he	goes to the restaurant he
'He brings coffee.'	'He goes to the restaurant.'

   i) Draw tree diagrams to show the phrase structure for each of the Malagasy sentences.
   ii) Do complements precede or follow their heads in Malagasy?

14. Consider the following Selayarese data.
   a) Laʔallei doeʔ injo iBaso.
   took money the Baso
   'Baso took the money.'

b) nraʔbai sapon injo.
collapsed house the
'The house collapsed.'

c) Lataroi doeʔ injo ri lamari injo iBaso.
put money the in cupboard the Baso
'Baso put the money in the cupboard.'

i) Draw a tree structure for each of these sentences.
ii) How does the phrase structure schema for Selayarese differ from English?

15. The following data is from Korean. You may ignore the nominative (subject) and accusative (direct object) markers for the purposes of this question.

a) Terry-ka ku yeca-lul coahanta.
Terry-Nom that girl-Acc likes
'Terry likes that girl.'

b) I noin-i hakkyo ey kassta.
this man-Nom school to went
'This man went to school.'

c) Sue-ka chinkwu eykey chayk-ul ilkessta.
Sue-Nom friend to book-Acc read
'Sue read the book to a friend.'

i) Draw the tree structure for each of the Korean sentences.
ii) What is the phrase structure schema for Korean?

16. The following data illustrate the formation of *yes-no* questions in German.

a) Das Kind wird die Schwester lehren.
the child will the sister teach
'The child will teach the sister.'

b) Wird das Kind die Schwester lehren?
will the child the sister teach
'Will the child teach the sister?'

c) Der Mann liebt die Frau.
'The man loves the woman.'

d) Liebt der Mann die Frau?
loves the man the woman
'Does the man love the woman?'

Assuming that German makes use of the same Inversion transformation as English (i.e., "Move I to the C position"), does the above data tell us whether German employs the Verb Raising transformation? Be sure to include the tree structures for *b* and *d* in your answer.

17. The following sentences contain modifiers of various types. For each sentence, first identify the modifier(s), then draw the tree structures.

a) A large iguana suddenly appeared.
b) The principal made an important announcement after the class.
c) An unusual event occurred before the game.
d) The very hazardous waste seeped into the ground quickly.
e) A huge moon hung in the black sky.
f) Timothy drew an enormous map during the afternoon.

18. The following Russian sentences contain several different forms for the pronoun 'I'—*ja, m^{j}en^{j}a, mnoj,* and *mn^{j}e* (^{j} is palatalization).

NOMINATIVE

a) ja pon^{j}imaju urok
I understand lesson
'I understand the lesson.'

b) ja viʒu joʒika
I see hedgehog
'I see the hedgehog.'

ACCUSATIVE

c) on uv^{j}id^{j}el m^{j}en^{j}a
he saw me
'He saw me.'

d) on^{j}i vstr^{j}et^{j}il^{j}i m^{j}en^{j}a
they met me
'They met me.'

INSTRUMENTAL

e) vi poʃl^{j}i so mnoj
you went with me
'You went with me.'

f) on^{j}i pogovor^{j}il^{j}i so mnoj
they spoke with me
'They were talking with me.'

DATIVE

g) on^{j}i poʃli ko mn^{j}e
they arrived to me
'They came to my place.'

h) on podoʃol ko mn^{j}e
he approached to me
'He approached me.'

i) Draw the tree structure for each of these sentences, and make a statement about the context in which each case form occurs.
ii) Does the complement of a preposition receive the same case as the complement of a verb?
iii) Is the case assigned to the complement of a preposition the same for the two prepositions found in the data?

19. In each of the following sentences, indicate above each NP whether it is subject, direct object, or oblique, and indicate below each NP whether it is agent or theme.

a) Marie purchased a present.
b) The class was conducted by an expert.
c) Those books were read by young children.
d) An expert conducted the class.
e) A present was purchased by Marie.

For the Student Linguist

BACKWARDS

Sometimes poetry frustrates me because of all the seemingly nonsensical sentence bits I get after my brain automatically inserts a dramatic pause at the end of each line. Because I'm stuck, waiting for my eyes to get to the next line, as I try to figure out what's so incredibly significant about a line consisting of "Eskimo" or "his amber eyes" or "detritus" and nothing else. But I really like Lesléa Newman's work because the line divisions actually seem meaningful and because she seems to be having so much fun arranging these sentence bits.

Tiff and I*

Tiff and I sit
in Tompkins Square Park
reading poetry
under a sky
full of clapping pigeons.
He calls them flying rats
but I think
the pink and green circles
around their necks
like greasy oil puddles are
beautiful.
Tiff says
all my poems sound better
backwards.

Backwards
all my poems sound better
Tiff says.
Beautiful
like greasy oil puddles
around their necks are
the pink and green circles
but I think
he calls them flying rats.
Full of clapping pigeons
under a sky
reading poetry
in Tompkins Square Park
Tiff and I sit.

If you read the poem as if it were prose, I think the first half sounds pretty bland and the second half is just plain loopy:

Tiff and I sit in Tompkins Square Park reading poetry under a sky full of clapping pigeons. He calls them flying rats but I think the pink and green circles around their necks like greasy oil puddles are beautiful. Tiff says all my poems sound better backwards.

Backwards all my poems sound better Tiff says. Beautiful like greasy oil puddles around their necks are the pink and green circles but I think he calls them flying rats. Full of clapping pigeons under a sky reading poetry in Tompkins Square Park Tiff and I sit.

In fact, I can't read the second half in prose format without imagining flying poems that have greasy pink and green circles around their necks, a sky that is reading poetry, and two people who've spent the afternoon eating live pigeons.

What is it about the change from prose to poetry that makes this string of words interesting and meaningful? (We've got to drudge through some syntax here, but trust me, it's relatively painless and worth it.) Assume that the first half of the poem has three untransformed sentences, and the second half has sentences that have undergone transformations. Also notice that one word—*are*—gets switched into a different line in the second stanza. It shouldn't be too hard to draw tree structures for the sentences in the first stanza *if* you do it line by line (i.e., first draw the tree for "Tiff and I sit," then for "in Tompkins Square Park," etc., and then hook them together).

The sentences in the second stanza will be harder to draw trees for, but if you do the first stanza line by line, those parts will be the same, except for where the word *are* is switched. So all you really need to do is figure out which parts of the trees got moved, and in which order. Actually, that's not even too hard to do, since only constituents can be moved.

You've probably figured out by now why this poem is in the syntax chapter: it does a good job of showing off what constituents are and of showing how the same words, even the same phrases, can have a different meaning when they're moved. However, this poem does more than show off constituents. I also like the rhythm of the poem—the way some of the lines seem to invite me to pause after them, and other lines lead me quickly on to the next line. Take a look at the subcategorizations of the last word of each line. Some of them lead you to expect a complement and others don't. Try reading the poem again and see if the subcategorization frames make a difference in how much emphasis you put on each line.

Finally, look at some other poetry that you love or hate and see what sort of match there is between grouping in lines or stanzas and grouping into constituents. Look at some different types of writing and their phrase structures; since punctuation is sadly limited in how well it can show pauses or emphasis or any sort of complex tone, the actual structure of the sentence can be crucial if the sentence is to be read with the right emphasis. And look in particular at some of your own writing and at how transformations of sentences could make a difference in their clarity. All of this theory might actually improve your writing.

*Newman, Lesléa, "Tiff and I," in *Sweet Dark Places* (Santa Cruz, CA: HerBooks, 1991).

six

SEMANTICS: THE ANALYSIS OF MEANING

William O'Grady

. . . in every object there is inexhaustible meaning.

– THOMAS CARLYLE

OBJECTIVES

In this chapter, you will learn:

- how we derive meaning from words and sentences
- how different languages encode concepts in words and sentences
- how we use sentence structure to produce and understand meaning
- how speaker beliefs and attitudes, setting, and context contribute to meaning

Up to now, this book has focused on the form of utterances—their sound pattern, morphological structure, and syntactic organization. But there is more to language than just form. In order for language to fulfill its communicative function, utterances must also convey a message; they must have content. Speaking very generally, we can refer to an utterance's content as its **meaning**.

This chapter is concerned with **semantics**, the study of meaning in human language. Because some work in this complicated area of linguistic analysis presupposes considerable knowledge of other disciplines (particularly logic, mathematics, and philosophy), not all aspects of contemporary semantics are suitable for presentation in an introductory linguistics textbook. We will restrict our attention here to four major topics in semantics: (1) the nature of meaning, (2) some of the properties of the conceptual system underlying meaning, (3) the contribution of syntactic structure to the interpretation of sentences, and (4) the role of nongrammatical factors in the understanding of utterances.

1 THE NATURE OF MEANING

Long before linguistics existed as a discipline, thinkers were speculating about the nature of meaning. For thousands of years, this question has been considered central to philosophy. More recently, it has come to be important in other disciplines as well, including psychology and sociology in addition to linguistics. Contributions to semantics have come from a diverse group of scholars, ranging from Plato and Aristotle in ancient Greece to Bertrand Russell in the twentieth century. Our goal in this section will be to consider in a very general way what this research has revealed about meaning in human language. We will begin by considering some of the basic analytic notions used in evaluating the meanings of words and sentences.

1.1 Semantic relations among words

Words and phrases can enter into a variety of semantic relations with each other. Because these relations help identify those aspects of meaning relevant to linguistic analysis, they constitute a good starting point for this chapter.

Synonymy

Synonyms are words or expressions that have the same meaning in some or all contexts. The following pairs of words in Table 6.1 provide plausible examples of synonymy in English.

Table 6.1 Some synonyms in English

filbert	hazelnut
youth	adolescent
automobile	car
remember	recall
purchase	buy
big	large

Because it would be inefficient for a language to have two words or phrases with absolutely identical meanings, perfect synonymy is rare, if not impossible. For example, although *youth* and *adolescent* both refer to people of about the same age, only the latter word can be used to imply immaturity—as in *What adolescent behavior!*

Antonymy

Antonyms are words or phrases that are opposites with respect to some component of their meaning. The pairs of words in Table 6.2 provide examples of antonymy. In each of these pairs, the two words contrast with respect to at least one aspect of their meaning. For instance, the meanings of *boy* and *girl* are opposites with respect to gender, although they are alike in other respects (both are human). Similarly, *come* and *go* are opposites with respect to direction, although both involve the concept of movement.

Table 6.2 Some antonyms in English

dark	light
boy	girl
hot	cold
up	down
in	out
come	go

Polysemy and homophony

Polysemy occurs in situations in which a word has two or more related meanings. Table 6.3 contains some examples of polysemous words in English.

Table 6.3 Some polysemous words in English

Word	*Meaning a*	*Meaning b*
bright	'shining'	'intelligent'
to glare	'to shine intensely'	'to stare angrily'
a deposit	'minerals in the earth'	'money in the bank'

If you consult a reasonably comprehensive dictionary for any language, you will find numerous examples of polysemy. For example, my dictionary lists several related meanings for the word *mark*.

1)

Polysemy in the meaning of *mark*

- a visible trace or impression on something (*The tires left a mark on the road.*)
- a written or printed symbol (*You need a punctuation mark here.*)
- a grade, as in school (*He got a good mark on the math test.*)
- a target (*She hit the mark every time.*)
- an indication of some quality or property (*The mark of a good diplomat is the ability to negotiate.*)

Homophony exists in words in which a single form has two or more entirely distinct meanings (see Table 6.4). In such cases, it is assumed that there are separate words with the same pronunciation rather than a single word with different meanings.

Table 6.4 Some homophones in English

Word	*Meaning a*	*Meaning b*
light	'not heavy'	'illumination'
bank	'a financial institution'	'a small cliff at the edge of a river'
club	'a social organization'	'a blunt weapon'
pen	'a writing instrument'	'an enclosure'

Homophones need not have identical spellings—*write* and *right* are homophones, as are *piece* and *peace*.

Polysemy and homophony create **lexical ambiguity** in that a single form has two or more meanings. Thus, a sentence such as *2* could mean either that Liz purchased an instrument to write with or that she bought an enclosure.

2)

Liz bought a pen.

Of course, in actual speech the surrounding words and sentences usually make the intended meaning clear. The potential lexical ambiguity in sentences such as the following therefore normally goes unnoticed.

3)

He got a loan from the *bank*.

4)

Because Liz needed a place to keep her goat, she went downtown and bought a *pen* for $100.

1.2 Semantic relations involving sentences

Like words, sentences have meanings that can be analyzed in terms of their relation to other meanings. Three such relations—paraphrase, entailment, and contradiction—are particularly important.

Paraphrase

Two sentences that can have the same meaning are said to be **paraphrases** of each other. The following pairs of sentences provide examples of paraphrase.

5)

a. The police chased the burglar.
b. The burglar was chased by the police.

6)

a. I gave the summons to Erin.
b. I gave Erin the summons.

7)

a. It is unfortunate that the team lost.
b. Unfortunately, the team lost.

8)

a. Paul bought a car from Sue.
b. Sue sold a car to Paul.

9)

a. The game will begin at 3:00 P.M.
b. At 3:00 P.M., the game will begin.

The *a* and *b* sentences in each of the above pairs are obviously very similar in meaning. Indeed, it would be impossible for one sentence to be true without the other also being true. Thus, if it is true that the police chased the burglar, it must also be true that the burglar was chased by the police. (Sentences whose meanings are related to each other in this way are said to have the same **truth conditions**.)

For some linguists, this is enough to justify saying that the two sentences have the same meaning. However, you may notice that there are subtle differences in emphasis between the *a* and *b* sentences in *5* to *9*. For instance, it is natural to interpret *5a* as a statement about what the police did and *5b* as a statement about what happened to the burglar. Similarly, *9b* seems to place more emphasis on the starting time of the game than *9a* does. As is the case with synonymy, many linguists feel that languages do not permit two or more structures to have absolutely identical meanings and that paraphrases are therefore never perfect.

Entailment

When the truth of one sentence guarantees the truth of another sentence, we say that there is a relation of **entailment**. This relation is mutual in the case of examples *5* to *9* since the truth of either sentence in the pair guarantees the truth of the other. In examples such as the following, however, entailment is asymmetrical.

10)

a. The park wardens killed the bear.
b. The bear is dead.

11)

a. Prince is a dog.
b. Prince is an animal.

If it is true that the park wardens killed the bear, then it must also be true that the bear is dead. However, the reverse does not follow since the bear could be dead without the park wardens having killed it. Similarly, if it is true that Prince is a dog, then it is also true that Prince is an animal. Once again though, the reverse does not hold: even if we know that Prince is an animal, we cannot conclude that he is a dog rather than a horse or a cat.

Contradiction

Sometimes it turns out that if one sentence is true, then another sentence must be false. This is the case with the examples in *12*.

12)

a. Charles is a bachelor.
b. Charles is married.

If it is true that Charles is a bachelor, then it cannot be true that he is married. When two sentences cannot both be true, we say that there is a **contradiction.**

1.3 WHAT IS MEANING?

Although it is relatively easy to determine whether two words or sentences have identical or different meanings, it is much more difficult to determine precisely what meaning is in the first place. In fact, despite many centuries of study, we still know very little about the nature of meaning or how it is represented in the human mind. Nonetheless, it is worthwhile to review briefly some of the better known proposals and the problems that they encounter.

Connotation

One notion that is closely linked with the concept of meaning is **connotation**, the set of associations that a word's use can evoke. For most Minnesotans, for example, the word *winter* evokes thoughts of snow, bitter cold, short evenings, frozen fingertips, and the like. These associations make up the word's connotation, but they cannot be its meaning (or at least not its entire meaning). The word *winter* does not become meaningless just because it is a mild year or because one moves to Florida in November. We must therefore look beyond connotation for our understanding of what meaning is.

Denotation

One well-known approach to semantics attempts to equate the meaning of a word or phrase with the entities to which it refers—its **denotation**, or **referents**. The denotation of the word *winter*, for example, corresponds to the season between autumn and spring (regardless of whether it is cold and unpleasant). Similarly, the denotation of the word *dog* corresponds to the set of canines, and so on.

Although a word's denotation is clearly connected to its meaning in some way, they cannot be one and the same thing. This is because there are words such as *unicorn* and phrases such as *the present king of France* that have no referents in the real world, even though they are far from meaningless.

A problem of a different sort arises with expressions such as *the Prime Minister of England* and *the leader of the Labour Party*, both of which refer (in 2000, at least) to Tony Blair. Although these two expressions may have the same referent, it seems wrong to say that they mean the same thing. Thus, we would not say that the phrase *Prime Minister of England* is defined as 'the leader of the Labour Party' or that the definition of the phrase *leader of the Labour Party* is 'Prime Minister of England'.

Extension and intension

The impossibility of equating an element's meaning with its referents has led to a distinction between **extension** and **intension**. Whereas an expression's extension corresponds to the set of entities that it picks out in the world (its referents), its intension corresponds to its inherent sense—the concepts that it evokes. Thus, the extension of *woman* is a set of real world entities (women) while its intension involves notions like 'female' and 'human'. Similarly, the phrase *Prime Minister of England* has as its extension an individual (Tony Blair), but its intension involves the concept 'leader of the governing party' (see Table 6.5).

Table 6.5 Extension versus intension

Phrase	*Extension*	*Intension*
Prime Minister of England	Tony Blair	leader of the governing party
Wimbledon champion (2000)	Venus Williams	winner of the women's tennis championship
Capital of Missouri	Jefferson City	city containing the state legislature

The distinction between intension and extension does not allow us to resolve the question of what meaning is. It simply permits us to pose it in a new way: what are intensions?

One suggestion is that intensions correspond to mental images. This is an obvious improvement over the referential theory, since it is possible to have a mental image of a unicorn or even of the king of France, although there are no such entities in the real world. However, problems arise with the meanings of words such as *dog*, which can be used to refer to animals of many different sizes, shapes, and colors. If the meaning of this word corresponds to a mental image, that image would have to be general enough to include Chihuahuas and St. Bernards, yet still exclude foxes and wolves. If you try to draw a picture that satisfies these requirements, you will see just how hard it is to construct an image for word meanings of this sort.

Componential analysis

Still another approach to meaning tries to represent a word's intension by breaking it down into smaller semantic components. Sometimes known as **componential analysis** or **semantic decomposition**, this approach has often been used to analyze the meaning of certain types of nouns in terms of **semantic features**. The analysis in Figure 6.1 for the words *man*, *woman*, *boy*, and *girl* illustrates how this works. (Nothing depends on the choice of feature names here; the analysis would work just as well with the feature ±FEMALE as ±MALE.)

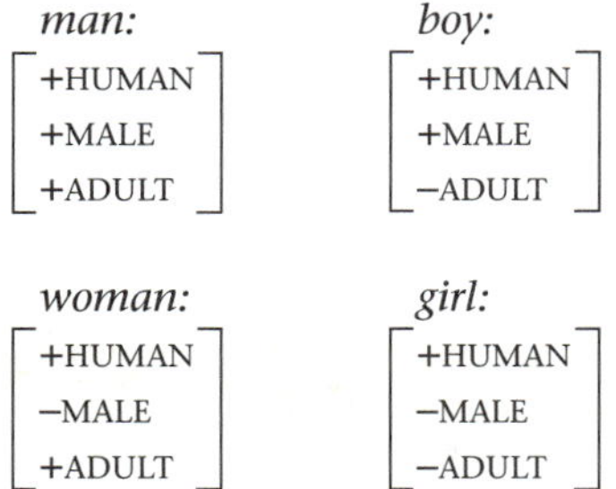

Figure 6.1 Semantic feature composition for *man, woman, boy, girl*

An obvious advantage of this approach is that it allows us to group entities into natural classes (much as we do in phonology). Hence, *man* and *boy* could be grouped together as [+HUMAN, +MALE] while *man* and *woman* could be put in a class defined by the features [+HUMAN, +ADULT].

This in turn can be useful for stating generalizations of various sorts. For instance, there are certain verbs, such as *marry*, *argue*, and the like, that we expect to find only with subjects that are [+HUMAN]. Moreover, within the English pronoun system, *he* is used to refer to [+HUMAN] entities that are [+MALE] while *she* is used for [+HUMAN] entities that are [–MALE].

There are limits on the insights into word meaning offered by componential analysis. What value, for example, is there in characterizing the meaning of *dog* as [+ANIMAL, +CANINE] as long as there is no further analysis of these features? Similarly, do we say that the meaning of *blue* consists of the feature [+COLOR] and something else? If so, what is that other thing? Isn't it blueness? If so, then we have not really broken the meaning of *blue* into smaller components, and we are back where we started.

To date, componential analysis has given its most impressive results in the study of verb meaning. A typical component of verb meaning is the concept GO, which is associated with change of various sorts. (The components of verb meaning tend not to be binary features.)

13)

manifestations of the concept GO:

a. positional change:
Harvey went from Chicago to Dubuque.

b. possessional change:
The inheritance went to Marla.

c. identificational change:
Max went from being a rational gentleman to being a stark raving lunatic.

Despite their somewhat different senses, all three uses of the verb *go* have something in common that can be traced to the GO component of their meaning—they typically occur with a phrase that denotes the entity undergoing change (e.g., the subject in these examples) and with a phrase expressing the endpoint of that change (the *to* complements).

The GO concept is manifested in the meaning of verbs other than just *go*. For instance, positional GO is present in the meaning of *fly* ('go through the air'), *walk* ('go on foot'), *crawl* ('go on hands and knees'), and so forth. Possessional GO is manifested in the meaning of *give*, *buy*, and *inherit*, all of which involve a change of possession, while identificational GO shows up in *become* and *turn into*. Consistent with this fact, each of these verbs is typically used with a phrase denoting the entity undergoing the change (marked below by a single underline) and a phrase denoting the endpoint of that change (marked by a double underline).

14)

a. positional GO:
The bird flew to its nest.

b. possessional GO:
The coach gave a new ball to the children.

c. identificational GO:
The caterpillar turned into a butterfly.

Sometimes quite surprising features of verb meaning can be relevant to the choice of accompanying phrases. Consider, for instance, the contrast between the verbs in list *a*, which can occur with two NP complements, and the verbs in list *b*, which cannot.

15)

a. throw [$_{NP}$ the boy] [$_{NP}$ a ball]	*b.* *push [$_{NP}$ the boy] [$_{NP}$ a ball]
toss	*pull
kick	*lift
fling	*haul

Can you see the semantic difference? The verbs in list *a* all denote ballistic motion that results from the instantaneous application of force to an object at its point of origin. (When we throw something, for example, we thrust it forward and then release it.) In contrast, the verbs in list *b* all denote motion that is accompanied by the continuous application of force to the object as it moves from one point to another. (Pulling, for instance, typically involves the extended use of force as the object moves, rather than a single quick motion.)

Now think about the contrast between the following two sets of verbs.

16)

a. fax [$_{NP}$ Helen] [$_{NP}$ the news]	*b.* *murmur [$_{NP}$ Helen] [$_{NP}$ the news]
radio	*mumble
email	*mutter
phone	*shriek

Once again, componential analysis reveals a subtle semantic contrast. The first group of verbs (*phone*, *radio*, etc.) have meanings that include the means by which a message was communicated (by phone, by radio, and so on). In contrast, the verbs in the second group all have meanings that describe the type of voice that was used to communicate the message (murmuring, mumbling, shrieking, etc.). For reasons that are not yet fully understood, meaning differences like these help determine the type of complements that particular verbs can select.

2 THE CONCEPTUAL SYSTEM

Underlying the use of words and sentences to express meaning in human language is a conceptual system capable of organizing and classifying every imaginable aspect of our experience, from inner feelings and perceptions, to cultural and social phenomena, to the physical world that surrounds us. This section focuses on what the study of this conceptual system reveals about how meaning is expressed through language. We will begin by considering some examples that illustrate the way in which these concepts are structured, extended, and interrelated.

2.1 FUZZY CONCEPTS

We tend to think that the concepts expressed by the words and phrases of our language have precise definitions with clear-cut boundaries. Some concepts may indeed be like this. For example, the concept expressed by the phrase *senator* seems to have a clear-cut definition: one is a senator if and only if one is duly elected to a particular legislative body; no other person can truthfully be called a senator.

But are all concepts so straightforward? Consider the concept associated with the word *rich*. How much does a person have to be worth to be called rich? Five hundred thousand dollars? Eight hundred thousand? A million? Is there any figure that we can give that would be so precise that a person who is short by just five cents would not be called rich? It seems not. While one could miss out on being a senator by five votes, it does not seem possible to miss out on being rich by just five cents. Moreover, whereas some people clearly qualify as rich and others uncontroversially do not, an indefinitely large number of people fall into the unclear area at the borderline of the concept and it is just not possible to say definitively whether or not they count as rich. This is because the notion of 'richness' does not have clear-cut boundaries; it is what we call a **fuzzy concept**.

This type of fuzziness pervades the human conceptual system. With only a little effort, you should be able to think of many everyday concepts whose boundaries are fuzzy—*tall, old, athlete, strong, gray-haired, genius, clean,* and *bargain* are just a few examples.

Graded membership

A second important fact about concepts is that their members can be **graded** in terms of their typicality. Consider first a fuzzy concept such as BASEBALL STAR. Even within the set of people who we can agree are baseball stars, some provide better examples of this concept than others. At the time of this writing, for instance, Sammy Sosa is a better example of a baseball star than is Darryl Strawberry. Although baseball fans agree that both players are stars, Sammy Sosa has hit more home runs, won more awards, set more records, received more media attention for his accomplishments, and so on. This makes him a better example of a star than Darryl Strawberry.

Even concepts whose boundaries can be scientifically defined exhibit this type of graded membership. A good example of this involves the concept BIRD. Even assuming that English speakers all think of birds as 'warm-blooded, egg-laying, feathered vertebrates with forelimbs modified to form wings' (the dictionary definition), they still feel that some of these creatures are more birdlike than others. For instance, robins and sparrows are intuitively better examples of birds than are hummingbirds, ostriches, or penguins.

Examples like these suggest that concepts have an internal structure, with the best—or **prototypical**—exemplars (Sammy Sosa in the case of BASEBALL STARS, robins in the case of BIRDS) close to the core, and less typical members arranged in successively more peripheral regions.

The existence of fuzzy concepts and of graded membership provides important insights into the nature of the human conceptual system. In particular, it seems that many (perhaps even most) concepts expressed in language are not rigid all-or-nothing notions with precise and clear-cut boundaries. Rather, they are characterized by an internal structure that recognizes degrees of typicality as well as by fuzzy boundaries that sometimes overlap with those of other concepts.

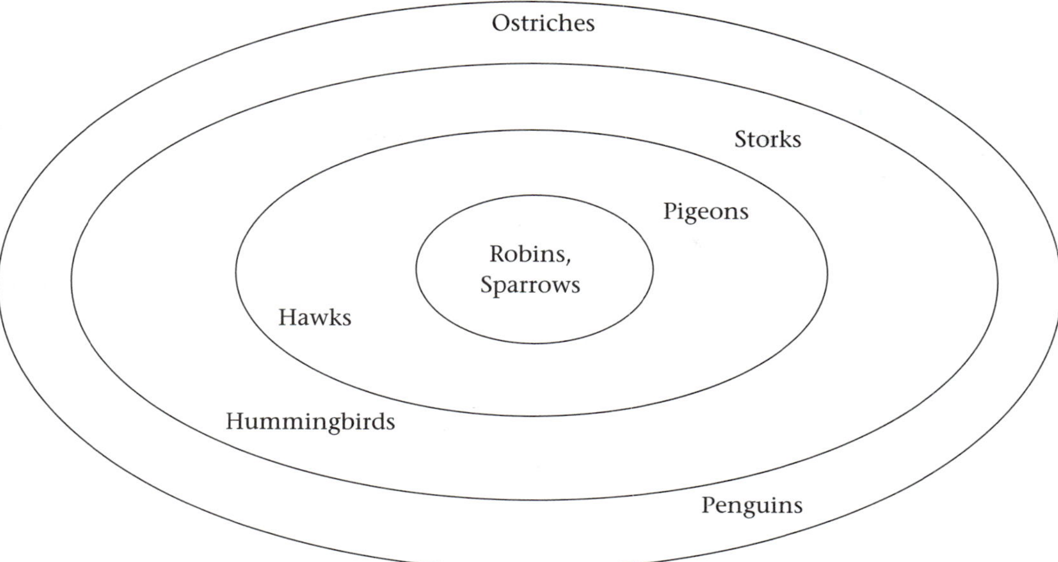

Figure 6.2 Internal structure of the concept BIRD

2.2 Metaphor

The concepts expressed by language make up a giant network, with many interconnections and associations. A good example of these interconnections involves **metaphor**, the understanding of one concept in terms of another.

Many people think of metaphor as a literary device reserved for the use of authors and poets. In fact, however, it has a prominent place in the conceptual system shared by all human beings. This can be seen in the way that we use language to talk about even commonplace notions such as time.

The dominant metaphor for talking about time involves treating it as if it were a concrete commodity that can be saved, wasted, and invested, just like other valuable things.

17)

a. You're *wasting* my time.
b. This gadget will *save* you hours.
c. How do you *spend* your time these days?
d. I have *invested* a lot of time in that project.
e. You need to *budget* your time.
f. Is that *worth* your while?
g. He's living on *borrowed* time.
h. You don't use your time *profitably*.

What is the basis for this metaphor? There is apparently no objective, inherent similarity between time and commodities such as gold or money. What brings these concepts together is the *perception*, based in part on culture and in part on feelings that all human beings share, that time is like a valuable commodity that can be gained and lost.

A spatial metaphor

Another very prevalent metaphor in our language involves the use of words that are primarily associated with spatial orientation to talk about physical and psychological states (see Table 6.6).

Table 6.6 Metaphorical use of spatial terms

Emotions: happy is up; sad is down	
I'm feeling *up*. That *boosted* my spirits. My spirits *rose*. You're in *high* spirits. the *height* of ecstasy That gave me a *lift*.	I'm feeling *down*. He *fell* into a depression. Her spirits *sank*. He's feeling *low*. the *depths* of depression
Physical health: health and life are up; sickness and death are down	
He's at the *peak* of health. Lazarus *rose* from the dead. He's in *top* shape.	He's *sinking* fast. He *fell* ill. He came *down* with the flu. Her health is *declining*. She's feeling *under* the weather.

The basis for these **spatial metaphors** appears to lie in our physical experience. Unhappiness and ill health tend to be associated with lethargy and inactivity, which often involve being on one's back (physically down). In contrast, happiness and good health are often correlated with energy and movement, which involve being on one's feet (physically up).

These few examples illustrate the more general point that the concepts expressed through language are interrelated in special and intriguing ways. By investigating phenomena such as the use of metaphor to represent abstract concepts in terms of more basic physical and cultural experience, we can gain valuable insights into how language is used to communicate meaning.

2.3 The lexicalization of concepts

Do all human beings share the same conceptual system? Do all languages express concepts in the same way? These are questions that have fascinated and puzzled researchers for many decades. At the present time, there is no reason to believe that human beings in different linguistic communities have different conceptual systems. But there is ample evidence that languages can differ from each other in terms of how they express particular concepts.

Lexicalization

A notorious example of how languages can supposedly differ from each other in the expression of concepts involves the number of words for snow in Inuktitut. Sometimes estimated to be in the hundreds, the number is actually much, much smaller. In fact, one dictionary gives only the four items in Table 6.7 (although other dictionaries give a few more, at least for some varieties of Inuktitut).

Table 6.7 Words for *snow* in Inuktitut

aput	'snow on the ground'
qana	'falling snow'
piqsirpoq	'drifting snow'
qimuqsuq	'snow drift'

As you can see, there is nothing particularly startling about this list of words. In fact, even in English there is more than just one word to describe snow in its various forms—*snow, slush, blizzard,* and *sleet* come to mind, for example.

These examples illustrate the phenomenon of **lexicalization**—the process whereby concepts are encoded in the words of a language. Thus, Inuktitut lexicalizes the concepts 'falling' and 'snow' in a single word (*qana*), while English uses two separate words. While some lexicalization differences may correlate with cultural factors (the relative importance of types of snow in traditional Inuit culture), this is not always so. For example, English has an unusually rich set of vocabulary items pertaining to the perception of light (see Table 6.8).

Table 6.8 Some verbs pertaining to 'light' in English

glimmer	glisten
gleam	glow
glitter	flicker
shimmer	shine
flare	glare
flash	sparkle

Although English speakers know and use the words in this list, it is hard to see how the variety found in this particular area of vocabulary can be correlated with any significant feature of culture or cognition.

As we have tried to emphasize throughout this book, linguistic analysis focuses on the *system* of knowledge that makes it possible to speak and understand a language. The fact that a particular language has more words pertaining to snow or light does not in and of itself provide any insight into the nature of the human linguistic system, and therefore does not merit special attention. However, as we shall see in the next subsection, certain lexicalization differences do shed light on how language expresses meaning.

Motion verbs

All languages have words that can describe motion through space (in English, *come, go,* and *move,* among many others). However, there are systematic differences in terms of how languages express motion and the concepts related to it. In English, for example, there are many verbs that simultaneously express both the concept of motion and the manner in which the motion occurs (see Table 6.9).

Table 6.9 Some verbs expressing motion and manner in English

The rock *rolled* down the hill.
The puck *slid* across the ice.
She *limped* through the house.
The smoke *swirled* through the opening.

Notice how each of these verbs expresses both the fact that something moved and the manner in which it moved (by rolling, sliding, limping, and so on). We describe this fact by saying that English lexicalization includes a **conflation pattern** that combines manner and motion into a single verb meaning.

Interestingly, Romance languages (descendants of Latin) cannot express motion events in this way. Thus, while Spanish has a verb *rodar* with the meaning 'to roll', it does not use this verb to express both manner and motion as English does.

18)

*La botella rodó en la cueva.
'The bottle rolled into the cave.'

Instead, the motion and its manner have to be expressed separately.

19)

La botella entró en la cueva, rodando.
'The bottle entered the cave, rolling.'

Although Spanish does not have the motion + manner conflation pattern, it does have verbs whose meaning brings together the concepts of motion and path (see Table 6.10). As the English translations show, Spanish verbs of motion express both the concept of movement and the direction of its path—down, up, back, across, out, and so forth. (English too has verbs that can express both motion and path—*descend, ascend, return,* and so on—but these words are not part of its native vocabulary; rather, they were borrowed into English from Latinate sources, usually through French.)

Table 6.10 Some verbs expressing motion and path in Spanish

El globo	*bajó*	por la chimenea.
'The balloon moved-down through the chimney.'		
El globo	*subió*	por la chimenea.
'The balloon moved-up through the chimney.'		
La botella	*volvió*	a la orilla.
'The bottle moved-back to the bank.'		
La botella	*cruzó*	el canal.
'The bottle moved-across the canal.'		
La botella	*salió*	de la cueva.
'The bottle moved-out from the cave.'		

Yet another conflation pattern is found in the Amerindian language Atsugewi (spoken in northern California), in which verbs can express both motion and the type of thing that moves (see Table 6.11).

Table 6.11 Some verb roots expressing motion and the thing moving in Atsugewi

lup	for movement of a small, shiny spherical object (a hailstone)
t	for movement of a smallish, flat object that can be attached to another (a stamp, a clothing patch, a shingle)
caq	for movement of a slimy, lumpish object (a toad, a cow dropping)
swal	for movement of a limp linear object, suspended by one end (a shirt on a clothesline, a hanging dead rabbit)
qput	for movement of loose, dry dirt
staq	for movement of runny, unpleasant material (manure, guts, chewed gum, rotten tomatoes)

We learn two things from these facts. First, the concept of motion is associated with a number of other concepts, including path, manner of movement, and moving thing. Second, the way in which these concepts are combined for the purposes of lexicalization can differ systematically from language to language. Languages such as English have verbs that conflate motion and manner while other languages have verbs that conflate motion and path (Spanish) or motion and the type of thing that moves (Atsugewi).

The general picture that is emerging from this type of work is consistent with the key idea underlying componential analysis (Section 1.3). In particular, it seems that at least within certain semantic domains, there may be a small universal set of concepts (motion, manner, path, thing that moves, and so on) and a small set of options for how these concepts can be combined for purposes of lexicalization (see Figure 6.3).

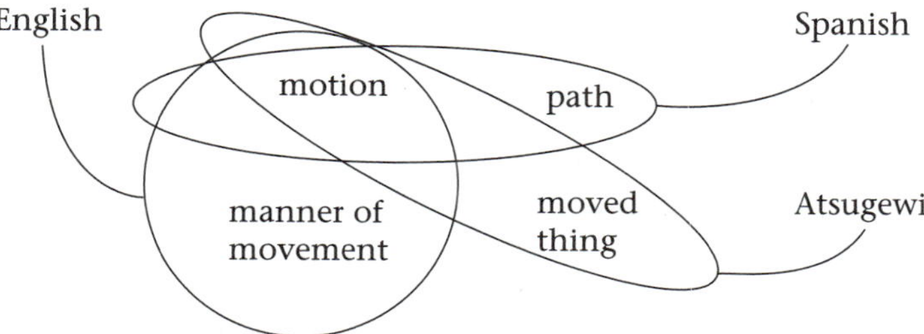

Figure 6.3 Systematic differences in conflation patterns

Unlike the lexicalization differences involving snow and light discussed earlier, these differences appear to be highly systematic and to reveal some general tendencies about the organization of the human conceptual system and the way in which meaning is expressed in language.

2.4 Grammaticization

Of the indefinitely large set of concepts expressible in human language, a relatively small subset enjoys a special status. These are the concepts that are lexicalized as affixes and nonlexical (functional) categories in one language or another. Some of the concepts that are treated this way in English are listed in Table 6.12.

Table 6.12 Some concepts associated with affixes and nonlexical categories in English

Concept	*Affix*
Past	*-ed*
More than one	*-s*
Again	*re-*
Negation	*in-, un-*
Concept	*Nonlexical category*
Obligation	*must*
Possibility	*may*
Definite, specific	*the*
Indefinite, nonspecific	*a*
Disjunction	*or*
Negation	*not*
Conjunction	*and*

Concepts that are expressed as affixes or nonlexical categories are said to have been **grammaticized**.

Some concepts, such as negation, tense, and number, are highly grammaticizable and are expressed as affixes or special nonlexical categories in most, if not all, of the world's languages. But grammaticization is not restricted to just these familiar concepts, as the example from the Siouan language Hidatsa in Table 6.13 illustrates.

Evidentiality in Hidatsa

In Hidatsa, each statement is accompanied by a morpheme to indicate the evidence for its truth. (Morphological contrasts of this sort express **evidentiality**.) Choice of the appropriate sentence-ender is extremely important in Hidatsa. Speakers who utter a false sentence marked by the morpheme *-ski* are considered to be liars. Had they used the morpheme *-c*, on the other hand, it would be assumed that they simply made a mistake.

While English has ways of indicating these contrasts (by using expressions such as *perhaps, I heard that,* and *I guess*), it does not have a grammatical system of morphemes that obligatorily encodes this information in every sentence. By investigating the grammaticization options found in different languages, it may eventually be possible to identify the factors that determine which concepts are singled out for association with affixes and nonlexical categories.

Table 6.13 Evidentiality morphemes in Hidatsa

ski	THE SPEAKER IS CERTAIN OF THE STATEMENT'S TRUTH Waceo iikipi kure heo -ski 'The man (definitely) carried the pipe.'
c	THE SPEAKER BELIEVES THE STATEMENT TO BE TRUE Waceo iikipi kure heo -c. 'The man (supposedly) carried the pipe.'
wareac	THE SPEAKER REGARDS THE STATEMENT TO BE COMMON KNOWLEDGE Waceo iikipi kure heo -wareac. 'The man carried the pipe (they say).'
rahe	THE STATEMENT IS BASED ON AN UNVERIFIED REPORT FROM SOMEONE ELSE Waceo wiira rackci heo -rahe. 'The man roasted the goose (it is rumored).'
toak	THE TRUTH OF THE STATEMENT IS UNKNOWN TO BOTH SPEAKER AND LISTENER Waceo cihpa rakci heo -toak. 'The man roasted the prairie dog (perhaps).'

3 SYNTAX AND SENTENCE INTERPRETATION

The two preceding sections have focused on the meaning conveyed by the individual words and phrases that make up a sentence. In this section, we turn to the problem of sentence interpretation, with an emphasis on how the positioning of words and phrases in syntactic structure helps determine the meaning of the entire sentence, consistent with the following principle.

20)

The Principle of Compositionality
The meaning of a sentence is determined by the meaning of its component parts and the manner in which they are arranged in syntactic structure.

Syntactic structure is relevant to meaning in a variety of ways. For purposes of illustration, we will consider four aspects of its contribution to the interpretation of sentences—constructional meaning, the representation of structural ambiguity, the assignment of thematic roles, and the interpretation of pronouns.

3.1 CONSTRUCTIONAL MEANING

There is reason to believe that structural patterns are themselves capable of carrying meaning above and beyond the meaning of their component parts. One example of this **constructional meaning** can be seen in "the caused-motion construction" exemplified in *21*.

21)

a. Seymour pushed the truck off the table.
b. Mabel moved the car into the garage.
c. Perry pulled the dog into the swimming pool.

As these examples help illustrate, the caused-motion construction consists of a structural pattern (NP V NP PP) that is used to express the meaning 'X causes Y to go somewhere'. Thus, the first sentence describes a situation in which Seymour causes the truck to go off the table by pushing it; the second sentence describes a situation in which Mabel causes the car to go into the garage; and so on.

22)

The caused-motion construction
FORM: NP V NP PP
MEANING: 'X causes Y to go somewhere'

Striking evidence for the existence of a constructional meaning comes from sentences such as the following.

23)

a. Boris sneezed the handkerchief right across the room.
b. The judges laughed the poor guy out of the room.
c. Morley squeezed the shirt into the suitcase.

There is clearly nothing in the meaning of verbs such as *sneeze*, *laugh*, and *squeeze* that implies caused motion. Yet, when they occur in the NP V NP PP pattern, the resulting sentence has a meaning in which X causes Y to go somewhere. Thus, sentence *23a* means that Boris caused the handkerchief to fly across the room by sneezing; *b* means that the judges forced someone out of the room by laughing at him; and so on.

How can this be? It seems that part of the meaning of these sentences comes from the construction itself: in *23a*, for instance, the verb *sneeze* provides the meaning 'involuntarily expel air from the mouth and nose', while the structural pattern tells us that this action caused the handkerchief to be propelled across the room. Without both types of information, the sentence could not mean what it does.

Another example of constructional meaning can be found in patterns such as the following.

24)

a. Jerry sent Lou a present.
b. The company gave its employees a bonus.
c. The secretary handed Mary a message.
d. Marvin threw Harry the ball.

These sentences are instances of the so-called ditransitive construction that is typically associated with the meaning 'X causes Y to have Z'. Thus *24a*, for instance, describes a situation in which Jerry causes Lou to have a present by sending it to her.

25)

The ditransitive construction
FORM: NP V NP NP
MEANING: 'X causes Y to have Z'

An indication that the structure itself contributes part of the meaning associated with ditransitive constructions comes from sentences such as *Jerry baked Lou a cake.* This sentence describes a situation in which Lou ends up with a cake, even though there is clearly nothing in the meaning of *bake* that implies that one person causes another person to have something. This part of the sentence's meaning comes from the structure itself—another example of constructional meaning.

3.2 STRUCTURAL AMBIGUITY

Some sentences are **structurally ambiguous** in that their component words can be combined in more than one way. A simple example of this is found in the phrase *wealthy men and women*, where 'wealthy' can be seen as a property of both the men and the women or of just the men alone. These two interpretations or **readings** are depicted in Figure 6.4 (Con = conjunction).

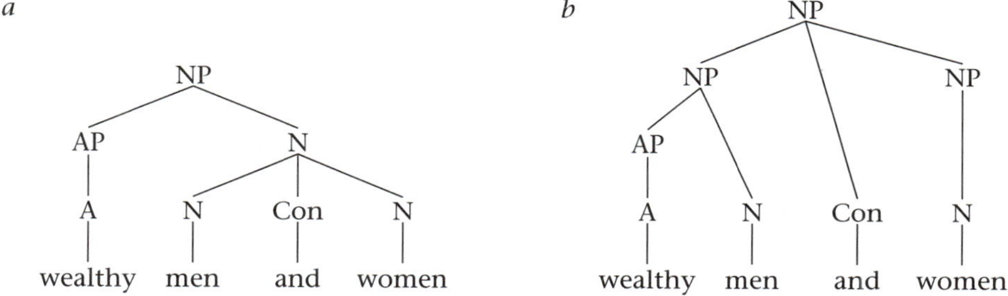

Figure 6.4 An ambiguous phrase. The structure on the left indicates that both the men and the women are wealthy; the structure on the right indicates that only the men are wealthy.

Figure 6.4a corresponds to the reading in which *wealthy* modifies both *men* and *women.* This is shown by having the adjective combine with a category that includes both nouns. In Figure 6.4b, on the other hand, the adjective combines only with the N *men.* This structure corresponds to the reading in which 'wealthy' applies only to the men.

Another case of structural ambiguity is found in sentences such as the following.

26)

Nicole saw the people with binoculars.

In one interpretation of *26*, the people had binoculars when Nicole noticed them (the phrase *with binoculars* modifies the noun *people*), while in the other interpretation, Nicole saw the people by using the binoculars (the PP modifies the verb). These two readings are represented in Figure 6.5.

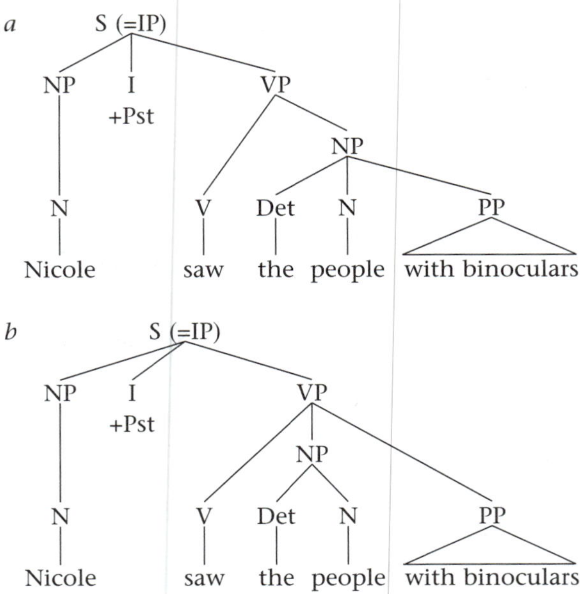

Figure 6.5 An ambiguous sentence. In the first structure, the people have the binoculars; in the second structure, Nicole uses the binoculars to see the people.

In Figure 6.5a, the PP *with binoculars* occurs with the N *people*, reflecting the first reading for this sentence. In Figure 6.5b, on the other hand, the PP is part of the VP headed by the verb *saw*. This corresponds to the interpretation in which *with binoculars* describes the way that Nicole saw the people.

In sum, the manner in which words are grouped together in syntactic structure reflects the way in which their meanings are combined. Sometimes, as in the examples we have just considered, identical strings of words can be combined in either of two ways, creating structural ambiguity that can be neatly captured with the help of tree structures.

3.3 Thematic roles

Another aspect of semantic interpretation involves determining the role that the referents of NPs play in the situations described by sentences. Consider in this regard the sentence in *27*.

27)

The courier carried the document from Boston to Seattle.

It would be impossible to understand this sentence if we could not identify the courier as the person who is responsible for carrying something, the document as the thing that is carried, Boston as the point of origin, and Seattle as the destination. Linguists often use **thematic roles** to categorize the relation between a sentence's parts and the event that it describes. In most linguistic analyses, the thematic roles listed in Table 6.14 are recognized.

Table 6.14 Thematic roles

Agent	the entity that performs an action
Theme	the entity undergoing an action or a movement
Source	the starting point for a movement
Goal	the end point for a movement
Location	the place where an action occurs

Examples of these thematic roles can be seen in sentences such as the following.

28)

a. The courier carried the document from Boston to Seattle.
agent theme source goal

b. The athletes practiced in the Astrodome.
agent location

The notion of movement used in the definition of **theme**, **source**, and **goal** is intended to involve not only actual physical motion but also changes in possession, as in *29*, and identity, as in *30*.

29)

Terry gave the skis to Mary.
agent theme goal

30)

The magician changed the ball into a rabbit.
agent theme goal

As you may recall, we observed a similar set of contrasts in the manifestation of the GO concept discussed in Section 1.3. This is no coincidence. Thematic roles can be traced to particular aspects of word meaning, and the presence of GO in a verb's meaning is specifically linked to the presence of a theme role and a goal role.

Thematic role assignment

How does the grammar ensure that the appropriate thematic role is associated with each NP in a sentence? As we have just seen, thematic roles originate in word meaning. Thus, if the sentence *Amber purchased a pencil at the bookstore* contains an **agent** and a theme, it is because the verb *purchase* has the type of meaning that implies an entity that does the purchasing (an agent) and an entity that gets purchased (a theme). Similarly, *the bookstore* is taken to denote the location of the action because of the meaning of the preposition *at*. Information about the thematic roles assigned by a particular lexical item is recorded in a **thematic grid**, as depicted in Table 6.15.

Table 6.15 Some words and the thematic roles implied by their meanings

purchase	<agent, theme>
walk	<agent>
to	<goal>
from	<source>
at	<location>

The thematic roles implied by the meanings of lexical items are assigned to NPs based on their position in syntactic structure, with each NP receiving a single role. As a first example of this, let us consider the complement of a preposition. In such cases, the process of thematic role assignment can be summarized as follows.

31)

A P assigns a thematic role to its complement NP.

The operation of this convention is illustrated in Figure 6.6.

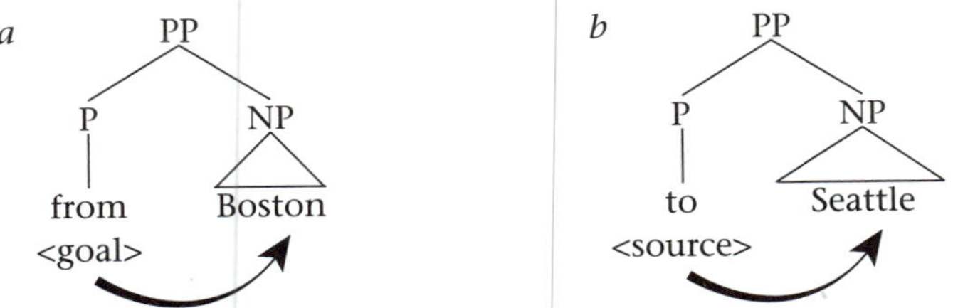

Figure 6.6 Thematic role assignment by prepositions

Matters are slightly more complicated in the case of Vs. Here we must distinguish between the theme role, which is assigned to the V's complement, and the agent role, which is assigned to its subject.

32)

A V assigns a theme role (if it has one) to its complement NP.
A V assigns an agent role (if it has one) to its subject NP.

This is exemplified in the structures in Figure 6.7.

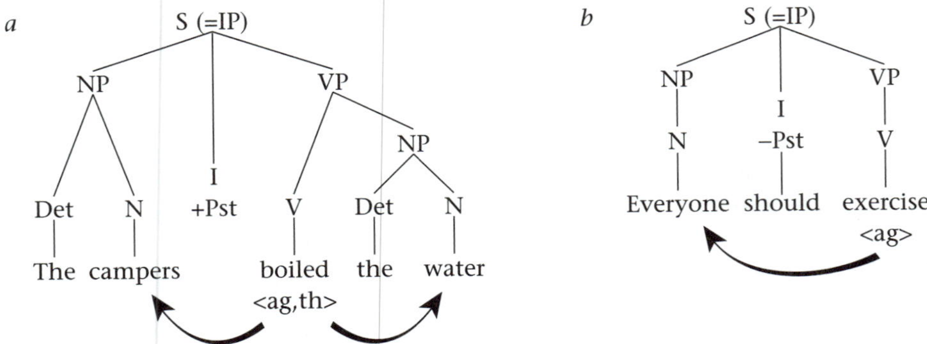

Figure 6.7 Thematic role assignment by verbs

In accordance with *32*, the theme role (where present) is assigned to the V's NP complement while the agent role is assigned to the subject.

The structure in Figure 6.8 illustrates the assignment of thematic roles in a sentence that contains a P in addition to a V.

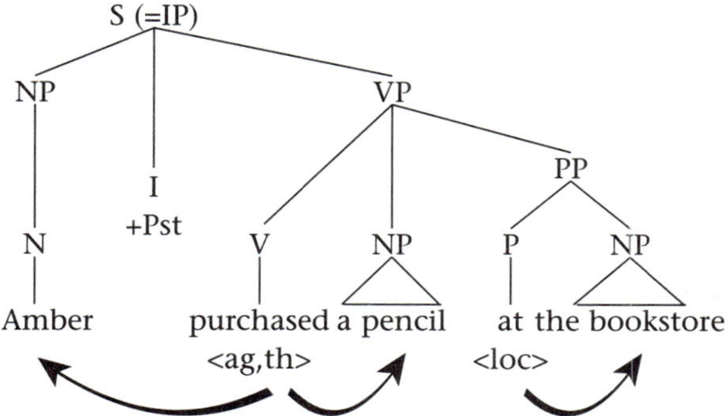

Figure 6.8 Thematic role assignment in a complex sentence

Here, the P *at* assigns its **location** role to its complement NP (*the bookstore*) while the verb *purchased* assigns its theme role to the complement *a pencil* and its agent role to the subject *Amber*.

Deep structure and thematic roles

In the examples considered to this point, it is unclear whether an NP receives its thematic role on the basis of its position in deep structure or surface structure. This is because our example sentences are all formed without the help of the Move operation, so that each NP occupies the same position in both deep structure and surface structure. But now consider a sentence such as *33*, which is formed with the help of *Wh* Movement.

33)

Which book should the students read?

This sentence has the deep structure depicted in Figure 6.9.

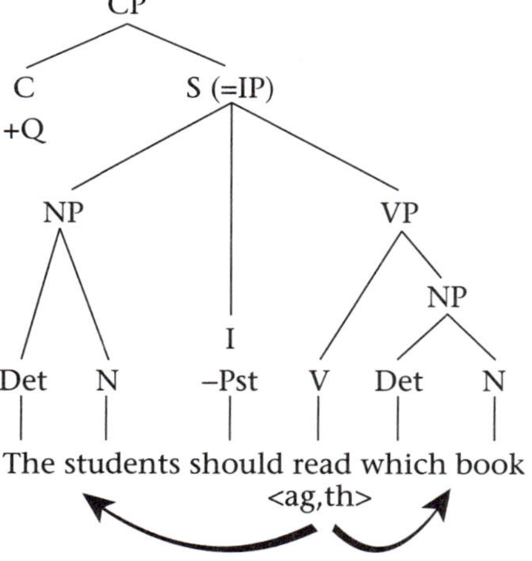

Figure 6.9 Thematic role assignment in a *wh* question

Since the theme role is assigned to the complement of V, it follows that the NP *which book* in the above example receives this role by virtue of its position in deep structure, not surface structure (where it occurs in the specifier of CP position).

In sum, an NP's initial position in syntactic structure (the result of the Merge operation) determines its thematic role. The Move operation may subsequently transport the NP to another position (as is the case with *wh* words), but the original thematic role remains unchanged. The relationship between syntactic structure and the part of a sentence's meaning represented by thematic roles is thus very intricate, reflecting the structural relations manifested in deep structure rather than position in surface structure.

3.4 The interpretation of pronouns *(Advanced)*

Syntactic structure also has an important role to play in the interpretation of **pronouns**, including **pronominals** such as *he, him, she,* and *her* and **reflexive pronouns** such as *himself* and *herself* (see Table 6.16).

Table 6.16 Subject and object pronouns in English

	Pronominals		*Reflexives*	
	SG	*PL*	*SG*	*PL*
1st person	I, me	we, us	myself	ourselves
2nd person	you	you	yourself	yourselves
3rd person	he, him		himself	
	she, her	they	herself	themselves
	it		itself	

A defining property of pronouns is that their interpretation can be determined by another element, called the **antecedent**. As the following sentences help show, pronominals and reflexive pronouns differ in terms of where their antecedents can occur.

34)

a. [$_S$ Claire knew that [$_S$ Alexis trusted *her*]].
b. [$_S$ Claire knew that [$_S$ Alexis trusted *herself*]].

Notice that *her* can refer either to Claire or to someone not mentioned in the sentence, but that *herself* refers only to Alexis. This reflects the fact that a reflexive pronoun must typically have an antecedent in the smallest S containing it.

A somewhat more abstract feature of syntactic structure enters into the interpretation of the reflexive pronouns in sentences such as *35*, which has the tree structure shown in Figure 6.10. (Pronouns are treated as N-type categories that head NPs; to save space, some word-level category labels are omitted. As noted in the previous chapter, possessor NPs occur in the specifier position within larger NPs.)

35)

That boy's teacher admires himself.

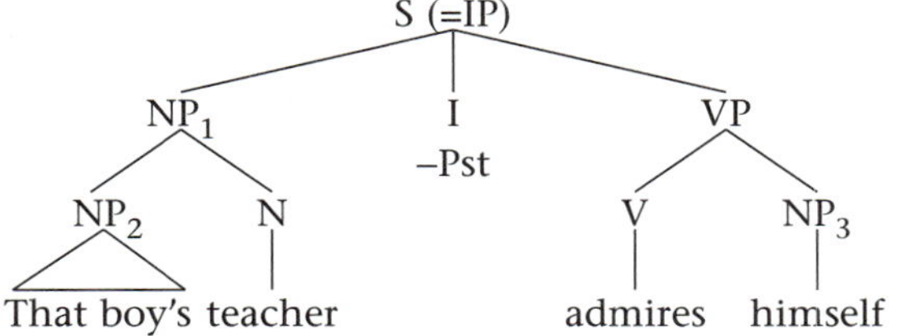

Figure 6.10 Structure containing a reflexive pronoun

Although there are two NPs in the same S as *himself* (namely, *that boy* (NP_2) and *that boy's teacher* (NP_1)), only one (*that boy's teacher* (NP_1)) can serve as antecedent for the reflexive pronoun (NP_3). Thus, the person who is admired in *35* must have been the boy's teacher, not the boy.

Principles A and B

The principle needed to ensure this interpretation makes use of the notion **c-command**, which is defined as follows.

36)

NP_a c-commands NP_b if the first category above NP_a contains NP_b.

Although c-command might appear to be a rather technical notion, the underlying idea is very simple. Figure 6.11 illustrates the type of configuration in which c-command occurs.

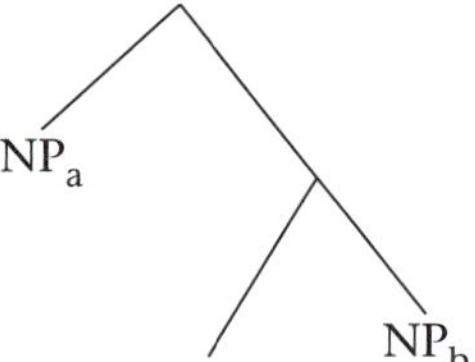

Figure 6.11 The c-command configuration

When trying to determine c-command relations, you can either use the definition in *36* or apply the template in Figure 6.11 to the tree structure being analyzed.

We can now formulate the constraint on the interpretation of reflexives, called **Principle A**, as follows.

37)

Principle A
A reflexive pronoun must have an antecedent that c-commands it in the same minimal S.

This means that the antecedent and reflexive pronoun should both be in the smallest S that contains the reflexive pronoun. When using Principle A, the key step involves determining whether a potential antecedent c-commands the reflexive pronoun. Compare in this regard the status of the NPs *that boy* and *that boy's teacher* in Figure 6.12.

Since the first category above *that boy's teacher* (namely, S) contains the reflexive, this NP c-commands *himself* according to our definition and can therefore serve as its antecedent. As we have already seen, the sentence has this interpretation.

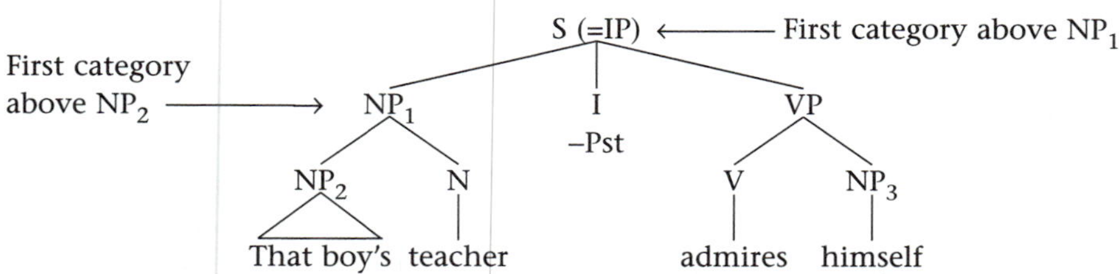

Figure 6.12 Structure illustrating c-command relations. NP_1 c-commands NP_3, but NP_2 does not.

In contrast, the first category above NP_2 (*that boy*) is NP_1, as illustrated in Figure 6.12. Since NP_1 does not contain *himself* (NP_3), *that boy* (NP_2) does not c-command *himself* (NP_3) according to our definition and therefore cannot serve as its antecedent.

Now let us consider the interpretation of pronominals. As the following example shows, the interpretation of the pronominal *him* contrasts sharply with that of the reflexive *himself* in the structure that we have been considering. Thus, *him* can refer to the boy but not to the boy's teacher—the opposite of what we observed for *himself.*

38)

That boy's teacher admires him.

How are we to account for these facts? The relevant constraint, called **Principle B**, is stated in *39*.

39)

Principle B

A pronominal must not have an antecedent that c-commands it in the same minimal S.

To see how this principle works, consider the structure in Figure 6.13.

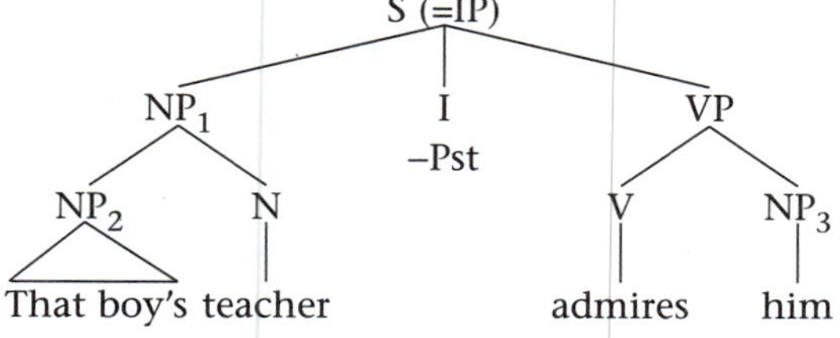

Figure 6.13 Structure containing a pronominal

In this structure, NP_1 (*that boy's teacher*) c-commands *him* since the first category above it (namely, S) also contains *him*. Principle B therefore prevents NP_1 from serving as antecedent for *him*. In contrast, NP_2 (*the boy*) does not c-command *him* since the first category above it (namely, NP_1) does not contain the pronoun. Thus, nothing prevents the interpretation in which *him* and *that boy* refer to the same person.

There is much more that can and should be said about the interpretation of pronouns. However, the examples we have just considered suffice to illustrate the crucial point in all of this, which is that syntactic structure plays an important role in the interpretation of both pronominals and reflexive pronouns.

4 OTHER FACTORS IN SENTENCE INTERPRETATION

Syntactic structure provides only a part of the information needed to interpret a sentence. Other necessary information comes from **pragmatics**, which includes the speaker's and addressee's background attitudes and beliefs, their understanding of the context in which a sentence is uttered, and their knowledge of how language can be used to inform, to persuade, to mislead, and so forth. This section focuses on the role of pragmatics in sentence interpretation.

4.1 THE ROLE OF BELIEFS AND ATTITUDES

As we saw in the preceding section, the grammar includes a structural principle (Principle B) that regulates the interpretation of pronominals such as *he* and *they*. However, as the following sentences show, nonlinguistic knowledge and beliefs can also play an important role in selecting the antecedent for a pronominal.

40)

a. The judge denied the prisoner's request because he was cautious.
b. The judge denied the prisoner's request because he was dangerous.

These two sentences have identical syntactic structures, differing only in the choice of the adjective in the second clause (*cautious* in the first sentence versus *dangerous* in the second). Yet most people feel that *he* refers to the judge in *40a* but to the prisoner in *40b*. Why should this be?

The crucial factor involves our beliefs about people in our society and their likely characteristics and behavior. All other things being equal, we are more likely to believe that a judge is cautious and a prisoner dangerous than vice versa. This in turn leads us to interpret the pronoun as referring to the judge in the first sentence in *40* but to the prisoner in the second.

Presupposition

There are many other ways in which a speaker's beliefs can be reflected in language use. Compare in this regard the following two sentences.

41)

a. Have you stopped exercising regularly?
b. Have you tried exercising regularly?

Use of the verb *stop* implies a belief on the part of the speaker that the listener has been exercising regularly. No such assumption is associated with the verb *try*.

The assumption or belief implied by the use of a particular word or structure is called a **presupposition**. The following two sentences provide another example of this.

42)

a. Nick admitted that the team had lost.
b. Nick said that the team had lost.

Choice of the verb *admit* in *42a* indicates that the speaker is presupposing the truth of the claim that the team lost. No such presupposition is associated with the choice of the verb *say* in *42b*, where the speaker is simply reporting Nick's statement without taking a position on its accuracy.

Still another type of presupposition is illustrated in *43*.

43)

a. Abraham Lincoln was assassinated in 1865.
b. Abraham Lincoln was murdered in 1865.

Notice that use of the verb *assassinate* in *43a* involves the assumption that Abraham Lincoln was a prominent person, but that no such presupposition is associated with the verb *murder*.

4.2 SETTING

As noted at the beginning of this section, the pragmatic factors relevant to sentence interpretation can include knowledge of the context in which a sentence is uttered, including its physical environment or **setting**.

All languages have forms whose use and interpretation depend on the location of the speaker and/or hearer within a particular setting. Called spatial **deictics**, these forms are exemplified in English by words such as *this* and *here* (proximity to the speaker) versus *that* and *there* (proximity to the hearer and/or distance from the speaker). Thus, if Steve and Brian are sitting across from each other at a table, each would refer to a plate directly in front of him as *this plate* and to a plate in front of the other or a plate distant from both as *that plate*. Without an understanding of how the setting in which a sentence is uttered can influence the choice of words such as *this* and *that*, it would be impossible for speakers of English to use or interpret these forms correctly.

As the preceding examples show, English makes a two-way distinction in its expression of deictic contrasts. However, many languages have a three-way system that may be sensitive to distance from the speaker, the addressee, or both (depending on the language). (See Table 6.17.)

Table 6.17 Languages with a three-way deictic distinction

Language	*'this'*	*'that'*	*'that over there'*
Spanish	este	ese	aquel
Japanese	kono	sono	ano
Korean	i	ku	ce
Palauan	tia	tilęcha	se
Turkish	/bu/	/ʃu/	/o/

An even more complex system is found in the Amerindian language Tlingit, which makes a four-way distinction: *yáa* 'this one right here', *héi* 'this one nearby', *wée* 'that one over there', and *yóo* 'that one far off'.

Determiners are not the only type of element whose use and interpretation require reference to features of the setting. In English, for example, deictic contrasts are also crucial to the understanding of such commonly used verbs as *come* and *go*. Notice in this regard the striking difference in perspective found in the following two sentences.

44)

a. The bear is coming into the tent!
b. The bear is going into the tent!

Whereas *come* with a third-person subject implies movement toward the speaker (hence we can infer that the person who utters *44a* is probably in the tent), *go* with the same type of subject suggests movement away from the speaker.

4.3 Discourse

An additional source of contextual information relevant to sentence interpretation can be found in **discourse**—the connected series of utterances produced during a conversation, a lecture, a story, or other speech event. The importance of discourse stems from the fact that individual sentences commonly include elements whose interpretation can only be determined with the help of information in preceding utterances. For instance, each of the italicized words in the following passage relies for its interpretation on information encoded in a preceding sentence. We interpret *there* with reference to *in the park*, *she* with reference to *a little girl*, and *it* with reference to *a rabbit*.

45)

A little girl went for a walk in the park. While *there*, *she* saw a rabbit. Since *it* was injured, *she* took *it* home.

One of the most important contrasts in the study of discourse involves the distinction between new and old information. **Old** (or **given**) **information** consists of the knowledge that the speaker assumes is available to the addressee at the time of the utterance, either because it is shared by both or because it has already been introduced into the discourse. In contrast, **new information** involves knowledge that is introduced into the discourse for the first time. Consider the contrast between the following two sentences.

46)

a. The man is at the front door.
b. A man is at the front door.

Choice of *the* as the determiner for *man* in *46a* suggests that the referent of the phrase is someone who has already been mentioned in the discourse and is therefore known to the addressee (old information). In contrast, choice of the determiner *a* in *46b* implies that the referent is being introduced into the discourse for the first time (new information).

Notice that both sentences in *46* use *the* as the determiner for *front door* and that the indefinite determiner *a* would not be natural in this context. This is because the setting for the conversation is likely to include only one front door. Since this information is likely to be known to both the speaker and the addressee (i.e., it is old information), *the* is the right determiner to use in this context.

Topics

Another important notion for the study of discourse is that of **topic**, which corresponds to what a sentence or a portion of the discourse is about. Consider the following passage.

47)

Once upon a time there was a merchant with two sons. The older son wanted to be a scholar. He spent his time reading and studying. As for the younger son, he preferred to travel and see the world.

The first sentence in this passage introduces a merchant and his two sons as new information. A topic (the older son) is selected in the second sentence and maintained in the third, in which *he* refers back to the older son. The final sentence then switches to a new topic (the younger son), providing some information about him. This switch is facilitated by the expression *as for*, which can be used in English to mark new topics.

There is a strong tendency in language to encode the topic as the subject of a sentence. This is why (as mentioned in Section 1.2) it is natural to interpret the active sentence in *48a* as being about the police and the passive sentence in *b* as being about the burglar (see also Section 6 of Chapter 5).

48)

a. The police chased the burglar.
b. The burglar was chased by the police.

In some languages, a special affix is used to identify the topic. The following sentences from Japanese illustrate this phenomenon (Nom = nominative, the subject marker; Top = topic marker; Ques = question marker).

49)

Speaker A:	Dare-ga kimasita-ka? Who-Nom came-Ques?
Speaker B:	John-ga kimasita. John-Nom came.
Speaker A:	John-wa dare-to kimasita-ka? John-Top who-with came-Ques? 'Who did John come with?'

The topic marker in Japanese (the suffix *-wa*) is distinguished from the subject marker (*-ga*) by its use to mark old or background information. This is why speaker B responds to A's first question by using the subject marker on the NP *John*. Because this NP provides new information (in answer to A's question), the topic marker would be inappropriate. However, once it has been established that John is the person who came, the corresponding NP can then bear the topic marker. This is precisely what happens in Speaker A's final utterance, in which the NP *John* (now associated with previously established information) is marked by the topic suffix *-wa*.

4.4 Conversational maxims

In addition to background beliefs, setting, and discourse, there is at least one other major type of information that enters into the interpretation of utterances. This information has to do with the "rules for conversation"—our understanding of how language is used in particular situations to convey a message. For example, if I ask you, *Would you like to go to a movie tonight?* and you respond by saying *I have to study for an exam*, I know that you are declining my invitation even though there is nothing in the literal meaning of the sentence that says so. Moreover, I recognize that this is a perfectly appropriate way to respond. (Notice that the same could not be said of a response like *I have to scratch my arm* or *It's a bit warm in here*.)

As speakers of a language, we are able to draw inferences about what is meant but not actually said. Information that is conveyed in this way is called **conversational implicature**. The ease with which we recognize and interpret implicature stems from our knowledge of how people in our linguistic community use language to communicate with each other.

The general overarching guideline for conversational interactions is often called the **Cooperative Principle**.

50)

The Cooperative Principle
Make your contribution appropriate to the conversation.

More specific **conversational maxims** or guidelines ensure that conversational interactions actually satisfy the Cooperative Principle, as shown in Table 6.18.

Table 6.18 Some conversational maxims

The Maxim of Relation
Be relevant.

The Maxim of Quality
Try to make your contribution one that is true. (Do not say things that are false or for which you lack adequate evidence.)

The Maxim of Quantity
Do not make your contribution more or less informative than required.

The Maxim of Manner
Avoid ambiguity and obscurity; be brief and orderly.

These maxims are responsible for regulating normal conversation but, as we will see, each can be suspended under certain circumstances to create particular effects.

Relation

The **Maxim of Relation** gives listeners a "bottom line" for inferring the intent of other speakers. For example, it is because of this maxim that we are able to interpret the utterance *I have to study for an exam* (in response to the question *Would you like to go to a movie?*) as a 'no'.

Failure to respect the Maxim of Relation creates a peculiar effect. For example, if someone asks you *Have you finished that term paper yet?* and you respond *It's been raining a lot lately, hasn't it?* you violate the Maxim of Relation by not responding in a relevant way. But by giving this response, you signal that you want to change the topic of conversation.

Quality

The **Maxim of Quality** requires that the statements used in conversations have some factual basis. If, for example, I ask *What's the weather like?* and someone responds *It's snowing*, I will normally assume that this statement provides reliable information about the current weather.

In order to achieve irony or sarcasm, however, it is sometimes possible to abandon the Maxim of Quality and say something that one knows to be false. Thus, if two people live in the middle of a sweltering desert and one person insists on asking every morning *What's the weather like?* it might be appropriate for the other person to respond sarcastically *Oh, today it's snowing, as usual*, perhaps with a particular facial expression or intonation to indicate that the statement was not intended as a true report of the facts.

Considerations of politeness can also justify suspension of the Maxim of Quality. For instance, in order to avoid hurt feelings, you might congratulate a fellow student on a presentation, even though you thought that it was the worst thing you ever heard.

Quantity

The **Maxim of Quantity** introduces some very subtle guidelines into a conversation. Imagine, for example, that someone asks me where a famous American author lives. The nature of my response will depend in large part on how much information I believe to be appropriate for that point in the conversation. If I know that the other person is simply curious about which part of the country the author lives in, it might suffice to respond *in Mississippi*. On the other hand, if I know that the person wants to visit the author, then much more specific information (perhaps even an address) is appropriate.

The Maxim of Quantity can be suspended in order to mislead a conversational partner. For example, if someone asks me where Mary is and I know that Mary does not want any visitors, I might respond by saying *I think she went downtown or something* even though I know precisely where she is. In responding in this way, I am not being untruthful since I have said nothing false, but by giving less information than is appropriate, I am violating the Maxim of Quantity and hence being misleading.

Manner

The **Maxim of Manner** imposes several constraints on language use, two of which will be exemplified here. First, imagine that I refer to a particular person as *the man who Mary lives with*. A listener would be justified in concluding that the man in question is not Mary's husband. This is because, by the Maxim of Manner, a briefer and less obscure description, *Mary's husband*, would have been used if it could have correctly described Mary's companion.

Second, imagine that an employer asks me about a former student of mine who has applied for a job and I say, with some sarcasm, *You will be fortunate indeed if you can get him to work for you*. By using a sentence that can be interpreted in two very different ways ('You will be glad to have him on your staff' versus 'It is not easy to get him to do any work'), I violate the Maxim of Manner by using an ambiguous structure. Since the maxims are violated only for specific purposes, the employer would be justified in doubting the sincerity of my recommendation.

Summing up

The study of **semantics** is concerned with a broad range of phenomena including the nature of **meaning**, the role of syntactic structure in the interpretation of sentences, and the effect of **pragmatics** on the understanding of utterances. Although much remains to be done in each of these areas, work in recent years has at least begun to identify the type of relations, mechanisms, and principles involved in the understanding of language. These include the notions of **extension** and **intension** in the case of word meaning, **thematic roles** in the case of NPs, and **c-command** in the case of pronouns. Other factors known to be involved in an utterance's interpretation include **constructional meaning**, the speaker's and hearer's background beliefs (as manifested, for example, in **presuppositions**), the context provided by the setting and the **discourse**, and the **maxims** associated with the **Cooperative Principle**.

Key terms

General terms

meaning
semantics

Terms concerning semantic relations among words

antonyms
homophony
lexical ambiguity
polysemy
synonyms

Terms concerning semantic relations in sentences

contradiction
entailment
paraphrases
truth conditions

Terms concerning meaning

componential analysis
connotation
denotation
extension
intension
referents
semantic decomposition
semantic features

Terms concerning how concepts are encoded

conflation pattern
evidentiality
fuzzy concept
graded (membership)
grammaticized (concepts)
lexicalization
metaphor
prototypical
spatial metaphors

General terms concerning the interpretation of sentences

constructional meaning
readings
structurally ambiguous

Terms concerning thematic roles in sentences

agent
goal
location
source
thematic grid
thematic roles
theme

Terms concerning the interpretation of pronouns

antecedent
c-command
Principle A
Principle B
pronominals
pronouns
reflexive pronouns

Terms concerning pragmatics

conversational implicature
conversational maxims
Cooperative Principle
deictics
discourse
Maxim of Manner
Maxim of Quality
Maxim of Quantity
Maxim of Relation
new information
old (given) information
pragmatics
presupposition
setting
topic

Sources

Surveys of the nature of word meaning and semantic relations can be found in many introductory books on semantics, including those recommended below. A prominent advocate of componential analysis is Ray Jackendoff, whose book *Semantic Structures* (Cambridge, MA: MIT Press, 1991) reviews earlier ideas in addition to offering new proposals. The discussion of a semantic constraint on double object patterns draws on the proposal put forward by Steven Pinker in *Learnability and Cognition* (Cambridge, MA: MIT Press, 1989). The discussion of fuzzy categories and graded membership in Section 2 draws from Part 1 of *Women, Fire, and Dangerous Things* by G. Lakoff (Chicago: University of Chicago Press, 1987) and the references cited there. The discussion of metaphor takes as its starting point the book *Metaphors We Live By*, cited below. The four Inuktitut words for *snow* in Table 6.7 are from *The Handbook of American Indian Languages* by F. Boas (Washington: Smithsonian Institution, 1911); for a longer list of words for *snow*, see *Dictionnaire français-eskimau du parler de l'Ungava* (Québec: Presses de l'Université Laval, 1970); see also "The Great Eskimo Vocabulary Hoax" by G. Pullum in *Natural Language and Linguistic Theory* 7 (1989): 275–81. The discussion of verbs of motion is based on the paper "Lexicalization Patterns: Semantic Structure in Lexical Form" by L. Talmy in *Language Typology and Syntactic Description*, Vol. 3, edited by T. Shopen (New York: Cambridge University Press, 1985), pp. 57–149. Data on Hidatsa evidentiality morphemes in the same section is from *Hidatsa Syntax* by G.H. Matthews (The Hague: Mouton, 1965).

The treatment of structural ambiguity, thematic role assignment, and pronoun interpretation in this chapter presents slightly simplified versions of views widely held within generative grammar in the early 1990s. For a summary of the last two issues, see *Introduction to Government and Binding Theory*, 2nd ed., by L. Haegeman (Cambridge, MA: Blackwell, 1994). The discussion of constructional meaning is based on *Constructions: A Construction Grammar Approach to Argument Structure* by A. Goldberg (Chicago: University of Chicago Press, 1995).

The data used in the discussion of deictics and in question 15 come from "Deixis" by S. Anderson and E. Keenan in *Language Typology and Syntactic Description*, Vol. 3, edited by T. Shopen (New York: Cambridge University Press, 1985), pp. 259–308. The discussion of topicalization draws on the "Major Functions of the Noun Phrase" by A. Andrews in *Language Typology and Syntactic Description*, Vol. 1, edited by T. Shopen (New York: Cambridge University Press, 1985), pp. 62–154. The discussion of the

Cooperative Principle and the maxims of conversation is based primarily on "Logic and Conversation" by Paul Grice in *Syntax and Semantics*, Vol. 3, edited by P. Cole and J. Morgan (New York: Academic Press, 1975), pp. 41–58, and the paper by L. Horn cited below.

The exercises for this chapter were prepared by Joyce Hildebrand.

Recommended reading

Chierchia, Gennaro, and Sally McConnell-Ginet. 1990. *Meaning and Grammar.* Cambridge, MA: MIT Press.

Horn, Laurence. 1988. "Pragmatic Theory." In *Linguistics: The Cambridge Survey*. Vol. 1. Edited by F. Newmeyer, 113–45. New York: Cambridge University Press.

Ladusaw, William. 1988. "Semantic Theory." In *Linguistics: The Cambridge Survey*. Vol. 1. Edited by F. Newmeyer, 89–112. New York: Cambridge University Press.

Lakoff, George, and Mark Johnson. 1982. *Metaphors We Live By*. Chicago: University of Chicago Press.

Lappin, Shalom (ed.). 1997. *The Handbook of Contemporary Semantic Theory.* Boston: Blackwell.

McCawley, James. 1993. *Everything That Linguists Have Always Wanted to Know about Logic*. 2nd ed. Chicago: University of Chicago Press.

Prince, Ellen. 1988. "Discourse Analysis: A Part of the Study of Linguistic Competence." In *Linguistics: The Cambridge Survey*. Vol. 2. Edited by F. Newmeyer, 164–82. New York: Cambridge University Press.

Saeed, John. 1996. *Semantics*. Boston: Blackwell.

Schiffrin, Deborah. 1993. *Approaches to Discourse: Language as Social Interaction.* Boston: Blackwell.

Questions

1. Two relations involving word meanings are antonymy and synonymy. Which relation is illustrated in each of the pairs of words below?

a) flourish-thrive	e) uncle-aunt
b) intelligent-stupid	f) intelligent-smart
c) casual-informal	g) flog-whip
d) young-old	h) drunk-sober

2. It was noted in this chapter that a single form can have two or more meanings. Depending on whether these meanings are related to each other, this phenomenon involves polysemy or homophony. Which of these two relations is exemplified by the forms below?

a) grass:	herbage used for grazing animals; marijuana
b) *leech:*	a bloodsucking worm; a hanger-on who seeks advantage
c) *range:*	a cooking stove; a series of mountains
d) *key:*	an instrument used to apply to a lock; an answer sheet for a test or assignment
e) *steal/steel*:	rob; a type of metal

f) *race:* the act of running competitively; people belonging to the same genetic grouping

g) *flower/flour:* a blossom; finely ground wheat

3. Three semantic relations among sentences were covered in this chapter: paraphrase, entailment, and contradiction. Which of these relations is exemplified in each of the following pairs of sentences?
   a) I saw Timothy at the anniversary party.
      It was Timothy that I saw at the anniversary party.
   b) Jules is Mary's husband.
      Mary is married.
   c) My pet cobra likes the taste of chocolate fudge.
      My pet cobra finds chocolate fudge tasty.
   d) Vera is an only child.
      Olga is Vera's sister.
   e) It is fifty miles to the nearest service station.
      The nearest service station is fifty miles away.
   f) My cousin Bryan teaches at the community college for a living.
      My cousin Bryan is a teacher.

4. In discussing the nature of meaning, we noted that it is necessary to distinguish between intension and extension. Describe the intensions and the extensions of each of these phrases.
   a) the President of the United States
   b) the Queen of England
   c) the capital of Canada
   d) women who have walked on the moon
   e) my linguistics professor

5. In our discussion of semantic decomposition, we noted that at least some words have meanings that can be represented in terms of smaller semantic features. Four such words are *dog, puppy, cat,* and *kitten.*

   i) Attempt to provide the semantic features associated with each of these words.
   ii) How are the pairs *dog-puppy* and *cat-kitten* different from *man-boy* and *woman-girl*?
   iii) Try to provide semantic features for the words *circle, triangle,* and *quadrangle.* What problems do you encounter?

6. Each of the following words is associated with a concept.

a) island	e) food
b) soft	f) husband
c) white	g) baseball bat
d) wristwatch	h) mountain

   i) Which of these examples are fuzzy concepts?
   ii) Choose one of the fuzzy concepts above. Name one prototypical member of that concept and one member that is closer to the concept boundary.
   iii) Draw a diagram for the concept 'dwelling' similar to that of Figure 6.2 in this chapter. Do the same for the concept 'vehicle'.

7. Examine the following sets of sentences, each of which includes words or phrases used metaphorically.
   a) She gave him an icy stare.
      He gave her the cold shoulder.
      He exudes a lot of warmth toward people.
      They got into a heated argument.
   b) He drops a lot of hints.
      The committee picked up on the issue.
      She dumps all her problems on her friends.
      Although he disagreed, he let it go.
   c) the eye of a needle
      the foot of the bed
      the hands of the clock
      the arm of a chair
      the table legs
   d) This lecture is easy to digest.
      He just eats up the lecturer's words.
      Chew on this thought for a while.
      Listen to this juicy piece of gossip.

   For each set of sentences:
   i) Identify the words or phrases that are used metaphorically in each sentence.
   ii) Determine the basis for each of these metaphor sets.
      Use the pattern: "The metaphors in (x) describe _____ in terms of _____."
      Example: The metaphors in (a) describe human relationships in terms of temperature.

8. The section on lexicalization of concepts discussed how some languages simultaneously express motion and path, motion and movement, and/or motion and thing moving in motion verbs. Change the sentence *He moved the goods by truck to the warehouse* so that both movement and vehicle used to move are lexicalized in one verb. What other verbs express a similar combination of concepts?

9. Consider the following Fijian pronouns.

au	1st person singular 'me'
iko	2nd person singular 'you'
koya	3rd person singular 'him/her/it'
kedaru	1st person dual 'you and me'
keirau	1st person dual 'one other (not you) and me'
kemudrau	2nd person dual 'you (two)'
rau	3rd person dual 'them (two)'
kedatou	1st person trial 'two others (including you) and me'
keitou	1st person trial 'two others (excluding you) and me'
kemudou	2nd person trial 'you (three)'
iratou	3rd person trial 'them (three)'
keda	1st person plural 'us (more than three, including you)'
keimami	1st person plural 'us (more than three, excluding you)'
kemuni:	2nd person plural 'you (more than three)'
ira	3rd person plural 'them (more than three)'

i) Some concepts are grammaticized in the Fijian pronoun system but not grammaticized in the English pronoun system. Can you identify them?

ii) Which concept is grammaticized in the English pronoun system but not in the Fijian system?

10. Each NP in the following sentences has a thematic role that represents the part that its referent plays in the situation described by the sentence.
    a) The man chased the intruder.
    b) The cat jumped from the chair onto the table.
    c) Aaron wrote a letter to Marilyn.
    d) The governor entertained the guests in the lounge.
    e) Henry mailed the manuscript from Atlanta.

    Using the terms described in this chapter, label the thematic role of each NP in these sentences and identify the assigner for each thematic role.

    Example: Bill wrote a novel in the park.

11. Each of the following sentences has undergone a movement transformation.
    a) What should Larry give to the bride?
    b) Who will Liane kiss?
    c) Which house will the group leave from?
    d) What might Marvin forget on the bus?
    e) The necklace was stolen by the burglar.
    f) The ball was thrown to Evan by Louise.

    Write out the deep structure string for each of these sentences and mark all thematic roles and thematic role assigners.

    Example: a) Larry should give what to the bride

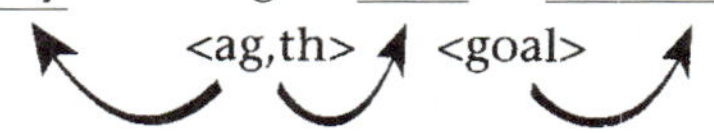

12. One of the relations involved in the interpretation of pronouns is that of c-command. Examine the following tree structure for the sentence *Marie's sister gave herself a haircut.*

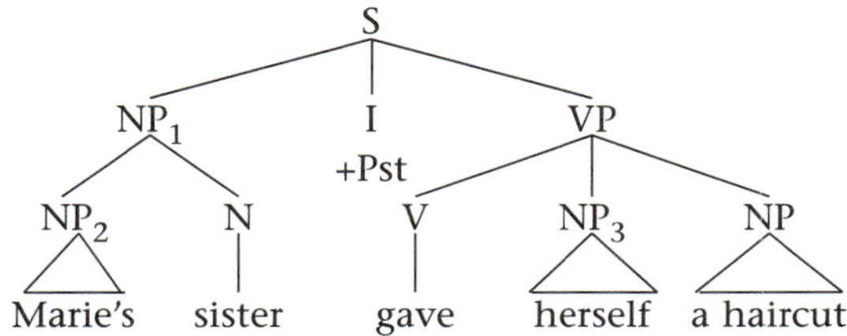

i) Who does *herself* refer to in this sentence?

ii) Does NP_2 c-command NP_3?

iii) How does your answer to *ii* relate to your answer to *i?*

iv) Does the antecedent change if you change *herself* to *her*? Why?

13. In the following sentence, the pronoun *she* could, according to Principle B, refer to either *the architect* or *the secretary*.
    The architect gave the secretary a raise after she typed the report.
    i) Which interpretation for *she* comes to mind first?
    ii) Why?
    iii) What happens to the pronoun's interpretation if you change the word *secretary* to *janitor*?

14. In the following pairs of sentences, one of the two sentences contains a presupposition relating to the truth of the complement clause.
    a) John regrets that Maria went to the graduation ceremony.
       John believes that Maria went to the graduation ceremony.
    b) The captain thought that the ship was in danger.
       The captain realized that the ship was in danger.
    c) It is significant that the criminal was sentenced.
       It is likely that the criminal was sentenced.

    For each pair:
    i) Identify the sentence that contains this presupposition and state what the presupposition is.
    ii) What word is responsible for the presupposition?

15. In Malagasy, the use of the deictics *ety* 'here' and *aty* 'there' depend on whether the object in question is visible to the speaker.
    a) *Ety ny tranony.* 'Here is his house (visible to the speaker).'
    b) *Aty ny tranony.* 'There is his house (not visible to the speaker).'
       How does this differ from the English use of *here/there*?

16. The syntactic construction *It was* _____ *that* _____ is called a 'cleft construction' and is used in certain discourse contexts. Consider the following conversations involving cleft constructions.
    a) *A:* Did Sally claim that she saw a flying saucer last night?
       B: No, it was a meteorite that Sally claimed she saw last night.
    b) *A:* Did Sally claim that she saw a flying saucer last night?
       B: No, it was Sally that claimed she saw a meteorite last night.
    c) *A:* Did Sally claim that she saw a flying saucer last night?
       B: No, it was last week that Sally claimed she saw a flying saucer.

    i) Is B's response equally acceptable in all three interactions?
    ii) Choose one of the discourses in which B's response is appropriate. How do the underlined parts correspond to new and old information?
    iii) For the discourse in which B's response is unacceptable, explain why it is unacceptable.
    iv) In addition to the cleft construction, identify the way in which new information is marked phonetically in B's responses.

17. Each of the following examples contains a conversational implicature.
    a) *A:* Have you washed the floor and done the dishes?
       B: I've washed the floor.
    b) *A:* Did you get hold of Carl yet?
       B: I tried to call him yesterday.

c) *A:* What did you think of the movie?
 B: Well, the supporting actor was great.
d) *A:* Do you have any pets?
 B: Yes, I have two cats.

What is the implicature for each example?

For the student linguist

ELVIS'S BIGGEST FAN CLEANS OUT BANK—ACCOMPLICE LAUNDERS THE DOUGH

PEORIA—Blanche VanBuren, an old Elvis fan from Oneida, Illinois, cleaned out the Peoria Institution for Savings yesterday with nothing but a sawed-off broom and old shotgun.

Darrel Apley, the owner of Union Electric and a shocked witness who preferred to remain anonymous said, "Blanche should be at home at this time of the day. Her favorite soap is on the TV."

A teller said, "Someone came in a truck. I heard some screams coming from inside. People were rolling on the floor. Then it was over and I smoked a pack of cigarettes on the way home."

By the time the Bureau had been hauled in, the local pigs had decided someone else had done it. But the tip-off, by Oneida Otters star center Billie Jones, was about her partner. "Everyone thought two people were involved from the beginning," Jones claimed. "But it was when I saw the suds in the record store behind the pizzeria that it all came together."

The King could not be reached for comment by press time.

It's surprisingly easy to write an article in which every sentence is ambiguous. It's much harder—maybe even impossible—to write one that isn't ambiguous, or to write anything that isn't ambiguous. Maybe this explains why legal language is so tedious in its attempt to be unambiguous and why our court system is so clogged (obstructed, that is, not filled with Dutch wooden shoes), and why multiple-choice exams are so awful.

To show that the sentences in this article really are ambiguous, I'll attempt to disambiguate the first couple of paragraphs of Blanche's story in painstaking detail. By the time I'm done, you'll probably be able to see ambiguity everywhere you go.

Blanche VanBuren is an elderly Elvis aficionado who resides in Oneida, Illinois. And she's just plain old, all would agree (see tree *1B*). Or, when considering Elvis fans from Oneida, she's getting up in years (see tree *1A*), but in some other context she'd be considered pretty young (because most of the Elvis fans in Oneida are teeny-boppers, whereas Blanche is pushing thirty). Maybe Blanche has been an Elvis fan for a long time (*1B*). Or maybe, just maybe, most Oneidan Elvis fans are new to their admiration of him (it began with the postage stamp), but Blanche has loved Elvis since 1984, when she encountered him on a spaceship, and is therefore, comparatively speaking, an old Elvis-fan-from-Oneida (tree *1A*). Of course, she could also be a fan of only the *old* Elvis—that is, she liked his Vegas days but hated the early stuff. You can figure out the tree for this reading.

Let's assume Blanche is elderly. And a neat freak, because she washed the Peoria Institution for Savings from top to bottom (taking the shotgun to teach a lesson to litterbugs). Then again, she might be an incredibly compulsive cleaner in her own house and spend so much money on lemon-scented antiseptics that she robbed the P.I.S. and took along that sawed-off broom because she was delirious from inhaling ammonia all day. Let's consider her implements. The shotgun was old. The broom was sawed-off. Was the broom old? We don't know; the story doesn't provide information on its age. Was the shotgun sawed-off? This is a classic case of structural ambiguity, made famous by the example "the old men and women," and the answer should be obvious by now (but see trees *2A* and *2B* for confirmation).

The article does make clear that the event of interest took place yesterday, but I'm wondering whether Blanche habitually cleans out banks, and it just happened to be the P.I.S. yesterday, or if this was an out-of-the-blue cleaning or what. Could be that she cleans the P.I.S. every day, but usually she has more equipment than a broom and a gun.

Then there's the possibility that Blanche is an early model electric cooling device (or an antique paper and balsa wood construction), once owned (and affectionately named) by Elvis, which either: (a) blew all the dirt out of the bank or (b) was brought to life and performed the robbery. You never know.

What about Darrel Apley? If the writer of this article had any ethics, he (Darrel) is not the person who owns Union Electric, nor is he (Darrel) a shocked witness who preferred to remain anonymous. If the writer had ethics there would have to have been three different people who all said "Blanche should be at home . . ." and one of them is Darrel, one's the owner of U.E., and the third is shocked and prefers anonymity (tree *3A*). However, sloppy writing and broken promises are everywhere, and it's quite possible that *the owner of Union Electric* and *a shocked witness who preferred to remain anonymous* are actually intended to describe Darrel (tree *3B*).

"Blanche should be at home at this time of the day." Should? As in, given her normal patterns, the most likely case is that Blanche is at home? Or *should* as in if that lowdown, bank-thieving woman knew what was good for her she'd be at home watching *All My Children*?

"Her favorite soap is on the TV." This one's easy; it's nothing but lexical ambiguity. Her favorite soap could be Ivory Family Size or the aforementioned *All My Children*. If this were spoken instead of written, we'd have to explore the option that her favorite soap is called "On the TV," and actually, considering the doubts you might have about the writer's integrity, that could have been what Darrel (and maybe two others) meant. Of course, "on" is ambiguous between "being broadcast" or "on top of" but enough is enough.

The rest of the article you can disambiguate on your own. It's useful to draw trees for the structurally ambiguous parts and make sure the different interpretations match the trees. Every *written* sentence—every portion of material from one period to another—is ambiguous, but not every *S* in the technical, linguistic sense is ambiguous. Be sure to look for lexical ambiguity, structural ambiguity, and pronouns that could refer to a few different people. Also look carefully at Jones's quote—this one is hard but interesting. Finally, check out your local newspaper. I predict that many of the sentences in it are as ambiguous as the ones in this article. You could even examine the instructions for your next linguistics homework assignment and (politely) tease your instructor if they're not crystal clear. Be careful, though—he or she might hold you to the same standard in your writing.

TREES:

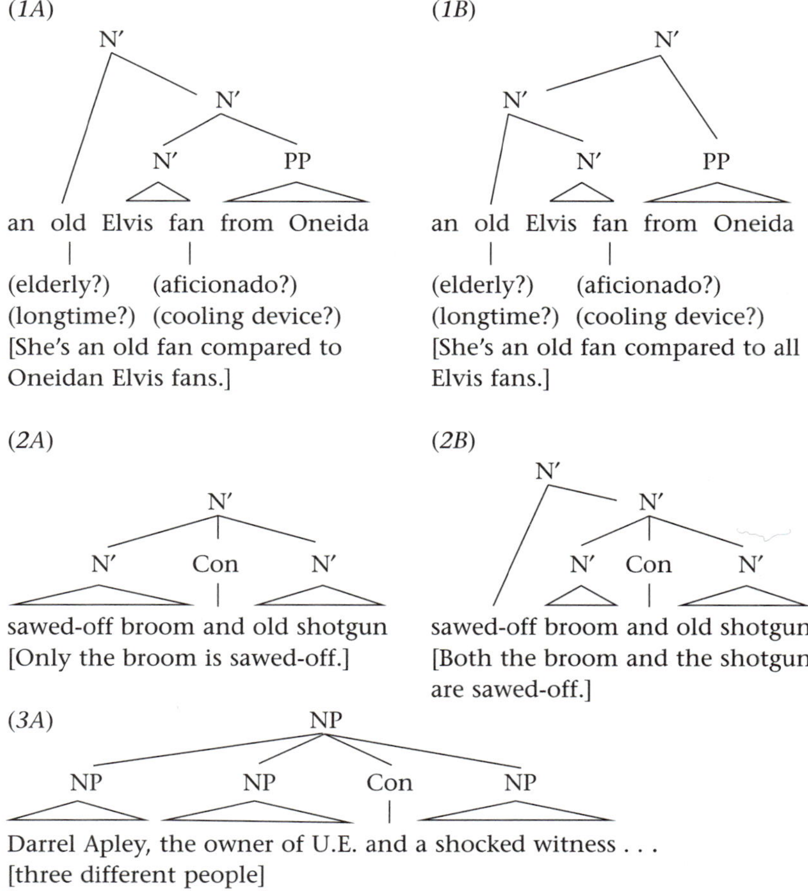

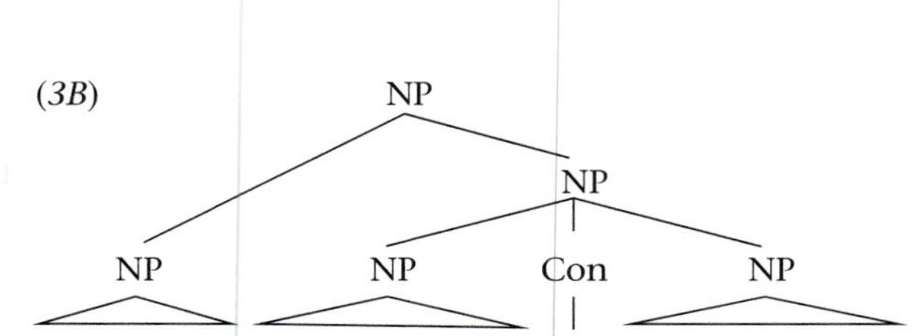

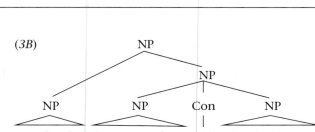

Darrel Apley, the owner of U.E. and a shocked witness . . .
[One person: "Darrell Apley, (who is) the owner . . . ," after "who is" has been deleted. Don't worry about the details of this structure.]

seven

HISTORICAL LINGUISTICS: THE STUDY OF LANGUAGE CHANGE

Robert W. Murray

Many men sayn that in sweveninges
Ther nys but fables and lesynges;
But men may some swevenes sene
Whiche hardely that false ne bene,
But afterwarde ben apparaunt.

– CHAUCER, *The Romance of the Rose* (c. 1370)

OBJECTIVES

In this chapter, you will learn

- how and why languages change over time
- how and why sound changes occur
- what kinds of changes occur in morphology and syntax
- ways in which words and their meanings change
- how linguists can reconstruct languages spoken in earlier times, based on the existing languages that are descended from them

Language change is both obvious and rather mysterious. The English of the late fourteenth century, for example, is so different from Modern English that without special training it is difficult to understand the opening lines to *The Romance of the Rose* cited above. Not only would these sentences have a foreign sound, but words and structures such as *sweveninges*, *lesynges*, and *false ne bene* are unfamiliar.[1] The existence of such differences between early and later variants of the same language raises questions as to how and why languages change over time.

Historical linguistics is concerned with both the description and explanation of language change. In this chapter we examine the nature and causes of language change and survey in some detail phonological, morphological, syntactic, lexical, and semantic change. We also explore techniques used to reconstruct linguistic prehistory and briefly discuss interrelated research into language acquisition and linguistic universals.

1 THE NATURE OF LANGUAGE CHANGE

All languages undergo change over time. English has undergone continuous and dramatic change throughout its three major periods: Old English (roughly from 450 to 1100), Middle English (from 1100 to 1500), and Modern English (from 1500 to the present). While Chaucer's Middle English is at least partially comprehensible today, Old English looks like a completely foreign language. The following is an extract from an eighth-century Old English document, a translation of Bede's Latin history of England. (The letter þ, called *thorn*, represented the phoneme /θ/ in Old English; here and elsewhere in this chapter ¯ marks a long vowel in the orthography.)

1)

and Seaxan þā sige geslōgan.
and Saxons the victory won
'And the Saxons won the victory.'

þā sendan hī hām ǣrenddracan.
then sent they home a messenger
'Then they sent home a messenger.'

These Old English sentences differ from their Modern English counterparts in many respects. In terms of pronunciation, for instance, the Old English word *hām* [haːm] 'home' in the second sentence became [hɔːm] in Middle English, and then [howm] in Modern English. In its morphology, Old English differed significantly from Modern English. The suffix *-an* on the Old English word for 'sent' indicates both past tense and plurality of the subject (*hī* 'they'). Differences in word order are also readily apparent, with the verb following both the subject and the direct object in the first sentence and preceding both the subject and the direct object in the second. Neither of these word orders would be acceptable in the Modern English forms of these sentences.

In addition, some Old English words have disappeared from use, as the unfamiliar *ǣrenddracan* 'messenger' and *sige* 'victory' indicate. Still other words have been maintained, but with a change in meaning. For example, the Old English word *geslōgan* (which we translated as 'won') is the past tense of the verb *slēan*, the Old English predecessor of our word *slay*. Although the Modern English meaning of this word in normal usage is restricted to the act of killing, the Old English verb could also mean 'to strike, beat, coin (money), and forge (weapons)'. As these examples imply, all components of the grammar from meaning (semantics) to individual sounds (phonology) are subject to change.

1.1 Systematicity of language change

A striking fact about language change in general is its regularity and systematicity. For example, the development of a fixed subject-verb-direct object (SVO) word order in English did not affect just a few verbs; all verbs in Modern English appear before rather than after the direct object. Similarly, the changes affecting the vowel in the word *hām* did not occur in that word only; they represent the regular development of the Old English vowel *ā* ([aː]) (see Table 7.1).

Table 7.1 Changes affecting Old English [aː]

Old English	*Middle English*	*Modern English*	
[baːt]	[bɔːt]	[bowt]	'boat'
[aːθ]	[ɔːθ]	[owθ]	'oath'
[staːn]	[stɔːn]	[stown]	'stone'

1.2 Causes of language change

The inevitability of language change is guaranteed by the way in which language is passed on from one generation to the next. Children do not begin with an intact grammar of the language being acquired but rather must construct a grammar on the basis of the available data (see Chapter 10). In such a situation it is hardly surprising that differences will arise, even if only subtle ones, from one generation to the next. Moreover, since all children use the same physiological and cognitive endowment in learning language, it is to be expected that the same patterns of change will be consistently and repeatedly manifested in all languages. Following is a brief overview of the principal causes of language change.

Articulatory simplification

As might be expected, most sound changes have a physiological basis. Since such sound changes typically result in **articulatory simplification**, they have traditionally been related to the idea of ease of articulation. Although this notion is difficult to define precisely, we can readily identify cases of articulatory simplification in our everyday speech, such as the deletion of a consonant in a complex cluster or, in some dialects, the insertion of a vowel to break up a complex cluster (see Table 7.2).

Table 7.2 Simplification of complex clusters

Deletion of a consonant			
[fɪfθ̲s]	→	[fɪfs]	'fifths'
Insertion of a vowel			
[æθlit]	→	[æθə̲lit]	'athlete'

Spelling pronunciation

Not all changes in pronunciation have a physiological motivation. A minor, but nevertheless important, source of change in English and other languages is **spelling pronunciation**. Since the written form of a word can differ significantly from the way it is pronounced, a new pronunciation can arise that seems to reflect more closely the spelling of the word. A case in point is the word *often*. Although this word was pronounced with a [t] in earlier English, the voiceless stop was subsequently lost, resulting in the pronunciation [ɔfən] (compare *soften*). However, since the letter *t* was retained in the spelling, [t] has been reintroduced into many speakers' pronunciation of this word.

Another case in point is the pronunciation of [s] in words such as *assume* and *consume*. Such words were originally pronounced with [s] as they are now, but **sound change** resulted in a pronunciation with [ʃ] (as in *assure*). Similar to the case of *often*, a pronunciation with [s] has been reintroduced into many dialects on the basis of the spelling (which remained unchanged even after the sound change took place). Since spelling tends to remain stable even though sound changes have occurred (English spelling began stabilizing more than three hundred years ago), spelling pronunciation can reintroduce a pronunciation that was earlier altered through sound change.

Analogy and reanalysis

Cognitive factors also play a role in change in all components of the grammar. Two sources of change having a cognitive basis are **analogy** and **reanalysis**. Analogy reflects the preference of speakers for regular patterns over irregular ones. It typically involves the extension or generalization of a regularity on the basis of the inference that if elements are alike in some respects, they should be alike in others as well. Both phonological and semantic characteristics can serve as a basis for analogy. For example, on the basis of its phonological similarity with verbs such as *sting/stung* and *swing/swung*, in some dialects *bring* has developed a form *brung*, as in *I('ve) brung it into the house*. The effects of analogy can also be observed in the speech of children, who often produce past tense forms such as *goed* and *knowed* analogous to *flowed* (see Chapter 10). As we will shortly see, analogy plays a very important role in morphological change as well.

Reanalysis is particularly common in morphological change. Morphological reanalysis typically involves an attempt to attribute a compound or root + affix structure to a word that was not formerly broken down into component morphemes. A classic example in English is the word *hamburger*, which originally referred to a type of meat patty deriving its name from the city of Hamburg in Germany. This word has been reanalyzed as consisting of two components, *ham* + *burger*. The latter morpheme has since appeared in many new forms, including *fishburger*, *chickenburger*, and even as a free morpheme *burger*. Note that the resulting reanalysis need not be correct. (There is usually no ham in a burger!)

Language contact

Another cause of language change is **language contact**. Language contact refers to the situation in which speakers of a language frequently interact with the speakers of another language or dialect. As a consequence, extensive **borrowing** can occur, particularly where there are significant numbers of bilinguals or multilinguals. Although borrowing can affect all components of the grammar, the lexicon is typically most affected. English, for example, has borrowed many Amerindian words, including *Mississippi*, *moccasin*, *totem*, *tomahawk*, *pecan*, *moose*, and *skunk*.

Among the effects that borrowing can have on the sound system are the introduction of new phonemes or allophones and changes in their distribution. For example, some English speakers pronounce the name of the classical composer *Bach* with the final velar fricative [x] found in the German pronunciation. If there is a significant number of borrowings from another language, the borrowed foreign segment can eventually become a new phoneme. In the early Middle English period, the London dialect had [f] but not [v] in word-initial position. The [v] was later introduced as a result of contact with other English dialects and with French, in which it did occur word-initially. This contact was a factor in the development of a contrast between /f/ and /v/ word-initially, as found in Modern English pairs such as *file* and *vile*.

Language (as well as dialect) contact also results in another minor but nevertheless important source of language change, **hypercorrection**. Hypercorrection occurs when a speaker who is attempting to speak another dialect or language overgeneralizes particular rules. For example, most Americans speak a dialect in which no distinction is made between intervocalic [t] and [d], so that words such as *latter* and *ladder* are both pronounced with an intervocalic flap [ɾ] (see Chapter 2). If a speaker from such a dialect attempts to emulate the pronunciation of a speaker from another dialect who does distinguish the two stops intervocalically, hypercorrection could result in the use of intervocalic [t] in words where [d] should be used—for example, the pronunciation *pro[t]igy* for *pro<u>d</u>igy*.

Another example of hypercorrection is the use of *I* in constructions such as *He saw John and I*. This usage is an overgeneralization of the rule that only *I* should be used in subject position, never *me*. According to this rule, *John and I are going* is correct but *John and me/me and John are going* is incorrect. For some speakers, hypercorrection has resulted in the inference that all coordinate phrases containing *me* (such as *John and me*) are incorrect, even when they serve as direct object (complement) of the verb. Note that even a person who says *He gave it to John and I* would not say *He saw I*.

2 SOUND CHANGE

Although all components of the grammar are susceptible to change over time, some types of change yield more obvious results than others. Variation and change are particularly noticeable in the phonology of a language. Several common types of sound change can be distinguished.

Most sound changes begin as subtle alterations in the sound pattern of a language in particular phonetic environments. The linguistic processes underlying such **phonetically conditioned change** are identical to the ones found in the phonology of currently spoken languages (see Chapter 2, Section 9). The application of such processes usually brings about an articulatory simplification, and over time significant changes in the phonology of a language can result.

Although all aspects of a language's phonology (e.g., tone, stress, and syllable structure) are subject to change over time, we will restrict our attention here to change involving segments. Since most sound changes involve sequences of segments, the main focus will be on **sequential change**. However, we will also discuss one common type of **segmental change** involving the simplification of an affricate. In addition, in order to demonstrate that more than just articulatory factors play a role in sound change, we will discuss a case of sound change based on auditory factors. All important sound changes discussed in this section and referred to in this chapter are found in the catalog of sound changes in Table 7.3.

Table 7.3 Catalog of sound changes

Sequential change	*Sequential change cont.*
Assimilation	Consonants
Place and/or manner of articulation	Deletion
Palatalization/affrication	Degemination
Nasalization	Frication
Umlaut	Voicing
Dissimilation	Rhotacism
Epenthesis (segment addition)	Consonantal strengthening
Metathesis (segment movement)	Glide strengthening
Weakening and deletion	*Segmental change*
Vowels	Deaffrication
Apocope	*Auditorily based change*
Syncope	Substitution
Vowel reduction	

2.1 SEQUENTIAL CHANGE

Assimilation

The most common type of sequential change is **assimilation**, which has the effect of increasing the efficiency of articulation through a simplification of articulatory movements. We will focus here on the four main types indicated in the catalog.

Partial assimilation involving place or manner of articulation is a very common change, which, over time, can result in **total assimilation**. In the Spanish and Latin examples in Table 7.4, the nasal assimilated in place of articulation to the following consonant.

Table 7.4 Assimilation in place of articulation in Spanish and Latin[2]

Old Spanish	semda	Modern Spanish	senda	'path'
Early Latin	inpossibilis	Later Latin	impossibilis	'impossible'

The first of the Old English examples in Table 7.5 shows voicing assimilation and the second shows the assimilation of nasality.

Table 7.5 Assimilation in manner of articulation in Old English

Early Old English	*Later Old English*	
slǣpde	slǣpte	'slept'
stefn	stemn	'stem (of a tree)'

In the Italian examples in Table 7.6, a stop assimilates totally to a following stop.

Table 7.6 Total assimilation in Italian

Latin	*Italian*	
octo (*c* = [k])	otto	'eight'
septem	sette	'seven'
damnum	danno	'damage'

Another type of assimilation is **palatalization**—the effect that front vowels and the palatal glide [j] typically have on velar, alveolar, and dental stops, making their place of articulation more palatal. If you compare your pronunciation of *keep* as opposed to *cot*, you will notice that the pronunciation of [k] in the former is much more palatal than in the latter due to the influence of [i]. Palatalization is often the first step in **affrication**, a change in which palatalized stops become affricates, either [ts] or [tʃ] if the original stop was voiceless or [dz] or [dʒ] if the original stop was voiced (see Table 7.7).

Table 7.7 Palatalization/affrication induced by front vowels and [j]

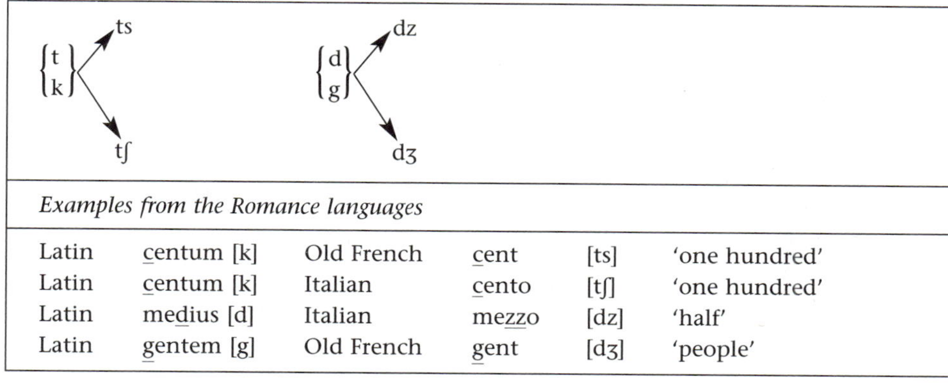

Examples from the Romance languages					
Latin	centum [k]	Old French	cent	[ts]	'one hundred'
Latin	centum [k]	Italian	cento	[tʃ]	'one hundred'
Latin	medius [d]	Italian	mezzo	[dz]	'half'
Latin	gentem [g]	Old French	gent	[dʒ]	'people'

Nasalization refers to the nasalizing effect that a nasal consonant can have on an adjacent vowel. This change occurred in both French and Portuguese, with the subsequent loss of the nasal consonant. (The pronunciation of the vowels in the examples in Table 7.8 underwent additional changes in height and backness in French.)

Table 7.8 Nasalization in Portuguese and French

Latin	*Portuguese*	*French*	
bon-	bom [bõ]	bon [bɔ̃]	'good'
un-	um [ũ]	un [œ̃]	'one'

Although assimilation is probably most common in the case of adjacent segments, it can also apply at a distance. A case in point is **umlaut**, the effect a vowel or sometimes a glide in one syllable can have on the vowel of another syllable, usually a preceding one. Umlaut (resulting in front rounded vowels [y] and [ø]) played an important role in Old English and is the source of irregular plurals such as *goose/geese* and *mouse/mice* in Modern English. For example, as Table 7.9 shows, the plural of the pre–Old English words gōs 'goose' and mūs 'mouse' was formed by adding a suffix -[i]. As a result, umlaut of the vowel in the preceding syllable occurred in the plural forms (see pre–Old English stages 1 and 2) but not in the singular forms. By early Old English, the suffix -[i] had been lost in a separate change leaving the umlauted vowel as the marker of the plural form. (Subsequent changes included the derounding of the umlauted vowels [ȳ] and [ø̄] yielding [ī] and [ē] respectively by Middle English, and the Great Vowel Shift as described in Section 2.4.

Table 7.9 Umlaut in English

Pre–Old English 1		*Pre–OE 2*		*Early OE*		*Subsequent changes*	
[gōs]	>	[gōs]	>	[gōs]	>	[gus]	'goose'
[gōsi]	>	[gø̄si]	>	[gø̄s]	>	[gis]	'geese'
[mūs]	>	[mūs]	>	[mūs]	>	[maws]	'mouse'
[mūsi]	>	[mȳsi]	>	[mȳs]	>	[majs]	'mice'

Dissimilation

Dissimilation, the process whereby one segment is made less like another segment in its environment, is much less frequent than assimilation. This type of change typically occurs when it would be difficult to articulate or perceive two similar sounds in close proximity. The word *anma* 'soul' in Late Latin, for example, was modified to *alma* in Spanish, thereby avoiding two consecutive nasal consonants. Like assimilation, dissimilation can also operate at a distance to affect nonadjacent segments. For instance, the Latin word *arbor* 'tree' became *árbol* in Spanish and *albero* in Italian, thereby avoiding two instances of [r] in adjacent syllables. (By contrast, dissimilation did not occur in French, where *arbre* has retained both instances of [r].)

Epenthesis

Another common sound change, **epenthesis**, involves the insertion of a consonant or vowel into a particular environment (see Table 7.10). In some cases, epenthesis results from the anticipation of an upcoming sound.

Table 7.10 Epenthesis in Old English

Earlier form	*Change*	*Later form*	
ganra	VnrV > VndrV	gandra	'gander'
simle	VmlV > VmblV	simble	'always'
ǣmtig	VmtV > VmptV	ǣmptig	'empty'

In these examples, the epenthetic [d], [b], or [p] has the place of articulation of the preceding nasal but agrees with the following segment in terms of voice and nasality. The epenthetic segment therefore serves as a bridge for the transition between the segments on either side, as is shown in Table 7.11.

Table 7.11 The nature of epenthesis

[m]	*[b]*	*[l]*	*[m]*	*[p]*	*[t]*
labial	labial	nonlabial	labial	labial	nonlabial
nasal	nonnasal	nonnasal	nasal	nonnasal	nonnasal
voiced	voiced	voiced	voiced	voiceless	voiceless

In other cases, vowel epenthesis serves to break up a sequence of sounds that would otherwise be difficult to pronounce or even inconsistent with the phonotactic patterns of the language. As mentioned above, some English speakers avoid [θl] clusters by inserting an epenthetic [ə] in their pronunciation of words, such as pronouncing *athlete* as *ath*[ə]*lete*. In the history of Spanish, word-initial [sk] clusters were avoided by inserting a vowel before the cluster (see Table 7.12).

Table 7.12 Examples of epenthesis

Latin	schola [sk]	Spanish	escuela [esk]	'school'
Latin	scrībere [sk]	Spanish	escribir [esk]	'write'

Metathesis

Metathesis involves a change in the relative positioning of segments. This change, like assimilation and dissimilation, can affect adjacent segments or segments at a distance (see Table 7.13).

Table 7.13 Metathesis of adjacent segments in Old English

Earlier form	*Later form*	
wæps	wæsp	'wasp'
þridda	þirdda	'third'

Metathesis at a distance is found in the change from Latin *mīrăculum* 'miracle' to Spanish *milagro*, in which [r] and [l] have changed places although they were not originally adjacent (see Figure 7.1).

Figure 7.1 Metathesis of nonadjacent segments in Spanish

Weakening and deletion

Both vowels and consonants are also susceptible to outright **deletion**, as well as to various **weakening** processes. We will first treat the effects of these processes on vowels and then turn to their effects on consonants.

Vowel deletion may involve a word-final vowel (**apocope**) or a word-internal vowel (**syncope**) (see Table 7.14). A vowel in an unstressed syllable is particularly susceptible to deletion, especially when a neighboring syllable is stressed.

Table 7.14 Vowel deletion in French

Apocope		
Latin	*French*	
cū́ra ōrnā́re	cure [kyʁ] orner	'cure' 'decorate'
Syncope		
Latin	*French*	
pḗrdere vī́:vere	perdre vivre	'lose' 'live'

The effects of syncope are also apparent in the loss of the medial vowel in Modern English words such as *vegetable*, *interest*, and *family*, which are frequently pronounced as [vɛ́dʒtəbl̩], [íntrɛst], and [fǽmli].

Vowel deletion is commonly preceded by **vowel reduction**, in which a full vowel is reduced to a schwa-like (i.e., short, lax [ə]) vowel. Vowel reduction typically affects short vowels in unstressed syllables and may affect all or only a subset of the full vowels (see Figure 7.2).

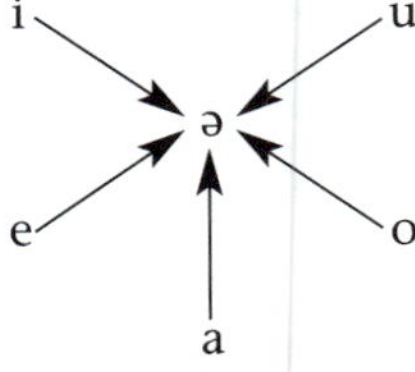

Figure 7.2 Vowel reduction

Vowel reduction with subsequent deletion (apocope and syncope) occurred in Middle English and Early Modern English, as shown in Table 7.15.

Table 7.15 Vowel reduction and deletion in English

Apocope					
Old English		*Middle English (vowel reduction)*		*Early Modern English (apocope)*	
nama	[a]	name	[ə]	name	Ø
talu	[u]	tale	[ə]	tale	Ø
Syncope					
Old English		*Middle English (vowel reduction)*		*Early Modern English (vowel deletion)*	
stānas	[a]	stones	[ə]	stones	Ø
stānes	[e]	stones	[ə]	stone's	Ø

Consonant deletion is also a very common sound change. For example, the word-initial cluster [kn] was found in Old and Middle English, as the spelling of such words as *knight*, *knit*, *knot*, and *knee* implies, but the [k] was subsequently lost, giving us our modern pronunciation. The loss of word-final consonants has played a major role in the evolution of Modern French. The final letters in the written forms of the words in Table 7.16 reflect consonants that were actually pronounced at an earlier stage of the language.

Table 7.16 Consonant loss in French

French spelling (masculine form)	*Current pronunciation*	
gros	[gro]	'large'
chaud	[ʃo]	'warm'
vert	[vɛʁ]	'green'

Just as vowel reduction can be identified as a weakening process, since it represents an intermediate step on the pathway from a full vowel to deletion of the vowel, so too can pathways of **consonant weakening** be identified. The scale of **consonantal strength** in Figure 7.3 can be helpful in identifying cases of weakening.

Consonantal strength

stronger ↑ voiceless stops
voiceless fricatives, voiced stops
voiced fricatives
nasals
liquids
weaker ↓ glides

(*Note:* Geminate consonants are stronger than their nongeminate counterparts.)

Figure 7.3 Scale of consonantal strength

Accordingly, geminates weaken to nongeminates (**degemination**), stops weaken to fricatives (**frication**), and voiceless stops or voiceless fricatives weaken to voiced stops or voiced fricatives, respectively (**voicing**). Weakening can ultimately result in the deletion of the consonant. Figure 7.4 is a typical pathway of weakening.

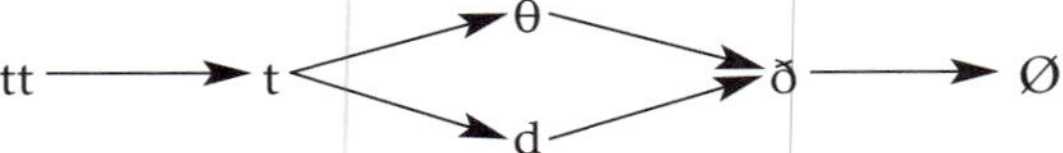

Figure 7.4 Typical pathway of consonant weakening

Consonants are particularly subject to weakening between vowels. Parts of the pathway of consonantal weakening are exemplified with developments from the Romance languages shown in Table 7.17.

Table 7.17 Consonantal weakening in Romance

Degemination (tt > t):	Latin	mittere	Spanish	meter	'to put'
Voicing (t > d):	Latin	mātūrus	Old Spanish	maduro	'ripe'
Frication (d > ð):	Old Spanish	maduro	Spanish	maduro [ð]	'ripe'
Deletion (ð > Ø):	Old French	[maðyr]	French	mûr	'ripe'

Rhotacism is a relatively common type of weakening that typically involves the change of [z] to [r]. Often rhotacism is preceded by a stage involving the voicing of [s] to [z]. Within the Germanic family of languages, for instance, [s] first became [z] in a particular intervocalic environment. This [z] remained in Gothic but became [r] in other Germanic languages such as English, German, and Swedish. The effects of the latter part of this change can be seen in the standard spellings of the words in Table 7.18.

Table 7.18 Rhotacism in English, German, and Swedish

Gothic	*English*	*German*	*Swedish*
maiza	more	mehr	mera
diuzam	deer	Tier	djur
huzd	hoard	Hort	—

In Modern English, rhotacism is the source of the alternation between [z] and [r] in *was* and *were*. The [r] resulted from the earlier [z], which was originally intervocalic.

Consonantal strengthening

Just as consonants weaken, they can also strengthen. **Glide strengthening** (the strengthening of a glide to an affricate) is particularly common, especially in word-initial position. In the Italian examples in Table 7.19, the glide [j] has been strengthened to [dʒ].

Table 7.19 Glide strengthening in Italian

Latin	iūdicium	[j]	Italian	giudizio	[dʒ]	'justice'
Latin	iuvenis	[j]	Italian	giovane	[dʒ]	'young'

2.2 Segmental change

Segments such as affricates are considered phonologically complex because they represent the fusing of a stop plus a fricative into a single segment, [dʒ] or [ts]. Such complex segments are commonly subject to simplification. A very common type of segmental simplification is **deaffrication**, which has the effect of turning affricates into fricatives by eliminating the stop portion of the affricate (see Table 7.20).

Table 7.20 Deaffrication in French

Old French	cent [ts]	French	cent [s]	'one hundred'
Old French	gent [dʒ]	French	gent [ʒ]	'people, tribe'

Since deaffrication of [tʃ] (as well as of [dʒ]) has not occurred in English, early borrowings from French maintain the affricate, while later borrowings have a fricative (see Table 7.21).

Table 7.21 Borrowing from French

Early borrowing (before deaffrication occurred in French)	
Old French [tʃ]	*English* [tʃ]
chaiere	chair
chaine	chain
(*Note:* Compare Modern French [ʃ] in chaire 'throne, seat' and chaîne 'chain'.)	
Later borrowings (after deaffrication occurred in French)	
Modern French [ʃ]	*English* [ʃ]
chandelier	chandelier
chauffeur	chauffeur

2.3 Auditorily based change

Although articulatory factors (particularly relating to "ease of articulation") are of central importance in sound change, as indicated in the preceding discussion, auditory factors also play a role. **Substitution** is a type of auditorily based change involving the replacement of one segment with another similar-sounding segment. A common type of substitution involves [f] replacing either [x] or [θ]. Earlier in the history of English, [f] replaced [x] in some words in standard varieties of English while [f] replaced [θ] in Cockney, a nonstandard dialect spoken in London (see Table 7.22).

Table 7.22 Auditorily based substitution

[x] > [f]	Middle English	laugh [x]	Modern English	laugh [f]
[θ] > [f]	Standard English	thin [θ]	Cockney	[fɪn]

So far we have treated sound changes without consideration of their effect on the sound pattern of the particular language as a whole. All of the foregoing sound changes can lead both to new types of allophonic variation and to the addition or loss of phonemic contrasts. Examples of such cases are presented in the next section.

2.4 Phonetic versus phonological change

The sound changes outlined in the previous sections can affect the overall sound pattern (phonology) of a language in different ways. Commonly, the first stage of a sound change results in the creation of a new allophone of an already existing phoneme. The term **phonetic sound change** can be used to refer to this stage.

A good example of phonetic sound change involves the laxing of short high vowels that has developed in Canadian French (see Table 7.23). This change can be seen in closed word-final syllables, among other environments.

Table 7.23 Vowel laxing in Canadian French

European French	*Canadian French*	
Closed syllable		
[vit]	[vɪt]	'quick'
[libʁ]	[lɪb]	'free'
[ekut]	[ekʊt]	'listen'
[pus]	[pʊs]	'thumb'
Open syllable		
[vi]	[vi]	'life'
[li]	[li]	'bed'
[vu]	[vu]	'you'
[lu]	[lu]	'wolf'

Whereas Canadian French has the lax vowels [ɪ] and [ʊ] in closed final syllables, European French has kept the tense vowels [i] and [u]. Both dialects of French retain [i] and [u] in open syllables. This suggests that Canadian French has developed the rule in Figure 7.5.

$$\begin{bmatrix}\text{V} \\ \text{+high} \\ \text{–long}\end{bmatrix} \rightarrow [\text{–tense}] \; / \; \underline{\quad} \; \text{C}]_{\sigma}$$

Figure 7.5 Vowel laxing rule in Canadian French

While this rule did introduce an allophone not present in European French, it did not create any new phonemes since there was no contrast between lax vowels and their tense counterparts in Canadian French. (However, a fully phonemic contrast between lax and tense vowels appears to be developing in Canadian French, partially under the influence of borrowings from English.)

Splits

Sometimes sound change can lead to changes in a language's phonological system by adding, eliminating, or rearranging phonemes. Such **phonological change** can involve **splits**, **mergers**, or **shifts**.

In a phonological split, allophones of the same phoneme come to contrast with each other due to the loss of the conditioning environment, with the result that one or more new phonemes are created. The English phoneme /ŋ/ was the result of a phonological split (see Table 7.24). Originally, [ŋ] was simply the allophone of /n/ that appeared before a velar consonant. During Middle English, consonant deletion resulted in the loss of [g] in word-final position after a nasal consonant, leaving [ŋ] as the final sound in words such as *sing*.

Table 7.24 Phonological split resulting in /ŋ/

Original phonemic form	/sɪŋg/
Original phonetic form	[sɪŋg]
Deletion of [g]	[sɪŋg] > [sɪŋ]
New phonemic form	/sɪŋ/

The loss of the final [g] in words created minimal pairs such as *sin* (/sɪn/) and *sing* (/sɪŋ/), in which there is a contrast between /n/ and /ŋ/. This example represents a typical phonological split. When the conditioning environment of an allophonic variant of a phoneme is lost through sound change, the allophone is no longer predictable and thus itself becomes phonemic. The original phoneme (in Figure 7.6 /n/) splits into two phonemes (/n/ and /ŋ/).

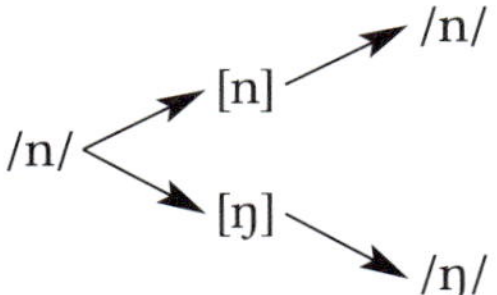

Figure 7.6 A phonological split

Mergers

In a phonological merger, two or more phonemes collapse into a single one, thereby reducing the number of phonemes in the language. The case of auditorily based substitution discussed above has this effect in Cockney English, in which all instances of the interdental fricative /θ/ have become /f/ (see Figure 7.7). Consequently, the phonemes /θ/ and /f/ have merged into one (/f/), and words such as *thin* and *fin* have the same phonological form (/fɪn/). Similarly, /v/ and /ð/ have merged (e.g., /smuv/ for *smooth*).

Figure 7.7 Phonological mergers

Shifts

A phonological shift is a change in which a series of phonemes is systematically modified so that their organization with respect to each other is altered. A well-known example of such a change is called the **Great English Vowel Shift**. Beginning in the Middle English period and continuing into the eighteenth century, the language underwent a series of modifications to the long vowels (see Table 7.25).

Table 7.25 The Great English Vowel Shift

Middle English	*Great Vowel Shift*			*Modern English*	
[tiːd]	[iː]	>	[aj]	/tajd/	'tide'
[luːd]	[uː]	>	[aw]	/lawd/	'loud'
[geːs]	[eː]	>	[iː]	/gis/	'geese'
[sɛː]	[ɛː]	>	[iː]	/si/	'sea'
[goːs]	[oː]	>	[uː]	/gus/	'goose'
[brɔːkən]	[ɔː]	>	[oː]	/brokən/	'broken'
[naːmə]	[aː]	>	[eː]	/nem/	'name'

Figure 7.8 illustrates the changes that gradually affected the English long vowels.

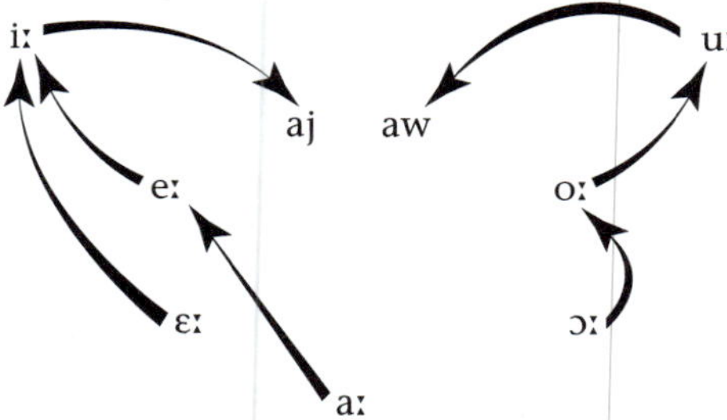

Figure 7.8 Changes brought about by the Great English Vowel Shift

2.5 Explaining phonological shift

The causes and even the details of the Great English Vowel Shift still remain unclear. In fact, the causes of phonological shift in general are not well understood. A possible motivation in some cases appears to involve the phonemic system itself, where the notion of phonological space plays a role. As in the case of "ease of articulation," phonological space is difficult to define precisely. For our purposes and with a focus on vowels only, we can consider the vowel quadrangle (a schematicization of the oral cavity) as the phonological space that vowels must occupy. Although the vowel systems of languages can be arranged in various ways (see Chapter 8), there is a tendency for languages to maximize the use of space in the quadrangle. Accordingly, if a language has only three vowels, they will likely be [i], [a], and [o] or [u], not (for example) [i], [e], and [ɛ]. Similarly, if a language has five vowels, they will be distributed throughout the phonological space typically as [i], [e], [a], [o], [u] rather than [u], [ʊ], [o], [ɔ], [a] for example (see Figure 7.9).

a Typical distribution of vowels in phonological space

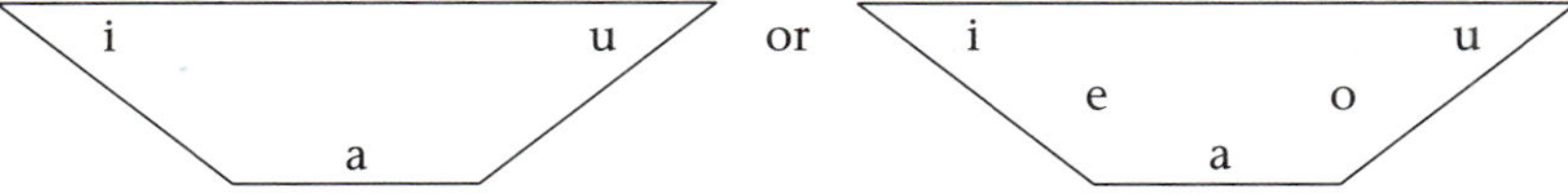

b Atypical distribution of vowels in phonological space

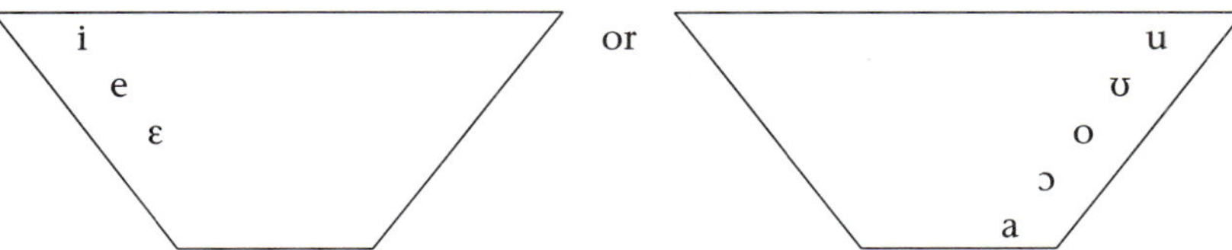

Figure 7.9 Vowel distribution

Languages with seven (or more) vowels (e.g., English at the starting point of the Great English Vowel Shift in Figure 7.8) often undergo **diphthongization**. This can be seen as a reaction to the overcrowding of the phonological space, since the effect of the diphthongization of a pair of vowels is to reduce a seven-vowel system to a five-vowel system. (Think of the two diphthongs as not infringing on the space of the simple vowels.)

Overcrowding appears to have resulted in diphthongization in many languages, including Old High German and Spanish (see Table 7.26). The diphthongization in these two languages differs from that of the Great English Vowel Shift in two ways. The mid vowels and not the high vowels are affected, and different sets of diphthongs result. Nevertheless, in terms of phonological space, all these cases of diphthongization achieve the same result: namely, a reduction of the overcrowded seven-vowel system. Although the Great English Vowel Shift was complicated by other developments, diphthongization resulting from overcrowding appears to have been a contributing factor.

Table 7.26 Diphthongization in Old High German and Spanish

Old High German diphthongization			*Spanish diphthongization*		
iː	uː		i	u	
iaː	uaː		e je	we o	
eː ↗	↖ oː		ɛ ↗	↖ ɔ	
ɛː	ɔː		a		
aː					
Old High German			*Latin*	*Spanish*	
Earlier	*Later*				
heːr	hiar	'here'	petra	piedra	'stone'
floːt	fluat	'flood'	mortem	muerte	'death'

2.6 Sound change and rule ordering

In describing language change, it is often crucial to identify the relative chronology, or times at which different changes have occurred. Three important changes in the history of English can be given as the (somewhat simplified) rules in Figure 7.10.

1) Voicing
   C → [+voice] / [+voice] ___ [+voice]

2) Syncope
   V → Ø / ___ C #
   [–stress]

3) Assimilation
   C → [+voice] / C + ___
   [+voice]

Figure 7.10 Three rules in the history of English

These changes have played an important role in the evolution of English plural forms such as *hooves* (versus *hoof*) and *wolves* (versus *wolf*). Of the possible orderings of these three rules, only one will derive the contemporary pronunciation from the earlier (Old English) phonemic form. Two of the possible orderings are given in Table 7.27.

Table 7.27 Rule ordering in the history of English

Hypothesis A		*Hypothesis B*	
Original phonemic form	/wulfas/	Original phonemic form	/wulfas/
Voicing	wulvas	Voicing	wulvas
Syncope	wulvs	Assimilation	(cannot apply)
Assimilation	wulvz	Syncope	wulvs (incorrect)

If we assume hypothesis A with the ordering voicing, syncope, and assimilation, we can account for the [vz] in the modern pronunciation of a word such as *wolves*. By contrast, the ordering proposed in hypothesis B would not account for the present pronunciation.

3 Morphological change

In this section we discuss morphological changes resulting from analogy and reanalysis as well as changes involving the addition or loss of affixes.

3.1 Addition of affixes

Borrowing has been a very important source of new affixes in English. During the Middle English period, many French words containing the suffix *-ment* (e.g., *accomplishment, commencement*) made their way into the language. Eventually, *-ment* established itself as a productive suffix in English and was used with bases that were not of French origin (e.g., *acknowledgment, merriment*). The ending *-able*, which converts a verb into an adjective (e.g., *readable, lovable*, etc.), followed a similar pattern. Although words with this ending (e.g., *favorable, conceivable*) were initially borrowed into English as whole units, eventually the suffix became productive and was used with new bases.

Not all new affixes are the result of borrowing. Lexical forms can become grammatical forms over time through a process called **grammaticalization.** Grammaticalized forms often undergo dramatic phonological reduction as well as semantic change, in which they can lose much of their original content. In the case where two words are frequently adjacent, over time they can become fused together to form a single unit consisting of a base and an affix. **Fusion** refers to this specific type of grammaticalization in which words develop into affixes (either prefixes or suffixes) (see Table 7.28).

Table 7.28 Fusion

word word	>	base + affix (suffixation)
word word	>	affix + base (prefixation)

A number of Modern English suffixes are derived from earlier words by means of fusion (see Table 7.29).

Table 7.29 English suffixes resulting from fusion

Suffix	*Old English word*	
-hood (childhood)	hād	'state, condition, rank'
-dom (freedom)	dōm	'condition, power'
-ly (fatherly)	(ge-)līc	'similar, equal, like'

Another case of fusion is the development of the future tense affixes in Italian, which are derived from various forms of the Latin word *habere* 'to have.' For example, the Latin word *habeo* '(I) have, hold, grasp' is the source of the Italian future suffix *ō* (see Table 7.30).

Table 7.30 Fusion resulting in a future tense affix in Italian

Latin	*Italian*	
amāre + habeō	amerò	'I will love'
amāre + habēmus	ameremo	'we will love'

3.2 Loss of affixes

Just as affixes can be added to the grammar, they can also be lost. Sometimes affixes simply fall into disuse for no apparent reason. For example, a number of Old English derivational affixes, including -*bǣre* and -*bora*, are no longer used (see Table 7.31).

Table 7.31 Affixes no longer found in English

N + bǣre	→	A	(e.g., lustbǣre 'pleasant, agreeable' from *lust* 'pleasure')
N + bora	→	N	(e.g., mundbora 'protector' from *mund* 'protection')

It is also very common for affixes to be lost through sound change. For example, Old English had a complex system of affixes marking case and gender. Nouns were divided into three gender classes—masculine, neuter, and feminine. Assignment to a class was not based on sex (natural gender) but on grammatical gender; for example, the word for *stone* (Old English *stān*) and even a word for *woman* (*wīfmann*) were masculine, the word for *sun* (*sunne*) was feminine, and another word for *woman* (*wīf*) was neuter. Each gender class was associated with a different set of case endings (see Table 7.32).

The following Old English sentence contains all four case categories.

2)

Se cniht	geaf	gief-e	þæs hierd-es	sun-e
the youth-Nom	gave	gift-Acc	the shepherd-Gen	son-Dat

'The youth gave a gift to the shepherd's son.'

Table 7.32 Old English case affixes

	Masculine		*Neuter*		*Feminine*	
Singular						
	hund	'dog'	dēor	'animal'	gief	'gift'
Nominative	hund		dēor		gief-u	
Accusative	hund		dēor		gief-e	
Genitive	hund-es		dēor-es		gief-e	
Dative	hund-e		dēor-e		gief-e	
Plural						
Nominative	hund-as		dēor		gief-a	
Accusative	hund-as		dēor		gief-a	
Genitive	hund-a		dēor-a		gief-a	
Dative	hund-um		dēor-um		gief-um	

By the fifteenth century, English case endings had changed radically. Consonant deletion resulted in the loss of the earlier [m] of the dative plural suffix, and through vowel reduction, all the unstressed vowels of the case endings were reduced to the short, lax vowel [ə] (which was later lost through vowel deletion). Consequently, many of the earlier case and gender distinctions were obliterated. (The examples in Table 7.33 also include changes to the base-internal vowels as the result of various processes, including the Great English Vowel Shift.) Whereas Old English had five distinct affixes for cases, Middle English had only two suffixes, *-e* and *-es,* which, with the loss of schwa, were ultimately reduced to a single suffix *-s*, still used in

Table 7.33 The loss of case affixes through sound change (in English *hound*)

	Old English	*Middle English (e = [ə])*	*Modern English*
Singular			
Nominative	hund	hund	hound
Accusative	hund	hund	hound
Genitive	hund-es	hund-(e)s	hound's
Dative	hund-e	hund-(e)	hound
Plural			
Nominative	hund-as	hund-(e)s	hounds
Accusative	hund-as	hund-(e)s	hounds
Genitive	hund-a	hund-(e)	hounds'
Dative	hund-um	hund-(e)	hounds

Modern English for the plural and the possessive. This represents a typical example of how sound change can result in modification to the morphological component of the grammar.

3.3 From synthetic to analytic to synthetic

Since languages vary greatly in the complexity of their morphology, linguists often make a distinction between **analytic** and **synthetic languages** (see Chapter 8). Whereas analytic languages have very few inflectional affixes (for example, Modern English), synthetic languages have many (for example, Latin, Old English).

Even in the absence of borrowing, sound change and fusion ensure that there is constant flux in the morphology of a language over time. As we have seen, due to the loss of case endings through sound change, English has developed from a synthetic language with many inflectional affixes to an analytic one with very few, as the previous discussion of nouns such as *hound* indicates.

By contrast, fusion ensures the rise of new synthetic forms. Fusion can be observed in some Modern English dialects in forms such as *coulda* (e.g., *I coulda won*), which represents the fusion of *could* and *have*. For many speakers, the *-a* is treated as a suffix that is no longer related to *have*, as evident in spellings such as *could of*, which result from confusion over how to represent the pronunciation of *coulda* in written English. Through fusion, a language with an analytic morphology can become more synthetic over time.

3.4 Analogy

The drastic effects that sound change can have on the morphology of a language are often alleviated through analogy. For example, the plural of Old English *hand* 'hand' was *handa*. Vowel reduction and apocope applying to *handa* would have yielded a Modern English plural form identical to the singular form, namely *hand* (see Table 7.34).

Table 7.34 Sound changes applied to Old English *handa* 'hands'

handa	
handə	vowel reduction
hand	apocope

Obviously, then, the Modern English plural *hands* cannot be the consequence of sound change. Rather, it is the result of earlier analogy with words such as Middle English *hund* 'hound' (see Table 7.33), which did form the plural with the suffix *-s*. This suffix, whose earlier form *-as* was predominant even in Old English, was extended by analogy to all English nouns with a few exceptions (*oxen, men, geese,* etc.). Other plural forms besides *hands* that were created on the basis of analogy include *eyes* (*eyen* in Middle English) and *shoes* (formerly *shooen*).

Continuing analogy along these lines is responsible for the development of the plural form *youse* (from *you*) in some English dialects. Each generation of English-speaking children temporarily extends the analogy still further by producing forms such as *sheeps, gooses,* and *mouses*. To date, however, these particular innovations have not been accepted by adult speakers of Standard English and are eventually abandoned by young language learners.

3.5 REANALYSIS

As mentioned in Section 1.2, reanalysis can result in a new morphological structure for a word. It can affect both borrowed words and, particularly in cases where the morphological structure of the word is no longer transparent, native words. Reanalysis can result in new productive patterns—as in the case of (-)*burger*—or it can remain quite isolated, affecting perhaps only one word. Since the type of reanalysis exemplified by *hamburger* is not based on a correct analysis of a word (at least from a historical perspective) and does not usually involve a conscious or detailed study of the word on the part of the speaker, it is often called **folk etymology**.

In the case of *hamburger*, the only evidence of folk etymology is the productive use of (-)*burger* as an independent word and in compounds like *fishburger*. However, in other cases, folk etymology commonly involves changes in pronunciation that reflect the new morphological analysis. For example, our word *earwig* derives from Old English *ēarwicga* [ǣərwiʤa], a compound consisting of 'ear' and 'insect'. Taking into consideration sound change alone, the expected Modern English pronunciation of this word would be *earwidge* [irwiʤ]. However, the second part of the compound was lost as an independent word by Middle English, so speakers could no longer associate it with the meaning of 'insect'. Subsequently, reanalysis related the second part of the compound to the verb 'wiggle', resulting in Middle English *arwygyll* (literally 'ear + wiggle'). The end result is Modern English *-wig* and not *-widge*. More examples of folk etymology are found in Table 7.35.

Although reanalysis of individual words is common, affixes can also be affected, sometimes with new productive morphological rules developing as a result. This is the case of the Modern English adverbial suffix *-ly*, which developed from Old

Table 7.35 Folk etymology in English (native words and borrowings)

Modern word	*Source*
belfry	Middle English *berfrey* 'bell tower' (unrelated to *bell*)
bridegroom	Middle English *bridegome* (unrelated to *groom*) (compare Old English *brȳd* 'bride' and *guma* 'man')
muskrat	Algonquian *musquash* (unrelated to either *musk* or *rat*)
woodchuck	Algonquian *otchek* (unrelated to either *wood* or *chuck*)

English *-lic(e)*. In Old English, adjectives could be derived from nouns by adding the suffix *-lic*. Adverbs, in turn, could be derived by adding the suffix *-e* to adjectives (including those derived with *-lic*) (see Table 7.36).

Table 7.36 The derivation of Old English adjectives and adverbs

Formation of an adjective from a noun				
$[\text{dæg}]_N$	+ lic	→	$[\text{dæglic}]_A$	'daily' (e.g., as in 'daily schedule')
Formation of an adverb from an adjective				
$[\text{dēop}]_A$	+ e	→	$[\text{dēope}]_{Adv}$	'deeply'
Formation of an adverb from a derived adjective with -lic				
$[\text{dæg+lic}]_A$	+ e	→	$[\text{dæglice}]_{Adv}$	'daily' (e.g., as in 'she ran daily')

At some point, the entire complex suffix *-lic+e* was reanalyzed as an adverbial suffix (rather than as an adjectival suffix *-lic* plus an adverbial suffix *-e*). It was then used by analogy to derive adverbs from adjectives in forms where it was not used before, resulting in Modern English *deeply* and other such words.

4 SYNTACTIC CHANGE

Like other components of the grammar, syntax is also subject to change over time. Syntactic changes can involve modifications to Merge or Move operations, as the following examples illustrate.

4.1 WORD ORDER

All languages make a distinction between the subject and direct object. This contrast is typically represented through case marking or word order. Since Old English had an extensive system of case marking, it is not surprising that its word order was somewhat more variable than that of Modern English. In unembedded clauses, Old English placed the verb in second position (much like Modern German). Thus we find subject-verb-object order in simple transitive sentences such as the following.

3)

S	V	O	
Hē	geseah	þone	mann
'He	saw	the	man.'

When the clause began with an element such as *þa* 'then' or *ne* 'not', the verb was still in second position but now preceded the subject, as in the following example.

4)

	V	S	O	
þa	sende	sē cyning	þone	disc
then	sent	the king	the	dish

'Then the king sent the dish.'

Although this word order is still found in Modern English (as in *5*), its use is very limited and subject to special restrictions, unlike the situation in Old English.

5)

	V	S	O
Rarely	has	he ever deceived	me.

When the direct object was a pronoun in Old English, the subject-object-verb order was typical.

6)

S	O	V
Hēo	hine	lǣrde
She	him	advised

'She advised him.'

The subject-object-verb order also prevailed in embedded clauses, even when the direct object was not a pronoun.

7)

	S	O	V	
þa	hē	þone cyning	sōhte,	hē bēotode
when	he	the king	visited,	he boasted

'When he visited the king, he boasted.'

Since case markings were lost during the Middle English period through sound change, fixed subject-verb-object order became the means of marking grammatical relations. As Table 7.37 shows, a major change in word order took place between 1300 and 1400, with the verb-object order becoming dominant.

Table 7.37 Word order patterns in Middle English

Year	*1000*	*1200*	*1300*	*1400*	*1500*
Direct object before the verb (%)	53	53	40	14	2
Direct object after the verb (%)	47	47	60	86	98

From SOV to SVO

Just as languages can be classified in terms of their morphology, languages can also be grouped on the basis of the relative order of subject (S), object (O), and verb (V) in basic sentences. Almost all languages of the world fall into one of three types: SOV, SVO, or VSO, with the majority of languages being one of the first two types. Just as languages change through time from one morphological type to another, they can also change from one syntactic type to another. A case in point is found in the history of English, which shows the development from SOV to SVO syntax.

Evidence indicates that the earliest form of Germanic from which English descended was an SOV language. One of the earliest recorded Germanic sentences, for example, has this word order. The sentence in *8* was inscribed on a golden horn (now called the Golden Horn of Gallehus) about sixteen hundred years ago.

8)

Horn of Gallehus

S		O	V
ek HlewagastiR	HoltijaR	horna	tawido
I Hlewagastir	of Holt	horn	made

'I, Hlewagastir of Holt, made the horn.'

Another type of evidence for an earlier SOV order is found in morphological fusion (see Section 3.1). Since fusion depends on frequently occurring syntactic patterns, it can sometimes serve as an indicator of earlier syntax. The OV compound, very common in Old English (as well as in Modern English), likely reflects an earlier stage of OV word order (see Table 7.38).

Table 7.38 Old English compounds with OV structure

manslæht	'man' + 'strike'	'manslaughter, murder'
æppelbǣre	'apple' + 'bear'	'apple-bearing'

If the earliest Germanic language was SOV and Modern English is firmly SVO, then Old English represents a transitional syntactic type. In developing from SOV syntax to SVO syntax, languages seem to follow similar pathways. For example, Modern German, which developed from the same Germanic SOV source as English, shares two of Old English's distinguishing characteristics. First, the verb is typically placed in the second position of the sentence in main clauses, preceded by the subject or some other element (such as an adverb). Secondly, the SOV order is employed for embedded clauses.

9)

Modern German word order

a. Verb in second position in unembedded clauses
(Compare the Old English sentences in *4*.)

	V	S	O
Gestern	hatte	ich	keine Zeit
yesterday	had	I	no time

'I had no time yesterday.'

b. SOV in embedded clauses
(Compare the Old English sentences in *7*.)

	S	O	V
Als	er	den Mann	sah . . .
when	he	the man	saw

'When he saw the man . . .'

The change from SOV to SVO is not restricted to English and other Germanic languages. The same change is evident in completely unrelated languages, such as those of the Bantu family of Africa. Since linguists are still not sure why languages change from one syntactic type to another, the causes of such change will undoubtedly remain an important area of investigation, especially since the relative order of verb and object (OV versus VO) has been closely linked with other word-order patterns (see Chapter 8).

4.2 Inversion in the history of English

In Old and Middle English the Move operation called Inversion (see Chapter 5) involved in the formation of *yes-no* questions could apply to all verbs—not just auxiliaries—yielding forms that would be unacceptable in Modern English.

10)

Speak they the truth?

During the sixteenth and seventeenth centuries, the Inversion rule was changed to apply solely to auxiliary verbs.

11)

Inversion *(old form)*
The V moves in front of the subject
They speak → Speak they?
They can speak → Can they speak?

Inversion *(new form)*
The Aux moves in front of the subject
They speak → *Speak they?
They can speak → Can they speak?

With this change, structures such as *Speak they the truth?* were no longer possible. The corresponding question came to be formed with the auxiliary *do* as in *Do they speak the truth?*

5 LEXICAL AND SEMANTIC CHANGE

Another obvious type of language change involves modifications to the lexicon. Since we have already dealt with some changes relating to derivational and inflectional morphology in Section 3, the main focus here will be on lexical change involving entire words. Simply stated, there are two possible types of lexical change—addition and loss. The addition or loss of words often reflects cultural changes that introduce novel objects and notions, and eliminate outmoded ones.

5.1 Addition of lexical items

Addition is frequently the result of technological innovations or contact with other cultures. Such developments result in **lexical gaps** that can be filled by adding new words to the lexicon. New words are added either through the word formation processes available to the language or through borrowing.

Word formation

The most important word formation processes are compounding and derivation, although other types including conversion, blends, backformation, clipping, and acronyms (see Chapter 4) can play a significant role.

Compounding and derivation have always been available to English speakers for the creation of new words. In fact, much of the compounding and derivation in Old English seems very familiar (see Table 7.39).

Table 7.39 Compounding and derivation in Old English

Noun compounds			
N + N		sunbēam	'sunbeam'
A + N		middelniht	'midnight'
Adjective compounds			
N + A		blōdrēad	'blood-red'
A + A		dēadboren	'stillborn'
Derived nouns			
$[\text{bæc}]_V$ + ere	→	bæcere	'baker'
$[\text{frēond}]_N$ + scipe	→	frēondscipe	'friendship'
Derived adjectives			
$[\text{wundor}]_N$ + full	→	wundorfull	'wonderful'
$[\text{cild}]_N$ + isc	→	cildisc	'childish'

Just as speakers of Modern English can use compounding and derivational rules to create new words (e.g., the N + N compound *airhead*), so could Old English speakers create new words such as the poetic N + N compound *hwǣlweg*—literally 'whale' + 'path' means 'sea'.

Note however that even though many Old English compounding and derivational patterns have been maintained in Modern English, words that were acceptable in Old English are not necessarily still in use in Modern English, even though many of them are quite understandable (see Table 7.40).

Table 7.40 Old English compounds and derived words that are no longer used

Noun compounds				
N + N	bōccræft ('book' + 'craft')			'literature' (compare *witchcraft*)
A + N	dimhūs ('dim' + 'house')			'prison'
Adjective compounds				
N + A	ælfscīene ('elf' + 'beautiful')			'beautiful as a fairy'
A + A	eallgōd ('all' + 'good')			'perfectly good'
Derived nouns				
$[\text{sēam}]_V$ + ere		→	sēamere	'tailor' (compare *seamster, seamstress*)
$[\text{man}]_N$ + scipe		→	manscipe	'humanity' (compare *friendship*)
Derived adjectives				
$[\text{word}]_N$ + full		→	wordfull	'wordy' (compare *wonderful*)
$[\text{heofon}]_N$ + isc		→	heofonisc	'heavenly' (compare *childish*)

In addition, not all word formation processes available to Modern English speakers were found in Old English. For example, conversion (as in Modern English $[\text{summer}]_N \rightarrow [\text{summer}]_V$) was not possible in Old English. In fact, conversion is typically not available to (synthetic) inflectional languages such as Old English since change in a word category in such languages is usually indicated morphologically, and conversion, by definition, does not involve the use of affixes.

Borrowing

As discussed in Section 1.2, language contact over time can result in an important source of new words—borrowing. Depending on the cultural relationship holding between languages, three types of influence of one language on another are traditionally identified: **substratum**, **adstratum**, and **superstratum influence**.

Substratum influence is the effect of a politically or culturally nondominant language on a dominant language in the area. Both American and Canadian English and Canadian French, for instance, have borrowed vocabulary items from Amerindian languages (see examples in Section 1.2). From a much earlier period in the history of English, the influence of a Celtic substratum is also evident, particularly in place names such as *Thames*, *London*, and *Dover*. Substratum influence does not usually have a major impact on the lexicon of the borrowing language. Borrowed words are usually restricted to place names and unfamiliar items or concepts. This situation reflects the fact that it is usually the speakers of the substratum language who inhabited the area first.

Superstratum influence is the effect of a politically or culturally dominant language on another language or languages in the area. For example, the Athapaskan language Gwich'in (Loucheux, spoken in Canada's Northwest Territories) has borrowed a number of governmental terms and expressions from English, including *bureaucratic*, *constituents*, *program*, *business*, *development*, and *political*.

In the case of English, Norman French had a superstratum influence. The major impact of French on the vocabulary of English is related to a historical event—the conquest of England by French-speaking Normans in 1066. As the conquerors and their descendants gradually learned English over the next decades, they retained French terms for political, judicial, and cultural notions (see Table 7.41). These words were in turn borrowed by native English speakers who, in trying to gain a place in the upper middle class, were eager to imitate the speech of their social superiors. Not surprisingly, borrowing was especially heavy in the vocabulary areas pertaining to officialdom: government, the judiciary, and religion. Other areas of heavy borrowing included science, culture, and warfare.

Table 7.41 Some French loan words in English

Government	tax, revenue, government, royal, state, parliament, authority, prince, duke, slave, peasant
Judiciary	judge, defendant, jury, evidence, jail, verdict, crime
Religion	prayer, sermon, religion, chaplain, friar
Science	medicine, physician
Culture	art, sculpture, fashion, satin, fur, ruby
Warfare	army, navy, battle, soldier, enemy, captain

In some cases, French loan words were used in conjunction with native English words to convey distinctions of various sorts. For a minor crime, for example, the English word *theft* was employed, but for a more serious breach of the law, the French word *larceny* was used. The English also kept their own words for domesticated animals but adopted the French words for the meat from those creatures (see Table 7.42).

Table 7.42 French loan words used in conjunction with native English words

English origin	*French origin*
cow	beef
calf	veal
sheep	mutton
pig	pork

Adstratum influence refers to the situation where two languages are in contact and neither one is clearly politically or culturally dominant. In a city such as Montreal with its large number of bilingual speakers, English and French inevitably influence each other (see Table 7.43).

Table 7.43 French influence on Montreal English

Montreal English	
subvention	'subsidy'
metro	'subway'
autoroute	'highway'

Earlier in the history of English, when the Scandinavians settled part of England beginning in A.D. 800, there was substantial contact between the speakers of English and Scandinavian, resulting in an adstratum relationship. As evident in the examples in Table 7.43 and Table 7.44 below, adstratum contact usually results in the borrowing of common, everyday words. In fact, without consulting a dictionary, most English speakers could not distinguish between borrowings from Scandinavian and native English words.

Table 7.44 Some loan words from Scandinavian

anger, cake, call, egg, fellow, gear, get, hit, husband, low, lump, raise, root, score, seat, skill, skin, take, their, they, thrust, ugly, window, wing

Borrowed words from many other languages attest to various types of cultural contact and serve often to fill the lexical gaps such contact inevitably brings (see Table 7.45).

Table 7.45 Some lexical borrowings into English

Italian	motto, artichoke, balcony, casino, mafia, malaria
Spanish	comrade, tornado, cannibal, mosquito, banana, guitar, vigilante, marijuana
German	poodle, kindergarten, seminar, noodle, pretzel
Dutch	sloop, cole slaw, smuggle, gin, cookie, boom
Slavic languages	czar, tundra, polka, intelligentsia, robot
Amerindian languages	toboggan, opposum, wigwam, chipmunk, Chicago, Missouri
Hindi	thug, punch (drink), shampoo, chintz

Although borrowing has been a very rich source of new words in English, it is noteworthy that loan words are least common among the most frequently used vocabulary items. This reflects a general tendency for highly frequent words to be relatively resistant to loss or substitution (see Table 7.46).

Table 7.46 Origin of the 5,000 most frequently used words in English

Degree of frequency	*Source language (%)*			
	English	*French*	*Latin*	*Other*
First 1,000	83	11	2	4
Second 1,000	34	46	11	9
Third 1,000	29	46	14	11
Fourth 1,000	27	45	17	11
Fifth 1,000	27	47	17	9

5.2 Loss of lexical items

Just as words can be added to the lexicon, they can also be lost. Changes in society play an important role in the loss of words, since words are often lost because the object or notion they refer to has become obsolete (see Table 7.47).

Table 7.47 Some Old English words lost through cultural change

dolgbōt	'compensation for wounding'
þeox	'hunting spear'
eafor	'tenant obligation to the king to convey goods'
flȳtme	'a blood-letting instrument'

5.3 Semantic change

Although changes in word meaning take place continually in all languages, words rarely jump from one meaning to an unrelated one. Typically, the changes are step by step and involve one of the following phenomena.

Semantic broadening is the process in which the meaning of a word becomes more general or more inclusive than its historically earlier meaning (see Table 7.48).

Table 7.48 Semantic broadening

Word	*Old meaning*	*New meaning*
bird	'small fowl'	'any winged creature'
barn	'place to store barley'	'farm building for storage and shelter'
aunt	'father's sister'	'father's or mother's sister'

Semantic narrowing is the process in which the meaning of a word becomes less general or less inclusive than its historically earlier meaning (see Table 7.49).

Table 7.49 Semantic narrowing

Word	*Old meaning*	*New meaning*
hound	'any dog'	'a hunting breed'
meat	'any type of food'	'flesh of an animal'
fowl	'any bird'	'a domesticated bird'
disease	'any unfavorable state'	'an illness'

In **amelioration**, the meaning of a word becomes more positive or favorable. In the opposite change, **pejoration**, a word becomes less favorable in meaning (see Tables 7.50 and 7.51).

Table 7.50 Amelioration

Word	*Old meaning*	*New meaning*
pretty	'tricky, sly, cunning'	'attractive'
knight	'boy'	'a special title or position'

Table 7.51 Pejoration

Word	*Old meaning*	*New meaning*
silly	'happy, prosperous'	'foolish'
wench	'girl'	'wanton woman, prostitute'

Given the propensity of human beings to exaggerate, it is not surprising that the **weakening of meaning** frequently occurs. For example, the word *soon* used to mean 'immediately' but now simply means 'in the near future'. Other examples are included in Table 7.52.

Table 7.52 Weakening

Word	*Old meaning*	*New meaning*
wreak	'avenge, punish'	'to cause, inflict'
quell	'kill, murder'	'to put down, pacify'

Semantic shift is a process in which a word loses its former meaning and takes on a new, but often related, meaning (see Table 7.53).

Table 7.53 Semantic shift

Word	*Old meaning*	*New meaning*
immoral	'not customary'	'unethical'
bead	'prayer'	'prayer bead, bead'

Sometimes a series of semantic shifts occurs over an extended period of time, resulting in a meaning that is completely unrelated to the original sense of a word. The word *hearse,* for example, originally referred to a triangular harrow (a farm implement). Later, it denoted a triangular frame for church candles and later still was used to refer to the device that held candles over a coffin. In a subsequent shift it came to refer to the framework on which curtains were hung over a coffin or tomb. Still later, *hearse* was used to refer to the coffin itself before finally taking on its current sense of the vehicle used to transport a coffin.

One of the most striking types of semantic change is triggered by **metaphor**, a figure of speech based on a perceived similarity between distinct objects or actions. (See Chapter 6 for a discussion of metaphor.) Metaphorical change usually involves a word with a concrete meaning taking on a more abstract sense, although the word's original meaning is not lost. The meanings of many English words have been extended through metaphor (see Table 7.54).

Table 7.54 Some examples of metaphor in English

Word	*Metaphorical meaning*
grasp	'understand'
yarn	'story'
high	'on drugs'

6 THE SPREAD OF CHANGE

Up to this point, we have been concerned with the causes and description of linguistic change. Still to be dealt with is the question of how linguistic innovations spread. This section focuses on two types of spread—one involving the way in which an innovation is extended through the vocabulary of a language, and the other the way in which it spreads through the population.

6.1 Diffusion through the language

Some linguistic change first manifests itself in a few words and then gradually spreads through the vocabulary of the language. This type of change is called **lexical diffusion**. A well-attested example in English involves an ongoing change in the stress pattern of words such as *convert*, which can be used as either a noun or a verb. Although the stress originally fell on the second syllable regardless of lexical category, in the latter half of the sixteenth century three such words, *rebel*, *outlaw*, and *record*, came to be pronounced with the stress on the first syllable when used as nouns. As Figure 7.11 illustrates, this stress shift was extended to an increasing number of words over the next decades.

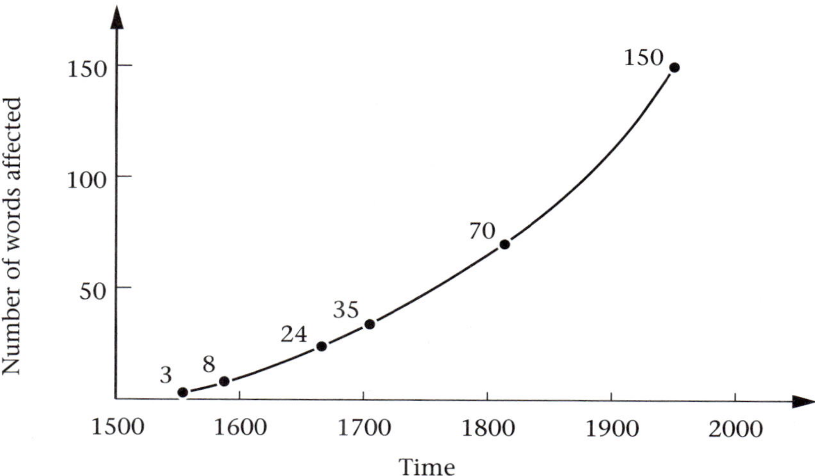

Figure 7.11 Diffusion of stress shift in English

This change has still not diffused through the entire vocabulary of English. There are about a thousand nouns of the relevant sort that still place the stress on the second syllable (e.g., *report*, *mistake*, and *support*). Table 7.55 illustrates the spread of this change to date.

Table 7.55 Stress shift in English (nouns)

Before the 16th century	*During the 16th century*	*During the 18th century*	*Today*
rebél	rébel	rébel	rébel
affíx	affíx	áffix	áffix
récess	récess	récess	récess
mistáke	mistáke	mistáke	mistáke

This ongoing change can still be observed today. The noun *address*, for example, is pronounced by many people as [ǽdrɛs], with stress on the first syllable, although the older pronunciation [ədrɛ́s] is still heard. Some speakers alternate between the two pronunciations. This change may continue to work its way through the language until all nouns in the class we have been considering are stressed on the first syllable.

The changes discussed in the section on analogy also spread word by word. For example, the transition of strong (irregular) verbs (the *sing/sang/sung* type) to the weak verb class (regular verbs with past tense *-ed*) is an ongoing change. Both strong and weak past tense forms of original strong verbs such as *dive* and *shine* are heard in current English: *dove/dived* and *shone/shined*.

However, not all linguistic change involves gradual diffusion through the vocabulary of a language. Sound changes typically affect all instances of the segment(s) involved. For example, in some dialects of Spanish (such as Cuban), the consonantal weakening of [s] to [h] in syllable-final position affects all instances of *s* in those positions. The relevant rule can be stated as in Figure 7.12.

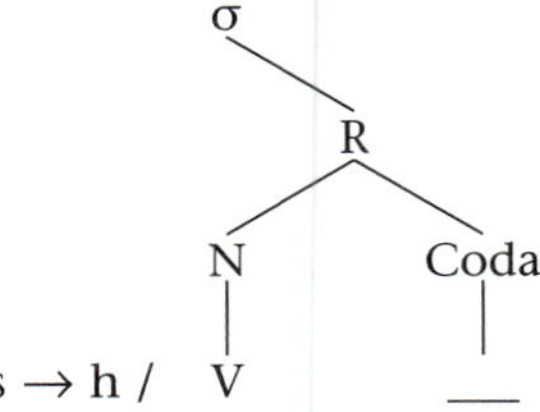

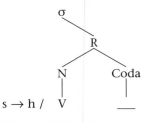

Figure 7.12 Consonant weakening of [s] to [h] in certain Spanish dialects

This rule has resulted in changes such as those exemplified in Table 7.56.

Table 7.56 The effects of the [s] to [h] change in Spanish dialects

Standard pronunciation	*New pronunciation*	
[felismente]	[felihmente]	'happily'
[estilo]	[ehtilo]	'type'
[espaɲa]	[ehpaɲa]	'Spain'

This change is entirely regular, affecting all instances of syllable-final [s] in the speech of individuals who adopt it.

Accordingly, two types of language change can be identified. One, exemplified by the stress shifts in bisyllabic English nouns of the type we have discussed, affects individual words one at a time and gradually spreads through the vocabulary of the language. The other, exemplified by the consonant weakening of syllable-final [s] to [h] in some dialects of Spanish, involves an across-the-board change that applies without exception to all words.

6.2 Spread through the population

For a language change to take place, the particular innovation must be accepted by the linguistic community as a whole. For example, although children acquiring English typically form the past tense of *go* as *goed* instead of *went*, *goed* has never received widespread acceptance. Doubtless the verb form in *he throve on fame* would be equally unacceptable to most speakers today. In earlier English, however, *throve* was the past tense form of *thrive* (compare *drive/drove*). At some point in the past, then, the novel form *thrived* received general acceptance.

Just as change sometimes begins with a small number of words, effects of a change often appear first in the speech of only a small number of people. Social pressures often play an important role in whether a particular innovation will spread through the entire linguistic community. Since speakers can consciously or unconsciously alter the way they speak to approximate what they perceive to be a more prestigious or socially acceptable variety of speech, once a change has taken hold in the speech of a high prestige group, it may gradually spread to other speakers and ultimately affect the entire linguistic community.

There have been numerous examples of this in the history of English, notably the loss of postvocalic [r] along the east coast of the United States. This change, which resulted in an "*r*-less" pronunciation of words such as *far* [fa:], originated in parts of England in the seventeenth and eighteenth centuries. At that time, postvocalic [r] was still pronounced throughout English-speaking settlements in North America. Two factors accounted for its loss in parts of this continent. First, the children of the New England gentry picked up the new pronunciation in British schools and subsequently brought it back to the colony. Second, the speech of newly arrived immigrants, including colonial administrators and church officials who enjoyed high social status in the colony, typically lacked the postvocalic [r]. As a result, the innovation was widely imitated and ultimately spread along much of the east coast and into the south.

Social pressures were also involved in limiting the spread of this innovation. It did not penetrate Pennsylvania or the other Midland states since the most prestigious group of settlers there were Quakers from northern England, an area which retained the postvocalic [r]. Similarly, in Canada, the influence of Scottish and Irish settlers, whose dialects did not undergo the change in question, helped ensure the survival of postvocalic [r] in all but a few areas where contact with New England was strongest, most notably in parts of Nova Scotia and in some areas of New Brunswick. More recently the "*r*-less" pronunciation has become stigmatized—even in areas where it was previously firmly entrenched—and we now see a trend to restoration of [r] in environments where it had been deleted.

7 LANGUAGE RECONSTRUCTION

When we compare the vocabulary items of various languages, we cannot help but notice the strong resemblance certain words bear to each other. By systematically comparing languages, we can establish whether two or more languages descended from a common parent and are therefore **genetically related** (see Chapter 8). The **comparative method** refers to the procedure of reconstructing earlier forms on the basis of a comparison of later forms. By means of such **comparative reconstruction**, we can reconstruct properties of the parent language with a great degree of certainty.

7.1 Comparative reconstruction

The most reliable sign of family relationships is the existence of **systematic phonetic correspondences** in the vocabulary items of different languages. Many such correspondences can be found in the sample of vocabulary items in Table 7.57 from English, Dutch, German, Danish, and Swedish, all of which are members of the Germanic family of languages.

Table 7.57 Some Germanic cognates

English	*Dutch*	*German*	*Danish*	*Swedish*
man	man	Mann	mand	man
hand	hand	Hand	hånd	hand
foot	voet	Fuß (ß=[s])	fod	fot
bring	brengen	bringen	bringe	bringa
summer	zomer	Sommer	sommer	sommar

Since the relationship between the phonological form and meaning of a word is mostly arbitrary, the existence of systematic phonetic correspondences in the forms of two or more languages must point toward a common source. Conversely, where languages are not related, their vocabulary items fail to show systematic similarities. This can be seen by comparing words from Turkish, which is not related to the Germanic languages, with their Germanic counterparts (Table 7.58).

Table 7.58 Some words in Turkish, a non-Germanic language (phonemic transcription)

adam	'man'
el	'hand'
ajak	'foot'
getir	'bring'
jaz	'summer'

Words that have descended from a common source (as shown by systematic phonetic correspondences and, usually, semantic similarities) are called **cognates**. Cognates are not always as obvious as the Germanic examples in Table 7.57. Where languages from the same family are only distantly related, the systematic correspondences may be considerably less striking. This is exemplified in the data in Table 7.59 from English, Russian, and Hindi, all of which are distantly related to each other. Forms from the unrelated Turkish are included to emphasize the similarities among the first three languages.

Once the existence of a relationship between two or more languages has been established, an attempt can be made to reconstruct the common source. This reconstructed language, or **proto-language**, is made up of **proto-forms**, which are written with a preceding * (e.g., **hand*) to indicate their hypothetical character as reconstructions of earlier forms that have not been recorded or are not directly observable.

Table 7.59 Some distantly related cognates compared to nonrelated Turkish

English	*Russian*	*Hindi*	*Turkish (phonemic transcription)*
two	dva	dō	iki
three	tri	tīn	ytʃ
brother	brat	bhāī	kardeʃ
nose	nos	nahī̃	burun

7.2 Techniques of reconstruction

Reconstruction can be undertaken with some confidence because (as discussed in the previous sections) the processes underlying language change are systematic. Once the processes are uncovered by linguists, they can be reversed, allowing us to infer earlier forms of the language. Although it is possible to reconstruct all components of a proto-language (its phonology, morphology, syntax, lexicon, and semantics), we will focus on phonological reconstruction—the area in which linguists have made the most progress.

Reconstruction strategies

Reconstruction of a proto-form makes use of two general strategies. The most important one is the **phonetic plausibility strategy**, which requires that any changes posited to account for differences between the proto-forms and later forms must be phonetically plausible. Secondarily, the **majority rules strategy** stipulates that if no phonetically plausible change can account for the observed differences, then the segment found in the majority of cognates should be assumed. It is important to note that the first strategy always takes precedence over the second; the second strategy is a last resort.

Consider the cognates (somewhat simplified) in Table 7.60 from members of the Romance family.

Table 7.60 Romance cognates

French	*Italian*	*Rumanian*	*Spanish*	
si	si	ʃi	si	'yes'

The data exemplify a correspondence between [s] and [ʃ] before the vowel [i]. To account for this, we could assume either that Rumanian underwent a change that converted [s] to [ʃ] before [i] or that the other three languages underwent a change converting [ʃ] to [s] before [i] as shown in Figure 7.13.

Hypothesis A
Proto-form: *si
Sound change (Rumanian only): *s > ʃ / ___ i

Hypothesis B
Proto-form: *ʃi
Sound change (French, Italian, and Spanish): *ʃ > s / ___ i

Figure 7.13 Romance cognates

Both reconstruction strategies favor hypothesis A. Most importantly, the phonetic change needed to account for the Rumanian pronunciation involves palatalization before [i]. Since palatalization in this context is a very common phenomenon in human language, it is reasonable to assume that it occurred in Rumanian. It would be much more difficult to argue that the proto-language contained [ʃ] before [i] and that three languages underwent the change posited by Hypothesis B, since depalatalization before [i] would be an unusual phonetic process. (The reconstructed **s* posited in hypothesis A is also compatible with the majority rules strategy, since three of the four languages in the data have [s] before [i].)

Reconstruction and the catalog of sound changes

Although there are factors that can confound our attempt to determine the relative plausibility of various sound changes, the changes listed in the catalog in Table 7.3 can generally be considered highly plausible. Table 7.61 lists some plausible versus less plausible or even implausible changes based on that catalog.

Table 7.61 Different rules in terms of their plausibility based on the catalog

Rule	*Name of sound change in the catalog*
High probability	
t > tʃ / __ i	palatalization
n > m / __ b	assimilation (place of articulation)
t > d / V __ V	voicing (assimilation)
k > Ø / V __ st	consonant deletion
Low probability	
tʃ > t / __ i	(does not correspond to any listed change)
m > n / __ b	(does not correspond to any listed change)
d > t / V __ V	(does not correspond to any listed change)
Ø > k / V __ st	(does not correspond to any listed change)

Reconstructing Proto-Romance

Consider now the slightly more complex example in Table 7.62 involving data from several languages of the Romance family.

Table 7.62 Some Romance cognates

Spanish		*Sardinian*	*French*		*Portuguese*	*Rumanian*	*Original meaning*
ri<u>b</u>a	[β]	ripa	rive	[ʁiv]	riba	rîpă	'embankment'
ami<u>g</u>a	[ɣ]	amica	amie	[ami]	amiga	—	'female friend'
copa		cuppa	coupe	[kup]	copa	cupă	'cup, goblet'
gota		gutta	goutte	[gut]	gota	gută	'drop'

(*Note*: Orthographic *c* represents [k] in all the above examples. Rumanian ă and î represent the central vowels [ə] and [ɨ], respectively. [β] is a voiced bilabial fricative and [ɣ] a voiced velar fricative. Some details of vowel quality have been ignored.)

Our goal here is to reconstruct the proto-forms for these words in Proto-Romance, which stands very close to Latin and is the parent language of the Modern Romance languages.

Let us first consider the reconstruction of the Proto-Romance form for 'embankment' (see Table 7.63). Since the first two segments are the same in all the cognate languages, we can reconstruct Proto-Romance **r* and **i* on the basis of the majority rules strategy. In the case of the second consonant, however, there are differences between the cognates.

Table 7.63 Systematic correspondences in the cognates for 'embankment'

Spanish	*Sardinian*	*French*	*Portuguese*	*Rumanian*
-β-	-p-	-v	-b-	-p-

It is most important that we first think in terms of phonetic plausibility. In the absence of evidence to the contrary, we will assume that one of the segments found in the cognates ([p], [b], [v], or [β]) should be reconstructed for Proto-Romance. Logically possible changes ranked with respect to their phonetic plausibility are found in Table 7.64.

Table 7.64 Changes based on phonetic plausibility

Change in V__V	*Name of change based on catalog*	*Phonetic plausibility*
p > b	voicing	high
p > v	voicing (p > b) and frication (b > v)	high
p > β	voicing (p > b) and frication (b > β)	high
b > p	—	low
β > p	—	low
v > p	—	low

In terms of plausibility, the only possible reconstruction for Proto-Romance is **p*. Proto-Romance **p* underwent no change in Sardinian and Rumanian, but in Portuguese it underwent intervocalic voicing and in Spanish it underwent both voicing and frication (that is, weakening) (see Table 7.65). (We assume that voicing preceded frication since Portuguese shows voicing but no frication.) If we assume that the final vowel of the proto-form was still present in French when the consonant changes took place, we can conclude that voicing and frication occurred in this language as well. (In its written form, *rive* retains a sign of the earlier reduced vowel [ə].) These changes are phonetically plausible and thus expected.

Table 7.65 Summary of the changes affecting Proto-Romance **p*

*p > p /V__V	no change in Sardinian or Rumanian
*p > b /V__V	voicing in Portuguese
*p > b > β /V__V	voicing and frication in Spanish
*p > b > v /V__V	voicing and frication in French

Turning now to the final vowel, we note that three languages have full vowels, Rumanian has [ə], and French has no vowel (see Table 7.66). Since vowel reduction and apocope are identified as phonetically plausible changes in the catalog, it is appropriate to posit a full vowel for the proto-language. Furthermore, since the three languages with a full vowel all have [a], we can posit this vowel on the basis of the majority rules strategy. Accordingly, the reconstructed proto-form is **ripa*.

Table 7.66 Summary of the changes affecting Proto-Romance **a*

Language	*Change (word final)*	*Name of change(s)*
Rumanian	*a > ə	vowel reduction
French	*a > ə > Ø	vowel reduction and deletion

We can now outline the evolution of the word in French, which has the most complicated development of the six languages (see Table 7.67).

Table 7.67 Evolution of French *rive* from **ripa*

Change	**ripa*	*Name of change*
p > b / V__ V	riba	voicing
b > v / V __ V	riva	frication
a > ə / __ #	rivə	vowel reduction
ə > Ø / __ #	riv	apocope

In the case of the cognates for 'female friend' (the second row of Table 7.62), the first three segments are the same in all the languages in the data. According to the majority rules strategy we can reconstruct the first three segments as **ami-*. In the reconstruction of the second consonant, however, we must appeal to our strategy of phonetic plausibility (see Table 7.68).

Table 7.68 Systematic correspondences in the second consonant of the cognates for 'female friend'

Spanish	*Sardinian*	*French*	*Portuguese*	*Rumanian*
-ɣ-	-k-	-Ø	-g-	—

Once again, since intervocalic voicing, frication, and deletion are phonetically plausible changes, it is most appropriate to posit **k* for the proto-form (see Table 7.69).

Table 7.69 Summary of the changes affecting Proto-Romance **k*

Language	*Change (in V_V)*	*Name of change(s)*
Portuguese	*k > g	voicing
Spanish	*k > g > ɣ	voicing and frication
French	*k > g > ɣ > Ø	voicing, frication, and deletion

In the case of the final vowel, we have the same situation we had in the previous form. The full vowel is found in Spanish, Sardinian, and Portuguese but there is no vowel in French. We can therefore assume the full vowel **a* for the proto-form, with subsequent vowel reduction and apocope in French. Consequently, we arrive at the proto-form **amika*.

Finally, applying the same procedure to the cognates in the final two rows of Table 7.62 yields the proto-forms **kuppa* 'cup' and **gutta* 'drop'. All the languages in the data retain the initial consonant of both proto-forms. The vowel **u* is reconstructed on the basis of the majority rules strategy, since we have no phonetic grounds for choosing either [u] or [o] as the older vowel. The systematic correspondences involving the intervocalic consonants are given in Table 7.70.

Table 7.70 Systematic correspondences of the medial consonants of **kuppa* and **gutta*

Spanish	*Sardinian*	*French*	*Portuguese*	*Rumanian*
-p-	-pp-	-p	-p-	-p-
-t-	-tt-	-t	-t-	-t-

Regardless of whether we are dealing with original **pp* or **tt,* the same pattern is evident in the case of both geminate types. There is a geminate stop consonant in Sardinian and a single consonant in Spanish, French, Portuguese, and Rumanian. Since degemination is an expected sound change (see the catalog in Table 7.3), we assume that the proto-forms contained geminate consonants that underwent degemination except in Sardinian. This is an example of a case in which the phonetic plausibility strategy overrules the majority rules strategy (since four of the five languages have [p]/[t] whereas only one language has [pp]/[tt]). As far as the final vowels are concerned, the same pattern found in the previous examples is once again evident. Proto-Romance **a* was retained in Spanish, Sardinian, and Portuguese; reduced to [ə] in Rumanian; and deleted in French (see Table 7.66).

Of the languages exemplified here, Sardinian is considered the most conservative since it has retained more of the earlier consonants and vowels. (In fact, the Sardinian words in the examples happen to be identical with the proto-forms, but this degree of resemblance would not be maintained in a broader range of data.) In the case of the other Romance languages and changes we have discussed, the most to least conservative are: Portuguese (degemination and voicing) and Rumanian (degemination and vowel reduction); Spanish (degemination, voicing, and frication); and French (degemination, voicing, frication, consonant deletion, vowel reduction, and apocope).

Although there is no reason to expect Proto-Romance to be identical with classical Latin, close similarity is expected. Accordingly, the fact that our reconstructions are so close to the Latin words gives us confidence in our methods of reconstruction (see Table 7.71).

Table 7.71 Comparison of Latin and Proto-Romance forms

Latin	*Proto-Romance form*
rīpa	*ripa
amīca (c = [k])	*amika
cuppa	*kuppa
gutta	*gutta

Notice that it is sometimes not possible to reconstruct all the characteristics of the proto-language. For example, on the basis of our data we were not able to reconstruct vowel length (Latin had a distinction between long and short vowels), since there was no evidence of this characteristic in the cognate forms.

It is also worth noting that we are not always so fortunate as to have written records of a language that we expect to be very close to our reconstructed language. In the case of the Germanic languages, for example, there is no ancient written language equivalent to Latin. We must rely completely on our reconstruction of Proto-Germanic to determine the properties of the language from which the modern-day Germanic languages descended. Furthermore, for many languages of the world, we have no written historical records at all, and for other languages, such as the Amerindian languages of North America, it is only very recently that we have written records.

In summary, when the forms of two or more languages appear to be related, we can, through a consideration of systematic phonetic correspondences among cognates, reconstruct the common form from which all the forms can be derived by means of phonetically plausible sound changes. Genetically related lexical forms of different languages are called cognates, while the reconstructed forms are called proto-forms and a reconstructed language, a proto-language.

7.3 Internal reconstruction

Sometimes it is possible to reconstruct the earlier form of a language even without reference to comparative data. This technique, known as **internal reconstruction**, relies on the analysis of morphophonemic variation within a single language. The key point is that the sound changes that create allomorphic and allophonic variation can be identified and then used to infer an earlier form of the morpheme. The data in Table 7.72 are from French; because of borrowing, English exhibits a parallel set of contrasts involving [k] and [ʃ].

Table 7.72 [k] / [s] correspondence in French

maʒik	'magic'	maʒis-jɛ̃	'magician'
lɔʒik	'logic'	lɔʒis-jɛ̃	'logician'
myzik	'music'	myzis-jɛ̃	'musician'

The root morpheme in each row exhibits two forms, one ending in [k], the other ending in [s]. The same methods and principles used in comparative reconstruction can be applied here to reconstruct the historically earlier form of the root morpheme. If a root ending in **s* is posited, no phonetically plausible change can account for the [k] in the left-hand column. By contrast, if a root-final **k* is posited, the [s] can be accounted for by assuming that the **k* was fronted under the influence of the high front vowel of the suffix (palatalization) and became an affricate [ts] (affrication), which was later simplified to a fricative [s] (deaffrication). All of these changes are phonetically plausible and listed in the catalog in Table 7.3. Accordingly, internal reconstruction indicates that at an earlier point in the development of French, the root morphemes in Table 7.72 contained the consonant **k*.

7.4 The discovery of Indo-European

The late eighteenth-century discovery that Sanskrit (the ancient language of India) was related to Latin, Greek, Germanic, and Celtic revolutionized European linguistic studies. Sir William Jones, a British judge and scholar working in India, summed up the nature and implications of the findings in his 1786 address to the Royal Asiatic Society, a part of which follows:

> The Sanskrit language, whatever be its antiquity, is of a wonderful structure; more perfect than the Greek, more copious [having more cases] than the Latin, and more exquisitely refined than either, yet bearing to both of them a stronger affinity, both in the roots of the verbs and in the forms of the grammar, than could possibly have been produced by accident; so strong indeed, that no philologer could examine them all three, without believing them to have sprung from some common source, which, perhaps, no longer exists; there is a similar reason . . . for supposing that both the Gothic and the Celtic . . . had the same origin with the Sanskrit; and the old Persian might be added to the same family . . .

This discovery led to several decades of intensive historical-comparative work and to important advances in historical linguistics during the nineteenth century. By studying phonetic correspondences from an ever increasing number of languages, linguists eventually ascertained that most of the languages of Europe, Persia (Iran), and the northern part of India belong to a single family, now called Indo-European. By applying the techniques of the comparative method, they began reconstructing the grammar of the proto-language from which these languages evolved—**Proto-Indo-European (PIE)**.

A number of individuals advanced this research. In 1814, the Danish linguist Rasmus Rask carefully documented the relationships among cognates in a number of Indo-European languages, and at the same time established the methods that would govern the emerging science of historical-comparative linguistics. He wrote:

> When agreement is found in [the most essential] words in two languages, and so frequently that rules may be drawn up for the shift in letters [sounds] from one to the other, then there is a fundamental relationship between the two languages; especially when similarities in the inflectional system and in the general make-up of the languages correspond with them.

Rask worked without access to Sanskrit. The first comparative linguistic analysis of Sanskrit, Greek, Persian, and the Germanic languages was done by the German scholar Franz Bopp in 1816. In 1822 another German, Jakob Grimm, extended Rask's observations and became the first person to explain the relationships among the cognates noted by Rask in terms of a **sound shift**, the systematic modification of a series of phonemes. Some of the correspondences on which he based his work are given in Table 7.73.

Table 7.73 Some Indo-European phonetic correspondences

Greek	*Latin*	*English*
patḗr	pater	father
treîs	trēs	three
hekatón	centum	hundred

The crucial observation is that where English has [f], [θ], and [h] (indicated here by underlining), Greek and Latin have [p], [t], and [k]. Grimm tabulated a series of consonant shifts for Proto-Germanic that differentiated it from other Indo-European languages. **Grimm's Law** is the name given to the consonant shifts that took place between Proto-Indo-European and Proto-Germanic (see Table 7.74).

Table 7.74 The sound shifts underlying Grimm's Law

Proto-Indo-European	p	t	k	b	d	g	bh	dh	gh
Germanic	f	θ	x	p	t	k	b	d	g

Some additional examples of the relationships captured by these shifts are below in Table 7.75. The Proto-Indo-European consonants were either maintained in Sanskrit, Greek, and Latin or in some cases underwent changes different from those found in Germanic.

Table 7.75 Some examples of the consonant shifts underlying Grimm's Law

Shift in Germanic	*Sanskrit*	*Greek*	*Latin*	*English*
p > f	pād-	pod-	ped-	foot
t > θ	tanu-	tanaós	tenuis	thin
k > x	çatam	hekatón	centum	hundred
b > p	—	—	lūbricus	slippery
d > t	daça	déka	decem	ten
g > k	ajras	agrós	ager	acre
bh > b	bhrātā	phrā́tēr	frāter	brother
dh > d	vidhavā	ēítheos	vidua	widow
gh > g	hansas	khḗn	(h)ānser	goose

Although there appeared to be exceptions to Grimm's Law, they turned out to be systematic and could be traced to specific environments. For example, voiceless stops were not subject to Grimm's Law when they were immediately preceded by *s* (see Table 7.76).

Table 7.76 A systematic exception to Grimm's Law

Original s + voiceless stop			
Latin	stāre	English	stand [st] (not [sθ])

A particularly important discovery was made by Karl Verner, who traced a group of exceptions to Grimm's Law to the original accentual pattern of Proto-Indo-European. In a generalization that came to be known as **Verner's Law**, he proposed that a voiceless fricative resulting from Grimm's Law underwent voicing if the original Proto-Indo-European accent did not immediately precede it. Since stress came to be fixed on the root syllable in Germanic subsequent to the changes covered by Verner's Law, the original environment was obscured. However, Sanskrit provides very direct evidence for Verner's claim, since it was very conservative in its maintenance of the original Proto-Indo-European stress. Although the English forms are complicated by other developments, the effects of Verner's Law are apparent in the Gothic examples in Table 7.77. In the Gothic word for *brother*, PIE **t* becomes [θ] according to Grimm's Law, whereas in the word for *father* it becomes [ð] in accordance with both Grimm's and Verner's Law.

Table 7.77 Verner's Law

PIE	*Sanskrit*	*Grimm's Law*	*Verner's Law*	*Gothic*	
*t	bhrā́tā	*t > θ	—	[bro:θar]	'brother'
*t	pitā́	*t > θ	θ > ð	[faðar]	'father'

It should also be noted here that borrowing is an important factor that must be taken into consideration when comparative reconstruction is being carried out. For example, English has many words that do not show the effects of Grimm's Law (see Table 7.78).

Table 7.78 English words not showing the effects of Grimm's Law

Expected by Grimm's Law	*Latin*	*English*
p > f	ped-	pedestrian
t > θ	tenuis	tenuous
k > h	canalis	canal

The apparent failure of Grimm's Law here stems from the fact that the English words were borrowed directly from Latin or French many centuries after the sound shifts described by Grimm's Law had taken place. The task of reconstruction can often be complicated by such borrowings.

Subsequent developments

By the middle of the nineteenth century, the study of language had made great strides—especially in the field of phonetics, which opened the way for the detailed comparison of linguistic forms. One influential hypothesis at that time was that sound laws operated without exception. A group of linguists known as the Neogrammarians adopted this idea and made many important contributions to the fledgling science of linguistics by applying it to new and more complicated data. Although such factors as lexical diffusion and social pressures were more or less ignored by the Neogrammarians, their hypothesis represented an important and daring advance in the scientific study of language.

The nineteenth century also saw major advances in the classification of languages. A German scholar, August Schleicher, developed a classification for the Indo-European languages in the form of a genealogical tree. This type of genetic classification is discussed in much more detail in the chapter on language typology that follows.

Work in comparative reconstruction is far from finished. In particular, linguists are now considering the possibility of superfamilies. One such proposed family is Nostratic, which includes Indo-European, Afro-Asiatic (e.g., Arabic, Hebrew), Altaic (e.g., Japanese, Korean, Turkic), and Uralic (e.g., Finnish, Hungarian). (See Chapter 8 for further discussion.) Comparative reconstruction is also playing an important role in determining the genetic relationships of the hundreds of North American indigenous languages—a topic that still remains highly controversial.

7.5 Reconstruction and typology

Since the 1800s, when the reconstruction of Proto-Indo-European was carried out, linguists have accumulated vast amounts of information on thousands of languages. This is in part due to the explosion of studies in the field of linguistic typology, which is concerned with the investigation of structural similarities among languages that are not genetically related. Even languages that do not belong to the same family can have striking similarities. For example, in addition to shared word-order patterns (see Section 2.3 in Chapter 8), SOV languages commonly exhibit a strong tendency toward agglutinating morphology (a type of complex affixation; see Chapter 8) and vowel harmony. Typological studies play an important role in the linguist's search for universals of language—statements that are true for all languages.

The extensive information on the languages of the world available to modern linguists was, of course, not available at the time the original reconstruction of Proto-Indo-European was undertaken. Modern linguists involved in comparative reconstruction now take a keen interest in typological studies and the role of **typological plausibility** in reconstruction has become an important topic. For example, a linguist would be very reluctant to propose a reconstruction that violated a universal property of language or that had no parallel in any known language.

Some linguists have argued that the traditional reconstruction of the PIE consonant system (given in Table 7.79) should be rejected on the basis of typological plausibility.

Table 7.79 The traditional reconstruction of the Proto-Indo-European consonants

p	t	ḱ	k	k^w	(voiceless stops)
(b)	d	ǵ	g	g^w	(voiced stops)
bh	dh	ǵh	gh	g^wh	(voiced aspirated stops)
	s				

(*Note: ḱ, ǵ,* and *ǵh* are palatal stops and ^{w} indicates a labialized consonant.)

This reconstruction is typologically questionable in at least two respects. First, reconstructed forms with PIE **b* are extremely rare, almost as if there were a gap in the labial system. Such a gap is very uncommon in the languages of the world. Typically if there is a missing labial stop, it is the voiceless stop that is missing, not the voiced counterpart. Second, the traditional reconstruction posits a series of voiced aspirated stops but no corresponding series of voiceless aspirated stops, even though some typologists have argued that all languages that have a voiced series also have a voiceless one.

Such facts have led some linguists to propose what they believe is a more typologically plausible reconstruction of Proto-Indo-European involving a voiceless stop series, an ejective series (produced by a closing of the glottis and raising of the larynx), and a voiced stop series (as well as **s* as in the traditional reconstruction) (see Table 7.80).

Table 7.80 A recent reconstruction of the Proto-Indo-European consonants

p	t	ḱ	k	k^w	(voiceless stops)
(p')	t'	ḱ'	k'	k'^w	(ejectives)
b	d	ǵ	g	g^w	(voiced stops)
	s				

Not only does this reconstruction avoid the problem with aspirates, but it also accounts for the missing labial, in that it is common for languages with an ejective series to lack the labial. From this perspective, this reconstruction seems much more plausible than the traditional one.

Both reconstructions have their supporters, and it is difficult to come to a definitive decision on the basis of typological considerations, since it is common for a proposed universal to have exceptions. For example, a few languages have been found with the characteristics attributed to Proto-Indo-European by the traditional reconstruction. These languages have labial gaps in the voiced series (e.g., Amerindian languages of the Athapaskan and Caddoan families) and a voiced aspirate series but no voiceless counterpart (Madurese, an Indonesian language). Accordingly, as long as the traditional reconstruction is linguistically possible, it would not seem possible to reject it simply because the phonological system proposed would be a rare one.

Typological plausibility will likely continue to play a secondary role in reconstruction until linguists can draw a clear line between what is linguistically possible and what is not possible. Nevertheless, as our knowledge and understanding of language universals continues to improve, it is certain that linguists involved in the reconstruction of proto-languages will maintain an interest in typological plausibility.

8 LANGUAGE CHANGE AND NATURALNESS

A striking fact about language change is that the same patterns of change occur repeatedly, not only within the same language at different periods in its history but also across languages. Both the similarity of changes across languages as well as the directionality of language change suggest that some changes are more natural than others. This notion of **naturalness** is implicit in the phonetic plausibility strategy introduced in the section on comparative reconstruction.

If naturalness is a factor in language change, its manifestations should also be found in the language acquisition process and in language universals. This does seem to be the case. As a specific example, let us consider the frequently made claim that the CV syllable is the most natural of all syllable types. At least three different kinds of evidence can be brought forth in support of this claim.

First, in terms of universals, all languages of the world have CV syllables in their syllable type inventory. Second, a variety of sound changes have the effect of reducing less natural syllable types to the more natural CV type (see Table 7.81).

Table 7.81 Sound changes yielding CV syllables

Deletion								
CCV	>	CV	Old English	cnēow	English	knee	/ni/
CVC	>	CV	Old Spanish	non	Spanish	no	
Vowel epenthesis							
CCVCV	>	CVCVCV	Italian	croce	Sicilian	kiruci	'cross'

By contrast, note that such changes rarely if ever apply to a CV syllable to yield a different syllable type. Deletion of the C in a word-initial CV syllable is extremely rare, as is vowel epenthesis in a CV syllable or a sequence of CVCV syllables.

Third, in terms of language acquisition, the CV syllable type is one of the first syllable types to be acquired, and many phonetic processes found in child language have the effect of yielding CV syllables, just like the sound changes listed in Table 7.81 (see Chapter 10 on language acquisition; see Table 7.82).

Table 7.82 Phonetic processes in language acquisition yielding CV syllables

CCV → CV	tree → [ti]	(simplification of consonant clusters)
CVC → CV	dog → [dɑ]	(deletion of final consonants)

It is clear, however, that it is inappropriate to take a simplistic view of linguistic naturalness. For example, some sound changes produce less natural syllables. Thus, syncope has the effect of reducing a sequence of CVCVCV syllables to the less natural CVCCV. Usually in such cases a different motivation can be identified, such as the preference for shorter phonological forms over longer forms. But given the complexity of human language, not to mention human behavior in general, it should not be surprising that there are many different parameters of linguistic naturalness and that these can, in turn, lead to apparently conflicting changes in language over time. It remains an important task of the linguist to identify, rank, and ultimately explain relations of linguistic naturalness. The study of language change will continue to make an important contribution to this area.

Summing up

Historical linguistics studies the nature and causes of language change. The causes of language change find their roots in the physiological and cognitive makeup of human beings. Sound changes usually involve articulatory simplification as in the case of the most common type, **assimilation**. **Analogy** and **reanalysis** are particularly important factors in morphological change. **Language contact** resulting in **borrowing** is another important source of language change. All components of the grammar, from phonology to semantics, are subject to change over time. A change can simultaneously affect all instances of a particular sound or form, or it can spread through the language word by word by means of **lexical diffusion**. Sociological factors can play an important role in determining whether or not a linguistic innovation is ultimately adopted by the linguistic community at large. Since language change is systematic, it is possible, by identifying the changes that a particular language or dialect has undergone, to reconstruct linguistic history and thereby posit the earlier forms from which later forms have evolved. Using sets of **cognates**, **comparative reconstruction** allows us to reconstruct the properties of the parent or **proto-language** on the basis of **systematic phonetic correspondences**.

Studies in historical linguistics can provide valuable insights into relationships among languages and shed light on prehistoric developments. Furthermore, historical studies of language are of great importance to our understanding of human linguistic competence. In fact, it has often been stated that language change provides one of the most direct windows into the workings of the human mind. Furthermore, the study of language change contributes to our understanding of how social, cultural, and psychological factors interact to shape language. Finally, the integration of studies on language change, language acquisition, and language universals remains one of the most important challenges facing linguists today.

Key terms

General terms and terms concerning the nature of change and its spread

analogy
articulatory simplification
borrowing
historical linguistics
hypercorrection
language contact

lexical diffusion
reanalysis
sound change
spelling pronunciation

General terms concerning sound change

assimilation
consonantal strength
deaffrication
dissimilation
epenthesis
glide strengthening
metathesis
phonetic sound change
phonetically conditioned change
segmental change
sequential change
substitution
weakening

Terms concerning sound change by assimilation

affrication
nasalization
palatalization
partial assimilation
total assimilation
umlaut

Terms concerning sound change by weakening

apocope
consonant deletion
consonant weakening
degemination
deletion
frication
rhotacism
syncope
voicing
vowel reduction

Terms concerning phonological change

diphthongization
Great English Vowel Shift
mergers
phonological (sound) change
shifts
splits

Terms concerning morphological and syntactical changes

analytic languages
folk etymology
fusion
grammaticalization
synthetic languages

Terms concerning changes in words and their meanings

adstratum influence
amelioration
lexical gaps
metaphor
pejoration
semantic broadening
semantic narrowing
semantic shift
substratum influence
superstratum influence
weakening of meaning

Terms concerning genetic relationships and reconstruction

cognates
comparative method
comparative reconstruction
genetically related (languages)
Grimm's Law
internal reconstruction

majority rules strategy
naturalness
phonetic plausibility strategy
proto-forms
Proto-Indo-European (PIE)
proto-language
sound shift
systematic phonetic correspondences
typological plausibility
Verner's Law

Notes

1 The translation for the passage is as follows:
Many men say that in dreams
There is nothing but talk and lies
But men may see some dreams
Which are scarcely false
But afterward come true.

2 In these and other examples throughout this chapter, orthographic forms are given where these clearly reflect the sound change(s) in question. If required, partial or full phonetic transcriptions are provided.

Sources

The textbooks (cited under Recommended Reading) by Anttila, Campbell, Hock, Labov, and Trask provide much more detailed discussions of most of the major topics in this chapter. They are also excellent sources for references relating to particular topics. Hock is particularly important for providing detailed discussions of syntactical change and the role of typology in reconstruction.

Overviews of historical linguistics as it applies to the development of English are presented in the books by Blake, Millward, and Smith cited under Recommended Reading.

The catalog of sound changes is adapted from catalogs proposed by Theo Vennemann in the article "Linguistic Typologies in Historical Linguistics" in *Società di linguistica italiana* 23 (1985): 87–91 and a book entitled *Preference Laws for Syllable Structure and the Explanation of Sound Change* (Amsterdam: Mouton de Gruyter, 1988). Section 2 has also benefited from unpublished material (particularly the manuscript *Linguistic Change*) kindly made available by Theo Vennemann (University of Munich) to the author during his stay in Munich from 1980 to 1985.

The data on vowel laxing in Canadian French are from Douglas C. Walker's book *The Pronunciation of Canadian French* (Ottawa: University of Ottawa Press, 1984). The data on word order in Old and Middle English come from the book by Joseph Williams, *Origins of the English Language: A Social and Linguistic History* (New York: Free Press, 1975). The examples of English loan words in Gwich'in (Loucheux) are given in *Dene* 1:1 (1985), published by the Dene Language Terminology Committee, Yellowknife, Northwest Territories. The discussion of borrowing and semantic change in English draws on materials in the book by Williams.

The table depicting lexical diffusion of the stress change in English nouns derived from verbs is taken from the book by Jean Aitchison, *Language Change: Progress or*

Decay? (New York: Universe Books, 1985). Aitchison's remarks are based on the article by M. Chen and W. Wang, "Sound Change: Actuation and Implementation," *Language* 51 (1975): 255–81. The data on the realization of [s] as [h] in Spanish were provided by Herbert Izzo of the University of Calgary.

The Germanic cognates used to illustrate family relationships are based on Leonard Bloomfield's classic work *Language* (New York: Holt, Rinehart and Winston, 1933). Some of the Romance cognates in this section come from *Proto-Romance Phonology* by Robert A. Hall, Jr. (New York: Elsevier, 1976). The quote from Jones is taken from *A Reader in Nineteenth-Century Historical Indo-European Linguistics,* edited and translated by Winfred P. Lehmann (Bloomington, IN: Indiana University Press, 1967), and the quote from Rask is taken from Holger Pedersen's book *The Discovery of Language: Linguistic Science in the Nineteenth Century* (Bloomington, IN: Indiana University Press, 1959).

Question 2 is based on data provided by Dr. George Patterson, whose generosity we hereby acknowledge. The data for questions 3 and 4 are from F. Columbus's *Introductory Workbook in Historical Phonology* (Cambridge, MA: Slavica, 1974). Question 10 is based on data provided by David Bellusci. The data for question 18 are drawn from *Source Book for Linguistics* by W. Cowan and J. Rakusan (Philadelphia: John Benjamins, 1987).

Recommended reading

Anttila, Raimo. 1989. *Historical and Comparative Linguistics.* 2nd ed. Amsterdam: John Benjamins.

Blake, N. F. 1996. *A History of the English Language.* Houndmills, Basingstoke, Hampshire: Macmillan.

Campbell, Lyle. 1999. *Historical Linguistics: An Introduction.* Cambridge, MA: MIT Press.

Hock, Hans Heinrich. 1992. *Principles of Historical Linguistics.* 2nd ed. Amsterdam: Mouton de Gruyter.

Hock, Hans Heinrich, and Brian D. Joseph. 1996. *Language History, Language Change, and Language Relationship: An Introduction to Historical and Comparative Linguistics.* New York: Mouton de Gruyter.

Hopper, Paul J., and Elizabeth Closs Traugott. 1993. *Grammaticalization.* Cambridge: Cambridge University Press.

Koerner, E. F., and R. E. Asher, eds. 1995. *Concise History of the Language Sciences: From the Sumerians to the Cognitivists.* New York: Pergamon.

Labov, William. 1994. *Principles of Linguistic Change: Internal Factors.* Oxford: Blackwell.

Lass, Roger. 1997. *Historical Linguistics and Language Change.* Cambridge: Cambridge University Press.

Lehmann, Winfred P. 1992. *Historical Linguistics.* 3rd ed. New York: Routledge.

McMahon, April M. S. 1994. *Understanding Language Change.* Cambridge: Cambridge University Press.

Millward, C. M. 1996. *A Biography of the English Language.* 2nd ed. New York: Holt, Rinehart and Winston.

Smith, Jeremy. 1996. *An Historical Study of English: Function, Form and Change.* New York: Routledge.
Trask, R. L. 1996. *Historical Linguistics.* London: Arnold.

Questions

1. Identify the following sound changes with reference to the catalog of sound changes provided in Table 7.3. In each pair of examples, focus on the segment(s) in bold only. The form on the left indicates the original segment(s) before the change, and the form on the right indicates the segment(s) after the change. (Note that * stands for hypothetical representation.)

a)	Sanskrit	**sn**eha	Pali	**sin**eha	'friendship'
b)	Old English	**hl**āf	English	**l**oaf	
c)	Latin	**i**uvenis [j]	Italian	**gi**ovane [dʒ]	'young'
d)	English	tria**thl**on	dialect	tria**th[ə]l**on	
e)	Latin	vi**du**a [dw]	Spanish	vi**ud**a [wd]	'widow'
f)	Sanskrit	sa**pt**a	Pali	sa**tt**a	'seven'
g)	Latin	tu**r**tu**r**	English	tu**r**t**l**e	
h)		*ve**nr**é	Spanish	ve**ndr**é	'I will come'
i)	Italian	mu**nd**o	Sicilian	mu**nn**u	'world'
j)	Old French	**c**ire [t^s]	French	**c**ire [s]	'wax'
k)	Latin	p**ān**-	French	p**ain** [ɛ̃]	'bread'
l)	Latin	**mul**gēre	Italian	**mun**gere	'to milk'
m)	Latin	pa**c**āre [k]	Italian	pa**g**are	'to pay'
n)	Old Spanish	ni**d**o	Spanish	ni**d**o [ð]	'nest'
o)	Latin	pe**cc**ātum [kk]	Spanish	pe**c**ado [k]	'sin'
p)		*honō**s**is	Latin	honō**r**is	'honor (gen sg)'
q)	English	ra**ge**	French	ra**ge** [ʒ]	'rage'
r)	English	co**ff**ee	Chipewyan	[ka**θ**i]	
s)	Latin	mar**e**	Portuguese	mar	'sea'
t)	Latin	vīcīn**i**tās	Spanish	vecindad	'neighborhood'
u)	Gothic	**þ**liuhan [θ]	English	**f**lee	
v)	Old English	(ic) sing**e**	English	(I) sing	
w)	Latin	su**mm**a	Spanish	su**m**a	'sum, gist'
x)	Latin	ōrn**ā**mentum	Old French	orn**e**ment [ə]	'ornament'
y)		*l**ū**si	Old English	l**ȳ**s [yː]	'lice'

2. *i)* Describe the difference between the two French dialects in the following data. Assume that the data are in phonetic transcription.
   ii) What sound change would you posit here? Why?
   iii) State the sound change in the form of a rule.

	European French	*Acadian French*	
a)	okyn	otʃyn	'none'
b)	kør	tʃør	'heart'
c)	ke	tʃe	'wharf'
d)	kɛ̃ːz	tʃɛ̃ːz	'fifteen'

e)	akyze	atʃyze	'accuse'
f)	ki	tʃi	'who'
g)	kav	kav	'cave'
h)	kɔr	kɔr	'body'
i)	kurir	kurir	'run'
j)	ɑ̃kɔːr	ɑ̃kɔːr	'again'

3. *i)* What sound changes differentiate Guaraní from its parent language, Proto-Tupí-Guaraní, in the following data?
   ii) State these changes in rule form.

	Proto-Tupí-Guaraní	*Guaraní*	
a)	jukɨr	jukɨ	'salt'
b)	moajan	moajã	'push'
c)	puʔam	puʔã	'wet'
d)	meʔeŋ	meʔẽ	'give'
e)	tiŋ	tʃĩ	'white'
f)	potiʔa	potʃiʔa	'chest'
g)	tatatiŋ	tatatʃĩ	'smoke'
h)	kɨb	kɨ	'louse'
i)	men	mẽ	'husband'

4. *i)* Describe the three changes that took place between Proto-Slavic and Bulgarian in the following data. (The symbol ˘ over a vowel indicates that it is short.)
   ii) State these changes as rules and indicate, as far as possible, the order in which they must have applied.
   iii) Apply these rules to the Proto-Slavic word for 'adroit' to show how the Bulgarian form evolved.

	Proto-Slavic	*Bulgarian*	
a)	gladŭka	glatkə	'smooth'
b)	kratŭka	kratkə	'short'
c)	blizŭka	bliskə	'near'
d)	ʒeʒĭka	ʒeʃkə	'scorching'
e)	lovŭka	lofkə	'adroit'
f)	gorĭka	gorkə	'bitter'

5. For each word, list all the sound changes required to derive the later form from the proto-form. Where necessary, give the chronology of the sound changes.

a)	*feminam	Old French	femme (final e =[ə])	'woman'
b)	*lumine	Spanish	lumbre	'fire'
c)	*tremulare	Spanish	temblar	'tremble'
d)	*stuppam	Spanish	estopa	'tow'
e)	*populu	Rumanian	plop	'poplar'

6. Taking into consideration the Great Vowel Shift, give all the changes necessary to derive the Modern English forms from the Old English forms. (*Note:* Assume, simplifying somewhat, that the Old English forms were pronounced as they are written.)

	Old English	*Modern English*	
a)	brōde (sg acc)	brood	[brud]
b)	cnotta (c = [k])	knot	[nɑt]
c)	wīse	wise	[wajz]
d)	hlǣfdige	lady	[lejdi]

7. Place names are often subject to spelling pronunciation. Transcribe your pronunciation of the following words and then compare your pronunciation with that recommended by a good dictionary. Do you think any of your pronunciations qualify as spelling pronunciations?
   a) Worcestershire
   b) Thames
   c) Edinburgh (Scotland; compare Edinburgh, Texas)
   d) Cannes (France)
   e) Newfoundland

8. Compare the Old English singular and plural forms:

Singular	*Plural*	
bōc	bēc	'book(s)'
āc	ǣc	'oak(s)'

   Although the Old English words have an umlaut plural (as in Old English gōs/gēs 'goose/geese'), the Modern English forms do not. Explain how the change in plural formation could have come about.

9. As evident in the following sentence, Shona, a modern Bantu language, has SVO word order. (*Note:* The morpheme *ano-* marks present tense.)

mwana	anotengesa	miriwo
child	sells	vegetables

   'The child sells vegetables'

   By contrast, Shona's morphology reflects a different pattern, as evidenced in the following examples.

mwana	ano**mu***ona*
child	**him**+*see*

   'The child sees him'

mukadzi	ano**va***batsira*
woman	**them**+*help*

   'The woman helps them'

   What do these examples indicate about earlier Shona or possibly Proto-Bantu word order?

10. All of the following English words at one time had meanings that are quite different from their current ones. Identify each of these semantic changes as an instance of narrowing, broadening, amelioration, pejoration, weakening, or shift.

	Word	*Earlier meaning*
a)	moody	'brave'
b)	uncouth	'unknown'
c)	aunt	'father's sister'

d) butcher 'one who slaughters goats'
e) witch 'male or female sorcerer'
f) sly 'skillful'
g) accident 'an event'
h) argue 'make clear'
i) carry 'transport by cart'
j) grumble 'murmur, make low sounds'
k) shrewd 'depraved, wicked'
l) praise 'set a value on'
m) ordeal 'trial by torture'
n) picture 'a painted likeness'
o) seduce 'persuade someone to desert his or her duty'
p) box 'a small container made of boxwood'
q) baggage 'a worthless person'
r) virtue 'qualities one expected of a man'
s) myth 'story'
t) undertaker 'one who undertakes'
u) hussy 'housewife'
v) astonish 'strike by thunder'
w) write 'scratch'
x) quell 'kill'

11. Look up the following words in a good dictionary. Discuss any semantic changes that have affected the underscored portions since Old English. Do you think speakers of Modern English have reanalyzed any of these forms in terms of folk etymology?
    a) wed<u>lock</u>
    b) witch<u>craft</u>
    c) stead<u>fast</u>
    d) after<u>ward</u>

12. The following line is from *Troilus and Criseyde V* by Geoffrey Chaucer.
    His lighte goost ful blisfully is went.
    [hɪs liçtə gɔːst fʊl blɪsfʊlli ɪs wɛnt] ([ç] is a voiceless palatal fricative.)
    His light spirit has gone very blissfully.
    i) How has the meaning of the word *ghost* changed since Chaucer's time?
    ii) Describe the changes that have taken place in the pronunciation of *light* and *ghost*.

13. Consider the following lyrics from the Middle English song "Sumer is i-cumen in." Compare the Middle English lyrics with the Modern English translation and answer the questions that follow.

Original text	*Transcription*
Sumer is i-cumen in;	[sʊmər ɪs ɪkʊmən ɪn
Lhude sing, cuccu!	luːdə sɪŋg kʊkku
Grōweþ sēd, and blōweþ mēd,	grɔːwəθ seːd and blɔːwəθ meːd
And springþ þe wude nū.	and sprɪŋgθ ðə wʊdə nuː]

Translation
'Summer has come in;
Loudly sing, cuckoo!
Seed grows and meadow blooms
And the wood grows now.'

i) What affix converted the adjective *loud* into an adverb in Middle English?
ii) What accounts for the difference between the Middle English and Modern English pronunciation of the vowel in *loud*?
iii) What other words in this poem reflect this general shift?
iv) How has the relative ordering of the subject and verb changed since this was written?
v) How has the third person singular present tense suffix changed since Middle English?

14. The following Cree words were borrowed from French as the result of contact between the two groups on the Canadian prairies. (Notice that the French determiner was not treated as a separate morpheme and was carried along with the borrowed word.) What types of considerations could one plausibly assume played a role in the borrowing of these words into Cree?

	Cree	*French*	
a)	labutōn	le bouton	'button'
b)	lībot	les bottes	'boots'
c)	lamilās	la mélasse	'molasses'
d)	lapwīl	la poêle	'frying pan'
e)	litī	le thé	'tea'

15. The following Latin roots are found in words that have been borrowed into English. Since these words were borrowed after Grimm's Law had applied, they do not show its effects. All of these roots, however, do have Germanic cognates that did undergo Grimm's Law. On the basis of your knowledge of this law and the meaning of the borrowing, try to determine the Modern English (Germanic) cognate for each root. Consult a good dictionary if you need help. (*Note:* Focus on the portion of the Latin word in bold only; vowel changes must also be taken into consideration.)

	Latin root	*Related borrowing*	*English cognate*
a)	**ped**is	pedestrian	*foot*
b)	**nep**os	nepotism	___________
c)	**pisc**es	piscine	___________
d)	**ten**uis	tenuous	___________
e)	**corn**u	cornucopia	___________
f)	**duo**	dual	___________
g)	**ed**ere	edible	___________
h)	**gen**us	genocide	___________
i)	**ager**	agriculture	___________

16. Attempt to reconstruct the Proto-Germanic form for each pair of cognates. Focusing on the vowels, describe the changes that affected the Old English forms. (*Note:* y = [y], œ = [ø], and j = [j].)

	Gothic	Old English	
a)	kuni	cyn	'kin'
b)	badi	bed	'bed'
c)	dōmjan	dœ̄man	'to judge'
d)	sōkjan	sœ̄can	'to seek'
e)	bugjan	bycgan	'to buy'
f)	nati	net	'net'

17. Reconstruct the Proto-Romance form for each set of cognates. Give all the changes necessary to derive each of the modern forms from the proto-forms. If you are not sure how to proceed, return to Section 7. (*Note:* The Spanish and Rumanian spelling 'ie' represents the sequence /je/, and the Rumanian spelling 'ia' represents the sequence /ja/.)

	Spanish	Sardinian	Rumanian	
a)	vida	bita	vită (ă = [ə])	'life'
b)	sí	si	şi (ş = [ʃ])	'yes'
c)	riso	rizu	rîs	'laugh'
d)	miel	mele	miere	'honey'
e)	hierro	ferru	fier	'iron'
f)	piedra	pedra	piatră (ă = [ə])	'stone'
g)	hierba	erva	iarbă (ă = [ə])	'grass'
h)	oso	ursu	urs	'bear'
i)	roto	ruttu	rupt	'broken'
j)	lecho	lettu	—	'bed'

eight

THE CLASSIFICATION OF LANGUAGES

Aleksandra Steinbergs

Everything it is possible for us to analyze depends on a clear method which distinguishes the similar from the not similar.
– LINNAEUS, *Genera Plantarum* (1754)

OBJECTIVES

In this chapter, you will learn

- how different languages can be classified according to similarities in their phonology, morphology, and syntax
- how languages are related to one another genetically
- what the major language families of the world are, and some representative languages of each family
- how language families may be grouped into larger phyla

In the world today there are thousands of different languages, each with its own sound patterns, grammar, and vocabulary. Regardless of how different these languages are, they have important similarities that allow linguists to arrange them into a fairly small number of groups. This chapter describes the methods of classification linguists use, and some of the findings that have resulted from this type of research.

1 SOME PRELIMINARIES

We will begin by considering two topics—the problem of distinguishing between a language and a **dialect**, and the chief methods of language classification used in linguistics today.

1.1 Dialect and language

It is often difficult to determine whether two linguistic communities speak different languages or merely different dialects of the same language. One test that linguists use to decide this involves the criterion of **mutual intelligibility**. Mutually intelligible varieties of the same language can be understood by speakers of each variety. According to this criterion, the English of Toronto, the English of Milwaukee, and the English of London qualify as dialects of the same language. On the other hand, if two speakers cannot understand one another, then linguists normally conclude that they are speaking different languages. The Italian of Florence and the French of Paris are examples of varieties of speech that are not mutually intelligible.

Political, cultural, social, historical, and religious factors frequently interfere when determining linguistic boundaries. (In fact, it is sometimes said that a language is just a dialect with an army and a navy!) For example, Serbs and Croats, with their different histories, cultures, and religions, often claim that they speak different languages. However, even though they use different alphabets, Serbian and Croatian are actually mutually intelligible dialects of the same language, which linguists call Serbo-Croatian. In contrast, we often speak of Chinese as if it were a single language, even though it is actually a number of individual, mutually unintelligible languages (Cantonese, Mandarin, Hakka, and so on), each with a multitude of dialects of its own.

In addition to the problems presented by these nonlinguistic considerations, complications also arise when we try to divide a continuum of mutually intelligible dialects whose two end points are not intelligible. Dutch and German, for example, are mutually intelligible around the border area between Germany and Holland; however, the Dutch of Amsterdam and the German of Munich are not. Similarly, Palestinian Arabic and Syrian Arabic are mutually intelligible, but Moroccan Arabic and Iraqi Arabic are not.

Taking these considerations into account, how many languages are there in the world today? The best available estimate places the current figure at about six thousand five hundred. However, many of these languages have only a few hundred speakers and many others are in grave danger of demise, as indigenous peoples throughout the world lose their traditional cultures and homelands. Indeed, according to one estimate, only about three hundred of the world's languages have a secure future. The threat of such a massive loss of the world's linguistic diversity is of great concern to linguists, many of whom are actively involved in recording and studying languages on the verge of extinction and in finding ways to improve the prospects for endangered languages.

Section 3 of this chapter presents an overview of a few hundred languages and the families to which they belong. First, however, we will turn our attention to some of the methods that are used for classifying languages into a manageable number of types.

1.2 Types of classification

Within the field of linguistics, three different approaches to language classification are used.

Genetic classification categorizes languages according to their descent. Languages that developed historically from the same ancestor language are grouped together and are said to be **genetically related**. This ancestor may be attested (that is, texts written in this language have been discovered or preserved, as in the case of Latin), or it may be a reconstructed proto-language for which no original texts exist (as is the case for Indo-European). Genetic classification is discussed further in Section 3.

Although genetically related languages often share structural characteristics, they do not necessarily bear a close structural resemblance. For example, Latvian and English are genetically related (both are descended from Indo-European), but their morphological structure is quite different. An English sentence like *It has to be figured out* can be expressed in Latvian by a single word.

1)

ja:izgudro
(one) must out figure (it)
'One must figure it out.'

Of course, Latvian and English are very distantly related, and languages that are more closely related will typically share a larger number of similarities. On the other hand, it is also necessary to recognize that even languages that are totally unrelated may share some structural similarities. Thus, English and Swahili, which are unrelated, both employ subject-verb-object word order in simple declarative sentences.

2)

Maria anapenda Anna
'Maria likes Anna.'

For this reason, another approach to language classification is useful. Known as **linguistic typology**, it classifies languages only according to their structural characteristics, without regard for genetic relationships. Thus typologists might group together languages with similar sound patterns or, alternatively, those with similar grammatical structures. Typological studies also endeavor to identify **linguistic universals**—that is, structural characteristics that occur in all or most languages. We discuss linguistic typology further in Section 2.

Finally, **areal classification** identifies characteristics shared by languages that are in geographical contact. Languages in contact often borrow words, sounds, morphemes, and even syntactic patterns from one another. As a result, neighboring languages can come to resemble each other, even though they may not be genetically related. Because of space considerations, this chapter will not deal with areal classification specifically; however, borrowing is discussed in Sections 1.2 and 5.1 of Chapter 7.

2 TYPOLOGICAL CLASSIFICATION

As just noted, the classification of languages according to their structural characteristics is known as linguistic typology. Typological studies group together languages on the basis of similarities in their syntactic patterns, morphological structure, and/or phonological systems. An important area of research within the study of linguistic typology is the search for linguistic universals. Structural patterns and traits that occur in all languages are called **absolute universals**, while those that simply occur in most languages are known as **universal tendencies**.

Many typological generalizations involve **implicational universals**, which specify that the presence of one trait implies the presence of another (but not vice versa). For instance, languages with fricative phonemes (such as /f/ and /s/) will also have stop phonemes (such as /p/ and /t/), although the reverse is not necessarily true.

Another way to analyze linguistic universals is through **markedness theory**. Within this theory, **marked traits** are considered to be more complex and/or universally rarer than **unmarked** characteristics. In addition, a marked trait is usually found in a particular language only if its unmarked counterpart also occurs. Thus, markedness theory is closely related to the study of implicational universals.

An example can provide some clarification of these terms. Nasalized vowels are said to be marked, while nonnasalized (oral) ones are said to be unmarked. Phonologically, oral vowels can be considered less complex: oral vowels allow the airstream to exit only through the mouth, while nasalized vowels allow air to escape from both the mouth and the nose.

Cross-linguistically, we find that all languages have oral vowels, while only some languages have nasalized vowels. Even in the languages that have both, there are usually fewer nasalized vowels than oral ones. Thus, nasalized vowels (which are considered to be marked) are both rarer and phonologically more complex than (unmarked) oral vowels.

The following sections present some of the typological generalizations and universals that have been proposed in the areas of phonology, morphology, and syntax.

2.1 PHONOLOGY

In this section, we represent all vowel and consonant systems phonemically. This simplifies their presentation; note, however, that the exact phonetic realization of these systems may vary in the individual languages.

Vowel systems

Languages are often classified according to the size and pattern of their vowel systems. The most common vowel system has five phonemes—two high vowels, two mid vowels, and one low vowel (see Figure 8.1). The front vowels are unrounded, as is the low vowel, and the back vowels are rounded.

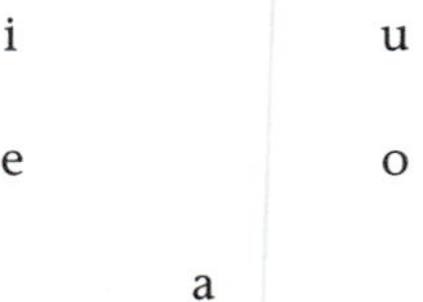

Figure 8.1 The most common vowel system

About half the world's languages, including Basque, Hawaiian, Japanese, Spanish, and Swahili, have such a system.

The majority of the world's other languages have vowel systems with three, four, six, seven, eight, or nine different vowels (disregarding contrasts based on length or nasalization, which can double or triple the number of phonemic vowels). Languages with fewer than three or more than nine distinctive vowels are rare. Some typical vowel systems are presented in Figure 8.2.

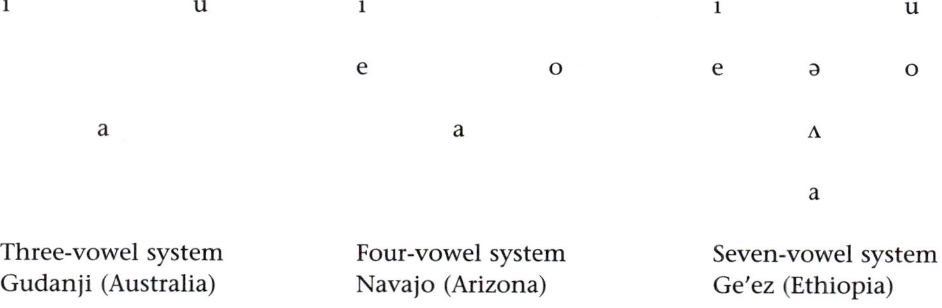

Figure 8.2 Common vowel systems

Analysis of many languages has led to the discovery of a number of universal tendencies pertaining to vowel systems. Some of these tendencies are listed here, along with a description of the most commonly occurring vowels.

- The most commonly occurring vowel phoneme is /a/, which is found in almost all of the languages of the world. The vowels /i/ and /u/ are almost as common as /a/.
- Front vowel phonemes (/i, e, ɛ, æ/) are generally unrounded, while nonlow back vowel phonemes (/ɔ, o, u/) are generally rounded.
- Low vowels (/æ, a, ɑ/) are generally unrounded.

Although English has an above-average number of vowels, they all conform to the above tendencies. Thus, English has only front unrounded vowels, all the low vowel phonemes are unrounded, and all of the back, nonlow vowels are rounded. The English vowel system is represented in Figure 8.3.

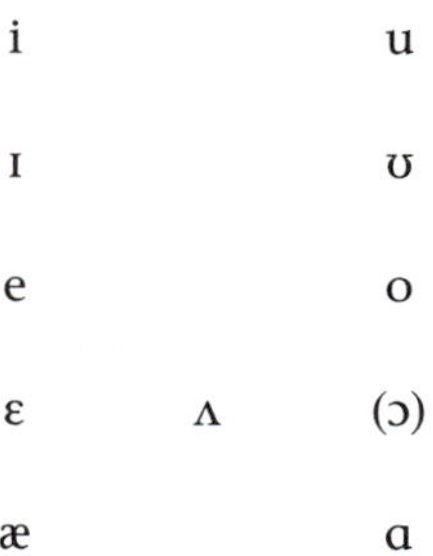

Figure 8.3 The English vowel system

The relationship between contrasting vowel types (such as oral versus nasal, and long versus short) can also be expressed in terms of implicational universals, since the presence of one vowel phoneme type implies the presence of another (but not vice versa).

- If a language has contrastive nasal vowels, then it will also have contrastive oral vowels. For example, French contrasts different nasal vowels (/lɔ̃/ 'long' and /lã/ 'slow'), and contrasts oral vowels with nasal vowels (/la/ 'weary' and /lã/ 'slow'). Predictably, French also contrasts different oral vowels, as in /klo/ 'shut' and /klu/ 'nail'. English shows contrasts among oral vowels but does not contrast nasal vowels with oral vowels. There are no contrasts in English like /bɔt/ 'bought' and */bɔ̃t/.
- If a language has contrasting long vowels, then it will also have contrasting short vowels. For example, Finnish shows contrasting long vowels and, predictably, contrasting short vowels (see Table 8.1).

Table 8.1 Finnish vowel contrasts

Long versus long	/viːli/	'junket'	/vaːli/	'election'
Short versus short	/suka/	'bristle'	/suku/	'family'
Short versus long	/tuli/	'fire'	/tuːli/	'wind'

The reverse is not necessarily the case. English has contrast between short vowels (/bɪt/ vs. /bɛt/) but does not contrast long vowels with short ones, since vowel length in English is predictable.

Consonant systems

It is not particularly useful to classify languages according to the number of consonants that they contain, since languages may have as few as eight consonant phonemes (as in Hawaiian) or more than ninety. (!Kung, a language spoken in Namibia, has ninety-six consonant phonemes.) Nevertheless, typological analysis of consonant systems has produced a number of well-substantiated universals:

- All languages have stops.
- The most common stop phonemes are /p, t, k/. Very few languages lack any one of these, and there are no languages that lack all three. If any one of these three stops is missing, it will probably be /p/; for example, Aleut, Nubian, and Wichita have no /p/ phoneme. The most commonly occurring phoneme of the three is /t/.
- The most commonly occurring fricative phoneme is /s/. If a language has only one fricative, it is most likely to be /s/. It is the only fricative found in Nandi (a language of Kenya) and Weri (a language of New Guinea). The next most common fricative is /f/.
- Almost every known language has at least one nasal phoneme. In cases where a language has only one nasal phoneme, that phoneme is usually /n/ (as in Arapaho, spoken in Wyoming). If there are two contrasting nasals, they are normally /m/ and /n/.

- The majority of languages have at least one phonemic liquid. However, a small number of languages have none at all—for example, Blackfoot, Dakota, Efik (spoken in Nigeria), and Siona (found in Ecuador). English, of course, has two: /l/ and /r/.

Consonant phonemes are also subject to various implicational universals:

- If a language has voiced obstruent phonemes (stops, fricatives, or affricates), then it will also have voiceless obstruent phonemes. The reverse is not necessarily true; for example, Ainu (a language of northern Japan) has only voiceless obstruent phonemes: /p, t, k, tʃ, s/.
- Sonorant consonants are generally voiced. Very few languages have voiceless sonorants; those that do always have voiced sonorants as well. For example, Burmese contrasts voiced and voiceless nasals and laterals.
- If a language has fricative phonemes, then it will also have stop phonemes. There are no languages that lack stops; however, there are some languages that lack fricatives. For example, Gilbertese (Gilbert Islands), Kitabal (eastern Australia), and Nuer (southeastern Sudan) have no fricatives.
- Languages that have affricates will also have fricatives and stops. This is not surprising, since an affricate is, in essence, a sequence of a stop followed by a fricative. However, many languages lack affricates altogether. Note that while European French, for example, has fricatives and stops but no affricates, English has all three.

Suprasegmental systems

Languages can also be classified according to their suprasegmental (or prosodic) type. Languages that use pitch to make meaning distinctions between words are called **tone languages**. (The phonetics and phonology of tone were introduced in Chapters 2 and 3.)

A great many of the world's languages are tone languages. Mandarin Chinese, for instance, has four contrastive tones (see Table 8.2).

Table 8.2 Tone contrasts in Mandarin Chinese

High tone	dā	'build'
Low rising tone	dá	'achieve'
Falling-rising tone	dǎ	'hit'
High falling tone	dà	'big'

The other Chinese languages—as well as many languages of Southeast Asia, Africa, and the Americas—are also tone languages. A few tone languages are also found in Europe; for example, one of the dialects of Latvian makes a three-way tonal distinction (see Table 8.3).

As noted in the chapter on phonetics, there are two types of tones: level tones and contour tones. Tone languages most often contrast only two tone levels (usually

Table 8.3 Tone contrasts in Latvian

Falling tone	loks	[lùoks]	'arch, bow'
Level (high) tone	loks	[lūoks]	'green onion'
Rising-falling (broken) tone	loks	[lûoks]	'window'

high and low). However, contrasts involving three tone levels (such as high, low, and mid tones) are also relatively common. Five or more levels of tonal contrast are extremely rare.

Tone systems, too, exhibit various universal tendencies:

- If a language has contour tones (such as rising tone or falling tone), then it will also have level tones (such as high, mid, or low tone). Burmese, Crow, Latvian, and Mandarin are examples of languages that fit this pattern. The reverse pattern (languages with contour tones but no level tones) is extremely rare (although Dafla, spoken in northern India, has such a system).

- If a language has complex contour tones (such as rising-falling or falling-rising), then it will also have simple contour tones (like rising or falling). Both the Mandarin and Latvian examples fit this pattern.

Differences in stress are also useful in classifying languages. **Fixed stress languages** are those in which the position of stress on a word is predictable. For example, in Modern Hebrew and K'iché (a Mayan language), stress always falls on the last syllable of a word; in Polish, Swahili, and Samoan, stress falls on the penultimate (second-to-last) syllable of a word; while in Czech, Finnish, and Hungarian, the stressed syllable is always the first syllable of a word. In **free stress languages**, the position of stress is not predictable and must be learned for each word. Free stress is also called phonemic stress because of its role in distinguishing between words. Russian is an example of a language with free stress, as shown in Table 8.4.

Table 8.4 Stress contrasts in Russian

múka	'torture'	muká	'flour'
zámok	'castle'	zamók	'lock'
rúki	'hands'	rukí	'hand's' (genitive singular)

Syllable structure

All languages permit V and CV syllable structures (where V normally stands for a vowel, and C for a consonant). These syllable types are unmarked, in the sense that they are permitted in all languages. They are also simpler than most other syllable structures, such as CVC or VCC. Note, however, that VC is just as simple a structure as CV, but that only the latter is universally permitted. The presence of an onset (as in a CV syllable) is apparently more valued than the presence of a coda (as in a VC syllable), perhaps because an onset may help to signal the beginning of a new syllable.

In any given language, onsets may be structured differently from codas. For example, in English, a nasal + stop sequence is permitted in the coda (in a word like *hand*), but not in the onset (there are no English words that begin with the sequence *nd*). However, Swahili has precisely the opposite restrictions: the *nd* sequence is permitted in onset position (in words like *ndizi* 'banana'), but not in coda position. In fact, Swahili syllables are coda-less—they can only end in vowels.

Differing syllable structure constraints can have interesting consequences when languages come in contact. For example, in Hawaiian only V and CV syllables are permitted. Thus, when a word is borrowed from a language like English, which allows more complicated syllable structures, vowels are inserted to produce the only allowed syllable structures. For example, when the phrase *Merry Christmas* was borrowed into Hawaiian, it was reformulated as follows: *mele kalikimaka*. (Of course, some consonant changes were made as well, since Hawaiian lacks /r/ and /s/ phonemes.)

Two examples of implicational universals for syllable structure are presented below. Both deal with the structure of onsets as opposed to codas.

- If a language permits sequences of consonants in the onset, then it will also permit syllables with single consonant onsets and syllables with no onset at all.
- If a language permits sequences of consonants in the coda, then it will also permit syllables with single consonant codas and syllables with no coda at all.

2.2 Morphology

Both words and morphemes are found in all languages. However, there are clear differences in the ways in which individual languages combine morphemes to form words. Four types of systems can be distinguished.

The isolating type

A language that is purely an **isolating** or **analytic language** would contain only words that consist of a single (root) morpheme. In such a language there would be no affixes, and categories such as number and tense would therefore have to be expressed by a separate word. In Mandarin Chinese, which is primarily an isolating language, the morpheme *le* is often used to indicate a past or completed action. Although this morpheme is thus semantically similar to a past tense, it acts just like an independent word, since its position in the sentence may vary:

3)

Tā chī fàn *le*
he eat meal past
'He ate the meal.'

Tā chī *le* fàn
he eat past meal
'He ate the meal.'

Other languages that are primarily isolating include Cantonese, Vietnamese, Laotian, and Cambodian.

The polysynthetic type

In a **polysynthetic language**, single words can consist of long strings of roots and affixes that often express meanings that are associated with entire sentences in other languages. The following word from Inuktitut illustrates this.

4)

Qasuiirsarvigssarsingitluinarnarpuq
Qasu -iir -sar -vig -ssar -si -ngit-luinar -nar -puq
tired not cause-to-be place-for suitable find not completely someone 3.SG
'Someone did not find a completely suitable resting place.'

Polysynthesis is common in many native languages of North America, including Inuktitut, Cree, and Sarcee to name but a few.

The terms *isolating* and *polysynthetic* refer to two extremes: words consisting only of single morphemes versus words that can be complete sentences. Few if any languages are either purely isolating or purely polysynthetic. Instead, the vast majority of languages are **synthetic languages**, in that they permit multimorphemic words.

Next we present two other morphological types that are sometimes distinguished.

The agglutinating type

An **agglutinating language** has words that can contain several morphemes, but the words are easily divided into their component parts (normally a root and affixes). In such languages, each affix is clearly identifiable and typically represents only a single grammatical category or meaning. The following examples are from Turkish (in standard Turkish orthography).

5)

a. köy
'village'

b. köy-ler
village-plural
'villages'

c. köy-ler-in
village-pl-genitive
'of the villages'

Turkish words can have a complex morphological structure, but each morpheme has a single, clearly identifiable function. In *5c*, for instance, *-ler* marks plurality and *-in* marks the genitive case, giving the meaning 'of the villages'.

The fusional type

Words in a **fusional** or **inflectional language** can also consist of several morphemes. However, in contrast to agglutinating systems, the affixes in fusional languages often mark several grammatical categories simultaneously. In Russian, for example, a single inflectional affix simultaneously marks the noun's gender class (masculine, feminine, or neuter), its number (singular or plural), and its grammatical role (subject, direct object, and so on). This is illustrated in *6* for the suffix *-u*.

6)

mi vid^{j}im ruk-u
we see hand-fem/SG/Accusative
'We see a/the hand.'

The distinction between agglutinating and fusional is sensitive to the number of semantic "bits" of information normally packed into an affix. In an agglutinating language, each affix normally contains only one element of grammatical or lexical meaning, while in a fusional language, affixes often denote several simultaneous functions.

Mixed types

Many (perhaps most) languages do not belong exclusively to any of the four categories just outlined. For example, English employs isolating patterns in many verbal constructions, where each notion is expressed by a separate word. The future, for instance, is indicated by the independent word *will* (rather than by an affix) in structures such as *I will leave*. On the other hand, English also exhibits considerable agglutination in derived words, such as *re-en-act-ment*, which consist of a series of clearly identifiable morphemes, each with its own unique meaning and function. However, the English pronoun system is largely fusional, since a single form can be used to indicate person, number, gender, and case. The word *him*, for instance, is used to express a third-person singular masculine direct object.

Since many, if not most, of the world's languages exhibit mixed patterns of this type, it has been suggested that terms like isolating, agglutinating, and fusional should be used to refer not to a language as a whole but to particular structures within a language.

It is also important to recognize that these classifications do not take into consideration morphological processes such as compounding (e.g., English *greenhouse*), reduplication (e.g., Tagalog *sulat* 'write' versus *susulat* 'will write'), grammatical use of stress or tone (e.g., the noun *présent* versus the verb *presént* in English), and internal word change (e.g., vowel ablaut, as in English *run* versus *ran*).

Implicational universals: morphology

A variety of generalizations can be made about word structure in human language.

- If a language has inflectional affixes, it will also have derivational affixes. For example, English not only has inflectional affixes such as the past tense *-ed* and possessive *-'s*, but it also contains derivational affixes like *un-* (*unhappy, unwanted*) and *-ly* (*quickly, slowly*).
- If a word has both a derivational and an inflectional affix, the derivational affix is closer to the root (DA = derivational affix; IA = inflectional affix) (see Table 8.5).

Table 8.5 The ordering of derivational and inflectional affixes

English					
friend-ship-s			*friend-s -ship		
Root DA IA			Root IA DA		
Turkish					
iʃ	-tʃi	-ler	*iʃ	-ler	-tʃi
work	-er	-pl	work	-pl	-er
Root	DA	IA	Root	IA	DA

- If a language has only suffixes, it will also have only postpositions. (As noted in Chapter 5, postpositions are the equivalent of prepositions in languages that place the head at the end of the phrase.) Turkish, for example, has only suffixes; as expected, it also has postpositions rather than prepositions. This is illustrated in the following sentence.

7)

Ahmet Ajʃe itʃin kitab-ɨ al-dɨ
Ahmet Ayshe for book-Acc bought
'Ahmet bought a book for Ayshe.'

2.3 Syntax

Because we lack detailed descriptions for most of the world's languages, much of the work on syntactic universals has been restricted to the study of word order in simple declarative sentences such as *The men built the house*. Patterns are classified in terms of the order of the subject (S), direct object (O), and verb (V). The three most common word orders (in descending order of frequency) are SOV, SVO, and VSO. Over 95 percent of the world's languages use one of these patterns as their basic word order.

8)

SOV (Turkish, in standard orthography):
Hasan öküz-ü al-dı
Hasan ox-Acc bought
'Hasan bought the ox.'

9)

SVO (English):
The athlete broke the record.

10)

VSO (Welsh, in standard orthography):
Lladdodd y ddraig y dyn
killed the dragon the man
'The dragon killed the man.'

SOV, SVO, and VSO patterns all have one common trait: the subject appears before the direct object. The prevalence of the SO pattern may be due to the fact that the subject usually coincides with the topic of the sentence (i.e., what the sentence is about; see Chapter 6, Section 4.3), and therefore is more useful at an early point in the utterance.

While an overwhelming majority of the world's languages place the subject before the direct object in their basic word order, this pattern is not universal. There are a small number of VOS languages, of which the best-known example is Malagasy.

11)
VOS (Malagasy):
Nahita ny mpianatra ny vehivavy
saw the student the woman
'The woman saw the student.'

As well, there are a very few OVS or OSV languages, all of which seem to be spoken in South America:

12)
OVS (Hixkaryana):
Kana yanɨmno bɨryekomo
fish caught boy
'The boy caught a fish.'

13)
OSV (Apuriña)
Anana nota apa
pineapple I fetch
'I fetch a pineapple.'

Word-order universals

Sometimes the order of elements within one kind of structure has implications for the order of elements in other structures. Many of these implications concern the relationship between the verb and its (direct) object.

- If a language has VO word order, then it will have prepositions rather than postpositions. Languages of this type include Berber (spoken in Morocco), Hebrew, Maori (spoken in New Zealand), Maasai (spoken in Kenya), Welsh, and Irish Gaelic.

14)
Irish Gaelic
a. VSO pattern:
Chonaic mé mo mháthair
saw I my mother
'I saw my mother.'
b. Preposition pattern:
sa teach
in house
'in the house'

- If a language has OV word order, then it will probably have postpositions rather than prepositions. Languages with this structural pattern include Basque, Burmese, Hindi, Japanese, Korean, Quechua, Turkish, and Guugu Yimidhirr, an aboriginal language of Australia (Erg = Ergative).

15)

Guugu Yimidhirr

a. SOV pattern:
Gudaa-ngun yarrga dyinday
dog-Erg boy bit
'The dog bit the boy.'

b. Postposition pattern:
yuwaal nganh
beach from
'from the beach'

- PPs almost always precede the verb in OV languages, and usually follow the verb in VO languages (Nom = Nominative; Acc = Accusative).

16)

Japanese

a. SOV pattern:
Gakusei-ga hon-o yonda
student-Nom book-Acc read
'The student read a book.'

b. PP precedes verb:
Taroo-ga [$_{PP}$ nitiyoobi ni] tsuita.
Taroo-Nom Sunday on arrived
'Taroo arrived on Sunday.'

17)

English

a. SVO pattern:
I like candy.

b. PP follows verb:
George left [$_{PP}$ on Sunday].

- Manner adverbs overwhelmingly precede the verb in OV languages and generally follow the verb in VO languages.

18)

Japanese (SOV pattern, as seen in *16a*):
Manner adverb precedes verb:
hayaku hasiru
quickly run
'run quickly'

19)

English (SVO pattern, as seen in *17a*):
Manner adverb follows verb:
John runs well.

- With respect to possessive structures, there is an overwhelming preference for Genitive + N order in OV languages, and a (somewhat weaker) preference for N + Genitive order in VO languages.

20)

Japanese (SOV pattern, as seen in *16a*):
Genitive structure precedes head N:
Taroo-no hon
Taroo-Gen book
'Taroo's book'

21)

French

a. SVO pattern:
Pierre aime Marie.
'Pierre likes Marie.'

b. Genitive structure follows head N:
la maison de Marie
the house of (Gen) Marie
'Marie's house'

English, although an SVO language, exhibits both Genitive + N and N + Genitive patterns:

22)

a. Genitive + N pattern:
the country's laws

b. N + Genitive pattern:
the laws of the country

Examples such as this are rare, however, and do not invalidate the universal tendencies we have been considering.

Grammatical hierarchies

Implicational universals are often stated in terms of **hierarchies** of categories or relations. One of the most important hierarchies of this type refers to the grammatical relations of subject and direct object (see Chapter 5). Hierarchies represent degrees of markedness, with the least marked option at the top and the most marked at the bottom. According to the hierarchy in Figure 8.4, then, a process that applies only to subjects is less marked than a process that applies to direct objects, and so on. Given the definition of markedness outlined at the beginning of Section 2, it follows that if a particular phenomenon applies to direct objects, it should also apply

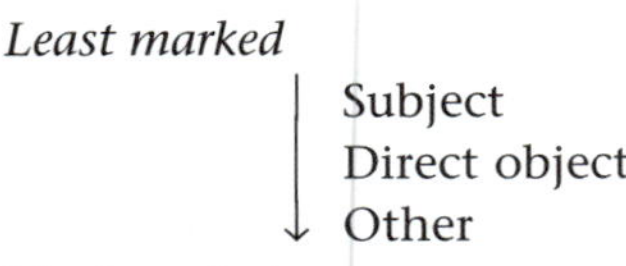

Figure 8.4 Hierarchy of grammatical relations

to subjects. The opposite, however, need not be true: it would not be surprising to find a process that applies to subjects but not to direct objects.

Among the many typological phenomena that conform to this hierarchy is verb agreement, first mentioned in Chapter 4 (Section 6.4). As the following examples show, there are languages in which the verb agrees only with the subject, and there are languages in which it agrees with both the subject and the direct object (3 = 3rd person, SG = singular, PL = plural, Pst = past).

23)

Agreement with subject only (Spanish):

Subject
Juan parti-ó
Juan leave-3.SG.Pst
'Juan left.'

24)

Agreement with subject and direct object (Swahili):

Subject				*Direct object*
Juma	a-	li-	wa- piga	watoto
Juma	3.SG	Pst-	3.PL-hit	children

'Juma hit the children.'

However, as predicted by the hierarchy, there are no languages in which the verb agrees only with the direct object.

2.4 Explaining universals

Linguists are still uncertain about how to explain the existence of many linguistic universals. Nonetheless, a number of interesting proposals have been made, and it is worthwhile to consider some of them here.

Phonology

Perceptual factors play a role in shaping phonological universals. For example, the fact that /s/ is the most commonly occurring fricative may have to do with its acoustic prominence: varieties of /s/ are inherently louder than other kinds of fricatives.

Vowel systems (discussed in Section 2.1) develop so as to keep vowel phonemes as different from each other as possible. A three-vowel system such as the following allows for plenty of "space" around each vowel, which probably makes each vowel easier to distinguish from the others.

i		u
	a	

Figure 8.5 A three-vowel system

The same holds true for the distribution of stop phonemes. It may be that /p/, /t/, and /k/ are the three most common stops, because they occur at three maximally distant places of articulation within the supralaryngeal vocal tract. These three stops are much easier to distinguish perceptually than a sequence of dental, alveolar, and palatal stops, for example, all of which are produced in the central region of the oral cavity (i.e., in the center of the mouth).

It has been recently suggested that consonant systems in general respond to the articulatory pressures that give rise to unmarked sounds and systems. Basic obstruents such as [p], [t], and [k] are found much more commonly than more complex articulations such as [tɬ] and [qʷ]. Table 8.6 shows the set of obstruents that is most widely used across human languages.

Languages tend to have consonant systems that consist of about 70 percent obstruents and 30 percent sonorants no matter what the total size of their consonant inventories may be. These figures reflect the articulatory possibilities available for contrast: more distinctions can be made among obstruents than among sonorants. There are, for example, no nasal fricative sonorants, because the air pressure needed to force air through a narrow opening (which is necessary for the production of fricatives) cannot be built up when so much air is flowing through the nasal passage at the same time. For reasons such as this, the number of obstruent consonants in any language is potentially much larger than the number of possible sonorant consonants. This is just one example of how considerations involving articulation can play a role in the shaping of consonant systems.

Table 8.6 Obstruents most often found cross-linguistically

p	t	k	ʔ
b	d	g	
f	s		h
	tʃ		

Morphology

Other types of explanations are appropriate for morphological universals. For example, the fact that languages with suffixes but no prefixes always have postpositions (Section 2.2) may have a historical explanation. In these languages, some postpositions became attached to a preceding word and were thereby converted into suffixes. Because suffixes in such languages evolved from postpositions, the link between the two elements can be traced to their common origin.

An example of this very phenomenon can be seen in the closely related languages Finnish and Estonian. The ancestor language (Proto-Baltic-Finnic) contained a postposition **kanssa* 'with', which is still evident in Standard Finnish but has evolved into a suffix in Estonian (see Table 8.7).

Table 8.7 Proto-Baltic-Finnic postposition *kanssa* becomes suffix *-ga*

Standard Finnish: postposition *kanssa* 'with'				
poika	'boy'	poja-n boy+Gen	kanssa with	'with the boy'
Estonian: case suffix *-ga*				
poeg	'son'	poja-ga son+Committative		'with the son'

The requirement that derivational affixes occur closer to the root than inflectional affixes has another type of explanation. As noted in the morphology chapter, derivation typically forms new words, while inflection marks the subclass (for example, plural for Ns, past tense for Vs) to which a word belongs. Given that a word must be formed before its subclass can be determined, it follows that derivational processes will precede inflection. This is reflected in word structure, where derivational affixes appear closer to the root than inflectional markers. In Figure 8.6, for instance, the verbal root *treat* is converted into a noun by the affix *-ment* before the plural inflectional marker is added.

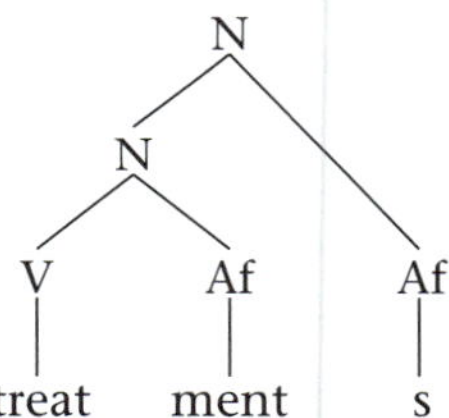

Figure 8.6 The structure of a word containing a derivational affix and an inflectional affix

Syntax

At least some syntactic universals may be explained in terms of the way that the human brain processes sentence structure. Consider the summary of word order patterns in Table 8.8, which is based on the implicational universals discussed in Section 2.3.

Table 8.8 Word-order patterns

Constituents	*Order in VO language*	*Order in OV language*
P & NP	preposition-NP	NP-postposition
V & PP	verb-PP	PP-verb
V & manner Adv	verb-manner Adv	manner Adv-verb
N & Gen	noun-genitive	genitive-noun

One recent explanation as to why the word-order properties in the second and third columns cluster together involves the contrast between right-branching and left-branching languages. In right-branching languages, the more elaborate part of a phrase's structure occurs on its right branch; in left-branching languages, it occurs on the left. Thus, a verb-object pattern is right-branching since a phrasal constituent (an XP) appears on its right branch, but an object-verb pattern is left-branching, as shown in Figure 8.7.

a. Right-branching (VO)

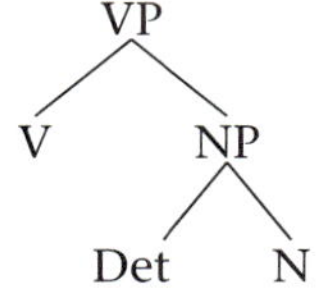

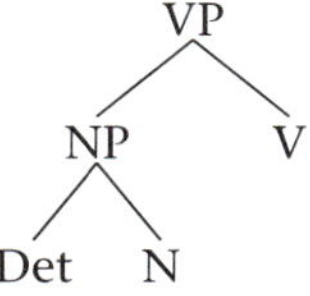

Figure 8.7 Right-branching and left-branching patterns

As you can easily determine for yourselves, the P-NP, V-PP, V-Adv, and N-Gen patterns commonly associated with VO languages are also all right-branching (both genitives and adverbials are a type of phrase). In contrast, the NP-P, PP-V, Adv-V, and Gen-N patterns typically found in OV languages are all left-branching. In other words, it seems that languages are fairly consistent in using one or the other type of branching structure. This sort of uniformity may make it easier for speakers and hearers to process syntactic structure. Thus, just as some human beings are right-handed and others left-handed, it appears that some languages prefer to use consistently right-branching systems, while others prefer consistently left-branching systems.

The study of linguistic typology and language universals is a relatively new field within linguistics. There is obviously much still to be learned about linguistic universals, and it must be admitted that some of the current work is speculative and incomplete. No doubt many interesting new facts will eventually come to light.

3 GENETIC CLASSIFICATION

The world's languages can be grouped into a relatively small number of language families. However, genetic classification is sometimes difficult for a number of reasons.

Perhaps the biggest problem is simply the amount of data that must be collected before linguists can be confident about the status of a group of languages. It is only in the last two or three decades, for example, that enough information has been accumulated to propose a detailed classification of the languages of Africa. Moreover, many of the languages of South America, New Guinea, and Australia are still relatively unknown.

In many cases, linguists face the problem of establishing the tests or criteria to be used in proposing genetic relationships. There is some disagreement over the degree of similarity that should exist among languages before a genetic relationship can be proposed. This issue arises because unrelated languages are often typologically similar (that is, share some structural characteristics). This is particularly likely if languages have been in contact long enough to have borrowed a large number of words, sounds, morphemes, or syntactic structures from one another.

Additional difficulties stem from the fact that genetically related languages need not be typologically similar. This is especially true if the relationship is a distant one, as is the case with English and Russian. Russian has numerous inflectional affixes, an extensive case system, and free word order, while English has relatively few inflectional affixes, virtually no case marking, and fixed word order. Yet, both belong to the **Indo-European family**.

To complicate matters even further, linguists also disagree as to how much evidence is required in order to establish a genetic relationship between languages. The more distant the genetic relationship between languages, the less likely it is that a large number of obvious cognates will be found, especially since sound changes can obscure similarities between cognate words. English and Latin are related (though distantly), but the similarity between cognates like Latin *unda* 'wave' and English *water* is certainly not striking.

Research is also hampered by the fact that words that may be excellent indicators of a genetic relationship can drop out of the lexicon. For example, Old English had a word *leax* 'salmon' (which was cognate with German *Lachs* and Yiddish *lox*), but this lexical item has since been lost from the native English lexicon (although *lox* has, of course, been borrowed back into some varieties of English as the name for a popular delicatessen food).

Since word loss is a common historical event, linguists prefer to use the oldest available form of a language for their research; thus, our knowledge of Proto-Indo-European is drawn from the study of Old English, Sanskrit, Latin, etc., rather than English, Hindi-Urdu, French, and their other modern descendants. Of course, languages that are genetically related do share many similarities, particularly if their common ancestor is not too distant.

Some language families contain many hundreds of languages. In other cases, only one language may remain to represent a family. In still other cases, families have become extinct. The following sections present some information about the makeup and membership of a few of the language families represented in the world today.

3.1 The Indo-European family

With only about a hundred languages, Indo-European is not a large family in terms of the total number of languages. However, it is the largest language family in the world in terms of the total number of speakers: there are about 1.7 billion native speakers of an Indo-European language.

If we consider only living languages, the Indo-European family currently has nine branches, which are listed in Table 8.9.

Table 8.9 Main branches of the Indo-European family

Germanic	Hellenic	Baltic
Celtic	Albanian	Slavic
Italic	Armenian	Indo-Iranian

Germanic

The Germanic branch of Indo-European can be divided into three sub-branches: East, North, and West. The East Germanic branch included Gothic, the oldest Germanic language for which written texts exist (dating from the fourth century A.D.). Gothic and any other languages belonging to this branch of Germanic have long been extinct.

The North Germanic (or Scandinavian) branch originally included Old Norse (also known as Old Icelandic)—the language of the Vikings and the ancestor of modern Icelandic, Norwegian, and Faroese (spoken on the Faroe Islands, north of Scotland). Swedish and Danish are two other familiar North Germanic languages.

The West Germanic branch includes English, German, Yiddish, Dutch, Frisian, and Afrikaans. Afrikaans is descended from the Dutch spoken by seventeenth-century settlers (known as Boers) in South Africa.

Frisian is the language most closely related to English. It is spoken on the north coast of Holland, on the Frisian Islands just off the coast, as well as on the northwestern coast of Germany. English descended from the speech of the Angles, Saxons, and Jutes—Germanic tribes who lived in northern Germany and southern Denmark (in an area just east of the Frisians) before invading England in A.D. 449 and settling there.

The organization of the Germanic family of languages is illustrated in Table 8.10. (In this and other tables, parentheses are used to indicate languages that no longer have any native speakers. The tables are intended to illustrate the membership and organization of the families; they do not necessarily provide a complete list of the languages in each family.)

Table 8.10 The Germanic family

(East Germanic)	*North Germanic*	*West Germanic*
(Gothic)	Icelandic	English
	Faroese	German
	Norwegian	Yiddish
	Swedish	Dutch
	Danish	Frisian
		Afrikaans

Celtic

The Celtic branch of Indo-European (see Table 8.11) has two main sub-branches: Insular and Continental (now extinct). Gaulish, a member of the Continental branch, was once spoken in France (the Gauls were the tribe Julius Caesar defeated), but it has long been extinct.

The Insular sub-branch can be subdivided into two groups of languages: Brythonic and Goidelic. Brythonic languages include Welsh and Breton (which is spoken in northwestern France) as well as Cornish, which was formerly spoken in southwest Britain but no longer has any native speakers. The Goidelic branch contains Irish (or Irish Gaelic), which is still spoken natively in the western parts of Ireland, and Scots Gaelic, which is native to some of the northwestern parts of Scotland (especially the Hebrides Islands) and, to a lesser extent, Cape Breton Island in Nova Scotia.

Table 8.11 The Celtic family

Insular		*Continental*
Brythonic	*Goidelic*	
Welsh Breton (Cornish)	Irish [= Irish Gaelic] Scots Gaelic	(Gaulish)

Italic

The Italic family originally had a number of branches, which included several now-extinct languages spoken in the area corresponding roughly to modern-day Italy. However, the only Italic languages that are presently spoken are all descended from Latin, the language of the Roman Empire (hence the term "Romance languages").

These languages can be divided into an Eastern group, consisting of Italian and Rumanian, and a Western group, containing all of the other Romance languages except Sardinian, which stands alone.

The Western group is further divided into Ibero-Romance (Spanish, Portuguese, and Catalan—the latter is spoken in northeastern Spain, around Barcelona) and Gallo-Romance, which includes French, Occitan (spoken in southern France), and Romansch (one of the four official languages of Switzerland). These divisions are illustrated in Table 8.12.

Table 8.12 The Romance family

Eastern	*Western*		
	Ibero-Romance	*Gallo-Romance*	*Sardinian*
Italian Rumanian	Spanish Portuguese Catalan	French Occitan Romansch	Sardinian

Hellenic

The Hellenic branch of Indo-European has only one living member, Greek. All modern Greek dialects are descended from the classical dialect known as Attic Greek, which was the speech of Athens during the Golden Age of Greek culture (approximately 500 to 300 B.C.).

Hellenic Greek, which was used in subsequent centuries, was the language of commerce throughout the Middle East. (Hellenic Greek was also Cleopatra's native language; she was descended from one of Alexander the Great's generals.)

Albanian

The Albanian branch of Indo-European has only one member—Albanian—which is spoken not only in Albania but also in parts of the former Yugoslavia, Greece, and Italy.

Armenian

The Armenian branch also has only one member—Armenian. This language is centered in the Republic of Armenia (once part of the former Soviet Union and located between the Black Sea and the Caspian Sea) but is also spoken in Turkey, Iran, Syria, Lebanon, and Egypt.

Baltic

The Baltic branch contains only two surviving languages—Latvian (or Lettish) and Lithuanian. They are spoken in Latvia and Lithuania (located just west of Russia and northeast of Poland). Lithuanian has an elaborate case system, which resembles the one proposed for Proto-Indo-European.

Slavic

The Slavic branch of Indo-European can be divided into three sub-branches: East, West, and South. The East Slavic branch is made up of Russian (also called Great Russian), Ukrainian, and Byelorussian (or White Russian). The latter is spoken in Byelorussia, which is just east of northern Poland. The West Slavic branch includes Czech, Slovak, and Polish.

The South Slavic branch consists of Bulgarian, Macedonian, Serbo-Croatian, and Slovene (or Slovenian). The latter three languages are all spoken in the former Yugoslavia. Note that although Alexander the Great was king of Macedonia, he spoke Hellenic Greek, not (Slavic) Macedonian; Slavic-speaking tribes did not move into that area until several centuries later.

The organization of the Slavic group of languages is represented in Table 8.13.

Table 8.13 The Slavic family

East Slavic	*West Slavic*	*South Slavic*
Russian	Czech	Bulgarian
Ukrainian	Slovak	Macedonian
Byelorussian	Polish	Serbo-Croatian
		Slovene

Indo-Iranian

The Indo-Iranian branch of Indo-European is divided into the Iranian and Indic sub-branches. The Iranian sub-branch contains about two dozen different languages, including Modern Persian (also called Parsi or Farsi, spoken in Iran), Pashto (the principal language of Afghanistan), and Kurdish (found in Iran, Iraq, Turkey, and Syria). Other Iranian languages are spoken in Pakistan, southern parts of the former Soviet Union, and China.

There are about thirty-five different Indic languages. Most of the languages spoken in northern India, Pakistan, and Bangladesh belong to this branch of Indo-European. Some of the most widespread (in terms of number of speakers) are Hindi-Urdu, Bengali, Marathi, and Gujarati. Although Hindi and Urdu are two dialects of the same language, they have totally different writing systems and are associated with different cultures; Urdu is spoken principally in Pakistan by Muslims while Hindi is spoken primarily in India by Hindus.

Less well known as an Indic language is Romany, or Gypsy. It is now believed that the Gypsies (or Roma) fled to Turkey from northwestern India during the Middle

Ages, after being defeated by Islamic invaders. Subsequently they spread throughout Europe: Gypsies are found as far west as Ireland and as far east as Russia. Many now live in North America. Romany contains many borrowed words—particularly from Greek, which was the language primarily spoken in Turkey during the Middle Ages.

Table 8.14 depicts the organization of Indo-Iranian.

Table 8.14 The Indo-Iranian family

Iranian	*Indic*
Persian [= Farsi]	Hindi-Urdu
Pashto	Bengali
Kurdish	Marathi
	Gujarati
	Romany [= Gypsy]

The map in Figure 8.8 illustrates the geographic location of the Indo-European families identified in this chapter.

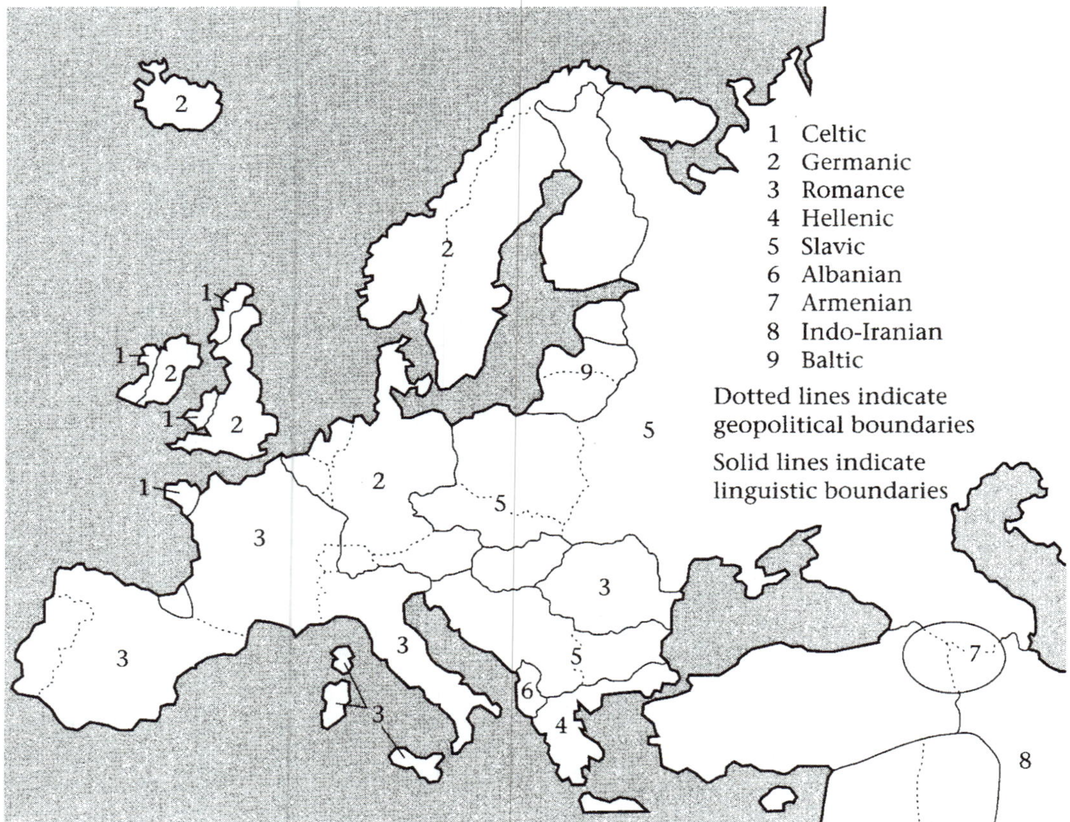

Figure 8.8 Location of Indo-European languages

3.2 Some other families

Although no introductory text could hope to present a complete survey of all of the world's language families, some further discussion of this topic is worthwhile in order to illustrate the extraordinary variety of human language.

Uralic

The Uralic family (see Table 8.15) contains about twenty languages and has approximately twenty-two million speakers. Uralic languages are spoken in a band across the northern part of Europe, all the way from northern Norway to Siberia. Uralic has two major branches: Samoyed and Finno-Ugric. The Samoyed branch contains a handful of languages spoken in northern Russia, particularly in areas around the Ural mountains, and also in Siberia.

The most widely spoken Finno-Ugric language is Hungarian. Other Finno-Ugric languages are Finnish, Lapp (also known as Lappish or Saame, spoken in northern Scandinavia and northwestern Russia), Estonian (Estonia), Livonian (Latvia), Karelian (eastern Finland and northwestern Russia), Erzya, and Cheremis (both spoken in the former Soviet Union).

Table 8.15 The Uralic family

Finno-Ugric		*Samoyed*
Finnic	*Ugric*	
Finnish	Hungarian	Nganasan
Lapp [= Saame]		Selkup
Estonian		Nenets
Livonian		Enets
Karelian		
Erzya		
Cheremis [= Mari]		

Uralic languages are primarily agglutinating, and most have postpositions with SOV or SVO word order. The nouns often have many cases (Finnish has fifteen), which appear to have developed historically from postpositions that became attached to nouns as suffixes.

Altaic

Languages belonging to the Altaic family are spoken in a continuum from Turkey to Siberia, as well as in China. The membership of the Altaic family (see Table 8.16) includes three main branches—Turkic, Mongolian, and Tungusic. Recent scholarship has collected evidence that Korean and Japanese are also members of the Altaic family.

The best-known Turkic language is Turkish, which is spoken by over fifty million people. Other Turkic languages (most of which are spoken in central Asia in the former Soviet Union) include Uzbek (Uzbekistan), Azeri (Azerbaijan Republic and Iran), Kazakh (Kazakhstan, China, and Mongolia), Uighur (China and Kazakhstan), and Volga Tatar (also called Tatar, in the Tataristan Republic, Kazakhstan, and China).

Table 8.16 The Altaic family

Turkic	*Mongolian*	*Tungusic*	*Korean*	*Japanese*
Turkish	Khalkha	Evenki	Korean	Japanese
Uzbek	Buriat	Manchu		Ryukyuan
Azeri [= Azerbaijani]	Chakhar	Even		
Kazakh	Kalmyck	Nanai		
Uighur	Monguor	Orik		
Volga Tatar [= Tatar]				

The Mongolian languages are spoken by around ten million people, primarily in Mongolia and China, while the Tungusic languages are spoken by approximately 50,000 people in central and east Siberia and Mongolia.

Altaic languages are usually agglutinating, often with several suffixes in the same word. They normally employ SOV word order and typically use postpositions rather than prepositions. Many Altaic languages have vowel harmony—a phonological phenomenon in which all vowels of a word share certain features, such as [round] or [back].

Caucasian

The languages that are normally grouped together as Caucasian have not yet been assigned to families in a definitive way. These languages are primarily found in northeastern Turkey and in the former Soviet Union (between the Black Sea and the Caspian Sea, in and around the Caucasus Mountains). The best evidence so far points to three distinct language families—South Caucasian, Northwest Caucasian, and Northeast Caucasian (see Table 8.17).

Table 8.17 The Caucasian languages

The South Caucasian (Kartvelian) family
Georgian Laz [= Mingrelian] Svan
The Northwest Caucasian family
Adyghe [= West Circassian] Kabardian [= East Circassian]
The Northeast Caucasian family
Chechen Lezghian Avar [= Daghestani]

South Caucasian (sometimes called Kartvelian) consists of Georgian, Laz (also called Mingrelian), and Svan. Georgian has the largest number of speakers. It was also the native language of Joseph Stalin, dictator of the former Soviet Union in the

1930s and 1940s. Northwest Caucasian contains a handful of languages, including Adyghe and Kabardian (also called West Circassian and East Circassian, respectively). Northeast Caucasian consists of about two dozen languages. Of these, Chechen, Lezghian, and Avar have the largest number of speakers.

Altogether there are about thirty-five languages in the three separate families, with a total of approximately five million speakers. Although no genetic relationship has been proven to exist between these three families, they do seem to share a number of areal features (probably brought about through mutual borrowing): many Caucasian languages have glottalized consonants, complex consonant clusters, a very large consonantal inventory, but very few vowel phonemes. It has recently been claimed that the Northwest and Northeast Caucasian languages are part of a single family, but this grouping is not yet widely accepted among Caucasianists.

Dravidian

There are twenty-five Dravidian languages (see Table 8.18), which are primarily found in the southern half of India, but also in Sri Lanka, Pakistan, and Nepal. About 175 million people are native speakers of a Dravidian language. The most widely spoken languages in this family are Telugu, Tamil, Kannada, and Malayalam. Dravidian languages are normally SOV. They are agglutinating and nontonal, and usually have initial stress.

Table 8.18 The Dravidian family

North	*Central*	*South-Central*	*South*
Kurux	Kolami	Telugu	Tamil
Malto	Naiki	Savara	Kannada
Brahui	Parji	Konda	Malayalam
	Gadaba	Gondi	Tulu

Austroasiatic

The Austroasiatic family of languages (see Table 8.19) consists of about 150 languages with approximately fifty million speakers.

Mon-Khmer is the largest branch of Austroasiatic and contains languages such as Vietnamese, Cambodian (also called Khmer), and many other languages of India, Cambodia, Vietnam, Burma, and southern China. The Munda branch of Austroasiatic includes languages spoken in central and northeastern India, such as Mundari and Santali. Other Austroasiatic languages are spoken in Malaysia and on the Nicobar Islands (northwest of Sumatra).

Table 8.19 The Austroasiatic family

Mon-Khmer	*Munda*
Vietnamese	Mundari
Cambodian [= Khmer]	Santali
Mon	
Parauk	

Some Austroasiatic languages are tonal (for example, Vietnamese) and some are characterized by large and complex vowel systems. Word order is generally SVO or SOV.

Tai-Kadai

The Tai-Kadai family includes Thai (formerly called Siamese), Laotian, Shan (spoken in Burma and Thailand), and several other languages of China, Thailand, and Vietnam. Typical salient features of these languages include SVO order, a general lack of inflectional morphemes, and the widespread use of tone (with the number of contrasting tones varying from three to nine).

Sino-Tibetan

In terms of numbers of speakers, the Sino-Tibetan family (see Table 8.20) is the largest language family after Indo-European. There are about three hundred Sino-Tibetan languages, with well over a billion native speakers.

Table 8.20 The Sino-Tibetan family

Tibeto-Burman	*Sinitic*						
	Mandarin	*Wu*	*Min*	*Yue*	*Xiang*	*Hakka*	*Gan*
Tibetan Burmese Yi [= Nyi] Sharpa	Mandarin	Wu	Taiwanese Amoy Hokkian Fukian	Cantonese	Hunan	Hakka	Gan

There are two major branches: Tibeto-Burman and Sinitic. The first branch includes Tibetan, Burmese, and many other languages spoken in northeastern India, Nepal, Burma, Tibet, and China. For the most part, these languages employ SOV word order.

The Sinitic branch contains several different subgroupings, including Mandarin (with major dialects in and around Beijing, Szechuan, and Nanking), Wu (with dialects in Shanghai and Suchow), Min (which includes Taiwanese, Amoy, Hokkian, and Fukian), Yue (Cantonese), Xiang, Hakka, and Gan. The Sinitic languages typically have SVO order and are usually tonal. They are predominantly isolating, having many monomorphemic (and usually monosyllabic) words. Consonant clusters are normally avoided.

The Sinitic family of languages is sometimes referred to as "Chinese" by nonlinguists, as if it were a single language with several dialects rather than a group of related, mutually unintelligible languages. This confusion is based on the fact that the same writing system is used across China and can be understood by speakers of different Chinese languages (see Chapter 15, Section 4.1).

Austronesian

The Austronesian family (see Table 8.21) contains approximately one thousand languages, which are spoken from the island of Madagascar halfway across the world to Southeast Asia, Hawaii, Easter Island, and New Zealand. Some of the languages of Taiwan belong to the Formosan branch of this family; however, Taiwanese, which is spoken by most of the island's residents, is a Sinitic language (see above).

Table 8.21 The Austronesian family

Formosan	*Malayo-Polynesian*	
	Western	*Oceanic*
Paiwan	Malagasy	Samoan
Amis	Malay [= Indonesian]	Tahitian
Atayal	Tagalog [= Pilipino]	Maori
Seediq	Javanese	Hawaiian
	Sundanese	Fijian
	Balinese	Motu
		Ponapean

The largest branch within the Austronesian family is Malayo-Polynesian, which contains all the Austronesian languages outside of Taiwan. These include Malagasy (spoken on Madagascar), Malay (and the mutually comprehensible Indonesian), Tagalog (the basis for Pilipino, the official language of the Philippines), Javanese, and many other languages spoken in the Philippines, Malaysia, Indonesia, Vietnam, Cambodia, Taiwan, and the islands of the Pacific Ocean.

The Polynesians were intrepid ocean travelers who colonized Hawaii, Easter Island, and New Zealand sometime between A.D. 500 and 1000. Well-known Polynesian languages include Samoan, Tahitian, Maori, and Hawaiian (which now has only a few hundred first-language native speakers, although efforts are underway to revive it).

A characteristic feature of Austronesian languages is the extensive use of reduplication. Many of these languages also make liberal use of infixes, which are extremely rare in other language families. Word order is usually SVO, although VSO is more prevalent in the Austronesian languages spoken in Taiwan, the Philippines, Northern Borneo, and Polynesia.

Some research has attempted to link the Austronesian family with the Austroasiatic family of India and Southeast Asia, forming a larger Austric family. However, this relationship is still very tentative.

Indo-Pacific

Indo-Pacific (or Papuan) languages are all spoken on the island of New Guinea, on nearby islands such as New Britain or Bougainville, or on the Andaman Islands (just southwest of Burma). Little is known about many of these languages, but they appear to be about seven hundred in number, with just under three million speakers.

Two languages with relatively large speaker populations are Enga (165,000 speakers, spoken in the western highlands of New Guinea) and Bunak (50,000 speakers, spoken on the island of Timor, west of New Guinea).

Indo-Pacific languages are normally tone languages. Nouns are often marked for case but not always for number. Word order is usually SOV.

Australian

Recent studies have established that all of the aboriginal languages of Australia belong to the same family. There are about 170 such languages, but many have very few speakers. There are currently only about thirty thousand speakers of aboriginal Australian languages.

The majority of Australian languages are spoken in Arnhem Land (north central Australia) and the northern part of Western Australia. The languages with the largest number of speakers are Mabuiag (seven thousand speakers on the Torres Straits Islands, north of Australia) and the Western Desert Language (five thousand speakers in Western Australia).

Australian languages are characterized by simple vowel systems. Nouns are normally marked for case, sometimes in unusual and intricate ways, and word order can be very free.

Afroasiatic

Afroasiatic languages (see Table 8.22) are spoken primarily in a band across the northern half of Africa and in the Middle East. There are about 250 Afroasiatic languages and 175 million speakers of these languages.

Table 8.22 The Afroasiatic family

(Egyptian)	*Cushitic*	*Berber*	*Chadic*	*Semitic*
(Coptic)	Somali	Tachelhit	Hausa	(Babylonian)
	Oromo	Tamazight		(Assyrian)
		Kabyle		(Old Canaanite)
		Riff		(Moabite)
		Tuareg		Aramaic
				Arabic
				Amharic
				Modern Hebrew

Afroasiatic has five main branches, one of which—Egyptian—no longer contains any living languages. Although Old Egyptian was spoken from 3000 B.C. onward (including during the time of Rameses II [1290–1224 B.C.], who was probably Pharaoh at the time of the Exodus), it has long been extinct. Its descendant, Coptic, is now used only as the liturgical language of the Coptic Church.

A second branch of Afroasiatic is Cushitic, whose member languages are spoken in Somalia, Kenya, Ethiopia, and the Sudan. A third branch, Berber, includes several languages of Algeria, Morocco, and Niger, such as Tamazight and Tuareg. Still another branch, Chadic, contains many of the languages of Chad and Nigeria, such as Hausa. Unlike other Afroasiatic languages, Chadic languages are tonal.

The fifth and largest branch of Afroasiatic (in terms of number of speakers) is the Semitic branch. Many (now extinct) languages mentioned in the Bible were of Semitic origin, such as Babylonian, Assyrian, (Old) Canaanite, Moabite, Classical Hebrew, and Biblical Aramaic. Biblical (or Palestinian) Aramaic was spoken in Palestine at the time of Jesus, and may have been his native language.

Classical Hebrew died out several centuries before the birth of Jesus, although it was maintained as a written language within Judaism. Modern (or Israeli) Hebrew is not directly descended from Classical Hebrew; rather, it was created (or re-created) at the beginning of this century by regularizing some aspects of Classical Hebrew and adding new vocabulary. Modern Hebrew has only had a community of native speakers for the past few decades.

Still another Semitic language, Arabic, has various dialects (not all of which are mutually intelligible) spoken across North Africa and throughout the Middle East. All of these are descended from Classical Arabic, which was the language of Mohammed, the founder of Islam, and is the language of the Koran, the holy book of Islam.

The Semitic languages are characterized by a system of consonantal roots. Most roots consist of three (sometimes two) consonants, with vowels being inserted to indicate various inflectional and derivational categories (see Chapter 4, Section 1.3). For example, Arabic has the root *k-t-b* (denoting the concept of writing) from which a variety of words can be formed, including *kitaabun* 'book', *kaatibun* 'writer', *kataba* 'he wrote', and *yaktubu* 'he is writing'. The Semitic languages frequently have complex consonant clusters and pharyngeal or pharyngealized consonants.

Niger-Congo

Most of the languages spoken in sub-Saharan Africa belong to the Niger-Congo family of languages (see Table 8.23). In all, this family contains over nine hundred languages, with a total of (approximately) 180 million speakers. There are three major branches: Kordofanian, Mande, and Atlantic-Congo.

Table 8.23 The Niger-Congo family

Kordofanian	*Mande*	*Atlantic-Congo*	
Tegali	Maninka	Swahili	Xhosa
Koalib	Bambara	Shona	Yoruba
Katla	Mende	KinyaRwanda	Igbo
		Zulu	Wolof

The Kordofanian branch includes only a handful of languages spoken in the Sudan, such as Tegali, Koalib, and Katla. The Mande branch contains a number of families of languages spoken in West Africa, such as Maninka, Bambara, and Mende. (Alex Hailey's famous African ancestor, described in the novel *Roots*, was probably a speaker of Maninka.)

Atlantic-Congo, on the other hand, is much larger and can be divided into several branches and numerous sub-branches. One of the largest sub-branches contains the more than one hundred languages of the Bantu family, with about fifty-five million speakers. Some of the principal Bantu languages are Swahili (Tanzania and Kenya), Shona (Zimbabwe and Zambia), KinyaRwanda (Rwanda, Uganda, and Congo), Zulu (South Africa and Lesotho), and Xhosa (South Africa). Other Atlantic-Congo languages include Yoruba (Nigeria, Togo, and Benin), Igbo (Nigeria), and Wolof (Senegal).

Niger-Congo languages are typically SVO and usually have tone systems (with the notable exception of Swahili). The Bantu languages are usually agglutinating with verb-subject and verb-direct object agreement. Languages in the Bantu group also exhibit a complex system of noun classes, each of which is marked by a separate set of prefixes.

Nilo-Saharan

The Nilo-Saharan family is primarily found in eastern and central Africa and includes approximately 120 languages, with about thirty million speakers. Languages

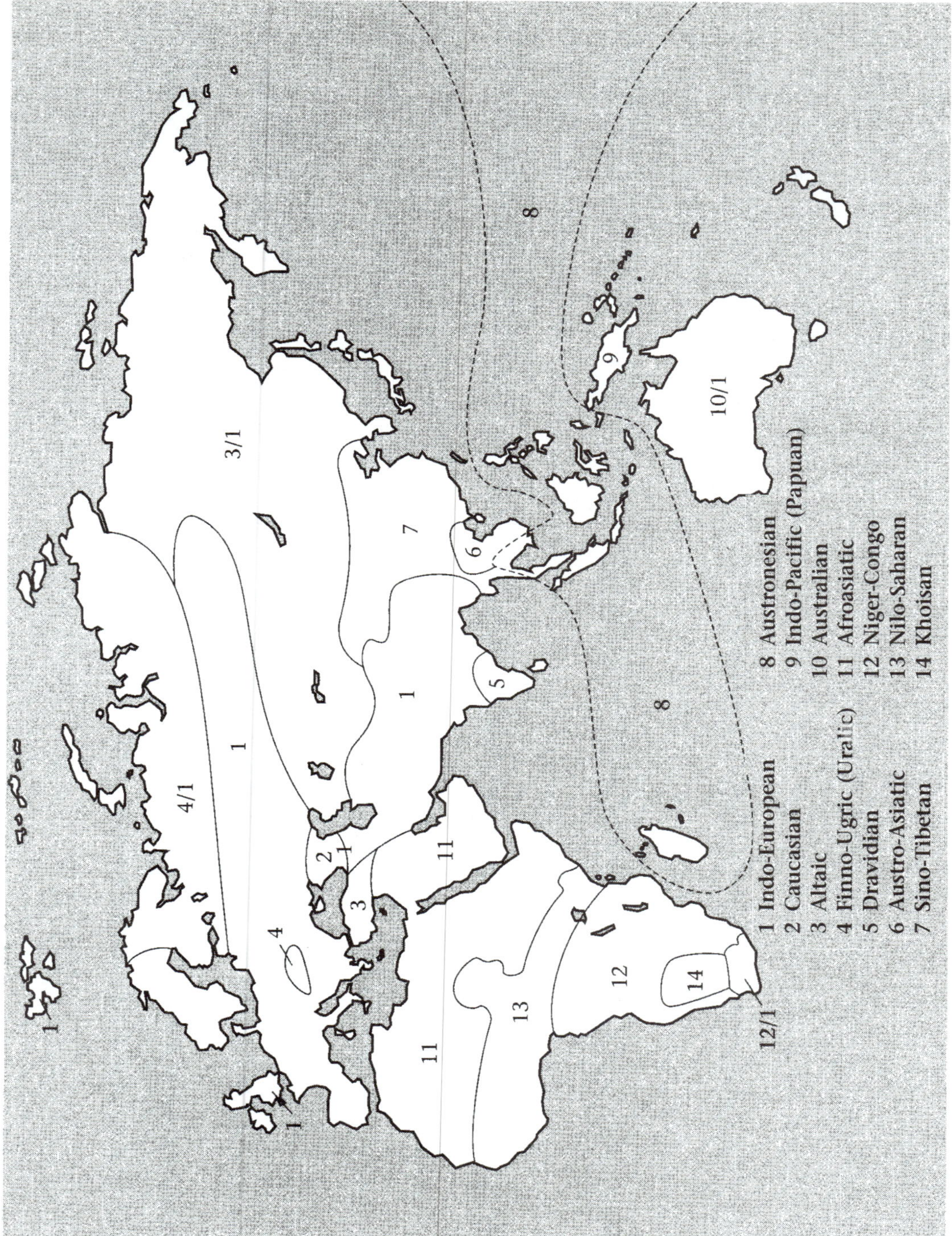

Figure 8.9 Location of some major language families

in this family include Luo and Maasai (both spoken in Kenya), Dinka (Sudan), Kanuri (Nigeria), and Nuer (Sudan and Ethiopia).

Nilo-Saharan languages generally have tonal systems, and nouns are usually marked for case and often use internal change (as in English *foot* vs. *feet*).

Khoisan

The Khoisan family is quite small, containing only about thirty languages spoken by 120,000 speakers. The majority of Khoisan languages are spoken in the southern and southwestern areas of Africa.

Some Khoisan languages are Hottentot (= Nama), !Kung, and Sandawe (one of only two Khoisan languages spoken in east Africa). Khoisan languages have unusual click sounds in their consonantal systems. These clicks have been borrowed by a few neighboring Bantu languages, such as Zulu and Xhosa.

3.3 North, Central, and South America

Contrary to popular belief, not all native American Indian (usually called **Amerindian**) languages belong to the same family. Although many of the genetic relationships are still unclear, it appears that there are well over a dozen different language families in the Americas (see Table 8.24). (Languages in parentheses in Table 8.24 are extinct.)

Table 8.24 North, Central, and South American families

Language family	*Some member languages*
Eskimo-Aleut	Inuktitut [= Inuit]
Athabaskan	Navajo, Apache, Chipewyan, Dogrib, Slavey
Algonquian	Blackfoot, Micmac, Cree, Ojibwa, (Mohican)
Siouan	Dakota, Lakota, Winnebago, Crow
Iroquoian	Cherokee, Mohawk, Cayuga, (Huron)
Caddoan	Caddo, Witchita, Pawnee
Wakashan	Nootka, Kwakiutl, Nitinat
Salish	Flathead, Halkomelem, Okanagan, Shuswap
Klamath-Sahaptin	Yakima, Nez Perce, Sahaptin, Klamath
Penutian	Patwin, Wintu, Nomlaki
Muskogean	Choctaw, Muskogee
Hokan	Diegueno, Yuma, Mohave
Coahuiltecan	Comecrudo, Cotoname, Pakawa, Carrizo
Uto-Aztecan	Hopi, Nahuatl, Papago, (Classical Aztec)
Oto-Manguean	Mazahua, Zapotec, Mixteco, Otomi
Mayan	Yucatec, Kekchi, Maya, Tzeltal, Tojolabal
Andean-Equatorial	Quechua, Aymara, Arawak, Guarani
Ge-Pano-Carib	Carib, Bororo, Witoto, Mataco
Macro-Chibchan	Cuna, Cayapa, Epera, Warao, Talamanca

Figure 8.10 shows the location of groups found in North and Central America.

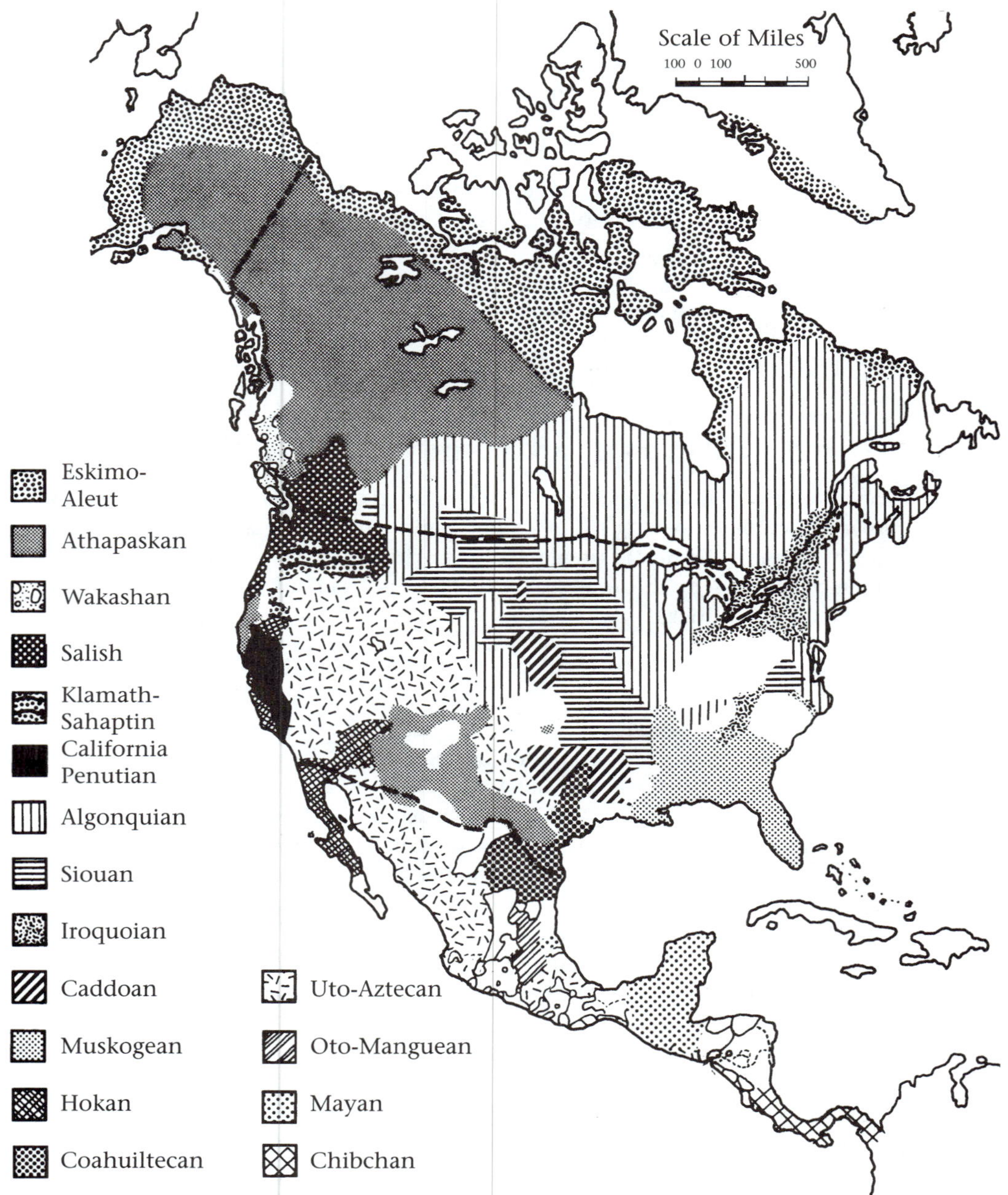

Figure 8.10 North and Central American language groups

Since the next chapter describes the native languages of the United States in some detail, it necessarily includes discussion of many of the Amerindian language families of North America. Therefore, we will restrict our focus here to some facts about a few of the indigenous languages of South America.

There are at least six hundred different Amerindian languages spoken in South America, by about eleven million people. However, our knowledge of these languages is often minimal, and some linguists estimate that there may be over a thousand South American Amerindian languages. Most of these languages belong to one of three subfamilies: Andean-Equatorial, Ge-Pano-Carib, and Macro-Chibchan.

The Andean-Equatorial subfamily contains languages that are found throughout South America, and may have as many as ten million speakers all together. The principal language in this family is Quechua, which has over six million speakers. Dialects of Quechua are spoken in Peru, Ecuador, and Bolivia. This was the language of the Inca empire, which reached its height in the sixteenth century A.D., before being destroyed by the Spanish conquistadors. Other languages belonging to this family are Aymara (Peru), Arawak (Surinam), and Guaraní (the major language of Paraguay). An interesting typological feature of some Andean-Equatorial languages is that they have no lateral consonants whatsoever.

The Ge-Pano-Carib subfamily is also spread over much of South America. Some of the languages belonging to this family are Carib (Surinam), Bororo (Brazil), Witoto (Peru), and Mataco (Argentina). Languages of the Ge-Pano-Carib family also often lack laterals; the dominant word order in these languages is usually SOV.

Languages of the Macro-Chibchan subfamily are found in Central America and the northwestern part of South America. Some languages belonging to this family are Cuna (Panama), Cayapa (Ecuador), Epera (Colombia), and Warao (Venezuela). Macro-Chibchan languages generally have SOV word order.

3.4 LANGUAGE PHYLA

In recent years attempts have been made to group many of the language families presented in Sections 3.1, 3.2, and 3.3 into even larger groupings called **phyla** (singular phylum) or **macrofamilies**. These attempts are controversial, as they challenge established views within linguistics. However, they also afford a number of intriguing possibilities. In this section we will attempt to provide a balanced view of these ventures into long-range comparison.

One of the best known of the proposed phyla is called Nostratic (also called Eurasiatic). It includes Indo-European, Uralic, Altaic, and (depending on the linguist) various other languages and language families. A number of reconstructed forms have been proposed for this phylum; two of the most convincing are the reconstructed first- and second-person singular pronouns: **m-* 'I' and **t-* 'you (sg)'. These forms are particularly persuasive, since pronoun systems are normally extremely stable and, thus, are among the most likely forms to have remained constant for the extended period of time since the existence of Proto-Nostratic (about 20,000 years ago).

Another proposed phylum is Dene-Caucasian. It includes Sino-Tibetan, Na-Dene (which includes Athabaskan), North Caucasian, and a number of other individual languages. A third proposed phylum is Austric (mentioned in Section 3.2), which includes at least Austroasiatic and Austronesian, and perhaps Daic (the family to which Thai belongs) and the Hmong-Mien (Mia-Yiao) group of languages of southern China and southeast Asia.

If all the phyla proposed to date were to be accepted by linguists, the total number of linguistic groupings would be reduced to a mere twelve (as opposed to the fifty or more that have previously been proposed) (see Table 8.25).

Table 8.25 Twelve phyla of the world's languages

1. Khoisan	7. Dene-Caucasian:	11. Nostratic/Eurasiatic:
2. Niger-Congo	a) Sino-Tibetan	a) Indo-European
3. Nilo-Saharan	b) Na-Dene	b) Uralic
4. Australian	c) North Caucasian	c) Altaic
5. Indo-Pacific	d) Nahali	d) Korean-Japanese-Ainu
6. Austric:	e) Basque	e) Gilyak
a) Austroasiatic	f) Yeniseian	f) Chuckchi-Kamchatkan
b) Austronesian	g) Burushaski	g) Eskimo-Aleut
c) Daic	8. Afroasiatic	12. Amerind
d) Hmong-Mien	9. Kartvelian (South Caucasian)	
	10. Dravidian	

Venturing still further, some linguists have even gone so far as to reconstruct a single, common ancestor for all human languages, which has been called Proto-World, or Proto-Sapiens. This ancestor language would have been spoken approximately 60,000 to 70,000 years ago. For the sake of interest, we provide a (simplified) example of one of the more than two dozen Proto-World etymologies that have been reconstructed to date:

> *Proto-World* *mena *'to think (about)'* Proposed cognates: Latin *men(s)* 'mind', Basque *munak* (pl) 'brains', Hungarian *mon(-d)* 'say', Telugu *manavi* 'prayer, humble request', Shawnee *menw* 'prefer, like', Bambara *mɛ* 'know', Tumale *aiman* 'think', Songhai *ma* 'understand', Masa *min* 'wish'.

It is certainly possible that all human languages have descended from a single ancestor language. It is generally agreed, for example, that all human beings are closely biologically related, and recent genetic studies have even proposed that all living human beings are descended from a particular *Homo sapiens* woman (dubbed "Eve") who lived in Africa some 200,000 years ago.

Most linguists would probably agree that all human languages must have descended from a small number of languages, if not a single mother language. However, many believe that the tools used for reconstruction (the historical-comparative method) are not able to provide any linguistic evidence for long-range comparisons that go back more than about 8,000 or 10,000 years. There are a number of reasons for this.

First, the pronunciation and meaning of words can change so radically over even a much shorter period of time that cognates can become completely unrecognizable. Thus, Latin *aqua* [akwa] 'water' developed into French *eau* [o] 'water' in less than 2,000 years, Proto-Indo-European (PIE) **dwo* 'two' developed into Armenian *erku* 'two' in approximately 5,000–8,000 years, and Old English *hūswīf* 'housewife' radically changed its meaning, to become *hussy* 'a strumpet, or trollop' in less than 1,500 years. Of course, as noted in Section 3, languages also lose words altogether, which can make it all the more difficult to uncover the cognates needed to establish a genetic relationship.

Another argument against long-range comparison has to do with the complications introduced by borrowings. For instance, for many years Thai was thought to be a Sino-Tibetan language because it contained so many Chinese loan words. However, painstaking research has finally made it clear that Thai is not Sinitic but belongs to the Daic family.

A further difficulty arises when words that appear to be cognates may have evolved independently as instances of onomatopoeia. Since onomatopoeic words (e.g., *cuckoo*, *vroom*) are intended to sound like real world noises, it would not be surprising to find such similar words even in unrelated languages.

Another argument against long-range comparison is that certain cross-linguistic similarities among sounds may stem from the fact that all human beings have the same vocal tract configuration. Thus, the presence of universally common sounds like /p, t, k, s, i, a, u/ in suspected cognates may be due not to a shared ancestor but rather to the fact that these sounds have articulatory and acoustic properties that favor their frequent use.

In defense of their endeavor, supporters of long-range comparison claim that loan words and onomatopoeic words are easily identifiable by the experienced researcher and can thus be easily discounted. Furthermore, language change need not affect all of the words of a language; some words retain a similar meaning and pronunciation for thousands of years. Thus, Old English *fisc* [fɪʃ] apparently had the same pronunciation and the same meaning as modern English *fish* [fɪʃ], despite a lapse of 1,500 years; the meaning and pronunciation of Latin *aqua* [akwa] 'water' have been maintained in Italian *acqua* [akːwa] 'water' (2,000 years); Proto-Indo-European **dwo* 'two' changed very little in pronunciation in Latin *duo* 'two' (about 6,000 years); and Proto-Indo-European **nepot* 'nephew, grandson' had a meaning and pronunciation almost identical to those of its descendant *nepot* 'nephew, grandson' in modern Rumanian (about 8,000 years).

Supporters of long-range comparison claim that both anthropological and biological evidence show that all human beings are at least distantly related and that it is therefore plausible to believe that all human languages must be related as well. It only remains, they claim, for linguists to determine the degree of relationship among the individual language families.

This controversy is far from being resolved, and it is fair to say that most linguists remain very skeptical about the evidence and conclusions associated with comparative research involving a time depth greater than 8,000 or 10,000 years. Nonetheless, the debate has presented new and intriguing possibilities in the study of linguistic classification.

Summing up

The focus of this chapter is on the criteria that linguists use to classify languages and on the enormous variety of languages found throughout the world. Linguists sometimes attempt to classify languages solely in terms of their structural similarities and differences (that is, in terms of their **linguistic typology**). Analysis of cross-linguistic data has identified a number of **linguistic universals**, indicating the most common characteristics of human language. The other major type of classificatory work in linguistics is concerned with **genetic relationships**—establishing language families whose members are descended from a common ancestor. While research in this area is hampered both by the large number of languages involved and the scarcity of the available data, a sizable portion of the world's several thousand languages has been placed in families. Finally, we present the controversial work recently done on linguistic **phyla** or **macrofamilies**. Research in these areas can shed light on the nature of language change, as well as the movement of peoples throughout the world.

Key terms

General terms and terms concerning types of classification

areal classification
dialect
genetic classification
genetic relationships
genetically related (languages)
linguistic typology
linguistic universals
mutual intelligibility

Terms concerning typological classification

absolute universals
agglutinating language
analytic language
fixed stress languages
free stress languages
fusional language
hierarchies
implicational universals
inflectional language
isolating language
markedness theory
marked traits
polysynthetic language
synthetic languages
tone languages
universal tendencies
unmarked

Terms concerning genetic classification

Amerindian (languages)
Indo-European family

Terms concerning larger groupings of language families

macrofamilies
phyla

Sources

The estimate that approximately sixty-five hundred languages are spoken in the world today comes from the Web site of the Foundation for Endangered Languages at <www.bris.ac.uk/Depts/Philosophy/CTL/FEL/> (email: nostler@chibcha.demon.co.uk). The suggestion that only three hundred of these languages have a secure future is due to K. Hale, professor of linguistics at MIT, cited in *Time* magazine (23 September

1991, p. 48). For further discussion, see "Endangered Languages" by K. Hale et al., *Language* 68 (1992): 1–42.

The section on linguistic typology draws on data from the books by B. Comrie and J. Greenberg cited in Recommended Reading. Other material for this section comes from *Tone: A Linguistic Survey*, edited by V. Fromkin (New York: Academic Press, 1978); J. Hawkins's "On Implicational and Distributional Universals of Word Order," *Journal of Linguistics* 16 (1980): 193–235; M. Dryer's "The Greenbergian Word Order Correlations," *Language* 68 (1992): 81–138; *Patterns of Sounds* by I. Maddieson (Cambridge: Cambridge University Press, 1984); M. Ruhlen's *A Guide to the Languages of the World* (Stanford, CA: Language Universals Project: Stanford University, 1976); *The World's Major Languages*, edited by B. Comrie (Oxford: Oxford University Press, 1990); and the four-volume series *Universals of Human Language*, edited by J. Greenberg (Stanford, CA: Stanford University Press, 1978).

The discussion of morphological typology draws on information presented in B. Comrie's book cited below. The estimate of the relative frequency of languages in which the subject precedes the direct object is based on information in the book by W. Croft cited below. The data on OVS and OSV languages are from "Object-Initial Languages" by D. Derbyshire and G. Pullum, *International Journal of American Linguistics* 47 (1981): 192–214. The discussion of consonant systems in Section 2.4 is based on "Phonetic Universals in Consonant Systems" by B. Lindblom and I. Maddieson, *Language, Speech and Mind: Studies in Honor of Victoria Fromkin*, edited by L. Hyman and C. Li (New York: Routledge & Kegan Paul, 1988), pp. 62–78.

The section on language families is based on B. Comrie's book *The Languages of the Soviet Union* (London: Cambridge University Press, 1981); J. Greenberg's *The Languages of Africa* (Bloomington, IN: Indiana University Press, 1966); the book by M. Ruhlen cited previously; another book by Ruhlen entitled *A Guide to the World's Languages, Volume 1: Classification* (Stanford, CA: Stanford University Press, 1987); and C. F. and F. M. Voegelin's *Classification and Index of the World's Languages* (cited below). Additional data derive from C. D. Buck's *A Dictionary of Selected Synonyms in the Principal Indo-European Languages* (Chicago: University of Chicago Press, 1949); *The American Heritage Dictionary of Indo-European Roots*, revised and edited by C. Watkins (Boston: Houghton Mifflin Company, 1985); the three-volume *Russisches Etymologisches Wörterbuch,* compiled by M. Vasmer (Heidelberg: Carl Winter Universitätsverlag); "Syntactic Reconstruction and Finno-Ugric," an article by L. Campbell in *Historical Linguistics* (1987), edited by H. Andersen and K. Koerner (Amsterdam: John Benjamins, 1990); and the Proto-Baltic dictionary database developed by the author of this chapter. The maps in Figures 8.8 and 8.9 are adapted from *Problems in the Origin and Development of the English Language*, 3rd ed., by John Algeo, copyright © by Harcourt Brace & Company, reprinted by permission of the publisher. The map in Figure 8.10 is adapted from *A Guide to the World's Languages, Vol. 1*, by M. Ruhlen (Stanford, CA: Stanford University Press, 1987).

The section on language phyla is based on the book by M. Ruhlen (cited below) and on *Sprung from Some Common Source*, edited by S. Lamb and E. Mitchell (Stanford, CA: Stanford University Press, 1991).

The data for exercises 1 to 3 are found in *A Guide to the Languages of the World* by M. Ruhlen. The data for exercise 6 are from *Malagasy: Introductory Course* by C. Garvey (Washington: Center for Applied Linguistics, 1964).

Recommended reading

Comrie, Bernard. 1989. *Language Universals and Linguistic Typology*. 2nd ed. Oxford: Blackwell.

Croft, William. 1990. *Typology and Universals*. New York: Cambridge University Press.

Greenberg, Joseph, ed. 1966. *Universals of Language*. 2nd ed. Cambridge, MA: MIT Press.

Lyovin, Anatole V. 1997. *An Introduction to the Languages of the World*. New York: Oxford University Press.

Ruhlen, Merritt. 1994. *On the Origin of Languages*. Stanford, CA: Stanford University Press.

Voegelin, C. F., and F. M. Voegelin. 1977. *Classification and Index of the World's Languages*. New York: Elsevier.

Questions

1. Which tendencies and universals are manifested in the following vowel systems? (*Hint:* Look at the pattern of the vowel systems and at rounding.)
   a) Afrikaans (South Africa) ([y] and [ø] are front rounded vowels)

   i y u
   ø ə o
   ɛ ɔ
   a

   b) Squamish (Washington State)

   i u
   ə
   a

2. As noted in Section 2.1, the presence of long and nasal vowel phonemes is governed by implicational universals. In what ways do the vowel systems below comply with the implicational universals that make reference to length and nasality?

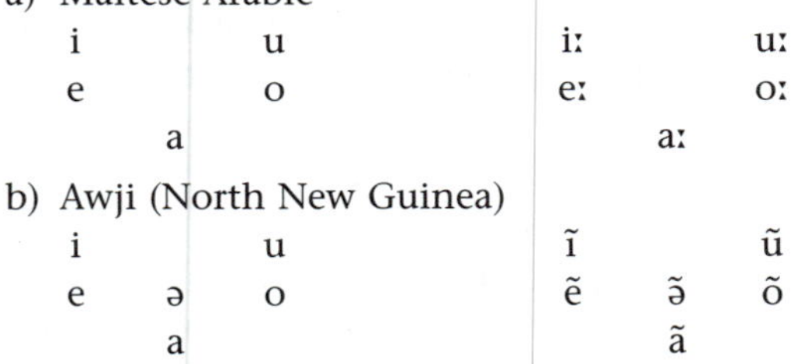

   a) Maltese Arabic

   i u iː uː
   e o eː oː
   a aː

   b) Awji (North New Guinea)

   i u ĩ ũ
   e ə o ẽ ə̃ õ
   a ã

3. Consider the following consonant systems. Do these consonant systems comply with the implicational universals mentioned in this chapter? Explain your answer.
   a) Tahitian (Tahiti)

p	t	ʔ
f		h
v	r	
m	n	

   b) Palauan (Palau Islands)

	t	k	ʔ
b			
	ð		
	s		
m		ŋ	
	l, r		

   c) Nengone (Loyalty Islands, South Pacific)—stop and nasal system only

pʰ	tʰ	ʈʰ		kʰ	ʔ
b	d	ɖ		g	
m	n		ɲ	ŋ	
m̥	n̥			ŋ̊	

   (*Note:* [ʈ] and [ɖ] are retroflex consonants; [̥] marks a voiceless nasal; [ɲ] represents a palatal nasal.)

   d) Mixe (South Mexico)

p	t		k	ʔ
	d		g	
	ts	tʃ		
	s		x	h
v			ɣ	
m	n			

4. Morphological phenomena can be classified into four types: analytic, polysynthetic, agglutinating, and fusional. Which type does each of the following languages belong to? Why?
   a) Siberian Yupik

   Angya-ghlla-ng -yug -tuq
   boat -big -get-want-3SG
   'He wants to get a big boat.'

   b) Latvian

las-u	las-ām	rakst-u	rakst-ām
read-1SG.Pres	read-1PL.Pres	write-1SG.Pres	write-1PL.Pres
'I read'	'we read'	'I write'	'we write'

   c) Japanese

   gakusei-wa homer-are-na-i
   student-Topic praise-Pass-neg-Pres
   'The student is not praised.'

5. Do a morphological analysis of the following data from Latvian. Single out each morpheme and identify its meaning. After you have segmented and identified the morphemes, describe how the data reflect the implicational universals in Section 2.2.

   a) lidotājs — 'aviator (nominative)'
   b) lidotāju — 'aviator (accusative)'
   c) lidotājam — 'to the aviator (dative)'
   d) lidot — 'to fly'
   e) rakstītājs — 'writer (nominative)'
   f) rakstītāja — 'writer's (genitive)'
   g) rakstīt — 'to write'

6. Note the following data from Malagasy, an Austronesian language spoken on the island of Madagascar. Does Malagasy comply with all the word-order tendencies mentioned in Section 2.3?

   a) amin' ny restauranta
      'to the restaurant'
   b) Enti'n ny labiera ny mpiasa.
      brings the beer the waiter
      'The waiter brings the beer.'
   c) Avy any Amerika izy.
      come from America he
      'He comes from America.'

7. For each of the following languages on the left, determine which of the languages on the right is most closely related to it. Use the information presented in Section 3, and give reasons for your answers.

   i) Macedonian — a) Albanian, b) Ukrainian, c) Greek
   ii) Gypsy — a) French, b) Old Egyptian, c) Egyptian Arabic
   iii) French — a) Spanish, b) Italian, c) Romansch
   iv) Irish — a) English, b) Icelandic, c) Breton
   v) Vietnamese — a) Laotian, b) Mundari, c) Burmese
   vi) Modern Hebrew — a) Turkish, b) Somali, c) Yiddish

8. To which families do the following languages belong?

a)	Gujarati	j)	Yuma
b)	Hakka	k)	Volga Tatar
c)	Lapp	l)	Georgian
d)	Uzbek	m)	Mohican
e)	Sandawe	n)	Aramaic
f)	Quechua	o)	Flathead
g)	Faroese	p)	Telugu
h)	Maninka	q)	Javanese
i)	Santali	r)	Navajo

9. Make a list of up to fifteen languages spoken by friends and acquaintances, and identify the language family to which each belongs.

nine

Indigenous Languages of North America

Victor Golla

The condition of American languages is . . . an epitome of that of the language of the world in general.
– William Dwight Whitney, *Life and Growth of Language* (1875)

Objectives

In this chapter, you will learn

- how many indigenous languages there are in North America
- where they may have come from
- what their historical relationships to one another are
- what their important phonetic characteristics are
- what their important grammatical characteristics are
- what is happening to them today

For the purposes of this chapter, North America includes the United States (except for Hawaii), Canada, and Greenland, as well as the northern states of Mexico. The indigenous peoples of North America are usually known as Indians in the United States and First Nations in Canada, except for the Aleuts and the Eskimos (the latter called Inuit in Canada), who are designated separately. In the United States, Native Americans is used as the general term for all indigenous peoples, including Indians, Aleuts, Eskimos, and Native Hawaiians.

Of the approximately 6,500 languages in the world, about 325 are (or once were) spoken by the indigenous peoples of North America. Although they account for only 5 percent of the languages of humankind, the impact of North American languages on linguistic theory has been disproportionately great. This is largely due to historical circumstances. Some North American languages were among the few non-European languages for which extensive and relatively accurate information was available to

European scholars before 1800. When the modern disciplines of linguistics and anthropology were established at the beginning of the twentieth century, North American languages continued to be a rich source of data on the diversity and variability of human speech, attracting the research interest of such influential figures as Franz Boas, Edward Sapir, Leonard Bloomfield, and Benjamin Whorf. Sapir's *Language* (1921), which was among the most influential books on language in the first half of the twentieth century, made extensive use of data from the North American languages Sapir had studied, such as Yana, Takelma, and Nootka.

Although enormously diverse in their structure, North American languages represent points on the same continuum of variation that is characteristic of all human languages. Taken as a whole, they are no more out-of-the-ordinary than a similar number of languages from New Guinea or the Sudan. However, since many widespread phonetic, morphological, and lexical features that are rare in European languages—for example, glottalization, incorporation, and polysynthesis—were first described in various North American languages, there is a lingering tendency to regard these languages as especially complex and difficult. This is especially true in popular culture, where such myths as the "thousands" of Eskimo words for snow, or the utter impenetrability of Navajo to a nonnative speaker, are deeply rooted. In truth, North American languages are no more and no less peculiar or inaccessible than the languages of Europe—just different.

1 ORIGIN AND CLASSIFICATION

1.1 Ultimate origins

Perhaps the oldest and most persistent question that has been asked about North American languages—and all of the languages of the Western Hemisphere—concerns their ultimate origin. Linked to this is the question of their historical relationship to one another: Is there an all-encompassing "American" linguistic stock?

During the past decade, the origin and historical uniqueness of indigenous American languages have once again become topics of heated debate. On the one hand, a few historical linguists—most notably Joseph Greenberg—have made a number of far-reaching proposals concerning historical connections among the languages of the world (see Chapter 8). In Greenberg's view, all American languages, with the exception of the Eskimo-Aleut and Na-Dene families in northwestern North America, are historically distinct from the rest of the world's languages and constitute a **stock** that he calls Amerind. Most other linguists who specialize in American languages believe that the historical diversity of languages in the Western Hemisphere is deep and fundamental, and that they are divided into a number of historically unrelated units. Some see as few as a dozen large stocks; others, using the strictest of criteria for historical relationship, count more than 180 historically distinct **language families** and unclassifiable languages in the hemisphere. Still other estimates lie between these extremes.

These differing interpretations of indigenous American linguistic diversity tend to be allied with different theories of the populating of the New World. Although most archaeologists and biological anthropologists believe that humans have lived in the Western Hemisphere since the end of the Pleistocene (approximately 12,500 years ago), there is no agreement on how long before that date the first humans arrived, or on whether the initial migration from the Eastern Hemisphere was followed by significant secondary migrations. Greenberg's hypothesis of "Amerind" unity appeals to prehistorians who favor a single founding migration, perhaps as recently as 12,500 years ago. On the other hand, the view that the languages of the hemisphere are deeply diverse appeals to prehistorians who favor multiple migrations over a long period, beginning perhaps as early as 35,000 years ago.

At the present time, the evidence is too weak and too susceptible to multiple interpretations to allow these debates to be resolved on purely linguistic grounds. Indeed, many historical linguists believe that any claim of a linguistic relationship older than six to eight thousand years is unprovable by the available tools of historical-comparative linguistics, so that hypotheses such as the Amerind one must always lie beyond scientific validation. On the other hand, since no linguistic relationship between an Asiatic and an American language has yet been shown to exist by these tools, nearly all linguists agree that even the most recent migrations of peoples across the Bering Strait must have taken place well before six thousand years ago.

1.2 Historical relationships in North America

Whatever their ultimate relationship to one another, the current standard classification of indigenous North American languages as shown in Table 9.1 divides them into 61 groups, including 33 established language families and 28 single-language **isolates**, whose further historical affilation cannot be readily determined. This classification ultimately derives from the work of John Wesley Powell, the late-nineteenth-century scientist and explorer. Powell's criteria for establishing a language family were strict, and very few of the families he proposed in his 1891 classification have been disproven by later work. However, the possibility of interpreting the data less strictly and arriving at wider schemes of relationship has appealed to many scholars. Scores of stocks and phyla have been proposed since Powell's day, but only a few have gained wide acceptance.

The American linguist Edward Sapir (1884–1939) was especially interested in reducing the number of language families in North America. He proposed six "super-stocks": Eskimo-Aleut, Na-Dene, Algonkian-Wakashan, Hokan-Siouan, Penutian, and Uto-Aztecan-Tanoan. Of these, only Eskimo-Aleut has won universal acceptance. Na-Dene (including Haida) and Penutian are still viable hypotheses but are far from universally accepted. The other four of Sapir's proposals are considered unlikely by most scholars today, although some of their components continue to be explored (most importantly, the Hokan component of Hokan-Siouan).

It is useful to make a distinction between language families that are geographically widespread (e.g., Algic, represented on the Pacific and Atlantic coasts, on the Plains, and around the Great Lakes) and those that are confined to one small region (e.g., Wakashan, on Vancouver Island and the adjoining coast of northern British Columbia). The former are often associated with (although not necessarily confined to) areas in which the aboriginal population was sparse and the lifestyle nomadic,

Table 9.1 Standard classification of North American languages (after Goddard 1996)

1. ESKIMO-ALEUT (13)
2. ALGIC
    - ALGONQUIAN (43)
    - RITWAN (2)
3. NA-DENE
    - Tlingit
    - ATHABASKAN-EYAK (46)
4. Haida
5. WAKASHAN (6)
6. CHIMAKUAN (2)
7. SALISHAN (23)

(8–18) Proposed PENUTIAN Superfamily

8. TSIMSHIANIC (2)
9. CHINOOKAN (3)
10. ALSEAN (2)
11. Siuslaw
12. COOSAN (2)
13. TAKELMAN (4)
14. WINTUAN (2)
15. MAIDUAN (3)
16. UTIAN
    - MIWOKAN (7)
    - COSTANOAN (8)
17. YOKUTS (6)
18. PLATEAU PENUTIAN
    - Klamath
    - SAHAPTIAN (2)
    - Molala

(19–28) Proposed HOKAN Superfamily

19. Karuk
20. Chimariko
21. SHASTAN (4)
22. PALAIHNIHAN
    - Achumawi
    - Atsugewi
23. POMOAN (7)
24. Yana
25. SALINAN (2)
26. COCHIMI-YUMAN (14)
27. Seri
28. Washo
29. YUKIAN
    - Yuki
    - Wappo
30. Esselen
31. CHUMASHAN (6)
32. UTO-AZTECAN*
    - NUMIC (7)
    - Tubatulabal
    - TAKIC (7)
    - Hopi
    - TEPIMAN (4)
    - TARACAHITAN (5)
    - Tubar
33. KIOWA-TANOAN (7)
34. KERESAN (2)
35. Zuni
36. Guaicura
37. Coahuilteco
38. COMECRUDAN (3)
39. Cotoname
40. Aranama
41. Solano
42. Maratino
43. Quinigua
44. Naolan
45. Karankawa
46. Kootenai
47. Cayuse
48. SIOUAN-CATAWBA
    - SIOUAN (15)
    - CATAWBAN (2)
49. Tonkawa
50. CADDOAN (6)
51. Adai
52. ATAKAPAN (2)
53. Chitimacha
54. Tunica
55. MUSKOGEAN (7)
56. Natchez
57. Yuchi
58. TIMUCUAN (2)
59. Calusa
60. IROQUOIAN (11)
61. Beothuk

Language families are in capitals, with the number of languages included shown in parentheses.

*Two additional branches of Uto-Aztecan are found only in Mesoamerica and are not included here—CORACHOL (two languages: Cora and Huichol) and AZTECAN (two languages: Nahuatl-Pipil and Pochutec). Nahuatl-Pipil, which was the language of the pre-Columbian Aztecs and was also used for administrative purposes in Colonial Mexico, remains one of the most widely spoken American Indian languages.

while the latter are frequently found in areas that were more heavily populated and characterized by sedentary cultures. Widespread language families can also sometimes be connected with the diffusion of an innovative technology, as with the bow and arrow in the case of the Athabaskan family (within Na-Dene) or the cultivation of squash and maize in the case of the Siouan family (within Siouan-Catawba).

Two regions of the continent—the Pacific Coast from southern Alaska to California, and the Gulf Coast from southern Texas to Florida—are remarkable for the number of unrelated languages and small language families they contained at the time of European contact. This mosaic-like linguistic diversity appears to have been correlated in both regions with village-level societies focused on the use of the rich local resources. On the other hand, many of the Pacific Coast language groups appear to some linguists to be related at a deeper level in the Penutian and Hokan superfamilies, indicating that at an earlier date the population of this area may have been considerably more mobile than in the contact period.

2 PHONETICS AND PHONOLOGY

Several speech sounds that are rare in Europe and Asia are frequently encountered in indigenous North American languages; most of these are consonants.

2.1 VELAR, UVULAR, AND PHARYNGEAL ARTICULATIONS

In addition to the velar stop [k] found in most of the world's languages, the majority of North American languages also have the less common velar fricative, often both voiceless and voiced ([x] and [ɣ]). In addition, stops and fricatives articulated with the back of the tongue touching the uvula (see Chapter 2) are found in about one-third of North American language groups, most of them in the northern and western parts of the continent. Uvular sounds have the quality of "deep-throated" velar sounds. In a few languages of the Northwest, most notably Nuuchahnulth (Nootka) and some Salishan languages, pharyngeal fricatives (as in Arabic) are also distinguished. (The symbols used for these sounds are shown in Table 9.2. It should be noted that here, and in several other cases, linguists who work with North American languages often use symbols that differ from the standard IPA symbols.)

Table 9.2 Velar, uvular, and pharyngeal consonants

	Velar	*Uvular*	*Pharyngeal*
Stops	k	q	
Fricatives			
Voiceless	x	x̣	ḥ
Voiced	ɣ	ɣ̣	ʕ

2.2 LATERAL FRICATIVES

The lateral fricative [ɬ] is characteristic of the Na-Dene and Salishan families and many other languages of the Northwest, and is also found in Muskogean, Tonkawa, and Zuni. The voiceless affricate formed with the lateral fricative [tɬ] is also frequent in these languages.

2.3 Glottalized stops and affricates (ejectives)

At least half of the language groups of North America have consonants with a complex type of coarticulation (see Chapter 2) known as **glottalization**. The most common glottalized consonants (also called **ejectives**) are voiceless stops or affricates that are articulated simultaneously with a closure of the glottis, accompanied by a constriction of the throat. The oral closure is released slightly before the glottis is opened, so that the sound is characterized by a distinctive "pop" or "crack." As Table 9.3 shows, glottalization is usually represented by an apostrophe above or following the phonetic symbol for the underlying stop or affricate (or other consonant).

Table 9.3 Glottalized (ejective) consonants

	Bilabial	*Dental/ alveolar*	*Lateral*	*Palatal*	*Velar*	*Uvular*
Stops	p'	t'			k'	q'
Affricates		ts'	tɬ' (ƛ̓)	tʃ' (č')		

In a few languages, fricatives, nasals, liquids, and even glides can also be accompanied by a closure of the glottis and throat constriction, and although the phonetic result differs from that heard in glottalized stops and affricates, these articulations are also usually considered to be glottalization.

2.4 Vowels and suprasegmental features

In the majority of indigenous North American languages, short and long vowels are phonemically distinct (e.g., [a] vs. [aː]). An oral/nasal distinction is also widespread, particularly in the eastern half of the continent and in the Pueblo Southwest. (Nasal vowels are usually represented in indigenous American languages with a hook beneath the vowel symbol rather than a tilde above—e.g., [ą] rather than [ã].) In some languages, such as Cherokee, a single nasal vowel of mid quality—that is, a nasalized schwa [ə̨]—contrasts with the oral vowels. In a number of languages, pitch differences between syllables are structurally significant, although in most cases the tone system is relatively simple—high versus low, or high versus mid versus low. (Phonemic high and low pitch are usually represented in indigenous American languages by acute and grave accents—e.g., [á] high vs. [à] low.) Tone systems are found in many languages of the Athabaskan branch of Na-Dene, in many Iroquoian languages, and in Kiowa-Tanoan.

Of particular typological interest is the tendency in some languages of the Northwest—most notably the Salishan family—to permit words and phrases with long clusters of consonants. These usually result from the morphological juxtaposition of a string of monosyllabic morphemes, with the vowel dropping out of the syllables not stressed. Thus, while the underlying structure of the Thompson Salish word that means 'you point a gun at him' is *čúɬ-aqs-xi-t-exw,* with four (potential) syllables, the word is actually pronounced as a single syllable, *čúɬqsxtxw,* with the only vowel phonetically realized being the one in the underlying stressed syllable.

2.5 Sounds not frequently found

Several speech sounds that are relatively common elsewhere are rarely found among indigenous North American languages. These include all voiced stops and affricates. In several groups—most notably Iroquoian, Na-Dene, Caddoan, and Salishan—the bilabial stop articulation [p] is generally lacking.

3 MORPHOLOGY AND SYNTAX

3.1 The structure of words

Polysynthesis

As far as grammatical structure is concerned, the most distinctive characteristic of many (although far from all) indigenous North American languages is their complex morphology. Unlike the moderately complex (synthetic) morphology of the verbal and nominal word classes in Indo-European languages, the morphological complexity of many North American languages focuses on a single word class, usually identified as the verb although its grammatical function is often like that of a sentence. This type of morphology is often called **polysynthetic**. (See also Chapter 4.)

Fully inflected complex words in a language with polysynthetic morphology typically have formal markers of grammatical relations such as subject, object, and indirect object; of various adverbial categories (particularly direction of motion); and of various inflectional categories such as tense, mode, and aspect. Such words are often semantically equivalent to sentences in languages such as English.

Yana, a Hokan language of northeastern California, has a typical polysynthetic morphology. Most polysynthetic Yana words are formed by suffixing up to half a dozen derivational and inflectional affixes to a root. Some typical formations are illustrated in Table 9.4.

Nuuchahnulth (Nootka), a Wakashan language of the west coast of Vancouver Island, has an especially well-developed polysynthetic morphology that greatly obscures the distinction between nouns and verbs. Except for a small number of interjections and particles, most Nuuchahnulth words are morphologically complex, consisting of at least two elements—a lexical stem and a word suffix. There are about a dozen of the latter, serving to determine the basic semantic and syntactic function of the word. They fall into two groups: predicational suffixes, which combine with the stem to form verbs; and relational suffixes, which form nouns, adverbs, or subordinate clauses.

Stems are semantically quite diverse. Some stems have meanings that are typically verb-like:

tɬ'i-   'shoot'
mamo:k-   'work'

Table 9.4 Polysynthetic words in Yana

puy-ru-walti-si-numa with.the.feet-into.fine.pieces-down.to.the.ground-PRES-2sg 'You mash it by stepping on it'
ni:na-ha-nča mother-PAST-1sg 'My mother is deceased; my late mother'
pay-ru-tʰpa-si-nča deer-going.in.pursuit.of-to.the.south-PRES-1sg 'I'm hunting deer to the south'
ni-wul-ha-numa one.male.goes-into.the.house-PAST-2sg 'You (a man) went into the house'
wa-tʰi:-walti-ha-nča with.the.buttocks-bending.(it)-down.to.the.ground-PAST-1sg 'I bent it down to the ground by sitting on it'

Other stems express meanings more frequently associated with nouns, adjectives, prepositions, and adverbs:

qo:ʔas- 'man'
tɬ'os- 'herring'
ʔiḥ- 'large'
ya:ɬ- 'there'
ʔokwiɬ- 'with respect to'

Although there are some restrictions, there is no general rule specifying which suffixes can be used with which stems. Thus, stems with verbal meanings can take predicational suffixes and form verbs:

tɬ'i-maḥ 'I shoot' (-(m)aḥ, indicative suffix, 1st-person form)
tɬ'i-ḥa 'is he shooting?' (-ḥa, interrogative suffix, 3rd-person form)

But so can stems with much less obviously verbal meanings:

q'oʔoc-aḥ 'I am a man'
ya:ɬ-ḥa 'is he there?'

Similarly, stems with nominal or relational meanings can take relational suffixes and form nouns, adverbs, and other non-verb words:

tɬ'os-ʔi '(that which is) a herring' (-ʔi, relative subject suffix, 3rd-person form)
q'o:ʔas-qa 'since he is a man; that he is a man' (-qa, general subordinate suffix, 3rd-person form)
ʔo:kwiɬ-ʔi 'with respect to him'

But so can stems with verbal meanings:

tł'i-ʔi 'he who shoots; shooter'
mamoːk-qa 'since he works; that he works'

In Nuuchahnulth, furthermore, stems are often complex. Stems can take suffixes that add a verbal idea to a noun-like stem (*-nakw-* 'have', *-ʔis-* 'eat') as well as suffixes that are typically locative or directional in their semantics (*-ił-* 'in the house', *-is-* 'on the beach'). Thus:

tł'os-ʔis-aḥ 'I am eating herring'
q'oʔac-ił-ʔi '(he who is) a man in the house'
yaːł-is-ḥa 'is he there on the beach?'

To sum up, in Nuuchahnulth, Yana, and many other North American languages, roots and affixes are linked together in "sentence-words" by a word-internal syntax that is the functional equivalent of at least some of the relationships marked in the sentences of European languages. However, there is often no semantic equivalence between the morphological elements that enter into these polysynthetic words and the familiar European word classes—noun, verb, adjective, and so on. While speakers of polysynthetic languages can undoubtedly express all of the concepts expressed by English speakers, they do so by taking a very different structural route.

It should be kept in mind, however, that not all North American languages are polysynthetic, and that among polysynthetic languages there are many—such as those belonging to the Eskimo-Aleut and Iroquoian families—that clearly distinguish nouns and verbs. In a few cases, moreover, polysynthesis occurs only in some languages of a historically related group. Thus, the Chinookan languages are polysynthetic, while many of the other languages that are commonly assigned to the Penutian superfamily more closely resemble European languages in their morphological and syntactic structures.

Noun incorporation

Compound verbs formed by the combination of a verb root with a noun (or an affix derived from a noun) are found in many of the world's languages (see Chapter 4). However, this process of deriving complex verb stems, usually called **noun incorporation**, is especially common in North America. Many polysynthetic North American languages use noun incorporation, as do a number of others, including many Siouan languages, Zuni, and Takelma. Some examples from Lakota, a Siouan language, are shown in Table 9.5.

Table 9.5 Lakota noun incorporation

šųŋʔakąyąka 'to ride horseback' = 'to on-horse-sit' < šųka 'horse' + aką 'on' + yąka 'sit'

ločʰį 'to be hungry' = 'to food-want' < lo- 'food' (nominal affix) + čʰį 'want'

wakšiyužaža 'to wash dishes' = 'to dish-wash' < wakšiča 'dishes' + yužaža 'wash'

ipuza 'to be thirsty' = 'to be mouth-dry' < i 'mouth' + puza 'be dry'

As the Lakota examples illustrate, the grammatical relationship of the noun to the verb can include that of subject ('mouth [is] dry' = 'be thirsty') and object ('want food' = 'be hungry'), as well as locative and other relationships ('sit on [a] horse' = 'ride horseback'). These morphological constructions differ from the syntactic ones on which they are based, however, in their often idiomatic reference.

3.2 Grammatical categories

Case relationships

The major grammatical categories expressed in a sentence—particularly the relationship of participants (subjects, objects, etc.) to states or actions—are encoded in various ways in the languages of the world. In some languages these **case** relationships between an entity and a state or action are marked by an affix on the noun (a case marker). In other languages, other grammatical devices (such as word order) are used to mark these relationships. However they are marked, case relationships usually follow one of three fundamental patterns.

In the **nominative-accusative pattern** (which is found in all the familiar European languages), the subject of a state or an intransitive action ('the man is old', 'the man walks') is formally identified with the **agent** of a transitive action ('the man sees the dog'). This nominative case is formally distinct from the object of a transitive action ('the dog sees the man'), the accusative case. (In English, these case distinctions are marked by word order: the nominative phrase precedes the verb, the accusative follows.)

By contrast, in the **ergative-absolutive pattern**, the agent of a transitive action (the **ergative** case) is formally distinct from the the subject of a state or intransitive action, which is marked in the same way as the object of a transitive action (the **absolutive** case). Although relatively rare among the world's languages, the ergative-absolutive pattern is well represented in North America. In the Eskimo languages, an ergative-absolutive case system is marked by suffixes on nouns, illustrated in Table 9.6 with examples from Central Alaskan Yupik.

Table 9.6 Ergative-absolutive case marking in Central Alaskan Yupik

nayiq cikkuuq	'the seal (abs) is frozen'
nayiq kittuq	'the seal (abs) sinks'
aŋuːtəm nayiq nəɣ̣ɣ̣aa	'the man (erg) eats the seal (abs)'
nayim nəqaq nəɣ̣ɣ̣aa	'the seal (erg) eats the fish (abs)'
aɣ̣naq ənəmmətuq	'the woman (abs) is in the house'
aɣ̣nam taŋx̣aa	'the woman (erg) sees him'

A third configuration of categories, the **agent-patient pattern**, formally distinguishes the subject of an intransitive action and the agent of a transitive action (the agent case) from the subject of a state and the object of a transitive verb (the **patient** case). The agent-patient pattern is especially widespread in North America, particularly in the languages that Sapir considered to be members of the Hokan-Siouan superstock (see Section 1.2), from the Iroquoian and Muskogean families in the east, to Yuki and various Hokan-affiliated languages in California. The basic pattern can be illustrated by the marking of pronominal categories in verbs in Tuscarora, a northern Iroquoian language, illustrated in Table 9.7.

Table 9.7 Agent and patient pronominal markers in Tuscarora

k-	1 SG agent	
	k-aʔnà:wə̨s	'I'm swimming'
	k-arè:rúheʔ	'I'm running'
	k-túhar	'I'm washing something'
	k-rì:yus	'I'm killing it'
wak-	1 SG patient	
	wak-ə̨́hré:tis	'I'm hungry'
	wak-nə̨́:hraraʔr	'I'm dirty'
	wak-rì:yus	'it's killing me'
	wak-yetkáhneʔ	'it's chasing me'

In some languages with an agent-patient pattern of case relationships, these categories interact with a semantic distinction between actions that are under the control of the participant and those that are uncontrollable. In Central Pomo, a language of northern California, speakers can sometimes indicate the degree of control that a participant has by choosing between agent and patient case marking:

ʔa: maṭ'ém	'I (agent) stepped on it (intentionally)'
to: maṭ'ém	'I (patient) stepped on it (accidentally)'
ʔa: k'lú:k'lu:w	'I (agent) coughed (intentionally)'
to: k'lú:k'lu:w	'I (patient) coughed (involuntarily)'

Evidentials

Many indigenous North American languages have grammatical expressions representing the speaker's source of information for the statement he or she is making. In many languages, these expressions (frequently enclitic particles) are ubiquitous in discourse, if not grammatically obligatory. The most common types of **evidentials** are (1) firsthand personal experience, (2) hearsay (often used to indicate that the speaker is quoting another's words), (3) nonverbal auditory evidence, and (4) inference from other evidence.

In Central Pomo, seven evidential categories are marked by enclitics, as shown in Table 9.8.

Table 9.8 Central Pomo evidential enclitics

čʰé mul=ʔma	'it rained' (it's an established fact)
čʰé mul=ya	'it rained' (I was there and saw it)
čʰé mul=ʔdo:	'it rained' (I was told)
čʰé mul=nme:	'it rained' (I heard the drops)
čʰé mul=ʔka	'it must have rained' (because everything is wet)
dačé:w=la	'I caught it' (I know because I did it)
dačé:w=wiya	'I got caught' (I know because it happened to me)

Aspect and tense

A popular misconception about indigenous American languages is that they are "timeless"—that is, that they do not concisely mark the categories of past, present, and future tense that are nearly universal in European languages. This is emphatically not true for a number of North American languages (see the discussion of Wishram Chinook tenses below), although there are many languages on the continent in which grammatical contrasts in **aspect**—the manner in which an action takes place, regardless of whether it is in the past, present, or future—are of equal or greater importance than contrasts in tense.

In the Athabaskan languages, verbs are obligatorily marked for several aspectual categories by intricate combinations of prefixes and stem variation. Typical of the aspectual variants in Hupa (an Athabaskan language of northern California) are the following forms (W represents a voiceless [w]):

yantiW	'you're picking it up' (continuously)
ya:ʔantiW	'you pick it up' (habitually)
ya:nta:n	'you pick it up' (at a specific time)
ya:ntiWiɬ	'you pick it up' (repeatedly)

In contrast to the morphological complexity of aspectual marking, **tense** is marked only by two optional enclitics, *-neʔin* 'past' and *-te* 'future':

yantiW-neʔin	'you were picking it up' (continuously)
ya:ʔantiW-neʔin	'you picked it up' (habitually)
yantiW-te	'you will be picking it up' (generally)
ya:ntan-te	'you will pick it up' (at a specific time)

These tense enclitics are not part of the inflectional system of Hupa verbs, but are markers of time past and time yet to come that can also be used with nouns and other parts of speech:

Wiʔad	'my wife'
Wiʔad-te	'my fiancée, my wife-to-be'
Wiʔad-neʔin	'my late wife'

Although aspectual marking is more often emphasized, grammatical contrasts in tense—particularly gradations of past tense—are quite elaborately marked in some North American languages. In Wishram Chinook, four past tenses are distinguished by prefixes:

Distant past	ga(l)-:	ga-yúya 'he went (a year or more ago)' (also used in reciting myths)
Indefinite past	ni(g)-:	ni-yúya 'he went (more than a couple of days ago, but less than a year)'
Recent past	na(l)-:	na-yúya 'he went (yesterday)'
Immediate past	i(g)-:	i-yúya 'he went (earlier today)'

A verb without a past tense prefix but with suffixed *-t* refers to an action now going on but soon to be completed:

yúi-t 'he is looking at him (just now)'

There is only one future tense, marked with *a(l)-*:

a-yúya 'he will go'

In addition, Wishram verbs can also take one of two directional prefixes, *u-* 'in that direction, thither', and *t-* 'in this direction, hither'. Speakers commonly make even finer tense distinctions by using these directional markers in combination with the tense markers:

gal-u-yúya 'he went (in the mythic age)'
ga-t-yúya 'he went (a few years ago)'

nig-u-yúya 'he went (last season)'
ni-t-yúya 'he went (last week)'

a-t-yúya 'he will go (immediately)'
al-u-yúya 'he will go (eventually)'

3.3 Noun classification

The classification of nouns into gender categories or similar selectional classes is a widespread phenomenon (see Chapter 4). Among North American languages, gender in the European sense (masculine/feminine/neuter) is rarely used to distinguish classes of nouns (the clearest cases are Tunica in the Southeast and Chimakuan, Salishan, and Chinookan in the Northwest), but classification by alienability of possession, animacy, and shape and texture is frequent.

Alienability of possession

The most common classification of nouns in North American languages—found in the majority of them—divides nouns into two groups: **inalienably possessed nouns**, which must always have a pronominal possessor indicated (usually by an affix), and all other nouns. Inalienably possessed nouns typically refer to things that are inherently connected to the possessor and that cannot be acquired or given away. The class of inalienably possessed nouns is sometimes quite small, but often includes most terms for parts of the body ('my head', 'his head', but never simply 'head') and for kinship relationships ('my father', 'his father', but never simply 'father'). In some languages, inalienably possessed nouns that have no identifiable possessor are marked with a special possessor that is not used with other nouns. This is the case in Yurok, an Algic language of northern California, as shown in Table 9.9.

Table 9.9 Possessed nouns in Yurok

Inalienably possessed		Other	
(*lin)		tepo	'tree'
ne-lin	'my arm'	ne-tepo	'my tree'
k'e-lin	'your arm'	k'e-tepo	'your tree'
we-lin	'his, her arm'	we-tepo	'his, her tree'
me-lin	'somebody's arm; an arm'	(*me-tepo)	

Animacy

In some North American languages, the degree of **animacy** of a noun—its relative semantic closeness to a sentient living being—plays an important grammatical role.

In all Algonquian languages, nouns belong to one of two classes, **animate** or **inanimate**, depending on the plural marker they take (*-ak* or *-a*) and which of two sets of verbal subject and object affixes are used to refer to them. Table 9.10 illustrates the animate and inanimate noun classes of Cree, an Algonquian language of Canada. (The conventional spelling of Cree words is used. Vowels with a macron (ā, ī, etc.) are long. Inalienably possessed nouns are shown with an initial hyphen.)

Table 9.10 Animate and inanimate nouns in Cree

	Animate class		*Inanimate class*	
A.	atihkamēk	'whitefish'	asiskiy	'mud, clay'
	cīpay	'ghost'	iskotēw	'fire'
	iskwēw	'woman'	kīsikaw	'day'
	ililiw	'person, Indian, Cree'	maskēk	'swamp, muskeg'
	maskwa	'bear'	mēskanaw	'road'
	mistik	'tree'	mistik	'stick, pole'
	mōs	'moose'	nipiy	'water'
	-tōtēm	'friend, guardian spirit'	pihkotēw	'ashes'
	-ōkom	'grandmother'	pīwāpisk	'metal'
	sīsīp	'duck'	sākahikan	'lake'
B.	asām	'snowshoe'	ācimōwin	'story'
	asiniy	'stone, rock'	astotin	'hat'
	askihk	'kettle, pail'	maskisin	'shoe, moccasin'
	āsokan	'wharf, jetty'	mīcim	'food'
	cīstēmāw	'tobacco'	mīnis	'berry'
	kōna	'snow'	-spiton	'arm'
	ospwākan	'(tobacco) pipe'	-tēhi	'heart'
	palacīs	'trousers'	pīskākan	'jacket'
	pīsim	'sun'	wāskāhikan	'house'
	siklētk	'cigarette'	wāwi	'egg'

The assignment of a Cree noun to one or the other class is often semantically arbitrary, just as with masculine and feminine classes in European languages. In the nouns of Group A, there is a clear semantic contrast between the animate and inanimate classes (note how *mistik* changes its meaning—'tree' or 'stick, pole'—according to which class it is treated as belonging to). The nouns of Group B, however, show no such obvious contrast.

Shape and texture classes

In Athabaskan languages, every noun belongs to one of several classes (in some languages a dozen or more), depending on which of a set of otherwise semantically identical stems is used when it is the object of a verb of moving or handling, or the subject of a stative verb. The verb stems that are matched with these noun classes are usually referred to as **classificatory verbs**. In Navajo, there are eleven basic classificatory categories, illustrated in Table 9.11 by the variants in the stative verb stem. (Each of the verb forms means 'it lies/they lie motionless'. They are cited in the standard Navajo orthography.) As can be seen, the noun classes are primarily distinguished by shape and texture.

Table 9.11 Classificatory categories in Navajo

Category	*'it lies there'*	*Typical Nouns in Category*
1. Solid or compact roundish object	si-'ą́	rock, box
2. Noncompact matter	shi-jool	wool, wig
3. Mushy matter	si-tłéé'	dough, pitch
4. Single flat flexible object	si-łtsooz	sheet of paper, shirt
5. Slender flexible object	si-lá	string of beads, snake
6. Slender stiff object	si-tą́	log, cigarette
7. Single animate object	si-tį́	baby, grandmother
8. Load, pack, or burden	si-yį́	load of trash, sack of apples
9. Anything in an open container	si-ką́	bowl of soup, box of apples
10. Plural (countable) objects	si-nil	dishes, children
11. Plural (granular) objects	shi-jaa	seeds, dirt

As with the animate/inanimate classification in Cree, not all Navajo nouns fall naturally into one of these classes, and a number of assignments are arbitrary or rest on metaphor or cultural assumptions. Thus, a lake or puddle is assigned to the "load, pack, or burden" class; a word or utterance to the "slender flexible object" class; and anything that comes in pairs (like socks, shoes, and scissors) to the "slender flexible object" class.

4 THE FUTURE OF INDIGENOUS NORTH AMERICAN LANGUAGES

Although this chapter has been written in the present tense, many indigenous North American languages have become extinct in recent generations (Yana, for example, has not been in use since the 1930s), and nearly all of those that remain are losing speakers and facing extinction. Only in a few remote communities in the United States and Canada (such as the Crow Reservation in Montana, various Cree settlements in the Canadian north, and in parts of the Navajo Nation) are indigenous languages still being routinely acquired by children as their first tongue. Even Navajo, which was vigorously prospering as late as 1970, is now the first language of only a minority of Navajo children.

This trend is part of a worldwide phenomenon. Languages of small and sociopolitically weak communities have been under threat since the beginning of the

European expansion in the late fifteenth century, a trend that has accelerated in recent decades with the development of satellite television and the Internet. If any but a handful of the indigenous languages of North America are to survive another century, deliberate efforts will have to be made to transmit them to new speakers. Ironically, the same electronic media that are now speeding the demise of so many languages and cultures may offer the best hope of creating new modes of transmission for these languages—and new, virtual communities in which they can meaningfully thrive.

Meanwhile, the linguistic repertoires of the most fluent surviving speakers should be documented with the best available tools, and analytic work should be carried out on as many languages as possible. Despite several centuries of work by linguists, anthropologists, and other skilled observers, the accumulated record of indigenous North American languages still has many gaps and inadequacies, and the need for well-trained descriptive linguists to work in this field remains acute.

Summing up

This chapter provides an overview of the approximately 325 languages spoken in North America at the time of European contact. More than sixty **language families** or **isolates** are recognized, and although they have been grouped into a smaller number of **stocks**, these remain controversial. Several otherwise rare speech sounds are common in North America, most notably the **glottalization** of stops and affricates. Many North American languages have a complex morphological structure usually referred to as **polysynthetic**. Many are also characterized by **noun incorporation**, by **ergative-absolutive** or **agent-patient** patterns of case marking, and by the use of **evidentials** to indicate the speaker's source of information. A grammatical distinction between **animate** and **inanimate** nouns is sometimes encountered, as are **classificatory verbs**. Unfortunately, much of this rich heritage of linguistic diversity is in imminent danger of disappearing as languages cease to be spoken.

Key terms

absolutive
agent
agent-patient pattern
animacy
animate
aspect
case
classificatory verbs
ejectives
ergative
ergative-absolutive pattern
evidentials
glottalization
inalienably possessed nouns
inanimate
incorporation
isolates
language family
nominative-accusative pattern
noun incorporation
patient
polysynthetic (languages)
stock
tense

Sources

The discussion of the origin and history of indigenous American languages is based in part on Campbell's book cited below. The classification given is, with one exception, the one outlined in Table 3, "Consensus Classification of the Native Languages of North America," on pp. 4–8 of the *Languages* volume of the *Handbook of North American Indians* cited below.

Yana examples are based on data in Edward Sapir, *The Fundamental Elements of Northern Yana,* University of California Publications in American Archaeology and Ethnology, 13 (1922): 215–34. Nuuchahnulth data are from Edward Sapir and Morris Swadesh, *Nootka Texts* (Philadelphia: Linguistic Society of America, 1939). Examples of Lakota noun incorporation come from "Sketch of Lakhota, a Siouan Language," by David S. Rood and Allan R. Taylor, pp. 440–82 in the 1996 *Handbook* volume cited below, and examples of Eskimo case marking are taken from Osahito Miyaoka's "Sketch of Central Alaskan Yupik, an Eskimoan Language," pp. 325–63 in the same volume. The examples of Wishram Chinook tenses, Central Pomo evidentials, and Tuscarora and Central Pomo grammatical roles are taken from pp. 163–64, 181, and 209–21 of the book by Mithun cited below. Yurok data are from R. H. Robins, *The Yurok Language,* University of California Publications in Linguistics, 15 (1958). Particulars on Cree animate and inanimate nouns are derived from H. C. Wolfart and J. Carroll's *Meet Cree: A Guide to the Cree Language* (Edmonton: University of Alberta Press, 1981), and from H. C. Wolfart and Freda Ahenakew, *The Student's Dictionary of Literary Plains Cree,* Algonquian and Iroquoian Linguistics, memoir 15 (1998). The data on classificatory categories in Navajo come from pp. 2–16 in *The Navajo Verb System: An Overview,* by Robert W. Young (Albuquerque: University of New Mexico Press, 2000). Data on Hupa are from the author's notes.

The alarming statistics on the decline of indigenous languages in North America are documented in two chapters of the collection *Endangered Languages,* edited by R. H. Robins and E. M. Uhlenbeck (New York: Berg, 1991): Ofelia Zepeda and Jane H. Hill, "The Condition of Native American Languages in the United States" (pp. 135–55), and M. Dale Kinkade, "The Decline of Native Languages in Canada" (pp. 157–76).

Recommended reading

Campbell, Lyle. 1997. *American Indian Languages: The Historical Linguistics of Native America.* Oxford Studies in Anthropological Linguistics, vol. 4. Oxford: Oxford University Press.

Goddard, Ives, ed. 1996. *Handbook of North American Indians.* Vol. 17, *Languages.* Washington: Smithsonian Institution.

Mithun, Marianne. 1999. *The Languages of Native North America.* Cambridge: Cambridge University Press.

Silver, Shirley, and Wick R. Miller. 1997. *American Indian Languages: Cultural and Social Contexts.* Tucson: University of Arizona Press.

ten

First language acquisition

William O'Grady
Sook Whan Cho

Human brains are so constructed that one brain responds in much the same way to a given trigger as does another brain, all things being equal. This is why a baby can learn any language; it responds to triggers in the same way as any other baby.

– D. Hofstadter

Objectives

In this chapter, you will learn

- how first language acquisition is studied
- how children learn to understand and pronounce the sounds of their language
- how children develop a vocabulary
- how children's morphology develops
- what stages children go through in their production of sentences
- what factors influence first language acquisition

Nothing is more important to a child's development than the acquisition of language. Most children acquire language quickly and effortlessly—giving the impression that the entire process is simple and straightforward. However, the true extent of children's achievement becomes evident when we compare their success with the difficulties encountered by adults who try to learn a second language (see Chapter 11). Understanding how children the world over are able to master the complexities of human language in the space of a few short years has become one of the major goals of contemporary linguistic research.

This chapter provides a brief overview of the progress that has been made in this area. We will begin by considering the research strategies used by linguists and psychologists in the study of linguistic development. We will then describe some of the major findings concerning children's acquisition of the various parts of their language—phonology, vocabulary, morphology, syntax, and semantics. The chapter concludes with a brief examination of the contribution of the linguistic environment to language acquisition, the relationship between the emergence of language and cognitive development, and the possible existence of inborn linguistic knowledge.

1 THE STUDY OF LANGUAGE ACQUISITION

Although we commonly refer to the emergence of language in children as "language acquisition," the end result of this process is actually a **grammar**—the mental system that allows people to speak and understand a language. There are at least two reasons for believing that the development of linguistic skills must involve the acquisition of a grammar.

First, as noted in Chapter 1, mature language users are able to produce and understand an unlimited number of novel sentences. This can only happen if, as children, they have acquired the grammar for their language. Simple memorization of a fixed inventory of words and sentences would not equip learners to deal with previously unheard utterances—a basic requisite of normal language use.

A second indication that children acquire grammatical rules comes from their speech errors, which often provide valuable clues about how the acquisition process works. Even run-of-the-mill errors such as **doed*, **runned*, and **goed* can be informative. Since we know that children don't hear adults produce words like these, such errors tell us that they have formulated a general rule that forms the past tense by adding *-ed* to the verb stem.

Because language acquisition involves the emergence of a grammar, its study is closely tied to the type of linguistic analysis with which we have been concerned in preceding chapters. Indeed, linguists and psychologists studying language acquisition must often look to the study of phonology, syntax, and other components of the grammar for help in identifying and describing the grammatical system that children acquire during the first years of life.

1.1 METHODS

The majority of research on the acquisition of language focuses on children's early utterances, the order in which they emerge, and the kinds of errors they contain. Two complementary methods of data collection are used—naturalistic observation and experimentation.

Two approaches

In the **naturalistic approach**, investigators observe and record children's spontaneous utterances. One type of naturalistic investigation is the so-called **diary study**, in which a researcher (often a parent) keeps daily notes on a child's linguistic progress. Alternatively, a researcher may visit individual children on a regular basis and record (or videotape) a sample of their utterances. In both cases, attention is paid to the context in which children's speech occurs, the toys they are playing with, the pictures they are looking at, and the like.

Naturalistic data collection provides a great deal of information about how the language acquisition process unfolds, but it also has its shortcomings. The most serious of these is that particular structures and phenomena may occur rarely in children's everyday speech, making it difficult to gather enough information from natural speech samples to test hypotheses or draw firm conclusions. This problem is further compounded by the fact that speech samples from individual children capture only a small portion of their utterances at any given point in development. (Because of the amount of time required to transcribe and analyze recordings, researchers typically have to be content with hour-long samples taken at weekly or biweekly intervals.)

In **experimental studies**, researchers typically make use of specially designed tasks to elicit linguistic activity relevant to the phenomenon that they wish to study. The child's performance is then used to formulate hypotheses about the type of grammatical system acquired at that point in time.

Experimental research is typically **cross-sectional** in that it investigates and compares the linguistic knowledge of different children (or groups of children) at a particular point in development. A typical cross-sectional study might involve conducting a single experiment with a group of two-year-olds, a group of four-year-olds, and a group of six-year-olds—taking each of these groups to be representative of a particular stage, or "cross-section," of the developmental process. In contrast, naturalistic studies tend to be **longitudinal** in that they examine language development in a particular child or group over an extended period of time (sometimes as long as several years). As the name suggests, longitudinal studies take a long time to conduct, but unlike cross-sectional studies, they have the advantage of permitting researchers to observe development as an ongoing process in individual children.

Type of experimental studies

Experimental studies usually employ tasks that test children's comprehension, production, or imitation skills. One widely used method for testing children's comprehension makes use of a picture selection format. For example, in order to test the interpretation of reflexive pronouns, an experimenter might show children a picture of Big Bird scratching himself as Cookie Monster looks on and a picture of Big Bird scratching Cookie Monster, and then ask which picture goes with the sentence *Big Bird is scratching himself.* A second method involves supplying children with an appropriate set of toys and then asking them to act out the meaning of a sentence—perhaps a passive structure such as *The truck was bumped by the car.* Children's responses can provide valuable clues about the type of grammatical rules being used to interpret sentences at particular stages of development.

In a typical production task, the child is shown a picture and asked to describe it. Although production tasks can be useful for assessing certain types of linguistic knowledge, there are many structures (such as passives) that are hard to elicit even from adults, since they are used only in special contexts. Moreover, because children's ability to comprehend language is often more advanced than their ability to produce sentences of their own, production tasks can provide an overly conservative view of linguistic development unless they are accompanied by other types of tests.

Experiments that have children imitate model sentences can also provide important clues about children's grammatical development. Although imitation might appear to be easy, it has been found that children's ability to repeat a particular structure provides a good indication of how well they have mastered it. For instance, a child who has not yet acquired auxiliary verbs can be expected to have difficulty repeating a sentence such as *The doggie has been barking a lot.*

The principal advantage of the experimental approach is that it allows researchers to collect data of a very specific sort about particular phenomena or structures. Experimentation is not without its pitfalls, however. In addition to the difficulty of designing a good experiment, there is always the possibility that children's performance will be affected by extraneous factors, such as inattention, shyness, or a failure to understand what is expected of them. Nonetheless, by using experimental techniques along with naturalistic observation, linguists and psychologists have made significant progress in the study of the language acquisition process. Much of this chapter is devoted to a survey of this progress, beginning with the development of speech sounds.

2 PHONOLOGICAL DEVELOPMENT

Children seem to be born with a perceptual system that is especially designed for listening to speech. Newborns respond differently to human voices than to other sounds; they show a preference for the language of their parents over other languages by the time they are two days old, and they can recognize their mother's voice within a matter of weeks.

From around one month of age, children exhibit the ability to distinguish among certain speech sounds. In one experiment, infants were presented with a series of identical [ba] syllables. These were followed by an occurrence of the syllable [pa]. A change in the children's sucking rate (measured by a specially designed pacifier) indicated that they perceived the difference between the two syllables, and were therefore able to distinguish between [p] and [b].

Even more amazing is the fact that infants are able to distinguish between sounds in unfamiliar languages. In one experiment, for instance, six- to eight-month-old infants who were being raised in English-speaking homes could hear contrasts among unfamiliar consonants in Hindi and Nthlakampx (an Amerindian language spoken on parts of Canada's west coast). By the time they were ten to twelve months old, though, this ability had begun to diminish.

Despite this early sensitivity to contrasts among speech sounds, children cannot initially distinguish between meaningful words. The emergence of this ability has been examined in a task in which children are presented with two toy animals named *bok* and *pok* (for instance) and are asked to respond to sentences such as *Show me pok*. To respond correctly, children must not only hear the difference between [p] and [b] but also recognize that it is linguistically significant—that it is used to distinguish between words in their language. Children under eighteen months have little success in this type of task.

2.1 BABBLING

The ability to produce speech sounds begins to emerge around six months of age, with the onset of **babbling**. It is likely that babbling provides children with the opportunity to experiment with and begin to gain control over their vocal apparatus—an important prerequisite for later speech. Children who are unable to babble for medical reasons (because of the need for a breathing tube in their throat, for example) can subsequently acquire normal pronunciation, but their speech development is significantly delayed.

Despite obvious differences among the languages to which they are exposed, children from different linguistic communities exhibit significant similarities in their babbling. The tendencies in Table 10.1 are based on data from fifteen different languages, including English, Thai, Japanese, Arabic, Hindi, and Mayan. (We focus here on consonant sounds, for which the data is somewhat more reliable than it is for vowels.)

Table 10.1 Cross-linguistic similarities in babbling

Frequently found consonants	*Infrequently found consonants*
p b m	f v θ ð
t d n	ʃ ʒ tʃ dʒ
k g	l r ŋ
s h w j	

Such cross-linguistic similarities suggest that early babbling is at least partially independent of the particular language to which children are exposed. In fact, even deaf children babble, although their articulatory activity is somewhat less varied than that of hearing children.

2.2 THE DEVELOPMENTAL ORDER

Babbling increases in frequency until the age of about twelve months, at which time children start to produce their first understandable words. Babbling may overlap with the production of real words for several weeks before dying out. By the time children have acquired fifty words or so, they begin to adopt fairly regular patterns of pronunciation.

Although there is a good deal of variation from child to child in terms of the order in which speech sounds are mastered in production and perception, the following general tendencies seem to exist.

- As a group, vowels are generally acquired before consonants (by age three).
- Stops tend to be acquired before other consonants.
- In terms of place of articulation, labials are often acquired first, followed (with some variation) by alveolars, velars, and alveopalatals. Interdentals (such as [θ] and [ð]) are acquired last.
- New phonemic contrasts manifest themselves first in word-initial position. Thus, the /p/-/b/ contrast, for instance, will be manifested in pairs such as *pat-bat* before *mop-mob*.

By age two, a typical English-speaking child has the inventory of consonant phonemes shown in Table 10.2.

Table 10.2 Typical consonant inventory at age two

Stops			*Fricatives*	*Other*
p	b	m	f	w
t	d	n	s	
k	g			

By age four, this inventory is considerably larger and typically includes the sounds shown in Table 10.3.

Table 10.3 Typical consonant inventory at age four

Stops			*Fricatives*		*Affricates*		*Other*	
p	b	m	f	v	tʃ	dʒ	w	j
t	d	n	s	z			l	r
k	g	ŋ	ʃ					

Still to be acquired at this age are the interdental fricatives [θ] and [ð] and the voiced alveopalatal fricative [ʒ].

In general, the relative order in which sounds are acquired reflects their distribution in languages of the world (see Chapter 8). The sounds that are acquired early are generally found most widely in the world's languages while the sounds that are acquired late tend to be less common across languages.

2.3 Early phonetic processes

Children's ability to perceive the phonemic contrasts of their language develops well in advance of their ability to produce them. So even children who are unable to produce the difference between words like *mouse* and *mouth*, *cart* and *card*, or *jug* and *duck* may nonetheless be able to point to pictures of the correct objects in a comprehension task. Moreover, as the following experimenter's report vividly illustrates, children distinguish phonemes they hear even when they cannot yet produce them.

> One of us, for instance, spoke to a child who called his inflated plastic fish a *fis*. In imitation of the child's pronunciation, the observer said: "This is your *fis?*" "No," said the child, "my *fis*." He continued to reject the adult's imitation until he was told, "That is your fish." "Yes," he said, "my *fis*."

The child's reaction to the adult's initial pronunciation of *fish* shows that he could perceive the difference between /s/ and /ʃ/ and that he had correctly represented the word as /fiʃ/ in his lexicon even though he could not yet produce it himself.

What precisely is responsible for the special character of the sound patterns in children's early speech? The key seems to lie in the operation of a limited number of universal phonetic processes that replace certain sounds with others that children find easier to produce and/or perceive.

Syllable deletion

Because syllables bearing primary or secondary stress are more noticeable than their unstressed counterparts, they tend to be more salient to children in the early stages of the language acquisition process. As a result, they are retained in children's pronunciation while unstressed syllables are often deleted (see Table 10.4).

Table 10.4 Deletion of unstressed syllables

Word	*Child's pronunciation*
hip po pó ta mus	[pɑs]
spa ghé tti	[gɛ]
hé li còp ter	[ɛlkɑt]
kan ga róo	[wu]

However, unstressed syllables in final position tend to be retained, probably because the ends of words are easier to notice and remember (see Table 10.5).

Table 10.5 Retention of unstressed syllables in final position

Word	*Child's pronunciation*
po tá to	[tejdo]
ba ná na	[ænə]
to má to	[mejdo]
él e phànt	[ɛlfən]

Syllable simplification

Another frequent process in children's speech involves the systematic deletion of certain sounds in order to simplify syllable structure. In the data in Table 10.6, typical

Table 10.6 Reduction of consonant clusters

[s] + stop (strategy: delete [s])
stop → [tɑp]
small → [mɑ]
desk → [dɛk]

stop + liquid (strategy: delete liquid)
try → [taj]
crumb → [gʌm]
bring → [bɪŋ]

fricative + liquid (strategy: delete liquid)
from → [fʌm]
sleep → [sip]

nasal + voiceless stop (strategy: delete nasal)
bump → [bʌp]
tent → [dɛt]

of the speech of two- and three-year-old children, consonant clusters are reduced by deleting one or more segments.

Yet another common deletion process in early language acquisition involves the elimination of final consonants, as in the following examples.

1)

dog	[dɑ]
bus	[bʌ]
boot	[bu]

Both the reduction of consonant clusters and the deletion of final consonants have the effect of simplifying syllable structure—bringing it closer to the CV template that is universally favored by children and that is generally the most widely found pattern in human language.

Substitution

One of the most widespread phonetic processes in early language involves substitution—the systematic replacement of one sound by an alternative that the child finds easier to articulate (see Table 10.7). Common substitution processes include **stopping**, the replacement of a fricative by a corresponding stop; **fronting**, the moving forward of a sound's place of articulation; **gliding**, the replacement of a liquid by a glide; and **denasalization**, the replacement of a nasal stop by a nonnasal counterpart.

Table 10.7 Substitution in early speech

Process	*Example*	*Change*
Stopping	sing → [tɪŋ]	s → t
(continuant → stop)	sea → [ti]	s → t
	zebra → [dibrə]	z → d
	thing → [tɪŋ]	θ → t
	this → [dɪt]	ð → d, s → t
	shoes → [tud]	ʃ → t, z → d
Fronting	ship → [sɪp]	ʃ → s
	jump → [dzʌmp]	dʒ → dz
	chalk → [tsɑːk]	tʃ → ts
	go → [dou]	g → d
Gliding	lion → [jajn]	l → j
	laughing → [jæfɪŋ]	l → j
	look → [wʊk]	l → w
	rock → [wɑk]	r → w
	story → [stowi]	r → w
Denasalization	spoon → [bud]	n → d
	jam → [dæb]	m → b
	room → [wub]	m → b

Assimilation

Still another widespread phonetic process in child language is assimilation—the modification of one or more features of a segment under the influence of neighboring sounds. In the following examples, initial consonants have been voiced in anticipation of the following vowel.

2)

tell	[dɛl]
pig	[bɪg]
push	[bʊs]
soup	[zup]

Assimilation is also observed in children's tendency to maintain the same place of articulation for all of the consonants or vowels in a word. This can lead to the pronunciation of *doggy* as [gɑgi] (with two velar stops). Other examples include [fɛlf] for *self* (with identical consonants), [bibi] for *baby* (with identical vowels in both syllables), [kæklin] for *Cathleen* (with identical velar stops), and [næns] for *dance* (with identical nasal consonants).

3 VOCABULARY DEVELOPMENT

By age eighteen months or so, the average child has a vocabulary of fifty words or more. Common items include the words listed in Table 10.8.

Table 10.8 Common items in the first fifty words

Entities
Words referring to people: *daddy, mommy, baby* food/drink: *juice, milk, cookie, water, toast, apple, cake* animals: *dog, cat, duck, horse* clothes: *shoes, hat* toys: *ball, blocks* vehicles: *car, boat, truck* other: *bottle, key, book*
Properties
hot, all-gone, more, dirty, cold, here, there
Actions
up, sit, see, eat, go, down
Personal-social
hi, bye, no, yes, please, thank-you

As this table shows, noun-like words make up the single largest class in the child's early vocabulary, with verb- and adjective-like words being the next most frequent category types. Among the most frequent individual words are expressions for displeasure or rejection (such as *no*) and various types of social interaction (such as *please* and *bye*). Over the next months this vocabulary grows rapidly, sometimes by as much as ten or twelve words a day. By age six, most children have mastered about thirteen thousand words.

Children seem to differ somewhat in the types of words that they focus on, especially in the early stages of language acquisition. One of these differences is reflected in the number of nouns in early vocabulary. Whereas some children have a relatively high proportion of such words (75 percent or more) by age two, other learners exhibit a much lower percentage of nouns (50 percent or less). Making up for the smaller number of nouns is a larger vocabulary of socially useful expressions such as *bye, go-away, stop-it, thank-you, I-want-it*, and so on. (Hyphens are used here to indicate that these expressions are not yet segmented into their component words.)

3.1 Strategies for acquiring word meaning

Children seem to draw on special strategies when trying to determine the meaning of a new word. This is perhaps easiest to illustrate in the case of noun-type meanings, for which the following strategies seem to be employed.

3)

Three strategies for learning the meanings of new words.

The Whole Object Assumption
A new word refers to a whole object.

The Type Assumption
A new word refers to a type of thing, not just to a particular thing.

The Basic Level Assumption
A new word refers to types of objects that are alike in basic ways.

To see how these strategies work, imagine that a mother and her eighteen-month-old daughter are driving through the countryside and they encounter a sheep munching on the grass. The mother points to the animal and says "sheep." What does the child think that the word means? Does it mean 'white'? Or does it mean 'woolly'? Does it refer to the animal? Or to parts of the animal? Or does it refer to the fact that a particular animal is munching on grass?

The Whole Object Assumption allows the child to infer that the word *sheep* refers to the animal itself, not to its parts, not to whiteness, and not to woolliness. The Type Assumption allows her to infer that *sheep* refers to a type of animal, not to just one particular sheep. And the Basic Level Assumption leads her to guess that *sheep* is used to refer just to white, four-legged, woolly animals, and not animals in general.

The fact that so many of children's first words are names for types of whole objects suggests that language learners rely heavily on strategies such as these in the early stages of word learning. Of course, these strategies don't always give the right result. Some words do in fact refer to parts of things (*toe, fingernail, eyeball*), to properties (*white, woolly*), to individuals (*Susie, Mr. Jones*), and to broad classes (*animal, plant*). Nonetheless, the strategies we have been considering provide children with a good way to get started, postponing the acquisition of certain types of words in favor of more basic vocabulary items.

Contextual clues

Another major factor in vocabulary development is the child's ability to make use of contextual clues to draw inferences about the category and meaning of new words. For instance, from early in the language acquisition process, children can use the presence or absence of determiners in English to distinguish between names and ordinary nouns. Two-year-old children who are told that a new doll is a *dax* will apply this label to similar-looking dolls as well. However, if they are told that the new doll is *Dax*, they will restrict use of the new word to the doll they have actually been shown. Like adults, these children treat *dax* as an ordinary noun when it is preceded by *a*, but as a name when there is no determiner.

In another experiment, three- and four-year-old children were asked to act out the meaning of sentences such as *Make it so there is* tiv *to drink in this glass (of water)*. The only clues about the interpretation of the nonsense word *tiv* came from the meaning of the rest of the sentence and from the child's understanding of the types of changes that can be made to a glass of water. Not only did more than half the children respond by either adding or removing water, but some even remembered what *tiv* meant two weeks later.

3.2 Meaning errors

The meanings that children associate with their early words sometimes correspond closely to the meanings employed by adults. In many cases, however, the match is less than perfect. The two most typical semantic errors involve overextension and underextension.

Overextensions

In cases of **overextension**, the meaning of the child's word is more general or inclusive than that of the corresponding adult form. The word *dog*, for example, is frequently overextended to include horses, cows, and other four-legged animals. Similarly, *ball* is sometimes used for any round object, including a balloon, an Easter egg, a small stone, and so on. As many as one-third of children's words may be overextended at the fifty-word stage of vocabulary development (see Table 10.9).

The evidence collected to date suggests that perceptual properties are the critical factor in children's first hypotheses about word meanings. As a result, children often overextend a word to include a set of perceptually similar objects that they know to have diverse functions. For example, one child used the word *moon* for the moon, grapefruit halves, and a crescent-shaped car light. Another child used the word *money* for a set of objects ranging from pennies to buttons and beads. If you reconsider the examples of overextension given in Table 10.9, you will see that they too are more plausibly explained in terms of perceptual similarities than a shared function.

Table 10.9 Additional examples of overextension

Word	*First referent*	*Subsequent extensions*
ticktock	watch	clocks, gas meter, fire hose on a spool, scale with round dial
fly	fly	specks of dirt, dust, small insects, child's toes, crumbs of bread
quack	duck	all birds and insects, flies, coins (with an eagle on the face)
candy	candy	cherries, anything sweet
apple	apples	balls, tomatoes, cherries, onions, biscuits
turtle	turtles	fish, seals
cookie	cookies	crackers, any dessert
kitty	cats	rabbits, any small furry animal
box	boxes	elevators
belt	belts	watch strap

There is reason to believe that many overextensions may be deliberate attempts to compensate for vocabulary limitations. One indication of this is that particular overextensions often disappear as soon as children learn the right word for the objects that they have been mislabeling. For example, two-year-old Allen was using the word *dog* for dogs, cats, sheep, and other four-legged mammals, but he stopped doing so as soon as he learned the words *cat* and *sheep*. If he thought that *dog* meant 'animal', he could still have sometimes referred to cats and sheep as *dogs* (just as adults sometimes refer to them as animals). The fact that he didn't suggests that he never thought *dog* meant 'animal'; he had just been "borrowing" it until the right word came along.

A further indication that many overextensions are designed to compensate for vocabulary limitations comes from the fact that children seem to overextend more in their production than in their comprehension. In one study, for instance, five children who were overextending words were given a naming task in which they were shown pictures and asked to name them. Overextensions were identified and then used to design a comprehension test. For example, if the child overextended *doggie* to include cows and horses on the naming test, the comprehension test would include pictures of these animals as well as a dog. The child would then be asked "Show me the doggie," "Show me the cow," and so on. The results were quite dramatic, revealing that overextensions in comprehension were much less frequent than in production. This is not the result that one would expect if children thought that *doggie* meant 'animal'.

Underextensions

Another possible type of word-meaning error in early language involves **underextension**—the use of lexical items in an overly restrictive fashion. Thus, *kitty* might be used to refer to the family pet, but not to any other cats. Or the word *dog* might be used for collies, spaniels, and beagles, but not for Chihuahuas.

Underextension errors often reflect children's propensity to focus on prototypical or core members of a category. As noted in Section 2.1 of Chapter 6, the potential referents of many words differ in terms of how well they exemplify the properties associated with a particular concept. For example, among the potential referents of the word *dog*, collies and spaniels have more of the properties associated with the concept DOG (long hair, relative size, type of bark, and so on) than do Chihuahuas. While the preference for a prototype can be overruled by factors such as the presence of a nontypical category member in the child's everyday experience (e.g., a Chihuahua as a family pet), the internal structure of concepts can have an important influence on semantic development.

Verb meanings

Meaning errors are also common for verbs. For example, many preschool children believe that *fill* means 'pour' rather than 'make full'. So, when asked to decide which of the two series of pictures in Figure 10.1 is an example of filling, they choose the second series—even though the glass ends up empty!

Figure 10.1 Sample pictures used to test children's understanding of *fill*. Some children believe that the action depicted in the bottom series of pictures involves filling, even though the glass remains empty.

Not surprisingly, there is a tendency for children who make this sort of mistake to use *fill* in the wrong syntactic patterns as well.

4)

I filled the grain up. (Adam, age 4 yrs. 11 mos.)
And fill the little sugars up in the bowl. (Mark, age 4 yrs. 7 mos.)
I didn't fill water up to drink it. (E, age 4 yrs. 1 mo.)
Can I fill some salt into the [salt shaker]? (E, age 5 yrs.)

These errors disappear as children come to realize that *fill* means 'make full' rather than 'pour'.

Dimensional terms

Terms describing size and dimension are acquired in a relatively fixed order, depending on their generality (see Table 10.10). The first adjectives of this type to be acquired, *big* and *small,* are the most general in that they can be used for talking about any aspect of size (height, area, volume, and so on). In contrast, the second group of adjectives to emerge—*tall, long, short, high,* and *low*—can only be used for a single dimension (height-length). The remaining modifiers (*thick-thin, wide-narrow,* and *deep-shallow*) are still more restricted in their use since they describe the secondary or less extended dimension of an object. For instance, the dimension of a stick that we describe in terms of width or thickness is almost always less extended than the dimension that we describe in terms of height or length, which tends also to be perceptually more salient.

Table 10.10 Order of acquisition for dimensional adjectives

Step	*Words*	*What they descriibe*
1	*big-small*	any aspect of size
2	*tall-short, long-short, high-low*	a single dimension
3	*thick-thin, wide-narrow, deep-shallow*	a secondary dimension

The difficulty of dimensional adjectives for children is also evident on experimental tasks. For instance, in one experiment, children aged three to five were shown pairs of objects—sometimes a big one and a tall one and sometimes a big one and a long one (see Figure 10.2).

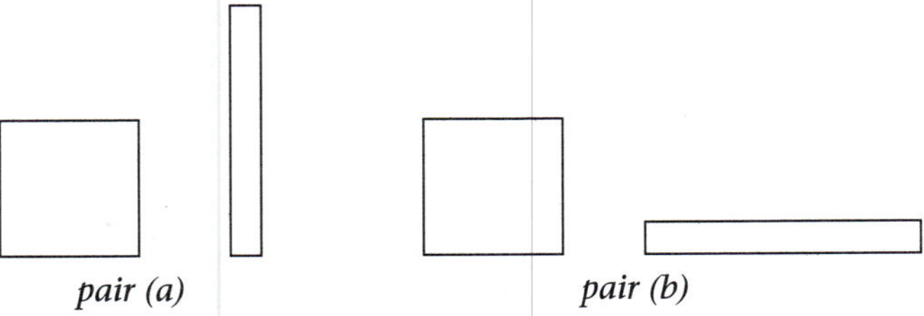

Figure 10.2 *big-tall* versus *big-long*

Younger children do well when asked to choose "the big one." However, when asked to choose "the tall one" or "the long one," they often pick the big one instead. This suggests that they are initially more sensitive to overall size than to a single dimension like height or length.

4 MORPHOLOGICAL DEVELOPMENT

As is the case with the sound pattern of language and with vocabulary, the details of morphological structure emerge over a period of several years. Initially, the words produced by English-speaking children seem to lack any internal morphological structure. Affixes are systematically absent and most words consist of a single root morpheme.

4.1 OVERGENERALIZATION

Because English has many examples of irregular inflection (*men* as the plural of *man*, *ran* as the past of *run*), children sometimes begin by simply memorizing inflected words on a case-by-case basis without regard for general patterns or rules. As a result, they may initially use irregular forms such as *men* and *ran* correctly. However, when they subsequently observe the generality of *-s* as a plural marker and *-ed* as a past tense marker (usually around age two and a half), they sometimes use these suffixes for the irregular forms—producing words such as *mans* and *runned.* (Errors that result from the overly broad application of a rule are called **overgeneralizations** or **overregularizations**.) Even occasional mixed forms such as *felled,* a blend of *fell* and *falled,* may occur during this period (see Table 10.11).

Table 10.11 The development of affixes

Stage 1:	case-by-case learning
Stage 2:	overuse of general rule
Stage 3:	mastery of exceptions to the general rule

One of the best indications that children have mastered an inflectional rule comes from their ability to apply it to forms they have not heard before. In a classic experiment, children were shown a picture of a strange creature and told, "This is a wug." A second picture was then presented and the children were asked the following type of question (see Figure 10.3).

a. This is a wug.

b. Now, there's another wug.
There are two of them.
Now, there are two . . . ?

Figure 10.3 The "wug" test

Even four- and five-year-old children did well with the plural forms of *wug* words, demonstrating that the general rules for inflection have been learned by that time, despite the occurrence of occasional errors.

Recent work has shown that inflectional overgeneralization, which can last into the school years, is much less frequent than previously thought: preschool children seem to overregularize verbs less than 25 percent of the time at any point in development. This suggests that the overgeneralization errors observed in early speech reflect lapses in accessing the appropriate irregular form from the lexicon rather than the failure to learn irregular forms per se.

4.2 A developmental sequence

An important result of child language research during the 1970s was the discovery that the development of bound morphemes and functional categories (such as determiners and auxiliaries) takes place in an orderly sequence with relatively little variation from child to child. In a pioneering study of three children between the ages of twenty and thirty-six months, the **developmental sequence** in Table 10.12 was found to be typical.

Table 10.12 Typical developmental sequence for nonlexical morphemes

1. *-ing*	5. past tense *-ed*
2. plural *-s*	6. third-person singular *-s*
3. possessive *-'s*	7. auxiliary *be*
4. *the, a*	

An interesting feature of this developmental sequence is that it seems to be largely unrelated to the frequency of the different morphemes in the speech heard by children (see Table 10.13). For example, the determiners *the* and *a* are the most frequent morphemes in the children's environments, even though they are acquired relatively late.

Table 10.13 Typical relative frequency of morphemes in parental speech

1. *the, a*	5. possessive *-'s*
2. *-ing*	6. third-person singular *-s*
3. plural *-s*	7. past tense *-ed*
4. auxiliary *be*	

This shows that frequency by itself cannot explain developmental order, although it may have some role to play in conjunction with other factors. (It's also clear that pronunciation by itself is not the key factor either, since the three '*-s*' morphemes are acquired at different times.)

Some determining factors

What, then, determines the order of acquisition of nonlexical categories and bound morphemes? Research on a variety of languages suggests that several factors are involved.

1. *Frequent occurrence in utterance-final position* Children show a greater tendency to notice and remember elements that occur at the end of the utterance than those found in any other position.
2. *Syllabicity* Children seem to take greater notice of morphemes such as *-ing*, which can constitute syllables on their own, than the plural or possessive suffix *-'s*, whose principal allomorphs (/s/ and /z/) are single consonants.
3. *Absence of homophony* Whereas the word *the* functions only as a determiner in English, the suffix *-s* can be used to mark any one of three things: singular number in nouns, third-person singular in verbs, or possession. The resulting complication in the relationship between form and meaning may impede acquisition.
4. *Few or no exceptions in the way it is used* Whereas all singular nouns form the possessive with *-'s*, not all verbs use *-ed* to mark the past tense (*saw, read, drove*). Such exceptions hinder the language acquisition process.
5. *Allomorphic invariance* Whereas the affix *-ing* has the same form for all verbs, the past tense ending *-ed* has three major allomorphs—/t/ for verbs such as *chase*, /d/ for forms such as *play*, and /əd/ for verbs such as *want*. This type of allomorphic variation, which also occurs with the plural, possessive, and third-person singular affixes in English, slows morphological development.
6. *Clearly discernible semantic function* Whereas morphemes such as plural *-s* express easily identifiable meanings, some morphemes (such as the third-person singular *-s*) make no obvious contribution to the meaning of the sentence. Acquisition of this latter type of morpheme is relatively slow.

The status of the English morphemes whose developmental order we have been considering is indicated in Table 10.14; as before, morphemes are listed in typical order of emergence. (The ± symbol in the second column indicates that the morphemes in question have both syllabic and nonsyllabic allomorphs. The plural suffix, for example, is realized as /s/ in some contexts but as /əz/ in others.)

Table 10.14 Factors affecting development

Morphemes	*Determining Factors*					
	1	*2*	*3*	*4*	*5*	*6*
-ing	+	+	+	+	+	+
plural *-s*	+	±	+	+	–	+
possessive *-'s*	–	±	+	+	–	+
the, a	–	+	+	+	–	–
past tense *-ed*	+	±	+	–	–	+
third-person singular *-s*	–	±	–	+	–	–
auxiliary *be*	–	±	–	+	–	–

As Table 10.14 helps show, the morphemes that are acquired first generally exhibit more of the properties just outlined than those that emerge at a later point.

4.3 Word-formation processes

The major word-formation processes in English—derivation and compounding—both emerge early in the acquisition of English. The first derivational suffixes to show up in children's speech are the ones that are most common in the adult language (see Table 10.15).

Table 10.15 Suffixes in the speech of Damon prior to age four

Ending	*Meaning*	*Example*
-er	'doer'*	walker
-ie	'diminutive'	doggie
-ing	'activity'	Running is fun.
-ness	'state'	bigness

(Note: *-*er* also has an 'instrument' meaning [as in *cutter* 'something used for cutting'], but this is less frequent in children's early speech.)

Moreover, children as young as three demonstrate an ability to use derivation to make up names for agents and instruments when presented with questions such as the following:

> "I've got a picture here of someone who crushes things. What could we call someone who crushes things? Someone who crushes things is called a . . ."

> "I've got a picture here of something that cuts things. What could we call something that cuts things? Something that cuts things is called a . . ."

Children also exhibit a propensity for forming compounds, especially of the N-N type, both in experimental settings where they are asked to make up words (e.g., "What would you call a boy who rips paper?") and in their own spontaneous speech. Some of the compounds found in the speech of three- and four-year-olds do not follow the usual pattern for English compounds (e.g., **open man* for someone who opens things and **cutter grass* for 'grass cutter'), but these disappear by age five. Other early compounds have the right structure but are inappropriate because English already has words with the intended meaning (see Table 10.16).

Table 10.16 Some innovative compounds

Child's word	*Intended meaning*
car-smoke	'exhaust'
cup-egg	'boiled egg'
firetruck-man	'firefighter'
plant-man	'gardener'
store-man	'clerk'

Children's creativity with compounds points to a preference for building words from other words, perhaps because this places less demand on memory than does learning a new simple word for each concept.

Even the subtlest properties of word formation seem to be acquired in the preschool years. One such property, first discussed in Section 3.1 of Chapter 4, involves the fact that an inflectional suffix such as the plural cannot occur inside compounds (compare **dogs catcher* with *dog catcher*). In one study, children as young as three years of age produced compounds that obeyed this constraint. Thus, when asked a question such as "What do you call someone who eats cookies?" they responded with *cookie eater* rather than **cookies eater*.

5 SYNTACTIC DEVELOPMENT

Like phonological and morphological development, the emergence of syntactic structure takes place in an orderly manner and reveals much about the nature of the language acquisition process. We will briefly survey some of the milestones in this developmental process here.

5.1 The one-word stage

As noted earlier, children begin to produce one-word utterances between the ages of twelve and eighteen months. A basic property of these one-word utterances is that they can be used to express the type of meaning that is associated with an entire sentence in adult speech. Thus, a child might use the word *dada* to assert 'I see Daddy', *more* to mean 'Give me more candy', and *up* to mean 'I want up'. Such utterances are called **holophrases** (literally 'whole sentences').

In forming holophrastic utterances, children seem to choose the most informative word that applies to the situation at hand. A child who wanted candy, for example, would say *candy* rather than *want*, since the former word is more informative in this situation. Similarly, a child who notices a new doll would be more likely to say *doll* than *see*, thereby referring to the most novel feature of the situation he or she is trying to describe.

Table 10.17 lists some of the semantic relations that children commonly express during the **one-word stage**.

Table 10.17 Semantic relations in children's one-word utterances

Utterance	*Situation*	*Semantic relation*
Dada	as father enters the room	agent of an action
Down	as child sits down	action or state
Door	as father closes the door	theme
Here	as child points	location
Mama	as child gives mother something	recipient
Again	as child watches lighting of a match	recurrence

5.2 The two-word stage

Within a few months of their first one-word utterances, children begin to produce two-word "mini-sentences." Table 10.18 provides a sampling of these utterances and the types of meaning they are commonly used to express. (Although these examples are from English, similar patterns are found in the early development of all languages.)

Table 10.18 Some patterns in children's two-word speech

Utterance	*Intended meaning*	*Semantic relation*
Baby chair	'The baby is sitting on the chair.'	agent-location
Doggie bark	'The dog is barking.'	agent-action
Ken water	'Ken is drinking water.'	agent-theme
Hit doggie	'I hit the doggie.'	action-theme
Daddy hat	'Daddy's hat'	possessor-possessed

It is unclear whether children have acquired syntactic categories such as noun, verb, and adjective at this point in their development. This is because the markers that help distinguish among syntactic categories in adult English (e.g., inflection such as the past tense suffix and minor categories such as determiners and auxiliary verbs) are absent during this period. To complicate matters further, the relative shortness of the utterances produced during the **two-word stage** means that the positional differences associated with category distinctions in adult speech are often not manifested. Thus, words such as *busy* (an adjective in adult speech) and *push* (a verb) may appear in identical patterns.

5)

Mommy busy.
Mommy push.

While this does not show that children lack syntactic categories, it makes it difficult to demonstrate that they possess them. For this reason, linguists and psychologists are split over whether to describe children's utterances in terms of the semantic relations that they express (as in Table 10.18) or the syntactic categories of adult speech.

A notable feature of children's two-word utterances is that they almost always exhibit the appropriate word order. This suggests a very early sensitivity to this feature of sentence structure, but there is reason to believe that children do not initially have a general word-order rule. Rather, they may have a separate rule for each verb (e.g., "Put the subject in front of *push*"; "Put the subject in front of *read*"; and so on). In one experiment, for instance, children aged two to four were taught made-up verbs (such as *tam, gop,* and *dack*) for novel actions involving puppet characters. Each verb was presented in one of the following orders:

6)

subject-verb-object order: Elmo tammed the apple
subject-object-verb order: Elmo the apple gopped
verb-subject-object order: Dacked the apple Elmo

The two- and three-year-old children were willing to learn word-order patterns not found in English and would often employ the subject-object-verb and verb-subject-object order for new verbs if that was what they had been exposed to. In contrast, the four-year-olds used the subject-verb-object order regardless of what the experimenter had said, which suggests that they had acquired a general word-order rule for English that they automatically extended to new verbs.

5.3 The telegraphic stage

After a period of several months, during which their speech is limited to one- and two-word utterances, children begin to produce longer and more complex grammatical structures (see Table 10.19). Some representative utterances from the first part of this period are given in *7*.

7)

Chair broken.
Daddy like book.
What her name?
Man ride bus today.
Car make noise.
Me wanna show Mommy.
I good boy.

At first, these utterances lack bound morphemes and most nonlexical categories. Because of the resemblance to the style of language found in telegrams, this acquisitional stage is often dubbed the **telegraphic stage**.

The telegraphic stage is characterized by the emergence of phrase structure. As the examples in *7* help show, the Merge operation can form phrases consisting of a head and a complement (*like book, ride bus, show Mommy*), phrases that include a modifier (such as *today* and *good*), and even full-fledged sentences.

Table 10.19 The development of phrase structure

Stage	*Approx. age*	*Developments*
Holophrastic	1–1.5 yrs.	single word utterances; no structure
Two-word	1.5–2 yrs.	early word combinations; presence of syntactic categories unclear
Telegraphic	2–2.5 yrs.	emergence of phrase structure, especially head-complement and subject-VP patterns

Language development from this point onward is rapid. As the examples in Table 10.20 help illustrate, children move from relatively primitive two- and three-word utterances at the beginning of the telegraphic stage to a broad range of syntactically intricate sentence types that include affixes and nonlexical categories in the space of just a few months.

Table 10.20 Sample utterances from a child's speech over a 12-month period

Age	*Sample utterances*
28 mos.	Play checkers. Big drum. I got horn. A bunny-rabbit walk.
30 mos.	Write a piece of paper. What that egg doing? I lost a shoe. No, I don't want to sit seat.
32 mos.	Let me get down with the boots on. Don't be afraid of horses. How tiger be so healthy and fly like kite? Joshua throw like penguin.
34 mos.	Look at that train Ursula brought. I simply don't want put in chair. Don't have paper. Do you want little bit, Cromer? I can't wear it tomorrow.
36 mos.	I going come in fourteen minutes. I going wear that to wedding. I see what happens. I have to save them now. Those are not strong mens. They are going sleep in wintertime. You dress me up like a baby elephant.
38 mos.	So it can't be cleaned? I broke my racing car. Do you know the lights went off? What happened to the bridge? Can I put my head in the mailbox so the mailman can know where I are and put me in the mailbox?

5.4 LATER DEVELOPMENT

In the years following the telegraphic stage, children continue to acquire the complex grammar that underlies adult linguistic competence, including the Move operations outlined in Chapter 5.

Inversion

In the very early stages of language acquisition, children signal *yes-no* questions by means of rising intonation alone. (Recall that auxiliary verbs are a relatively late development.)

8)

See hole?
I ride train?
Ball go?
Sit chair?

Even after individual auxiliary verbs appear in child language, there is often a delay of a few months before they appear at the beginning of the sentence in *yes-no* questions. In one study, for example, a young boy began using the auxiliary verb *can* at age two years five months, but it did not undergo Inversion in questions until six months later.

An interesting—but infrequent—error in children's early use of Inversion in both *yes-no* and *wh* questions is exemplified in *9*.

9)

Can he *can* look?
What *shall* we *shall* have?
Did you *did* came home?

In these sentences, the auxiliary verb occurs twice—once to the left of the subject (in the position that it occupies after Inversion) and once to the right (in the position it occupies in deep structure). It has been suggested that this pattern reflects an error in the application of the Inversion transformation in that a copy of the moved auxiliary is left behind in its original position.

Wh questions

Wh questions emerge gradually between the ages of two and four. The first *wh* words to be acquired are typically *what* and *where,* followed by *who, how,* and *why; when, which,* and *whose* are relatively late acquisitions.

10)

Where that?
What me think?
Why you smiling?
Why not me drink it?

With the acquisition of auxiliary verbs, Inversion becomes possible. Interestingly, some children appear to find it easier to carry out the Inversion operation in *yes-no* questions, where it is the only Move operation, than in *wh* questions, where *Wh* Movement must also apply. They go through a stage where Inversion is more common in *yes-no* questions than in *wh* questions.

11)

Yes-no questions (with Inversion):
Did Mommy pinch her finger?
Can't you fix it?
Do I have it?
Will you help me?
Is Mommy talking to Robin's grandmother?

12)

Wh questions (no Inversion):
What I did yesterday?
Why Kitty can't stand up?
Where I should put it?
Where I should sleep?
Why you are smiling?

5.5 The interpretation of sentence structure (Advanced)

As noted in Chapter 6, the interpretation of sentences draws heavily on various features of syntactic structure. In this section we will briefly consider some aspects of the acquisition of two interpretive phenomena that rely on information about syntactic structure.

Passives

Children learning English are able to associate thematic roles with particular structural positions at a very early point in the acquisition process. By the time their average utterance length is two words, they are able to respond correctly about 75 percent of the time to comprehension tests involving simple active sentences such as *13*, in which *the truck* is the agent and *the car* is the theme.

13)

The truck bumped the car.

However, children find it much harder to interpret certain other types of sentences correctly. This is especially true for passive sentences such as the one in *14*, which contains no semantic clues about which NP is agent and which one is theme. (Note that it makes just as much sense for the car to bump the truck as it does for the truck to bump the car. Such sentences are said to be "reversible.")

14)

The car was bumped by the truck.

Although children produce passive sentences in their own speech from around age three, they have continuing difficulty responding appropriately to passive constructions in comprehension tests (see Table 10.21).

Table 10.21 Comprehension of reversible passive constructions

Group	*Percentage correct*
Nursery school	20
Kindergarten	35
Grade 1	48
Grade 2	63
Grade 3	88

Why should this be so? One possibility is that children expect the first NP in a sentence to bear the agent role and the second NP to bear the theme role. This is sometimes called the **canonical sentence strategy** (see Figure 10.4).

NP ... V ... NP is interpreted as:
agent – action – theme

Figure 10.4 The canonical sentence strategy

The canonical sentence strategy works for active, transitive sentences but not for passive sentences, where the first NP is the theme and the second NP is the agent.

15)

Active sentence:	The truck	bumped	the car.
	agent		*theme*
Passive sentence:	The car	was bumped	by the truck
	theme		*agent*

Not surprisingly, the most common error made by children employing this strategy is to treat the first NP in passive sentences as the agent and the second NP as the theme.

As the data in Table 10.21 show, the canonical sentence strategy is applied much less consistently by first graders, who have evidently begun to realize that there is no simple correlation between linear position and thematic role. A year or so later, children's scores start to rise dramatically, indicating that they have come to recognize the special properties of the passive construction.

Pronominals and reflexives

In Chapter 6, we saw that a reflexive pronoun (*myself, himself, herself,* and so on) must have a "higher" (i.e., c-commanding) antecedent in the minimal clause containing it.

16)

a. Reflexive pronoun with a higher antecedent in the same clause
I hurt *myself* with the knife.

b. Reflexive pronoun without a higher antecedent in the same clause
*You hurt *myself* with the knife.

In contrast, a pronominal (*me, him, her*) cannot have a higher antecedent in the same minimal clause.

17)

a. Pronominal with a higher antecedent in the same clause
*I hurt *me* with the knife.

b. Pronominal without a higher antecedent in the same clause
You hurt *me* with the knife.

Despite the intricacy of the principles involved here, children appear not to have trouble distinguishing between pronominals and reflexive pronouns in their own speech. In one study of the use of *me* and *myself* in speech transcripts from three children aged two to five, researchers found only a few errors of the following type.

18)

Sample pronoun errors:

Mistake involving *me:* I see *me.* (Adam, age 34 mos., looking through a telescope)

Mistake involving *myself:* Don't you drop me . . . you hurt *myself.* (Abe, age 34 mos.)

Overall, though, the children misused *me* only about 5 percent of the time and made mistakes using *myself* less than 1 percent of the time. We will return to this point in Section 6.4.

6 WHAT MAKES LANGUAGE ACQUISITION POSSIBLE?

In the preceding sections, we have seen that the language acquisition process extends over a period of several years. It is relatively easy to describe what takes place during these years, but it is much more difficult to explain *how* it happens. The sections that follow focus on some of the factors that may contribute to an eventual understanding of how the language acquisition process works.

6.1 THE ROLE OF ADULT SPEECH

At one time, it was widely believed that children learn language simply by imitating the speech of those around them. This cannot be true, however. Not only do children tend not to repeat the speech of others, but they are typically unable to imitate structures that they have not yet learned. For instance, a child who has not yet acquired the Inversion operation will imitate sentence *19a* by producing *19b*.

19)

a. *Model sentence*: What can you see?
b. *Child's imitation*: What you can see?

A child's own grammar, not the model provided by adult speech, determines what she or he will say at any given point of development.

Of course, language learners must be sensitive in some way to the language in their environment. After all, children who are exposed to English learn to speak English, those exposed to Spanish learn Spanish, and so forth. It seems, though, that the relationship between input (the language children hear) and acquisition is subtler and more complicated than one might think.

Caregiver speech

A good deal of recent work has been devoted to the search for a possible relationship between language acquisition and the type of speech that is typically addressed to young language learners. Such speech is often called **motherese** or **caregiver speech**. Table 10.22 summarizes the principal features of the caregiver speech used by middle-class English-speaking mothers with their children.

Table 10.22 Some features of English caregiver speech

Phonetic
Slow, carefully articulated speech Higher pitch Exaggerated intonation and stress Longer pauses
Lexical and semantic
More restricted vocabulary Concrete reference to here and now
Syntactic
Few incomplete sentences Short sentences More imperatives and questions
Conversational
More repetitions Few utterances per conversational turn

Caregiver speech could be helpful to children in a variety of ways. For example, exposure to slow, carefully articulated speech may make it easier for children to pick out words and to learn their pronunciation. (Remember that sentences consist of a continuous stream of speech sounds; there are no pauses between words.) Moreover, the acquisition of meaning may be facilitated by the fact that maternal speech tends to concentrate on the here and now, especially the child's surroundings, activities, and needs. The examples in Table 10.23 help illustrate this.

Table 10.23 Some examples of maternal speech

Mother's utterance	*Context*
That's right, pick up the blocks	the child is picking up a box of building blocks
That's a puppy.	the child is looking at a young dog
The puppy's in the basket.	the child is examining a puppy in a basket

Exposure to language of this type may well make it easier to match morphemes, words, and phrases with meanings—a major part of the language acquisition process.

Although potentially *helpful*, caregiver speech may not actually be *necessary* to the language acquisition process. In some cultures, for instance, children are not considered to be potential conversation partners until they are fluent speakers. Little speech is addressed directly to them, although they do spend a lot of time with their mothers and are exposed to a good deal of conversation among adults. The fact that these children learn language in a normal fashion indicates that exposure to the speech style typical of middle-class mothers in North American society is not necessary for language acquisition.

Moreover, even in cultures where it is common, caregiver speech seems to have very selective effects on child language. For instance, the number of *yes-no* questions in caregiver speech seems to be correlated with the rate at which auxiliary verbs develop—apparently because auxiliaries occur in the salient sentence-initial position in *yes-no* questions (*Can Jennifer go?*). At the same time, though, many other features of caregiver speech seem not to affect child language. As we saw earlier (Section 3.1), for example, the relative frequency of bound morphemes and nonlexical categories in caregiver speech apparently does not determine their order of acquisition.

In and of itself, then, caregiver speech cannot explain how language acquisition occurs. However, research into this subject may contribute to this goal in less direct ways by helping determine the types of linguistic experience that are most valuable to children. This in turn could help linguists identify the types of mechanisms and strategies involved in language acquisition.

6.2 The role of feedback

It is sometimes suggested that parents provide children with direct linguistic training by correcting ill-formed utterances. However, studies of actual interactions between parents and children point in a quite different direction. In general, parents tend to be more concerned with the truth of children's utterances than with their grammaticality. For example, one transcript of a parent-child conversation includes *That's right* as a response to the grammatical monstrosity *Mama isn't boy, he's a girl!*

Moreover, even when adults do attempt to correct children's grammatical errors, their efforts often have little effect. The following exchange between a child and his father is typical in this regard.

20)

Child: Want other one spoon, daddy.
Father: You mean, you want the other spoon.
Child: Yes, I want other one spoon, please Daddy.
Father: Can you say "the other spoon"?
Child: Other . . . one . . . spoon.
Father: Say "other."
Child: Other.
Father: "Spoon."
Child: Spoon.
Father: "Other spoon."
Child: Other . . . spoon. Now give me other one spoon?

Interestingly, however, some research suggests that subtler forms of feedback may have a role to play in the language acquisition process.

Recasts

Adults often respond to a child's utterance by repeating it, while making adjustments to its form and/or content. (Responses of this sort are called **recasts**.)

21)

Child: Daddy here.
Mother: Yes, Daddy is here.

Child: Him go.
Mother: Yes, he is going.

Child: Boy chasing dog.
Mother: Yes, the boy is chasing the dog.

Child: The dog is barking.
Mother: Yes, he is barking at the kitty.

Recasts provide children with potentially useful information—adding a missing verb (*is* in the first example), changing the form of a pronoun (*him* to *he* in the second example), and so on. On the other hand, parents sometimes modify their children's grammatical utterances too (as in the final example), so recasts also have the potential to be misleading.

It is not yet clear what role recasts play in language learning, and studies to date have yielded conflicting results. For instance, a study of the acquisition of *the* and *a* by three children revealed no link between the frequency of recasts and the rate at which their use of determiners increased; no matter how many recasts children heard, their learning speed didn't seem to increase.

On the other hand, a quite different result emerged from an experiment in which four and five year olds were taught made-up verbs that have irregular past tense forms—for example, *pell* (with *pold* as its past tense). When the children first learned what the verbs meant (they were linked to various funny actions, such as hitting someone with a beanbag attached to a string), they heard only the "*-ing*" forms ("This is called *pelling*"). They therefore had no idea what the past tense forms should be and often produced "mistakes" such as *pelled* when using the new verbs to describe actions in the past tense. Interestingly, a single recast was often enough to permit learning of the "correct" form—which suggests that feedback of this type may have a role to play in the language acquisition process after all.

6.3 The role of cognitive development

Because there are dramatic changes in both linguistic and nonlinguistic abilities during the first years of life, it is tempting to think that the two are somehow linked. Indeed, prominent psychologists have suggested both that general cognitive development shapes language acquisition (a view put forward by the late Swiss psychologist Jean Piaget) and that language acquisition is crucial to other aspects of cognitive development (a position associated with the late Russian psychologist Lev Vygotsky).

There are many suggestive similarities between language acquisition and cognitive development. During the first two years of life, for example, several cognitive advances that could facilitate language acquisition take place. One of these involves the development of **object permanence**—the ability to recognize that objects have an existence independent of one's interaction with them. Prior to the development of this ability, children seem to assume that an object ceases to exist when it moves out of sight, and that it is a different entity when it reappears. They therefore do not know where to look for an object that they observe being hidden; from their perspective, it has apparently simply ceased to exist. Object permanence emerges around age eighteen months, just prior to a period of rapid growth in the child's vocabulary. The relative timing of these two events suggests a possible connection: children's ability to learn the names for objects increases dramatically once they understand that those objects have an independent existence.

Another possible link between cognitive development and language acquisition involves **seriation**, the ability to arrange elements (such as sticks) in order of increasing or decreasing size. Children who are unable to perform this type of task typically describe the objects on which they are working simply as *long* or *short*. In contrast, children who are capable of seriation (age five and older) use comparative terms such as *longer* and *shorter*. Here again there is an apparent connection between an aspect of language (the *-er* suffix for adjectives) and a more general cognitive skill (seriation).

Just as cognitive development may influence language acquisition, so the emergence of linguistic skills may have an effect on cognition. At the very least, language seems to provide its users with an enhanced capacity for complex reasoning. It is also conceivable that language may help draw children's attention to certain conceptual distinctions that would otherwise develop more slowly. For instance, in the course of learning words such as *father, mother, brother, uncle,* and so on, children may make discoveries about family relationships that would otherwise develop more slowly.

Selective impairment

These examples notwithstanding, there is good reason to believe that language acquisition is to a large extent independent of other types of cognitive development. One source of evidence for this conclusion comes from the study of individuals whose general cognitive development is deficient but whose language is highly developed.

One important study of this type focused on Rick, a severely retarded fifteen-year-old whose performance on a variety of nonlinguistic tasks suggests that his general cognitive level is that of a preschool child. Yet, as the following examples illustrate, Rick's speech shows signs of syntactic and morphological sophistication—with appropriate use of affixes, nonlexical categories, and word order.

22)

She must've got me up and thrown me out of bed.
She keeps both of the ribbons on her hair.
If they get in trouble, they'd have a pillow fight.
She's the one that walks back and forth to school.
I wanna hear one more just for a change.

Another celebrated case involves Christopher, a linguistic savant. Although mentally impaired due to early brain damage (his IQ is 56) and unable to care for himself, he has shown an obsession for language since he was six years old. Thanks solely to his own efforts, he is able to read, write, and communicate in fifteen to twenty different languages, taking particular delight in learning complex morphological paradigms.

On the other hand, there are also documented cases of people whose IQ is perfectly normal but who nonetheless have great difficulty with inflection for the past tense and plural, as illustrated by the examples in *23*. (There is reason to believe that this particular disorder is inherited, since it has been observed in some, but not all, members of three generations within a single family.)

23)

The boys eat four cookie.
It's a flying finches, they are.
The neighbors phone the ambulance because the man fall off the tree.

Case studies such as these suggest that certain aspects of language (in particular, morphology and syntax) are independent of nonlinguistic types of cognitive development. This in turn implies that the mental mechanisms responsible for the acquisition of those parts of the grammar are relatively autonomous and that their operation neither follows from nor guarantees general cognitive development.

6.4 The role of inborn knowledge

There can be no doubt that there is something special about the human mind that equips it to acquire language. The only real question has to do with precisely what that special thing is. A very influential view among linguists is that children are born with prior knowledge of the type of categories, operations, and principles that are found in the grammar of any human language. They therefore know, for example, that the words in the language they are acquiring will belong to a small set of syntactic categories (N, V, and so on) and that they can be combined in particular ways to create larger phrases (NP, VP, S, etc.). The set of inborn categories, operations, and principles common to all human languages makes up **Universal Grammar (UG)**, first mentioned in Chapter 5.

The view that certain grammatical knowledge is inborn is known as **nativism**. Although nativism has roots in philosophy that date back thousands of years, its popularity in linguistics is due largely to the influence of Noam Chomsky, a linguist at the Massachusetts Institute of Technology. Chomsky's basic claim is that the grammars for human language are too complex and abstract to be learned on the basis of the type of experience to which children have access. Therefore, he argues, significant components of the grammar must be inborn. To illustrate this, we must consider a relatively complex example involving the notion of c-command, introduced in Chapter 6 (Section 3.4).

Principles A and B *(Advanced)*

The interpretation of pronouns such as *himself* and *him* is regulated by the following two principles.

24)

Principle A
A reflexive pronoun must have an antecedent that c-commands it in the same minimal S.

Principle B
A pronominal must not have an antecedent that c-commands it in the same minimal S.

These principles have played an important role in the study of language acquisition, and three arguments have been put forward in support of the claim that they are inborn.

First, the notion of c-command is quite abstract. It is not the type of concept that we would expect young children to discover simply by listening to sentences. Since we also know that no one teaches them about c-command, it makes sense to think that this notion is inborn and therefore does not have to be discovered or taught.

Second, the c-command relation seems to be universally relevant to pronoun interpretation. Thus, there appears to be no language in which the equivalent of English *himself* can refer to the boy rather than the boy's father in sentences such as the following (see Chapter 6 for discussion).

25)

The boy's father overestimates himself.

The universality of this restriction would be explained if Principles A and B were innate and hence part of the inborn linguistic knowledge of all human beings.

Third, as we saw earlier in this chapter, Principles A and B seem to be available to children from a very early stage in their development—even three-year-olds appear to have mastered the distinction between reflexives and pronominals. Given the complexity of these principles, this provides additional evidence for the claim that they are inborn.

Parameters

Of course, not every feature of a language's grammar can be inborn. Its vocabulary and morphology must be learned, and so must at least part of its syntax. In the case of phrase structure, for example, UG stipulates that an XP constituent can include a head and its complements, but it does not specify the relative order of these elements. This differs from language to language, so that a child acquiring English must learn that heads precede their complements whereas a child acquiring Japanese must learn the reverse order. As noted in Section 4.1 of Chapter 5, UG includes a parameter for word order that offers a choice between head-initial and head-final order. (We ignore the positioning of specifiers for the purposes of this illustration in Table 10.24.)

Table 10.24 The word-order parameter

Stipulated by UG	*Resulting options*
XP → X, Complement	XP → X Complement [head-initial] XP → Complement X [head-final]

There are also phonological parameters: for example, languages can differ from each other in terms of whether they allow more than one consonant in the onset—English does (e.g., *gleam, print*) whereas Japanese does not.

Part of the language acquisition process involves **parameter setting**—that is, determining which of the options permitted by a particular parameter is appropriate for the language being learned.

6.5 Is there a critical period?

One of the most intriguing issues in the study of language acquisition has to do with the possibility that normal linguistic development is possible only if children are exposed to language during a particular time frame or **critical period**. Evidence for the existence of such a period comes from the study of individuals who do not experience language during the early part of their lives.

One such individual is the much discussed Genie, who was kept in a small room with virtually no opportunity to hear human speech from around age two to age thirteen. After many years of therapy and care, Genie's nonlinguistic cognitive functioning was described as "relatively normal" and her lexical and semantic abilities as "good." In terms of syntax and morphology, however, many problems remained, as evidenced in the sample utterances in Table 10.25.

Table 10.25 Some of Genie's utterances

Utterance	*Meaning*
Applesauce buy store	'Buy applesauce at the store.'
Man motorcycle have	'The man has a motorcycle.'
Want go ride Miss F. car	'I want to go ride in Miss F.'s car.'
Genie have full stomach	'I have a full stomach.'
Mama have baby grow up	'Mama has a baby who grew up.'

As these examples show, Genie makes word-order errors (the first two examples), and her speech does not contain nonlexical categories or affixes.

Another revealing case study involved Chelsea, a deaf child who was misdiagnosed as retarded and emotionally disturbed. Chelsea grew up without language and was not exposed to speech until the age of thirty-one, when she was finally fitted with hearing aids. After intensive therapy, she is able to hold a job and to live independently. However, her vocabulary consists of only 2,000 words, and her sentences are ill formed, as the following examples help show.

26)

The woman is bus the going.
Combing hair the boy.
Orange Tim car in.
The girl is gone the ice cream shopping buying the man.

Based on case studies such as these, it is now widely believed that the ability to acquire a first language in an effortless and ultimately successful way begins to decline from age six and is severely compromised by the onset of puberty.

Summing up

This chapter has been concerned with the problem of how children acquire the **grammar** of their first language. Research in this area deals with two major issues: the nature of the developmental sequence leading to the emergence of mature linguistic competence in the areas of phonology, vocabulary, morphology, and syntax, and the factors that make it possible for children to acquire a complex grammar. A number of factors may contribute to the child's acquisition of language, including the properties of **caregiver speech, recasts,** the effects of general cognitive development, and inborn linguistic knowledge (**Universal Grammar**). We look to future research for deeper insights into the precise role of these and other factors.

Key terms

General terms and terms concerned with research methods

cross-sectional
diary study
experimental studies
grammar
longitudinal
naturalistic approach

Terms concerning phonological development

babbling
denasalization
fronting
gliding
stopping

Terms concerning vocabulary development

overextension
overgeneralizations
overregularizations
underextension

Terms concerning morphological and syntactic development

canonical sentence strategy
developmental sequence
holophrases
one-word stage
telegraphic stage
two-word stage

Terms concerning factors contributing to language acquisition

caregiver speech
critical period
motherese
nativism
object permanence
parameter setting
recasts
seriation
Universal Grammar (UG)

Sources

Pioneering work on infant perception is reported in "Developmental Studies of Speech Perception" by P. Eimas in *Infant Perception*, edited by L. Cohen and P. Salapatek (New York: Academic Press, 1975). More recent work is reported by J. Mehler, E. Dupoux, T. Nazzi, and G. Dehaene-Lambertz, "Coping with Linguistic Diversity: The Infant's Viewpoint," and by J. Werker, V. Lloyd, J. Pegg, and Linda Polka, "Putting the Baby in the Bootstraps: Toward a More Complete Understanding of the

Role of the Input in Infant Speech Processing," both in *Signal to Syntax*, edited by J. Morgan and K. Demuth (Mahwah, NJ: Erlbaum, 1996). The ability to use phonetic contrasts to distinguish between words is examined in "Perception and Production in Child Phonology: The Testing of Four Hypotheses" by M. Edwards in *Journal of Child Language* 1 (1974): 205–19. The cross-linguistic data on babbling are summarized and discussed on pp. 9–11 of *Phonological Acquisition and Change* by J. Locke (San Diego: Academic Press, 1983); see also "Adaptation to Language: Evidence from Babbling and First Words in Four Languages" by B. de Boysson-Bardies and M. Vihman, *Language* 67 (1991): 297–319. For a recent discussion of the relevance of babbling to the development of control over the vocal tract, see S. Pinker's *The Language Instinct* (New York: Morrow, 1994), p. 266. Differences between children's production and perception of speech sounds are found in *The Acquisition of Phonology: A Case Study* by N. Smith (New York: Cambridge University Press, 1973); the "*fis* phenomenon" is reported in "Psycholinguistic Research Methods" by J. Berko and R. Brown in *Handbook of Research Methods in Child Development*, edited by P. Mussen (New York: John Wiley & Sons, 1960). David Ingram's *Phonological Disability in Children* (London: Edward Arnold, 1976) contains many useful examples of early phonetic processes. The discussion of syllable deletion draws on information in "A Role for Stress in Early Speech Segmentation" by C. Echols, in *Signal to Syntax*, edited by J. Morgan and K. Demuth (Mahwah, NJ: Erlbaum, 1996), and in "The Acquisition of Prosodic Structure: An Investigation of Current Accounts of Children's Prosodic Development" by M. Kehoe and C. Stoel-Gammon, *Language* 73 (1997): 13–44. The data on developmental order for speech sounds come from chapter 8 of *First Language Acquisition* by D. Ingram, cited below.

The sample fifty-word vocabulary in Section 3 is from p. 149 of the book by Ingram cited below. Differences among children in terms of the types of words in their early vocabulary were first noted by K. Nelson in "Structure and Strategy in Learning to Talk," *Monographs of the Society for Research in Child Development* 38: 149 (1973): 1–135. The "*dax* experiment" on proper and common nouns is reported by N. Katz, E. Baker, and J. Macnamara in their article "What's in a Name? A Study of How Children Learn Common and Proper Nouns," *Child Development* 45 (1974): 469–73; the "*tiv* experiment" is from "The Child as Word Learner" by S. Carey in *Linguistic Theory and Psychological Reality*, edited by M. Halle, J. Bresnan, and G. Miller (Cambridge, MA: MIT Press, 1978). The discussion of strategies for learning word meaning is based on the proposals outlined in *Categorization and Naming in Children: Problems of Induction* by E. Markman (Cambridge, MA: MIT Press, 1989). The contrast between overextension in production and comprehension is described on pp. 152–53 of the book by Ingram cited below. The report of overextension in the speech of Allen is based on the discussion on p. 92 of the book by Eve Clark recommended below. The experimental study on overextension was carried out by J. Thomson and R. Chapman and reported in "Who Is 'Daddy' Revisited: The Status of Two-Year-Olds' Over-extended Words in Use and Comprehension," *Journal of Child Language* 4 (1977): 359–75. The experiment on *pour* and *fill* can be found in "Syntax and Semantics in the Acquisition of Locative Verbs" by J. Gropen, S. Pinker, M. Hollander, and R. Goldberg, *Journal of Child Language* 18 (1991): 115–51. The experiment on dimensional terms was carried out by P. Harris and J. Morris and is reported in "The Early Acquisition of Spatial Adjectives: A Cross-linguistic Study," *Journal of Child Language* 13 (1986): 335–52.

The remarks on inflectional overgeneralization are based in part on *Overregularization in Language Acquisition* by G. Marcus, S. Pinker, M. Ullman, M. Hollander, T. Rosen, and F. Xu, *Monographs of the Society for Research in Child Development*, serial no. 228, vol. 57, no. 4 (1992). The pioneering work on the developmental order for English bound morphemes and lexical categories was done by R. Brown and reported in his book *A First Language: The Early Stages* (Cambridge, MA: Harvard University Press, 1973); see also "Universal and Particular in the Acquisition of Language" by D. Slobin in *Language Acquisition: The State of the Art*, edited by E. Wanner and L. Gleitman (New York: Cambridge University Press, 1982). The original "*wug* test" was done by J. Berko and is reported in her article "The Child's Learning of English Morphology," *Word* 14 (1958): 150–77. The work on the development of derivational affixes and compounding in English is based on information reported in the book by Eve Clark recommended below and in the article by E. Clark and B. Hecht, "Learning to Coin Agent and Instrument Nouns," *Cognition* 12 (1982): 1–24. The data on the acquisition of the prohibition against inflection within compounds is from "Level-Ordering in Lexical Development" by P. Gordon, *Cognition* 21 (1985): 73–93. Word-order errors within compounds are reported in "Coining Complex Compounds in English: Affixes and Word Order in Acquisition" by E. Clark, B. Hecht, and R. Mulford, *Linguistics* 24 (1986): 7–29.

The data in Table 10.14 in Section 4.3 are taken from S. Pinker, *The Language Instinct* (New York: Morrow, 1994), pp. 269–70. The data on the development of question structures are based on the classic article by E. Klima and U. Bellugi, "Syntactic Regularities in the Speech of Children" in *Psycholinguistic Papers*, edited by J. Lyons and R. Wales (Edinburgh: Edinburgh University Press, 1966). The auxiliary copying error in question structures is the subject of an experiment reported by M. Nakayama, "Performance Factors in Subject-Auxiliary Inversion," *Journal of Child Language* 14 (1987): 113–26. The developmental order for *wh* words is documented by L. Bloom, S. Merkin, and J. Wootten, "*Wh* Questions: Linguistic Factors That Contribute to the Sequence of Acquisition," *Child Development* 53 (1982): 1084–92. Other descriptions confirming the main points of this account can be found in chapter 9 of the book by Ingram cited below. The data on the acquisition of passive structures come from a study by E. Turner and R. Rommetveit, reported in their article "The Acquisition of Sentence Voice and Reversibility," *Child Development* 38 (1967): 650–60. The data on children's use of *me* and *myself* come from "Children's Knowledge of Binding and Coreference: Evidence from Spontaneous Speech" by P. Bloom, A. Barss, J. Nicol, and L. Conway in *Language* 70 (1994): 53–71.

The role of correction in language development is examined in "Derivational Complexity and the Order of Acquisition in Child Speech" by R. Brown and C. Hanlon in *Cognition and the Development of Language*, edited by J. Hayes (New York: John Wiley & Sons, 1970). The data on mothers' reactions to children's ungrammatical and grammatical utterances come from "Brown and Hanlon Revisited: Mothers' Sensitivity to Ungrammatical Forms" by K. Hirsh-Pasek, R. Treiman, and M. Schneiderman, *Journal of Child Language* 11 (1984): 81–88. The relationship between *yes-no* questions in caregiver speech and the development of auxiliaries is discussed by E. Newport, H. Gleitman, and L. Gleitman in their article, "Mother, I'd Rather Do It Myself: Some Effects and Noneffects of Maternal Speech Style" in *Talking to Children*, edited by C. Snow and C. Ferguson (New York: Cambridge University Press, 1977); see also the discussion in the book by Gallaway and Richards recommended below.

The "other one spoon" example is reported on p. 161 of an article by M. Braine, "The Acquisition of Language in Infant and Child" in *The Learning of Language*, edited by C. E. Reed (New York: Appleton-Century-Crofts, 1971). The recast experiment involving nonsense verbs is from "The Contrast Theory of Negative Evidence" by M. Saxton, *Journal of Child Language* 24 (1997): 139–61.

General reviews of the role of the cognitive development in language acquisition can be found in the book by D. Ingram cited below and in "Cognitive Prerequisites: The Evidence from Children Learning English" by J. Johnston in *The Crosslinguistic Study of Language Acquisition*, vol. 2, edited by D. Slobin (Hillsdale, NJ: Erlbaum, 1985), pp. 961–1004. The description of Genie and of Rick is based on "Abnormal Language Acquisition and the Modularity of Language" by S. Curtiss in *Linguistics: The Cambridge Survey*, vol. 2, edited by F. Newmeyer (New York: Cambridge University Press, 1988), pp. 96–116. Chelsea's case is discussed by S. Curtiss in "The Independence and Task-Specificity of Language" in *Interaction in Human Development*, edited by A. Bornstein and J. Bruner (Hillsdale, NJ: Erlbaum, 1989). Christopher is the subject of a book by N. Smith and I. Tsimpli, *The Mind of a Savant: Language Learning and Modularity* (Cambridge, MA: Blackwell, 1995). The examples of sentences produced by speakers who have problems with inflection are from p. 49 of *The Language Instinct* by S. Pinker, cited above.

Figure 10.1 is adapted from "Syntax and Semantics in the Acquisition of Locative Verbs" by Jess Gropen, Steven Pinker, Michelle Hollander, and Richard Goldberg, *Journal of Child Language* 18 (1991): 115–51. Figure 10.3 is adapted from *A First Language* by Roger Brown (Cambridge, MA: Harvard University Press). Exercises for this chapter were prepared by Joyce Hildebrand.

Recommended reading

Clark, Eve. 1993. *The Lexicon in Acquisition.* New York: Cambridge University Press.

Gallaway, Clare, and Brian Richards. 1994. *Input and Interaction in Language Acquisition.* New York: Cambridge University Press.

Ingram, David. 1989. *First Language Acquisition: Method, Description and Explanation.* New York: Cambridge University Press.

O'Grady, William. 1997. *Syntactic Development.* Chicago: University of Chicago Press.

Piattelli-Palmarini, Massimo, ed. 1980. *Language and Learning: The Debate between Jean Piaget and Noam Chomsky.* Cambridge, MA: Harvard University Press.

Vihman, Marilyn. 1996. *Phonological Development: The Origins of Language in the Child.* Cambridge, MA: Blackwell.

Questions

1. One piece of evidence that children acquire a grammar is their production of forms like *doed, leaved,* and *goed.* From recollections of your experience with children, what are some other forms (not related to the past tense rule) that children produce that indicate they are acquiring and overgeneralizing grammatical rules?

2. In one naturalistic study, a search for passive structures in a sample of 18,000 utterances from sixty children yielded only nineteen examples produced by twelve of the children.

i) Is this evidence that the other forty-eight children had not yet mastered the passive structure? Why or why not?
ii) How are the disadvantages of the naturalistic method exemplified here?

3. The following transcriptions represent the pronunciation of a two-year-old child. Indicate which phonetic processes have applied in each case.

a)	skin	[kɪd]	h)	tent	[dɛt]
b)	spoon	[bun]	i)	teddy	[dɛdi]
c)	zoo	[du]	j)	brush	[bʌt]
d)	John	[dɑn]	k)	bump	[bʌp]
e)	bath	[bæt]	l)	play	[pwej]
f)	other	[ʌdə]	m)	breakfast	[brɛkpəst]
g)	Smith	[mɪt]			

4. Drawing on the phonetic processes posited for the preceding exercise, predict one or more plausible immature pronunciations for each of the following words.

a) show	e) juice
b) please	f) thumb
c) spit	g) zebra
d) under	h) ring

5. Consider the following examples of overextensions, all of which have actually been observed in children's speech. What is the basis for each of these overextensions?

	Word	*First Referent*	*Overextensions*
a)	sch	sound of a train	music, noise of wheels, sound of rain
b)	bow-wow	dog	sheep, rabbit fur, puppet
c)	baby	baby	people in pictures
d)	sizo	scissors	nail file, knife, screwdriver, spoon
e)	policeman	policeman	mailman, sailor, doctor
f)	strawberry	strawberry	grapes, raspberry
g)	fireworks	fireworks	matches, light, cigarette
h)	Batman	Batman logo on a T-shirt	any logo on a T-shirt

6. Since children have a tendency to focus on the prototypical members of categories in the acquisition of words, how might you expect children to underextend the following words? What members of the category might you expect children not to include?
   a) car
   b) tree
   c) ball

7. Children acquire certain spatial terms like *behind* and *in front of* relatively late. They also acquire words like *those, this, here,* and *there* relatively late. What do all of these words have in common that delays their acquisition?

8. The allomorphic variation associated with the third-person singular verbal ending *-s* is identical to that found with plural *-s*.
   i) Make up a test parallel to the "*wug* test" discussed in Section 4.1.
   ii) If possible, give your test to children between the ages of three and seven. Are your results similar to the ones discussed in the chapter?

9. Based on the discussion in Section 4.2 about the developmental sequence of morpheme acquisition, consider the acquisition in other languages of the morphemes corresponding to those listed in Table 10.14. Would you predict that these morphemes would be acquired in exactly the same order as their English equivalents? Why or why not?

10. Considering children's tendency to overgeneralize morphological rules, what might we expect a young child to use in the place of the following adult words? Justify your choice in each case.

a)	fish (plural)	f)	geese
b)	went	g)	brought
c)	mice	h)	hit (past tense)
d)	ate	i)	himself
e)	has	j)	women

11. Each of the following utterances is from the speech of a child in the two-word stage. Identify the semantic relation expressed by each of these utterances.

	Intended meaning	*Child's utterance*
a)	Jimmy is swimming.	Jimmy swim
b)	Ken's book	Ken book
c)	Daddy is at his office.	Daddy office
d)	You push the baby.	push baby
e)	Mommy is reading.	Mommy read

12. Consider the following data from Jordie, a two-and-a-half-year-old child, in light of the list of morphemes in Table 10.14.

	Intended meaning	*Jordie's utterance*
a)	Where's my blanket?	Where my blanket?
b)	Does it go right here, Mommy?	Go right here, Mommy?
c)	It's running over.	Running over.
d)	Here, it goes here.	Here, go here.
e)	No, that's mine.	No, that mine.
f)	Dinosaurs say gronk.	Dinosaur say gronk.
g)	There's more.	There more.

i) Which of the morphemes in Table 10.14 are missing in Jordie's sentences but present in the equivalent adult utterance?

ii) List the morphemes that are present in both the adult interpretations and in Jordie's speech.

13. Now consider the following utterances from a child named Krista.

	Intended meaning	*Krista's utterance*
a)	My name is Krista.	Mine name Krista.
b)	My last name is Pegit.	Last name Pegit.
c)	The tape is right there.	Tape right there.
d)	Daddy's book	Daddy book
e)	I've got a book.	I'm got a book.
f)	Read me a story.	Read me story.
g)	I'll do it.	I'm do it.
h)	He went outside.	He went outside.
i)	Open the gate, please.	Open a gate, please.

j)	Gramma's house	Gramma's house
k)	Smell the flowers.	Smell flowers.
l)	Shoes on	Shoes on
m)	The wee boy fell down.	Wee boy fell down.
n)	That's my ball.	That's mines ball.

i) Which morphemes are missing in Krista's speech but present in the adult interpretations?
ii) Krista uses the past tense twice in the above utterances. Do you think this is evidence that she has acquired the past tense morpheme? Why or why not?
iii) Comment on Krista's difficulty with possessive pronouns.
iv) Do you think she has acquired possessive -*'s*? Why or why not?

14. The following utterances were produced spontaneously by Holly, age three years.
   a) I learned about loving moms.
   b) Put him in the bathtub.
   c) We eated gummy snakes.
   d) Thank you for giving these books us.
   e) I don't know.
   f) He bited my finger. (When corrected, she said: He bitted my finger.)
   g) I runned in the water.
   h) I rided on a elephant.

   i) Has Holly acquired the past tense morpheme? How do you know?
   ii) What is the evidence that words such as *eat*, *know*, and *ride* are verbs for Holly and that words such as *bathtub*, *books*, and *water* are nouns?
   iii) What is the evidence in Holly's speech that she has learned the phrase structure schema for English?

15. The following sentences were uttered by a child aged two and a half.
   a) What's this is called?
   b) Mom, what these is called?
   c) Did you don't go to school today?
   d) You gonna don't go to school?

   Considering these four sentences, describe the child's current knowledge of the Inversion transformation.

16. Consider the following speech sample from a child.
   a) What Evan will read?
   b) Where Evan will read?
   c) Why you see seal?
   d) Why she want to?

   i) Determine the stage of development of this child in terms of his acquisition of question structures.
   ii) What do we expect to happen next?

17. It has been reported that hearing children growing up in homes with non-speaking deaf parents cannot learn language from radio or even television (see p. 278 of *The Language Instinct* by S. Pinker [New York: Morrow, 1994]).

   i) Can you think of any reasons for this?
   ii) What are the implications of these findings for our understanding of the type of experience that is required for language acquisition?

eleven

SECOND LANGUAGE ACQUISITION

John Archibald

When we talk about acquisition in SLA research, we are not talking about acquisition in the sense that one acquires polo ponies, Lladró figurines, or CBS, but rather in the sense that one acquires vicious habits, a taste for Brie, or a potbelly.

– KEVIN R. GREGG

OBJECTIVES

In this chapter, you will learn

- how the learner's first language and the language being learned interact to influence changes in the learner's grammar as he or she progresses
- what characterizes the phonology, syntax, and morphology of a second language learner's grammar
- how nonlinguistic factors may influence second language acquistion
- how second language classrooms help the learner by modifying language and focusing on form

The field of **second language acquisition (SLA)** research investigates how people attain proficiency in a language that is not their mother tongue. Whether we are looking at someone learning to read Greek in college, or someone becoming fluent in a fifth language in their forties, or a child acquiring a new language after moving to a new country, we refer to it as second language acquisition. The interesting phenomenon of children simultaneously acquiring two languages is generally investigated in the field known as **bilingualism** (which may be thought of as a subdiscipline of SLA research). In this chapter, we will primarily be concerned with second language (L2) acquisition in adults.

Over the years, the study of second language acquisition has been undertaken from a variety of different perspectives. In the 1950s and 1960s the primary objective was pedagogic. Researchers were interested in trying to improve the way in which second languages were taught. Hence, they were interested in discovering how those languages were learned. From the 1970s on, the focus shifted from the teacher to the learner and the field of L2 instruction became somewhat separate.

The reason for this has something to do with what was going on in linguistics, psychology, and first language acquisition research. All three of these areas shifted focus from the external to the internal in the 1960s. Linguistics became concerned with the mental grammar of the speaker, not just the description of the linguistic structures of a given language. Psychology shifted from behaviorism (which denied the importance of mental representations) to cognitive psychology. And research on first language acquisition focused on children's internal grammars. These fields are also crucial to the study of SLA. Linguistics gives us a sophisticated and accurate description of what people are trying to learn (the second language), and what they already know (the first language). Psychology can provide us with a learning theory to account for how people acquire knowledge. Finally, the field of first language acquisition (which has been around longer than the field of second language acquisition) offers various findings that can be productively applied to SLA. For example, we know that children who are acquiring their first language (L1) have grammars that are systematic and that their utterances are not just bad imitations of the adult target. As we will see, second language learners, too, are developing a grammar that is systematic even if it is not nativelike.

1 THE STUDY OF SECOND LANGUAGE ACQUISITION

In the case of first language acquisition, we may ascribe the difference between child and adult grammars to either cognitive or biological immaturity in the child. In the case of second language learning by adults, however, we cannot say that the learners are either cognitively or biologically immature. Rather, they are subject to an influence that is absent from the child's situation: the first language itself. We can diagram the situation as shown in Figure 11.1.

L1 → Interlanguage Grammar ← L2

Figure 11.1 Influences on an interlanguage grammar

This diagram illustrates the fact that second language learners have a systematic **interlanguage (IL)** grammar—so called because it is a system of mental representations influenced by both the first and the second language, and has features of each.

1.1 The role of the first language

One of the most easily recognizable traits of a second language learner's speech is that it bears a certain resemblance to the first language. Thus, when speaking English, someone whose first language is French is likely to sound different from someone whose first language is German. Consider in this regard the typical pronunciation of the English word *have* by speakers of French and German, as shown in Table 11.1.

Table 11.1 Phonological transfer

English target	*French speaker*	*German speaker*
have [hæv]	[æv]	[hæf]

As Table 11.1 shows, the form produced by the French speakers reflects the fact that French lacks the phoneme /h/, while the pronunciation associated with German speakers can be traced to the fact that German includes a rule of Syllable-Final Obstruent Devoicing (which changes the [v] to a [f]). The term **transfer** is used to describe the process whereby a feature or rule from a learner's first language is carried over to the IL grammar. Other examples can be seen in Table 11.2.

Table 11.2 More phonological transfer

L1	*L2*	*Example*	*Comment*
Spanish	English	I espeak Espanish.	Spanish does not allow s + consonant sequences word-initially.
English	French	[ty] 'you' → [tu]	English does not have the front, rounded vowel [y]. The English speaker substitutes the [u] sound.
Quebec French	English	Over dere.	The [ð] sound is replaced by [d].
European French	English	Over zere.	The [ð] sound is replaced by [z].
English	Spanish	[paɾa] 'for' → [para]	As English does not have the tapped [ɾ] as an allophone of /r/, an [r] is substituted.

1.2 The role of the L2

The first language is not the only influence on the interlanguage grammar, since some properties of the IL can be traced to aspects of the L2. In the case of a German speaker who is learning English, for example, the IL grammar will contain some features of both German and English. Consider how a German speaker learning Canadian English might pronounce the word *eyes* (see Table 11.3). Here, the learner first applies the rule of Syllable-Final Obstruent Devoicing (transferred from German), changing /ajz/ to [ajs]. But the learner also has acquired some knowledge of the target language—in this case, the rule of Canadian Vowel Raising (discussed in Chapter 3), which states that [aj] becomes [ʌj] before a voiceless consonant in the same syllable. Thanks to application of the Syllable-Final Obstruent Devoicing rule, the input form now ends in a voiceless consonant ([s]), which triggers Canadian

Table 11.3 One possible pronunciation of the English word *eyes* by a German-speaking learner

Target form	*Result of Final Obstruent Devoicing*	*Result of Canadian Vowel Raising*
/ajz/	[ajs]	[ʌjs]

Raising. This example serves to show us something about the nature of an interlanguage: it contains features of both the L1 and the L2.

1.3 The nature of an interlanguage

The dual nature of IL grammars is captured in the **Ontogeny Model** of second language acquisition. According to this model, there are two types of error in an IL grammar: **transfer errors** and **developmental errors**. As we have seen, the former type of error reflects transfer from the L1. In contrast, developmental errors involve the same sort of mistakes that children make in acquiring their L1. For example, as we saw in Chapter 10, children learning English as a first language sometimes produce forms like *goed* and *breaked*, apparently overgeneralizing the regular rule for past tense formation. A similar developmental error has been observed in second language learners, who also overgeneralize rules as they acquire a grammar.

It is possible that the processes of transfer and overgeneralization in L2 learning are the result of a single cognitive strategy that could be informally stated as "use what you know." This predicts that the kind of errors made by second language learners will be dependent on their level of proficiency. Beginning learners may have nothing to draw on but their L1. However, more advanced learners have acquired a certain amount of knowledge about the L2, and this knowledge becomes a potential source of errors. This is illustrated in Table 11.4.

Table 11.4 Error patterns in L2 acquisition

Level of proficiency	*Transfer errors*	*Developmental errors*
Beginner	high	low
Intermediate	medium	high
Advanced	low	low

Graphically, the predictions of the Ontogeny Model are illustrated in Figure 11.2. The number of transfer errors should decrease over time while the number of developmental errors should initially be small, but then should increase before finally decreasing.

The IL grammar, then, is influenced by both the L1 and the L2, though the proportion of influence is dependent on the learner's level of overall proficiency. Note that advanced learners have low numbers of both transfer and developmental errors. Not all learners, however, reach this advanced stage. It is common in second language acquisition for learners to reach a plateau in their development. For example,

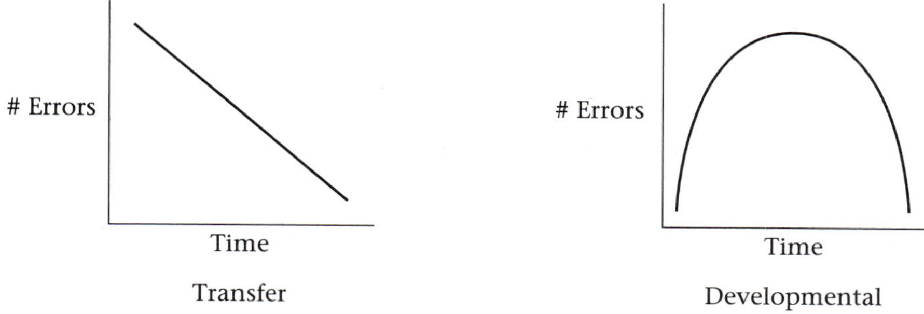

Figure 11.2 Error patterns predicted by the Ontogeny Model

even after many years of exposure to English, a second language learner may still produce sentences like *I don't know what should I do* (meaning 'I don't know what I should do'), in spite of hearing the grammatical version from native speakers and perhaps being corrected. When the interlanguage grammar stops changing, it is said to have **fossilized**.

Second language learners can exhibit nonnativelike characteristics in any linguistic domain, as can be seen in Table 11.5.

Table 11.5 Types of errors found in the acquisition of English

L1	*Example*	*Error type*	*Comment*
Spanish	My wife is embarrassed (meaning 'pregnant').	lexical	Spanish *embarazada* = 'pregnant'
Various	I live in a two-bedroom department.	lexical	Sometimes the wrong word can be chosen.
Various	I didn't took the car.	morphological	English doesn't mark the past tense on both auxiliary and main verbs.
Various	She get ups late.	morphological	The speaker adds the agreement marker to the particle not the verb.
French	He drinks frequently beer.	syntactic	French places the main verb before the adverb.
Various (e.g., Turkish, Arabic)	There's the man that I saw him.	syntactic	Some languages allow pronouns in this position in a relative clause.

1.4 The final state

So far we have been talking about the characteristics of the intermediate grammar. But a discussion of what an IL grammar looks like must consider the **target**—that is, what is to be acquired. The field of SLA, then, must address the issue of actual proficiency or **communicative competence**. While knowledge of a language's grammar allows us to distinguish between grammatical and ungrammatical sentences, successful communication requires much more than this. The learner must also be able to use the language in a way that is appropriate to the situation or context. As Figure 11.3 helps illustrate, both grammatical accuracy and communicative ability are part of communicative competence.

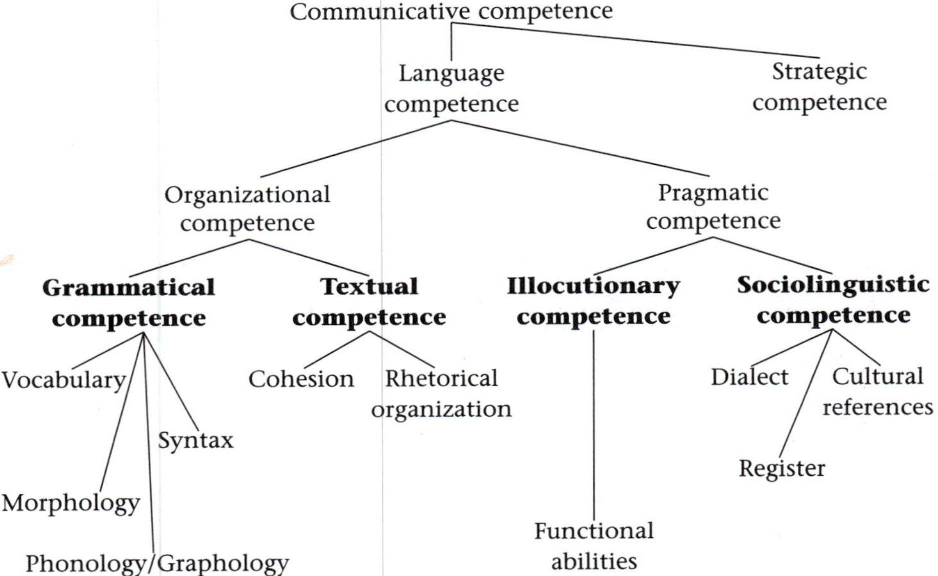

Figure 11.3 A model of communicative competence

Let us now briefly consider each of the major subparts of the model.

Grammatical competence

Grammatical competence has to do with knowledge of the core components of the grammar: phonetics, phonology, morphology, syntax, and semantics. We will address these areas in detail in Section 2.

Textual competence

Textual competence involves knowledge of well-formedness above the sentence level, including the rules that string sentences together to make a well-formed text in the spoken or written language. As the following examples help show, a text is not just a sequence of grammatical utterances.

1)

MGs can be very temperamental. MGs won't start if they are wet. When they work, MGs are fun to drive. They do not work often.

2)

Like most roadsters, MGs can be very temperamental. For example, they won't start if they are wet. However, on the rare days when they work, they are fun to drive.

The difference between the two texts does not involve the grammaticality of individual sentences but rather relates to differences in the use of intersentential links such as *like*, *for example*, and *however*. To be proficient, second language learners have to acquire the ability to organize and link sentences in this way.

Illocutionary competence

The meaning of an utterance is not always directly reflected in its surface structure. For example, when uttering the sentence *Have you ever considered professional help?* a speaker could have in mind a variety of intended meanings. He might mean 'I can't help you, but maybe somebody else could' or 'I think you are a truly disturbed individual; seek help.' The speaker's intent in producing an utterance is referred to as **illocutionary force**. **Illocutionary competence**, then, refers to the ability to comprehend a speaker's intent, and to produce a variety of syntactic structures to convey a particular intent in various circumstances (e.g., *Are you cold? Could I close the window? Why on earth is the window open?*). This, too, is something that second language learners need to acquire.

Sociolinguistic competence

As we will see in Chapter 14, language use can vary according to the context. For example, we use a different style of language in informal situations than we do in formal ones. This can affect phonology, syntax, and lexical choice, as can be seen in the following two utterances.

3)

I assume we will be working late again this evening? What a shame!

4)

We gotta work late again? Dammit!

In order to have **sociolinguistic competence**, second language learners need to be able to produce and comprehend a variety of social dialects.

In sum, communicative competence is a model of proficiency that allows us to measure second language knowledge and ability, to construct second language proficiency tests, and to design balanced second language courses.

1.5 Variation in performance

An important goal of L2 research is to integrate the study of **competence** (linguistic knowledge) and **performance** (actual language use in particular situations). One of the characteristics of the output of second language learners is that it is quite variable. For example, a learner might well produce the following sentence:

5)

I **didn't** like **th**at movie so I told her I **no** want to go **d**ere.

In this (hypothetical) example, the learner is inconsistent, getting one of the two negatives right and correctly pronouncing one of the interdental fricatives. The question that intrigues researchers has to do with what causes this sort of variation. We usually think of knowledge as fairly stable within an individual. So, for example, if you make a mistake while speaking in your native language, you tend not to question your competence in that language, but rather to assume that you made some kind of performance error. So how do we account for learners who behave as if they know how to negate a verb or pronounce [ð] on some occasions, but not others? Do they have the knowledge or don't they?

It is difficult to answer this question, in part because of considerations involving error frequency. If a second language learner gets something wrong 10 percent of the time, is it the same (in terms of competence) as getting it wrong 60 percent of the time? We would probably say that a nonnative speaker who gets the English past tense correct 10 percent of the time doesn't know it, and that someone who gets it right 90 percent of the time does. But what about someone who gets it right somewhere between those two scores? This is a complex research question. The (admittedly simplistic) view adopted in this chapter is that variation falls into the realm of linguistic performance.

Linguistic performance clearly involves the interaction of a number of cognitive systems and has much in common with other skills. A crucial notion for the study of how skills develop involves the distinction between controlled and automatic processing. When acquiring a new skill (e.g., playing golf), we begin by having to devote a lot of conscious or controlled processing to the activity: feet apart, head down, elbow straight, and so on. Once we become proficient, we just hit the ball; the activity has become automatic.

We need to shift processing from controlled to automatic because, as humans, we have a fixed processing capacity. We can't consciously process everything at once. Shifting some material into automatic processing frees up space for more controlled processing. Consider an example from reading. When we first learn how to read, we devote much of our cognitive processing to determining what the written symbols stand for. When we are focusing on decoding the letters, we do not have the processing capacity to deal with things like reading for prejudice or bias. After a time, though, letter recognition happens automatically in our first language, and learners can devote more of their cognitive capacity to higher level skills.

That native speakers do this kind of thing automatically can be seen by the difficulty we have in proofreading. It is hard to suppress the information we're getting from the context since the mind tries to make sense of what it's reading. Conversely, when we are forced by exceptional circumstances to devote a lot of energy to decoding the print (e.g., a bad photocopy or fax), our higher-level processing slows down; we can't focus as much on the message when we are focusing on the form.

All this is relevant to second language acquisition in that it can help explain the variable performance of L2 learners. When learners are focusing on the form of the L2 utterance, they may be able to produce it accurately. However, when there are extra demands, such as trying to communicate a complex thought or carry on a conversation in a noisy room, errors may occur. This suggests that the learner has a mental representation of the form in question (say a negated verb or a [ð]) but can have difficulty implementing or accessing it under certain conditions.

2 INTERLANGUAGE GRAMMARS

Let us turn now to a discussion of the specifics of what is acquired when learning the phonology, syntax, and morphology of a second language. The general question we are trying to answer here is "What is the structure of an interlanguage?" Second language learners are acquiring grammars, and those grammars involve mental representations. Therefore we can investigate the nature of those representations within the various subdomains of linguistic theory. We begin with phonology.

2.1 L2 PHONOLOGY

Let us consider what is to be acquired in the domain of phonology. Broadly speaking, we can distinguish between segmental and prosodic phonology. Segmental phonology has to do with the characteristics of phonological segments, like consonants (C) and vowels (V). Prosodic phonology, on the other hand, has to do with phonological phenomena that affect more than a single segment (e.g., syllables and stress).

Segmental phonology

As we saw in Chapter 3, languages vary in their segmental inventory in that they choose a subset of the sounds found in human languages. There is thus a good chance that a second language learner will have to learn to produce and perceive some new sounds when acquiring a second language.

One of the most obvious characteristics of adult second language speech is that it is accented, as the result of phonological and phonetic transfer from the native language. This is why native speakers of English can usually distinguish French-accented English from German-accented English. Consider the examples in Table 11.6.

Table 11.6 French- and German-accented English

English target		*Quebec French speaker*	*German speaker*
[ðə]	'the'	[də]	[zə]

As both French and German lack the interdental fricative [ð], native speakers of those languages substitute a sound from their L1 in place of the English sound. Generally, the learners substitute a sound that shares some features with the target sound. In Table 11.6, the Quebec French speaker substituted a voiced alveolar (coronal) stop, while the German speaker substituted a voiced alveolar (coronal) fricative for the English voiced, interdental (coronal) fricative. Particularly at a beginning level of proficiency, L2 learners pronounce words using their L1 phonological system.

A similar phenomenon can be seen in the phonology of loan words. When a language borrows a word from another language, it makes the word fit into its own phonological system. For example, as we saw in Chapter 3, when English borrowed the word *pterodactyl* from Greek, it reduced the onset cluster [pt], which is well-formed in Greek but not English. However, no such change was made in the word *helicopter* (also from Greek) since it already complied with the phonological pattern of English.

Markedness

One question that has received a lot of attention in SLA research is whether some sounds are harder to acquire in a second language than others. Perhaps some sounds are simpler than others. Or perhaps some sound systems are easier for speakers of a certain language to acquire. Would it be easier for a Japanese speaker to acquire English or Vietnamese? As might be expected, these are not simple issues. We cannot talk about the ease or difficulty of entire languages, but we may have something to say about individual sounds.

When linguists try to deal with the notions of ease or simplicity, they make use of the notion of **markedness**. Structures that are simple and/or especially common in human language are said to be **unmarked**, while structures that are complex or less common are said to be **marked**. So, we might say that a sound that is found in relatively few of the world's languages (e.g., [θ]) is marked while a sound that occurs in many of the world's languages (e.g., [t]) is unmarked.

Markedness is commonly approached from the perspective of language typology, which is concerned with the comparative study of similarities and differences among languages. As noted in Chapter 8, researchers have discovered certain implicational universals of the form "if a language has *x,* it will also have *y.*" For example, if a language has nasal vowels (e.g., [ã]), then it will also have oral vowels (e.g., [a]). Crucial to the understanding of implicational universals is the fact that the implication is unidirectional. Thus a language that has oral vowels does not necessarily have nasal vowels. This allows us to identify [a] as less marked than [ã], in accordance with the following generalization.

6)

X is more marked than *y* if the presence of *x* implies the presence of *y, but not vice versa.*

It is interesting to ask whether IL grammars obey such implicational universals and whether this can tell us something about the question of ease and difficulty of learning.

The **Markedness Differential Hypothesis** investigates second language acquisition by comparing the relative markedness of structures in the L1 and the L2. Remember the earlier example of Syllable Final Obstruent Devoicing in German, which explains why a word like *hund* 'dog' is pronounced with a [t] at the end. German speakers learning English typically transfer Syllable Final Obstruent Devoicing into their IL (producing [hæt] for [hæd] 'had') and must learn to make the contrast between [t] and [d] at the ends of words. We might be tempted to think that the principle underlying this phenomenon is something like "it's hard to learn to make contrasts that your L1 doesn't make." But when we look at another set of data, we see that this is not the case.

French makes a contrast between [ʃ] and [ʒ] word-initially, whereas English does not, as Table 11.7 indicates.

Table 11.7 The [ʃ]/[ʒ] contrast in English and French

	English [ʃ] / [ʒ]	*French [ʃ] / [ʒ]*
Initial	sure [ʃ] / * [ʒ]	chant ([ʃ]) / gens ([ʒ]) 'song' 'people'
Medial	assure ([ʃ]) / azure ([ʒ])	boucher ([ʃ]) / bouger ([ʒ]) 'to fill up' 'to budge'
Final	leash ([ʃ]) / liege ([ʒ])	hache ([ʃ]) / age ([ʒ]) 'h' 'age'

If it were invariably difficult for second language learners to make contrasts that are not found in their L1, we would expect English speakers to have difficulty learning to produce [ʒ] at the beginning of words. But they don't. English speakers seem able to learn to pronounce French words like *jaune* 'yellow' and *jeudi* 'Thursday' without trouble.

The notion of markedness can be used to explain why German speakers have difficulty making a new contrast in English, while English speakers don't have difficulty making a new contrast in French. The typological situation is as follows:

- There are languages that have a voicing contrast initially, medially, and finally (e.g., English).
- There are languages that have a voicing contrast initially and medially, but not finally (e.g., German).
- There are languages that have a voicing contrast initially, but not medially or finally (e.g., Sardinian).

These generalizations allow us to formulate the following implicational universal.

7)

The presence of a voicing contrast in final position implies the presence of a voicing contrast in medial position, which in turn implies the presence of a voicing contrast in initial position.

We can represent this universal graphically as follows:

8)

initial < medial < final
C B A

The presence of A implies the presence of B (but not vice versa), and the presence of B implies the presence of C (but not vice versa). Therefore A is the most marked and C is the least marked. This markedness differential explains the differing degrees of difficulty exhibited by the German and English L2 learners. The German speakers learning English are attempting to acquire a contrast in a universally more marked position (final), whereas the English speakers learning French are attempting to acquire a contrast in a universally unmarked position (initial).

Another way of looking at the similarity/difference question, though, is not in terms of ease or difficulty of acquisition but rather in terms of *rate* of acquisition. The **Similarity Differential Rate Hypothesis** (SDRH) makes the claim that the rates of acquisition for dissimilar phenomena are faster than for similar phenomena. In other words, all other things being equal, learners will learn something that is unlike their first language structure *faster* than something that is similar to (and hence could be confused with) a first language structure. The data shown in Figure 11.4 describe the acquisition of English [r] (in word-initial position) and English velarised [ɫ] (in word-final position) by a native speaker of Haitian Creole that has a uvular [ʁ] and only a clear alveolar [l]. Note that there is virtually no acquisition of the velarised [ɫ] and little change in rate, whereas the rate of change for [r] is much more dramatic. The dissimilar [r] is acquired at a faster rate that the similar [l].

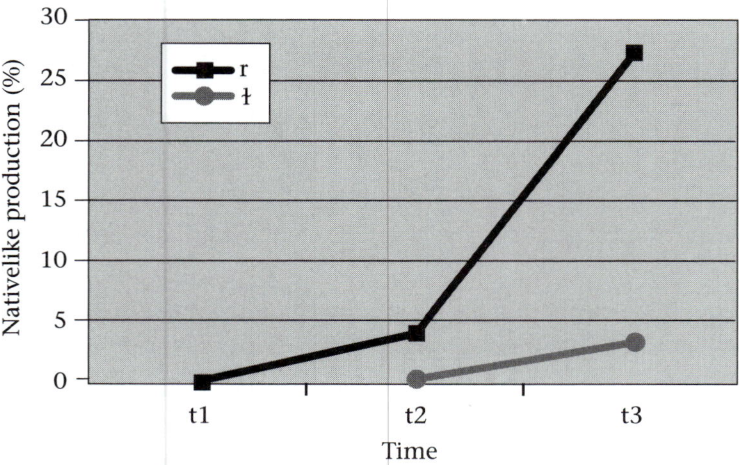

Figure 11.4 Differential rates of acquisition

Of course, the question of how to determine whether two features are similar or dissimilar is not always straightforward. To test this hypothesis, we would need to look at perceptual, phonetic, phonological, and even orthographic factors that could affect this judgment. Here we will just accept that the two *l*'s are more similar than the two *r*'s.

In addition to the segmental inventory, second language learners also have to acquire the prosodic phonology of the target language. For example, they have to acquire the principles of syllabification and stress assignment. We will now look at each in turn.

L2 syllabification

We saw in Chapter 3 that syllables have the hierarchical structure shown in Figure 11.5.

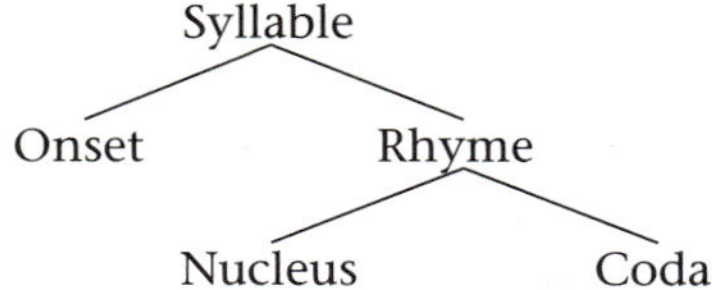

Figure 11.5 The internal structure of the syllable

The languages of the world vary according to such things as whether syllabic nodes can be complex. Some languages (e.g., Japanese) do not allow clusters in onsets or codas. Ignoring some complexities, let us assume that all syllables must be CV or CVC. More complex syllables such as CCVCC are not allowed. A common phenomenon in second language learning involves modifying an L2 word so that it fits the L1 syllable structure. Consider the following words spoken by someone whose L1 is Arabic:

9)

English target	*Nonnative speaker's version*
plant	pilanti
Fred	Fired
translate	tiransilet

Arabic does not allow clusters in onsets or codas, so an English word like *plant* cannot be mapped onto a single Arabic syllable. A characteristic of Arabic is that illicit consonant clusters are broken up by an epenthetic [i].

With this in mind, let us look at the steps that an Arabic speaker would go through in syllabifying 'plant'.

Step 1 *Initial syllabification:* Assign vowels to a nucleus (N) and the nucleus to a rhyme (R).

Step 2 Assign allowable onset (O) consonants (in Arabic, one).

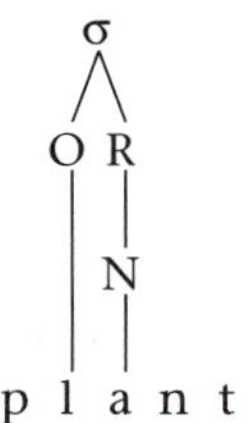

Step 3 Assign allowable coda (Co) consonants (in Arabic, one).

Step 4 Insert an epenthetic [i] to the right of an unsyllabified consonant.

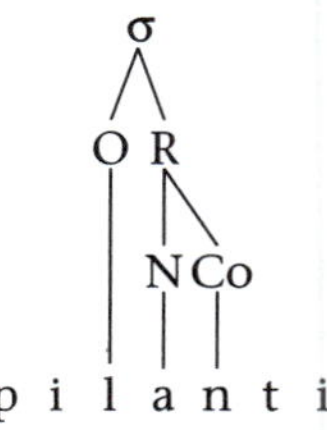

Step 5 Assign vowels to a nucleus and the nucleus to a rhyme.

Step 6 Assign allowable onset consonants (in Arabic, one).

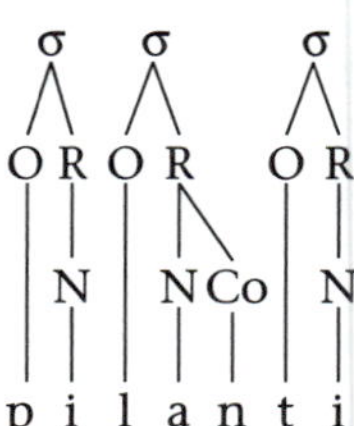

As this example helps show, we can explain why Arabic speakers pronounce English words in the way that they do by investigating the principles of syllabification in the L1. Especially at the beginning levels of proficiency, the structure of the IL is influenced by the structure of the L1.

Stress assignment

L2 learners also have to acquire the stress patterns of the language they are trying to learn. Consider an example from Polish. Polish is a language in which word-level stress is assigned to the penultimate syllable (regardless of syllable weight). These metrical principles transfer and result in one of the characteristics of a Polish accent in English: the tendency to place stress on the penultimate syllable regardless of syllable weight. Remember from Chapter 3 that in English, heavy syllables tend to attract stress (e.g., aróma, agénda). The following examples illustrate a nonnative stress pattern in which the second to last syllable is always stressed.

10)

English target	*Nonnative form*
astónish	astónish
maintáin	máintain
cábinet	cabínet

2.2 L2 SYNTAX

L2 learners also have to acquire the syntax of their new language. In this section, we will look at two facets of syntactic structure: the null subject parameter and verb movement.

Null subjects

As we saw in Chapter 5, Universal Grammar includes universal principles (that account for what all natural languages have in common) as well as parameters (that account for cross-linguistic variation). Parameters are like linguistic switches (often binary) that can be set to a particular value as a result of the linguistic input. One of the first parameters to be proposed was the **Null Subject** (or pronoun-drop) **Parameter**. Essentially, this parameter is designed to account for the contrast between languages like French and English, which require overt grammatical subjects (e.g., *He speaks French/*Speaks French*), and languages like Spanish and Italian, which allow subjects to be omitted (e.g., Spanish *Él habla español/Habla español* '[S/he] speaks Spanish').

11)

The Null Subject Parameter

The subject of a clause with a verb marked for tense {may/may not} be null.

Languages that allow null subjects tend to have other grammatical traits associated with them. For one, they tend to allow declarative sentences with the word order Verb + Subject as well as Subject + Verb, as in the following examples from Spanish.

12)

a. Juan llegó.
John arrived.

b. Llegó Juan.
arrived John.

Secondly, they tend to allow sentences like the following, in which a complementizer (here *que* 'that') is immediately followed by the trace of a moved *wh* word.

13)

Quién dijo usted que t llegó?
who said you that arrived
'Who did you say arrived?'

As the following example shows, such sentences are unacceptable in Standard U.S. English.

14)

*Who did you say [$_{CP}$ that [$_S$ t arrived]]?
(deep structure = *you did say that who arrived*)

In other words, languages like Standard English ([–null subject]) do not allow *that*-trace sequences, whereas languages like Spanish ([+null subject]) do.

Studies on L2 learners of English show that Spanish speakers are more likely to judge subjectless English sentences to be grammatical than are French speakers. This is consistent with the assumption that L1 parameter settings are transferred into the IL grammar, at least in the early stages. Learning a second language can be seen as involving the resetting of parameters that have different values in the L1 and the L2.

Moreover, when Spanish subjects are given a task that requires them to change a declarative sentence into a question, they are more likely to produce a sentence that contains a *that*-trace sequence than are French subjects. For example, if Spanish subjects are given a sentence like *Joshua believed that his father would be late* and have to form a question asking about the underlined element, they are more likely than French subjects to produce a sentence like **Who did Joshua believe that t would be late?* This points toward the possibility that the admissibility of null subjects and the acceptability of *that*-trace sequences are somehow both related to the Null Subject Parameter (i.e., speakers of null subject languages are more likely to permit *that*-trace sequences).

However, there are complications. Remember that the study just described had the Spanish and French speakers form new sentences. Another study had both French and Spanish subjects judge the grammaticality of English sentences with a *that*-trace violation. Both groups were quite able to reject those sentences as ungrammatical. For some reason, there is a stronger L1 influence when learners have to form new sentences themselves.

Verb movement

French and English differ in the setting of the **Verb Movement Parameter**.

15)

The Verb Movement Parameter
V {raises/does not raise} to I.

We saw in Chapter 5 that the transformation of verb movement takes a verb from within the VP and moves it up in I (see Figure 11.6). Simplifying slightly, let us say that English does not allow verb movement but French does. Thus, in French the verb raises

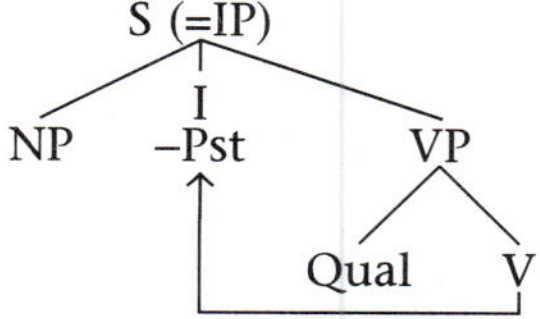

Figure 11.6 Verb movement

to I past a preverbal qualifier, but in English it does not. This difference can be seen in the following sentences, in which movement of the verb over the qualifier separating it from the I position gives a bad result in English but a good result in French.

16)

a. *Marie watches often *t* television.
b. Marie regarde souvent *t* la télévision.

Studies have shown that French speakers learning English initially assume that English allows verb raising. In order to learn English, they have to reset the value of their verb raising parameter.

Markedness and the Subset Principle

Another interesting facet of a parameter-setting approach to SLA has to do with whether adult L2 learners can reset their parameters, and whether the notion of directionality of difficulty captured by the Markedness Differential Hypothesis (see Section 2.1) can be captured in a parameter-setting model. The Null Subject Parameter can be used to address these questions. To understand how, we must first consider how a parameter-setting model instantiates the notion of markedness.

If we consider the two settings of the Null Subject Parameter (+/–), we can see that the different values generate different grammars, as shown in the following sentences from English and Spanish.

17)

[–null subject]:	I	speak	Spanish.
[+null subject]:	Yo	hablo	español.
		Hablo	español.

As you can see, the [+null subject] setting generates more grammatical utterances than does the [–null subject] setting. Therefore the [–] setting is said to be a subset of the [+] setting. Graphically, this can be represented as shown in Figure 11.7.

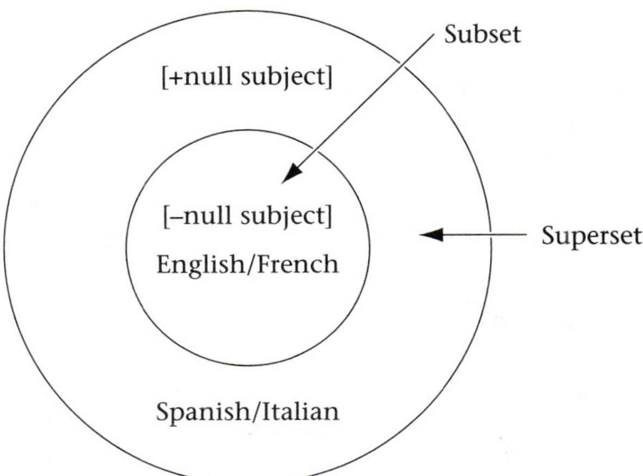

Figure 11.7 Subset/superset relation for the Null Subject Parameter

The **Subset Principle** stipulates that for first language learners, the initial or default setting will be the subset value (i.e., [–null subject]) in the case of the Null Subject Parameter.

Second language learners may have to reset their parameters. When attempting to reset from subset to superset or from superset to subset, learners have access to different types of evidence. Imagine a speaker of English (who has the [–] setting) trying to learn Spanish. The learner's initial assumption will be the L1 parameter setting, which leads to the expectation that all sentences will have overt subjects. When faced with Spanish input, the learner will be exposed to grammatical utterances in the L2 that do not have overt subjects (e.g., *Hablo español* '[I] speak Spanish'), which indicates that the L1 setting is incorrect and needs to be reset. Data like these, which involve grammatical utterances to which one is actually exposed, are referred to as **positive evidence**.

Now imagine someone whose L1 is Spanish ([+]) trying to learn English ([–]). The learner's initial assumption will be that English should be [+null subject], like the L1. The learner's IL grammar will allow both sentences with overt subjects and sentences without. Crucially, there will be no positive evidence in the English input directed at this learner to show that the L1 parameter setting is wrong. The learner will hear sentences with overt subjects, which are sanctioned by the current IL grammar, but there will be no direct indication that sentences with null subjects are not allowed. There is no pressure to reset the parameter. In this case, the learner will have to rely on **negative evidence** (i.e., observations about what is missing or ungrammatical in the data) to reset the parameter. In particular, the learner would either have to be explicitly told what is ungrammatical (**direct negative evidence**) or have to infer that it is ungrammatical on the basis of the fact that no one else ever says it (**indirect negative evidence**).

Given that direct positive evidence is available in one case (English → Spanish) and negative evidence is required in the other (Spanish → English), we might predict that it is harder for Spanish speakers to learn the English value of the Null Subject Parameter than vice versa. In fact, the prediction is borne out. Studies have shown that it is easier for English speakers to reset to the Spanish value of the Null Subject Parameter than it is for Spanish subjects to reset to the English setting.

Let us now consider how an approach based on typological universals would treat the same phenomenon. The presence of null subjects implies the presence of overt subjects, but not vice versa.

18)

overt subjects > null subjects

Therefore, null subjects would be thought of as more marked and, consequently, more difficult to acquire. The Markedness Differential Hypothesis predicts that structures that are more marked typologically will cause difficulty in SLA because they are more marked. The Subset Principle, on the other hand, predicts that structures that are more marked will not cause difficulty because there will be clear evidence that the L1 setting is wrong. Although only the Subset Principle seems to make the correct prediction in the case of the null subjects, further research is necessary in order to see which approach is better able to handle a wider range of data.

2.3 L2 MORPHOLOGY

The study of second language morphology has a slightly different flavor than the study of either L2 phonology or syntax. L2 phonology has been studied for a long time, though the analyses have changed to reflect changes in linguistic theory. L2 syntax is a much younger field, and much of it has been informed by current linguistic theory. By contrast, L2 morphology has been studied more or less in a theoretical vacuum. In the 1970s, a number of studies collected data on the accuracy of second language learners on a variety of morphemes. This research drew on previous studies in the field of first language acquisition that had attempted to determine the order of acquisition of morphemes in L1 development. The developmental sequence shown in Table 11.8 was found.

Table 11.8 Developmental sequence for first language acquisition

1. *-ing*	The present participle affix (e.g., she is work*ing*)
2. Plural *-s*	(e.g., bottle*s*)
3. Irregular past	(e.g., she *taught* French)
4. Possessive *-s*	(e.g., a child'*s* toy)
5. Copula *be*	(e.g., I *am* happy)
6. Articles	(e.g., *a*, *the*)
7. Regular past	(e.g., she walk*ed* quickly)
8. Third person *-s*	(e.g., she walk*s* quickly)
9. Auxiliary *be*	(e.g., She *is* working)

Research on second language acquisition focused on whether the developmental sequence in L2 learning was the same as for L1 learning. The order shown in Table 11.9 was found.

Table 11.9 Developmental sequence for second language acquisition

1. *-ing*	4. Auxiliary *be*	7. Regular past
2. Copula *be*	5. Plural *-s*	8. Third person *-s*
3. Articles	6. Irregular past	9. Possessive *-s*

There are many similarities but there are also some differences. For example, note that auxiliary and copula *be* are acquired at a relatively earlier point in L2 than in L1, and that the possessive morpheme *-'s* is acquired later in L2 than in L1. To attempt to explain these patterns, we need to look a little more closely at the structures that are involved in inflectional morphology.

In the syntax section we saw that in English, main verbs do not raise to I. Now we note that the verb *be* does raise to I if no modal is present (see Section 4.2 in Chapter 5).

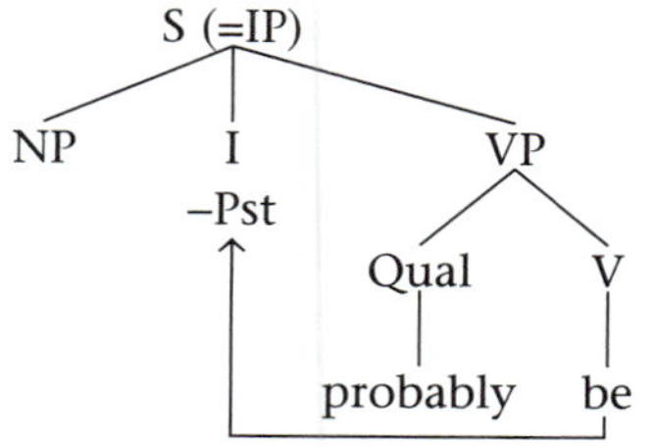

Figure 11.8 Raising of *be* to I

19)

a. No modal is present: the auxiliary verb moves from inside the VP to I.
He is [$_{VP}$ probably *t* eating].

b. A modal is present: the auxiliary verb does not raise.
He should [$_{VP}$ probably be eating].

c. Regular verbs do not raise.
He [$_{VP}$ probably likes eating] vs. *He likes [$_{VP}$ probably *t* eating].

Children acquire *be* as a main verb before they acquire *be* as an auxiliary verb. So, children start by producing sentences that are simpler in that they have only a copula verb (e.g., *He is hungry*) before they begin producing sentences that include an auxiliary plus a main verb (e.g., *He was working*), as shown in the following trees:

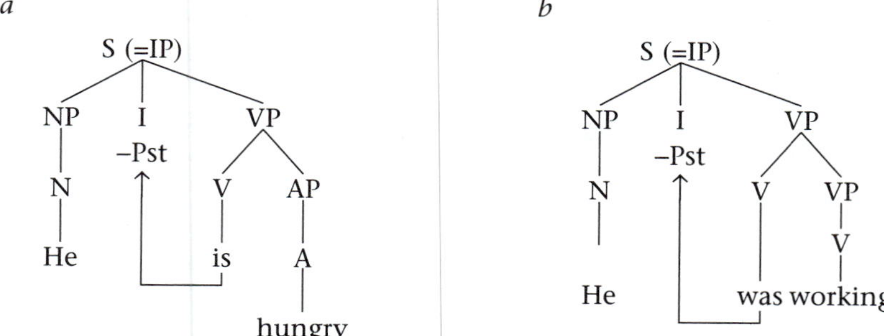

Figure 11.9 Copula versus auxiliary *be*

The structure in *b* has an extra level of complexity in that it has a complex verb phrase (one VP within another). Adult second language learners, on the other hand, appear to be able to use both the simple copula and auxiliary verbs early on. Whether this difference is because of the adult's greater ability to handle complexity in general cognitive terms or because children's linguistic systems are still maturing remains a controversial and unresolved issue.

In addition, note that children acquiring English as their first language acquire the three *-s* morphemes in the following order: plural, possessive, third person. Phonetically, these morphemes have the same realization, so we can't say that the order reflects phonological complexity. The order might be explained by noting that plural is a word-level phenomenon (e.g., *dogs*), possessive is a phrase-level phenomenon (e.g., [*the king of England*]*'s horse*, not *[*the king*]*'s of England horse*), and third person marking involves a relation between the verb and a phrase (the subject) elsewhere in the sentence (e.g., [*That man*] *usually thinks too much*). Like the pattern noted for the development of copula and auxiliary *be*, children seem to be acquiring structures in order of complexity, as shown in the following trees:

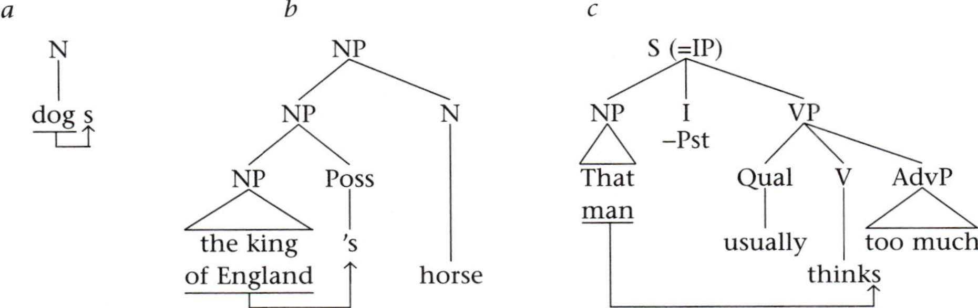

Figure 11.10 Three types of -*s* affix

In contrast, adults acquire the plural quite early, but then seem to get both the possessive and the third person marking quite late—perhaps for reasons involving processing. (When concentrating on getting the words right, we do not always have the processing capacity to produce well-formed higher-level structures.) Interestingly, adults do not seem to find interphrasal morphology (like *c* above) more difficult than phrasal morphology (like *b* above). This may be because the adults have already acquired the grammar for their first language and that grammar most likely has both phrase-level and interphrasal morphological phenomena. In contrast, children have to set up a hierarchical structure of a grammar for the first time, and could conceivably be building the structure from the bottom up (words → phrases → sentences).

In summary, we note that the order of acquisition data are intriguing in both first and second language acquisition, even though we await a conclusive explanation of the facts.

3 FACTORS AFFECTING SLA

So far, we've looked at some of the characteristics of an IL grammar. Now let's turn to a variety of factors that can influence second language acquisition. It is clear that there is much more variation in the grammars of people learning second languages than in the grammars of people learning first languages. This brings us to the question of what factors might help to account for that variation.

3.1 AGE

One of the obvious ways that language learners vary is in their age. People start learning second languages at different points in their lives. Could the age of onset of L2 learning cause different levels of final proficiency?

This is a question usually considered under what is known as the **critical period hypothesis** (see Chapter 10, Section 6.5). We know that biologically based critical periods exist in other species. For example, some birds can learn the song of their species only if exposed to it during a particular window of opportunity. If they hear the song too early or too late, learning will not take place. (See Chapter 16 for further discussion.)

Is second language learning like this? Is there an optimal time (or critical period) to acquire a second language? The answer appears to be yes and no. As the discussion of communicative competence in Section 1.4 indicates, proficiency in a language is a remarkably complex thing. Usually, discussion of a possible critical period focuses on the area of phonological competence. While people who begin SLA as adults tend to retain nonnativelike phonology in the target language, it is much more difficult to predict knowledge or ability in any of the other areas of communicative competence (syntax, cohesion, sociolinguistics, etc.) based upon age of acquisition.

In fact, even L2 phonology is not as straightforward as it might first appear to be. We can predict with fair certainty that people who start learning their L2 before the age of seven will have nativelike L2 speech and that people who start learning after fourteen or fifteen will probably not have nativelike speech. But the results of people who start learning between the ages of seven and fourteen are much more varied. Some end up with accents, and some do not.

There is no current evidence of anything biological that prevents adults from acquiring proficiency in a second language. Factors that have been considered in the past (e.g., brain lateralization—see Chapter 13) are now thought to be of little predictive value in determining L2 ability. The question of "ultimate attainment" in L2 acquisition is still hotly debated, and the literature has cited cases of adult L2 learners who apparently perform virtually identically to native speakers in a variety of domains (including phonology).

Currently, the critical period debate in SLA research is usually couched in terms of the question, "Do adults have access to Universal Grammar?" Rather than looking for changes in the brain that coincide with aging, researchers now look to see whether IL grammars are governed by the same constraints as first languages (e.g., Russian, Yoruba). If adults are engaged in the same kind of development process as children, then we would expect their IL grammars to be describable in terms of the same principles and parameters of UG that we use to describe first languages. Conversely, if adults are acquiring their second languages using qualitatively different learning mechanisms than are used to acquire an L1 (e.g., if they use general problem-solving abilities), then we might expect them to adopt hypotheses that are not sanctioned by Universal Grammar. Something like this may in fact happen in the acquisition of gender in French. Children learning French as a first language seem to have very little trouble learning gender as they learn the words themselves (e.g., *le livre*, 'the book' is masculine; *la table*, 'the table' is feminine). On the other hand, adults whose first language does not have gender often have great difficulty learning French gender. They seem to set up complex (but incorrect) rules for predicting the gender of a given noun. For example, they may assume that words naming colors (or some other semantic category) are of one gender, or that words that end with a certain sound sequence are of another. Rules like this sometimes allow nonnative speakers to guess the gender correctly, but they still perform significantly differently from native speakers. This is an example of how adults' greater capacity to formulate general rules can sometimes lead them down the wrong path.

3.2 Individual differences

Learners vary in ways other than age. Broadly speaking, the researcher asks the question, "If learners have a particular quality *x*, does this make them better at second language acquisition?" For example, we might look at the effect of inhibition, left-handedness, or some other individual trait on L2 ability. As intuitively appealing as this avenue is, it is one that must be taken carefully. In particular, there are three points on which we must be explicit:

1. how we define and measure *x*;
2. what it means to be *better*;
3. what aspect of communicative competence we are referring to.

Consider in this regard a trait like empathy. It has been argued that people who are empathetic are better language learners. This is an intuitively appealing notion. People who are empathetic can imagine what it feels like to be in someone else's shoes, and can look at things from another perspective. Second language learning certainly involves looking at things from a different perspective, but in SLA research, we need to find a more precise way to evaluate this hypothesis.

There are tests that claim to measure a person's empathy, but is this notion really a well-defined construct? Is one simply empathetic or not, or are there degrees of empathy? If there are degrees, do we see a correlation between degree of empathy and degree of success? And what does it mean for empathetic learners to be better language learners than people who aren't empathetic? Do they make fewer errors? Less serious errors? Should we expect people with greater empathy to be better at everything in the L2? Or maybe just at phonology and sociolinguistic competence? On what basis could we make a prediction? These are not simple issues. We raise them not to argue that research in individual variation is misguided, but to show some of the complex areas that need to be addressed before we can hope to establish a causal connection between a particular personality trait and success at second language learning.

We can distinguish between two kinds of factors in terms of which individuals can vary: affective factors and cognitive factors. First we will look at the role of affect.

Affective factors

Affective factors have to do with the emotional side of learning a second language. Clearly there is a great deal at stake emotionally when learning a second language, and it is possible that emotions affect how successful a second language learner is. Affective factors that have been studied include empathy, anxiety, inhibition, and risk-taking. In this section we will look at one such factor: motivation.

Learners can vary with respect to the amount or type of motivation they have to learn a second language. If someone is highly motivated to learn, will that person do better at learning? In order to answer this question, we need to say a bit more about what it means to be motivated.

Traditionally, two types of motivation have been proposed: **instrumental** and **integrative**. Instrumental motivation involves wanting to learn the L2 for a specific goal or reason. For example, someone might need to pass a language requirement in order to get a graduate degree or a job with a government agency. Integrative motivation, on the other hand, involves wanting to learn the L2 in order to learn more about a particular culture or fit into it better. For instance, someone might want to learn Japanese in order to learn more about a fascinating culture.

Studies have shown that the degree of integrative motivation correlates with the degree of success in language learning. That is to say, subjects who score high on tests of integrative motivation do better on certain language tests than comparable subjects who score low on the same tests. However, subjects with instrumental rather than integrative motivation can also do well if their level of motivation is high. One study found that subjects who were offered a cash reward if they obtained a certain score on a language test performed much the same as subjects with high integrative motivation. All this seems to suggest that degree of motivation is a better predictor of future learning success than is type of motivation.

Cognitive factors

While affective factors have something to do with the emotional side of learning, cognitive factors involve the mechanics of how an individual learns something. Different people seem to learn via different cognitive styles and different learning strategies. We will first address cognitive style.

As individuals, we tend to tackle mental tasks using a particular **cognitive style**. In contrast with an affective factor like motivation, which may vary from domain to domain (e.g., someone might be more motivated to learn French cooking than to learn the French language), cognitive style is a stable trait across domains.

The study of cognitive style often focuses on a contrast between **field dependence** and **field independence**. Learners who are field independent are not distracted by irrelevant background information when trying to learn something. These are people who can see the trees without being distracted by the forest. On the other hand, learners who are field dependent tend to see the forest but may miss the characteristics of individual trees. Of course, this is not to say that one trait is good and the other is bad. Field-dependent learners are probably able to synthesize the overall picture better than field-independent learners, but field-independent learners are probably better able to pick out relevant facts.

In terms of second language acquisition, it seems that field-independent learners do better on language tests that focus on analytic tasks such as providing the correct grammatical form in a given sentence:

20)

Yesterday, we ___ the kids to the zoo. (take)

In contrast, field-dependent learners tend to do better on tasks that involve synthesizing their knowledge. For example, they may demonstrate broader communicative competence in that they are more concerned with getting the message across than with the grammatical accuracy of the sentences they use to form their message.

Ultimately, the proficient L2 learner needs to be concerned with both **accuracy** and **fluency**. Broadly speaking, accuracy has to do with whether the learner has the correct representation of a particular linguistic structure (i.e., *knowledge*). Fluency, on the other hand, has to do with the rapid retrieval or processing of those representations (i.e., *skill*). Someone who is not fluent may have accurate representations but take considerable time and energy to retrieve them. Different learners will most likely have a natural affinity to emphasize either accuracy or fluency, depending perhaps on their individual cognitive style.

While cognitive styles appear to be relatively stable traits in individuals, there are elements of learning that we have some control over. Each of us has certain **learning strategies** that we can employ to try to fill gaps in our linguistic knowledge. These strategies can be contrasted with **communication strategies**, which are designed to keep communication happening in spite of gaps in knowledge—as when someone uses paraphrase to describe an object for which he or she has no vocabulary item (e.g., *Could you pass me the thing you use for hitting nails?*). In contrast, a learning strategy is used to discover something new about the L2.

Many different learning strategies have been proposed. For example, using the strategy of directed attention, learners may decide in advance to focus on particular aspects of a task and to ignore others. So, when reading a text or listening to a lecture, they might decide to focus only on the main points. Another strategy involves repetition: to retain a lexical item or to improve the pronunciation of a sequence of sounds, the learner may repeat a word or phrase over and over. A third strategy makes use of clarification requests (to the teacher, a peer, or the others in a conversation) about something that is not understood (e.g., How come *stood* doesn't rhyme with *food*? What's a *liege*?). Under this view, learners have a variety of strategies at their disposal and have to discover which ones work best for them.

3.3 The good language learner

The question of individual variation in second language learning has received quite a bit of attention under the heading of "the good language learner." What makes a good language learner? One researcher has presented the following list of characteristics. (For the most part, this list is concerned with the learning strategies that people invoke in an attempt to acquire L2 knowledge and ability.)

Table 11.10 Characteristics of the "good language learner"

1. Has an effective personal learning style or positive learning strategies.
2. Has an active approach to the learning task.
3. Has a tolerant and outgoing approach to the target language and empathy with its speakers.
4. Has technical know-how about how to tackle a language.
5. Has strategies of experimentation and planning with the object of developing the new language into an ordered system and revising this system progressively.
6. Is consistently searching for meaning.
7. Is willing to practice.
8. Is willing to use the language in real communication.
9. Has self-monitoring ability and critical sensitivity to language use.
10. Is able to develop the target language more and more as a separate reference system and is able to learn to think in it.

By focusing on such characteristics, the learning strategy approach seeks to account for differences in L2 proficiency by referring to the way in which individuals try to acquire new knowledge. Some people have gone so far as to suggest that this type of research will make it possible to teach not-so-good language learners the learning strategies necessary to be good language learners.

This brings us to the interesting question of second language learning in classrooms and the effect that instruction has on L2 learning. Is it really possible to teach someone a second language? Or can you just create an environment in which second language learning can take place? We turn now to the research that has looked specifically at L2 classrooms.

4 THE L2 CLASSROOM

It has been flippantly said that people have been successfully acquiring second languages for thousands of years, but when teachers get involved, the success rate plummets. This comment is probably more a reflection of people's unfortunate experience in certain types of language classrooms (that may have been dull or even physically threatening, depending on the century) than it is a statement about general pedagogic utility. However, the fact remains that language classrooms can be sheltered environments where students can be given the opportunity to learn and practice without being subject to the penalties for failure that can be imposed outside the classroom.

We should acknowledge at this point that there is really no such thing as *the* second language classroom. In reality, all classrooms are different because they have different people in them (both students and teachers). Nevertheless, there are certain statements that can be made. Here we will explore three relevant characteristics of a second language classroom:

1. modified input,
2. modified interaction,
3. focus on form.

4.1 MODIFIED INPUT

In Chapter 10 it was noted that adults do not talk to children in the same way that they talk to other adults. Just as the input directed to children has certain simplifying characteristics, so speech directed at nonnative speakers tends to be simplified compared to the speech directed at native speakers. In all communicative situations—whether dealing with a child or an adult, a nonnative speaker or a native speaker—we seem to make a rapid assessment of the level of proficiency or background knowledge of the listener, and adjust the input accordingly.

The input aimed at nonnative speakers is referred to as **foreigner talk**. The subset of this speech that takes place in classrooms is known as **teacher talk**. Teacher talk tends not to be as evenly matched to the proficiency of the listener as foreigner talk is, for the simple reason that teachers are usually addressing a class rather than an individual. As a result, some learners may find the modified speech too hard or too easy.

The pedagogic goal of teacher talk is crystal clear: make sure the students know what is being talked about by providing **comprehensible input**. Perhaps surprisingly, this idea has generated an extraordinary amount of conflict in the field of SLA research. Although it seems to be useful to provide learners with comprehensible input, teachers must guard against simplifying too much, which might give the appearance of patronizing the learners or talking to them as if they were stupid rather than on their way to becoming bilingual.

4.2 Modified interaction

Second language classrooms also differ from the outside world in terms of the kind of interactions that go on there. However, the difference appears to be mainly one of degree, not quality. Inside a classroom, the teacher may engage in the following kinds of strategies:

- more comprehension checks, e.g., *Do you understand? OK?*
- more prompting, e.g., *Who knows where Council Bluffs is?*
- more expansions, e.g., Student: *Me red sweater.*
Teacher: *Yes, you're wearing a red sweater, aren't you?*

This modified interaction appears to be one of the characteristics that differentiates classrooms from other communicative settings. While all these devices (e.g., comprehension checks) occur in nonclassroom discourse as well, they appear to occur more frequently in second language classrooms. Assuming that the teacher realizes that the purpose of the classroom is to prepare the student to understand input and interaction outside of the classroom as well, modified interaction is beneficial.

4.3 Focus on form

The final characteristic of the second language classroom to be discussed here involves **focus on form**. The term *focus on form* encompasses two distinct practices that tend to occur in most L2 classrooms: instruction about the language and explicit correction.

Most second language classes present the students with some sort of information about the language—noting, for example, "The English sound [θ] is produced by placing the tongue between the teeth," or "The *on* in French *bon* is pronounced as a nasal vowel." Instruction of this type is designed to improve the form (or accuracy) of the student's L2. In all likelihood, other activities that happen in the class will focus on giving the student a chance to improve fluency or particular sociolinguistic skills.

Error correction is also designed to improve the form of the student's L2. Regardless of the methodology used in most classes today, there is some focus on form and some error correction. The interesting research question is whether either of these practices can be shown to have a positive effect on the learner. Do students who get corrected do better than students who don't?

The question may not be as straightforward as it appears. Remember that it has frequently been argued in first language acquisition research that attempts at error correction are relatively infrequent and don't really affect children's grammars. Could it be different for adult second language learners? The learning environment is different in that adult learners (unlike children) are usually exposed to a fair amount of error correction. But does that make a difference? Not surprisingly, this question is difficult to answer. Some studies have argued that second language learners who receive correction develop at about the same pace as those who do not. Other studies have shown certain increases in accuracy as the result of correction.

These results may not be as contradictory as they seem. The areas where correction seems to be most useful involve lexical items. When people try to learn particular properties of a lexical item, they benefit from feedback. However, feedback concerning certain structural phenomena may not be as effective. For example, the previously mentioned study of French speakers learning about the lack of verb movement in English (see Section 2.2) found that while there were short-term improvements in the subjects who were explicitly taught the relevant facts, there were no significant long-term effects. When the subjects were tested a year later, they were found to have reverted to their pre-instructional performance.

This doesn't necessarily mean that students should not be corrected or that there should be no focus on form in the second language classroom. If a balance is struck between classroom activities that focus on form and those that focus on meaningful communication, then there is certainly no evidence that feedback causes any problems. Indeed, to the contrary, there is evidence that students in classes that focus primarily on communication but also include some instruction on form are significantly more accurate than students who are exposed only to instruction that focuses on communication.

Most of the studies to date have considered focus on form within a pedagogical framework (i.e., how it affects the learner or the classroom), but there are more recent studies that are couched within a cognitive framework. Under this approach, the following questions could be asked: (TL = target language.)

1. *The noticing issue:* Do learners have the cognitive resources to notice the gap between their IL utterances and the TL utterances around them?

   This is a very complex question that involves the details of how memory (working, short-term, and long-term) works. Learners would have to have the coordinated working and long-term memory resources to enable the cognitive comparison of the IL and TL sentences. This sort of comparison eventually leads to knowledge restructuring. Studies suggest that learners do have the cognitive resources to engage in this type of comparison, especially if they are comparing TL utterances that have occurred recently in the discourse.

2. *The interruption issue:* Is pedagogical intervention that does not interrupt the learner's own processing for language learning even possible?

   Focus on form should be carried out in response to the learner's needs. If (a) the primary focus of the lesson is on meaning, (b) the focus-on-form targets arise incidentally, and (c) the learner shifts attention briefly, then the focus-on-form activity will be relatively unobtrusive. Indeed, rather than being an unwanted interruption, focus-on-form may allow the learner to pay selective attention to a structure for a short period of time, which would be beneficial.

3. *The timing issue:* If so, then precisely when, in cognitive terms, should the pedagogical intervention occur?

   Learners appear to benefit from being prepared in advance for some focus-on-form activities. If they know what is coming, it helps them to notice the relevant features in the input. One of the most promising types of intervention is an immediate recast. A corrective recasting involves the repetition of an error plus a recast, as shown below:
   Student: *I think that the worm will go under the soil.*
   Teacher: *I think that the worm will go under the soil?...I thought that the worm would go under the soil.*

In sum, adult students usually expect error correction, and teachers are accustomed to providing it. Assuming that the class is not devoted entirely to instruction that focuses on form (with no opportunity for meaningful practice), error correction doesn't seem to cause any harm. In a class with activities that focus on both form and fluency, the students tend to emerge with greater accuracy. Certain types of classroom activities seem to be able to engage the cognitive abilities of adult second language learners and allow them to continue to advance their L2 proficiency.

4.4 Bilingual education

We will conclude this chapter with a discussion of two types of bilingual education programs: minority language maintenance programs and **immersion** programs. Both are designed to produce bilingual children, but there are important differences. French immersion programs in Canada, for example, involve children from a majority language (English) being immersed in a minority language (French). As English-speaking children, they are in no danger of losing their first language since it is so dominant in the culture. Their situation is clearly different from that of children who speak a minority language (e.g., Spanish or Chinese in the United States) and are submersed in the majority language (English). Not only are these children in some danger of losing their first language, but the sink-or-swim approach can have strongly negative consequences on their future in school. For these reasons, it should be emphasized that even if we argue for the benefits of immersing English-speaking children in French classrooms, it does not follow that we should submerse speakers of other languages in English classrooms.

Let us look in more detail at some of the issues surrounding bilingual education. We begin with minority language maintenance programs.

Minority language maintenance programs

Minority language maintenance programs, which are also known as heritage language programs or L1 maintenance programs, have been introduced around the world to try to address the fact that minority language children often have difficulty in majority language schools. Even with separate classes of instruction, these children tend to have more than their share of problems later in school (including a higher than expected drop-out rate). One reason for this becomes evident when one thinks of what these children face. Up until the age of five, they are exposed to a language at home (say, Russian). Then they are put into an English-speaking school in a class of primarily native English speakers. Typically, they do not understand everything that the teacher is saying, and they do not have the opportunity to develop the basic cognitive skills necessary for functioning in school. These children may thus suffer a setback from which they will never recover.

This poor beginning can lead to minority language students being placed in classes not designed for students intending to pursue postsecondary education, which in turn can lead to an exit from the educational system. To try to change this recurring pattern, a number of bilingual education programs have been set up in places like Canada, Finland, England, and the United States. In all of these programs, the children of minority language background receive their initial instruction in the minority language. Over the years of their elementary education, instruction in the majority language is gradually introduced, so that by grades three to six, the children receive about half of their instruction in the majority language.

The question raised in evaluating these programs (and indeed the question that led policymakers to adopt the competing sink-or-swim approach to minority language education) is, "What is the effect on the children's English?" Obviously, knowledge of English in places like the United States and Canada is essential. But is submersion in English the only way to acquire proficiency in English? It would seem that the answer is no, since children can become bilingual with relative ease. In virtually all of the bilingual education programs studied, the subjects ended up performing as well as their monolingual L1 and L2 peers by the end of grade six. So, for example, a child who received all instruction in Cree for the first couple of years of schooling and was getting 50 percent English and 50 percent Cree instruction by the end of grade six would be performing in Cree like a monolingual Cree speaker and in English like a monolingual English speaker.

Thus, receiving instruction in the L1 does not have negative consequences on the L2. On the contrary, it seems to have significant positive effects on success in school, on linguistic proficiency, and even on the family situation of the students. The students can understand the teacher (which helps them at school), and they can understand their parents and grandparents (which helps them at home).

Immersion programs

Another kind of bilingual education program involves immersing a majority language student in a minority language class, as is the case with French immersion programs in Canada. Immersion differs from traditional foreign language instruction and from submersion programs. It is different from a traditional foreign language course in that French is the medium of communication, not the subject of the course. It is teaching *in* French, not teaching *of* French. In a traditional foreign language course, French is just another subject (about 40 minutes a day). In French immersion, all of the instruction is in French, even when the content is geography or music.

Immersion is different from submersion in that no one in the class is a native speaker of the medium of instruction, so all the students are starting from approximately the same place. Contrast this with the experience of a native Chinese speaker who is thrown into an English-only class with a large number of native speakers of English.

The positive features of French immersion programs as they have been implemented in Canada can be stated as follows. Children who emerge from French immersion suffer no negative effects on their English, do well in school, outperform their monolingual counterparts in a number of ways, and know a lot of French.

Given the success of immersion programs in Canada, one might ask why similar programs are not popular in the United States. The simple answer is that bilingualism is not, by and large, considered worth the cost of immersion education. There are a few prestigious private schools in this country in which French immersion is practiced with success. However, setting up what is essentially an entirely separate school curriculum is quite costly, and only a small number of English-speaking parents strongly want their children to be bilingual. In the United States, no single foreign language is perceived as important enough to justify the cost involved.

Summing up

This chapter has dealt with a number of issues in the field of second language acquisition. We investigated the notion of an **interlanguage** and the influence of both the source and target languages on this grammar in terms of **transfer** and **developmental errors**. Proficiency in a second language requires both knowledge and ability, something captured in a model of **communicative competence**. Someone must acquire knowledge in all linguistic domains (phonetics, phonology, morphology, syntax, and semantics) as well as the ability to use that knowledge in a variety of social contexts.

What is easy or difficult to acquire in a second language has been investigated from a variety of perspectives. We focused on Universal Grammar (the **Subset Principle**) and typological universals (the **Markedness Differential Hypothesis**). However, it is not just universals that influence second language learning; the specific characteristics of an individual can also affect the process. Affective factors and cognitive factors both influence second language learning. So too do factors such as modified input, modified interaction, focus on form, and bilingual education.

The field of second language acquisition is remarkably diverse, in part because of what is involved in L2 learning. Someone who is attempting to learn an additional language must develop new mental representations, and develop facility at accessing those representations in a variety of circumstances. The field of SLA research must therefore draw on philosophy (theories of mind), psychology (theories of learning, theories of performance), linguistics (theories of linguistic structure), and pedagogy (theories of instruction). This is probably the main reason why we have not established anything like a comprehensive theory of how second languages are learned. But bit by bit, piece by piece, we're starting to put together some pieces of the puzzle.

Key terms

General terms concerning the study of second language acquisition

bilingualism
developmental errors
fossilized
interlanguage (IL)
Ontogeny Model
second language acquisition
target
transfer
transfer errors

Terms concerning second language proficiency

communicative competence
competence
grammatical competence
illocutionary competence
illocutionary force
performance
sociolinguistic competence
textual competence

Terms concerning interlanguage grammars

direct negative evidence
indirect negative evidence
marked
markedness
Markedness Differential Hypothesis
negative evidence
Null Subject Parameter
positive evidence
Similarity Differential Rate Hypothesis
Subset Principle
unmarked
Verb Movement Parameter

Terms concerning other factors affecting second language acquisition

accuracy
cognitive style
communication strategies
critical period hypothesis
field dependence
field independence
fluency
instrumental (motivation)
integrative (motivation)
learning strategies

Terms related to the second language classroom

comprehensible input
focus on form
foreigner talk
immersion
teacher talk

Appendix: L2 pedagogy

It has probably become clear that this chapter (and the field of second language acquisition research) is not directly concerned with second language *teaching*. Anyone interested in a catalog of approaches to language teaching could consult *Approaches and Methods in Language Teaching* by J. C. Richards and T. S. Rodgers (Cambridge: Cambridge University Press, 1986).

Historically, there have been a number of specific methods proposed as the best way to teach a language. There have been methods that emphasize physical activity (Total Physical Response), and methods that emphasize relaxed learning (Suggestopedia). Some methods encourage translation (Grammar-Translation) while others discourage it (Direct Method). There are approaches that encourage repetitive drilling (Audiolingualism) and others that discourage it (Communicative Language Teaching).

Recent trends in second language pedagogy have tended to downplay the idea that a single method of instruction will work for all people. As second language acquisition research identified the large number of ways in which second language learners can vary, it became evident that not everybody learns in the same way. Therefore, not everybody can be taught in the same way.

Currently, teachers tend to adopt an eclectic approach to second language instruction. What this means is that a variety of methods and approaches are utilized. A class may include some time for drilling and some time for physical activity (just to name two possibilities). The metaphor of multiple bridges may help to explain the rationale of this eclectic approach. If teachers want to get as many students as possible to a particular destination (call it proficiency), they have a better chance if there are multiple bridges (i.e., techniques) than if there is only one bridge (i.e., a single methodology).

The activities that make up a class will be determined by the needs and preferences of the learners, as well as by the experience and preferences of the teacher. Together they attempt to negotiate a program of instruction that is best-suited for all concerned.

Sources

The Ontogeny Model was proposed by R. Major in "A Model for Interlanguage Phonology" in *Interlanguage Phonology*, edited by G. Ioup and S. Weinberger (New York: Newbury House/Harper & Row, 1987), 101–24. The model of communicative competence is an adaptation of L. Bachman's *Fundamental Considerations in Language Testing* (Oxford: Oxford University Press, 1990). The Markedness Differential Hypothesis was developed by F. Eckman in "Markedness and the Contrastive Analysis Hypothesis," *Language Learning* 27 (1977): 315–30. The discussion of the Similarity Differential Rate Hypothesis comes from R. Major, "Further Evidence for the Similarity Differential Rate Hypothesis," in J. Leather and A. James, eds., *New Sounds 97* (Klagenfurt, Austria: University of Klagenfurt, 1997).

The data from Arabic syllabification come from E. Broselow, "Prosodic Phonology and the Acquisition of a Second Language," in S. Flynn and W. O'Neil, eds., *Linguistic Theory in Second Language Acquisition* (Dordrecht: Kluwer, 1988). The stress data were reported in J. Archibald, *Language Learnability and L2 Phonology* (Dordrecht: Kluwer, 1993). The null subject analysis is drawn from L. White, *Universal Grammar and Second Language Acquisition* (Amsterdam: John Benjamins, 1989). The verb movement study can be found in L. White, "Adverb Placement in Second Language Acquisition: Some Effects of Positive and Negative Evidence in the Classroom," *Second Language Research* 7 (1991): 133–61.

The L2 morphology data can be found in H. Zobl and J. Liceras, "Functional Categories and Acquisition Order," *Language Learning* 44:1 (1994): 159–80. The French gender information is discussed in S. Carroll, "Second-Language Acquisition and the Computational Paradigm," *Language Learning* 39:4 (1989): 535–94. The instrumental/integrative distinction comes from R. Gardner, J. B. Day, and P. D. MacIntyre,

"Integrative Motivation, Induced Anxiety and Language Learning in a Controlled Environment," *Studies in Second Language Acquisition* 14:2 (1992): 197–214.

The good language learner profile of Table 11.10 can be found in H. H. Stern, "What Can We Learn from the Good Language Learner?" *Canadian Modern Language Review* 34 (1975): 304–18, but see also J. Rubin, "What the 'Good Language Learner' Can Teach Us," *TESOL Quarterly* 9:1 (1975): 41–51, and R. Ellis, *Understanding Second Language Acquisition* (Oxford: Oxford University Press, 1986). The L2 classroom discussion owes much to R. Allwright and K. Bailey, *Focus on the Language Classroom: An Introduction to Classroom Research for Language Teachers* (Cambridge: Cambridge University Press, 1991). The evidence from focus on form was presented by P. Lightbown and N. Spada, "Focus-on-Form and Corrective Feedback in Communicative Language Teaching: Effects on Second Language Learning," *Studies in Second Language Acquisition* 12:4 (1990): 429–48. The discussion of focus-on-form draws on C. Doughty, "Cognitive Underpinnings of Focus on Form," in *Cognition and Second Language Instruction*, Cambridge Applied Linguistics Series (Cambridge: Cambridge University Press, forthcoming). Bilingual education and French immersion programs are discussed in J. Cummins and M. Swain, *Bilingual Education* (New York: Longman, 1986).

Recommended reading

Archibald, J., ed. 1999. *Second Language Acquisition and Linguistic Theory*. Oxford: Blackwell.

Cummins, J., and M. Swain. 1986. *Bilingual Education*. London: Longman.

Flynn, S., G. Martohardjono, and W. O'Neil, eds. 1998. *The Generative Study of Second Language Acquisition*. Mahwah, NJ: Lawrence Erlbaum.

Leather, J., and A. James. 1997. *New Sounds 97*. Klagenfurt, Austria: University of Klagenfurt.

Long, M., and D. Larsen-Freeman. 1991. *Second Language Acquisition Research*. London: Longman.

Sharwood Smith, M. 1994. *Second Language Learning: Theoretical Foundations*. London: Longman.

White, L. 1989. *Universal Grammar and Second Language Acquisition*. Philadelphia: John Benjamins.

Questions

1. Some dialects of Arabic break up clusters by inserting an epenthetic vowel to the *left* of an unsyllabified consonant (unlike the dialect discussed in this chapter). How would a speaker of this dialect pronounce the words *plant*, *transport*, and *translate*? Draw the necessary syllable structures.

2. The following is a sample of nonnative writing. The assignment was to write about whether you prefer to live in the city or the country. Look through the sample and "correct" the errors. Compare your corrected copy with that of

someone else in the class and see if you agree on the corrections. What are three or four problems this learner should work on?

> Are you among the number of people who have to choose their place to live? Whenever they have to move from another country, they even change the profession, they want to have a house outside the big city, or they can't find a place in Downtown.
>
> Its possible to move as well as you are supported by some essential condition of life I've mention in the following lines.
>
> Most of people are living in the Big city to have many of the opportunities that offer the Downtown lifestyle, jobs, studies, activities or whatever but nowadays for instance in [Toronto] its really difficult to find a place to live because the percentage of vacancy is slightly under 0% so many people are constrained to move on the suburb, by this way some of these get along this phenomene because they want to avoid the noise, the smog of the city and even they try to find their own place to live with garden and everything, actually to invest money to owe their house which is better than to rent an apartment in downtown, therefore they have to consider the transportation problem to reach the city even to have a car or use the public transportation.
>
> to have your own house outside the city required a great initial capital that you have to draft from any bank or you dispose in your account but afterwhat the house become your possession with the years and couple of more will increase the house value, although it is expensive furthermore it should be a great benefit for the owner even though he decided to rent the unoccupied room into the house.
>
> Moreless the frienship beetween the person in the subrub is closer they are ore contact with each other and maybe can meet themselves doing yardwork or other kind of activities belong to the suburb lifestyle.
>
> But in another [illegible] it should be difficult for the people who haven't ever lived in the suburb to move from th big city because they have to adapt their habits but they can fin amonst a great number of things that they use to have in the city. Otherwise during the last 15 years the business activites has developing around the city quickly in the North America also the supermarket company, manufacture and so on offered the job opportunity to the people outside the big aglomeration in that way it was created some apartments vacaint in the city.
>
> For me I don't even care where I have to live but I will observe which part could be the less expensive as well as transportation to reach my job but I will be sure that I'd like to live outside the downtown.

3. Given what you know about implicational universals, do you think it would be easier for an English speaker to acquire French nasal vowels (e.g., *gant* [gã], 'glove') or for French speakers to acquire English oral vowels? Explain your answer.

4. What explanation would you give for a native speaker of French who produced the English sentence *I drink frequently coffee*. How could you explain the fact that when the same speaker produces the sentence *He is frequently late*, it is grammatical? What other English verbs have the same properties as *be*?

5. Which of the following sentences would you classify as positive evidence and which as negative evidence for the learner:
   a) Nonnative Speaker (NNS): He study a lot.
      Native Speaker (NS): He *studies* a lot.
   b) NS: What kind of books do you like to read?
      NNS: Mysteries.
   c) NNS: I was born in Munich.
      NS: Pardon me?
   d) NNS: I goed to Washington on the weekend.
      NS: Remember that *go* has an irregular past.

6. Discuss why second language learners, regardless of their first language, might produce forms such as *goed, sheeps,* and *he felts,* given that they never hear these forms in input from native speakers of English. Give some other forms analogous to the above that might be generated.

7. What factors can you think of that might influence fossilization? In other words, do you think that some people are more likely to fossilize than others? Do you think it can be reversed? How?

8. Acquiring a second language involves both knowing something about the language and being able to do something with the language. Do you think that knowledge and skills are related? Can you see any trade-off between accuracy and fluency?

9. Why do you think that nonnative speakers of English would be more at risk of leaving the education system than native speakers?

10. Respond to the following statement:

    It's the school system's job to make sure that nonnative speakers of English learn English. They need English in order to be able to succeed in this country. We want them to succeed. If we encourage them to speak their own language, then ghettoes will form and they'll never learn English. And if we want them to learn English, then obviously they need to be exposed to more English. What good is it knowing how to speak another language in North America? What they need is English, English, and more English.

twelve

PSYCHOLINGUISTICS: THE STUDY OF LANGUAGE PROCESSING

Gary Libben

Leaving one still with the intolerable wrestle
With words and meanings

– T. S. ELIOT

OBJECTIVES

In this chapter, you will learn

- what methods psycholinguists use to study language processing
- how linguistic concepts and principles contribute to understanding language comprehension and production
- how psycholinguistic models are used to explain language processing

We engage in language processing almost every day of our lives. This processing takes place when we watch television, listen to the radio, read a passing billboard while driving, or discuss the weather. Usually these language activities are carried out with great ease and in a completely subconscious manner. We might sometimes be aware that we are searching for a word, composing a sentence, or straining to understand someone else, but we are never aware of the actual mechanisms and operations involved in producing and understanding language.

Psycholinguistics is the study of these language processing mechanisms. Psycholinguists study how word meaning, sentence meaning, and discourse meaning are computed and represented in the mind. They study how complex words and sentences are composed in speech and how they are broken down into their constituents in the acts of listening and reading. In short, psycholinguists seek to understand how language is done.

This chapter introduces the field of psycholinguistics by first discussing some methods used by psycholinguists to probe language representation and processing in the mind. This is followed by a summary of recent research on language processing in the domains of phonetics, phonology, morphology, and syntax. Finally, we will discuss how these various aspects of linguistic processing work together to make the everyday acts of speaking, listening, and reading appear so simple and effortless.

1 METHODS OF PSYCHOLINGUISTIC RESEARCH

As was noted, language users are not able to introspect on the details of language processing. Simply paying attention to what you are doing will not provide reliable insights into how you access words or build sentences. Perhaps the reason for this is that, in normal use, language processing must occur very quickly. By shielding mental linguistic operations from the conscious mind, it is possible that the language processing system is maximizing its ability to operate with speed and efficiency.

In order to get a sense of just how subconscious language processing is, you might try the following exercise: Give a friend a page of text to read silently and sit opposite him or her. Carefully observe your friend's eyes as they move across the text. You will notice that the eyes do not move smoothly from left to right but rather proceed in a series of jerks called **saccades**. Like most of us, your friend probably has the subjective impression that his or her eyes are moving very evenly across the page. But that subjective impression is incorrect. It seems that we are simply not constructed to be able to monitor many of our automatic activities, including language processing.

A substantial additional challenge for the psycholinguistic researcher is presented by the fact that most of language processing does not involve observable physical events such as eye movement, but rather involves mental events that cannot be observed directly. Research in this field therefore requires that mental language-processing events be inferred from observable behavior. Consequently, a large part of psycholinguistic research is concerned with the development of new (and often very clever) techniques to uncover how language processing is accomplished. Some of these techniques are presented in the following sections.

1.1 SLIPS OF THE TONGUE

Some of the earliest and most influential studies of language processing examined the spontaneous slips of the tongue produced during speech. Slips of the tongue are also known as **Spoonerisms**, after Reverend William A. Spooner who was head of New College Oxford between 1903 and 1924. Reverend Spooner was famous for producing a great many, often humorous, speech errors. Some of his more well-known mistakes are presented below.

1)

What he intended:	You have missed all my history lectures.
What he said:	You have hissed all my mystery lectures.

2)

What he intended: Noble sons of toil
What he said: Noble tons of soil

3)

What he intended: You have wasted the whole term.
What he said: You have tasted the whole worm.

4)

What he intended: The dear old Queen
What he said: The queer old dean

Beginning in the 1960s Victoria Fromkin began to study these and other naturally occurring slips of the tongue and noted that they can be very revealing of the manner in which sentences are created in speech. For instance, as can be seen in the examples, the characteristic pattern in Reverend Spooner's errors is a tendency to exchange the initial consonants of words in the utterance. When these segment exchanges create new words (as opposed to nonwords such as *fire and brimstone* → *bire and frimstone*), the result is often humorous. But here's the important psycholinguistic point: in order for these exchanges to occur, the entire sentence would have to be planned out before the person begins to say it. Otherwise, how would it be possible in example *1* for the first segment of the sixth word *history* to be transported backward so that it becomes the first segment of the third word (*missed* → *hissed*)?

Another important observation that Fromkin made was that speech errors also often involve "mixing and matching" morphemes within words. Consider the following slips of the tongue from Fromkin (1993):

5)

Intended: rules of word formation
Produced: words of rule formation

6)

Intended: I'd forgotten about that.
Produced: I'd forgot aboutten that.

7)

Intended: easily enough
Produced: easy enoughly

All these errors involve morphemes being exchanged within a sentence. As is the case for sound exchange errors, these slips of the tongue provide evidence that a sentence must be planned out before speech begins. They also provide evidence that the morpheme rather than the word is the fundamental building block of English sentence production. Note how in example *5*, although the nouns *rule* and *word* are exchanged in the sentence, the inflectional suffix *-s* remains in its original position. In examples *6* and *7*, it is the suffixes that move while the stems remain in their original positions. These examples all suggest that morphological components of words can function independently during sentence planning (and of course also in sentence misplanning).

As can be seen from these examples, slips of the tongue can offer a fascinating window to the mechanisms involved in language production and to the role that linguistic units such as phonemes and morphemes play in that production. But because slips of the tongue are naturally occurring events, the researcher has no control over when and where they will occur and must simply wait for them to happen. In this way, the analysis of slips of the tongue is a **field technique** and differs from the experimental paradigms discussed in the following sections. In these **experimental paradigms**, the researcher takes an active role in controlling the circumstances under which language is processed, the stimuli to which the experimental subjects are exposed, and the ways in which subjects may respond to these stimuli.

1.2 Experimental methods: words in the mind

One of the most intense areas of psycholinguistic research has been the investigation of how words are organized in the mind. We are all in possession of a vocabulary that forms the backbone of our ability to communicate in a language. In many ways, this vocabulary must be used as a normal dictionary is used. It is consulted to determine what words mean, how they are spelled, and what they sound like. But the dictionary in our minds—our mental lexicon—must also be substantially different from a desktop dictionary. It must be much more flexible, accommodating the new words that we learn with ease. It must be organized so that words can be looked up extremely quickly—word recognition takes less than one-third of a second and the average adult reads at a rate of about 250 words per minute. It must allow us to access entries in terms of a wide variety of characteristics. **Tip-of-the-tongue phenomena**, in which we are temporarily unable to access a word, are particularly revealing of how flexible access to the mental lexicon can be—we have all experienced episodes in which we eventually retrieve words on the basis of their meaning, sound, spelling, or first letter, or even what they rhyme with.

Many psycholinguists conceive of the mental lexicon as a collection of individual units, as in Figure 12.1. In this figure, the lexicon is shown as a space in which entries of different types are stored and linked together. The main questions that are asked about the mental lexicon are: (1) How are entries linked? (2) How are entries accessed? (3) What information is contained in an entry?

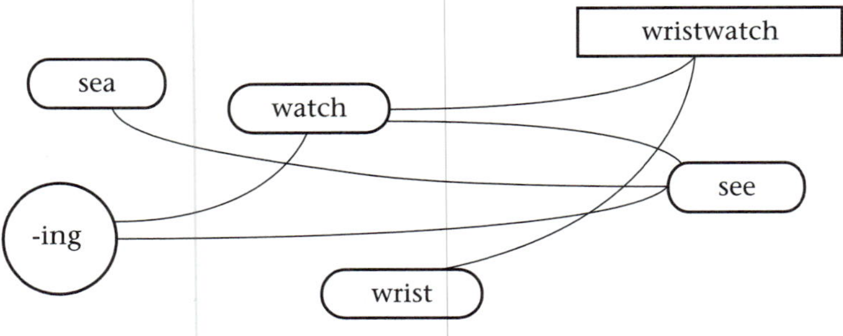

Figure 12.1 Units in the mental lexicon

Although these questions are simple and straightforward, there is no way to answer them directly because the human mental lexicon cannot be observed. So the psycholinguist must use special experimental methods to understand how words are organized, accessed, and represented in the mind. We will briefly discuss the two most common of these methods—**lexical decision** and **priming**.

Lexical decision

In the lexical decision paradigm, the experimental subject (in this example, a native speaker of English) is seated in front of a computer screen. A word appears in the middle of the screen and the subject must judge as quickly as possible whether or not the word is a real English word by pressing a button labeled "yes" or a button labeled "no" (see Figure 12.2).

Figure 12.2 A lexical decision experiment

This task is very easy for subjects to carry out. They typically see and judge hundreds of words in a single fifteen-minute lexical decision experiment. In most lexical decision experiments there are two **dependent variables**—that is, things that are being measured: (1) the time that it takes for a subject to respond (**response latency**) and (2) whether or not the subject's judgment is correct (**response accuracy**). A response is judged as correct if a subject responds "yes" to a real word such as *glove* or *sadness* and "no" to a nonword such as *blove* or *sadding*.

Lexical decision experiments usually involve comparing subjects' performance on one set of stimuli (e.g., nouns) to their performance on another set of stimuli (e.g., verbs). The key to the importance of the experimental paradigm is that in order for a subject to respond "no" to a stimulus such as *blove* or "yes" to a real word such as *glove*, the subject's mental lexicon must be accessed. The lexical decision task can therefore be used to measure the speed and accuracy with which words in the mental lexicon are accessed. It has been found in many experiments, for example, that subjects take about half a second (500 milliseconds) to press the "yes" button for frequently used words such as *free*, but almost three-quarters of a second to press the "yes" button for less common words such as *fret*. This finding has been called the **frequency effect**. Assuming that longer response times reflect processing that is more difficult or complex, this finding suggests that our mental dictionaries are organized so that words that we typically need more often (the frequent words) are more easily and quickly available to us.

Another way in which the lexical decision task can be used to explore language representation and processing is to investigate the speed and accuracy with which subjects press the "no" button for different types of stimuli. It has been found, for example, that pronounceable nonwords such as *plib* show slower "no" response times than unpronounceable nonwords such as *nlib*. Thus subjects' lexical decisions seem to take into account the phonotactic constraints of the language. It has also been found that nonwords that sound like real words (e.g., *blud*, *phocks*) take longer to reject than stimuli that are nonwords both visually and phonologically. Again this tells us that aspects of phonology are automatically activated during word reading (note that in the lexical decision task, the subject never has to pronounce the word).

The priming paradigm

The priming paradigm very often involves the lexical decision task and can be considered an extension of it. Recall that in lexical decision tasks different categories of stimuli (e.g., concrete versus abstract words) are compared in terms of subjects' response latency and accuracy. Priming experiments typically involve the same procedure as the lexical decision task except that the word to be judged (now called the **target**) is preceded by another stimulus (called the **prime**). What is measured is the extent to which the prime influences the subject's lexical decision performance on the target stimulus.

The priming paradigm is an excellent technique for probing how words are related in the mind. One of the first experiments using this paradigm showed that response time is faster when a target is preceded by a semantically related prime (e.g., *cat-dog*) as compared to when it is preceded by an unrelated prime (e.g., *cat-pen*). Results of this sort lead us to the view that words are related in the mind in terms of networks. On the basis of evidence from these priming experiments, psycholinguists reason that when a word such as *cat* is seen, its image is activated in the mind and that activation spreads to other words in the lexical network that are semantically related (e.g., *dog*). Now, because the mental representation for *dog* has already been activated through the prime, it is in a sense "warmed up" so that when the subject later sees it on the screen as the target, response time is faster than it otherwise would have been. This is called the **priming effect**.

In recent years, the priming paradigm has been used to explore many aspects of the representation of words in the mind, and researchers have explored many types of priming in addition to the semantic priming above. For example, priming effects have been found for orthographically related words (e.g., *couch-touch*), for phonologically related words (e.g., *light-bite*), and between word roots and complex forms (e.g., *legal-illegality*). This last finding suggests that words are represented in the mind in terms of their constituent morphemes, and will be discussed further in Section 2.2.

1.3 Experimental methods: sentence processing

The lexical decision and priming paradigms discussed above offer interesting insights into how words are processed, but are of limited use in exploring the processing of sentences. The main reason for this is that the types of questions asked about sentence processing tend to be different from those asked about the mental lexicon. The vast majority of the sentences that we hear are unique events. Therefore, sentence processing must fundamentally be a process that relies on a particular type of computation (as opposed to a particular type of storage in the case of words in the mind). It is presumed that in sentence processing (i.e., in reading or listening), a sentence is understood through the analysis of the meanings of its words and through the analysis of its syntactic structure. Psycholinguists refer to this type of unconscious automatic analysis as **parsing**. Much of the research on sentence processing is concerned with the principles and steps in sentence parsing, the speed of parsing, and the manner and conditions under which parsing can break down.

In this section, we review two groups of experimental paradigms that have been used extensively to study sentence processing. These are timed-reading experiments and eye-movement experiments.

Timed-reading experiments

Timed-reading experiments begin with the assumption that the more difficult sentence processing is, the longer it should take. Therefore, by timing how long it takes subjects to read particular sentence types or parts of sentences, we can study the determinants of sentence-processing difficulty.

One of the more common and revealing timed-reading experimental paradigms is the bar-pressing paradigm, in which subjects are seated in front of a computer screen and read a sentence one word at a time. The subject begins by seeing the first word of the sentence in the middle of the screen. When the subject presses a bar on the keyboard, the first word disappears and the second word of the sentence appears in its place. This process continues until the subject has read all the words in the sentence.

The dependent variable in these experiments is the amount of time it takes subjects to press the bar after seeing a particular word (i.e., the amount of time they need to process that word in the sentence).

Bar-pressing experiments can be very revealing of the manner in which sentence processing occurs. Subjects do not show equal bar-pressing times across a sentence, but rather a pattern that reflects the syntactic structure of the sentence. An example of such a pattern is shown in Figure 12.3, which displays bar-pressing times for the sentence *The Chinese, who used to produce kites, used them in order to carry ropes across the rivers.*

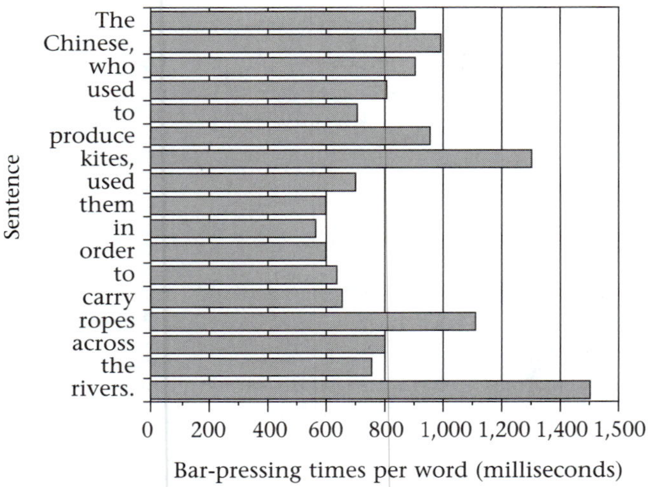

Figure 12.3 Bar-pressing times in sentence reading (adapted from Stine 1990)

As can be seen in Figure 12.3, subjects show longer bar-pressing times for processing content words such as nouns and verbs and relatively less time for function words such as determiners, conjunctions, and prepositions. What is particularly interesting is how subjects pause at the end of clause boundaries. This increased processing time is interpreted as reflecting the extra amount of time required to integrate preceding information into a complete clause structure. Thus the greatest bar-pressing time is required for *rivers*, the final noun in the sentence.

Eye-movement experiments

We have already noted that sentence reading involves a series of jerky eye movements called saccades. A number of events occur during these jerky movements. When the eyes are at rest, they take a "snapshot" of two or three words. These snapshots usually last from 200 to 250 milliseconds. While the snapshot is being taken, the language-processing system calculates where to jump to next. During a jump to the next fixation location (usually about eight letters to the right), the subject is essentially blind.

The details of eye movements in sentence reading are studied with sophisticated laboratory procedures in which a subject is seated in front of a computer screen on which text is displayed. A low-intensity infrared beam of light is bounced off the subject's eyeball and registered on a video camera. The image from the video camera is fed to a computer that calculates where on the screen the subject is currently fixating.

This technique has revealed that fixation times are typically longer for less-frequent words, and the points of fixation are typically centered on content words such as nouns and verbs rather than on function words such as determiners and conjunctions. Difficult sentence structures create longer fixation times as well as many more **regressive** (backward) **saccades**. Regressive saccades are backward jumps in a sentence and are usually associated with misparsing or miscomprehension. On average, backward saccades make up 10 to 15 percent of the saccades in sentence reading. But syntactically complex sentences and semantically anomalous sentences (e.g., *The pizza was too hot to drink*) create many more regressive saccades. It has also been found that poor readers jump back and forth through sentences much more often than good readers do.

1.4 Brain activity: event-related potentials

Perhaps the most exciting new technique to be used in psycholinguistic research is the study of **event-related potentials** (**ERPs**) produced by the brain during language processing. As a research technique, the ERP paradigm has the same basic advantage as eye-movement studies. The subject simply sits in front of a computer screen and reads. This is a relatively natural language-processing activity that, unlike lexical decision or bar pressing, is similar to what subjects do in normal language-processing situations.

ERP experiments measure electrical activity in the brain. Electrodes are placed on a subject's scalp and recordings are made of voltage fluctuations resulting from the brain's electrical activity. The difference between ERP recordings and the more familiar EEG recordings is that in the EEG, all the electrical activity of the brain is recorded. This electrical activity results from a very large number of continuous background brain activities. The advantage of the ERP approach is that it uses a computer to calculate what part of the electrical brain activity is related to a stimulus event (in our case words or sentences on a screen). This is done by a process of averaging. The computer records the instant at which a stimulus is presented and compares the voltage fluctuation immediately following the stimulus presentation to the random background "noise" of the ongoing EEG. By repeating this process many times with stimuli of a particular type, random voltage fluctuations are averaged out and the electrical potentials related to that stimulus type can be extracted. The resulting wave forms are called the event-related potentials.

The ERP pattern is typically depicted in a line graph, in which time is shown from left to right and voltage is shown on the vertical axis with negative values on top and positive values on the bottom. An example of an ERP graph is provided in Figure 12.4. This figure also displays one of the most interesting psycholinguistic findings using ERPs. It turns out that in the processing of sentences, the brain displays a characteristic ERP sign of surprise. Consider the following sentences:

8)

a. The pizza was too hot to eat.
b. The pizza was too hot to drink.
c. The pizza was too hot to cry.

The sentences in *8* are arranged in order of semantic plausibility. In the first case, the last word fits in perfectly well with the sentence and would typically be expected by the reader. As can be seen in Figure 12.4, the ERP for this sentence shows a positive voltage associated with the last word. In the case of *8b*, however, in which the last word does not make sense (people do not drink pizza), the ERP is much more negative. As is shown in the horizontal axis, this negative spike occurs 400 milliseconds after the onset of the word. For this reason, this signal of semantic anomaly is called the N400 (negative spike at 400 milliseconds after stimulus presentation). Note how the N400 is even stronger in the case of sentence *8c,* which is less congruent with the sentence context (*drink* is at least associated with food).

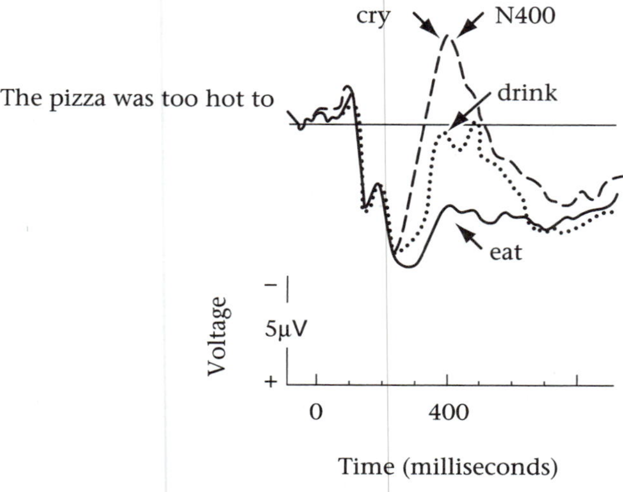

Figure 12.4 ERPs elicited by sentence-final words that are congruent, incongruent, and very incongruent with the sentence context

The N400 effect can be obtained not only at the ends of sentences but in any sentence position. This fact suggests that sentence processing is immediate and on-line. When reading a sentence, we do not wait until the entire string is complete but rather constantly build interpretations of the sentence as it unfolds. Whenever what we see or hear contradicts our expectations based on our ongoing interpretative processes, an N400 ERP spike is observed.

2 LANGUAGE PROCESSING AND LINGUISTICS

In the preceding sections we discussed some of the methods that psycholinguists use to investigate the manner in which language is processed. One of the most important results of such psycholinguistic investigations has been that many of the concepts and principles used by linguists to describe and understand the structure of language in terms of phonetics, phonology, morphology, and syntax have been found to also play an important role in the understanding of how language is produced and comprehended during activities such as speaking, listening, reading, and writing. In this section we will focus on these points of contact between theoretical linguistics and psycholinguistics. In doing so, we will also highlight the correspondence between the study of language processing and the concepts discussed in Chapters 1 through 5 of this book.

2.1 Phonetics and phonology

The study of phonetics and phonology reveals that the sound system of language is richly structured and contains different levels of representation. Thus, as is discussed in Chapters 2 and 3, individual segments can be characterized in terms of place and manner of articulation or with respect to a matrix of phonological features. Sequences of sounds can be grouped into syllabic structures, and allophonic variation can be described in terms of underlying phonemes and surface allophones. How much of this structure plays a role in language processing? The simple answer to this question is: "All of it!" The more complex and more accurate answer is that language processing shows evidence that features, phonemes, and syllable structure all capture some aspects of the way in which we process language, but that speech production and perception are complex activities that involve much more than these phonetic and phonological representations.

To see why this is the case, consider what might occur when you hear the sentence *The dog bit the cat.* Because the utterance unfolds in time, you will first hear the segment /ð/ and then the segment /ə/. (In fact, you do not hear these segments separately but rather you create them out of a continuous sound stream.) As soon as these segments are identified, you have already accessed the representation for the word *the* in your mental lexicon. When the next segment comes up in the sound stream, you already know that it is the beginning of a new word and you also know that this word must be a noun or an adjective. The phonetic analysis that follows identifies the segments *d-o-g* and the corresponding lexical entry. Now come the first segments of the word *bit.* In principle the first two phonemes /bɪ/ could be the first two segments of the word *believe,* but you are not likely to consider this possibility because your developing interpretation of the sentence is biasing you toward the word *bit,* which is associated in your mind with *dog.*

As can be appreciated from this example, language processing involves the interplay of information that develops simultaneously at many different levels of analysis. The person hearing the sentence *The dog bit the cat* is performing a phonetic analysis to isolate phonemes and word boundaries and to relate these to representations in the mental lexicon. This inductive analysis is referred to as **bottom-up processing**. But we do not wait until we have analyzed all the phonemes in a sentence before we begin to try to understand it. Rather, we begin interpretation of a sentence spontaneously and automatically on the basis of whatever information is available to us. For this reason, by the time we get to the word *bit* in the sentence, we are not only recognizing it using bottom-up processing but are also employing a set of expectations to guide phonetic processing and word recognition. This is called **top-down processing**. In normal language use we are always engaged in both bottom-up and top-down activities. We never just process features or phonemes or syllables. We process language for the purposes of understanding each other.

In Section 3 of this chapter we will discuss how phonetic and phonological analysis fits into other processes involved in speaking and listening. For now, however, we will concentrate on three levels of linguistic structure that seem fundamental to phonetic and phonological representation: features, phonemes, and syllables.

Features

In both linguistics and psycholinguistics, the term *feature* is used to refer to the most basic level of representation. It is therefore always associated with bottom-up processing in language. In the processing of sound, it refers to characteristics of individual phonemes (e.g., ± voice, ± continuant, etc.). The most straightforward evidence concerning the role of such features comes from the analysis of slips of the tongue. Some examples of these slips are presented in Table 12.1.

Table 12.1 The role of features in speech errors

	Intended	*Actually produced*
a)	big and fat	pig and vat
b)	Is Pat a girl?	Is bat a curl?
c)	Cedars of Lebanon	Cedars of Lemmanon

The errors in Table 12.1 follow a pattern, but that pattern can only be understood with reference to a system of phonological features. In all three examples in this table, the errors involve a phonological feature. In example *a* the feature [voice] has been exchanged between the words *big* and *fat* to create the new words *pig* and *vat* (note that /b-p/ and /f-v/ only differ in the feature [voice]).

This same pattern of voice feature exchange can be seen in example *b*, where *Pat* becomes *bat* and *girl* becomes *curl*. Finally, the error in *c* is particularly intriguing because we normally think of /b/ and /m/ as completely different phonemes. In fact, however, they are both voiced bilabial stops that only differ in terms of the feature ± nasal. Changing the /b/ in *Lebanon* from [–nasal] to [+nasal] creates the error *Lemmanon*. These examples offer evidence that language production makes use of the individual feature components of phonemes and that the phonemes that we produce in speech may actually be put together "on the fly" out of bundles of such features.

Phonemes

We have seen in Section 1.1 that Spoonerisms show evidence of entire phonemes being misplaced during sentence planning. The phonemic unit of representation also plays a central role in psycholinguistic models of speech processing such as the **cohort model**, proposed by William Marslen-Wilson. This model states that in word comprehension, words are analyzed by hearers from beginning to end. So, for example, when we hear the word *glass*, we initially consider all the words that begin with the sound [g]. When the next sound [l] is recognized, the number of possible words (the **cohort**) is reduced to those words that begin with [gl]. This process continues until the cohort of possible words is reduced to one—the word that is being recognized. In a number of experiments, Marslen-Wilson investigated whether this beginning-to-end analysis of spoken words proceeds one phoneme at a time, one cluster at a time, or one syllable at a time. He and his colleagues found that the phoneme seems to be the fundamental unit of auditory word recognition.

Syllables

Although in the cohort model the phoneme rather than the syllable seems to be the fundamental unit of auditory word recognition, there is other evidence that the syllable plays an important role in speech perception. In one study, subjects were presented with disyllabic words (e.g., *bullet*) and disyllabic nonwords (e.g., *sullet*) and were asked to press a button if a particular target unit was in the stimulus. The target units were either syllables (e.g., *let*) or segments (e.g., *t*). It was found for both words and nonwords that subjects were significantly faster at identifying syllable targets than at identifying single segment targets. It was concluded that syllable identification was faster because in normal auditory analysis, subjects break down stimuli first into syllables and then into individual segments, as the situation demands.

Another source of evidence on the role of the syllable in language processing comes from observing subjects' performance on word-blending tasks. In such a task, subjects are given two words such as *bug* and *cat* and are required to blend the words together to make a new word. Now, what sounds better: (*bug* + *cat* = *bat*) or (*bug* + *cat* = *but*)? The difference between these two possibilities is that the first one takes the onset of the first syllable and combines it with the rhyme of the second syllable. The other possibility does not split the words in a natural point of English syllable structure. As you might expect, subjects are much better at creating word blends that correspond to the syllable structure of their language and prefer such blends when presented with a choice. The fact that English speakers find such onset-rhyme divisions

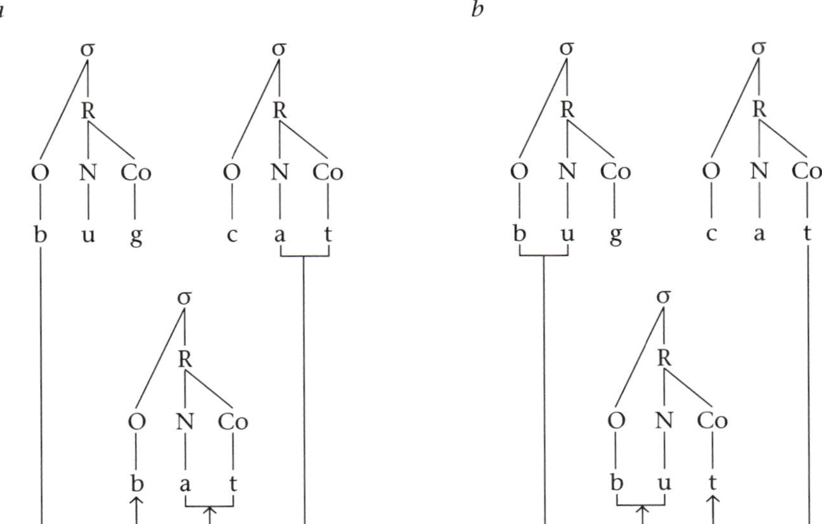

Figure 12.5 Speakers of English find the word blend in *a* easier and more natural than the word blend in *b* because *a* involves breaking the words at natural syllable-structure boundaries.

easier and more natural suggests that the sound of words is represented in speakers' minds in terms of their syllables and syllable constituents (e.g., onset and rhyme).

2.2 Morphological processing

Morphology is the study of word structure. It seeks to characterize the system of categories and rules involved in word formation and interpretation. The psycholinguistic study of morphological processing seeks to understand how this word structure plays a role in language processing. In the following sections, we will summarize some psycholinguistic research that reveals how morphological structures and principles play a substantial role in the representation of words in the mind and in word recognition.

Morpheme activation

Words such as *blackboard*, *happiness*, and *watching* are made up of two morphemes. In the case of the compound *blackboard*, both of the morphemes are roots. In the case of *happiness*, one morpheme is a root and the other is a derivational suffix. Finally, in the case of *watching*, one morpheme is a root and the other is an inflectional affix. The first question we will address is whether the individual morphological components of words play a role in processing.

The answer to this question seems to be a straightforward yes. For most multimorphemic words, individual morphemes are automatically activated during word recognition. One source of evidence for this conclusion comes from priming experiments in which it is found that words like *happiness* will prime their constituents and vice versa in a lexical decision experiment. In other words, when a subject is exposed to a multimorphemic word such as *happiness*, the activation of that word in the mind automatically activates the lexical entry for its root *happy*, which results in its showing a faster response time as the target in a lexical decision task.

Another source of evidence for this view comes from semantic priming lexical decision experiments with compounds in which it is found that presentation of a compound such as *crowbar* will produce a priming effect for the subsequent lexical decision time for a word such as *bird*. For this priming effect to take place, the morpheme *crow* would have to be individually activated during word recognition because as a whole, the compound *crowbar* has nothing to do with birds.

Selectional restrictions

As discussed in Chapter 4, one of the properties of English morphology is that not all affixes can attach to all stems. For example, the suffix *-ize* attaches to adjectives or nouns to form verbs; for this reason, English morphological constraints would not allow a word such as **understandize* because *understand* is already a verb. Now the question for psycholinguistic research is: Do these formal restrictions play a role in the way in which native speakers of English process new words?

In a recent experiment in morphological processing, subjects were presented with nonsense roots (e.g., *birm*) that had prefixes and suffixes attached to them. Because they contained nonsense roots, none of these words made much sense (e.g., *re-birmable*, *re-birmize*, *re-birmity*). But notice that as is shown in Figure 12.6, *re-birmable*

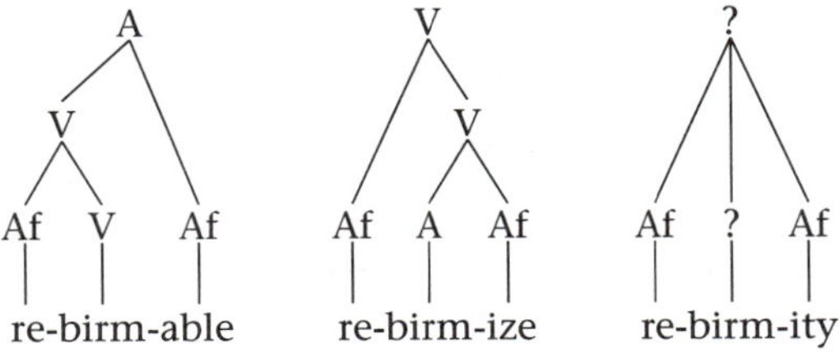

Figure 12.6 Morphologically legal and illegal affixed nonsense roots

and *re-birmize* are morphologically legal whereas *re-birmity* violates a morphological constraint—the prefix *re-* must attach to a verb and the suffix *-ity* must attach to a noun. The construction is illegal because the nonsense root *birm* cannot be both at the same time. In experiments with these sorts of stimuli, it was found that processing times were significantly longer for the illegal nonsense words than for the morphologically legal words. These results suggest that knowledge of the selectional restrictions of affixes does indeed form part of the word-processing system.

Hierarchical structure

In Figure 12.6, trimorphemic words are represented in terms of a tree diagram in which constituent morphemes are arranged in a hierarchy. The last question we will consider in our discussion of morphological processing is whether there is evidence that the representation of multimorphemic words in the mind includes a representation of hierarchical structure.

This question has been investigated in priming experiments that use lexical decision response times as the dependent variable. These experiments compare stimuli such as *refillable*, which have a structure in which the left branch is complex, to stimuli such as *unbearable*, which have a structure in which the right branch is complex (see Figure 12.7). This means that for the word *refillable*, the substring *fillable* is not a morphological component of the tree structure (even though it is a real word of English). However, because the word *unbearable* is right-branching, its final two morphemes (*bear* and *-able*) make up a component of the morphological tree.

In the priming experiments, subjects were first shown the right substrings such as *fillable* and then the full trimorphemic word (e.g., *refillable*). Priming effects were measured in terms of the lexical decision response times for the full word. It was found that those substrings that were real morphological constituents produced a significantly larger priming effect than those that were not.

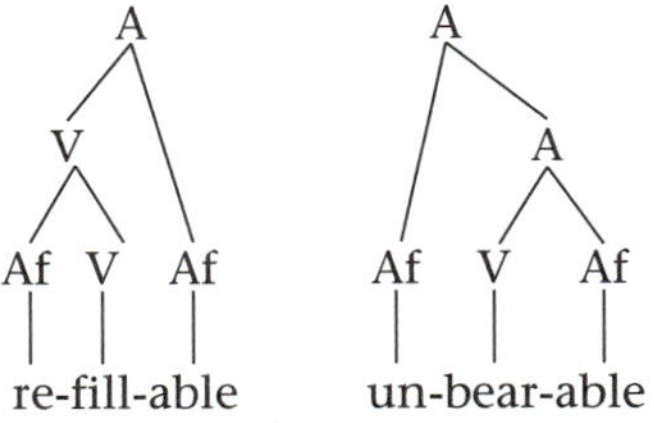

Figure 12.7 Complex words with different structures

Note that if hierarchical structure were not part of the representation of multimorphemic words in the mind—that is, if these words were simply strings of morphemes (e.g., *re + fill + able*)—there would be no difference between the priming effects for stimuli in which the left branch is complex versus those in which the right branch is complex. The fact that such priming effects were observed is evidence that our representation of complex words is organized in terms of hierarchical morphological structure.

2.3 Syntax

Syntax is the system of rules and categories that underlies sentence formation in human language. One of the fundamental insights in the study of syntax is that sentences are unique events. That means that virtually all of the sentences that you read in this chapter are sentences that you have never encountered before. They are typically made up of familiar words, but the arrangement of those words into a syntactic structure is unique to each sentence. The question that we will consider in this section is: How are these syntactic structures created during sentence processing?

The syntax module

One very simple possibility for how sentences are processed is that production and comprehension employ the system of rules that are used by syntacticians to describe sentence structure. This possibility suggests that speakers would begin with deep structure representations and employ a series of transformations to derive the surface structure characteristics of a sentence. Many psycholinguistic experiments examined this possibility by testing, for example, whether sentences with many transformations take longer to process than sentences with fewer transformations. It turned out that the number of transformations in a sentence did not predict processing time. Researchers concluded that there is at least some difference between the rules that native speakers use to generate and comprehend sentences and the rules that linguists use to characterize the linguistic knowledge of native speakers. It was therefore necessary to postulate a special module for sentence processing and another for grammatical knowledge. This processing module is called the **syntactic parser**.

The parser is understood to be the system that makes use of grammatical knowledge but also contains special procedures and principles that guide the order in which elements of a sentence are processed and the manner in which syntactic structure is built up. Because our parsing ability is based on our grammatical knowledge of our language, it is usually the case that there is a close correspondence between sentence parsing and grammatical structure. However, because the parsing module has its own set of principles, sentences that are grammatically complex are not necessarily difficult to parse and some sentences with relatively simple syntactic structure can create substantial parsing problems.

It should be noted that in discussing how processing takes place, the term **module** has a special meaning. It refers to a unit of processing that is relatively autonomous from other processing units. The idea of processing modules has been very important and controversial in many domains of human information processing. To get a sense of how processing may involve the coordination of separate modules, consider what occurs when you watch a movie. The movie director, in order to obtain a variety of effects, relies on processing modularity. The director knows that in watching an adventure film, your stomach will take a dip when the airplane on the screen goes into a dive or when the canoe goes over the falls. He or she knows that you cannot stop this from happening even though you are aware that you are sitting in a chair that is not moving. Similarly, you will be frightened by the sudden appearance of a monster, even though you know that you are really in no danger. All these effects result from processing modularity. The bottom-up information that comes from processing modules cannot be turned off by the top-down information that you are seated in a stationary and safe movie-theater environment.

A variety of psycholinguistic studies have investigated whether this same sort of modularity is present in syntactic processing. In other words, they look at whether syntactic parsing operates in an automatic and obligatory manner that is relatively independent of the activity of other processing systems. Two sources of evidence have been very important in the exploration of the principles of modularity of sentence processing. These are garden path sentences and sentence ambiguity, which are discussed below.

Garden path sentences

Some sentences are extraordinarily difficult to understand even though they are not very complex syntactically. These sentences are called **garden path sentences** because they lead the syntactic parser down the garden path to the wrong analysis. Perhaps the most famous garden path sentence is the one given in *9* below.

9)

The horse raced past the barn fell.

This sentence is perfectly grammatical, but almost impossible to understand. The reason for this is that as we read the sentence, we build up a syntactic structure in which *the horse* is the subject of the sentence and *raced past the barn* is the main VP. When we get to the word *fell*, we are surprised because the sentence we have built up has no room for an extra VP. The correct interpretation for the sentence requires that *fell* be the head of the main VP and that *raced past the barn* be a clause that attaches to the NP *the horse* (see Figure 12.8).

The ways in which native speakers misunderstand garden path sentences reveal how the parser might work. It seems that we construct syntactic representations

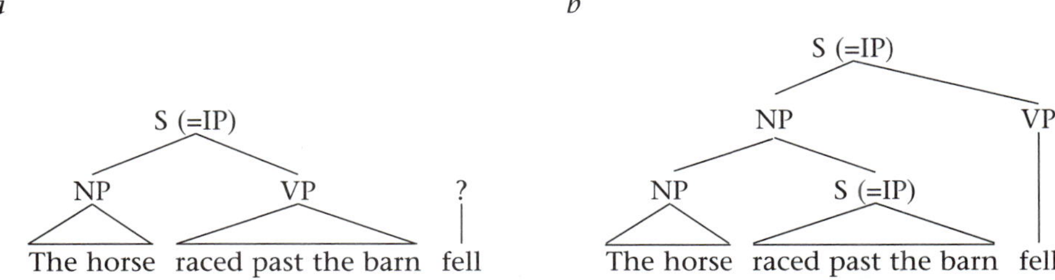

Figure 12.8 A garden path sentence. The garden path effect is shown in *a*. The correct interpretation is represented in *b*.

from the beginning of the sentences to the end and that our sentence parsers are organized so that we make a number of assumptions about how a sentence will proceed. This can be seen by considering the garden path sentence in *10*.

10)

Since Jay always walks a mile seems like a short distance to him.

This sentence is not as difficult to process as the sentence in *9*, but you probably noticed yourself having to backtrack after an initial misanalysis. Your parser is inclined to build a single VP out of the string *walks a mile*, when in fact they belong to different clauses. This tendency has been extensively studied by psycholinguists. The backtracking that you might have noticed in your own reading shows up significantly in eye-movement studies in which it is found that subjects show more regressive saccades for these sentences as well as longer fixation times.

It has been claimed by Lynn Frazier and her colleagues that the garden path effect results from two principles of parsing. These are **minimal attachment** and **late closure**. The principle of minimal attachment states that we do not postulate new syntactic nodes (like the extra embedded S in Figure 12.8b) unless it is clear that we absolutely have to. The principle of late closure states that we prefer to attach new words to the clause currently being processed as we proceed through a sentence from beginning to end. The result of late closure can be discerned in sentence *10*, where we are inclined to add the NP *a mile* to the VP headed by *walk* rather than beginning a new clause.

There is one last point to be made concerning what garden path sentences can tell us about how people process sentences. Try reading the sentence in *10* again. You should find that although you now know the correct analysis for the sentence, you misread it the second time just as you did the first time. This suggests that the parsing system is in fact a module that operates automatically and independently.

Sentence ambiguity

Another important clue to how syntactic processing is accomplished comes from the study of **sentence ambiguity**. Consider the sentence in *11*.

11)

They all rose.

In fact the last word in *11* is ambiguous. The word *rose* can either be related to *stand* or be related to *flower*. However, the sentence context leads us clearly to favor the *stand* version of the word. Does the sentence context therefore inhibit activation of the other meaning of *rose*? This question was investigated in a lexical decision experiment in which the sentence in *11* served as the prime. After seeing the sentence, subjects were presented with either the word *flower* or the word *stand*. The researchers found that the sentence facilitated lexical decision response times to both words. That is, both meanings for the word *rose* in the sentence were activated, even though the sentence clearly presented a bias in favor of one reading over the other.

This experimental finding is one of many that reveal a fundamental property of human language processing. We create all representations possible and then discard the ones that are either incorrect or unnecessary. This last characteristic was found in a follow-up priming experiment that was identical to the one just described except that there was a pause of several hundred milliseconds between the prime and the target. When the pause was present, the priming effect disappeared for the meaning that was unrelated to the sentence context (i.e., *flower*). This suggests that, in fact, sentence processing proceeds in two stages. In the first stage, all possible representations and structures are computed. In the second stage, one of these structures is selected and all others are abandoned. Of course all this happens very quickly and subconsciously so that we as native speakers of a language are never aware that for a sentence such as *12*, we compute two possible interpretations.

12)

The tuna can hit the boat.

In reading this sentence, you either ended up imagining:

a. tuna meat that is packed in a small round can

b. a large fish swimming toward a boat

The point of the psycholinguistic experiments just described is this: no matter which interpretation you arrived at (*a* or *b*), you probably considered both of them, chose one, discarded the other, and forgot about the whole thing in less than a second.

3 PUTTING IT ALL TOGETHER: PSYCHOLINGUISTIC MODELING

Up to this point, our discussion of psycholinguistic research has been restricted to examining characteristics of phonetic, phonological, morphological, and syntactic processing and the relation between the concepts used in theoretical linguistics and in psycholinguistics. It is important to note, however, that research in language processing seeks to discover not only which types of representations play a role in language processing but also how these representations and processes fit together to make activities such as speaking, listening, reading, and writing possible.

Psycholinguistic researchers present their ideas of how "language is done" in terms of models. A **psycholinguistic model** incorporates the results of experiments into a proposal of how processing takes place. In other words, it is a statement of what happens when.

Suppose, for example, we wished to present the finding discussed in Section 2.3 that a sentence such as *They all rose* will prime both *flower* and *stand*. The model might look like Figure 12.9.

For our present purposes, it is not important whether this model is actually correct. The purpose of the model is simply to illustrate how psycholinguistic statements can be represented. This model, which looks very much like a computer flow chart, shows that when processing a sentence such as *They all rose*, we first perform phonological analysis. This is followed by lexical access, in which all words with

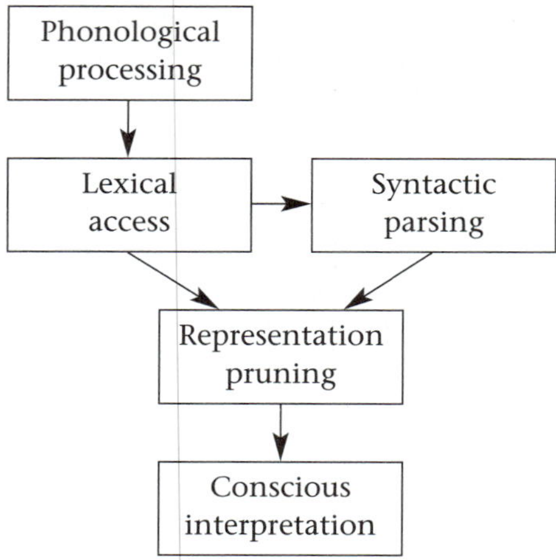

Figure 12.9 A serial psycholinguistic model of sentence processing

matching phonological representations are accessed (including the two words *rose*). Information from lexical access "feeds" the syntactic parsing module, and information from both the lexical access module and the parsing module are fed to the representation pruning module (the module that discards multiple representations). Finally, the model states that interpretation only becomes conscious in the final stage of analysis and that there is only one-way information flow to conscious interpretation (in other words, the conscious mind cannot "peek" at how things are going).

You will note that in creating this model, we have taken two kinds of shortcuts. First, we have created a novel name (representation pruning) to describe an operation that has been deduced from the results of psycholinguistic experimentation. Second, our model uses the box notation as a shorthand for a constellation of processes. Thus, it is understood that as the model becomes more elaborate, each one of the boxes in Figure 12.9 would be expanded into a flow chart of its own.

As you inspect the model in Figure 12.9 you should find that it is really very inadequate. It is missing much important detail, it seems to characterize only one aspect of sentence processing, and it avoids any mention of how meaning is accessed or how sentence interpretation actually takes place. In other words, to be a model of any real value, it would have to be much more elaborate.

Indeed, the types of psycholinguistic models that have been proposed in recent years are very elaborate. This is a good thing. We want models to be as detailed and comprehensive as possible, to take a great deal of experimentation into account, and, perhaps most importantly, to show how linguistic and nonlinguistic operations work together in the processing of language.

3.1 The use of metaphors in psycholinguistic modeling

Perhaps the most important characteristic of the model presented in Figure 12.9 is the fact that it obviously could not reflect what really happens in the mind of a language user. It is exceedingly unlikely that our minds possess boxes and arrows (or their equivalents). This model, like all psycholinguistic models, employs metaphors for language representations and language processing. The value of these metaphors is that they allow researchers to make specific claims about how language processing works, which can then be tested. For example, through its architecture, the model in Figure 12.9 claims that phonological processing precedes lexical access, which in turn precedes syntactic processing. This claim can easily be tested in an experiment that investigates whether all phonological processing is complete before syntactic processing begins.

We see then that psycholinguistic models have dual functions. They summarize specific research findings and generate specific hypotheses. They also have the very important function of embodying general perspectives on how language processing works. This is again accomplished through the use of metaphors. These metaphors have the effect of shaping how we conceive of language in the mind and what kinds of questions are asked by psycholinguistic researchers. Finally, these metaphors provide the means by which major families of models can be contrasted in order to test which most accurately describes language processing. In the following sections, we review three of the most important current contrasts in psycholinguistic modeling: serial versus parallel processing models; single-route versus dual-route models; and, finally, symbolic versus connectionist models.

Serial versus parallel processing models

Let us return to Figure 12.9. By employing the metaphor of a computer program that operates sequentially, the **serial processing model** in Figure 12.9 not only makes a claim about sentence processing but also claims that language processing proceeds in a step-by-step manner. In contrast, a **parallel processing model** would claim that phonological, lexical, and syntactic processes are carried out simultaneously. Figure 12.10 represents an example of a parallel processing model. Here information does not flow in a sequential manner. Rather, all modules operate simultaneously and share information. The model in Figure 12.10 claims, therefore, that when we hear a sentence, we begin phonological, lexical, and syntactic processes at the same time. As each type of processing proceeds, it informs the other.

In recent research, serial and parallel processing models have been central to our ability to understand the extent to which bottom-up and top-down processing interact. Serial models correctly characterize those aspects of language processing that are

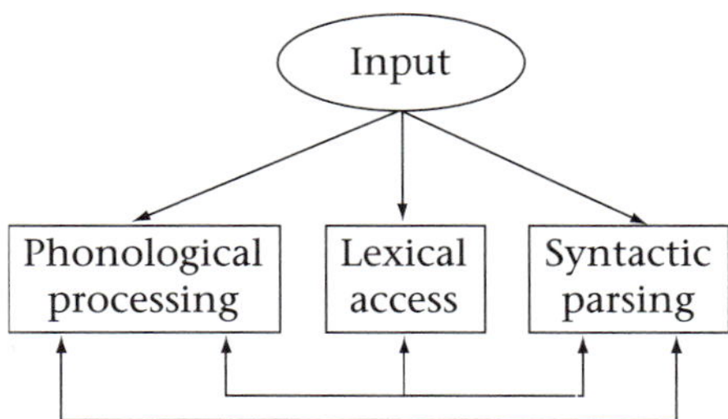

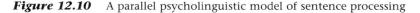

Figure 12.10 A parallel psycholinguistic model of sentence processing

modular and are driven by strict bottom-up procedures. Parallel processing models, on the other hand, are more effective than serial models at characterizing complex processes such as sentence comprehension.

Single-route versus dual-route models

Put most directly, **single-route models** claim that a particular type of language processing is accomplished in one manner only. Dual-route models, on the other hand, claim that a language-processing task is accomplished through (usually two) competing mechanisms. Consider, for example, the task of reading English words. Here there are three possibilities: (1) we always read a word by looking it up in our mental lexicon directly based on its visual characteristics; (2) we convert a visual input into a phonological representation first, and this phonological representation becomes the basis for comprehension; and (3) we do both at the same time. Options (1) and (2) represent single-route models in the sense that they claim that reading is accomplished in one way. Option (3), which is represented in Figure 12.11, represents a **dual-route model** in that it claims that both mechanisms are employed. Usually such dual-route models employ the additional metaphor of a horse race by claiming that for some words (e.g., very frequent short words), the direct route is faster, but for others (e.g., rare words), the phonological conversion route is faster and "wins the horse race."

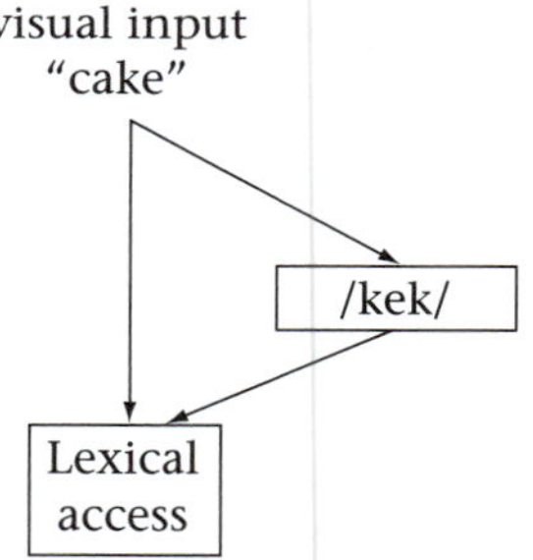

Figure 12.11 A dual-route model of word reading

In recent psycholinguistic investigations, the dual-route model has been very influential in modeling, whether multimorphemic words are decomposed into their constituent morphemes during word recognition or are accessed as whole words. It has been found that although both procedures are active all the time, the whole-word recognition route wins the race for frequent bimorphemic words such as *blackboard*. However, in the case of less frequent words such as *breadboard* or novel multimorphemic forms such as *blueboard*, the morphological decomposition route is the one that provides the basis for comprehension.

Symbolic versus connectionist models

The final modeling contrast that we review in this section is the contrast between symbolic and connectionist models. These types of models represent fundamentally different views about the nature of mental representations. **Symbolic models** (which include all the ones we have discussed so far) claim that models of linguistic knowledge must make reference to rules and representations consisting of symbols, such as phonemes, words, syntactic category labels, and so forth. **Connectionist models**, on the other hand, claim that the mind can best be modeled by reference to large associations of very simple units (often called **nodes**), which more closely approximate the kinds of processing units (i.e., neurons) that we know the brain to be composed of. Connectionist models do not typically contain direct representations for language units such as words, but rather represent these as an association of nodes. This difference is exemplified in Figure 12.12.

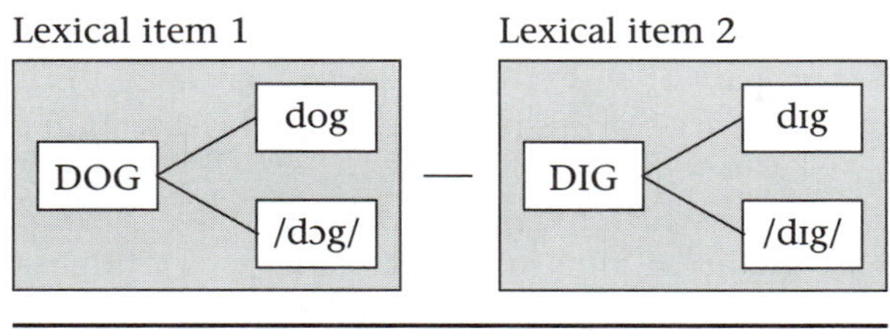

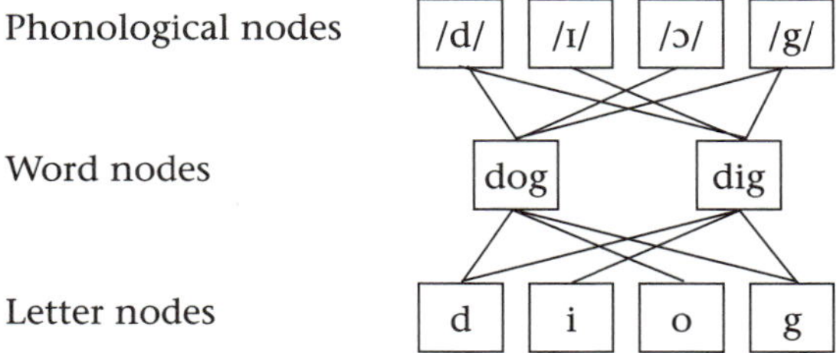

Figure 12.12 Symbolic versus connectionist representations of the words *dog* and *dig* in the mind

In one sense, the two kinds of representations in Figure 12.12 represent exactly the same information—namely the phonological and graphemic makeup of the words *dog* and *dig*. In another sense, however, they are very different. The connectionist representation shows words as having "reality" only in the sense that they are bundles of associations between phonological and graphemic nodes. (In some connectionist approaches, the word *nodes* would not exist at all.) In the symbolic representation, on the other hand, words do indeed have discrete representations in the mind and each representation contains information regarding the word's sound and spelling.

3.2 Which model is right?

Almost certainly, none of the models that we have discussed is correct. All models represent a researcher's claim about the most current version of the truth. Because psycholinguistics is a very young field, we can expect that any "current version of the truth" will be very far from the real truth (if there is one). Perhaps this is the reason that psycholinguistic models are so important. They give us the vocabulary with which to ask major questions about mental processing. For example, do our representations consist of symbols corresponding to phonemes, words, and phrases, or are mental representations distributed over a large number of nodes? Does the mind settle into a best way to perform a task, or are all processes horse races between alternative ways to solve a problem? Do mental operations proceed in a step-by-step manner?

These are all big questions and big issues, and language research is at the center of them. The more we investigate the details of language processing, the more we realize that it offers the best clues to the secrets of human cognition and the more we appreciate how well guarded those secrets are. In the past quarter-century of psycholinguistic research, we have learned a great deal about language representation and processing. In the first part of this chapter, we concentrated on the research techniques that have made these advances possible. In this final section of the chapter, we have focused on the yet unresolved major issues. Although we do not yet know which models are right or which hybrids will be most effective in our evolving understanding of human cognition, one thing is certain: psycholinguistic research has been and will continue to be critical to that understanding.

Summing up

Psycholinguistics is the study of language processing. The field is defined both by an area of subject matter and a particular methodology. Psycholinguists study how people perform the functions of language comprehension and production. They seek to discover the nature of the mental representations that serve these functions and the nature of the cognitive operations and computations that are employed when we understand and produce language.

Because language processing involves computations and representations that cannot be observed and measured directly, psycholinguists have devised special experimental techniques to investigate language processing. Some of these techniques, such as **lexical decision** and **priming**, measure a subject's response time and response accuracy to linguistic stimuli. Other techniques measure eye movement while subjects are reading silently, and still others measure electrical activity in the brain during language processing.

Language processing involves many processing modules that are specialized for a particular language processing task and interact with other modules in restricted ways. Thus, language processing involves a constant interplay between **bottom-up** and **top-down processing**. We process phonetic features, phonemes, and words all at the same time. We construct syllable representations, morphological representations, and syntactic representations in a spontaneous and obligatory manner. As conscious beings we are aware of the results of our processing but not of the processing itself.

In general, psycholinguistic studies have revealed that many of the concepts employed in the analysis of sound structure, word structure, and sentence structure also play a role in language processing. However, an account of language processing also requires that we understand how these linguistic concepts interact with other aspects of human processing to enable language production and comprehension.

Psycholinguists typically present their views of how language production and comprehension are achieved in terms of processing models. These models are at the heart of research in psycholinguistics and allow researchers to express the significance of particular research findings, to predict the outcomes of future experiments, and to debate the fundamental characteristics of human cognition.

Key terms

General terms and terms concerning psycholinguistic methods

dependent variables
event-related potentials (ERPs)
experimental paradigms
field technique
frequency effect
lexical decision
parsing
prime
priming
priming effect
psycholinguistics
regressive saccades
response accuracy
response latency
saccades
Spoonerisms
target
tip-of-the-tongue phenomena

Terms concerning language processing

bottom-up processing
cohort
cohort model
garden path sentences
late closure
minimal attachment
module
sentence ambiguity
syntactic parser
top-down processing

Terms related to psycholinguistic models

connectionist models
dual-route model
nodes
parallel processing model
psycholinguistic model
serial processing model
single-route models
symbolic models

Sources

In recent years, many new books on psycholinguistics have appeared. These include *Psycholinguistics* by Joseph Kess (Philadelphia: John Benjamins, 1992) and *Psycholinguistics* by Jean Berko-Gleason and Nan Bernstein Ratner (Philadelphia: Harcourt Brace, 1993). Another excellent source is the *Handbook of Psycholinguistics*, edited by Morton Ann Gernsbacher (New York: Academic Press, 1994). Some of the "slip of the tongue" material in Section 1.1 is drawn from Victoria Fromkin's chapter on speech production (pp. 272–300) in the Berko-Gleason and Ratner volume cited above.

The experiment in which bar-pressing times were found to correspond to clause boundaries was reported by E. A. Stine in an article titled "On-Line Processing of

Written Text by Younger and Older Children," *Psychology and Aging* 5 (1990):68–78 and is discussed in Arthur Wingfield's chapter "Sentence Processing" in the Berko-Gleason and Ratner text. (Copyright © 1990 by the American Psychological Association. Adapted with permission.)

The discussion of eye-movement data in psycholinguistics was based on the article by K. Rayner and S. Sereno, "Eye Movements in Reading," in the *Handbook of Psycholinguistics*, edited by M. A. Gernsbacher, as well as in the book by K. Rayner and A. Pollatsek, *The Psychology of Reading* (Englewood Cliffs, NJ: Prentice-Hall, 1989).

The material on event-related potentials is discussed in an excellent review article by Marta Kutas and Cyma Van Petten in Gernsbacher's *Handbook of Psycholinguistics* cited above (pp. 83–133); see p. 103 for a discussion of Figure 12.4. The syllable-processing experiment cited in the syllable section was reported in "Phoneme Monitoring, Syllable Monitoring, and Lexical Access" by J. Segui, U. Frauenfelder, and J. Mehler, *British Journal of Psychology* 72 (1981):471–77 and is discussed by R. E. Remes in "On the Perception of Speech" in the Gernsbacher *Handbook*.

The word-blending studies are reported in a series of studies conducted by Rebecca Treiman; see "The Structure of Spoken Syllables: Evidence from Novel Word Games," *Cognition* 15 (1983):49–74. A cross-linguistic study using a forced-choice version of these word games is reported in G. E. Wiebe and B. L. Derwing's paper, "A Forced-Choice Blending Task for Testing Intra-syllabic Break Points in English, Korean, and Taiwanese," in *The Twenty-First LACUS Forum* (Chapel Hill, NC: LACUS, 1994).

The morphological priming experiments are summarized in an article by William Marslen-Wilson, Lorraine Komisarjevsky Tyler, Rachelle Waksler, and Lianne Older, "Morphology and Meaning in the English Mental Lexicon," *Psychological Review* 101 (1994):3–33. The experiments on selectional restrictions and hierarchical structure are reported in Libben's "Are Morphological Structures Computed During Word Recognition?" *Journal of Psycholinguistic Research* 22 (1993):535–44 and in Libben's "Computing Hierarchical Morphological Structure: A Case Study," *Journal of Neurolinguistics* 8 (1994):49–55.

The section on the processing of garden path sentences is taken from Lynn Frazier's article, "Sentence Processing: A Tutorial Review," in *Attention and Performance (XII): The Psychology of Reading*, edited by M. Coltheart (London: Lawrence Erlbaum, 1987), 559–96. These sentence types are also discussed in David Caplan's *Language: Structure Processing and Disorders* (Cambridge, MA: MIT Press, 1994).

The study of sentence ambiguity was conducted by M. K. Tannenhaus, G. N. Calson, and M. S. Seidenberg in "Do Listeners Compute Linguistic Representations?" in *Natural Language Parsing*, edited by D. R. Dowty, L. Karttunen, and A. M. Zwicky (New York: Cambridge University Press, 1985).

Recommended Reading

Berko-Gleason, J., and Nan Bernstein Ratner. 1993. *Psycholinguistics*. Philadelphia: Harcourt Brace.

Gernsbacher, M. A. 1994. *Handbook of Psycholinguistics*. New York: Academic Press.

Kess, J. 1992. *Psycholinguistics*. Philadelphia: John Benjamins.

QUESTIONS

1. How do psycholinguistic investigations of language differ from theoretical linguistic investigations?

2. Consider the following slips of the tongue. What does each reveal about the process of language production?
   a) They *laked* across the *swim*.
   b) The spy was *gound* and *bagged*.
   c) I will *zee* you in the *bark*.

3. Imagine that a psycholinguist has reported on an experiment in which a priming effect was found for morphological roots on suffixed past tense forms in a lexical decision task.
   i) State the dependent variable in the experiment.
   ii) Give an example of a prime stimulus.
   iii) Give an example of a target stimulus.

4. Imagine that ERP researchers find that a positive spike is consistently observed half a second after the presentation of a particular sentence type. What do you think this new ERP spike would be called?

5. Complete the following sentences by filling in the blanks. In each case, what type of top-down processing and bottom-up processing guided your decision?
   a) The children ______ running in the park.
   b) All ______ movies I like have happy endings.
   c) He tends to see everything as ______ and white.

6. Recall that according to the cohort model, a word is recognized from beginning to end, one phoneme at a time. According to the cohort model, how many phonemes of each of the following words would have to be processed before a hearer would be sure which word had been spoken?
   a) giraffe
   b) splat
   c) computerize

7. Write the garden path sentences in examples *10* and *11* of this chapter on separate index cards. Take a few other cards and write an unambiguous sentence on each of them. Now, have some friends try to read aloud the sentences on the cards. Do they show evidence that the garden path sentences are more difficult to process? If so, what is the evidence?

8. What is a processing model? Try to describe the process of reading single words in terms of a processing model that contains specific modules.

9. In this chapter, parsing has been discussed in the context of sentence processing. The notion of parsing, however, can also be used to describe how morphologically complex words are parsed. Describe, in terms of parsing, how you think the following multimorphemic words would be processed.

a) bookmark
b) unredoable
c) overbearing

10. Imagine yourself as a psycholinguist trying to devise experiments to investigate how people do language. What experiments would you make up to address the following questions? Be as specific as possible about how you would interpret the question and about what you would do to try to find an answer through psycholinguistic experiment.
    a) Are semantically abstract words easier to process than semantically concrete ones?
    b) Are simple clauses more difficult to understand than conjoined clauses?
    c) Do people read words from beginning to end?
    d) Do people with different degrees of education process language in fundamentally different ways?
    e) Does the way you parse a sentence depend on what language you speak?

thirteen

BRAIN AND LANGUAGE

Gary Libben

The goal of neurology is to understand humanity.

– WILDER PENFIELD

OBJECTIVES

In this chapter, you will learn

- how the human brain is structured as it relates to language
- how neurolinguists have investigated the brain and language
- what studies of brain damage tell us about the brain and language

In this chapter we will be concerned with the branch of neuroscience that has as its goal the understanding of how language is represented and processed in the brain. This field of study is called **neurolinguistics**. Although the study of the relationship between brain and language is still in its infancy, much has already been learned about which parts of the brain are involved in various aspects of language production and comprehension. The field of neurolinguistics has also done much to deepen the way we think about the nature of linguistic competence.

The chapter provides a brief survey of brain structure and the methods that are currently available to study the brain. This is followed by a discussion of the different types of language disturbance that result from brain damage and by a discussion of how phonology, morphology, syntax, and semantics may be represented in the brain. The chapter concludes by reviewing the current answers to the important neurolinguistic question, "Where is language?"

1 THE HUMAN BRAIN

Contained within your skull are about 1,400 grams of pinkish-white matter. It may be the most complex 1,400 grams in the galaxy. For most of human history, however, the role of the brain as the center of mental life remained completely unknown. Even the Greek philosopher Aristotle believed that its primary function was to cool the blood.

We now know much more about the structure and functioning of the brain. But in many ways we are still like Aristotle, finding it hard to believe that this wrinkled mass of nerve cells could be the stuff that dreams, fears, and knowledge are made of. Nevertheless, it is, and the task of brain science (or **neuroscience**) is to understand how the breadth and depth of human experience is coded in brain matter.

The brain is composed of nerve cells or **neurons** that are the basic information-processing units of the nervous system. The human brain contains about 10 billion neurons that are organized into networks of almost unimaginable complexity. This complexity results from the fact that each neuron can be directly linked with up to 10 thousand other neurons. But the brain is not simply a mass of interconnected neurons. It is composed of structures that seem to play specific roles in the integrated functioning of the brain. The following sections provide a brief overview of these structures.

1.1 The cerebral cortex

The brain encompasses all the neurological structures above the spinal cord and appears to have evolved from the bottom up. The lower brain structures are shared by almost all animals. These structures are responsible for the maintenance of functions such as respiration, heart rate, and muscle coordination that are essential to the survival of all animals. As we move farther away from the spinal cord, however, we begin to find structures that have developed differently in different species. At the highest level of the brain—the **cerebral cortex**—the differences are most pronounced. Reptiles and amphibians have no cortex at all, and the progression from lower to higher mammals is marked by dramatic increases in the proportion of cortex to total amount of brain tissue. The human brain has the greatest proportion of cortex to brain mass of all animals.

In humans, the cortex is a gray wrinkled mass that sits like a cap over the rest of the brain. The wrinkled appearance results from the cortex being folded in upon itself. This folding allows a great amount of cortical matter to be compressed into the limited space provided by the human skull (in much the same way as the folding of a handkerchief allows it to fit into a jacket pocket). It has been estimated that up to 65 percent of the cortex is hidden within its folds.

It is the human cortex that accounts for our distinctness in the animal world, and it is within the human cortex that the secrets of language representation and processing are to be found. The remainder of our discussion of brain structure, therefore, will focus on the features of the cerebral cortex.

1.2 The cerebral hemispheres

The most important orientation points in mapping the cortex are the folds on its surface. The folds of the cortex have two parts: sulci (pronounced /sʊlsaj/; singular:

sulcus), which are areas where the cortex is folded in, and gyri (singular: **gyrus**), which are areas where the cortex is folded out toward the surface.

Figure 13.1 shows a human brain as seen from above, illustrating the many sulci and gyri of the cortex. A very prominent feature is the deep sulcus (in this case called a **fissure** because of its size), which extends from the front of the brain to the back. This fissure, which is known as the **longitudinal fissure**, separates the left and right **cerebral hemispheres**. In many ways, the cerebral hemispheres can be considered to be separate brains and indeed are often referred to as the left brain and the right brain. There are two main reasons for this.

First, the hemispheres are almost completely anatomically separate. The main connection between them is a bundle of nerve fibers known as the **corpus callosum**, whose primary function is to allow the two hemispheres to communicate with one another.

The other reason for considering the hemispheres to be separate brains is that they show considerable functional distinctness. In terms of muscle movement and sensation, each hemisphere is responsible for half the body—oddly enough, the opposite half. Thus the left hemisphere controls the right side of the body and the right hemisphere controls the left side of the body. These **contralateral** (*contra* = 'opposite', *lateral* = 'side') responsibilities of the cerebral hemispheres account for the fact that people who suffer damage to one hemisphere of the brain (as a result of a stroke or accident) will exhibit paralysis on the opposite side of the body.

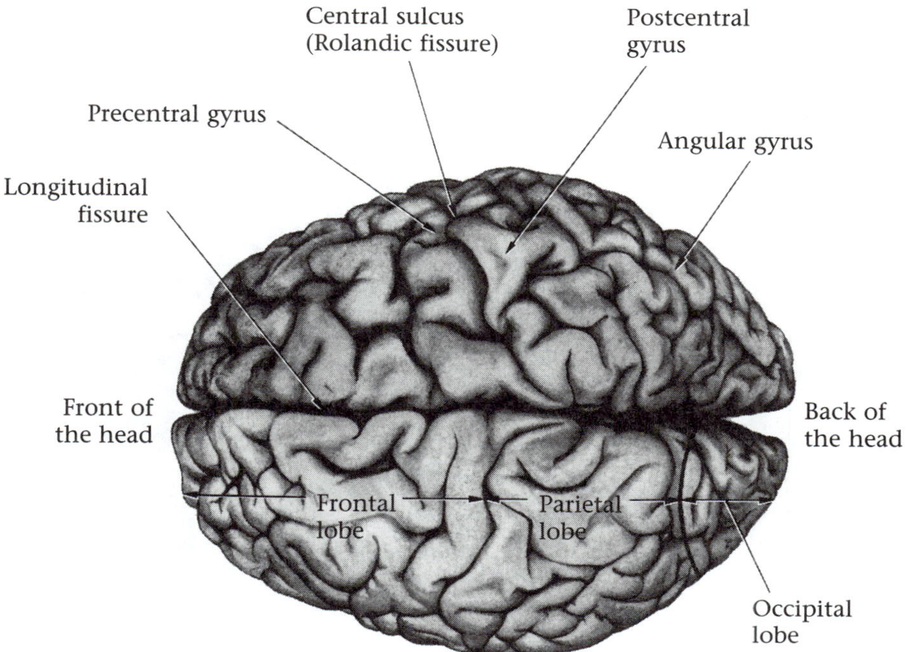

Figure 13.1 The cerebral hemispheres seen from above the head. Note the many fissures and gyri of the cortex and the prominence of the longitudinal fissure that separates the left and right hemispheres.

The hemispheres also show functional distinctness with respect to higher cognitive functions. In general, the left hemisphere seems to excel in analytic tasks such as arithmetic, whereas the right hemisphere excels in tasks that require an overall appreciation of complex patterns such as the recognition of familiar faces and melodies.

Despite the fact that the hemispheres show such specialization, we should be cautioned against sweeping generalizations about left-brain versus right-brain abilities or strategies. In all probability, complex mental activities involve the coordinated functioning of both hemispheres. The representation of language in the brain provides a useful example of this.

Most right-handed individuals have language represented in the left cerebral hemisphere and are therefore said to be left **lateralized** for language. But not every aspect of language is represented in the left hemisphere of right-handers. Adults who have had their left cerebral hemispheres surgically removed lose most but not all of their linguistic competence. They typically lose the ability to speak and process complex syntactic patterns but retain some language comprehension ability. Clearly, it must be the right hemisphere that is responsible for whatever language-processing ability remains (see Figure 13.2).

It has also been reported that right-handed patients who suffer damage to the right cerebral hemisphere exhibit difficulty in understanding jokes and metaphors in everyday conversation. These patients are able to provide only a literal or concrete interpretation of figurative sentences such as *He was wearing a loud tie*. They frequently misunderstand people because they cannot use loudness and intonation as cues to whether a speaker is angry, excited, or merely joking. Thus the right hemisphere has a distinct role to play in normal language use.

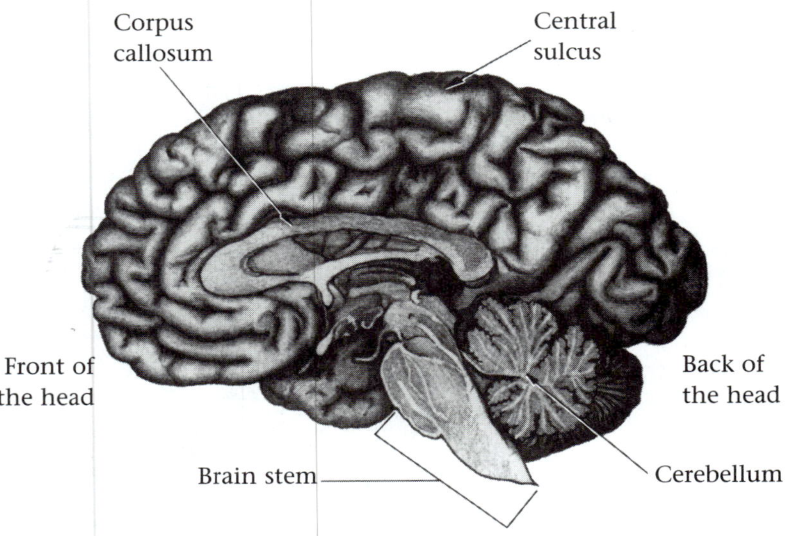

Figure 13.2 The right hemisphere seen from the inside. In this picture the corpus callosum has been cut so that one hemisphere may be separated from the other. Note how the gray cortex caps the lower structures (the brain stem and cerebellum), which are whitish in color.

Finally, consideration of language representation in the brains of left-handers makes matters even more complex. Contrary to what might be expected, few left-handers have a mirror image representation for language (that is, language localization in the right hemisphere). Rather, they tend to show significant language representation in both hemispheres. Thus, left-handers are generally less lateralized for language.

To sum up, although the left and right hemispheres have different abilities and different responsibilities, complex skills such as language do not always fall neatly into one hemisphere or the other. Research into why this is the case constitutes an important part of neuroscience. This research promises to reveal much about the cerebral hemispheres and about the individual representations and processes that constitute language.

1.3 The lobes of the cortex

We have seen that the cerebral hemispheres make distinct contributions to the overall functioning of the brain. In addition, each hemisphere contains substructures that appear to have distinct responsibilities. The substructures of the cortex in each hemisphere are called **lobes**. Like the hemispheres, the lobes of the cortex can be located with reference to prominent fissures, sulci, and gyri, which are useful as orientation points in much the same way that rivers and mountain ranges are useful in finding particular locations on a map. As can be seen in Figure 13.3, the **central sulcus** (also called the Rolandic fissure) extends from the top of the cortex to another

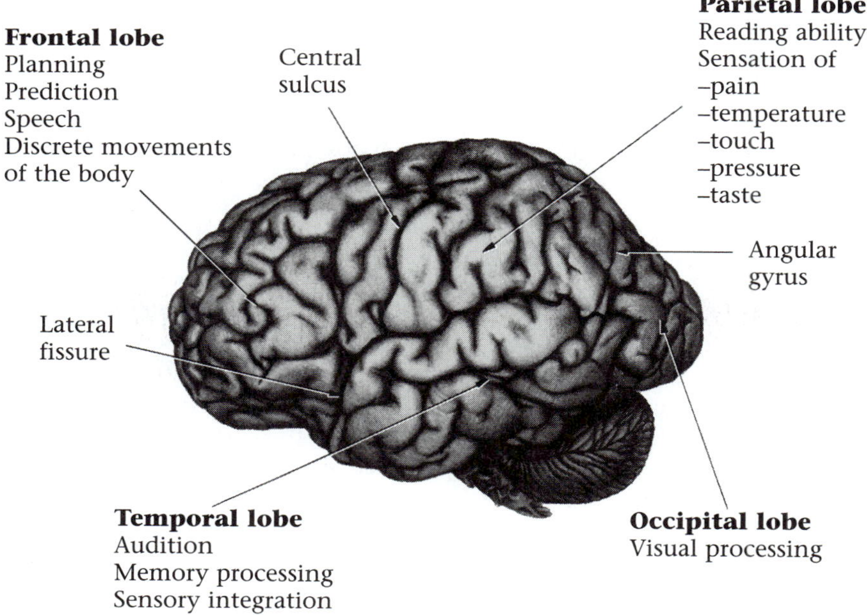

Figure 13.3 The left hemisphere seen from the outside

groove known as the **lateral fissure** (also called the Sylvian fissure). These two features are important in the delineation of the cerebral lobes. The **frontal lobe** lies in front of the central sulcus and the **parietal lobe** lies behind it. The **temporal lobe** is the area beneath the lateral fissure. The fourth lobe, the **occipital lobe**, is not clearly marked by an infolding of the cortex, but can be identified as the area to the rear of the **angular gyrus** (which has been found to play an important role in reading).

Figure 13.3 shows the left hemisphere of the brain. It indicates the location of each lobe and its specialized functions. Assuming that this is the brain of a right-hander, it is also possible to identify those areas of the cortex that have a particular role to play in language processing, as we will see.

2 INVESTIGATING THE BRAIN

Imagine that you could open the top of a living human being's skull and observe the brain while the individual is engaged in activities such as reading, writing, watching a football game, or having a heated argument. What would you see? The answer is—nothing! To the outside observer, the working brain shows no evidence of its activity. This is clearly a problem for the field of neurolinguistics, which requires the use of special investigative techniques to uncover the secrets of where and how language is processed in the brain. In addition, these special techniques must meet the ethical requirements of research with human subjects. While other neuroscientists are able to do much of their research using animal subjects, this option is not available to neurolinguists.

Imposing as they may be, the problems of investigating the processing of language in the brain are not insurmountable. Recent decades have seen a number of technological advances that have greatly facilitated the investigation of the question, "What is going on in the brain when people are engaged in language behavior?" In the following sections, we discuss some of the techniques of neurolinguistic investigation.

2.1 Autopsy studies

Until recently the only way to study the brain was through **autopsy studies**. This technique was most often carried out with patients who were admitted to hospitals after displaying a neurological disorder. Careful observations were made of a patient's behavior, and subsequent to his or her death, the brain was examined to determine which areas were damaged. By comparing the area of brain damage and the type of disorder the patient displayed while alive, neurologists could develop theories about the role of the damaged brain parts in normal brain functioning.

A famous example of this type of analysis comes from the work of Paul Broca, a nineteenth-century French neurologist. In 1860, Broca observed a patient who had been hospitalized for over twenty years in Paris. For most of his hospitalization, the patient was almost completely unable to speak, but appeared to understand everything that was said to him. Toward the end of his life (he died at age fifty-seven), he also developed a paralysis of the right arm and leg. Immediately after the patient's death (as a result of an unrelated infection), Broca examined the brain. It showed severe damage (called a **lesion**) in the lower rear area of the left frontal lobe. Broca concluded that because the patient was unable to speak, this part of the frontal lobe must normally be responsible for speech production. Since that time, many other autopsy studies have supported Broca's conclusions. This lower rear portion of the left frontal lobe is now called **Broca's area** (see Figure 13.4, which shows this and other language-processing areas of the left hemisphere). As will be discussed in Section 3.1, the impairment of the ability to speak as a result of damage to Broca's area is called Broca's aphasia.

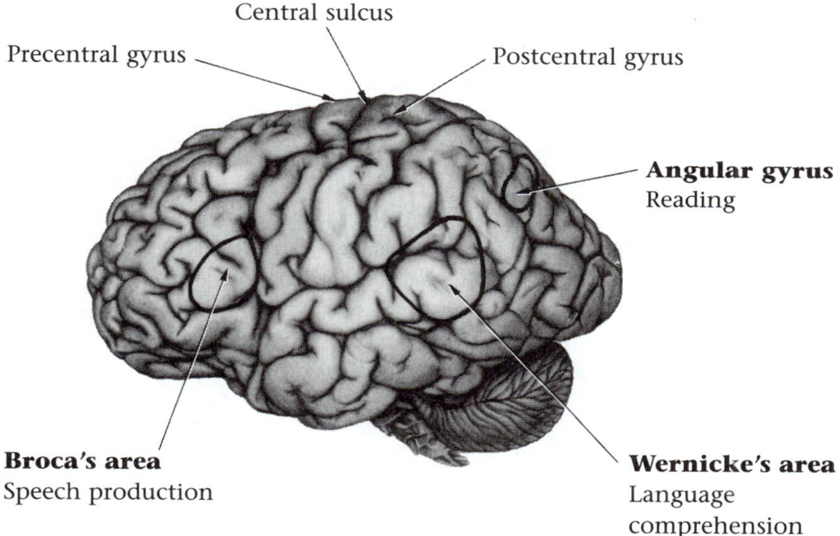

Figure 13.4 Language processes in the left hemisphere. Damage to Broca's area is usually associated with nonfluent speech and difficulty processing complex syntactic patterns. Damage to Wernicke's area (see Section 3.2) is usually associated with comprehension disturbances. Damage to the area around the angular gyrus results in reading impairment.

2.2 Images of the Living Brain

Autopsy analysis has been and continues to be an important tool in the understanding of the brain. But an autopsy can be carried out only after the patient's death. Therefore, whatever information it reveals about the nature and extent of the patient's brain damage can no longer be of any use in treatment.

Computerized axial tomography (also called **CT scanning**) is a relatively new technique that uses a narrow beam of X-rays to create brain images that take the form of a series of brain slices. CT scans have offered neuroscientists their first opportunity to look inside a living brain. However, like autopsy, CT scanning provides a static image of the brain. It is most useful in identifying brain lesions and tumors.

Recently a number of new techniques have emerged that make it possible to study the brain in action. One such technique is **positron emission tomography** (**PET**).

The technique capitalizes on one of the brain's many interesting properties—it is extremely hungry for glucose and oxygen. Although the brain accounts for only about 2 percent of total body weight, it consumes about 20 percent of the oxygen the body uses while at rest. This oxygen is, of course, carried to the brain by the blood.

In the PET technique, positron-emitting isotopes, which function as radioactive tracers, are injected into the arteries in combination with glucose. The rate at which the radioactive glucose is used by specific regions of the brain is recorded while the subject is engaged in various sorts of cognitive activities. These recordings are used to produce maps of areas of high brain activity associated with particular cognitive functions. Examples of such PET maps are represented in Figure 13.5.

Another dynamic brain-imaging technique that has become increasingly important over the past few years is **functional magnetic resonance imaging** (**fMRI**). This technique yields information on areas of high brain activity during the performance of cognitive tasks but is somewhat less invasive because it does not require the injection of radioactive compounds. The fMRI technique allows many measurements to be taken in a single testing session and offers a good measure of how brain activity changes during language comprehension and production. At present, however, the best fMRI machines employ high-field permanent magnets and require expensive installations not currently available at most research centers.

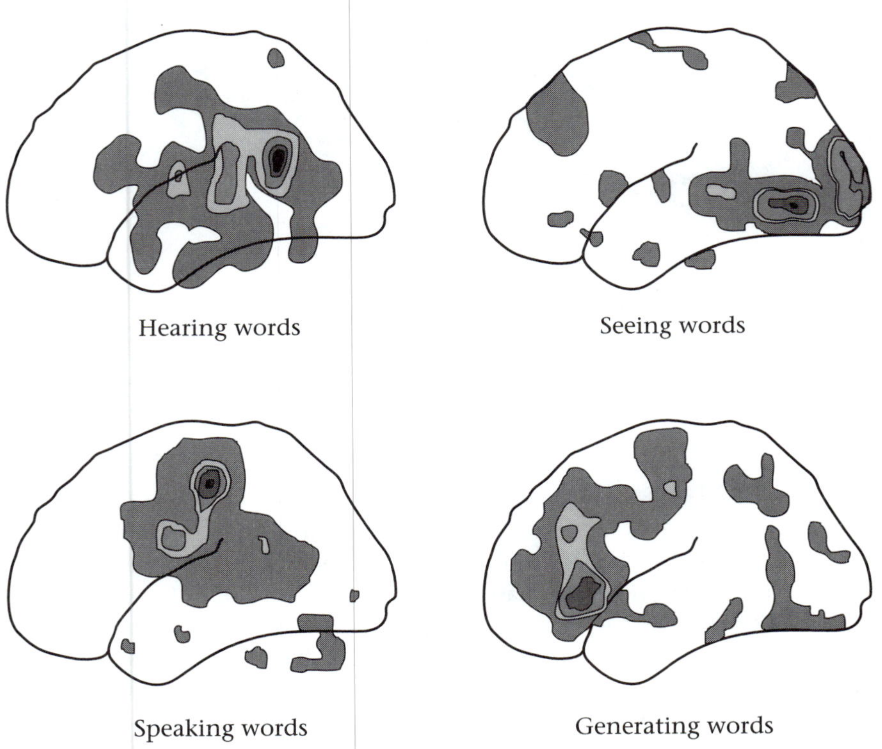

Figure 13.5 PET scans show how blood flow to the brain shifts to different locations depending on which task is being performed.

PET and fMRI studies have greatly increased our knowledge of where language processing takes place in the brain. It has been found, for example, that when subjects speak, much blood flows to the left hemisphere of the cortex and to Broca's area in particular. When subjects read, much blood flows to the occipital lobe (because it is responsible for visual processing), to the angular gyrus (which has a special role to play in reading), and to other areas of the left hemisphere. These observations support the view that the left hemisphere is primarily responsible for language and that there are specific language areas within the left hemisphere.

Finally, fMRI studies are playing an important role in increasing our understanding of the differences that might exist between language processing in a mother tongue and language processing in a second language. Second-language processing has been shown to involve a wider variety of cortical sites, which supports the view that the less automatic nature of language use in a second language requires the involvement of diverse mental processes in addition to those specifically dedicated to language.

2.3 Learning from hemispheric connections and disconnections

In the techniques that have been described, information about language representation in the brain is gained through an investigation of the brain itself. In this section, we review an alternate approach—one which examines behavior that can be associated with a particular brain hemisphere.

Dichotic listening studies

Dichotic listening studies have been extremely important in the accumulation of the knowledge we possess about the specialization of the cerebral hemispheres. The technique capitalizes on the property of the brain that we have discussed in Section 1.2—namely that each hemisphere is primarily wired to the opposite side of the body (including the head). So most of the input to your right ear goes to the left hemisphere of your brain. Now, if the left cerebral hemisphere is indeed specialized for language processing in right-handers, these individuals should process language better through the right ear.

If you are right-handed, you will most probably be able to verify this by observing the difference between holding a telephone receiver to your right ear and holding it to your left ear during a conversation. When the receiver is held to the right ear, it will appear that the speech is louder and clearer. This phenomenon is known as the **right ear advantage (REA)**. In the laboratory technique, stereo earphones are used and different types of stimuli are presented to each ear. In general, the right ear shows an advantage for words, numbers, and Morse code, whereas the left ear shows an advantage for the perception of melodies and environmental sounds, such as bird songs.

Split brain studies

If the left hemisphere is wired to the right ear, why is it possible to understand speech presented to the left ear? There are two reasons for this. The first is that the auditory pathways to the brain are not completely crossed—there are also secondary links between each hemisphere and the ear on the same side of the body. The second is that after the right hemisphere receives information from the left ear, that information can be transferred to the left hemisphere via the corpus callosum—the bundle of fibers that connects the two hemispheres.

Evidence concerning the crucial role that the corpus callosum plays in normal brain functioning is from the study of patients who have had this pathway surgically severed in a rare procedure used to treat severe forms of epilepsy. Studies that have investigated the effects of this surgery on cognition are referred to as **split brain experiments**. They have provided dramatic illustrations of what happens when the hemispheres cannot communicate with one another.

It appears from the behavior of split brain patients that although the right hemisphere does show some language understanding, it is mute. In one of many split brain experiments, a patient is blindfolded and an object (e.g., a key) is placed in one hand. When the key is held in the right hand, the patient can easily name it because the right hand is connected to the left hemisphere, which can compute speech output. However, when the key is placed in the left hand, the patient cannot say what it is. The right hemisphere, which receives information from the left hand, knows what is there, but it can neither put this into words nor transfer the information across the severed corpus callosum to the left brain.

Split brain experiments have presented new and important knowledge about the functioning of the brain. In terms of overall investigative methodology, however, they are not quite as exotic as they seem. In fact, the logic of split brain experiments is identical to the logic employed by Broca in 1860. In both cases the researcher endeavors to learn how the normal brain works by examining which functions are lost as a result of the brain damage. In the case of split brain studies, the damage is surgically induced. In the case of Broca's aphasia, disease caused an "experiment in nature." In the following section, we return to these experiments in nature and examine what they reveal about language representation in the brain.

3 APHASIA

Occasionally, humans suffer damage to particular parts of their brains. The most common cause of such brain damage is a **stroke** (also called a **cerebrovascular accident**). A language deficit caused by damage to the brain is called **aphasia**. The study of aphasia is by far the most important tool in the investigation of language in the brain. By observing and documenting the varieties of aphasic symptoms, neurolinguists have the best chance of identifying the major components of language in the brain.

In general, the amount and type of aphasic disturbance that a patient will exhibit depends on how much the brain is damaged and where it is damaged. There are many varieties of aphasia. In the following sections, we will describe some of the more important types.

C. S. Moss was a psychologist who became aphasic subsequent to a stroke. He later wrote a book about the experience entitled *Recovering with Aphasia*. The following is an excerpt from that book:

> I recollect trying to read the headlines of the *Chicago Tribune* but they didn't make any sense to me at all. I didn't have any difficulty focusing; it was simply that the words, individually or in combination, didn't have meaning, and even more amazing, I was only a trifle bothered by that fact.
>
> The second week I ran into a colleague who happened to mention that it must be very frustrating for me to be aphasic since prior to that I had been so verbally facile. [I] later found myself wondering why it was not. I think part of the explanation was relatively simple. If I had lost the ability to converse with others, I had also lost the ability to engage in self-talk. In other words, I did not have the ability to think about the future—to worry, to anticipate or perceive it—at least not with words.
>
> It took a great deal of effort to keep an abstraction in mind. For example, in talking with the speech therapist I would begin to give a definition of an abstract concern, but as I held it in mind it would sort of fade, and chances were that I would end up giving a simplified version rather than the one at the original level of conception. It was as though giving an abstraction required so much of my added intelligence that halfway through the definition I would run out of energy available to me and regress to a more concrete answer.

A consideration of Moss's recollections leads to some provocative questions about the relationship between language and thought. Is it possible that the ability to think about the future is dependent on language? Does language support abstract thought?

The type of aphasia that Moss reports involves a mixture of deficits—speaking, listening, reading, and writing. Some other forms of aphasia, however, are much more specific. In these more specific forms, particular skills are lost, and others remain intact. The study of the specific aphasias can tell us much about the building blocks of language in the brain. Sections 3.1 and 3.2 discuss the two most important specific aphasias.

3.1 Nonfluent aphasia

Nonfluent aphasia (also called **motor aphasia**) results from damage to parts of the brain in front of the central sulcus. Recall that an important part of the frontal lobe is concerned with motor activity and that the bottom rear portion of the frontal lobe (Broca's area) is responsible for the articulation of speech (see Figure 13.4). Not surprisingly, therefore, nonfluent patients show slow effortful speech production (hence the term *nonfluent*). The most severe form of nonfluent aphasia is **global aphasia**. In this type of aphasia, the patient is completely mute. Of the less severe forms, **Broca's aphasia** is the most important.

The speech of Broca's aphasics is very halting. Patients have great difficulty in accurately producing the needed phonemes to say a word. For example, a patient who wishes to produce the sentence in *1a* would be likely to produce the utterance in *1b*.

1)

a. It's hard to eat with a spoon.

b. [... hɑr it ... wɪt ... pun]

The ellipsis dots (...) between the words in *1b* indicate periods of silence in the production of the utterance. Sentences produced at this slow rate tend to also lack normal sentence intonation. This is a common characteristic of the speech of Broca's aphasics and is called **dysprosody**. Note how the patient simplifies the consonant clusters in the words *hard* and *spoon* and changes the /θ/ to /t/ in the word *with*. The speech errors that result from these sorts of phonemic errors are called **phonemic paraphasias**.

It is tempting to think that the impairment of speech production in Broca's aphasia is caused by the fact that Broca's area is adjacent to the motor strip that controls movement of the facial muscles. The problem with this hypothesis is that damage to Broca's area usually only produces mild weakness of the muscles on the opposite side of the face and no permanent damage. Yet for some reason even people who can still control the muscles used in speech cannot use language properly after damage to Broca's area. This suggests that Broca's area has a language-specific responsibility.

Broca's aphasia as a syntactic disorder

Returning to the utterance in *1b*, note that the patient also omits a number of words that would normally be used in this utterance. The words that are omitted are *it, is, to, a*—the sorts of words that we too would be likely to omit if we were writing a telegram (for example, *I will meet you in the airport lounge → Meet you in airport lounge*). These "little words" are often called **function words** and their omission in the speech of Broca's aphasics has been referred to as **telegraphic speech**. (We will return to the problem of determining which items belong to the set of function words in Section 5.)

One possible account of the speech of Broca's aphasics is that it results from an economy of effort. Speech production is very effortful for these patients so they use as few words as possible because, like telegram writers, they are "paying" by the word. But there are other characteristics of their linguistic abilities that point to a deeper cause—the disturbance of syntactic competence.

In addition to omitting function words, Broca's aphasics tend to omit inflectional affixes such as *-ing, -ed,* and *-en* in words such as *running, chased,* and *broken*. They also show difficulty judging the grammaticality of sentences. For example, given sentences such as the ones in *2*, Broca's aphasics will not always be able to determine which ones are grammatical and which ones are not.

2)

a. The boy ate it up.
b. *The boy ate up it.
c. *Boy ate it up.
d. The boy ate up the cake.

Finally, a close examination of the comprehension of Broca's aphasics offers further support to the view that there is a syntactic component to the disorder.

3)

a. The mouse was chased by the cat.
b. The dog was chased by the cat.
c. The cat was chased by the mouse.

Broca's aphasics tend to interpret sentences such as *3a* correctly. In a sentence such as this, knowledge about the behavior of cats and mice helps the patient to guess correctly at the meaning of the sentence. For sentences such as *3b*, however, in which knowledge of the world is not a reliable guide to comprehension, patients are unsure about the meaning. Finally, Broca's aphasics tend to interpret a sentence such as *3c* as though it had the same meaning as *3a*. When we read a sentence like *3c*, we recognize it as describing an unlikely event, but our interpretation is driven by the syntax of the sentence, not by our knowledge of the world. Many Broca's aphasics appear not to have this ability.

These sorts of observations have led many neurolinguists to reconsider the traditional view that Broca's aphasia is simply a production deficit. The possibility that Broca's aphasia also involves some central disturbance of syntactic competence is intriguing and may lead to a deeper understanding of how syntactic knowledge is represented in the brain. We will return to this question in Section 4.

A final point about Broca's aphasia is of a less technical nature but is of great importance to the understanding of the syndrome as a whole. Unlike patients such as C. S. Moss, Broca's aphasics are acutely aware of their language deficit and are typically very frustrated by it. It is as though they have complete understanding of what they should say but, to their constant dismay, find themselves unable to say it. This plight of Broca's aphasics is consistent with our understanding of the role of the frontal lobe, which is usually the site of lesion in the syndrome. Broca's area of the frontal lobe plays an extremely important role in language; however, it does not seem to be involved in the semantic relationships between words and the relationship between units of language and units of thought. The neurological basis of these meaning relationships remains almost entirely unknown. From the analysis of nonfluent aphasia in general and Broca's aphasia in particular, however, we suspect that these semantic relationships are the responsibility of areas of the brain that lie behind the central sulcus—in the temporal and parietal lobes of the brain (see Figure 13.3). This suspicion is supported by the type of language deficits associated with damage to the temporal-parietal lobes.

3.2 Fluent aphasia

The type of aphasia that results from damage to parts of the left cortex behind the central sulcus is referred to as **fluent aphasia** (or **sensory aphasia**). This type of aphasia stands in sharp contrast to nonfluent aphasia. Fluent aphasics have no difficulty producing language, but have a great deal of difficulty selecting, organizing, and monitoring their language production.

The most important type of fluent aphasia is called **Wernicke's aphasia**. The syndrome is named after the German physiologist Carl Wernicke, who, in 1874, published a now famous report of a kind of aphasia that was almost the complete opposite of Broca's aphasia. It was determined from autopsy data that this type of aphasia was associated with a lesion in the temporal lobe just below the most posterior (rear) portion of the lateral fissure. In severe cases, the lesion could also extend upward into the lower portion of the parietal lobe. This area of the brain is now known as **Wernicke's area** (see Figure 13.4).

In contrast to Broca's aphasics, Wernicke's aphasics are generally unaware of their deficit. Their speech typically sounds very good: there are no long pauses; sentence intonation is normal; function words are used appropriately; word order is usually syntactically correct. The problem is that the patient rarely makes any sense. The following is a conversation between an examiner (E) and a Wernicke's patient (P).

4)

E: How are you today, Mrs. A?
P: Yes.
E: Have I ever tested you before?
P: No. I mean I haven't.
E: Can you tell me what your name is?
P: No, I don't I . . . right I'm right now here.
E: What is your address?
P: I cud /kʌd/ if I can help these this like you know . . . to make it.
We are seeing for him. That is my father.

The patient in this conversation produces a number of errors. But note that most of these errors are different from the kinds of errors made by Broca's aphasics. While the patient is able to produce some well-formed structures (e.g., *no, I don't*), these structures appear intermittently amidst various unrelated fragments. Not only are these constructions unrelated to each other but they are also unrelated to the examiner's questions. It appears that the patient has no understanding of the questions being asked.

This patient displays a significant but not severe form of Wernicke's aphasia. Her speech appears to result from a semi-random selection of words and short phrases. In very severe cases of this syndrome, phonemes are also randomly selected and the result is speech that has the intonational characteristics of English but actually contains very few real words of the language. This is termed **jargonaphasia**.

The type of deficit found in Wernicke's aphasia leads us to a greater understanding of the role of the temporal-parietal area of the brain known as Wernicke's area and to a deeper consideration of the nature of language comprehension. Wernicke's aphasia is primarily a comprehension deficit. But as we have seen, when comprehension breaks down, most of what we call language ability breaks down with it. Patients cannot express themselves because they cannot understand what they have just said and use that understanding in the planning of what to say next. In a very real sense, these patients have lost contact with themselves (and therefore with the rest of the world). Wernicke's patients cannot have coherent trains of thought—the brain damage does not allow the elements of the train to be connected, and this extends to more general sequenced behavior such as buying groceries or getting home by bus.

In summary, our discussion of fluent and nonfluent aphasia has demonstrated how normal language use is a marriage of content and form. In the case of nonfluent aphasia, form is compromised but the content of language remains relatively intact. In contrast, fluent aphasia is characterized by a rapid flow of form with little content.

4 ACQUIRED DYSLEXIA AND DYSGRAPHIA

Reading and writing skills involve a complex array of perceptual and motor skills. In this section we will consider impairments of reading and writing that are caused by damage to the brain. The impairment of reading ability is called **acquired dyslexia** (or acquired alexia). The impairment of writing ability is called **acquired dysgraphia** (or acquired agraphia). In both cases the term *acquired* indicates that the patient possessed normal reading and/or writing ability prior to brain damage and distinguishes the syndromes from developmental dyslexia and developmental dysgraphia, which deal with disturbances of reading and writing development in children.

4.1 Reading and writing disturbances in aphasia

Acquired dyslexia and dysgraphia typically accompany the aphasic syndromes that we considered in Section 3. Most Broca's aphasics show writing disturbances that are comparable to their speaking deficits. In other words, a patient who cannot pronounce the word *spoon* will also not be able to write it correctly. The resulting error in writing (e.g., *poon*) is called a **paragraphia**. In spontaneous writing, Broca's aphasics also tend to omit function words and inflectional affixes. Finally, while the silent reading of Broca's aphasics is very good, their reading aloud shows the same telegraphic style as their spontaneous speech. These observations reinforce the view that the deficit in Broca's aphasia is much more than a speech articulation deficit. It is a production deficit at a very deep level of language planning.

Wernicke's aphasics also show reading and writing deficits that match their deficits in speaking and listening. The writing of Wernicke's aphasics is formally very good. They typically retain good spelling and handwriting. However, like their speaking, what they write makes little sense. Reading comprehension is also severely impaired in Wernicke's aphasia. Like C. S. Moss, patients can see the letters and words, but cannot make any sense of them. Again the conclusion to be drawn is that Wernicke's aphasia, like Broca's aphasia, involves a central disturbance of language competence—the knowledge that underlies language functioning. In such cases of central language disturbance, whatever impairment the patient has in listening and speaking will be matched in reading and writing.

4.2 Acquired dyslexia as the dominant language deficit

In addition to the reading and writing deficits that accompany aphasia, there are many cases in which the disruption of reading and writing ability is the dominant symptom. This typically follows damage in and around the angular gyrus of the parietal lobe. An analysis of these types of disabilities has led to some very interesting theories about the nature of reading (at least in English).

Before we begin our discussion of two contrasting types of acquired dyslexia, it might be worthwhile to reflect on the abilities involved in the reading of words. Up to this point in the chapter you have read over five thousand words. Some of these words (such as the function words) are very familiar to you and you probably recognized them as wholes. But others, such as *angular gyrus*, are words that you probably read for the first time. How then could you know how to pronounce them? Many theorists believe that readers maintain a set of spelling-to-sound rules that enable them to read new words aloud. These rules are important in the development of reading ability and in the addition of new words to our reading vocabulary.

Phonological dyslexia is a type of acquired dyslexia in which the patient seems to have lost the ability to use spelling-to-sound rules. Phonological dyslexics can only read words that they have seen before. Asked to read a word such as *blug* aloud, they either say nothing or produce a known word that is visually similar to the target (e.g., *blue* or *bug*).

Surface dyslexia is the opposite of phonological dyslexia. Surface dyslexics seem unable to recognize words as wholes. Instead they must process all words through a set of spelling-to-sound rules. This is shown by the kinds of errors they make. Surface dyslexics do not have difficulty reading words such as *bat* that are regularly spelled. They read irregularly spelled words such as *yacht*, however, by applying regular rules and thus producing /jɑtʃt/. The most interesting aspect of surface dyslexics' reading ability is that they understand what they produce, not what they see. For example, a surface dyslexic would be likely to read the word *worm* as /wɑrm/ (and not /wərm/). When asked what the word means, the patient would answer: the opposite of *cold*.

Data from acquired dyslexia allow researchers to build models that specify the components of normal reading ability and their relationship to each other. Clearly, this type of analysis plays a very important role in the development of our understanding of language, the mind, and the brain.

5 LINGUISTIC THEORY AND APHASIA

Looking at aphasia in terms of linguistic theory gives us a new perspective on language in the brain. Linguistic theory has been traditionally concerned with the structure of language, not with how it is used in the processes of listening, speaking, reading, and writing. In contrast, the traditional way of looking at aphasia has been in terms of what the patient can and cannot do. The involvement of theoretical linguists in the study of aphasia has caused a minor revolution in the field. Aphasia researchers have begun to think about the deficit in terms of the loss of semantic features, phonological rules, and perhaps syntactic tree structures. Theoretical linguists have also found that the study of aphasia offers an important area for testing theoretical distinctions such as the one between derivational suffixes and inflectional suffixes. In this section, we will look at some of the areas in which the marriage of theoretical linguistics and neurolinguistics has been most fruitful. This fruitfulness has usually meant an increase in the sophistication of the questions that are asked about aphasia. It has also meant the discovery of new and often bizarre aphasic phenomena.

5.1 Features, rules, and underlying forms

In the area of phonology, we have found that the phonemic paraphasias of Broca's aphasics usually differ from the target phoneme by only one distinctive feature (recall example *1* in Section 3.1: *with* → /wɪt/) and can therefore be easily described by phonological rules. Observations such as these lead us to believe that phonological features and rules might be good tools to characterize how language is represented and produced.

In the area of morphology, the study of aphasia has offered empirical support for the theoretical distinction between inflection and derivation. As we have discussed, Broca's aphasics show a sensitivity to this distinction in their omission of affixes in speech. Inflectional affixes are commonly dropped, but derivational affixes are usually retained. Perhaps most interesting is the tendency of some aphasics to produce underlying forms of morphemes in reading and repetition. Asked to repeat the word *illegal*, for example, some aphasics will produce *inlegal*, using the underlying form of the negative prefix rather than the allomorph that should occur before a base beginning with /l/. Again, errors such as these point to the possibility that phonological processes such as nasal assimilation and the notion of underlying form not only are an elegant way to represent linguistic competence but also are relevant to the processing of language in the brain.

The study of aphasia also stands to shed light on the nature of semantic representations. Most of the work in this area has concentrated on the many subvarieties of acquired dyslexia. In a syndrome known as **deep dyslexia**, patients produce reading errors that are systematically related to the word that they are asked to read (in the sense that they share some semantic features but not others). Given the word *mother*, for example, a deep dyslexic is likely to read *father*.

The detailed study of semantic deficits associated with brain damage has also led to some very surprising discoveries. Most aphasics and dyslexics find abstract words much more difficult to process than concrete words. But there have been reports of concrete word dyslexia in which the patient shows exactly the opposite problem (having difficulty with concrete words such as *table)*. There has even been a report of a patient who shows a selective inability to read words that refer to fruits and vegetables.

5.2 Agrammatism

In Section 3.1 we observed that many theorists now believe that Broca's aphasia involves a central syntactic deficit. The syndrome that is characterized by telegraphic speech has been given the name **agrammatism**—to indicate that grammatical ability has been lost. Agrammatism is the aphasic disturbance that has been most studied by linguists. As was discussed in Section 3.1, it is characterized by the omission of function words such as *it, is, to,* and *a*; by the omission of inflectional affixes; and by comprehension deficits in cases where the correct interpretation of a sentence is dependent on syntax alone.

In recent years, many linguists have become involved in the problems of characterizing the agrammatic deficit. These problems have raised both specific questions such as, What exactly is a function word?; and general questions such as, Is it possible to lose syntax? The involvement of linguists has also generated cross-linguistic studies of agrammatism that provide interesting insights into the interaction between characteristics of the syndrome and characteristics of particular languages.

5.3 Function words

Intuitively, function words are grammatical words that can be distinguished from content words such as nouns, verbs, and adjectives. In terms of formal syntax, however, they are quite heterogeneous. They include pronouns, auxiliaries, determiners, and prepositions—items that do not fall into any single syntactic category. Much of the recent work in this area by linguists has concentrated on working out what exactly the so-called function words have in common. Some researchers have suggested that they form a phonological group—they are all words that do not normally take stress. Others have pointed to the fact that function words do not normally take affixes and therefore form a morphological group. Still others have suggested that syntactic theory should be modified so that all the words that are lost in agrammatism fall under the functional category heading (this would involve changing the status of prepositions, which are currently treated as lexical categories—see Chapter 5).

Whatever the outcome of this debate, it is clear that neurolinguistic evidence has presented a new set of challenges to the field of formal linguistics. One of these challenges is to build bridges between normal and pathological linguistic competence by finding units of analysis that are appropriate to both.

5.4 The loss of syntactic competence

Another much more general challenge is to define what it means to possess syntactic competence such that we can speak of its loss. This challenge has forced researchers to address the question, What is the essence of syntactic knowledge? Is it the hierarchical arrangement of elements? Is it the representation of abstract entities such as empty categories and traces?

Some researchers have suggested that agrammatism involves the loss of the ability to form hierarchical representations. They claim that agrammatics interpret sentences as strings of content words and assign thematic roles to nouns (as opposed to NPs) according to a default strategy that treats the first noun as the agent (for example). This strategy works reasonably well for simple sentences in which the first noun can be assigned the thematic role of agent and the second noun can be assigned the role of theme, as in sentence *5a*. It results in miscomprehension, however, for sentences such as *5b* and *5c*, in which the first noun does not have the role of agent.

5)

a. The girl kissed the boy.
b. The girl was kissed.
c. It was the girl that the boy kissed.

Other researchers have argued that agrammatism does not involve the loss of syntactic competence but rather an alteration of that competence. They have claimed that agrammatics have hierarchical syntactic structures but can no longer represent the traces that indicate an NP's position in deep structure. As a result, they are unable to recognize that the subject NP bears the theme role since they do not realize that it is the complement of the verb in deep structure (see Section 3 of Chapter 6).

5.5 Agrammatism in other languages

Data from other languages have suggested that the original characterization of agrammatism as a syndrome in which function words and inflectional affixes are lost may not reflect the true nature of the deficit but rather reflects the fact that the English language normally allows such deletions.

In English, affixes are typically attached to a base that is itself a free form. The past form of the verb *watch*, for example, is created by the addition of *-ed*; the third-person singular is created by the addition of *-s*. However, not all languages work this way. In Semitic languages, such as Hebrew, the base is typically a string of three consonants, which is unpronounceable in its uninflected form. Inflections are produced by inserting vowels into this triconsonantal "skeleton." For example, the Hebrew root for the verb *to write* is /ktv/. The masculine third-person present form of the verb is /kɔtɛv/, and the masculine third-person past form is /katav/. If Hebrew agrammatics simply "lose" inflectional affixes the way they do in English, they should not be able to produce any verbs. As it turns out, Hebrew agrammatics do produce verbs, but instead of dropping inflectional forms, they choose randomly among them. This sort of evidence has provided a convincing argument against the view that agrammatic language results from a simple economy of effort. Rather, it seems that it is a linguistic deficit that involves the mis-selection of linguistic forms. It is only in languages such as English, where the base is also a legal free form, that the agrammatism is characterized by affix omission.

6 WHERE IS LANGUAGE?

In this chapter we have outlined some important findings that have greatly increased our understanding of the types of language disturbances that result from damage to the brain, as well as our understanding of the association between specific areas of the brain and particular language functions. We have seen that Broca's area plays a crucial role in the articulation of speech and in the ability to create syntactic representations. Wernicke's area plays a key role in language comprehension, and the area surrounding the angular gyrus plays a special role in reading.

On the other hand, we have seen that, in an important sense, normal language use involves the integrated functioning of the entire cortex. Even right-handers who are strongly left lateralized for language show some language deficit in cases of damage to the right hemisphere. In addition, virtually all forms of aphasia are accompanied by word-finding difficulties. This observation suggests that the storage and retrieval of word forms may be diffusely represented in the brain.

There is, therefore, no simple answer to the question, "Where is language?" Even if there were, the task of neurolinguistics would be far from done, for the truly important question concerning language in the brain is not "Where is it?" but "What is it?" Indeed, the answer to the first question may have little to do with the answer to the second question. Consider, by analogy, the goal of understanding the American Congress: To what extent does the knowledge that Congress is to be found in Washington advance the understanding of how it works?

Ultimately, the goal of neurolinguistics is to understand in neurological terms what language is. The field of neurolinguistics is still a long way from being able to specify how syntax is coded in brain matter, or even how a word is represented. Nevertheless, as our discussion of agrammatism has revealed, recent work by neurolinguists has resulted in important new perspectives on the nature of language competence.

Summing up

This chapter is concerned with how language is represented and processed in the human brain. **Dichotic listening** studies and **split brain** studies have shown that the left hemisphere of the brain carries most of the responsibility for language processing in right-handed individuals. Neuroscientists have also used **autopsy studies**, **computerized axial tomography**, **positron emission tomography**, and **functional magnetic resonance imaging** to determine the relationship between particular areas of the left hemisphere and specific language functions. It has been found that **Broca's area** is primarily responsible for speech production, **Wernicke's area** is primarily responsible for language comprehension, and the area surrounding the **angular gyrus** plays an important role in reading. Most of our knowledge concerning language representation in the brain comes from the study of **aphasia**—language disturbance resulting from damage to the brain. **Neurolinguists**, trained in both linguistics and neuroscience, carefully examine the manner in which linguistic competence is affected by brain damage. Their goal is to increase our understanding of how linguistic knowledge is coded in brain matter and how this knowledge is used in the processes of language comprehension and production.

Key terms

General terms

neurolinguistics
neuroscience

Terms concerning the structure of the brain

angular gyrus
Broca's area
central sulcus
cerebral cortex
cerebral hemispheres
contralateral
corpus callosum
fissure
frontal lobe
gyrus
lateral fissure
lateralized
lobes
longitudinal fissure
neurons
occipital lobe
parietal lobe
sulcus
temporal lobe
Wernicke's area

Terms concerning how language in the brain is studied

autopsy studies
Broca's aphasia
computerized axial tomography (CT scanning)
dichotic listening studies
functional magnetic resonance imaging (fMRI)
lesion
positron emission tomography (PET)
right ear advantage (REA)
split brain experiments

Terms concerning language deficit caused by brain damage

acquired dysgraphia
acquired dyslexia
agrammatism
aphasia
Broca's aphasia
cerebrovascular accident
deep dyslexia
dysprosody
fluent aphasia
function words
global aphasia
jargonaphasia
motor aphasia
nonfluent aphasia
paragraphia
phonemic paraphasias
phonological dyslexia
sensory aphasia
stroke
surface dyslexia
telegraphic speech
Wernicke's aphasia

Sources

David Caplan's 1996 book *Language: Structure, Processing, and Disorders* (Cambridge, MA: MIT Press) offers a comprehensive overview of the breakdown of language in aphasia and its relation to normal processing. His 1987 book *Neurolinguistics and Linguistic Aphasiology: An Introduction* is an excellent introduction to the field and provides important historical background. A more practical approach to aphasia and its treatment is to be found in J. C. Rosenbek, L. L. Lapointe, and R. T. Wertz's *Aphasia: A Clinical Approach* (Boston: Little Brown, 1989). The discussion of agrammatism was drawn from the rich literature that includes M.-L. Kean's edited volume *Agrammatism* (New York: Academic Press, 1985) and Yosef Grodzinsky's challenging proposals in *Theoretical Perspectives on Language Deficits* (Cambridge, MA: MIT Press, 1990). An alternative approach to Grodzinsky's is well represented by David Caplan and Nancy Hildebrandt's *Disorders of Syntactic Comprehension* (Cambridge, MA: MIT Press, 1988).

C. S. Moss's autobiographical account of his aphasic experience is to be found in *Recovery with Aphasia* (Urbana, IL: University of Illinois Press, 1972). Another book that offers an experiential perspective on aphasic disturbance is Howard Gardner's *The Shattered Mind* (New York: Knopf, 1975).

The material on acquired dyslexia is drawn from the volumes *Deep Dyslexia* and *Surface Dyslexia* (see Recommended Reading) as well as Y. Zotterman's *Dyslexia: Neuronal, Cognitive, and Linguistic Aspects* (Oxford: Pergamon Press, 1982). Figure 13.5 is adapted from Gerald D. Fischbach's "Mind and Brain," *Scientific American* (September 1992).

Finally, an excellent overview of recent developments in the field of neurolinguistics as a whole is available in the *Handbook of Neurolinguistics*, edited by B. Stremmer and H. Whitaker (New York: Academic Press, 1998).

Recommended reading

Caplan, D. 1987. *Neurolinguistics and Linguistic Aphasiology: An Introduction.* New York: Cambridge University Press.

Caplan, D. 1996. *Language: Structure, Processing, and Disorders.* Cambridge, MA: MIT Press.

Coltheart, M., J. Patterson, and J. C. Marshall (eds.). 1980. *Deep Dyslexia.* London: Routledge & Kegan Paul.

Patterson, K. E., J. C. Marshall, and M. Coltheart (eds.). 1986. *Surface Dyslexia.* Hillsdale, NJ: Lawrence Erlbaum.

Rosenbek, J. C., L. L. Lapointe, and R. T. Wertz. 1989. *Aphasia: A Clinical Approach.* Boston: Little Brown.

Segalowitz, S. 1983. *Two Sides of the Brain.* Englewood Cliffs, NJ: Prentice-Hall.

Questions

1. What distinguishes the human brain from a nonhuman brain?
2. In what ways can the cerebral hemispheres be considered to be two separate brains?
3. Below is an unlabeled diagram of the left hemisphere. Choose four contrasting colors and color each lobe of the cortex. Use arrows to point to the central sulcus, the lateral fissure, and the angular gyrus. Finally, use a pencil to indicate areas of lesion that would result in Broca's aphasia, Wernicke's aphasia, and acquired dyslexia. Label these lesions.

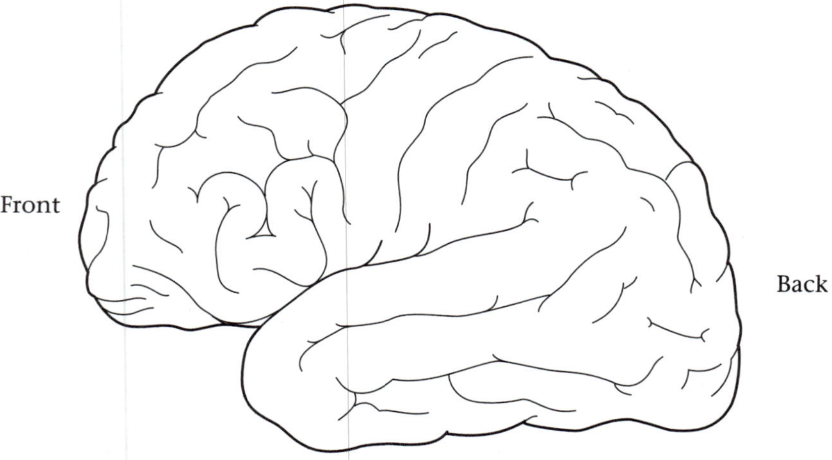

4. What are the relative advantages and disadvantages of the various techniques used to investigate the brain? Consider ethics, cost, intrusiveness, and type of information yielded.

5. What do dichotic listening tests tell us about the specialization of the cerebral hemispheres? Can you think of types of stimuli that would be interesting to present dichotically?

6. Do you think it is possible to learn how the normal brain functions by studying brain-damaged patients? What can the study of aphasia tell us about normal language competence?

7. Contrast the differences in behavior between fluent and nonfluent aphasics. What could explain these differences?

8. Describe the differences between phonological and surface dyslexia.

9. Reread Section 3. What do you think Moss's account tells us about the relationship between language and thought?

10. Many researchers have claimed that agrammatism involves a loss of syntactic knowledge. Imagine a type of aphasia that involves a loss of *phonological* knowledge. How would patients with this type of aphasia behave?

fourteen

LANGUAGE IN SOCIAL CONTEXTS

Marjory Meechan
Janie Rees-Miller

The real linguistic fact is the full utterance within its context of situation.

– BRONISLAW MALINOWSKI

OBJECTIVES

In this chapter, you will learn

- how social conventions influence speech interactions, and how these interactions are studied
- how speech marks a speaker's social identity
- how speech variation is studied
- how factors such as region, social class, and ethnicity affect American speech
- what happens to languages when they come into contact

Language is a tool for social interaction and it should not be surprising to learn that it can be affected by different social contexts. The study of language in social contexts, termed **sociolinguistics**, focuses on the relationship between linguistic behavior and social situations, roles, and functions. Rather than concentrating on individuals, sociolinguistics is centered on the **speech community**, defined as any group of people who share some set of social conventions, or **sociolinguistic norms**, regarding language use.

Speech communities may be distinguished by differing sociolinguistic norms at almost any level of language. Distinctions may be limited to minor phonetic differences in pronunciation, as when two groups have different **accents** or when differences in grammatical structure may be evident. For example, in some parts of the United States, the words *caught* and *cot* contain two different vowel phonemes, while in many other areas of the United States and in Canada, they are homophones. In other words, where the phoneme inventory of one community has two vowels, the other has only one. Differences in norms between communities may also show up as different preferences for particular morphemes or words or even different orderings of words. Where there is a systematic difference between varieties, the two varieties are generally considered to be different **dialects**.

There are cases where the degree of structural difference between dialects is so extensive that speakers from each community no longer have **mutual intelligibility**. In other words, they can no longer understand one another. Although it might seem that in these cases the dialects should then be classified as different languages, their speakers may still consider themselves to speak the same language, as, for example, when they are all citizens of the same country or members of the same ethnic group. In these cases, even radically distinct varieties may be classified as dialects of the same language. This situation holds for many varieties of Chinese.

Of course, groups will vary widely as to the degree to which they differ, and where it is not clear whether their speech involves an accentual, dialectal, or even language difference, the term **speech variety** is used as a cover term to merely indicate that some set of sociolinguistic norms are present. It can refer to accentual differences, dialectal differences or language differences. Essentially, a dialect shows systematic linguistic distinctions from some other variety of the same language and is spoken by a socially identifiable subgroup of some larger speech community. Dialects that are strongly associated with some social group are referred to as **sociolects**. An **ethnic dialect**, in which the accent is associated with a particular ethnic group, is a type of sociolect. **Regional dialects** occur when the speakers are associated with a particular geographical area.

Sociolinguistic norms are not only important for distinguishing speech communities but may also be relevant to language behavior within the community. There are two aspects of the social context that are important. On the one hand, differing sociolinguistic norms can serve to express a speaker's social identity or membership in the community. This can be referred to as the **sociolinguistics of society**. On the other hand, sociolinguistic norms can determine how language is structured depending on the social circumstances in which it is used. This can be referred to as the **sociolinguistics of language**.

1 THE SOCIOLINGUISTICS OF LANGUAGE

Conventions associated with social situations can have an influence on the structure of individual speech interactions. These can include anything from conventions for beginning a casual conversation to conventions for asking a question of a teacher in a formal classroom setting or even conventions for writing a technical manual or a novel. Almost any interaction can be the focus of sociolinguistic study. No matter what sort of interaction is involved, it is a representation of some type of **discourse**.

1.1 Discourse analysis

Analysis of the structure of discourse concentrates on how **utterances** are put together by speakers in individual interactions. Language in natural conversations is not always produced in complete sentences (*Do you want a cookie?*), so elliptical sentences (*Want a cookie?*) and even single words (*Cookie?*) can also be considered utterances. Both written and spoken discourse can be subjected to **discourse analysis** using one of various methods. Among these are analyses using **speech act theory** and the study of pragmatics, which have been described in previous chapters and will not be expanded on here. Other methods include **ethnography of communication, ethnomethodology**, and **text analysis**.

The ethnography of communication

The ethnography of communication method analyzes discourse using the same approach as anthropologists might use to study other cultural institutions such as medical practices or religious practices. Discourse studied using this approach is called a **speech event** and appears within a **speech situation**, which is any circumstance that may involve the use of speech. Speech events are subject to cultural rules of usage that are determined by the speech situation.

Ethnography of communication analysis involves the identification of individual components of the speech event and how they are realized. Eight basic components relevant to every speech event have been identified using the mnemonic SPEAKING, as shown in Table 14.1, which also includes sample analysis of a local telephone call.

Comparisons of these components across speech events shows that in order for speakers to function effectively in any speech situation, they must be aware of more than just the grammatical rules for language. They must also have access to all the rules of communication, or **communicative competence** (as discussed in Chapter 11). For example, if the receiver in the example in Table 14.1 had failed to answer the caller's complaint with an apology, the goal of the receiver would have been compromised. Conversely, if the receiver's goal had been to get rid of the caller in the most expeditious way, an apology might not have been indicated.

Instrumentalities can also be important for achieving specific outcomes and goals. For example, if the receiver wishes to appease the caller, it is important for her to show the caller that she views her with respect and takes her concerns seriously. To achieve this in North American society, she adopts a formal **style** or **register** during the conversation. Although these two terms are very similar in meaning and are often used interchangeably, they do differ. A speech style is defined in terms of formality of situation, and its values range along a continuum from relatively informal to formal. A register is more often directly associated with a specific speech situation that may or may not also be associated with some specific degree of formality. In both cases, they are characterized by a range of phonological, lexical, and syntactic properties. As example *1a* shows, the register used in newspaper headlines tends to omit small function words such as the determiners *the* or *a* and the copula *be*. Ritualistic register, as in *1b*, often includes archaic forms such as *ye* and *thou*. Recipes, as in *1c*, have a recognizable structure in their frequent omission of both subject and object pronouns as well as determiners. All these contrast with more formal registers, such as the technical writing in *1d*.

1) Examples of register

a. *Newspaper headlines*
Safety group to rate autos on rollover risk
Drink helps active dogs replace bodily fluids
Loaded gun found in bathroom of commercial jet

Table 14.1 SPEAKING mnemonic indicating components of a speech event

Component	*Explanation*	*Sample analysis*
Setting or locale	Scientific information about where it occurred (place, time)	Seattle at ten A.M. on May 3, 2000
Scene or situation	Generic information about the social occasion	Telephone call
Participants	Who was there (addressor/addressee, performer/audience, questioner/answerer	Caller—Ms. J. Smith Receiver—Ms. E. Jones, manager of a department store
Ends Outcomes—	Purpose of the event (transfer of knowledge, exchange of goods)	Complaint
Goals—	Purpose of the participants (impart knowledge, minimize price)	Caller—to register a complaint Receiver—to appease the caller
Act sequences	Content and forms particular to its use	Content: complaint about a malfunctioning toaster Form: tirade
Key	Tone or mood	Angry, sarcastic
Instrumentalities	Type of discourse or channel (spoken, written, recitation, etc.)	Spoken over a telephone line (only speech communication cues)
	Types of speech (dialect, style)	Formal standard business English
Norms Interaction—	Conventions of the interaction	After the conventional greeting, the caller speaks first giving complaint, receiver says she is sorry and offers to refund the money, etc.
Interpretation—	Normal interpretation	Receiver recognizes that the caller is angry and must be appeased while the caller recognizes that the receiver is making an attempt to do so.
Genres	Category of event (poem, story, conversation)	Conversation

b. *Rituals*
With this ring, I thee wed.
Hear ye, hear ye, the court of Judge John Smith is now in session.

c. *Recipes*
DINO-GETTI ON TOAST:
INGREDIENTS:
2 slices bread (white or brown, must fit in toaster)
butter or margarine
1 can 16 oz dino-getti

INSTRUCTIONS:

Pour contents of dino-getti tin into medium-size saucepan. Place on medium heat. Stir ever so gently, so as not to disfigure any of the dinosaur pasta shapes. Taste occasionally, and remove from heat when desired temperature is reached. While the dino-getti is being heated, carefully place bread in the toaster and press down on the handle. Bread will automatically pop up when done. At this time delicately spread a small amount of butter on *one* side of the toast. Place toast on plate (butter side up), and gingerly pour dino-getti on top.

d. Technical writing

Developers used several different languages to generate project code.

Patients who recovered either through cognitive-behavior therapy (CBT; N = 25) or through pharmacotherapy (PT; N = 29) completed self-reported ratings of dysfunctional attitudes before and after a negative mood induction procedure.

When a register is connected to a particular profession or activity, it may also be characterized by specific vocabulary items known as **jargon**. Jargon may involve specialized meanings for existing lexical items, as in the specialized use of the word *language* to mean programming language in *1d*. There also may be new terms coined specifically for that register, as in the psychological term *pharmacotherapy* for a treatment involving drugs. Jargon is interesting because although it is generally developed to facilitate communication within the group, it can also be used to indicate membership in the group. Jargon is not always viewed positively by all members of the community. For example, in the computer field, advanced developers will often dismiss jargon-filled sales and managerial reports with little real technical content as *technobabble*.

Slang, a common register found in a number of languages, is also a well-known vehicle for demarking group membership. The term *slang* refers to the use of faddish or nonstandard lexical items. Since slang is sensitive to current styles, it changes rapidly. Most slang terms will either disappear from use within a generation or become standardized and, therefore, no longer slang. Words like *dwindle, fan,* and *mob* were all once slang terms.

Slang is generally considered to be a low or vulgar form of the language and is most consistently associated with younger speakers. The form of any particular slang will differ according to the interests of the group that employs it. For example, high school students usually group themselves according to their interests and goals. Most high school communities include a popular group sometimes called Jocks (or also Preppies, Collegiates, or Soc's [sowʃəz]) and a rebellious group sometimes called Burnouts (or Hoods or Greasers). Anyone not falling into either group can be considered a Lame. Of course, some high schools are not necessarily limited to these three although, in some sense, they do tend to be universal.

For example, in one Calgary (Canada) high school in the early 1980s, as many as seven groups could be identified (Jocks, Freaks or Heads, Punks or Rockers, Snobs, Preppies, Brown-Noses or Homework Gang, and Nerds or Hosers). Some groups were more closely linked than others and shared some slang features. Freaks and Punks both used many terms for drugs. Jocks and Preppies employed a kind of California "Valley Girl" speech (for example, extreme shifts in pitch or frequent use of *like*) in their slang. Special high school cliques can be formed on the basis of whatever brings the group together, and in most cases, they will employ some slang. Slang is always an informal register and its use in a speech situation requiring a more formal register would be viewed negatively by other participants in the speech event.

A study of slang at a major American university (UCLA) produced a dictionary that included details of syntax and word formation as well as some indications of the origins of many of the slang expressions. For example, *homeboy* 'very close male friend' came from African American English; *mazeh* 'gorgeous guy' from Hebrew; and *happa* 'half-Asian person' from Japanese.

The students were also found to use particular word-formation processes in producing slang, as Table 14.2 shows.

Table 14.2 Processes of word formation in UCLA slang

Slang	*Meaning*	*Source*	*Process*
sucky	'awful'	suck	derivation [V → Adj]
mazehette	'gorgeous girl'	mazeh	derivation [N → N]
gork	'nerd'	**g**eek + d**ork**	blending
cas [kæʒ]	'all right'	**cas**ual	clipping
T.F.A.	'great!'	**T**otally **F**ucking **A**wesome	acronymy
fake-bake	'tanning salon'	fake + bake	compounding

In addition to these morphological techniques of word formation there was substantial use of the semantic technique of metaphor, in which an existing lexical item is replaced by another which suggests an image similar to that associated with the item replaced. Often the new coinage can be seen as more dramatic than the original. A typical instance of this process is seen in the phrase *blow chunks* 'vomit'. This replaces the older phrase *throw up* with a new phrase that has greater impact.

Although speakers of this slang can be expected to exhibit phonological variability with respect to (ing) in their usual speech, they consistently realize (ing) as [ɪn] in the slang word *bitchin'* 'good, excellent' so that there is no **bitching* alternating with it.

Interestingly, the slang items gathered in this study had a relatively limited semantic range. That is, the overwhelming majority of forms referred to comparatively few concepts. Many concerned the appearance of males (most were flattering, such as *hoss* 'stud; muscular male'; only a few were not: *eddie* 'ugly guy'). A large proportion of the terms referring to women were denigrating (as, *wilma* 'ugly girl', or *turbobitch* 'crabby female'). Some descriptive labels were gender-neutral (e.g., *studmuffin,* both 'strong, muscular person' and 'cute person; achiever'; and *gagger* 'disgusting person or thing'). Other frequently attested semantic domains in the UCLA slang included aspects of university life, sexual relations, and bodily functions.

Ethnography of communication can be an important tool for those who need to translate speech situations across cultures. For example, second language teachers want to educate students in both the grammatical and communicative rules of the language in question if the students are to function effectively in the second language society. Even in situations in which the participants are all native speakers of the same language, differences in communicative competence can lead to difficulties. English speakers with only one register or who lack the knowledge of where each register is appropriate would find it difficult to function in a wide variety of speech situations. Furthermore, the rules may change across cultures.

A great deal of international business is now carried out in English, yet there is no guarantee that characteristics of the components of a speech event conducted in an American setting will be the same as those occurring in other English-speaking regions such as Ghana, India, or England. For example, the standard response to *thank you* is *you're welcome,* but in parts of the United States, a convenience store clerk may give the reply *uh huh*. In Barbados, in the West Indies, the response is frequently *alright*. An American traveling in areas where other responses besides *you're welcome* are perfectly acceptable may get the erroneous impression that people in this place are rude and respond in kind. It is obvious that violating the often unspoken rules of communication can lead to errors in interpretation, which can have embarrassing and even costly consequences.

Ethnomethodology

Ethnomethodology, also called **conversation analysis**, is another approach to the study of discourse interactions. By identifying different types of utterances and isolating recurring patterns for their distribution in large corpora of tape-recorded natural conversations, many rules for the organization of conversation have been discovered. One very common structure that has been identified is the **adjacency pair**. This is an ordered pair of adjacent utterances spoken by two different speakers. Once the first utterance is spoken, the second is required. A few of the many adjacency pairs that have been identified are shown in *2*.

2)
Summons—answer
Can I get some help here?
On my way.

Offer—refusal
Sales clerk: May I help you find something?
Customer: No thank you, I'm just looking.

Compliment—acceptance
Your hair looks lovely today.
Thank you. I just had it cut.

Conversation analysis also tries to identify discourse units within a conversation. For example, most conversations will include an **opening**, or a beginning section, and these frequently include the "greeting–response" adjacency pair, as in example *3*.

3)
How are you?
Fine, thank you.

How these openings are structured affects which participant will introduce the first topic of conversation and even if the conversation will proceed at all. For example, speakers will conventionally respond by saying they are fine even if they are not. Someone who responds with a detailed description of their health has taken control of the conversation. Another common part of a conversation is a **closing** section, which signals the end of the conversation.

Between the opening and closing, speakers participate in the conversation in turns. The study of **turn-taking** is a central interest in conversation analysis. Three basic rules for turn-taking have been isolated based on the observation that at the end of a turn, a speaker may either select the next speaker (for example, by asking him or her a question) or not.

4) Turn-taking rules

a. If the next speaker in the conversation is selected, then only that person has either a "right" or an "obligation" to speak.

b. If no particular speaker is selected, then any other participant in the conversation may "self-select."

c. If no other speaker opts to take a turn, then the original speaker may continue.

Conversation analyses have shown that there are cues in the discourse that tell speakers where potential transition points occur in conversation. Besides being triggered by direct questions, transition points can be identified by intonational cues and even pause durations. For example, in 5, the tag question *don't you think* followed by a pause invites other participants to take a turn. If the discourse marker *but* occurs before another speaker takes a turn, the speaker shows that she is continuing her turn.

5)

He's a nice guy, don't you think, . . . but I don't think I'll go out with him.

Interestingly, cross-linguistic studies have shown that there are culture-specific conventions for turn-taking. For example, in some communities—as is generally the case for standard North American varieties of English—turns generally do not overlap. In other communities where speakers show a **high involvement style**, such as Eastern European Jews in New York, beginning a turn before the previous speaker is finished is not only acceptable but desired. In these cases, turns are not so much offered as taken, using strategies such as finishing another's sentence or other **cooperative overlaps**. Failure to do so may give the initial speaker the impression that the other participants are not involved or interested in the conversation.

Even where overlaps are desired, there are culture-specific differences in the meaning of transition point cues. For example, the pause signaling a transition point in Cree discourse is far longer than that found in standard English. Someone using standard English pause lengths as cues for transition points in other communities would either fail to take their turn when obligated (as in New York conversation) or be constantly interrupting other speakers' turns (as in Cree conversation). In both of these cases, the conversational flow would be disrupted.

Text analysis

The types of discourse analysis mentioned so far focus on the roles and obligations of speakers in conversation as controlled by aspects of their social and cultural environments. Text analysis, both written and oral, concentrates on the linguistic structure of discourse—both within and between utterances. These kinds of studies include analyses of pragmatics and speech act theory discussed in earlier chapters. A prominent sociolinguistic approach to text analysis uses variationist methodology. The variationist approach to discourse operates under the assumption that although a variety of structures may be used to fulfill any one discourse function, patterns in the variation found in natural conversational speech show that there is structure in discourse.

An important tool in variationist analysis is the **sociolinguistic variable** which, roughly speaking, represents alternative ways of saying the same thing. In example *6*, the variable is a question, and to show that it is a variable, it is enclosed in parentheses. This is a standard convention of variationist sociolinguistics. Any form put into parentheses is a variable.

6)

(Questions)
Wanna drive?
You want to drive?
Do you want to drive?

In the study of structure in discourse, any set of utterances with equivalent discourse functions can constitute a variable. To determine which utterances are functionally equivalent, utterances in specific types of discourse units—such as narratives or lists—are analyzed to isolate their function. For example, **narratives** are composed of several different clause types. **Abstract clauses**, which contain a general summary of the experience to be narrated, will sometimes appear at the beginning of the narrative. More often, **orientation clauses** will begin the narrative by giving the background to the story, such as who was involved as well as where and when it took place. **Complicating action clauses** describe the events of the story, and each event generally appears in the order it took place. **Evaluation clauses** consist of comments regarding the events. Finally, the narrative may end with a **coda clause** that serves to shift the time of the narrative back to present time. Example *7* shows a narrative analysis with most of these elements. (A *coulee* in *f* is a ditch.)

7)

Narrative example from southern Alberta English corpus (Cass 12, Spkr 011, 1.01.00)

a. Abstract	**Well**, there was one time
b. Orientation	when I was driving with my mom.
c. Orientation	I just—just got my learner's,
d. Orientation	we're going to my—had a banquet—hockey banquet
e. Orientation	**and** it was snowing outside, everything
f. Complicating action	**and all of a sudden**, I just lost control of the car going down into a coulee.
g. Orientation	Car's slowly going over
h. Orientation	**and** I'm just turning it this way,
i. Complicating action	slammed on the brakes.
j. Orientation	There's my mom

k.	Orientation	**just** looking,
l.	Orientation	just praying, **eh**
m.	Complicating action	**and** I w—I just—I missed the barricade by this much
n.	Complicating action	**and then** I came to a complete stop in an in—into a—an approach.
o.	Evaluation	It was close.
p.	Complicating action	I sa—I got out of the car,
q.	Complicating action	I said, "Mom, you're driving now."
r.	Evaluation	I think that was the closest thing
s.	Evaluation	that I came to even experiencing anything
t.	Evaluation	that would be—even be close to death.

This approach to discourse can be very valuable for examining the role of **discourse markers**. These are elements that bracket utterances and organize the sequence and relationship between events and participants in the discourse. In *7*, there are numerous examples of discourse markers (shown in bold). For example, *well* in utterance *7a*, *eh* in *7l,* and *and then* in *7n* are all discourse markers, and there are numerous other examples in this short narrative such as *just, and, and all of a sudden,* etc. Speakers are not generally aware of discourse markers but they are important signals in discourse. For example, the discourse in *7* was given in response to a question asking if the speaker had ever been in serious danger of death. Speakers will often use *well* to soften responses to questions. In *7a*, the speaker's use of *well* may be expressing the feeling that while the experience was harrowing, there was never really any strong danger of death.

The study of discourse markers is closely connected to a central interest of many variationist analyses of discourse. One frequently noted function of discourse markers is to provide additional temporal organization or cohesion to clauses. The discourse marker *then* has been shown to signal some point of achievement in discourse. In *7*, the speaker is describing the experience while the car was out of control and uses *then* to signal how it ended. This shows the importance of **cohesive devices** in discourse. For example, discourse markers like *well, then,* and *and* link utterances in discourse and provide information about how they relate to one another. This gives coherence to the discourse. To see this, try removing the discourse markers from the example in *7*; it will it be obvious how the flow of discourse is interrupted.

Cohesive devices are also important for tracking participants and events in discourse, as an examination of temporal and spatial reference clearly shows. For example, in *7*, there is variation in the speaker's reference to the car. In *7f* it is referred to as *the car*, in *7g* the speaker just says *car*, in *7h* the car is designated by the pronoun *it,* and in *7p* the speaker again refers to *the car*. Pragmatic and discourse analysis of this has revealed that speakers have conventions for reference in discourse. For example, the pronoun *it* is generally found after the full noun phrase *the car* in discourse. This is called **anaphoric reference**. In less frequent cases, a pronoun may precede the full noun phrase and is then called **cataphoric reference**. In *7g*, for example, the speaker might have used the clause in *8*.

8)

It's slowly going over, **the car**.

The function and structure of discourse marking is still not very well understood. For example, the study of *eh* in Canadian English has focused almost completely on its use as a questioning form, although its use in example *7l* is clearly not of this type. As this shows, one of the problems of studying discourse markers is the fact that they often will perform multiple functions depending on the type of clause or adjacency pair in which they are found and their position in the clause. For example, the use of *then* depends on the type of discourse, what kind of clause it appears in, and its position in relation to the clause—initial or final. Quantitative variationist analysis takes these factors into account and avoids the dangers of ad hoc explanations as found in many anecdotal studies. It also accounts for the fact that choice of discourse markers can be a signal of group identity, which explains why a particular marker may occur less often and in a more restricted number of positions in the speech of one speaker as opposed to another. For example, the use of *eh* in New Zealand English is most frequent among Maori men and operates as a mark of Maori identity for these speakers. In fact, discourse markers are just one device that speakers may use to mark relationships of solidarity and power.

1.2 Solidarity and Power

Language use can reflect not only the identity of a speaker but also relationships between speakers. For example, language behavior can reflect differences in **power** between speakers in that some individuals have some degree of control over the behavior of others. In addition, speakers can either show **solidarity** by using forms of language that emphasize some degree of closeness or intimacy, or register difference by avoiding them. Solidarity and power are frequently invoked as explanations for linguistic behavior. Examination of politeness in language can illustrate how this occurs.

Politeness

Politeness can be expressed in many ways in language and is culture-specific. This is illustrated very clearly in ethnomethodology studies of the compliment–response adjacency pair. In North American culture, one polite response to a compliment is **self-praise avoidance**, as in example *9*.

9)

a. What a nice dress!
b. This old thing?

In other cultures, avoidance of self-praise may be considered rude. There may also be other responses unrelated to self-praise. For example, in some cultures, the response to *9a* is to offer the item that was praised as a gift, as is the case in traditional Cree society and in some African societies.

Politeness is related to the notions of solidarity and power. Standards of politeness are determined by both the power relationship between speakers and the degree of solidarity between them. Speakers with a high degree of solidarity are most likely to observe the conventions of politeness as determined by relative differences of power between speakers since this emphasizes shared attitudes and values. Where these are used to express regard and consideration for other participants, it can be considered **positive politeness**. Speakers wishing to show distance and/or lack of regard will employ these conventions to show rudeness. For example, a Cree speaker who overtly compliments someone on an expensive or otherwise valued item that they know the recipient would not like to give up would be expressing rudeness. Another example of this involves register choice in speaker interactions. If standards of politeness require a formal register and a speaker with control over both formal and informal registers chooses to be informal, he is using politeness conventions deliberately to be impolite. Notice that this is different from incorrect use or failure to use conventions due to ignorance or other reasons. In these cases, the speaker is not employing politeness conventions at all.

Another effect of politeness on language use is the avoidance of certain topics of conversation that are deemed by societal convention to be impolite. Words used to refer to these are frequently considered **taboo** by some or all members of the community. What is considered taboo is culture-specific. For example, in Western society, speakers will frequently avoid words relating to bodily functions. This results in the use of **euphemisms** as shown in *10*, where the top word is the most taboo and the bottom is the least.

10)

piss
pee
urinate

Euphemisms are also used when the common word for some item or activity has possible negative associations that the speaker wishes to avoid. For example, the U.S. military uses the term *collateral damage* to mean civilian casualties as a result of its actions. After a Stealth fighter crashed during the NATO bombing of Belgrade, U.S. military spokesmen suggested that at the time the airplane went down, the pilot was *task saturated.* In fact, special care needed to be taken during operation of the aircraft due to its sophisticated and complicated engineering and the pilot was merely busy.

Perhaps a more obvious example of the role of politeness and avoidance strategies in discourse is found in the employment of different forms of address.

Forms of address

Address terms are the forms that speakers use to address and refer to each other. Some types of address in English are shown in Table 14.3.

Table 14.3 Types of address terms in English

Term	*Example*
First name (N)	Mary
Title + last name (TLN)	Mr. Jones
Title alone (T)	Nurse
Last name (LN)	Jones

Which form of address is chosen is heavily dependent on both power and solidarity relationships between speakers as well as on conventions for usage in each culture. For example, the use of a particular form indicates the degree of solidarity the speaker feels with the addressee (person spoken to). With a friend, speakers are more likely to be on a first name basis while more distant relationships involve the use of a title and last name. In the case of a friendship, speakers are likely to address each other reciprocally, each using the other's first name. In relationships where there is a perceived power distinction, such as between age groups or work associates, addressing may be nonreciprocal. For example, students will usually refer to their teachers as Ms. Smith or Professor Smith whereas the teacher will use the students' first names. In some cases, power and solidarity relationships between individuals can conflict for the use of address forms. For example, newlyweds will often have difficulty deciding what to call their in-laws. *Mother* may seem too familiar while the use of a first name might seem disrespectful. However, title and last name is too formal; it implies that the speaker is unwilling to form a close relationship. In this situation, speakers may engage in what is called **no-naming**: they avoid naming their in-laws at all.

In English, it is possible to avoid directly naming someone because unlike other European languages, English has lost a formality distinction in the pronoun system. In languages in which distinctions in pronouns still exist, no-naming is more difficult. For example, in most French communities the standard rule is that between speakers of roughly equal status, reciprocal pronouns are used. To express solidarity, as in relationships between family members and friends, the form *tu* is used. If the addressee is someone of roughly equal status with whom the speaker shares no feeling of solidarity, the form *vous* is used. Where one speaker is in a position of power over another, pronouns are employed nonreciprocally, with the more powerful participant addressed as *vous* and the less powerful as *tu*.

Studies of *tu/vous* usage patterns in Quebec French found that rural areas showed more usage of nonreciprocal *vous* within the family than did urban areas. In other words, in rural families, elders were more likely to be addressed as *vous* and younger people as *tu*. It has been suggested that increased use of pronouns as solidarity markers rather than markers of power in urban areas may indicate that there is a de-emphasis of the power relationship in modern society. However, variationist studies comparing *tu/vous* use in Montreal over a period of thirteen years found that there was no clear evidence that *vous* was disappearing, indicating the continued use of *tu/vous* as markers of both power and solidarity.

Pronoun usage to express solidarity is not restricted to Indo-European languages. In Bislama, a creole spoken in the Republic of Vanuatu in the Pacific, there is a distinction between inclusive and exclusive first-person pronouns (pronouns that distinguish whether the hearer is included or not), as shown in Table 14.4.

Table 14.4 Some pronoun contrasts in Bislama

	Singular	*Plural*
1st (inclusive)	—	yumi
1st (exclusive)	mi	mifala
2nd	yu	yufala

In addition to marking addressee participation in the event described, these pronouns are also used as signals of solidarity between the speaker and addressee. Speakers of Bislama will use the inclusive forms like *yumi* in the presence of someone with whom they want to show solidarity, even if that person was not actually a participant in the activity described, and an exclusive form like *mifala* to express distance.

In Javanese discourse, solidarity marking is not limited to address terms or pronoun choice but also involves sharp morphological and lexical differences across registers. Table 14.5 shows examples of high and low registers found in the most standard dialect. In fact, these do not exhaust all of the distinctions available to a speaker of Javanese for indicating differences of solidarity and power.

Table 14.5 Dialect of the Prijajis (Javanese)

Level	*'are*	*you*	*going*	*to eat*	*rice*	*and*	*cassava*	*now'*
High	menapa	pandjenengan	baḍé	ḍahar	sekul	kalijan	kaspé	semanika
Low	apa	sampéjan	arep	neda	sega	lan	kaspé	saiki

As with address terms, speakers can show reciprocal use of the low register indicating strong solidarity and equivalent status, reciprocal use of higher registers showing distance but equivalent status, or nonreciprocal use, in which each speaker uses forms that reflect the status of the addressee. In other words, a lower status person would address a higher status person using the higher form and would be answered in the lower form.

Address forms are also a commonly noted source of distinction between the sexes in a number of societies. For example, in Japanese, there are differences in the pronoun systems of the speech of men and women, as shown in Table 14.6.

Table 14.6 Japanese nonformal personal pronouns

	Men's speech	*Women's speech*
First person	boku	watasi
Second person	kimi	anata

Language and sex

In most societies, the language of men and women differs. Among the Gros Ventre tribe in Montana, women consistently pronounce some words differently than men. For example, the word for *bread* is pronounced /kjá tsa/ by the women and /dʒá tsa/ by the men. In Koasati, a Muskogean language found in Louisiana, verb forms differ depending on the sex of the speaker, as shown in Table 14.7 (ˆ marks falling pitch stress; ´ marks high pitch stress).

Table 14.7 Gender-exclusive verb forms in Koasati

Women	*Men*	*Gloss*
lakawwîl	lakawwís	'I am lifting it'
lakáwtʃ	lakáwtʃ	'You are lifting it'
lakáw	lakáws	'He is lifting it'
lakáwwilit	lakáwwilitʃ	'I lifted it'

Types of differences such as those found in Koasati and Japanese are considered **gender-exclusive** in that there are strong social prohibitions against using forms associated with the opposite sex.

Although most examples of gender-exclusive differentiation come from non-European languages, differences between sexes have also been noted in European languages. In most cases, these are exhibited as tendencies rather than categorical distinctions. For example, women in North American society tend to possess a wider variety of color terms than men. Men, on the other hand, tend to have more terms relating to sports. Men and women may also differ in rates of usage of variable grammatical forms, as discussed later in the chapter. This kind of differentiation is called **gender-variable** because it involves overall rates rather than absolute distinctions.

Despite the strong correlation between sex of the speaker and language differences, the wide variety of distinctions argues against a biological explanation. There is no genetic reason for men and women to be different in terms of how they use language. Clearly these differences are related to gender roles in these societies. There are two basic views for explaining the relationship between language and gender. One claims that these differences reflect the inherent differences between the sexes in society; the other claims that these differences may indicate that language operates as a tool for one group to establish and maintain power over another group. This latter view is often held by feminists.

This is a classic point of contention in linguistics. Does language determine society or does society determine language? Some linguists have found that women are more likely to use **verbal hedges** such as *perhaps, you know, sort of,* etc., than are men. It has been suggested that this indicates unassertiveness of women as a result of their relatively powerless position in society. However, a study of the verbal hedge *you know*, which distinguished between its use as an expression of uncertainty—as in example *11a* where there is rising intonation (´)—and its use as a mark of confidence—as in *11b* with falling intonation (`)—found that women are more likely to use *you know* to express confidence than are men.

11)

a. well it was all very embarrassing *you knów.*

b. and that way we'd get rid of exploitation of many by many all that stuff *you knòw* you've heard it before.

Thus, the existence of increased amounts of verbal hedges in women's speech is not necessarily proof that they are unassertive. Furthermore, other studies of gender-variable differences in language have found that upper-middle-class speakers tend to show the greatest differences across genders. Since upper-middle-class women are arguably the *most* powerful women in society, power differential as an explanation for gender difference is probably an overly simplistic explanation.

Even so, it is undoubtedly the case that women, as a group, *do* occupy less powerful positions in most societies. On average, women in full-time employment earn less than men, and fewer women than men hold managerial positions. This difference between the sexes is reflected both in the way women's speech is described and in how men and women are referenced. In English, what is considered "correct" can frequently be traced back to an androcentric bias on the part of grammarians in that characteristics of men's speech have been considered desirable and those of women are traditionally denigrated. A fourteenth-century grammar of English noted that the noun phrase in *12a*, which places the woman before the man, should be considered less "correct" than that in *12b*.

12)

a. My mother and father
b. My father and mother

Difference in speech as it correlates with gender of the speaker is only one side of the coin. There are numerous examples in language relating to differences between how men and women are referred to.

Correlation of language behavior with gender roles is also connected to another kind of gender in language—that of grammatical gender. In particular, the use of masculine gender as a generic or unmarked form shows a male bias. As mentioned in earlier chapters, many languages use a noun classification system that puts nouns into different classes; in European languages this is called gender, partly because nouns with female referents take one grammatical gender and those with male referents take another, although as the Spanish data in *13* shows, sex is not the only consideration.

13)

Feminine		*Masculine*	
la mujer	'the woman'	**el** hombre	'the man'
la casa	'the house'	**el** edificio	'the building'

English has lost most of its grammatical gender, with only a few vestiges of the system remaining—particularly in the pronoun system. However, androcentric grammatical "correctness" has influenced pronoun choice in situations where the sex of the referent is not specified. For instance, *14a*, which uses the masculine pronoun, has traditionally been considered more correct by prescriptive grammarians than *14b*, which uses a gender-neutral pronoun.

14)

a. Someone left a message, but he forgot to leave his name.
b. Someone left a message, but they forgot to leave their name.

Of course, not all gender distinction in language is the result of androcentric bias. Gender differences in many languages may have also arisen due to differences in what was considered taboo for each sex. The avoidance of taboo words by one sex and not the other may have led to differences in word choice. In any case, the study of gender differences in language can provide a revealing glimpse into the structure of any society.

Accommodation

Another important aspect of interpersonal relationships related to solidarity and power is that of linguistic **accommodation,** in which speakers will modify their language patterns in interactions to make them more like those of the people with whom they are speaking. Speakers' language may **converge** syntactically, morphologically, and even phonologically during the course of the conversation. For example, a study comparing conversations between a travel assistant in Wales and several of her clients according to the social class of the client to whom she was speaking found that the assistant tended to use phonological characteristics such as /h/ deletion, *-in'* versus *-ing,* etc., more often when speaking to clients of lower socioeconomic classes whose speech is also characterized by these forms. In other words, her speech became more like that of those with whom she was speaking.

Conversely, speakers may also make modifications that cause their language patterns to **diverge** or become more unlike each other. Studies in Catalonia (in Spain) and in Japan have found that some speakers, when addressed in their native language by foreigners, will often shift into the foreigner's language even though the foreigner's speech may be perfectly understandable and even technically "correct." Accommodation theory suggests that speakers converge in order to show solidarity and diverge to show distance. This is important for analyzing style differences between speakers but may also be related to how they express their identity linguistically in relation to others in society.

2 THE SOCIOLINGUISTICS OF SOCIETY

The sociolinguistics of society relates to the way language behavior operates as a mark of a speaker's social identity. Since any individual speaker may at the same time have any number of identities related to her sex, age, ethnic background, or social class, the investigation of the sociolinguistics of society can be complex. A central issue is the notion of what sociolinguistic norms are guiding speakers with respect to their choices for linguistic behavior.

2.1 Sociolinguistic norms

Numerous studies have found that patterns within individual social groups reflect perceived societal norms for the entire community. How subgroups pattern for mainstream norms may reflect their participation (or lack of it) in the society. Linguistic patterns across social groups form an **orderly heterogeneity** in that even though subgroups show varying degrees of use of particular variants, similar overall patterns of variability within each group reveal shared linguistic systems and social norms. Distinct behavior can reveal both distinctions in linguistic systems as well as the ways language use can construct social barriers.

Standard varieties

Most speech communities feature more than one language variety. In a number of situations, prescriptive grammarians and other language purists may hold up one variety as the "correct" **standard** or way of speaking. Language standardization is largely limited to international and colonial languages like English or French and classical languages such as Arabic. Despite the strong belief in the "correctness" of the standard, it is an idealization created as a result of social and historical pressures associated with the growth of nation-states and colonial empires.

The intangibility of the standard is most clearly shown by the fact that in both the United States and Canada, when linguists have come together to define standard

American and Canadian English, the attempt has failed because of lack of agreement on how a standard variety arises and how it should be defined. This situation also holds with French in North America where the principal debate is the existence of a standard form of Quebec French that is distinct from standard European French. Is the standard merely the most frequent form or that which most people consider most prestigious, or is it some collection of grammatical rules imposed on a community by "experts"?

In fact, the standard variety, as defined by grammarians, does not really exist. Speakers in any community will adopt many of its features according to their social status, their level of education, and the situation in which they find themselves; even in the written form, any sizable stretch of discourse may violate someone's idea of correct or standard language, since grammarians often disagree. For example, a survey of English professors found that there was quite a bit of disagreement about the acceptability of some commonly noted grammatical "errors," as shown in Table 14.8.

Table 14.8 Sample results: survey of English professors

	Frequency (%) (as estimated by the English professors)				*Acceptability (%)*		
	Rare	*Moderately frequent*	*Very frequent*	*Can't say*	*Yes*	*No*	*Can't say*
Everyone volunteered but they all failed to appear. (agreement error)	0	25	63	12	19	81	0
Jane Austen now feels that it is necessary to partially clarify Frank Churchill's relationship to Jane. (split infinitive)	0	16	74	10	17	72	11
Considering how little satisfaction she obtained from it, it was just a waste. (dangling participle)	12	47	35	6	35	59	6

A more reasonable way of thinking of the standard is to consider it to be the variety that has the most features that are conventionally believed in society to be prestigious. In fact, in popular use, the standard variety is usually the one that is taught in the schools, and its features are found more frequently in the speech of the upper classes, politicians, and the news media. In this sense, there are a number of ways of establishing what features characterize the standard of any given speech community.

Language attitudes

One way of determining which variety is looked on as more standard in any community is through attitude studies. Generally, people tend to believe they use more standard forms than they actually do in practice. However, in some cases, speakers are painfully aware of the gap between the way they speak and the standard. For example, a study of **linguistic insecurity** in New York City used a list of words with variable pronunciations to test the relationship between usage and speakers' intuitions of "correctness," or standard language. Table 14.9 shows the list of items tested.

Participants were asked to listen to two possible pronunciations and mark on a questionnaire which one was "correct" and which one they usually used. Interestingly, lower-middle-class speakers (as opposed to working-class, lower-class, and upper-middle-class speakers) were most likely to show a high degree of linguistic insecurity, since they were much more likely than other groups to identify a difference between what they said and what they perceived as correct. Similarly, women were more likely than men to manifest linguistic insecurity in this way. A similar study conducted in Winnipeg in Canada confirmed the relatively higher degree of linguistic insecurity for lower-middle-class speakers.

Table 14.9 Items on the linguistic insecurity test given to New Yorkers

Token	*Form 1*	*Form 2*	*Token*	*Form 1*	*Form 2*
Joseph	[dʒowsɪf]	[dʒowzɪf]	length	[lɛnθ]	[lɛŋθ]
catch	[kætʃ]	[kɛtʃ]	February	[fɛbruɛri]	[fɛbjuɛri]
tomato	[təmejto]	[təmɑto]	ketchup	[kætʃəp]	[kɛtʃəp]
diapers	[dajpɚz]	[dajəpɚz]	escalator	[ɛskəlejtɚ]	[ɛskjulejtɚ]
aunt	[ɑnt]	[ænt]	new	[nu]	[nju]
often	[ɔftən]	[ɔfən]	tune	[tjun]	[tun]
garage	[gərɑdʒ]	[gərɑːʒ]	avenue	[ævənu]	[ævənju]
humorous	[hjumərəs]	[jumərəs]	because	[bikɔs]	[bikɔz]
vase	[vejz]	[vɑːz]	half	[hæf]	[haf]

Another method for determining speakers' attitudes to particular varieties and languages is the **matched guise test**. In this test, participants are asked to listen to recordings of two speakers and then give the speakers ratings according to characteristics like intelligence, likability, and social class. In reality, the participants are listening to the same speaker speaking two different varieties. Studies in Britain found that, as expected, the variety taught in school—received pronunciation (RP)—was ranked as most standard. The RP-accented speaker was felt to have more characteristics associated with success, such as intelligence, height, and high socioeconomic status. Matched guise tests have been used extensively since the early sixties to investigate attitudes toward French and English in Quebec. Early studies found that both anglophone and francophone Canadians ranked speakers more positively when they were speaking English.

Another type of attitude test that originated in the Netherlands and Japan but is also used in both the United States and Canada asks participants to rate the accents of different geographical areas according to perceptual categories such as "pleasantness," "correctness," and "similarity" to the participants' own speech. In the United States, residents of Michigan rated their own speech highest with respect to values connected to "correctness" but ranked the speech of southerners higher for categories connected to "pleasantness."

Nonstandard varieties

The existence of standard forms of a language implies that all other forms are somehow not standard or even "substandard." However, this is not the case. There are many forms that are proscribed by grammarians but are commonly used throughout the community without sanction. An excellent example is the use of the pronoun *they* discussed in the section on language and gender to refer to referents that are unspecified for gender. Widely used forms that carry no negative connotations are not necessarily nonstandard. The use of the term **nonstandard** merely indicates that the form lacks positive prestige in the community. However, in no way does it mean that the forms are somehow defective.

Prescriptivists often claim that nonstandard forms show an inherent illogic or lack of systematicity. The so-called double negative, seen in *15a*, is a prime example.

15)

a. She didn't see nobody.
b. She didn't see anybody.
c. She saw somebody.
d. She saw nobody.

From a prescriptivist point of view, where a sentence is marked for negation twice as in *15a*, the double negative will give the sentence an affirmative meaning, as in *15c*. However, as everyone knows, this is patently false. Both *15a* and *15b* are universally recognized by even highly standard speakers as having the meaning in *15d*. In fact, both negative sentences, standard and nonstandard, show parallel grammatical marking; it is just the form that differs. In *15a*, the pronoun is marked with *no-*, and in *15b*, it is marked with *any-*. In both cases, the negative pronoun differs from that found in an affirmative sentence such as *15c*. Neither *15a* nor *15b* is any more or less logical than the other. Furthermore, while the double negative construction is considered nonstandard in modern English, it is the standard form in many other languages such as Spanish, as shown in *16a*.

16)

Ella	no	vió	nada
She	neg	saw	nothing

'She didn't see anything.'

In other words, nonstandard varieties are not grammatically less valued, but since they generally represent the speech of a politically less powerful group, they may be socially less valued. However, it is possible that two relatively standard varieties can coexist in one community.

Where two varieties are used in sharply distinguished situations or **domains of use** in a particular speech community, the relationship between varieties is known as **diglossia**. One variety is used in more formal situations or in the written form and is called the high variety, while the other is used in less formal situations and is referred to as the low variety. Table 14.10 shows some uncontroversial cases of diglossia.

In most communities, use of informal language features is restricted in formal situations. This differs from what is generally considered diglossia in that the differences in features between formal and informal registers indicate a clear difference in varieties. Furthermore, in situations of diglossia, each variety can be considered the standard or correct variety for its particular domain of use.

Table 14.10 Recognized situations of diglossia

Country	*High*	*Low*
Switzerland	Standard German	Swiss German
Haiti	French	Haitian creole
Greece	Katharévusa	Demotic Greek

Official languages and language planning

The issue of standard and nonstandard varieties is also connected to the notion of **official language**. An official language differs from a standard language in that it has been declared the language of a particular region or country as a result of legislation. Designation of an official language has implications for the political and economic power of ethnic groups, and is often a reaction to a perceived increase in power of a minority group by the majority. Currently, about half of the United States has some sort of law giving English official status. In Canada, there are two designated official languages at the federal level—English and French. However, most individual provinces conduct official business in one or the other. Governments are not the only institutions concerned with language use. Use of particular languages can be dictated by the official policies of any organization; determining what policies are to be followed is called **language planning**.

Official language designation usually puts speakers of nonofficial languages at a disadvantage because their access to legal or other documents and their participation during official business may be restricted if they have a reduced ability in the official language. They may have less access to educational opportunities and, hence, less advancement in society. In the past, language planning has even resulted in speakers' being banned from using their language at all. This was the case in the earlier part of the twentieth century when native languages such as Lakota and Apache were banned at residential schools for Native Americans, with harsh punishments dealt out to offenders. In more recent years, attempts have been made to ban languages other than English. For example, in 1988, Spanish-speaking clerks of the municipal court in Huntington Park, California, challenged the English-only rule in their workplace. Although the clerks involved were hired because of their expertise in Spanish and ability to deal with Spanish-speaking members of the public, they were forbidden to use Spanish among themselves. The case was heard by a U.S. Court of Appeals, and the English-only rule was struck down. The court cited Equal Employment Opportunity Commission guidelines that prohibit language restrictions except in narrowly defined cases of business necessity.

Restricting language use is not the only possible outcome of language planning. For example, regulations can also be enacted to increase minority language rights, such as access to education in the minority language as well as access to official government processes like driver's license examinations. The 2000 U.S. census forms, for example, were available in Spanish, Chinese, Korean, Tagalog, and Vietnamese, and assistance guides in more than forty languages were available on the Internet. The 1974 U.S. Supreme Court decision in *Lau v. Nichols* and policies emitting from both the legislative and executive branches of the government have established safeguards for speakers of minority languages. Thus, voting materials must be made available in significant minority languages, and school boards must plan for the education of non-English-speaking children in ways that take into account their differing native languages.

Language planning is not restricted to multilingual situations; it can also have an effect on which variety of a language is deemed acceptable for official use. For example, in 1961, the *Office de la langue française* was formed in Quebec to regulate the use of Quebec French, protect a standardized Quebec French, and give advice to Quebecers and others on the correct use of the language. A similar watchdog on the French language also exists in France. Although there are no equivalent government regulators on the quality of the English language, recognized authorities on English such as the *Oxford English Dictionary* and numerous published grammars and style manuals serve a similar purpose.

Language planning can be a particularly hot issue in the field of education. There has been a great deal of debate over whether it is preferable to educate minority groups using their native languages, at least at the primary levels, or to force assimilation of the group by eliminating minority-language education. This is the main issue surrounding the debate over the use of **ebonics**, or **African American Vernacular English (AAVE)**, as a tool for minority education in the Oakland, California, school system. Many people mistakenly believed that the Oakland school system was considering *teaching* students to speak ebonics rather than merely *recognizing* the variety and incorporating it into the teaching of standard English (among other topics). In other words, they were proposing an attempt to reduce the disadvantage of speaking a nonstandard variety. A portion of the official statement of the Linguistic Society of America on the issue is shown in *17*.

17)

There is evidence from Sweden, the U.S., and other countries that speakers of other varieties can be aided in their learning of the standard variety by pedagogical approaches which recognize the legitimacy of the other varieties of a language. From this perspective, the Oakland School Board's decision to recognize the vernacular of African American students in teaching them Standard English is linguistically and pedagogically sound.

Wherever nonstandard or nonofficial languages exist side-by-side with a standard national language, this issue arises. For example, many African nations have adopted a colonial language such as English or French as their official language, partly because of access to international trade and partly because in many of these countries, there are a number of ethnic languages, and choosing an international language minimizes ethnic disputes. In many countries, despite the fact that most citizens are native speakers of an indigenous language, most education takes place in the colonial language. This issue is also highly relevant to addressing possible education problems among Native Americans who may speak Navajo, Cherokee, or any one of a number of indigenous languages as their first language.

Identification and status of a language variety can affect what form of the language will be spoken in any one situation and if it will be considered as standard. What is considered prestigious for one community may not be so considered for another, and speakers will vary their language depending on the situation and their need to express their social identity. In order to determine how language is structured as a function of these social considerations, special methodologies have been developed for the study of variation.

2.2 Methods of studying variation

One problem in determining the relationship between form, function, and social identity in language is that it is highly variable. The fact that language is variable is relatively uncontroversial. Any short discourse will reveal variability. For example, *18* shows five words ending in *-ing*. Two are pronounced [ɪŋ], two are pronounced [ən], and one is pronounced [in].

18)

Stocks and investments and stuff like that in math but no, they don't do noth*en'*. Like, I don't do anyth*ing*. We were talk*en'* about school and I don't do anyth*ing* that I've learned from school. Noth*een*. (Alberta English Corpus; Cass 26, Spkr 023, 22.08)

Where fields of linguistics differ is in how this variation is to be interpreted and even if it is to be interpreted at all. Most studies of the rules governing phonology, morphology, and syntax attempt to factor out unexplained variation. The variationist approach to language is unique in that it takes as its starting point the tenet that language is inherently variable. Variation like this, in which the appearance of different variants is regulated by one variable linguistic system, is a classic example of inherent variability.

As noted in the section on discourse, the central focus of interest to variationist analysis is the sociolinguistic variable. This is a set of forms, or **variants**, that can all be used to say the same thing. A phoneme, a morpheme, or a set of syntactic structures operating over some semantic or functional domain can each be considered a variable if at least some of their surface structures cannot be explained using **categorical**, or invariant, rules. By counting each possible variant of a variable and finding out what percentage occur in each possible conditioning environment, patterns in the variation can be discovered. For example, variationist analyses of the example in *18* comparing the percentage of *-in'* versus *-ing* in casual registers to that found in formal registers in a number of communities have usually found that formality is a factor in determining which variant is used.

Data culled from speaker intuitions are prohibited in variationist study of the sociolinguistics of society because the researcher can never be sure what speaker intuitions about variable patterns represent. Some people have very strong attitudes about language. The "Letters to the Editor" column in the magazine *Organic Gardening* provides an excellent example. When the magazine hired a new editor who adopted a more casual style, a controversy began that ran for well over three years, with many readers voicing strong objections, as shown in *19*.

19)

I suspect you view yourself as a breath of fresh air to this encrusted old publication. I view your insistence on fracturing the written English language as a blast of pollution. (January 1992, p. 14)

Sociolinguistic studies have found that speakers who believe a particular form to be "slang" or "incorrect" will often deny using it even though subsequent examination of their recorded speech shows that they do. Thus, only corpora of natural conversational speech are acceptable for examining variation.

Since the rarity of some variant may merely reflect the rarity of the structure where it is most likely to occur, there is no infallible way, using conversational data, to determine when a form is completely prohibited. Instead, variation studies compare overall rates of occurrence and cooccurrences of variants to determine which linguistic or social contexts favor or disfavor any one form. To obtain this information, a quantitative analysis is required.

Indexing analysis

When a variable is continuous, one method of quantifying the variation is by **indexing analysis**—that is, assigning an index value to points along a continuum. Each **token**, or instance, of the variable uttered by the speaker is given a value based on where it falls along the continuum. For instance, in William Labov's investigation of speech in New York City, one of the variables was production of θ and ð in contexts such as that in *20*:

20)

There's something strange about that—how I can remember everything he did: this thing, that thing, and the other thing.

Labov noted that the θ and ð sounds could be produced as the standard fricatives or as nonstandard stops (the stereotypical *dese* and *dose* instead of *these* and *those*). Sometimes, however, they were produced as affricates—an intermediate stage between fricative and stop. Each possible pronunciation was assigned a numerical value reflecting how closely it approximated the standard. These values are shown in Table 14.11.

Table 14.11 Interdental fricative index

Value	*Phonetic form*	
0	θ, ð	fricative
1	tθ, dð	affricate
2	t, d	stop

Each speaker's individual score was computed with the numerical values for the possible pronunciations, using the formula in *21*:

21)

$$\left[\frac{(\text{number of stops} \times 2) + (\text{number of affricates} \times 1)}{\text{total number of pronunciations of variable}}\right] \times 100$$

Thus, an individual who produced all stops and no fricatives or affricates would have a score of 200, whereas an individual who produced all fricatives would have a score of 0. Indexing scores for individuals and for groups can then be compared. Table 14.12 shows the index scores for stopping of the interdental fricative by two individual

New Yorkers: Bennie N. was a truck driver who had not finished high school, and Miriam L. was a practicing lawyer who had completed college and law school.

Table 14.12 Index scores for stopping of interdental fricatives in two individuals in casual style

Sound	*Bennie N. (truck driver)*	*Miriam L. (lawyer)*
θ	168	00
ð	153	25

As Table 14.12 indicates, Miriam L. always produced θ as an interdental fricative and almost always produced ð as a fricative. In contrast, Bennie N. was much more likely to produce a nonstandard stop or affricate instead of a fricative for θ and ð. Index analysis of a random sample of New Yorkers revealed that use of a stop or affricate instead of the standard interdental fricative was sharply stratified according to socio-economic class.

Indexing analysis was also used in a study of /aw/ fronting in Canada. The initial portion of the diphthong is sometimes produced with a more forward articulation than at other times. The /aw/ in such words as *crowd, out,* and *now* can be produced as back [ɑw] or [ɔw]; as central [aw]; or as front [æw] or [ɛw]. When data from informants in Toronto and Vancouver were sorted according to age, indexing analysis revealed that younger speakers were far more likely than older speakers to front the /aw/.

This methodology is most valuable in cases where the variation operates along a continuum. However, in cases where the variation involves a choice between discrete categories—such as syntactic structures, as in *22a*—or where the opposition is between presence and absence—as in *22b*, where the final [t] of *past* may be deleted—indexing is not appropriate.

22)

a. The cat bit the dog.
The dog was bitten by the cat.

b. The time is half past one.
The time is half pasØ one.

In these situations, other types of analysis can be employed.

Marginal analysis

In **marginal analysis**, the overall percentages of occurrence for each variant in relevant linguistic and social contexts are reported, as shown in Table 14.13 for /aw/ fronting in southern Alberta.

Table 14.13 Percentage of variants of /aw/ by age group in Lethbridge, Alberta

Age group	*% front*	*% mid*	*% back*
18–25	22	41	37
30–42	16	41	43

In fact, this is probably the best way to determine rates and occurrences of variants by context. However, since this variation may be subject to so many possibly interconnected factors, more sophisticated statistical methodology serves as a valuable tool for determining (1) whether distinctions are significant, and (2) whether cross-cutting factors are falsely inflating or obscuring variation. Variable rule analysis is ideal for this purpose.

Variable rule analysis

Variable rule analysis is an important and frequently employed tool in the study of variation. Using statistical procedures specifically adapted for linguistic data, it indicates not only the probability that one variant or another will occur in any context but also whether there is a statistically significant difference between those contexts. More importantly, we can also find out which of a number of (possibly conflicting) explanations is most likely in accounting for any variation. Thus, a variety of social factors and linguistic factors can be simultaneously taken into account. As an example, a variable rule analysis of /aw/ fronting in southern Alberta showed that at least seven different factors, both linguistic and social, played a role in determining whether or not a speaker would front. These included the height of the onset vowel, relative stress, sex, age, and style.

Principal components analysis

Principal components analysis is markedly different from other methods of studying variation in that instead of correlating particular variants of individual variables with predefined categories, a number of variables are examined simultaneously to see if any groups of speakers share linguistic features. A **principal component** is a set of variables that gives the best fit for the data with respect to how test items group together. In the Puerto-Rican Spanish speech community in New York City, principal components analysis was used to determine if factors like gender, widespread usage, or phonological and/or morphological integration were all relevant in loan-word assimilation. Studies of speech communities in Sydney, Australia, and St. John's, Newfoundland, have studied the grouping of speakers with respect to their use of designated variables. Thus, which features are important and the social divisions that they mark fall out from the data rather than any specified social category. This has the advantage of revealing social distinctions that might not have been isolated if only correlations were examined.

In St. John's, six variables were found to make up one principal component. These are shown in Table 14.14. The speakers with the highest rate of nonstandard variants for the variables in this component were found to be the older men in the community. No other social factors were discovered.

A second principal component included the variables in Table 14.15. In the second component, it was speakers with high rates of standard features who formed a cluster, and these were predominantly women and speakers from higher socioeconomic classes. The differing groups of speakers isolated for each component show the conflict between standard and local nonstandard language varieties and the importance of social identity in accounting for variation.

Table 14.14 Phonological variables in Newfoundland English PC1

Variable	*Word*	*Phonetic realization*
/e/	bay	*a.* standard [ej] *b.* nonstandard [eː]
/o/	boat	*a.* standard [ow] *b.* nonstandard [oː]
/θ/	three	*a.* standard [θ] *b.* nonstandard [t]
/l/ (postvocalic)	mole	*a.* standard dark [ɫ] *b.* Irish-like clear [l] *c.* vocalic [ɤ] (a high, back, unrounded, lax vowel)
/ɔr/	bore	*a.* standard [ɔr] *b.* nonstandard [ar]
/ð/	them	*a.* standard [ð] *b.* nonstandard [d] or flap

Table 14.15 Phonological variables in Newfoundland English PC2

Variable	*Word*	*Phonetic realization*
/ɪŋ/	fishing	*a.* standard [ɪŋ] *b.* nonstandard/casual [ɪn]
/ð/	them	*a.* standard [ð] *b.* nonstandard [d] or flap
/θ/	three	*a.* standard [θ] *b.* nonstandard [t]

2.3 Social influence on variation

Although almost any social characteristic that plays a role in the formation and maintenance of group identities could hypothetically be a factor in variation, there are six main types of social influence that have been studied extensively. These are: geographical or regional location, socioeconomic class, social network, age, gender, and ethnicity.

Geographical or regional location

Perhaps the most well-known factor affecting variation is geographical location. Most early work in sociolinguistics was in the field of **dialectology**, which allowed historical linguists to track sound changes across space, although it quickly expanded to the study of differences in other levels of grammar—particularly the lexicon.

Dialectology studies usually involve **atlas surveys** of large numbers of speakers over wide areas, designed to establish the geographical range and distribution of dialect difference. They are called atlas surveys because ultimately the variation is charted on a map. There are a number of methods by which data are collected for an atlas survey. The predominant method is a personal interview conducted by a field-worker. Based on available information regarding social practice and likely areas of distinction between regions, the field-worker follows an interview schedule constructed to elicit terms and pronunciations considered of interest. The interview includes both casual conversation on preselected topics or specific language questions like those in *23*.

23)

a. Do you pronounce *news* like *cues* or *coos*?

b. "There is a chicken in the yard." Please repeat this sentence substituting the phrase "three chickens" for "a chicken."

Since the main goal of a regional dialect study is to speak to people from as many areas as possible, a limited number of speakers are interviewed in each area. In early studies, only one male lifelong resident of the area was chosen. Unfortunately, this resulted in problems related to representativeness, since it ignored or disregarded many social influences in the community. For example, it provided little data on the speech of women. More recent studies include at least one woman and one man from each area, and other possible social influences are noted. For example, The Phonological Atlas of North America, a study currently underway at the University of Pennsylvania, samples two speakers from cities with populations under 1,000,000 and four from larger centers. Prior to the widespread use of tape recorders, data were hand-transcribed by trained field-workers. Now, all interviews are tape-recorded.

Besides using direct interviews, researchers can also gather data over the telephone and by various written means. The Phonological Atlas of North America uses **telephone survey** methods for some data collection. In cases in which the interview schedule does not require access to recordings of the speakers, other methods can be used. For example, written questionnaires can be sent out. This kind of survey is called a **postal survey**. Although the lack of direct contact with each speaker is a drawback, a postal survey has the advantage of more easily reaching a larger number of people than is possible with face-to-face interviews. Informal surveys are also conducted by newspapers, often with the assistance of linguists. Some questions that appeared in a survey conducted by the *Wichita Eagle* appear in *24*:

24)

a. Do you pronounce these words the same or differently?
pin / pen
crayon / crown

b. Do these pairs of words rhyme in your speech?
roof / goof
greasy / easy

Although a newspaper survey is not respresentative in the same way that a random sample is, tendencies can nevertheless be noted. Responses to the survey in *24*, for example, indicated that Kansans generally rhyme *greasy* with *easy* and tend to merge the [ɪ] and [ɛ] sounds before a nasal (as most southerners do). Furthermore, respondents under the age of twenty were more likely than older respondents to rhyme *goof* and *roof* and to pronounce *crayon* and *crown* the same (see the section on age-grading on p. 574).

Surveys done over the Internet may also be valuable in the future, but since Internet access is still somewhat limited to more affluent, educated people, **Internet surveys** do not reach the entire population. Thus, they are not widely used, although a survey is currently underway for the Linguistic Atlas Project based at the University of Georgia at <http://hyde.park.uga.edu/survey.html>.

Once the data have been collected, they are reported in a document called a dialect atlas. This document summarizes the responses to each item of interest from the interviews, and plots them on a map such as that shown in Figure 14.1.

Maps show either that different communities share features or that they are distinguished by different features. The map in Figure 14.1 shows that there are similarities in vocabulary between francophone fishing villages in Atlantic Canada and a dialect in western France. Similarities between areas indicate some relationship between speakers, either because one community migrated from another area or because the areas are in close contact due to connecting trade routes or other lines of communication.

In many cases, it is possible to find distinct boundaries between areas that are shown on maps in the form of lines called **isoglosses**. A single isogloss indicates one point of distinction between areas. Where several isoglosses occur in roughly the same area on the map, it is referred to as an **isogloss bundle**. The larger the

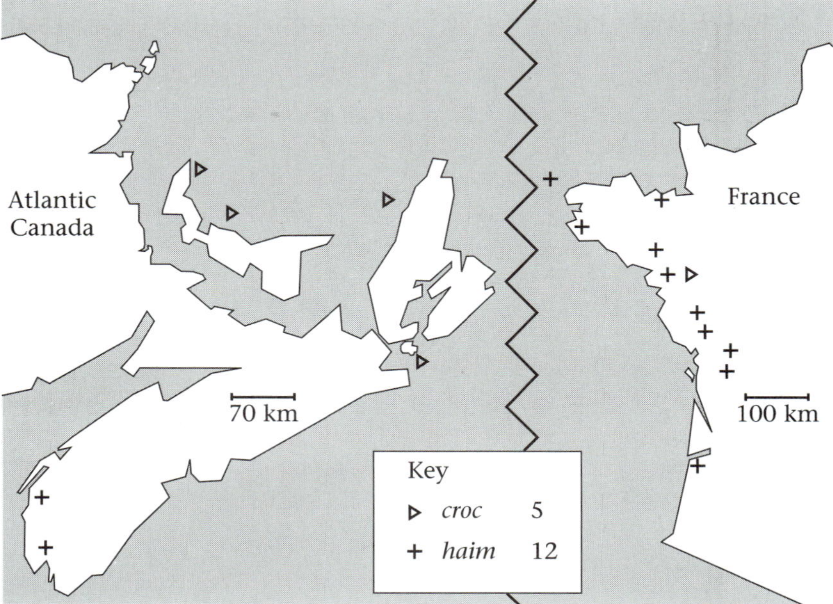

Figure 14.1 Words for 'fishhook' [Standard French *hameçon*] in French dialects of Atlantic Canada and western France (Péronnet and Arsenault, 1990)

isogloss bundle, the more likely a true systematic difference among areas exists, and in that case, there are usually two distinct regional dialects. Isogloss bundles are also interesting for historical reasons because they often reveal a great deal about changing patterns of movement and communication among communities. For example, a study of isogloss bundles in Louisiana found that earlier patterns corresponded to the river systems, consistent with the fact that most transportation in that area of North America was along the water, whereas modern patterns correspond to road systems.

In fact, much of the existing dialect patterns in North America can be traced to routes of trade and immigration. Figure 14.2 shows the major dialect areas of the United States and routes of immigration.

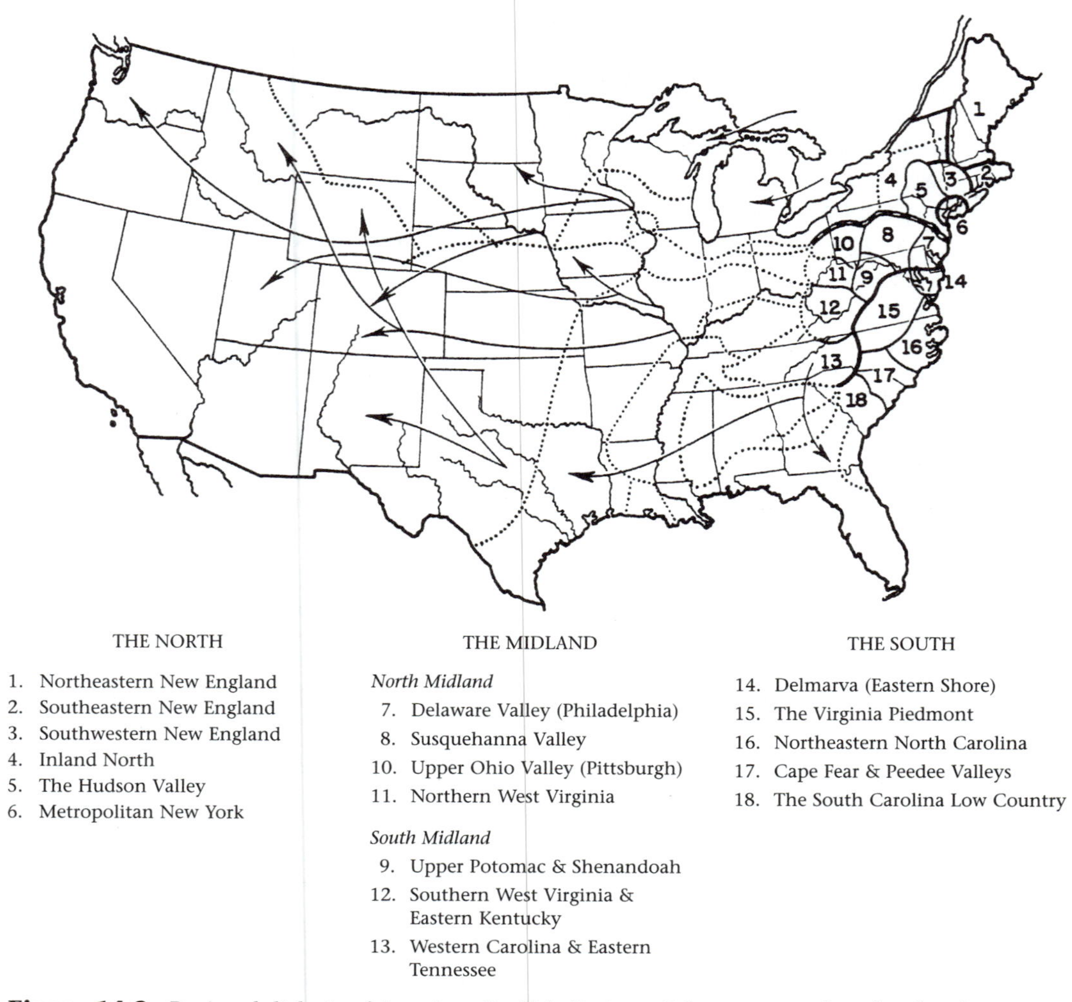

Figure 14.2 Regional dialects of American English. Eastern dialects are numbered; other (more tentative) dialect boundaries are indicated by dotted lines. Arrows indicate direction of major migrations.

The northern dialect area reflects patterns of migration and settlement from western New England and northern New York State along the southern shores of the Great Lakes. This route followed the Erie Canal west across New York State to the area around Cleveland known as the Western Reserve and westward to Detroit. From there, settlement fanned out into the upper Midwest and the West. The North Midland region follows the migration route from Philadelphia and the Delaware valley across Pennsylvania and west along the old National Road (along the approximate route of present-day Interstate 70). The South Midland region spreads out from the Upper Potomoac and Shenandoah Valley into the mountains of southern West Virginia, eastern Kentucky, and Tennessee. The dividing line between North and South Midland is roughly the Ohio River, with South Midland extending northward into Indiana in what is known as the Hoosier Apex. The southern dialect area reflects migration and settlement patterns starting in the Chesapeake Bay and tidewater Virginia and sweeping southward through western North Carolina and north Georgia. Another source of migration began on the coast, especially around Charleston, South Carolina, and spread westward across Georgia, Alabama, and Mississippi.

Regional variation in the United States

The preceding discussion suggests a far simpler picture of regional dialects in the United States than is actually the case. In fact, how dialect boundaries are drawn depends in part on what kinds of data are collected and who the informants are. As the following sections will explain, when updated work conducted on lexical variation is compared with a recent phonological survey, somewhat different dialect boundaries are drawn.

Lexical variation in the United States

In the first half of the twentieth century, when a majority of the U.S. population lived in or close to rural areas, dialectologists believed that isolated rural speech was purer and more interesting than urban speech. Numerous questions on dialect surveys elicited agricultural terms, such as names for farm equipment, terms for livestock, and words used when calling horses, sheep, and cattle. For example, a dialect boundary was drawn across eastern Pennsylvania based on a bundle of isoglosses, including an isogloss separating alternative terms for the pivot bar on a horse-drawn wagon. Today, however, most Americans would probably not even be able to visualize parts of a horse-drawn wagon, much less name the pivot bar with a regionally distinctive word such as *whiffletree*, *whippletree*, or *swingletree* (see Figure 14.3).

Nevertheless, regional differences in lexical items certainly exist today. For example, a carbonated soft drink is called *soda* in the Northeast, *pop* in the inland and northwest, *tonic* in eastern New England, and *soda pop* in parts of the southern Midland. Similarly, a sandwich on a large roll with a variety of meats and cheeses may be called a *grinder*, a *hero*, a *sub(marine)*, a *hoagy*, or a *poorboy*, depending on the region of the country. Some other lexical variants are displayed in Table 14.16.

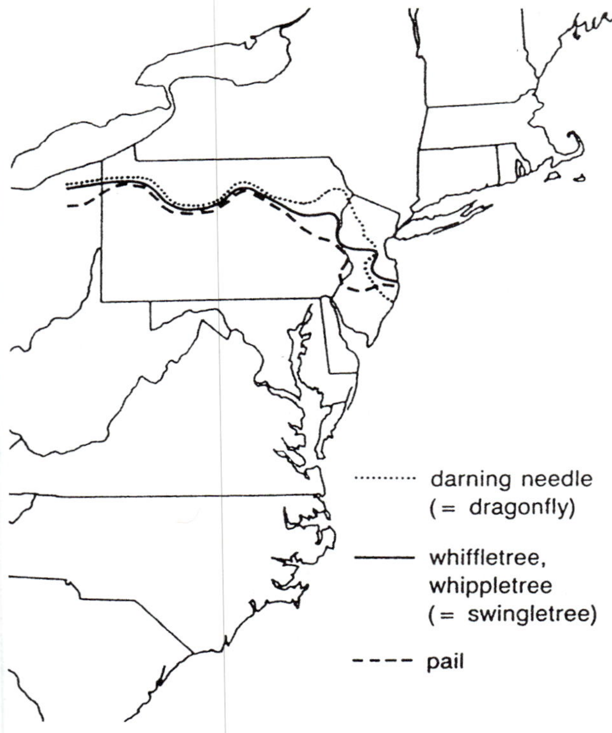

Figure 14.3 An isogloss bundle across eastern Pennsylvania

Table 14.16 Some regional variants

North	*Midland*	*South*	*Meaning*
angleworm	fishing worm	mud worm, wiggler	worm used as fishing bait
darning needle	snake feeder	mosquito hawk	dragonfly
mud wasp (NE)	mud dauber	dirt dauber	wasp that builds a mud nest
bag (upper North)	sack, poke (Appalachian)	sack	paper container

On the basis of lexical variation, it has been suggested that there are really only two main dialect areas: North and South, with the dividing line roughly along the Ohio River. The North is further divided into the upper North and New England, the lower North (previously North Midland), and the West. The South is divided into lower South and upper South (previously South Midland). These divisions and dialect layers are illustrated in Figure 14.4.

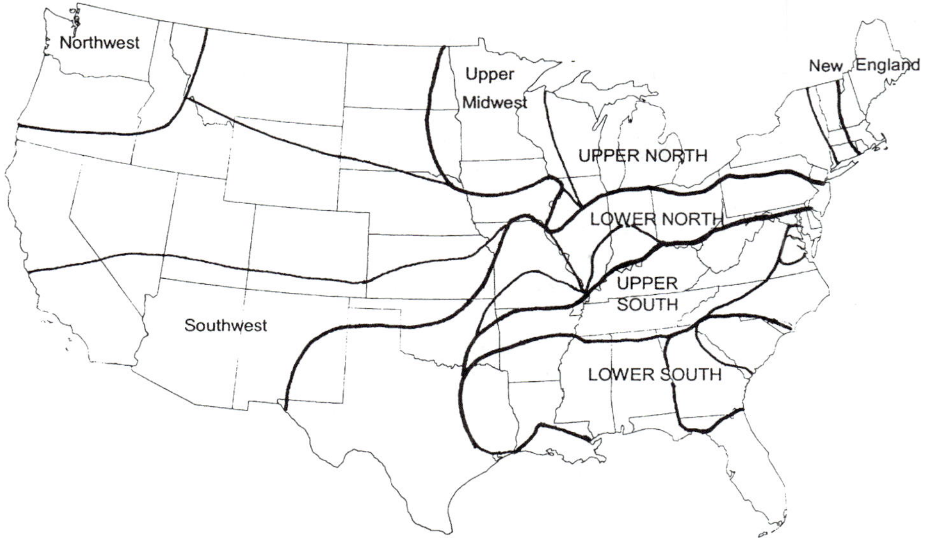

Figure 14.4 Dialect regions of the United States based on lexical items

Phonological variation in the United States

One distinctive characteristic that distinguishes North from South is the pronunciation of the word *greasy*. In the North, it is said with [s], whereas in the South, it is pronounced with [z]. This distinction, while long recognized, does not suggest any systematic differences, and it is to more systematic differences that we now turn.

One of the most notable regional differences is the presence or absence of **postvocalic r**. In the South, in New England, and as a stigmatized variant in the New York metropolitan area, [r] is deleted when it is in the syllable coda following a vowel. Where postvocalic r is deleted, words such as *car* [kɑr] and *cork* [kɔrk] become [kɑ] and [kɔk], respectively. The [r] is retained but somewhat weakened and less retroflex in a broad swath extending northwest from Texas to Washington State.

In fact, liquids and nasals systematically affect the preceding vowels in ways that are dialectally distinctive. For instance, there is considerable dialectal variation in how [ej], [ɛ], and [æ] are pronounced when followed by [r] in words such as *Mary* [mejri], *merry* [mɛri], and *marry* [mæri]. In much of the Midwest, for example, the distinction among [ej], [ɛ], and [æ] is neutralized to [ɛ] when the vowel is followed by [r]. Thus, *Mary*, *merry*, and *marry* all sound the same, as do *Harry* and *hairy*, *Barry* and *berry*, *fairy* and *ferry*.

Another dialectal difference is the effect that a nasal has on preceding vowels. Throughout the South and into southern Ohio, central Indiana, Illinois, Missouri, and Kansas, the vowels [ɪ] and [ɛ] have merged as [ɪ] before [n] or [m]. Thus, both *him* and *hem* are pronounced as [hɪm], and one must specify whether a [pɪn] is for sticking (*pin*) or for writing (*pen*). This merger of [ɪ] and [ɛ] before a nasal had its origins in the southern states, and seems to be in the process of spreading northward and westward.

Another dialectal change in progress is the merger of [ɔ] and [ɑ] in words such as *caught* and *cot*, *hawk* and *hock*, and *dawn* and *Don*. Although the two sounds remain distinct in much of the Midwest, the South, and the mid-Atlantic states, they have merged in northeastern New England, in western Pennsylvania and central Ohio, in northern Minnesota, and throughout the West (with the possible exception of the large cities of San Francisco, Los Angeles, and Denver). One sign that this merger is in the process of expanding is that it is more strongly represented by younger speakers than by older speakers.

Finally, two separate vowel shifts have been tracked over the past quarter century. A **vowel shift** occurs when a series of vowel phonemes undergo reorganization (see Chapter 7, Section 2.4). The **Northern Cities Shift** began in the metropolitan areas of Chicago, Detroit, Cleveland, and Buffalo and may now be spreading to smaller cities around the Great Lakes. In order to understand the changes taking place in the Northern Cities Shift, see Figure 14.5.

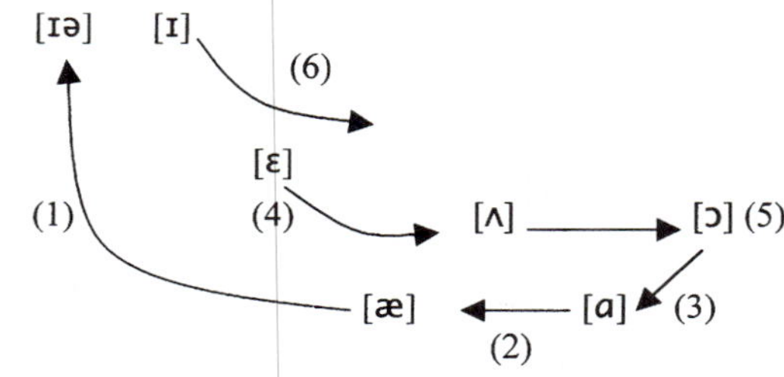

Figure 14.5 The Northern Cities Shift

First, the [æ] in words like *cad* was raised and diphthongized to become [ɪə]. Then, the [ɑ], as in *cod*, *Don*, *pop*, and *hot*, was fronted to become closer to [æ]. The [ɔ], as in *dawn* and *cawed*, was then lowered to become more like [ɑ]. The [ɛ], as in *Ked*, was backed, which in turn pushed the [ʌ], as in *cud*, farther back. In parallel with the backing of [ɛ], [ɪ], as in *kid*, also moved back.

A quite different vowel shift is in progress in the South and extends northward through eastern Tennessee and Kentucky and into southern West Virginia. In this shift, known as the **Southern Shift**, the vowels are rotating quite differently from those in the Northern Cities Shift (see Figure 14.6).

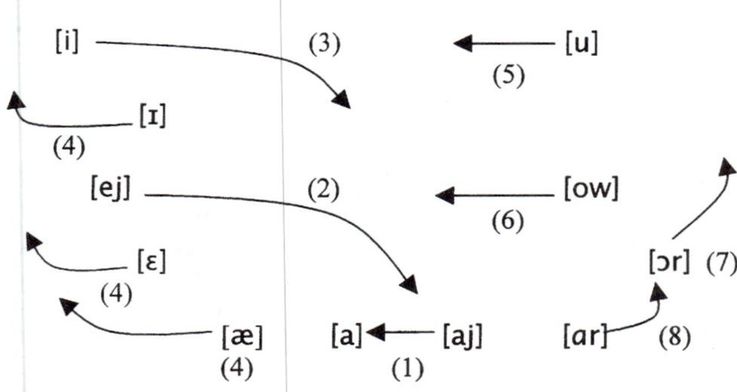

Figure 14.6 The Southern Shift

In the Southern Shift, the [aj] in words like *I* and *time* is monophthongized to [a] and fronted. The [ej], as in *made*, is lowered and backed to sound almost like [aj]. In parallel, the [i], as in *heed*, is also lowered and backed. The remaining front vowels are raised and in some cases become diphthongized so that *bed*, for example, sounds more like [bɪəd]. The nonlow back vowels [u] and [ow] are fronted, and [ɑr] and [ɔr] move upward.

When dialectal differences based on lexicon are superimposed on dialectal differences based on phonology, the results are actually remarkably similar, as is shown in Figure 14.7.

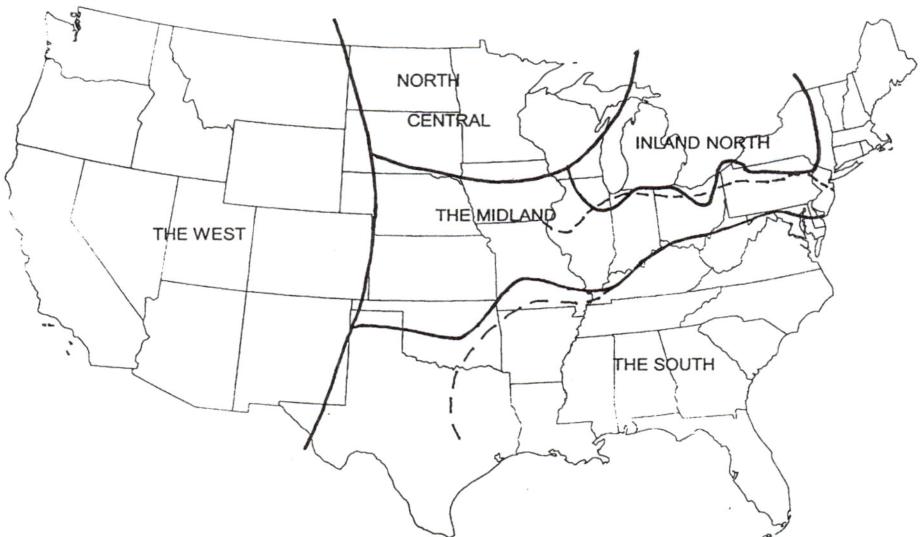

Figure 14.7 Dialect boundaries based on lexical items and a phonological survey. (The solid line represents dialect boundaries found in the Phonological Atlas survey; the dashed line represents dialect boundaries based on lexical items.)

Regional differences in morphology and syntax

Regional differences in morphology and syntax are relatively few, and this section will present examples primarily from southern English and Appalachian English. Two distinctive markers of southern English are the use of double modals and the extension of the pronoun system to include a second person plural. Whereas most dialects of American English have but one *you* to denote both singular and plural, southern English distinguishes between *you* (singular) and *you-all* or *y'all* (plural). Another distinctive grammatical feature in the South is the use of double modals such as *might could* or *might should*, where *might* is used to mean "perhaps."

Appalachian English shares a number of features with southern English but also preserves some **relic forms**—forms of older English that have become obsolete in standard American English (although Appalachian English is not unaltered Elizabethan English, as is sometimes claimed!). One such relic form is **a-prefixing** on verbs in the progressive aspect or on adverbial complements to V, as in *25*.

25)

The dog came up just a-prancin'.
The wind was a-comin' on strong.

Other forms in Appalachian English include counterfactual *liketa*, as in *I laughed so hard I liketa died*, and the use of *right* as a degree word, as in *It's right nice weather today*. A couple of interesting syntactic differences exist between standard American English and Appalachian English in relative clauses. In most dialects of American English, the complementizer *that* and the trace of a *wh-* element moved from subject position are not acceptable in sentences such as *26*.

26)

* Who did you say that (t) called?

However, this type of structure is perfectly acceptable in Appalachian English. Interestingly, in some areas of Appalachia and in other southern-based dialects, it is possible to delete the relative pronoun even when it is the subject of a relative clause:

27)

That man lives down the road is crazier than a loon.

As this discussion shows, geographical area can be a factor in explaining patterns of variation. However, other factors within regional dialects can also play a role.

Socioeconomic class

Patterning of variants according to socioeconomic class can give valuable clues to how language behavior reflects social mobility. The theory is exemplified by studies of variation in New York City and rests on two basic findings: (1) the upper classes tend to use linguistic variants with higher prestige; and (2) speakers from the lower middle class show the most linguistic insecurity. Because lower-middle-class speakers may not have internalized norms of "correctness," they tend to adopt variants that they believe to be "correct," even though these variants are not standard. This pattern is called **hypercorrection**. Table 14.17 shows some examples of hypercorrection.

Table 14.17 Examples of hypercorrection

Standard	*Hypercorrection*
often pronounced as [ɔfən]	spelling pronunciation [ɔftən]
Who did you say was calling?	Whom did you say was calling?
between you and me	between you and I

Certain phonological and grammatical variants may be associated with socioeconomic class. In a now famous study entitled "The Social Stratification of r in New York City Department Stores," William Labov hypothesized that the presence or absence of postvocalic r in New York City speech was linked to social class. To test his hypothesis, he chose three department stores catering to different clientele: Saks

Fifth Avenue for the upper end of the social scale; S. Klein, a now defunct bargain basement, for the lower end; and Macy's for middle-class shoppers. In each store, Labov asked employees questions that would elicit the response "fourth floor." When he tabulated the percentages of employees who pronounced postvocalic r some or all of the time in their responses, he indeed found social stratification: 62 percent of the employees at Saks produced postvocalic r all or some of the time and 51 percent of Macy's employees did so, but only 20 percent of the employees of S. Klein pronounced the postvocalic r.

However, just because a society can be grouped into classes on the basis of some objective socioeconomic criteria does not indicate that social class is necessarily the prime factor in determining the behavior of individuals. Other societies may be organized according to different criteria even in Western culture.

Another way to determine the standard variants in a community is with **linguistic market analysis**. Speakers can be ranked according to the degree to which they need the standard language for their work or hobbies and not necessarily according to their economic status. For example, two computer programmers could make the same salary but one might be required by her job to promote products at sales meetings whereas the other might not. The speakers' jobs may also not be the most important aspect of their linguistic life. Speakers may be very active in their community, making public speeches before government committees or corporate sponsors. Studies of Montreal French have shown that linguistic market not only is a good predictor of linguistic behavior but also is closely tied to speakers' "symbolic orientation" (i.e., individual preferences, social values, attitudes, etc.)—some of the very attributes that social class is purported to reflect. Speakers ranking higher for linguistic market are more likely to use standard variants—particularly in more formal styles.

Of course, social class may also have an effect because people associate more with those in their own socioeconomic class. To examine possible effects of social association, a more direct approach uses social network analysis.

Social network

Individual social relationships can be examined as an explanation for patterns of variation by counting the ties between speakers according to relevant social network clusters, such as family, neighborhood, employment, religion, and friendships. This is called **social network analysis**.

The basic idea behind social network analysis is that people who talk to one another often are more likely to have the same speech patterns. Speakers are given individual network scores according to both the kinds of network ties they have and the density of the networks in which they are involved. Dense social networks are those in which a large number of the speakers are interconnected. For example, a study investigating the language of African American youth in New York City revealed that the greater the participation in street culture—including gang membership—the greater the use of vernacular speech forms. However, fewer vernacular forms were used by those youths who were on the peripheries of street culture for whatever reason.

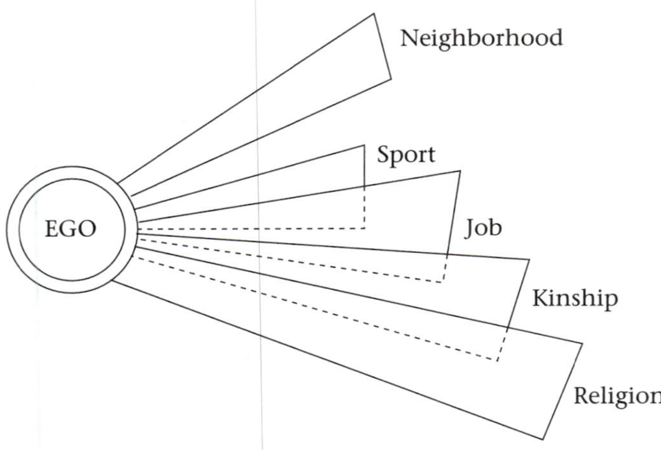

Figure 14.8 Social networks

Multiplex networks are those in which the relationships are formed on the basis of several clusters, or kinds, of relationships. In Northern Ireland, dense social networks act to enforce community norms, so that speakers who are most closely integrated into the network show the highest rate of variants associated with it. Their relationships constrain their linguistic behavior in much the same way as those in closely knit communities act to restrain other types of social behavior, such as moral values and work ethics. Recent work on the island of Ocracoke on North Carolina's Outer Banks has shown that select distinctive features of the endangered local dialect are most strongly maintained by a group of middle-aged men with dense multiplex networks. They play poker together several times a week, generally work in fishing or other marine activities, and share strong local loyalty and pride. In the face of loss of the island dialect through contact with tourists and with the mainland, the poker players assert their island identity through their speech.

The precise calculation of social network scores varies depending on the community, since some types of network ties may be more important in one community than in another. For example, a study of a small Newfoundland fishing village found that ties related to traditional employment associations, such as fishing or shopkeeping, were the most important for predicting language behavior, whereas in Northern Ireland, personal relationships and neighborhood associations were the most important ties for maintaining local forms.

Age

Differences across age groups are another important social factor. When younger speakers use more new variants than older speakers, it may indicate the presence of natural changes in the language. However, age differences may have other explanations. In some cases, differences are merely the result of **age-grading**. Speakers may have different language behavior depending on social situations associated with age. For example, as noted earlier, slang expressions are more closely associated with younger speakers. Furthermore, there may be differences associated with the aging process. Age also interacts with gender in cases where the language is changing.

Gender

One of the most widely reported social factors in linguistic variation is that of gender. Cross-linguistically and cross-culturally, we find that the speech of men and women tends to differ. Two tendencies have been frequently observed:

29)

I. When variation is stable (no change is occurring), men use more nonstandard forms than do women.
II. When variation is leading to a change in the language, women use more of the incoming forms than do men.

In general, it has been observed that women are most often associated with greater use of variants that carry prestige, but agreement has not been reached as to the explanation for these tendencies. A number of theories have been suggested.

One possibility is that gender differences result from local network density. However, this is difficult to uphold since social groups always include members of both sexes. Even so, men and women will often form distinct social networks within social groups. As discussed earlier, linguistic differences related to sex may also be the result of power differentials in society associated with gender roles.

One extremely compelling explanation is associated with the observation that women tend to lead in situations where change is in progress. This is attributed to their role as child caregivers. Small children in the early stages of acquisition would be more likely to hear advanced forms produced by women than by men; thus, the change is advanced because it is transmitted to the younger generation. Where men are in the lead, their limited contact with the next generation during the formative years limits the probability that their speech patterns will be passed on.

Ethnicity

In multicultural settings, ethnicity can be expressed linguistically either by the use of different languages or by means of phonological or other grammatical distinctions among varieties in the same language. A group's ancestral language or dialect may have an effect on its variety. The speech of subordinate ethnic groups may feature speech markers due to direct influences from the substrate language or dialect. The study of ethnic variation in the English of Irish and Italian Americans in Boston, Cajuns in Louisiana, and Hispanic Americans in other parts of the United States has confirmed this.

However, an appeal to linguistic origin does not account for why ethnic variation persists or, for that matter, why other potential transfer items do not. It has been suggested that the persistence of ethnic languages and dialects is related to their degree of **ethnolinguistic vitality**. Such factors as the number of speakers in a community; the degree to which the ethnic group and the language it speaks has institutional support from government, schools, church, mass media, and culture; as well as pride in the community may result in retention of ethnic varieties in a community.

The study of ethnicity is complicated because it is frequently entangled with a complex of social characteristics, any or all of which may influence variation. For example, proposing ethnicity to explain African American Vernacular English (AAVE) as a distinct variety of American English has been confounded by the possible effects of geographical distribution and social class.

AAVE (African American Vernacular English)

Despite the caveat against generalizing about AAVE as a distinct variety of American English, some common characteristics of AAVE are agreed upon. However, the origins of AAVE are still a topic of vigorous debate among linguists. Among the questions under investigation are the possible origins of AAVE as a creole (Section 2.4), the extent to which present-day features can be traced to origins in African languages, and the extent to which AAVE both influenced and was influenced by white southern speech.

Some of the characteristics of AAVE, particularly where phonology is concerned, are shared with other dialects of American English, and it is difficult to point to single features as characteristic of AAVE and AAVE only. However, the list in Table 14.18, while not exhaustive, is illustrative of some of the phonological features of AAVE.

Table 14.18 Some phonological features of AAVE

Phonological feature	*Example*
Consonont cluster reduction word-finally	test → tes, desk → des
Deletion of postvocalic liquids	help → [hɛp], ball → [bɔ], car → [kɑ]
Stopping of θ, ð word-initially	I think → I [tɪŋk] the man → [də] man
Change of θ to f, and ð to v word-medially and -finally	mouth → [mawf] the brother → [də brʌvə]

Consonant cluster reduction word-finally is quite regular and can be formulated as a rule:

29)

Rule for consonant cluster reduction

$$\begin{matrix} \text{C} \\ [\alpha\ \text{voice}] \end{matrix} \rightarrow \varnothing \ / \ \begin{matrix} \text{C} \\ [\alpha\ \text{voice}] \end{matrix} \_\_\#$$

In other words, the second element in a cluster is deleted word-finally if it shares the same [± voice] feature with the preceding consonant. Thus, *test* becomes *tes*, *desk* becomes *des*, *hand* becomes *han*, but *pant* does not become **pan*. The deletion rule operates before the addition of the plural suffix, since the plural of *tes* is *tesses* and the plural of *des* is *desses*. Although other varieties of English simplify consonant clusters word-finally, AAVE is more likely than other varieties to delete the second consonant even when a vowel follows, as in *lif up* (for *lift up*).

The morphosyntactic features of AAVE illustrate the rule-governed and systematic nature of AAVE. Some of these features are listed in Table 14.19.

Table 14.19 Some morphosyntactic features of AAVE

Morphosyntactic feature	*Example*
absence of possessive -*s*	John hat, Byron car
absence of 3 SG present -*s*	she talk, he sing
absence of PL -*s* when quantifier given	three dog, some cat
multiple negation	He don' know nothin'.
inversion with indefinite negative subject	Don' nobody talk like that.
stressed *bín* for state begun in remote past and still continuing	She bín married. I bín known him.
habitual *be*	The coffee be cold (= always). He be tired out (= habitually).
copula deletion	She nice. He in the kitchen. He tired out (= temporarily).
come to express indignation	She come goin' in my room.

The -*s* morph marking the possessive, the third-person singular present, and the plural may be absent. AAVE shares with some other varieties of English (including the English written by Chaucer) the possibility for multiple negation, but it also allows inversion when the subject of the sentence is an indefinite negative:

30)

Don't nobody talk like that.
'Absolutely no one talks like that.'
*Don't John talk like that.
*Don't everybody talk like that.

As the starred examples in *30* show, when the subject of the sentence names a specific person, the inversion is unacceptable; likewise, it is unacceptable when the subject is not a negative.

AAVE has a much richer aspectual system (the forms that indicate duration or type of activity of the verb) than standard English, and the examples listed in Table 14.19 are not exhaustive. In AAVE, the stressed *bín* denotes a state, condition, or activity begun in the remote past and continued to the present. It is not simply a deletion of the standard English auxiliary verb *have* with the same meaning as in standard English *have/has been*. For an AAVE speaker, *She bín married* means that she got married a long time ago and is still married, whereas most non-AAVE speakers would interpret it as meaning that she is no longer married.

The use of **habitual (invariant) *be*** to mark a habitual or repeated state, condition, or action is illustrated in *31*.

31)

a. This room be cold.
*This room be cold today.

b. He be tired out.
*He be tired out right now.

As the starred examples show, the use of habitual *be* means that the state is constant or habitual, not one that is a temporary condition or one-time occurrence. Conversely, copula deletion may be used for a temporary or one-time state of affairs. Thus, *He tired out* can mean that he is tired out today or right now, but not necessarily as a habitual state.

Another aspectual marker in AAVE is *come* used to express indignation. Although other varieties of English have similar structures with *come*, it is obviously not a verb of motion in this AAVE structure when it is used as in *32*.

32)

She come goin' into my room without knockin'.

As this sentence illustrates, *come* and *go* cannot both be verbs of motion. Instead, *come* expresses the speaker's annoyance.

The lists given here of AAVE features are not meant to be exhaustive, nor are they meant to suggest that all speakers of AAVE use exactly these forms. Just as speakers of Appalachian English will differ according to their specific geographical origin, level of education, and socioeconomic status, so too will speakers of AAVE. Similarly, it must be remembered that speakers of any variety of English may be bidialectal or multidialectal and will accommodate to a greater or lesser extent to the setting in which they find themselves and the interlocutors with whom they are speaking.

2.4 Variable use of varieties

Lingua francas

Wherever there is social and commercial interaction between groups of people who speak different languages, we frequently find that speakers will maintain their own languages for interaction within the group and designate one semi-official language for the purpose of communicating between groups. A language used for this purpose is called a **lingua franca**. A lingua franca may be the native language of one of the interacting groups or it may be a "neutral" language in that none of the groups speaks it natively. For example, in many colonized countries, where more than one language group exists, a European language—spread by traders and then adopted by local groups as a convention—may operate as the lingua franca. However, there are other ways for a lingua franca to arise.

Pidgins and creoles

Contact situations where speakers have restricted access to each other's language can sometimes lead to the formation of a **pidgin**—a rudimentary language with minimal grammatical rules and a small lexicon. By definition, a pidgin has no native speakers and many pidgins are predominantly used as a lingua franca. In fact, the term *lingua franca* comes from the name of a pidgin trade language spoken in the eastern Mediterranean in the Middle Ages. Example *33* shows two examples of English-based pidgins.

33)

a. Neo-Melanesian
mi stap lɔŋ bɪglajn, mi kətɪm kopra
'I was in the work-group, cutting copra.'

b. Hawaii Pidgin English
wok had dis pipl
'These people work hard.'

Exactly how pidgins form is a controversial question. Pidgin languages are distinguished from other languages in that they have only a small number of grammatical categories and very little grammatical complexity. For example, pidgins generally do not have complement clauses, agreement marking, or tense marking. Temporal reference is frequently achieved by use of adverbs or aspect markers. Some have suggested that pidgins arise as a result of foreigner talk (discussed in Chapter 11), which is also a simplified form of language. This suggestion, of course, assumes that native speakers of the **lexifier language**—the language from which the pidgin takes most of its words—who came into contact with speakers of other languages spoke to them using this reduced form of their language.

Pidgins tend to originate in two main social situations. One common place where pidgins are found is in areas where there was a great deal of trade between groups of people who spoke different languages. Many known examples of pidgins were lexified by European or other internationally spoken languages—as in the case of Australian Pidgin English, Russonorsk, Chinese Pidgin Portuguese, and Pidgin Arabic—as a result of contact with traders. For example, Russonorsk arose in the early 1800s between Russian and Norwegian fishermen working on the Arctic coast of Norway. Apparently, both groups were under the impression that they were speaking the other's language, partly due to the accidental fact that the word /pɔ/ 'in' had the same meaning in both base languages. As a result, Russonorsk had dual variants for many words, some lexified from Russian and some from Norwegian, as well as a few words of Dutch or English origin.

There are also several examples of pidgins formed from non-European languages as a result of trade, as in Chinook Jargon—a trading language of North American natives in the Pacific northwest—and Sango—a pidgin form of Ngabandi, a language of west central Africa. Pidgins have also frequently been found in situations where people from a large number of language backgrounds come together as laborers, either as slaves or as indentured workers, on large agricultural plantations.

Pidgins tend to be very short-lived for two reasons. They are generally held in great disdain by native speakers of the lexifier language, so it is socially advantageous for pidgin speakers to learn the standard form of the language when communicating with its speakers. Only in situations where the pidgin operates as a lingua franca between speech communities does it tend to endure for some time. In other cases, speakers of numerous languages have either come together in unified communities as a result of urbanization or were forced into such communities, as in the case of slave segregation. If their children then learn the pidgin as a first language and it is adopted as the native language of the new community, it becomes a **creole** and is no longer considered a pidgin.

When a pidgin becomes a creole, its inventory of lexical items and grammatical rules expands dramatically, usually in only one or two generations. Furthermore, creoles worldwide have remarkably similar grammatical characteristics. There are two basic theories for why this should occur. Some people believe that creoles either (l) originated from a single, common proto-pidgin, with different lexical items taken from each individual lexifier language, or (2) are based on one or more of the native languages originally spoken by the founders of the community. The fact that creoles have many similarities simply reflects universal features of language, and differences are accounted for by differences in the **substrate**—or base—languages. This is called the **relexification hypothesis**.

The other prevailing theory is the **language bioprogram hypothesis**, which claims that similarities among creoles reflect universal properties of an innate biological program found in the mental makeup of every human being that guides language acquisition. This theory has evolved, and more recent versions of the bioprogram hypothesis are similar to the Universal Grammar (UG) hypothesis (see Chapters 5 and 12). The bioprogram hypothesis is supported by studies of Tok Pisin, a recently formed creole in New Guinea, that have shown that there is a sharp difference in grammatical structure between the generation that speaks pidgin and the one that speaks creole. According to the theory, since the first generation of children who acquired the creole must have done so on the basis of an impoverished input, any grammatical structure found in the newly formed creole must have come from their innate language program.

Both these theories have been criticized, and the available evidence is not sufficient to decide unequivocably between the two. Critics of relexification note that there are too many differences across the possible substrate languages to account for the similarities in creoles. Furthermore, in slave populations, people who spoke a common language were often separated from each other to avoid rebellion, casting doubt on the possibility that one base language would have predominated. However, there have been studies of Pacific creoles that are consistent with the relexification hypothesis. The main problem in resolving the issue is that there are no current situations where both the resulting creole and the pidgin input can be observed, so even conclusions based on detailed quantitative comparative analysis are still subject to doubt. One difficulty is that creoles are not static in their development.

In most areas, creoles exist alongside a local version of the standard language, which is termed the **acrolect**. As in most other nonstandard language situations, the creole is highly variable and a number of stages or varieties of the creole can be identified. The variety that is least like the standard is called the **basilect**, while varieties intervening between the basilect and acrolect are termed **mesolects**. Therefore, grammatical features of some creoles may also have arisen from contact from the lexifier language.

In all the previous situations described, it is the speakers of each individual language who are in contact, so that while elements of two languages may combine in a resulting variety, there is no clear indication that any "mixing" of languages is taking place. In the day-to-day use of bilinguals, two languages are used by a single speaker who may or may not combine languages in a number of ways.

Language mixture

In bilingual speech communities, speakers will often adopt a speech variety that involves alternation between languages in the same discourse. Where there is evidence that the grammatical systems of both languages are in operation during this alternation, this type of discourse, as shown in example *34*, is referred to as **code-switching**.

34) Examples of code-switching

a. *Acadian French-English*
Pis, elle est toute seule, comme c'est ('well, it is all alone as if it's') *in the middle of nowheres.*

b. *Puerto Rican Spanish-English*
Why make Carol *sentarse atrás pa' que* ('sit in the back so') everybody has to move *pa' que se salga* ('for her to get out')?

c. *Fongbe-French*

mɛ́ɖé	lɛ́	nɔ́	ɖò	*gravement*	*blessés.*
someone	PL	HAB	be	seriously	hurt

'Some are seriously hurt.'

Not all utterances that contain elements from two languages necessarily involve code-switching. In example *35*, where a single word from one language is embedded in the syntax of another language, the speaker may merely be **borrowing** a word from one language into another.

35) Examples of borrowing

a. J'ai ramassé une *bathtub,* pis j m'ai viré de bord avec la *bathtub.* (French-English)

b.

Näitä	kaks,	kolme *bypassia*	sillä	on.
these-PL	two	three -PL	he-AD	is

'He has two, three bypasses.' (Finnish-English)

c.

dartha	f'	l'	*couloir*	u	ɣadi
put it (I)	in	the	hallway	and	left (I) ...

'I put it in the hallway and I left' (Arabic-French)

This is particularly true when the word in question shows phonological, morphological, and syntactic properties of the host language, although borrowing does not always involve full integration on all these levels.

Another important question in the study of code-switching—besides that of distinguishing it from borrowing—is why speakers choose to do it. In some communities, the mere act of code-switching operates as a discourse mode and can signal solidarity between speakers in the same way as any other register of language. This is the case in the Puerto Rican Spanish-English community in New York City and may also be true of French-English bilinguals in New Brunswick. Some researchers have suggested that code-switching may operate metaphorically to express solidarity with or distance from one community. When this occurs, it is called **metaphorical code-switching**.

When people switch from one code to another for clearly identifiable reasons, it is referred to as **situational code-switching**. For example, in some bilingual societies, one language may be more closely associated with government functions while the other is more closely associated with casual conversations. In this situation, a speaker may begin a conversation with an acquaintance at a government office in one language, and when the conversation turns to more bureaucratic topics, the participants may switch to another language.

Studies of code-switching as a discourse mode have found that, contrary to popular belief, the ability to produce code-switching smoothly requires a great deal of language ability and counters any suggestion that code-switching is somehow degenerate and not "real" language, as derogatory terms like *Franglais* and *Spanglish* may imply.

SUMMING UP

The study of **sociolinguistics** is concerned with language in its social context within the **speech community**, involving both the **sociolinguistics of language** as well as the **sociolinguistics of society**. How language is used in discourse is affected by the **speech situation** and its components. Any given discourse can be analyzed and its overall structure identified. These structures can provide clues to the function of linguistic behavior. Language is an important tool in the expression of **solidarity** and **power** between individuals. Sociolinguistic norms for language use can also give indications of how power is distributed in society in general.

The relationship between language and society is clearly shown by the existence of **standard** and **nonstandard** language varieties. Whether or not a language or structure is considered standard depends on attitudes of speakers and not on any inherent "correctness." In order to determine what features of each variety are affected by these attitudes, some form of variation analysis such as **indexing**, **variable rule analysis**, or **principal component analysis** can be used. Factors such as region, social class, social network, age, gender, and ethnicity may all have an effect on whether or not a form is considered nonstandard. The designation of **official languages** and **language planning** are political ways for either reducing disadvantage for speakers of nonstandard varieties or promoting varieties in the interest of increased power for speakers of standard varieties. Speakers can also vary between varieties for political reasons. A **lingua franca** can be used in societies where many languages are spoken to communicate between groups. Where communication is limited, a **pidgin** or **creole** language may arise. In groups where speakers are multilingual, speakers may **code-switch** between languages for a number of reasons. At the very least, a language contact situation usually results in the **borrowing** of words between linguistic groups.

By confronting variation and studying its properties (both linguistic and social), more than thirty years of research has confirmed that linguistic variation is not "free" but rather shows complex, probabilistic patterns of social and linguistic conditioning that form a sociolinguistic structure reflecting the sociolinguistic competence and, in most cases, the social identity of speakers. Speakers will behave in a manner consistent with their own identity and according to the perceived identity of others.

Key terms

General terms

accents
dialects
ethnic dialect
mutual intelligibility
regional dialects
sociolects
sociolinguistic norms
sociolinguistics
sociolinguistics of language
sociolinguistics of society
sociolinguistic variable
speech community
speech variety

Terms concerning discourse analysis and ethnography of communication

communicative competence
discourse
discourse analysis
ethnography of communication
jargon
register
slang
speech act theory
speech event
speech situation
style
text analysis
utterances

Terms concerning ethnomethodology

adjaceny pair
closing
conversation analysis
cooperative overlaps
ethnomethodology
high involvement style
opening
turn-taking

Terms concerning text analysis: narratives

abstract clauses
coda clause
complicating action clauses
evaluation clauses
narratives
orientation clauses

Terms concerning text analysis: discourse markers

anaphoric reference
cataphoric reference
cohesive devices
discourse markers

Terms concerning power and solidarity

accommodation
address terms
converge
diverge
euphemisms
gender-exclusive (differentiation)
gender-variable (differentiation)
no-naming
positive politeness
power
self-praise avoidance
solidarity
taboo
verbal hedges

Terms concerning the standard and linguistic attitudes

diglossia
domains of use
linguistic insecurity
matched guise test
nonstandard
orderly heterogeneity
standard

Terms concerning language planning

African American Vernacular English (AAVE)
ebonics
language planning
official language

Terms concerning methods of studying variation

atlas surveys
categorical (rules)
dialectology
indexing analysis
Internet surveys
marginal analysis
postal survey
principal component
principal components analysis
telephone survey
token
variable rule analysis
variants

Terms concerning regional variation

a-prefixing
isogloss bundle
isoglosses
Northern Cities Shift
postvocalic r
relic forms
Southern Shift
vowel shift

Terms concerning language and social class

hypercorrection
linguistic market analysis
multiplex networks
social network analysis

Terms concerning age and ethnic variation

age-grading
ethnolinguistic vitality
habitual (invariant) *be*

Terms related to languages in contact

acrolect
basilect
borrowing
code-switching
creole
language bioprogram hypothesis
lexifier language
lingua franca
mesolects
metaphorical code-switching
pidgin
relexification hypothesis
situational code-switching
substrate (language)

SOURCES

The discussion of dialect and the terms *sociolinguistics of language* and *sociolinguistics of society* are adapted from R. Fasold, *The Sociolinguistics of Society* (Oxford: Blackwell, 1984) and R. Fasold, *Sociolinguistics of Language* (Oxford: Blackwell, 1990). The discussion of discourse analysis was informed by D. Schiffrin, *Approaches to Discourse* (Oxford: Blackwell, 1994). Examples of register were taken from R. Grable, J. Jernigan, C. Pogue, and D. Divis, "Metrics for Small Projects: Experiences at the SED," *Software* 16 (1999): 21–29, and from Z. Segal, M. Gemar, and S. Williams, "Differential Cognitive Response to a Mood Challenge Following Successful Cognitive Therapy or Pharmacotherapy for Unipolar Depression," *Journal of Abnormal Psychology* 108 (1999): 3–10.

The recipe for Dino-gettis on toast comes from *Time . . . in the Kitchen*, a cookbook compiled for the United Way by the 25th Anniversary Committee of Time Air; recipe contributed by Mike Exner, p. 117. Information about UCLA slang is from Pamela Munro, ed., *U.C.L.A. Slang: A Dictionary of Slang Words and Expressions Used at U.C.L.A., Occasional Paper in Linguistics #8* (1989). The study of slang in a Calgary high school is from J. P. Bowes, "Teenage Labelling: 'Are You a Jock or a Freak?'" *Calgary Working Papers in Linguistics* 9 (1983): 7–16.

The discussion of solidarity and power is partly based on the discussion in J. Holmes, *An Introduction to Sociolinguistics* (New York: Longman and Brown, 1992), and in R. Brown and A. Gilman, "The Pronouns of Power and Solidarity," in *Style in Language*, edited by T. Sebeok (Cambridge, MA: MIT Press, 1960), pp. 253–76. Examples from Koasati come from M. Haas, "Men's and Women's Speech in Koasati," *Language* 20 (1944): 142–49. Examples from Bislama come from M. Meyerhoff, "Accommodating Your Data: The Use and Misuse of Accommodation Theory in Sociolinguistics," *Language and Communication* 18 (1998): 205–25. Examples from the Prijajis come from C. Geertz, "Linguistic Etiquette," in *Sociolinguistics,* edited by J. B. Pride and J. Holmes (New York: Penguin Books, 1972), pp. 167–79. Examples from Japanese are from S. Ide, "How and Why Do Women Speak More Politely in Japanese?" in *Aspects of Japanese Women's Language*, edited by S. Ide and N. H. McGloin (Tokyo: Kurosio Publishers, 1991), pp. 63–79. Discussion of gender and language, including some examples, comes from J. Coates, *Women, Men and Language* (New York: Longman, 1993).

The discussion of standard and nonstandard language comes from I. Pringle, "The Complexity of the Concept of Standard," in *In Search of the Standard in Canadian English*, edited by W. C. Lougheed (Kingston, ON: Queen's University, 1985), pp. 20–38, and W. Labov, "The Logic of Non-standard English," in *Georgetown Monographs on Languages and Linguistics,* edited by J. Alatis (Washington, DC: Georgetown University Press, 1970), pp. 1–43.

The original study of linguistic insecurity in New York City is found in William Labov, *The Social Stratification of English in New York City* (Washington, DC: Center for Applied Linguistics, 1966). Canadian studies discussed in the section on attitudes are by T. W. Owens and P. M. Baker, "Linguistic Insecurity in Winnipeg, Canada: Validation of a Canadian Index of Linguistic Insecurity," *Language in Society* 13 (1984): 337–50, and M. McKinnie and J. Dailey-O'Cain, *A Perceptual Dialectology of Anglophone Canada from the Perspective of Young Albertans and Ontarians* (Paper presented at NWAVE 27, University of Georgia, 1998). Excerpts of the Court of Appeal's decision on English-only in the workplace can be accessed through James Crawford's Web site at <http://ourworld.compuserve.com/homepages/JWCRAWFORD/rights.htm>. The New York City indexing analysis is from William Labov, *The Social Stratification of English in New York City* (Washington, DC: Center for Applied Linguistics, 1966). The computation of the indexing analysis is summarized in Gregory Guy, "The Quantitative Analysis of Linguistic Variation," in *American Dialect Research*, edited by Dennis R. Preston (Amsterdam and Philadelphia: John Benjamins, 1993), pp. 223–49. Results on /aw/ fronting in Toronto and Vancouver come from J. K. Chambers and M. Hardwick, "Comparative Sociolinguistics of a Sound Change in Canadian English," *English World-Wide* 7 (1986): 23–46. The newspaper survey was the work of Hal Edwards and was reported by Donald William in "The Latest Word on How Kansans Pronounce Things," *Wichita Eagle*, 24 Nov. 1996, 25A.

The discussion of principal components analysis and reported figures are from S. Clarke, *Problems in the Analysis of Sociolinguistic Variability: From Social to Linguistic Groupings* (Paper presented at NWAVE 19, University of Pennsylvania, 1990). The map in Figure 14.1 comes from L. Péronnet and P.-A. Arsenault, "Linguistic Atlas of French Maritime Terminology," *Journal of English Linguistics* 22 (1990): 25–29. The study of water isoglosses in Louisiana is reported in C. Bodin, *Water-Based Isoglosses in Louisiana Acadian French* (Paper presented at Methods IX, University of Wales, Bangor, 1996). The discussion of regional dialects makes use of a number of sources: Wolfram and Schilling-Estes (listed in the Recommended Reading); Carver (listed in the Recommended Reading); and the Web site of the Phonological Atlas of North America, which can be accessed at <http://www.ling.upenn.edu/phono_atlas/home.html>.

The New York department store survey is found in William Labov, *Sociolinguistic Patterns* (Philadelphia: University of Pennsylvania Press, 1972). The social network discussion comes from L. Milroy, *Language and Social Networks* (Baltimore: University Park Press, 1980), with figures and examples from J. Boissevain, *Friends of Friends: Networks, Manipulators and Coalitions* (Oxford: Blackwell, 1974). Information on the Ocracoke dialect is found in W. Wolfram and N. Schilling-Estes, "Moribund Dialects and the Endangerment Canon: The Case of the Ocracoke Brogue," *Language* 71 (1995): 696–721. The study of African American youth in New York is the subject of William Labov's *Language in the Inner City* (Philadelphia: University of Pennsylvania Press, 1972). The section on African American Vernacular English is based on W. Wolfram and N. Schilling-Estes (cited in Recommended Reading); papers on John Rickford's Web site devoted to ebonics at <http://www.stanford.edu/~rickford/ebonics/>; and an untitled column by Jack Sidnell in *Anthropology Newsletter* 38:3 (1997): 8. The section on lingua franca, pidgins, and creoles is based on a number of sources including R. A. Hall, Jr., *Pidgin and Creole Languages* (Ithaca, NY: Cornell University Press, 1966); D. Bickerton, "The Language Bioprogram Hypothesis," *Behavioral and Brain Sciences* 7 (1984): 173–221; and G. Sankoff and S. Laberge, "On the Acquisition of Native Speakers by a Language," in *Pidgins and Creoles: Current Trends and Prospects*, edited by D. DeCamp and I. F. Hancock (Washington, DC: Georgetown University Press, 1974), pp. 73–84. The section on language mixture is informed by S. Poplack, "Sometimes I'll Start a Sentence in Spanish y Termino en Español: Toward a Typology of Code-Switching," *Linguistics* 18 (1980): 581–618, as well as by J. Holmes, *An Introduction to Sociolinguistics* (New York: Longman and Brown, 1992). Additional examples come from D. Turpin, "'Le français c'est le last frontier': Le syntagme nominal dans le discours bilingue français/anglais" (MA thesis, University of Ottawa, 1995); M. Meechan and S. Poplack, "Orphan Categories in Bilingual Discourse: Adjectivization Strategies in Wolof-French and Fongbe-French," *Language Variation and*

Change 7 (1995): 169–94; S. Poplack, S. Wheeler, and A. Westwood, "Distinguishing Language Contact Phenomena: Evidence from Finnish-English Bilingualism," in *The Nordic Languages and Modern Linguistics*, edited by P. Lilius and M. Saari (Helsinki: University of Helsinki Press, 1987), pp. 33–56; and M. Naït M'Barek and D. Sankoff, "Le discours mixte arabe/français: des emprunts ou des alternances de langue?" *Revue Canadienne de Linguistique* 33 (1988): 143–54.

Recommended reading

Carver, C. M. 1989. *American Regional Dialects: A Word Geography.* Ann Arbor: University of Michigan Press.

Chambers, J. K. 1995. *Sociolinguistic Theory.* Oxford: Blackwell.

Downes, W. 1998. *Language and Society.* Cambridge: Cambridge University Press.

Fasold, R. 1984. *The Sociolinguistics of Society.* Oxford: Blackwell.

Fasold, R. 1990. *Sociolinguistics of Language.* Oxford: Blackwell.

Holmes, J. 1992. *An Introduction to Sociolinguistics.* New York: Longman and Brown.

Schiffrin, D. 1994. *Approaches to Discourse.* Oxford: Blackwell.

Wolfram, W., and N. Schilling-Estes. 1998. *American English: Dialects and Variation.* Oxford: Blackwell.

Questions

1. Choose a speech situation and analyze it using the components discussed in the section on ethnography of communication.

2. Focusing on a particular adolescent or young adult social group in your community, make a list of slang terms that they use. Using this list, question an older member of the community and determine how terms differ and how they are the same.

3. Using the adjacency pair greeting–response, choose a specific situation and question four people from different cultural backgrounds to determine if there are any differences in kinds of utterances they would use.

4. Observe the way people around you close conversations. Make a list of some examples of closings. What made a closing particularly effective? Were any ineffective, and why?

5. Examine the news articles in a newspaper or television news report and isolate any examples of euphemisms. Try to determine why the euphemism was employed. For example, was it used to avoid a taboo word or was the word it replaced avoided for some other reason?

6. Find some example of narrative discourse in a contemporary play, a television show, a book, or another source. Narrative involves the telling of the sequential events of a story. If it is not written down, transcribe it. Make a list of all the discourse markers and try to determine their function. For example, are they limited to bracketing any particular clause type?

7. Considering the discussion of language and gender, find three books on the prescriptive rules of English grammar and look for two examples of androcentric bias therein. Try to choose books from three different time frames—such as one from the early 1900s—as opposed to books that have been published more recently. Are all three books in agreement regarding the rules you have isolated? What might this indicate about the representation of gender in language?

8. *i.* The examples given in Table 14.9 in the section on language attitudes were given to subjects in New York City. Make your own list of ten words with alternative pronunciations that could be used to test linguistic insecurity. Justify your choice of each word.
   ii. Comparing your list of ten words from *i* with lists from your classmates, compile a class list of ten words.
   iii. Ask ten people to give you their preferred pronunciation of the words. Then, ask each person which is more "correct." Are there any discrepancies in their answers? What do the results say about the possible linguistic insecurity of the people you talked to?

9. Based on observation of people in your community, construct a questionnaire for eliciting terms, structures, and pronunciations that you have noticed are variable.

10. Words that have been borrowed into English may not always be completely integrated into English grammar. In that case, speakers may vary their pronunciation or use irregular morphology such as deleted plurals or determiners. Make a list of borrowed words in your dialect that show signs of variable integration.

FOR THE STUDENT LINGUIST

WHEN LANGUAGE GOES BAD

Nothing shows more clearly how many rules and norms we have about language use than when something goes awry. The following example, from Tom Stoppard's *Rosencrantz and Guildenstern Are Dead,* would probably be an interactional sociolinguist's worst nightmare.

In case you haven't read the play or seen the movie, Rosencrantz and Guildenstern (whom you may recall as two minor characters from *Hamlet*) are killing time and decide to play a game. The rules of the game are actually straightforward. Unfortunately for the poor interactional sociolinguist, the guys aren't too consistent with their application of the rules. Thus, some of the statements they make about the game (e.g., "Cheating!") aren't scored as part of the game while others are (e.g., "I hadn't started yet.").

The speech norms seem even more dubious when you look at Rosencrantz and Guildenstern's decisions about what does (and does not) count as a synonym, as a non sequitur, or as rhetoric. However, it's surprising to me that many of the components of this speech situation are relatively easily identifiable in spite of this being such an absurd discourse. After you've identified the components, you might want to experiment with making just one or two of them absurd (choosing different ones than Stoppard did) while keeping the others logical, and see if there's any sort of system or pattern to effective humor. Then again, too much analysis always kills a joke. Maybe you should just rent the video, make some popcorn, and put off your homework for tonight.

ROS: We could play at questions.
GUIL: What good would that do?
ROS: Practice!
GUIL: Statement! One-love.
ROS: Cheating!
GUIL: How?
ROS: I hadn't started yet.
GUIL: Statement. Two-love.
ROS: Are you counting that?
GUIL: What?
ROS: Are you counting that?
GUIL: Foul! No repetitions. Three-love. First game to . . .
ROS: I'm not going to play if you're going to be like that.
GUIL: Whose serve?
ROS: Hah?
GUIL: Foul! No grunts. Love-one.
ROS: Whose go?
GUIL: Why?
ROS: Why not?
GUIL: What for?
ROS: Foul! No synonyms! One-all.
GUIL: What in God's name is going on?
ROS: Foul! No rhetoric. Two-one.
GUIL: What does it all add up to?
ROS: Can't you guess?
GUIL: Were you addressing me?
ROS: Is there anyone else?
GUIL: Who?
ROS: How would I know?
GUIL: Why do you ask?
ROS: Are you serious?
GUIL: Was that rhetoric?
ROS: No.
GUIL: Statement! Two-all. Game point.
ROS: What's the matter with you today?
GUIL: When?

ROS: What?
GUIL: Are you deaf?
ROS: Am I dead?
GUIL: Yes or no?
ROS: Is there a choice?
GUIL: Is there a God?
ROS: Foul! No non sequiturs, three-two, one game all.
GUIL: (*seriously*) What's your name?
ROS: What's yours?
GUIL: I asked you first.
ROS: Statement. One-love.
GUIL: What's your name when you're at home?
ROS: What's yours?
GUIL: When I'm at home?
ROS: What home?
GUIL: Haven't you got one?
ROS: Why do you ask?
GUIL: What are you driving at?
ROS: (*with emphasis*) What's your name?
GUIL: Repetition. Two-love. Match point to me.
ROS: (*seizing him violently*) WHO DO YOU THINK YOU ARE?
GUIL: Rhetoric! Game and match!

fifteen

Writing and Language

Michael Dobrovolsky
William O'Grady

Outside of a dog, a book is man's best friend; inside of a dog, it's too dark to read.

– Groucho Marx

Objectives

In this chapter, you will learn

- how different types of writing systems have evolved from earliest times
- how different types of alphabetic systems emerged
- how various types of non-European writing systems developed
- how historical factors have led to the modern English spelling system
- how writing and reading are related

Speaking and writing are different in both origin and practice. Our ability to use language is as old as humankind and reflects the biological and cognitive modification that has occurred during the evolution of our species. **Writing**—the symbolic representation of language by graphic signs or symbols—is a comparatively recent cultural development, having occurred within the past five thousand years and only in certain parts of the world. The contrast between speech and writing comes into sharper focus when we consider that spoken language is acquired without specific formal instruction, whereas writing must be taught and learned through deliberate effort. There are entire groups of people in the world today, as well as individuals in every literate society, who are unable to write. While spoken language comes naturally to human beings, writing does not.

1 TYPES OF WRITING

As different as they are, speech and writing share one major characteristic: just as spoken language shows an arbitrary link between sound and meaning, so too written language exhibits an arbitrary link between symbol and sound.

All writing can be grouped into two basic types—logographic and phonographic—depending on the technique that it uses to represent language.

1.1 Logographic writing

Logographic writing (from Greek *logos* 'word') refers to a type of writing in which symbols represent morphemes or even entire words.

Logograms

Logographic writing is the oldest type of genuine writing. Ancient Mesopotamian cuneiform inscriptions, Egyptian hieroglyphics, and primordial Chinese characters were all highly logographic in their early stages. In fact, all writing systems maintain some logographic writing. Conventional abbreviations such as &, %, $, and the like are **logograms**, as are the symbols for numerals. To a certain extent, logographic writing can be read independently of its language of origin. For example, the Arabic numbers 1, 2, 7, 10, and so on can be read in any language.

1.2 Phonographic writing

No writing system can be purely logographic, however, since using a separate symbol to write each word in a language is simply too cumbersome. Throughout human history, writing systems have always evolved signs that represent some aspect of pronunciation. In **phonographic writing** (from Greek *phōnēs* 'sound'), symbols represent syllables or segments. There are two principal types of phonographic writing systems—syllabic and alphabetic.

Syllabic writing

As the name suggests, **syllabic writing** employs signs to represent syllables (a set of syllabic signs is called a **syllabary**). Languages with relatively simple syllabic structures such as CV or CVC (Japanese and Cree, for example) are well suited to this type of writing, since they contain a relatively limited number of syllable types. In Japanese, for example, the word *kakimashita* '(s/he) wrote' can be written with the five syllabic signs か, き, ま, し, and た: かきました.

Alphabetic writing

Alphabetic writing represents consonant and vowel segments. Unlike the International Phonetic Alphabet, which is devised expressly to represent details of pronunciation, ordinary alphabets generally ignore nonphonemic phenomena. Thus, the spelling of the English words *pan* and *nap* represents the phonemes /p/, /n/, and /æ/ but ignores consonant aspiration, vowel nasalization, stress, and other sub-phonemic variation. As we will see in Section 4 of this chapter, some spelling systems also capture certain morphophonemic alternations.

Writing systems emerged and spread around the world over a long period of time. Though we can trace the spread of some systems over a wide area, writing may have emerged independently in several different places. The next sections trace the development of some writing systems from their pictorial origins.

2 THE EARLY HISTORY OF WRITING

It is surprising that we cannot say with certainty how a comparatively recent cultural phenomenon like writing originated. We do know that writing developed in stages, the earliest of which involves direct representation of objects. This stage is sometimes called **prewriting**.

2.1 PREWRITING

Figures and scenes depicted on cave walls and rock faces in the Americas, Africa, and Europe twelve thousand years ago—and perhaps even earlier—may have been forerunners of writing. Some of these petroglyphs (scenes painted on stone) may represent a type of preliterate stage that did not evolve into a full-fledged writing system.

These drawings depict a wide range of human and animal activity and may even have been intended for purposes of linguistic communication. Some illustrations were doubtless a form of religious magic to guarantee a successful hunt or other benefits, and some may have been purely for aesthetic expression. Still others, such as those depicting the phases of the moon, may have been part of some form of record keeping. Figure 15.1a shows a pair of elk from a rock wall drawing in Sweden dating from the Old Stone Age (Paleolithic) period, perhaps as far back as 20,000 B.C. Figure 15.1b shows an incised eagle bone from Le Placard, France, that dates back some 13,000 to 15,000 years. The incisions, which vary subtly, have been analyzed as a record of lunar phases. Pictorial records thus link the origins of writing with the history of representative art.

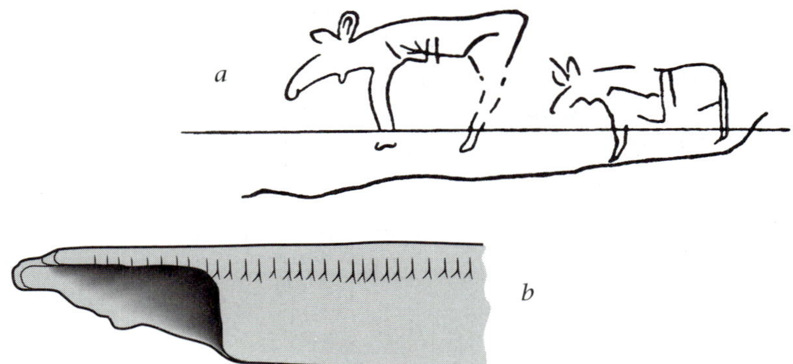

Figure 15.1 *a*. Paleolithic drawing, Sweden; *b*. Le Placard eagle bone

An even more direct connection links the origin of writing with record keeping. It has been suggested that the idea of writing had its origin in small clay tokens and counters that were used in record keeping and business transactions in the ancient Middle East. These small, fire-baked pieces of clay were apparently used for thousands of years before writing emerged (see Figure 15.2). Counters representing cattle and other goods were stored on shelves or in baskets. Eventually, people began to make an impression of the tokens on soft clay tablets rather than storing and shipping the tokens themselves. This may have led to the idea that other objects and events in the world could be represented symbolically in graphic form.

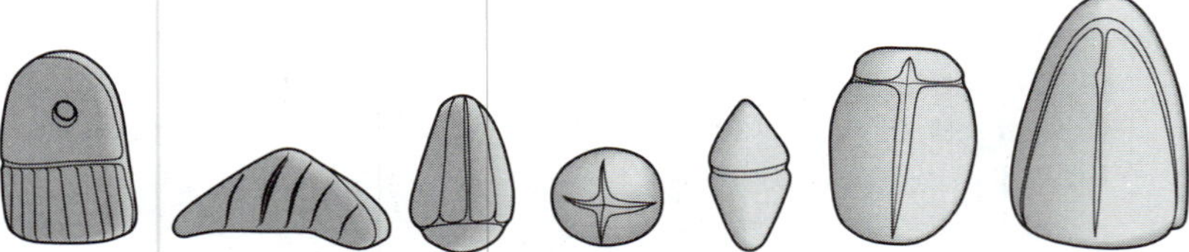

Figure 15.2 Ancient Mesopotamian tokens

2.2 Pictograms

Whatever their purpose, there is no doubt that pictures were among the precursors of the written word. Early writing systems all evolved from pictorial representations called **pictograms**, or picture writing. Each pictogram was an image of the object or concept that it represented and, as far as we know, offered no clues to pronunciation. Pictorial representations of this sort have been found among people throughout the ancient and modern world. Figure 15.3 is an example of Amerindian picture

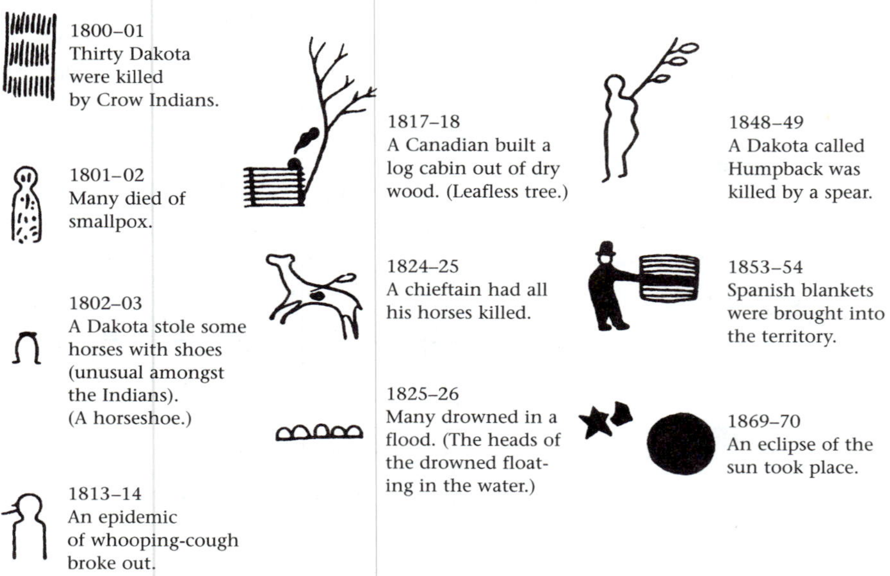

1800–01
Thirty Dakota were killed by Crow Indians.
1801–02
Many died of smallpox.
1802–03
A Dakota stole some horses with shoes (unusual amongst the Indians). (A horseshoe.)
1813–14
An epidemic of whooping-cough broke out.
1817–18
A Canadian built a log cabin out of dry wood. (Leafless tree.)
1824–25
A chieftain had all his horses killed.
1825–26
Many drowned in a flood. (The heads of the drowned floating in the water.)
1848–49
A Dakota called Humpback was killed by a spear.
1853–54
Spanish blankets were brought into the territory.
1869–70
An eclipse of the sun took place.

Figure 15.3 Amerindian pictography: a Dakota record of significant events

writing taken from a record kept by a Dakota named Lonedog; these pictures served as a kind of memory aid and not as a detailed record of events.

Like any other product of culture, pictography requires a knowledge of the conventions used by the author. Lonedog's record, for example, lists thirty Dakotas killed, but there are only twenty-four short vertical lines. To interpret the record correctly, it is necessary to know that the frame around the short lines consists of six additional joined lines.

Pictograms are still used today, often reflecting the function of this form of prewriting as a memory aid. Signs indicating roadside services or information in parks are all pictographic in nature, as are the standardized set of symbols developed by the Olympic Association to indicate sporting events (see Figure 15.4).

Figure 15.4 Contemporary pictograms: Olympic signs for sporting events

A contemporary and very sophisticated development of pictographic writing, **Blissymbolics** (originally called semantography), was developed by Charles K. Bliss. It makes use of a number of recombinable symbols that represent basic units of meaning, as the example in Figure 15.5 illustrates.

Figure 15.5 Blissymbolics

Though Blissymbolics was intended as a means of international, cross-linguistic communication by its inventor, its primary use today is as a means of communication for nonspeaking individuals. The Blissymbolics Communication Institute of Toronto sets the standard for the training and application of Blissymbols for this specialized purpose.

As we consider developments that emerge from pictographic representation, it is important to remember that pictograms are not writing in any sense of the word. They do not represent linguistic elements such as segments, syllables, morphemes, or words; they are not written in a sequence that matches the language's word order; and they typically lend themselves to more than one interpretation, often providing only limited clues about their intended meaning.

3 THE EVOLUTION OF WRITING

The earliest known pictographic writing came from Sumeria, from where it spread to surrounding areas about five thousand years ago. Over time, inherently ambiguous pictograms came to be used to represent abstract notions, as their use was extended to include related concepts. In Figure 15.6, for example, the pictogram for 'fire' was also used for 'inflammation', the pictogram for 'hand' was employed to signify 'fist' as well as a particular unit of measurement, and the symbol for 'foot' came to stand for 'go', 'move', and 'go away'.

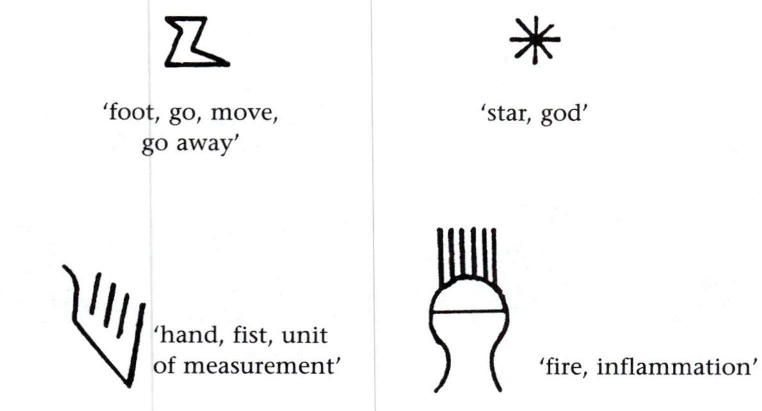

Figure 15.6 Sumerian logograms

Sumerian writing also combined signs to express abstract meanings. For example, a head with fire coming out of the crown indicated 'anger'.

Figure 15.7 The Sumerian logogram for 'anger'

Although its evolution was gradual, we can state with some certainty that Sumerian writing was logographic because, from a fairly early stage, it was written in a consistent linear order that appears to reflect the order of words in speech. We cannot say with certainty at what date pictures began to be read as words, but once this practice took hold, the stage was set for the evolution to phonographic writing.

3.1 Rebuses and the emergence of writing

Phonographic writing made its appearance around 3000 B.C. with the first use of Sumerian symbols to represent sound rather than just meaning. This major development in the history of writing was made possible by the use of the **rebus principle**, which allows a symbol to be used for any word that was pronounced like the word whose meaning it originally represented. In the inscription of an economic transaction in Figure 15.8, for example, the symbol in the upper left-hand corner was originally used to represent the word *gi* 'reed', but here represents a homophonous word with the meaning 'reimburse'.

Figure 15.8 Sumerian rebus inscription (c. 3000 B.C.)

Thanks to the rebus principle, concepts that could not be directly depicted by a pictogram/logogram could be represented in writing. Thus, the sign for the word *ti* 'arrow', ⟶ , was also used for the word *ti* 'life'.

3.2 Toward syllabic writing

Once the breakthrough toward phonographic writing had been made, it did not take long (in historical terms) before syllabic writing began to emerge. Within about five hundred to six hundred years, signs that clearly represented not just homophonous words but parts of words—specifically, syllables—had become well established in Sumerian writing. For example, the word *kir* was represented by the syllabic signs for *ki* and *ir*, written in sequence. (By allowing the function of the symbols to overlap in this way, the need for a special sign for *r* was avoided.) Figure 15.9 illustrates this with the help of Sumerian cuneiform signs, which are discussed in more detail in the following section.

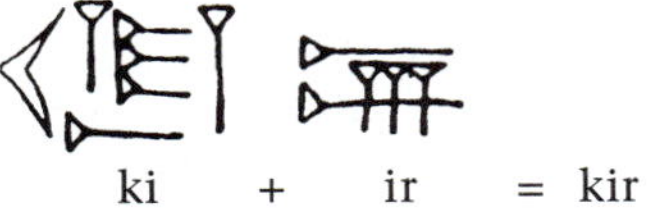

Figure 15.9 Overlapped Sumerian syllabic signs

Sumerian writing never developed into a pure syllabary. Logographic elements were interspersed with syllabic ones, and many syllabic signs were used to represent syllables with other pronunciations as well.

Cuneiform

Over the centuries, Sumerian writing was simplified and eventually came to be produced with the use of a wedge-shaped stylus that was pressed into soft clay tablets.

This form of writing, initiated in the fourth millennium B.C., has come to be known as **cuneiform** (from Latin *cuneus* 'wedge'). In time, a change in writing practices led the cuneiform signs to be rotated 90° to the left. This resulted in their bearing even less resemblance to their pictographic origins than before. Figure 15.10 illustrates this development in two forms.

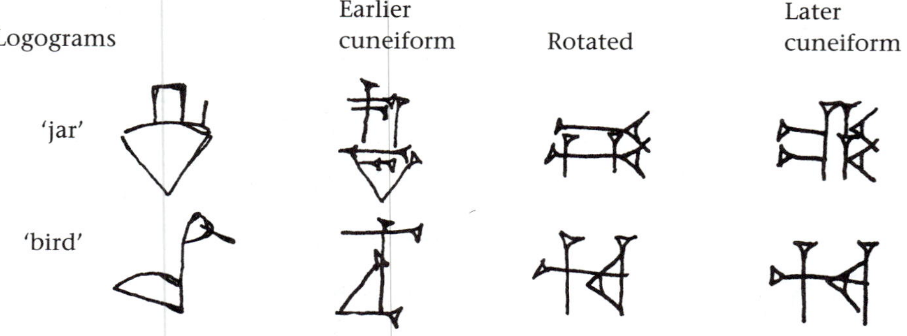

Figure 15.10 Changes in cuneiform writing

The cuneiform system was borrowed in the third millennium B.C. by the Elamites and Akkadians, a little later by the Persians, and in the second millennium B.C. by the Hittites far to the north in the ancient region of Anatolia (modern Asian Turkey).

Cuneiform writing persisted until about the first few centuries of the Christian era in some areas and then disappeared from use, not to be rediscovered until the nineteenth century. It was first deciphered from Old Persian texts, a breakthrough that led to the deciphering of Akkadian, Sumerian, and Hittite, among other languages that employed it. This script was used for thousands of years but then was generally replaced by systems of writing employed by the Semitic peoples of the Eastern Mediterranean.

3.3 Another Middle Eastern writing system: hieroglyphics

At about the time Sumerian pictography was flourishing, a similar system of pictorial communication was in use in Egypt. The Egyptian signs have become known as **hieroglyphics** (meaning 'sacred inscriptions' in Greek). The earliest texts display about five hundred such symbols. Like Sumerian pictograms, the hieroglyphic signs at first represented objects, but later they became logographic as they began to be associated with words.

Egyptian hieroglyphics developed into a mixed system of both word writing and phonographic writing. For example, the sign for a lute was a picture of a lute: 𓄤; this represented the word itself: *nfr*. (Only the consonants of words represented by hieroglyphics are known with certainty. The Egyptians did not represent vowels—these can only be partially reconstructed from transcriptions in Greek and other languages that were made much later.) Eventually, the sign for 'lute' came to be dissociated from the word it represented, and was used to transcribe other words that consisted of or included the same sounds, such as the word for 'good', which also contained the consonants *nfr*.

Hieroglyphic symbols eventually came to be used to represent individual consonant phonemes by application of what is called the **acrophonic principle** (from Greek *acros* 'extreme'): sounds are represented by pictures of objects whose pronunciation begins with the sound to be represented. In this way, the first consonant of a word-sign came to be what the sign stood for. For example, the hieroglyph for 'horned viper':

is read logographically as *f(V)t*. Thanks to the acrophonic principle, this sign is also used to represent the phoneme /f/ in spellings such as *fen* 'pleasant'.

As we will see in Section 3.4, the acrophonic principle was crucial to the development of true alphabets. In Egyptian writing, however, it was only part of a system that mixed logographic and phonographic elements.

Figure 15.11 provides some additional examples of hieroglyphics. (Throughout this chapter, a macron indicates a long vowel.) Hieroglyphics continued in decreasing use to Christian times. By the second century A.D., Egyptian began to be written with Greek letters, and by the third century A.D., hieroglyphics had been replaced by the Greek alphabet.

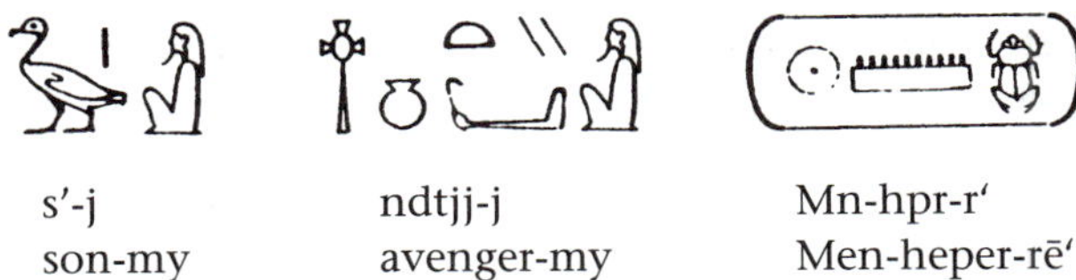

Figure 15.11 Egyptian hieroglyphics (c. 2000 B.C.)

3.4 The emergence of alphabets

Alphabetic writing emerged slowly from mixed writing systems over a long period in the Middle East. Building on this tradition, the Semitic peoples of ancient Phoenicia (modern Lebanon) devised a writing system of twenty-two consonantal signs as early as 1000 B.C. This system was written horizontally, right to left, as had been common in earlier scripts. It ultimately led to the development of many alphabetic writing systems, including both the Greek and Latin alphabets.

The pictorial (and eventually logographic) origins of the Phoenician alphabet are evident in some of its symbols. Figure 15.12 illustrates the development of logograms for a stylized ox's head, a throwing stick, and a wavy flow of water into alphabetic symbols.

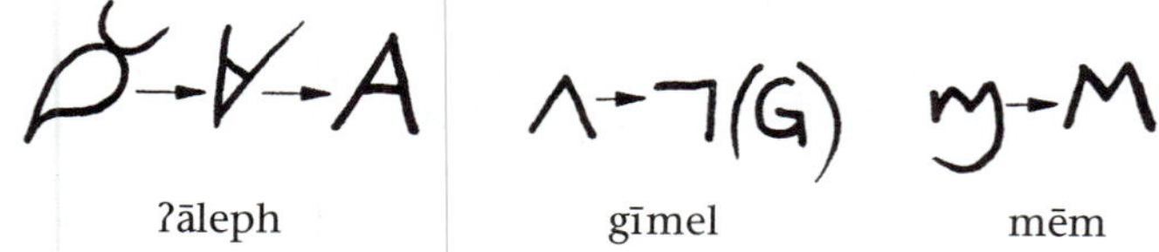

Figure 15.12 Pictorial and logographic origins of some signs in the Phoenician alphabet

These symbols eventually came to be used to represent the consonant phonemes of words by application of the acrophonic principle (see Section 3.3). In this way, *ʔāleph* was used to represent a glottal stop; *gīmel*, a /g/; and *mēm*, an /m/. Some of the symbols of the Phoenician alphabet had developed from Egyptian hieroglyphics, and, as in hieroglyphic writing, vowels were not represented (see Figure 15.11).

The Phoenicians were a trading people, and their alphabetic writing spread to adjacent countries and beyond. Eventually, the Greeks acquired and adapted the Phoenician alphabet.

The Greek alphabet

The Greeks developed the Phoenician writing system into a full alphabet: each sign represented one phoneme and all phonemes were recorded by a sign. The Greeks were aware that some of the Phoenician symbols represented consonant sounds that were not found in Greek. Some of these symbols were adapted to represent Greek vowels, and other unneeded consonant signs were eventually dropped. Figure 15.13 illustrates the evolution of the Classical Greek and ultimately the Latin alphabet from the original Phoenician consonantal signs.

As we have seen, Phoenician *ʔāleph* represented a glottal stop. Since Greek had no such phoneme, the *ʔāleph* was employed to represent the vowel /a/ in Greek. Phoenician (*h*) was used to represent the Greek vowel /e/, and other signs were added to the system by the Greeks, including Φ/f/, X/x/, Ψ/ps/, and Ω/ō/.

The Semitic names for the letters (*aleph, beth, gimel, daleth,* and so on) were maintained by the Greeks (as *alpha, beta, gamma, delta,* and so on), but the possible pictorial origins had been lost and the names carried no other meaning. In ancient Greek, the direction of writing was often reversed at the end of each line. If the first line of a text was written right to left, the next line continued left to right, then right to left, and so on. This practice was typical of many old writing systems and is known as **boustrophedon** (Greek for 'as the ox turns'), since it was said to resemble the pattern made by plowing a field. The writing system itself gained its name—alphabet—from the first two letters of the series.

The Roman alphabet

When Greek colonists occupied southern Italy in the eighth and seventh centuries B.C., they took their alphabet with them. It was in turn taken up and modified by the Etruscan inhabitants of central Italy—a non-Latin-speaking people who were a political and cultural power before the rise of Rome. It is believed that the Romans acquired their alphabet through the Etruscans. As the Romans grew in power and

Symbols			Greek			Latin	
Phoenician	Hebrew name	Phonetic value	Early	Classical	Name	Early	Monumental (Classical)
𐤀	'Aleph	ʔ	Α	Α	Alpha	A	A
𐤁	Beth	b	Β	Β	Beta		B
𐤂	Gimel	g	Γ	Γ	Gamma		C
𐤃	Daleth	d	Δ	Δ	Delta	D	D
𐤄	He	h	Ǝ	Ε	Epsilon	Ǝ	E
𐤅	Waw	w	Ϝ		Digamma	Ϝ	F
							G
𐤆	Zayin	z	I	Ζ	Zeta		
𐤇	Ḥeth	ħ	Η	Η	Ēta	Η	H
𐤈	Teth	ŧ	⊗	Θ	Theta		
𐤉	Yod	j	Ι	Ι	Iota	I	I
							(J)
𐤊	Kaph	k	Κ	Κ	Kappa	K	K
𐤋	Lamed	l	Λ	Λ	Lambda		L
𐤌	Mem	m	Μ	Μ	Mu	M	M
𐤍	Nun	n	Ν	Ν	Nu	N	N
𐤎	Samekh	s					
𐤏	'Ayin	ʕ	Ο	Ο	Ŏmicron	O	O
𐤐	Pe	p	Π	Π	Pi		P
𐤑	Tsade	s	Ϻ		San		
𐤒	Qoph	q	Ϙ		Qoppa		Q
𐤓	Reš	r	Ρ	Ρ	Rho		R
𐤔	Šin	ʃ-s	Σ	Σ	Sigma	S	S
𐤕	Taw	t	Χ		Tau		T
				Υ	Upsilon	V	V
				Χ	Chi		X Y
				Ω	Omega		Z

Figure 15.13 Evolution of the Greek and Latin alphabets

influence during the following centuries, first as masters of Italy and later of Europe, the Roman alphabet spread throughout their empire.

Under the Romans, the Greek/Etruscan alphabet was again modified, this time with some symbols influenced by the Etruscans. The *G* in Greek writing developed into both *C* for the phoneme /k/ and *G* for /g/. The oldest inscriptions also retained

K for /k/ in some words, but it was generally replaced by *C*. Similarly, *Q* was retained before /u/. Roman script also employed Greek *U* (= V), *X*, *Y*, and *Z* and moved *Z* to the end of the alphabet. The symbols Φ, Θ, Ψ, and Ω were among those discarded, and *H* was converted back to a consonant symbol.

Some subsequent changes were made in the alphabet as it was adapted by various peoples of the Roman Empire. In English, for example, *W* was created from two juxtaposed *V*s. Spanish employs a tilde (˜) over *n* (ñ) to signify a palatal nasal, as in *año* /aɲo/ 'year', and French uses a cedilla under c (ç) to indicate the dental fricative /s/, as in the spelling of *français* /frãsɛ/ 'French'.

3.5 Other developments, East and West

A large number of alphabetic systems other than those of Greek and Rome evolved and flourished in Europe and the Middle East. In this section, we briefly present some of these that are of historical significance or interest.

Runic writing

Germanic tribes occupying the north of Italy developed an early offshoot of the Greek/Etruscan tradition of writing into a script known as **Runic writing**. This system emerged shortly after the beginning of the Christian era, and its developments were eventually found as far north as Scandinavia. Runic writing persisted until the sixteenth century in some areas before giving way to the Roman alphabet.

Figure 15.14 illustrates some signs from one of the oldest known Runic inscriptions, which dates from about the third century A.D. The angular style of the letters arose because the alphabet was carved in wood or stone, the former especially not readily lending itself to curved lines. The script is read from right to left.

= harigasti ['the warriors' guest']
(epithet for the god Odin)

Figure 15.14 Runic script

Cyrillic script

Another offshoot of the Greek script was created for the Slavic peoples in the ninth century A.D. The Greek missionary brothers Constantine (Cyril) and Methodius introduced a writing system for the translation of the Bible that is now known as **Glagolitic script**. A later development, which combined adaptations of Glagolitic letters with Greek and Hebrew characters, has come to be known as the **Cyrillic alphabet**. The current Russian, Byelorussian, Ukrainian, Serbian, Macedonian, and Bulgarian alphabets, as well as those used to represent many non-Slavic languages spoken in the former Soviet Union, have evolved from this early Cyrillic script. Some examples of its development and adaptation are given in Figure 15.15, followed by a short passage in contemporary Russian Cyrillic, which is transliterated for its letter values. (The apostrophe is the traditional transliteration for palatalization in Slavic languages.)

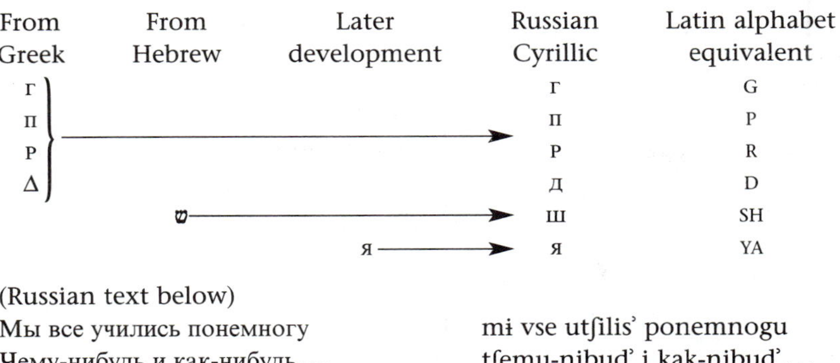

(Russian text below)

Мы все учились понемногу	mɨ vse utʃilis' ponemnogu
Чему-нибудь и как-нибудь...	tʃemu-nibud' i kak-nibud'...

'We all pick up our education
In bits and pieces as we can . . .'
Pushkin, *Eugene Onegin*, I.5

Figure 15.15 Contemporary Russian Cyrillic transliterated

Two Semitic alphabets

Both Arabic and Hebrew are written with alphabets that descend from or are closely related to Phoenician script. Both are essentially consonant-writing systems (vowels are indicated by diacritics), and both are written from right to left.

The contemporary Arabic alphabet is the most widespread of all the descendants of Middle Eastern writing except the Roman alphabet. The earliest inscription dates back to the fourth century A.D. In the latter half of the seventh century, this script was used to write the Koran—the sacred text of Islam—and its use spread rapidly along with the Islamic religion over the next centuries.

The Arabic alphabet contains twenty-eight consonants, with vowels indicated by diacritics above and below the consonants. An interesting feature of this alphabet is that twenty-two of its twenty-eight signs have different forms, depending on their position in (or outside of) a word. Figure 15.16 illustrates the forms of the letters *b* and *k* in initial, medial, and final position, as well as their forms when written in isolation.

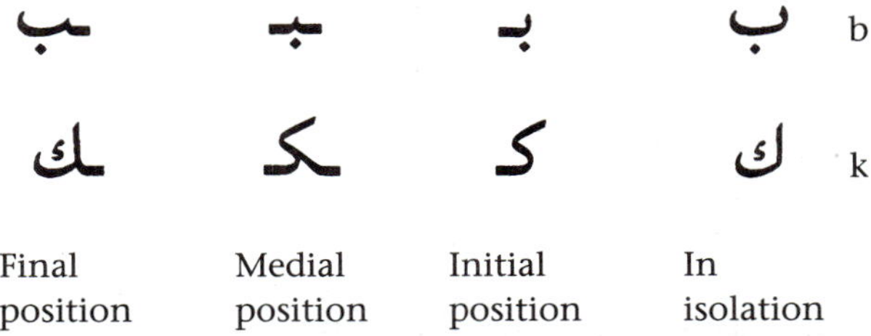

Figure 15.16 Variation in two Arabic letters according to position

The similarities among the symbols in Figure 15.17 demonstrate the link between Phoenician script and the Hebrew and Arabic scripts.

Hebrew Letter name	Phonetic value	Phoenician	Modern Hebrew	Modern Arabic
'Aleph	ʔ	𐤀	א	ا
Beth	b	𐤁	ב	ب
Gimel	g	𐤂	ג	ج
Daleth	d	𐤃	ד	د
He	h	𐤄	ה	ه
Waw	w	𐤅	ו	و
Zayin	z	𐤆	ז	ز
Ḥeth	ħ	𐤇	ח	ح
Ṭeth	ŧ	𐤈	ט	ط
Yod	j	𐤉	י	ي
Kaph	k	𐤊	כ	ك
Lamed	l	𐤋	ל	ل
Mem	m	𐤌	מ	م
Nun	n	𐤍	נ	ن
Samekh	s	𐤎	ס	س
'Ayin	ʕ	𐤏	ע	ع
Pe	p	𐤐	פ	ف
Tsade	ʂ	𐤑	צ	ص
Qoph	q	𐤒	ק	ق
Reš	r	𐤓	ר	ر
Šin	ʃ-s	𐤔	ש	ش
Taw	t	𐤕	ת	ت

Figure 15.17 The Phoenician, Hebrew, and Arabic alphabets

Other descendants of Middle Eastern systems

Early Middle Eastern scripts gave rise to Aramaic, Old Hebrew, and South Arabic scripts, which, in turn, led to a host of further writing systems eventually stretching across the Near East and North Africa from India to Morocco. Figure 15.18 illustrates this widespread diffusion on a time scale.

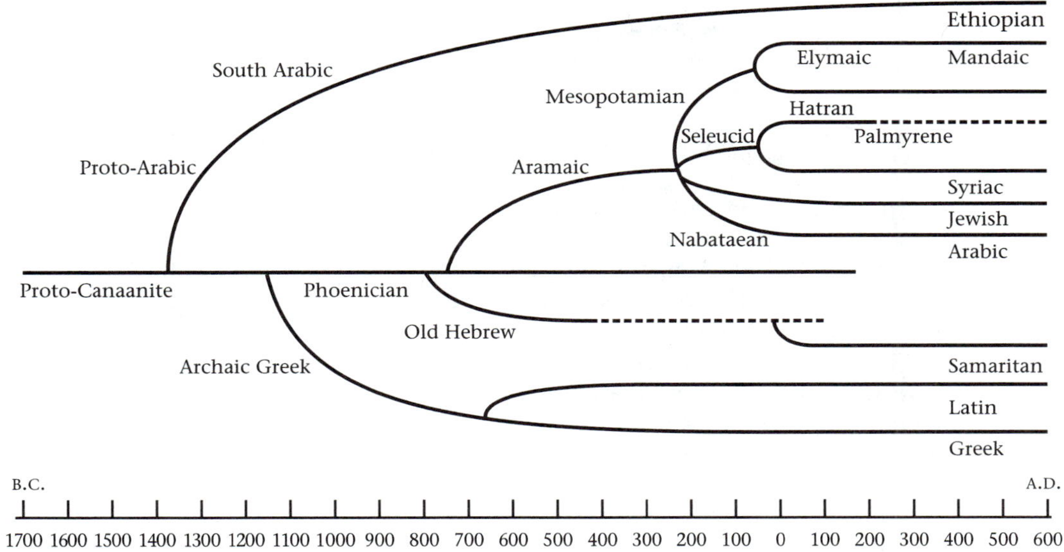

Figure 15.18 Development of writing systems (dotted lines indicate that the line of development is hypothetical)

4 SOME NON-EUROPEAN WRITING SYSTEMS

This section focuses on the nature and development of writing systems that originated outside the Middle East. While some of these systems emerged in response to external influences, others seem to have been entirely independent innovations.

4.1 Chinese writing

The Chinese system of writing developed out of pictograms that eventually came to represent morphemes (most of which are also words). The oldest inscriptions are the oracle texts, written on animal bones and tortoise shells and dating back to about twelve hundred B.C. These include many recognizable images, such as ⊙ 'sun' and ☽ 'moon'.

A change toward more **symbolic signs** began at an early date, as more abstract notions were symbolized, such as 'above' and 'below'. Symbols were also combined to extend meanings metaphorically. For example, the sign for 'to tend' 牧 is composed of 牛 'cow' and 支 'hand and whip'. 'To follow' 从 is two men in sequence, and so on. In time, the characters became more abstract. Figure 15.19 shows the historical development of the symbol for 'dog'.

Calligraphy is an ancient and respected art in China, and Chinese writing exists in a number of styles. The script is usually written from left to right along a horizontal axis, although newspapers and older texts begin in the right-hand margin and are read downward.

Figure 15.19 Historical development of the Chinese symbol for 'dog'

The units of contemporary Chinese writing are called **characters**. Many monosyllabic words are presented in true logographic fashion by a character consisting of a single symbol. For example, the Mandarin words [ʃǒw] 'hand' and [mǎ] 'horse' are written 手 and 馬, respectively. However, the overwhelming majority of characters (one estimate is 99 percent) consist of two parts.

The main component of a multi-element character, called the **phonetic determinative**, provides information about the pronunciation of the corresponding morpheme. Although about four thousand different phonetic determinatives are used in Chinese writing, they represent pronunciation very imperfectly. Tone, which is contrastive in Chinese (see Chapter 2), is not represented at all, and many phonetic determinatives indicate only part of the morpheme's pronunciation. For instance, the determinative 敖 is used for a wide variety of words ending in *ao* regardless of whether the initial consonant is *j, n, r,* or some other element. Furthermore, due to sound changes over the last centuries, about one-third of all phonetic determinatives provide little or no useful information about current pronunciation. Finally, because Chinese has many homophones, even the most informative phonetic determinatives can be used for many different words.

Chinese characters also include a semantic component, called the **radical** or key, which provides clues about the morpheme's meaning. There are about two hundred different radicals in contemporary Chinese writing. Table 15.1 provides examples of some of the characters that can be formed by combining phonetic determinatives with radicals.

Table 15.1 Some Chinese characters

		Phonetic determinatives			
		A	*B*	*C*	*D*
Semantic radical		敖 (*áo*)	參 (*cān*)	堯 (*yāo*)	甫 (*fǔ*)
1	亻 'person'	傲 (*ào:* 'proud')	傪 (*cān:* 'good')	僥 (*jiǎo:* 'lucky')	俌 (*fù:* 'help')
2	扌 'hand'	摮 (*ào:* 'shake')	摻 (*shán:* 'seize')	撓 (*nǎo:* 'scratch')	捕 (*bǔ:* 'catch')
3	木 'wood'	木敖 (*āo:* 'barge')	槮 (*shēn:* 'beam')	橈 (*náo:* 'oar')	木甫 (*fú:* 'trellis')
4	氵 'water'	滶 (*ào:* 'stream')	滲 (*shèn:* 'leak')	澆 (*jiāo:* 'sprinkle')	浦 (*pǔ:* 'creek')

Notice that only the phonetic determinative in column A indicates the precise pronunciation (ignoring tone) of the four characters in which it appears. The other determinatives supply helpful, but incomplete, phonetic information. For instance, the determinative *yao* (column C) has a pronunciation that rhymes with that of the four morphemes it helps to represent.

The usefulness of the information supplied by the radicals also varies. The characters in row 1 represent morphemes whose meaning is at best indirectly associated with that of the radical ('person'), but the radicals in rows 2, 3, and 4 are much more informative. For example, the characters in row 2 all denote actions involving the hand, those in row 3 all refer to things made of wood, and those in row 4 all have something to do with liquids.

Although neither phonetic determinatives alone nor semantic radicals alone suffice to identify the morphemes that they are used to represent, they are more than adequate when used in conjunction with each other. Despite these complexities—one authority has described the system as "outsized, haphazard, inefficient, and only partially reliable"—Chinese writing provides its users with an effective way to represent the words and morphemes of the language. Moreover, the lack of efficiency is offset by the fact that the same literary script can be understood by speakers of different Chinese languages. Although a speaker of Mandarin and a speaker of Cantonese may pronounce the word for 'fire' differently—/xwǒ/ and /fɔ̀/, respectively—both can read it from the same character (火), since Chinese writing does not directly represent a word's phonemic segments.

In recent times, the government of the People's Republic of China has introduced simplified characters (some newly invented) in an attempt to promote literacy. At the same time, a system of writing Mandarin with a modified Latin alphabet, called **pinyin**, has also been introduced. Pinyin is used as a subsidiary system for writing such things as street signs, addresses, and brand names, as well as for teaching children how to pronounce characters. It is also used for word processing and other computer-related activities, including electronic mail.

4.2 Japanese writing

The writing system of modern Japanese is arguably the most complicated in the entire world. Its use requires knowledge of three distinct scripts, including a pair of syllabaries—**hiragana** and **katakana**—which were created by modifying Chinese characters (see Table 15.2).

Although Japanese can be written exclusively with either syllabary, normal writing involves the use of Chinese characters (called **kanji** in Japanese) in addition to hiragana and katakana. Kanji symbols are typically used to represent all or part of a word's root while affixes are represented by hiragana symbols. The phrase *the man's car*, for example, can be written as in Figure 15.20, with the roots 'man' and 'car' represented by kanji, and the possessive morpheme *no* written in hiragana.

The katakana syllabary, whose symbols are less rounded than their hiragana counterparts, is used to write onomatopoeic words as well as words borrowed into Japanese from other languages. In addition, it is employed in advertising and in telegrams.

Table 15.2 Hiragana and katakana syllabaries and their phonetic values. (The conventions for representing voicing, vowel length, and gemination are not indicated here.)

Hiragana chart

COLUMN / LINE	A	I	U	E	O
SINGLE VOWEL	あ A	い I	う U	え E	お O
K	か KA	き KI	く KU	け KE	こ KO
S	さ SA	し SHI	す SU	せ SE	そ SO
T	た TA	ち CHI	つ TSU	て TE	と TO
N	な NA	に NI	ぬ NU	ね NE	の NO
H	は HA	ひ HI	ふ FU	へ HE	ほ HO
M	ま MA	み MI	む MU	め ME	も MO
Y	や YA		ゆ YU		よ YO
R	ら RA	り RI	る RU	れ RE	ろ RO
W	わ WA				を O
N (in a coda)	ん N				

Katakana chart

COLUMN / LINE	A	I	U	E	O
SINGLE VOWEL	ア A	イ I	ウ U	エ E	オ O
K	カ KA	キ KI	ク KU	ケ KE	コ KO
S	サ SA	シ SHI	ス SU	セ SE	ソ SO
T	タ TA	チ CHI	ツ TSU	テ TE	ト TO
N	ナ NA	ニ NI	ヌ NU	ネ NE	ノ NO
H	ハ HA	ヒ HI	フ FU	ヘ HE	ホ HO
M	マ MA	ミ MI	ム MU	メ ME	モ MO
Y	ヤ YA		ユ YU		ヨ YO
R	ラ RA	リ RI	ル RU	レ RE	ロ RO
W	ワ WA				ヲ O
N (in a coda)	ン N				

hito no	kuruma de
人 の	車 で
man Genitive	car Locative
kanji hiragana	kanji hiragana

Figure 15.20 A phrase written in a mixture of kanji and hiragana

Finally, it should be noted that the Roman alphabet, which the Japanese call *romaji*, is also making inroads. It is not unusual to see all four writing systems used together, especially in advertising.

New Tomato

ほんのり 甘味 さらっと あと 味
(honnori amami saratto ato aji)
'Subtle sweetness and light after taste.'

トマト の 新しい ジュース です
(tomato no atarashi juusu desu)
'It's a new tomato juice.'

——— --Hiragana
〰〰 --Katakana
═══ --Kanji

Figure 15.21 Kanji, hiragana, katakana, and romaji in a Japanese advertisement

Learning to read Japanese is a formidable task, in part because of the way the various scripts are intermingled and in part because of complexities in the use of kanji symbols, which can have more than one pronunciation depending on whether they are used to represent a word of Chinese or Japanese origin. (For example, Japanese has two morphemes with the meaning 'mountain'—/san/, which is of Chinese origin, and the native Japanese /yama/; both are written with the kanji character 山.)

4.3 Korean writing

Korean was once written with Chinese characters, which had been introduced in the first centuries A.D. However, Korean suffixes could not be easily represented by Chinese writing. Various devices were used to alleviate this problem, but inadequacies persisted. Finally, King Sejong (1419–52) commissioned an alphabetic script, called **hangul**. After some modifications over the centuries, it became the standard Korean writing system. An especially interesting feature of hangul is that symbols are grouped together into syllable-sized clusters (see Figure 15.22).

Hangul symbols

ㅂ	ㅜ	ㄹ	ㄱ	ㅗ	ㅣ
/p/	/u/	/l/	/k/	/o/	/i/

Grouped symbols

불	고기
'fire' /pul/	'meat' /koki/

Written form

불고기

'barbecued meat' *pulkoki*

Figure 15.22 Korean hangul

Like Japanese, Korean makes use of Chinese characters (called **hanja**), although in a more restricted way. Slightly more than half the vocabulary of contemporary Korean is of Chinese origin, and many words of this type are written with the help of Chinese characters in newspapers and in scientific articles. However, this practice has been reduced somewhat in recent years in South Korea, and it has been eliminated entirely in North Korea.

4.4 American scripts

A number of major civilizations developed on the American continents. In Mesoamerica alone, more than eighteen writing systems have been discovered, including those of the Mayans of the Yucatan and the Aztecs of Mexico. In both systems, we can see the evolution of pictograms toward phonetic word signs, as with the Egyptian hieroglyphics illustrated in Section 3.3.

Mayan symbols are called **glyphs** (see Figure 15.23). Although some were read as word signs (logograms), they had other uses as well. The rebus principle was employed, although sometimes only partially, as in the use of the symbol for a smoking bundle of pine, /taaʒ/, to represent the locative preposition /ta/ in a form of

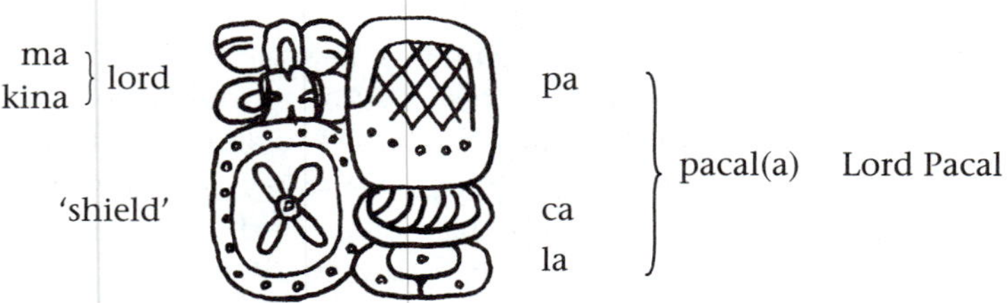

Figure 15.23 Six Mayan glyphs spelling *Lord Pacal*

syllabic writing. Glyphs that mix syllabic writing with logographic representation are also found.

Cherokee

Some American writing systems are of more recent origin. After the colonization of North America by Europeans, a number of scripts were developed to provide native peoples with a form of written communication. In one well-known case, the Cherokee leader Sikwayi (Sequoia) devised a syllabic script of more than eighty symbols, some based on the shapes of English letters and others newly invented (see Table 15.3).

Table 15.3 Some Cherokee syllabic symbols

Symbol	Value	Symbol	Value	Symbol	Value	Symbol	Value	Symbol	Value
Ꭰ	*a*	Ꭱ	*e*	Ꭲ	*i*	Ꭳ	*o*	Ꭴ	*u*
Ꭶ	*ga*	Ꭸ	*ge*	Ꭹ	*gi*	Ꭺ	*go*	Ꭻ	*gu*
Ꭽ	*ha*	Ꭾ	*he*	Ꭿ	*hi*	Ꮀ	*ho*	Ꮁ	*hu*
Ꮃ	*la*	Ꮄ	*le*	Ꮅ	*li*	Ꮆ	*lo*	Ꮇ	*lu*
Ꮉ	*ma*	Ꮊ	*me*	Ꮋ	*mi*	Ꮌ	*mo*	Ꮍ	*mu*

Cree

Professional linguists have often played a role in the development of American scripts, as have missionaries. The syllabic script of the Cree Indians was the creation of a missionary, J. Evans, in the nineteenth century. It was employed for religious literature, and by 1861 the entire Bible appeared in the Cree syllabary. Today, in somewhat modified form, this script is used by Cree speakers across Canada.

Cree morphemes are made up of syllables that combine one of ten initial consonants with one of seven vowels; in some cases, there is also a postvocalic consonant. The Cree writing system provides a separate symbol for each V and CV syllable. As in syllabaries in general, the symbols representing the CV syllables bear no resemblance to those representing syllables consisting of a single vowel; there is no connection, for instance, between the symbols for the syllable /ki/ ᑭ and the syllable /i/ ᐃ. However, the Cree system is not wholly syllabic since consonants that occur at the end of a syllable must be represented by a separate symbol.

A striking feature of the Cree syllabary is its phonetic symbolism. Vowels are indicated by the direction in which a syllabic symbol faces. Symbols that face "south" (downward on the printed page) contain /eː/; those facing "north" (upward) contain /i/ or /iː/; those pointing "east" (rightward) have /o/ or /oː/, and those looking to the "west" (leftward) contain /a/ or /aː/. Vowel length is indicated by a superposed dot, as in ᓰ = /siː/.

Plains Cree, a variety of Cree spoken in Western Canada, is written with the symbols in Table 15.4 (other dialects use slightly different ones). The examples in Figure 15.24 illustrate the use of the Cree syllabary.

Table 15.4 Western Cree syllabary

ᐃ	i, ī	ᐁ	ē	ᐅ	o, ō	ᐊ	a
ᐱ	pi, pī	ᐯ	pē	ᐳ	po, pō	ᐸ	pa
ᑎ	ti, tī	ᑌ	tē	ᑐ	to, tō	ᑕ	ta
ᒋ	ci, cī	ᒉ	cē	ᒍ	co, cō	ᒐ	ca
ᑭ	ki, kī	ᑫ	kē	ᑯ	ko, kō	ᑲ	ka
ᒥ	mi, mī	ᒣ	mē	ᒧ	mo, mō	ᒪ	ma
ᓂ	ni, nī	ᓀ	nē	ᓄ	no, nō	ᓇ	na
ᓯ	si, sī	ᓭ	sē	ᓱ	so, sō	ᓴ	sa
ᔨ	yi, yī	ᔦ	yē	ᔪ	yo, yō	ᔭ	ya

Finals

ᑊ p ᐟ t ᐨ c ᐠ k ᒼ m ᐢ s ᐣ n ᐧ y ᐤ w ᐦ h ᕽ hk ᓬ l ᕒ r

ᓃᐱ		ᓂᐱ		ᓰᐱ	
nīpi	'leaf'	nipi	'water'	sīpi	'river'

Figure 15.24 Three words in Western Cree syllabary

Some other American scripts

The Cree syllabary, appropriately modified, is used by the Inuit of Baffin Island, Canada to represent their language, which is unrelated to Cree. A word-writing system developed by Alaskan Inuit toward the end of the nineteenth century eventually evolved into a partially syllabic system, although it did not become fully syllabic. A number of different systems are in use in regions of Alaska, and in some, tendencies toward alphabetization are discernible.

4.5 Some African scripts

In the past several centuries, societies in Central Africa have also produced syllabic scripts, which have either been invented as such or developed through stages from pictograms to refined syllabaries. Although the idea of writing appears to have been imported into these societies, the development of the various systems was indigenous.

The first sub-Saharan African writing seems to have been that of the Vai peoples in the region of Sierra Leone and Liberia. In the nineteenth century, a native of the area developed a syllabary from a system of picture communication. The new system, which grew to consist of 226 syllabic symbols plus a few logographic symbols, appears to have spawned a number of imitations throughout the area.

The writing of the Bamum people in the Cameroons was invented at the end of the nineteenth century by a native leader. The current seventy syllabic symbols show tendencies toward alphabetization.

The only sure example of alphabetic writing developed in modern times among African peoples is the Somali alphabet. The originator, acquainted with Arabic and Italian, devised an alphabet composed of nineteen consonants and ten vowels. The symbols themselves appear to have been invented, but their names are based on those used for the letters of the Arabic alphabet and are listed and recited in the same order.

4.6 Some Indian scripts

A pictorial script appears to have had an independent origin in northern India, where inscribed seals, pottery, and copper tablets dating back to the third millennium B.C. have been unearthed. The system seems to have consisted of about 250 symbols such as , , and but died away long before another writing system, seemingly derived from Semitic (see Figure 15.25), was employed in the middle of the first millennium B.C. to record the ancient Sanskrit language.

The date of the first appearance of Indian Sanskrit symbols cannot be ascertained, but they resemble Aramaic and appeared as a full system of writing in the edicts of Ašoka (who ruled from 272 to 231 B.C.). They occurred in two types of writing—Kharosthi and Brahmi. The former continued in use until about the fifth century A.D. in northern India. The Brahmi script gave rise to all later varieties of Indian writing.

One of these varieties, a cursive type called the Gupta script, was later employed to write Tocharian, Saka, and Turkish manuscripts discovered in eastern Turkestan. In India, it evolved into the Devanagari script, which became the most widespread type of writing in the subcontinent and which was used to record the voluminous literature of the Sanskrit language. Inscriptions in Devanagari are found throughout Southeast Asia, Indonesia, and as far afield as the southern Philippines.

a
व्यवहारान्नृपः पश्येद्विद्वद्भिर्ब्राह्मणैः सह ।
धर्मशास्त्रानुसारेण क्रोधलोभविवर्जितः ॥१॥

b
ਕਿਉਂਕਿ ਪਰਮੇਸੁਰ ਨੇ ਜਗਤ ਨੂੰ ਅਜਿਹਾ ਪਿਆਰ
ਕੀਤਾ ਜੋ ਉਸ ਨੇ ਆਪਣਾ ਇਕਲੌਤਾ ਪੁਤ੍ਰ ਦਿੱਤਾ ਤਾਂ
ਹਰੇਕ ਜੋ ਉਸ ਉੱਤੇ ਨਿਹਚਾ ਕਰਦਾ ਹੈ ਉਹਦਾ ਨਾਸ
ਨਾ ਹੋਵੇ ਸਗੋਂ ਸਦੀਪਕ ਜੀਉਣ ਪਾਵੇ।

c
തന്റെ ഏകജാതനായ പുത്രനിൽ വിശ്വ
സിക്കുന്ന ഏവനും നശിച്ചു പോകാതെ നിത്യ
ജീവൻ പ്രാപിക്കേണ്ടതിന്നു ദൈവം അവനെ
നല്കുവാൻ തക്കവണ്ണം ലോകത്തെ സ്നേഹിച്ചു.

d ตาอ่อนเป็นคนจน บ้านอยู่ใกล้ๆป่า

Figure 15.25 *a*. Devanagari; *b*. Gurmuki; *c*. Modern Malayalam; *d*. Modern Thai

Varieties of Indian writing were carried abroad by Buddhist missionaries and influenced writing systems in Tibet and Central and Southeast Asia. The Dravidian peoples of southern India also developed a number of scripts under the influence of the northern varieties. Another ancient Indian script, called Pali, gave rise to a number of Southeast Asian writing systems, including those used for Thai and Cambodian. Figure 15.25 illustrates Devanagari and some of the many other scripts found in India and Southeast Asia.

The examples cited in this chapter only touch on the variety of writing systems past and present that scholars have investigated (the index of one standard work lists 470 scripts). Many of these systems are historically related, but the number nonetheless testifies to human ingenuity and creativity in devising writing systems.

5 ENGLISH ORTHOGRAPHY

The set of conventions for representing language in written form is called an **orthography**. English employs an alphabetic orthography in which symbols are used to represent individual consonants and vowels rather than syllables or words. In this section, we will consider the nature and history of English orthography. Section 6 examines the relationship between writing and reading.

5.1 Irregularities

A frequently expressed complaint about English orthography is that it does not establish a one-to-one relationship between symbols and phonological segments. Table 15.5 lists some well-known examples of this.

Table 15.5 Some problems with English orthography

Problem	*Examples*
Some letters do not represent any segments in a particular word.	through, sign, give, comb
A group of two or more letters can be used to represent a single segment.	think /θ/, ship /ʃ/, philosophy /f/
A single letter can represent a group of two or more segments.	saxophone /ks/, exile /gz/
The same letter can represent different segments in different words.	*o* in rot /ɑ/, bone /ow/, son /ʌ/, one /wʌ/
The same segment can be represented by different letters in different words.	/u/ in rude, loop, soup, new, sue, to, two

The following excerpt from a poem by Richard Krogh vividly illustrates the extent to which English orthography departs from the principle of one sound, one letter (one segment, one symbol).

Beware of heard, a dreadful word
That looks like beard and sounds like bird.
And dead; it's said like bed, not bead;
For goodness sake, don't call it deed!
Watch out for meat and great and threat
(They rhyme with suite and straight and debt).
A moth is not a moth in Mother,
Nor both in bother, broth in brother.

Historical factors

The relationship between symbol and segment in English orthography has not always been so indirect. In fact, the spelling system used throughout England during the Old English period provided a regular set of direct symbol-segment correspondences. The foundation for today's system, it lacked the symbols *j, v,* and *w* but made use of four symbols that are not part of our current alphabet.

Table 15.6 Old English symbols not found in Modern English spelling

Symbol	*Name*	*Segment(s) it represented*
æ	ash	[æ]
ð	eth	[θ] and [ð]
þ	thorn	[θ] and [ð]
ƿ	wynn	[w]

The relationship between symbol and segment in English orthography was significantly disturbed in the Middle English period, as the phonological pattern of the language began to change. To see an example of this, we need only consider the Great Vowel Shift, which dramatically altered the pronunciation of long vowels—converting /iː/ into /aj/, /eː/ into /i/, /aː/ into /e/, and so on (see Chapter 7). Because Old English orthography used the same symbol for long and short vowels, complications arose when the former vowels changed. Thus, the letter *i*, which had formerly been used only to represent the phonetically similar /iː/ and /i/, ended up representing the very dissimilar /aj/ (the descendent of /iː/) and /ɪ/ (the descendant of /i/). The end result can be seen in the spelling of *hide* and *hid, write* and *written, ride* and *ridden, wide* and *width,* and many other words.

Additional complications arose following the invasion of England by French-speaking Normans in the eleventh century. The use of English in official documents declined and regional orthographies developed in the absence of a national standard. To make matters worse, scribes who were trained primarily to write French and Latin introduced a number of conventions from those languages into English spelling. Among those that have survived are the use of *ch* rather than *c* for /tʃ/ (*cheese, chin*), *th* rather than þ (thorn) and ð (eth) for /θ/ and /ð/ (*thin, this*), and *c* rather than *s* for /s/ (*ice, mice*).

Toward the end of the fifteenth century, yet another trend developed—the practice of spelling words in a manner that reflected their etymological origin. Enduring examples of this influence are found in the spelling of the words *debt, doubt, receipt,* and *salmon* (formerly spelled *dette, doute, receite,* and *samon*), all of which were given a "silent" consonant to make them look more like the Latin words from which they descended.

By the 1500s English orthography had become increasingly irregular and idiosyncratic, with many different spellings in use for the same word. The word *pity*, for example, could be spelled *pity, pyty, pitie, pytie, pittie,* and *pyttye*. As printing presses came into greater use and books became more widely available, the need to reform and regularize English orthography became apparent. In the late 1500s and early 1600s, a number of individuals (most notably Richard Mulcaster and Edmond Coote) formulated and published spelling rules, which were gradually adopted by printers and other literate speakers of English. While these rules retained many of the practices discussed above, they at least had the effect of stabilizing English spelling. By the 1700s, English orthography was more or less fixed.

The vast majority of the spelling conventions introduced during this period are still in use today. One of the most famous, proposed by Mulcaster in 1582, involves the use of "silent" *e* at the end of words to indicate a preceding long (tense) vowel, as in *name, same,* and *mate*. Even here, though, there are complications and exceptions. In an earlier period, word-final *e* had represented [ə]. Following the loss of this sound in this position in the fourteenth century, final *e* was used quite haphazardly and was often added to words that would otherwise end in a single consonant. The *e* in the modern spelling of *have, done,* and *gone,* which contain lax vowels, reflects this practice and has survived even though it does not comply with Mulcaster's rule.

5.2 Obstacles to reform

Over the years, there have been numerous proposals for the reform of English orthography, including those put forward by Benjamin Franklin, George Bernard Shaw, and Noah Webster. However, far-reaching reforms are unlikely for a variety of reasons. For one thing, they would require a long and difficult period of transition. As the following letter to *The Economist* by M. J. Shields illustrates, reform would not be painless even if it took place over a period of many years.

> For example, in Year 1 that useless letter "c" would be dropped to be replased either by "k" or "s," and likewise "x" would no longer be part of the alphabet. The only kase in which "c" would be retained would be the "ch" formation, which will be dealt with later. Year 2 might reform "w" spelling, so that "which" and "one" would take the same konsonant, wile Year 3 might well abolish "y" replasing it with "i" and Iear 4 might fiks the "g-j" anomali wonse and for all.
>
> Jenerally, then, the improvement would kontinue iear bai iear with Iear 5 doing awai with useless double konsonants, and Iears 6–12 or so modifaiing vowlz and the rimeining voist and unvoist konsonants. Bai Iear 15 or sou, it wud fainali be posibl tu meik ius ov thi ridandant leterz "c," "y" and "x"—bai now jast a memori in the maindz of ould doderers—tu replais "ch," "sh" and "th" rispektivli.
>
> Fainali, xen, after sam 20 iers ov orxogrephikl riform, we wud hev a lojikl, kohirnt speling in ius xrewawt xe Ingliy spiking werld . . .

People who knew only the reformed spelling system proposed in this letter would have difficulty reading books written in traditional orthography. Those who wished to read any of the millions of books or articles currently in print would therefore have to either learn the traditional spelling system or have the documents that interested them converted into the new orthography.

A second factor militating against serious orthographic reform has to do with the dialectal variation found within English. Because English is spoken in more parts of the world than any other language, it has many different dialects. Any attempt to establish an orthography based on a principle of one segment, one symbol, would result in serious regional differences in spelling. For instance, speakers of Boston English would write *far* as *fa*, since they do not pronounce syllable-final /r/. Speakers of some dialects of Irish English would write both *tin* and *thin* as *tin* and *day* and *they* as *day* since they have no /t/-/θ/ or /d/-/ð/ distinction. Moreover, while many Americans would have identical spellings for *cot* and *caught* (since these words are homophonous in their speech), speakers of English in many other parts of the world pronounce them differently and would therefore spell them differently as well.

Other considerations

Even if considerations relating to practicality and dialectal variation did not rule out major reforms to our orthography, there might still be reasons for retaining at least some of the current spelling conventions.

One advantage of the contemporary system is that it often indicates derivational relationships among words. For instance, if the words *music* and *musician* or *sign* and *signature* were spelled phonetically, it would be difficult to perceive the relationship between them, since the root is pronounced differently in each case (see Table 15.7).

1)

music	[mjuzɪk]	musician	[mjuzɪʃ-ən]
sign	[sajn]	signature	[sɪgn-ɪtʃər]

There are many other cases where English orthography ignores differences in pronunciation so that a morpheme can have the same or nearly the same spelling in different words.

Table 15.7 Some cases in which English orthography provides a single spelling for roots with different pronunciations

electric – electricity	[k] and [s] represented as *c*
insert – insertion	[t] and [ʃ] as *t*
right – righteous	[t] and [tʃ] as *t*
bomb – bombard	Ø and [b] as *b*
damn – damnation	Ø and [n] as *n*
impress – impression	[s] and [ʃ] as *ss*
allege – allegation	[ɛ] and [ə] as *e*; [dʒ] and [g] as *g*
resign – resignation	[aj] and [ɪ] as *i*; Ø and [g] as *g*
chaste – chastity	[ej] and [æ] as *a*
produce – productive	[u] and [ʌ] as *u*
please – pleasant	[i] and [ɛ] as *ea*

Examples such as these show that English orthography does not simply represent phonemic contrasts. Often, it provides a single representation for the variants of a morpheme, even if this means ignoring morphologically conditioned alternations among phonemes. (For this reason, some linguists have concluded that English orthography is a type of *morphophonemic* spelling system; see Chapter 4, Section 7 for a discussion of morphophonemic alternations.) Once this fact is taken into account, it is possible to see the usefulness of orthographic conventions that allow *c* to stand for either /k/ (*electric*) or /s/ (*electricity*) and *t* to represent /t/ (*react*) or /ʃ/ (*reaction*).

Morphological considerations are reflected in English orthography in other ways as well. Consider the spelling of the following words.

2)

mess	lapse
crass	dense
kiss	house
gloss	mouse

Although these words all end in the phoneme /s/, this segment cannot be represented as a simple *s*. Instead, the *s* is either doubled to *ss* (when preceded by a lax vowel, as in the first column) or followed by an *e* (all other cases, as exemplified in the second column). This reflects a general rule of English orthography, which reserves word-final *s* for inflectional suffixes (particularly, the plural and the third-person singular). Thus, word-final *s* is permitted in the word *laps* (the plural of *lap*) but not in *lapse*.

Another example of morphological influence is found in the rule that prohibits a final *ll* in polysyllabic words—*plentiful, excel, repel,* and so on. As the following examples show, this rule is systematically suspended in two morphological patterns: compounds (the first column) and derivations consisting of a prefix and its base (the second column).

3)

baseball	unwell
spoonbill	resell
landfill	recall

Yet another morphologically constrained rule of English orthography converts postconsonantal *y* to *i* in front of a suffix.

4)

carry	carri-ed
merry	merri-ly
marry	marri-age
candy	candi-es
beauty	beauti-ful

The existence of conventions and practices such as these demonstrates that English orthography is much more than a system for phonemic transcription. Its intricacies can be understood only through the careful study of the history and structure of the linguistic system that it is used to represent.

6 WRITING AND READING

The three types of writing described earlier in this chapter represent different types of linguistic units—morphemes and words in the case of logographic systems, syllables in the case of syllabaries, and consonants and vowels in the case of alphabets. Because of these differences, each orthography places different demands on readers. We know that different parts of the brain are used for reading logographic writing systems and phonographic orthographies such as syllabaries and alphabets. Because phonological structure is largely irrelevant to logographic writing, people suffering from Broca's aphasia (see Chapter 13) typically do not lose the ability to write and read logograms. However, the use of syllabaries and alphabets can be severely disrupted by this type of brain disorder. There are reports of Japanese patients suffering from Broca's aphasia who are unable to use hiragana or katakana (the Japanese syllabaries), but retain mastery of kanji (the logographic writing system).

Further information about the relationship between language and writing systems comes from the study of the congenitally deaf. Because they have never heard speech, congenitally deaf individuals have little or no understanding of the phonological units that alphabets represent. Significantly, they have a great deal of difficulty learning to read English.

The type of linguistic unit represented by an orthography also has an effect on how children with normal hearing learn to read. Each system has its own advantages and disadvantages. Children learning Chinese characters, for instance, have little difficulty understanding what each symbol represents, but it takes them many years to learn enough symbols to be able to write and read all the items in their vocabulary. (Knowledge of several thousand separate symbols is required just to read a newspaper.) Even educated people typically know only a few thousand characters and must use dictionaries for new or unfamiliar words.

This problem does not arise in syllabic and alphabetic orthographies. Because languages have far fewer syllables and phonemes than morphemes or words, the entire inventory of symbols can be learned in a year or two and then used productively to write and read new words. This is the major advantage of sound-based orthographies over word-based writing systems.

There is reason to believe that children find syllabaries easier to master than alphabets. Children learning syllabaries (such as Japanese hiragana) are reported to have fewer reading problems than children learning alphabetic orthographies. Although at least some difficulties encountered by children learning to read English may be due to the complexity of English spelling conventions, Italian and German children learning to use their relatively regular alphabetic orthographies also have reading problems.

The advantage of syllabaries over alphabets for young readers apparently stems from the fact that children have less difficulty identifying syllables than phonemes.

One study revealed that 46 percent of four-year-olds and 90 percent of six-year-olds can segment words into syllables. In contrast, virtually no four-year-olds and only about two-thirds of all six-year-olds can segment words into phoneme-sized units. Since learning to read involves an understanding of the type of unit represented by written symbols, it is not surprising that syllabaries are generally easier for young children to learn.

Of course, it must be remembered that syllabaries may have disadvantages of other sorts. While syllabic writing is feasible for languages such as Japanese that have a relatively small number of syllable types, it would be quite impractical in English, where there are dozens of different syllable structures. Ultimately, an orthography must be judged in terms of its success in representing language for the purpose of reading and writing. There is no doubt that an alphabetic orthography is superior to a syllabary for representing the phonological structure of English.

Summing up

The development of writing has been one of humanity's greatest intellectual achievements. From **pictograms** and **logograms**, the graphic representation of language has developed through syllabic writing to the **alphabet**. This was achieved through the discovery of the relationship between graphic symbols and sounds.

Many of the large number of writing systems found throughout the modern world owe their origin directly or indirectly to the Semitic writing systems of the eastern Mediterranean. As the idea of writing spread, new forms of the signs were independently invented and sound-symbol correspondences were altered to accommodate individual languages. Some writing systems derived from the Greco-Phoenician tradition are today scarcely recognizable as such, since so little remains of the original symbols. In cases where the entire system was invented, perhaps only the idea of writing is traceable to the early traditions.

In all cases, the historical line of development is clear. There seems to be no evidence of a culture that has developed an alphabet and then followed this with the development of, for example, a logographic script. But this cultural line of development does not imply that earlier forms of writing are inferior to alphabetic writing. In the case of languages such as Japanese or Cree, the syllabic writing system is as well suited to the phonological structure of the language as an alphabetic script would be.

Key terms

Terms concerning types of writing

alphabetic writing
logograms
logographic (writing)
orthography
phonographic writing
syllabary
syllabic writing
writing

Terms related to the history and evolution of writing

acrophonic principle
Blissymbolics
cuneiform
hieroglyphics
pictograms
prewriting
rebus principle

Terms concerning alphabetic writing systems

boustrophedon
Cyrillic alphabet
Glagolitic script
Runic writing

Terms related to non-European writing systems

characters
glyphs
hangul
hanja
hiragana
kanji
katakana
phonetic determinative
pinyin
radical
symbolic signs

Sources

Comprehensive surveys of the development of writing and of the world's writing systems are found in Jensen, Gelb, and DeFrancis (all cited below). The possibility that pure syllabaries may not exist was called to the authors' attention by Prof. W. Poser of the University of British Columbia (personal communication). The idea that writing may have originated in record keeping with clay tokens is taken from Schmandt-Besserat (cited below). The following Figures are adapted from Jensen: 15.1a, 15.3, 15.6, 15.11, 15.14, Table 15.3, Figure 15.25; from Marshack, *The Roots of Civilization* (New York: McGraw-Hill, 1972): Figures 15.1b; from Schmandt-Besserat: 15.2; from René Labat, *Manuel d'Epigraphie Akkadienne,* 5th ed. (Paris: P. Geuthner, 1976): 15.6; from DeFrancis (see Labat, further references to origins of these figures therein): 15.8, 15.9, 15.13, 15.17, Table 15.4 (adapted from *Visible Speech: The Diverse Oneness of Writing Systems* and reprinted by permission of the University of Hawaii Press); from Wayne M. Senner, "Theories and Myths on the Origins of Writing: A Historical Overview," in Senner (cited below and reprinted by permission of the University of Nebraska Press): Figures 15.10; from Sampson (cited below): 15.12; from Frank Moore Cross, "The Invention and Development of the Alphabet," in Senner, p. 89 (cited below and reprinted by permission of the University of Nebraska Press): 15.18. The sport pictograms in Figure 15.4 are courtesy of the Olympic Trust of Canada, ™Official Mark © Canadian Olympic Association, 1972. Figure 15.5 is courtesy of the Blissymbolics Communication Institute, exclusive licensee, 1982, and is derived from the symbols described in the work *Semantography*, original copyright C. K. Bliss, 1949.

The discussion of Arabic writing is based on "The Arabic Alphabet" by James A. Bellamy in the book by Senner (cited below). John DeFrancis (University of Hawaii), Robert Fisher (York University), and Brian King (University of British Columbia) all provided insightful and helpful comments (especially regarding Chinese writing)—

so many, in fact, that we were not able to make use of all of them here. Their views are not necessarily those reflected in the chapter, however. The discussion of Chinese writing is derived from DeFrancis (cited below), as is Table 15.1; Figure 15.19 was adapted from Jerry Norman, *Chinese* (Cambridge: Cambridge University Press, 1988); Chinese characters were kindly provided by Lin Zhiqiu. The presentation of Japanese writing is also indebted to DeFrancis, as well as to M. Shibatani, *The Languages of Japan* (Cambridge: Cambridge University Press, 1990). The hiragana and katakana charts (Table 15.2) are adapted from Len Walsh's *Read Japanese Today* (Tokyo: Charles E. Tuttle, 1971) and reprinted by permission of the publisher; Japanese examples were provided by Kazue Kanno. For a discussion of Cherokee writing, see "Native American Writing Systems" by W. Walker, in *Language in the USA*, edited by C. Ferguson et al. (New York: Cambridge University Press, 1981). Our presentation of the Cree syllabary is adapted from D. Pentland, *Nēhiyawasi-nahikē-win: A Standard Orthography for the Cree Language* (Saskatoon: Saskatchewan Indian Cultural College, 1977). David H. Kelley of the University of Calgary provided corrective and helpful advice on Mayan and other Mesoamerican writing. The examples of northern Indian pictorial script are from John Marshall, *Mohenjo-Daro and the Indus Civilization* (London: A. Probsthain, 1931).

The discussion of the history of English spelling is based on *A History of English Spelling* by D. G. Scragg (New York: Barnes & Noble, 1974). The examples of spelling rules sensitive to morphological structure come from the book by D. W. Cummings cited below. Data on children's ability to segment words into syllables and phonemes come from I. Y. Liberman, reported in the book by Gibson and Levin cited below. John Sören Pettersson of Uppsala University helped us by commenting extensively on an earlier version of this chapter.

Recommended reading

Cummings, D. W. 1988. *American English Spelling*. Baltimore: Johns Hopkins University Press.

DeFrancis, John. 1989. *Visible Speech: The Diverse Oneness of Writing Systems*. Honolulu: University of Hawaii Press.

Gelb, I. 1952. *A Study of Writing*. Chicago: University of Chicago Press.

Gibson, E., and H. Levin. 1975. *The Psychology of Reading*. Cambridge, MA: MIT Press.

Gleitman, L., and P. Rozin. 1977. "The Structure and Acquisition of Reading I: Relations Between Orthographies and the Structures of Language." In *Toward a Psychology of Reading*. Edited by A. Reber and D. Scarborough, 1–53. Hillsdale, NJ: Lawrence Erlbaum.

Jensen, H. 1970. *Sign, Symbol and Script*. Translated by G. Unwin. London: George Allen and Unwin.

Sampson, G. 1985. *Writing Systems: A Linguistic Introduction*. Stanford, CA: Stanford University Press.

Schmandt-Besserat, Denise. 1989. "Two Precursors of Writing: Plain and Complex Tokens." In *The Origins of Writing*. Edited by W. M. Senner, 27–42. Lincoln, NE: University of Nebraska Press.

Senner, W. M., ed. 1989. *The Origins of Writing*. Lincoln, NE: University of Nebraska Press.

Wallace, Rex. 1989. "The Origins and Development of the Latin Alphabet." In *The Origins of Writing*. Edited by W. M. Senner, 121–36. Lincoln, NE: University of Nebraska Press.

QUESTIONS

1. Suppose you are the user of a pictographic writing system that can already represent concrete objects in a satisfactory way. Using the pictographic symbols of your system, propose ideographic extensions of these symbols to represent the following meanings.

a) hunt	f) cook
b) cold	g) tired
c) fast	h) wet
d) white	i) angry
e) strength	j) weakness

2. Construct a syllabary for English that can be used to spell the following words. What problems do you encounter?

foe	law	shoe
slaw	slow	slowly
lee	day	daily
sue	pull	shop
ship	loop	food
lock	shock	unlock
locked	shocked	pulled
shops	locker	shod
float	splint	schlock

3. How does English orthography capture the morphophonemic alternations in the following words? Begin your analysis with a phonemic transcription of the forms.

a) hymn	hymnal	
b) part	partial	
c) recite	recitation	
d) reduce	reduction	
e) design	designation	
f) critical	criticize	criticism
g) analog	analogous	analogy

4. After discussing the forms in question 3, consider the following forms. Does the spelling system treat all cases of allomorphic variation the same way?

a) invade	invasion
b) concede	concession
c) assume	assumption
d) profound	profundity

5. Briefly outline the advantages and disadvantages of the three major types of writing that have evolved throughout history.

sixteen

Animal Communication

Michael Dobrovolsky

As I listened from a beach-chair in the shade
To all the noises that my garden made,
It seemed to me only proper that words
Should be withheld from vegetables and birds.

– W. H. Auden

Objectives

In this chapter, you will learn

- how animals communicate nonvocally
- what types of signs are used in communication
- how bees, birds, and nonhuman primates communicate
- what arguments are made for and against linguistic ability in nonhuman primates
- how the communication systems of humans and animals may be compared

Communication—the passing on or exchange of information—distinguishes what is living from what is nonliving in nature. Communication is found even in the apparently passive world of plants; trees, for example, have been found to pass on information about advancing predators by means of chemical signals. Animals communicate among themselves and with humans so effectively that they are often said to use "language." But the words *communication* and *language* do not mean the same thing. Human language is a specific way of representing the world and passing on information. From the linguist's point of view, not just any communication qualifies as language as it is defined in this book.

A question that therefore interests many linguists is whether animals make use of any system of communication that genuinely resembles or approximates human language. Just as the use of communication sets what is living apart from what is nonliving, the use of language is often said to set humans apart from all other animals. If animals communicate with a system that is structured like human language, then language as we know it is not the unique property of our species, and we will have to look for other ways of defining what it means to be human. This chapter investigates the ways in which animal communication is like human language and the ways in which it is different.

1 NONVOCAL COMMUNICATION

One of the most striking things about animal communication is the variety of means with which it is carried out. Animals communicate not only with sounds but with scent, light, ultrasound, visual signs, gestures, color, and even electricity. From the slime mold to the giant blue whale, all living things appear to have some means of communication. Some nonvocal modes of communication are described here.

Scent Chemicals used by animals specifically for communicative purposes are called **pheromones**. Pheromones are used by species as different as molds, insects, and mammals. A female moth signals its reproductive readiness through the release of a pheromone into the air. Only a few of these molecules need to be sensed by a male moth for it to start flying zigzag upwind toward its potential mate. Dogs and other canines leave a urine-based pheromone as an identification mark to stake out their territory, and many nonhuman primates have specialized scent glands for the same purpose.

Light Probably the most well-known light user in North America is the firefly or lightning bug. This small flying beetle uses light flashes in varying patterns to signal its identity, sex, and location. Different species of these insects have different and distinguishing light patterns.

Electricity Certain species of eels in the Amazon River basin communicate their presence and territoriality by means of electrical impulses at various frequencies. Each species signals at a specific frequency range, and the transmitting frequencies, like those of radio and television stations, do not overlap.

Color The color (or color pattern) of many animals plays an important role in their identification by members of their own species and other animals. The octopus changes color frequently and this coloring is used for a range of messages that include territorial defense and mating readiness.

Posture This is a common communicative device among animals. Dogs, for example, lower the front part of their bodies and extend their front legs when they are being playful. They lower their whole bodies to the ground when they are being submissive. Postural communication is found in both human and nonhuman primates as well.

Gesture A gesture may be defined as active posturing. Humans wave their arms in recognition or farewell, dogs wag their tails in excitement, and cats flick their tails when irritated. Many birds perform elaborate gestures of raising and lowering the head or racing back and forth across the water in their mating rituals. Some fish, such as the male stickleback, perform a series of distinct movements in the water as part of their mating ritual.

Facial expressions These are specific types of communicative gestures. When a male baboon yawns, bares its fangs, and retracts its eyebrows, it is indicating a willingness to fight. A wide and recognizable variety of facial expressions is found among chimpanzees, a number of which are shown in Figure 16.1. Experiments have shown that humans can classify the meanings of these expressions quite accurately. For example, when humans draw back the corners of their mouths into a smile, they are generally indicating cooperation. A nonhuman primate's smile also indicates nonaggressiveness.

Figure 16.1 Some chimpanzee facial expressions: *a.* anger; *b.* fear-anger; *c.* affection; *d.* frustration-sadness; *e.* playfulness

2 COMMUNICATION STRUCTURE: THE STUDY OF SIGNS

Certain common elements underlie the bewildering variety of communicative methods found in nature. An understanding of these is necessary for comparing the differences and similarities among systems of communication.

2.1 Signs

Communication relies on using something to stand for something else. Words are an obvious example of this: you do not have to have a car, a sandwich, or your cousin present in order to talk about them—the words *car, sandwich,* and *cousin* stand for them instead. This same phenomenon is found in animal communication as well. Instead of fighting over territory, for example, many animals produce sounds or make gestures that threaten and intimidate intruders—the message replaces the attack. Birds utter warning calls that represent the presence of a threat. A threatening animal or human need not be seen by other birds before they take flight—perception of the warning call replaces visual perception of the threat.

Each of these things that stand for other things is technically known as a **sign**. The sign is a unit of communication structure that consists of two parts: a **signifier**—be it a word, a scent, a gesture, or an electrical frequency—and the thing **signified**—something that exists in the real world and that is being mentally represented by the sign's conceptual content. The real world can be thought of as either external, mental, or emotional, and so what is signified by a sign can be as diverse as a tree, an abstract idea, a perception, or a feeling. Because their content is conceptual, all signs are associated with some **meaning**, such as "danger," or "item of furniture with legs and a flat top." Individual instances of signs are called **tokens**. For example, in the sentence *The baby threw the rattle,* there are five word tokens but only four signs; *the* occurs twice as a token, but it is the same sign in both instances. Figure 16.2 illustrates these distinctions.

The study of signs is known as **semiotics**. Semiotics is a field of study that links many diverse disciplines, among them linguistics, anthropology, philosophy, zoology, genetics, literary study, and computer science. An understanding of signs is essential for understanding how messages are transmitted. So that we can understand signs better before proceeding to an analysis of animal communication, the next section examines their structure in more detail.

The signifier

A signifier is that part of a sign that stimulates at least one sense organ of the receiver of a message. The phonological component of the word *tree,* represented as /tri/ and pronounced [tr̥i], is a typical linguistic signifier. A signifier can also be a picture, a photograph, a sign language gesture, or one of the many other words for *tree* in different languages.

The signified

The signified component of the sign refers to both the real-world object it represents and its conceptual content.

The first of these is the real-world content of the sign—its extension or referent (Chapter 6, Section 1.3) within a system of signs such as English, avian communication, or sign language. In our example, the referent is represented by a drawing, since there is no room to include a real tree between the pages of this book. (Of course, the signifier /tri/ could also have a picture of a tree as its referent.) It is easiest to think of referents as concepts or persons or things, but they may be ideas or feelings as well.

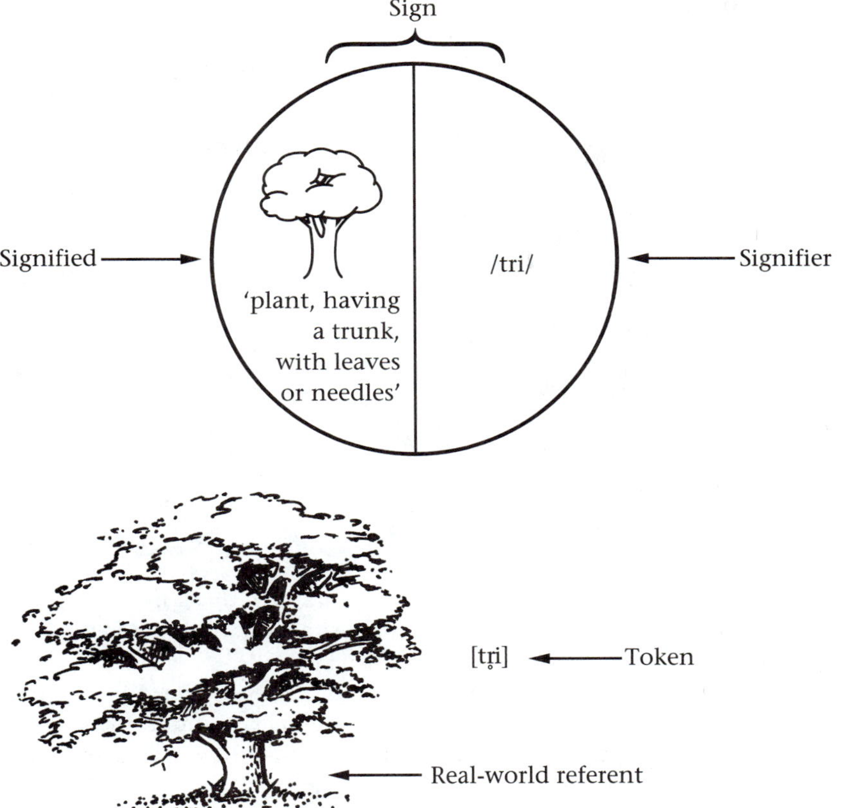

Figure 16.2 A sign

The signified component of a sign also evokes an intension (Chapter 6, Section 1.3) to users of the system in question. A word for *tree* evokes concepts that probably include 'plant,' 'having a trunk,' and 'bearing leaves or needles' in the minds of speakers of any language who are familiar with trees. Some animals appear to conceptualize in terms of classes or categories as well. Certain monkeys, for example, distinguish among various types of predators on the basis of size, shape, and motion (see Section 5.3).

2.2 Types of signs

Signs can be divided into three basic types, depending on (1) whether the signifier naturally resembles its referent, (2) whether the signifier is directly linked with the referent in a physical or mechanical sense, or (3) whether signifier and referent are arbitrarily associated.

Iconic signs

Iconic signs, or **icons**, always bear some resemblance to their referent. A photograph is an iconic sign; so too is a stylized silhouette of a female or a male on a restroom door. A baboon's open-mouth threat is iconic, resembling as it does the act of biting. Onomatopoeic words like *buzz, splat,* and *squish* in English and their counterparts in other human languages are also iconic in that they somewhat resemble what they signify. Because of this inherent resemblance to these referents, icons are considered nonarbitrary signs.

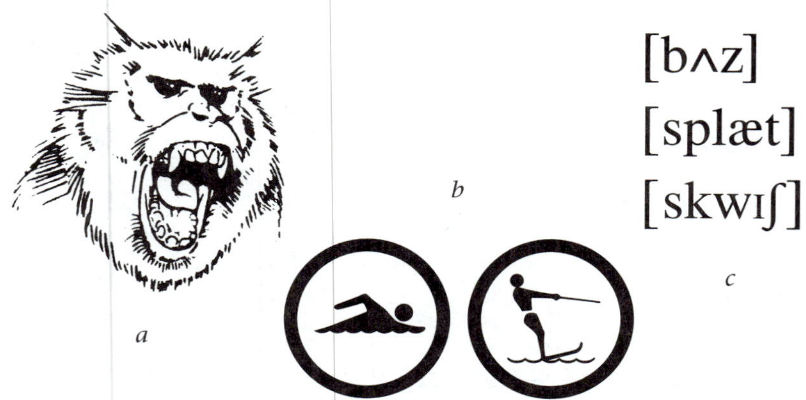

Figure 16.3 Some iconic signs: *a.* open-mouth threat by a Japanese macaque (*Macaca fuscata*); *b.* park recreation signs; *c.* onomatopoeic words in English

Icons are widespread in the communication systems of all animals; many postures and gestures that are critical to animal communication are iconic, as are the postures and gestures used by humans. Human linguistic communication, however, does not make extensive use of iconic signs.

Indexical signs

An **indexical sign**, or **index**, fulfills its function by "pointing out" its referent, typically by being a partial or representative sample of it. Indexes are not arbitrary, since their presence has in some sense been caused by their referent. For this reason it is sometimes said that there is a causal link between an indexical sign and its referent. The track of an animal, for example, points to the existence of the animal by representing a part of it. The presence of smoke is an index of fire.

Most important for our discussion here is a specific kind of indexical sign called a **symptomatic sign**, or symptom. Symptomatic signs spontaneously convey the internal state or emotions of the sender and thus represent the sender in an indexical manner. For example, the fact that our body temperature rises when we are ill is a spontaneous reflection of our internal state. When someone steps on our foot and we cry out, the cry is a spontaneous reflection of our internal state (surprise and pain) and thus constitutes a symptomatic sign.

Since symptomatic signs are spontaneous, we do not consider them to be deliberately selected by the sender for purposes of communication. We do not choose to cry out in pain in the same way as we might, for example, decide to call our dwelling place a *house, home, dwelling,* or *residence* in the appropriate circumstances. As forms of communication, symptomatic signs are therefore used primarily by the receiver of a message to assess the internal state of the sender. Since senders do not deliberately choose to transmit the sign, the message is assumed to be essentially beyond their control.

Symbolic signs

Symbolic signs bear an arbitrary relationship to their referents and in this way are distinct from both icons and indexes. Human language is highly symbolic in that the vast majority of its signs bear no inherent resemblance or causal connection to their referents, as the following words show.

hana	=	?
mazə	=	?
talo	=	?
kum	=	?
berat	=	?

Figure 16.4 Arbitrary sound-meaning correspondence in language

No phonological property of the words in Figure 16.4 gives you any hint as to their possible meaning. (*Hana* means 'flower' or 'nose' in Japanese, *mazə* is 'forest' in Kabardian, *talo* is 'house' in Finnish, *kum* means 'sand' in Turkish, and *berat* means 'heavy' in Indonesian.)

We encounter many other symbolic signs in everyday life. The octagonal shape of a stop sign is symbolic; it bears no inherent connection with the message it helps to communicate. The colors used in traffic signals are symbolic as well; red has no more inherent connection with the act of stopping than does yellow.

Mixed signs

Signs are not always exclusively of one type or another. Symptomatic signs, for example, may have iconic properties, as when a dog opens its mouth in a threat to bite. Symbolic signs such as traffic lights are symptomatic in that they reflect the internal state of the mechanism that causes them to change color. Still, we classify a sign according to its major property: if it resembles its referent, it is iconic; if it is linked to its referent in some causal way or represents it partially in some nonarbitrary way, it is indexical (and symptomatic if it spontaneously expresses some internal state); and if its relationship to its referent is arbitrary, it is a symbol.

Signals

All signs can act as **signals** when they trigger a specific action on the part of the receiver, as do traffic lights, words in human language such as the race starter's "Go!" or the warning calls of birds. Typically, a signal releases more energy in the receiver than it takes for the transmitter to send it. For example, the simple release of a mating pheromone into the wind by a female moth (a symptomatic sign and also a signal) can cause the male to fly as much as six kilometers in search of her. Signals are very common in animal communication, but only a limited subset of human linguistic activity consists of signaling.

2.3 Sign structure

No matter what their type, signs show different kinds of structure. A basic distinction is made between graded and discrete sign structure.

Graded signs

Graded signs convey their meaning by changes in degree. A good example of a gradation in communication is voice volume. The more you want to be heard, the louder you speak along an increasing scale of loudness. There are no steps or jumps from one level to the next that can be associated with a specific change in meaning.

Gradation is common in many forms of communication. The hands of most clocks move (or appear to move) in a graded manner, as does the needle of an automobile speedometer. Many animal signs, such as the barking of dogs, are graded as well. A goose has essentially one type of honk, which may become louder and faster as it takes off in flight but does not become another kind of honking. The gradually increasing fear in the facial expression of the monkey depicted in Figure 16.5 is also a graded sign.

Figure 16.5 Some graded signs: the facial expressions *a*, *b*, and *c* of the macaque monkey represent just three points on a continuum expressing fear; *a* is a neutral face; *b* expresses slight fear; and *c* expresses extreme fear. Each expression grades into the next. The hands of the clock in *d* express minutes and hours in a graded manner.

Discrete signs

Discrete signs are distinguished from each other by categorical (stepwise) differences. There is no gradual transition from one sign to the next. The words of human language are good examples of discrete signs. There is no intermediate stage between the words *stop* and *go* in English except that which can be expressed by other discrete words or combinations of words, such as *start to go*. The digital displays of watches are discrete as well, since they progress from one minute (or even second) to the next with no gradation. Traffic lights, too, are discrete signs; there is no gradual shifting from green to yellow to red.

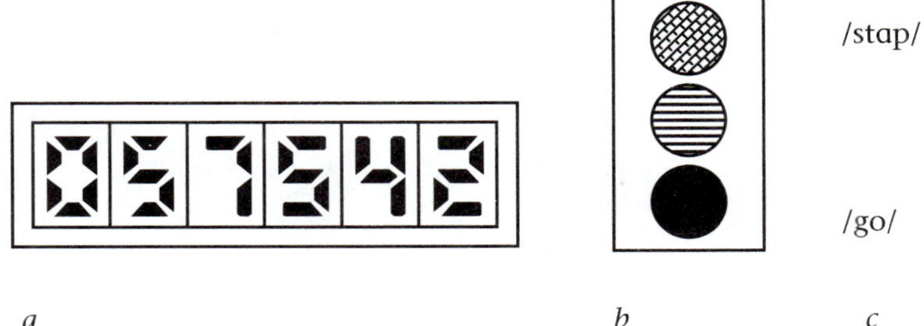

Figure 16.6 Some discrete signs: *a,* odometer; *b,* traffic lights; *c,* words of a human language

Sign types and structure

All three types of signs—iconic, indexical/symptomatic, and symbolic—can be graded or discrete. A photograph is iconic and discrete, but a threatening canine's gradual baring of its fangs is iconic and graded. Morse code is symbolic and discrete, but a slowly dimming light that signals the beginning of a theatrical performance is symbolic and graded. Symptomatic signs, too, may be discrete (the traffic light again) or graded (the crying of a child or the act of blushing).

It is possible for a discrete sign to be internally graded, and even to slip over into another type by degrees. Human crying, for example, is interpreted by experimental subjects as becoming gradually more like screaming as the audible intake of breath between sobs becomes shorter and shorter. Figure 16.7 illustrates this phenomenon.

At the extreme ends of the continuum, there is no difficulty interpreting the sound as one or the other, although it is difficult to say precisely when a sob becomes a scream. Thus we can say that sobbing and screaming are discrete symptomatic signs, but each of them is internally graded, and their gradations overlap. The same is true of many vocalizations in animal communication.

2.4 A VIEW OF ANIMAL COMMUNICATION

> They're like Swiss watches . . . they just react. Their genes and hormones and experience tell them what to do. They don't think about it.
>
> Zookeeper Ben Beck (on golden lion tamarin monkeys)

Most animal communication, it is claimed, shows little arbitrariness. It is said to be largely iconic and symptomatic and hence not deliberate or conscious in intent, nor symbolic in its sign repertoire. For example, if a monkey gives a certain cry in the presence of danger, it is assumed that the monkey is spontaneously signaling its fear by vocalizing, but is not deliberately warning other group members of the danger. The symptomatic vocalization is interpreted and used by other members of a troop for their own benefit.

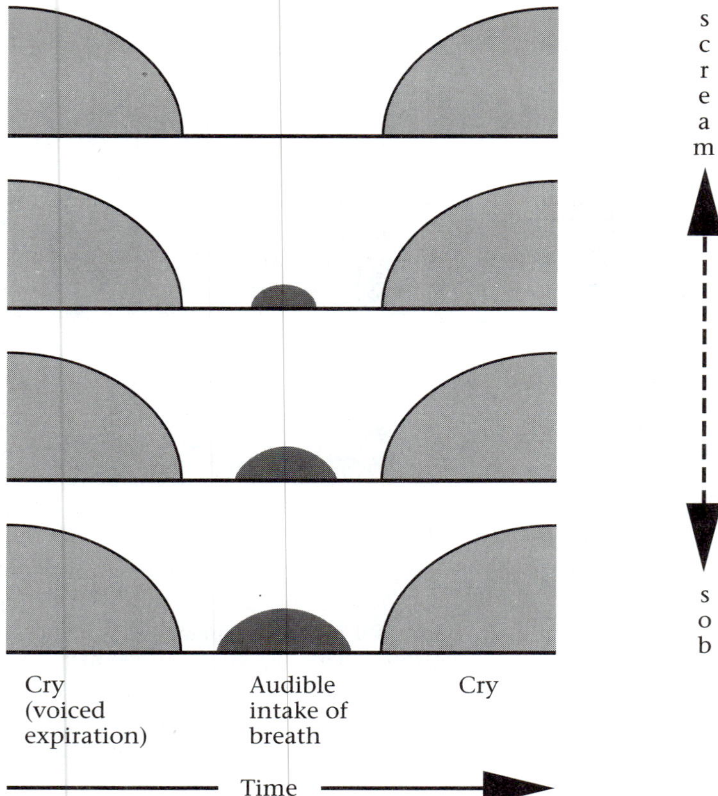

Figure 16.7 The graded continuum from sobbing to screaming (the height of the stippled and blackened areas represents the audibility of the vocalization and the width, its time): both sob and scream are discrete signs, even though each grades into the other.

It follows from this view of animal communication that the acquisition of communicative systems by animals was in the past assumed to be largely devoid of learning and experience. Rather, it was claimed that the systems are rather strictly limited by genetic inheritance, and in this sense are radically unlike human language, the acquisition of which requires exposure to a mature system. This limitation certainly appears to be true in some cases. When raised in isolation, animals as diverse as the fox, the elephant seal, the cat, and certain monkeys develop the full range of vocalizations typical of their species. However, as we will see in Section 4 of this chapter, the situation can be more complex than this.

It is further claimed that animal communication is neither conscious nor deliberate. It is not widely believed, for example, that a monkey assesses a situation and then deliberately chooses to warn group members of danger by selecting a sign from a repertoire of meaningful sound symbols at its disposal. For this reason, the term **stimulus-bound** is also used to describe animal communication, since it is often claimed that animal communication only occurs when it is triggered by exposure to a certain stimulus or for certain specific ends. Animals do not communicate about anything but the here and now. As the philosopher Bertrand Russell once noted, "No matter how eloquently a dog may bark, it cannot tell you that its parents were poor but honest."

With respect to structure, animal communication is said to show few traces of discrete structuring beyond the obvious fact that one group of symptomatic, graded signals may sound very different from another. Whining in dogs, for example, is clearly different from barking, but both are assumed to be symptomatic, and the two may grade into each other. Combining and recombining of discrete units of structure such as phonemes, morphemes, and words is not characteristic of the way animals communicate. Dogs do not combine whines and barks to produce novel messages.

This does not mean that animal communication consists of random emotional outbursts. Nor does it mean that animal communication does not show structure. Animal communication is both complex and organized. Evolutionary pressure has guaranteed that animal communication is optimally in tune with the survival requirements of each species. The electrical communication of Amazonian eels is an excellent means of communication in muddy waters. The danger whistle of a small, tree-dwelling primate like the galago is ideal for nocturnal communication in a dense forest. Small jungle frogs in South America communicate by sticking out their long and colorful legs, ideal for sending messages in the dim and noisy jungle. But jungle frogs do not try new combinations of leg movements in order to come up with an original message any more than the electric eel recombines frequencies in order to signal something it has never conveyed before. Animal communication appears to be limited in the messages it can convey.

But is animal communication so very unlike human language in all respects? Recent work on animal communication has often focused on its relationship to human linguistic communication. The next sections examine the communication systems of several kinds of animals and compare them with human language.

3 THE BEES

> I have no doubt that some will attempt to "explain" the performances of the bees as the results of reflexes and instincts . . . for my part, I find it difficult to assume that such perfection and flexibility in behavior can be reached without some kind of mental processes going on in the small heads of the bees.
>
> August Krogh, *Scientific American*

3.1 THE SYSTEM

Forager bees display a remarkable system of communicating the location of a food source to other bees in their hive. When a food source has been discovered, the forager flies back to the hive and communicates information about it by performing special movements (which humans call dancing) before other members of the hive. The dancing conveys information about the location of the food source, its quality, and its distance from the hive.

Distance

Distance is conveyed by one of three different dances performed on the wall or floor of the hive (some species have only two different dances, and so may be said to have a different "dialect"). In doing the round dance, the bee circles repeatedly. This indicates a food source within five meters or so of the hive. The sickle dance indicates a food source from five to twenty meters from the hive. It is performed by the bee dancing a curved figure eight. The tail-wagging dance indicates distances farther than twenty meters. In this dance, the bee wags its abdomen as it moves forward, circles to the right back to its starting point, repeats the wagging forward motion, and circles left. The cycle then begins again.

Direction

The round dance does not communicate direction, presumably since the food source is so close to the hive. The direction of more distant food sources is indicated in the other two types of dance.

As the bee performs the sickle and tail-wagging dances, it is simultaneously indicating the direction of the food source. Bees orient themselves in flight relative to the angle of the sun. When danced on the floor of the hive, the angle of the open side of the sickle dance's figure eight or the angle of the wagging path during the tail-wagging dance indicates the direction of flight. When the dancing is performed on the vertical wall of the hive, it is apparently "understood" that the top of the hive wall represents the current position of the sun in the sky. During the sickle dance, the angle of the open side of the figure eight relative to the hive's vertical alignment indicates the direction of flight toward the food source relative to the sun. When the bee performs the tail-wagging dance, the angle of its wagging path relative to the hive's vertical angle indicates the path of flight toward the food source relative to the sun. Figure 16.8 illustrates the dances and their manner of indicating the direction of the food source.

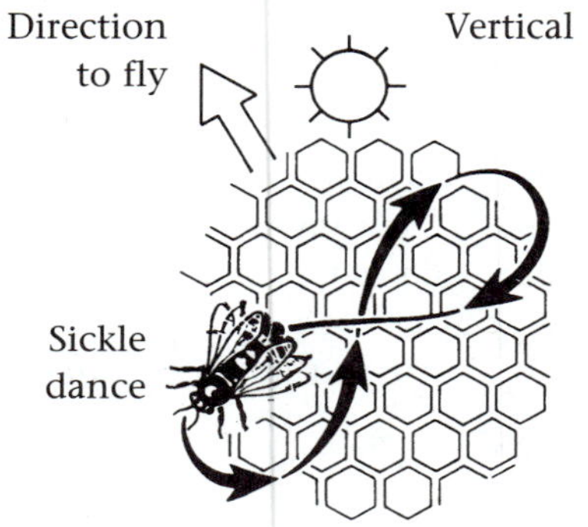

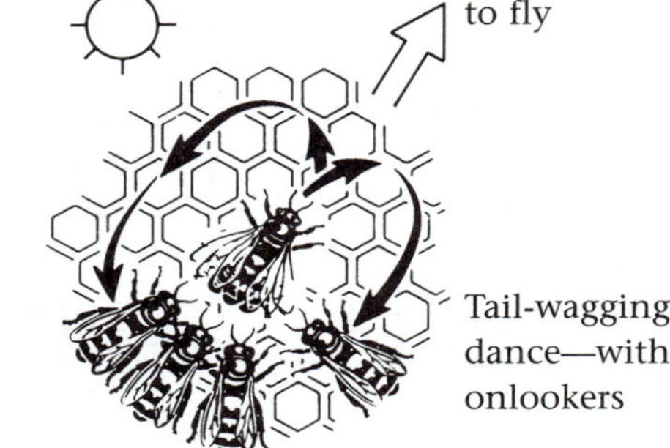

Figure 16.8 Bee dancing

Quality

Quality of the food source is indicated by the intensity of the dancing and the number of repetitions of the circling movements. As the food source is depleted, the dance is performed with less vivacity.

Other factors

These messages are not communicated with perfect accuracy, nor are they the only ones involved in bee communication. Bees also leave a hive-specific pheromone trace at the site of the food source, thereby directing their fellow foragers to the precise location. The bees also carry back traces of the food-source odors, which further aid other bees in the search. A complex of communicative modes operating on different channels—a constellation—is thus employed in bee communication. The use of different modalities to communicate the same information is called **redundancy**. Redundancy helps guarantee that communication will succeed in the event that one or another modality fails or is imperfectly transmitted. All communication systems make use of redundancy, and human language is no exception. For example, the presence of allophonic features such as voicelessness and aspiration of syllable-initial voiceless stops, or both length and quality differences of vowels provides redundancy that assists in decoding the signals.

3.2 Bees and humans

How does bee communication compare with human language? The three patterns that the bees dance are not obviously connected with the messages they communicate and so are symbolic in nature (though it is possible to argue that relative distance is iconically represented in that a greater distance covered by the bee in each cycle of the dance corresponds to a greater distance of the nectar source from the hive). The communication of direction is indexical when carried out on the hive floor (in the sense that it points in the direction of flight), and in this sense may be comparable to a human gesture. Bees are, however, capable of transforming this information into a symbolic representation, since they transfer the horizontal flight path to a vertical representation on the hive wall. The expression of food source quality is, in all probability, symptomatic: the more stimulated a bee is by the quality of the food source, the faster it dances.

The total communicative constellation involves other, redundant sources of communication as well, such as pheromones and food-source samples. The performance even involves audience participation. During its dance, the returning bee is expected to provide samples from the food source. If it fails to do so, it may be stung to death.

Bee communication, then, like human language, shows symbolic, indexical, and symptomatic traits, as well as interaction between sender and receiver of the messages. But there is a major difference between the two systems of communication. The topic of bee language is severely constrained. Bees communicate only about food sources. Furthermore, their potential for communication is very limited. Only certain locations of food sources can be conveyed. Bees cannot communicate the notion of up or down. They can easily be tricked into communicating the wrong direction of the food source if a strong light source is placed in an incorrect position with relation to the food source. They can also be tricked into giving the wrong information about distance to the food source if they are forced to walk or stop several times during their trip. This indicates that they gauge distance by time. The bees show no means of assessing varying information and communicating this fact. Their system of communication appears to be close-ended and limited to a specific number of facts about a specific type of information.

It also appears that bee language is largely innate—that is, there is very little need for a new forager bee to be exposed to the system in the presence of other bees. Foragers on their first flight perform the appropriate dances, although they refine their performance to some extent with time and exposure to other dancing. Their flight orientation to the sun is imperfect at first, but it develops within a few hours. However, there seems to be varying ability among individuals, as some dancers communicate more effectively than others.

The innateness of bee dancing has been tested by cross-breeding Austrian bees, which do not perform the sickle dance to express intermediate distance of the food source from the hive, with Italian honeybees, which do. The results of such experiments further support a genetic interpretation of bee communication. In the cross-breeding experiment, the bees that bore a physical resemblance to their Italian parent performed the sickle dance to indicate intermediate distance 98 percent of the time. The bees that bore a physical resemblance to their Austrian parent performed the round dance to indicate intermediate distance 96 percent of the time; they did not perform the sickle dance at all. The dance pattern used in a specific situation appears to be inherited from a certain parent along with other more obvious genetic traits.

In 1948, when the Danish physiologist August Krogh made the statement quoted at the beginning of this section, he struck at the widely accepted notion that animal behavior was either the result of some kind of conditioning or, in some ill-defined way, instinctive. Much has been learned since then about the enormous quantity of information imparted by genetic transfer. It is now possible to state with a fair degree of certainty that the complex and sophisticated behavior of bees and other equally remarkable insects is in all probability largely genetically predetermined and, unlike human language, relies very little on exposure to the mature system in order to be acquired.

4 THE BIRDS

> How intelligent is a creature that can amuse himself for 15 minutes by uttering, over and over, the following sounds: uhr, uhr, uhr, Uhr, URH, URH, Wah, Wah, wah, wah, wah.
>
> Jake Page (on his Amazon Parrot)

4.1 BIRD VOCALIZATION

Birds, as Jake Page later found out, can do a lot more than utter sounds over and over. Even the parrot, which has been labeled for years as nothing but a stimulus-bound mimic, has been shown to have some capacity for meaningful labeling. The parroting of trained birds is generally accepted to be nothing more than nonintentional response to external stimuli arrived at through repetitive conditioning. But recently, it has been claimed that certain kinds of parroting have cognitive underpinning of a type shared with primates and perhaps even humans (although it took one test parrot four years to acquire a vocabulary of eighteen nouns). Research on natural communication among birds has already shed light on certain parallels in human linguistic communication.

Bird vocalization can be divided into two types, **call** and **song**. Calls are typically short bursts of sound or simple patterns of notes. Songs are lengthy, elaborate patterns of mostly pitched sounds.

Calls

Calls serve very specific functions in the bird community. They typically warn of predators, coordinate flocking and flight activity, express aggression, and accompany nesting or feeding behavior. The cawing of crows is a typical call. It appears to convey a generalized mobilization to possible danger. When a crow hears cawing, it flies up to a tree if it is on the ground, or flies higher in a tree—or to another tree—if it is already in one. (If there are crows in your neighborhood, you can test this yourself, as cawing is easy to imitate.)

In some birds, individual calls are associated with specific activities; a danger call is quite different from a call given when birds are grouped in flight. A flight call is generally short, crisp, and easy to locate by other group members. The honking of geese in flight is a typical example of this sort of call. Because it is loud and easy to locate, it is well suited to enable the bird flock to stay together. The call given by small birds when larger avian predators threaten them is very different. It is typically thin and high-pitched. This kind of sound is difficult to locate, and so can be given as a warning without revealing the position of the caller. Such functional utility is typical of bird calls, and in fact, calls that serve the same communicative purpose are often remarkably similar among different species of birds.

Song

Birdsong is different from calling. Although calls are produced year-round, singing is largely limited to spring, summer, and autumn. Furthermore, it is generally only male birds that sing.

The main purposes of song are, as far as we know, to announce and delimit the territory of the male and to attract a mate. Birds establish territory for breeding purposes and defend it vigorously. Across the country, it is a common sight in the spring to see a red-winged blackbird (*Agelaius phoeniceus*) and its mate team up to drive away a male of their species that has strayed into their territory. The use of song enables male birds to establish and maintain this territory without constant patrolling and fighting. Moreover, once a bird has established its territory, its song serves to attract and maintain contact with a mate. It follows that birdsong is unique from species to species, and even varies to some degree from bird to bird within the same species, since its purposes require species and individual recognition.

In some species, songs are nothing more than a successive repetition of calls. In others, songs consist of complex patterns of pitches—sometimes called syllables—that form longer repeated units or themes. The sometimes elaborate complexity of song structure reflects individual variation among the singers and, as pointed out previously, serves a specific purpose. Figure 16.9 shows a **spectrogram** (an acoustic recording that shows pitch and intensity of sound along a time axis) of the song of the European robin (*Erithacus rubecula*). Note how the different subsections of the song are distinct and recognizable. There is also some evidence that sections of a song are combined in different orders by certain birds, but there is no evidence that recombination is associated with different meanings.

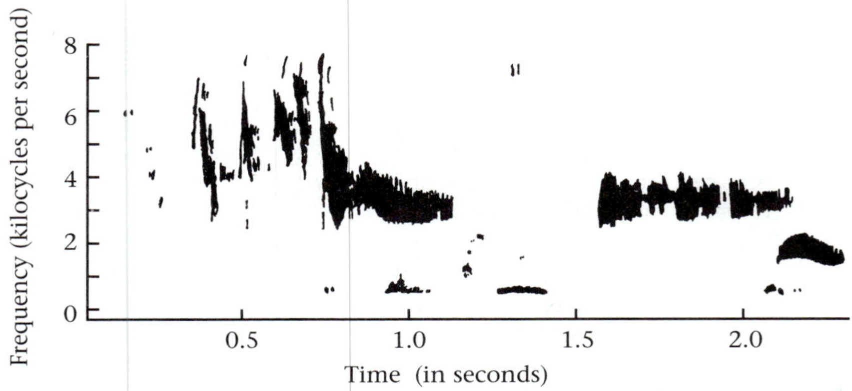

Figure 16.9 Spectrogram of a robin song; pitch is shown vertically along the L-R time axis, intensity by greater darkness

Avian dialects

There is evidence for both song and call dialects among bird species. Researchers even speak of avian isoglosses (lines drawn on a map to indicate shared characteristics among dialects; see Chapter 14, Section 2.3) that are based on variations in the melody of song "syllables" or themes (see Figure 16.10). The reason for the existence of dialects is still unclear; it may be no more than a reflection of individual avian variation in song and call learning. If it is, we are led to an intriguing issue in the relationship of bird vocalization to human language—the question of how bird vocalizations are acquired.

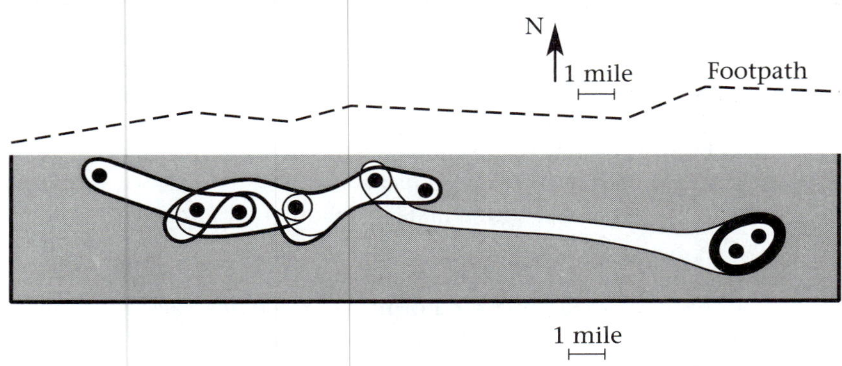

Figure 16.10 Avian isoglosses: call patterns of male Hill Mynahs (black dots show mynah groups; the shaded area shows forested hills and the unshaded area, open plain; the heavier the black lines, the more song characteristics are shared by the group within its boundaries)

4.2 Birds and humans

The acquisition of call and song by birds shows interesting parallels with recent hypotheses about the acquisition of language by human children (see Chapter 10). Though a great deal of bird vocalization—particularly calling—appears to be innate, there is much that appears to be acquired. Studies of avian dialects have shown that birds reared in the same nest acquire different song dialects when they live in different dialect areas. It also appears to be the case that singing ability is lateralized in the left brains of birds, as is linguistic ability in humans. Still more significant for linguistic study is the fact that some birds must acquire the species-specific characteristics of their song within a certain time span or critical period. A number of bird species do not develop fully characteristic songs if they are deprived from hearing them during the early stages of their lives. The chaffinch (*Fringilla coelebs*) is one such bird. If chaffinches are reared in isolation they sing, but replicate only in a general way the typical song of the species. If young chaffinches are reared away from fully developed singers but with other young chaffinches, the entire experimental community develops an identical song. Finally, chaffinches that have been exposed to only some part of the fully developed song (those that are captured in the autumn of the first year of life) will, the following spring, develop a song that is partially typical but not completely well formed.

These experiments indicate that there are some songbirds that have both an innate and a learned component in their song. The innate component predisposes them to perform a general song that is extremely simplified. This has been called a **template** or a blueprint. Only exposure to the fully formed song of the species will enable them to produce the correct song. (Exposure to another song causes some species to imitate in this direction; other species simply do not acquire anything they are exposed to unless it is their own species-characteristic song.) Finally, it is clear that certain birds do not acquire their characteristic song in a brief span of time, requiring several seasons of exposure to do so. The evidence from songbird studies, while not transferable directly to humans, gives strong support to the idea that a combination of innate and acquired components is one way that the acquisition of complex behavior takes place in nature.

5 NONHUMAN PRIMATES

> Some animals share qualities of both man and the four-footed beasts, for example, the ape, the monkey, and the baboon.
>
> Aristotle, *On Animals*

Fascination with nonhuman primates goes far back in human history. Their social behavior has long been seen as an amusing (and sometimes instructive) parody of human behavior. Since the recent establishment of the fact that we are closely related genetically to these animals—some 99 percent of our genetic matter is shared with chimpanzees and gorillas—the resemblance of their behavioral, social, and communicative traits to ours has been seen as more than an amusing counterpart to human activity. Recently, the question of our shared cognitive—and especially linguistic—

ability has become more important; it is thought that a better understanding of nonhuman primates may shed light on the evolution of human social and cognitive abilities.

Primates form a large class of mammals, which range from the tiny tarsier to the imposing mountain gorilla. Among the nonhuman primates, some are nocturnal and some diurnal in their activity cycle. Some are solitary and some form part of complex social groups. Many are tree-dwelling, and many are ground-dwelling. Some are quadrupeds, and some show periods of bipedal locomotion. Figure 16.11 shows one widely accepted classification of the primates.

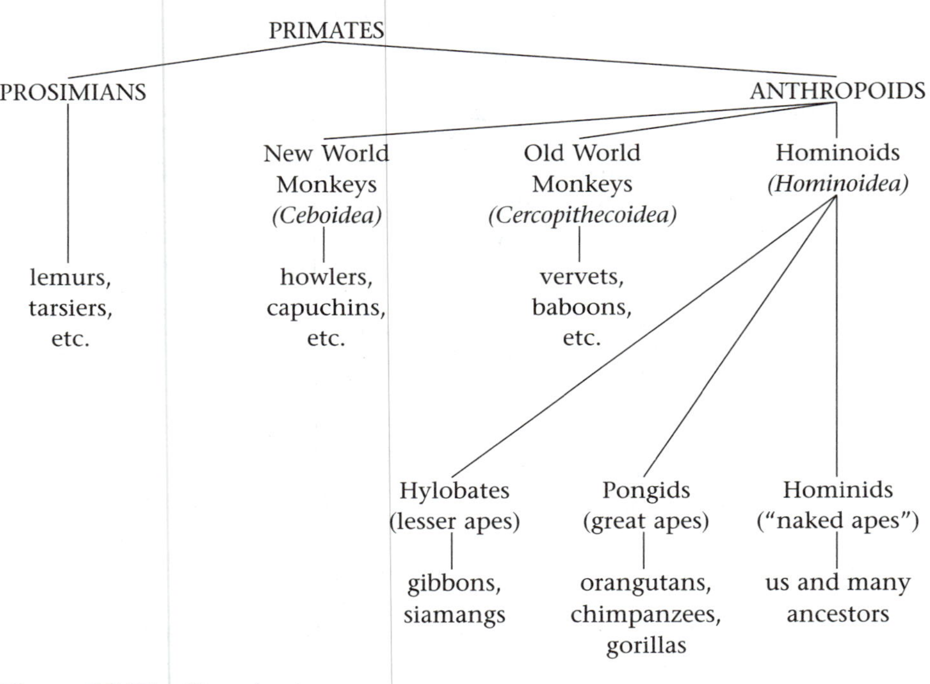

Figure 16.11 The primates

The prosimians are an evolutionarily early group found on the island of Malagasy, in sub-Saharan Africa, and in Southeast Asia. New World Monkeys range from Mexico through South America. Among them are the only primates with prehensile (grasping) tails. Old World Monkeys include the many tree- and ground-dwelling species of Africa and the Far East. The larger nonhuman primates—baboons, chimpanzees, and gorillas—are not native to North and South America. Baboons—large, mainly ground-dwelling primates—are found from central to northern Africa. They show a high degree of social organization, intelligence, and aggressiveness. The hominoids include the agile gibbons, solitary orangutans (both found only in Southeast Asia), the large but peaceful gorillas, the chimpanzees, and humans.

The validity of studies of communication among captive primates has been criticized because the animals' social existence is highly limited and compromised in zoos. Studies of nonhuman primate communication have largely left the zoo and laboratory and moved into the animals' natural habitat. While careful observation of nonhuman primate communication is still the basis of this work, the use of playback experiments—in which tape recordings of natural calls are played back over hidden loudspeakers—has led to a greater understanding of the communicative systems of these animals.

In the next section, we first turn our attention to nonhuman primate communication in the wild. It is there that we can gain an initial understanding of how forms of nonhuman primate communication resemble or differ from our own in terms of function and structure.

5.1 Some functions of nonhuman primate communication

Although the social life of even the most gregarious nonhuman primate is relatively simple when compared to that of humans, primates, like humans, communicate for many different reasons.

Typical nonhuman primate communication serves to mark and announce territory, to warn other group members of danger, to seek or maintain contact with a mate or other members of the species, and to interact with members of the troop or species in various ways we can call "socializing." Socializing vocalizations are particularly important in mother-child bonding and in primate groups with a complex and hierarchical social structure. In these groups, it is important to know which members have a higher or lower rank so that group members can behave accordingly in their presence. Vocalization is a key factor in maintaining this behavior.

As we briefly survey some aspects of the structure of nonhuman primate communication systems, we will also refer to the ways in which structure and function are linked.

5.2 Prosimian communication

Prosimian communication shows a small repertoire of sounds that are patterned into discrete groups. The lemur (*Lemur catta*) of Malagasy is a typical prosimian with respect to its vocal communication system. It has been described as making essentially two types of vocalization—noises and calls—each of which shows some grading. The vocalizations appear to be symptomatic. They are classified in Table 16.1; quasi-phonetic descriptions like *spat* should be interpreted as onomatopoeic.

Table 16.1 Lemur vocalization

Noises		*Calls*	
Sound	*Context*	*Sound*	*Context*
Single click	In response to strange objects	Light spat (yip)	When driving off threatening inferiors
Clicks, grunts	During locomotion or for friendly greeting	Spat	When crowded or handled roughly
Purr	While grooming	Bark	When startled

Each graded set of sounds is used in a circumscribed range of situations. The calls, in particular, are limited to threat or fear encounters. They seem to form a graded series, ranging from the light spat to the bark in intensity. A small repertoire of distinct vocalizations is the norm among prosimians. The slow loris (*Nycticebus coucang*), an Asian prosimian, is reported to have no more than five calls.

5.3 Monkeys

The study of communication among the many varieties of New and Old World Monkeys is too vast for this chapter. An oversimplified picture reflects what most researchers agree is primarily a symptomatic system but one that shows a larger number of signs, with more gradation among them, than does the communication of prosimians.

One study of the bonnet macaque (*Macaca radiata*), a South Asian monkey, presents a system of twenty-five different basic patterns that are used in various social interactions, including contact, agonistic encounters, foraging, greeting, sexual contact, and alarm giving. These vocalizations are determined by correlating observation with spectrographic analysis; descriptive labels are also given to the vocalizations, such as *whoo, rattle, growl, whistle,* and *bark*. These basic patterns are described as grading into each other. It is also claimed that they occur in combinations. There is no evidence, however, that these recombinations mean anything novel when they occur.

The communication systems of many monkeys appear to be genetically determined. This has been established by raising newborns in isolation. However, this statement cannot be made for all monkeys. For some monkeys, input from the adult system appears to be required. The study of one small monkey has suggested that not all monkey vocalizations are symptomatic, and that experience and learning can play a role in the acquisition of the communicative system.

The East African vervet monkey (*Cercopithecus aethiops*) is said to have three distinctive and arbitrary calls that announce the presence of either eagles, snakes, or large terrestrial mammals posing a threat. These calls are associated with different responses by the monkeys. When they hear the eagle call, the monkeys look up or run into the bushes. The snake call causes them to look down at the ground near them. The mammal alarm sends them running up into the trees, or climbing higher in a tree if they are already in one.

These findings, which appear to have been well established by playback experiments since they were first reported in 1967, suggest that not all nonhuman primates rely strictly on symptomatic signals to communicate or to trigger behavior in others. It is claimed rather that the vervets assess the potential danger situation and then choose a specific call with a clearly defined referent to announce the danger. Furthermore, each call is a vocalization signifier that is arbitrarily linked with its referent. Other monkeys respond appropriately to the calls without necessarily observing the danger themselves. All this taken together suggests a cognitive ability for classification of objects in the world, and an ability to link this classification system to arbitrary sounds for purposes of intentional communication (see Figure 16.12).

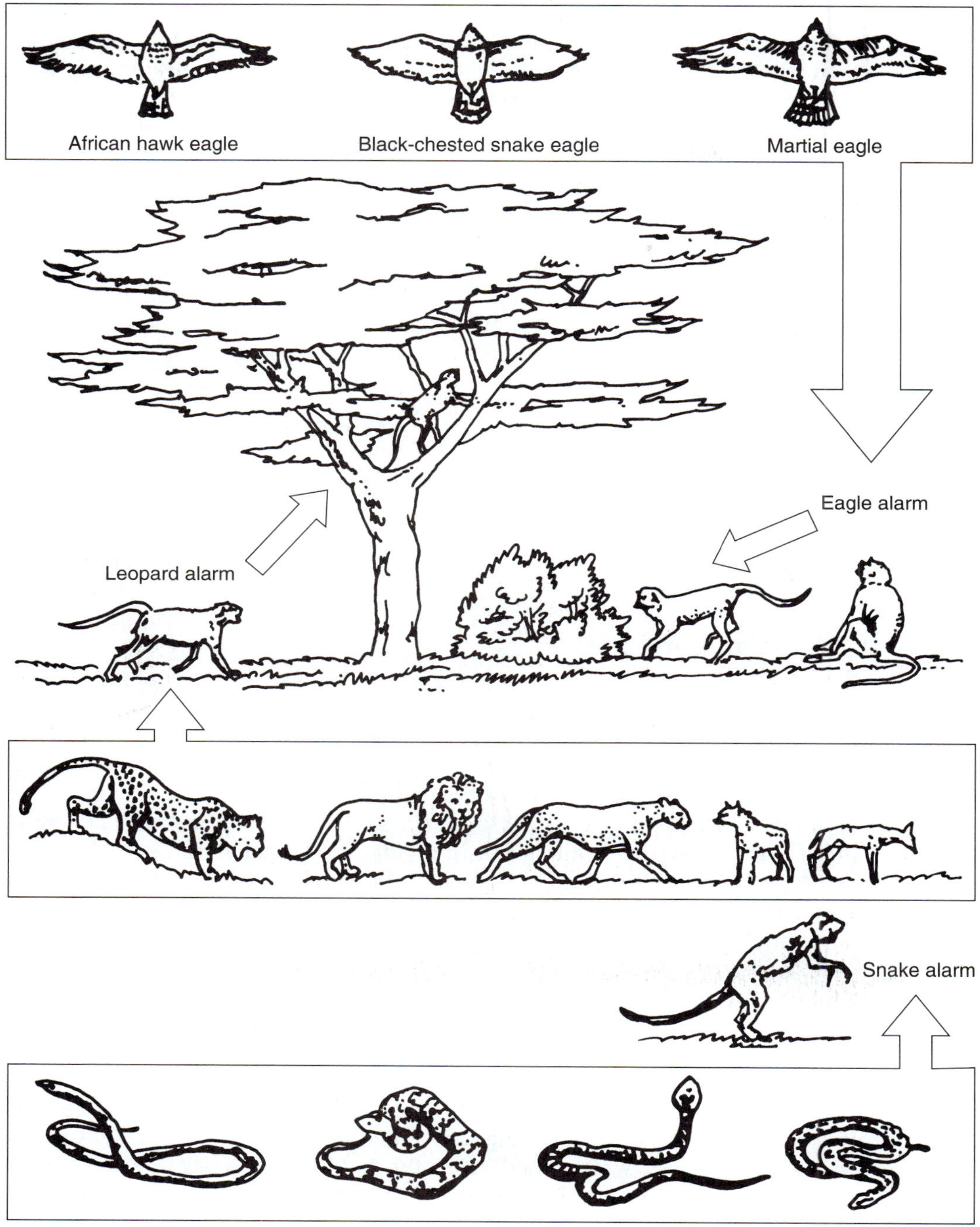

Figure 16.12 Response of vervet monkeys to specific predators

The vervet may not be an isolated case. Goeldi's Monkey (*Callimico goeldii*), found in South America, is said to have five different alarm calls, three of which are used when terrestrial predators approach, and two of which have been heard in the presence of large birds. Such observations support the claim that certain monkeys have the cognitive capacity to associate perceptual categories with vocalizations.

The acquisition of these signals among vervets is interesting. Infant vervets appear to distinguish innately among broad classes of mammals, snakes, and birds, but they also give the eagle call when other birds appear and the leopard call when other terrestrial mammals appear. Adults distinguish between leopards and less dangerous mammals, and eagles and less dangerous birds (as well as between snakes and sticks), and it is claimed that this ability must be perfected through experience. This once again suggests that a mixture of innate components and learning is typical of the way some communication systems are naturally acquired.

5.4 Gibbons, orangutans, and chimpanzees

Since the higher primates are close genetic relatives of humans, it is natural to expect their vocal communication to resemble that of humans. Perhaps surprisingly, communication among the higher primates does not show much indication of discrete vocal signs that could be interpreted as resembling human words. Rather, the communication systems of these animals are made up of groups of graded vocal signs.

Gibbons and orangutans

Gibbons display an interesting form of vocal interaction known as **duetting**. This is the interchange of calls in a patterned manner between two members of a species, and is found among certain birds, bats, and even antelopes. Duetting is, however, atypical of primate communication—among the hominoids, only gibbons perform it. Recent playback experiments show that duetting among gibbons serves to maintain spacing among territories much as does birdsong (see Section 4.1). Playback of duetting within a gibbon's territory will cause it to approach the apparent source of the vocalizations, possibly with the intent of driving the intruders out. Playback of singing and duetting from outside a group's territory only infrequently evokes a response. Recognition of individuals does not appear to play a role in these vocalizations.

Unlike gibbons, which live in family groups, orangutans largely keep to themselves (except for mother-child pairs). Some sixteen distinct vocalizations have been identified, many of them straightforwardly symptomatic. Among the solitary forest males, loud calls up to three minutes long serve a territorial and spacing function. These calls also identify the individuals who produce them. High-ranking males approach calls, presumably to confront the intruder, while low-ranking males stay away from areas where they hear the calls of high-ranking males. These calls are, in other words, indexes, which stand in for the individual animals themselves, and orangutans must identify and assess each of these calls before acting on them.

Chimpanzees

Chimpanzees vocalize with a number of graded calls. As many as thirty-four distinct calls have been reported for one species (*Pan troglodytes*). Some of these appear to show rather specific referents. Chimps typically hoot to signal location (a sound that carries well in dense forest). Hooting is also used in greeting or when chimps are excited about something. Another typical vocalization is known as rough grunting and is given in the presence of a favorite food source. Pant grunting appears to be used by lower-ranking animals in the presence of higher-ranking ones, signaling and reinforcing social hierarchy. A recent experiment has led to the claim that transmission of signs from one generation to the next plays a role in the acquisition of certain signs among chimpanzees. (For more on tradition, see Section 7.1, number 10.)

"Language" in the wild?

Especially among highly socialized species, nonhuman primate vocalizations show a great deal of variation. There is every indication that their vocalizations form part of a constellation of redundant communicative acts including gesture, posture, gaze (eye "pointing"), and the expression of affect, all of which must be interpreted by other troop members. The obvious complexity of communication systems among these animals suggests that the level of mental activity devoted to communicative behavior is sophisticated and well developed.

But despite the high degree of intelligence and social organization these animals demonstrate, there is very little evidence for arbitrary relationships between sound and meaning among apes. Even more significantly, there is no evidence of recombining various sections of a message to form new messages. Nothing that parallels the phonemic or morphological recombination of human language has been discovered in the natural communication systems of nonhuman primates.

It is possible that this lack of parallels in communication with species so closely related to our own may be because of the nature of their social organization. The small groups or family units typical of chimpanzees and gorillas living in a food-rich environment may not have required the development of any other mode of communication. What has evolved is suited to their needs. This does not mean, however, that our near relatives do not possess any of the cognitive abilities necessary for using a system of communication akin to human language. There is some evidence, for example, of left-hemisphere development of the type associated with human linguistic ability. A number of recent experiments with nonhuman primates have attempted to determine the extent—if any—of their linguistic abilities.

6 TESTING NONHUMAN PRIMATES FOR LINGUISTIC ABILITY

Much attention has been paid in recent years to nonhuman primates who communicate with humans through the use of sign language.

Controlled testing of the possible shared linguistic abilities of nonhuman primates and humans goes back to 1948, when two psychologists attempted to train Viki, a young chimpanzee, to say meaningful words in English. With great effort, Viki learned to approximate the pronunciations of a few words like *cup* and *papa* over a period of fourteen months. Unfortunately, the experiment was doomed to failure from the start, since the vocal-fold structure and supralaryngeal anatomy of the chimpanzee is unsuited for producing human sounds.

Chimpanzee vocal folds are fatty and less muscular than those of humans, and the neurological pathways between the brain and vocal folds are less developed than in humans. The chimpanzee's epiglottis extends well up into the throat cavity, which lessens the range of sounds it can produce. Finally, the whole larynx-tongue linkage rests higher in the chimpanzee throat than in humans, which results in limitations on its human-like sound production as well. In short, chimpanzee anatomy is unsuited for human speech, and concentrating effort on teaching one to articulate words was distracting from the more provocative question: To what extent is a chimp mentally capable of linguistic behavior?

6.1 Some experiments

An experiment conducted from 1965 to 1972 by Allen and Beatrice Gardner with a young female chimpanzee named Washoe created a new perspective on nonhuman primate linguistic abilities. The Gardners attempted to raise Washoe much as a human child would be raised, and to teach her American Sign Language (ASL), on the assumption that it was a genuinely linguistic form of communication (of which there is no doubt). Given the known manual dexterity of chimpanzees, it was felt that sign language might provide a window on chimpanzee linguistic abilities.

Washoe

The Gardners' reports claim that Washoe communicates intentionally with arbitrary signs in a creative manner, and thus shows the rudiments of human linguistic ability. Washoe learned to produce approximately 130 signs over a period of three years, and she recognized many more. Most significantly, it is claimed that Washoe spontaneously combined these signs to form novel utterances. She is reported to have signed WATER BIRD (in this chapter, signs are indicated by capital letters) on seeing ducks. Washoe also is said to have spontaneously produced BABY IN MY CUP when her toy doll was placed in her drinking cup and she was asked WHAT THAT?

Washoe was the first but not the only chimpanzee to be taught sign language. The results have suggested to some linguists that chimpanzees show greater ability to associate arbitrary tokens with referents than was earlier believed, and that they demonstrate rudimentary syntactic behavior. Other chimps, gorillas, and an orangutan that have been taught ASL since the pioneering Washoe experiment are reported to have performed even better.

Nim

Still other experiments in teaching chimpanzees sign language have produced contradictory results. The achievements of a chimpanzee named Nim have been interpreted by his teachers as consisting of frequent repetitions of a small number of all-purpose signs (NIM, ME, YOU, EAT, DRINK, MORE, and GIVE) that were largely appropriate to any context. These signs are said to have made up almost 50 percent of Nim's production. Furthermore, there are no reports of his engaging in creative combining of signs.

6.2 Nonsigning experiments

Much of the criticism leveled at Washoe's performance centered on the relative informality of her training and claims at the time that ASL is a loose communicative system that does not require a strict adherence to syntactic rules (though we now know ASL to be a rule-governed natural language). Two very different experiments with chimpanzees attempted to forestall such criticism.

Lana

A chimpanzee called Lana was trained to fulfill her needs for food, fresh air, grooming, and entertainment (in the form of slide shows) by requesting these from a computer-controlled apparatus. Communication with the computer was carried out by means of a simple rule-governed language of nine arbitrary symbols. The symbols were on buttons that lit up and activated the computer when pressed. Any deviation from the syntactic rule system invented for the experiment failed to get the desired responses from the computer. Human experimenters communicated directly with the chimpanzee through use of the same symbols. Lana learned to label and request food and other amenities through the computer. The experiment with Lana was criticized because she was said to have learned simple reflex associations among symbol, sequence, and reward. There was no evidence that she had acquired the rules underlying the sequences, and so she could not be said to have displayed linguistic abilities.

Sarah

Another well-known experiment involved training a young female chimp named Sarah to manipulate arbitrary plastic symbols in a predetermined manner in order to obtain rewards. Sarah had to learn to use word order correctly, since only the following order would obtain a banana.

Figure 16.13 Arbitrary symbols used in experiments with the chimpanzee Sarah

She also seemed to show sensitivity to more abstract words like *if/then* in sentences like those shown in Figure 16.14. But was Sarah learning aspects of human language or was she, too, trained? Humans who are taught similar skills perform them as well as Sarah but find it difficult to translate them into human language. They approach the exercise of moving plastic symbols around to obtain a reward as a puzzle that is not necessarily associated with language. It has been suggested that Sarah was performing the same kind of puzzle-solving and not demonstrating human-like linguistic capacities.

Interest in human-animal communications is not new. Language-using dogs, cats, pigs, and even turtles have been reported for thousands of years. The basis of much of the current criticism of these ancient reports and contemporary experiments rests on the performance of a horse in Germany at the turn of the last century.

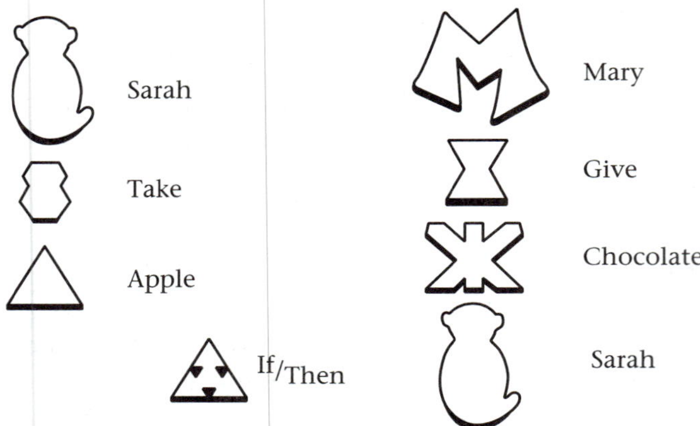

Figure 16.14 A "sentence" understood by Sarah

6.3 The Clever Hans controversy

When I play with my cat, who is to say that my cat is not playing with me?
Michel de Montaigne, *Essays*

In 1904, a Berlin schoolteacher named Wilhelm von Osten claimed to possess a horse that showed evidence of a human-like capacity to think. His horse, **Clever Hans** (*der kluge Hans*), could supposedly calculate and convey messages by tapping out numbers or numbered letters of the alphabet with a front hoof or by nodding its head.

Experimentation by a skeptical scientist, Oskar Pfungst, eventually showed that Clever Hans was not so much a creative thinker as a careful observer: the horse perceived cues that indicated that he had performed correctly. For example, von Osten involuntarily moved his head very slightly when a correct answer had been reached. This movement (less than five millimeters) was outside the normal perceptual range of human observers, but the horse had learned to associate it with the correct answer. When observers did not know the answer to a question or when Clever Hans was blindfolded, he failed to perform his miracles.

Clever Hans's performance resulted from **dressage**, a type of interaction between trainer and animal that depends on the animal's interpreting subtle cues given by the trainer. The Clever Hans phenomenon is an excellent example of dressage, which need not involve conscious communication on the part of humans. The highly developed perceptual ability displayed by Clever Hans is common to many animals. Many scientists believe that chimpanzees and gorillas that use sign language and perform other language-like tasks are demonstrating nothing more than the Clever Hans phenomenon.

The position is explained as follows. Human trainers want very much for their animal charges to succeed. This desire is translated into involuntary actions, which can be seized on by the animal because of its keen perceptual abilities; it is these cues that determine the animal's performance. A typical example of this is pointed out in Washoe's signing of BABY IN MY CUP, which has been recorded on film (*First Signs of Washoe*). A careful examination of this interchange shows that the human repeatedly holds out the object to be signed and then points rapidly at the cup. Probably none of this cueing was intentional on the human's part.

Some so-called linguistic activity may be the result of factors other than the Clever Hans effect. Some reports of creative signing, such as Washoe's WATER BIRD, are dismissed as reflex signing that shows no intention of forming combinations on the part of the chimp. Reports of the gorilla Koko's displays of wit (she occasionally produces the opposite sign of the one requested, such as UP for DOWN) are also considered to be exaggerated or simply wishful thinking by researchers.

Some reports of linguistic behavior are attributed to nonsystematic or inaccurate observing. (For example, if Washoe answered WHAT THAT with any noun sign, the answer was considered correct.) Other reports are attributed to overoptimistic interpretation of signs. (Koko is reported to intentionally produce "rhyming" signs—those that are very similar to the ones asked for or expected.) In short, those who do not view chimpanzee signing and symbol manipulation as linguistically relevant claim that this behavior is more simply explained as arising from straightforward response-reward association and/or from dressage, and not a reflection of linguistic competence. As one researcher noted, training two pigeons to bat a Ping-Pong ball across a net does not mean that the birds know the rules of Ping-Pong.

6.4 The great ape debate

> We believe that . . . there is no basis to conclude that signing apes acquired linguistic skills.
>
> Mark S. Seldenberg and Laura Petitto

> When these projects [Washoe, Lana, Sarah, and Nim] are taken together, it can be seen that chimpanzees are within the range of language behavior of humans and therefore have the capacity for language.
>
> Roger Fouts

Researchers involved with the chimpanzees and gorillas who are being taught to sign attest to the emotional bonds they form with them, and also emphasize that in using human language, such bonds are a prerequisite to normal communication. They strongly insist that apes communicate spontaneously and creatively with humans. Roger Fouts, who has spent many years in close contact with Washoe and other chimpanzees, puts the case this way.

> I reject the notion that there is some ultimate cut-and-dried criterion that distinguishes language from all other social and cognitive behaviors, or that distinguishes human communication and thought from that of all other species.

It is important to emphasize that most researchers sympathetic to the idea that apes show human linguistic abilities employ a broader definition of language than many of their critics. For these researchers, language use includes socialization and the use of communicative constellations.

For many linguists critical of these projects, a definition of language that rests on its social or functional aspects is unacceptable. In much current linguistic thinking, language is viewed as independent of the purposes it serves. This view, sometimes called the linguistic autonomy hypothesis, equates language with grammar—the "mental system that allows human beings to form and interpret the sounds, words, and sentences of their language," to quote from Chapter 1 of this text. It follows from this definition that linguistic ability in nonhuman primates can only be claimed to exist if the animals produce, at the very least, spontaneous and intentional symbolic signs that are manipulated in a rule-governed manner.

Symbol use

All researchers who support the claim that nonhuman primates can employ intentional symbolic communication deny that cueing is a major factor in the apes' abilities, although most admit that it might be present on occasion. In order to refute charges of the Clever Hans effect, researchers employ a strict form of experimentation.

Primate sign-language researchers try to avoid cueing by using a **double-blind test**. In this test, a researcher first shows the ape objects or pictures of objects that are invisible to a second human researcher. The ape's signing is then recorded by the second researcher and the record is interpreted by a third researcher who has not seen the signing. In this way, unintentional cueing is said to be avoided.

Critics of this research claim that even double-blind tests can be affected by human-animal interaction. First, the apes must be taught to perform the task. During this process they may be conditioned to provide certain responses. Second, it is difficult to avoid any human-animal interaction during these tests, and this could lead to subliminal cueing. As we have also seen, many claims for symbolic behavior on any ape's part have been dismissed as stimulus-response conditioning—the mere aping of behavior in order to obtain a reward. We still have no way of knowing whether Washoe's use of a sign sequence like TIME–EAT indicates that she has a concept of time.

Ongoing work with two chimpanzees named Sherman and Austin has led to their exchanging signed information about classes of objects such as tools and food. These experiments are claimed to have circumvented any reliance on the Clever Hans effect and shown that signing apes can communicate about whole referential classes of items rather than be bound to simple stimulus-response association with individual items such as a banana and ice cream.

Careful control of experiments has convinced some linguists that limited symbol use has been exhibited by some apes, perhaps even up to the level of a two-year-old human child. But some linguists who allow that a level of symbolic signing has been achieved have also denied that this is a critical feature for defining language. Rather, rule-governed, creative symbol combinations and syntactic behavior are said to be the critical features.

Creative signing?

A feature of language that sets it apart from most animal communication is its creativity—the fact that humans can use language to create novel messages. Sign researchers claim that such creativity is present in the many instances of novel combinations signed by the animals.

An early and famous instance of alleged creative signing was Washoe's WATER BIRD (referred to in Section 6.3), which she signed on seeing a duck in the water for the first time. Such alleged compound signing behavior has been noted in various signing apes. Some of the gorilla Koko's novel combinations are provided in Table 16.2.

Table 16.2 Some sign combinations produced by Koko

Compound	*Referent*
MILK CANDY	rich tapioca pudding
FRUIT LOLLIPOP	frozen banana
PICK FACE	tweezers
BLANKET WHITE COLD	rabbit-fur cape
NOSE FAKE	mask
POTATO APPLE FRUIT	pineapple

Critics say either that such combinations are accidental or that the ape produces the two signs independently of each other and thus does not display true compounding. There is no doubt that Washoe signed both WATER in the presence of water and BIRD in the presence of the bird, but there is no consistent indication from her other output that she has a rule of compound formation.

It has been claimed that in more recent and carefully controlled experiments with a pygmy chimpanzee (*Pan pansicus*) named Kanzi, statistically significant differences in the spontaneous ordering of symbols have been observed. The conclusion that has been drawn from this is that Kanzi has exhibited a form of grammatical rule. For example, Kanzi frequently used combinations of signs that link two actions, such as CHASE HIDE, TICKLE SLAP, and GRAB SLAP. In fifty-four out of eighty-four cases, the first sign corresponded to the invitation to play and the second to the type of play requested.

Is there syntax?

Claims for syntactic behavior among signing apes have also been made. Even though it has been claimed that the general (though flexible) syntax of ASL is copied by the apes, reports on the signing chimp Nim (Section 6.1) showed that the animal had no consistent word-order patterning. In fact, Nim's syntactic output was structurally incoherent. His longest sentence is reported as GIVE ORANGE ME GIVE EAT ORANGE ME EAT ORANGE GIVE ME EAT ORANGE GIVE ME YOU.

Koko is said to have developed her own word order in noun phrases—the adjective consistently follows the noun it modifies. It is difficult to prove claims for syntactic behavior in animal signing because all signing forms constellations with facial expression and gestures and so may be said to reduce the need for rigorous syntax. Koko, for example, can sign a meaning like 'I love Coca-Cola' by hugging herself (the sign for *love*) while signing *Coca-Cola* at the same time with her hands.

In spite of what is now widely considered to be the disappointment of the earlier studies (possibly because they expected too much), some controlled experimentation continues. Recently, the pygmy chimpanzee Kanzi is reported to have produced significant (though not wholly consistent) differences in the placement of animate agents in sign combinations. When another chimpanzee named Matata was grabbed, Kanzi produced GRAB MATATA, but when Matata performed an action such as biting, Kanzi produced MATATA BITE.

Lingering doubts

As we have seen, supporters of language use among apes have not yet proved to the satisfaction of all their critics that genuine symbolic behavior is occurring, much less anything resembling rule-governed creativity in compounding or syntactic patterning.

Researchers who see the results of ape studies as positive evidence for linguistic ability in these animals claim that their opponents keep raising the stakes every time a chimp or a gorilla accomplishes something that could be interpreted as linguistic behavior. Possible evidence of symbol use or creative signing to indicate linguistic ability is dismissed by these opponents as unsurprising or irrelevant. Supporters of ape studies note that such critics are motivated by a long tradition of viewing animals as "organic machines" that are locked into specific behavioral and communicative repertoires by their genetic inheritance, and that can therefore only respond automatically to a given situation with a narrow range of signs. Their own view, they claim, is at once more ancient and more modern in granting animals a certain as yet unknown degree of intentionality and cognitive ability in their behavior.

In general, recent experiments have established more convincingly than earlier ape studies that symbol use and referential behavior form part of the cognitive makeup of some nonhuman primates. Taken together with naturalistic studies, they help circumvent the claim that all evidence of symbol use among nonhuman primates is caused by the Clever Hans phenomenon.

Nonetheless, questions about creative sign combination and syntactic use still remain. Kanzi's alleged rules have been equated with those of a two-year-old child. But the major difference between a chimpanzee and a child at that point in their lives is that the elementary grammar of a two-year-old is the first hint of a full system that is rapidly developing and that will be in place in a matter of a few more years. While Kanzi's communicative behavior constitutes interesting evidence for a chimpanzee's awareness of the world, it does not unequivocally imply a system of grammar. It has been noted, for example, that Kanzi's rules are often bound up with a natural order of action or relationships (as when the sign GRAB precedes the sign SLAP).

To critics of these experiments, the apparent lack of rule-governed behavior among signing apes (especially in the realm of syntax) remains the linguistic hurdle that the animals have not overcome. It is certain that apes do not show syntactic behavior to any degree that humans do (for example, embedding is completely lacking), and many linguists claim that without such behavior, the apes cannot be said to be using language. Syntax, in the strict linguistic sense, provides a system of rules capable of producing a sentence of potentially infinite length (even though in practice this is never required). There is no evidence that primates have shown this ability.

6.5 Implications

Critics of the ape studies have at this time carried the day. Many funding sources for ape-human research have dried up, and most of the subjects have lost their privileged relationships with humans and been returned to zoos. But the severe reaction to the apparent failure of ape-human linguistic communication research has had positive effects on the field as well. Recent trends—the number of experiments on animal cognition in the wild, and the more carefully controlled experiments with apes like Kanzi—are slowly leading us closer to new evidence that bears on this age-old issue.

The real significance of these experiments in ape-human linguistic communication goes far beyond popular enthusiasm about what an ape might say to us if it could talk. It has often been pointed out that an animal's view of the world must be totally unlike our own. It is perhaps not surprising that apes appear to communicate largely about their fundamental emotions and such basic needs as food and play.

In time, this research may help illuminate what is truly unique about human linguistic ability. As we have seen, many linguists claim that there is no connection between the communicative behavior of nonhuman primates and the complex structures of human language. The opposing view claims that the capacity for true grammatical activity can be found in nonhuman primates. This implies that what we call language reflects a cognitive difference in *degree* and not in *kind* between humans and these animals. The optimistic view is that such research may ultimately shed light on the evolutionary origins of our species and its language use by demonstrating the degree of shared cognitive abilities between ourselves and our nearest genetic relatives.

7 COMPARING COMMUNICATION SYSTEMS: DESIGN FEATURES

Throughout this chapter, we have emphasized the distinction between communication and language. In this final section, we will compare human linguistic communication with what we have learned about systems of animal communication.

Differences and similarities between human language and natural animal communication systems can be highlighted by comparing essential characteristics of the systems. These characteristics are called **design features** and are set up (perhaps unfairly) with reference to human language. Since this book emphasizes the essentially mental nature of linguistic ability, the design features that follow do not include the traditional reference to vocal-auditory transmission. What is emphasized is the nature of the semantic and organizational structuring of each system. These design features represent an adaptation of those of Charles Hockett and W. H. Thorpe, as noted at the end of this chapter.

1. *Interchangeability* All members of the species can both send and receive messages.

   This is obviously true of human language. It is not the case with bee dancing (performed only by foragers) or birdsong (performed only by males). Nonhuman primate vocalizations appear to be largely interchangeable.

2. *Feedback* Users of the system are aware of what they are transmitting.

   Humans monitor their linguistic output and correct it. It is debatable whether bees do so when they dance, or whether birds monitor their calls. It is not known if birds monitor their song; it is likely that they do.

3. *Specialization* The communication system serves no other function but to communicate.

Human language represents reality—both external (real world) and internal (states, beliefs)—symbolically in the mind. Manifested as speech, language serves uniquely as a communicative system. Bee dancing and birdsong also appear to be specialized communicative activities. Alarm calls of any species may be symptomatic but at the same time are specialized for different types of predators. Symptomatic tokens, on the other hand, are unspecialized. Crying is a symptomatic sign that may be interpreted by someone else and thus function communicatively, but its primary purpose is physiological (the clearing of foreign matter from the eye, the release of emotional tension). If animal communication is primarily symptomatic—a claim that is hotly disputed by specialists in animal communication—then it would not qualify as a specialized communicative system.

4. *Semanticity* The system conveys meaning through a set of fixed relationships among signifiers, referents, and meanings.

   Human language conveys meaning through arbitrary symbols. Bee dancing conveys meaning, but within a very limited range, as do bird calls and song. The range of meaning is broader and more subtle in nonhuman primate vocalizations. Although we cannot claim to know the minds of such near relations as chimpanzees and gorillas, it appears that the range of meanings suggested by their behavior in the wild does not approach the vastness of human semanticity (see feature 8).

5. *Arbitrariness* There is no natural or inherent connection between a token and its referent.

   This is true of human language, with the possible exception of a few onomatopoeic terms. Bee dancing shows arbitrariness in that there may be no connection between the form of the dance and the distance from the hive. Expressions of food-source quality and direction are not arbitrary, however. Many bird calls are highly suited for their purpose, such as danger calls that are difficult to locate, and in this sense are not arbitrary. Most nonhuman primate vocalization appears to be equally adaptive, though arbitrariness has been claimed for vervet monkey alarm calls.

6. *Discreteness* The communication system consists of isolable, repeatable units.

   Human language shows distinctive features, phonemes, syllables, morphemes, words, and still larger combinations. There are two (three, in some dialects) discrete types of bee dances, but these dances are not combined in various ways to produce novel messages. There is some evidence for subunits in birdsong. They are also present in primate call systems.

7. *Displacement* Users of the system are able to refer to events remote in space and time.

   Bee dancing shows displacement. No evidence for displacement is found in bird calls or songs. Baboons occasionally produce threat and fight vocalizations long after an aggressive encounter, but there is no evidence that this is reflecting displacement; it probably reflects a slow winding down of the animal's emotional state. Among apes, it is not yet clear whether some degree of displacement is a feature of either their communication in the wild or the systems they have learned from humans. Nonhuman primates do not appear to communicate about imaginary pasts or futures, which humans are able to do with language.

8. *Productivity* New messages on any topic can be produced at any time.

   This is obviously true of human language. Bees show limited productivity. Bird calls show none. Birdsong shows evidence of recombination (the songs of laughing gulls are well documented in this respect), but it is doubtful whether these recombinations transmit novel messages. This is also true of recombination in the calls of certain monkeys, such as macaques.

9. *Duality of patterning* Meaningless units (phonemes) are combined to form arbitrary signs. These signs in turn can be recombined to form new, meaningful larger units.

   In human language, phonemes can be combined in various ways to create different symbolic tokens: *spot*, *tops*, *opts*, and *pots*. These tokens in turn can be combined in meaningful ways: *Spot the tops of the pots*. There is no evidence of this type of patterning in any known animal communication system.

10. *Tradition* At least certain aspects of the system must be transmitted from an experienced user to a learner.

    This is obviously a factor in the acquisition of human language. It is possibly present in a very limited way in bee communication, and it is definitely present in the acquisition of birdsong for some species. As noted in Section 5.4, there is some recent evidence for a degree of tradition among chimpanzees.

11. *Prevarication* The system enables the users to talk nonsense or to lie.

    Undoubtedly, this property is found in human language. There are specialized mimics among birds, fishes, and even insects. A few examples of animal deception have been noted among the arctic fox and among vervets, but it is not clear whether this is normal species-specific behavior or the acts of a few isolated individuals. The question of intentionality is crucial here. Current work with birds suggests that some species learn as many songs as possible and use this repertoire to maintain territorial advantage by "impersonating" other species. This may well be purely genetically determined behavior, but in any event, it is highly complex.

12. *Learnability* A user of the system can learn other variants.

    Humans can learn a number of different languages. Bees are limited to their own genetically specified dialect. Bird calls are apparently limited in this same way. As noted previously, some birds learn the songs of other species, but this may well be simply mimicry. Nonhuman primates seem restricted to their own systems in the wild.

13. *Reflexiveness* The ability to use the communication system to discuss the system itself.

    No evidence exists that any other species writes grammars or linguistics textbooks.

Tables 16.3 and 16.4 summarize this survey of design features.

Table 16.3 Summary of design features for bees and birds

Design feature	*Bees*	*Birds*
1. Interchangeability	no; foragers only	no; only males sing
2. Feedback	?	?
3. Specialization	yes	yes
4. Semanticity	yes, very limited	yes, limited
5. Arbitrariness	yes, for expressing distance	yes, though highly adaptive
6. Discreteness	in a limited way	yes, in song
7. Displacement	yes	no
8. Productivity	yes, very limited	possibly
9. Duality of patterning	no	no
10. Tradition	possibly, but highly limited	yes, limited
11. Prevarication	no	possibly
12. Learnability	no	possibly
13. Reflexiveness	no	no

Table 16.4 Summary of design features for nonhuman primates and humans

Design feature	*Nonhuman primates*	*Humans*
1. Interchangeability	yes	yes
2. Feedback	probably	yes
3. Specialization	in part	yes
4. Semanticity	yes	yes
5. Arbitrariness	limited confirmation; selectively adaptive	yes
6. Discreteness	in call systems	yes
7. Displacement	no	yes
8. Productivity	possibly	yes
9. Duality of patterning	no	yes
10. Tradition	possibly	yes
11. Prevarication	possibly	yes
12. Learnability	no	yes
13. Reflexiveness	no current evidence	yes

Summing Up

This brief overview of animal communication systems emphasizes that human language is one communication system among the many that life forms on this planet employ.

Communication can be described with reference to the **sign**, which is composed of two components, a **signifier** and that which is **signified**. Tokens may be **iconic**, **symbolic**, or **indexical** (the latter including the **symptomatic** token), and structured as **graded** or **discrete** types. Most animal communication has traditionally been viewed as symptomatic, though studies of communication among birds and bees suggest symbolic signs are used. A significant innate component may interact with some exposure to the communication system, especially among birds. Nonhuman primate communication consists of graded series of vocalizations and appears to show little arbitrariness, though some has been reported for the alarm calls of several monkeys.

Experiments with nonhuman primates have created controversy over whether chimpanzees and gorillas have shown symbolic behavior and a capacity for linguistic behavior. Many researchers have dismissed the work as an example of **dressage** or the **Clever Hans** phenomenon.

Human language and systems of animal communication share certain **design features**. Humans, however, lack many communicative skills that animals possess. We are hopelessly inadequate at following scent trails, a feat that prosimians accomplish with ease; we cannot change color for communicative purposes with the facility of an octopus; and we are not as gifted as horses and many other mammals at assessing and interpreting subtle body gestures. Humans do possess an ability to symbolize that far exceeds that of chimpanzees and gorillas (our nearest genetic relatives), even allowing for the most generous interpretation possible of recent experiments. Human language is also more flexible and productive in manipulating these symbols than any known animal communication system. Language is as suited for and as much a part of human life patterns as the communication systems of our fellow creatures are for their modes of existence.

Key terms

Terms concerning nonvocal communication and signs used in communication

discrete signs
graded signs
iconic signs
icons
index
indexical sign
meaning
pheromones
semiotics
sign
signals
signified
signifier
stimulus-bound
symbolic signs
symptomatic sign
tokens

Terms related to communication of birds and bees

(bird) call
(bird) song
redundancy
spectrogram
template

Terms concerning communication of nonhuman primates

Clever Hans
design features
double-blind test
dressage
duetting

Picture credits

Chimpanzee facial expressions in Figure 16.1 and question 3, and monkey facial expressions in Figure 16.5 are adapted from S. Chevalier-Skolnikoff's "Facial Expression and Emotion in Nonhuman Primates," in *Darwin and Facial Expression,* edited by E. Ekman (New York: Academic Press, 1973), pp. 11–90. The Japanese macaque open-mouth threat in Figure 16.3 is adapted from a photograph in K. R. L. Hall and I. DeVore's "Baboon Social Behavior," in *Primate Behavior,* edited by I. DeVore (Toronto: Holt, Rinehart and Winston, 1965), pp. 53–110; park information signs in Figure 16.3 are courtesy of Alberta Provincial Parks. Figure 16.7 is adapted from D. Todt's "Serial Calling as a Mediator of Interaction Processes: Crying," in *Primate Vocal Communication,* edited by D. Todt, D. E. Goedeking, and D. Symmes (Berlin: Springer-Verlag, 1988), pp. 88–107, and reprinted by permission of the publisher. Bee dancing (Figure 16.8) is adapted from K. von Frisch's *The Dance Language and Orientation of Bees,* p. 57 (cited in sources). Copyright © 1967, 1993 by the President and Fellows of Harvard College. Reprinted by permission of Harvard University Press. The spectrogram of the robin song (Figure 16.9) is from *Bird-Song* by W. H. Thorpe (cited in sources), copyrighted and reprinted with the permission of Cambridge University Press. Avian isoglosses in Figure 16.10 are from Paul Mundinger's "Microgeographic and Macrogeographic Variation in Acquired Vocalizations of Birds," in *Acoustic Communication in Birds,* edited by D. E. Kroodsma, E. H. Miller, and H. Ouellet, vol. 2 (New York: Academic Press, 1982), pp. 147–208, and reprinted by permission. Figure 16.12 illustrating the response of vervet monkeys to predators is taken from *Animal Language* by Michael Bright (cited in recommended reading). Tokens used in the Sarah experiments (Figures 16.13 and 16.14) are taken from D. Premack and A. J. Premack as cited on p. 179 in E. Linden's *Apes, Men, and Language* (Baltimore, MD: Pelican Books, 1974).

Sources

The theory of semiotics outlined in this chapter is drawn from several recent works on semiotics, including T. Sebeok's *Contributions to the Doctrine of Signs, Studies in Semiotics* 5 (Bloomington, IN: Indiana University Press, 1976); *I Think I Am a Verb* (New York: Plenum Press, 1986); and U. Eco's *Semiotics and the Philosophy of Language* (Bloomington, IN: Indiana University Press, 1984). Bee communication is drawn from K. von Frisch's "Dialects in the Language of the Bees," *Scientific American* 202 (1962): 78–87, and his work *The Dance Language and Orientation of Bees,* translated by C. E. Chadwick (Cambridge, MA: Harvard University Press, 1967). Bird vocalization is based largely on W. H. Thorpe's *Bird-Song* (Cambridge, MA: Cambridge University Press, 1961). Jake Page's parrot is reported in *Science* (1982). Lemur vocalizations in Table 16.1 are drawn from A. Jolly's *Lemur Behavior* (Chicago: University of Chicago Press, 1966). Vervet communication is drawn from D. L. Cheney and R. M. Seyfarth's *How Monkeys See the World* (cited below). Much information on primate communication in the wild was provided by Hugh Notman. Creative signing by Koko is reported in F. Patterson and E. Linden's *The Education of Koko* (New York: Holt, Rinehart and Winston, 1981). The reference to cultural transmission of signs among chimpanzees is drawn from Michael Tomasello's "Cultural Transmission in the Tool

Use and Communicatory Signaling of Chimpanzees?" in Parker and Gibson (cited below), pp. 274–311; some of the material on invented rules by the pygmy chimpanzee Kanzi is drawn from Patricia Marks Greenfield and E. Sue Savage-Rumbaugh's "Grammatical Combination in *Pan paniscus*," also in Parker and Gibson, pp. 540–76; this volume contains a number of other articles relevant to the question of nonhuman primate cognitive and linguistic abilities. Some question material is drawn from various articles in *How Animals Communicate*, edited by Thomas A. Sebeok (Bloomington, IN: Indiana University Press, 1977).

Recommended reading

Bright, Michael. 1984. *Animal Language*. London: British Broadcasting Corporation.

Cheney, Dorothy L., and Robert M. Seyfarth. 1991. *How Monkeys See the World*. Chicago: University of Chicago Press.

de Luce, Judith, and Hugh T. Wilder, eds. 1983. *Language in Primates: Perspectives and Implications*. New York: Springer-Verlag.

Hauser, M. 1996. *The Evolution of Communication*. Cambridge, MA: MIT Press.

Hockett, Charles. 1960. "The Origin of Speech." *Scientific American* 203 (3): 88–96.

Lieberman, Philip. 1998. *Eve Spoke*. New York: W. W. Norton.

Parker, Sue Taylor, and Kathleen Rita Gibson. 1990. *"Language" and Intelligence in Monkeys and Apes: Comparative Developmental Perspectives*. Cambridge: Cambridge University Press.

Pinker, Steven. 1994. *The Language Instinct*. New York: Harper Perennial.

Sebeok, Thomas A., and Jean Umiker-Sebeok. 1980. *Speaking of Apes*. New York: Plenum Press.

Sebeok, Thomas A., and Robert Rosenthal, eds. 1981. *The Clever Hans Phenomenon: Communication with Horses, Whales, Apes, and People*. Annals of the New York Academy of Sciences, 364. New York: New York Academy of Sciences.

Snowden, C. T., C. H. Brown, and M. R. Petersen, eds. 1982. *Primate Communication*. London: Cambridge University Press.

Thorpe, W. H. 1974. *Animal Nature and Human Nature*. Garden City, NY: Doubleday.

Questions

1. The following signs are all symptomatic.
   a) Dogs wag their tails when happy; cats flick their tails when irritated.
   b) An octopus, when showing aggressive behavior, becomes bright red.
   c) The Canada goose shows aggressive intentions by opening its mouth, coiling its neck, and directing its head toward an opponent. When it is unlikely to attack, its mouth is closed, its head is horizontally extended, and its head is directed away from an opponent.
   d) Tree leaves change color in the fall.
   e) The presence of stratocumulus clouds accompanies good weather.

   i) Why is this designation appropriate in each case?
   ii) State which of these signs—in addition to being symptomatic—are primarily *iconic*, which are primarily *symbolic*, and which are primarily *indexical*.

2. Find two examples each of *iconic, symbolic,* and *indexical* signs you encounter in the course of a day. Is it possible to classify unambiguously each sign as to type? If not, state why in each case.

3. What do the following chimpanzee facial expressions convey? Using a mirror, try to imitate the facial expressions; does this make it easier for you to label them? What characteristics of the signs led you to your conclusion in each case?

4. Observe an animal in a zoo or at home for at least a half hour. Try to discover at least three unambiguous signs the animal employs to communicate. Describe each one in terms of both *signifier* and *signified.* (A good way to do this is to note carefully the context in which the sign is given, to whom it is addressed, and what the receiver's response is to the communication.)

5. Add two columns to the list of design features presented in Tables 16.3 and 16.4. For one column, take the perspective of a researcher who believes that apes show true linguistic ability in their signing, and fill in the column from this point of view. Fill in the other column from the perspective of a researcher who does not believe such ability has been shown. Be sure to comment on each design feature.

6. Now that you have been exposed to both sides of the ape language issue, summarize your own conclusions about it. Do you believe that human language is different in degree or in kind from the communicative behavior of the great apes? Why?

Answers to question 3: *a)* submission; *b)* excitement, perhaps affection; *c)* desiring, perhaps mixed with frustration.

seventeen

COMPUTATIONAL LINGUISTICS

Judith Klavans

How comes it that human beings, whose contacts with the world are brief and personal and limited, are nevertheless able to know so much as they do know?

– BERTRAND RUSSELL

OBJECTIVES

In this chapter, you will learn

- what is involved in computer synthesis and recognition of human speech
- how computers can recognize and generate morphological permutations of words
- why analyzing and generating sentences is a complex task for a computer
- the kind of information that computer programs must include on how words are combined to make sense
- how computational linguistics can be applied to practical problems

Imagine that your computer can speak and understand language. Imagine a wireless device you carry in your pocket that can read communications—for example, email or messages from another wireless—and truly understand them. Such a device could actually decide what to answer, generate the answer, and beam it in fluent and natural-sounding English to the sending machine. You would merely have to provide a few ideas or basic concepts, and the device would create a message to be sent. Alternatively, the device could dictate your personalized message in a completely natural-sounding foreign language, be it French, Chinese, or Swahili, even though you may not speak a word of that language.

While the study of linguistics is centuries old, **computational linguistics** has only been studied for some decades. In the 1990s, computational linguistics as a field made rapid strides as the Internet, formerly accessible only to select scientists and researchers and to the military, became available to the public. This single development has rapidly increased the impact of computational linguistic research and applications so that even novice users of the World Wide Web are influenced by this impact, often without knowing it.

The central question in computational linguistics is this: What would a computer program have to capture to enable a robot, another device, or the computer itself to analyze, understand, and create sentences, paragraphs, or even entire essays? Sentences could be either spoken or written. This is something that we humans achieve effortlessly. However, consider the amount and type of information that a computer would have to know about language in order to understand a simple sentence like this:

1)

The essay reads well and provides strong arguments.

First, the computer would have to understand the meaning and use of each of the words. For example, the computer would need to know that when the determiner *the* is used, it indicates a specific essay. The determiner *a* or *an* would indicate that it is the class of items or entities known as essays that read easily; this is the kind of usage found in a sentence like *An apple a day keeps the doctor away.* Since the subject of the sentence, *essay*, is a singular noun, the computer would have to know that the verb must be singular, in order to avoid sentences like **The essay read well.* But this is only true in the present tense; in the past tense, the verb *read* would serve both for singular and plural, as in *Yesterday's essay read well* and *Yesterday's essays read well*, because *read* is an irregular verb, with homophonous verb forms (as discussed in Chapter 4 on morphology, and Chapter 6 on semantics). So the computer would have to know that **The essay read well* is in the present tense, not the past.

In addition to this **grammatical knowledge** about *the*, about tense (present or past), and about agreement between subject and verb (singular or plural), humans have a great deal of other information about the sentence in example *1*. For instance, we know that essays are written and thus are likely to be read, and that essays are likely to contain arguments to prove a point. This is called **real-world knowledge**, as distinct from grammatical knowledge. For example, although telephone and email messages are written and are likely to be read, they are unlikely to contain arguments. Furthermore, when analyzed carefully, the verb *read* has several uses. One is the transitive use, in which the subject is the agent (the entity that performs the action), as in *The professor read forty essays*. Another is the intransitive use, in which the subject of the sentence, *essay* in example *1*, is the theme (the entity undergoing the action).

In example *1*, the agent is not explicit; we do not know who is doing the reading. These two ways of using the verb *read* are related, but their interpretation is quite different. Finally, the word *strong*, like many adjectives, has many different meanings in context. Most often, *strong* is used to mean 'physically powerful' (as in *strong muscles*); it can also be used in other ways (e.g., *strong odor*). The interpretation of the word *strong* depends on the noun it describes; in example *1*, it refers to the fact that arguments have a gradation of effectiveness, measured from weak or unconvincing to strong or persuasive.

What sort of knowledge about pronunciation would a computer need to know to utter this sentence? The rules of pronunciation, like the rules of grammar, are different for each language and even for dialects within the same language. Pronunciation is likely to vary within the same language, depending on many factors. For example, the vowel in *the* when preceding a consonant is pronounced as a schwa /ə/ as in *the book* (see Chapter 2), whereas when preceding a vowel, it is pronounced as /i/ as in "the apple." English speakers know that the letter *e* in *the* is to be pronounced differently depending on the initial phoneme in the word that follows, but this is not true for every word ending in the sound /i/. For example, the words *we* and *flea* do not change pronounciation so drastically according to the word that follows, although there is always some adjustment in spoken language. Another fact of pronunciation concerns the verb *read*: Is this present or past tense? Of course, there is more to pronunciation than just converting letters to sounds, as was shown in Chapters 2 and 3 and will be discussed in later sections of this chapter.

These examples are sufficient to illustrate the quantity and variety of information that humans know about language. We take this knowledge for granted; it is so obvious to us that even to write about it sometimes seems trivial. Until we try to write computer programs to understand or generate even the most simple sentences, there is no need to pick apart the knowledge about language that we possess. However, computers are only as capable as the humans who program them, so it is the task of the computational linguist to spell out this knowledge for the computer. This is a major undertaking, involving all aspects of knowledge of language.

Computational linguistics is a relatively new discipline that lies at the intersection of the fields of linguistics and computer science. It is but one of many new hybrid disciplines involving computers that require computational expertise as well as background in another field. The term *computational linguistics* covers many subfields. It sometimes refers to the use of computers as a tool to understand or implement linguistic theories. This means that linguists and computer scientists can gain a better understanding of the scientific and research questions by using computers. On the other hand, the term is sometimes used to refer to working systems or applications in which linguistic knowledge is needed. In this case, the questions and issues are usually ones of software engineering as well as theory.

This chapter is organized around subfields of linguistics that are discussed in other chapters in this book: phonetics and phonology, morphology, syntax, and semantics. There is also a section on computational lexicology. The first part of the chapter shows how each linguistic subfield is used as the basis for a computational linguistics subfield. The second part of the chapter shows some ways in which these various subsystems are combined to create computer systems that use language, such as talking books, smart Internet search engines, and automatic summarization systems.

1 COMPUTATIONAL PHONETICS AND PHONOLOGY

1.1 THE TALKING MACHINE: SPEECH SYNTHESIS

At the 1939 World's Fair in New York, a device called a vocoder was displayed. The machine, developed by scientists at Bell Laboratories, reconstructed the human voice by producing a sound source that was then modified by a set of filters. The settings for the filters were derived from the analysis of human speech. The vocoder system consisted of a source of random noise for unvoiced sound, an oscillator to give voicing, a way to control resonance, and some switches to control the energy level. This was to simulate the vowel sounds and fricatives (see Chapter 2). Then there were controls for the stop consonants /p, b/, /t, d/, and /k, g/. An amplifier then converted the modified source signal into sound resembling the human speech it was modeled after.

The vocoder was nicknamed the Talking Machine. It was a crude device, but it demonstrated that good speech synthesis could indeed be achieved, given the right values for the major frequencies and the right methods of concatenating and modifying adjacent values. Early systems used different technology from that used today, but the principles remain the same. The goal is to replicate the waveforms that reflect those of human speech in order to produce speech that, at the very least, will be intelligible and aesthetically pleasing and that, in the ultimate, could not be distinguished from the speech of a human being.

Chapter 2 gave a summary of articulatory phonetics—that is, how sounds are made when humans speak. Chapter 3 covered some aspects of sound systems. Speech recognition and speech synthesis rely on a detailed knowledge of acoustic phonetics as well as articulatory phonetics, although there are correlations between the acoustic and articulatory properties of sounds. Acoustic phonetics is the study of the structure of the waveforms that constitute speech. As was explained in Chapter 2, the lungs push a stream of air through the trachea. The airstream is modified first at the glottis and then by the tongue and lips.

Each sound can be broken down into its fundamental waveforms, as shown in Figure 17.1. The figure shows a spectrographic analysis, or **spectrogram**, of the words *heed, hid, head, had, hod, hawed, hood,* and *who'd* as spoken by a British speaker. The diagrams give a visual representation of the duration of the utterance on the horizontal axis, and the different frequencies in the waveform on the vertical axis. The main frequencies, or **formants**, show up because they have more intensity than other frequencies. Note the different locations of the formants along the frequency dimension for the different vowels. The sound /h/ is only slightly visible as fuzzy lines across the spectrum because /h/ is a voiceless fricative with little or no glottal constriction (see Chapter 2, Section 5). The acoustic effect is weak white noise resembling fuzz or static. The /d/ is a stop, so there is just a low-frequency voice bar resulting from the vibrations in the glottis, but there are no vowel formants for the period of closure since the airflow is blocked. This shows up as blank space on the spectrogram. For speech synthesis, the first three formants are the most critical for identifying different vowels. The others add some refinement to the sound, but they do not determine intelligibility or naturalness with the same significance as the first three basic formants.

Since different vowels are composed of different frequencies, the task of the speech synthesizer in theory is simply to replicate those vowel sounds, put in a few consonants, and string them together just as letters are strung together to make words and sentences. Unfortunately, the matter is not so simple, since sounds are not fixed but rather vary according to the segments that surround them. Effects occur on adjacent segments and across groupings, sometimes as far as six phonemes

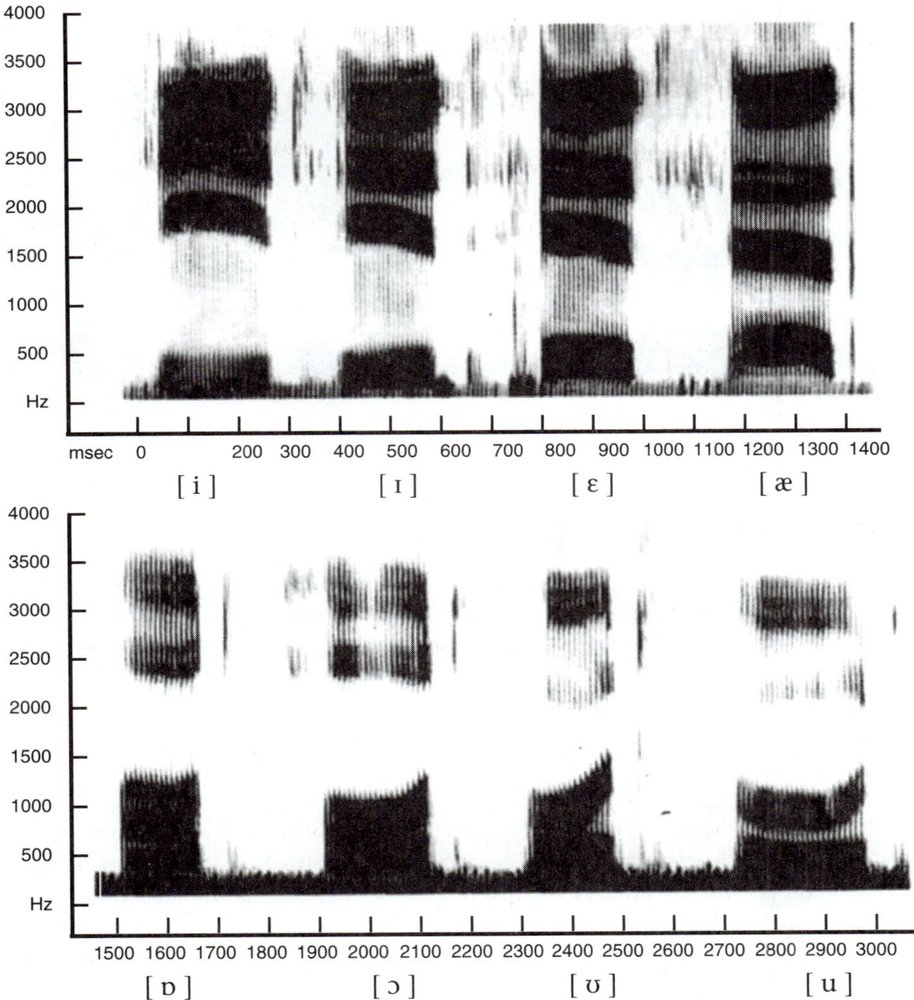

Figure 17.1 Spectrograms of vowels

away. For example, Figure 17.2 shows the same phonetic vowel [æ], but notice the rises and slumps in the formants. The figure shows how adjacent consonants can modify vowels. Similarly, vowels modify consonants, and nasal sounds modify larger chunks of surrounding speech. On top of these local changes, there are changes to entire phrases based on suprasegmental features such as stress and intonation (see Chapter 2, Section 8).

Many steps are involved in achieving speech synthesis, and there are many different choices to be made in ordering these steps. The text to be spoken has to be analyzed syntactically, semantically, and orthographically. Pronunciations for exceptional words such as *have* /hæv/ or *four* /fɔr/ must be found. These words do not

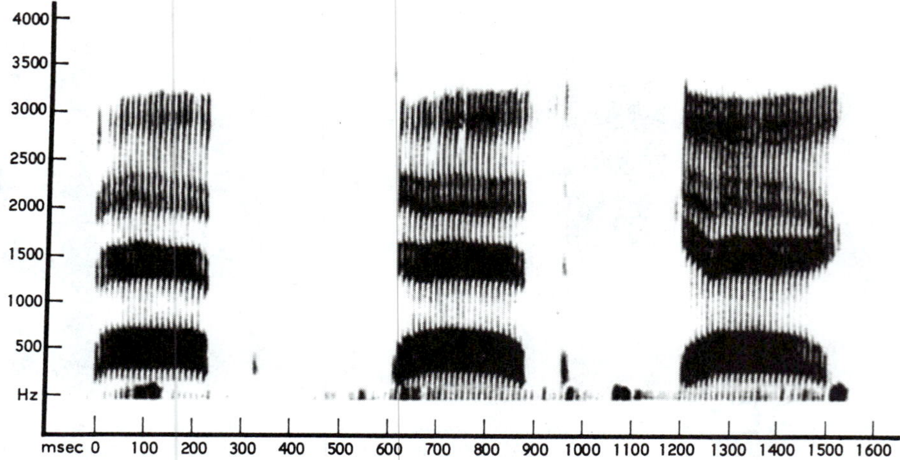

Figure 17.2 Spectrograms of the words *bab, dad, gag*

follow the predictable letter-sound correspondences of English: *have* does not rhyme with *nave* or *rave*, and *four* does not rhyme with *sour* or *glamour*. Contrastive sounds need to be assigned based on the letters in the word as well as other information about the word. After the correct phoneme is chosen, a system must look at the environment to see which allophone of the phoneme to choose. For example, to return to Figure 17.2, if the system were trying to pronounce *bab* /bæb/, the vowel /æ/ corresponding to the labial onset and labial offset would be chosen, since labials tend to lower adjacent formants.

A syntactic analysis of a sentence permits a system to identify words that might go together for phrasing. This is particularly important for noun compounds in English. As many as six nouns can be strung together, and the pronunciation of the compound can change the listener's interpretation of the meaning. For example, the phrase *Mississippi mud pie* could have two interpretations, depending on its structure. The most likely interpretation is shown in Figure 17.3, in which the mud pie is Mississippi style, as opposed to New York style.

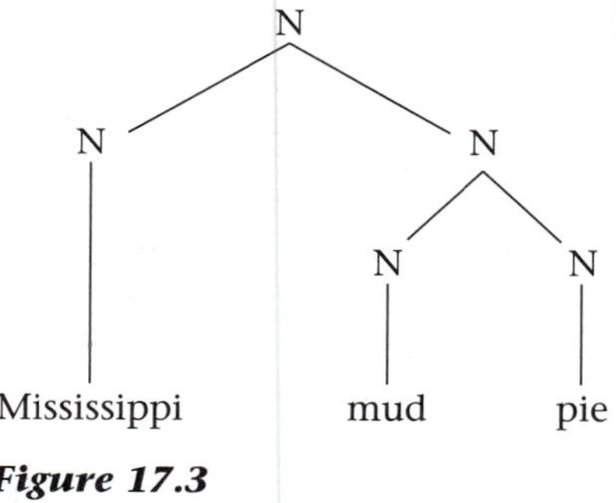

Figure 17.3

Alternatively, the pie could be made of mud from Mississippi (and not from Alabama), in which case the syntax of the phrase is different, as shown in Figure 17.4, and so is the pronunciation. Syntactic analysis can also determine the part of speech for noun/verb pairs that are spelled the same but pronounced differently, such as the verb *record* /rəkɔ́rd/ and the noun *record* /rɛ́kərd/.

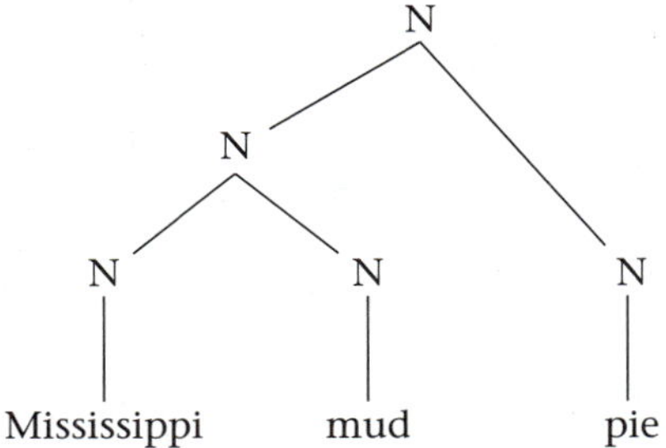

Figure 17.4

Also, parentheticals will be identified, as in these examples:

2)

Here are the apples, as you can see.

3)

He said, although I don't believe it, that he was a good driver.

Parentheticals are typically pronounced at a lower pitch and loudness. When pronounced with main phrase intonation, they are difficult to understand. Finally, a semantic analysis of a sentence, and of a text, gives an idea of focus and stress. These features must be translated into duration (length), pitch, and loudness in order for synthetic speech to sound completely natural.

Given advances in computer technology along with advances in electronics and acoustics, intelligible speech synthesis has already been achieved. However, anyone who has seen popular science fiction films knows that even now, synthetic speech still sounds synthetic. In addition to the syntactic and semantic issues raised here, a number of difficult problems remain, such as improving individual sounds and incorporating intonational variety into the rules to eliminate the droning quality of synthesized speech.

1.2 Speech recognition or speech analysis

As we have seen, speech consists of very complex waveforms changing rapidly across time and in subtle ways, which can affect the perception of a message. The task of **speech recognition** is to take these waveforms as input and decode them. This is exactly what we humans do when listening to speech. The waveform that reaches the ear is a continuous stream of sound; we segment this sound into words, phrases, and meaningful units so we can determine the meaning of an utterance. The task of a speech-recognition system is to teach a computer to understand speech, whether the system models human mechanisms or not.

Even though human beings have no trouble decoding speech waveforms, computers do. The problems are immense. First of all, as was shown in Chapter 2, Section 9, speech sounds are modified by adjacent sounds in natural speech. The faster and more informal the speech, the more sounds are merged and dropped. Guessing what sounds have been dropped based on faulty and limited input is an extremely difficult task. Knowledge of context, syntactic structure, and probabilities of occurrence is helpful, but it doesn't solve the problem.

Since decoding of continuous speech presents such problems, some systems impose the requirement that words be pronounced slowly and separated by a slight pause. The pause gives a clear cue that the word has ended, so a system has much less guesswork to do. Also, if the speech is said more slowly, fewer sounds will be dropped. In addition to the constraint of pronouncing words in isolation, limiting a system's vocabulary means that the recognition machine will have less guesswork to do. Finally, yet another way to reduce the guesswork is to require that an individual user "train" the system to be tailored to his or her voice alone. Anyone who is skilled at recognizing voices or accents can attest to the fact that no two people sound alike. The purpose of training a computer is to familiarize it with the unique and distinguishing features of the user's voice.

Another very difficult problem for speech recognition is what is called the **cocktail party effect**, such as that of being in a crowded room. Even though there is much noise from other people, from music, or from the street, humans manage to filter out the background noise and focus on a particular sound or conversation. Everyone has had the experience of not hearing a sound, such as a leaking faucet, until someone points out the sound. After that the annoying sound suddenly becomes impossible to ignore. Whatever mechanisms were used to suppress the noise of the faucet were deactivated when the sound was brought to the listener's attention. Computer recognition systems have difficulty distinguishing speech signals from background noise, so they perform poorly in noisy environments. Thus, another condition—a reasonably quiet environment—is often imposed on systems in order for them to function adequately.

Each of these constraints can be imposed to result in more reliable systems, but the overall research problem still remains: Why is it that humans are so adept at decoding speech, yet computers cannot be easily taught to do so?

2 COMPUTATIONAL MORPHOLOGY

Morphology is the study of the internal structure of words, covering such topics as affixation, compounding, and infixation (see Chapter 4). Most research in computational morphology arose as a by-product of developing **natural language processing systems**. Looking up words in a computational dictionary for these systems turned out to be more complicated than expected, precisely because of morphological processes that can conceal the base word. For example, if a dictionary has the word *book*, the word *books* will not necessarily be found by a simple search. Unless a system is explicitly told that *book* is related to *books* by a productive and regular rule of inflectional morphology, it will not be able to infer that the words are related. Thus, a program needs to include the rule of pluralization in English as well as other rules in order to recognize or generate the morphological permutations of words.

2.1 Morphological processes

Most morphologically conditioned changes in written English involve spelling, with some changes in stems. Examples are *stop/stopped, sing/sang,* and *tolerate/tolerant.* In general, morphological variations in English are not as opaque as in other languages. Some languages, such as German, have very productive compounding, whereas others have infixation and reduplication, or complex stem changes. Words altered by morphological processes cannot be easily recognized by a natural language processor unless they are properly related to their bases for lexical lookup.

Implementing morphological processes: method one

Broadly speaking, there are two approaches to computational morphology. Historically, the first was called a **stemming algorithm**, or **stripping algorithm**. An algorithm is a set of rules for solving a problem; the term was first used in mathematics to describe the rules for solving mathematical problems. Since algorithmic procedures usually involve a sequence of repeated steps, the term is naturally suited to computer programs in general, and to programs for computational linguistics in particular. In the stemming, or stripping, algorithm, affixes are recursively stripped off the beginnings and ends of words, and base forms are proposed. If the base form is found in the base-form dictionary, then the word is analyzable. Successful analyses provide information about the internal structure of the word as well as whatever other information is produced by the rule for a given affix, such as part-of-speech change, inherent semantic changes (e.g., *-ess* is +feminine), or other information (e.g., abstract, Latinate, singular, plural). Most of these systems are sensitive to constraints on affix ordering, such as those described in Chapter 4. Inflectional affixes occur outside of derivational affixes, and there may be some derivational affixes that occur outside of other derivational affixes.

Two different types of dictionaries are possible with the stemming approach: word-based and stem-based. A word-based system has a dictionary with words only. For word generation, all input to morphological rules must be well-formed words in order for all output to be well-formed words. For word analysis, all proposed stems will be words. The word-based system has proven to be very useful for projects that use large machine-readable dictionaries, since dictionaries list words, not stems. A machine-readable dictionary is a dictionary that appears in computer form, such as that available in a spelling checker or thesaurus. Machine-readable dictionaries have definitions, pronunciations, etymologies, and other information, not just the spelling or synonyms. (See Section 4 for more on machine-readable dictionaries.)

Table 17.1 presents an example of the type of analysis given by a word-based stemming system. To analyze *conceptualize* as an infinitive verb (V form(inf)), first *conceptual* must be analyzed as an adjective (A). This would be done by a rule stating

Table 17.1 Input word: conceptualize

Analysis	*Part of speech*	*Features*
concept	N	num(sing)
-ual	A	
-ize	V	form(inf)

that the suffix *-ize* can attach to certain adjectives to create verbs. *Conceptual* can be analyzed as an adjective if *concept* can first be analyzed as a singular noun (N num(sing)). This would be done by a rule for *-ual* stating that the suffix *-ual* can attach to certain nouns to create adjectives. *Concept* is stored in the dictionary as a singular noun, so this lexical lookup serves as the final step of the analysis. The analyses shown here actually result from recursive calls to the morphological rules. Each rule has conditions that restrict its operation. In this example, the *-ual* rule states that the base must be a singular noun. The condition for the *-ize* rule is that the base must be an adjective (but compare *terrorize* and *hospitalize*, where in each case the base, namely *terror* and *hospital*, is a noun). Since each condition is met, an analysis is possible. The word *conceptualize* is deemed a well-formed infinitive verb.

How would the system analyze a more complex form? Consider the analyses in Table 17.2 of the word *conceptualizations*, which is based on the previous example.

Table 17.2 Input word: conceptualizations

Analysis	*Part of speech*	*Features*
concept	N	num(sing)
-ual	A	
-ize	V	form(inf)
-ation	N	num(sing)
-s	N	num(plur)

In this example, the suffix *-ation* attaches to infinitival verbs. Notice that when *-ation* attaches to *conceptualize*, there is a spelling change. If no spelling rules were written, then the word **conceptualizeation* would be allowed by the system. Finally, the plural marker *-s* is attached at the outside of the noun. For the plural suffix *-s*, there is no change in the part of speech, only in the number feature of the word from singular to plural. Observe that these examples illustrate a word-based system. Both the dictionary entry, in this case *concept*, and the complex words *conceptualize* and *conceptualizations* are well-formed words of English.

How would this system differ if it were stem-based? For this example, the morpheme *-cept* might be listed in a stem dictionary, due to its presence in other words in English, such as *reception, conception, inception,* and *perception*. Since *-ceive* and *-cept* are related in a regular way, this relationship might also be given in the stem dictionary, or the words could be related by rule. Consider again *conceptualizations*, analyzed down to a stem in Table 17.3. In this example, the prefix *con-* attaches to *-cept*.

Table 17.3 Input word: conceptualizations

Analysis	*Part of speech*	*Features*
con-		
-cept	N	num(sing)
-ual	A	
-ize	V	form(inf)
-ation	N	num(sing)
-s	N	num(plur)

The point was made earlier that a word-based morphology system can use a regular dictionary as its lexicon, but no such convenience exists for a stem-based system. In order for stem-based morphology to get wide coverage, a large dictionary of stems is required. (More on this topic is found in Section 4 on computational lexicology later in this chapter.)

Implementing morphological processes: method two

The other common approach to computational morphology, the two-level approach, is fundamentally different from the stemming approach. This results in basic differences in computational properties. Both systems contain a lexicon, or dictionary, although two-level morphology requires a stem-based lexicon. Both systems have rules, but the rules are very different. In two-level morphology, the rules define correspondences between lexical and surface representations; they specify whether a correspondence is restricted to, required by, or prohibited by a particular environment. *Lexical* roughly translates to 'underlying', whereas *surface* usually means 'orthographic' but sometimes 'phonemic'. In Figure 17.5, the lexical representation of *try* followed by the +*s* is compared with a surface representation *tries*.

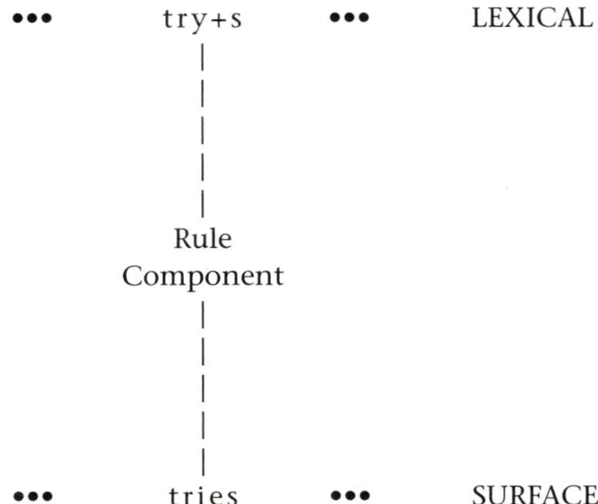

Figure 17.5

Lexical and surface representations are compared using a special kind of rule system called finite-state transducer. Simply put, the rules would decide whether the lexical *y* could correspond to the surface *i* based on information the rules have already seen. The rules that compare lexical and surface form move from left to right, so when a successful correspondence is made, the rule moves along. One of the claimed strengths of this method is that since the procedure moves from left to right, it accurately reflects the way that people process words. Since people hear and read English from left to right (i.e., the beginning of the word is encountered before the end), a system that incorporates this directionality might be an actual model of processing. Furthermore, since the two-level system processes from left to right for morphological analysis, it can easily be reversed and function from right to left for morphological generation. The primary drawback of the two-level system is that it requires a specialized stem dictionary, complete with restrictions on the stems so that not all affixes attach without restrictions. For example, a dictionary would need to include *-cept* or *-mit* (for *transmit, submit, permit,* and so on).

2.2 Some problems in computational morphology

Compounding is a particularly thorny problem since it tends to be so productive that compounds are often not listed in a dictionary. Until recently the word *bookworm*, for example, did not appear in *Merriam Webster's Collegiate Dictionary*. A good morphological analyzer should be able to analyze *bookworm* as shown in Table 17.4. However, what about a word like *accordion*?

Table 17.4 Input word: bookworm

Analysis	*Part of speech*	*Features*
book	N	num(sing)
worm	N	num(sing)

The analysis in Table 17.5 shows that *accordion* could be composed of the noun *accord* plus the noun *ion*. This is obviously incorrect because *accordion* is not a compound analogous to *bookworm*. Since *accordion* does not ever have this analysis, it might be marked as an exception to morphological decomposition.

Table 17.5 Input word: accordion

Analysis	*Part of speech*	*Features*
accord	N	num(sing)
ion	N	num(sing)

A related problem arises from overenthusiastic rule application. Table 17.6 presents an analysis of *really*. Here *really* is analyzed as [*re-* [*ally-* $_{\text{verb}}$]$_{\text{verb}}$], meaning 'to ally oneself with someone again'. This analysis is correct, although highly improbable. Cases like that of *re-* in *really* bring up a difficult issue. Should a word like *really* be specially marked in the dictionary as a nonanalyzable word, an exception to the rules that would apply to regular formations like *reapply, redo,* and *reduplicate*? Or should the rules be allowed to apply freely? What about a word like *resent*, which could either be [*re-*[*sent*$_{\text{verb}}$]$_{\text{verb}}$], as in *She didn't get my letter, so I resent it,* or [*resent*$_{\text{verb}}$], as in *Did he resent that nasty comment*? The spelling of this word is truly ambiguous, so a decision about its analyzability requires knowledge of syntactic and semantic

Table 17.6 Input word: really

Analysis	*Part of speech*	*Features*
re-		
ally	V	form(inf)

features in the sentence and context. Usually the decision is driven by practical concerns. A system that is designed to implement a theory but that does not need to perform well on a task that applies the theory would probably allow the rules to apply freely. A system that needs to perform accurately on large texts would probably mark *really* and *resent* as nonanalyzable words, even though strictly speaking they are not.

3 COMPUTATIONAL SYNTAX

Research in computational syntax arose from two sources. One was the practical motivation resulting from attempts to build working systems to analyze and generate language. Some of these systems, such as machine translation and question-answering systems, are discussed in Section 6. The other motivation was a desire on the part of theoretical linguists to use the computer as a tool to demonstrate that a particular theory is internally consistent. In this case, less value was given to efficiency or broad coverage, since this was not the goal. The emphasis was instead on theory testing and on formal issues in natural language analysis. Recently, builders of practical systems have taken greater advantage of theoretical insights, and linguistic theoreticians have paid more attention to practical problems. This has also been the case in research on syntactic parsing, although this is a fairly new friendship.

3.1 Natural language analysis

Parsers and grammars

Chapter 5 showed how sentences can be analyzed by rules into substructures such as noun phrases, verb phrases, prepositional phrases, and so on, as shown in Figure 17.6. Given a system of rules, an analyzer will be able to break up and organize a sentence into its substructures. A grammar can be viewed as the set of rules that define a language. These rules can be of different types, which accordingly give them different

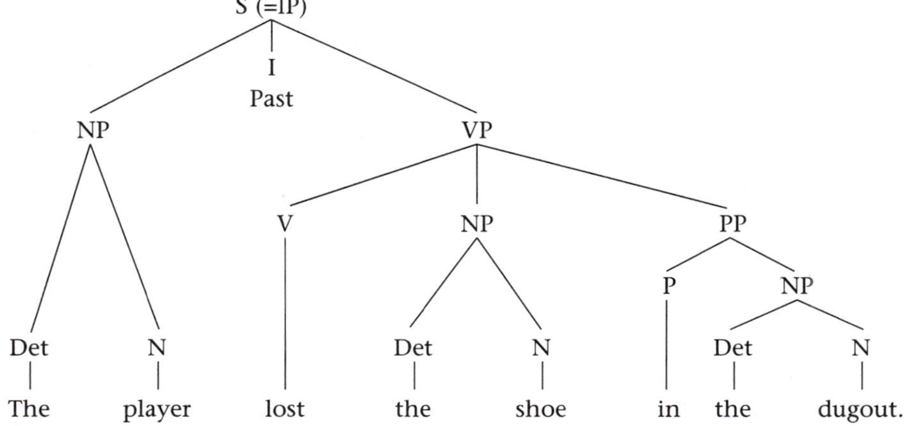

Figure 17.6 A syntactic analysis done by a parser

properties. A **parser** is the machine or engine that is responsible for applying these rules. A parser can have different strategies for applying rules. Chapter 5 showed how the rules for sentence structure differ among languages. These differences are reflected in the grammars of these languages, although the parser that drives the grammars can remain constant. (Recall the discussion of the role of parsers in language processing in Chapter 12.)

Determinism versus nondeterminism

Any time a syntactic parser can produce more than one analysis of an input sentence, the problem of backtracking is raised. For example, if the beginning of the sentence in Figure 17.7 is read word by word, there is more than one possible ending.

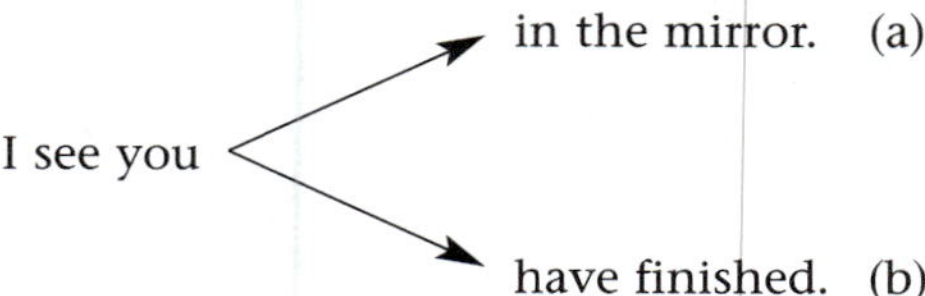

Figure 17.7

In choice (a), "I see you in the mirror," the word *you* is the object of the main verb *see.* For (b), "I see you have finished," the word *that* has been left out, as is permitted in English, so the word *you* is the subject of the clause *you have finished.* If the parser follows path (a), and if that path turns out to be the wrong one, how can the situation be rectified to get the right analysis? Or can choices be controlled so that a parser never has to undergo the time-consuming task of going back and starting over? This problem for computational analyzers is the very problem that humans have. If a sentence leads to a false path, it is called a garden path sentence, as discussed in Chapter 12.

Nondeterministic parsing may refer to going back or backtracking if an initial analysis turns out to be incorrect. It may also mean following multiple paths in parallel, meaning that both analyses are built at the same time but on separate channels. By contrast, **deterministic parsing** means that the parser has to stick to the path it has chosen. There have been many proposals about controlling the backtracking of parsers. The problem is a serious one since the number of alternatives increases as the coverage of a system increases. The result is that as an analyzer improves, it becomes more and more cumbersome because it is increasingly presented with more and more options.

Top-down versus bottom-up parsing

Consider the following phrase structure rules for English (introduced in Chapter 5):

4)

a. S (=IP) → NP I VP
b. NP → (Det) (AP) N (PP)
c. VP → V (NP) (PP)
d. PP → P NP

There are two ways to build an analysis of a sentence using just these rules. This section illustrates the principles of what are called **top-down parsing** and **bottom-up parsing**. Working systems may not be built to function exactly like this, but the principles are the same.

In addition to the rules in *4*, we also need to give some lexical items, or **terminal nodes**, for each category of nonterminal nodes.

5)

N	→	Larry
I	→	past
V	→	sat
P	→	on
Det	→	the
N	→	grass

Generally speaking, a nonterminal is not a word in the language. Rather, it is a category or a phrase, such as N or NP. A terminal can be thought of as a word (although sometimes a terminal is a part of a word or several words). In top-down parsing, the analyzer always starts with the topmost node, in this case S, and finds a way to expand it. The only rule in example *4* for S (=IP) is shown in Figure 17.8. The next

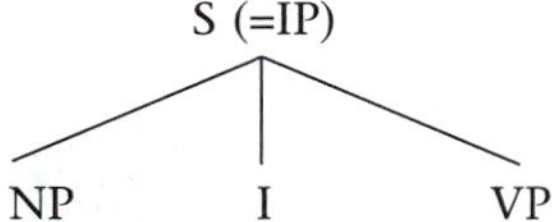

Figure 17.8 Top-down parsing: first step starts with S

rules to apply are the NP expansion rule and the VP expansion rule. Both NP and VP are **nonterminal nodes**. Although N is a nonterminal, it has no expansions, so we move right along to the VP rule (results are shown in Figure 17.9). If the subject of the sentence had been *the batter*, then the NP would have been expanded to Det and N. This process continues until no more expansions could apply, and until all the lexical items or words in *5* occur in the correct position to match the input sentence *Larry sat on the grass*. Top-down parsers suggest a hypothesis that a proposed structure is correct until proven otherwise.

Figure 17.9

In contrast, bottom-up parsers take the terminals (words) of a sentence one by one, replace the terminals with proposed nonterminal or category labels, and then reduce the strings of categories to permissible structures. For the same example, the analysis would be built as follows: first the word *Larry* would be assigned to the category N; then *sat* would be assigned to V, and so on. The partial analysis up to this point is shown in Figure 17.10. None of the rules in *4* permits the combination of N

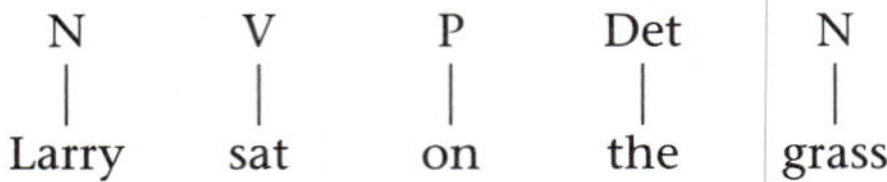

Figure 17.10

and V; none permits V and P nor P and Det to combine. But the NP rule does combine Det and N to build up a structure, as shown in Figure 17.11. This continues until the structure of a sentence is built. It has been proposed that the building of the structure from the **terminal nodes** up to the topmost S (=IP) node from left to right reflects the way human beings process sentences more accurately than does the top-down approach, but this is a controversial issue.

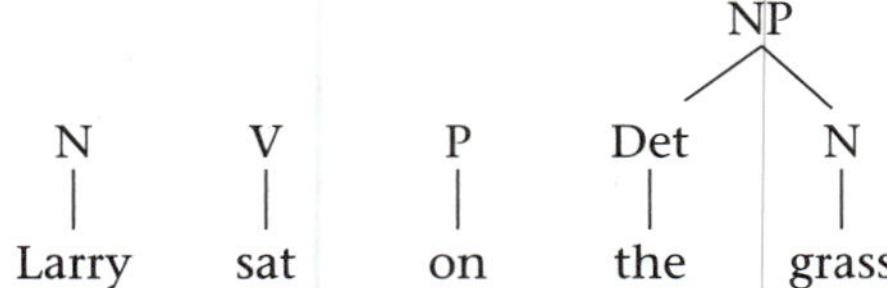

Figure 17.11

Generative capacity

The term *generative* in this context refers to formal properties of grammars as mathematical systems. It does not refer to language generation, which is discussed in Section 3.2. Recall that a grammar consists of a set of rules that describe a language. Assume also some finite set of symbols, V, to be the vocabulary of a language. For English, examples of V would be:

6)

V_L = [*player, shoe, child, lost, a* . . .]

In the vocabulary V are other symbols and categories, such as N and Det. Formally, a language L over V is a finite set of strings of symbols taken from V. Informally, a language consists of items from the vocabulary. Of course, a sentence is more than just a string of words, as shown in Chapter 5. Furthermore, the set of strings is greater than the set of well-formed sentences, as examples *7* through *9* show. Even though the vocabulary V may be a finite list, the language L may be finite or infinite. This is because of recursion, a very powerful property of natural languages. (Chapter 5, Section 2.3 contains a discussion of recursive rules.) The application of a finite number of recursive rules results in languages that can contain an infinite number of well-formed strings.

The following sentences consist of vocabulary from the set in *6*. While *7* is a well-formed sentence in English, *8* and *9* are not.

7)

A child lost a shoe.

8)

*child shoe a.

9)

*Lost a shoe a child.

Although *9* is not in the language L for English, it could be found in the language L for Spanish, given the same vocabulary.

10)

Perdió un zapato un niño.
lost a shoe a child

The grammar of English would give a correct description of *7*, but not *8* or *9*. On the other hand, the grammar of Spanish would allow both *7* and *9*, but not *8*. The goal of an implemented grammar is exactly the same. An **implementation** is simply a practical system. The grammar rules are programmed into a computer, and the computer program then decides if the string is permitted in the language. If the string is permitted, it then has the task of giving the sentence the correct description.

Natural languages (as opposed to computer languages) are highly complex, since there are many ambiguities and subtleties, so discovering the correct grammar for a given language is an extremely difficult task. The complexity and subtlety of natural languages continue to present a challenge to linguists. There are many competing theories of what the "correct" grammar of natural languages will be like. Even the grammar for English, a very well-studied natural language, is not at all well understood. One issue that all theories agree on, however, is that a grammar should have certain properties. Grammars should give a correct description of the following:

A. The strings of a language L

B. The structures corresponding to the strings in L

Property A is called **weak generative capacity**. Property B is called **strong generative capacity**.

To explain, Figure 17.6 shows an analysis in which the first two words—*the* and *player*—are joined into a noun phrase (NP). I is dominated by S (=IP). The verb phrase (VP) is described by the grammar as consisting of a verb (V), followed by a noun phrase (NP), followed by a prepositional phrase (PP). These three constituents are immediately dominated by the VP node. What if a different grammar were to claim a different structure for this sentence? Consider the structure in Figure 17.12. This analysis makes different claims about the structure of the sentence, but the actual string of words stays the same. The tree in Figure 17.12 has two levels of verb phrase. One is VP^1, which dominates everything in the predicate of the sentence

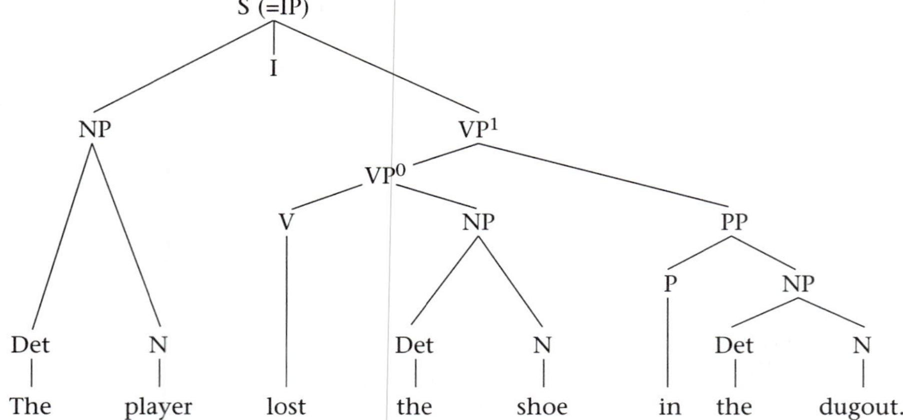

Figure 17.12

(everything in the sentence except the subject and I). The other is VP⁰, which dominates only the main verb and the direct object. The grammar generating the structure in Figure 17.12 differs in strong generative capacity from the grammar for Figure 17.6 (on p. 675). However, both grammars may have the same weak generative capacity since they both have the ability to describe the string *The player lost the shoe in the dugout.*

The role of syntax and semantics

The preceding section dealt with syntactic analyzers, but it is important to note that the division between what should be handled by the syntactic component of a system and what is properly in the semantic component is a matter of great debate. For example, some systems might claim that selection of prepositions by verbs, often considered a syntactic property, is actually dependent on the semantic category of the verb. For example, not all verbs can take the instrumental, as in the reading of *11* in which the bone was used to reward the dog.

11)

He rewarded the dog with a bone.

If a different VP is substituted for *rewarded the dog,* would the sentence be semantically or syntactically ill-formed?

12)

*He told his story with a bone.

Some systems assume that a syntactic analysis precedes a semantic one, and that the semantics should be applied to the output of syntactic analyses. This is the position of the earliest transformational models, which were incorporated into many computational systems. Some systems perform syntactic and semantic analyses hand-in-hand. Other systems ignore the syntactic, viewing it as a second-step derivative from semantic analyses.

3.2 Natural language generation

What is generation?

To utter a sentence, a speaker must first decide on goals, then plan the information to be included, and finally express that information in a sentence of his or her language. The language generation problem is often viewed as the reverse of the language analysis problem, but this is not accurate. In the same way, the generation of speech, discussed in Section 6, is in no way simply the reverse of speech recognition. Certain problems are the same, but many are not. In language analysis, the linguist is given a set of data (i.e., strings of the language) with which to work. For language generation, the linguist has ideas and plans that need to be turned into language. A language generator must be able to make decisions about the content of the text, about issues of discourse structure, and about cohesion of the sentences and paragraphs. In contrast, a language analyzer might be invoked to make proposals about discourse and content, but the raw material on which guesses are based is already there. For the language generator, only concepts and ideas are available to work with. Choices of words (lexical items) and syntactic structures are part of decisions to be made in building a text.

As with syntactic analyzers, there are two approaches to generation: top-down and bottom-up. In the top-down approach, a very high-level structure of the output text is determined, along with very abstract expressions of meaning and goals. Then lower levels are filled in progressively. Subsections are determined, and examples of the verbs with their subjects and objects, if any, are proposed. This is refined until the prefinal stage, when lexical items are chosen from the dictionary. After all sentences have been decided on and all lexical items have been inserted, there is a component to "smooth" and provide low-level coherence to the text. This component makes sure that pronouns are used correctly, for example, and that connecting phrases such as *in the preceding paragraph* or *on the other hand* are used correctly. In contrast, the bottom-up approach builds sentences from complex lexical items: words to achieve the goals are hypothesized, sentences are composed, and finally high-level paragraph and text coherence principles are applied.

The generation lexicon

The **lexicon** is just one link in many difficult steps involved in generating natural and cohesive text for an underlying set of goals and plans. Imagine that you have determined an underlying message, plan, or goal. In order to figure out how to translate the underlying message into some actual words in a language, your generation system will have to figure out such matters as what verbs to pick and how to pick the subjects and objects, if any, for those verbs.

Suppose you want to express how fast time is going by in your life. You might use the verb *elapse*. *Elapse* is said to be a one-place predicate or a one-place verb. It is intransitive, so it takes just one argument—the subject. (The term *argument* here refers to grammatical dependents of a verb.) If you want to talk about baseball, you need to describe the action. You might use the verb *hit*. *Hit* is transitive; it takes two arguments. *Hit* is also often used with an instrumental—a phrase that tells what the subject hit with, as in *with a bat*. In this case, *hit* can take three arguments. Finally, a verb like *give* takes an agent, theme, and goal, and those three arguments can be expressed as a subject, object, and indirect object, indicated by *to*, as in *13*. Alternatively, *give* can undergo what is called dative movement, as in *14*, in which case the indirect object *dog* appears next to the verb and is not preceded by the preposition *to*.

13)

He gave a stick to the dog.

14)

He gave the dog a stick.

Often verbs with very close meanings take different numbers of arguments and in different orders. For example, *give* can also mean *donate*, but *donate* does not permit the same alternations as *give*.

15)

He donated a stick to the dog.

16)

*He donated the dog a stick.

A system must be capable of deciding what the meaning to be conveyed is, and then it must be capable of choosing very similar words to express that meaning. The lexicon or dictionary must supply items to instantiate the link between meaning and words.

The design and content of the generation lexicon is one of the most difficult areas in language generation. The lexicon needs to contain many different types of information, such as syntactic facts about verbs, facts about usage and focus, and facts about types of modifiers. Building lexicons for generation is one of the goals of computational lexicology, as discussed in the following section.

4 COMPUTATIONAL LEXICOLOGY

Since phrases, sentences, and paragraphs are composed of words, computer systems need to contain detailed information about words. The section on morphology dealt with the structure and analyses of word forms, but there is more to know about words than this, and this is the purview of **computational lexicology**.

Computational linguists are realizing that an analyzer or generator is only as good as its dictionary or lexicon. The lexicon is the repository of whatever information about words a particular system needs. The individual words in the lexicon are called lexical items. Chapter 5, Section 2, showed how lexical insertion occurs in syntactic structure. For example, in order for a bare structure such as Figure 17.13 to be "filled

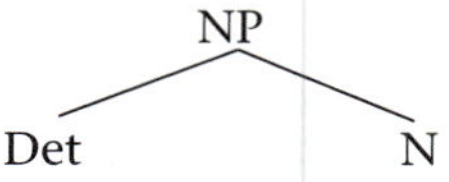

Figure 17.13

out" with real words, a program would need to have a match between a word marked Det (determiner) in the lexicon and the slot in the tree requiring a Det. The same goes for any part of speech, such as noun, verb, or adjective. Given the items in *5*, a valid match for Figure 17.13 would be Figure 17.14. Figure 17.15 would not be a valid match. Notice that the preposition *on* occurs under the determiner node, and the verb *sat* occurs under the noun node. At the very least, the condition of matching part of speech has to be met.

Figure 17.14 ***Figure 17.15***

A computer program would need to know more than just part of speech to analyze or generate a sentence correctly. Subcategorization—that is, the number of arguments a verb can take—must be considered (see Chapter 5, Section 2). Knowledge of thematic roles, such as agent, patient, and goal, is also needed (see Chapter 6, Section 3.3). A syntactic analyzer would also need to know what kinds of complements a verb can take (see Chapter 5).

17)

I decided to go.

18)

*I decided him to go.

19)

*I persuaded to go.

20)

I persuaded him to go.

The verb *decide* can take the infinitive *to go* as in *17*, but it cannot take an NP object and then the infinitive, as in *18*. The verb *persuade* is the opposite. It cannot take the infinitive *to go* as in *19*, but it must have an NP object before the infinitive, as in *20*.

The lexicon needs to know about the kinds of structures in which words can appear, about the semantics of surrounding words, and about the style of the text. For example, the sentence in *21* is strange in meaning, but the structure is fine.

21)

I broke the concept.

The verb *break* is transitive and so can take an object; the problem here is the type of noun. Only concrete objects are breakable unless the meaning is metaphorical, as in *The disease broke his will to live.* (See Chapter 6 for more discussion of semantics.)

What does a computational lexicon look like? So far the list of information includes:

22)

Lexical Entry
1. Part of speech
2. Sense number
3. Subcategorization
4. Semantic properties

Keeping in mind that a computational lexicon has to contain as much information as possible in order to correctly analyze and generate phrases, sentences, and text, the following are also needed:

22) (continued)

5. Pronunciation
6. Context and style
7. Etymology
8. Usage (e.g., taboos)
9. Spelling (including abbreviations)

The task of collecting all the important information for every existing word in the English language is overwhelming. In addition, given that the kind of information needed cannot be found in conventional dictionaries, how are computational lexicons built? There are several approaches. One is to hand-build a lexicon, specifying only those features that a given system needs and using only the lexical items that are most likely to occur. For example, assume that an analyzer is reading the *Wall Street Journal,* and assume that the sentence to be analyzed is *His stock is high.* If the analyzer is to assign a meaning to this sentence, it has to know at least the information below.

Word: *stock*^{1}

1. Part of speech: noun
2. Semantic properties: [+concrete], . . .
3. Context: financial

In just this usage, there is no reason to know about any other meanings of *stock*, as in *vegetable stock*. The lexical entry for this other sense would include the information below.

Word: *stock*^{2}

1. Part of speech: noun
2. Semantic properties: [+concrete], . . .
3. Context: food

Most words have many different senses, and sometimes the different senses have very different grammatical behavior. If a new word with a new feature is added to the lexicon, the dictionary builder will have to go back through the lexicon and modify every word to match the new expanded word. When *stock*^{2} was added to the dictionary, new features had to be added, namely that *stock*^{1} does not have a context "food" and that *stock*^{2} does not have a context "financial." One of the major problems in building computational dictionaries is extensibility. The problem is how to add new information and modify old information without starting over each time.

Another option in building large lexicons is to use two resources: the power of the computer and the data of machine-readable dictionaries. A **machine-readable dictionary (MRD)** is a conventional dictionary, but it is in machine-readable form (i.e., on the computer) rather than on the bookshelf. Many examples of dictionaries can be found on the Internet at Web sites where people often go for clarification or translation. MRDs are useful in building large lexicons because the computer can be used to examine and analyze automatically information that has already been organized by lexicographers, the writers of dictionaries. Unfortunately, the type of information that is needed by a computational dictionary is not always easy to find in a conventional dictionary. However, with some clever approaches to exploiting the hidden information in conventional MRDs, it appears that many important facts can be pulled out and put into a computational lexicon.

For example, the knowledge that a word has a sense that is [+human] is needed in a computational lexicon for both syntactic and semantic reasons. The tenth edition of *Merriam-Webster's Collegiate Dictionary*, which has about seventy thousand headwords, has just over a thousand nouns that are defined in terms of the word *person*. Some examples are given below:

accessory

a *person* not actually or constructively present but contributing as an assistant or instigator to the commission of an offense—called also accessory before the fact

acquaintance

a *person* whom one knows but who is not a particularly close friend

intellectual

a very intelligent or intellectual *person*

scatterbrain

a giddy, heedless *person*: FLIBBERTIGIBBET

unbeliever

one that does not believe: an incredulous *person*: DOUBTER, SKEPTIC

Notice that each word can have other senses. *Accessory*, for example, can mean an object or device that is not essential but that enhances the main object. Programs can be written to extract these words. The headwords are then marked [+human], and synonyms such as *flibbertigibbet, doubter,* and *skeptic* can also be marked [+human] in one sense.

Although this approach is appealing, caution is in order. In the first place, lexicographers are people, and dictionaries are huge undertakings written by many different contributors. Therefore, there is less internal consistency than would be ideal. Finally, and most seriously, there is the problem that most words have more than one sense. Keeping track of which senses have which features is not an easy task. Furthermore, the decision on what is a sense is also not clear-cut. The problem of extensibility enters into play again. Even with all these restrictions, however, the use of machine-readable dictionaries as a resource for constructing large lexicons has been widespread.

Another approach to building large lexicons for natural language analysis and generation is **corpus analysis**. The larger the corpus, or text, the more useful it is, since the chances of covering the language as it is actually used increase. In addition to size, a good corpus should include a wide variety of types of writing, such as newspapers, textbooks, popular writing, fiction, and technical material. As an example of the way large corpora (the plural of *corpus*) are useful, consider the verb of movement *flounce*. The definitions given for the verb in the tenth edition of *Merriam-Webster's Collegiate Dictionary* are:

flounce[1]

to move with exaggerated jerky or bouncy motions
to go with sudden determination

These definitions tell nothing about likely subjects. Looking at corpus data will yield this information. From a large corpus, about twenty occurrences of the verb *flounce* were extracted. Thirteen had subjects that were female, as in examples *23* and *24*.

23)

Carol flounced out to the kitchen for an apron.

24)

She flounced off with a following of hens behind her.

Four had subjects that were clothing:

25)

The white cashmere dressing-gown flounced around her.

One had horses as the subject, and the others had pronouns as subjects. The point is that, given a good parser, it would be possible to extract automatically all the subjects of a given verb, and then to look for properties of those subjects. For *flounce*, that information would appear in the lexicon as:

Word: *flounce*[1]

1. Part of speech: Verb
2. Subcategorization: Intransitive
3. Semantic properties: Female human subject

Word: *flounce*[2]

1. Part of speech: Verb
2. Subcategorization: Intransitive
3. Semantic properties: Clothing subject

Using computers to extract linguistically useful information from dictionaries and texts for the purpose of constructing large lexicons is a growing field within computational linguistics. The use of statistical methods to analyze language has seen great advances in recent years, giving promise to solving the difficult but fundamental problem of building computational lexicons out of already existing resources. At this point, clever programs give large and comprehensive lists of words with a potential characteristic, but human judgments are still necessary. If the computer is viewed as a tool to be used in collecting lists of words, then the endeavor is successful. If the goal is to view the computer as the only tool, and to eliminate the human judge, then computational lexicon builders have a long way to go.

5 COMPUTATIONAL SEMANTICS

So far in this chapter, we have focused on structure—the structure of sentences and words. However, in order to understand what a word, sentence, or text means, a computer program has to know the semantics of words, sentences, and text. This section treats briefly some of the semantic representations and processes that have been proposed in computational linguistics.

Semantic issues were touched on in the preceding section. The lexical item contains a field for semantic information, such as what kind of semantic features a verb requires for its subject or which thematic roles a verb requires or permits. The semantic fields for the two senses of *flounce* are:

Word: *flounce*^{1}

Semantic restrictions: Female human subject

Word: *flounce*^{2}

Semantic restrictions: Clothing subject

Although the semantics of words is an important component of any language system, there is yet a broader issue: the semantics of sentences and paragraphs.

Broadly speaking, two approaches to semantics and language analysis have been proposed: syntactically based systems and semantically based systems. Considering for the moment the analysis of sentences, in the first approach the sentence is assigned a syntactic analysis, much in the way outlined in Chapter 5 and earlier in this chapter. A semantic representation is built after the syntactic analysis is performed (see Figure 17.16). The problems arise in getting from one representation to

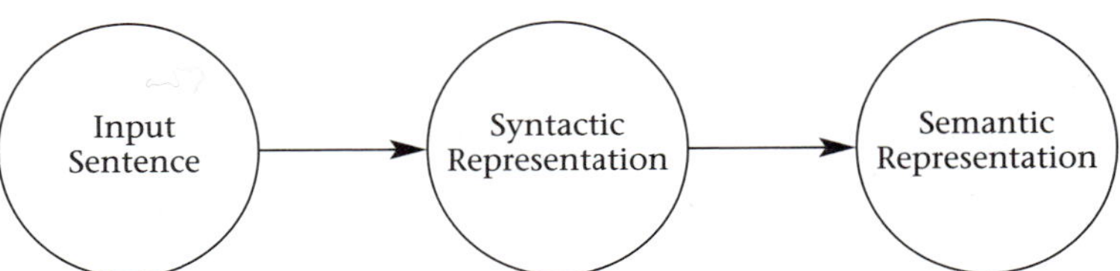

Figure 17.16 Syntactically based systems

the other. This is sometimes called the mapping problem. However, in the semantically based system, first a semantic representation is built. Sometimes there is no syntactic analysis at all (see Figure 17.17).

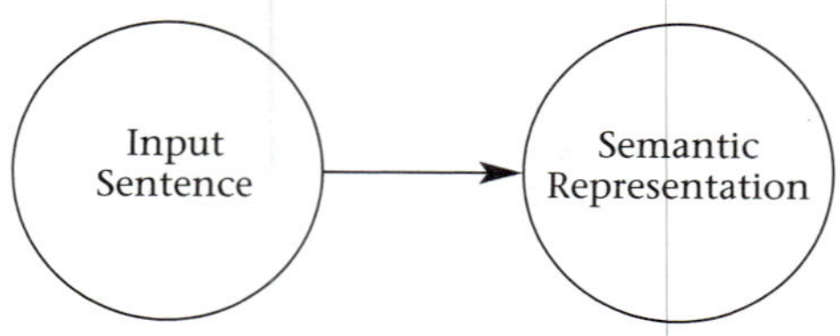

Figure 17.17 Semantically based systems

Consider a response to the question *Who got the coffee today?*

26)

The new student went.

A syntactic analysis of the sentence would show that *the new student* is the first NP directly dominated by S (=IP) (see Figure 17.18). From there, the parser might guess that the subject is *the new student*. This is often true in English, although it is not always the case.

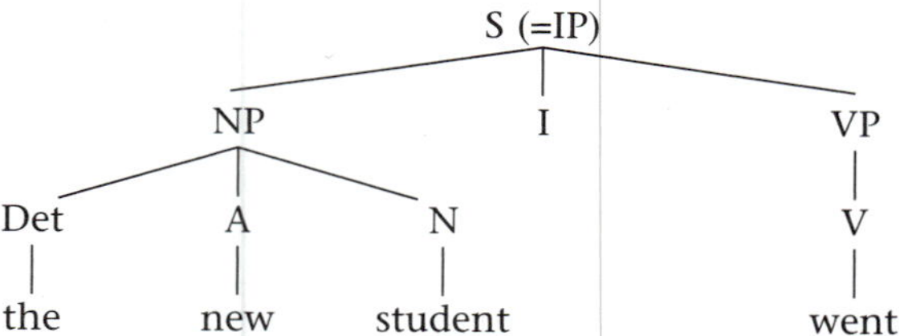

Figure 17.18

Still, nothing is said about the fact that the subject is the actor (i.e., the one who performs the action) with a verb like *go*. Compare this to the intransitive version of the verb *open*.

27)

The door opened.

In this case, the subject *door* is not performing an action; something or someone opened the door. A syntactically based system obtains this knowledge about a sentence after a structure is built.

In contrast, a semantically based system builds a semantic representation first. For sentence *26*, it might look something like the one in Figure 17.19.

Go — Actor
NP
went the new student

Figure 17.19

The word order is not represented, but the underlying semantic information is expressed. The semantic representation of related sentences might be the same.

28)

It was the new student who went.

The mapping into the various syntactic forms of what is basically the same sentence occurs after the semantic representation is decided on. Semantically based systems have been used for text and discourse analysis, such as for understanding stories.

Both approaches still need to accomplish the same goal, namely that of assigning word meaning, sentence meaning, and text meaning. The problem of semantic representation will not be covered here. However, it must be mentioned that determining matters like reference, as in *29*, and scope, as in *30* through *32*, are part of what needs to be achieved.

29)

Chris wants to marry an Australian.

30)

Pregnant women and children get out first.

31)

Ripe apples and peaches make a good fruit salad.

32)

Every person speaks two languages.

For *29*, is this a specific Australian, or would any Australian do? For *30*, what is the scope of *pregnant*? Is it pregnant women and pregnant children? This is unlikely. But in *31*, a sentence that should be interpreted exactly as its syntactic twin *30*, the likely interpretation is exactly the opposite—that is, *ripe apples and ripe peaches*. Finally, in *32*, does every person speak the same two languages or a different two languages?

5.1 Pragmatics

Pragmatics is the study of how language is used in communication. Consider the following telephone conversation. (See Chapter 6, Section 4.)

33)

Caller: Is George at home?
Answer: Yes.

This dialogue is amusing because the answerer has broken some basic conversational principles. The caller is not really asking the literal question *Is George at home?* although the semantic analysis of the sentence would indicate that this is a request for information about whether or not George is at home. The syntactic form of the question requires the answers yes or no, but nothing else. The dialogue in *34* does not have the amusing quality of *33*.

34)

Caller: Are you tired?
Answer: Yes.

Conversational principles (see Chapter 6) require that an answer be as informative as possible. This is not the case in *33*, which violates the maxim of quantity. Other examples of conversational principles are illustrated in *35* and *36*.

35)

Sue got on the horse and rode into the sunset.

36)

Sue rode into the sunset and got on the horse.

Why is *36* strange? The coordinating conjunction *and* should just be a simple joining of two like parts. For example, the nouns from *31* could be reversed with no strange result (the scope problem remains unsolved, however):

37)

Ripe peaches and apples make a good fruit salad.

The reason for the problem in *36* is that the word *and* is often given a temporal interpretation. That is, the first sentence usually occurs before the second one in time. This may not be part of the meaning of *and* but rather a matter of how it is used.

Whether pragmatics is a subfield of semantics is controversial, but there is no disagreement over the fact that knowledge of pragmatic principles is necessary to understanding and generating language.

6 PRACTICAL APPLICATIONS OF COMPUTATIONAL LINGUISTICS

The previous sections of this chapter have shown how the use of computers has forced linguists to formulate rigorous statements of theory and facts, because all of the implicit knowledge that humans have about language has to be made explicit. Theories become testable in a concrete way. Implementations of practical systems tend to force researchers (and students) to understand a particular language process in very detailed terms. Since related skills are needed both for linguistic analysis and for programming, the field of computational linguistics has flourished. This section discusses some specific types of computer systems that involve using linguistically sophisticated programs.

An **application** can be defined as the use to which a program or set of programs is put—for example, a payroll application, an airline reservation application, or a word-processing application. Most early applications in computational linguistics fell into three categories: indexing and concordances, machine translation, and information retrieval. Other applications include speech synthesis and recognition, summarization, and query systems for databases.

6.1 INDEXING AND CONCORDANCES

Indexing means finding, identifying, and usually counting all occurrences of a certain word in large texts. This application of computers to language study does exactly what computers are best at doing: locating a word, recording the location by line or sentence number, and counting how many times it appears. The examples of the use of the word *flounce* in the lexicology section were extracted from text using an indexing program. The program searched text on the computer to find any occurrence of the string *flounce, flouncing, flounced,* or *flounces*. When the string was found, the computer program took out the sentence and saved it in a separate file. A tally was kept of each time a targeted word was found.

A **concordance** tells which words occur near other words. Concordance and indexing programs are used widely in literary analysis. Some authors seem to favor using certain words in the context of other words. Concordance programs can find these relationships. A concordance program could tell, for example, how many times the word *she* occurred next to *flounce*.

Perhaps the most widely used word count was performed by Henry Kucera and Nelson Francis in 1962 on a corpus of one million words. The corpus is referred to as the Brown corpus, since the work was completed at Brown University. Kucera and Francis took fifteen different texts and wrote a program to count the number of times each word appeared. The ten most frequent words of English from this study are:

the	69,971
of	36,411
and	28,852
to	26,149
a	23,237
in	21,341
that	10,595
is	10,099
was	9,816
he	9,543

The numbers after the words indicate how many times they appeared in the one-million-word corpus. Word-frequency lists derived from these data have been useful to psycholinguists who need to pay attention to frequency when designing experiments.

These early applications are still very useful, but they are not linguistic in nature. They used the power of the computer to count and categorize words, so the results were of use to the linguist, but they did not rely on any linguistic knowledge. For example, to find *flounce*, the related words *flounced, flounces,* and *flouncing* also had to be looked for. Early systems were not endowed with morphological knowledge, so they could look only for the exact string given. The program could not figure out that *flounce* and *flouncing* were related forms. Furthermore, all occurrences of the strings *flounce, flounces,* and so on were pulled out, without regard to part of speech. Since the goal was to look at subjects of verbs, it was necessary to distinguish between the verb *flounce* and the noun *flounce,* as in *They always flounce out* and *The chair had a lacy flounce around the bottom*. Notice the implications of this: two of the top ten most frequent words are forms of the verb *be,* but since the system counted only strings, the forms *is* and *was* were counted separately. The inability of early systems to relate words had other problems. Note the following example:

minute	53
min	5
min.	1
min,	1

The above are probably all variations of the word *minute,* although this would have to be verified by checking the original text. The count of *minute* is 53, but it should really be 60. Note, however, that there is a possible complication: some of the occurrences of *minute* may be examples of the noun *minute* meaning 'memorandum' rather than '60 seconds', or of the unrelated, differently pronounced adjective *minute* [majnút] meaning 'very small'; they could also be an abbreviation of *minister, ministry, minimum,* or *minim* (a fluid measure roughly equivalent to a drop). We cannot be sure.

Most current concordance and indexing programs have solved some of the easier problems such as abbreviations and acronyms. For example, the abbreviation *CIA* could stand for either Central Intelligence Agency or Culinary Institute of America. Without adequate context to tell which organization the abbreviation refers to, it would be difficult for a computational linguistic system to make a reliable guess. Much larger bodies of text are now being used to overcome some of the problems of sparse and limited data, and more sophisticated statistical techniques are being employed. Yet most of the harder problems still remain. First of all, morphological knowledge is needed in order to relate various forms of the same word to just one base word. Second, syntactic knowledge is needed in order to establish the part of speech of the word in a sentence and in order to determine the arguments of the verb, such as subject and object. Finally, semantic knowledge is needed to know the thematic roles of the arguments and to know which meaning of a word is intended.

6.2 Information accessing and retrieval

The development of Internet browsers has enabled the creation of a growing body of text, image, sound, and video that can easily be searched. Furthermore, there are dozens of freely available search systems or engines for roaming through titles, articles, captions, and text. However, anyone who has ever tried to search for articles on a particular topic has had the frustrating experience of having to wade through masses of irrelevant material to find what was wanted. For example, when the word *morphology* was searched for in a library index of book titles, the following titles were among the results:

Principles of Polymer Morphology
Image Analysis and Mathematical Morphology
Drainage Basin Morphology
French Morphology

If a linguistically sophisticated program had been used to retrieve these titles, it is likely that they would have been divided according to the semantic subject field. Thus a chemist would not get titles on French, just as a linguist would not get titles on chemistry.

What linguistic expertise could text-retrieval systems use? Again, as with indexing and concordance, the three critical subareas are computational morphology, syntax, and semantics. For example, someone wanting to know about the theory of light might want to find all references to the word *light* in an encyclopedia. Searching for the string *light* anywhere in the text might yield *lightning, enlightenment,* and *lighthearted,* but also *delight* and *candlelight.* On the other hand, if the user searched only for *light* surrounded by blanks, then words like *lighting* or *lights* would be missed. The user might want to find synonyms or related words, such as *colorless* or *clear* for the adjective, or *illuminate* for the verb. Without a parser and semantics, an automatic search system has no clue about the real meaning of the word *light* when it is found in text.

Several creative solutions to this problem are currently being developed—approaches that for the time being build on computational linguistic knowledge rather than on more complex knowledge built into the system. These systems use shallow parsing combined with some statistical analysis, and this is how they work. First, very frequent words such as those in the list given in Section 6.1 are filtered out, since they have low information value. This speeds up a computational linguistic system considerably, since it can remove nearly half the words. Next, word frequency and cooccurrence are computed. Cooccurrence refers to determining whether words are likely to occur together. For example, the phrase *bad weather* is more common than *clarified weather,* even though both *bad* and *clarified* are adjectives. Similarly, the phrase *clarified butter* is more frequent than *tart butter,* even though both *clarified* and *tart* are adjectives. This permits the application of statistical computational linguistic methods to determine whether an article is about a topic that appears frequently in the collection or whether it is about an unusual topic. For example, newspapers on a certain day tend to have a set of articles on the breaking news, so cooccurrences from these articles will rise to the top. Occurrences of a phrase such as *Argentina bombing* might peak on certain days, whereas unfortunately occurrences of a phrase such as *hunger in Africa* will tend to be more constant.

In addition to the use of statistical computational linguistic techniques such as cooccurrence and deviation over the normal occurrence of words as a measure of what an article is truly about, more theoretical linguistic techniques involving shallow parsing are also used. For example, programs that determine all the noun phrases (see Chapter 5) can extract and list these NPs, both from within articles and across articles. Once the noun phrases are extracted, they can be sorted and organized according to the head of the phrase and according to modifiers. Given that the goal of information retrieval is to determine who did what to whom, it is a well-known fact that *who, what,* and *whom* are usually found in the noun phrases of a text. Highlighting just these noun phrases without the verbs tends to give a sensible overview of the essence of an article. Sorting, counting, and applying statistical manipulation to these phrases is another way to represent the true meaning of text, and thus gives a more principled and computationally smart way to retrieve and present text that truly answers a particular question.

6.3 Machine translation

The purpose of a **machine translation** system is the same as that of any translation system: taking text written or spoken in one language and writing or speaking it in another (see Figure 17.20). Translation poses challenging problems both for the human translator and for the machine attempting to do what the human does. Projects in machine translation in the 1940s and 1950s spawned much of the early research in computational linguistics. Consider the written case first, and think of a single institution like the United Nations. Every day millions of words need to be translated from one language to another. Add to that other political and scientific institutions, plus businesses and publishers. This results in an overwhelming need for help in translation, since the process, when done correctly, is time consuming and mentally demanding. Since computers are suited to tasks requiring memory, it would seem that, with careful programming, the problem of translating by computer could be solved.

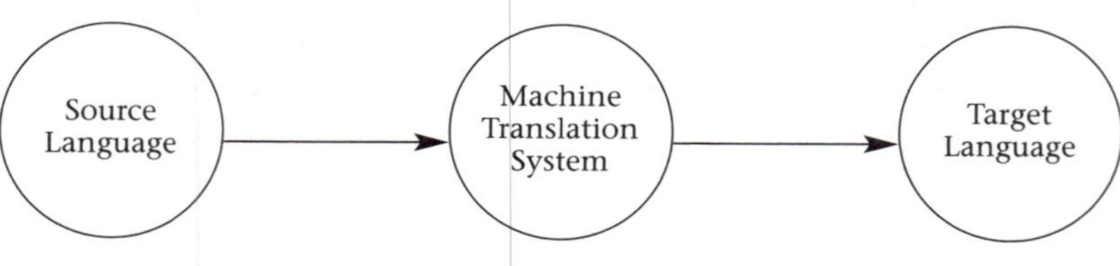

Figure 17.20

This was the thinking of computer scientists and linguists, but the problems turned out to be far more difficult than was imagined. Much government money was poured into the machine translation task from the late 1940s to the early 1960s, but results were slow to emerge due to the complexity of unforeseen problems. The subtlety of language—the nuances and lack of precision—caused problems because computers are suited to mathematical computation where subtleties do not prevail. Funding agencies became disillusioned, and although most researchers were still hopeful, they were humbled by the difficulties encountered in early years.

Researchers are now more realistic about their goals. Rather than attempting to build full-fledged machine translation systems that automatically convert a text from one language to another, some projects are aiming toward machine-assisted translation. In these projects, the computer is viewed as a tool to aid the translator. The computer makes suggestions, but the human translator makes final decisions. Another simplification is to aim the translation at a specific subject area; this way, word ambiguities are reduced to a minimum. For example, in the financial domain, the word *vehicle* is probably an investment device, but in the automobile domain, *vehicle* is most likely a device for driving. Still other projects are developing ways to take texts and pass them through a preprocessor—a system that looks at sentences and figures out which ones might present problems. The computer can identify the problem and then ask the original writer to clarify. Take the following example:

38)

Many elephants smell.

Since this sentence could be confusing due to the ambiguousness of the verb *smell* (is the intended interpretation that many elephants stink or that many elephants are capable of perceiving odors?), it might be sent back to the writer for clarification.

Machine translation applications encompass many aspects of computational linguistics. For this reason, the venture is one of the more challenging to researchers. In addition, the notion of a machine that is capable or nearly capable of mimicking a very complex and subtle human activity constitutes an intriguing enterprise. The source language needs to be analyzed syntactically and semantically. Lexical items need to be matched—a particularly difficult task, for not only do words in one language often not exist in another but sometimes several words are used for one. One example involves the German words *essen* and *fressen*. Both words mean 'eat' in English, but the verb *essen* is used for humans, whereas *fressen* is used for animals. If the system made the mistake of using *fressen* for people, the usage would be insulting. Syntax can also be a problem. An example from Spanish concerns a missing word, as shown in *39* and *40*. Sentence *41* gives the word-by-word translation of the Spanish in *40*.

39)

The elephants slept but didn't snore.

40)

Los elefantes durmieron pero no roncaron.

41)

*The elephants slept but not snored.

The word-by-word translation in *41* is not English. What's wrong? In English, a negative sentence without an auxiliary verb needs the properly inflected form of the verb *do* to be inserted. Since *39* is in the past tense and since the subject is plural, the correct form is *did*. There is no word for *did* in the Spanish version of the same sentence. Just as the human translator has to know this fact, so does the machine translation system. If the input language were Spanish and the input sentence were *40*, then the English generation system would need to know to insert the verb *do*, properly inflected, and not to inflect the main verb. The difficulties increase with languages that are fundamentally different in nature, such as English and Japanese, or Spanish and Finnish, or French and Chinese. If the machine translation system is required to take spoken language as input and give spoken language as output, then the system becomes even more complex, as is shown in Figure 17.21.

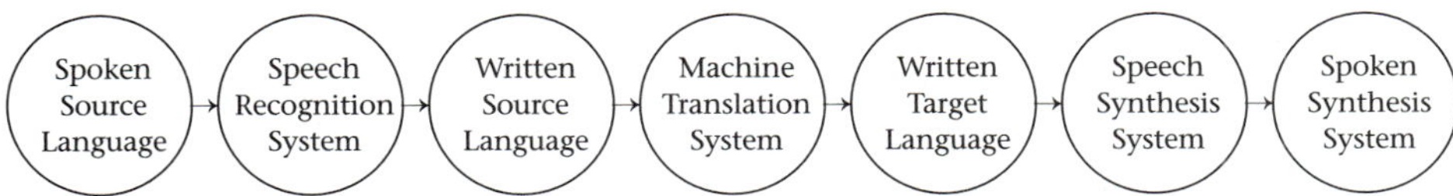

Figure 17.21

Recent research in machine translation has given new impetus to this field. This resurgence is attributed to two reasons. First, pressure from the global economy is creating a need for international cooperation that in turn requires communication across language barriers. Second, advances in computational methods for language analysis and generation are bringing the hope of computer translation of natural languages closer to reality.

6.4 Automatic summarization

A relatively new application using computational linguistic techniques is **automatic summarization**. Summarization refers to the process of automatic analysis of either a single article (single-document summarization) or a set of articles (multi-document summarization) and the creation of an abstract reflecting the key ideas in a concise and coherent way. With the rise in information overload, the need for summarization systems has become increasingly pressing since many people do not have the time to keep up with so much reading. At times, a summary will suffice as a way of screening a set of documents so the user can decide which ones to read in depth and which ones to ignore.

Two approaches to summarization currently prevail. First is the purely statistical approach, a method based on techniques developed in the 1950s. The words in a document are listed by frequency (except the most frequent words such as those listed in Section 6.1), and then sentences that contain these frequent words are extracted from the article. This technique is crude but somewhat effective; its main drawbacks are that it allows limited analysis of the articles, and that the sentences, when strung together, can be choppy and difficult to read. The other approach now being developed is based on computational linguistic analysis of articles to extract key concepts. With the help of language generation, an entirely new abstract is created from the concepts. This approach creates a coherent and fluent summary that captures the key ideas, both for single- and multi-document summarization.

6.5 Speech recognition

A **speech recognition system** takes spoken language as input and understands it (see Figure 17.22). The result could be the written text of what was said, or it could be orders to another machine. For example, a smart typewriter equipped with a recognition device will take an order to delete a line. The typewriter follows the order and the words *delete line* will not be written. Speech recognition is a process that humans perform effortlessly, but teaching computers to recognize speech has turned out to be more difficult than was originally thought. Some of the linguistic problems involved were outlined in the section on computational phonetics and phonology (Section 1).

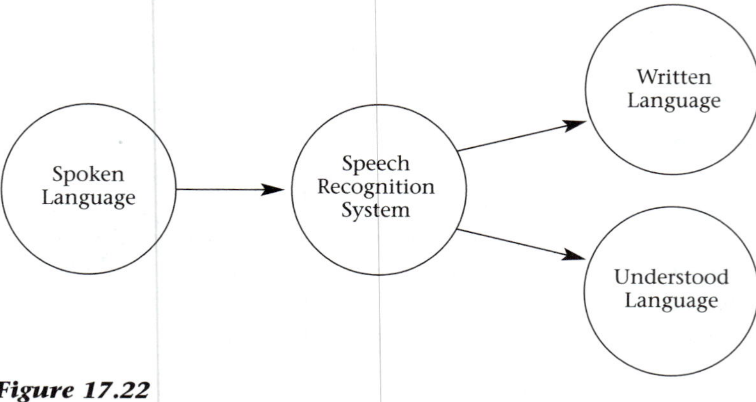

Figure 17.22

What are some applications that would benefit from a speech recognition system? One that has been explored is in the area of medical record keeping. Writing down details of examinations is time consuming; often doctors leave out critical information due to these time pressures. With a speech recognition system, the doctor would simply talk while doing an examination. The speech would automatically and instantly be translated into text, which could be printed out immediately. In this way, the doctor could examine the report with the patient there to make sure everything had been covered. Medical terminology is fairly controlled, so the computer would have an advantage in guessing words. The examination room is relatively quiet, reducing the problem of background noise. Finally, a speech recognition system would allow the doctor to use both hands while speaking. Medical records could immediately go into a central library, which could be referred to by researchers studying symptoms and treatments. Last but not least, no one would ever have to struggle to read the doctor's illegible handwriting.

Such a system would have to be absolutely perfect. However, it is easier to correct an error in a report than to write one from scratch. Other applications that have been explored include quality control devices for inspecting assembly lines. For example, a worker would be able to say "pass" or "fail," and the machine would then know whether to accept the part or refuse it. A very important application of speech recognition is in developing aids for the physically disabled. These include devices such as voice-operated appliances, machines, and tools.

6.6 Speech synthesis

A **speech synthesis system** has the opposite goal from a speech recognition system (see Figure 17.23). Applications for speech synthesis systems abound. One of the most important uses is "reading" to the visually impaired. Previously this required a human either to do the actual reading or to prerecord books and other material. Both processes are not only expensive but also limiting, since what the person wants or needs to read may not be available on tape. Another important application of speech synthesis is as a talking aid for the vocally handicapped. Communication boards and talking typewriters show the value of converting text to spoken language.

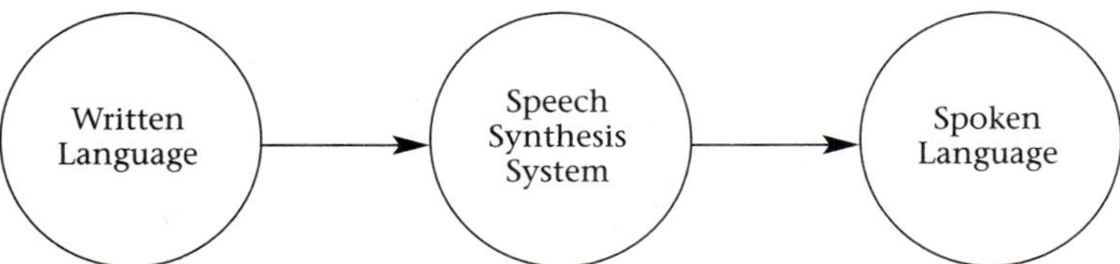

Figure 17.23

Still another fairly common application is in an area called database query. A database is a large source of information, such as bank records, billing records, airline schedules, and theater and movie schedules. Imagine wanting to find out about ticket availability for the theater, movies, or other cultural events. This information is constantly changing as people buy tickets and agencies release them. When you call, the text-to-speech machine can read the information aloud directly out of the database. No one has had to record it, which would be time consuming and expensive. Furthermore, the information is completely up-to-date. Other applications include use in machine translation systems, for robots, for expert systems, and for novel medical applications.

Summing up

This chapter has covered the relatively new field of **computational linguistics**, which is the application of computers to the study of linguistic problems. There are two goals in computational linguistics. One is to use the computer as a tool to build programs that model a particular linguistic theory or approach. For this goal, the computer becomes a testing ground for the theory. The other goal is to build working systems that use linguistic information. The chapter covers the fields of computational phonetics and phonology, morphology, syntax, lexicology, and semantics and pragmatics. A section on **applications** presents some of the devices that have incorporated linguistic tools, such as **machine translation** systems, automatic summarizers, and reading machines for the visually impaired.

Key terms

General terms

computational linguistics
grammatical knowledge
real-world knowledge

Terms concerning computational phonetics, phonology, and morphology

cocktail party effect
formants
spectrogram
speech recognition
stemming/stripping algorithm

Terms concerning computational syntax

bottom-up (parsing)
deterministic (parsing)
implementation
natural language processing systems
nondeterministic (parsing)
nonterminal nodes
parser
strong generative capacity
terminal nodes
top-down (parsing)
weak generative capacity

Terms concerning computational lexicology and computational semantics

computational lexicology
corpus analysis
lexicon
machine-readable dictionary (MRD)
pragmatics

Terms concerning practical applications of computational linguistics

applications
automatic summarization
concordance
indexing
machine translation
speech recognition system
speech synthesis system

Recommended reading

Allen, James. 1995. *Natural Language Understanding*. 2nd ed. Menlo Park, CA: Benjamin/Cummings.

Biber, Douglas, Susan Conrad, and Randi Reppen. 1998. *Corpus Linguistics: Investigating Language Structure and Use*. Cambridge: Cambridge University Press.

Cole, Ronald, Joseph Mariani, Hans Uszkoreit, Giovanni Battista Varile, Annie Zaenen, and Antonio Zampolli. 1998. *Survey of the State of the Art in Human Language Technology*. Cambridge: Cambridge University Press.

Dutoit, Thierry. 1997. *An Introduction to Text-to-Speech Synthesis*. Norwell, MA: Kluwer Academic Publishers.

Grishman, Ralph. 1986. *Computational Linguistics: An Introduction*. Cambridge University Studies in Natural Language Processing. Cambridge: Cambridge University Press.

Journal of the Association for Computational Linguistics 13 (3–4).

Journal of Machine Translation. Norwell, MA: Kluwer Academic Press.

Klavans, Judith, and Philip Resnick. 1996. *The Balancing Act*. Cambridge, MA: MIT Press.

Levinsohn, Stephan E., and Mark Y. Liberman. "Speech Recognition by Computer." *Scientific American* (April 1981).

Manning, Christopher, and Hinrich Schütze. 1999. *Foundations of Statistical Natural Language Processing*.

Pullman, Steve. 1997. *Computational Linguistics*. Cambridge: Cambridge University Press.

Savitch, Walter J., Emmon Bach, William Marsh, and Gila Safran-Naveh, eds. 1987. *The Formal Complexity of Natural Language*. New York: D. Reidel/Kluwer.

Strzalkowski, Tomek, ed. 1999. *Natural Language Information Retrieval*. Norwell, MA: Kluwer Academic Publishers.

Questions

1. What kinds of problems might a computer have with these sentences?
   a) Sue bought red apples and plums.
   b) It was a large animal house.
   c) Susan baked in the kitchen.
   d) Susan baked in the sun.
   e) Susan baked.

2. What are the main uses of a text-to-speech system? What information does the computer need to know in order to pronounce these sentences in informal style?
   a) What are you doing tonight?
   b) The woman was delighted.
   c) That article misled me.
   d) That's a new car, isn't it?
   e) It was a tough test, although I did well.
   f) Can't you sing better?

3. What rules are necessary for a computer program to analyze these words? (Hint: First figure out the prefixes and suffixes. Refer to Chapter 4 if necessary.)
   a) kindness
   b) kindly
   c) kindnesses
   d) nationalism
   e) countability
   f) nontransformational
   g) reusable

4. What different structures might a syntactic analyzer propose for the following ambiguous sentences?
   a) She saw the man with a telescope.
   b) Watch dogs bark.
   c) Broadcast programs like *60 Minutes.*

5. Think of a word that has many different meanings, such as *bank* or *interest.* Then give information about that word using the categories discussed in Section 4. Give at least two senses for each part of speech. The following example has one sense for the noun part of speech, and two senses for the verb part of speech.

   WORD: *bank*
   a) Part of speech: Noun
   b) Sense number: 1
   c) Semantic properties: Of a river
   d) Pronunciation: [bæ̃ŋk]
   e) Context and style: Normal
   f) Example: The bank of the river was grassy.

   WORD: *bank*
   a) Part of speech: Verb
   b) Sense number: 1
   c) Subcategorization: Transitive, requires the preposition *on*
   d) Semantic properties: Object of preposition is either a person or a thing
   e) Pronunciation: [bæ̃ŋk]
   f) Context and style: Informal
   g) Example: I can't bank on him to do it.

   WORD: *bank*
   a) Part of speech: Verb
   b) Sense number: 2
   c) Subcategorization: Transitive
   d) Semantic properties: Object is money
   e) Pronunciation: [bæ̃ŋk]
   f) Context and style: Normal
   g) Example: She banks her money at the local branch.

6. List three applications of computational linguistics. How can these systems improve the quality of life for people with physical disabilities?

7. The use of the Internet and the World Wide Web has changed the way people access information. In the context of requesting information from an electronic source:
   i) List three cases where linguistic information would help you to find your way around the Internet. For example, if you are looking for information on *attorney*, it would help in your search to know that the British equivalents are *barrister* and *solicitor*.
   ii) List three cases where linguistic ambiguity would hurt you in your search for information electronically. For example, in looking for articles on the word *bank*, you will find articles on rivers and financial institutions. What are some words and phrases that would give you problems? For each example, explain what the problem is and how you could solve it.

FOR THE STUDENT LINGUIST

ONE SECOND

Mike is driving the kids to the game. It's a simple sentence; you probably have no problem understanding it and can do so within the few seconds it takes to utter it. But by now you've learned something about phonetics, phonology, morphology, and syntax, and so you can recognize that there's a lot of structure hidden inside this seemingly simple sentence. In computational linguistics, we deal with the ways in which individual components of grammar interact. One place where this happens is during parsing.

I think parsing is one of the most fascinating parts of language. To illustrate how complex parsing can be, I've listed some of the steps your brain might be following as you hear this sentence. Imagine how much work you'd have to do for a more complicated sentence.

M

As soon as you hear the first sound, you're already coming up with possible words:

my	Mabel	microphone	magazine	meat
music	Midol	migraine	mine	mud
might	make	mat	miss	mice
Mike	mascara	moped	mitochondria	model

Mi

Each new sound eliminates some possibilities and makes others more likely.

my	Midol	mine
might	microphone	mitochondria
Mike	migraine	mice

Mike

Already there's a conflict: this string of sounds could be *my* plus another word (starting with [k]), or *Mike, microphone,* etc.

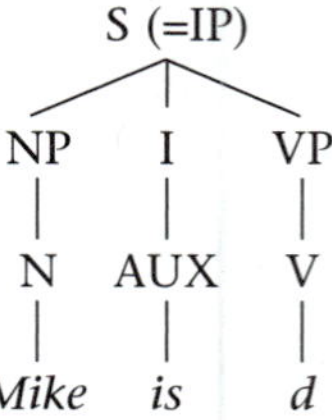

By now these sounds are probably identified as *Mike is . . . ,* since a possibility like *My kismet . . .* is ruled out by the [d] and *my* followed by some unknown word has a low probability. So syntax can kick in and start making tree structures. You might wonder when your brain knows it's going to get a sentence. It might assume it right away and postulate an S (IP) node as soon as the first word starts. Or maybe it waits until it hears something verb-like. What do you think? Let's assume that as soon as it hears a noun or a determiner, it knows it's going to get an NP, and as soon as it gets an AUX or a verb, it knows it's going to get a VP.

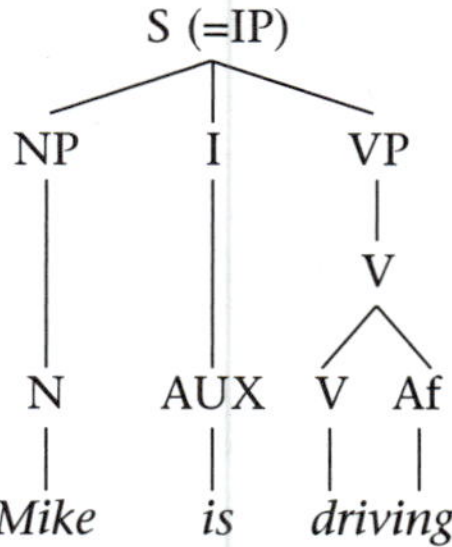

The morphology component of the parser didn't have to do much with the first two words, but once it reaches *driving* it has to identify the verb stem and the affix. Meanwhile, phonology and morphology together have to rule out something like *Mike is dry . . . ving. . . .* Notice how misleading it could be to pick the first legitimate-sounding sequence as the real sequence; it's *Mike,* not *My k . . . ;* it's *Mike is driving,* not *Mike is dry.* So your brain has to delay decisions a bit, until it has confirmation that it has made the right choice.

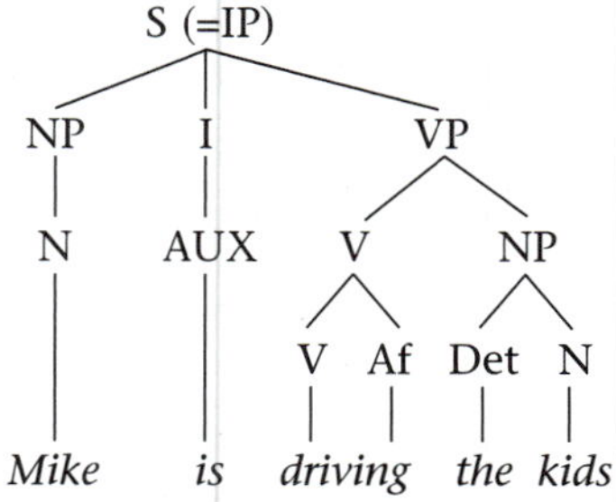

Now the morphology component has a dilemma. *Kids* could be plural or possessive (remember, you're hearing this, so you can't see any punctuation), so the morphology and syntax components can't tell whether the NP is complete (if it's just *the kids*) or to expect more material in the NP, waiting for whatever object follows *the kid's* or *the kids'*.

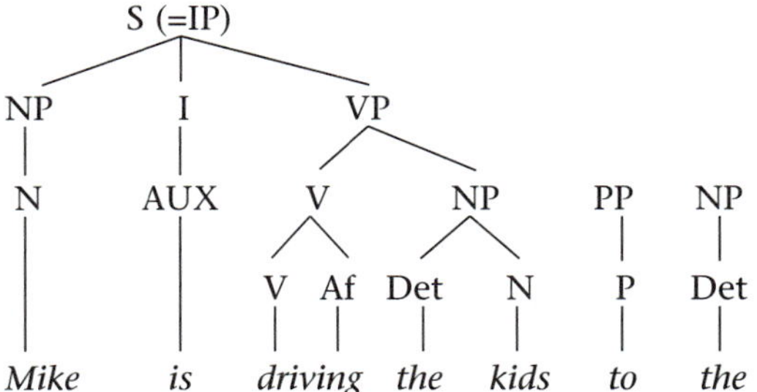

Once you hear *the*, you can rule out something like *the kid's two cars . . .* or *the kids' two cars . . .* and "close" the NP (decide that it's complete). Or can you? What if the PP following *kids* modifies it (and therefore the PP for *to the game* is a sister of the N for *kids* instead of a sister of the NP *the kids*)? Again, the different components have to interface to determine the structure as quickly as possible without locking into an incorrect decision prematurely.

Why am I emphasizing the need to figure out when you've reached the end of some phrase? Because it might require more memory to hold a group of words as an open, active unit than to declare it a complete constituent. The situtation is like having a limited amount of desk space; it's easier to file away things you know you're done with than to keep them spread all over your desk surface and in your way.

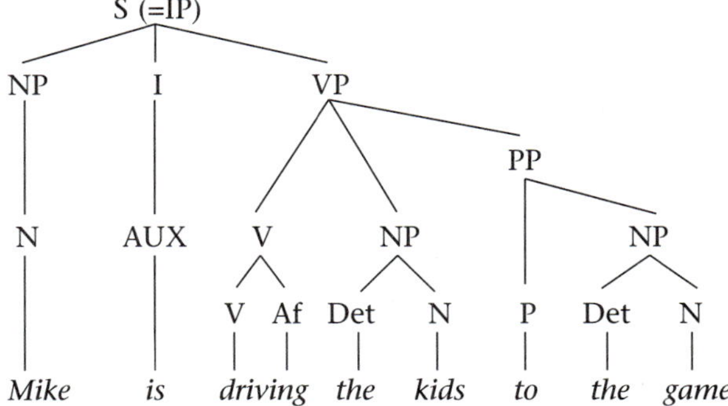

And finally you're done. Pretty amazing that you can do all that parsing in a few seconds, isn't it? Now you can try to explain why sentences like the following are so hard to understand. Good luck.

The dog walked past the kennel barked.

Since Sheila kept on eating the brownies burned.

The reporter that the dog that Mary owns bit last week slept late.

GLOSSARY

Ablaut A vowel alternation that marks a grammatical contrast (e.g., *mouse/mice*).

Absolute universals Patterns or traits that occur in all languages.

Absolutive In some languages, the **case** associated with both the direct object of a transitive verb and the subject of an intransitive verb.

Abstract Hypothetical, not phonetically realized. *See* **Underlying**.

Abstract case Case that need not be expressed as inflection.

Abstract clause A type of narrative utterance that sometimes appears at the beginning of a narrative to provide a general summary of the story to be told.

Abstract representation A phonological description that is to a greater or lesser degree distinct from its phonetic realization.

Accent Phonetic qualities of a language variety that identify it to speakers of other varieties as different from their own.

Accidental gaps Nonoccurring but possible forms of a language (e.g., in English, *blork*).

Accommodation The modification of speech patterns to match those of other participants in a discourse.

Accuracy Second language production in which the structures are nativelike.

Acoustic phonetics An approach to phonetics that is concerned with measuring and analyzing the physical properties of sound waves produced when we speak.

Acquired dysgraphia The impairment of writing ability in patients who previously possessed normal writing ability (also called acquired agraphia).

Acquired dyslexia The impairment of reading ability in patients who previously possessed normal reading ability (also called acquired alexia).

Acrolect A creole variety that is relatively similar to the standard language from which it arose. (*See also* **Basilect** and **Mesolect**.)

Acronym A word that is formed by taking the initial letters of (some or all) of the words in a phrase or title and pronouncing them as a word (e.g., *NATO* for *North Atlantic Treaty Organization*).

Acrophonic principle The representation of sounds by pictures of objects whose pronunciation begins with the sound to be represented (e.g., the sound [b] might be represented by a picture of a bird).

Active sentence A sentence in which the NP with the **agent** role is the subject (e.g., *Helen painted the room*).

Address terms The various forms that are used to address people, indicating something of one's relationship to the individual addressed (e.g., in English, *Ms. Callaghan, Professor Van Haar, Jake*).

Adjacency pair An ordered pair of utterances spoken by two different participants in a conversation.

Adjective (A) A **lexical category** that designates a property that is applicable to the entities named by nouns, can often take comparative and superlative endings in English, and functions as the **head** of an adjective phrase (e.g., *red, obese, hearty*).

Adstratum influence The mutual influence of two equally dominant languages on each other (e.g., the influence of English and French on each other in Montreal).

Adverb (Adv) A **lexical category** that typically names properties that can be applied to the actions designated by verbs (e.g., *quickly, fearfully*).

Affix (Af) A bound morpheme that modifies the meaning and/or syntactic (sub)category of the stem in some way (e.g., *un-* and *-able* in *unreadable*).

Affixation The process that attaches an affix to a base.

Affricates Noncontinuant consonants that show a slow release of the closure (e.g., [tʃ, dʒ]).

Affrication A process in which stops become affricates.

African American Vernacular English (AAVE) A cover term describing distinctive varieties of English spoken by Americans of African descent.

Age-grading The correlation of a particular linguistic variant with social situations that are closely associated with a particular age group.

Agent The **thematic role** of the doer of an action (e.g., *Marilyn* in *Marilyn fed the dolphin*).

Agent-patient pattern Sentence pattern in which the **agent** role is assigned to the subject of an **intransitive verb** and the agent subject of a **transitive verb**; the **patient** role is assigned to the object of a transitive verb or the subject of a state.

Agglutinating languages Languages in which words typically contain several morphemes, of which usually only one is a lexical category. The others are clearly identifiable affixes, each of which typically encodes a single grammatical contrast.

Agrammatism An aphasic disturbance characterized by the omission of function words and inflectional affixes and by syntactic comprehension deficits.

Agreement The result of one category being inflected to mark properties of another (e.g., the verb marked for the person and/or the number of the subject).

Allomorphs Variants of a **morpheme** (e.g., [-s], [-z], and [-əz] are allomorphs of the English plural morpheme).

Allophones Variants of a **phoneme**, usually in complementary distribution and phonetically similar (e.g., voiced and voiceless *l* in English).

Allophonic distribution The set of distinct phonetic environments in which variants of a phoneme occur.

Alpha notation In stating phonological rules, the use of a conventional formula in which variables (α, β, etc.) are introduced to represent the value of distinctive features.

Alpha rules Phonological rules stated in a conventional formula in which variables (α, β, etc.) are introduced for the value of distinctive features.

Alphabetic writing A type of writing in which symbols represent consonant and/or vowel segments.

Alveolar ridge The small ridge just behind the upper front teeth.

Alveopalatal (area) The area just behind the alveolar ridge where the roof of the mouth rises sharply (also called **palatoalveolar**).

Amelioration The process in which the meaning of a word becomes more favorable (e.g., *pretty* used to mean "tricky, sly, cunning").

Amerind The group into which all the Native American languages (except for Na-Dené and Eskimo-Aleut stocks) have been placed, according to one controversial classification system.

Amerindian languages Languages spoken by the aboriginal peoples of North, South, and Central America.

Analogy A source of language change that involves the generalization of a regularity on the basis of the inference that if elements are alike in some respects, they should be alike in others as well (e.g., *bring* becoming *brung* by analogy with *ring/rung*).

Analytic languages *See* **Isolating languages**.

Anaphoric reference The use of a pronoun that refers to an NP earlier in the discourse (e.g., *her* in *Hilary ate her dinner*).

Angular gyrus An area of the brain that plays an important role in reading.

Animacy *See* **Animate**.

Animate In some languages, a class consisting of nouns, most of which have living referents.

Antecedent The element that determines the interpretation of a pronoun (e.g., *Jeremy* in *Jeremy looked at himself in the mirror*).

Anterior A place feature that characterizes sounds articulated in front of the alveopalatal region.

Antonyms Words or phrases that are opposites with respect to some component of their meaning (e.g., *big* and *small*).

Aphasia A language deficit caused by damage to the brain.

Application The use to which a computer program is put.

Apocope The deletion of a word-final vowel (e.g., *name* used to be pronounced with a word-final schwa).

A-prefixing A **relic form** in Appalachian English in which *a-* may be attached to the front of verbs in the progressive aspect *(She's a-coming)* or the front of adverbial complements to the verb *(He sat there a-thinking)*.

Arbitrariness A property of communication whereby there is no natural or inherent connection between a sign and its referent.

Areal classification An approach to language classification that identifies characteristics shared by languages that are in the same geographical area.

Articulatory phonetics An approach to phonetics that studies the physiological mechanisms of speech production.

Articulatory simplification A process that facilitates acquisition (e.g., by deleting a consonant in a complex cluster or inserting a vowel to break up a cluster).

Arytenoids Two small cartilages in the larynx that are attached to the vocal folds, enabling the vocal folds to be drawn together or apart.

Aspect In syntax and morphology, an inflectional category indicating the manner in which an action or event takes place, in particular its duration in time (punctual, repetitive, etc.).

Aspiration The lag in the onset of vocalic voicing—accompanied by the release of air—that is heard after the release of certain stops in English (e.g., the first sound of *top* is aspirated).

Assimilation The influence of one segment on another, resulting in a sound becoming more like a nearby sound in terms of one or more of its phonetic characteristics (e.g., in English, vowels become nasal if followed by a nasal consonant).

Association line A line linking a symbol that represents a sound segment with a symbol that represents a tone or feature.

Atlas survey A linguistic survey that samples speakers according to regional speech communities.

Audiolingualism A method of second language teaching based on the notion that second language learning should be regarded as a mechanistic process of habit formation.

Automatic summarization An **application** of **computational linguistics** in which a computer uses key ideas to create an abstract of an article or set of articles.

Autopsy studies Studies based on a postmortem examination.

Autosegmental (notation) The type of notation in phonology that links segments with tones or individual features by **association lines**.

Autosegmental principles Rules that account for phonological processes, including rules that associate **features** to **segments** and segments to features, and rules that prohibit the crossing of **association lines**.

Autosegmental representation A means of illustrating how phonological **features** are organized and how they change as a result of phonological **processes**. (*See also* **Autosegmental (notation)** and **Autosegments**.)

Autosegments Phonological features (such as **manner features** and **place features**) that operate more or less autonomously.

Auxiliary verb (Aux) A verb in the I position that must occur with a main verb (e.g., *was* in *was talking*).

Babbling Speech-like sounds produced as babies acquire and exercise articulatory skills.

Back A feature of sounds articulated behind the palatal region in the oral cavity.

Back (of the tongue) The part of the tongue that is hindmost but still lies in the mouth.

Back vowel A vowel that is made with the tongue positioned in the back of the mouth (e.g., the vowel sounds in *hoot* and *board*).

Backformation A word-formation process that creates a new word by removing a real or supposed affix from another word in the language (e.g., *edit* came from *editor* through the removal of *-or*).

Base The form to which an affix is added (e.g., *book* is the base for the affix *-s* in *books*, *modernize* is the base for the affix *-ed* in *modernized*).

Basilect A creole variety that shows the least influence from the standard language from which it arose. (*See also* **Acrolect** and **Mesolect**.)

Bilabial Involving both lips (e.g., *p*, *b*, and *m* are all bilabial consonants).

Bilingualism The state of possessing knowledge of two languages; the discipline devoted to the study of the simultaneous acquisition of two languages by children.

(Bird) call *See* **Call**.

(Bird) song *See* **Song**.

Blade (of the tongue) The area of the tongue just behind the tip.

Blend A word that is created from parts of two already existing items (e.g., *brunch* from *breakfast* and *lunch*).

Blissymbolics A contemporary development of pictographic writing that uses a number of recombinable symbols representing basic units of meaning; primarily used for nonspeaking individuals.

Body (of the tongue) The main mass of the tongue.

Borrowing A source of language change that involves adopting aspects of one language into another.

Bottom-up parsing A method of speech analysis that starts with individual words and builds structures upward in successively larger units.

Bottom-up processing A type of mental processing in which more complex representations (e.g., words) are accessed through simpler constituent representations (e.g., phonemes).

Bound morpheme A morpheme that must be attached to another element (e.g., the past tense marker *-ed*).

Boustrophedon The practice of reversing the direction of writing at the end of each line, which was typical of many old writing systems.

Broca's aphasia A **nonfluent aphasia** in which speech is very halting, there are numerous phonemic errors, and there is a lack of intonation.

Broca's area The area in the lower rear portion of the left frontal lobe of the brain that plays an important role in language production.

Bundles of isoglosses *See* **Isogloss bundle**.

Call In avian communication, a short burst of sound or simple patterns of notes, typically used as warnings or other group-related signals.

Canonical sentence strategy A processing strategy that leads children to expect the first NP in a sentence to bear the agent role and the second NP to bear the theme role.

Caregiver speech *See* **Motherese**.

Case A morphological category that encodes information about an element's grammatical role (subject, direct object, and so on) (e.g., the contrast between *he* and *him*).

Case Filter, The The requirement that every NP in a grammatical sentence be assigned a case feature.

Cataphoric reference The use of a pronoun that refers to an NP later in the discourse (e.g., *she* in *When she heard the news, Ann smiled*).

Categorical (rules) Rules that always apply.

Category change A change in the part of speech of a word as a result of **affixation** (e.g., adding *-ize* to *modern,* an adjective, makes it into a verb, *modernize*).

C-command A syntactic notion that is involved in pronoun interpretation and is formulated as: NP_a c-commands NP_b if the first category above NP_a contains NP_b.

Central sulcus The fold that extends from the top of the **cerebral cortex** to the lateral fissure (also called the fissure of Rolando).

Cerebral cortex The grey wrinkled mass that sits like a cap over the rest of the brain and is the seat of cognitive functioning.

Cerebral hemispheres The left and right halves of the brain, separated by the longitudinal fissure.

Cerebrovascular accident *See* **Stroke**.

Characters The units of the contemporary Chinese writing system, many of which consist of two parts—a phonetic **determinative** and a **radical**.

Class 1 affixes A group of affixes that (in English) often trigger changes in the consonant or vowel segments of the base and may affect the assignment of stress.

Class 2 affixes A group of affixes that tend to be phonologically neutral in English, having no effect on the segmental makeup of the base or on stress assignment.

Class node A label that represents each phonological feature grouping in the feature hierarchy (also called simply a **node**).

Class (sound) A group of sounds that shares certain phonetic properties (e.g., all voiced sounds).

Classificatory verbs In Athabaskan languages of North America, verb stems that are matched with noun classes on the basis of the type of movement or handling involved in the verb meaning.

Clever Hans A horse that seemed to have a human-like capacity to think.

Clipping A word-formation process that shortens a polysyllabic word by deleting one or more syllables (e.g., *prof* from *professor*).

Clitic A word that is unable to stand alone as an independent form for phonological reasons.

Cliticization The process by which a **clitic** is attached to a word.

Closed syllable A syllable with a coda (e.g., both syllables in *camping*).

Closing A discourse unit conventionally used to end a conversation.

Coarticulation An articulation in which phonemes overlap to a certain extent.

Cocktail party effect The ability to filter out background noise and pick out a particular sound.

Coda (Co) The elements that follow the nucleus in the same syllable (e.g., [rf] in *surfboard*).

Coda clause A type of narrative utterance sometimes found at the end of a narrative that shifts the time of the narrative into the present.

Code-switching The systematic alternation between language systems in discourse.

Cognates Words of different languages that have descended from a common source, as shown by systematic phonetic correspondences (e.g., English *father* and German *Vater*).

Cognitive development The emergence of the various mental abilities (such as language) that make up the human intellect.

Cognitive style The way in which we are predisposed to process information in our environment.

Cohesive device A device that establishes a connection among two or more elements in the discourse (e.g., anaphoric reference, cataphoric reference, lexical cohesion, ellipsis, and so on).

Cohort In a psycholinguistic model of spoken-word recognition, a set of possible words. (*See also* **Cohort model**.)

Cohort model A model of spoken-word recognition according to which word recognition proceeds by isolating a target word from a set of words that share initial segments.

Coinage *See* **Word manufacture**.

Communication strategies Strategies used by L2 learners when they are lacking the necessary linguistic knowledge to say what they want to say (e.g., paraphrasing).

Communicative competence A speaker's underlying knowledge of the linguistic and social rules or principles for language production and comprehension in particular speech situations.

Comparative method In historical linguistics, the reconstruction of properties of a parent language through systematic comparison of its descendant languages.

Comparative reconstruction The reconstruction of properties of a parent language through comparison of its descendant languages.

Competence The mental system that underlies a person's ability to speak and understand a given language; distinguished from **performance**.

Complement A syntactic constituent that provides information about entities and locations implied by the meaning of the **head**.

Complement clause A sentence-like construction that is embedded within a larger structure (e.g., *that his car had been totaled* in *Jerry told Mary that his car had been totaled*).

Complementary distribution The distribution of allophones in their respective phonetic environments such that one never appears in the same phonetic context as the other (e.g., the distribution of long and short vowels in English).

Complementizer (C) A **functional category** that takes an S complement, forming a CP (complementizer phrase) (e.g., *whether* in *I wonder whether Lorna has left*).

Complex word A word that contains two or more morphemes (e.g., *theorize, unemployment*).

Complicating action clause A type of narrative utterance that describes the events in a story.

Componential analysis The representation of a word's **intension** in terms of smaller semantic components called features.

Compound word A word made up of two or more words (e.g., *greenhouse, pickpocket*).

Compounding The combination of lexical categories (N, V, A, or P) to form a larger word (e.g., *fire + engine*).

Comprehensible input The linguistic input to which the L2 learner is exposed that is slightly beyond his or her competence in the target language (i+1).

Computational lexicology The subfield of **computational linguistics** that deals with words in the **lexicon** (e.g., their parts of speech, **subcategorization**, semantic properties).

Computational linguistics The area of common interest between linguistics and computer science.

Computational system The syntactic component of grammar that can combine and arrange words in particular ways.

Computerized axial tomography A technique for observing the living brain that uses a narrow beam of X-rays to create brain images that take the form of a series of brain slices (also called **CT scanning**).

Concatenative A term used for the morphological process that builds word structure by assembling morphemes in an additive, linear fashion.

Concordance An index of words showing every occurrence of each word in its context.

Conditioned allomorphs The different forms of a **morpheme** whose distribution depends on the phonological and morphological environment in which they occur (e.g., the English plural has several allomorphs whose distribution depends on phonological and morphological factors).

Conflation pattern A class of meanings created by combining semantic elements such as manner and motion or direction and motion.

Conjugation The set of inflected forms associated with a verb (also called a verbal paradigm).

Conjunction (Con) A **functional category** that joins two or more categories of the same type, forming a coordinate structure (e.g., *and* in *a man and his dog*).

Connectionist model A psycholinguistic theory built around the claim that the mind can be best modeled by reference to complex associations of simple units that approximate neurons.

Connotation The set of associations that a word's use can evoke (e.g., in Wisconsin *winter* evokes ice, snow, bare trees, etc.). (*See also* **Denotation**.)

Conservative language A language that shows comparatively few changes over time.

Consonant deletion A phonetic process that deletes a consonant (e.g., the deletion of [θ] in *sixths*).

Consonant weakening A lessening in the time or degree of a consonant's closure.

Consonantal A major class feature that characterizes sounds produced with a major obstruction in the vocal tract.

Consonantal strength Increasing time or degree of a consonant's closure.

Consonants Sounds that are produced with a narrow or complete closure in the vocal tract.

Constellation A complex of communicative modes operating on different channels.

Constituent One or more words that make up a syntactic unit (e.g., *the apple* in *the apple fell onto the floor*). (*See also* **Coordination test, Substitution test**, and **Movement test**.)

Constricted glottis ([CG]) A laryngeal feature that characterizes sounds made with the glottis closed (in English, only [ʔ]).

Constructional meaning The meaning associated with a structural pattern above and beyond the meaning of its component words.

Continuant A manner feature that characterizes sounds made with free or nearly free airflow through the oral cavity: vowels, fricatives, glides, and liquids.

Continuants Sounds that are produced with a continuous airflow through the mouth.

Contour tone A tone that changes pitch on a single syllable.

Contradiction A relationship between sentences wherein the truth of one sentence requires the falsity of another sentence (e.g., *Raymond is married* contradicts *Raymond is a bachelor*).

Contralateral The control of the right side of the body by the left side of the brain and vice versa.

Contrast Segments are said to contrast when their presence alone may distinguish forms with different meanings from each other (e.g., [s] and [z] in the words *sip* and *zip*).

Converge *See* **Convergence**.

Convergence The modification of language so that it becomes more similar to that of another speaker or group of speakers.

Conversation analysis *See* **Ethnomethodology**.

Conversational implicature Information that is understood through inference but is not actually said.

Conversational maxims *See* **Maxims**.

Conversion A word-formation process that assigns an already existing word to a new syntactic category (also called **zero derivation**) (e.g., *nurse* [V] from *nurse* [N]).

Cooperative overlaps Overlapping of turns in a high-involvement-style conversation according to mutually held conventions of the participants.

Cooperative Principle, The The general overarching guideline thought to underlie conversational interactions: Make your contribution appropriate to the conversation.

Coordinate structure A phrase that is formed by joining two (or more) categories of the same type with a conjunction such as *and* or *or* (e.g., *those men and that woman*).

Coordination The process of grouping together two or more categories of the same type with the help of a conjunction (e.g., *Mary and the white horse*).

Coordination test A test used to determine if a group of words is a **constituent** by joining it to another group of words with a conjunction such as *and* or *or*.

Coronal A place feature that characterizes sounds made with the tongue tip or blade raised (e.g., [t, d, s, θ]).

Corpus analysis A technique for building lexicons by means of automated analysis of a body of texts.

Corpus callosum The bundle of nerve fibers that serves as the main connection between the cerebral hemispheres, allowing the two hemispheres to communicate with one another.

Creativity The characteristic of human language that allows novelty and innovation in response to new thoughts, experiences, and situations.

Creole A language that originated as a **pidgin** and has become established as a first language in a speech community.

Cricoid cartilage The ring-shaped cartilage in the larynx on which the thyroid cartilage rests.

Critical period A particular time frame during which children have to be exposed to language if the acquisition process is to be successful.

Critical period hypothesis The hypothesis that achievement of nativelike proficiency in a second language depends on age of acquisition and is rarely attainable unless the learner begins second language acquisition during the **critical period**.

Cross-sectional (research) Research that investigates and compares subjects selected from different developmental stages.

CT scanning *See* **Computerized Axial Tomography**.

Cuneiform Writing invented in the fourth millenium B.C. and produced by pressing a wedge-shaped stylus into soft clay tablets.

Cyrillic alphabet An alphabet that combined adaptations of **Glagolitic script** with Greek and Hebrew characters, evolving into the alphabets that are currently used to represent some of the languages spoken in the former Soviet Union and in the Balkans.

Deaffrication A type of segmental simplification that turns affricates into fricatives by eliminating the stop portion of the affricate (e.g., [dʒ] becoming [ʒ]).

Declension *See* **Nominal paradigm**.

Deep dyslexia A type of **acquired dyslexia** in which the patient produces a word that is semantically related to the word he or she is asked to read (e.g., producing *father* when asked to read *mother*).

Deep structure The structure generated by the phrase structure rules in accordance with the subcategorization properties of the heads.

Degemination The weakening of a geminate consonant to a nongeminate consonant (e.g., [tt] becoming [t]).

Degree word (Deg) A **functional category** that serves as the specifier of a preposition or an adjective (e.g., *quite* in *quite tired*, *very* in *very near the house*).

Deictics Forms whose use and interpretation depend on the location of the speaker and/or addressee within a particular setting (e.g., *this/that, here/there*).

Delayed release A manner feature that refers to the release of the stop in affricate consonants.

Deletion A process that removes a segment from certain phonetic contexts (e.g., the pronunciation of *fifths* as [fɪfs]).

Denasalization A common substitution process in child language acquisition that involves the replacement of a nasal stop by a nonnasal counterpart (e.g., *come* is pronounced [kʌb]).

Denotation Entities that a word or expression refers to (also called its **referents** or **extension**).

Dentals Sounds made with the tongue placed against or near the teeth.

Dependent variable In an experiment, the behavior or event that is measured.

Derivation (a) In morphology, a word-formation process by which a new word is built from a stem—usually through the addition of an affix—that changes the word class and/or basic meaning of the word. (b) The set of steps or rule applications that results in the formation of a sentence in syntax or of a phonetic representation from an underlying form in phonology.

Derived (phonology) Resulting from the application of phonological rules to underlying representations.

Descriptive (grammar) A grammar that seeks to describe human linguistic ability and knowledge, not to prescribe one system in preference to another. (*See also* **Prescriptive [grammar]**.)

Design features Essential characteristics of communication systems that have been established with reference to human language.

Determiner (Det) A **functional category** that serves as the specifier of a noun (e.g., *a, the, these*).

Deterministic parsing A means of processing sentences in which no more than one analysis at a time is pursued.

Developmental errors Errors that occur in language acquisition and provide evidence of the learner's attempts to create a grammatical system based on his or her hypotheses about the target language (e.g., *why didn't he came to work?*).

Developmental sequences The stages of linguistic development that are relatively invariant across language learners.

Devoicing Voicing assimilation in which a sound becomes voiceless because of a nearby voiceless sound (e.g., the *l* in *place* is devoiced because of the voiceless stop preceding it).

Diacritic A mark added to a phonetic symbol to alter its value in some way (e.g., a circle under a symbol to indicate voicelessness).

Dialect A regional or social variety of a language characterized by its own phonological, syntactic, and lexical properties.

Dialectology A branch of linguistics concerned with the analysis and description of regional varieties of a language.

Diaphragm The large sheet of muscle that separates the chest cavity from the abdomen and helps to maintain the air pressure necessary for speech production.

Diary study A type of naturalistic investigation in which a researcher (often a parent) keeps daily notes on a child's linguistic progress.

Dichotic listening studies Research based on an experimental technique in which the subject listens to different sounds in each ear.

Diglossia The relationship between multiple varieties spoken by one speech community but with sharply distinct domains of use.

Diphthong A vowel that shows a noticeable change in quality within a single syllable (e.g., the vowel sounds in *h<u>ou</u>se* and *r<u>i</u>de*).

Diphthongization A process in which a monophthong becomes a diphthong (e.g., [i:] became [aj] during the Great English Vowel Shift).

Direct negative evidence Language instruction involving correction or focus on form.

Direct object The NP **complement** of a verb (e.g., *a fish* in *Judy caught a fish*).

Discourse A set of utterances that constitute a speech event.

Discourse analysis The field that deals with the organization of texts, including ways in which parts of texts are connected and the devices used for achieving textual structure.

Discourse markers Expressions that bracket utterances in discourse, separating one "unit of talk" from a previous one (e.g., *well, y'know*).

Discrete sign A sign that is distinguished from other signs by stepwise differences (e.g., voiced and voiceless sounds, the numbers of a digital clock).

Displacement A property by which the users of the communication system are able to refer to events that are remote in space and time.

Dissimilation A process whereby one segment becomes less like another segment in its environment (e.g., *anma* 'soul' in a form of Latin became *alma* in Spanish).

Distinctive feature A feature that serves to distinguish contrastive forms (e.g., the feature [voice] is distinctive in English because it underlies the contrast between /p/ and /b/, /t/ and /d/, etc.).

Distribution The set of elements with which an item can cooccur.

Diverge *See* **Divergence**.

Divergence The modification of language so that it becomes more different from that of another speaker or group of speakers.

***Do* insertion** The syntactic rule that places *do* into an empty I position, making **inversion** possible in English questions.

Domains of use Speech situations in which a particular variety is commonly used.

Dorsal A place feature that represents sounds produced when the body of the tongue is involved (e.g., vowels and [k, g]).

Dorsum (of the tongue) The body and back of the tongue.

Double-blind test A test in which a subject's responses are interpreted independently by someone other than the administrator of the test.

Downdrift The maintenance of a distinction among the pitch registers of an utterance even as the overall pitch of the utterance falls.

Dressage Interaction between trainer and animal in which the animal responds to subtle cues given by the trainer.

D-structure *See* **Deep structure**.

Dual-route model A psycholinguistic theory built around the claim that a particular type of language processing can be accomplished in more than one manner.

Duality of patterning A property of communication systems in which meaningless units are combined to form arbitrary signs that, in turn, are recombined to form new larger signs.

Duetting The interchange of calls in a patterned manner between two members of a species.

Dysprosody The lack of sentence intonation, a common characteristic of the speech of Broca's aphasics.

Ebonics *See* **African American Vernacular English (AAVE)**.

Economy constraint A grammatical constraint whose effect is to reduce the computational cost of derivations.

Ejectives Stops or affricates that are made with simultaneous closure of the glottis and constriction of the throat, producing a distinctive "popping" sound.

Enclitic A **clitic** that attaches to the end of a word.

Endocentric compound A compound word in which one member identifies the general class to which the meaning of the entire word belongs (e.g., *dogfood* is a type of food in English). (*See also* **Exocentric compound**.)

Entailment A relation between sentences in which the truth of one sentence necessarily implies the truth of another (e.g., *Gary is Bernice's husband* entails the sentence *Bernice is married*).

Environment The phonetic context in which a sound occurs.

Epenthesis A process that inserts a segment into a particular environment (e.g., the insertion of a schwa in the pronunciation of *athlete* as [æθəlit]).

Ergative The case associated with the subject of a **transitive verb** (but not that of an **intransitive verb**).

Ergative-absolutive pattern Sentence pattern in which **ergative** case is assigned to the **agent** of a **transitive verb**, but **absolutive** case is assigned to the subject of an **intransitive verb** or the object of a transitive verb.

Ethnic dialect A dialect spoken by a particular ethnic group.

Ethnography of communication A type of discourse analysis that concentrates on how language is used to achieve communicative goals in particular social situations.

Ethnolinguistic vitality The strength of an ethnic group identity and the variety of language associated with it as measured by the number of people in the group relative to the majority, the degree of institutional support they receive, and their relative pride in their identity.

Ethnomethodology A type of discourse analysis that focuses on the structural relationship between utterances in conversations.

Euphemism A word or phrase that is less direct than the taboo word it replaces and is considered to be more socially acceptable (e.g., *passed away* for *died*).

Evaluation clause A type of narrative utterance that gives comments or evaluations regarding the events being narrated.

Event-related potentials (ERP) A measurement of electrical activity in the brain that is correlated with the presentation of particular stimulus events.

Evidentiality A system of morphological contrasts indicating the type of evidence for the truth of a statement.

Evidentials Morphological or syntactic elements (frequently **enclitic** morphemes) that indicate the speaker's source of information for the statement he or she is making.

Exclusive A type of first-person plural pronoun whose referents do not include the addressee. (*See also* **Inclusive**.)

Exocentric compound A compound whose meaning does not follow from the meaning of its parts (e.g., *redneck*, since its referent is not a type of neck).

Experimental paradigm A method of investigation that involves a particular way of presenting stimuli and a particular way of measuring responses.

Experimental studies Studies in child language in which researchers make use of specially designed tasks to elicit linguistic activity relevant to a particular phenomenon.

Extension The set of entities to which a word or expression refers (also called its **denotation** or **referents**).

Feature hierarchy A hierarchical representation of how features are related to each other.

Feature (phonetic) The smallest unit of analysis of phonological structure, combinations of which make up segments (e.g., [nasal], [continuant]).

Features (semantic) The semantic components that make up a word's **intension**.

Feeding (rule order) A rule ordering where the first rule makes the application of the following rule possible.

Field dependence A learning style in which the learner operates holistically, perceiving the "field" as a whole rather than in terms of its component parts.

Field independence A learning style in which the learner operates analytically, perceiving the "field" in terms of its component parts rather than as a whole.

Field technique A method of study that does not involve manipulation and control of factors in a laboratory, but rather involves observing phenomena as they occur.

Fissure A relatively deep **sulcus** of the cerebral cortex.

Fixed stress Stress whose position in a word is predictable.

Fixed stress languages Languages in which the position of stress in words is predictable. (*See also* **Fixed stress**.)

Flap A sound commonly identified with *r* and produced when the tongue tip strikes the alveolar ridge as it passes across it (e.g., in North American English, the medial consonant in *bi<u>tt</u>er* and *bi<u>dd</u>er*).

Flapping A phonetic process in which an alveolar stop is pronounced as a voiced flap between vowels, the first of which is generally stressed (e.g., [bʌ́tr̩] → [bʌ́ɾr̩]).

Fluency Second language speech that is produced automatically and without noticeable hesitation.

Fluent aphasia The **aphasia** that occurs due to damage to parts of the left cortex behind the central sulcus, resulting in fluent speech but great difficulty selecting, organizing, and monitoring language production (also called **sensory aphasia**).

Focus on form In second language teaching, the practice of giving explicit instruction about the second language and overtly correcting errors.

Folk etymology Reanalysis of a word that is based on an incorrect historical analysis (e.g., *hamburger* being reanalyzed into two morphemes, *ham* and *burger*).

Foreigner talk The type of speech that is typically addressed to second language learners, characterized by such properties as simple word order and more common vocabulary items (also called **teacher talk**).

Formants The main frequencies of a speech wave.

Fossilized Characteristic of an **interlanguage** grammar that has reached a plateau, i.e., ceased to improve.

Free form An element that can occur in isolation and/or whose position with respect to neighboring elements is not entirely fixed.

Free morpheme A **morpheme** that can be a word by itself (e.g., *fear*).

Free stress Stress whose position in a word is not predictable and must be learned on a case-by-case basis.

Free stress languages Languages in which the position of stress in words is not predictable. (*See also* **Free stress**.)

Free variation The free alternation of allophones and/or phonemes in a given environment (e.g., *sto*[pˀ], *sto*[p]; /ɛ/*conomics*, /i/*conomics*).

Frequency effect The common experimental finding that words that occur more frequently in a language are processed more quickly and more accurately.

Frication The weakening of a stop to a fricative (e.g., [d] becoming [ð]).

Fricatives Consonants produced with a continuous airflow through the mouth, accompanied by a continuous audible noise (e.g., [f], [ʃ]).

Front *See* **Front vowel**.

Front vowel A vowel that is made with the tongue positioned in the front of the oral cavity (e.g., the vowel sounds in *s<u>ea</u>l* and *b<u>a</u>t*).

Frontal lobe The lobe of the brain that lies in front of the central sulcus and in which Broca's area is located.

Fronting A common substitution process in child language acquisition that involves the moving forward of a sound's place of articulation (e.g., *cheese* pronounced as [tsiz]).

Full reduplication A morphological process that duplicates the entire word (e.g., in Turkish, tʃabuk 'quickly'/tʃabuk tʃabuk 'very quickly').

Function words Words such as determiners and conjunctions that specify grammatical relations rather than carry semantic content.

Functional analysis An approach to syntactic analysis that attempts to understand syntactic phenomena in terms of their communicative function.

Functional category A word-level syntactic category whose members specify grammatical relations rather than carry semantic content (e.g., auxiliary verbs, conjunctions, determiners, and degree words) (also called **nonlexical category**).

Functional Magnetic Resonance Imaging (fMRI) A brain imaging technique that yields information on areas of high brain activity during the performance of cognitive tasks.

Fusion A morphological change where a word becomes an affix (e.g., English affixes such as *-hood, -dom,* and *-ly* used to be words).

Fusional languages Languages in which words typically consist of several morphemes and the morphemes that are affixes often mark several grammatical categories simultaneously (e.g., Russian).

Fuzzy concepts Concepts that do not have clear-cut boundaries that distinguish them from other concepts (e.g., the concept POOR).

Garden path sentence A sentence that is difficult to process and interpret because its structure biases sentence parsing toward an incorrect analysis.

Gender *See* **Noun class**.

Gender-exclusive differentiation A type of social differentiation in which the use of some linguistic forms depends on the gender of the speakers.

Gender-variable differentiation The relative frequency with which men and women use certain features of language.

Genetic classification The categorization of languages according to the ancestor languages from which they developed.

Genetic relationships Relationships among languages that have descended from a common ancestor language. (*See also* **Genetic classification** and **Genetically related languages**.)

Genetically related languages Languages that have descended from a common parent (e.g., German and Italian have both descended from Indo-European).

Given information Knowledge that the speaker assumes is available to the addressee at the time of the utterance, either because it is shared by both or because it has already been introduced into the discourse (also called **old information**).

Glagolitic script A script that was introduced in Slavic-speaking areas in the ninth century A.D. for the translation of the Bible.

Glide strengthening The strengthening of a glide to an affricate (e.g., [j] becoming [dʒ]).

Glides Sounds that are produced with an articulation like that of a vowel, but move quickly to another articulation (e.g., [j], [w]).

Gliding A common substitution process in child language acquisition that involves the replacement of a liquid by a glide (e.g., *play* is pronounced [pwej]).

Global aphasia The most severe form of **nonfluent aphasia**, in which the patient is completely mute.

Glottalization A consonant that is made with simultaneous closure of the glottis and constriction of the throat. Glottalized stops and affricates (**ejectives**) are the most common glottalized consonants.

Glottals Sounds produced by using the vocal folds as the primary articulators (e.g., [h], [ʔ]).

Glottis The space between the vocal folds.

Glyphs The symbols used in Mayan writing.

Goal A **thematic role** that describes the end point for a movement (e.g., *Mary* in *Terry gave the skis to Mary*).

Graded (concept) A concept whose members display varying degrees of the characteristics that are considered typical of the concept.

Graded sign A sign that conveys its meaning by changes in degree (e.g., voice volume, a blush).

Grammar The mental system of rules and categories that allows humans to form and interpret the words and sentences of their language.

Grammatical (sentence) A sentence that speakers judge to be a possible sentence in their language.

Grammatical competence Competence in the structural aspects at or below the sentence level.

Grammatical hierarchy A hierarchy of grammatical relations such as subjects and objects in terms of markedness.

Grammatical knowledge Knowledge of the meaning and use of words in sentences. (Compare **real world knowledge**.)

Grammaticalization The change of a lexical form into a grammatical form (e.g., an **affix** or member of a **functional category**).

Grammaticized concepts Concepts that are expressed as affixes or nonlexical categories (e.g., the concept of OBLIGATION as expressed by the auxiliary verb *must*).

Great English Vowel Shift A series of nonphonetically conditioned modifications to long vowels that occurred from the Middle English period to the eighteenth century.

Grimm's Law A set of consonant shifts that took place between Proto-Indo-European and Proto-Germanic.

Gyrus An area where the cerebral cortex is folded out.

Habitual (invariant) be Uninflected *be* used to indicate a habitual state or action in **African American Vernacular English** (e.g., *The coffee be cold* means 'the coffee is usually cold').

Hangul The alphabetic script used to represent Korean, the symbols of which are grouped to represent the syllables of individual morphemes.

Hanja The Korean word for the Chinese characters used in Korean writing.

Head (of a phrase) The **lexical category** around which a phrasal category is built (e.g., V is head of VP, N is head of NP, A of AP, P of PP).

Head (of a word) The morpheme that determines the category of the entire word (e.g., *bird* in *blackbird*).

Hierarchies In the classification of languages, the degrees of **markedness** of particular structures in the world's languages, going from least marked (i.e., most common) to most marked (i.e., least common).

Hieroglyphics An Egyptian pictorial writing system, which later developed into a mixed writing system.

High A dorsal feature that characterizes sounds produced with the tongue body raised.

High involvement style A style of turn-taking in a conversation in which speaker turns overlap.

High vowel A vowel that is made with the tongue raised (e.g., the vowel sounds in *beat* and *lose*).

Hiragana The Japanese syllabary that is used in conjunction with katakana and kanji to write Japanese.

Historical linguistics The linguistic discipline that is concerned with the description and the explanation of language change over time.

Holophrases Utterances produced by children in which one word expresses the type of meaning that would be associated with an entire sentence in adult speech (e.g., *up* used to mean 'Pick me up').

Homophony The situation in which a single form has two or more entirely distinct meanings (e.g., *club* 'a social organization', *club* 'a blunt weapon').

Host The element to which a **clitic** is attached.

Hypercorrection Overgeneralization of particular rules in a language in an attempt to speak (or write) "correctly."

Iconic sign A sign that bears some resemblance to its referent (e.g., a picture of a woman on a washroom door).

Illocutionary competence The ability to understand a speaker's intent and to produce a variety of forms to convey intent.

Illocutionary force The intended meaning of an utterance.

Immersion A method of teaching a second language to children in which students are given most of their content courses and school activities in the target language.

Implementation A practical application of a formal system.

Implicational universals A universal of language that specifies that the presence of one trait implies the presence of another (but not vice versa).

Inalienably possessed nouns Nouns that must always have a pronominal possessor indicated; usually parts of the body or kinship terms.

Inanimate A noun class category in some languages generally assigned to nonliving referents. (*See also* **Animate**.)

Inclusive A contrast in some languages that indicates that the addressee is to be included in the interpretation of the first-person plural morpheme. (*See also* **Exclusive**.)

Incorporation The combination of a word (usually a noun) with a verb to form a compound verb.

Indexical sign A sign that fulfills its function by pointing out its referent, typically by being a partial sample of it (e.g., the track of an animal).

Indexing Finding, identifying, and counting all occurrences of a word in large texts.

Indexing analysis A means of analyzing sociolinguistic variation by putting each instance of a variable on a continuum; used especially to evaluate degree and direction of vowel movement.

Indirect negative evidence The assumption that nonoccurring structures in the linguistic environment are ungrammatical.

Indo-European family The **language family** that includes most of the languages in a broad curve from northern India through western Asia (Iran and Armenia) to Europe.

Infix An **affix** that occurs within a base.

Inflection The modification of a word's form to indicate the grammatical subclass to which it belongs (e.g., the *-s* in *books* marks the plural subclass).

Inflectional language *See* **Fusional languages** and **Synthetic language**.

Insertion rule An operation that adds an element to a tree structure.

Instrumental motivation The desire to achieve proficiency in a new language for utilitarian reasons, such as job promotion.

Integrative motivation The desire to achieve proficiency in a new language in order to participate in the social life of the community that speaks the language.

Intension An expression's inherent sense; the concepts that it evokes.

Intercostals The muscles between the ribs that help to maintain the air pressure necessary for speech production.

Interdentals Sounds made with the tongue placed between the teeth (e.g., [θ], [ð]).

Interlanguage The changing grammatical system that an L2 learner is using at a particular period in his or her acquisition of a second language as he or she moves toward proficiency in the target language.

Internal change A process that substitutes one nonmorphemic segment for another to mark a grammatical contrast (e.g., *sing, sang, sung*).

Internal reconstruction The reconstruction of a **proto-language** that relies on the analysis of morphophonemic variation within a single language.

International Phonetic Alphabet (IPA) A system for transcribing the sounds of speech that attempts to represent each sound of human speech with a single symbol.

Internet survey A linguistic survey completed by subjects who happen to access a given Web site, Internet bulletin board, or special interest list on the Internet.

Intonation Pitch movement in spoken utterances that is not related to differences in word meaning.

Intransitive verb A verb that does not take a direct object (e.g., *sleep*).

Inversion A **transformation** that moves the element in the I position to a position in front of the subject, formulated as: Move I to C.

Isogloss bundle Convergence of several lines drawn on a dialect map to represent boundaries between dialects.

Isoglosses Lines drawn on a dialect map to represent boundaries between dialects.

Isolate A language that is not known to be related to any other living language (e.g., Basque, Kutenai).

Isolating languages Languages whose words typically consist of only one morpheme (e.g., Mandarin). (Also called **analytic languages**.)

Jargon Vocabulary peculiar to some field; also called occupational sociolect.

Jargonaphasia A symptom of severe cases of Wernicke's aphasia in which speech contains very few real words of the language.

Kanji The Japanese word for the Chinese characters used to write Japanese.

Katakana The Japanese syllabary that is used in conjunction with **hiragana** and **kanji** to write Japanese.

Labial A place feature that characterizes sounds articulated with one or both lips.

Labials Sounds made with closure or near closure of the lips (e.g., the initial sounds of *win* and *forget*).

Labiodentals Sounds involving the lower lip and upper teeth (e.g., the initial sounds of *freedom* and *vintage*).

Labiovelars Sounds made with the tongue raised near the velum and the lips rounded at the same time (e.g., the initial sound of *wound*).

Language bioprogram hypothesis The hypothesis that similarities among creoles reflect linguistic universals both in terms of first language acquisition and with respect to processes and structures that are innate.

Language contact Interaction between speakers of one language and speakers of another language or dialect.

Language family In language classification, a group of languages with a historical origin in the same **proto-language**.

Language planning Official policy with the goal of increasing or limiting the domain of use of a particular language or languages.

Laryngeal features Phonological features that represent laryngeal states (e.g., [voice], [spread glottis], and [constricted glottis]).

Laryngeal node A node in the feature geometry in autosegmental phonology that dominates laryngeal features such as voicing, spread glottis, and constricted glottis.

Larynx The box-like structure located in the throat through which air passes during speech production; commonly known as the voicebox.

Late closure A parsing principle that claims that in sentence comprehension, humans prefer to attach new words to the clause currently being processed.

Lateral (sound) A sound made with the sides of the tongue lowered (e.g., varieties of [l]).

Lateral fissure The fissure that separates the temporal lobe from the frontal and parietal lobes in the brain.

Lateral fricative A **lateral sound** made with a narrow enough closure to be classified as a fricative.

Lateralization The unilateral control of cognitive functions by either the left or the right side of the brain (e.g., language is lateralized to the left hemisphere in most people).

Lateralized *See* **Lateralization**.

Laterals Sounds made with the sides of the tongue lowered (e.g., varieties of *l*).

Lax vowel A vowel that is made with a placement of the tongue that results in relatively less vocal tract constriction (e.g., the vowel sounds in *hit* and *but*).

Learning strategies The ways in which language learners process language input to develop linguistic knowledge.

Length The subjective impression of time occupied by the duration of a **phone**.

Lesion Severe damage to the brain.

Lexical ambiguity A situation in which a single form has two or more meanings (e.g., a *trunk* is a 'piece of luggage' or an 'elephant nose').

Lexical category The word-level syntactic categories noun (N), verb (V), adjective (A), and preposition (P).

Lexical decision An experimental paradigm in which a person sees or hears a stimulus and must judge as quickly as possible whether or not that stimulus is a word of his or her language.

Lexical diffusion Linguistic change that first manifests itself in a few words and then gradually spreads through the vocabulary of the language.

Lexical gaps Gaps in the lexicon that result from technological innovation or contact with another culture.

Lexicalization The process whereby concepts are encoded in the words of a language (e.g., the concepts of MOTION and MANNER are both encoded by the word *roll*).

Lexicon A speaker's mental dictionary, which contains information about the syntactic properties, meaning, and phonological representation of a language's words.

Lexifier language The language that provides most of the lexical items to a contact variety.

Lingua franca A language that is used when speakers of two or more different languages come into contact and do not know each other's languages.

Linguistic competence Speakers' knowledge of their language, which allows them to produce and understand an unlimited number of utterances, including many that are novel.

Linguistic insecurity The degree to which speakers believe that their own variety is not standard.

Linguistic market analysis The analysis of linguistic variation according to the degree to which speakers need the standard language in their everyday lives.

Linguistic typology An approach to language classification that classifies languages according to their common structural characteristics without regard for **genetic relationships**.

Linguistic universals Structural characteristics that occur across the languages of the world.

Linguistics The discipline that studies the nature and use of language.

Liquids A class of consonants containing *l* and *r* sounds and their variants.

Lobes Substructures of the hemispheres of the brain that appear to have distinct responsibilities (e.g., **frontal lobe**, **temporal lobe**).

Location A **thematic role** that specifies the place where an action occurs (e.g., *the SkyDome* in *The athletes practiced in the SkyDome*).

Logogram A written symbol representing a morpheme or word.

Logographic writing A type of writing in which symbols represent morphemes or even entire words.

Longitudinal fissure The fissure that extends from the front of the brain to the back and separates the left and right cerebral hemispheres.

Longitudinal studies Studies that examine language development over an extended period of time.

Loudness The subjective impression of a speech sound's volume relative to the sounds around it.

Low (sound) A sound made with the tongue lowered (e.g., [a], [ɑ], [æ]).

Low vowel A vowel that is made with the tongue lowered (e.g., the vowel sounds made in the words *c<u>a</u>t* and *t<u>o</u>p*).

Machine translation The process by which a machine (e.g., a computer) takes text spoken or written in one language and translates it into another language.

Macrofamilies *See* **Phyla**.

Major class features Phonological features that represent the classes consonant, obstruent, nasal, liquid, glide, and vowel.

Majority rules strategy A secondary strategy used to reconstruct proto-forms, which stipulates that the segment found in the majority of cognates should be assumed to be part of the **proto-form**. (*See also* **Phonetic plausibility strategy**.)

Manner features Phonological features that represent manner of articulation.

Manners of articulation The various configurations produced by positioning the lips, tongue, velum, and glottis in different ways (e.g., nasal, fricative, liquid).

Marginal analysis Analysis of sociolinguistic data in which overall percentages of occurrences in relevant linguistic and social contexts are reported for each variant.

Marked Occurring less commonly in world languages. (*See also* **Marked traits** and **Markedness theory**.)

Marked traits Complex or less common features or characteristics of languages.

Markedness The quality of being relatively complex or rare in world languages. (*See also* **Marked traits** and **Markedness theory**.)

Markedness Differential Hypothesis The hypothesis that L2 elements that are different and more **marked** than the L1 elements will cause difficulty in learning L2.

Markedness theory A theory that classifies traits or patterns of languages as marked (those that are considered to be more complex and/or universally rarer) and unmarked (those that are considered to be less complex and/or universally more common).

Matrix A representation of sounds, in which all the relevant distinctive features and their values are placed in an array.

Matrix clause The larger S in which a complement clause occurs.

Maxim of Manner A principle that is thought to underlie the efficient use of language and is formulated as: Avoid ambiguity and obscurity; be brief and orderly.

Maxim of Quality A principle that is thought to underlie the efficient use of language and is formulated as: Try to make your contribution one that is true. (Do not say things that are false or for which you lack adequate evidence.)

Maxim of Quantity A principle that is thought to underlie the efficient use of language and is formulated as: Do not make your contribution more or less informative than required.

Maxim of Relation A principle that is thought to underlie the efficient use of language and is formulated as: Be relevant.

Maxims The specific principles that ensure that conversational interactions satisfy **The Cooperative Principle.**

Meaning The message or content that a sign or utterance conveys.

Mental lexicon See **Lexicon**.

Merge A syntactic operation that combines elements to create phrases and sentences.

Merger A change in a phonological system in which two or more phonemes collapse into one, thereby reducing the number of phonemes in that language.

Mesolect A creole variety that falls between an **acrolect** and a **basilect** in terms of the amount of influence from the standard language.

Metaphor The understanding of one concept in terms of another, sometimes responsible for language change (e.g., "argument" understood in terms of "war": *She annihilated him in the debate*).

Metaphorical code-switching The use of code-switching to express solidarity with or distance from the speech communities associated with the languages being switched.

Metathesis A process that reorders a sequence of segments (e.g., in child language, pronouncing *spaghetti* as [pəskɛɾi]).

Mid vowel A vowel that is made with the tongue neither raised nor lowered (e.g., the vowel sounds in *set* and *Coke*).

Minimal attachment A proposed parsing principle that claims that, in sentence comprehension, humans tend to attach incoming material into phrase structure using the fewest nodes possible.

Minimal pair Two forms with distinct meanings that differ by only one segment found in the same position in each form (e.g., [ʃɪp] and [ʃip]).

Mixed type language A language that simultaneously has some characteristics of two or more morphological types such as isolating, polysynthetic, agglutinating, and fusional types.

Modifier An optional element that describes a property of a **head** (e.g., *blue* in *that blue car,* or *that Gloria likes* in *the car that Gloria likes*).

Module A unit of processing that is relatively autonomous from other processing units.

Morph A meaningful sequence of sounds that cannot be divided into smaller meaningful component parts. Morphs that have the same meaning and are in **complementary distribution** are members of the same **morpheme** (e.g., the English plural morpheme includes a number of morphs, including /z/, /s/, /əz/, and /ən/).

Morpheme The smallest unit of language that carries information about meaning or function (e.g., *books* consists of the two morphemes *book* + *s*).

Morphology The system of categories and rules involved in word formation and interpretation.

Morphophonemics Rules that account for alternations among **allomorphs**.

Morphophonology *See* **Morphophonemics**.

Motherese The type of speech that is typically addressed to young children (also called **caregiver speech**).

Motion verbs Words that can describe motion through space (e.g., *come, go,* and *move* in English).

Motor aphasia *See* **Nonfluent aphasia**.

Move A syntactic operation that transports an element to a new position within a particular sentence.

Movement test A test used to determine if a group of words is a **constituent** by moving it as a single unit to a different position within the sentence.

MRD Machine-readable dictionary.

Multiplex networks Social networks where the connections are based on several kinds of relationships.

Murmur The glottal state that produces voiced sounds with the vocal folds relaxed enough to allow enough air to escape to produce a simultaneous whispery effect (also called **whispery voice**).

Mutual intelligibility The criterion that is sometimes used to distinguish between language and dialect: Mutually intelligible varieties of a language can be understood by speakers of each variety and are therefore dialects of the same language.

Narrative A type of discourse unit that tells a story.

Nasal A manner feature that characterizes any sound made with the **velum** lowered.

Nasal phone Sound produced by lowering the velum, allowing air to pass through the nasal passages.

Nasal vowels Vowels produced with a lowered **velum** so that air passes through the oral and nasal cavities at the same time.

Nasalization The nasalizing effect that a nasal consonant can have on an adjacent vowel.

Native speaker One who has acquired a language as a child in a natural setting.

Nativism The view that certain grammatical knowledge is inborn.

Natural class A class of sounds that shares a **feature** or features (e.g., voiced stops).

Natural language processing systems Computer systems that can process human language.

Naturalistic approach An approach to investigating child language in which researchers observe and record children's spontaneous verbal behavior.

Naturalness A criterion that guides language reconstruction by determining whether or not changes are natural.

Near-minimal pair Two forms with distinct meanings that contrast segments in nearly identical environments.

Negative evidence Information as to the ungrammatical nature of utterances.

Neurolinguistics The study of how language is represented and processed in the brain.

Neurons The basic information-processing units of the nervous system, also called nerve cells.

Neuroscience The scientific study of the brain.

New information Knowledge that is introduced into the discourse for the first time.

Node *See* **Class node**.

Nominal paradigm The set of related forms associated with a noun (also called a **declension**).

Nominative-accusative pattern Sentence pattern in which the subject of the sentence is identified by nominative **case**, and the direct object is marked by accusative **case**.

No-naming The practice of avoiding address terms when participants are unsure which term to use.

Nondeterministic parsing A means of processing sentences in which more than one analysis at a time can be pursued.

Nonfluent aphasia Aphasia that results from damage to parts of the brain in front of the central sulcus and is characterized by slow, effortful speech production (also called **motor aphasia**).

Nonlexical category *See* **Functional category**.

Nonstandard (dialect) A variety of language that differs from the standard dialect in systematic ways.

Nonstridents Coronal fricatives and affricates that have less acoustic noise than **stridents** ([θ, ð] are nonstridents).

Nonsyllabic (sounds) Sounds that do not act as syllable peaks, as distinguished from **syllabic** sounds.

Nonterminal (intonation) contour Rising or level intonation at the end of an utterance, often signaling that the utterance is incomplete.

Nonterminal nodes Parts of a structure that are not lexical items, for example VP, NP, Det, N. Compare with **terminal nodes**.

Northern Cities Shift The systematic change in vowel sounds taking place in cities around the Great Lakes. (*See also* **Shift**.)

Noun (N) A **lexical category** that typically names entities, can usually be inflected for number and possession (in English), and functions as the **head** of a noun phrase (e.g., *key*, *Bob*, *perception*).

Noun class A grammatical category dividing nouns into classes often based on shared semantic properties (also called **gender**).

Noun incorporation *See* **Incorporation**.

NP Movement A transformation that moves a noun phrase into the subject position.

Nucleus (N) A vocalic element that forms the core of a syllable (e.g., the vowel [æ] is the nucleus of the first syllable of *Patrick*).

Null Subject Parameter A cross-linguistic variation that allows some languages to drop subject pronouns, while other languages require an overt grammatical subject.

Number The morphological category that expresses contrasts involving countable quantities (e.g., in English, the two-way distinction between singular and plural).

Object permanence A developmental milestone characterized by the child's ability to recognize that objects have an existence independent of one's interaction with them.

Oblique NP A noun phrase that combines with a preposition.

Obstruent Any nonsonorant consonant: fricatives, affricates, oral stops.

Occipital lobe The area of the brain to the rear of the angular gyrus in which the visual cortex is located.

Official language A language that has been designated by political or other official authorities as the working language of a region, nation, or other group.

Old information *See* **Given information**.

One-word stage A stage of first language acquisition at which children characteristically produce one-word utterances.

Onomatopoeic words Words that sound like the thing that they name (e.g., *plop*, *hiss*).

Onset The portion of a syllable that precedes the nucleus (e.g., /spl/ in *spleen*).

Ontogeny Model Predicts that during the course of SLA, transfer errors start out high in number and subsequently decrease, while developmental errors start out low in number, then increase, and finally decrease.

Open syllable A syllable that is not closed by a consonant.

Opening A discourse unit conventionally used to begin a conversation.

Oral phones Sounds produced with the velum raised and the airflow through the nasal passage cut off.

Orderly heterogeneity Variation in use of language among groups (e.g. social groups) such that members from one group can be distinguished from members of other groups on the basis of linguistic **variants**.

Orientation clause A type of narrative utterance that gives background information to the story; e.g., the time and place where it occurred.

Orthography A set of conventions for representing language in written form.

Overextension A developmental phenomenon in which the meaning of a child's word overlaps with that of the equivalent adult word, but also extends beyond it (e.g., *dog* is used to refer to other animals as well as dogs).

Overgeneralization A developmental phenomenon that results from the overly broad application of a rule (e.g., *falled* instead of *fell*).

Overregularization *See* **Overgeneralization**.

Palatalization The effect that front vowels and the palatal guide [j] typically have on velar, alveolar, and dental stops, making their place of articulation more palatal (e.g., the first sound of *k̲eep* is palatalized).

Palatals Sounds produced with the tongue on or near the palate (e.g., [j]).

Palate The highest part of the roof of the mouth.

Palatoalveolar *See* **Alveopalatal (area)**.

Paragraphia Writing errors made by Broca's aphasics that have characteristics corresponding to their speech.

Parallel processing model A psycholinguistic theory built around the claim that phonological, lexical, and syntactic processes are carried out simultaneously.

Parameter The set of alternatives for a particular phenomenon made available by **Universal Grammar** to individual languages.

Parameter setting The determination of which option permitted by a particular **parameter** is appropriate for the language being learned.

Paraphrases Two sentences that have the same basic meaning (e.g., *A Canadian wrote that book* is a paraphrase of *That book was written by a Canadian*).

Parietal lobe The lobe of the brain that lies behind the central sulcus and above the temporal lobe.

Parser A program or mental process for doing grammatical analysis.

Parsing The procedure through which speech or text is analyzed by assigning categories to words and structure to strings of words.

Partial assimilation A phonological process by which neighboring segments become more like each other, e.g., by sharing the same **place of articulation** or the same **manner of articulation**.

Partial reduplication A morphological process in which part of a stem is repeated to form a new word (e.g., in Tagalog, *takbuh* 'run' and *tatakbuh* 'will run').

Partial suppletion A morphological process that marks a grammatical contrast by replacing part of a morpheme (e.g., *think/thought*).

Passive sentence A sentence whose **theme** is encoded as grammatical subject (e.g., *The report was prepared by the committee members*).

Patient The recipient of an action (e.g., *dolphin* in *Marilyn fed the dolphin*).

Pejoration A semantic change in which the meaning of a word becomes more negative or unfavorable (e.g., the meaning of *wench* used to be 'girl').

Performance Actual language use in particular situations.

Person A morphological category that typically distinguishes among the first person (the speaker), the second person (the addressee), and the third person (anyone else) (e.g., in English, the difference between *I*, *you*, and *she/he/it*).

Pharyngeals Sounds made through the modification of airflow in the **pharynx** by retracting the tongue or constricting the pharynx.

Pharynx The area of the throat between the **uvula** and the **larynx**.

Pheremones Chemicals used by animals specifically for communicative purposes.

Phoenician script An early writing system, which had twenty-two consonantal signs, devised by the Semitic peoples of ancient Phoenicia as early as 1000 B.C.

Phone Any sound used in human language (also called a **speech sound**).

Phoneme A contrastive segmental unit with predictable phonetic variants.

Phonemic level *See* **Phonemic representation**.

Phonemic paraphasias Speech errors that result from phonemic substitutions and omissions (e.g., *spoon* may be pronounced as *poon*).

Phonemic representation The representation that consists of the phonemes to which allophones belong; predicable phonetic information is not represented.

Phonemic transcription A type of transcription of sounds where phonetic details are ignored and only phonemic contrast is recorded.

Phonetic determinative The part of a Chinese character that provides information about the pronunciation of the corresponding morpheme.

Phonetic level *See* **Phonetic representation**.

Phonetic plausibility strategy The primary strategy used to reconstruct protoforms that requires any sound changes posited to be phonetically plausible. (*See also* **Majority rules strategy**.)

Phonetic representation The representation that consists of predictable variants or allophones.

Phonetic sound change A sound change that results in a new allophone of an already existing phoneme.

Phonetic transcription A type of transcription of sounds in which not only phonemic differences but also phonetic details are recorded.

Phonetically conditioned change Sound change that begins as subtle alterations in the sound pattern of a language in particular phonetic environments.

Phonetics The study of the inventory and structure of the sounds of language.

Phonographic writing A type of writing in which symbols represent syllables or segments.

Phonological dyslexia A type of acquired dyslexia in which the patient seems to have lost the ability to use spelling-to-sound rules and can only read words that they have seen before.

Phonological processes *See* **Processes**.

Phonological representation *See* **Phonemic representation**.

Phonological rules Rules that relate the underlying forms of words to their phonetic forms.

Phonological sound change A sound change that results in the addition, elimination, or rearrangement of phonemes (e.g., splits, mergers).

Phonology The component of a grammar made up of the elements and principles that determine how sounds pattern in a language.

Phonotactics The set of constraints on how sequences of segments pattern.

Phrase A unit of syntactic structure that is built by combining words together so that the phrase consists of a head and an optional specifier and/or complement (e.g., *the apple, Bob, hurried to class*).

Phrase structure rule A rule that specifies how a syntactic **constituent** is formed out of other smaller syntactic constituents (e.g., S → NP VP).

Phrase structure schema The blueprint for the internal structure of phrases.

Phyla The groups into which purportedly related language **stocks** are placed (also called superstocks).

Pictograms Pictorial representations of objects or events.

Pidgin A **lingua franca** with a highly simplified grammatical structure that has emerged as a mixture of two or more languages and has no native speakers.

Pinyin The system of writing Mandarin with a modified Latin alphabet, used for such things as street signs and brand names.

Pitch The auditory property of a sound that enables us to place it on a scale that ranges from low to high.

Place features Phonological features that represent place of articulation.

Place node A node in the feature geometry in autosegmental phonology, which dominates major place features.

Places of articulation The points at which the airstream is modified in the vocal tract to produce **phones** (also called *points of articulation*).

Plural An inflectional category associated with nouns with more than one referent.

Politeness formulas Modifications of a simple expression so that it can convey politeness (e.g., *Open the window!* → *Please open the window.*).

Polysemy The situation in which a word has two or more related meanings (e.g., *bright* 'intelligent', *bright* 'shining').

Polysynthetic languages Languages in which single words can consist of long strings of lexical categories and affixes, often expressing the meaning of an entire sentence in English (e.g., Inuktitut).

Positive evidence Grammatical utterances in the learner's linguistic environment.

Positive politeness The use of politeness conventions to express regard and solidarity with other participants in discourse.

Positron emission tomography (PET) A brain imaging technique that uses radioactive isotopes to measure changes in brain metabolism associated with particular cognitive and behavioral tasks.

Postal survey A linguistic survey given in the form of a written questionnaire and distributed by mailing batches of questionnaires to selected intermediaries in the community who then pass them on to subjects.

Postposition A P that occurs after its complement. (*See* **Preposition**.)

Postvocalic r An *r* that occurs after a vowel in the same syllable (e.g., the *r* in *core* or *darling*).

Power The degree of control that one group or individual may hold over another.

Pragmatics Speakers' and addressees' background attitudes and beliefs, their understanding of the context of an utterance, and their knowledge of how language can be used for a variety of purposes.

Predicate A traditional term for the verb phrase in a sentence.

Prefix An **affix** that is attached to the front of its base (e.g., *re-* in *replay*).

Preposition (P) A minor **lexical category** whose members typically designate relations in space or time (e.g., *in*, *before*); they come before the NP complement with which they combine to form a PP.

Prescriptive (grammar) A grammar that aims to state the linguistic facts in terms of how they should be. (*See also* **Descriptive**.)

Presupposition The assumption or belief implied by the use of a particular word or structure.

Prewriting Possible forerunners of writing, such as incised bone or clay counters used to keep records.

Primary stress The most prominent stress of a word.

Prime In a priming experiment, this is the stimulus that is expected to affect a subject's **response accuracy** and **latency** to the following stimulus.

Priming A situation in which the presentation of a stimulus makes it easier to process the following stimulus.

Priming effect In a priming experiment, this is the extent to which a priming stimulus facilitates the processing of the next stimulus.

Principal component A set of variables that when taken together, show patterns of variation that provide the best statistical fit for determining how test subjects should be grouped together.

Principal components analysis (PCA) An approach to studying social differentiation in which the statistical investigation of a large number of linguistic variants precedes determining what social similarities are shared among them.

Principle A The syntactic principle that constrains the interpretation of reflexive pronouns and is formulated as: A **reflexive pronoun** must have an antecedent (within the same clause) that c-commands it.

Principle B The syntactic principle that constrains the interpretation of pronominals and is formulated as: A **pronominal** must not have an antecedent (within the same clause) that c-commands it.

Principle of Compositionality, The A principle underlying sentence interpretation that is formulated as: The meaning of a sentence is determined by the meaning of its component parts and the manner in which they are arranged in syntactic structure.

Processes Articulatory adjustments that occur during the production of speech (e.g., **deletion**, **epenthesis**, **assimilation**).

Proclitic A **clitic** that attaches to the beginning of a word.

Productivity In morphology, the relative freedom with which affixes can combine with bases of the appropriate category.

Progressive assimilation Assimilation in which a sound influences a following segment (e.g., liquid-glide devoicing).

Pronominal A pronoun whose interpretation may, but does not have to, be determined by an antecedent in the same sentence (e.g., *he*, *her*).

Pronoun (Pro) A minor **lexical category** whose members can replace a noun phrase and look to another element for their interpretation (e.g., *he*, *herself*, *it*).

Prosodic properties *See* **Suprasegmental properties**.

Proto-form The form that is reconstructed as the source of cognate words in related languages.

Proto-Indo-European (PIE) The proto-language from which evolved most of the languages of Europe, Persia (Iran), and the northern part of India.

Proto-language The reconstructed language that is presumed to be the common source for two or more related languages (e.g., Proto-Indo-European).

Prototypes The best exemplars of a concept (e.g., robins or sparrows are prototypes of the concept BIRD).

Psycholinguistic model A schematic representation based on experimental results of how language is processed mentally.

Psycholinguistics The study of the mental processes and representations involved in language comprehension and production.

Q feature In syntax, a feature in the **complementizer** position that marks a sentence as a question and that may attract elements (such as an **auxiliary verb**) to the complementizer position.

Qualifier (Qual) A **nonlexical category** for a type of adverb that can appear in the **specifier** position of the verb phrase.

Radical The part of a Chinese character that provides clues about the morpheme's meaning (also called a **key**).

Reading The interpretation for a particular utterance.

Real-world knowledge Knowledge of what is likely in real life.

Reanalysis A source of language change that involves an attempt to attribute an internal structure to a word that formerly was not broken down into component morphemes (e.g., *ham* + *burger*).

Rebus principle In writing, the use of a sign for any word that is pronounced like the word whose meaning the sign represented initially.

Recast A repetition of a child's utterance that includes adjustments to its form and/or content.

Reduced A phonological characteristic of schwa [ə], indicating a weakly articulated, unstressed variant of stressed vowels.

Reduced vowel *See* **Schwa**.

Redundancy The use of different modalities to convey the same information.

Reduplication A morphological process that repeats all or part of the base to which it is attached. (*See also* **Partial reduplication** and **Full reduplication**.)

Referents The set of entities to which a word or expression refers (also called its **denotation** or **extension**).

Reflexive pronoun A pronoun that must have a c-commanding antecedent, usually in the same clause (e.g., *himself, herself*).

Regional dialect A speech variety spoken in a particular geographical area (e.g., Appalachian English).

Register A speech variety appropriate to a particular speech situation (e.g., formal versus casual).

Register tone A tone that has a stable pitch over a single syllable.

Regressive assimilation Assimilation in which a sound influences a preceding segment (e.g., **nasalization** in English).

Regressive saccades Eye movements in which the eyes dart backward to a section of text that has been previously read.

Relational analysis A syntactic analysis in which phenomena are described in terms of grammatical relations such as **subject** and **direct object** rather than morphological patterns or the order of words.

Relexification hypothesis The hypothesis that **creoles** are formed by using words from one language and the grammatical system of another.

Relic forms Forms that used to be widespread in a language but have survived only in a particular dialect (e.g., **a-prefixing** is a relic form in Appalachian English).

Representations Models of one aspect of language (e.g., phonological representation, syntactic representation).

Response accuracy The correctness of a subject's responses to particular stimuli in an experiment.

Response latency The amount of time taken by a subject in an experiment to respond to a stimulus.

Retroflex Sounds produced by curling the tongue tip back into the mouth (e.g., American English [r]).

Rhotacism A type of weakening that typically involves the change of [z] to [r].

Rhyme (R) The **nucleus** and the **coda** of a syllable (e.g., [uts] in the word *boots*).

Right ear advantage A phenomenon where speech is louder and clearer when it is heard in the right ear than in the left ear for right-handed people.

Root (of a word) In a complex word, the morpheme that remains after all affixes are removed (e.g., *mind* in *unmindfulness*).

Root (of the tongue) The part of the tongue that is contained in the upper part of the throat.

Root node The highest node of the feature hierarchy.

Round A place feature that characterizes sounds made by protruding the lips (e.g., [ɔ], [w]).

Rounded (sounds) Sounds made with the lips protruding (e.g., [ow], [ɔ]).

Rounding The act of protruding the lips to make **rounded sounds**.

Runic writing A writing system that was developed shortly after the beginning of the Christian era by Germanic tribes and that lasted until the sixteenth century.

Saccades The quick and uneven movements of the eyes during reading.

Schwa The mid lax unrounded vowel that is characterized by briefer duration than any of the other vowels (also called a **reduced vowel**) (e.g., the underlined vowels in *Canada*, *suppose*).

Second language acquisition (SLA) The acquisition of a language that is not one's native language.

Secondary stress The second most prominent stress in a word.

Segmental change A sound change that affects a segment.

Segments Individual speech sounds.

Self-praise avoidance The use of self-deprecating expressions in response to a compliment.

Semantic broadening The process in which the meaning of a word becomes more general or more inclusive than its historically earlier form (e.g., the word *aunt* used to mean only 'father's sister').

Semantic decomposition *See* **Componential analysis**.

Semantic features The components of meaning that make up a word's **intension** (e.g., *man* has the feature [+human]; *dog* has the feature [-human]).

Semantic narrowing The process in which the meaning of a word becomes less general or less inclusive than its historically earlier meaning (e.g., the word *meat* used to mean any type of food).

Semantic shift The process in which a word loses its former meaning, taking on a new, often related meaning (e.g., *immoral* used to mean 'not customary').

Semantics The study of meaning in human language.

Semiotics The study of signs.

Sensory aphasia *See* **Fluent aphasia**.

Sentence (S) A syntactic unit consisting of a noun phrase and a verb phrase.

Sentence ambiguity The possibility that a sentence can be interpreted in more than one way.

Sequential change Sound change that involves sequences of segments (e.g., **assimilation**).

Serial processing model A psycholinguistic theory built around the claim that language processing proceeds in a step-by-step manner.

Seriation A child's ability to arrange objects in order of increasing or decreasing size.

Setting Contextual information having to do with the physical environment in which a sentence is uttered.

Shift A change in a phonological system in which a series of phonemes is systematically modified so that their organization with respect to each other is altered (e.g., the **Great English Vowel Shift**).

Shortest move The requirement in syntax that constituents should be moved the shortest possible distance from their original position.

Sibilants *See* **Stridents**.

Sign A unit of communication structure that consists of two parts: a **signifier** (such as a sequence of sounds [tri]) and something **signified** (such as a tree in the real world).

Signal A sign that triggers a specific action on the part of the receiver (e.g., traffic lights).

Signified The real-world object that a sign represents, as well as the sign's conceptual content.

Signifier That part of a sign that stimulates at least one sense organ of the receiver of a message.

Similarity Differential Rate Hypothesis The hypothesis that claims that the rates of acquisition for dissimilar phenomena in two languages are faster than for similar phenomena.

Simple vowels Vowels that do not show a noticeable change in quality during their production (also called monophthongs) (e.g., the vowel sounds of *cab* and *get*).

Simple word A word that consists of a single **morpheme** (e.g., *horse*).

Single-route model A psycholinguistic theory built around the claim that a particular type of language processing is accomplished in one manner only.

Singular An inflectional category associated with nouns with a single referent.

Situational code-switching Switching between languages for clearly identifiable reasons, such as when reporting the speech of another or when the topic of conversation switches from personal to business affairs.

Slang An informal nonstandard speech variety characterized by newly coined and rapidly changing vocabulary.

Social network analysis An approach to sociolinguistic research in which the researcher is a participant-observer of a social group and interprets linguistic variation in terms of the kinds and densities of relationships experienced by speakers.

Sociolect A speech variety spoken by a group of people who share a particular social characteristic, such as socioeconomic class, ethnicity, or age.

Sociolinguistic competence The ability to understand and produce a variety of social dialects in appropriate circumstances.

Sociolinguistic norms Conventions for use of language structures in particular social situations.

Sociolinguistic variables Alternative ways of saying the same thing.

Sociolinguistics The study of the social aspects of language.

Sociolinguistics of language The study of how language structures are associated with particular social circumstances.

Sociolinguistics of society The study of how language structures are related to a speaker's social identity.

Solidarity The degree of intimacy or similarity that one group or individual may feel for another.

Song In bird communication, lengthy, elaborate patterns of mostly pitched sounds.

Sonorant A major class feature that characterizes all and only the "singables": vowels, glides, liquids, and nasals.

Sonorous Characterized by a relatively open vocal tract with relatively little obstruction of airflow as a sound is made (e.g., vowels are sonorous sounds).

Sound change A systematic change of sounds that took place over a long period.

Sound class *See* **Class (sound)**.

Sound shift The systematic modification of a series of phonemes (e.g., Grimm's Law).

Source A **thematic role** that describes the starting point for a movement (e.g., *Maine* in *The senator sent the lobster from Maine to Nebraska*).

Southern Shift The systematic change in pronunciation of vowels in the southern states of the United States. (*See also* **Shift**.)

Spatial metaphor Use of a word that is primarily associated with spatial orientation to talk about physical and psychological states.

Specifier A word that helps to make more precise the meaning of the **head** of the phrase and that occurs immediately beneath XP (e.g., *the* in *the book*).

Spectrogram An acoustic recording that graphically shows the frequency, intensity, and time of sounds.

Speech act theory A theory explaining how speakers use language to accomplish intended actions and how hearers infer intended meaning from what is said.

Speech community A group whose members share both a particular language or variety of language and the norms for its appropriate use in social context.

Speech event An identifiable type of discourse associated with a particular speech situation.

Speech recognition The ability (e.g., of a computer) to decode the wave forms that constitute spoken language.

Speech recognition system A computerized system that uses spoken language as input and decodes it to produce a written text or to give orders to another machine.

Speech situation The social situation in which language is used.

Speech sound *See* **Phone**.

Speech synthesis system A computerized system (sometimes called text-to-speech synthesis) that converts written text to spoken language (e.g., reading aloud to the visually impaired).

Speech variety The language or form of language used by any group of speakers.

Spelling pronunciation One factor in sound change, where a new pronunciation reflects the spelling of the word (e.g., *often*).

Split brain experiments Studies that investigate the effects of surgically severing the **corpus callosum**.

Splits Phonological changes in which two allophones become separate phonemes due to the loss of the conditioning environment.

Spoonerisms A type of speech error, named after Reverend William A. Spooner, in which words or sounds are rearranged with often humorous results.

Spread Glottis ([SG]) A laryngeal feature that refers to the position of the **vocal folds** and that distinguishes unaspirated from aspirated sounds.

Spreading Association of a feature to neighboring segments in autosegmental phonology.

S-structure *See* **Surface structure**.

Standard language The prestige variety of a language that is employed by the government and media, is used and taught in educational institutions, and is the main or only written variety.

Stem The base to which an inflectional **affix** is added (e.g., *modification* is the stem for *-s* in the word *modifications*).

Stemming (or stripping) algorithm A computer program for doing automated morphological analysis.

Stimulus-bound communication Communication that only occurs when it is triggered by exposure to a certain stimulus or for certain specific ends (e.g., the warning call of a bird).

Stocks In language classification, groups of related language families.

Stopping In child language acquisition, the replacement of a fricative by a corresponding stop (e.g., *zebra* is pronounced [dibrə]).

Stops Sounds made with a complete and momentary closure of airflow through the vocal tract (e.g., [p], [t], [k]).

Stress *See* **Stressed vowels**.

Stressed vowels Vowels that are perceived as relatively more prominent due to the combined effects of pitch, loudness, and length.

Strident A manner feature of fricatives and affricates characterized by greater acoustic noise (in English, [s, z, ʃ, ʒ, tʃ, dʒ]).

Stridents The noisier coronal fricatives and affricates (in English, [s, z, ʃ, ʒ, tʃ, dʒ]) (also called **sibilants**).

Stroke A hemorrhage in the brain or the blockage or rupture of an artery, causing brain damage (also called a **cerebrovascular accident**).

Strong generative capacity Capacity to describe correctly the structures of the strings of a language.

Structurally ambiguous A property of phrases or sentences whose component words can be combined in more than one way (e.g., *fast cars and motorcyles*).

Style The level of formality associated with a linguistic structure or set of structures classified along a continuum from most informal to most formal.

Subcategorization The classification of words in terms of their complement options (e.g., the verb *devour* is subcategorized for a complement NP).

Subject The NP occurring immediately under S (e.g., *Irene* in *Irene is a tailor).*

Subject Constraint, The A constraint on transformations that prevents elements from being moved out of a subject phrase.

Subset Principle, The The initial or default setting of a parameter will correspond to the option that permits fewer patterns.

Substitution (of sounds) Replacement of one segment with another similar sounding segment.

Substitution test A test used to determine if a group of words is a syntactic **constituent** by replacing it with a single word.

Substrate language A language hypothesized to have supplied the basic grammatical structure for a contact variety.

Substratum influence The influence of a politically or culturally nondominant language on a dominant language in the area (e.g., the borrowing of words into English from Amerindian languages).

Suffix An **affix** that is attached to the end of its base (e.g., *-ly* in *quickly*).

Sulcus In the brain an area where the **cerebral cortex** is folded in.

Superstratum influence The influence of a politically or culturally dominant language on a less dominant language in the area (e.g., the effects of Norman French on English during the Middle English period).

Suppletion A morphological process that marks a grammatical contrast by replacing a morpheme with an entirely different morpheme (e.g., *be/was*).

Suprasegmental Above the individual speech sound. (Syllables are suprasegmental.)

Suprasegmental properties Those properties of sounds that form part of their makeup no matter what their place or manner of articulation: pitch, loudness, and length (also called **prosodic properties**).

Surface dyslexia A type of acquired dyslexia in which the patient seems unable to recognize words as wholes, but must process all words through a set of spelling-to-sound rules (e.g., *yacht* would be pronounced /jætʃt/).

Surface representation *See* **Phonetic representation**.

Surface structure The structure that results from the application of whatever transformations are appropriate for the sentence in question (also called **S-structure**).

Syllabary A set of signs used for writing the syllables of a language.

Syllabic A major phonological class feature assigned to segments that function as the nuclei of syllables (vowels and liquids).

Syllabic (sounds) Sounds that could be peaks of syllables (e.g., vowels in English).

Syllabic liquids Liquids that function as syllabic nuclei (e.g., the *l* in *bottle*).

Syllabic nasals Nasals that function as syllabic nuclei (e.g., the *n* in *button*).

Syllabic writing A type of writing in which each symbol represents a syllable.

Syllable A unit of linguistic structure that consists of a syllabic element and any segments that are associated with it. (*See also* **Onset**, **Nucleus**, **Coda**.)

Symbolic model A psycholinguistic theory built around the claim that models of linguistic knowledge make reference to rules and representations consisting of symbols, such as phonemes, words, syntactic category labels, and so forth.

Symbolic sign A sign that bears an arbitrary relationship to its referent (e.g., nononomatopoeic words, a stop sign).

Symptomatic sign A sign that spontaneously and involuntarily conveys an internal state or an emotion (e.g., crying).

Syncope The deletion of a word-internal vowel (e.g., the deletion of the schwa in *police*).

Synonyms Words or expressions that have the same meanings in some or all contexts (e.g., *buy* and *purchase*).

Syntactic category The category into which an element is placed depending on the type of meaning that it expresses, the type of affixes it takes, and the type of structure in which it occurs (includes both lexical and functional categories).

Syntactic parser The theoretical construct that accounts for the human ability to assign grammatical categories and hierarchical structure to elements in a stream of language input.

Syntax The system of rules and categories that underlies sentence formation in human language.

Synthetic language A language that makes extensive use of polymorphemic words (e.g., words containing a root and one or more affixes) (also called an **inflectional language**) (e.g., Spanish).

Systematic gaps Nonoccurring forms that would violate the phonotactic constraints of a language (e.g., in English **mtlow*).

Systematic phonetic correspondences Sound correspondences between two or more related languages that are consistent throughout the vocabularies of those languages.

Taboo Expressions that are seen as offensive and are therefore often euphemized.

Target In a priming experiment, this is the stimulus to which a subject must respond and for which response accuracy and latency are measured.

Teacher talk *See* **Foreigner talk**.

Telegraphic speech Speech lacking functional categories and bound morphemes.

Telegraphic stage The stage in child language acquisition in which children's utterances are generally longer than two words but lack bound morphemes and most functional categories.

Telephone survey A linguistic survey conducted over the telephone.

Template The innate blueprint of bird song that predisposes birds to perform a general song that is extremely simplified.

Temporal lobe The lobe of the brain that lies beneath the lateral fissure and in which Wernicke's area is located.

Tense (feature) A dorsal feature that expresses the distinction between **tense** and **lax vowels**.

Tense (verb) In syntax and morphology, an inflectional category indicating the time of an event or action relative to the moment of speaking.

Tense vowel A vowel that is made with a relatively tense tongue and greater vocal tract constriction than a **lax vowel** (e.g., the vowel sounds in *heat* and *boat*).

Terminal (intonation) contour Falling intonation at the end of an utterance, signaling that the utterance is complete.

Terminal nodes The lexical items or prefixes, suffixes, stems, or words of a language.

Text analysis A type of discourse analysis that studies how linguistic structures are used to perform particular discourse functions.

Textual competence Competence in the organization of language beyond the sentence.

Thematic grid The part of a word's lexical entry that carries information about the thematic roles that it assigns.

Thematic role The part played by a particular entity in an event (e.g., agent, theme, source, goal, location).

Theme The **thematic role** of the entity directly affected by the action of the verb (e.g., *the ball* in *Tom caught the ball*).

Thyroid cartilage The cartilage that forms the main portion of the larynx, spreading outward like the head of a plow.

Tier A level of phonological description in which only certain phonological elements are represented (e.g., a syllabic tier, a tonal tier).

Tip (of the tongue) The narrow area at the front of the tongue.

Tip-of-the-tongue phenomena Instances of temporary inability to access a word in the mental lexicon.

Token An individual instance of a variable or sign.

Tone Pitch differences that signal differences in meaning.

Tone language A language in which differences in word meaning are signaled by differences in pitch.

(Tongue) back *See* **Back**.

(Tongue) blade *See* **Blade**.

(Tongue) body *See* **Body**.

(Tongue) root *See* **Root**.

(Tongue) tip *See* **Tip**.

Top-down parsing A method of sentence analysis in which the entire sentence is considered first, before its component parts.

Top-down processing A type of mental processing using a set of expectations to guide phonetic processing and word recognition.

Topic What a sentence or group of sentences is about.

Total assimilation The **assimilation** of all the features of neighboring segments.

Trace The empty element, marked by the symbol *t*, that is left in syntactic structure after an element has been moved.

Trachea The tube below the larynx through which air travels when it leaves the lungs, commonly known as the windpipe.

Transfer The process by which the first language (L1) influences the interlanguage grammar of the learner of a second language.

Transfer error An error made by a second language learner that can be traced to the first language.

Transformation A type of syntactic rule that can move an element from one position to another.

Transformational grammar A widely accepted approach to syntactic analysis in which syntactic phenomena are described in terms of building phrase structures and moving elements (transformations) as a result of **Merge** and **Move** operations.

Transitive *See* **Transitive verb**.

Transitive verb A verb that takes a **direct object** (e.g., *hit*).

Tree structure A diagram that represents the internal organization of a word, phrase, or sentence.

Trill An *r*-like sound that is made by passing air over the raised tongue tip, allowing it to vibrate.

Truth conditions The circumstances under which a sentence is true.

Turn-taking The change-over between speakers' turns in a conversation.

Two-word stage A stage of first language acquisition in which children normally utter two succeeding words.

Typological plausibility A criterion that guides language reconstruction by referring to universals or existing properties of language.

Umlaut The effect that a vowel (or sometimes a glide) in one syllable can have on the vowel of another (usually preceding) syllable.

Underextension A developmental phenomenon in which a child uses a lexical item to denote only a subset of the items that it denotes in adult speech (e.g., *car* used to refer to only moving cars).

Underlying Unpredictable and basic (e.g., features of a phonemic segment before **derivation**).

Underlying representation In phonology, a form from which phonetic forms are derived by rule.

Universal Grammar The system of categories, operations, and principles shared by all human languages and considered to be innate.

Universal tendencies Patterns or traits that occur in all or most languages.

Unmarked Tending to be relatively common in world languages and/or less complex. (*See also* **Unmarked traits**.)

Unmarked traits Those characteristics of language that are considered to be less complex and/or universally more common in languages.

Unordered rule application In a phonological **derivation**, an application of rules in which the outcome will be the same regardless of the order in which rules are applied.

Utterance Any bit of talk produced by a speaker that is distinct from other bits of talk in a speech situation.

Uvula The small fleshy flap of tissue that hangs down from the velum.

Uvulars Sounds made with the tongue near or touching the **uvula**.

Variable rule analysis Method of analyzing sociolinguistic data in which statistical procedures allow a variety of social and linguistic factors to be considered simultaneously.

Variant One of a set of several possible forms that can be used to express the same function or meaning.

Velars Sounds made with the tongue touching or near the **velum** (e.g., [ŋ], [k]).

Velum The soft area toward the rear of the roof of the mouth.

Verb (V) A **lexical category** that typically designates actions, sensations, and states; can usually be inflected for **tense**; and functions as the **head** of a verb phrase (e.g., *see, feel, remain*).

Verb Movement Parameter A cross-linguistic variation involving whether the verb does or does not raise to I.

Verb raising A syntactic rule that moves the verb to the I position in **S-structure** in languages such as French.

Verbal hedges Words or phrases that make statements less assertive (e.g., *maybe, sort of*).

Verbal paradigm The set of inflected forms associated with a verb (also called a **conjugation**).

Verner's Law A generalization made by Karl Verner, which states that a word-internal voiceless fricative resulting from **Grimm's Law** underwent voicing if the original Proto-Indo-European accent did not immediately precede it.

Vocal cords *See* **Vocal folds**.

Vocal folds A set of muscles inside the larynx that may be positioned in various ways to produce different glottal states (also called **vocal cords**).

Vocal tract The oral cavity, nasal cavity, and pharynx.

Voice A laryngeal feature that distinguishes between **voiced** and **voiceless** sounds.

Voiced The glottal state in which the vocal folds are brought close together but not tightly closed, causing air passing through them to vibrate (e.g., [æ], [z], [m] are voiced).

Voiceless The glottal state in which the vocal folds are pulled apart, allowing air to pass directly through the glottis (e.g., [t], [s], [f] are voiceless).

Voicing A historical process of **consonant weakening** in which voiceless stops or fricatives become voiced.

Voicing assimilation Assimilation in which one segment becomes more like a nearby segment in terms of voicing (e.g., liquid-glide devoicing).

Vowel qualities Vowel sounds.

Vowel reduction A process that converts a full vowel, typically unstressed, to the short, lax **schwa**.

Vowel shift *See* **Shift**.

Vowels Resonant, syllabic sounds produced with less obstruction in the vocal tract than that required for glides.

Weak generative capacity Capacity to describe properly all the strings of a language.

Weakening (phonetic) A type of assimilation in which a lessening in the time or degree of a consonant's closure occurs (also called lenition).

Weakening of meaning The process in which the meaning of a word has less force (e.g., *soon* used to mean 'immediately' but now means 'in the near future').

Wernicke's aphasia The **aphasia** that results in fluent but nonsensical speech, sometimes characterized by **jargonaphasia**.

Wernicke's area The area of the brain involved in the interpretation and the selection of lexical items.

***Wh* movement** A **transformation** that moves a *wh* phrase to the beginning of the sentence, formulated as: Move a *wh* phrase to the specifier position under CP.

***Wh* question** A sentence that begins with a *wh*-word such as *who, what, where, when* (e.g., *Who did you see?*).

Whisper The glottal state in which the **vocal folds** are adjusted so that the front portions are pulled close together, while the back portions are apart.

Whispery voice *See* **Murmur**.

Word The smallest free form found in language.

Word manufacture The creation of a word from scratch, sometimes with the help of a computer (also called **coinage**) (e.g., *Kodak*).

Word-based morphology Morphology that can form a new word from a base that is itself a word (e.g., *re-do* and *treat-ment* in English).

Writing The representation of language by graphic signs or symbols.

X′ rule A phrase structure rule that deals with intermediate categories, which states that an intermediate category X′ consists of a head, X, and any optional complements.

XP rule A phrase structure rule that deals with maximal categories, which states that a maximal category XP consists of an optional specifier and an X′.

Yes-no questions Questions that require an answer of either "yes" or "no" (e.g., *Is linguistics interesting? Do you speak a second language?*).

Zero derivation *See* **Conversion**.

Acknowledgments

Pages 179–181: Douglas Campbell Coupland. Excerpts from *Generation X* by Douglas Campbell Coupland. Copyright © 1991 by Douglas Campbell Coupland. Reprinted by permission of St. Martin's Press Paperbacks.

Pages 242–244: Leslie Newman. "Tiff and I." From *Sweet Dark Places* by Leslie Newman. Copyright © 1991 Leslie Newman. Reprinted by permission of the author.

Page 492: Figure 12.3. Bar-pressing times in sentence reading. Adapted from chart by Elizabeth Stine-Morrow in "On-Line Processing of Written Text by Younger and Older Adults" in *Psychology and Aging* 5: 68–78. Copyright © 1990 by The American Psychological Association. Adapted with permission from the author and The American Psychological Association.

Page 568: Figure 14.3. An isogloss bundle across eastern Pennsylvania. Map adapted from data on page 12 in *American Regional Dialects: A Word Geography* by Craig M. Carver. Copyright © 1987 by Craig M. Carver. Reprinted by permission of the University of Michigan Press.

Page 569: Figure 14.4. Dialect regions of the United States based on lexical terms. Map adapted from data on page 248 in *American Regional Dialects: A Word Geography* by Craig M. Carver. Copyright © 1987 by Craig M. Carver. Reprinted by permission of the University of Michigan Press.

Page 571: Figure 14.7. Dialect boundaries based on lexical items and a phonological survey. Map adapted from data on National Map. Web site:www.ling.epenn.edu/phono_atlas/National Map. Reprinted by permission.

Pages 589–590: Tom Stoppard. Excerpt from *Rosencrantz and Guildenstern Are Dead* by Tom Stoppard. Copyright © 1967 by Tom Stoppard. Used by permission of Grove/Atlantic, Inc.

Page 598: Fig. 15.10. Changes in cuneiform writing. Adapted from fig. 6, page 49 by M.W. Green in *The Origins of Writing* by Wayne M. Senner. Copyright © 1989 by the University of Nebraska Press. Reprinted by permission of the University of Nebraska Press.

Page 605: Figure 15.18. Development of writing systems. Adapted from "Family tree of early alphabetic scripts" as drawn by Joseph Naveh for "The Invention and Development of the Alphabet" by Frank Moore Cross, reprinted in *The Origins of Writing* edited by Wayne M. Senner, University of Nebraska Press (1970), page 89. Reprinted by permission of Joseph Naveh.

Page 625: W.H. Auden. "Their Lonely Betters" first verse from page 583 in *W.H. Auden: Collected Poems,* edited by Edward Mendelson. Copyright © 1940; renewed 1968 by W.H. Auden. Reprinted by permission of Random House, Inc.

Pages 627, 632, and 662: Figures 16.1, 16.2 (a–c) and q.3 w/figures. From "Facial Expressions of Emotion in Nonhuman Primates" (fig. 21, a, c, f, i, k on page 73; fig. 4, a, e, g, on page 27; and fig. 21, d, i, g on page 73) by S. Chevalier-Skolnikoff in *Darwin and Facial Expression: A Century of Research in Review* edited by Paul Ekman. Copyright © 1973 by Academic Press. Reproduced by permission of the publisher. All rights of reproduction in any form reserved.

Page 640: Figure 16.10. Avian isoglosses. Adapted from "Microgenographic and Macrogenographic Variation in Acquired Vocalizations of Birds" by Paul Mundiger in *Acoustic Communication in Birds* edited by D.E. Kroodsma, E.H. Miller, and H. Ouellet, vol. 2 (1982), pages 147–208. Published by Academic Press. This is a modified version by B. Bertram from "The vocal behavior of the Indian Hill Mynah, *Gracula religiosa." Anim. Behav. Monagr.* 3, (1970) pp. 81–192.

Page 643: Table 16.1. Lemur vocalization. Adapted from data in *Lemur Behavior* by A. Jolly (1966) Reprinted by permission of The University of Chicago Press.

Pages 649–650: Figures 16.13 and 16.14. Adapted from data cited on page 179 (D. Premack and A. J. Premack) in *Apes, Men and Language* by Eugene Linden. Copyright © 1974 by Eugene Linden. Reprinted by permission of Russell & Volkening, Inc.

Page 653: Table. 16.2. Some sign combination produced by Koko. Adapted from data in *The Education of Koko* by Francine Patterson and E. Linden. Copyright © 1981 by F. Patterson and E. Linden. Reprinted by permission of the authors.

LANGUAGE INDEX

Acadian French-English, 581
Adyghe, 373
African American English, 542
African American Vernacular English (AAVE), 558, 575–78
Afrikaans, 367
Afroasiatic languages, 376
Ainu, 353, 382
Albanian, 366, 368
Aleut, 352, 379, 380, 382, 391–93, 399
Altaic languages, 334, 371–72
American English, 31, 33–36, 48, 67, 554, 566, 571, 572, 576. *See also* English
  phonetic transcription of consonants and vowels, 36–38
  variations of, 564
    lexical variation in the United States, 567–68
    phonological variation in the United States, 569–71
    regional differences in morphology and syntax, 571–72
    regional variation in the United States, 567
    social network analysis, 573–74
Amerind, 392, 393
Amerindian (American Indian) languages, 53, 293, 316, 318, 335, 379–81, 384, 394, 412, 594. *See also* North American indigenous languages
Andean-Equatorial languages, 381
Appalachian English, 571, 572, 578
Arabic, 24, 138–40, 348, 376, 377, 386, 395, 413, 453, 461, 462, 553, 579, 581, 592, 603, 604, 613
  alphabet, 603–4
Aramaic, 376, 604
Arapaho, 352
Arawak, 381
Armenian, 366, 368–69, 382
Athabaskan (Athapaskan) languages, 39, 134, 154, 316, 335, 379–81, 395, 396, 402, 404–5
Atlantic-Congo languages, 377
Atsugewi, 259, 394
Attic Greek, 368
Australian languages, 375–76
Austric phylum, 381
Austroasiatic languages, 373–74, 381
Austronesian languages, 374–75, 381
Avar, 373
Aymara, 381
Azeri, 371

Baltic, 366, 369
Bantu languages, 377
Basque, 161, 350, 360, 382
Bengali, 369, 370
Berber, 359, 376
Berber languages, 376
Bini, 40
Bislama, 549–50
Blackfoot, 353, 379
Bororo, 381
Breton, 367, 368
Brythonic languages, 367
Bulgarian, 369
Bunak, 375
Burmese, 353, 354, 360, 374
Byelorussian, 369, 602

Caddoan languages, 397
Cambodian (Khmer), 76, 355, 373, 614
Canadian English, 72–74, 316, 451, 547, 554
Canadian French, 50, 124, 125, 302, 316
Cantonese, 348, 355, 374, 607
Carib, 381
Catalan, 368, 553
Caucasian languages, 372–73
Cayapa, 381
Celtic, 316, 331, 366–68
Central Pomo, 401
Chadic languages, 376
Chechen, 373
Cheremis, 371
Cherokee, 396, 558, 611
ChiBemba, 164, 173
Chinese, 216
  writing system, 605–7
Chinookan languages, 399
Chinook Jargon, 579
Chukchee, 150, 151
Cockney English, 301, 303
Coptic, 376
Cornish, 367, 368
Cree, 42, 404, 405, 478, 544, 547, 548, 592, 611–12, 620
Croatian, 348
Crow, 354, 379, 405
Cuna, 381
Cushitic languages, 376
Czech, 354, 369

Dafla, 354
Daic languages, 381, 383
Dakota, 353, 379, 594, 595
Danish, 324, 331, 367
Dene-Caucasian phylum, 381
Dinka, 379
Dravidian languages, 373
Dutch, 47, 285, 324, 348, 367, 579
Duwai, 115, 116

East Circassian, 373
Efik, 353
Enga, 375
English
  African American, 542
  African American Vernacular English (AAVE), 558, 575–78
  American. *See* American English
  Appalachian, 571, 572, 578
  aspiration in, 87–88
  Canadian, 72–74, 316, 451, 547, 554
  case in, 162
  Cockney, 301, 303
  compounds in, 147–51
  consonants, 32
    affricates, 27–28
    aspirated and unaspirated consonants, 28–30
    fricatives, 26–27
    glides, 31–32
    liquids, 30–31

English, consonants *(continued)*
phonetic and phonemic inventories of, 78
phonetic transcription of, 36–38
places and manners of articulation, 32
stop consonants, 26
strident fricatives and affricates, 28
syllabic liquids and nasals, 31
derivational affixes in, 143–46
diffusion of stress shift in, 321–22
features of, 95–100
inflection in, 155–56
liquid-glide devoicing in, 110, 114–15
Middle, 290, 291, 293, 296, 299, 301, 303, 304, 306, 308–12, 314, 615
negative constructions in, 9
Newfoundland, 562, 563
"nonstandard" varieties of, 7
Old, 290, 291, 295–97, 299, 306–16, 319, 336, 383, 615
onsets in, 81–82
orthography, 614–19
phonetic transcription of American consonants and vowels, 36–38
pidgin, 578–80
rules in the history of, 306
spread of change in, 321–23
stops and their transcription, 25–26
stress placement in, 43
syllables in, 79–81
stress and, 89–91
vowel-glide combinations in, 74
vowels, 33–36, 74, 351–52
Great English Vowel Shift, 304, 305, 308
phonetic and phonemic inventories of, 78
phonetic length, 88–89
phonetic transcription of, 36–38
Epera, 381
Erzya, 371
Eskimo-Aleut languages, 393
Eskimo languages, 400
Estonian, 363, 364, 371
Eurasiatic phylum, 381

Faroese, 367
Farsi (Parsi), 369
Finnish, 42, 67, 68, 151, 155, 160, 334, 352, 354, 363, 364, 371, 581, 631, 695
Finno-Ugric languages, 371
Fongbe-French, 581
French, 50, 51, 53, 54, 66, 83, 137, 139, 140, 159, 217–21, 258, 293, 295, 296, 298–302, 306, 307, 317, 318, 325–31, 333, 345, 348, 352, 361, 366, 368, 382, 451, 453, 475–79, 549, 553–55, 557, 558, 565, 573, 581, 602, 615, 692, 695
Canadian, 50, 124, 125, 302, 316
Quebec, 457, 549, 554, 555, 558
second language acquisition and, 451, 453, 457, 459, 460, 463–65, 467, 470, 472
tu/vous use in, 549
Frisian, 367

Gaelic
Irish, 359, 367, 368
Scots, 47, 75, 114, 367, 368
Gallo-Romance, 368
Gan, 374
Gaulish, 367, 368
Ge'ez, 351
Georgian, 372
Ge-Pano-Carib languages, 381
German, 42, 48, 50, 53, 140, 151, 160, 161, 240, 293, 300, 305, 311, 313, 324, 348, 366, 367, 451, 452, 457–59, 557, 619, 671, 695, 708
second language acquisition and, 451–52, 457–59
Germanic languages, 140, 313, 314, 324, 330–33, 340, 345, 366, 367, 602
Gilbertese, 353
Goidelic languages, 367
Gothic, 300, 331, 333, 367
Greek, 43, 82, 111, 154, 331, 332, 368–70, 458, 557, 598–603
alphabet, 600
Guarani, 381
Gudanji, 351
Gujarati, 369, 370
Guugu Yimidhirr, 360
Gwich'in (Loucheux), 316
Gypsy (Romany), 369–70

Haitian Creole, 460, 557
Hakka, 348, 374
Hawaiian, 350, 352, 355, 375, 391
Hebrew, 354, 359, 376, 531, 542, 602–4
Hellenic Greek, 368
Hellenic languages, 366, 368, 369
Hidatsa, 260–61
Hindi, 51, 52, 133, 318, 324, 325, 360, 366, 369, 370, 412, 413
Hindi-Urdu, 366, 369, 370
Hmong-Mien languages, 381
Hokan, 393
Hottentot, 379
Hungarian, 42, 334, 354, 371, 382
Hupa, 402

Ibero-Romance, 368
Igbo, 41, 42, 377
Indic languages, 369
Indo-European languages, 366–70
Indo-Iranian languages, 369
Indo-Pacific (Papuan) languages, 375
Inuktitut, 51, 158, 161, 173, 256, 257, 356, 379
Irish Gaelic, 359, 367, 368
Iroquoian languages, 397
Italian, 42, 51, 53, 162, 163, 295, 296, 300, 307, 318, 325, 336, 348, 368, 383, 463, 575, 613, 619, 638
Italic languages, 366, 368

Japanese, 52, 67, 68, 82, 133, 136, 154, 155, 161, 214–16, 273–75, 334, 350, 360, 361, 371, 372, 382, 387, 413, 440, 441, 458, 461, 472, 542, 550, 551, 553, 592, 607–10, 619, 620, 631, 695

writing, 607–9
Javanese, 375, 550

Kabardian, 373
Kannada, 373
Kanuri, 379
Karelian, 371
Kazakh, 371
Khmer (Cambodian), 76, 355, 373, 614
Khoisan languages, 379
K'iché, 354
KinyaRwanda, 377
Kitabal, 353
Koasati, 550
Kordofanian languages, 377
Korean, 216, 273, 334, 360, 371, 372, 557, 609, 610
writing, 609–10
!Kung, 352, 379
Kurdish, 369, 370

Lakota, 399–400
Laotian, 355, 374, 388
Lapp, 371
Latin, 294–98, 300, 305, 307, 309, 318, 327, 329–33, 368
Latvian, 349, 353, 354, 369, 387
Laz, 372
Lezghian, 373
Lithuanian, 163, 164, 369
Livonian, 371
Loucheux (Gwich'in), 316
Luo, 379

Maasai, 359, 379
Macedonian, 369, 602
Macro-Chibchan languages, 381
Madurese, 335
Malagasy, 359, 375
Malay, 75–77, 94, 152, 375
Malayalam, 373, 613
Malayo-Polynesian languages, 375
Mandarin Chinese, 39, 40, 173, 229, 348, 353–55, 374, 606, 607
Mande languages, 377
Maninka, 377
Maori, 359, 375, 547
Marathi, 369, 370
Mataco, 381
Mayan, 413, 610
Mazatec, 39
Mende, 39, 128, 377
Mia-Yiao languages, 381
Middle English, 290, 291, 293, 296, 299, 301, 303, 304, 306, 308–12, 314, 615
Min, 374
Mongolian languages, 372
Mon-Khmer languages, 373
Mono-Bili, 141, 142
Munda languages, 373
Mundari, 373
Muskogean, 395

Na-Dene languages, 381, 393, 395, 397
Nancowry, 158
Nandi, 352
Navajo, 6, 351, 379, 392, 405
Newfoundland English, 562, 563
New York English, 53, 555, 560, 561, 569, 572, 573, 581
Ngabandi, 579
Niger-Congo languages, 377
Nilo-Saharan languages, 377–79
North American English. *See* American English
North American indigenous languages, 391–406
future of, 405–6
morphology and syntax of, 397–405
alienability of possession, 403
animacy, 404
aspect and tense, 402–3
case relationships, 400–401
evidentials, 401
noun classification, 403–5
noun incorporation, 399–400
polysynthesis, 397–99
shape and texture classes, 404–5
origin and classification of, 392–95
phonetics and phonology of, 395–97
North Caucasian, 381
Northeast Caucasian languages, 372, 373
Northwest Caucasian languages, 372, 373
Nostratic phylum, 334, 381
Nubian, 352
Nuer, 353, 379
Nuuchahnulth (Nootka), 395, 397, 399

Occitan, 368
Old Egyptian, 376
Old English, 290, 291, 295–97, 299, 306–16, 319, 336, 383, 615
Old Hebrew, 604
Old Icelandic, 367
Old Norse, 367

Palauan, 43, 273
Parsi (Farsi), 369
Pashto, 369, 370
Penutian languages, 393, 399
Phoenician, alphabet, 603–4
Pilipino, 375
Plains Cree, 611
Polish, 51, 354, 369, 462
Ponapean, 150, 151, 375
Portuguese, 51, 295, 296, 327–29, 368
Proto-Baltic-Finnic, 363, 364
Proto-Germanic, 332
Proto-Indo-European (PIE), 331–35, 366, 369, 382, 383
Proto-Romance, reconstruction of, 326–30
Proto-World (Proto-Sapiens), 382
Puerto Rican Spanish-English, 581

Quebec French, 457, 549, 554, 555, 558
Quechua, 360, 379, 381

Romance languages, 258, 295, 300, 325–30, 368
Romansch, 368
Romany (Gypsy), 369–70
Rumanian, 50, 160, 325–29, 346, 368, 383
Russian, 43, 80–81, 83, 140, 159, 161, 324, 325, 354, 356, 366, 369, 579
Cyrillic alphabet, 602–3

Saame, 371
Salishan languages, 395–97
Samoan, 354, 375
Samoyed languages, 371
Sandawe, 379
Sango, 579

Sanskrit, 331–33, 613
Santali, 373
Sarcee, 39, 356
Sardinian, 326–29, 346, 368
Scandinavian, 318, 367
Scots Gaelic, 47, 75, 114, 367, 368
Semitic languages, 376, 377
Serbian, 348, 602
Serbo-Croatian, 51, 53, 348, 369
Shan, 374
Shona, 377
Sinitic languages, 374
Sino-Tibetan languages, 374, 381, 383
Siona, 353
Siouan languages, 395, 399
SiSwati, 159
Slavey, 154, 379
Slavic languages, 366, 369, 602
Slovak, 369, 602
Slovene (Slovenian), 369
South Arabic, 604
South Caucasian languages, 372
Spanish, 51–53, 82, 136, 140, 163, 164, 258, 259, 273, 294, 296–98, 300, 305, 318, 322, 325–29, 336, 340, 350, 362, 368, 434, 451, 453, 463–66, 477, 552, 556, 557, 562, 581, 602, 679, 695
  second language acquisition and, 451, 453, 463–66
Svan, 372
Swahili, 6, 155, 349, 350, 354, 355, 362, 377, 470, 663
Swedish, 300, 324, 367

Tagalog, 138, 140, 141, 150, 154, 161, 357, 375, 557
Tahitian, 375
Tai-Kadai languages, 374
Taiwanese, 374
Takelma, 399
Tamil, 216, 217, 373
Tatar, 371
Telugu, 373, 382
Thai, 83, 134, 189, 215–17, 374, 381, 383, 413, 613, 614
Tibetan, 374
Tibeto-Burman languages, 374
Tlingit, 273, 394
Tok Pisin, 580
Tonkawa, 395
Tungusic languages, 372
Turkic languages, 371
Turkish, 42, 49, 50, 67, 86, 141, 160, 161, 172, 173, 273, 324, 325, 356, 358, 360, 371, 372, 453, 613, 631, 714
Tuscarora, 401
Tzotzil, 151, 228, 230

Uighur, 371
Ukrainian, 369, 602
Uralic languages, 371
Urdu, 369, 370
Uzbek, 371

Vietnamese, 355, 373, 374, 388, 458, 557
Volga Tatar, 371

Walbiri, 6, 11
Warao, 381
Welsh, 53, 220, 221, 358, 359, 367, 368
Weri, 352
West Circassian, 373
Wichita, 352
Wishram Chinook, 402–3
Witoto, 381
Wolof, 377
Wu, 374

Xhosa, 377, 379
Xiang, 374

Yana, 397–99, 405
Yap, 42
Yiddish, 367
Yoruba, 377
Yue, 374
Yupik, 400
Yurok, 403

Zulu, 377, 379
Zuni, 396, 399

INDEX

Ablaut, 140
Absolute universals, 350
Abstract clauses, 545
Accidental gaps, 82–83
Accommodation, 552–53
Accuracy, second language acquisition and, 472–73
Acoustic phonetics, 16
Acrolects, 580
Acronyms, 154
Acrophonic principle, 599
Active sentences, 227–31
Acute accent, as primary stress mark, 43
Address terms, 548–49
Adjacency pairs, 543
Adjective phrases, 221–22
Adjectives, 185
Adstratum influence, 317–18
Adverbs, 185
Affective factors, second language acquisition and, 471–72
Affixes, 135–36, 138–39
  addition of, 306–7
  derivational, 146–47
    in English, 143–46
  inflectional, 155–56
  loss of, 307–9
Affricates, 27–28
  in languages other than English, 53
  in North American languages, 396
Affrication, 295
African scripts, 612–13
Age
  second language acquisition and, 469
  variants and, 574
Agent-patient pattern, 400–401
Agglutinating languages, 356
Agrammatism, 529–31
  in languages other than English, 531
Agreement, person and number, 162–63
Alienability of possession, in North American languages, 403
Allomorphs, 134–35
  deriving, 165–67
Allophones, 69–79
  language-specific variation in distribution of, 76
Allophonic nasalization, language-specific variation in, 75
Allophonic variation, 76
  features and, 94–95
Alphabet(s)
  Arabic, 603–4
  Cyrillic, 602
  emergence of, 599–602
  Greek, 600
  Hebrew, 603–4
  Phoenician, 603–4
  phonetic, 16–17
  Roman, 600–602
  Somali, 613
Alphabetic writing, 592–93
Alpha rules (alpha notation), 111
Alveolar fricatives, 26
Alveolar ridge, 24
Alveolar sounds, 24
Alveolar stops, 25
Alveopalatal sounds, 24
Ambiguity
  lexical, 248
  sentence, 502–3
  structural, 263–64
Amelioration, 319
American scripts, 610–12
Amerindian pictography, 594–95
Analogy
  language change and, 292
  morphological change and, 309–10
Analytic languages, 309, 355
Animal communication, 625–58
  bees, 635–38
  human linguistic communication compared to, 655–58
  nonhuman primates. *See* Primates, nonhuman
  as stimulus-bound, 634–35
Animate nouns, 404
Antecedents, of pronouns, 268
Antonyms, 246–47
Aphasia, 522–26
  Broca's, 523–25, 527, 529
  fluent, 525–26
  linguistic theory and, 528–31
  nonfluent, 523–25
  reading and writing disturbances in, 527
  Wernicke's, 525–26
Apocope, 298
A-prefixing, 571–72
Areal classification, 349
Articulation, 21
  of consonants, 22–24
  manners of, 25–32
  places (points) of, 22–24
  of vowels, 21, 33–34
Articulation features, place of, in English, 97–100
Articulatory phonetics, 16
Articulatory processes, 46–50
Articulatory simplification, language change and, 291
Arytenoids, 19
Aspiration, 28–30
  in English, 87–88
Assimilation, 46–48, 294–96
  in early speech, 417
  feature hierarchy and, 113
  laryngeal, 114–15
  progressive, 47, 48
  regressive, 47
  tonal, 115–16
  voicing, 47
Association, 113–14
Association line, 39
Atlas surveys, 563–64
Attitudes
  sentence interpretation and, 271–72
  toward varieties and languages, 554–55
Auditorily based change, 301–2
Automatic summarization, 696
Autopsy studies, 518–19
Autosegmental notation, 39, 113–15
Autosegmental representation, 113
Auxiliary verbs, 185
Avian dialects, 640

Babbling, 413
Backformation, 153
Bamum people, writing of, 612
Bases, 136

Basic Level Assumption, 418
Basilects, 580
Bees, communication system of, 635–38
Beliefs and attitudes, sentence interpretation and, 271–72
Bilabial fricatives, 52
Bilabial sounds, 23
Bilabial stops, 25
Bilingual education, 477–79
Bilingualism, 449
Bird calls, 639
Birds, 638–41
Birdsong, 639–40
Blends, 152–53
Bliss, Charles K., 595
Blissymbolics, 595
Blueprint (phrase structure schema), 190–93
Bopp, Franz, 332
Borrowing (loan words), 293, 306, 316–18
  interlanguage (IL) grammars and, 457–58
Bottom-up parsing, 677
Bottom-up processing, 495
Boustrophedon, 600
Brahmi script, 613
Brain, the, 514–22. *See also* Aphasia
  aphasia, 522–26
  autopsy studies, 518–19
  dichotic listening studies, 521
  imaging techniques, 519–21
  reading and writing impairments caused by damage to, 527–28
  split brain studies, 521–22
Broca, Paul, 518
Broca's aphasia, 523–25, 527, 529
Broca's area, 519
Brown corpus, 691

Calls, bird, 639
Canadian Vowel Raising, 72–74, 77, 451–52
Caregiver speech, first language acquisition and, 434–36
Case, 160–62, 223–26
  in English nouns and pronouns, 162
  ergative case marking, 161
  in North American languages, 400–401
Case Filter, 224–26
Categories, syntactic, 184–96
  phrases, 187–91
  sentences, 192–93
  words, 185–87
  X', 194–96
Category change, inflection and, 156–57
C-command, 269
Central sulcus, 517–18
Cerebral cortex, 514
  lobes of, 517–18
Cerebral hemispheres, 514–17
Children. *See* First language acquisition
Chimpanzees, 646–49, 651, 653
Clarity, processes and, 46
Class 1 affixes, 146
Class 2 affixes, 146–47
Classification of languages, 347–83
  genetic, 348–49
  types of, 348–49
  typological, 349–65
    consonant systems and, 352–53
    morphology and, 355–58
    phonology, 350–55
    suprasegmental systems, 353–54
    syntax and, 358–62
    vowel systems and, 350–52
Classificatory verbs, 405
Class nodes, in feature hierarchy, 105
Clauses, complement, 200–202
Clever Hans effect, 650, 652, 654
Clipping, 152
Cliticization, 139
Clitics, 139
Closing section, in conversations, 544
Coarticulation, 44–45
Cocktail party effect, 670
Coda clause, 545
Coda of syllables, 79, 80, 84–90, 95
Code-switching, 581–82
Cognates, 324, 325
Cognitive development, first language acquisition and, 437–39
Cognitive factors, second language acquisition and, 472–73
Cohort model, 496
Coinage (word manufacture), 154–55
Communication
  animal, 625–58
    bees, 635–38
    human linguistic communication compared to, 655–58
    nonhuman primates. *See* Primates, nonhuman
    as stimulus-bound, 634–35
  language distinguished from, 625
  nonvocal, 626–27
  signs and, 628–33
Communication strategies, second language acquisition and, 473
Communicative competence, 454–55, 539
Comparative method, 323
Comparative reconstruction, 323–25
Complementary distribution, 68–71, 119, 120
Complement clauses, 200–202
Complements
  phrase structure and, 189–90
  syntactic options for, 196–202
    adjectives, 199
    clauses, 200–202
    nouns, 199
    prepositions, 199
    verbs, 197–98
Complicating action clauses, 545
Componential analysis, 251–53
Compositionality, principle of, 261
Compounding, 137, 147–51
Compound words (compounds), 147–51
  endocentric and exocentric, 149–50
  in languages other than English, 150–51
Comprehensible input, 475
Comprehension, testing children's, 411
Computational linguistics, 663–98
  lexicology, 682–87
  morphology, 670–75
  phonetics and phonology, 665–70
  practical applications of, 690–98

automatic summarization, 696
indexing and concordances, 691–92
information accessing and retrieval, 692–93
machine translation, 693–95
speech recognition, 696–97
speech synthesis, 697–98
semantics, 687–90
syntax, 675–82
Computational system, 184
Computerized axial tomography (CT scanning), 519
Concordance applications, 691–92
Conjugation, 162
Conjunctions, 185
Connectionist models, 507
Connotation, 250
Consonantal strength, scale of, 299
Consonant deletion, 299
Consonants, 21, 22
affricates, 27–28, 53
articulation of, 22–24
aspirated and unaspirated, 28–30
coarticulation with vowels, 45
epenthesized, 49
fricatives, 26–27
glides, 31–32, 54
glottalized, 396
in languages other than English, 51–54
laterals, 30
liquids, 53–54
nasal, 25, 75, 76, 113, 120, 164, 295, 296, 303
obstruent, 79, 89, 92, 93, 95, 96, 101, 107, 111, 146, 353, 363, 451, 452, 458
pharyngeal, 395
uvular, 395
velar, 395
Consonant systems, typological classification of languages and, 352–53
Consonant weakening, 299–300
Constructional meaning, 261–63
Contextual clues, vocabulary development and, 419
Continuants, 26
Contour tones, 39
Contradiction, 249
Contrastive segments, 65–68
Conversational implicature, 275
Conversational maxims, 275–77
Conversation analysis, 543–44
Conversion, 151–52
Cooperative overlaps, in conversations, 544
Cooperative Principle, 275
Coordinate structures, 194
Coordination test, 194
Coote, Edmond, 616
Corpus callosum, 515
Creativity of language, 3–5
Creoles, 578–80
Cricoid cartilage, 19
Critical period
first language acquisition and, 441
second language acquisition and, 470
Cross-sectional studies, 411
Cuneiform, 597–98
Cyrillic alphabet (script), 602–3

Deaffrication, 301
Deep dyslexia, 529
Deep structure (D-structure), 211–13
thematic roles and, 267–68
Degemination, 300
Degree words, 185
Deletion, 48–49, 298–300
consonant, 299
as a rule, 110–11
syllable, in early speech, 415
vowel, 298–99
Denasalization, 416
Denotation, 250
Dental sounds, 24
Derivation(s), 106–8, 142–47
of allomorphs, 165
complex, 144–45
constraints on, 145–46
inflection versus, 156–58
zero, 151
Derivational affixes, 146–47
in English, 143–46
Design features, 655
Determiners, 185
Deterministic parsing, 676
Devanagari script, 613, 614
Developmental errors, in interlanguage (IL) grammars, 452
Developmental sequence, for nonlexical morphemes, 424–25
Devoicing
deriving allomorphs and, 166–67
liquid-glide, in English, 110, 114–15
Dialectology, 563
Dialects, 538. *See also* Variation (variants)
avian, 640
languages distinguished from, 348–49
Diaphragm, 19
Diary study, 410–11
Dichotic listening studies, 521
Diffusion, 321
Diglossia, 556–57
Dimensional terms, vocabulary development and, 422–23
Diphthongization, 305
Diphthongs, 33
Direct negative evidence, 466
Direct object, 190
Discourse, sentence interpretation and, 273–75
Discourse analysis, 538–47
ethnography of communication and, 539–43
ethnomethodology and, 543–44
text analysis and, 544–47
Discourse markers, 546
Discrete signs, 632–33
Dissimilation, 48, 296
Distinctive features, 94
Distribution, categories of words and, 187
Do insertion, *yes-no* questions and, 206–7
Downdrift, 41
Dressage, 650
Dual-route models, 506
Duetting, 646
Dyslexia, acquired, 527–28

Ebonics, 558
Egyptian hieroglyphics, 598–99
Ejectives, 396
Enclitics, 139
Endocentric compounds, 149–50
English, errors found in the acquisition of, 453

Entailment, 249
Environment, 66
Epenthesis, 49, 111, 296–97
  vowel, 112
Ergative-absolutive pattern, 400
Ergative case marking, 161
Ethnic dialects, 538
Ethnicity, 575–76
Ethnography of communication, 539–43
Ethnolinguistic vitality, 575
Ethnomethodology, 543–44
Etruscans, 600
Euphemisms, 548
Evaluation clauses, 545
Event-related potentials (ERPs), 493–94
Evidentiality, in Hidatsa, 260–61
Evidentials, in North American languages, 401
Evolution, 2
Exocentric compounds, 149–50
Expanded XP Rule, 222
Experimental methods, in psycholinguistic research, 488–91
Experimental studies, 411–12
Extension, 250–51
Eye-movement experiments, 492

Facial expressions, 627
Feature hierarchy, 103–6
  assimilation and, 113
Feature representations, 95–103
  determining, 100–103
Features, 17, 64, 65, 91–106
  allophonic variation and, 94–95
  in Broca's aphasia, 529
  distinctive, 94
  of English, 95–100
  as independent and coordinated phonetic elements, 91–92
  laryngeal, 97, 101
  manner, 96
  natural classes and, 92–94
  place of articulation, 101
    in English, 97–100
  reasons for using, 91–95
  speech errors and, 496
  spreading of, 112–14, 116, 118
Feedback, first language acquisition and, 436–37
Feeding, 109
Field dependence/field independence, 472–73
First language acquisition, 409–41
  adult speech and, 434
  cognitive development and, 437–39
  critical period in, 441
  feedback and, 436–37
  inborn knowledge and, 439–41
  morphological development, 423–27
  phonological development and, 412–17
    babbling, 413
    developmental order, 413–14
    early phonetic processes, 414–17
  study of, 410–12
  syntactic development, 427–34
    interpretation of sentences, 432–34
    later development, 430–32
    one-word stage, 427
    telegraphic stage, 429–30
    two-word stage, 427–29
  vocabulary development, 417–23
    contextual clues and, 419
    meaning errors and, 419–23
    strategies for acquiring word meanings, 418–19
Fissure, 515
Fixed stress languages, 354
Flapping, 48
Flaps, 31
Fluency, second language acquisition and, 472–73
Fluent aphasia, 525–26
FMRI (functional magnetic resonance imaging), 520–21
Foreigner talk, 474
Forms of address, 548–50
Fouts, Roger, 651
Francis, Nelson, 691
Frazier, Lynn, 502
Free stress languages, 354
Frication, 300
Fricatives, 26–28
  alveolar, 26
  in languages other than English, 52
  lateral, 53, 395–96
Fromkin, Victoria, 487
Fronting, 416
Full reduplication, 141
Functional analysis, 230–31
Functional categories, 185
Functional magnetic resonance imaging (fMRI), 520–21
Function words, 524, 530
Fusion, 307
Fusional languages, 356–57
Fuzzy concepts, 253–54

Gaps, accidental and systematic, 82–83
Garden path sentences, 501–2
Gardner, Allen and Beatrice, 648
Gender differences, 550–52
Generation, natural language, 681
Generative capacity, 678–80
Genetically related languages, 323, 349
Genetic classification of languages, 348–49, 365–83
  phyla, 381–83
Geographical location, variation and, 563–67
Gestures, 626–27
Gibbons, 646
Glagolitic script, 602
Glides, 21, 22, 31–32
  in languages other than English, 54
  nasal, 75
Glide strengthening, 300
Gliding, 416
Global aphasia, 523
Glottalization, in North American languages, 396
Glottalized consonants, 396
Glottals, 24
Glottal states, 19–21
Glottal stops, 25–26
Glottis, 19
  coarticulation and, 45
Glyphs, 610
Gorillas, 651
Gould, Edward S., 10
Graded membership, 254
Graded signs, 632
Grammar(s)
  acquisition of, 410, 411
  components of, 5
  defined, 6
  as essentially equal, 7–8
  as feature of all languages, 6–7

interlanguage, 450, 452–53, 457–69
markedness and, 458–60
phonology and, 457–63
mutability of, 9–10
natural language analysis and, 675–76
similarities among, 8–9
subconscious knowledge of, 10
transformational, 184
Grammatical, defined, 184
Grammatical competence, second language acquisition and, 454
Grammaticalization, 307
Grammatical knowledge, 664
Grammaticization, 260–61
Grave accent, as secondary stress mark, 43
Great English Vowel Shift, 304, 305, 308, 615
Greenberg, Joseph, 392, 393
Grimm, Jakob, 332
Grimm's Law, 332, 333
Gupta script, 613

Hangul, 609
Hanja, 610
Heads of phrases, 188
Heavy syllables, 90
Hierarchies, 361–62
Hieroglyphics, 598–99
High involvement style, in conversations, 544
Hiragana, 607, 608
Historical linguistics, 289–337. *See also* Language change
Hockett, Charles, 655
Homophones, 247
Hypercorrection, 293, 572

Iconic signs, 633
Iconic signs (icons), 629–30
Illocutionary competence, second language acquisition and, 455
Illocutionary force, 455
Immersion programs, bilingual education, 478–79
Implicational universals, 350, 351, 353, 355, 357, 361, 364
Inanimate nouns, 404
Inborn knowledge, first language acquisition and, 439–41
Incorporation, 150, 151
Indexical signs, 630–31, 633
Indexing analysis, 560–61
Indexing applications, 691–92
Indian scripts, 613–14
Indirect negative evidence, 466
Infixes, 138
Inflection (inflectional affixes), 155–58
case, 160
categories of words and, 186–87
derivation versus, 156–58
noun class, 159
number, 158–59
person and number agreement, 162–63
Inflectional languages, 356–57
Information accessing and retrieval, 692–93
Insertion rule, 206–7
Instrumental motivation, second language acquisition and, 472
Integrative motivation, second language acquisition and, 472
Intension, 250–51
Intercostals, 19
Interdental sounds, 24
Interlanguage (IL) grammars, 450, 452–53, 457–69
markedness and, 458–60
phonology and, 457–63
Internal change, 139–40
Internal reconstruction, 330–31
International Phonetic Alphabet (IPA), 16
Intonation, 40–42
Inversion operation, 205–6, 314
early language acquisition and, 430–32, 434
Isogloss bundle, 565–66
Isoglosses, 565–66
Isolating languages, 355

Jargon, 541
Jargonaphasia, 526

Kanji, 607, 608
Kanzi (chimpanzee), 653–55
Katakana, 607, 608
Kharosthi script, 613
Koko (gorilla), 651, 653
Krogh, August, 635
Kucera, Henry, 691

Labial sounds, 23
Labiodentals, 23
Labiovelar sounds, 24
Labov, William, 560, 572–73
Lana (chimpanzee), 649
Language(s)
classification of (*See* Classification of languages)
communication distinguished from, 625
dialects distinguished from, 348–49
Language acquisition. *See* First language acquisition; Second language acquisition
Language bioprogram hypothesis, 580
Language change, 289–323
analogy and, 292
causes of, 291–93
language contact and, 292–93
naturalness and, 336–37
reanalysis and, 292
reconstruction, 323–36
sound change(s), 292, 293–306
auditorily based change, 301–2
phonetic versus phonological change, 302–4
phonological shift, 304–5
rule ordering and, 306
segmental change, 301
sequential change, 294–300
spread of, 320–23
syntactic change, 311–14
systematicity of, 291
Language contact, language change and, 292–93
Language mixtures, 581–82
Language planning, 557–59
Language reconstruction, 323–36
Laryngeal assimilation, 114–15
Laryngeal features, 97, 101
Laryngeal nodes, 105
Larynx, 18–20, 24
Late closure, 502
Lateral fissure, 518
Lateral fricatives, 53, 395–96
Laterals, 30, 53

Lax vowels, 35
Learning strategies, second language acquisition and, 473
Length, 38, 42
Lexical ambiguity, 248
Lexical categories, 185
Lexical change, 314–19
Lexical decision, 489–90
Lexical diffusion, 321–22
Lexical gaps, 315
Lexicalization of concepts, 256–59
Lexicology, computational, 682–87
Lexicon, 131, 184
  addition of words to, 315–18
  loss of words from, 318–19
  natural language generation and, 681–82
Lexifier language, 579
Lingua francas, 578
Linguistic Atlas Project, 565
Linguistic change. *See* Language change
Linguistic competence, 5
Linguistic insecurity, 555
Linguistic market analysis, 573
Linguistics
  computational. *See* Computational linguistics
  as descriptive, not prescriptive, 8
  historical, 289–337. *See also* Language change
Linguistic typology, 349
Linguistic universals, 349
Lips, coarticulation and, 44
Liquid-glide devoicing, in English, 110, 114–15
Liquids, 30–31
  in languages other than English, 53–54
  syllabic, 31
Lobes of the cortex, 517–18
Logograms, 592
Logographic writing, 592
Lonedog, 595
Longitudinal fissure, 515
Longitudinal studies, 411
Loudness, 38
Lungs, 18–19

Machine translation, 693–95
Macrofamilies of languages, 381–83
Majority rules strategy, 325
Manner, Maxim of, 277
Manner features, 96
Marginal analysis, 561–62
Markedness, 465
  interlanguage (IL) grammars and, 458–60
Markedness Differential Hypothesis, 458, 465
Markedness theory, 350
Marked traits, 350
Marslen-Wilson, William, 496
Matched guise test, 555
Matrix, 91
Matrix clause, 200
Maxims, conversational, 275–77
Meaning(s)
  categories of words and, 186
  componential analysis and, 251–53
  conceptual system and, 253–61
  connotation and, 250
  denotation and, 250
  extension and intension, 250–51
  first language acquisition and erprors, 419–23
    strategies for acquiring meaning, 418–19
  fuzzy concepts and, 253
  grammaticization and, 260–61
  lexicalization of concepts and, 256–59
  metaphors and, 255–56
  nature of, 246–53
  signs and, 628
  syntax, sentence interpretation, and, 261–71
    constructional meaning, 261–63
    pronouns, 268–71
    structural ambiguity, 263–64
    thematic roles, 264–68
  weakening of, 320
Merge operation, 184
Mergers, 303
Mesolects, 580
Metaphorical code-switching, 581
Metaphors, 255–56, 320
  in psycholinguistic modeling, 504–7
  spatial, 256
Metathesis, 49–50, 297–98
Mid vowels, 34
Minimal attachment, 502
Minimal pairs, 65–67, 71
Minority language maintenance programs, 477–78
Mixed signs, 631
Mixtures, language, 581–82
Modifiers, 221–23
Modules, 500
Monkeys, communication among, 644–46
Morphemes, 133–35
  allomorphs of, 134–35
  free and bound, 133–34
Morphological change, 306–11
  addition of affixes, 306–7
  analogy and, 309–10
  in analytic and synthetic languages, 309
  loss of affixes, 307–9
  reanalysis and, 310–11
Morphological development, 423–27
  developmental sequence for nonlexical morphemes, 424–25
  overgeneralization and, 423–24
  word-formation processes, 426–27
Morphological processing, 498–500
Morphological universals, 363–64
Morphology, 131–73. *See also* Words
  case and, 223
  computational, 670–75
  regional differences in, 571–72
  second language, 467–69
Morphophonemics (morphophonology), 164–69
  conditioning by morphological class, 167–69
  deriving allomorphs, 165–67
Moss, C. S., 522–23
Motherese, 435
Motion verbs, 257–59
Motivation, second language acquisition and, 471–72
Motor aphasia, 523–25
Movement test, 194
Move operation, 184, 203, 216–21

Mulcaster, Richard, 616
Multiplex networks, 574
Murmur, 20
Mutual intelligibility, 538

Narratives, 545
Nasal consonants, 75, 76, 113, 120, 164, 295, 296, 303
Nasal glides, 75
Nasalization, 47, 113, 295
  allophonic, language-specific variation in, 75–76
Nasal phones, 25
Nasals, syllabic, 31
Nasal stops, 25
Nasal vowels, 51, 75, 77, 352, 396, 458
Native speakers, 3
Natural classes, 92–94
Naturalistic approach to language acquisition, 410–11
Natural language analysis, 675–80
Natural language generation, 681
Natural language processing systems, 670
Naturalness, language change and, 336–37
Near-minimal pairs, 66, 71
Negative evidence, 466
Neurolinguistics, 513–32. *See also* Brain
Neurons, 514
New information, discourse and, 274
Nim, 648
Nodes, 507
No-naming, 549
Nondeterministic parsing, 676
Nonfluent aphasia, 523–25
Nonlexical categories, 185
Nonstandard varieties, 556–57
Nonstridents, 28
Nonsyllabic sounds, 21–22
Nonterminal (intonation) contour, 40
Nonterminal nodes, 677
Nonvocal communication, 626–27
North American indigenous languages, 391–406
  future of, 405–6
  morphology and syntax of, 397–405
    alienability of possession, 403
    animacy, 404
    aspect and tense, 402–3
    case relationships, 400–401
    evidentials, 401
    noun classification, 403–5
    noun incorporation, 399–400
    polysynthesis, 397–99
    shape and texture classes, 404–5
  origin and classification of, 392–95
  phonetics and phonology of, 395–97
Northern Cities Shift, 570
Noun class, inflectional affixes and, 159
Noun incorporation, in North American languages, 399–400
Nouns, 185
  animate, 404
  inanimate, 404
  in North American languages, 403–6
  used as verbs, 3
Nuclei of syllables, 21, 79, 80, 84, 86, 90
Null Subject Parameter, 463–66
Null subjects, second language acquisition and, 463–64
Number, inflection and, 158
Number agreement, 162–63

Obstruents, 79, 89, 92, 93, 95, 96, 101, 107, 111, 146, 353, 363, 451, 452, 458
Official languages, 557–59
Old information, discourse and, 273–74
One-word stage, 427
Onomatopoeia, 154
Onset of syllables, 79–89
  constraints on, 80–82
Ontogeny Model of second language acquisition, 452–53
Opening, in conversations, 543–44
Oral sounds, 25
Oral stops, 25
Orangutans, 646
Order, inflectional affixes and, 157
Orientation clauses, 545
Orthography, English, 614–19
  irregularities, 614–16
Osten, Wilhelm von, 650
Overextensions, 419–20
Overgeneralization, first language acquisition and, 423–24

Page, Jake, 638
Palatalization, 295
Palatal sounds, 24
Palate, 24
Pali script, 614
Paragraphia, 527
Parallel processing model, 505–6
Parametric variation, 214–21
Paraphrases, 248
Parroting, 638–39
Parsers, 675–76
Parsing, 491
  deterministic, 676
  nondeterministic, 676
  top-down versus bottom-up, 676–78
Partial reduplication, 141
Partial suppletion, 141
Passive sentences, 227–31, 432–33
Pejoration, 319
Person agreement, 162–63
PET (positron emission tomography), 519–21
Pfungst, Oskar, 650
Pharyngeal consonants, 395
Pharyngeal sounds, 24
Pharynx, 18
Pheromones, 626
Phoenician alphabet, 599–600
Phonemes, 66, 69–79
  in psycholinguistic models of speech processing, 496–97
Phonemic inventory, 78
Phonemic representations, 69–70, 107
Phonemic transcription, 76–78
Phones, 15
  nasal versus oral, 25
Phonetically conditioned change, 293
Phonetically conditioned variation, 68–76
Phonetic determinative, 606
Phonetic inventory, 78
Phonetic length, in English vowels, 88–89

Phonetic plausibility strategy, 325
Phonetic representations, 69–70, 107
Phonetics, 15–54
  acoustic, 16
  articulatory, 16
Phonetic sound change, 302–4
Phonetic transcription (phonetic alphabet), 16–17, 76–78
  of American English consonants and vowels, 36–38
  length in, 42
  stress in, 43
Phonographic writing, 592–93, 596
Phonological Atlas of North America, 564
Phonological change, 303
Phonological development, 412–17
  babbling, 413
  developmental order, 413–14
  early phonetic processes, 414–17
Phonological dyslexia, 528
Phonological processes, 107
Phonological representations, 107
Phonological rules. *See* Rules, phonological
Phonological shift, 304
Phonological transfer, 451
Phonological universals, 362–63
Phonology, 63–116
  classes and generalization in, 71–72
  contrastive segments, 65–68
  derivations and rules, 106–12
  features, 91–106
  phonetically conditioned variation, 68–76
  phonetic and phonemic transcription, 76–78
  syllabic, 87–91
  syllables and, 79–91
Phonotactics, 81–82
  language-specific, 83
Phrase structure, 187–91
  blueprint (phrase structure schema), 190–91
  complements, 189–90
  development of, 429
  heads, 188
  rules of, 190–91
  specifiers, 188–89
  tests for, 193–94
  variation in, 214–16
Phyla of languages, 381–83
Pictograms, 594–95
Pidgins, 578–80
Pinyin, 607
Pitch, 38–42
Place nodes, 105
Place of articulation features, 97–101
Plural. *See also* Number
Politeness, 547–48
Polysemy, 247
Polysynthesis, in North American languages, 397–99
Polysynthetic languages, 356
Positive evidence, 466
Positron emission tomography (PET), 519–21
Possession, alienability of, in North American languages, 403
Postpositions, 214
Posture, 626
Powell, John Wesley, 393
Power, language behavior and, 547
Pragmatics, 271, 689–90
Prefixes, 138. *See also* Affixes
Prephonation, 21
Prepositions, 185
Presupposition, 271–72
Prewriting, 593–94
Primates, nonhuman, 641–55
  chimpanzees, 646–47
  gibbons and orangutans, 646
  monkeys, 644–46
  prosimians, 642–44, 659
  testing, for linguistic ability, 647–55
    creativity, 652–53
    definition of language, 651–52
    experiments with signing, 648
    nonsigning experiments, 649–50
    symbol use, 652
    syntax, 653
Priming paradigm, 490–91
Principal components analysis, 562–63
Principle A, 269–70
Principle B, 270–71
Processes, 43–50, 116
  articulatory, 46–50
  clarity and, 46
  efficiency and, 45–46
  phonological, 107
Proclitics, 139
Production tasks, 411–12
Productivity, inflectional affixes and, 157–58
Progressive assimilation, 47, 48
Pronominals
  language acquisition and, 433–34
  meaning and interpretation of, 268–71
Pronouns
  meaning and interpretation of, 268–71
  reflexive
    language acquisition and, 433–34
    meaning and interpretation of, 268–71
Pronunciation, spelling, 292
Prosimians, 642–44, 659
Prosodic properties, 38
Proto-forms, 324
Proto-language, 324
Psycholinguistic modeling, 503–8
  metaphors in, 504–7
  serial versus parallel processing models, 505–6
  single-route versus dual-route models, 506
  symbolic versus connectionist models, 506–7
Psycholinguistics, 485–508
  defined, 485
  language processing and linguistics, 494–503
    features, 496
    morphological processing, 498–500
    phonetics and phonology, 495–98
    syntax, 500
  methods of research in, 486–94
    lexical decision experiments, 489–90
    priming paradigm, 490–91
    sentence processing and, 491–93

slips of the tongue, 486–88
tip-of-the-tongue phenomena, 488–89

Q feature, 204
Quality, Maxim of, 276
Quantity, Maxim of, 277
Questions
intonation in, 41
wh, 207–10, 216–17
yes-no, 203–7, 216

Rask, Rasmus, 331, 332
REA (right ear advantage), 521
Reading, writing and, 619–20
Real-world knowledge, 664
Reanalysis
language change and, 292
morphological change and, 310–11
Rebuses, 596–97, 610
Reconstruction, 323–36, 382
catalogue of sound changes and, 326
comparative, 323–25
internal, 330–31
of Proto-Romance, 326–30
strategies of, 325–26
techniques of, 325–30
typology and, 334–36
Redundancy, 637
Reduplication, 141
Referents, 250
Reflexive pronouns
language acquisition and, 433–34
meaning and interpretation of, 268–71
Regional dialects, 538
Registers, 539–41
Register tones, 39
Regressive assimilation, 47
Regressive saccades, 493
Relation, Maxim of, 276
Relational analysis, 228–30
Relexification hypothesis, 580
Relic forms, 571
Representation(s), 112–16
feature, 95–103
phonemic, 69–70, 107
phonetic, 69–70, 107
phonological, 107
tonal assimilations as, 115–16
Rhotacism, 300
Rhyme of syllables, 79, 80, 84
Right ear advantage (REA), 521
Rolandic fissure, 517–18
Romaji, 609
Roman alphabet, 600–602
Root nodes, 105
Roots of words, 135–36
Rules, 190
phonological, 106–12, 116
alpha (alpha notation), 111
application of, 108–9
form and notation of, 109–12
that refer to syllable structure, 111–12
phrase structure, 190–91
Runic writing, 602
Russell, Bertrand, 635

Saccades, 486
regressive, 493
Sapir, Edward, 392, 393
Sarah (chimpanzee), 649
Scent, 626
Schleicher, August, 334
Schwa, 35
deletion of, in English, 110–11
vowel reduction and, 50
Scripts. *See* Writing
Second language acquisition, 449–79
bilingual education and, 477
classrooms, 474–79
communicative competence and, 454–55
error patterns in, 452
factors affecting, 469–74
age, 469–71
individual differences, 471–73
first language's role in, 450–51
good language learners and, 473–74
interlanguage (IL) grammars and, 452–53, 457–69
markedness, 458
phonology and, 457–63
segmental phonology, 457–58
stress assignment, 462–63
syllabification, 460–62
morphology and, 467–69
role of the second language (L2), 451–52
study of, 450–57
syntax and, 463–67
variation in performance and, 455
Segmental change, 301
Segmental phonology, interlanguage (IL) grammars and, 457–58
Segments, 17, 64, 65
contrastive, 65–68
Self-praise avoidance, 547
Semantic broadening, 319
Semantic change, 319–20
Semantic decomposition, 251
Semantic narrowing, 319
Semantics, 245–77. *See also* Meaning(s)
computational, 687–90
natural language analysis and, 680
Semantic shift, 320
Semivowels and semiconsonants, 22. *See also* Glides
Sensory aphasia, 525–26
Sentence ambiguity, 502–3
Sentence interpretation, 271–77
beliefs and attitudes and, 271–72
conversational maxims and, 275–77
discourse and, 273–75
meaning and, 261–71
constructional meaning, 261–63
pronouns, 268–71
structural ambiguity, 263–64
thematic roles, 264–68
setting and, 272–73
topics and, 274–75
Sentences, 192–93
processing of, 491–93
semantic relations involving, 248–49
Sentence structure. *See also* Syntax
interpretation of, 268–71
language acquisition and, 432–34
Sequential change, 294–300
assimilation, 294–96
consonantal strengthening, 300
dissimilation, 296
epenthesis, 296–97
metathesis, 297–98
weakening and deletion, 298–300

Serial processing model, 505
Setting, sentence interpretation and, 272
Shields, M. J., 616
Shifts, 304
Sibilants, 28
Signals, 631–32
Signified, 628–29
Signifier, 628
Signs, 628–33
  discrete, 632–33
  graded, 632
  iconic, 629–30, 633
  indexical, 630–31, 633
  mixed, 631
  symbolic, 631, 633
  symptomatic, 633
Similarity Differential Rate Hypothesis (SDRH), 460
Simplification, articulatory, 291
Single-route models, 506
Situational code-switching, 582
Slang, 541
Slips of the tongue, 17, 486
Social network analysis, 573–74
Socioeconomic class, variants and, 572–73
Sociolects, 538
Sociolinguistic competence, second language acquisition and, 455
Sociolinguistics, 537–82
  of language, 538–53
    accommodation, 552–53
    discourse analysis, 538–47
    forms of address, 548–50
    gender, 550–52
    politeness, 547–48
    solidarity and power, 547–53
  of society, 538, 553–82
    age, 574
    attitudes, 554
    ethnicity, 575–76
    gender, 575
    indexing analysis, 560–61
    lexical variation in the United States, 567–68
    marginal analysis, 561–62
    methods of studying variation, 559–63
    nonstandard varieties, 556–57
    norms, 553–59
    official languages and language planning, 557–59
    phonological variation in the United States, 569–71
    principal components analysis, 562–63
    regional differences in morphology and syntax, 571–72
    regional variation in the United States, 567
    social network analysis, 573
    socioeconomic class, 572–73
    standard varieties of languages, 553–54
    variable rule analysis, 562
Sociolinguistic variable, 545
Solidarity, 547
Somali alphabet, 613
Sonorants, 79
Sonority, 21
Sound change(s), 292, 293–306
  auditorily based change, 301–2
  phonetic versus phonological change, 302–4
  phonological shift, 304–5
  rule ordering and, 306
  segmental change, 301
  sequential change, 294–300
Sound classes, 21
Sound-producing system, 18–21
Spatial metaphors, 256
Specifiers, 188–89
Spectrograms, 666, 667
Speech act theory, 539
Speech community, 537
Speech events, 539
Speech organs, 2
Speech recognition (speech analysis), 669–70, 696–97
Speech situations, 539
Speech sounds, 15–16
Speech synthesis, 665–69, 697–98
Speech variety, 538
Spelling, English orthography, 614–19
Spelling pronunciation, 292
Split brain studies, 521–22
Splits, 303
Spoonerisms, 486
Spreading, of features, 112–14, 116, 118
Standard varieties of languages, 553–54
Stemming algorithm, 671
Stems, 155
Stopping, 416
Stops, 25–26, 51–52, 352
  grid for, 26
Stress, 42–43
  classification of languages and, 354
  in English syllables, 89–91
  placement of, 141–42
  second language acquisition and assignment of, 462–63
Stress shift in English, 321–22
Stridents, 28
Stripping algorithm, 671
Strong generative capacity, 679
Structural ambiguity, 263–64
Subcategorization, 196–97, 199
Subset Principle, 466
Substitution
  auditorily based, 301–2
  in early speech, 416
Substitution test, 193–94
Substrate languages, 580
Substratum influence, 316
Suffixes, 138. *See also* Affixes
  case, 160
  inflectional, 155–56
Sumeria, 595–97
Summarization, automatic, 696
Superstratum influence, 316–17
Suppletion, 140–41
  partial, 141
Suprasegmentals (prosodic properties), 38–43
  pitch, 38–42
Suprasegmental systems, classification of languages and, 353–54
Surface dyslexia, 528
Surface representations (or forms), 107. *See also* Phonetic representations
Surface structure (S-structure), 211–13
Swift, Jonathan, 9–10
Syllabary, 592
Syllabic liquids, 31
Syllabic nasals, 31
Syllabic sounds, 21–22
Syllabic writing, 592, 597–98
Syllabification, second language acquisition and, 460
Syllable deletion, in early speech, 415
Syllable Final Obstruent Devoicing, 451, 458

Syllables, 17, 64–65, 79–91
coda of, 79, 80, 84–90, 95
defining, 79–80
in English, 79–81
stress and, 89–91
heavy, 90
language processing and, 497–98
nuclei of, 21, 79, 80, 84, 86, 90
onset of, 79–89
rules that refer to structure of, 111–12
setting up, 83–87
as suprasegmental, 79
Syllable simplification, in early speech, 415–16
Syllable structure, classification of languages and, 354–55
Sylvian fissure, 518
Symbolic models, 506–7
Symbolic signs, 631, 633
Symptomatic signs, 630, 633
Syncope, 298
Synonyms, 246
Syntactic categories, 184–96
phrases, 187–91
sentences, 192–93
words, 185–87
X′, 194–96
Syntactic change, 311–14
inversion in the history of English, 314
word order, 311–14
Syntactic development, 427–34
interpretation of sentences, 432–34
later development, 430–32
one-word stage, 427
telegraphic stage, 429–30
two-word stage, 427–29
Syntactic parser, 500
Syntactic universals, 364–65
Syntax, 183–231. *See also* Sentence structure
Broca's aphasia as a syntactic disorder, 524–25
case and, 223
complement options, 196–202
computational, 675–82
functional analysis and, 230–31
language processing and, 500–503
loss of syntactic competence, 530–31
modifiers and, 221–23
nonhuman primates and, 653
regional differences in, 571–72
relational analysis and, 228–30
second language acquisition and, 463–67
sentence interpretation and, 261–71
transformational analysis and, 227–28
transformations, 202–14
typological classification of languages and, 358–62
Synthetic languages, 309, 356
Systematic gaps, 82–83
Systematic phonetic correspondences, 324

Teacher talk, 474–75
Telegraphic speech
in Broca's aphasics, 524
in children, 429–30
Tense, 163–64
Tenses, tones and, 40
Tense vowels, 35
Terminal (intonation) contour, 40
Terminal nodes, 677, 678
Text analysis, 544–47
Textual competence, second language acquisition and, 454–55
Thematic grid, 265
Thematic roles, 264–68
Thorpe, W. H., 655
Thyroid cartilage, 19
Timed-reading experiments, 491–92
Tip-of-the-tongue phenomena, 488–89
Tonal assimilation, 115–16
Tone, 38–40
intonation and, 41–42
placement of, 141–42
Tone languages, 38, 353
Tongue
as articulating organ, 22–23
coarticulation and, 44
vowel articulation and, 33–35
Top-down parsing, 677
Top-down processing, 495–96
Topics, sentence interpretation and, 274–75
Trachea (windpipe), 19
Transcription. *See also* Phonetic transcription
phonetic (phonetic alphabet), 16–17, 76–78
of American English consonants and vowels, 36–38
length in, 42
stress in, 43
Transfer, phonological, 451
Transfer errors, in interlanguage (IL) grammars, 452
Transformational analysis, 227–28
Transformational grammar, 184
Transformations, 202–14
constraints on, 213–14
variation in the use of, 216–21
Verb Raising, 217
wh movement, 207–10, 216–17
yes-no questions, 203–7, 216
Transitive verbs, 190
Translation, machine, 693–95
Trill, 53
Truth conditions, 249
Turn-taking, in conversations, 544
Two-word stage, 427–29
Type Assumption, 418
Typological classification of languages, 349–65
consonant systems and, 352–53
morphology and, 355–58
phonology, 350–55
suprasegmental systems, 353–54
syntax and, 358–62
vowel systems and, 350–52
Typological plausibility, 334–36
Typology
linguistic, 349
reconstruction and, 334–36

Umlaut, 140, 296
Underextensions, 420–21
Underlying representations (or forms), 107. *See also* Phonemic representations
abstract, 168–69
Universal Grammar (UG), 184, 214–21
Universals, 362–65
morphological, 363–64

Universals *(continued)*
phonological, 362–63
syntactic, 364–65
Universal tendencies, 350
Unmarked characteristics, 350
Unordered rule application, 108–9
Uralic, 334
Uvular consonants, 395
Uvular sounds, 24

Vai peoples, writing system of, 612
Variable rule analysis, 562
Variation (variants)
allophonic, 76
features and, 94–95
lingua francas, 578
methods of studying, 559–60
parametric, 214–21
phrase structure, 214–16
pidgins and creoles, 578–80
social influence on, 563–78
AAVE (African-American Vernacular English), 575–78
age, 574
ethnicity, 575–76
gender, 575
geographical or regional location, 563–67
lexical variation in the United States, 567–68
regional differences in morphology and syntax, 571–72
regional variation in the United States, 567
social network, 573–74
socioeconomic class, 572–73
Varieties, nonstandard, 556–57
Velar consonants, 395
Velar fricatives, 52
Velar sounds, 24
Velar stops, 25
Velum
coarticulation and, 45
oral versus nasal phones and, 25
Verbal hedges, 551
Verbal paradigm, 162
Verb-initial languages, 220–21
Verb Movement Parameter, 464–65
Verb Raising transformation, 217–19
Verbs, 185
auxiliary, 185
classificatory, 405
meaning errors made by children, 421–22
motion, 257–59
nouns used as, 3
Verner, Karl, 333
Verner's Law, 333
Vocabulary development, 417–23
contextual clues and, 419
meaning errors and, 419–23
strategies for acquiring word meanings, 418–19
Vocal folds (vocal cords), 18–20, 24, 26
Vocal tract, 18
Vocoder, 665–66
Voiced sounds, 20, 21
Voice lag, 28
Voicelessness, 20
Voiceless sounds, 21
Voicing, 20, 300
Voicing assimilation, 47
Vowel contrasts, in English, 66–67
Vowel deletion, 298, 299
Vowel epenthesis, 112
Vowel reduction, 50, 298–99
Vowels, 21, 32–36. *See also* Diphthongs
articulation of, 21
basic parameters for describing, 33–35
consonant coarticulation with, 45
English, 33–36, 74, 351–52
Great English Vowel Shift, 304, 305, 308
phonetic and phonemic inventories of, 78
phonetic length, 88–89
phonetic transcription of, 36–38
epenthesized, 49
in languages other than English, 50–51
lax, 35
length of, 42
mid, 34
nasal, 51, 75, 77, 352, 396, 458
simple, 33
as sonorous (acoustically powerful), 21
as syllabic nuclei, 21
tense, 35
Vowel systems, typological classification of languages and, 350–52

Washoe (chimpanzee), 648, 651, 653
Weakening, 298
consonant, 299–300
of meaning, 320
Weak generative capacity, 679
Wernicke, Carl, 525
Wernicke's aphasia, 525–26
Wernicke's area, 525
Whisper, 20
Whispery voice, 20
Whole Object Assumption, 418
Whorf, Benjamin, 392
Wh questions, 207–10, 216–17
in early language acquisition, 431–32
Word formation, 315–16
in early speech, 426–27
Word manufacture (coinage), 154–55
Word order, 311–14
in Old English, 290
typological classification of languages and, 359–61
Words, 132–42. *See also* Lexicon; Meaning(s); Semantics; Vocabulary development
compound, 147–51
defined, 132
function, 530
semantic relations among, 246–48
structure of, 135–37
syntactic categories, 185
Word structure, 132–42
acronyms, 154
affixes, 135–36, 138–39
backformation, 153
bases, 136
blends, 152–53
clipping, 152
cliticization, 139
common morphological phenomena, 137–42
compounding, 137, 147–51
conversion, 151–52
internal change, 139–40
morphemes, 133–35
morphophonemics, 164–69

in North American languages, 397–400
onomatopoeia, 154
problematic cases, 136–37
reduplication, 141
roots, 135–36
suppletion, 140–41
Writing (scripts), 591–620. *See also* Alphabets
African, 612–13
alphabetic, 592–93
American, 610–12
Chinese, 605–7
cuneiform, 597–98
early history of, 593–95
evolution of, 595–605
hieroglyphics, 598–99
Indian, 613–14
Japanese, 607–9
Korean, 609–10
logographic, 592
phonographic, 592–93, 596
reading and, 619–20
Runic, 602
syllabic, 592, 597–98

X′ categories, 194–96

Yes-no questions, 203–7, 216
in early language acquisition, 430–31

Zero derivation, 151